FIFTH EDITION

Concepts of Chemical Dependency

FIFTH EDITION

Concepts of Chemical Dependency

Harold E. Doweiko

BROOKS/COLE

THOMSON LEARNING

Australia • Canada • Mexico • Singapore • Spain • United Kingdom • United States

BROOKS/COLE

THOMSON LEARNING

Sponsoring Editor: *Julie Martinez*
Marketing Team: *Caroline Concilla, Megan Hansen*
Editorial Assistant: *Cat Broz*
Project Editor: *Janet Hill*
Production Service: *Scratchgravel Publishing Services*
Cover Design: *Irene Morris*
Cover Photos: *Corbis; Science/Photo Researchers;*
  Sharpshooters; Francisco Cruz/Superstock;
  Lisette Le Bon/Superstock

Print Buyer: *Jessica Reed*
Typesetting: *Scratchgravel Publishing Services*
Cover/Interior Printing and Binding: *R. R. Donnelley*
  and Sons, Crawfordsville

For more information about this or any other Brooks/Cole product, contact:
BROOKS/COLE
511 Forest Lodge Road
Pacific Grove, CA 93950 USA
www.brookscole.com
1-800-423-0563 (Thomson Learning Academic Resource Center)

For permission to use material from this work, contact us by
www.thomsonrights.com
fax: 1-800-730-2215
phone: 1-800-730-2214

Printed in the United States of America

10   9   8   7   6   5   4   3

Library of Congress Cataloging-in-Publication Data
Doweiko, Harold E., [date]–.
    Concepts of chemical dependency / Harold E. Doweiko.—5th ed.
       p. cm.
    Includes bibliographical references and index.
    ISBN 0-534-53722-7 (alk. paper)
     1. Substance abuse. I. Title.

RC564 .D68 2001
362.29—dc21
                                    2001025823

In loving memory
of my wife, Jan

Contents

Preface

There have been a number of major advances in our understanding of the addictive disorders since the last edition of *Concepts of Chemical Dependency* was published. To keep this text as current as possible, several hundred changes have been made. Numerous references have been deleted because ongoing research has made them obsolete. New discoveries in the fields of neurology, neuropsychology, and neuropsychopharmacology have provided new insights into the effects of recreational chemicals upon the user's brain, how drugs of abuse disrupt the normal functions of the central nervous system, and the social problem of recreational drug abuse.

The pace of discovery in the field of addictions has been so fast that the latest text is barely in print when new research makes some of it obsolete. Thus, although every effort has been made to keep this text current, there is, of necessity, a lag between announcement of discoveries in the press or professional journals and incorporation of this research into an edition of *Concepts of Chemical Dependency*. This is one reason why the field of addictive medicine is so exciting: It is constantly changing. There are few generally accepted answers, a multitude of unanswered questions, and, in comparison to the other branches of science, few interdisciplinary boundaries to limit one's exploration of the field.

New in This Edition

This new edition of *Concepts of Chemical Dependency* includes significant changes. Older references have

been deleted, and new reference material has been added for each of the drugs of abuse. The text now identifies some of the more significant drug interactions for each major drug of abuse, showing how different agents might interact and affect the drug abuser in unanticipated ways. A glossary has been included at the end of the book to help students understand the more technical terms.

Several chapters have been revised, if not entirely rewritten. For example, Chapter 18 has been revised to include information on ketoprofen, the latest NSAID agent to be released as an over-the-counter medication in modified dosage form. This chapter was rewritten to allow a more concise review of the normal dosage levels and the complications brought on by the use of each over-the-counter analgesic.

Chapter 10, which addresses benzodiazepine use and abuse, has been revised to provide information on Rohypnol, as well as the latest information on the non-benzodiazepine hypnotics introduced in the last years of the 20th century.

Chapter 11 has been entirely rewritten to provide an overview of the CNS stimulants as they are used in medical practice and, in a separate section, the abuse of the CNS stimulants. This chapter includes expanded information on ephedrine, methylphenidate, and methamphetamine, both in the first half of the chapter (in the "Medical Uses" section) and in the section on the abuse of these and other CNS stimulants.

Another extensively revised chapter is Chapter 20, which addresses the impact of maternal chemical abuse on neonatal growth and development. This chapter provides a drug-by-drug summary of what is known about prenatal exposure to the drugs of abuse, as well as the latest information on the controversy surrounding maternal cocaine abuse during pregnancy.

Chapter 22, which concerns the "dual diagnosis" client, was rewritten with an emphasis on the interaction between such conditions as ADHD and substance abuse, as well as obsessive-compulsive disorder and chemical use problems.

Chapter 33, which addresses infectious disease as a consequence of drug abuse, has been expanded to include the latest information on hepatitis (all known subforms), HIV-1 infection, pneumonia, and tuberculosis.

These are some of the major changes made in the fifth edition, in addition to the hundreds of smaller changes made to include new information that reflects the latest discoveries in the field of substance abuse.

Disclaimer

This text was written in an attempt to share the author's knowledge and experience with others interested in the field of substance abuse. While every effort has been made to ensure that the information reviewed in this text is accurate, this book is not designed for, nor should it be used as, a guide to patient care. Furthermore, this text provides a great deal of information about the current drugs of abuse, their dosage levels, and their effects. This information is provided not to advocate or encourage the use or abuse of chemicals. Rather, this information is reviewed to inform the reader of current trends in the field of drug abuse and addiction. This text is not intended as a guide to self-medication, and neither the author nor the publisher assumes any responsibility for individuals who attempt to use this text as a guide for the administration of drugs to themselves or to others or as a guide to treatment.

Acknowledgments

It would not be possible to mention each and every person who has helped to make this book a reality. However, I must mention the library staff at Lutheran Hospital–La Crosse for their continued assistance in tracking down many obscure references, many of which have been utilized in this edition of *Concepts of Chemical Dependency*.

I would like to thank the reviewers who read the manuscript, offering valuable suggestions and insights: Cathy Carlson, Carleton College; David Elias, Antelope Community College; Harold Engen, University of Iowa; James Fuller, Indiana Wesleyan University; Leonard Hamilton, Rutgers University; Phyllis Marley, Texarkana Community College; Maria Saxionis, Bridgewater State College; Ron Solinski, Lethbridge Community College; and Annie M. Wells, Alabama A&M University.

Also, I would like to point out that without the support of my late wife, Jan, the earliest editions of this text would never have been published. Until her untimely death, she happily read each chapter of each edition. She corrected my spelling (many, many times over) and encouraged me when I was up against the brick wall of writer's block. I received her feedback with the same openness with which any author receives "constructive criticism." Despite that, she persisted with her feedback on each edition and was right more often than not. She was indeed my best friend and my "editor-in-chief." I have attempted to complete the revisions to the fifth edition in such a manner as to remain true to what I think she would have liked, and I hope she would have approved of this edition of *Concepts of Chemical Dependency*. I miss her input.

Harold E. Doweiko

FIFTH EDITION

Concepts of Chemical Dependency

CHAPTER ONE

Why Worry about Recreational Chemical Use in the United States?

Introduction

It is virtually impossible to find a country on this planet that does not struggle with an alcohol/drug abuse problem of some kind (United Nations, 1997). Here in the United States, we have been waging a "war" against recreational chemical use for more than a century. Every U.S. president during the last half of the 20th century has either declared or renewed the "war" against drug abuse, maintaining that uncounted hundreds of billions of dollars have been spent in an effort to eliminate recreational chemical use/abuse. Even so, at the start of the 21st century, virtually every drug that has ever been discovered is available to recreational chemical users in the United States (Hopkins, 1998).

One must wonder why, if alcohol/drug abuse is so deeply ingrained in the social life of the United States, this nation tries to resist the use of recreational chemicals. The answer to this question is that the abuse of alcohol and/or drugs is intermixed with every other problem society faces at the start of the 21st century. For example, the challenge of providing affordable, effective health care services has been compounded by alcohol and drugs:

- Approximately 21% of patients admitted to a hospital Intensive Care Unit are there because of alcohol use (Lieber, 1998).
- The medical treatment of alcoholism and drug addiction, in combination with the various psychiatric consequences of these disorders, accounts for up to 60% of hospital usage in the United States (Ciraulo, Shader, Ciraulo, Greenblatt, & von Moltke, 1994a).
- Either directly or indirectly, substance abuse is *the* most common "disease" encountered by the modern physician (American Medical Association, 1993), yet most alcohol and/or drug abuse problems are not recognized by physicians (O'Brien & McLellan, 1997).
- The abuse of illicit drugs is a major cause of ischaemic stroke in adults, increasing the individual's risk of such an event 1100% (Martin, Enevoldson, & Humphrey, 1997).

Recreational drug use is a drain not only on the general medical resources of the United States, but also on specialized components of the health care industry. For example,

- The most common cause of psychotic conditions in young adults is alcohol/drug abuse (Cohen, 1995).
- Alcohol use is a known risk factor in suicide attempts. In one study, 62% of suicide attempters were found to have consumed alcohol prior to their suicide attempt (Lester, 2000).
- Suicide is 30 times as common among alcoholics as among the general population (Mosier, 1999). In one study, 33% of completed suicides were found to have alcohol in their bodies (Lester, 2000).[1]

[1]Although these figures would seem to contradict each other, there is a simple explanation. Many people who are not alcohol-dependent drink heavily before attempting suicide. Thus alcohol *use* is a factor in 50% of all suicides, whereas alcohol *dependency* is a factor in 25% of all suicides in the United States.

- Suicide is the cause of death in 35% of all intravenous drug abusers (Neeleman & Farrell, 1997).

The problem of interpersonal violence has contributed to untold suffering in the United States for generations. Fully 56% of all assaults are alcohol-related (Dyehouse & Sommers, 1998), and 60–70% of men with a history of domestic assault are intoxicated on alcohol when they attack their partner (Gortner, Gollan, & Jacobson, 1997). Substance use disorders are involved in 89% of substantiated cases of child abuse involving a child under the age of 12 months (Evans, 1998).

There is a known relationship between substance abuse and homicide (Rivara, Mueller, Somes, Mendoza, Rushforth, & Kellerman, 1997). The authors found that illicit drug use in the home increased 28-fold a woman's chances of being murdered by a significant other, even if she herself was not using drugs. Alcohol alone is implicated in half of all homicides committed in the United States (National Foundation for Brain Research, 1992). Further, the role of alcohol/drugs in victimization has been underscored by study after study:

- The team of Liebschutz, Mulvey, and Samet (1997) found that 42% of a sample of 2322 women who were seeking treatment for substance use problems had a history of having been physically or sexually abused at some point in their lives. A quarter of these women said that they were in danger of being victimized again, in the near future.
- Of a sample of 802 inpatients being treated for alcoholism, 49% of the women and 12% of the men reported that they had been the victim of some form of sexual abuse (Windle, Windle, Scheidt, & Miller, 1995).

The impact of alcohol/drug abuse on the health care crisis facing the United States is not limited to the problem of interpersonal violence. For example, between 40% (Liu, Siegel, Brewer, Mokdad, Sleet, & Serdula, 1997) and 60% (Hingson, 1996) of the U.S. population will be involved in an alcohol-related motor vehicle accident at some point in their lives. The list goes on and on. Either directly or indirectly, recreational substance abuse continues to extract a terrible toll from every individual living in the United States.

Who "Treats" Those Who Abuse or Are Addicted to Chemicals?

Although the media speak knowingly of the "disease" of addiction, and the medical profession pays lip service to the addictive disorders by classifying them as diseases, as a general rule, health care professionals are not trained to intervene and treat those who abuse and/or are addicted to chemicals. This was clearly demonstrated by a recent study by the National Center on Addiction and Substance Abuse at Columbia University (2000), which surveyed a national sample of 648 physicians. Each physician was presented with case histories of patients in which alcohol and/or illicit drug abuse was a possible diagnosis. The study found that 94% of the physicians failed to identify alcohol abuse as a possible cause of the patient's illness when they reviewed the case histories presented to them. Further, less than 20% of the physicians surveyed considered themselves prepared to deal with alcohol-dependent patients and that less than 17% thought that they had the skills necessary to deal with prescription drug abusers.

These findings are understandable in light of the fact that "[few] medical schools or residency programs have an adequate required course in addiction" and "most physicians fail to screen for alcohol or drug dependence during routine examinations. Many health professionals view such screening efforts as a waste of time" (McLellan, Lewis, O'Brien, & Kleber, 2000, p. 1689).

An example of the outcome of this process of neglect is seen in Bernstein, Tracey, Bernstein, and Williams (1996). The authors examined the Emergency Department physicians to detect alcohol-related problems in over 210 patients. The patients completed an evaluation process that included three different tests: the Ever A Problem (EAP) quiz, the CAGE (discussed in Chapter 26), and the QED Saliva Alcohol Test (SAT). Forty percent of the patients were found to have an alcohol use problem on at least one of the three measures utilized, yet less than a quarter of them were referred for further evaluation or treatment. This result was interpreted as evidence that professionals believe it is hopeless to intervene when a patient has an alcohol abuse problem.

In spite of the known relationship between alcohol use and traumatic injury, almost three-quarters of the trauma centers reviewed do not screen for alcohol abuse/addiction when treating patients (Gentillelo, Donovan, Dunn, & Rivara, 1995). Although the benefits of professional treatment of alcohol abuse/addiction have been demonstrated time and again, many physicians continue to consider alcohol and illicit drug use to be virtually untreatable (National Center on Addiction and Substance Abuse at Columbia University, 2000). As a result of such unfounded pessimism, only 40% of general-practice physicians are motivated to work with the alcoholic patient (Alexander & Gwyther, 1995).

However, this diagnostic blindness is not limited to physicians. The typical training program for registered nurses includes less than 2–4 hours of classwork on addictive diseases, and many programs have no formal training at all on this disorder (Coombs, 1997). Further, in spite of the fact that alcohol use/abuse is a known risk factor for violence within the family, marital/family therapists only rarely ask the proper questions to identify alcohol/drug abuse/dependence. When a substance use problem within a marriage or family is not uncovered, therapy proceeds in a haphazard fashion. Vital clues to a very real illness within the family are missed, and the attempt at family or marital therapy is ineffective unless the addictive disorder is identified and addressed.

In spite of the obvious relationship between substance abuse and the various forms of psychopathology, 74% of the psychologists surveyed admitted that they had no formal education in the area of the addictions (Aanavi, Taube, Ja, & Duran, 2000). Whether substance abuse/addiction is a true "disease" or not, the health care and mental health professions have not trained practitioners either how to recognize this disorder or how to treat it. Perhaps this is because the problem of drug use/abuse in the United States has not been perceived as serious. In the next section, the scope of the problem of substance abuse/addiction will be examined, and you can decide whether it warrants the serious attention of large numbers of professionals in health care.

The Scope of the Problem of Chemical Abuse and Addiction

There are a number of reasons why it is difficult to identify the full scope of the problem of recreational substance misuse in the United States. First, the very nature of the problem of drug/alcohol abuse means that people will tend to hide evidence that they abuse recreational chemicals. For example, 70% of those people who used illicit drugs in 1997 had full-time jobs ("Report: Typical drug user not poor," 1999) and thus were unlikely to call attention to their use of illegal chemicals. This makes it difficult for researchers, or the general public, to comprehend easily the trends in drug use as they evolve.

Second, there is the nature of the news media, which is devoted to "breaking" news, not long-term problems. If a dam bursts, sending a flood of water downstream to destroy an unsuspecting village, dozens of reporters would converge at the scene of the disaster. But how many reporters would take the time to document the slow deterioration of the dam in the months and years before the final moments in which it failed? The same process is at work when the media devote their attention to the problem of substance abuse: They focus only on the dramatic new developments. Drug abuse trends emerge over months and years—time frames far too long for the news media to address the problem in depth. Also, the news media seldom devote sustained attention to any single subject; to do so would be to risk boring some of those who read the newspapers or listen to news programs on the radio or television.

Third, it may be hard for the average "person on the street" to understand how scientists might reach opposite conclusions on the basis of their respective research samples. The dialectic approach to research, where conflicting theories are examined and revised over time, is unfamiliar to the average person. Thus, when two scientists disagree over the same data, or, when their respective research projects yield conflicting results, many people become confused and tend to discount both the theories and the scientists who developed them.

Finally, the public has become increasingly skeptical, convinced that many "problems" are really just media-generated fads. Yet, as we will see in later chapters, the abuse of legal and illegal substances has caused tens of thousands of deaths in the United States in just the past decade and constitutes one of the major drains on the health care resources in this country. It is hardly a passing fad, even if it is not the most important news story of the day.

A word about demographic research. Students who review research based on demographic data frequently wonder how it is possible for different researchers to reach such disparate conclusions. The answer to this problem is simple: Because the population is so large, researchers must limit themselves to information drawn from small samples.

Consider the story about the four blind men in India, who encounter an elephant for the first time. One of the men, holding the elephant's trunk, concluded that an elephant is very much like a snake. Another, feeling the elephant's leg, disagrees, stating that the elephant resembles a tree. The third man, feeling the flank of the elephant, maintains that the elephant is similar to a wall. The last man, holding on to the tail, insists that an elephant is like a rope. These men were all feeling the same animal, and yet arrived at a different conclusion on the basis of his "sample" (what he could feel). However, if 50 blind men were to touch the same elephant, the summary of all 50 samples would give a good approximation of what the creature looks like.

Thus, this text will review a large number of studies. In spite of what some students might think, this is not done to overwhelm the reader. Rather, by considering a summary of a large number of research studies, each of which draws on a small sample of subjects, we should be able to gain an impression of the overall pattern of the alcohol/drug use trends in the United States at this time.

The scope of the problem. One of the most dramatic and frightening estimates of the scope of substance use problems in the past century was offered a decade and a half ago (Franklin, 1987). At the height of the drug use "crisis" of the 1980s, the author suggested that when drug rehabilitation professionals examined the statistics on alcohol and illegal drug abuse, combined with the abuse of prescription drugs, they found that "perhaps one in every five Americans [is] hopelessly addicted to something—and another one or two [are] steady users" (p. 59). If Franklin's estimate was accurate, then at that time, approximately 53 million of the some 265 million people in the United States were addicted to chemicals, and another 53–106 million people were steady users. These alarming figures are consistent with the findings of some research studies (Kessler, McGonagle, Zhao, Nelson, Hughes, Eshleman, Hans-Ulrich, & Kendler, 1994; Kessler, Crum, Warner, Nelson, Schulenberg, & Anthony, 1997). The data from each of these studies were based on the responses of a sample of 8098 individuals who took part in the National Comorbidity Sur-

vey. The sample was selected in such a way as to approximate the characteristics of the population of the United States as a whole, providing an overview of the population that would meet diagnostic criteria for a diagnosis of one of 14 separate psychiatric conditions both in the preceding 12 months, and, during the respondent's lifetime.

Kessler *et al.* (1994) drew several conclusions:

1. More than 14% of their respondents had a lifetime history of alcohol dependence.
2. More than 7% of their sample had been dependent on alcohol in the past 12 months.
3. More than 4% of their sample had used a drug for recreational purposes at some point in their lives but were not dependent on chemicals,
4. More than 7% of their sample would meet the diagnostic criteria for a diagnosis of drug dependency at some point in their lives.

However, Kessler *et al.* (1997) observed that the earlier team's interpretation of the data obtained from the National Comorbidity Survey was based on a rather liberal definition of alcohol/drug abuse and addiction and that other researchers might reach different conclusions from the same data if they used different criteria to define the problem behaviors being studied.

In a similar study, Warner, Kessler, Hughes, Anthony, and Nelson (1995) found that 51% of their sample admitted to having used an illicit chemical at least once, although only 15% had done so in the preceding 12 months. Because homeless people tend to be under-represented in their research sample, and because there is a known relationship between homelessness and chemical abuse, the authors suggested that the percentage of American adults who had ever used an illicit substance might actually be higher than the 51% that they found in their research sample.

Most certainly, the results obtained by Werner *et al.* (1995) and Kessler *et al.* (1994) were significantly different from those suggested by the *Harvard Mental Health Letter* (1995a). This publication suggested that 5–10% of the adults in the United States had a "serious alcohol problem" (p. 1) and that another 1–2% had a "serious illicit drug problem" (p. 1). Yet at the height of the last wave of drug abuse in this country a decade ago, Regier, Farmer, Rae, Locke, Keith, Judd, and Goodwin (1990) attempted to examine the lifetime prevalence rates of various forms of mental illness, including alcohol and substance use disorders, in the United States. Their findings suggested that at any given time, only 2.8% of the population would meet diagnostic criteria for a diagnosis of either alcohol abuse or alcohol dependency. Another 1.3% of the population would meet the diagnostic criteria for a drug abuse or dependency problem at any given time (Regier *et al.* 1990).

The authors also concluded that 13.5% of the population would, at some time in their lives, meet the criteria for alcohol abuse or dependency. Another 6.1% of the population would meet the criteria for a diagnosis of substance abuse or dependency, according to Regier *et al.* (1990). If we assume that the population of the United States is approximately 265 million persons, and if we apply the figures suggested by Regier *et al.* (1990) and Kessler *et al.* (1994), we reach some interesting conclusions. On the basis of the study by Regier *et al.* (1990), it would appear that at any given time, about 7.4 million Americans would meet the diagnostic criteria for alcohol abuse or dependency. Another 3.4 million Americans would qualify for a diagnosis of drug abuse or dependency.

In contrast to these estimates, the conclusions of Kessler *et al.* (1994) suggested that (given a population estimate of 265 million people) 18.2 million people in the United States had been physically dependent on alcohol at some point in the preceding 12 months and that 10.4 million Americans had used a recreational chemical other than alcohol in the same 12-month period. This latter estimate was slightly below *Playboy's* (1995b) estimate of 11.8 million Americans who were thought to have used an illicit drug in the last 30 days. Kessler *et al.* (1994) also suggested that 35.8 million Americans would become physically dependent on alcohol, and 16.2 million Americans on a recreational drug, at some point in their lives. Now compare these estimates with what researchers have found out about the drug abuse problem in the United States. Nationally, it is estimated that 70 million people have used an illicit substance at least once (Leshner, 1997b) but that only 12 million people might be classified as "frequent users" (White, 1993, p. 26A). This estimate did not attempt to separate those who are addicted to one or more drugs from those who are simply drug *abusers*.

The intravenous drug addict often is seen as a stereotype of the addicted person, and yet there are only between 1.1 and 1.8 million intravenous drug users in the United States (Selwyn, 1993), less than 1% of the estimated population. These estimates, and the predictions reviewed earlier in this chapter, are significantly lower than the estimate of 20% of the population (or a possible 53 million Americans) that Franklin (1987) presumed to be addicted to chemicals and the additional 20% of the population that he suggested were abusing chemicals at the height of the last wave of cocaine addiction. The reader might consider Franklin's (1987) figures as a "worst case" estimate, which has not been supported by the research data.

The wide differences among the various estimates of the scope of substance abuse/addiction in this country underscore one serious shortcoming in the field of substance abuse rehabilitation: the lack of clear data. Depending on the research study being cited, substance abuse is or is not a serious problem, is or is not getting worse (or better), will or will not be resolved in the next decade, and is something that parents should or should not worry about. The truth is that large numbers of people use one or more recreational chemicals but that only a small percentage of people who use them will ultimately become addicted to the chemical(s) being abused (Peele, Brodsky, & Arnold, 1991). For example, only 1 in every 4 drug abusers was classified as a "hardcore" user by the Office of National Drug Control Policy (1996). The next section offers an overview of the problem of substance abuse in this country.

Overview

Estimates of the problem of alcohol use, abuse, and addiction. Surprisingly, the use of alcohol in the United States has declined about 15% since 1980 (Musto, 1996). But alcohol remains a popular recreational chemical in the United States; just under 90% of the adults in the United States have consumed it at least once (Schuckit, 2000), and half of the adults in this country use it on a regular basis (Lieber, 1995).

When it is used to excess, alcohol becomes a drug of abuse. Those who abuse alcohol tend to consume a disporportionate amount of this chemical, as evidenced by the fact that only 34% of the population in this country consumes 62% of all the alcohol used. Approximately 10% of those who drink alcohol on a regular basis will become alcohol-dependent (Kotz & Covington, 1995). However, estimates of the scope of the problem of alcohol addiction in this country range from 9 million (Ordorica & Nace, 1998) or 12 million (L. Siegel, 1989) to as many as 20 million (Lieber, 1995; Kotz & Covington, 1995) adults.

The majority of those who abuse or are addicted to alcohol in the United States are male. But this does not mean that alcohol abuse/addiction is exclusively a male problem. The ratio of male to female alcohol abusers/ addicts is thought to fall between 2:1 and 3:1 (Hill, 1995; Blume, 1994; Cyr & Moulton, 1993). These figures suggest that significant numbers of women are also abusing or are addicted to alcohol. Because alcohol can be legally purchased by adults over the age of 21, many people tend to forget that it too is a drug. However, the grim reality is that this "legal" chemical makes up the greatest part of the drug abuse/addiction problem in this country. Franklin (1987) stated, for example, that alcoholism alone accounts for 85% of the problem of drug addiction in the United States. This is not surprising, for alcohol is the most commonly abused chemical in the world (Lieber, 1995).

Estimates of the problem of narcotics abuse and addiction. Narcotics, especially heroin, are the drugs many people think of when they hear the term "drugs of abuse." Although narcotic analgesics have the reputation of being quite addictive, only about half of the people who abuse these drugs become addicted to them (Jenike, 1991). However, addiction to heroin is a very real problem in the United States. The Office of National Drug Control Policy (1996) estimated that 500,000 people in the United States use heroin at least once a week and that an additional 229,000 use this chemical less often. This yields a total that is very close to the estimate of 1 million Americans who use heroin at least once a week offered by Kaufman and McNaul (1992). Another estimate of between 500,000 and 1,000,000 heroin-addicted people was suggested by Warner, Kosten, & O'Connor (1997). About half of the people addicted to heroin in the United States are thought to live in New York City (Kaplan, Sadock, & Grebb, 1994; Witkin & Griffin, 1994). A significant percentage of those addicted to heroin are women. Indeed, Kaplan and Sadock (1991) suggest a ratio of three male heroin addicts for every female. Given an estimate of 800,000 heroin addicts, this would mean that there

are approximately 200,000 women addicted to heroin in the United States. Unfortunately, the methodology used by the federal government to estimate the number of "hard core" drug users is flawed. The journal *Alcoholism & Drug Abuse Week* (1997) reported that the federal government's estimates are based on telephone surveys and home visits. When special efforts were made to include the homeless population in the research sample, government researchers found that there were *three times* as many "hardcore" drug users in the Chicago area as had previously been thought.

There is another hidden population of opiate users in the United States: those individuals who have regular jobs, and thus have private health care insurance, but who abuse or are addicted to opiates. Fully 7.7% of the adults between the ages of 18 and 49 who were surveyed admitted to having used an illicit substance at least once in the month preceding the survey, and 70% of these individuals were employed on a full-time basis ("Report: Typical drug user not poor," 1999). It is unlikely that these individuals will appear in estimates of drug addiction; they constitute a "hidden" population of drug abusers and addicts about which very little is known. There are other aspects of opiate abuse/addiction that have never been studied. For example, it is known that some pharmaceutical narcotic analgesics are diverted to the illicit drug market. However, we have almost no information about the scope of the problem of pharmaceutical diversion, nor do we know whether the person who abuses pharmaceuticals is similar to, or markedly different from, the person who abuses illicit narcotics. Thus the figure of 500,000–1,000,000 intravenous heroin addicts must be accepted as only a minimal estimate of the narcotics abuse/addiction problem in the United States.

Estimates of the problem of cocaine abuse and addiction. Although there is evidence to suggest that cocaine abuse peaked in the mid-1980s, it still remains a popular drug of abuse. Angell and Kassirer (1994) estimated that 1.6 million Americans use cocaine on a regular basis. However, these authors did not differentiate between people who were addicted to the drug and those who used cocaine infrequently. Cornish, McNicholas, and O'Brien (1995) offered a different estimate of the number of people using cocaine in the United States. The authors suggested that there were 3 million cocaine users in this country, of whom approximately 855,000 used the drug at least once a week. The Washington-based research group Abt Associates, Inc. (1995a) suggested that there were 2.1 million "hardcore" cocaine users (those who used cocaine more than twice a week) and 4 million occasional users. Surprisingly, in spite of its reputation as an addictive substance, only a fraction of those who use cocaine ever actually become addicted to it. Researchers now believe that only between 3 and 20% of those who use cocaine go on to become addicted to this substance (Musto, 1991). Of the 3 million Americans who were thought to use cocaine at the time, only 855,000 did so once a week or more (Cornish, McNicholas, & O'Brien, 1995). Other researchers have suggested that only 1 cocaine user in 6 (Peele, Brodsky, & Arnold, 1991) to 1 in 12 (Peluso & Peluso, 1988) was actually addicted to the drug.

Estimates of the problem of marijuana abuse and addiction. Marijuana is the most commonly abused *illegal* drug in the United States (Kaufman & McNaul, 1992), as well as in Canada (Russell, Newman, & Bland, 1994). It is estimated that more than 68 million (Kaufman & McNaul, 1992) people in the United States have used marijuana at some point in their lives. This number means that approximately 25% of the entire population has used marijuana at least once. It is estimated that there are 9 million "regular" users of marijuana in this country (Angell & Kassirer, 1994, p. 537). However, the authors did not specify what they meant by "regular" marijuana users.

Estimates of the problem of hallucinogenics abuse. As with marijuana, there are questions about whether one can become addicted to hallucinogenics. For this reason, this text speaks of the "problem of hallucinogenics abuse." Perhaps as many as 20% of Americans below the age of 25 have used hallucinogenics at one time or another (Kaplan & Sadock, 1996). However, hallucinogenics use is actually quite rare, and of those young adults who have used hallucinogenic drugs, only 1 or 2% will have done so in the past 30 days, according to the authors. These data suggest that *addiction* to hallucinogenics, even if it is possible, is exceedingly rare.

Estimates of the problem of tobacco addiction. Tobacco is a special product. Like alcohol, it is legally sold to adults. Unfortunately, tobacco products are also readily obtained by adolescents, who make up a significant proportion of those who use tobacco. Researchers estimate that approximately 46 million Americans smoke cigarettes (Brownlee, Roberts, Cooper, Goode, Hetter, & Wright, 1994). Of this number, an estimated 24 million smokers are male, 22.3 million female.

The Cost of Chemical Abuse and Addiction in the United States

Although the total number of people in this country who abuse recreational chemicals or are addicted to them is limited, recreational substance use still takes a terrible toll on society. It has been suggested that the annual financial impact of substance use disorders in the U.S. (including alcohol and tobacco) is $510 billion (Evans, 1998). Nationally, it is estimated that 420,000 smokers die each year from tobacco-related illness, and an additional 56,000 nonsmokers die each year as a result of their exposure to cigarette smoke generated by other people (Benson & Sacco, 2000). Each year, an estimated 100,000 (Lewis, 1997) to 200,000 (Hymen & Cassem, 1995; Kaplan, Sadock, & Grebb, 1994) die from alcohol-related illness. In contrast to these figures, only an estimated 5475 people die as a direct result of drug abuse each year in the United States (Evans, 1998). However, when one stops to consider the impact of drug-related infant deaths, overdose-related deaths, suicides, homicides, motor vehicle accident deaths, and the various forms of drug-abuse-related disease (such as hepatitis, HIV infection, pneumonia, and endocarditis), the true death toll from drug abuse/addiction in the United States might be more like 20,000 (Miller, 1999) to 30,000 (Prater, Miller, & Zylstra, 1999) people a year. Even this number is only $1/16$ as many people as are thought to die as a result of tobacco use each year in the United States, yet the use of tobacco remains legal for individuals over the age of 21.

Recreational chemical abuse accounts for between one-quarter and one-third of all deaths in the United States each year (Hurt, Offord, Croghan, Gomez-Dahl, Kottke, Morse, & Melton, 1996). But most of the substance-related deaths are caused by alcohol or tobacco. In contrast to the number of annual deaths attributable to these two legal substances, alcohol and drugs cause approximately 7600 premature deaths each year in the United States, whereas heroin and morphine abuse resulted in 6500 deaths. Cocaine is estimated to cause 8100 deaths each year in the United States (Hilts, 1996). As these figures suggest, chemical use or abuse is a significant factor in premature death, illness, loss of productivity, and medical expenses. However, because chemical abuse/addiction has so many hidden facets, behavioral scientists believe that these are only rough estimates of the annual impact of problems with alcohol and drug use. Consider, for example, the hidden facet of substance abuse as a cause of traumatic injuries. For example, one study showed that 71% of those patients admitted to a major trauma center had evidence of alcohol/illicit drugs in their bodies when they were hospitalized for their injuries (Cornwell, Blezberg, Velmahos, Chan, Demetriades, Stewart, Oder, Kahuku, Chan, Asensio, & Berne, 1998).

The cost of alcohol abuse. A number of factors must be considered in any effort to calculate the annual financial impact of alcohol abuse and addiction in this country. They include not only direct but also indirect costs, such as the cost of alcohol-related criminal activity, motor vehicle accidents, and destruction of property; the cost of social welfare programs; private and public hospitalization costs for alcohol-related illness; and the cost of public and private treatment programs. Collectively, the direct and indirect costs of United States medical and social services for alcohol dependence are thought to total between $99 billion (Olmedo & Hoffman, 2000) and $166 billion (Garbutt, West, Carey, Lohr, & Crews, 1999) per year.

In recent years, politicians have spoken at length about the need to control the rising cost of health care in the United States. Alcohol use disorders are significant factors in the growing health care financial crisis. Although only 5–10% of the general population has an alcohol use problem, 10–20% of the ambulatory patients and 25–40% of the patients in hospitals suffer from some complication of alcohol use or abuse (Weaver, Jarvis, & Schnoll, 1999; Blondell, Frierson, & Lippmann, 1996). Further, between 15 and 30% of the nursing home beds in this country are occupied by individuals whose alcohol use has contributed to their need for placement in a nursing home (Schuckit, 2000). Many of these nursing home beds are supported in part by public funds, so chronic alcohol abuse is a major factor in the growing cost of nursing home care for the elderly.

There is another way in which alcohol abuse and addiction increase the cost of health care: Alcohol use was a factor in 41% of motor vehicle accident deaths in 1995 (Hingson, 1996) and in 25–60% of all traumatic injuries (Dyehouse & Sommers, 1998). Each year, an estimated 200,000 people in this country lose their lives because of alcohol use/abuse (Mosier, 1999); this means that alcohol figures in 5% of the annual death toll in the United States (Miller, 1999).

Individuals who have been injured as a result of alcohol use/abuse require medical treatment. Ultimately, this medical treatment is paid for by the public in the form of higher insurance costs and higher taxes. Indeed, alcohol use disorders are thought to account for 15% of the money spent for health care in the United States each year (Schuckit, 2000; McCrady & Langenbucher, 1996). Yet in spite of the pain and suffering that alcohol causes each year, only 5% (Prater, Miller, & Zylstra, 1999) to 10% of alcohol-dependent individuals are *ever* identified and referred to a treatment program (Wing, 1995).

Kales, Barone, Bixler, Miljkovic, and Kales (1995) examined the problems of mental illness and substance use in a rural sample of homeless people. The authors found almost 60% of their sample of 110 individuals to have had either an alcohol or a recreational drug use problem at some time in their lives. While the authors admitted that their sample was drawn from a rural setting rather than a large city, their findings were consistent with earlier studies based on urban samples of homeless people. Thus it would seem that substance use problems often coexist with homelessness.

The cost of tobacco use. Although it is legally produced and may be consumed by adults without legal problems, tobacco use extracts a terrible penalty. The annual cost of direct health care for cigarette smokers, combined with lost productivity as a result of smoking-related illness, has been estimated as between $100 billion (Hogan, 2000) and $130 billion (Leistikow, 2000) per year in the United States. Fully 19% of the annual death toll in this country can be traced to smoking-related disease (Miller, 1999).

The cost of illicit substance abuse. The factors that must be included in any estimate of recreational drug use include the estimated financial impact of premature death or illness caused by substance abuse, wages lost by those who lose their jobs as a result of substance abuse, the financial losses incurred by victims of drug-related crimes and the expected costs of drug-related law enforcement activities, among others. With this in mind, researchers have suggested that the annual economic cost of recreational chemical use in the United States is approximately $383 per person (Swan, 1998). The total annual economic impact of illicit chemical use/abuse is estimated at between $109.8 billion (Swan, 1998) and $276 billion per year (Stein, Orlando, & Sturm, 2000). No matter which of these estimates you accept, it is clear that drug abuse is an expensive luxury.

Drug use as an American way of life. Note that in the last paragraph, drug abuse was identified as a luxury. To illustrate how much we, as a nation, have come to value recreational chemical use, consider that money spent on illicit recreational chemicals is not used to buy medical care, food, shelter, or clothing, but simply on illegal chemicals that are used for personal pleasure. The annual expenditure for illicit recreational chemicals in the United States is a sum greater than *the total combined income* of the 80 poorest "Third World" countries (Corwin, 1994).

In conclusion, there is no possible way to gauge accurately the personal, economic, and social impact that these various forms of chemical addiction have had on society. Only by considering the economic impact of medical costs incurred, lost productivity, and other indirect costs of "hidden" drug abuse and addiction can one begin to appreciate the impact that chemical abuse and addiction have had.

Why Is It So Difficult to Understand the Drug Abuse Problem in the United States?

For the past two generations, politicians have spoken about society's war on drug use/abuse. One of the basic strategies of this ongoing "war" has been exaggeration of the dangers associated with chemical use (Peele, 1994; Musto, 1991). This technique is known as *disinformation*, and distorting and exaggerating the scope of the problem and the dangers associated with recreational drug use seem almost to have been an unofficial government policy.

An excellent example of this "disinformation" appears in a statement made by U.S. Representative Vic Fazio, who, in calling for legislation to control access to certain chemicals that might be used to manufacture illicit methamphetamine, spoke of "a generation of meth-addicted crank babies . . . rapidly filling our nation's hospitals" (*Forensic Drug Abuse Advisor*, 1996j, p. 70). This statement came as a surprise to health care

professionals: There was no epidemic of babies addicted to methamphetamine. But that did not prevent this false statement from being offered as a "fact" in the United States House of Representatives.

For more than two generations, the media have presented drugs in such a negative light that ". . . anyone reading or hearing of them would not be tempted to experiment with the substances" (Musto, 1991, p. 46). Unfortunately, such "scare tactics" have not been found to work. For example, in the mid-1980s, the media presented report after report of the dangers of chemical addiction, yet they consistently failed to point out that only 5½ million Americans (about 2% of the current population of approximately 260 million) was addicted to illegal drugs (Holloway, 1991).

It is not the goal of this text to advocate substance use, but there are wide discrepancies between the scope of recreational drug use as reported in the mass media and that revealed by scientific research. For example, Franklin (1987), in his widely read series of newspaper articles on the addictive disorders, stated that 20% of the population was addicted to chemicals and another 20% were on the verge of addiction. Yet scientific research articles, which are read only by a small minority of the population, suggested that only a small percentage of the population of the United States was using illicit chemicals. Given these wide discrepancies, it is clear that much of what has been said about the drug abuse "crisis" in the United States has been tainted by misinformation or outright falsity. To understand the problem of recreational chemical use/abuse, it is necessary to look beyond the "sound bytes" and "factoids" of the mass media and the politicians.

Summary

It has been estimated that at any point in time, between 2 and 10% of American adults either abuse or are addicted to illegal drugs. This percentage suggests that large numbers of people are using illicit chemicals in this society, but also that the drugs of abuse are not universally addictive. We also noted in this chapter that the various forms of chemical abuse/addiction are different manifestations of a unitary disorder: chemical abuse/addiction. Finally, although drug addiction is classified as a disease, most physicians are ill-prepared to treat substance-abusing patients.

In this chapter, we examined the problem of recreational drug use and tried to assess its impact on society. In later sections of this book, we will find detailed information on the various drugs of abuse, their effects on the user, the consequences of their use, and the reha-bilitation process for those who are abusing or addicted to chemicals. This information should help you better understand the problem of recreational substance use in this country.

CHAPTER TWO

What Do We Mean When We Say Substance Abuse and Addiction?

Introduction

In the previous chapter, we saw that substance abuse/addiction is an under-recognized social problem. Like many problem areas, the world of substance abuse and drug rehabilitation has its own language. In this chapter, we will discuss some of the more common concepts and terms used in the field of substance abuse and chemical dependency treatment.

The Continuum of Chemical Use

It is surprising how often people confuse chemical *use* with *abuse* and *addiction*. Indeed, these terms are often mistakenly used as though they were synonymous, even in clinical research studies (Minkoff, 1997). In reality, recreational alcohol/drug use, like most forms of human behavior, falls on a continuum (Kaminer, 1999). Complete abstinence is one end of the continuum, and physical addiction to a chemical is the opposite end point (McCrady & Epstein, 1995). Between these two extremes are various patterns of chemical use, which differ in the intensity with which the person engages in substance use and in the consequences of this behavior for the individual. In their discussion of illegal substance use, Cattarello, Clayton, and Leukefeld (1995) suggested that

> people differ in their illicit drug use. Some people never experiment; some experiment and never use again. Others use drugs irregularly or become regular users, whereas others develop pathological and addictive patterns of use. (p. 152)

In this statement, the authors identified five different patterns of recreational chemical use: (1) total abstinence, (2) a brief period of experimentation, followed by a return to abstinence, (3) irregular, or occasional, use of illicit chemicals, (4) regular use of chemicals, and (5) the pathological or addictive pattern of use that is the hallmark of the physical dependency on chemicals.

Even the stage of addiction to alcohol/drugs is not uniform. Rather, the addictive use of alcohol/drugs might range from "from moderate excess to severe compulsion" (Peele, Brodsky, & Arnold, 1991, p. 133). Further, there are no firm boundaries between the points on a substance use continuum (Sellers *et al.*, 1993). Only the end points—total abstinence and active physical addiction to chemicals—remain relatively fixed. The main advantage a drug use continuum such as the one suggested by Cattarello, Clayton, and Leukefeld (1995) is that it allows the classification of chemical use in terms of various intensities and patterns. Drug use/abuse/addiction thus becomes a behavior, not a "condition" that merely either is or is not present. A continuum also allows us to assign behavior to a number of possible intermediate steps between the two extreme points of total abstinence and physical addiction. For the purpose of this text, we will view the phenomenon of recreational alcohol/drug use along the continuum shown in Figure 2.1.[1]

---

[1]The team of Carey, Cocco, & Simons (1996) utilized a similar continuum in their work with dual-diagnosis clients (discussed in Chapter 22). But they suggested that the assessor evaluate the client's alcohol use and other drug use separately.

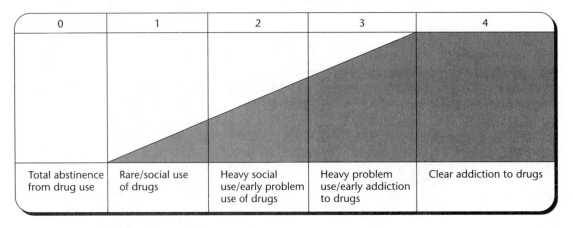

FIGURE 2.1   The continuum of chemical use.

The first point on the continuum presented in Figure 2.1 is *Level 0: Total abstinence*. Individuals whose substance use falls in this category abstain from all recreational use of alcohol and chemicals, and they present no immediate risk for substance use problems (Isaacson & Schorling, 1999).

The second category is *Level 1: Rare/social use*. Individuals at this level of experimental use present a low risk for a substance use disorder on the continuum suggested by Isaacson & Schorling (1999). Individuals in this category only rarely use alcohol or chemicals for recreational purposes. This person does not experience any of the social, financial, interpersonal, medical, or legal problems that are the hallmark of the pathological use of chemicals. People whose substance use falls at this level do not demonstrate a loss of control over their chemical use, and their chemical use does not result in any form of danger to their lives.

Level 2: Heavy social use/early problem use of drugs. A person whose chemical use falls at this point on the continuum (a) is using alcohol/drugs in a manner that is clearly above the norm for society, and/or (b) begins to experience various combinations of legal, social, financial, occupational, and personal problems associated with chemical use. Individuals whose substance use fall in this range can be classified as being "at risk" for a substance use disorder (Isaacson & Schorling, 1999), as substance abusers, or as "problem drinkers."

Individuals in this category are more numerous than those who are clearly addicted to chemicals. Sobell and Sobell (1993) found, for example, that problem drinkers were 4 times as numerous as alcohol-dependent individuals. At this level of chemical use, the individual begins to manifest symptoms of a behavioral disorder by making poor choices about the recreational use of one or more chemicals, but she or he may still be able to control the use of the substance(s) (Minkoff, 1997). The individual might try to hide, or deny, the problems that arise as a result of chemical use. Fortunately, many of those whose chemical use reaches this point in the drug use continuum learn from their experience and alter their chemical use so that they are unlikely to have future problems. Thus, at this level of chemical use, the individual is not addicted to chemicals.

Level 3: Heavy problem use/early addiction. This person's alcohol or chemical use has reached the point where there clearly is a problem. Indeed, these people may have become addicted to chemicals, although they may argue this point. The person whose chemical abuse falls at this level has started to experience medical complications associated with chemical use, as well as to undergo classic withdrawal symptoms when unable to continue the use of drugs/alcohol. On their continuum, Isaacson & Schorling (1999) classify individuals who fall at this level as engaging in "problem use." Individuals at this level are often preoccupied with substance use, and have *lost control* over their chemical use (Brown, 1995; Gordis, 1995). Shute and Tangley (1997) estimated that 40 million people in the United States abuse alcohol but are not dependent on it. Such individuals fall into category 3 on this continuum.

Level 4: Clearly addicted to drugs. At this point on the continuum, the person demonstrates all the symptoms of the classic addiction syndrome, in combination with multiple social, medical, legal, financial, occupational, and personal problems that are the hallmark of an alcohol/drug dependency. A person whose chemical use falls at this point on the continuum clearly exhibits the physical disorder of alcohol/drug dependency (Minkoff, 1997). Even at this level of substance use, the addicted individual may try to rationalize away or deny problems associated with his or her alcohol or drug use. More than one elderly alcoholic, for example, has tried to explain away abnormal liver function as the aftermath of a childhood illness. However, to an impartial assessor, the person at this level is clearly addicted to alcohol or drugs.

This classification system, like all others, is imperfect. The criteria used to determine at what level an individual might fall are arbitrary and subject to discussion. It is often "the variety of alcohol-related problems, not any unique criterion, that captures what clinicians really mean when they label a person alcoholic" (Vaillant, 1983, p. 42). However, as we shall see in later chapters of this book, even in the case of the opiates, there are individuals who use these drugs, perhaps even on a regular basis, but do not become *addicted* to narcotics. Physical addiction to a chemical is just one extreme on the continuum of drug use styles.

Definitions of Terms to Be Used in This Book

In order to understand each other when they consult about cases, individuals who study substance abuse need a common language. Unfortunately, because the world of substance abuse seems to have a language all its own, drug abuse terminology can be rather confusing to the newcomer.

Social use. The "social use" of a substance is defined by traditional social standards. *Social use* might be further subdivided into *occasional* and *regular* patterns of use (Herscovitch, 1999). Currently, alcohol is the chemical most frequently used within a social context; it is often used in religious or family functions. In some circles, marijuana is also used within a social context,

although it is a controlled substance,[2] and thus its use is less acceptable than the use of alcohol.

Substance abuse. Substance abuse occurs when an individual is using a drug when there is no legitimate medical need to do so. In the case of alcohol, the person is drinking in excess of accepted social standards (Schuckit, 1995). Thus the definition of *substance abuse* is based on current social standards. The individual who abuses a chemical might be said to have made *poor choices* regarding his or her use of that substance but is not addicted to it (Minkoff, 1997).

Drug of choice. At one time, clinicians spoke about the individual's *drug of choice* as an important component of the addictive process. It was assumed that the drug(s) people would use if they had a choice was an important clue to the nature of their addiction. Now, however, clinicians no longer put much emphasis on the individual's drug of choice (Walters, 1994). One reason for this change is that in this era of polypharmacology,[3] it is rare for a person to be addicted to just one chemical. For example, many stimulant users also drink alcohol or use benzodiazepines to control the side effects of the cocaine or amphetamines.

Addiction. Morse and Flavin (1992) offered an updated definition of alcoholism that might be viewed as a model for all forms of drug addiction. In their opinion, alcoholism is

> a primary, chronic disease with genetic, psychosocial and environmental factors influencing its development and manifestations. The disease is often progressive and fatal. It is characterized by impaired control over drinking, preoccupation with the drug alcohol, use of alcohol despite adverse consequences, and distortions in thinking. . . . (p. 1013)

In this definition, one finds all of the core concepts used to define drug addiction. Each form of drug addiction is viewed as (1) a primary disease, (2) with multiple manifestations in the person's social, psychological, spiritual, and economic life, (3) which is often progressive, (4) is potentially fatal, and is marked by (5) an inability to control the use of the drug(s) and (6) preoccupation with chemical use. Further, in spite of the many

[2] See Appendix 3.
[3] See the Glossary.

consequences inherent in the use of the chemical(s), (7) the individual develops a distorted way of looking at the world that supports his or her continued chemical use. Addiction to a chemical is also marked by (8) the development of *tolerance* to the effects of that chemical and, (9) a *characteristic withdrawal syndrome* when the drug is discontinued (Schuckit, 1995). Let's look at these two additional symptoms of addiction in more detail.

Tolerance develops over time, as the individual's body struggles to maintain normal function in spite of the presence of one or more foreign chemicals. Technically, there are several different types of tolerance. In this text, we will limit our discussion to just two types of tolerance: *metabolic tolerance* and *pharmacodynamic tolerance.*

Metabolic tolerance develops when the body becomes more effective at biotransforming a chemical into a form that can be easily eliminated from the body. (The process of biotransformation will be discussed in more detail in Chapter 3). The liver is the main organ in which this process is carried out. In some cases, the constant exposure to a chemical causes the liver to become more efficient at breaking down the drug, which makes a given dose less effective over time.

Pharmacodynamic tolerance is the increasing insensitivity of the central nervous system to the drug's effects. When the cells of the central nervous system are continuously exposed to a chemical, they often "try" to maintain normal function by making minute changes in their cell structure to compensate for the drug's effects. The cells of the central nervous system then become less sensitive to the effects of that chemical, and the person must use more of the drug to achieve the initial effect.

When they are used long enough, the major recreational chemicals bring about a *withdrawal syndrome.* The exact nature of the withdrawal syndrome varies, depending on what class of drugs is being used, how long the individual has used that chemical, and other factors, such as the individual's state of health. But withdrawal from each group of drugs produces certain characteristic physical symptoms. A rule of thumb is that the withdrawal syndrome will include symptoms the opposite of those induced by the given chemical. In clinical practice, the existence of a withdrawal syndrome is evidence that pharmacodynamic tolerance has developed, because the withdrawal syndrome is caused by the absence of the chemical that the central nervous system had previously adapted to. When the drug is discontinued, the central nervous system goes through a period of readaptation, as it learns to function normally without the drug. During this period of time, the individual experiences the physical signs of withdrawal.

This process is clearly seen during alcohol withdrawal. Alcohol functions as a chemical "brake" on the cells of the central nervous system, much like the brakes on your car. If you attempted to drive with the brakes engaged, you might eventually be able to force the car to go fast enough to meet the posted speed limits. But if you then suddenly released the pressure on the brakes, the car would leap ahead because the brakes were no longer resisting the forward motion of the car. You would have ease up on the gas pedal so that the engine would slow down enough to keep you within the posted speed limit.

During that period of readjustment, the car would, in a sense, be going through a withdrawal phase. Much the same thing happens in the body, when the individual stops using drugs. The body must adjust to the absence of a chemical that it has learned will always be there. This withdrawal syndrome, like the presence of tolerance to the drug's effects, provides strong evidence that the individual is addicted to one or more chemicals.

The Growth of New "Addictions"

Just as the popular press tends to exaggerate the dangers associated with chemical abuse, there is a widespread, disturbing trend to speak of larger and larger numbers of people as "addicts." Many substance abuse professionals speak of "addiction" to food, sex, gambling, men, women, play, television, shopping, credit cards, making money, carbohydrates, shoplifting, unhappy relationships, the Internet, and a multitude of other non-drug-related behaviors and substances (Peele, 1989; Peele, Brodsky, & Arnold, 1991).

Fortunately, however, there is little evidence that non-drug-centered behaviors can result in physical addiction (Herscovitch, 1999). Because substance abuse often blends into addiction to that same chemical, this text will often use the terms *substance use, chemical dependency, substance abuse* and *addiction* interchangeably. But all these terms will be applied only to physical dependency on alcohol or drugs of abuse.

What Do We *Really* Know about the Addictive Disorders?

If you were to watch the television talk shows or read a small sample of the multitude of self-help books currently on the market, you would be left with the impression that researchers fully understand the causes and treatment of drug abuse. *Nothing could be further from the truth!* Much of what is "known" about addiction is based on mistaken assumptions, clinical theory, or incomplete data.

An excellent example of how incomplete data might influence the evolution of treatment theory is found in the fact that much of the research on substance abuse is based on a distorted sample of people: those who are in treatment for substance abuse problems (Gazzaniga, 1988). Virtually nothing is known about those people who use chemicals on a social basis but never become addicted or about those who are addicted to chemicals but recover from their chemical use problem(s) without formal intervention/treatment. A serious question that must be asked is whether individuals in treatment are representative of *all* the addicted.

For example, the individuals who seek treatment for a substance use disorder are quite different from those who do not (Carroll & Rounsaville, 1992). As a group, alcohol/drug-addicted persons who do not seek treatment seem better able to control their substance use, and have shorter drug use histories, than people who seek treatment for their substance use problem. This may be why the majority of those who abuse chemicals either stop or significantly reduce their chemical use without professional intervention (Humphreys, Moos, & Finney, 1995; Tucker & Sobell, 1992; Carroll & Rousaville, 1992; *Mayo Clinic Health Letter*, 1989; Peele, 1985, 1989). Thus only a minority of those who begin to use recreational chemicals lose control over their substance use and require professional intervention. Yet it is on this minority that much of the research into the recognition and treatment of substance abuse problems is based.

Consider, for a moment, the people known as "chippers." These people make up a subpopulation of drug users about which virtually nothing is known. Chippers seem to be able to use a chemical when they want to and then, even though the drug may be one thought quite addictive, discontinue using it at will. Researchers are not even able to make an educated guess as to their number. It is thought that chippers use chemicals in response to social pressure and then stop when the social need has passed. But this is only a theory, and it might not account for the phenomenon of chipping.

Yet another reason why much of the research in the field of substance abuse rehabilitation is flawed is that a significant proportion of this research is carried out in either Veterans Administration (VA) hospitals, or public facilities such as state hospitals. Individuals in these facilities are not necessarily representative of the "typical" alcohol/drug-dependent person. For example, to be admitted to a VA hospital, an individual must have successfully completed a tour of duty in the military. The simple fact that the individual was able to complete a term of military service means that she or he is quite different from those people who either never enlisted in the military or enlisted but were unable to complete a tour of duty. By the same token, the alcohol/drug addict who is employed and can afford treatment in a private treatment center might be far different from the indigent alcohol/drug-dependent person who must be treated in a publicly funded treatment program.

Another problem is that only a small proportion of the available literature on the subject of drug addiction addresses forms of addiction other than alcoholism. An even smaller proportion addresses the impact of recreational chemical use on women (Griffin, Weiss, Mirin, & Lange, 1989). Much of the research conducted to date has assumed that alcohol/drug use is the same for men and women and thus has overlooked possible differences in how men and women come to use chemicals, in how recreational chemicals affect them, and in what impact addiction might have on them.

As we will see in Chapter 21, the problem of child and adolescent drug and alcohol abuse is a serious one, yet there still is virtually no research on drug abuse/ addiction in children or adolescents. Children and adolescents are not simply small adults, and it is not possible to generalize automatically from research done on adults to the effects of substance abuse on children or adolescents.

Thus, much of what we think we know about addiction is based on research that is quite limited, and many important questions remain to be answered. Yet this is the foundation on which an entire "industry" of treatment has evolved. It is not our intent to deny that large numbers of people abuse drugs or that such drug abuse carries with it a terrible cost in personal suffering. Nor do we deny that many people are harmed by drug abuse. Rather, the purpose of this section is to make the reader aware of the shortcomings of the current body of research on substance abuse.

The State of the Art: Unanswered Questions, Uncertain Answers

As the reader has discovered by now, there is much confusion in the professional community over the problems of substance abuse/addiction. Even in the case of alcoholism, which is perhaps the most common of the drug addictions, there is uncertainty about what the essential features of alcoholism might be. For example, 30–45% of all adults will have at least one transient alcohol-related problem (blackout, legal problem, etc.) (Kaplan, Sadock & Grebb, 1994). Yet this does not mean that 30–45% of the adult population is alcohol-dependent! Rather, it underscores the need for researchers to identify more clearly the features that the potential alcoholic might exhibit.

What constitutes a valid diagnosis of chemical dependency? Another unanswered question is how to distinguish among casual use of a given chemical, problem use of the same chemical, and addiction to that substance. There are no clear lines that separate problematic and nonproblematic use of a recreational substance. Instead, as Vaillant (1983) suggested for the problem of alcoholism, "it is not who is drinking but *who is watching*" (p. 22, italics added) that defines whether a given person is alcohol-dependent. In the final analysis, a diagnosis of drug addiction may be called a value judgment. Forming this professional opinion might be made easier by lists of suggested criteria, such as the American Psychiatric Association's *Diagnostic and Statistical Manual of Mental Disorders*, 4th edition (*DSM-IV*), but even in rather advanced cases of drug dependency, it is not always clear whether the individual is addicted.

The Harvard Mental Health Letter (1995a) identified three elements necessary to the diagnosis of alcoholism or drug addiction:

1. *Compulsion/loss of control:* the person will use more of the chemical in question than she or he intended,

or is unable to cut back on the amount used, or is unable to stop using the chemical in question.
2. *Tolerance* to the effects of the chemical(s), including withdrawal symptoms when use of the chemical is stopped.
3. *Impairment:* a physical disease, which is to say one of many possible medical, social, psychological, legal, or vocational complications caused by use of the chemical. Included in this criterion is the concept of preoccupation with further use of the chemical and the organizing of one's recreational activities around the chemical.

The diagnosis of chemical dependency is still, in the final analysis, an opinion, formed by a professional, about another person's chemical use. The issue of assessing another individual's substance use pattern will be discussed in a later chapter. There is still much to be learned about how best to assess a person's chemical use pattern and arrive at an accurate diagnosis.

What is the true relationship between alcohol/drug use and violence within the family? In the last chapter, we noted that there is a relationship between alcohol/drug use and violence within the family. It is wrong automatically to assume, however, that the alcohol use *caused* the violence. Indeed, there is evidence that, at least in some families, the violence might have taken place even if one or more members of that family did not use alcohol (Steinglass, Bennett, Wolin, & Reiss, 1987). In such families, it is possible that both the alcohol use and the violence reflect the presence of yet another form of familial dysfunction that has yet to be identified. Behavioral science has a great deal more to learn about the true relationship between violence in the family and alcohol/drug abuse.

What is the role of news media in the development of new trends in chemical use? One of the most serious unanswered questions facing mental health and substance abuse professionals is whether the media exert a positive or a negative influence on those who have not started to experiment with alcohol or drugs. There is a prohibition against chemical use, coupled with legal sanctions against the importation or use of many drugs. Accordingly, the sale or use of drugs (or of alcohol, for those under the legal drinking age) is "newsworthy."

It is possible that media reports have served to make these drugs appear more attractive to many who might not otherwise have been motivated to try them. Media coverage of drug arrests, of the dangers associated with the use of various chemicals, and of the profits associated with the sale of controlled substances contributes to a certain aura of mystery and "charm" that surrounds the street drug world.

It is also possible that their being "forbidden fruit" enhances the appeal of drugs. The outcome of a Dutch experiment in dealing with the drug problem (see Chapter 35) supports the theory that when the legal sanctions against drug use are removed, they actually become *less* attractive to the average individual, and casual drug use declines. For many years in Holland, substance abuse was seen not as a legal problem but from a public health perspective. It was only after large numbers of foreign chemical users moved to Holland to take advantage of this permissiveness that Dutch authorities began to apply law enforcement as a means of controlling substance use.

Summary

In this chapter, the concept of a continuum of drug use was introduced. Research studies outlining the extent of the problem of the abuse of various drugs were reviewed, along with studies that identified the extent of the problem of addiction to different chemicals. The direct and hidden costs of chemical use/abuse were explored. Apart from economic impact of substance abuse, it is important that society not lose sight of the effect it has on the individual's spouse, on family members, and on the entire community. Unanswered questions about chemical abuse were raised, and we discussed the media's role in the evolution of the substance abuse problem.

CHAPTER THREE

The Medical Model of Chemical Addiction

Introduction

Later in this text, the various major drugs of abuse will be discussed. However, merely knowing what each drug of abuse might do to the user does not help us answer some crucial questions: (1) Why do people *begin* to use these chemicals? (2) Why do people *continue* to use recreational chemicals? (3) Why do people *become addicted* to them? In this chapter, we will examine these questions from the perspective of what has come to be known as the "medical," the "biomedical," or the "disease" model of addiction.

Why Do People Abuse Chemicals?[1]

At first, this question might seem rather simplistic. People use drugs because the drugs of abuse make them feel good. Because many continue to search for drug-induced pleasure, the drugs of abuse have become part of our environment. The prevailing atmosphere of chemical use/abuse then forces each one of us to decide whether to use recreational chemicals. For most of us, this choice is relatively simple. Usually the decision not to use chemicals did not even require conscious thought. But, whether or not the individual acknowledges the need to make a decision, each person is faced with the opportunity to use recreational chemicals each day and must decide whether to engage in recreational chemical use.

[1]This question refers not to those people who are addicted to chemicals but to those who use chemicals for recreational purposes.

Stop for a moment, and think: Where is the nearest liquor store? If you wanted to do so, where could you buy some marijuana? If you are above the age of about 15, the odds are very good that you can answer both of these questions. But why did you (or why didn't you) go out and buy any of these chemicals on your way to work, or to school this morning? Why did you (or why didn't you) buy a recreational drug or two on your way home last night? The answer is that you made a choice to do so (or not to do so). In one sense, then, the answer to the question of why people use the drugs of abuse is because they choose to. But there are a number of factors that influence the individual's decision whether to use recreational chemicals, and we will discuss these factors in the next section.

Factors That Influence Recreational Drug Use

The physical reward potential. Actually, the question of why a person might use alcohol or another drug of abuse is rather complex. The novice chemical user may make the decision to try one or more drugs in response to peer pressure, or, because that individual anticipates that the drug will have pleasurable effects. Researchers call this the "pharmacological potential," or the "reward potential" of the chemical (Meyer, 1989a). Not surprisingly, virtually all of the drugs of abuse have a high reward potential (Crowley, 1988), and the subjective experience of their use is pleasure or euphoria. To illustrate this point, consider that cocaine's effects have been likened to that of sexual orgasm by some users, and that the "rush" from intravenously administered heroin has been described in similar terms. Indeed, so powerful is cocaine for some users that they prefer the drug to a human lover!! On a similar note, it is not unusual for AA members to speak of alcohol as their "best friend" (Knapp, 1996, p. 96).

The basic laws of behavioral psychology hold that if something: (a) increases the individual's sense of pleasure, or (b) decreases his or her discomfort, then he or she is likely to repeat that behavior. This process is called *reward process*. In contrast to the reward process, if a certain behavior (c) increased the individual's sense of discomfort, or (d) reduced the person's sense of pleasure, he or she would be unlikely to repeat that behavior. This is called the *punishment potential* of the behavior in question. Finally, the immediate consequence (either reward or punishment) has a stronger impact on behavior than delayed consequence. When these rules of behavior are applied to the problem of substance abuse such as cigarette smoking, one discovers that the immediate consequences of chemical use (that is, the immediate pleasure) have a stronger impact on behavior than the delayed consequences (i.e. possible disease at an unspecified later date). Within this context, it should not be surprising to learn that, since many people find the effects of the drugs of abuse[2] pleasurable, they will be tempted to use them again and again.

The social-learning component of drug use. Individuals do not start life expecting to abuse chemicals. Consider marijuana abuse. First-time marijuana users must be taught by their drug-using peers (1) how to smoke it, (2) how to recognize the effects of the drug and (3) why marijuana intoxication is so pleasurable (Kandel & Raveis, 1989). The same learning process takes place with the other drugs of abuse, including alcohol. It is not uncommon for a novice drinker to become so ill after a night's drinking that he or she swears never to drink again. However, more experienced drinkers will help the novice learn how to drink, what effects to look for, and why these alcohol-induced physical sensations are so pleasurable. This feedback is often informal, and "drinking buddies," newspaper articles, advertisements, television programs, conversations with friends and coworkers, and casual observations of others who are drinking all contribute.

[2]Obviously, the OTC analgesics are exceptions to this rule, since they do not cause the user to experience "pleasure." However, they are included in this text because of their significant potential to cause harm.

Individual expectations as a component of drug use. The individual's expectations for a drug strongly influence how that person interprets the effects of that chemical. It has been found, for example, that drinkers' expectations for alcohol are more strongly influenced by the context in which they drank, and by cultural traditions, than by the pharmacological effects of the alcohol consumed (Lindman, Sjoholm and Lang (2000). The individual's expectations for alcohol are formed during childhood or in the early years of adolescence—well before she or he actually begins to experiment with chemicals (Smith, 1994).

During adolescence and early adulthood, these drug use expectations play a powerful role in shaping the individual's drug/alcohol use. For example, it has been found that those individuals who became "high-risk drinkers" (Werner, Walker, & Greene, 1995, p. 737) by the end of their junior year in college had significantly stronger expectations that alcohol use would be a positive experience for them than did nondrinkers or those whom the authors classified as "low-risk" (p. 737) drinkers. In the case of LSD abuse, novice LSD users are more likely to anticipate negative consequences from the drug than are more experienced users. This anxiety seems to help set the stage for the negative drug experience known as the "bad trip."

In some cases the individual's expectations about the use of a specific drug are so negative that she or he will not even contemplate using that compound. (This is often seen in cases of children who grew up with a violent, abusive, alcoholic parent and subsequently vowed *never* to use alcohol themselves. Although this is an extreme response to the issue of personal alcohol use, it is not uncommon. But more often than not, the individual's expectations about alcohol/drugs can be modified by both personal experience and social feedback. For example, an adolescent with initial misgivings about drinking who nevertheless found alcohol's effects pleasurable would be more likely to continue to use alcohol during adolescence (Smith, 1994). After their first use of a recreational chemical, people's preconceptions, combined with feedback from others, help shape their interpretation of the chemical's effects, and they become either more or less willing to engage in the use of that compound in the future.

Cultural/social influences on patterns of chemical use. The individual's decision whether to use a recreational chemical is made within the context of the community and the social group(s) to which she or he belongs (Rosenbloom, 2000). There are five levels at which the individual's cultural heritage might affect his or her chemical use (Pihl, 1999): the general cultural environment, the specific community in which the individual lives, subcultures within that specific community, family/peer influences, and the context within which alcohol/drugs are used. At each of these levels, factors such as the availability of recreational substances, combined with prevailing attitudes and feelings, combine to govern the individual's use of mood-altering chemicals (Kadushin, Reber, Saxe, & Livert, 1998; Westermeyer, 1995).

One indication of the powerful effect of cultural influences on the individual's chemical use is Peele's (1985) suggestion that

> [in] cultures where use of a substance is comfortable, familiar, and socially regulated both as to style of use and appropriate time and place for such use, addiction is less likely and may be practically unknown. (Peele, 1985, p. 106)

Unfortunately, in contrast to the rapid rate at which trends in drug use spring up, cultural guidelines might require generations or centuries to evolve (Westermeyer, 1995).

An interesting transition is emerging from the Jewish subculture, especially in the ultraorthodox sects. Only certain forms of alcohol are blessed by the local rabbi as having been prepared in accordance to Jewish tradition and thus are considered "kosher." Recreational drugs, on the other hand, are not considered kosher and are forbidden (Roane, 2000). Yet as the younger generation explores new behaviors, many are experimenting with the "unclean" chemicals that they hear about through non-Jewish friends and the mass media. Significant numbers of these individuals are becoming addicted to recreational chemicals, in spite of the religious sanction against their use, in large part because their education failed to warn them of the addictive powers of these compounds (Roane, 2000).

In the Italian-American subculture, drinking is limited mainly to religious or family celebrations, and excessive drinking is strongly discouraged. The "proper" (*i.e.*, socially acceptable) drinking behavior is modeled by the adults during religious or family activities, and there are strong familial and social sanctions against failing to follow these rules. As a result of this process of social instruction, the Italian-American subculture has a relatively low rate of alcoholism.

Kunitz and Levy (1974) explored the different drinking patterns of the Navaho and Hopi tribes. This study is significant in that these cultures live in close geographic proximity and share similar genetic histories. Navaho tribal customs hold that public group drinking is acceptable, whereas solitary drinking is a mark of deviance. For the Hopi, however, drinking is more likely to be a solitary experience, for alcohol use is not tolerated within the tribe, and those who drink are shunned. These two groups clearly demonstrate how different social groups develop different guidelines for alcohol use.

This discussion has been largely limited to the use of alcohol because alcohol is the recreational drug most commonly used in the United States. However, this is not always true for other cultural groups. For example, Native Americans of the southwestern United States frequently ingest mushrooms with hallucinogenic potential during religious ceremonies. In many cultures in the Middle East, alcohol is prohibited, but the use of hashish is quite acceptable. In both cultures, strict social rules exist that dictate when these substances may be used, under what conditions they may be used, and what the penalties for unacceptable substance use are.

The point to remember is that cultural rules provide the individual with a degree of guidance about acceptable/unacceptable substance use. But within each culture, there are various social groups that may adopt the standards of the parent culture only to a limited degree. The relationship between different social groups and the parent culture might be viewed as shown in Figure 3.1.

Social feedback mechanisms and drug use. A subtle and often overlooked feedback mechanism exists between individuals and the social groups they belong to. The individual's behavior is shaped, at least in part, by any social group to which he or she belongs, but the individual also helps shape the behavioral expectations of that social group by choosing to belong to it. In other words, individuals who abuse certain chemicals tend to associate with others who abuse those same compounds and to avoid people whose substance abuse pattern is different from their own. An example of this might be found in the pattern of cocaine abuse that has evolved

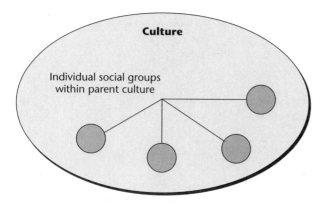

FIGURE 3.1 Relationship between different social groups and the parent culture.

in the United States: "Crack" cocaine is found mainly in the inner cities, whereas powdered cocaine is found more often in the suburbs.

Although most people do not think in terms of cultural expectations, their behavior *does* parallel these themes. Consider the "closet" alcohol abusers who go to a different liquor store each day to hide the extent of their drinking from sales staff (Knapp, 1996) or who sneak around the neighborhood at night hiding empty alcohol bottles in neighbors' trash cans. These individuals are attempting to project an image of their alcohol use that is closer to social expectations than to reality.

A fact often overlooked in substance abuse research is that chemical use patterns are not fixed. People often change their alcohol/drug use pattern over time. For example, if one were to question large numbers of those who used marijuana and hallucinogenics during the "hippie" era (the late 1960s to the mid-1970s), most of these former drug users would say something to the effect that this drug use was simply "a phase I was going through." Unfortunately, there are also those who find that the chemical's effects are desirable enough to encourage further abuse, in spite of social sanctions against its use. In such cases, it is not uncommon for such individuals to drift toward social groups wherein the use of that drug is encouraged and supported, in what amounts to either a conscious or an unconscious attempt to restructure their social environment so that it supports their chemical use.

Individual life goals as helping to shape chemical use. Another factor that influences the individual's decision whether to begin or continue the use of chemicals is whether the use of a specific drug or drugs is consistent with his or her long term goals or values. This is rarely a problem with socially approved drugs, such as alcohol and (to a lesser extent) tobacco. But consider the dilemma of a junior executive who has just won a much anticipated promotion, only to find that the new position is with a division of the company that has embraced a strict "no smoking" policy.

In this hypothetical example, the executive might find that giving up smoking was not as hard as she had once thought, if this was part of the price that she had to pay to accept the promotion. She has evaluated the issue of to what degree further use of tobacco is consistent with her life goal of achieving a major administrative position with a large company. An alternative would have been to search for a new position rather than accept the restriction on cigarette use. An individual who made that choice would have considered the promotion and decided that the cost of giving up cigarettes outweighed those of making a major lifestyle change. Figure 3.2 is a flow chart of the decision-making process a person might engage in when deciding whether to use alcohol/drugs.

Note, however, that we are discussing the individual's decision to use alcohol or drugs on a recreational basis. People do not plan to become addicted to alcohol or drugs. Thus the factors that *initiate* chemical use are not the same factors as those that *maintain* chemical use (Zucker & Gomberg, 1986). For example, a person might begin to abuse narcotic analgesics because these chemicals help him or her deal with painful memories. However, after that individual has become physically addicted to the narcotics, fear of withdrawal may be one reason why he or she continues to use the drugs.

What Do We Mean When We Say That Someone Is "Addicted" to Chemicals?

Surprisingly, in light of the ease with which people speak of the "medical model" of alcohol/drug addiction, there is no single definition of addiction to alcohol/drugs, and a universally accepted, comprehensive theory of addiction has yet to be developed. In this text, we define addiction in terms of the criteria outlined in the American Psychiatric Association's (2000)

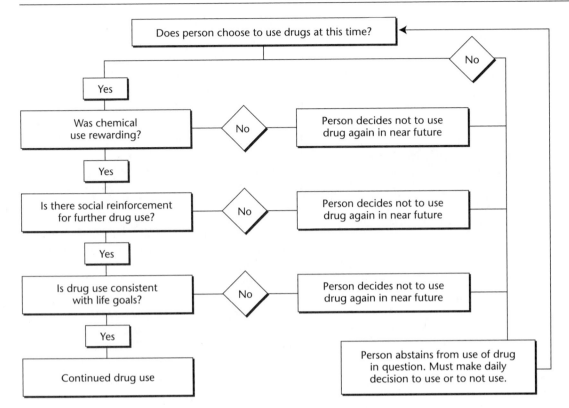

FIGURE 3.2   The chemical use decision-making process.

Diagnostic and Statistical Manual of Mental Disorders-TR (4th edition -Text Revision), or *DSM-IV-TR*. According to the *DSM-IV-TR*, the signs of alcohol/drug addiction include

1. *Preoccupation* with use of the chemical between periods of use.
2. *Using more of the chemical* than had been anticipated.
3. *The development of tolerance* to the chemical in question.
4. A *characteristic withdrawal syndrome* from the chemical.
5. *Use of the chemical to avoid or control withdrawal symptoms.*
6. *Repeated efforts to cut back or stop* the drug use.
7. *Intoxication at inappropriate times* (such as at work) or *withdrawal interfering with daily functioning* (as when a hangover makes a person too sick to go to work).

8. A *reduction in social, occupational, or recreational activities* in favor of further substance use.
9. *Continuation* of chemical use in spite of the individual having suffered social, emotional, or physical problems related to drug use.

Any combination of four or more of these signs is taken to indicate that the individual suffers from the "disease" of addiction. The "disease model" of substance abuse—or the "medical model," as it is also known—holds that (1) addiction is a medical disorder, as much as cardiovascular disease or a hernia, (2) there is a biological predisposition toward addiction, and (3) the disease of addiction is progressive. The "disease" model of drug addiction rests on the assumption that some people have a biological vulnerability to the effects of a certain chemical or chemicals, which is expressed as a loss of control over their use (Foulks & Pena, 1995).

The Medical Model of Drug Addiction

The medical model reflects the belief that much of behavior is based on the individual's biological predisposition. Thus, if the individual behaves in a way that society views as inappropriate, the medical model suspects that a biological dysfunction is responsible for this "pathology." However, there is no single, universally accepted disease model that explains alcohol/drug abuse. Rather, there are a group of loosely related theories postulating that alcohol and drug abuse and addiction are the outcome of an unproven biomedical or psychobiological process—and thus are "disease" states.

The disease model of chemical dependency has not met with universal acceptance. It has even been suggested that the issue of whether addiction is a true disease is nothing more than a "turf battle" between the mental health and medical professions (Goodwin & Warnock, 1991, p. 485). In spite of such criticism, however, the treatment of chemical addiction in the United States is considered to fall within the realm of medicine. In this section, we will discuss the disease model of addiction, along with some of the research that according to proponents of this treatment model, supports their belief that the compulsive use of chemicals is a true disease.

Jellinek's work. The work of E. M. Jellinek (1952, 1960) has had a profound impact on how alcoholism[3] has been viewed by physicians in the United States. Prior to the American Medical Association's decision to classify alcoholism as a formal disease in 1956, it was seen as a moral disorder. Alcoholics were viewed as immoral individuals both by society in general and by the majority of physicians. In contrast to this, Jellinek (1952, 1960) and a small number of other physicians argued that alcoholism was a disease, just like cancer or pneumonia. The characteristics of this disease, according to Jellinek, included the individual's loss of control over his or her drinking, a specific progression of symptoms, and the fact that if it was left untreated, alcoholism would result in the individual's death.

In an early work on alcoholism, Jellinek (1952) suggested that the addiction to alcohol progressed through four stages. The first of these stages, which he called the *prealcoholic* phase, was marked by the individual's use of alcohol for relief from social tensions encountered

[3]See Appendix 3.

during the day. In the prealcoholic stage, one sees the roots of the individual's loss of control over his or her drinking, in that the individual is no longer drinking merely on a social basis. The individual who continues to engage in "relief drinking" for an extended period of time enters the second phase of alcoholism, the *prodromal* stage (Jellinek, 1952). This second stage of alcoholism was marked by the development of memory blackouts, secret drinking (also known as hidden drinking), a preoccupation with alcohol use, and feelings of guilt over one's behavior while intoxicated.

With the continued use of alcohol, the individual eventually becomes physically dependent on alcohol, a hallmark of what Jellinek (1952) called the *crucial* phase. Other symptoms of this third stage of drinking were a loss of self-esteem, a loss of control over one's drinking, social withdrawal in favor of alcohol use, self-pity, and a neglect of proper nutrition while drinking. During this phase, the individual would attempt to reassert his or her control over alcohol by entering into periods of abstinence, only to return to the use of alcohol after short periods of time. Finally, with continued alcohol use, Jellinek (1952) thought the alcoholic would enter the chronic phase. The symptoms of the chronic phase included moral deterioration, drinking with social inferiors, the development of motor tremors, an obsession with drinking, and, for some, the use of substitutes (such as rubbing alcohol) when "safe" alcohol was not available. Figure 3.3 is a graphical representation of these four stages of alcoholism.

In 1960 Jellinek presented a theoretical model of alcoholism that was both an extension and a revision of his earlier work. According to Jellinek (1960), the alcoholic was often unable to predict in advance how much he or she would drink at any given time. Jellinek viewed alcoholism as having specific symptoms, which included the physical, social, vocational and emotional complications often experienced by the compulsive drinker. Further, Jellinek continued to view alcoholism as having a progressive course that, if not arrested, would ultimately result in the individual's death.

In his 1960 book, however, Jellinek also attempted to classify different patterns of addictive drinking. Like Dr. William Carpenter in 1850, Jellinek had come to view alcoholism as a disease that might be expressed in a number of different forms, or styles, of drinking (Lender, 1981). Unlike Dr. Carpenter, who thought

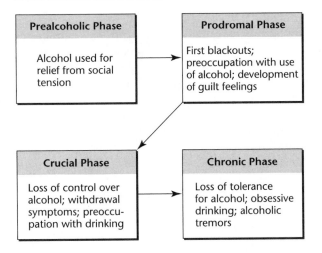

FIGURE 3.3   Jellinek's four stages of alcoholism.

that there were three types of alcoholics, Jellinek identified five subforms of alcoholism. Jellinek used the first five letters of the Greek alphabet to identify the most common forms of alcoholism found in the United States. Table 3.1 offers a brief overview of his theoretical system.

Advanced in an era when the majority of physicians viewed alcohol dependency as being caused by a moral weakness, Jellinek's (1960) model of alcoholism offered physicians a new paradigm. First, it provided a diagnostic framework, within which physicians could classify different patterns of drinking, to replace the restrictive dichotomous view in which the patient was simply alcoholic or not. Second, Jellinek's (1960) model of alcoholism as a physical disease made it worthy of study and made the person with this disorder worthy of "unprejudiced access" (Vaillant, 1990, p. 5) to medical treatment. Finally, the Jellinek model attributed the individual's use of alcohol not to a failure of personal will power but to the fact that the drinker suffered from a medical disorder (Brown, 1995).

Ever since the Jellinek (1960) model was introduced, researchers have struggled to determine whether it is valid. Sobell and Sobell (1993) found a clear-cut progression in the severity of the individual's drinking in only 30% of the cases they studied. In the same year, Schuckit, Smith, Anthenelli, and Irwin (1993) found that there *was* clear evidence of a progression in the severity of problems experienced by the alcohol-

dependent men in their research sample. But, the authors added, there was remarkable variation in the specific problems encountered by their subjects, which suggests that alcohol-dependent individuals do not exhibit a *single* progressive pattern. Thus the research data supporting the Jellinek model continues to be mixed.

The genetic inheritance theories. In the past 20 years, "compelling evidence" (Li, 2000, p. 5) of a genetic predisposition toward alcoholism has been uncovered. One such study was conducted by Tsuang, Lyons, Meyer, Doyle, Eisen, Goldberg, True, Lin, Toomey, and Eaves (1998), who concluded that both genetic and environmental factors predisposed their subjects toward the abuse of *classes* of chemicals. The authors also found that there were variations in the manner in which either the environment or genetic inheritance influenced the use of a specific compound. But each class of drug was associated with a unique genetic predisposition, which, according to the authors, may explain why different individuals seem "drawn" to very specific drugs of abuse.

In a study that underscored the impact of cultural expectations on genetics, Kendler, Thornton, and Pedersen (2000) utilized the growth records of Swedish twins raised together, and of twins raised apart, to determine whether there was evidence that tobacco use was genetically influenced. The authors found strong evidence of a genetic predisposition toward tobacco use in some of their subjects. In the case of Swedish women, the authors found that as the social restrictions against the use of tobacco products by women slowly relaxed, more and more women with the suspected genetic predisposition indulged in the use of tobacco products.

A landmark study still cited as evidence of genetic predispostion toward substance abuse is that of Cloninger, Gohman, and Sigvardsson (1981). Drawing on the records of 3000 individuals who were adopted, the authors discovered that the children of alcoholic parents were likely to grow up to be alcoholic themselves, even in cases where the children were reared by nonalcoholic adoptive parents almost from birth. The authors also found that the children who grew up to be alcoholic essentially fell into two groups. The first subgroup was made up of three-quarters of the children whose parents were alcoholic and who themselves went on to develop alcohol use disorders. During young adulthood, these individuals drank in

TABLE 3-1   Comparison of Jellinek's Drinking Styles

Type of alcoholism	Alpha	Beta	Delta	Gamma	Epsilon
Psychological dependence on alcohol?	Yes	Yes	Yes	Yes	Possibly, but not automatically
Do physical complications develop?	No	Yes	Minimal to no physical complications	Multiple and serious physical problems from drinking	Possibly, but rare because of binge pattern of alcohol use
Tolerance to the effects of alcohol?	No	No	Yes. Person will "crave" alcohol if forced to abstain from use.	Yes. Person will "crave" alcohol if forced to abstain from use.	Possibly, but rare because of binge pattern of alcohol use
Can the individual abstain from alcohol use?	For short periods of time, if necessary	For short periods of time, if necessary	No. Person has lost control over his or her alcohol use	No. Person has lost control over his or her alcohol use	Yes. Person is able to abstain during periods between binges
Is this pattern of drinking stable?	Yes	Yes	Yes	Yes	Unknown*
Is this pattern of drinking progressive?	In rare cases, but not automatically	Possibly, but not automatically	Strong chance of progression to gamma, but not automatic	No. This is an end-point style of drinking	Unknown*
If so, to what pattern will this style of drinking progress?	Gamma	Gamma	Gamma	Not applicable	Unknown*

*According to Jellinek (1960), the epsilon style of drinking was the least common in the United States and only limited information about this style of drinking was available to him.

moderation. It was only later in life that their drinking progressed to the point where they could be classified as alcohol-dependent. Even so, Cloninger, Gohman, and Sigvardsson (1981) found that these individuals tended to function within society and were rarely involved in antisocial behaviors. The authors classified these individuals as "Type I" (or "Type A" or "late onset") alcoholics (Gastfriend & McLellan, 1997; Goodwin & Warnock, 1991).

Cloninger, Gohman, and Sigvardsson (1981) found that there was a strong environmental impact on the possibility that the adopted child would be alcoholic. For example, the authors found that if they were adopted by a middle-class family in infancy, children of

alcoholic parents had only a 50–50 chance of being alcoholic in adulthood. Although this is markedly higher than what one would expect, given that only 3% of the general population is alcohol-dependent, it is lower than the outcome found for children of alcoholic parents who were adopted and raised by parents who were poor. The authors interpreted these findings as evidence of a strong environmental influence on the evolution of alcohol use, despite the individual's genetic inheritance.

The second, smaller group of alcoholics found by this research team were more violent, male alcoholics who were more likely to be involved in criminal activity. These individuals were classified as having "Type II" (or "male limited," "Type B", or "early onset") alcoholism (Gastfriend & McLellan, 1997; Goodwin & Warnock, 1991). A male child born to a "violent" alcoholic had nearly a 20% chance of himself becoming alcoholic, no matter what the social status of the child's adoptive parents. Because a male child whose father was a "violent" alcoholic stood a significantly greater chance of himself becoming dependent on alcohol than what one would expect on the basis of chance alone, the authors concluded that there was a strong genetic influence for this subgroup of alcoholics.

In 1996, Sigvardsson, Bohman, and Cloninger (1996) successfully replicated this earlier study on the heritability of alcoholism. The authors examined the adoption records of 557 men and 600 women who were born in Gothenburg, Sweden, and who were adopted at an early age by nonrelatives. The authors confirmed their earlier identification of two distinct subtypes of alcoholism for men. Further, they found that these two subtypes appear to be independent, but possibly related, forms of alcoholism. Where one would expect, on the basis of population statistics, 2–3% of their sample to have alcohol use problems, the authors found that 11.4% of their male sample fit the criteria for Type I alcoholism, and 10.3% of the men in their study fit the criteria for Type II alcoholism. However, in contrast to the original studies, which suggested that Type II alcoholism was limited to males, there is now evidence that a small percentage of alcohol-dependent women might also be classified as Type II alcoholics (Cloninger, Sigvardsson, & Bohman, 1996; Del Boca, & Hesselbrock, 1996).

The distinction between Type I and Type II alcoholics has lent itself to a series of research studies designed to identify possible personality traits unique to each group of alcohol dependency. Researchers have found that as a group, Type I alcoholics tend to engage in harm-avoidance activities, whereas Type II alcoholics tend to be high in the novelty-seeking trait (Cloninger, Sigvardsson, & Bohman, 1996). Other researchers have found that Type I and Type II alcoholics differ in brainwave activity on the electroencephalograph (EEG). Further, as a group, Type I alcoholics tend to have higher levels of the enzyme monoamine oxidase (MAO) than Type II alcoholics. It was hypothesized that this lower MAO level in Type II alcoholics might account for their tendency to be more violent than Type I alcoholics (Cloninger, Sigvardsson & Bohman, 1996).

Using a different methodology and a research sample of 231 substance abusers, 61 control subjects, and 1267 adult first-degree relatives of these individuals, Merikangas, Stolar, Stevens, Goulet, Preisig, Fenton, Zhang, O'Malley, and Rounsaville (1998) found evidence of "an 8-fold increased risk of drug [use] disorders among relatives of probands with drug disorders" (p. 977). According to the authors, there was evidence of familial predisposition toward the abuse of specific substances, although they did admit that the observed familial clustering of drug abuse "could be attributable to either common genetic or environmental factors" (p. 977). According to the authors, such environmental factors might include impaired parenting skills, marital discord, stress within the family unit, and/or physical/emotional/sexual abuse, as well as exposure to parental chemical abuse at an early age. These findings were supported by an independent study conducted by Bierut, Dinwiddie, Begleiter, Crowe, Hesselbrock, Nurnberger, Porjesz, Schuckit, and Reich (1998). These authors suggested that "a general addictive tendency" (p. 987) was transmitted within the family unit, but they could not be more specific about the nature of this genetic predisposition toward alcohol/substance abuse. Other researchers have concluded that 48–58% of the risk for alcoholism is based on the individual's genetic inheritance, at least for males (Prescott & Kendler, 1999). Researchers have also found evidence that within each family, forces are at work that seem to help shape the individual's choice of recreational chemical(s) to abuse (Merikangas *et al.*, 1998; Bierut *et al.*, 1998).

The biological differences theories. Over the past 50 years, a number of studies have suggested that those who are alcohol-dependent are somehow different biologically from those who are not. This research is far too extensive to discuss in detail, but in general it suggests that alcohol-dependent individuals metabolize alcohol differently from nondependent drinkers, that the site or mechanism of alcohol biotransformation is different in the alcoholic, or that alcoholics react differently than nonalcoholics to the effects of that chemical.

The implication that there is a biological difference between alcoholics and nonalcoholics has inspired a number of research studies conducted in an effort to determine what differences might exist between alcoholic and nonalcoholic individuals. One example is the study conducted by Ciraulo, Sarid-Segal, Knapp,

Ciraulo, Greenblatt, and Shader (1996). The authors selected a sample made up of 12 women who were adult daughters of alcoholic parents and 11 women whose parents were not alcohol-dependent. Then they administered to their subjects either a 1-mg dose of the benzodiazepine alprazolam or a placebo. The authors found that among the women who received the alprazolam, those who had alcoholic parents found it more enjoyable than did those whose parents were not alcohol-dependent. This finding, along with an earlier study conducted by the same team on male subjects, was consistent with the results of Tsaung *et al.* (1998), who found evidence of vulnerability to entire classes of recreational drugs rather than to specific chemicals.

In the 1990s, as the technology developed to the point where such research could be attempted, different teams of investigators explored the possibility that one of the five subtypes of the dopamine receptor might be involved in addiction to alcohol/drugs. Much of this research has focused on the *dopamine D_2 receptor gene* and on whether variations in this receptor site are associated with increased risk for alcoholism. In one such study, Blum, Noble, Sheridan, Montgomery, Ritchie, Jagadeeswaran, Nogami, Briggs, and Cohn (1990) examined the prevalence of the dopamine D_2 receptor gene in samples of brain tissue from 70 cadavers. Half of the brain tissue samples were from known alcoholics, half from individuals known not to have been addicted. The authors found that 77% of the alcoholics, but only 28% of the nonalcoholics, possessed the dopamine D_2 receptor gene, a result that suggests a genetic basis for alcohol use.

In an extension of the original research, Noble, Blum, Ritchie, Montgomery, and Sheridan (1991) examined tissue samples from the brains of 33 known alcoholics and a matched group of 33 nonalcoholic controls. On the basis of their "blind" study of the genetic makeup of the tissue samples,[4] the authors concluded that there was strong evidence of a genetic foundation, involving the D_2 dopamine receptor, for severe alcoholism. (As we shall see in the next chapter, however, these studies have been challenged by other researchers.) On the basis of this and subsequent research, Blum, Cull, Braverman, and Comings (1996) argued that such behavioral disorders as alcoholism, drug abuse/addiction, cigarette smoking, pathological gambling, Tourette's syndrome, and obesity were all reflections of a "reward deficiency syndrome" in which the brain's reward system failed to function appropriately. The authors hypothesized that a defect in the A_1 subtype of the dopamine D_2 receptor gene was pivotal in the development of the so-called reward deficiency syndrome, which expressed itself behaviorally as an inability on the part of the individual to derive pleasure from everyday activities.

Marc Schuckit (1994) used a different approach to try to identify biological predictors of alcoholism. In the early 1980s, the author tested 227 men who were the sons of alcoholics. He found that 40% of the sons of alcoholics, but only 10% of the men who did not have an alcoholic parent, were "low responders" to a standard dose of alcohol. The author found that the "low responders" did not seem to have been as strongly affected as the individuals in the control group by the alcohol they received. Ten years later, the author was able to contact 223 of the original sample of men who were raised by alcoholic parents. Of the men who had had an abnormally low response to the alcohol challenge test, 56% had become alcoholic. Of the men who were raised by alcoholic parents but had not demonstrated an abnormally low physiological response to a standard dose of alcohol, only 14% had become alcoholic in the decade since the original examination (Schuckit & Smith, 1996; Schuckit, 1994).

These data were interpreted to suggest that low responders were somewhat insensitive to the effects of alcohol and might therefore drink more often, and to consume more alcohol per session, than individuals who were not low responders (Schuckit, 1994). As will be discussed in the next chapter, however, although this study does seem to suggest some significant differences between those who do, and those who do not, become alcoholics, it does not reveal what biochemical factors predict the later development of alcoholism.

Researchers presently believe that there is strong evidence for a genetic predisposition toward addictive disorders but that environmental factors must interact with the individual's genetic heritage to allow that disorder to develop (Barondes, 1999). And so far, researchers have identified no *unequivocal* biochemical or biophysical difference between those who are and those who are not addicted to one or more chemicals.

[4]See the Glossary.

The Personality Predisposition Theories of Substance Abuse

Many researchers believe that substance abuse might be traced back to the individual's personality structure. This perspective is known as the *characterological model* of addiction (Miller & Hester, 1995). An example of this perspective on substance use disorders is the theory that the ego structure of some individuals would "predispose them to depend on substances" (Murphy & Khantzian, 1995, p. 1689). Proponents of this theory hold that the addictions are an unintended side effect of the process of self-medication, in which the individual uses recreational chemicals as a way of coping with emotional states that are overwhelming, confusing, or simply too painful to face, only to realize agonizingly at a later time that she or he has stumbled into physical dependence on that chemical (Shaffer & Robbins, 1995; Murphy & Khantzian, 1995).

An early proponent of this model was Karen Horney (1964), who spoke of alcohol as being a way to "narcotize" (p. 45) anxiety. "In other words," suggested Khantzian, Mack, and Schatzberg (1999),

> the more familiar pathways to stability and predictability in personality organization, whether healthy or pathological, have been supplanted by the stability of the moment that can be provided by the drug and all of the attendant rituals, practices and pseudo-culture that are involved with its use. (p. 24)

As a result of this process of seeking immediate relief at the expense of long-term adjustment, the addictive disorders evolve from the individual's attempts to control overwhelming feelings of helplessness and narcissistic rage (Murphy & Khantzian, 1995; Khantzian, Mack, & Schatzberg, 1999). Ultimately, people become addicted to the very chemical(s) that they had initially used to help them control these painful emotions. As shown in Table 3.2, other modern psychoanalysts interpret substance abuse as a way to counter a wide range of emotional states.

In support of the psychoanalytic model of addiction, there is an impressive body of evidence suggesting that individuals who abuse chemicals *have* suffered significant psychological trauma in their lives. For example, ongoing research suggests a relationship between the individual's having been physically and/or sexually

TABLE 3-2   Ego State and Drug of Choice

Class of chemical being abused	*Affective state that chemical of abuse is thought to control*
Alcohol and CNS depressants (barbiturates, benzodiazepines, etc.)	Loneliness, emptiness, isolation
Opiates (heroin, morphine, etc.)	Rage and aggression
CNS stimulants (cocaine, amphetamines, etc.)	Depression, a sense of depletion, anergia (sense of no energy), low self-esteem

Source: Based on Murphy & Khantzian (1995).

abused during childhood or adolescence and his or her later development of a substance use disorder (Miller & Downs, 1995). Such victimization is thought to contribute to the development of lifelong patterns of emotional distress, which the individual then attempts to self-medicate through the use of alcohol and/or chemicals (Kaufman, 1989).

Even if the child is not abused by his or her primary caregivers, the child's family might still be so dysfunctional that it virtually prevents normal development for its members. In such cases, the individual often finds that recreational chemical use provides a means to escape, if only for a short time, the shame experienced as a result of the emotional distress in the family (Bradshaw, 1988a). If the individual compulsively uses the same method to cope with emotional pain time after time, the seeds of addiction take root.

In order to explore the premise that there was a relationship between the father's alcohol dependency and early-onset alcohol abuse in boys, Dobkin, Tremblay, and Sacchitelle (1997) examined data from 13-year-old boys, some of whom had an alcoholic father and some of whom did not. The authors did not find that sons of male alcoholics were at increased risk for alcohol use problems at the age of 13. On the basis of their research, they concluded that the mother's parenting style and whether the boy engaged in disruptive behavior(s), but not the father's alcoholism, were indicative of increased risk for alcohol use disorders for the sample of 13-year-old boys in this study. These findings were supported, in part, by Masse and Tremblay (1997), who examined the personality characteristics of students at ages 6, age 10, and adolescence to see whether there were personality features that predicted which individuals would engage in recreational drug use. The authors found that those students who scored highest in the characteristic of novelty seeking and lowest in harm avoidance tended to be the individuals who, as adolescents, engaged in the use of cigarettes and recreational drugs. Low harm avoidance is a trait that might express itself through disruptive behaviors, providing partial support for the study completed by Dobkin, Tremblay, and Sacchitelle (1997).

The theory that some individuals are predisposed to abuse recreational chemicals as they try to come to terms with otherwise intolerable emotional states is intuitively appealing. According to this theory, those individuals who are prone to abuse narcotics tend, as a group, to suffer from an untreated depressive disorder that predisposes them to using narcotics (Franklin, 1987). Further, it is through the use of opiates that they are able to experience a more nearly normal emotional state. In this way, the narcotics provide these individuals with an illusion of control over their depression—at least until they discover that they are addicted to the substance that once allowed them to "control" their feelings.

Section summary. A number of researchers have suggested that there are certain personality characteristics that predispose the individual toward alcoholism or other forms of chemical abuse. Indeed, certain personality traits do appear to be associated with substance use disorders. However, it is difficult to determine whether these personality traits precede the development of drug dependency or result from the frequent use of illicit chemicals. No clearly identified causal factor has yet been found, and research into possible personality factors that might predispose one toward alcohol or substance abuse continues.

Summary

This chapter has explored some of the leading theories that attempt to answer the question of why people use recreational chemicals and why they become addicted to these drugs. Several factors that help to modify the individual's substance use pattern were explored, including the physical reinforcement value of the drugs being abused, their social reinforcement value, the cultural rules that govern recreational chemical use, and the individual's life goals.

The "medical" or "disease" model of addiction has come to play an important role in the treatment of substance abuse in this country. Based on the work of E. M. Jellinek, the "disease" model of alcoholism has come to be applied to virtually every other form of substance abuse as well. Jellinek viewed alcoholism as a disorder that progressed through specific stages. At a time when the alcoholic was regarded as a social failure who resorted to the bottle out of moral weakness, Jellinek suggested that the alcoholic suffered from a disease that, if not treated, would result in death. In time, the field of medicine came to accept this new viewpoint, and alcoholism came to be seen as a medical disorder.

Since the early work of Jellinek, other researchers have attempted to identify the specific biophysical dysfunction that forms the basis for the addictive disorders. Most recently, drawing upon medicine's growing understanding of human genetics, scientists have tried to identify the genetic basis for alcoholism and the other forms of drug addiction. To date, however, the exact biochemical or genetic factors that predispose one to become addicted have not been identified.

CHAPTER FOUR

Are People Predestined to Become Addicted to Chemicals?

Introduction

The disease model of substance addiction, which was discussed in the last chapter, has not met with universal acceptance. Indeed, there are many health care professionals and scientists who maintain that there are no biological or personality traits that *automatically* predispose the individual to abuse chemicals. Some researchers question the contention that alcohol/drug addiction is a true "disease." Others concede that there is evidence of biological or psychosocial predispositions toward substance abuse but maintain that certain environmental forces are needed to activate the biopsychosocial predisposition toward addiction. In this chapter, some of these reactions against the "disease" model of substance abuse will be examined.

Multiple Models

Although the medical model dominates the field of substance abuse rehabilitation in the United States, there are a number of other theoretical systems that also address the problem of alcohol/drug abuse. Some of them are reviewed in Table 4-1.

Reaction Against the Disease Model of Addiction

It is tempting to speak of the medical model, or "disease model," of alcohol/drug abuse as though there were a single, universally accepted definition of substance use problems. But in reality, there are philosophical differences in how physicians view the same disease. For example, treatment protocols for a condition such as a myocardial infarction (heart attack) might vary from one hospital to another, because of the differing treatment philosophies for that disorder at the different health care facilities.

Many of those who challenge the "disease" model of addiction focus their attack on how *disease* is defined. In the United States, *disease* is defined as reflecting a biophysical dysfunction of some kind that interferes with the normal functioning of the body. In an infectious process, a bacterium, virus, or fungus invading the host organism would be classified as a disease by this criterion. Another class of diseases are those occasioned by a genetic disorder that causes abnormal growth or functioning of the individual's body. A third class of diseases are those where the optimal functioning of the organism is disrupted by acquired trauma.

As noted in previous chapters, behavioral scientists largely agree that there is a genetic "loading" for alcoholism, although the exact nature of predisposition has not been clearly identified (Goodwin & Warnock, 1991). It is argued that if such a genetic predisposition exists for alcoholism, then one must exist for all forms of substance addiction, because alcohol is just one of a variety of recreational chemicals. If it is true that there is a genetic predisposition for addictive behaviors, then chemical dependency is very much like the other physical disorders where there is a genetic predisposition. In this sense, substance abuse might be said to be a "disease," which is what E. M. Jellinek proposed in 1960.

TABLE 4.1   Theoretical Models of Alcohol/Drug Abuse

	Moral model	*Temperance model*	*Spiritual model*	*Dispositional disease model*
Core	The individual is viewed as choosing to use alcohol in problematic manner.	This model advocates the use of alcohol in moderate manner.	Drunkenness is a sign that the individual has slipped from his or her intended path in life.	The person who becomes addicted to alcohol is somehow different from the non-alcoholic. The alcoholic might be said to be allergic to alcohol.
	Educational model	*Characterological model*	*General systems model*	*Medical model*
Core	Alcohol problems are caused by a lack of adequate knowledge about harmful effects of this chemical.	Problems with alcohol use are based on abnormalities in the personality structure of the individual.	People's behavior must be viewed within context of social system in which they live.	The individual's use of alcohol is based on biological predispositions, such as his or her genetic heritage, brain physiology, and so on.

Source: Chart based on material presented by Miller & Hester (1995).

Reaction to the Jellinek model.[1] Although the Jellinek (1960) model was a theoretical model of *alcoholism*, it has also been applied to virtually every other pattern of drug abuse/addiction. Yet, in addition to the fact that it never was designed as an comprehensive theory of addiction, there are serious flaws in the Jellinek model. One of the most striking flaws is that Jellinek based his work on surveys that were mailed out to members of Alcoholics Anonymous (AA). Only 98 of the 1600 copies of the surveys mailed out were returned (a return rate of just 6%). It was on the data generated from these 98 returned surveys that Jellinek based his model of alcoholism. In so doing, Jellinek violated several basic principles of behavioral research. First, he made the faulty assumption that those individuals who were members of AA were the same as nonmembers. There are differences between those who do, and do not, belong to this self-help organization. If one major difference between these two groups exists, then one must assume that there are other differences as well.

Second, one must not assume that individuals who volunteer to participate in a research study are representative of the population as a whole. The volunteers are different from those who were asked to participate, but who did not do so, if only by the fact that they *did* volunteer to take part in the research study. If there is one

major difference between groups, there may very well be other significant differences. Jellinek violated this rule of research by making the assumption that those individuals who participated in his study were the same as those who did not return the questionnaire.

Thus Jellinek's research was flawed from the start. It should not be surprising that researchers have started to question his conclusions. For example, one of the cornerstones of the Jellinek (1960) theory is that alcoholism is a progressive disorder. Other researchers, using different methodologies, have found mixed evidence and have not been able to confirm that alcoholism is progressive (Skog & Duckert, 1993). Researchers now believe that the progression of alcoholism suggested by Jellinek develops only in a minority (25–30%) of cases (Sobell & Sobell, 1993; Toneatto, Sobell, Sobell, & Leo, 1991). The reality seems to be that alcoholism is "often [but not automatically] progressive" (Morse & Flavin, 1992, p. 1013), with the alcohol-dependent individual alternating between periods of abusive and nonabusive drinking. Illicit drug use also tends to follow a variable course (Toneatto, Sobell, Sobell, & Rubel, 1999).

On the basis of the data generated by his 98 completed questionnaires, Jellinek assumed that the individual eventually experienced a *loss of control* over his or her alcohol use. Again, subsequent research has failed to support this conclusion, and researchers now believe that alcohol-dependent individuals tend to

[1] See Appendix 3.

demonstrate *in*consistent control over their drinking, rather than a loss of control (Toneatto, Sobell, Sobell, & Leo, 1991; Vaillant, 1990).

The genetic inheritance theories. In the last 35 years, a growing body of research has developed that suggests a *possible* biological predisposition toward alcohol/drug dependence. The research evidence is far from conclusive, and many researchers still question whether there is a genetic basis for even the most common form of drug dependency, alcoholism (Hill, 1995). In spite of this, proponents of the medical model point to research studies such as that of Cloninger, Gohman, and Sigvardsson (1981) to support their contention that there is a biological predisposition toward alcoholism.

Yet the methodology that was utilized by Cloninger, Gohman, and Sigvardsson (1981) was later found to be seriously flawed, casting doubt on the authors' conclusions concerning the heritability of alcoholism (Hall & Sannibale, 1996). For example, Cloninger *et al.* (1981) claimed that the alcohol-dependent males in their study fell into two different subgroups, the Type I/Type II typology discussed in the last chapter. However, Hall and Sannibale (1996) found that fully 90% of the alcohol-dependent individuals who are admitted to treatment actually have characteristics of *both* Type I *and* Type II alcoholics.

It should also be noted that although the original intent of the study by Cloninger, Gohman, and Sigvardsson (1981) was to explore the genetics of alcoholism, the authors also uncovered strong evidence suggesting that environmental forces help to shape alcohol use disorders. Even in cases where the child's genetic inheritance seemed to predispose him or her to alcoholism, if the child had been adopted by a middle-class family in infancy, the odds of the child's actually being alcoholic in adulthood were no greater than chance alone. However, if the child had been adopted into a poor family, the chances were greater that she or he would grow up to be an alcoholic. These findings suggest a strong environmental influence on the evolution of alcoholism, in spite of the individual's genetic inheritance, for Type I alcoholism. Because of this environmental influence, some researchers call Type I alcoholism *milieu-limited alcoholism.*

In contrast to the Type I alcoholics identified by Cloninger, Gohman, and Sigvardsson (1981) were the Type II, or *male-limited,* alcoholics. These individuals tend to be both alcoholic and involved in criminal behaviors. The male offspring of a "violent" alcoholic adopted in infancy ran almost a 20% chance of himself becoming alcohol-dependent regardless of the social status of his adoptive parents. However, here again the statistics are misleading. Although nearly 20% of the male children of a "violent alcoholic" themselves eventually became alcoholic, more than 80% of the male children born to these fathers did *not* follow this pattern. This would suggest that additional factors, such as environmental forces, may play a role in the evolution of alcoholism for Type II alcoholics.

Several teams of researchers have attempted to identify the degree to which the individual's genetic heritage influences the development of alcohol/drug use disorders. The results of these investigations consistently reveal that 40–60% of the individual's "risk" of developing an alcohol/drug use disorder appears to be mediated by genetics; the remainder is due to unidentified environmental forces (Prescott & Kendler, 1999; Kender, Heath, Neale, Kessler, & Eves, 1992; Pickens, Svikis, McGue, Lykken, Heston, & Clayton, 1991). To illustrate the impact of the environment on alcohol use disorders, consider the fact that there are significant variations in the male:female ratio of those who are alcohol-dependent in different cultures around the world. In the United States, the male:female ratio for alcohol use disorders is about 5.4:1. In Israel, this same ratio is approximately 14:1, whereas it is 9.8:1 in Puerto Rico, and 29:1 in Taiwan. In South Korea the male:female ratio for alcohol use disorders is 20:1, and it is 115:1 in the Yanbian region of China (Hill, 1995). These differing ratios underscore the strong impact that social/cultural forces have on the evolution of alcohol use disorders in various parts of the world.

On the basis of research to date, it is clear that *both* a biological predisposition toward alcohol addiction and strong environmental influences help to shape the individual's pattern of alcohol use. But there is still a great deal to be discovered about the evolution of substance use disorders, as evidenced by the fact that for reasons that are not understood, up to 60% of known alcoholics come from families where there is no prior evidence of alcohol dependency (Cattarello, Clayton & Leukefeld, 1995).

Does genetics rule? There has been a great deal of research conducted with the goal of isolating the "alcohol gene." Such a simplistic view of alcoholism as being caused by a genetic disorder serves only to confuse the average person. In reality, the individual's genetic heritage does not control his or her behavior; it guides the production of a protein or proteins within the cell (Sapolsky, 1997). Only rarely does one of these proteins "cause" a specific behavior. It is much more common for these genetically controlled proteins to produce a *tendency* for the individual to respond to the environment in a specific manner (Sapolsky, 1997).

Another misconception commonly encountered in the behavioral sciences is the belief that genetic predisposition is unalterable. In the field of substance abuse rehabilitation, for example, counselors speak knowingly of a patient's "genetic loading" for an addictive disorder because relatives are themselves addicted to alcohol/ drugs. In reality, the popular belief that "one gene = one unchangeable behavior" is a misconception (Alper & Natowicz, 1992; Sapolsky, 1997). The genetic predisposition toward a certain condition does not guarantee that it will develop (Sapolsky, 1998; Sapolsky, 1997; Holden, 1998). The evidence suggests that the genetic predisposition toward alcohol/drug addiction has "incomplete penetrance, which means you can have the genes but not be an alcoholic" (Holden, 1988, p. 1349). Thus, predisposition is not predestination (Gordis, 1996b; Cattarello, Clayton, & Leukefeld, 1995). Social, environmental, historical, and cultural forces all play a role in determining whether the genetic potential to develop alcohol/drug addiction will be activated.

In refuting the biological determinist theories of alcoholism, Greene and Gordon (1998) argued that "No 'alcoholism gene' has been discovered, just a bundle of biological risk factors that make alcoholism more or less likely" (p. 35). On a similar note, Tavris (1998) pointed out that "to say that some behavior is 'genetic' rarely means it is inevitable" (p. 42). Finally, even if a certain genetic pattern were found to predispose the individual toward addictive disorders, there would be no specific treatment to reverse or control the impact of that genetic inheritance on the individual (Chiauzzi, 1991). The identification of a genetic pattern predisposing the individual toward addictive disorders would simply serve to identify a *risk factor* for the development of a substance use disorder.

The dopamine D_2 receptor site connection. Researchers have uncovered mixed evidence suggesting that the dopamine D_2 receptor is involved in the development of alcohol/drug addiction (Volkow, Wang, Fowler, Logan, Gatley, Gifford, Hitzemann, Ding, & Pappas, 1999). These authors found that subjects who enjoyed the effects of a test dose of methylphenidate had lower levels of dopamine D_2 receptor sites in their brains than did those individuals who reported that the drug's effects were unpleasant. It was concluded that individuals with lower levels of dopamine D_2 receptor sites in their brains might be vulnerable to stimulant abuse problems, because they would find the drug's effects rewarding. The authors also concluded that individual variation in the number of dopamine D_2 receptor sites in the brain might account for the different responses that their volunteers had to the test dose of methylphenidate.

Even if the dopamine D_2 connection does play a major role in the biochemistry of addiction,

> Knowing that drug dependence has a neurochemical basis does not tell us why some people but not others use drugs regularly and heavily, why they use them in some circumstances and not others, and why different people prefer different drugs. (*The Harvard Mental Health Letter*, 1992a, p. 2)

Rather, the importance of the D_2 receptor gene theory must be viewed in light of the fact that

> finding genetic differences in susceptibility to drug abuse or addiction does not imply that there is an 'addiction gene' which dooms unfortunate individuals to become hopeless drug addicts. (George, 1999, p. 99)

In the last chapter, a recent study by Marc Schuckit (1994) was presented as evidence of a biological predisposition toward alcohol abuse/dependence on the part of certain men. In this study, the author reexamined 223 men who had, when tested a decade earlier, demonstrated an abnormally low physical response to a standard dose of an alcoholic beverage. At the time of his earlier study, Schuckit had found that fully 40% of the men who had been raised by alcoholic parents, but only 10% of the control group, demonstrated this unusual response.

A decade later, in 1993, the author found that 56% of the men who had the abnormally low physiological response to alcohol had progressed to the point of alcoholism. The author interpreted this finding as evidence that the abnormally low physical response he had found to a standard dose of an alcoholic beverage might serve as a biological "marker" for alcoholism. But only a minority of the men who had been raised by an alcoholic parent demonstrated this abnormally low physiological response to the alcohol challenge test. Only 91 men of the experimental group of 227 men had this abnormal response. Further, a full decade later, only 56% of these 91 men (just 62 men of the original sample) appeared to have become dependent on alcohol. Thus, although Schuckit's (1994) study is suggestive of possible biochemical mechanisms through which alcoholism might develop, it also illustrates quite clearly that biological predisposition does not predestine the individual to develop an alcohol use disorder.

Other challenges to the disease model of addiction. No matter how you look at it, addiction remains a most curious "disease." Even Vaillant (1983), who has long been a champion of the disease model of alcoholism, had to concede that alcoholism had to be "shoehorned" into the disease model (p. 4). Further, even if alcoholism is a disease, "both its etiology and its treatment are largely social" (Vaillant, 1983, p. 4). This trait would seem to suggest that alcohol dependency is an unusual disorder. For example, after following a group of alcoholic males for 50 years, Vaillant (1995) concluded that in at least some cases, genetics determines whether an individual is going to become dependent on alcohol, whereas the social environment determines when this transition may occur.

The possibility has been suggested that what we call "addictions" actually represent the misapplication of existing neurobiological reward systems (Rodgers, 1994). According to the author, evolution allowed for the development in animals of a "reward system" to reinforce behaviors that contributed to survival, such as eating, reproduction, and drinking water. This makes evolutionary sense: Those organisms that could reward themselves for doing something that enhanced survival would seem to be better likely to survive than animals who lacked this ability. Unfortunately, this reward system is sometimes fooled, by such chemicals as alcohol, opiates, and cocaine, into operating when survival-enhancing activities are not in progress. Sometimes, by coincidence, some chemical happens to be able to trig-

ger the reward system even when the person is not involved in a survival-enhancing activity.

> The inescapable fact is that nature gave us the ability to become hooked because the brain has clearly evolved a reward system, just as it has a pain system. (S. Childers, as quoted in Rodgers, 1994, p. 34)

From this perspective, we might all be said to have the potential to become addicted, because we are all biologically "wired" with a reward system. However, it is not yet known why some people are trapped more easily than others by the ability of chemicals to activate the reward system.

In the United States, the manufacturers of alcohol-containing beverages spend an estimated $1 billion a year to promote their products. If alcohol abuse/dependency is indeed a disease, then why is the use of the offending agent, alcohol, promoted through commercial means? The answer to this question raises some interesting questions about the role of alcohol within this society and about the classification of excessive alcohol use as a disease.

The medical model and individual responsibility. Modern medicine "always gives the credit to the disease rather than the person" (B. Siegel, 1989, p. 12), and this is certainly true for the addictive disorders (Tavris, 1990; Peele, 1989). For example, Pratt (1990) suggested that "Activation of the disease of addiction, once an individual is exposed to activating agents, is genetically predetermined" (p. 18). From this perspective, once the individual has been exposed to the "activating agents," he or she ceases to exist except as a genetically preprogrammed disease process! For example, in an article on an adolescent who developed a chemical use problem, it was noted that one parent was a pharmacist, the other a physician. The parents, identified as the "Lowells," were

> well-versed in the clinical aspects of substance abuse, [but were] . . . outmaneuvered by the cunning that so often accompanies addiction. (Comerci, Fuller, & Morrison, 1997, p. 64)

This quotation is an excellent example of how modern medicine tends to give credit to the disease rather than the person. Note that the adolescent substance abuser is totally absolved of any responsibility for attempting to manipulate his parents! The same assumption appears in the concept behind methadone maintenance. Proponents of methadone maintenance have suggested that even a single dose of narcotics would forever change the brain structure of the opiate-dependent individual, making him or her crave more opiates (Dole, 1988; Dole & Nyswander, 1965).

Now, if narcotics are so incredibly powerful, how can we account for the thousands of patients who receive doses of narcotics for the control of pain, for extended periods of time, without developing a "craving" for narcotics after their treatment is ended? Further, even patients who receive massive doses of narcotic analgesics only rarely report a sense of euphoria or feel the urge to continue their use of opioids (Rodgers, 1994). This would seem to cast some doubt on Dole and Nyswander's (1965) theory that exposure to narcotic analgesics causes changes in the people's brains that make them want to use these chemicals again. In addition to this, there are many individuals who "chip" (occasionally use) narcotics for years without becoming addicted to these drugs. Nevertheless, the whole concept upon which methadone maintenance is based is the belief that narcotics are so powerful that a single dose erases the individual's power of self-determination.

Another example of the manner in which the medical model makes the disease all-powerful appears in the following statement:

> Alcohol and a few other chemicals found in nature can stealthily commandeer the brain's pleasure center in some people, in effect robbing them of their willpower. (Kotulak, 1997, p. 1)

There are many who view the addictive disorders as being "a brain disease. The behavioral state of compulsive, uncontrollable drug craving, seeking, and use comes about as a result of fundamental and long-lasting changes in brain structure and function" (Leshner, 1997a, p. 691). Yet when one speaks with alcohol-dependent persons, they readily agree that they can resist the craving for alcohol *if the reward for doing so is high enough*. Many alcoholics successfully resist the desire to drink for weeks, months, years, or decades. If one can resist the impulse to use, *if the re-*

ward is high enough, does the substance rob the individual of his or her willpower?

One central feature of the medical model of illness is that once a person has been diagnosed as having a certain "disease," she or he is expected to take certain steps towards recovery. According to the medical model, the "proper way to do this is through following the advice of experts [e.g., doctors] in solving the problem" (Maisto & Connors, 1988, p. 425). Unfortunately, as we saw in Chapter 1, physicians are not required to be trained in either the identification or the treatment of the addictions. The medical model of addiction thus lacks internal consistency: although medicine claims that addiction is a "disease," it does not routinely train its practitioners in how to treat this ailment.

What Exactly *Are* the Addictive Disorders?

Proponents of the disease model often point out that Dr. Benjamin Rush first suggested that alcoholism was a disease 200 years ago. What they do not point out, however, is that the very definition of *disease* has changed since the time of Dr. Rush. In his day, a disease was anything classified as being able to cause an imbalance in the nervous system (Meyer, 1996). Alcohol is certainly capable of causing such an "imbalance," or disruption in the normal function of the CNS. Thus, by the standards applied by Benjamin Rush in the 1700s, alcoholism was indeed a disease.

However, by the criteria used by modern physicians, the issue is not so clear. Indeed, there still is no standard definition of what constitutes an addictive disorder. Further, some health care radicals question whether the compulsive use of a chemical can actually be said to be a disease. For example, the most common form of drug addiction, alcoholism, was called simply a "bad habit" by Thomas Szasz (1972, p. 84) a quarter of a century ago. The addictive use of chemicals has been described simply as "a bad habit that is especially difficult to change" (*The Harvard Mental Health Letter*, 1992b, p. 2). Admittedly, it is up to the individual to try to overcome bad habits, but this does not make such a habit a disease (Szasz, 1972). The author went on to warn that "if we choose to call bad habits 'diseases,' there is no limit to what we may define as a disease" (p. 84).

By the late 1980s, society had reached the point where there was no apparent limit on what might be called a disease. The addictions have been converted into diseases (alcoholism), [and] bad habits . . . upgraded and transformed into addictions (yesterday's hard-to-break smoking habit is today's nicotine addiction). (Leo, 1990, p. 16)

The outcome of this transformation has been the birth of a multitude of "pseudo ailments" (Leo, 1990, p. 16), through which people have been able to avoid admitting responsibility for a variety of socially unacceptable behaviors. Or, in the words of Gilliam (1998), we "have all become a nation of blamers, whiners, and victims, all too happy, when we get the chance, to pass the buck to someone else for our troubles" (p. 154).

Further, as Ehrenreich (1992) observed, one of the benefits of modern medicine is that although we might not "have a cure for every disease, alas, . . . there's no reason we can't have a disease for every cure" (p. 88). There are many examples of this process at work. For example, the concept of an "anxiety disorder" was only a theoretical construct of Freud's, first suggested in the era after World War II. Physicians in the 1950s expressed little interest in medication(s) that treated anxiety (Shenk, 1999). Then suddenly, a whole range of antianxiety agents, such as Miltown, Valium, and Xanax, were developed and aggressively marketed as treatments for this theoretical disorder, and within a single generation, one woman in five was taking a medication for control of her "anxiety disorder" (Shenk, 1999). In much the same manner, now that the treatment industry has established itself, why not discover other "diseases" for which the Twelve-Step model might be applied? Not surprisingly, this is just what has happened. The Twelve-Step model pioneered by AA has now been applied to more than 100 different conditions that at least some people believe are forms of addiction (*The Harvard Mental Health Letter*, 1992b). But this does not mean that all of these different socially inappropriate behaviors are actually diseases. Indeed, there are those who still challenge the concept that alcohol/drug use disorders themselves are diseases (Szasz, 1988; Kaiser, 1996).

A point that is often overlooked is that *neither alcohol nor drugs are the enemy*. By itself, a chemical has no inherent value (Shenk, 1999; Szasz, 1997, 1996, 1988). Drug molecules are neither good nor evil. *It is the way in which they are used by the individual* that determines whether they are helpful or harmful. To complicate

matters further, society has made an arbitrary decision to classify some drugs as dangerous, and others as acceptable for social use. The antidepressant medication Prozac (fluoxetine) and the hallucinogen MDMA both cause select neurons in the brain to release the neurotransmitter serotonin and then block its reabsorption. Surprisingly, although fluoxetine is an antidepressant, a small but significant percentage of those patients taking this drug do so because they desire its mood-enhancing effects rather than its antidepressant properties (*The Economist*, 1996). This raises a dilemma: If a pharmaceutical is being used by a person only because he or she enjoys its effects, where is the line between the legitimate need for that medication and its abuse?

The basis on which this distinction is made is often not scientific studies, but "religious or political (ritual, social) considerations" (Szasz, 1988, p. 316). Because it is apparent that people *desire* the recreational drugs for their effects, it would seem that the current "war" on drugs is really a "war on human desire" (Szasz, 1988, p. 322). The dilemma is not so much that people use chemicals, according to Szasz, but that people desire to use them for personal pleasure. Indeed, some find it "hard, in fact, to think of a single social ritual that does not revolve around some consciousness-altering substance" (Shenk, 1999, p. 43). Because of this fact,

[the] desire to take mood-altering substances is an enduring feature of human societies worldwide and even draconian legislation has failed to extinguish this desire—for every substance banned another will be discovered, and all are likely to have some ill-effect on health. ("Dangerous Habits" 1998, p. 1565)

Further evidence supporting Szasz's position might be found in the observation that 1 out of every 131 outpatient deaths in the United States are caused by "drug mistakes" (Friend, 1998). An estimated 300 deaths per day, or 125,000 deaths per year, occur in the United States as a result of adverse reactions to prescribed medications (Pagliaro & Pagliaro, 1998; Lazarou, Pomeranz, & Corey, 1998; Graedon & Graedon, 1996). Another 2.21 million people are injured each year in the United States as a result of mistakes made in the prescription of legitimate pharmaceuticals by health care professionals (Lazarou, Pomeranz, & Corey, 1998). The annual death toll of such "drug mistakes" is five times the number of deaths caused each year by recreational drug use. Yet hardly a whisper is heard from Washington about the impact of drug mistakes, whereas thousands of speeches have been made about the problem of drug misuse.

The unique nature of addictive disorders. In spite of all that has been written about the problem of alcohol/drug use/abuse over the years, researchers continue to overlook a very important fact. Unlike the other diseases, *the substance use disorders require the active participation of the "victim" in order to exist.* The capacity for addiction rests with the individual, not (as so many would have us believe) with the drug itself (Savage, 1993). The addictive disorders do not force themselves on the individual, in the same sense that an infection might. Alcohol and drugs do not magically appear in the individual's body. Rather, the "victim" of this disorder must go through several steps to introduce the chemical into his or her body.

Consider the case of heroin addiction. The addict must obtain the money necessary to buy the drug. Then he or she must find somebody who is selling heroin and actually buy some for use. Next, the "victim" must prepare the heroin for injection (mixing the powder with water, heating the mixture, and pouring it into a syringe), find a vein to inject the drug into, and then insert the needle into the vein. Finally, the individual must then actively inject the heroin into his or her own body. Each step of this rather complicated chain of events involves the active participation of the individual. If it took as much time and energy to catch a cold, pneumonia, or cancer, it is doubtful that any of us would ever be sick a day in our lives!

The team of O'Brien and McLellan (1996) offered a modified challenge to the disease model of the addictions as it now stands. The authors accepted that drug/alcohol addiction is a form of chronic "disease." But they went on to state that although the addictive disorders were chronic diseases like adult-onset diabetes or hypertension, there also were behavioral factors that helped to shape the evolution of these disorders. Thus,

> although a diabetic, hypertensive or asthmatic patient may have been genetically predisposed and may have been raised in a high-risk environment, it is also true that behavioral choices . . . also play a part in the onset and severity of their disorder. (p. 237)

It is the individual's behavior—the decisions that she or he makes, that will help to shape the evolution of the addictive disorders. Ultimately, individuals remain responsible for their behavior, even if they have a "disease" such as addiction (Vaillant, 1990, 1983).

In the past 60 years, proponents of the medical model of alcoholism have attempted to identify the biological foundation for abusive drinking. Over the years, a large number of research studies have been published, many of which have suggested that alcoholics: (1) seem to metabolize alcohol differently than nonalcoholics, or (2) seem to be relatively insensitive (or, depending on the research study, more sensitive) to the effects of alcohol, when compared to nonalcoholics. Proponents of the medical model of addiction often point to these studies as evidence of a biological predisposition toward alcoholism.

However, the truth is that in spite of a significant amount of research, no *consistent* difference has been found in the rate of metabolism, the route by which addicted and nonaddicted individuals biotransform chemicals, or the susceptibility of addicted and nonaddicted individuals to the effects of recreational chemicals. Although substance abuse rehabilitation professionals talk about the "genetic predisposition" toward alcohol/drug use disorders as though it were a proven fact, scientists still have virtually no idea how individual genes or groups of genes affect the individual's behavior (Siebert, 1996). In the words of David Kaiser (1996),

> modern psychiatry has yet to convincingly prove the genetic/biologic cause of any single mental illness. However, this does not stop psychiatry from making essentially unproven claims that . . . alcoholism . . . [is] in fact primarily biologic and probably genetic in origin, and that it is only a matter of time until . . . this is proven. (p. 41)

Thus, at this point, it does not appear that the disease model of addiction as it now stands provides the ultimate answer to the question of why people become addicted to chemicals.

The disease model as theory. In the time since it was first introduced, the disease model of drug addiction has experienced a remarkable metamorphosis: Although it was first introduced as a *theoretical* model of alcoholism, it has evolved into the standard model for the treatment of virtually all forms of drug addiction. Further, although the medical model of addiction is but one of several competing theoretical models, proponents speak of it not as a *theoretical* model but as an established fact.

Admittedly, the disease model might provide "a useful metaphor or reframe for many clients" (Treadway, 1990, p. 42), to help them understand their compulsion. But Treadway warned that mental health professionals become rather "uncomfortable when it is presented as scientific fact." In reality, the disease model reflects a theoretical tenet of modern medicine: *All forms of suffering are caused by physical disorder of some kind* (Breggin, 1998). In spite of rather vocal claims about the scientific nature of the medical model,

> psychiatrists as medical doctors have always claimed that everything they happen to be treating is biological and genetic. [These] claims, in other words, are nothing new. . . . They are inherent in the medical viewpoint. In reality, not a single psychiatric diagnosis, including schizophrenia and manic-depressive disorder, have been *proven* to have a genetic or biochemical origin. (Briggin, 1998, p. 173, italics added)

In spite of the lack of proof that the addictive disorders are physical disease states, the theory of the biogenetic foundation of alcoholism, and by extension the other forms of drug addiction, has become dogma. Unfortunately, dogmatists tend rarely, if ever, to question their basic assumptions (Kaiser, 1996). History has demonstrated that once a certain theoretical viewpoint has become established, proponents of that position work to protect that theory from both internal and external criticism (Astrachan & Tischler, 1984). This process may clearly be seen in the disease model of addiction. The current atmosphere is one in which legitimate debate over strengths and weaknesses of the different models of addiction is discouraged.

This tendency for proponents of the disease model to turn a deaf ear to other viewpoints is exacerbated by the fact that in this country, the disease model has become "big politics and big business" (Fingarette, 1988, p. 64). The "disease model" has formed the basis of a massive treatment industry, into which many billions of dollars,

and thousands of worker-years, have been invested. In a very real sense, the biogenetic model has taken on a life of its own (Vaillant, 1983).

In reality, what is surprising is not that the disease model exists but that it has become so politically successful in this country. Consider, for example, the fact that the treatment methods currently in use are those advocated by the proponents of the disease model. Yet these treatment methods have not changed significantly in 40 years (Rodgers, 1994). Imagine the uproar that would result if a physician were to be found using the technology of 40 years ago to treat a disorder such as cancer or cardiovascular disease. Yet in the field of substance abuse rehabilitation, treatment methods have remained essentially static for the past two generations.

Many current treatment methods in use in the field of substance abuse rehabilitation are based not on clinical research but on the somebody's belief that those treatment methods should work (Gordis, 1996a). Given this fact, it should not be surprising that there is strong evidence that current treatment methods for the addictions are less effective than doing *nothing* for the individual (Larimer & Kilmer, 2000).

Proponents of the medical model are hardly likely to go to insurance companies, or to the public, after 60-odd years of claiming that the addictions are diseases, and admit that treatment does not work. Rather, as Peele (1989) pointed out, when the "treatment" of an addictive disorder is unsuccessful, the patient is usually blamed: "She didn't really want to quit," or "He was still in denial" of having an addictive disorder, or any of a thousand other excuses. But the blame is never placed on the disease model, in spite of an extensive body of evidence that suggests that applying it has not been successful in the treatment of the addictive disorders.

Summary of reaction to the disease model of addiction. A welcome breath of fresh air was offered by Miller (1998), who observed that

> In the end, even in more biologically oriented treatment programs, clients in effect are left to use their rational capacities of deciding, accepting, choosing, and controlling themselves. And so they do, by the millions, with or more often without treatment. . . . Motivation [to quit using chemicals] does not seem to be a matter of insurmountable biology. (p. 122)

People in the United States seem to be fascinated with biological explanations for addictive disorders. The available data do seem to point to a biological contribution to substance abuse, but researchers have not been able to identify the specific biological mechanism or genetic pattern that seems to predispose the individual to the addictive use of chemicals. Indeed, in their summary of the current state of this research, Goodwin and Warnock (1991) stated that although alcoholism is known to run in certain families, "We do not believe that alcoholism definitely has been shown to be genetic . . ." (p. 485).

In spite of significant efforts to identify a personality or biological predisposition toward addiction, "there's no proof that anyone is chemically, genetically or psychologically doomed" (*The Wellness Letter*, 1990, p. 2). Increasingly, researchers in the field of behavioral genetics are viewing alcohol dependence as being "polygenic"—a behavior that reflects the input of a number of different genes (Gordis, 1996a). Each of these genes then adds a degree of risk to the individual's total potential for developing an addiction to alcohol. However, environmental influences are also thought to play a significant role in the development of alcohol dependency.

The Personality Predisposition Theories of Substance Abuse

It has long been suspected that personality factors play a role in the development of addiction (Jenike, 1991; Butcher, 1988). There are a number of variations on this "predisposing personality" theme, but all are strongly deterministic in the sense that the individual, because of his or her personality predisposition, is viewed as being powerless to avoid developing an addictive disorder if he or she is exposed to certain conditions.

For example, a number of studies have suggested that alcohol-dependent individuals were more impulsive, anxious, depressed, or prone to taking risks. These personality traits were then traced to disturbances in the dopamine utilization system in the brains of individuals who were alcohol abusers/addicts. To test this hypothesis, Heinz, Dufeu, Kuhn, Dettling, Graf, Kurten, Rommelspacher, and Schmidt (1996) examined the clinical progress of 64 alcohol-dependent individuals and attempted to assess their sensitivity to dopamine through various biochemical tests. In spite of the expected association among depression, anxiety, disturbances in dopamine utilization, and alcohol use problems, the authors found little evidence to support the popular beliefs that alcoholism is associated with depression, high novelty seeking, or anxiety.

The researcher C. R. Cloninger proposed what he termed a "unified biosocial" model of personality, in which certain individuals who were predisposed to exhibit a given personality characteristic (such as risk taking) could have that trait reinforced by social/environmental factors. In other words, Cloninger attempted to identify the interaction between genes and environment (Howard, Kivlahan, & Walker, 1997). Cloninger then applied his theory of personality to the evolution of alcohol use disorders, on the theory that individuals who were high on the traits of harm avoidance (HA), novelty seeking (NS), and reward dependence (RD) would be at risk for alcohol use disorders.

The team of Howard, Kivlahan, and Walker (1997) examined a series of research studies that attempted to relate Cloninger's theory of personality to the development of alcohol abuse/addiction. The authors found that even when a test specifically designed to test Cloninger's theory of personality was used, the results did not clearly support the theory that individuals high on the traits of HA and RD were significantly more likely to have an alcohol use disorder. To date, the personality predisposition theoretical models do not allow for more than a general statement that some personality characteristics might increase the long-term risk that a person will become addicted to chemicals. However, which personality characteristics might predispose the individual to become addicted to alcohol and/or drugs is still not clear. Indeed, in spite of a spirited search for the so-called "alcoholic personality" that has gone on for the past 50 years, such a personality pattern remains elusive at best (Schuckit, Klein, Twitchell, & Smith, 1994; Miller & Kurtz, 1994).

In spite of the fact that researchers have been unable to identify personality characteristics that consistently typify the person who is "at risk" for the development of an addictive disorder, certain clinical myths have developed within the field of substance abuse rehabilitation. For example, in spite of the fact that there is limited evidence to support these beliefs, clinicians continue to operate on the assumptions that (1) alcoholics are developmentally immature, (2) the experience of growing up in a disturbed family helps to shape the personality growth of the future alcoholic, and (3) alcohol-dependent individuals tend to overuse ego defense mechanisms such as denial.

Thus, much of what is called "treatment" in the United States rests on assumptions about the nature of the personality of addicted people that have not been supported in the clinical research. Indeed, in spite of a search that has lasted for more than half a century, researchers still have been unable to identify the characteristics of the "addictive personality" (Miller, 1995; Brown, 1995; Woody, McLellan, & Bedrick, 1995). Traits identified in one research study as being central to the personality of addicted people are found in subsequent studies to be of peripheral importance, and the "alcoholic personality" has been judged to be nothing more than a clinical myth (Stetter, 2000).

In the face of this evidence, one must ask how the myth of the "alcoholic personality" evolved. Nathan (1988) postulated that the characteristics of the so-called addictive personality that were found by earlier researchers actually might reflect a misdiagnosis. The author suggested that previous research confused the antisocial personality disorder (ASPD) (discussed in Chapter 22) with a prealcoholic personality pattern. This is possible, in light of the fact that 84% of those individuals with ASPD have some form of a substance use disorder (Ziedonis & Brady, 1997). Indeed, it has been suggested that substance abuse might be an unrecognized aspect of ASPD (Peele, 1989).

This is not to suggest that the antisocial personality disorder *caused* the substance use. Rather, ASPD and the addiction to chemicals are postulated to be two separate disorders that may coexist in the same individual (Stetter, 2000; Schuckit, Klein, Twitchell, & Smith, 1994). An alternative theory about how people began to believe that there was an addictive personality was suggested by Bean-Bayog (1988). After considering the available evidence, Bean-Bayog (1988) postulated that the so-called alcoholic personality emerged as a consequence of the effect of chronic alcohol use upon the individual's personality pattern, not the other way around. If this theory is true, then all of the research conducted to date on identified addicts has been based on the mistaken assumption that the personality characteristics thought to precede addiction are actually part

of the addictive process. It would be as though researchers had thought for years that the pain of a broken leg caused the injury to the bone, rather than that the pain was a signal of a broken limb!

Another theory suggesting that the "addictive personality" might be a research artifact was advanced by Pihl (1999). The author, drawing on earlier research, pointed out that 93% of the research studies conducted in an attempt to identify whether those persons who had substance use disorders shared common personality traits used samples composed of individuals in treatment for their chemical abuse problems. This suggests that the so-called addictive personality might more accurately be called the "treatment personality," because there is a very real chance that those individuals with an alcohol/drug addiction who do not enter treatment have far different personality traits from those who either ask for treatment or are coerced into seeking it.

At the present time, there is little conclusive evidence that there are personality characteristics that predispose the individual toward alcoholism or drug addiction (Stetter, 2000). However, the study of the whole area of personality growth and development—not to mention the study of those forces that initially shape and later maintain addiction—is still so poorly defined that it is quite premature to try to answer the question of whether there are personality patterns that may precede the development of substance use disorders.

The abuses of the medical model. Unfortunately, since the time of its introduction, the disease model of alcoholism has been misused, or perhaps "misapplied," to the point where

> Judges, legislators, and bureaucrats . . . can now with clear consciences get the intractable social problems caused by heavy drinkers off their agenda by compelling or persuading these unmanageable people to go elsewhere—that is, to get "treatment." (Fingarette, 1988, p. 66)

This is because the substance use disorders exist at the boundary between biological facts and social values (Wakefield, 1992). Indeed, it has been argued that

> [the term] "mental disorder" is merely an evaluation label that justifies the use of medical power (in the broad sense, in which all the professions concerned

with pathology, including psychiatry, clinical psychology, and clinical social work, are considered to be medical) to intervene in socially disapproved behavior. . . . (Wakefield, 1992, p. 374)

Thus the guardians of social order—the courts and the lawyers—have assumed the power to define who has the "disease" of addiction and how it is to be treated. As a result of this transformation of the medical model, it has been suggested that the "War on Drugs" that began in the early 1980s evolved as a politically inspired program to control those individuals who were defined by conservative Republicans as social deviants (Humphreys & Rappaport, 1993). According to Humphreys and Rappaport, the War on Drugs essentially served the Reagan administration as a "way to redefine American social control policies in order to further political aims" (p. 896). By shifting the emphasis of social control away from the community mental health center movement to the War on Drugs, the authors suggested, justification was also found for a rapid and possibly radical expansion of the government's police powers, and the "de facto repeal of the Bill of Rights" (Duke, 1996, p. 47).

Indeed, the charge has been made that the community mental health movement itself has been subverted by government rules and regulations until it has become little more than "an arm of government enforcement" (Cornell, 1996, p. 12). These rather disturbing articles raise serious questions about whether the social problem of chemical abuse and the medical model of addiction were used as an excuse to extend the government's police powers. Most certainly, drivers who operate motor vehicles while intoxicated present a very real problem of social deviance. However, one must question the wisdom of sending the chronic offender to "treatment" time and time again, when his or her acts warrant incarceration. As Peele (1989) has argued, incarceration may help bring about a greater behavior change in these people than would repeated exposure to short-term treatment programs.

In an ideal world, one question the courts would consider is "At what point should treatment be offered as an alternative to incarceration, and when should incarceration be imposed on the chronic offender?" Unfortunately, the courts all too often fail to consider this issue before sending the offender to "treatment" once more.

The Final Common Pathway Theory of Addiction

As should be evident by now, there have been strong challenges to the medical model of substance abuse. Indeed, in their review of the genetics of alcoholism, Crabbe and Goldman (1993) concluded that "there are many factors associated with whether a person becomes an alcoholic, one of which is genetics" (p. 297). At the same time, the psychosocial models of drug use also have been challenged as being too narrow in scope and as not being able to account for the phenomenon of drug/alcohol abuse/addiction.

But there is another viewpoint to consider, one called the *final common pathway* (FCP) theory of chemical dependency. In a very real sense, FCP is a nontheory: It is not supported by any single group or profession. However, the final common pathway perspective holds that substance use/abuse is not the starting point but, rather, a common *end point* of a unique pattern of growth. Thus the FCP theory holds that there is no single "cause" of drug dependency, but a multitude of different factors that may "cause" a given individual to become addicted. These might include social forces, psychological conditioning, an attempt on the part of the individual to come to terms with internal pain, a spiritual shortcoming, or some combination of other factors. The proponents of this position acknowledge a possible genetic predisposition toward substance abuse. But the FCP theory also suggests that people who lack this genetic predisposition to drug dependency may also become addicted to chemicals, if they have has the proper life experiences.

Strong support for the final common pathway model of addiction might be found in the latest neurobiological research results. Over time, evolution has equipped humans (and many other species) with a "reward system" that is activated when the individual engages in some activity that enhances survival (Nesse & Berridge, 1998). The drugs of abuse seem to activate this so-called "pleasure center" of the brain (Gardner, 1997). In effect, the various drugs of abuse "create a signal in the brain that indicates, falsely, the arrival of a huge fitness benefit" (Nesse & Berridge, 1998, p. 64).

An impressive body of research on both animals and humans suggests that the *nucleus accubens*, a subunit of the region of the brain known as the basal ganglia, is part of the brain's reward system (Salloway, 1998; O'Brien, 1997; Fleming, Potter, & Kettyle, 1996; Hyman, 1996; Blum, Cull, Braverman, & Comings, 1996; Restak, 1994). In support of this theory, Salloway (1998) observed that virtually all of the drugs of abuse, including nicotine, stimulate dopamine activity in the nucleus accumbens. But other researchers believe that recreational drugs are able to cause the user to feel pleasure by altering the function of the mesolimbic dopamine system of the brain (Leshner, 1998; Nestler, Fitzgerald, & Self, 1995). This also seems to be the region of the brain most involved in the individual's subjective experience of "craving" for his or her drug of choice, when he or she stops using it, and in drug-seeking behavior (O'Brien, 1997; Nutt, 1996; Anthony, Arria, & Johnson, 1995). Within the brain,

> [the] mesolimbic reward system . . . extends from the ventral tegmentum to the nucleus accumbens, with projections to areas such as the limbic system and the orbitofrontal cortex. (Leshner, 1998, p. 46)

Which is to say that the mesolimbic dopamine system seems to function as a focal point for the brain's reward system, projecting electrochemical messages to the limbic system (where emotions are thought to be generated) and to the frontal cortex (a region of the brain involved with consciousness and planning).

The confusion about the exact brain structures involved in the reward cascade is understandable, for many reasons. First, the human brain is an intricate, complicated organ that is poorly understood. Second, there are few clear boundaries between one brain region and another, which makes it difficult to identify the limits of any one region of the brain. Finally, all of the structures of the brain thought to be involved in the "reward system" are in close physical proximity. For example, the nucleus accumbens is near the striatum, the limbic system, and the base of the frontal lobes (Salloway, 1998).

There still is much to learn about how the drugs of abuse alter brain function. For example, it is known that the current drugs of abuse alter the function of a region of the brain known as the *locus ceruleus*. The locus ceruleus appears to be the region of the brain that coordinates the body's response to both novel external stimuli and internal stimuli that might signal a danger to the individual (Gourlay & Benowitz, 1995). Thus the locus ceruleus will respond to such internal stimuli as blood loss, hypoxia, and pain. The locus ceruleus is also involved in the "fight-or-flight" response of fear and in anxiety. This makes clinical sense, because in ages past, novel stimuli might prove dangerous to the individual (example: a mountain lion running at the observer). It also is not surprising that this region of the brain is involved in the body's response to the various drugs of abuse.

Although different researchers have suggested that different regions of the brain are involved in the addictive process, it is important to remember that they have all identified the *mesolimbic system* as being involved in the pleasure response induced by the various drugs of abuse. They are presently attempting to identify the sequence of brain regions activated by the drugs of abuse; however, the consensus is that the limbic system is one region of the brain where the recreational chemicals induce a feeling of pleasure.

The final common pathway model of addiction views alcohol addiction and drug addiction as common end points. There may be different routes, but eventually, the chemical result is the same: activation of the brain's "pleasure center." Each different class of recreational chemical might also affect other regions of the brain besides the pleasure center, but they all induce a state of pleasure by altering the function of at least part of the limbic system. This is not to say that the individual is just a helpless victim of his or her genetic vulnerability to the reinforcing properties of the drugs of abuse. Rather, *both* a genetic predisposition *and* environmental factors interact to bring about a state of vulnerability to drug abuse. If either element were missing, the individual would be unlikely to become addicted to recreational chemicals.

This, then, is the core element of addiction, according to the final common pathway theory of addiction: Addiction is the common end point for each individual who suffers from the compulsion to use chemicals. In order to treat the addiction, the chemical dependency counselor must identify the forces that brought about, and those that support, this individual's addiction to chemicals. On the basis of this understanding, the chemical dependency counselor might establish a treatment program that will help the individual abstain from further chemical abuse.

Summary

Although the medical model of drug dependency has dominated the treatment industry in the United States, this model is not without its critics. For each study that proports to identify a biophysical basis for alcoholism, or for other forms of addiction, other studies fail to document such a difference. For each study that claims to have isolated personality characteristics that seem to predispose one toward addiction, other studies fail to find these characteristics to have predictive value, or they find that the personality characteristic in question is brought about by the addiction, rather than preceding it.

The medical model of addiction may be useful as a metaphor through which people might better understand their problem behavior. However, the medical model of addiction is a theoretical model, a model that has not been proved. Nor does addiction fit easily into the concept of "disease" as medicine in this country understands the term. Indeed, it is the use to which people put the chemicals that is the problem, not the drugs themselves.

CHAPTER FIVE

Addiction as a Disease of the Human Spirit

Introduction

To some, addiction is best understood as a disease of the "spirit." For example, the concept of alcoholism as a spiritual disorder forms the basis of the Alcoholics Anonymous program (Miller & Hester, 1995; Miller & Kurtz, 1994). From this perspective, to understand the reality of addiction is ultimately to understand something of human nature. Unfortunately, modern society, especially Western medicine, tends to disparage matters of the spirit (Sims, 1994). When the subject is brought up, the "enlightened" person turns away, as though embarrassed by the need to discuss spiritual matters. To such a person, the spirit is viewed as a remnant of our specie's primitive past, much like spears or clothing made of animal skins.

The word "spirit" is derived from the Latin word *spiritus*, which means the divine, living force within each of us. In the human, life—spiritus—has become aware of itself as being apart from nature and from others (Fromm, 1956). But with self-awareness comes the painful understanding that we are all forever isolated from our fellows. Fromm termed this awareness of one's basic isolation an "unbearable prison" (1956, p. 7), in which are found the roots of anxiety and shame. "The awareness of human separation," wrote Fromm, "without reunion by love—is the source of shame. It is at the same time the source of guilt and anxiety" (p. 8).

A flower, a bird, or a tree cannot help but be what its nature ordains. A bird does not think about being a bird or what kind of a bird it might become. The tree does not reflect about being a tree. But each person possesses the twin gifts of self-awareness and self-determination. Each can, within certain limits, be aware of himself or herself, and decide his or her fate.

These gifts, however, carry a price. Fromm (1956, 1968) viewed people's awareness of their fundamental aloneness as being the price that they had to pay for the power of self-determination. We have come to know that we are different from the animal world and isolated from the rest of the universe. In becoming aware of "self," we came to know loneliness. It is only through the giving of "self" to another through love that Fromm (1956, 1968) envisioned people as transcending their isolation, to become part of a greater whole.

Merton (1978) came to take a similar view on the nature of human existence. Yet Merton clearly understood that one could not seek happiness through the compulsive use of chemicals. He discovered that "there can never be happiness in compulsion" (1978, p. 3). Rather, happiness may be achieved through the love that is shared openly and honestly with others. Martin Buber (1970) took an even more extreme view, holding that it is only through our relationships that our life has definition. Each individual stands "in relation" to another. The degree of relation, the relationship, is defined by how much of the "self" one offers to another and how much of another's "self" one receives in return.

The reader might question what relevance this material has to a text on chemical dependency. The answer is that the early members of Alcoholics Anonymous came to view alcoholism (and, by extension, the other forms of addiction) as a disease. However, they saw the disease of addiction to alcohol (and, by extension, to the other drugs of abuse) as unique. For in their wisdom, the early members of Alcoholics Anonymous came to view alcoholism as a disease not only of the body, but also of the spirit. In so doing, they transformed themselves from helpless victims of alcoholism into active participants in the healing process of recovery.

Out of this struggle, the early members of Alcoholics Anonymous came to share an intimate knowledge of the nature of addiction. They came to view addiction not as a phenomenon to be dispassionately studied, but as an elusive enemy that held each member's life in its hands. The early members of Alcoholics Anonymous struggled to understand and share in the healing process of sobriety. In so doing, the early pioneers of AA came to understand that recovery was a spiritual process through which the individual recovered the spiritual unity that he or she could not find through chemicals.

Self-help groups such as Alcoholics Anonymous and Narcotics Anonymous[1] do not postulate any specific theory of how chemical addiction comes about (Herman, 1988). Rather, it is simply assumed that any person whose chemical use interferes with his or her life has an addiction problem. The need to attend AA was, to its founders, self-evident to the individual, in that either one was addicted to alcohol or one was not.

Addiction itself was viewed as resting upon a spiritual flaw within the individual. The addicted person was viewed as being

> on a spiritual search. They really are looking for something akin to the great hereafter, and they flirt with death to find it. Misguided, romantic, foolish, needful, they think they can escape from the world by artificial means. And they shoot, snort, drink, pop or smoke those means as they have to leave their pain and find their refuge. At first, it works. But, then it doesn't. (Baber, 1998, p. 29)

In a very real sense, the drugs do not bring about addiction; rather, the individual comes to abuse or be addicted to drugs because of what he or she believes to be important (Peele, 1989). Such spiritual flaws are not uncommon, and they usually pass unnoticed in the av-

[1]Although there are many similarities between AA and NA, these are separate programs. On occasion, they might cooperate on certain matters, but, each is independent of the other.

erage person. But the alcohol/drug-addicted person's spiritual foundation is such that she or he deems chemical use acceptable, appropriate, and desirable as a means to reach a goal that is ill-defined, at best.

One expression of this spiritual flaw is the individual's hesitation to take responsibility for the "self" (Peele, 1989). Personal suffering is one way of owning responsibility for one's life. And because suffering is an inescapable fact of life, we are granted endless opportunities to take personal responsibility for our lives. Unfortunately, modern society looks down on the process of individual growth and the pain inherent in growth. It is preoccupied with individual happiness, and any pain is viewed as unnecessary, if not dysfunctional. Further, modern society advocates that pain *automatically* be eradicated through the use of medications, so long as the pills are prescribed by a physician (Wiseman, 1997).

A reflection of this modern neurosis is that many people are willing to:

> go to quite extraordinary lengths to avoid our problems and the suffering they cause, proceeding far afield from all that is clearly good and sensible in order to find an easy way out, building the most elaborate fantasies in which to live, sometimes to the total exclusion of reality. (Peck, 1978, p. 17)

In this, the addicted person is not unique. Many people find it difficult to accept the pain and suffering that life entails. We all must come to terms with personal responsibility and with the pain of our existence. But the addicted person chooses a different path from the average person. Addiction might be viewed as an outcome of a process through which the individual comes to utilize chemicals to avoid recognizing and accepting life's problems. The chemicals come to lead the individual away from what he or she believes is good and acceptable, in return for the promise of comfort and relief.

Diseases of the Mind and Diseases of the Spirit: The Mind-Body Question

As B. Siegel (1986) and many others have observed, modern medicine has come to enforce an artificial dichotomy between the individual's "mind," and the same individual's "body." As a result of this dichotomy, modern medicine has become rather mechanical, with the physician treating "symptoms," or "diseases," rather than the patient as a whole (Cousins, 1989; B. S. Siegel, 1989).

The modern physician might be said to be a very highly skilled technician, who often fails to appreciate the unique person who is now in the role of a patient. Diseases of the body are viewed as falling in the realm of physical medicine, diseases of the mind in the realm of the psychological sciences. Diseases of the human spirit, according to this view, are the speciality of clergy (Reiser, 1984). The problem with this perspective is that the patient is not merely a spiritual being or a psychosocial being or a physical being but a unified whole. Thus, when a person abuses chemicals, the drug use will affect that person "physically, emotionally, socially, and spiritually" (Adams, 1988, p. 20). Unfortunately, society has difficulty accepting that an affliction of the spirit—such as addiction—is just as real as a disease of the physical body.

We are indeed spiritual beings, and self-help programs such as Alcoholics Anonymous and Narcotics Anonymous view addiction to chemicals as being a spiritual illness. Their success in helping people to achieve and maintain abstinence would argue that there is some validity to this claim. However, in its commitment to the artificial mind-body dichotomy, society struggles to come to terms with the disease of addiction, which is neither totally a physical illness nor exclusively one of the mind.

The Growth of Addiction: The Circle Narrows

As the disease of alcoholism progresses, alcohol becomes the "axis" around which the alcoholic's life revolves (Brown, 1985, p. 79). Alcohol comes to assume a role of "central importance" (p. 78) for both the alcoholic and the family. It is difficult for those who have never been addicted to chemicals to understand the importance that addicts attach to their drug(s) of choice. The addicted person will demonstrate a preoccupation with chemical use and will protect his or her source of chemicals. To illustrate this point, it is not uncommon for cocaine addicts to admit that if it came down to a choice, they would choose cocaine over friends, lovers, or even family. In many cases, the drug-dependent person has already made this choice—in favor of the chemical(s).

The grim truth is that the active addict is, in a sense, insane. One reflection of this moral insanity is that other people and the addict's other commitments take on a role of secondary importance. Addicted persons might be said "never [to] seem to outgrow the self-centeredness of the child" (*The Triangle of Self-Obsession*, 1983, p. 1). In exploring this point, the book *Narcotics Anonymous* (1982) noted:

> Before coming to the fellowship of NA, we could not manage our own lives. We could not live and enjoy life as other people do. We had to have something different and we thought we found it in drugs. We placed their use ahead of the welfare of our families, our wives, husbands, and our children. We had to have drugs at all costs. . . . (p. 11)

As experienced mental health professionals can affirm, there are many people whose all-consuming interest is themselves. They care for nothing outside of that little portion of the universe known as "self." In this sense, chemical addiction might be viewed as a form of self-love or, perhaps more accurately, as a perversion of self-love. It is through the use of chemicals that the addicted seek to cheat themselves of the experience of reality, replacing it with the distorted desires of the self.

To say that the addicted person demonstrates an ongoing preoccupation with chemical use is something of an understatement. The addicted person may also demonstrate an exaggerated concern about maintaining a supply of the drug and may avoid those who might prevent further drug use. Consider an alcoholic who, with six or seven cases of beer in storage in the basement, goes out to buy six more cases, just to be sure of having an "adequate" supply. The addict views other people either as useful in the acquisition of chemicals or as impediments to drug use. It is for this reason that recovering addicts speak of their still addicted counterparts as morally insane.

The Circle of Addiction: Addicted Priorities

The authors of the book *Narcotics Anonymous* concluded that addiction was a disease composed of three elements. These were (1) a compulsive use of chemicals, (2) an obsession with further chemical use, and (3) a spiritual disease that is expressed through a total self-centeredness on the part of the individual. It is this total self-centeredness—the spiritual illness that causes the person to demand "what *I* want when *I want* it!"—that makes the individual vulnerable to addiction. But to admit to embracing this philosophy would be to face the need for change. Thus people who are addicted to chemicals will begin to use the defense mechanisms of denial, rationalization, projection, and/or minimization to justify their increasingly narrow range of interests both to themselves and to significant others.

To support his or her addiction, the individual must come to renounce more and more of his or her "self" in favor of new beliefs and behaviors that make it possible to continue to use chemicals. This is the spiritual illness that is found in addiction, for the individual comes to believe that "nothing should come between me and my drug use!" No price is too high, nor is any behavior unthinkable, if it allows for further drug use. The individual will lie, cheat, and steal to support his or her addiction. Many addicts have examined the cost of their drug use and have turned away from chemicals with or without formal treatment, but there are those who accept this cost willingly. These individuals will go to great pains to hide the evidence of their drug addiction so that they are not forced to look at the grim reality that they *are* addicted.

Although the alcohol/drug-dependent person is an active participant in this process, she or he is also blinded to its existence. If you were to ask the alcohol-dependent person why she or he uses alcohol, you would be unlikely to learn the real reason. "You have to understand," one individual said at the age of 73, "the reason why I drink now is that I had pneumonia when I was 3 years old." For her to say otherwise would have been to run the risk of admitting that she had a problem with alcohol, an admission that she had struggled very hard to avoid for most of her adult life.

As the addiction comes to control more and more of the individual's life, greater and greater effort must be expended by the addict to maintain the illusion of living a normal life. Gallagher (1986) related how one physician, addicted to a synthetic narcotic known as fentanyl, ultimately bought drugs from the street because it was no longer possible to divert enough drugs from hospital sources to maintain his drug habit. When the tell-tale scars from repeated injections of street drugs began to form, this same physician intentionally burned himself on the arm with a spoon to hide the scars.

The addicted person also finds that as the drug comes to control more and more of his or her life, significant effort must be invested in maintaining the addiction itself. More than one cocaine or heroin addict has had to engage in prostitution (homosexual or heterosexual) in order to earn enough money to buy more drugs. Everything is sacrificed in order to obtain and maintain what the addict perceives as an "adequate" supply of the chemicals.

Some Games of Addiction

One major problem in working with those who are addicted to chemicals is that these individuals will often seek out sources of legitimate pharmaceuticals either to supplement their drug supply or to serve as their primary source of chemicals. There are many reasons for this. First, as Goldman (1991) observed, pharmaceuticals can be legally purchased if there is a legitimate medical need for the medication. Armed with a legitimate prescription signed by a physician, the drug user does not need to fear arrest.

Second, for the drug-addicted person who is able to obtain pharmaceuticals, the medication is a known product at a known potency level. The drug user does not have to worry about low-potency street drugs, about the impurities that may be part of drugs purchased on the street (as when PCP is mixed with low-potency marijuana, for example), or about misrepresentation (as when PCP is sold as LSD, for example). Also, legitimate pharmaceuticals are usually much less expensive than street drugs. For example, the pharmaceutical analgesic hydromophone costs about $1 per tablet at a pharmacy. On the street, each tablet might sell for as much as $100 (Goldman, 1991).

In order to manipulate physicians into prescribing desired medications, addicts are likely to "use ploys such as outrage, tears, accusations of abandonment, abject pleading, promises of cooperation, and seduction" (Jenike, 1991, p. 7). The physician who works with an addicted person must keep in mind the fact that the latter cares little for the physician's feelings. For the alcohol/drug-dependent person, the goal is to obtain more drugs, at virtually any cost. One favorite manipulative "scam" is for the addict (or an accomplice) to visit the hospital emergency rooms (Klass, 1989) or the physician's office in an attempt to seek medication. Such addicts will either simulate an illness or, if they are lucky enough, use a real physical illness as an excuse to obtain desired medications. Sometimes the presenting complaint is "kidney stones" or a story about how other doctors or emergency rooms have not been able to help the patient or a story about how the individual "lost" his or her medication(s) or how "the dog ate it," etc.

Patients who have been asked to submit a urine sample for testing have been found to be secretly pricking their fingers with needles in order to squeeze some blood into the urine, to support their claim that they were passing a kidney stone. Others have inserted foreign objects into the urethra in order to irritate the tissues lining it and enable them to provide a bloody urine sample. The object is to obtain a prescription for narcotics from a sympathetic doctor who wants to treat the patient's obvious "kidney stone." Addicted individuals have also been known to go to an emergency room with a broken bone, have the bone set, and go home with a prescription for a narcotic analgesic (provided to help the patient deal with the pain of a broken bone). Once at home, the patient (the accomplice) then removes the cast so that the patient can go to yet another hospital emergency room to have yet another cast applied to the injured limb, in the process receiving yet another prescription for a narcotic analgesic. In a large city, this process might be repeated ten times or more (Goldman, 1991).

It is not unusual for addicted persons to study medical textbooks to learn what symptoms to fake and how to present these symptoms convincingly to health care professionals. In many cases, the addicted person knows more about the disorder she or he is trying to simulate than does the physician who is treating them!

A Thought on Playing the Games of Addiction

A friend who worked in a maximum-security penitentiary for men was warned by older, more experienced corrections workers not to try to "out-con a con." Which is to say that a person should not try to out-maneuver the individual whose entire life centers on the ability to manipulate others. "You should remember that while you have been home watching the evening news, or going out to see a movie, these people have been working on perfecting their game. It is their game, their rules, and in a sense their whole life." This is also a good rule to keep in mind at all times when working with the addicted person. Addiction is a lifestyle—one that involves manipulating others into supporting the addiction. This is not to say that the addict cannot, if necessary, change his ways, at least for a short time. This is especially true early in the addiction process and during the early stages of treatment.

Often, addicts will go "on the wagon" for a few days, or perhaps even a few weeks, in order to prove both to themselves and to others that they can "still control it." Unfortunately, addicts who do this overlook the fact that by attempting to "prove" their control, they actually demonstrate their lack of control over the chemicals. However, as the addiction progresses, it takes more and more to motivate the addict to give up the drug, even for a short time. Eventually, even "a short time" becomes too long.

There is no limit to the manipulations that the addicted person will use to try to support his or her addiction. Vernon Johnson (1980) spoke at length of how the addicted person will even use compliance as a defense against treatment. Overt compliance may be, and is often utilized as, a defense against acceptance of one's own spiritual, emotional, and physical deficits (Johnson, 1980).

Honesty as a Part of the Recovery Process

One of the core features of the physical addiction to a chemical is "a fundamental inability to be honest . . . with the *self*" (Knapp, 1996, p. 83). Honesty is the way to break through this deception, to bring the person face to face with the reality of addiction. The authors of the book *Narcotics Anonymous* (1982) warned that coming to understand that one is addicted is not easy. Indeed, self-deception is part of the price that the addict pays for addiction. According to the NA "Big Book," "Only in desperation did we ask ourselves, 'Could it be the drugs?'" (pp. 1–2).

Addicted persons will often speak with pride about how they have been more or less "drug free" for various periods of time. The list of reasons why the individual is drug-free is virtually endless. This person is drug free because his or her spouse threatened divorce if he or she continued using chemicals. (But he or she secretly longs to return to chemical use—and will if he or she can find a way to do so). Another person is drug-free because his or her probation officer has a reputation for sending people to prison if their urine sample (drawn under strict supervision) is positive for chemicals. (But he or she is counting the days until the probation period is over—and may even sneak an occasional drink or use a drug in spite of the risk.

In each instance, the person is drug-free only because of an external threat. In virtually every case, as soon as the external threat is removed, the individual gradually drifts back to chemicals. It is simply impossible for one person to provide the motivation for another person to remain drug-free forever. Many addicted people have admitted, after repeated and strong confrontation, that they have simply switched addictions in order to give the appearance of being drug-free. It is not uncommon for an opiate addict in a methadone maintenance program to use alcohol, marijuana, or cocaine. The methadone does not block the euphoric effects of these drugs as it does the euphoria of narcotics. Thus the addicted person can maintain the appearance of complete cooperation, showing up each day to take his or her methadone without protest, while still using cocaine, marijuana, or alcohol at will.

The addicted person has lost touch with reality. Over time, those who are addicted to chemicals come to share many personality traits. There is some question whether this personality type, the so-called "addictive personality" predates addiction or evolves as a result of the addiction (Bean-Bayog, 1988; Nathan, 1988). However, this chicken-or-the-egg question does not alter the fact that for the addict, addiction always comes first.

Many an addicted person has admitted to going without food for days on end, but very few would willingly go without using chemicals for even a short period of time. Cocaine addicts have spoken about how they would avoid sexual relations with their spouse or partner in order to continue using cocaine. Just as the alcoholic often sleeps with an "eye opener" (i.e., an alcoholic drink) already mixed by the side of the bed, addicts have spoken of having a "rig" (i.e., a hypodermic needle) loaded and ready for use so that they could inject the drug before they got out of bed for the day.

Many physicians have boasted of how the patients that they worked with had no reason to lie to them. One physician went so far as to boast that he knew that a certain patient did not have prescriptions from other doctors, because the patient told him so! The chemical dependency professional needs to keep in mind at all times the twin realities that for the person who is ad-dicted, the chemical comes first and that the addicted person organizes his or her life around the chemical. To lose sight of this reality is to run the danger of being trapped in the addict's web of fabrications, half-truths, manipulations, and lies.

Recovering addicts will speak of how manipulative they were and will often admit that they were their own worst enemy. For, as they move along the road to recovery, addicts come to recognize that they would also deceive themselves, as part of the addiction process. One inmate said that "Before I can run a game on somebody else, I have to believe it myself." As the addiction progresses, the addict does not question his or her perception but comes to believe what he or she needs to believe in order to maintain the addiction.

False Pride: The Disease of the Spirit

Every addiction is, in the final analysis, a disease of the spirit. Edmeades (1987) related a story of how, in the year 1931, Carl Jung was treating an American, Rowland H., for alcoholism. Immediately after treatment, Rowland H. relapsed, but he was not accepted back into analysis by Jung. His only hope of recovery, according to Jung, lay in a spiritual awakening, which he later found through a religious group in America.

Carl Jung identified alcoholism (and by implication all forms of addiction) as diseases of the spirit (Peluso & Peluso, 1988). The *Twelve Steps and Twelve Traditions of Alcoholics Anonymous* (1981) speaks of addiction as being a sickness of the soul. In support of this perspective, Kandel and Raveis (1989) found that a "lack of religiosity" (p. 113) was a significant predictor of continued use of cocaine and/or marijuana for young adults with previous experience with these drugs. For addicted individuals, a spiritual awakening appears to be an essential element of their recovery.

In speaking with addicted persons, one is impressed by how often the individual has suffered in his or her lifetime. It is almost as though one could trace a path from the emotional trauma to the addiction. Yet the addict's spirit is not crushed at birth, nor does the trauma that precedes addiction come about overnight. The individual's spirit comes to be diseased over time, as the addict-to-be loses his or her way in life.

Fromm (1968) observed that "we all start out with hope, faith and fortitude" (p. 20). However, the assorted insults of life often join forces to bring about disappointment and a loss of faith. The individual comes to feel an empty void within. It is at this point that if something is not found to fill the addict's "empty heart, he will fill his stomach with artificial stimulants and sedatives" (Graham, 1988, p. 14). An excellent example of this process might be seen in the Poland of a decade ago, where many of that country's young-adult "no future" generation, whose future has been throttled by years of economic hardship and the martial law of the 1980s, turned to heroin to ease their pain (Ross, 1991).

Few of us escape this moment of ultimate disappointment, or ultimate awareness (Fromm, 1968). It is at this moment that individuals are faced with a choice. They may come to "reduce their demands to what they can get and . . . not dream of that which seems to be out of their reach" (Fromm, 1968, p. 21). The Narcotics Anonymous pamphlet *The Triangle of Self-Obsession* (1983) observed that this process is, for most, a natural part of growing up. But the person who is in danger of addiction refuses to reduce those demands. Rather, the addicted person comes to demand "What *I* want when *I* want it!" Again, *The Triangle of Self-Obsession* (1983) noted that addicted persons tend to

> refuse to accept that we will not be given everything. We become self-obsessed; our wants and needs become demands. We reach a point where contentment and fulfillment are impossible. (p. 1)

Despair comes to exist when the individual views himself or herself as being powerless. Existentialists speak of the realization of ultimate powerlessness as awareness of one's nonexistence. In this sense, the individual comes to feel the utter futility of existence. When the person comes to face the ultimate experience of powerlessness, the individual is faced with a choice. He or she may either come to accept his or her true place in the universe or continue to distort his or her perceptions and thoughts to maintain the illusion of self-importance.

It is only when one accepts one's true place in the universe, along with the pain and suffering that life might offer, that one is capable of any degree of spiritual growth (Peck, 1978). Many choose to turn away from reality, for it does not offer them what they think they are entitled to. In so doing, these people become

somewhat grandiose and exhibit the characteristic false pride so frequently encountered in addiction.

One cannot maintain the illusion of being more than what one is without an increasingly large investment of time, energy and emotional resources. This lack of humility—the denial of what one *is* in order to give an illusion of being better than this—plants the seeds of despair (Merton, 1961). Humility implies an honest, realistic view of "self" worth. Despair proceeds from a distorted view of one's place in the universe. This despair grows with each passing day, as reality threatens, time and again, to force upon the individual an awareness of the ultimate measure of his or her existence.

In time, external supports are necessary to maintain this false pride. Brown (1985) identified one characteristic of alcohol as being its ability to offer the individual an illusion of control over his or her feelings. This is a common characteristic of every drug of abuse. If life does not provide the pleasure one feels entitled to, at least one might find this comfort and pleasure in a drug, or combination of drugs, which frees one from life's pain and misery . . . at least for a while.

When faced with this unwanted awareness of one's true place in the universe, the addicted person must increasingly distort his or her perception to maintain the illusion of superiority. Into this fight to avoid the painful reality of what is, the chemical injects the ability to choose one's feelings seemingly at will. The chemical, in effect, provides an illusion of control over the emotions—a kingly power to select what feeling one wishes to experience. What the individual does not realize, often not until after the seeds of addiction have been planted, is that the chemical offers an illusion only. There is no substance to the self-selected feelings brought about by the chemical, only a mockery of peace. The deeper feelings made possible through the acceptance of one's lot in life (which is humility) seem to be a mystery to the addicted person. "How can you be happy?" they ask "you're nothing like me! You don't use!!!"

Humility, as noted above, is the honest acceptance of one's place in the universe (Merton, 1961), including one's strengths and one's weaknesses. At the moment when the individual becomes aware of the reality of his or her existence, the individual chooses whether to accept his or her lot in life. When one struggles against this acceptance, one in effect places one self above all else, demanding "not as it is, but as I want it!" This is a cry against the ultimate knowledge of being lost that Fromm (1968) spoke of. This despair is often so all-inclusive that the "self" ultimately seems unable to withstand its attack. Addicts have described this despair as an empty, black void within. Then, as Graham (1988) noted, they have attempted to fill this void with the chemicals they find around them.

Twelve Steps and Twelve Traditions (1981) viewed false pride as a sickness of the soul. In this light, chemical use might be viewed as a reaction against the ultimate despair of encountering one's lot in life—the false sense of being that says "not as it is, but as I want it!" in response to one's discovery of personal powerlessness. Surprisingly, in light of this self-centered approach to life, various authors have come to view the substance-abusing person as essentially seeking to join with a higher power. But in place of the spiritual struggle that is necessary to achieve inner peace, the addicted person seems to take a shortcut through the use of chemicals (Chopra, 1997; Gilliam, 1998; Peck 1997b, 1993, 1978). Thus May (1988) was able to view alcohol/drug addiction as sidetracking "our deepest, truest desire for love and goodness" (p. 14). The individual organizes his or her life more and more around further chemical use, until at last the person believes that he or she cannot live without it. Further spiritual growth is impossible when the individual views chemical use as having the highest priority.

In the process of sidetracking her or his drive for truth and spiritual growth, the addict develops a sense of false pride. This false pride expresses itself almost as a form of narcissism. The clinical phenomenon of narcissism is itself a reaction against perceived worthlessness, loss of control, and an emotional pain so intense that it almost seemed physical (Millon, 1981). In speaking of the narcissistic personality, Millon (1981) observed that such persons view their own self worth in such a way that "they rarely question whether it is valid" (p. 167) and "place few restraints on either their fantasies or rationalizations . . . their imagination is left to run free."

Although drug-dependent persons are not usually narcissistic personalities in the pure sense of the term, there are significant narcissistic traits present in addiction. One finds that false pride, which is based on the lack of humility, causes addicted individuals to distort their perceptions not only of self but also of "other," in the service of their pride and their chemical use (Merton, 1961). In speaking of the normal division that takes place within the human soul, one must keep in mind that there are people whose entire life centers on their "self." Such people "imagine that they can only find themselves by asserting their own desires and ambitions and appetites in a struggle with the rest of the world" (Merton, 1961, p. 47).

In this quote, there are hints of the seeds of addiction, for the individual's chemical of choice allows the individual to impose his or her own desires and ambitions on the rest of the world. Brown (1985) speaks at length of the illusion of control over one's feelings that alcohol gives to the individual. May (1988) also speaks of how chemical addiction reflects a misguided attempt to achieve complete control over one's life. The drugs of abuse also give an illusion of control to the user, a dangerous illusion that makes the user's loss of control to the chemical a reality.

One often finds addicted persons speaking with pride of the horrors they have suffered in the service of their addiction. In such "euphoric recall," the addict selectively recalls mainly the pleasant aspects of drug use, while selectively forgetting the pain and suffering experienced as a consequence of chemical use (Gorski, 1993). In listening to alcohol/drug-addicted persons, one is almost left with the impression that they are speaking about the joys of a valued friendship rather than a drug of abuse (Byington, 1997). For example, they may expound at length on the quasi-sexual thrill that they achieved through cocaine or heroin, dismissing the fact that their abuse of this same drug cost them a spouse, a family, or several tens of thousand dollars.

There is a name for the distorted view of one's self, and of one's world, that comes about with chronic chemical use. It is called the insanity of addiction.

Projection, Denial, Rationalization, and Minimization: The Four Musketeers of Addiction

The traditional view of addiction is that all human behavior, including the addictive use of chemicals, rests upon a foundation of characteristic psychological defenses. In the case of chemical dependency, the defense mechanisms that are thought to be involved are the triad of denial, projection, and rationalization. These defense mechanisms, like all psychological defense of minimization that often accompanies them, are thought to operate unconsciously, in both the intrapersonal and interpersonal spheres. They exist to protect the individual from the conscious awareness of anxiety.

Often without knowing it, addicted individuals will utilize these defense mechanisms in an effort to avoid recognizing the reality of their addiction and, hence, the implicit social expectation that they will deal with their addiction. To understand addiction, then, one must also understand each of these characteristic defense mechanisms.

Clinical lore among substance abuse rehabilitation professionals holds that the individual's substance use problem hides behind a wall of *denial*. The characteristic denial of the individual's growing chemical dependency, and the impact of the chemical(s) on his or her life, is thought to be the most common reason why the individual fails to seek help for alcoholism (Wing, 1995). Simply, denial is "a disregard for a disturbing reality" (Kaplan & Sadock, 1996, p. 20). It is a form of unconscious self-deception used by the individual's unconscious to help him or her avoid anxiety and emotional distress (Shader, 1994). This is accomplished through a process of selective perception of the past and present, so that painful and frightening elements of reality are not recognized or accepted. AA calls it "tunnel vision." Denial is a primitive form of unconscious defense, usually found in the person who is experiencing significant internal and interpersonal distress (Perry & Cooper 1989).

Projection is an unconscious defense mechanism through which "what is emotionally unacceptable in oneself is unconsciously rejected and attributed to others" (Kaplan & Sadock, 1996, p. 20). Johnson (1980) defined projection differently, noting that the act of projection is the act of "unloading self-hatred onto others" (p. 31).

At times, the defense mechanism of projection expresses itself through the behaviors of misinterpreting the motives or intentions of others (Kaplan & Sadock, 1996). Young children will often cry out, "See what you made me do?" when they have misbehaved, in order to project responsibility for their action onto others. Individuals with substance use problems will often do this

as well, blaming others for their addiction or unacceptable aspects of their behavior.

Rationalization is the third common defense mechanism utilized by addicted individuals. Through rationalization, the "individual attempts to justify feelings, motives, or behavior that otherwise would be unreasonable, illogical or intolerable" (Kaplan & Sadock, 1996, p. 20). In a later work, these authors also noted that rationalization may express itself via the individual's "invention of a convincing fallacy" (p. 184) through which their behavior might seemingly be justified. Some of the examples of rationalization used by addicts include blaming their spouse or family ("If you were married to ——, you'd drink, too!") or blaming medical problems.

Minimization operates in a different manner than the three defensive operations reviewed above. Minimization resembles rationalization, but it is more specific. The addicted individual who uses minimization as a defense markedly reduces the amount of chemicals that he or she *admits to* using or otherwise understates the impact that chemical use has had on his or her life.

The alcohol-dependent individual, for example, might pour his or her drinks into an oversized container, perhaps the size of three or four regular glasses, and then claim to be having "only three drinks a night!" The individual might claim to "only drink four nights a week" and hope that the interviewer does not think to ask whether *a week* means a five-day work "week" or the full seven-day week. (In such cases, it is not uncommon to find that the client drinks four nights out of five during the work week and then is intoxicated from Friday evening until bedtime on Sunday, the final result being that the individual drinks six nights out of each full week.) Another expression of rationalization occurs when the individual claims time when he or she was in treatment, in jail, or hospitalized as "straight time," overlooking the fact that they were unable to get alcohol/drugs because they were incarcerated.[2]

Another common rationalization is that one can become addicted only to artificial chemicals, such as al-

---

[2] This is often classified as "situational" abstinence by rehabilitation professionals, especially if the client admits that she or he *would have* used chemicals during these "dry" periods if it had been possible to do so without being caught.

cohol, amphetamines, or heroin. Obviously, the addict rationalizes because marijuana is an herb that grows naturally, one cannot possibly become addicted to it. Another popular rationalization is that it is "better to be an alcoholic than a needle freak . . . after all, alcohol is legal!"

Reactions to the spiritual disorder theory of addiction. Although the traditional view of substance abuse in the United States has been that the defense mechanisms of denial, projection, rationalization, and minimization are traditionally found in cases of chemical dependency, this view is not universally accepted. A small, increasingly vocal minority has offered alternative frameworks within which substance abuse professionals might view the defense mechanisms that they encounter in their work with addicted individuals.

In the 1980s and 1990s, Stanton Peele proved to be a very vocal critic of the medical model of chemical dependency. In his (1989) work on the subject, he spoke at length of how treatment centers often utilize the individual's refusal to admit to his or her addiction as being a confirmation of the fact that the individual is addicted. The individual is automatically assumed to be "in denial" of his or her chemical abuse problem. A second possibility, all too often overlooked by treatment center staff according to Peele, is that the individual might not be addicted to chemicals to begin with!

The automatic assumption that the client is "in denial" might blind treatment center staff to the possibility that the individual's refusal to admit to being addicted to chemicals might reflect reality, not denial. This possibility underscores the need for an accurate assessment of the client's substance use patterns, in order to determine whether there really is a need for active intervention or treatment. Miller and Rollnick (1991) offered a theory that radically departs from the belief that addicts typically utilize denial as a major defense against the admission of being "sick." The authors suggest that alcoholics, as a group, do not utilize denial more frequently than any other group. Rather, the authors suggest that a combination of two factors has made it appear that addicts frequently utilize defense mechanisms such as denial, projection, rationalization, and minimization in the service of their dependency.

First, the authors suggest that the process of selective perception on the part of treatment center staff

makes it appear that addicts frequently use these defense mechanisms. The authors point to the phenomenon known as the "illusion of correlation" to support this theory. According to the illusion of correlation, human beings tend to remember information that confirms their preconceptions and to forget or overlook information that fails to meet their conceptual model. Substance abuse professionals are thus more likely to remember those clients who did use the defense mechanisms, because that is what they were trained to expect.

Second, Miller and Rollnick (1991) suggested that when substance abuse rehabilitation professionals utilize the wrong treatment approach for the client's unique stage of growth, the resulting conflict is interpreted as evidence of denial, projection, rationalization, or minimization. On the basis of their work with addicted individuals, Berg and Miller (1992) also suggested that "denial" is found when the therapist utilizes the wrong treatment approach for the client that he or she is working with. Thus both teams of clinicians have concluded that defense mechanisms such as "denial" are not a reflection of a pathological condition on the part of the client, but the result of the wrong intervention. These theories offer challenging alternatives to the traditional model of the addicted person exhibiting characteristic defense mechanisms.

Summary

Many human services professionals who have had limited contact with addiction tend to have a distorted view of the nature of drug addiction. Having heard the term *disease* applied to chemical dependency, the inexperienced human services worker may think in terms of more traditional illnesses and may thus be rudely surprised at the deception that is inherent in drug addiction. Although chemical dependency is a disease, it is a disease unlike no other. It is a disease that requires the active participation of the "victim." Further, self-help groups such as Alcoholics Anonymous and Narcotics Anonymous view addiction as a disease of the spirit and offer a spiritual program to help their members achieve and maintain their recovery.

Addiction is, in a sense, a form of insanity. The insanity of addiction rests upon a foundation of psychological defense mechanisms such as denial, projection, rationalization, and minimization. These defense mechanisms, along with self-deception, keep the person from becoming aware of the reality of his or her addiction until the disease has progressed quite far. To combat self-deception, Alcoholics Anonymous places emphasis on honesty, openness, and a willingness to try to live without alcohol. Honesty, both with self and with others, is the central feature of the AA program, which is designed to foster spiritual growth to help the individual overcome his or her spiritual weaknesses.

CHAPTER SIX

An Introduction to Pharmacology[1]

Introduction

It is virtually impossible to discuss the effects of the various drugs of abuse without touching on a number of basic pharmacological concepts. In this chapter, we will review some of the basic principles of pharmacology, which will help you better understand the impact that the different drugs of abuse may have on the user's body.[2]

There are many misconceptions about recreational chemicals. For example, many people believe that recreational chemicals are somehow unique. This is not true; they work in the same way that other pharmaceuticals do. Alcohol and the drugs of abuse act by changing (strengthening or weakening) a potential that already exists within the cells of the body (Williams & Baer, 1994; Ciancio & Bourgault, 1989). In the case of the drugs of abuse, all of which exert their desired effects in the brain, they modify the normal function of the neurons of the brain.

A second misconception is that the drugs of abuse are somehow different from legitimate pharmaceuticals. In fact, many of the drugs of abuse are—or were once—legitimate pharmaceuticals used by physicians to treat disease. Thus the drugs of abuse obey the same laws of pharmacology that apply to the other medications in use today.

The Prime Effect and Side Effects of Chemicals

One rule of pharmacology is that whenever a chemical is introduced into the body, there is an element of risk (Laurence & Bennett, 1992). *Every* chemical agent has the potential to harm the individual, although the degree of risk varies with the specific chemical being used, the individual's state of health, and so on. The localized treatment of an infection caused by, say, a fungus on the skin presents us with a localized site of action—that is, the surface the body. This makes it easy to limit the impact that a medication used to treat the infection might have on the organism as a whole. The patient is unlikely to need more than a topical medication that can be applied directly to the affected region. But compare the situation with the drugs of abuse. The site of action for each of the recreational chemicals lies deep within the central nervous system (CNS). There is increasing evidence that each of the various drugs of abuse ultimately affects the limbic system of the brain. However, the drugs of abuse are very much like a blast of shotgun pellets spewing from the end of a "scatter-gun": They will have an impact not only on the brain but also on many other organ systems in the body.

For example, cocaine causes the user to experience a sense of well-being, or euphoria. The euphoria and sense of well-being that might result from cocaine abuse are called the *primary effects* of the cocaine abuse. But the chemical has a number of side effects, including causing the coronary arteries of the user's heart to constrict. This is hardly a desired effect and may even be the

---

[1]This chapter is designed to provide the reader with a brief overview of some of the more important principles of pharmacology. It is not intended to serve, nor should it be used, as a guide to patient care.

[2]Individuals interested in reading more on pharmacology will find several good resources in any medical or nursing school bookstore.

cause of heart attacks in cocaine users.[3] Such unwanted effects of a chemical are often called *secondary effects* or *side effects*. The side effects of a chemical may range from simply making the patient feel uncomfortable precipitating to a life-threatening event.

A second example is aspirin, which inhibits the production of chemicals known as prostaglandins at the site of an injury. This helps to reduce the individual's pain. But the body also produces prostaglandins within the kidneys and stomach, where these chemicals help control the functioning of these organs. Because aspirin tends to block prostaglandin production nonselectively *throughout* the body, this unwanted side effect of aspirin may put the user's life at risk.

Finally, consider a person with a bacterial infection of the middle ear (a condition known as *Otitis media*). When the patient takes an antibiotic such as penicillin, the desired outcome is for the antibiotic to destroy the bacteria that cause the infection in the middle ear. The side effects, however, may include drug-induced diarrhea, as the antibiotic interferes with normal bacteria growth patterns in the intestinal tract.

Thus one needs to keep in mind that all pharmaceuticals, and all the drugs of abuse, have both desired effects and numerous—possibly undesirable—side effects.

Drug Forms and How Drugs Are Administered

A drug is, essentially, a foreign chemical that is introduced into the individual's body to bring about a specific response. Antihypertensive medications are used to control excessively high blood pressure, antibiotics to eliminate unwanted bacterial infections. The recreational drugs are introduced into the body, as a general rule, to bring about feelings of euphoria, relaxation, and relief from stress. The specific *form* in which a drug is administered has a major effect on the speed with which that chemical is able to work and the way the

chemical is distributed throughout the body. In general, the drugs of abuse are administered by either the *enteral* or the *parenteral* route.

Enteral Forms of Drug Administration

Medications that are administered by the enteral route are administered *orally, sublingually, or rectally* (Williams & Baer, 1994; Ciancio & Bourgault, 1989). The most common means by which medication is administered orally is the *tablet*. Essentially, a tablet is

> a compounded form in which the drug is mixed with a binding agent to hold the tablet together before administration. Most tablets are designed to be swallowed whole . . . (Shannon, Wilson & Stang, 1995, p. 8).

A number of the drugs of abuse are often administered in tablet form, including aspirin, the hallucinogens LSD and MDMA, and (on occasion) illicit forms of amphetamine. Amphetamine tablets are frequently made in illicit laboratories, and are known on the street by a variety of names (such as "white cross" and "cartwheels").

A second common form that oral medication may take is that of a *capsule*. Capsules are modified tablets, the inside medication being surrounded by gelatin. The capsule is designed to be swallowed whole, and once it reaches the stomach, the gelatin capsule breaks down, allowing the medication to be released into the gastrointestinal tract (Shannon, Wilson, & Stang, 1995).

There are many other forms that medication may take. Antibiotics and some over-the-counter analgesics often are administered in liquid form for oral use, especially when the patient is a very young child. Liquid forms of a drug make it possible to tailor each dose to the patient's weight and are ideal for patients who have trouble taking pills or capsules by mouth. Of the drugs of abuse, alcohol is perhaps the best example of a chemical that is administered in liquid form.

Some medications, and a small number of the drugs of abuse, can be absorbed through the blood-rich tissues under the tongue. This *sublingual* method of drug administration is a variation on the oral form. Certain drugs, such as nitroglycerin and fentanyl, are well ab-

---

[3]Shannon, Wilson, and Stang (1995) refer to a chemical's *primary effects* as the drug's *therapeutic effects* (p. 21). However, their text is devoted to medications and their uses, not to the drugs of abuse. To differentiate clearly between the use of a medication in the treatment of disease and the abuse of chemicals for recreational purposes, this text will use the term "primary effects."

sorbed by the sublingual method of drug administration. However, for the most part, the drugs of abuse are not administered sublingually.

Parenteral Forms of Drug Administration

The parenteral method of drug administration involves injecting the medication directly into the body. There are several forms of parenteral administration, which are commonly used both in the world of medicine and in the world of drug abuse. First, there is the *subcutaneous* method of drug administration. In this process, a chemical is injected just under the skin. Drugs administered in a subcutaneous injection do not pass through the stomach and gastrointestinal tract, but they are absorbed more slowly than chemicals injected either into muscle tissue or into a vein. As we will see in the chapter on narcotics addiction, heroin addicts will often use subcutaneous injections, a process they call "skin popping."

A second method of parenteral administration is the *intramuscular* injection of a medication. Muscle tissues have a good supply of blood, and medications injected into muscle tissue are absorbed into the general circulation more rapidly than those injected just under the skin. As we will see, it is quite common for individuals who abuse anabolic steroids to inject these chemicals into the muscle tissue.

The third method of parenteral administration is *intravenous* (IV) injection. Here the chemical is injected into a vein and thus is deposited directly into the general circulation (Schwertz, 1991). Among the drugs of abuse, heroin, cocaine, and some forms of amphetamine are often administered by IV injection. Because of the speed with which the chemical reaches the general circulation when administered by IV injection, there is great potential for undesirable reactions; the body has very little time to adapt to the arrival of the foreign chemical (Ciancio & Bourgault, 1989). This is one reason why users of intravenously administered chemicals, such as heroin, frequently experience a wide range of adverse effects in addition to the euphoria they seek.

Remember that the use of a parenteral method of drug administration does not necessarily mean that the chemical in question will have an instantaneous effect. The speed at which all forms of drugs begin to work is influenced by a number of factors, which we discuss later in this chapter, in the section on drug distribution.

Other Forms of Drug Administration

There are a number of additional methods of drug administration. Some chemicals might be absorbed through the skin, a *transdermal* method of drug administration. Eventually, chemicals absorbed transdermally reach the general circulation and are then distributed throughout the body. Physicians often take advantage of the potential offered by transdermal drug administration to provide the patient with a low, steady blood level of a chemical. Transdermal drug administration is a very slow way to introduce a drug into the body, but for certain agents, it is useful. An example is the "skin patch" used to administer nicotine to patients who are attempting to quit smoking. Some antihistamines are administered transdermally, especially when used for motion sickness. There also is a transdermal "patch" available for the narcotic analgesic fentanyl, although its success as a means of providing analgesia has been quite limited.

Occasionally, chemicals are administered *intranasally*. The intranasal administration of a chemical involves "snorting" the material in question, so that it is deposited on the blood-rich tissues of the sinuses. From that point, it is possible for many chemicals to be absorbed into the general circulation. For example, both cocaine and heroin powders are frequently "snorted."

The process of snorting is similar to *inhalation*, which is used by both physicians and illicit drug users. Inhalation of a compound takes advantage of the fact that the blood is separated from exposure to the air by a layer of tissue that is less than 1/100,000 of an inch (0.64 micron) thick (Garrett, 1994). Many chemical molecules are small enough to pass through the lungs into the general circulation, as is the case with surgical anesthetics. Some of the drugs of abuse, such as heroin and cocaine, are abused via inhalation when they are smoked. In another form of inhalation, the particles being inhaled are suspended in the smoke. These particles are small enough to reach the deep tissues of the lungs, where they are then deposited. In a brief period of time, the particles are broken down into smaller units, until they are small enough to pass through the walls of the lungs and to reach the general circulation. This is what occurs when tobacco products are smoked.

Each subform of inhalation takes advantage of the fact that the lungs offer a blood-rich, extremely large surface area through which chemical agents can be absorbed (Benet, Kroetz, & Sheiner, 1995). Further, depending on how quickly the chemical being inhaled can cross over into the general circulation, inhalation can introduce chemicals into the body relatively quickly. But for a number of reasons, the actual amount of a chemical absorbed through inhalation tends to be quite variable. First, the individual must inhale at just the right time to allow the chemical to reach the desired region of the lungs. Second, some chemicals pass through the tissues of the lung only very poorly and thus are not well absorbed by inhalation.

For example, as we will see when we discuss marijuana, the individual who smokes marijuana must use a different technique than the person who smokes tobacco, in order to get the maximal effect from the chemical. The variability in the amount of chemical absorbed through the lungs limits the utility of inhalation as a means of administering medications. However, for some of the drugs of abuse, inhalation is the preferred method of use. There are a number of other methods through which pharmaceuticals can be introduced into the body. For example, the chemical might be prepared in such a way that it could be administered rectally or through enteral tubes. However, because the drugs of abuse are generally introduced into the body by injection, orally, intranasally, or through smoking, we will not discuss these obscure methods of drug administration.

Bioavailability

In order to work, the drug(s) being abused must enter the body in sufficient strength to achieve the desired effect. Pharmacists refer to this strength as the *bioavailability* of the chemical. Bioavailability is the *concentration of the unchanged chemical at the site of action* (Loebl, Spratto, & Woods, 1994; Sands, Knapp, & Ciraulo, 1993). The bioavability of a chemical in the body is influenced, in turn, by the following factors of (Benet, Kroetz & Sheiner, 1995; Sands, Knapp & Ciraulo, 1993): absorption, distribution, biotransformation, and elimination.

Absorption

Except for topical agents, which are deposited directly on the site of action, chemicals must be absorbed into the body. Consequently, the concentration of a chemical in the serum, and at the site of action, is influenced by the process of absorption (Loebl, Spratto, & Woods, 1994). Absorption involves the movement of drug molecules from the site of entry, through various cell boundaries, to the site of action.

The human body is composed of layers of specialized cells, which are organized into specific patterns to carry out certain functions. For example, the cells of the bladder are organized in such a way as to form a muscular reservoir in which waste products can be stored and from which excretion can take place. The cells of the circulatory system are organized in such a manner as to form tubes (blood vessels) that contain the cells and fluids of the circulatory system.

As a general rule, each layer of cells through which the drug must pass to reach the general circulation will slow the absorption. For example, just one layer of cells separates the air in our lungs from the general circulation. Drugs that are able to pass across this boundary may reach the circulation in just a few seconds. By contrast, a drug that is ingested orally must pass through several layers of cells before being able to reach the general circulation from the gastrointestinal tract. Thus the oral method of drug administration is one of the slowest by which a drug might be admitted into the body.

There are a number of specialized *cellular transport mechanisms* that drug molecules can exploit to pass through the walls of the cells at the point of entry. These cellular transport mechanisms are quite complex, and they function at the molecular level. Some drug molecules simply diffuse through the cell membrane, a process that is known as *passive diffusion*, or *passive transport* across the cell boundary. This is the most common method of drug transport into the body's cells; it operates on the principle that chemicals tend to diffuse from areas of high concentration to areas of lower concentration. Other drug molecules take advantage of one of several molecular transport mechanisms, which move various essential molecules into (and out of) cells. Collectively, these different molecular transport mechanisms provide a system of *active transport* across cell boundaries and into the interior of the body.

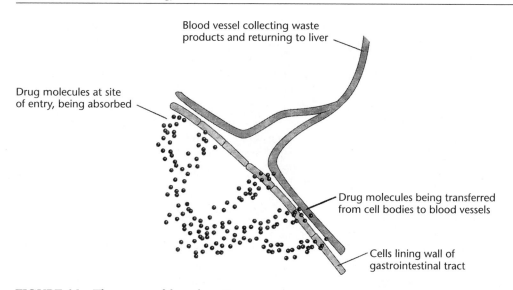

FIGURE 6.1 The process of drug absorption.

A number of variables influence the speed at which drugs can be absorbed from the site of entry. For example, there is the *rate of blood flow* at the site of entry and the *molecular characteristics of the drug molecule* being admitted to the body. However, for the purposes of this text, it is important simply to remember that the process of absorption refers to the movement of drug molecules from the site of entry to the site of action. In the next section, we will discuss the second factor that influences how a chemical acts in the body, its distribution.

Distribution

The process of *distribution* is the way the chemical molecules are moved about in the body. This includes both the process of drug transport and the pattern of drug accumulation within the body at normal dosage levels. As a general rule, very little is known about drug distribution patterns in the overdose victim (Jenkins & Cone, 1998). An example of drug distribution data is the fact that the hallucinogen PCP has been found to accumulate in the brain and in adipose (fat) tissue. Drug distribution is highly variable between individuals, being affected by such factors as the individual's sex, muscle/adipose tissue ratio, blood flow patterns to various body organs, the amount of water in different parts of the body, the individual's genetic heritage, and his or her age (Jenkins & Cone, 1998).

Drug transport. Once a chemical has reached the general circulation, that substance can then be transported to the site of action. But the main purpose of the circulatory system is not to provide a distribution system for drugs! Rather, a drug molecule is a foreign substance that takes advantage of the body's own chemical distribution system to move from the point of entry to the site of action. There are several different ways in which chemicals do this. Some chemicals, the *water-soluble* drugs, are able to mix freely with the blood plasma. Because water is such a large part of the human body, the drug molecules from water-soluble chemicals are rapidly and easily distributed throughout the fluid in the body. Alcohol is an excellent example of a water-soluble chemical. Shortly after gaining admission into the body, alcohol is rapidly distributed throughout the body to *all* blood-rich organs, including the brain.

Other drugs are transported differently. Their chemical structure allows them to "bind" to fat molecules known as *lipids* that are found floating in the general circulation. Chemicals that bind to these fat molecules are often called *lipid-soluble*. Because fat molecules are used to build cell walls within the body, lipids can move rapidly out of the circulatory system into the body tissues. Indeed, blood lipids are constantly passing out of the circulatory system and into the body tissues.

By this means, chemicals that are lipid-soluble are distributed throughout the body, especially to organs with a high concentration of lipids. In comparison to the other organ systems in the body, which are made up of between 6% and 20% lipid molecules, lipids account for fully 50% of the weight of the brain (Cooper, Bloom & Roth, 1986). Thus chemicals that are highly lipid-soluble tend to concentrate rapidly within the tissues of the brain. The short- and ultrashort-acting barbiturates are good examples of lipid-soluble drugs. The speed at which a given barbiturate begins to have an effect depends in part on its ability to form bonds with lipid molecules. The effects of the ultrashort-acting barbiturates might be felt within seconds of the time they are injected into a vein. This is one reason why they are so useful as surgical anesthetics.

Remember that drug molecules are foreign substances in the body. Their presence might be tolerated, but only until the body's natural defenses against chemical intruders are able to detoxify (biotransform) and/or eliminate them. One way that drugs are able to avoid biotransformation and/or elimination before they have an effect is to join with protein molecules that are normally present in human blood.

By coincidence, the chemical structures of many drugs enable the individual molecules to bind with protein molecules in the general circulation. This most often involves a protein known as *albumin*. Such chemicals are said to become "protein-bound" (or, if they bind to albumin, to become "albumin-bound").[4] While a drug molecule is protein-bound, it is difficult for the body to either biotransform or excrete it. Some drugs form stronger chemical bonds with protein molecules than do others, and the strength of this chemical bond determines how long the drug will remain in the body before it is eliminated. However, while they are protein bound, drug molecules are also unable to have any biological effect. To have an effect, the molecule must be free of chemical bonds (*unbound*).

Fortunately, although a chemical might be strongly protein bound, a certain percentage of the drug molecules will always be unbound. For example, if 75% of a given drug's molecules are protein-bound, then 25% of that drug's molecules are said to be unbound, or free.

It is this unbound fraction of drug molecules that will be biologically active. The protein-bound molecules are unable to have any effect at the site of action and are biologically inactive while bound (Shannon, Wilson, & Stang, 1995; Rasymas, 1992). Thus, for chemicals that are largely protein-bound, the unbound drug molecules must be extremely potent.

For example, the antidepressant amitriptyline is 95% protein-bound. This means that only 5% of a given dose of this drug is actually biologically active at any time (Ciraulo, Shader, Greenblatt, & Barnhill, 1995). Another drug that is strongly protein-bound is diazepam. Over 99% of the diazepam molecules that reach the general circulation become protein-bound. Thus the sedative effects of diazepam are actually caused by the small fraction (approximately 1%) of the diazepam molecules that remained unbound after the drug reaches the circulation.

As noted earlier, unbound drug molecules may easily be biotransformed and/or excreted. Thus one advantage of protein binding is that the protein-bound drug molecules form a "reservoir" of drug molecules that have not yet been biotransformed. These drug molecules are gradually released back into the general circulation as the chemical bond between the drug and the protein molecules weakens, or as other molecules compete with the drug for the binding site. The drug molecules that gradually are released back into the general circulation then replace those molecules that have been biotransformed and/or excreted. Thus, although the *amount* of chemical in the general circulation gradually diminishes as the body biotransforms or eliminates the unbound drug molecules, the *proportion* of bound to unbound drug molecules remains essentially unchanged.

Protein binding is related to another trait of a drug: the biological half-life of that chemical. This topic will be discussed in more detail later in this chapter. However, protein binding allows the drug in question to have a longer duration of effect. As the protein-bound molecules are gradually released into the general circulation, the total period of time during which that drug is present in sufficient quantities to remain biologically active is extended.

Biotransformation

Because drugs are foreign substances, the natural defenses launch an effort to eliminate the drug almost

---

[4]In general, acidic drugs tend to bind to albumin, and basic drugs tend to bind to alpha$_1$-acid glycoprotein (Ciancio & Bourgault, 1989).

immediately. In some cases, the body is able to eliminate the drug without modifying its chemical structure. Penicillin is an example of a drug that is excreted unchanged from the body. Many of the inhalants, as well as many of the surgical anesthetics, are also eliminated from the body without being metabolized to any significant degree. But as a general rule, the chemical structure of most chemicals must be modified before they can be eliminated from the body.

This is accomplished through what was once referred to as *detoxification*. However, as researchers have come to understand how the body prepares a drug molecule for elimination, the term "detoxification" has been replaced with the term *biotransformation*.[5] Drug biotransformation usually is carried out in the liver, although on occasion this process is also seen in other tissues of the body. The *microsomal endoplasmic reticulum* of the liver produces a number of enzymes[6] that transform toxic molecules into a form that is more easily eliminated from the body. Technically, the new compound that emerges from each step of the process of drug biotransformation is known as a *metabolite* of the chemical that was introduced into the body. The original chemical is occasionally called the *parent compound* of these metabolites.

In general, metabolites are less biologically active than the parent compound. However, there are exceptions. Depending on the substance being biotransformed, the metabolite might actually have a psychoactive effect of its own. On rare occasions, a drug might actually have a metabolite that is more biologically active than the parent compound.[7] This is why pharmacologists have come to use the term "biotransformation" rather than the older terms "detoxification" and "metabolism."

Although it is easier to speak of drug biotransformation as though it were a single process, there are really four different subforms of this procedure (Ciraulo, Shader, Greenblatt, & Barnhill, 1995): oxidation, reduction, hydrolysis, and conjugation. The complex specifics of each form of drug biotransformation are best reserved for pharmacology texts. It is enough for the reader to remember that many chemicals must go through more than one step in the biotransformation process before they are ready for the next step: *elimination*.

One major goal of the process of metabolism is to transform the foreign chemical into a form that can be rapidly eliminated from the body (Clark, Bratler, & Johnson, 1991). But this process does not take place instantly. Rather, the process of biotransformation is accomplished through chemical reactions facilitated by enzymes produced in the body. This process is carried out over a period of time, and depending on the drug involved, there are often a number of intermediate steps in the process of biotransformation before that chemical is ready for elimination.

Simply stated, the goal of the drug biotransformation process is to change the chemical structure of the foreign substance in such a way that it is less lipid-soluble and thus more easily eliminated from the body. There are two major forms of drug biotransformation. In the first subtype, a constant fraction of the drug is biotransformed in a given period of time, such as a single hour. This is called a *first order biotransformation* process. Certain antibiotics are metabolized in this manner. Other chemicals are eliminated from the body by what is known as a *zero order biotransformation* process. Such drugs are metabolized at a set rate, no matter how high the concentration of that chemical in the blood.

Alcohol is a good example of a chemical that is biotransformed through a zero-order biotransformation process. Alcohol is biotransformed at the rate of about one regular mixed drink, or one can of beer, per hour. It does not matter whether the person ingests just that one drink or 20 drinks in an hour. His or her body still biotransforms only the equivalent of one can of beer or one mixed drink per hour. This is what a zero-order biotransformation process means.

As a general rule, chemicals that are administered orally must pass through the stomach to the small intestine before they are absorbed. However, the human circulatory system is designed in such a way that chemicals absorbed through the gastrointestinal system are carried

---

[5]This process is inaccurately referred to as metabolism of a drug. Technically, the term "drug metabolism" refers to everything the drug undergoes in the body, including its absorption, distribution, biotransformation, and excretion.

[6]The most common of these routes is known as the P-450 metabolic pathway, or the microsomal P-450 pathway.

[7]For example, after gamma-hydroxybutyrate (GHB) was banned by the Food and Drug Administration, illicit users switched to the compound gamma-butyrol-actone (a compound with reported health benefits such as improved sleep patterns), which is biotransformed into the banned substance GHB in the user's body.

first to the liver, where the body is able to begin to break down any toxins in the substance before those toxins can damage other organ systems.

Unfortunately, one effect of this process is that the liver is often able to biotransform many medications that are administered orally before they have had a chance to reach the site of action. This *first-pass metabolism* is one reason why it is so hard to control pain via orally administered narcotic analgesic medications.

Elimination

In the human body, biotransformation and elimination are closely intertwined. Indeed, some authorities on the subject of pharmacology consider them to be a single process, because one goal of drug biotransformation is to change the foreign chemical into a water-soluble metabolite that can then be easily removed from the circulation (Clark, Bratler, & Johnson, 1991).

The organs most commonly used to eliminate drugs are the kidneys (Benet, Kroetz, & Sheiner, 1995). However, the biliary tract, lungs, and sweat glands may also play a role in the process of drug elimination (Shannon, Wilson, & Stang, 1995). For example, a small percentage of the alcohol that a person has ingested is excreted when that person exhales. A small percentage of the alcohol in the system is also eliminated through the sweat glands. These characteristics of alcohol contribute to the characteristic smell of the intoxicated individual.

Key Considerations in Assessing the Effects of Chemicals

The Drug Half-life

There are several different measures of *drug half-life*, all of which provide a *rough* estimate of the period of time that a drug remains active in the human body. The *distribution half-life* is the time that it takes for 50% of a drug to work its way from the general circulation into body tissues such as muscle and fat tissues (Reiman, 1997). This is important information in overdose situations, for example, where the physician treating the patient has to estimate the amount of compound(s) in the patient's circulation. Another measure of drug activity in the body is the *therapeutic half-life*, or the period of time that it takes for the body to inactivate 50% of a single dose of a compound. The therapeutic half-life is

intertwined with the concept of the *elimination half-life*. This is the time it takes for 50% of a single dose to be *eliminated* from the body.

For example, different chemicals might rapidly migrate from the general circulation into adipose or muscle tissues, with the result that that compound would have a short distribution half-life. THC, the active agent in marijuana, is one example of such a compound. For heavy users, however, a reservoir of unmetabolized THC forms in the adipose tissue, which is gradually released back into the user's circulation when she or he stops using marijuana. This gives THC a long elimination half-life in the chronic user, although the therapeutic half-life of a single dose is quite short.

In this text, we will lump all of these different measures of half-life together under the term *biological half-life* (or *half-life*) of that chemical. Sometimes, the half-life is abbreviated by the symbol $t_{1/2}$. The half-life of a chemical will be viewed as the period of time required for the individual's body to reduce the amount of active drug in the circulation by one-half (Benet, Kroetz, & Sheiner, 1995). The concept of $t_{1/2}$ is based on the assumption that the individual ingested only one dose of the drug, and the reader should keep in mind that the dynamics of a drug following a single dose are often far different from those for the same drug when it is used on a chronic basis. Thus, although the $t_{1/2}$ concept is often a source of confusion even among health professionals, it does allow health care workers to estimate how long a drug's effects will last when that chemical is used at normal dosage levels.

One popular misconception is that it takes only two half-lives for the body to eliminate a drug totally. In reality, 25% of the original dose remains at the end of the 2nd half-life period, and 12% of the original dose still is in the body at the end of three half-life periods. As a general rule, it takes five half-life periods for the body to eliminate virtually all of a single dose of a chemical (Williams & Baer, 1994). See Figure 6.2.

Generally, drugs with long half-life periods tend to remain biologically active for longer periods of time. The reverse is also true; that is, chemicals with a short biological half-life tend to be active for shorter periods of time. This is where the process of protein binding comes into play: Drugs with longer half-lives tend to become protein-bound. Protein binding allows a "reservoir" of an unmetabolized drug to be released gradually

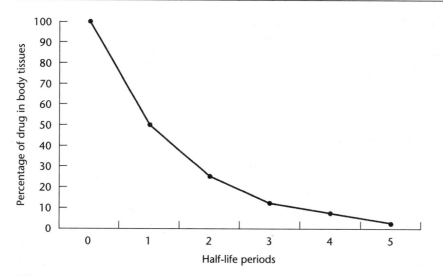

FIGURE 6.2   Drug elimination in half-life stages.

into the general circulation, as the drug molecules become "unbound." This enables a chemical to remain in the circulation at a sufficient concentration to have an effect for an extended period of time.

The Effective Dose

The concept of the *effective dose* (ED) is based on dose-response calculations, in which pharmacologists calculate what percentage of a population will respond to a given dose of a chemical. Scientists usually estimate the percentage of the population that is expected to experience an effect by a chemical at different dosage levels. For example, the ED_{10} is that dosage level where 10% of the population will experience the desired effects.

The ED_{50} is the dosage level where 50% of the population would experience the drug's effects. Obviously, for medications, the goal is to find a dosage level where the largest percentage of the population will respond to the medication. However, you cannot keep increasing the dose of a medication forever. Sooner or later you will raise the dosage level to the point where the drug will start to have toxic effects, and that patient may even die from the effects of the chemical.

The Lethal Dose Index

Drugs are, by their very nature, foreign to the body. By definition, drugs that are introduced into the body will disrupt the function of the body in one way or another.

Indeed, one common characteristic of both legitimate pharmaceuticals and the drugs of abuse is that the person who administered that chemical hopes to alter the body's function to bring about a desired effect. But chemicals that are introduced into the body have the potential to disrupt the function of one or more organ systems to the point where it is no longer possible for these systems to function normally. Chemicals may even disrupt the body's activities to the point where the very life of the individual is in danger.

Scientists express this continuum as a form of modified dose-response curve. However, whereas in the typical dose-response curve, scientists calculate the percentage of the population that would be expected to benefit from a certain exposure to a chemical, the calculation for a fatal exposure level is slightly different. In such a dose-response curve, scientists calculate the percentage of the general population that would, in theory, die as a result of being exposed to a certain dose of a chemical or toxin.

This figure is then expressed in terms of a *lethal dose* (LD) ratio. The percentage of the population that would die as a result of exposure to that chemical or toxin source is identified as a subscript to the LD heading. Thus, if a certain level of exposure to a chemical or toxin resulted in a 25% death rate, this level would be abbreviated as the LD_{25} for that chemical or toxin. A level of exposure to a toxin or chemical that resulted in a 50% death rate would be abbreviated as the LD_{50} for that substance.

For example, as we will discuss in the next chapter, a person with a blood alcohol level of 0.350 mg/mL would stand a 1% chance of death without medical intervention. Thus a blood level of 0.350 mg/mL is the LD_{01} for alcohol. It is possible to calculate the potential lethal exposure level for virtually every chemical. These figures give scientists a way to calculate the relative safety of different levels of exposure to chemicals or radiation—and a way to determine when medical intervention is necessary.

The Therapeutic Index

In addition to their potential to benefit the user, all drugs also have the potential to do harm if used in too great an amount.

Scientists have devised what is known as the therapeutic index (TI) as a way to measure the relative safety of a chemical. Essentially, the TI is the ratio of the ED_{50} to the LD_{50}. In other words, the TI is a ratio between the effectiveness of a chemical and the potential for harm inherent in using that chemical. A smaller TI means that there is only a small margin between the dosage level needed to achieve the therapeutic effects and the dosage level at which the drug becomes toxic to the individual. A large TI suggests that there is a great deal of latitude between the normal therapeutic dosage range and the dosage level at which that chemical might become toxic to the user.

Unfortunately, as we will see in the next few chapters, many of the drugs of abuse have a small TI. These chemicals are potentially quite toxic to the user. For example, as we will see when we discuss barbiturate abuse, the ratio between the normal dosage range and the toxic dosage range for the barbiturates is only about 1:30. In contrast to this, the ratio between the normal dosage range and the toxic dosage level for the benzodiazepines is estimated to be about 1:200. Thus, relatively speaking, the benzodiazepines are said to be much safer than the barbiturates.

Peak Effects

The effects of a chemical within the body develop over a period of time, until the drug reaches what is known as the *therapeutic threshold*. The therapeutic threshold is the point at which the concentration of a specific chemical in the body allows it to begin to have the desired effect on the user. The chemical's effects continue to become stronger and stronger until, finally, the strongest possible effects from a dose of that drug are reached. This is the period of *peak effects*. Then, gradually, the impact of the drug becomes less and less pronounced as the chemical is eliminated/biotransformed over a period of time. Eventually, the concentration of the chemical in the body falls below the therapeutic level. Scientists have learned to calculate dose-response curves in order to estimate the potential for a chemical to have an effect at any given time after it was administered. Figure 6.3 is an example.

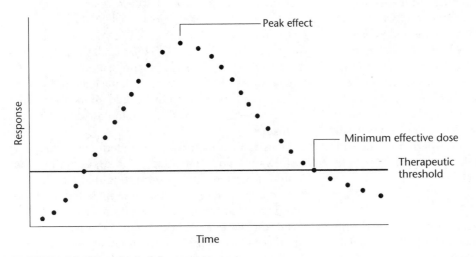

FIGURE 6.3 Hypothetical dose-response curve.

The period of peak effects following a single dose of a drug varies from one chemical to another. For example, the peak effects of an ultrashort-acting barbiturate might be achieved in a matter of seconds following a single dose, whereas the long-term barbiturate phenobarbital might take hours to achieve its strongest effects.

Sites and Structures of Special Importance in Pharamacology

The Site of Action

To illustrate the concept of the *site of action*, consider the case of a person with an "athlete's foot" infection. This condition is caused by a fungus that attacks the skin. Obviously, the individual who has such an infection will want to have it cured, and there are several excellent over-the-counter antifungal compounds available. In most cases, the individual need only select one, and then apply it to the proper area, in order to be cured of the infection.

At about this point, somebody is asking what antifungal compounds have to do with drug abuse. The example of the "athlete's foot" infection helps to illustrate the concept of the *site of action*. To put it simply, the site of action is where the drug being used will have its prime effect. In the case of the medication being used for the "athlete's foot" infection, the site of action is the infected skin on the person's foot. For the drugs of abuse, the central nervous system (CNS) will be the primary site of action.

Receptor Sites

The receptor site is the exact spot, either on the cell wall or within the cell itself, where the chemical exerts its main effects (Olson, 1992). Most drugs bind either to specific receptor sites on the cell wall or with one of various proteins within the cell. The receptor site is usually a pattern of molecules that, by coincidence, allows a single drug molecule to attach itself to the target portion of the cell at that point. For example, those forms of bacteria that are susceptible to the antibiotic penicillin have a characteristic "receptor site," the enzyme transpeptidase, that allows the antibiotic to work against that specific germ. This enzyme carries out an essential role in bacterial reproduction. By blocking the action of transpeptidase, penicillin prevents the bacteria cells from reproducing. Eventually, the bacteria cells are destroyed, as they continue to grow without being able to multiply.

In general, the drugs of abuse achieve their main effects by altering the function of the individual nerve cells (*neurons*) within specific regions of the CNS. The drugs accomplish this by either simulating or altering the action of chemical messengers, known as *neurotransmitters*, that pass between neurons. Neurotransmitters are the means by which neurons communicate with each other. By altering the action of certain neurotransmitters in specific regions of the brain, chemicals can alter the individual's subjective perception and feelings.

Although the adult human brain is perhaps the most complex, and is certainly the most compact, organ in the body, the individual neurons actually do not touch each other. Rather, microscopic examination of the brain reveals that the neurons are separated by small spaces known as *synapses*. To pass information across such a gap, one neuron will release a small amount of a chemical neurotransmitter from the end of its axon. Some of these molecules will drift across the synapse to receptor sites located on the cell wall of the next neuron in the circuit. The analogy of a key slipping into the slot of a lock is appropriate to understanding the "fit" between a neurotransmitter and its receptor site. If a sufficient number of receptor sites are occupied at the same instant, the electrical potential of the receiving neuron is changed, and it will pass the message on to the next cell.

Following the release of the neurotransmitter molecules, the first neuron activates molecular "pumps" that absorb, for reuse, as many as possible of the free-floating neurotransmitter molecules that were just released. At the same time, this neuron will also work to manufacture more of that neurotransmitter for future use, storing both the reabsorbed and the newly manufactured neurotransmitter molecules in special sacks within the nerve cell.

Essentially, all of the chemicals known to function as neurotransmitters within the CNS might be said to fall into two groups: those that stimulate the neuron to release a chemical "message" to the next cell and those that inhibit the release of neurotransmitters. By altering the flow of these two classes of neurotransmitters, the drugs of abuse alter the way the CNS functions.

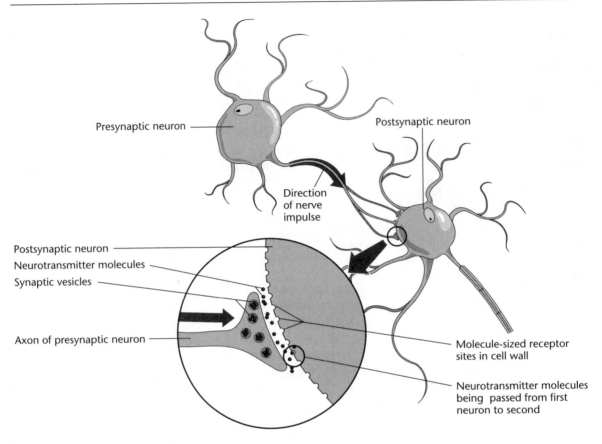

Presynaptic neuron

Postsynaptic neuron

Direction
of nerve
impulse

Postsynaptic neuron
Neurotransmitter molecules
Synaptic vesicles

Axon of presynaptic neuron

Molecule-sized receptor
sites in cell wall

Neurotransmitter molecules
being passed from first
neuron to second

FIGURE 6.4   Neurotransmitter diagram.

Upregulation and downregulation. The individual neurons of the CNS are not passive participants in the process of information transfer. Rather, each individual neuron is constantly adapting to the level of activity demanded of it by either increasing or decreasing the possible number of neurotransmitter receptor sites on the cell wall. If a neuron is subjected to high levels of a given neurotransmitter or a similar chemical, that nerve cell will respond by increasing the number of possible receptor sites in the cell wall. This will give the neurotransmitter molecules a larger number of possible "targets" (receptor sites), reducing the frequency with which that neuron will be required to "fire." Scientists call this process *upregulation,* and it is one reason why a person becomes tolerant to a drug's effects.

In many cases, if there is a significant drop in the number of neurotransmitter molecules being released by one neuron, the next neuron in line will decrease the total number of possible receptor sites by absorbing/inactivating some of the receptor sites in the cell wall. This is the process of *downregulation,* by which a neuron decreases the total number of receptor sites necessary to cause it to "fire." To understand the process of upregulation/downregulation, remember that for a given neuron to fire, a *certain percentage* of the receptor sites must be occupied at the same instant. If there is a surplus of neurotransmitter molecules arriving at the receptor sites, the neuron will be forced to fire frequently, possibly sending "false" signals. To reduce chances that this will occur, the neuron increases the total number of possible receptor sites, but the *critical percentage required to activate that neuron remains the same.*

For example, assume that 70% of the receptor sites must be occupied in the same instant before a given neuron can fire. Rather than a neuron having to fire every time 70% of 200 receptor sites are occupied by a neurotransmitter molecule, the process of upregulation allows a neuron to increase the number of receptor sites to perhaps 400. A larger number of neurotransmitter molecules would be necessary to reach the critical figure of 70% of these 400 receptor sites, allowing that neuron to reduce its firing rate. In other words, during periods of neurotransmitter surplus, neurons in many regions of the brain upregulate the number of receptor sites. During times of neurotransmitter deficit, these same neurons will tend to downregulate the number of receptor sites and hence maintain a relatively constant firing rate.

Tolerance and cross-tolerance. In brief, *tolerance* is a reflection of the body's ongoing struggle to maintain normal function. Because a drug is a foreign substance, the body will attempt to continue its normal function in spite of the presence of the chemical. Part of the process of adaptation in the CNS is the upregulation/downregulation of receptor sites, as the neurons attempt to maintain a normal level of firing.

As the body adapts to the effects of the chemical, the individual will no longer achieve the same effect from the original dose and must use larger and larger doses in order to maintain the original effect. When a chemical is used as a neuropharmaceutical (a drug that is intentionally introduced into the body by a physician to alter the function of the CNS in a desired manner), tolerance is often referred to as the process of *neuro-adaptation*. If the drug being used is a recreational substance, the same process is usually called tolerance. However, neuroadaptation and tolerance are essentially the same biological adaptation. The only difference is that one involves a pharmaceutical, the other a recreational chemical.

The concepts of a drug agonist and antagonist. To understand how the drugs of abuse work, it is necessary to grasp the twin concepts of a drug agonist and antagonist. These may be difficult concepts for students of drug abuse to understand. Essentially, a drug *agonist* mimics the effect(s) of a chemical that is naturally found in the body (Shannon, Wilson, & Stang, 1995). Either the agonist tricks the body into reacting as though the endogenous chemical were present, or it enhances the effect(s) of the naturally occurring chemical. For example, as we will see when we discuss the abuse of opiates, there are morphine-like chemicals found in the human brain that help to control the level

of pain the individual is experiencing. Heroin, morphine, and the other narcotic analgesics mimic the actions of these chemicals and, for this reason, might be classified as agonists of the naturally occurring painkilling chemicals.

The antagonist essentially blocks the effects of a chemical already working within the body. In a sense, aspirin might be classified as a prostaglandin antagonist, because aspirin blocks the normal actions of the prostaglandins. Antagonists may also block the effects of certain chemicals introduced into the body for one reason or another. For example, the drug Narcan blocks the receptor sites in the CNS that opiates normally bind to in order to exert their effect. Narcan thus is an antagonist for opiates and is of value in reversing the effects of an opiate overdose.

Because the drugs of abuse either simulate the effects of actual neurotransmitters or alter the action of existing neurotransmitters, they either enhance or retard the frequency with which the neurons of the brain "fire" (Ciancio & Bourgault, 1989). The constant use of any of the drugs of abuse forces the neurons to go through the process of neuroadaptation, as they struggle to maintain normal function in spite of the artificial stimulation/inhibition caused by the drug. In other words, depending on whether the drug of abuse causes a surplus or a deficit of neurotransmitter molecules, the neurons in many regions of the brain upregulate or downregulate the number of receptor sites, in an attempt to maintain normal function. This will cause the individual's responsiveness to that drug to be different over time, a process that is part of the development of tolerance.

When the body begins to adapt to the presence of one chemical, it will often also become tolerant to the effects of other drugs that have the same mechanism of action. This effect is called *cross-tolerance*. For example, a chronic alcohol user will often require higher doses of CNS depressants than a nondrinker in order to achieve a given level of sedation. Physicians have often noticed this effect in the surgical theatre: Chronic alcohol users require larger doses of anesthetics than nondrinkers to achieve a given level of unconsciousness. Anesthetics and alcohol are both classified as CNS depressants. The individual's tolerance to the effects of alcohol will, through the development of *cross-tolerance*, cause him or her to require a larger dose of many anesthetics, in order for the surgery to proceed.

The Blood-Brain Barrier

The blood-brain barrier (BBB) is a unique structure in the human body. Its role is to function as a "gateway" to the brain. In this role, the BBB will allow only certain molecules needed by the brain to pass through. For example, oxygen and glucose, both essential to life, pass easily through the BBB (Angier, 1990). But the BBB exists to protect the brain from toxins and infectious organisms. To this end, endothelial cells that form the lining of the BBB have established tight seals with overlapping cells.

Initially, students of neuroanatomy may be confused by the term blood-brain barrier, for when we usually speak of a barrier, we usually mean a single structure. The BBB, however, is the result of a unique feature of the cells that form the capillaries through which cerebral blood flows. Unlike capillary walls throughout the rest of the body, those of the cerebral circulatory system are securely joined together. Each endothelial cell is joined to its neighbors, forming a tight tube-like structure that protects the brain from direct contact with the general circulation. Thus many chemicals in the general circulation are blocked from entering the CNS. However, the individual cells of the brain require nutritional support, and some of the very substances that the brain needs, such as glucose and iron, are blocked by the endothelial cell boundary.

To overcome this problem, specialized transport systems, have evolved in the endothelial cells in the cerebral circulatory system. These transport systems selectively allow needed nutrients to pass through the lining of the endothelial cell to reach the brain (Angier, 1990). Each of these transport systems selectively admits one specific type of water-soluble molecule, such as a glucose.

But lipids also pass through the lining of the endothelial cells and are able to reach the CNS beyond. Lipids are basically molecules of fat. Lipids are essential elements of cell walls, which are made up of lipids, carbohydrates, and protein molecules, arranged in a specific order. As the lipid molecule reaches the endothelial cell wall, it gradually merges with the molecules of the cell wall and passes through into the interior of the endothelial cell. Later, it will also pass through the lining of the far side of the endothelial cell to reach the neurons beyond the lining of the BBB.

Summary

In this chapter, we have examined some of the basic components of pharmacology. It is not necessary for students in the field of substance abuse to have the same depth of knowledge possessed by pharmacists. However, it is important for the reader to understand at least some of the basic concepts of pharmacology, in order to understand how the drugs of abuse achieve their primary and their secondary effects. Hence this chapter offers basic information regarding drug forms, methods of drug administration, and biotransformation/elimination.

Other concepts discussed in this chapter include a drug's bioavailability, the therapeutic half-life of a chemical, the effective dose and lethal dose, the therapeutic dose ratio, and how drugs need receptor sites in order to work. The student should have at least a basic understanding of these concepts, before starting to review the different drugs of abuse discussed in the following chapters.

CHAPTER SEVEN

An Introduction to Alcohol

Introduction

Although scientists do not know when early humans discovered alcohol's intoxicating effects, the history of alcohol use is believed to date back at least 10,000–15,000 years (Potter, 1997). It is thought that prehistoric humans learned about the intoxicating effects of fermented fruit by watching animals eat such fruit from the forest floor and then act strangely. Curiosity may then have compelled one or two brave souls to try some of the fermented fruits that the animals seemed to enjoy (R. Siegel, 1986). Having discovered alcohol's intoxicating action, prehistoric humans started to experiment and eventually discovered how to produce alcoholic beverages.

It is not unrealistic to say that "alcohol and the privilege of drinking have always been important to human beings" (Brown, 1995, p. 4). Indeed, it has even been suggested that alcohol use is a "yardstick" by which cultural development can be measured:

> [V]irtually all cultures—whether hunter-gatherers or farmers; whether technologically advanced or primitive— share two universals: the development of a noodle and the discovery and use of the natural fermentation process. (Beasley, 1987, p. 17)

Some anthropologists now believe that early civilization came about in response to the need for a stable home base from which to ferment a form of beer known as *mead* (Stone, 1991). Most certainly, the brewing and consumption of beer were of considerable im-

portance to the inhabitants of Sumer,[1] for many of the clay tablets that have been found are devoted to the process of brewing beer (Cahill, 1998). If this theory is correct, then it would seem that human civilization owes much to alcohol, which is also known as ethanol, or *ethyl alcohol.*[2]

A Brief History of Alcohol

Historians believe that it was not until the 19th century that most Western countries could provide clean, safe water for people to drink (McAnalley, 1996). Prior to this, people used wine and various forms of beer to quench their thirst. The earliest written records of beer making date back only 4000 years, to approximately 1800 B.C. (Stone, 1991). However, historical evidence would suggest that a form of beer was in common use around the year 8000 B.C. (Ray & Ksir, 1993).[3] This form of beer was quite unlike modern beers. Its thick liquid was quite nutritious, providing many necessary vitamins and amino acids. Modern beer is very thin and almost anemic, compared to the beer of our prehistoric ancestors.

Beer and wine are also mentioned several times in the *Illiad* and the *Odyssey* of Homer, legends that date back thousands of years. The earliest written record of

---

[1]See the Glossary at the end of the book.

[2]At least 45 other forms of alcohol exist, but these are not normally used for human consumption and will not be discussed further in this text.

[3]Remember that 8000 B.C. was 10,000 years ago.

wine making is found in an Egyptian tomb from around the year 3000 B.C. (*Los Angeles Times,* 1996a), although scientists have uncovered evidence suggesting that ancient Sumerians may have used wine made from fermented grapes in the year 5400 B.C. (*Los Angeles Times,* 1996a). On the basis of these studies, it would appear that alcohol has been a part of human culture for a long, long time.

How Alcohol Is Produced

By whatever means, somehow humans discovered that if you crush certain fruits and allow them to stand for a period of time in a container, alcohol is produced. We now know that unseen microorganisms called yeast, which float in the air, settle on the crushed fruit, multiply, and begin to digest the sugars in the fruit through a chemical process called *fermentation.* The yeast breaks down the carbon, hydrogen, and oxygen atoms it finds in the sugar for food and, in the process, produces molecules of ethyl alcohol and carbon dioxide as waste. Waste products are often toxic to the organism that produces them, and so it is with alcohol. When the concentration of alcohol in a container reaches about 15%, it becomes toxic to the yeast, and fermentation stops. Thus the highest alcohol concentration that one might achieve by natural fermentation is about 15%.

Several thousand years passed before humans learned to obtain alcohol concentrations above this 15% limit. Then, around A.D. 800, the process of *distillation* was introduced. Somehow it was discovered that alcohol boils at a much lower temperature than water. Because this is true, when wine is boiled, some of the alcohol content boils off as a vapor, or steam. This steam contains more ethyl alcohol than water vapor, and if it is collected and allowed to cool down, the resulting liquid will have a higher concentration of alcohol, and a lower concentration of water, than did the original mixture. Over time, it was discovered that the cooling process could take place in a metal coil, allowing the liquid to drip from the end of the coil into a container of some kind. This device is the famous "still" of lore and legend.

Ethyl alcohol is an extraordinary source of energy. The human body is able to obtain almost as much energy from alcohol as from fat, and far more energy gram for gram than it can obtain from carbohydrates or pro-

teins (Lieber, 1998). It is for this reason that alcohol-containing beverages such as wine and beer were considered a part of the individual's diet for much of history.[4] Unfortunately, as a result of the process of distillation, many of the vitamins and minerals found in the original wine and beer are lost. This is why many dietitians refer to alcohol as a source of "empty" calories. Over time, the chronic ingestion of alcohol-containing beverages can contribute to a state of vitamin depletion called *avitaminosis,* which will be discussed in the next chapter.

Within two centuries of its discovery, the process of distillation had spread from Arabia, where is was developed, to Europe. It is reported that by A.D. 1000 Italian wine growers were using distillation to produce various drinks with higher concentrations of alcohol than natural wine. It was found that by mixing the obtained distilled "spirits" with various herbs and spices, one could produce different flavors in the fluids that resulted from this process. Many of these compounds were used for medicinal purposes by physicians of the era. Because of the widespread abuse of alcohol, a number of attempts have been made over the years to control or regulate alcohol use in Europe and the New World. These attempts at alcohol regulation have been almost uniformly unsuccessful.

Alcohol Today

Over the last 900 years since the development of the distillation process, various forms of fermented wines using various ingredients, different forms of beer, and distilled spirits combined with various flavorings have emerged. Surprisingly, no agreement has emerged about what constitutes a "standard" drink or what alcohol concentrations might be included in different alcoholic beverages (Duvour, 1999).

At this time most beer in the United States has an alcohol content of between 3.5% and 5% (Duvour, 1999; Herman, 1993). However, some brands of "light" beer might have less than 3% alcohol content, and "speciality" beers or malt liquors might contain up to 9% alcohol (Duvour, 1999). In the United States, wine contin-

---

[4]When the Puritans set sail for the New World, for example, they carried with them 14 tons of water and 42 tons of beer (Freeborn, 1996). The fact that they ran out of beer was one reason why they decided to settle where they did (McAnalley, 1996).

ues to be made by allowing fermentation to take place in vats containing various grapes or other fruits. Occasionally, especially in other countries, the fermentation involves products other than grapes, such as the famous "rice wine" from Japan called *sake*. In the United States, wine usually has an alcohol content of approximately 8% to 17% (Herman, 1993), although "light" wines might be about 7% alcohol, and wine "coolers" generally contain 5% to 7% alcohol (Duvour, 1999).

In addition to wine, there are the "fortified" wines, which are produced mixing distilled wine with fermented wine to raise the total alcohol content to about 20% to 24% (Duvour, 1999). Examples of fortified wines include sherry and port (Herman, 1993). Finally, there are the "hard liquors," the distilled spirits, which have generally 40% to 50% alcohol by volume (Duvour, 1999). However, there are exceptions to this rule, and some beverages contain 80% or higher alcohol concentrations, such as the famous "Everclear" distilled in the southern United States.

Scope of the Problem of Alcohol Use

Beverages that contain alcohol are moderately popular drinks. In 1998, 90.6% of the adults between the ages of 19 and 32 surveyed reported that they had consumed alcohol at least once (Johnston, O'Malley, & Bachman, 1999b). Given its current popularity, it is surprising to many people that alcohol consumption in the United States actually peaked almost two centuries ago, around the year 1830. At that time, the annual per capita consumption of alcohol was an estimated 7.1 gallons of pure alcohol (Musto, 1996; Heerema, 1990). In recent years, the per capita level of alcohol use in the United States has fallen from about 2.76 gallons of pure alcohol/person in 1980, to 2.43 gallons in 1989, to about 2.35 gallons per in 1996 (McAnalley, 1996; Musto, 1996).

In this country, just 10% of those who drink consume 50% of the alcohol ingested (Kaplan, Sadock, & Grebb, 1994). As the individual's frequency of alcohol use, and the amount of alcohol ingested, increase, she or he becomes more likely to develop some of the complications induced by excessive alcohol use. The impact of excessive alcohol use will be discussed in more detail in the next chapter. In this chapter, we will focus on the casual drinker.

The Pharmacology of Alcohol

Ethyl alcohol, or simply "alcohol," may be introduced into the body intravenously or inhaled as a vapor, but the most common means by which alcohol is taken into the body is by oral ingestion as a liquid. The alcohol molecule is quite small, and it is soluble in both water and lipids, although it shows a preference for the former (Jones, 1996). When consumed in sufficient quantities, alcohol molecules are rapidly distributed to all blood-rich tissues throughout the body, including the brain. Indeed, because alcohol is so readily soluble in lipids, high concentrations of alcohol in the brain are very rapidly achieved. Alcohol also diffuses into muscle and fat tissues, so very obese and very muscular persons normally have a slightly lower blood alcohol level than leaner persons after a given dose.

The main route of alcohol absorption is through the small intestine (Baselt, 1996). But when alcohol is ingested in the absence of food, about 10% (Kaplan, Sadock, & Grebb, 1994) to 25% (Baselt, 1996) of the alcohol is immediately absorbed through the stomach lining, the first molecules of alcohol appearing in the drinker's blood in as little as one minute (Rose, 1988). Although the liver is the primary organ where alcohol is biotransformed in the human body, an enzyme known as *gastric alcohol dehydrogenase* begins the process of alcohol biotransformation in the stomach (Frezza, DiPadova, Pozzato, Terpin, Baraona, & Lieber, 1990). The levels of gastric alcohol dehydrogenase are highest in occasional social drinkers; they are significantly lower in regular/chronic drinkers and in people who have taken an aspirin tablet before drinking (Roine, Gentry, Hernandez-Munoz, Baraona, & Lieber, 1990).

When alcohol is consumed on an empty stomach, the drinker experiences the peak blood levels of alcohol between 30 and 120 minutes after a single drink (Baselt, 1996). When consumed with food, alcohol is absorbed more slowly, and peak blood levels are not reached until 1 to 6 hours after a single drink was ingested (Baselt, 1996). However, all of the alcohol consumed is eventually absorbed into the drinker's circulation. Researchers have long known that men tend to have lower blood alcohol levels than women after consuming a given amount of alcohol. There are several reasons for this. First, males tend to produce more gastric alcohol dehydrogenase than women (Frezza, DiPadova, Pozzato, Terpin, Baraona, & Lieber, 1990. Also, women tend to have lower body weights, lower muscle-to-body-mass ratios, and 10% less water in their bodies (Zealberg & Brady, 1999).

In the brain, alcohol has a number of effects on the cellular and regional levels. On the cellular level, researchers have suggested several different theories to explain the effects of alcohol on the brain. It was once thought that alcohol's effects were caused by its ability to disrupt the structure and function of the lipids in the cell wall of the neurons. This *membrane fluidization theory*, or *membrane hypothesis*, dates back to the turn of the century (Tabakoff & Hoffman, 1992). This theory rests on the fact that alcohol is known to disrupt the structure of lipids, making it more difficult for the neurons to maintain normal function. However, researchers are still not sure which lipids are affected by alcohol or which components within the neuron are most sensitive to alcohol's effects. Indeed, there are strong reasons to question whether the membrane hypothesis can account for alcohol's observed effects.

Another theory suggests that alcohol disrupts the normal function of neurons by interacting with protein molecules within the cell walls of the neuron (Valenzuela & Harris, 1997; Tabakoff & Hoffman, 1992). These protein molecules help to form the ion channels and neurotransmitter receptor sites in the walls of neurons. Other protein molecules help to form some of the enzymes found in the brain (Tabakoff & Hoffman, 1992). Through this interaction with protein molecules at the neurotransmitter receptor sites, alcohol interferes with the normal function of the neuron, causing the characteristic feeling of intoxication.

One of the neurotransmitter receptor sites in the brain affected by alcohol is utilized by the amino acid *N-methyl-D-aspartate* (NMDA), which functions as an excitatory amino acid within the brain (Valenzuela & Harris, 1997; Hobbs, Rall, & Verdoorn, 1995). Alcohol blocks the influx of calcium atoms through the ion channels normally activated when NMDA binds at those sites. In a very real sense, alcohol might be said to be an NMDA antagonist (Tsai, Gastfriend, & Coyle, 1995). At the same time, alcohol enhances the influx of chloride atoms through an ion channel at the receptor site utilized by gamma-amino-butyric acid (GABA) (Valenzuela & Harris, 1997; Marshall, 1994). GABA is the main inhibitory neurotransmitter in the brain, and approximately 20% of all neurotransmitter recep-

tors in the brain are devoted to GABA (Mosier, 1999). Neurons that utilize GABA are found in the cortex,[5] the cerebellum, the hippocampus, the superior and inferior colliculi regions of the brain, the amygdala, and the nucleus accumbens.

By blocking the effects of the excitatory amino acid NMDA while facilitating the inhibitory neurotransmitter GABA in these various regions of the brain, alcohol is able to depress the action of the central nervous system. There is evidence that the pleasure, or euphoria, that some drinkers experience from alcohol is brought on by the ability of this chemical to activate the endorphin reward system within the brain (Nutt, 1996). However, other researchers believe that alcohol's euphoric effects are brought on by its ability to stimulate the release of the neurotransmitter dopamine. Some researchers believe that alcohol use interferes with the process of dopamine reuptake, forcing the neurons to empty their stores of dopamine back into the synaptic junction (Heinz, Ragan, Jones, Hommer, Williams, Knable, Gorey, Doty, Geyer, Lee, Coppola, Weinberger, & Linnoila, 1998). Alcohol is also known to cause the release of the neurotransmitter serotonin in many parts of the brain. Recently, researchers have discovered that when alcohol is used in low to moderate concentrations, it seems to potentiate the effects of serotonin at one of the subtypes of receptor sites used by this neurotransmitter (Hobbs, Rall, & Verdoorn, 1995). This receptor site is located on certain neurons that inhibit behavioral impulses, and it is this action that seems to account at least in part for alcohol's disinhibitory effects.

Scientists still do not completely understand, or agree, how alcohol affects the function of either individual neurons or different regions of the human brain. But researchers generally agree that alcohol is a potent drug of abuse that affects the normal function of virtually every neuron in the CNS.

The Biotransformation of Alcohol

Depending on the individual's blood alcohol level, between 2% to 10% of the alcohol ingested will be excreted unchanged through the lungs, skin, and urine, with higher percentages of alcohol being excreted unchanged in those individuals with greater blood alcohol

[5]See the Glossary.

levels (Schuckit, 1998). As is the case for most toxins that gain entry into the body, however, the liver is the primary site where this foreign chemical is broken down and removed from the blood (Brennan, Betzelos, Reed, & Falk, 1995). Alcohol biotransformation is accomplished in two steps. First, the liver produces an enzyme known as *alcohol dehydrogenase* (ADH), which breaks the alcohol down into acetaldehyde. It has been suggested that ADH evolved in our ancestors because it enables them to biotransform fermented fruits or the small amount of alcohol produced endogenously (Jones, 1996).

In high concentrations, acetaldehyde is quite toxic to the body, although there is evidence that small amounts might function as a stimulant (Schuckit, 1998). Fortunately, many different parts of the body produce a second enzyme, *aldehyde dehydrogenase*, which breaks acetaldehyde down into acetic acid.[6] Ultimately, alcohol is biotransformed into carbon dioxide, water, and fatty acids (carbohydrates).

The speed of alcohol biotransformation. There is some individual variation in the speed at which alcohol is biotransformed in the body (Garriott, 1996). However, a rule of thumb is that the liver can biotransform, each hour, about one mixed drink of 80 proof alcohol, 5 ounces of wine, or one 12-ounce can of beer (Maguire, 1990). As we saw in the last chapter, alcohol is biotransformed through a zero-order biotransformation process, and the rate at which alcohol is biotransformd by the liver is "independent of the concentration of alcohol in the blood" (Julien, 1992, p. 72). If a person consumes one standard drink per hour,[7] his or her body biotransforms the alcohol at a rate fairly close to the speed at which the alcohol is ingested. But if the person consumes *more* than one standard drink per hour, the amount of alcohol in his or her bloodstream increases, perhaps to the point where the drinker becomes intoxicated.

The alcohol-flush reaction. After drinking even a small amount of alcohol, a small group of people in this country, and perhaps 50% of the population of Asia, experience what is known as the *alcohol-flush reaction.* The alcohol-flush reaction is caused by a genetic mutation that is found predominantly in persons of Asian descent. Because of this genetic mutation, the liver is unable to manufacture enough aldehyde dehydrogenase to biotransform rapidly the acetaldehyde that is manufactured in the first stage of alcohol biotransformation.

Persons with the alcohol-flush syndrome experience symptoms such as facial flushing, heart palpitations, dizziness, and nausea, as the blood level of acetaldehyde climbs to 20 times that seen in normal individuals who have consumed the same amount of alcohol. As we have noted, acetaldehyde is a toxin. The person with significant amount of this chemical in his or her blood becomes quite ill. This phenomenon is thought to be one reason why heavy drinking is so rare in persons of Asian descent.

The Blood Alcohol Level

Because it is not yet possible to measure the alcohol level in the brain of a living person, physicians have to settle for a measure known as the *blood alcohol level* (BAL).[8] The BAL is a measure of the level of alcohol actually in a given person's bloodstream. It is reported in terms of milligrams of alcohol per 100 milliliters of blood (mg/mL). A BAL of 0.10 thus indicates one-tenth of a milligram of alcohol per 100 milliliters of blood.

The BAL provides a rough approximation of the individual's *subjective* level of intoxication. For reasons that are still not clear, the individual's subjective level of intoxication is highest when the BAL is still rising, a phenomenon known as the *Mellanby effect* (Garriott, 1996; Lehman, Pilich, & Andrews, 1994). Further, as we shall see in the next chapter, individuals who drink on a chronic basis become somewhat tolerant to the intoxicating effects of alcohol. Thus a person who is tolerant to the effects of alcohol might have a rather high BAL while appearing relatively normal.

The BAL measures for two people who consume the same amount of alcohol may differ because of a number of different factors, such as the individual's body size (or volume). To illustrate this confusing characteristic

---

[6]The medication Antabuse (disulfiram) works by blocking the enzyme aldehyde dehydrogenase. This allows acetaldehyde to build up in the individual's blood, causing the individual to become ill from the toxic effects of the acetaldehyde.

[7]Defined as 1.5 ounces of 80 proof distilled spirits, one 5-ounce glass of wine, or a 12-ounce can of 3.2% beer (Duvour, 1999).

[8]Occasionally, the term *blood alcohol concentration* (BAC) will be used in place of the blood alcohol level.

Weight (pounds)

		100	120	140	160	180	200	220
	2	0.07	0.06	0.05	0.05*	0.04	0.04*	0.03
	3	0.10	0.09	0.07	0.07*	0.06	0.05	0.05*
	4	0.14	0.11	0.10	0.08	0.08*	0.07	0.06
	5	0.18	0.14	0.12	0.11	0.10	0.08	0.08*
	6	0.20	0.18	0.14	0.12	0.12*	0.10	0.09
	7	0.25	0.20	0.18	0.16	0.12	0.12*	0.11
	8	0.30	0.25	0.20	0.18	0.16	0.14	0.12

Number of drinks in one hour

*Rounded off.   Level of legal intoxication with measured blood alcohol level of 0.10

FIGURE 7.1   Approximate blood alcohol levels.

of alcohol, consider the hypothetical example of a person who weighs 100 pounds and who consumed two regular drinks in an hour's time. Blood tests would reveal that this individual had a BAL of 0.09 mg/mL (slightly below legal intoxication in most states) (Maguire, 1990). After consuming the same amount of alcohol, an individual who weighed 200 pounds would have a measured BAL of only 0.04 mg/mL. Both drinkers would have consumed the same amount of alcohol, but it would be more concentrated in the smaller individual, resulting in a higher BAL.

A variety of other factors influence the speed with which alcohol enters the blood and the individual's blood alcohol level. Figure 7.1 provides a rough estimate of the blood alcohol levels that might be achieved through the consumption of different amounts of alcohol.[9] This chart is based on the assumption that one "drink" is either one can of standard beer or one regular mixed drink. It should be noted that although the

BAL provides an estimate of the individual's current level of intoxication, it is of little value in screening individuals for alcohol abuse problems (Chung, Colby, Barnett, Rohsenow, Spirito, & Monti, 2000).

Subjective Effects of Alcohol on the Individual

At Normal Doses in the Average Drinker

Both as a toxin and as a psychoactive agent, alcohol is quite weak. For example, to achieve effects equivalent to those of a 10-mg intravenous dose of morphine, the individual would have to ingest 15,000–20,000 mg of alcohol (Jones, 1996).[10] However, when it is consumed in sufficient quantities, alcohol does affect the user, and it is for its psychoactive effects that most people consume alcohol.

At low to moderate dosage levels, the individual's *expectations* play a role both in how a person interprets the effects of alcohol and in his or her drinking behavior (Smith, Goldman, Greenbaum, & Christiahnsen,

[9] This chart is provided only as an illustration, and is not sufficiently accurate to be used as a guide to "safe" drinking. Individual blood alcohol levels from the same dose of alcohol vary widely, and these figures merely provide an average blood alcohol level for an individual of a given body weight.

[10] This is the approximate amount of alcohol found in one standard drink.

1995; Brown, 1990). Indeed, it is now apparent that "expectancies are closely linked to actual drinking practices of both adolescents and adults" (p. 17). Unfortunately, some people begin to form expectations for alcohol in childhood, perhaps as early as 3 years of age, and such expectations may crystalize between the ages of 3 and 7 (Jones & McMahon, 1998). This is clearly seen in the observation that adolescents who abused alcohol were more likely than their nondrinking counterparts to anticipate a positive experience when they drank (Brown, Creamer, & Stetson, 1987).

After one or two drinks, alcohol has a second effect known as the *disinhibition effect*. Researchers now believe that the disinhibition effect is caused when alcohol interferes with the normal function of inhibitory neurons in the cortex. This is the part of the brain most responsible for "higher" functions, such as abstract thinking and speech. The cortex is also the part of the brain where much of our voluntary behavior is planned. As the alcohol interferes with cortical nerve function, the drinker tends temporarily to "forget" social inhibitions (Elliott, 1992; Julien, 1992). During periods of alcohol-induced disinhibition, the individual may engage in some behavior that he or she would never carry out under normal conditions. This disinhibition effect may contribute to the relationship between alcohol use and aggressive behavior, as illustrated by the fact that between 40% and 50% of those who commit homicide use alcohol before committing the murder (Parker, 1993). Individuals with either developmental or acquired brain damage are especially at risk for the disinhibition effects of alcohol (Elliott, 1992). Of course, individuals without any known neurological trauma may also experience alcohol-induced disinhibition.

At Intoxicating Doses in the Average Drinker

For a 160-pound person, two drinks in an hour's time would result in a BAL of 0.05 mg/mL. At this level of intoxication, the individual's reaction time and depth perception become impaired (Hartman, 1995). Four drinks in an hour's time will cause a 160-pound person to have a BAL of 0.10 mg/mL or higher (Maguire, 1990). At about this level of intoxication, the individual's reaction time is approximately 200% longer than it is for the nondrinker (Garriott, 1996), and he or she will have problems coordinating muscle actions (a condi-

tion called *ataxia*). Research has shown that individuals with a BAL between 0.10 and 0.14 mg/mL are 48 times as likely as nondrinkers to be involved in a fatal car accident (*Alcohol Alert*, 1996).

A person with a BAL of 0.15 mg/mL is above the level of legal intoxication in every state and will definitely experience some alcohol-induced physical problems. Also, because of alcohol's effects on reaction time, individuals with a BAL of 0.15 mg/mL are between 25 times (Hobbs, Rall, & Verdoorn, 1995) and 380 times (*Alcohol Alert*, 1996) as likely as a nondrinker to be involved in a fatal car accident. The person who has a BAL of 0.20 mg/mL experiences marked ataxia (Garriott, 1996). The person with a BAL of 0.25 mg/mL staggers around and has difficulty interpreting sensory data (Garriott, 1996; Kaminski, 1992). The person with a BAL of 0.30 mg/mL is stuporous and, although conscious, unlikely to remember what happened to him or her while intoxicated (Matuschka, 1985). With a BAL of 0.35 mg/mL, the stage of surgical anesthesia is achieved (Matuschka, 1985). At high dosage levels, alcohol's effects are analogous to those seen with the anesthetic ether (Maguire, 1990).

Unfortunately, the level of blood alcohol necessary to induce unconsciousness is only a little less than the level that constitutes a fatal overdose. This is because alcohol has a therapeutic index (TI) of between 1:4 and 1:10 (Grinspoon & Bakalar, 1993). In other words, the minimal effective dose of alcohol (the dose at which the user becomes intoxicated) is a significant fraction of the lethal dose. Thus a person who drinks to the point of losing consciousness is dangerously close to overdosing on alcohol. Because of alcohol's low TI, it is very easy to *die* from an alcohol overdose, or acute alcohol poisoning; this happens 200–400 times a year in the United States (Garrett, 2000). Even experienced drinkers have been known to die from an overdose of alcohol. About 1% of drinkers who achieve a BAL of 0.35 mg/mL die unless they get medical treatment (Ray & Ksir, 1993).[11] At or above a BAL of 0.35 mg/mL, alcohol is thought to interfere with the activity of the nerves that control respiration (Lehman, Pilich, & Andrews, 1994). *All cases of known or suspected alcohol overdose must be immediately treated by a physician.* A BAL of 0.40 mg/mL will result in about a 50% death rate from

[11] Thus the LD_{01} dosage level for alcohol is about 0.35 mg/mL.

TABLE 7.1   Effects of Alcohol on the Infrequent Drinker

Blood alcohol level (BAL)	Behavioral and physical effects
0.02	Feeling of warmth, relaxation
0.02–0.09	Skin becomes flushed. Drinker is more talkative, feels euphoria. At this level, psychomotor skills are slightly to moderately impaired, and ataxia develops. Loss of inhibitions, increased reaction time, and visual field disturbances
0.10–0.19	Slurred speech, severe ataxia, mood instability, drowsiness, nausea, staggering gait, confusion.
0.20–0.29	Lethargy, combativeness, stupor, incoherent speech, vomiting
0.30-0.39	Coma, respiratory depression
Above 0.40	Death

Sources: Based on material provided by Lehman, Pilich, & Andrews (1994), pp. 305–309; Morrison, Rogers, & Thomas (1995), pp. 371–389; and Baselt (1996).

alcohol overdose without medical intervention (Bohn, 1993). The LD_{50} is thus around 0.40 mg/mL.

Segal and Sisson (1985) reported that the approximate lethal BAL in humans was 0.5 mg/mL, whereas Lingeman (1974) notes that the fatal concentration of alcohol in the blood lies somewhere between 0.5 and 0.8 mg/mL. In theory, the LD_{100} is reached when the nondrinker has a BAL between 0.5 and 0.8 mg/mL. However, there are cases on record where an alcohol-tolerant person was still conscious and able to talk with a BAL as high as 0.78 mg/mL (Schuckit, 2000; Bohn, 1993). The effects of alcohol on the infrequent drinker are summarized in Table 7.1.

At high doses, the stomach begins to excrete higher levels of mucus than is normal and also closes the pyloric valve between the stomach and the small intestine to slow the absorption of the alcohol that is still in the stomach (Kaplan, Sadock, & Grebb, 1994). These actions contribute to feelings of nausea, which reduce the drinker's desire to consume more alcohol and may also contribute to the urge to vomit that many drinkers report they experience at the higher levels of intoxication. Vomiting enables the body to rid itself of the alcohol the

drinker has ingested. But alcohol interferes with the normal vomit reflex and may even cause the drinker to attempt to vomit when unconscious, which increases the risk that the drinker will aspirate some of the material being regurgitated. This can contribute to the condition known as *aspirative pneumonia* and can even cause death by blocking the airway with stomach contents.

Medical Complications of Alcohol Use in the Average Drinker

The hangover. Although there is evidence that humans have known about the alcohol-induced hangover for thousands of years, the exact mechanism by which alcohol causes the drinker to suffer a hangover is still unknown (Swift & Davidson, 1998). Indeed, researchers are still divided over whether the "hangover" is caused by the alcohol ingested by the drinker, a metabolite of alcohol (such as acetaldehyde), or some of the compounds found in the alcoholic beverage that give it flavor, aroma, and taste (called *congeners*) (Swift & Davidson, 1998). Some researchers believe that the hangover is a symptom of an early alcohol withdrawal syndrome (Swift & Davidson, 1998; Ray & Ksir, 1993). Other researchers suggest that the alcohol induced "hangover" is caused by the lower levels of ß-endorphin that result during alcohol withdrawal (Mosier, 1999).

What *is* known about the alcohol-induced hangover is that 75% of those individuals who drink to excess will experience a hangover at some point in their lives, although there is evidence that some drinkers are more prone that others to experience this aftereffect of alcohol use (Swift & Davidson, 1998). The physical manifestations of the alcohol hangover include fatigue, malaise, headache, sensitivity to light, thirst, tremor and nausea, dizziness, depression, and anxiety (Swift & Davidson, 1998). Although a severe hangover may make the victim wish for death (O'Donnell, 1986), there usually is little physical risk for the individual, and the symptoms generally subside in 8–24 hours (Swift & Davidson, 1998). Antacids, bed rest, solid foods, fruit juice, and OTC analgesics are usually all that is required to treat an alcohol-induced hangover (Swift & Davidson, 1998; Kaminski, 1992).

The effects of alcohol on sleep. Although alcohol, like the other CNS depressants, may bring about sleep, it interferes with the normal dream cycle. This effect is not noted for the person who drinks only on a social basis. However, in the chronic alcoholic, the cumulative effects can be quite disruptive. The impact of chronic alcohol use on the normal sleep cycle will be discussed in the next chapter.

Researchers have discovered that individuals who consumed moderate amounts of alcohol in the hours before going to sleep experienced twice as many episodes of sleep apnea[12] as when these same individuals abstained from alcohol use (*Science Digest*, 1989). Thus persons with a respiratory disorder, especially sleep apnea, should discuss their use of alcohol with their physician to avoid alcohol-related sleep breathing problems.

Alcohol use and cerebrovascular accidents (CVA). For reasons that are not understood, even light alcohol use (defined as the individual ingesting 1–14 ounces of pure alcohol per month) more than doubles the individual's risk for hemorrhagic stroke (or CVA) (Smith, 1997). It should be noted that the lower limit of this range of alcohol use, 1 ounce of pure alcohol per month, is less than the amount of alcohol found in a single can of beer.

Drug interactions involving alcohol.[13] There has been little research into the effects of moderate alcohol use (defined as 1–2 standard drinks per day) on the action of pharmaceutical agents (Weathermon & Crabb, 1999). As a CNS depressant, alcohol may potentiate the action of other CNS depressants such as antihistamines, opiates, barbiturates, anesthetic agents, and benzodiazepines. Thus alcohol should not be used by patients using these agents (Zernig & Battista, 2000; Weathermon & Crabb, 1999). Patients who take nitroglycerin, a medication often used in the treatment of heart conditions, frequently develop significantly reduced blood pressure levels, possibly to the point of dizziness and loss of consciousness, if they drink while using this medication (Zernig & Battista, 2000). Patients taking the antihypertensive medication propranolol should not drink, because the alcohol decreases the effectiveness of this antihypertensive medication (Zernig

& Battista, 2000). Patients taking the anticoagulant medication warfarin should not drink, because moderate to heavy alcohol use can cause the user's body to biotransform the warfarin more quickly than normal (Graedon & Graedon, 1995; *Alcohol Alert*, 1995).

There is some evidence that the antidepressant amitriptyline enhances alcohol-induced euphoria (Ciraulo, Creelman, Shader, & O'Sullivan, 1995). The mixture of alcohol and certain antidepressant medications, such as amitriptyline, desimipramine, and doxepin, might also cause the user to have trouble concentrating, because alcohol potentiates the sedation caused by these medications, and the interaction between alcohol and the antidepressant might contribute to rapid changes in blood pressure (Weathermon & Crabb, 1999).

Surprisingly, some animal research suggests that individuals who take beta carotene, and who drink to excess on a chronic basis, may experience more liver damage than heavy drinkers who do not take this vitamin supplement (Graedon & Graedon, 1995). When combined with aspirin, alcohol may contribute to bleeding in the stomach, because both alcohol and aspirin are irritants to the stomach lining (Sands, Knapp, & Ciraulo, 1993). Acetaminophen does not irritate the stomach lining, but the chronic use of alcohol causes the liver to release enzymes that transform the acetaminophen into a poison, even when the drug is used at recommended dosage levels (Zernig & Battista, 2000).

Patients taking oral medications for diabetes should not drink, because the antidiabetic medication may interfere with the body's ability to biotransform alcohol. This may result in acute alcohol poisoning from even moderate amounts of alcohol. Further, because the antidiabetic medication prevents the body from biotransforming alcohol, the individual will remain intoxicated far longer than he or she would normally. In such a case, the individual may underestimate the time before it is safe to drive a motor vehicle.

Patients who are on the antidepressant medications known as monoamine oxidase inhibitors (MAO inhibitors or MAOIs) should not consume alcohol under any circumstances. The fermentation process produces an amino acid, tyramine, along with the alcohol. Normally, this is not a problem. Indeed, tyramine is a necessary nutrient. But tryamine interacts with the MAO inhibitors, causing dangerously high — and possibly fatal—blood pressure levels. Patients who take MAO

[12]See the Glossary.

[13]The list of potential alcohol-drug interactions is quite extensive. Patients who are taking either a prescription or an over-the-counter medication should not consume alcohol without first checking with a physician or pharmacist to determine whether there is any danger of an interaction between the two substances.

inhibitators are provided a list of foods that they should avoid while they are taking their medication. These lists usually include alcohol.

Researchers have found that the calcium channel blocker Verapamil inhibits alcohol biotransformation, increasing the period of time in which alcohol might cause the user to be intoxicated. Although early research studies suggested that the medications Zantac (ranitidine)[14] and Tagamet (cimetidine) interfered with the biotransformation of alcohol, subsequent research failed to support this hypothesis (Jones, 1996).

Patients who are taking the antibiotic medications chloramphenicol, furazolidone, or metronidazole or the antimalarial medication quinacrine should not drink alcohol. The combination of these antibiotics with alcohol may produce a painful reaction very similar to that seen when the patient on disulfiram (to be discussed in a later chapter) consumes alcohol (Meyers, 1992). Individuals taking the antibiotic erythromycin should not consume alcohol; this medication can contribute to abnormally high blood alcohol levels because of enhanced gastric emptying (Zernig & Battista, 2000). Patients who are taking the antitubercular drug isoniazid (INH) should also avoid the use of alcohol. The combination of these two chemicals reduces the effectiveness of the isoniazid and may increase the individual's chances of developing hepatitis.

Although there has been little research into the possible interaction between alcohol and marijuana because using the latter substance is illegal, preliminary evidence suggests that alcohol's depressant effects exacerbate the CNS-depressant effects of marijuana (Garriott, 1996). Alcohol is a very potent chemical, and it is not possible to list all the potential interactions between alcohol and the various medications currently in use. Before mixing alcohol with any medication, one should consult a physician or pharmacist in order to avoid dangerous interactions between pharmaceutical agents and alcohol.

[14]The most common brand name is given first, with the generic name in parentheses.

Alcohol Use and Accidental Injury or Death

Advertisements in the media proclaim the benefits of recreational alcohol use at parties, social encounters, or as a way to celebrate good news, but they rarely mention alcohol's role in accidental injury. The grim reality is that there is a clear relationship between alcohol use and accidental injury. For example, in spite of a protracted campaign to reduce "drunk driving" in this country, alcohol-related motor vehicle accidents remain one of the leading causes of motor vehicle deaths. In addition to this, alcohol use has been found to be a factor in 60% of all boating fatalities (*Alcohol Alert*, 1994a), and an estimated 70% of the motorcycle drivers who are killed in an accident are thought to have been drinking prior to the accident (Colburn, Meyer, Wrigley, & Bradley, 1993).

Alcohol use is a factor in 17% to 53% of all falls and in 40% to 64% of all fatalities associated with fires (Lewis, 1997). Researchers have found that 52% of those individuals treated at one major trauma center had alcohol in their blood at the time of admission (Cornwell, Blezberg, Velmahos, Chan, Demetriades, Stewart, Oder, Kahuku, Chan, Asensio, & Berne, 1998). No matter how you look at it, even casual alcohol use carries with it a significantly increased risk of accidental injury or death.

Summary

This chapter provides a brief history of alcohol—the first recreational chemical. The process of distillation was discussed, as was the manner in which wine is obtained from fermented fruit. The use of distillation to achieve concentrations of alcohol above 15% was reviewed, and questions surrounding the use of alcohol were discussed. Alcohol's effects on the infrequent social drinker were reviewed, as well as some of the more significant interactions between alcohol and pharmaceutical agents. The role of alcohol in accidental injury and death was also considered.

Chronic Alcohol Abuse and Addiction

Introduction

The focus of the last chapter was on the acute effects of alcohol on the "average" or infrequent social drinker. Unfortunately, when used often enough and in sufficient quantity, alcohol has a very real potential to be abused, or even to cause the user to become physically addicted. Alcohol abuse/addiction causes a wide range of physical, social, financial, and emotional problems for the drinker. Indeed, given its potential for harm, one could argue that if alcohol had never been used before and were just discovered today, its use might never be legalized (Miller & Hester, 1995). In this chapter, some of the manifestations, and some of the consequences, of alcohol addiction will be discussed.

Scope of the Problem

Alcohol is the most commonly abused substance in the United States (Franklin, 1987). Although physical addiction to alcohol is only the most extreme form of alcohol use disorders, it is still the most common psychiatric disorder encountered by mental health professionals (Gold & Miller, 1997b). Alcohol abuse has been shown to affect the individual's social life, interpersonal relationships, and educational or vocational activities, as well as causing legal problems for the drinker. But not every person who experiences a *single* alcohol-related problem is *dependent* on this chemical. In fact, 60% of the men and 30% of the women who consume alcohol will have at least one transient alcohol-related problem (such as blackouts) without going on to become physi-

cally dependent on it (American Psychiatric Association, 2000; Kaplan, Sadock, & Grebb, 1994).

Unfortunately, population studies conducted a decade ago suggest that 13.5% of the population will either abuse or become physically dependent on alcohol at some point in their lives (Regier, Farmer, Rae, Locke, Keith, Judd, & Goodwin, 1990). Thus a significant minority of those who experience one symptom of alcohol use problems will go on to demonstrate additional symptoms, of which the physical addiction to alcohol (alcohol dependence, or alcoholism) is the most extreme example.

Estimates of the scope of alcohol use problems in the U.S. range from 9 million alcohol-dependent people in the United States, and another 6 million alcohol abusers (Ordorica & Nace, 1998), to 10–15 million Americans currently dependent on alcohol, with an additional 10 million being "on the cusp of alcoholism" (Beasley, 1987, p. 21)[1]. In the United States, alcoholism is predominantly a male disease, for alcohol-dependent males outnumber alcohol-dependent females about 2:1 (Blume, 1994).

Clinicians who specialize in the area of substance abuse often hear clients deny that they are alcoholic—rather, they are "only problem drinkers." Unfortunately, there is little evidence to suggest that "problem drinkers" are different from alcohol-dependent individuals (Prescott & Kendler, 1999; Schuckit, Zisook & Mortola, 1985). At best, research data suggests that the

[1]The abuse of, and addiction to, alcohol by children and adolescents will be discussed in Chapter 23.

so-called problem drinkers differ from the alcohol-dependent only in the number and severity of their alcohol-related problems. There is little evidence to support the theory that problem drinkers are significantly different from alcohol-dependent individuals (Schuckit, Zisook, & Mortola, 1985).

The progression to alcohol dependency usually takes between 10 (Meyer, 1994) and 20 years (Alexander & Gwyther, 1995) of heavy drinking. However, physical dependency on alcohol has lifelong implications for the individual. Once a person *does* become dependent on alcohol, even if that person should stop drinking for a period of time, he or she will again become dependent on alcohol "in a matter of days to weeks" if he or she resumes drinking (Meyer, 1994, p. 165).

The "Typical" Alcohol-Dependent Person

Alcohol abusers and addicts are frequently "masters of denial" (Knapp, 1996, p. 19), able to offer a thousand and one reasons why *they* cannot possibly have an alcohol use problem: They always go to work; they never go to the bar just to drink; they know ten people who drink more than they do; etc., etc., etc. One of the most common rationalizations offered by the person with an alcohol use problem is that she or he has nothing in common with the stereotypical "skid row" derelict. In reality, only about 5% of those people who are dependent on alcohol fit the image of the "skid row" alcoholic (Knapp, 1996). The majority of those with alcohol use problems might best be described as "high functioning" (Knapp, 1996, p. 12) individuals who have jobs, responsibilities, families, and public images to protect. In many cases, the individual's growing dependency on alcohol is hidden from virtually everybody in the alcoholic's world, including the drinker. It is only in secret moments of introspection that the alcohol-dependent person wonders why his or her alcohol use is somehow different from that of the nonalcoholic drinker.

Alcohol Tolerance, Dependency, and "Craving": Signposts of Alcoholism

There are certain symptoms that suggest the drinker has moved past the point of simple social drinking to the point of having an alcohol use problem, or even being physically dependent on alcohol and its effects. The first of these signs is *tolerance*.

As the individual repeatedly consumes alcohol, his or her body begins to make certain adaptations in order to try to maintain normal function in spite of the individual's use of alcohol. For one thing, the liver becomes more efficient at the biotransformation of alcohol. This improvement in the liver's ability to biotransform alcohol is seen in the earlier stages of the individual's drinking career and is known as *metabolic tolerance*. As the metabolic tolerance to alcohol develops, the drinker notices that she or he must consume more alcohol in order to achieve a desired level of intoxication (Nelson, 2000). In clinical interviews, such drinkers might admit that when they were 21, it took "only" 6–8 beers before they became intoxicated, whereas it now takes 12–15 beers consumed over the same period.

Another expression of tolerance to alcohol's effects is what is known as *behavioral tolerance*. Where a novice drinker might appear quite intoxicated after 5 or 6 beers, the experienced drinker might show few outward signs of intoxication even after consuming a significant amount of alcohol. On occasion, even skilled law enforcement and health care professionals are shocked to learn that an apparently sober person in their care has a BAL well into the range of legal intoxication. This is why objective test data are used to determine whether the individual is legally intoxicated at the time she or he is stopped by the police.

Pharmacodynamic tolerance is the last type of tolerance that we will discuss in this chapter. As the cells of the central nervous system attempt to carry out their normal function in spite of the continual presence of alcohol, they become less and less sensitive to the intoxicating effects of the chemical. Over time, the individual has to consume more and more alcohol to achieve the same effect on the CNS. As pharmacodynamic tolerance develops, the individual might switch from beer to "hard" liquor, or increase the amount of beer ingested, in order to achieve a desired state of intoxication.

If any of these subtypes of tolerance has developed, the patient is simply said to be tolerant to the effects of alcohol. Compare the effects of alcohol for the chronic drinker, shown in Table 8.1 with those shown in Table 7.1.

It should be pointed out that developing tolerance demands great effort on the part of the individual's body, and that eventually the different organs prove unequal to the task of maintaining normal function in

TABLE 8.1 Effects of Alcohol on the Chronic Drinker

Blood alcohol level (BAL)	Behavioral and physical effects
0.05–0.09	None to minimal effect
0.10–0.19	Mild ataxia, euphoria
0.20–0.29	Mild emotional changes, ataxia
0.30-0.39	Drowsiness, lethargy, stupor
Above 0.40	Coma, death

Sources: Based on material provided by Lehman, Pilich, & Andrews (1994), pp. 305–309; Morrison, Rogers, & Thomas (1995), pp. 371–389; and Baselt (1996).

the face of the constant presence of alcohol. When this happens, the individual actually becomes *less* tolerant to alcohol's effects. It is not uncommon for chronic drinkers to admit that, in contrast to the past, they now can become intoxicated on just a few beers or mixed drinks. An assessor would say that this individual's tolerance is "on the downswing"—a sign that the drinker has entered the later stages of alcohol dependence.

Another warning sign that the drinker is addicted to alcohol is his or her growing *dependency* on alcohol. There are two types of alcohol dependency. In *psychological dependency*, individuals repeatedly self-administer alcohol because they find it rewarding or because they believe that they need alcohol to socialize, relax, function sexually, or sleep better. This individual uses alcohol as a "crutch." Often, the alcohol-dependent person believes that she or he *deserves* to have a drink, for one reason or another.

The second form of dependence is known as *physical dependence*. Remember that the chronic use of alcohol forces the body to attempt to adapt to the constant presence of the chemical. Indeed, the body might be said now to need the foreign chemical in order to maintain normal function. When the chemical is suddenly removed from the body, the body goes through a period of readjustment as it relearns how to function without the foreign chemical. This period of readjustment is known as the *withdrawal syndrome.*

Like many drugs of abuse, alcohol has a characteristic withdrawal syndrome, but the alcohol withdrawal syndrome involves not only some degree of subjective discomfort for the individual, but also the potential for

life-threatening medical complications. It is for this reason that *all cases of alcohol withdrawal should be evaluated and treated by a physician.*

There are several factors that influence the severity of the alcohol withdrawal syndrome, including: how frequently the individual drank, in what amount the individual consumed alcohol, and his or her state of health. The longer the period of alcohol use and the greater the amount ingested, the more severe the alcohol withdrawal syndrome. The symptoms of alcohol withdrawal for the chronic alcoholic will be discussed in more detail later in this chapter.

Often, the recovering alcoholic will speak of a "craving" for alcohol that continues long after he or she has stopped drinking. Some alcoholics will talk about feeling "thirsty" or find themselves preoccupied with the possibility of having a drink. It is not known why alcoholics "crave" alcohol. However, preoccupation with alcohol use is a sign that the individual has become dependent on alcohol.

The TIQ hypothesis: In the late 1980s, Trachtenberg and Blum (1987) suggested that chronic alcohol use significantly reduces the brain's production of the endorphins, the enkephalins, and the dynorphins. These neurotransmitters function in the brain's pleasure center to help moderate an individual's emotions and behavior. It was also suggested that a by-product of alcohol metabolism combined with neurotransmitters normally found within the brain to form the compound *tetrahydroisoquinoline,* or TIQ (Blum, 1988). It was suggested that the TIQ was capable of binding to opiate-like receptor sites within the brain's pleasure center, causing the individual to experience a sense of well-being (Blum & Payne, 1991; Blum & Trachtenberg, 1988). However, TIQ's effects were thought to be short-lived, forcing the individual to drink more alcohol in order to regain or maintain the initial feeling of euphoria achieved through the use of alcohol.

Over time, the individual's chronic use of alcohol would cause his or her brain to reduce its production of enkephalins, as the ever-present TIQ was substituted for these naturally produced opiate-like neurotransmitters (Blum, & Payne, 1991; Blum & Trachtenberg, 1988). The cessation of alcohol intake was thought to result in a neurochemical deficit, which the individual would then attempt to relieve through further chemical use (Blum, & Payne, 1991; Blum & Trachtenberg, 1988). Subjectively, this deficit was experienced as the "craving" for alcohol commonly reported by recovering alcoholics. The TIQ theory had a number of strong adherents in the late 1980s and early 1990s, but it has gradually fallen into disfavor. A number of research studies have failed to find evidence to support the TIQ hypothesis, and there are now few researchers in the field of alcohol addiction who believe that TIQ plays a major role in the phenomenon of alcohol "craving."

Complications of Chronic Alcohol Use

Alcohol is a mild toxin, and over time, the chronic use of alcohol often results in damage to one or more organ systems. It is also important to recognize that chronic alcohol use includes "weekend" or "binge" drinking. Repeated episodes of alcohol abuse may bring about many of the same effects seen with chronic alcohol use. Unfortunately, there is no simple formula by which to calculate the risk of alcohol-related organ damage or determine which organs will be affected (Segal & Sisson, 1985). As these authors noted,

> Some heavy drinkers of many years' duration appear to go relatively unscathed, while others develop complications early (e.g. after five years) in their drinking careers. Some develop brain damage; others liver disease; still others, both. The reasons for this are simply not known. (p. 145)

However, chronic use of alcohol has the potential to affect virtually every system in the body.

Effects of Chronic Alcohol Use on the Digestive System

As we saw in the last chapter, during the distillation of wine, many of its vitamins and minerals are lost. Further, when the body breaks down alcohol, it finds "empty calories." That is, it obtains carbohydrates from the alcohol it metabolizes, but none of the proteins, vitamins, calcium, and other minerals the body needs. Also, the chronic use of alcohol interferes with the absorption of needed nutrients from the gastrointestinal tract and may cause the drinker to experience diarrhea. These factors may contribute to a state of vitamin depletion called *avitaminosis*, which will be discussed in more detail later in this chapter.

It has been known for many years that chronic drinkers have a higher risk of many forms of cancer than do social drinkers and nondrinkers. The chronic use of alcohol is associated with higher rates of cancer of the upper digestive tract, respiratory system, mouth, pharynx, larynx, esophagus, and liver (Garro, Espina, & Lieber, 1992). Alcohol use is associated with 75% of all deaths due to cancer of the esophagus (Rice, 1993). Further, although the research data are not clear at this time, there is also evidence suggesting a link between chronic alcohol use and cancer of the large bowel and cancer of the breast (Garro, Espina, & Lieber, 1992).

The combination of cigarettes and alcohol is especially dangerous. Alcoholics experience almost a 6-fold increase in their risk of developing cancer of the mouth or pharynx (Garro, Espina, & Lieber, 1992, p. 83). For comparison, consider that cigarette smokers have slightly over a 7-fold increased risk of developing cancer of the mouth or pharynx. Alcoholics who also smoke have a 38-*fold increased risk* of cancer in these regions.

The body organ most heavily involved in the process of alcohol biotransformation is the liver. Unfortunately, scientists do not know how to determine the level of exposure necessary to cause liver damage. It is known that the chronic exposure to even limited amounts of alcohol may result in damage to that organ (Lieber, 1996; Frezza, Di Padova, Pozzato, Terpin, Baraona, & Lieber, 1990; Schenker & Speeg, 1990). Chronic alcohol use is the most common cause of liver disease in the United States (Hill & Kugelmas, 1998) and the United Kingdom (Walsh & Alexander, 2000). Approximately 80–90% (Walsh & Alexander, 2000; Ordorica & Nace, 1998) of heavy drinkers develop the first manifestation of alcohol-related liver problems: a "fatty liver" (also called steatosis). This is a condition in which the liver becomes enlarged and does not function at full efficiency (Nace, 1987). Few symptoms of a fatty liver would be noticed without a physical examination, but blood tests would detect characteristic abnormalities in the patient's liver enzymes (Schuckit, 2000). This condition will reverse itself with abstinence (Walsh & Alexander, 2000).

Approximately 35% of those individuals with alcohol-induced "fatty" liver who continue to drink go on to develop a more advanced form of liver disease: *alcoholic hepatitis.* In alcohol-induced hepatitis, the cells of the liver become inflamed as a result of the body's continual exposure to alcohol. Symptoms of alcoholic hepatitis may include a low-grade fever, malaise, jaundice, an enlarged, tender liver, and dark urine (Nace, 1987). Blood tests would also reveal characteristic changes in the blood chemistry (Schuckit, 2000), and the patient might complain of abdominal pain (Hill & Kugelmas, 1998). Even with the best of medical care, 20–65% of the individuals with alcohol-induced hepatitis die (Bondesson & Saperton, 1996).

Doctors do not know why some alcohol abusers go on to develop alcohol-induced hepatitis and others do not. It is thought that genetic factors may mediate the individual's vulnerability to alcohol-induced liver damage, which usually develops after 15–20 years of heavy drinking (Walsh & Alexander, 2000). It is known that individuals who suffer from alcohol-induced hepatitis should avoid having surgery, if possible; they are poor surgical risks. Unfortunately, if the patient were to be examined by a physician who was not aware of his or her history of alcoholism, the abdominal pain might be misinterpreted as a symptom of another condition such as appendicitis, pancreatitis, or inflammation of the gall bladder.

Alcoholic hepatitis is "a slow, smoldering process that may proceed or coexist with" another form of liver disease known as *cirrhosis of the liver* (Nace, 1987, p. 25). The cells of the liver begin to die as a result of their chronic exposure to alcohol. Eventually, these dead liver cells are replaced by scar tissue. A physical examination of the patient with cirrhosis of the liver will reveal a hard, nodular liver, an enlarged spleen, "spider" angiomas on the skin, tremor, jaundice, mental confusion, signs of liver disease on various blood tests, and possibly a number of other symptoms such as testicular atrophy in males (Nace, 1987).

Although some researchers believe that alcoholic hepatitis precedes the development of cirrhosis of the liver, this has not been proved. Indeed, "alcoholics may progress to cirrhosis without passing through any visible stage resembling hepatitis" (*Alcohol Alert*, 1993a, p. 1). Thus many chronic alcoholics never appear to develop alcoholic hepatitis, and the first outward sign of serious liver disease is cirrhosis of the liver. Statistically, cirrhosis of the liver is the fourth leading cause of death for adults between the ages of 25 and 64 (Lieber, 1995). For reasons that are not fully understood, only 15–20% (Ordorica & Nace, 1998) to 30% (Hartman, 1995) of chronic drinkers develop cirrhosis of the liver.

Scientists are not certain how alcohol causes or contributes to liver damage. A number of different theories have been advanced to explain this phenomenon. One theory suggests that "free radicals" generated during the process of alcohol biotransformation contribute to the death of individual liver cells, initiating the development of alcohol-induced cirrhosis (Walsh & Alexander, 2000). It is known that as individual liver cells are destroyed, they are replaced by scar tissue. Over time, large areas of the liver may be replaced by scar tissue as significant numbers of liver cells die. Unfortunately, scar tissue is essentially nonfunctional, and as more and more liver cells die, the liver is no longer able to cleanse the blood effectively. This allows various toxins and poisons to build up in the individual's system. Some of these toxins, such as ammonia, are thought to then damage the cells of the CNS (Butterworth, 1995).

At one point, it was thought that malnutrition was a factor in the development of alcohol-induced liver disease. However, research has found that the individual's dietary habits do not seem to influence the development of alcohol-induced liver disease (Achord, 1995). Recently, scientists have developed blood tests capable of detecting one of the viruses known to infect the liver. The virus is Hepatitis Virus-C (or Hepatitis-C or HVC), and it normally is found in about 1.6% of the general population. This means that under normal conditions, less than 2% of the population is infected with HVC. However, between 25% and 60% of chronic alcohol users have been found to be infected with HVC (Achord, 1995). This fact suggests that HVC infection, chronic alcohol use, and the development of liver disease may be related.

Whatever its cause, cirrhosis itself can bring about severe complications, including liver cancer and sodium and water retention (Nace, 1987; Schuckit, 2000). As the toxins build up in the drinker's blood, they begin to add to the damage being done to the brain by the alcohol (Willoughby, 1984). At the same time, the now-enlarged liver squeezes the blood vessels that pass through it, causing the blood pressure to build up within the vessels and adding to the stress on the drinker's heart. This *portal hypertension* may in turn contribute to a swelling of the blood vessels in the esophagus. When the blood vessels in the esophagus swell, weak spots called *esophageal varices* form on the walls of the vessels. These weak spots may rupture. Ruptured esophageal varices constitute a medical emergency that, even with the most advanced forms of medical treatment, results in death for 30% of those who develop this disorder (Giacchino & Houdek, 1998). Between 50% and 60% of those who survive will develop a second episode of bleeding, resulting in an additional 30% death rate. Ultimately, 60% of those afflicted with esophageal varices will die as a result of blood loss from a ruptured varix[2] (Giacchino & Houdek, 1998).

As though that were not enough, alcohol has been implicated as one cause of a painful inflammation of the pancreas known as *pancreatitis*. Approximately 35% of all known cases of pancreatitis are alcohol-induced, and some research centers have suggested that alcoholism is the major cause of between 66% and 75% of the cases of pancreatitis (McCrady & Langenbucher, 1996; Steinberg & Tenner, 1994). Pancreatitis develops slowly, usually after "10 to 15 years of heavy drinking" (Nace, 1987, p. 26). Although pancreatitis can be caused by exposure to a number of toxic agents, such as the venom of scorpions and certain insecticides, chronic exposure to ethyl alcohol is the most common cause of toxin-induced pancreatitis in the United States (Steinberg & Tenner, 1994).

Even low concentrations of alcohol appear to inhibit the stomach's ability to produce enough prostaglandins to protect it from digestive fluids (Bode, Maute, & Bode, 1996), and there is evidence that beverages containing just 5–10% alcohol can damage the lining of the stomach (Bode, Maute, & Bode, 1996). This seems to be why about 30% of chronic drinkers develop *gastritis*,[3] as well as bleeding from the stomach lining and gastric ulcers (McAnalley, 1996; Willoughby, 1984). If an ulcer forms over a major blood vessel, the stomach acid eats through the stomach lining and blood vessel walls, causing a "bleeding ulcer." This is a severe medical emergency. Physicians may try to "seal" a "bleeding ulcer" by using laser beams, but in extreme cases, conventional surgery is necessary to save the patient's life. The surgeon may remove part of the stomach to stop the bleeding.

Unfortunately, the vitamin malabsorption syndrome that develops following the surgical removal of the majority of the individual's stomach (Willoughby, 1984) both contributes to a chronic state of malnutrition and makes the drinker a prime candidate for the development of tuberculosis (TB). Upwards of 95% of alcohol-dependent individuals who had had a portion of their stomach removed secondary to bleeding ulcers, and who continued to drink, ultimately developed TB (Willoughby, 1984).

The chronic use of alcohol can cause or contribute to a number of vitamin *malabsorption syndromes*, in which the individual's body is no longer able to absorb needed vitamins or minerals from food. The minerals that might not be absorbed by the body of the chronic alcoholic include zinc (Marsano, 1994), sodium, calcium, phosphorus, and magnesium (Lehman, Pilich, & Andrews, 1994). The chronic use of alcohol also interferes with the body's ability to absorb or properly utilize vitamin A, vitamin D, vitamin B-6, thiamine, and folic acid (Marsano, 1994).

Chronic drinking is known to cause a condition called *glossitis*,[4] as well as possible stricture of the esophagus (Marsano, 1994). Each of these conditions can indirectly contribute to a failure on the part of the individual to ingest an adequate diet, further contributing to alcohol-related dietary deficiencies in the drinker's body. Further, as we noted in the last chapter, alcohol-containing beverages are a source of "empty" calories. Many chronic drinkers obtain up to half of their daily caloric intake from alcoholic beverages, rather than from more traditional food sources (Suter, Schultz, & Jequier, 1992). Alcohol-related dietary problems can contribute to a decline in the immune system's ability to protect the individual from various infectious diseases such as pneumonia and tuberculosis (TB).

The chronic use of alcohol is a known risk factor in the development of a number of different metabolic disorders. For example, it interferes with the body's ability to control blood glucose levels (*Alcohol Alert*, 1993c). Research has shown that between 45% and 70% of alcoholics with liver disease are also either glucose-intolerant (a condition that suggests the body is having trouble dealing with sugar in the blood) or diabetic

[2]*Varix* is the singular form of *varicies*.
[3]See the Glossary.

[4]See the Glossary.

(*Alcohol Alert*, 1994b). Many heavy drinkers experience episodes of abnormally high (*hyperglycemic*) or abnormally low (*hypoglycemic*) blood sugar levels. These conditions are caused by alcohol-induced interference with the secretion of digestive enzymes from the pancreas (*Alcohol Alert*, 1993c, 1994b).

Further, chronic alcohol use may interfere with the way the drinker's body metabolizes fats. When the individual reaches the point where he or she obtains 10% or more of his or her daily energy requirements from alcohol rather than more traditional foods, the individual's body will go through a series of alcohol-induced changes (Suter, Schultz, & Jequier, 1992). First, the chronic use of alcohol slows the body's energy expenditure (metabolism), which in turn, causes the body to store the unused lipids as fatty tissue. This is the mechanism by which the so-called "beer belly" commonly seen in the heavy drinker is formed.

Effects of Chronic Alcohol Use on the Cardiopulmonary System

The *moderate* use of alcohol (1–2 drinks per day), especially wine, has been found to have a beneficial effect on the cardiovascular system. The consumption of *no more than* 2½ drinks per day seems to be associated with a significant reduction in the risk of heart attack in both men (Klatsky, 1990) and women (Doria, 1990). Although Kemm (1993) suggested that the safe limit was 21 "units" (p. 1373) of alcohol per week for males, and 14 units per week for females, the average of 2 drinks per day still appears valid. Kemm defined a "unit" of alcohol as ½ pint of beer, a 5-ounce glass of wine, or a standard mixed drink.

Within the body, alcohol inhibits the ability of blood platelets to "bind" together (Renaud & DeLorgeril, 1992). By inhibiting the action of blood platelets to start the clotting process, the moderate use of alcohol may result in a lower risk of heart attack and of certain kinds of strokes. This should not be surprising, because wine contains salicylic acid, the active ingredient of aspirin, which is known to interfere with blood clot formation (*Discover*, 1994). However, there is a fine line between "just enough" alcohol and too much (Herman, 1993). Indeed, the issue of possible health benefits from moderate alcohol use is quite controversial, and the World Health Organization (WHO) has denounced *any*

claims of health benefits from moderate alcohol use on the grounds that such claims may result in people drinking more alcohol (Craft, 1994).

However, although the moderate use of alcohol might provide a limited degree of protection against coronary artery disease, it also increases the individual's risk of developing alcohol-related brain damage (Karhunen, Erkinjuntti, & Laippala, 1994). Further, for women, drinking even one drink per day significantly increases the risk of breast cancer (Brody, 1993). Thus the role of alcohol in reducing the risk of heart attack is limited at best, and drinking carries with it other forms of health risks.

When used to excess, alcohol not only loses its protective action but may actually harm the cardiovascular system. The excessive use of alcohol results in the suppression of normal red blood cell formation, and both blood-clotting problems and anemia are common complications of alcoholism (Nace, 1987). Alcohol abuse is thought to be a factor in the development of cerebral vascular accidents (strokes, or CVAs). The light drinker (1–2 drinks per day) has a twofold higher risk of a stroke, and heavy drinking (4+ drinks per day) almost triples the risk of a CVA (Ordorica & Nace, 1998). Approximately 23,500 strokes each year in the United States are thought to be alcohol-related (Sacco, 1995).

In large amounts (more than 1–2 drinks per day), alcohol is known to be *cardiotoxic*. Indeed, chronic alcohol use is considered the most common cause of heart muscle disease (Rubin & Doria, 1990). Prolonged exposure to alcohol (6 beers per day or a pint of whiskey per day for 10 years) may result in permanent damage to the heart muscle tissue, hypertension (high blood pressure), inflammation of the heart muscle, and a general weakening of the heart muscle known as *alcohol-induced cardiomyopathy* (Figueredo, 1997).

Alcoholic cardiomyopathy actually appears to be a special example of a more generalized process in which chronic alcohol use results in damage to *all* striated muscle tissues, not just those in the heart muscle (Fernandez-Sola, Estruch, Grau, Pare, Rubin, & Urbano-Marquez, 1994). These investigators examined a number of men who were alcohol-dependent and a number who were not. They found that the alcoholic men in general had less muscle strength, and greater levels of muscle tissue damage, than the nonalcoholic men in this study. They concluded that alcohol is toxic to muscle tissue and that the chronic use of alcohol will result in a loss of muscle tissue throughout the body.

Cardiomyopathy itself develops in between 25% (Schuckit, 2000) and 40% of chronic alcoholic users (Figueredo, 1997) and accounts for 20–50% of all U.S. cases of cardiomyopathy (Zakhari, 1997). But even this figure might not reflect the true scope of alcohol-induced heart disease. Rubin and Doria (1990) suggested that the majority of alcoholics, which they defined as those individuals who obtained between 30% and 50% of their daily caloric requirement through alcohol, will ultimately develop "pre-clinical heart disease" (p. 279). Because of the body's compensatory mechanisms, many chronic alcoholics do not show evidence of heart disease except on special tests designed to detect this disorder (Figueredo, 1997; Rubin & Doria, 1990). However, about 50% of those individuals with alcohol-induced cardiomyopathy will die within 4 years, if they continue to drink (Figueredo, 1997).

Although many individuals take comfort in the fact that they drink to excess only occasionally, even "binge" drinking is not without its dangers. Binge drinking may result in a condition known as the "holiday heart syndrome" (Figueredo, 1997; Zakhari, 1997). Episodic drinkers, such as those who go on binges such as during the holiday season, are prone to develop an irregular heartbeat known as *atrial fibrillation.* Not every case of atrial fibulation is caused by alcohol abuse. However, the condition may be fatal, if it is not diagnosed and properly treated by a physician. Thus, even episodic alcohol use is not without some degree of risk.

Effects of Chronic Alcohol Use on the Central Nervous System

Alcohol is a neurotoxin. One example of the toxic effects of alcohol is the way alcohol interferes with memory formation. Neuropsychological testing has revealed that alcohol may begin to affect memory formation after a single drink, although one normally needs to consume more than 5 drinks in an hour's time before alcohol is able to affect the process of memory formation significantly (Browning, Hoffer, & Dunwiddie, 1993).

Memory problems are one of the most frequent symptoms experienced by the heavy drinker. The individual may find it impossible to remember events that took place while intoxicated—a condition commonly known as a *blackout.* These periods of alcohol-induced amnesia may last several days, although for the most part they involve shorter periods of time (Segal & Sisson, 1985; Willoughby, 1984). During a blackout, the individual may *appear* to be conscious, and is able to carry out many complex tasks. Afterwards, however, the drinker has no memory of what she or he did during the blackout. The alcohol-induced blackout is somewhat similar to a condition known as *transient global amnesia* (Kaplan, Sadock, & Grebb, 1994; Rubino, 1992).

Scientists believe that alcohol prevents the individual from being able to form (encode) memories during the period of acute intoxication (Browning, Hoffer, & Dunwiddie, 1993). The alcohol-induced blackout is "an early and serious indicator of the development of alcoholism" (Rubino, 1992, p. 360). When asked, the majority of heavy drinkers admit to having alcohol-induced blackouts (Schuckit, Smith, Anthenelli & Irwin, 1993). There are also indications that 15% of alcohol-dependent individuals show signs of alcohol-induced brain damage before demonstrating overt signs of alcohol-related liver damage (Bowden, 1994; Berg, Franzen, & Wedding, 1994; Volkow, Hitzemann, Wang, Fowler, Burr, Pascani, Dewey, & Wolf 1992).

Researchers still do not agree on the mechanism by which the chronic use of alcohol contributes to brain damage (Roehrs & Roth, 1995). However, the chronic use of alcohol has been called the single most preventable cause of dementia in this country (Beasley, 1987). Research suggests that up to 75% of chronic alcohol users show evidence of alcohol-induced cognitive impairment following detoxification (Hartman, 1995; Butterworth, 1995; Tarter, Ott, & Mezzich, 1991) and that 15–30% of all nursing home patients are there because of permanent alcohol-induced brain damage (Schuckit, 2000). It has also been estimated that alcohol-induced dementia is the "second most common adult dementia after Alzheimer's disease" (Nace & Isbell, 1991, p. 56).

A limited degree of improvement in cognitive function is possible in alcoholics who abstain from alcohol for extended periods of time, but not every alcoholic who abstains from alcohol achieves a complete recovery (Grant, 1987; Løberg, 1986). Research suggests that, following abstinence, only 20% of chronic alcohol users return to their previous level of intellectual function (Nace & Isbell, 1991). Some limited degree of recovery is possible in perhaps 60% of the cases, and virtually no recovery of lost intellectual function is seen in 20% of the cases, according to the authors. Another central nervous system complication seen as a result of chronic alcohol abuse is *vitamin deficiency amblyopia*. This condition will cause blurred vision, a loss of visual perception in the center of the visual field known as central scotomata, and, in extreme cases, atrophy of the optic nerve (Mirin, Weiss, & Greenfield, 1991). The alcohol-induced damage to the visual system may be permanent.

Wernicke-Korsakoff syndrome. Perhaps the most serious complication of chronic alcohol use is a form of brain damage once known as *Wernicke's encephalopathy* (Charness, Simon, & Greenberg, 1989), which develops in about 20% of chronic alcohol users (Bowden, 1994). Alcohol-induced avitaminosis is thought to be a major factor in the development of this condition. As a result of the alcohol-related reduced vitamin absorption, the reserves of thiamine (one of the "B" family of vitamins) in the individual's body are gradually depleted, causing various neurological problems. Even with the best of medical care, the mortality rate during the acute phase of Wernicke's encephalopathy is 15–20% (Zubaran, Fernandes & Rodnight, 1997; Ciraulo, Shader, Ciraulo, Greenblatt, & von Moltke, 1994b).

Chronic thiamine deficiency results in characteristic patterns of brain damage, which is often detected on physical examination of the brain following death. Patients suffering from Wernicke's encephalopathy often appear confused, possibly to the point of being delirious and disoriented. They are also apathetic and unable to sustain physical or mental activities (Victor, 1993). A physical examination reveals a characteristic pattern of abnormal eye movements known as *nystagmus* and such symptoms of brain damage as gait disturbances and ataxia (Lehman, Pilich, & Andrews, 1994).

Before physicians developed a method to treat Wernicke's encephalophy, up to 80% of the patients who developed this condition went on to develop a condition known as *Korsakoff's psychosis* or *syndrome*, also called the *alcohol amnestic disorder* (Victor, 1993; Charness, Simon, & Greenberg, 1989). Even when Wernicke's encephalophy is properly treated through the most aggressive thiamine replacement procedures known to modern medicine, fully 25% of the patients who develop it go on to develop Korsakoff's syndrome (Sagar, 1991).

For many years, scientists thought that Wernicke's encephalopathy and Korsakoff's syndrome were separate disorders. It is now known that Wernicke's encephalopathy is the acute phase of Wernicke-Korsakoff syndrome. One of the most prominent symptoms of the Korsakoff phase of this syndrome is a memory disturbance, wherein the patient is unable to remember the past accurately and has difficulty learning new information. This may be associated with the alcohol-related loss of brain cells that is clearly visible in magnetic resonance imaging (MRI) studies (Pfefferbaum, Sillivan, Rosenbloom, Mathalon, & Kim, 1998). The authors found that this loss of brain tissue is most conspicuous in the anterior superior temporal cortex region of the brain, which seems to correspond to the behavioral deficits observed in Wernicke-Korsakoff syndrome.

It is not unusual to observe that in spite of clear evidence of cognitive impairment, the patient frequently appears indifferent to his or her memory loss (Ciraulo, Shader, Ciraulo, Greenblatt, & von Moltke, 1994b). In the earlier stages, the person may be confused by his or her inability to remember the past clearly and often "fills in" these memory gaps by making up answers to questions. This *confabulation* is most common in the earlier stages of Korsakoff's syndrome (Victor, 1993; Parsons & Nixon, 1993). Later on, as patients adjust to their memory loss, they are less likely to use confabulation to cover up their memory problem (Blansjaar & Zwinderman, 1992; Brandt & Butters, 1986).

In rare cases, the individual loses virtually all memories after a certain period of her or his life and is almost "frozen in time." For example, Sacks (1970) described a man who, when examined in the 1960s would answer questions as though he were still living in the 1940s. This radical confabulation, though extremely rare, can result from chronic alcoholism. More frequent are the less pronounced cases, where significant portions of the memory are lost, but the individual retains some ability to recall the past.

Unfortunately, the exact mechanism of Wernicke-Korsakoff syndrome is unknown at this time. The characteristic nystagmus seems to respond to massive doses of thiamine, or vitamin B-1. It is possible that victims of Wernicke-Korsakoff syndrome possess a genetic susceptibility to the effects of the alcohol-induced thiamine deficiency (Parsons & Nixon, 1993). This theory is attractive in that it explains why some chronic alcoholics develop Wernicke-Korsakoff syndrome and others do not, but it remains just a theory.

Jensen and Pakkenberg (1993) offered a unique theory that relates the effects of alcohol to the physical structure of the brain. The authors performed a post-mortem examination of the brains of 55 individuals who had been active alcoholics. It was found that the chronic alcohol use did not cause the death of neurons so much as it caused them to become *disconnected* from their neighbors. The authors found evidence of degeneration *in specific regions of the nerve cells*—regions known as the axons and dendrites—rather than evidence that the entire nerve cells died as a result of chronic alcohol exposure. The authors suggested that the loss of intellectual function seen in chronic alcohol use might thus reflect the disruption of established nerve pathways.

These are only theories, which remain to be proved. It is known that, once Wernicke-Korsakoff syndrome has developed, only a minority of its victims escape without lifelong neurological damage. It is estimated that even with the most aggressive of vitamin replacement therapy, only 20% (Nace & Isbell, 1991) to 25% (Brandt & Butters, 1986) of its victims will return to their previous level of intellectual function. The other 75–80% will experience greater or lesser degrees of neurological damage. Further, very little is known about the process of rehabilitation or whether rehabilitation is even possible (Parsons & Nixon, 1993; Blansjaar & Zwinderman, 1992).

There is evidence that chronic alcohol abuse/addiction is a risk factor in the development of a movement disorder known as *tardive dyskinesia* (TD) (Lopez & Jeste, 1997). This condition may result from alcohol's neurotoxic effect, according to the authors. Although TD is a common complication in patients who have used neuroleptic drugs for the control of psychotic conditions for long periods of time, there are cases where the alcohol-dependent individual has developed TD in spite of having had no prior exposure to neuroleptic agents (Lopez & Jeste, 1997). The exact mechanism by which alcohol causes the development of tardive dyskinesia remains to be identified, and scientists have no idea why some alcohol-abusers develop TD and others do not. According to these investigators, TD usually develops in chronic alcohol users who have a history of drinking for 10–20 years.

Alcohol's effects on the sleep cycle. Alcohol is a CNS depressant that, although it might induce sleep, suppresses melatonin production in the brain, which in turn interferes with the normal sleep cycle (Pettit, 2000). Thus alcohol use/abuse is a known cause of sleep disturbance. Clinicians often encounter patients who complain of sleep problems without revealing their alcohol abuse. For example, the staff of one sleep disorders clinic found that 12% of the patients who were seen because of insomnia were found to have a history of alcohol abuse or alcohol dependence (Frederickson, Richardson, Esther, & Lin, 1990). Alcohol also interferes with the normal dream cycle by suppressing the rapid eye movement (REM) phase of sleep. There is a relationship between REM sleep and dreaming. When alcohol abusers stop drinking, they enter a period of abnormal sleep known as REM rebound.[5] The "rebound" dreams may be so frightening that the individual may return to the use of alcohol in order to "get a decent night's sleep." The phase of REM rebound can last for up to six months after the person has stopped drinking, and the effects of alcohol have been known to interfere with the normal sleep cycle for as long as two years after detoxification (Satel, Kosten, Schuckit, & Fischman, 1993; Fredrickson, Richardson, Esther, & Lin, 1990). Further, alcohol appears to trigger episodes of sleep apnea, which can continue for weeks after the individual's last drink (Le Bon, Verbanck, Hoffmann, Murphy, Staner, De Groote, Mampuza, Den Dulk, Vacher, Kornreich, & Pelc, 1997).

Effects of Chronic Alcohol Use on the Peripheral Nervous System

The human nervous system is usually viewed as two interconnected systems. The brain and spinal cord make up the central nervous system, and the nerves found in the outer regions of the body are classified as the peripheral nervous system. Unfortunately, the effects of alcohol-induced avitaminosis are sufficiently widespread to include the peripheral nerves, especially those in the hands and feet. *Peripheral neuropathy* is found in between 10% (Schuckit, 1995b) and 33% of chronic alcohol users (Monforte, Estruch, Valls-Sole, Nicolas, Villalta, & Urbano-Marquez, 1995). Its symptoms include weakness, pain, and a burning sensation in the

[5]See the Glossary.

afflicted region of the body (Lehman, Pilich, & Andrews, 1994). Eventually, the victim loses all feeling in the affected region. Approximately 30% of all cases of peripheral neuropathy are thought to be alcohol-induced (Hartman, 1995).

The exact cause of alcohol-induced peripheral neuropathies is not known. Some researchers believe that peripheral neuropathy is the result of a deficiency of the "B" family of vitamins in the body (Charness, Simon, & Greenberg, 1989; Nace, 1987; Beasley, 1987). But Monforte, Estruch, Valls-Sole, Nicolas, Villalta, and Urbano-Marquez (1995) suggested that peripheral neuropathies might be the result of chronic exposure to alcohol itself or its metabolites, some of which are themselves quite toxic. The authors failed to find evidence of a nutritional deficit for those hospitalized alcoholics who had developed peripheral neuropathies. But they did find a relationship between the amount of alcohol consumed and the development of peripheral neuropathies.

Surprisingly, in light of alcohol's known neurotoxic effects, there is evidence to suggest that at some doses it may suppress the involuntary movements of Huntington's disease (Lopez & Jeste, 1997). This effect of alcohol might account for the finding that patients with movement disorders such as essential tremor, or Huntington's disease, tend to abuse alcohol more often than close relatives who do not have a movement disorder.

Effects of Chronic Alcohol Use on the Person's Emotional State

The chronic use of alcohol can simulate the symptoms of virtually every form of neurosis, even those seen in psychotic conditions. These symptoms, which are thought to be secondary to the individual's malnutrition and to the toxic effects of chronic alcohol use (Beasley, 1987), include depressive reactions (Blondell, Frierson, & Lippmann, 1996; Schuckit, 1995b), generalized anxiety disorders, and panic attacks (Beasley, 1987).

There is a complex relationship between anxiety symptoms and alcohol use disorders. For example, without medical intervention, almost 80% of alcohol-dependent individuals experience panic episodes during the acute phase of withdrawal from alcohol (Schuckit, 2000). The chronic use of alcohol causes a paradoxical stimulation of the autonomic nervous system (ANS). The drinker often interprets this ANS stimulation as a

sign of anxiety and turns to alcohol or antianxiety medications to control it. Then the chronic use of alcohol sets the stage for further anxiety-like symptoms, resulting in the perceived need for more alcohol/medication. Stockwell and Town (1989) discussed this aspect of chronic alcohol use and concluded that "many clients who drink heavily or abuse other anixolytic drugs will experience substantial or complete recovery from extreme anxiety following successful detoxification" (p. 223). The authors recommend a drug-free period of *at least two weeks* in which to assess the need for pharmacological intervention for anxiety.

Of course, it is possible that the individual has both antianxiety disorder *and* an alcohol use disorder. Indeed, researchers have discovered that 10–40% of those who are alcohol-dependent also have an anxiety disorder of some kind and that between 10% and 20% of those patients being treated for some form of anxiety disorder also have some kind of alcohol use disorder (Cox & Taylor, 1999). For these individuals, the anxiety coexists with their alcohol use disorder and does not reflect alcohol withdrawal. The diagnostic dilemma is for the clinician to determine which patients have withdrawal-induced anxiety and which have a legitimate anxiety disorder in addition to their substance use problem. This determination is made more difficult by the fact that chronic alcohol use can cause drinkers to experience feelings of anxiety for many months after they stop drinking (Schuckit, 1998).

Differentiating between "true" anxiety disorders and alcohol-related anxiety-like disorders is thus quite complex. Kushner, Sher, and Beitman (1990) concluded that alcohol withdrawal symptoms may be "indistinguishable" (p. 692) from the symptoms of panic attacks and generalized anxiety disorder (GAD). One diagnostic clue is the observation that problems such as agoraphobia and social phobias usually predate alcohol use. Victims of these disorders usually attempt self-medication through the use of alcohol and only later develop alcohol use problems. On the other hand, Kushner, Sher and Beitman concluded that the symptoms of simple panic attacks and generalized anxiety disorder are more likely to reflect the effects of alcohol withdrawal than a psychiatric disorder.

Another form of phobia that frequently coexists with alcoholism is the *social phobia* (Marshall, 1994). Individuals with social phobias fear situations in which they are exposed to other people and are twice as likely to have alcohol use problems as people from the general population. However, in such cases the social phobia usually precedes the development of alcohol abuse/addiction.

It is not uncommon for alcohol-dependent individuals to complain of anxiety symptoms when they see their physician, who may then prescribe a benzodiazepine to control the anxiety. Unfortunately, this enables chronic drinkers to control their withdrawal symptoms during the day without having the smell of alcohol on their breath. (One alcohol-dependent individual explained, for example, that the effects of 10 mg of diazepam were similar to the effects of 3–4 quick drinks). Given this tendency for alcohol-dependent individuals to use benzodiazepines, it is not surprising that 25–50% of alcoholics are also addicted to these drugs (Miller & Gold, 1991b). If the physician fails to obtain an adequate history and physical (or if the patient lies about his or her alcohol use), there is also a risk that the alcohol-dependent person will combine the use of antianxiety medication with alcohol. Thus, the use of alcohol with CNS depressants such as the benzodiazepines and antihistamines presents a very real danger of overdose.

The interaction between benzodiazepines and alcohol has been implicated as one cause of the condition known as the *paradoxical rage reaction* (Beasley, 1987). This is a drug-induced reaction in which a CNS depressant brings about an unexpected period of rage in the individual. During the paradoxical rage reaction, individuals may engage in assaultive or destructive behavior toward themselves or others, and they later have no conscious memory of what they did (Lehman, Pilich, & Andrews, 1994).

If antianxiety medication is needed for long-term anxiety control in recovering drinkers, buspirone should be used first (Kranzler, Burleson, Del Boca, Babor, Korner, Brown, & Bohn, 1994). Buspirone is not a benzodiazepine and thus does not present the potential for abuse seen with the latter family of drugs. The authors found that those alcoholic subjects in their study who suffered from anxiety symptoms and received buspirone were more likely both to remain in treatment and to consume less alcohol than those anxious subjects who did not receive buspirone. This suggests that buspirone might be an effective medication in treating anxious alcoholics.

Chronic alcohol use has been known to interfere with sexual performance for both men and women (Schiavi, Stimmel, Mandeli, & White, 1995). Although the chronic use of alcohol has been shown to interfere with the erectile process for men, Schiavi, Stimmel, Mandeli, and White (1995) found that once the individual stopped drinking, the erectile dysfunction usually resolved itself. However, as noted in Chapter 32, there is evidence that disulfiram (often used in the treatment of chronic alcoholism) itself may interfere with the man's ability to achieve an erection.

There also is a relationship between alcohol use disorders and depression. Research has suggested that only 2–3% (Powell, Read, Penick, Miller, & Bingham, 1987) to perhaps as many as 5% (Schuckit, 2000) of the cases of depression seen in alcoholics represent a primary depression. But it has been estimated that 10–15% of individuals who are depressed will attempt to use alcohol to self-medicate their emotional distress (Campbell, 1992). Unfortunately, many people who are clinically depressed are unaware that although alcohol initially will "numb" feelings of depression, alcohol ultimately can contribute to the very depression that the person wishes to escape. Willoughby (1984) noted that the depressant effects from one drink may last as long as 96 hours. The depressant effects of an alcohol binge of even one or two days might last for several weeks after abstinence begins (Segal & Sisson, 1985).

Thus the use of alcohol as a form of "self-medication" for depression actually adds to the individual's feelings of depression. To further complicate the diagnostic picture, alcohol has been implicated as the cause of depressive reactions for chronic alcohol users. It has been suggested that during the first two weeks of treatment, most chronic drinkers will meet the diagnostic criteria for major depression (Wolf-Reeve, 1990, p. 72). However, in the vast majority of these cases, the individual will be found to suffer from an alcohol-induced depression. Such alcohol-induced depressive episodes usually clear after 2–5 weeks of abstinence and usually do not require formal treatment (Miller, 1994; Decker & Ries, 1993; Satel, Kosten, Schuckit, & Fischman, 1993). Decker and Ries (1993) noted that various experts in the field of psychiatry believe that waiting periods of between 4 weeks and several months (p. 704) are necessary after the person stops drinking, to determine whether the alcohol-induced depression will resolve itself. Thus there is no clear guideline for when antidepressant medication and/or psychiatric treatment may be needed to help the drinker recover from his or her depression.

However, Blume (1994) issued a note of caution concerning relationship between depression and alcohol use disorders. She noted that because most research into the effects of alcohol has been conducted using male subjects, there is little understanding of the effects of alcohol on women. In her exploration of those few studies that have addressed the impact of alcoholism in women, Blume (1994) suggested that in 60–65% of the cases where an alcoholic woman is depressed, the woman is experiencing a major depression that should be treated.

It *is* known that active alcohol abuse has a negative effect on the recovery from depression. Mueller, Lavori, Keller, Swartz, Warshaw, Hasin, Coryell, Endicott, Rice, and Akiskal (1994) examined the relationship between these two disorders and found that depressed individuals who were either: nonalcoholic, or abstinent alcoholics had twice the recovery rate from depression as did depressed active alcoholics. The authors also found evidence that other factors than alcohol use caused the depressive disorder. Once the depressive disorder was in place, however, the individual's alcohol use status was a major factor in whether he or she would recover from that depressive episode.

There is a strong relationship between depression and suicide (Hirschfield & Davidson, 1988). Because alcoholics tend to experience depressive symptoms either as a consequence of their drinking or because of a coexisting major depression, they are a high-risk group for suicide. Eighteen percent of all those who remain actively addicted to alcohol will eventually commit suicide (Bongar, 1997), and 25% of those who commit suicide each year in the United States are alcohol-dependent (Harwitz & Ravizza, 2000). It has been suggested that alcohol-related suicide is most likely to occur late in the course of alcoholism, when the individual first begins to experience alcohol-related medical complications, such as cirrhosis of the liver (Brent, Kupfer, Bromet, & Dew, 1988).

Murphy, Wetzel, Robins, and McEvoy, (1992) identified seven factors that seemed to predict suicide in the chronic male alcoholic:

1. Drinking heavily in the days and weeks just prior to the act of suicide
2. Talking about the possibility of committing suicide
3. Having little social support
4. Suffering from a major depressive disorder
5. Being unemployed
6. Living alone
7. Suffering from a major medical problem

Although the authors failed to find any single factor that seemed to predict suicide in the chronic male alcoholic, they did conclude that "as the number of risk factors increases, the likelihood of a suicidal outcome does likewise (p. 461). Roy (1993) also identified several factors that seemed to be associated with an increased risk of suicide in adult alcoholics:

1. *Gender.* Men tend to commit suicide more often than women, and the ratio of male:female suicides for alcoholics may be about 4:1.
2. *Marital status.* Single/divorced/widowed adults are significantly more likely to attempt suicide than are married adults.
3. *Coexisting depressive disorder.* Depression is associated with an increased risk of suicide.
4. *Adverse life events.* The individual who has suffered an adverse life event, such as the loss of a loved one, a major illness, or legal problems, is at increased risk for suicide.
5. *Recent discharge from treatment for alcoholism.* The first four years following treatment were found to be associated with a significantly higher risk for suicide.
6. *A history of previous suicide attempts.* Approximately one-third of alcoholic suicide victims had attempted suicide at some point in the past.
7. *Biological factors.* Such factors as decreased levels of serotonin in the brain are thought to be associated with increased risk for violent behavior, including suicide.

One mechanism through which chronic drinking might cause/contribute to depressive disorders is the fact that chronic alcohol use causes an increase in dopamine turnover in the brain and a downregulation in the number of dopamine receptors within the neurons (Heinz, Ragan, Jones, Hommer, Williams, Knable, Gorey, Doty, Geyer, Lee, Coppola, Weinberger, & Linnoila, 1998).

These investigators also found a 30% reduction in serotonin transporters in chronic drinkers. Low levels of both dopamine and serotonin have been implicated in causing depression, so that this mechanism might explain how depression evolves in heavy drinkers.

Alcohol Withdrawal for the Chronic Alcoholic

Each year, "millions" (Yost, 1996, p. 657) of episodes of mild to moderate alcohol withdrawal take place. In such cases, the symptoms of such alcohol withdrawal usually subside quickly, with no need for medical intervention, and might not even be attributed by the individual to the use of alcohol. But in 200,000–450,000 cases each year in the United States, the individual's alcohol withdrawal is life-threatening, and even with the best of medical care, there is a significant risk of death from alcohol withdrawal syndrome (AWS).

For reasons that are not known, chronic drinkers vary in their risk for developing AWS (Saitz, 1998). However, AWS may become progressively worse each time the individual goes through the cycle of alcohol dependency and withdrawal (Littleton, 1998). In 90% of the cases, the symptoms of AWS develop within 4–12 hours after the individual's last drink, although in some cases, AWS develops simply because a chronic drinker significantly reduces his or her level of drinking (Saitz, 1998). In a small percentage of cases, AWS symptoms do not appear until 96 hours after the last drink or the reduction in alcohol intake (Lehman, Pilich, & Andrews, 1994; Weiss & Mirin, 1988). In extreme cases, the person does not begin to experience the symptoms of AWS until 10 days after his or her last drink (Slaby, Lieb, & Tancredi, 1981).

AWS is an acute brain syndrome what might at first be mistaken for such conditions as subdural hematoma, pneumonia, meningitis, and a range of other infections (Saitz, 1998). The severity of AWS depends on (1) the intensity with which that individual used alcohol, (2) how long the individual drank, and (3) the individual's state of health. Symptoms of AWS include agitation, anxiety, tremor, diarrhea, hyperactivity, exaggerated reflexes, insomnia, vivid dreams, nausea, vomiting, loss of appetite, restlessness, sweating, tachycardia, headache, and vertigo (Saitz, 1998; Lehman, Pilich, & Andrews, 1994).

In the hospital setting, an instrument commonly used to assess the severity of the individual's withdrawal symptoms is the Clinical Institute Withdrawal Assessment for Alcohol–Revised (CIWA-Ar). This non-copyrighted tool measures 15 symptoms of alcohol withdrawal and takes 3–5 minutes to administer. It has a maximum score of 67 points, with each symptom being weighted in terms of severity. A score of 0–4 points indicates minimal withdrawal discomfort; 5–12 points, mild alcohol withdrawal; 13–19 points, moderately severe alcohol withdrawal; and 20+ points, severe alcohol withdrawal. The CIWA-Ar might be repeatedly administered over time to provide a baseline measure of the patient's recovery from the acute effects of alcohol intoxication.

Patients who earn a score of 0–4 points on the CIWA-Ar may experience few symptoms of alcohol withdrawal and, depending on their alcohol use history, they will either remain at this level of withdrawal discomfort or progress to more severe levels. In more advanced cases, the symptoms may become more intense over the first 6–24 hours following the individual's last use of alcohol. The patient may also begin to experience *alcoholic hallucinosis*. The hallmark of alcoholic hallucinosis is frightening hallucinations (both visual and auditory). In about 80% of the cases of severe alcohol withdrawal, these hallucinations occur after the individual has stopped drinking, but they can develop while the individual is still actively consuming alcohol (Olmedo & Hoffman, 2000).

In extreme cases of alcohol withdrawal, these symptoms will continue to become more intense over the next 24–48 hours, and by the third day following the last drink, the patient will start to experience fever, incontinence, and/or tremors as well. Approximately 10–16% of those individuals who go through severe alcohol withdrawal experience a seizure as part of the withdrawal syndrome (D'Onofrio, Rathlev, Ulrich, Fish, & Freedland, 1999; Lehman, Pilich, & Andrews, 1994; Nace & Isbell, 1991). In 90% of the cases, the first seizure takes place within 48 hours after the last drink, although in 2–3% of the cases, the seizure may occur as late as 5–20 days after the last drink (Trevisan, Boutros, Petrakis, & Krystal, 1998). Approximately 60% of those adults who experience alcohol withdrawal seizures have multiple seizures (D'Onofrio, Rathlev, Ulrich, Fish, & Freedland, 1999). Alcohol withdrawal seizures are seen both in individuals who do, and in those who do not, experience hallucinations as part of their withdrawal from this chemical.

In 5% (Lieveld & Aruna, 1991) to 10% (Weiss & Mirin, 1988) of the cases of alcohol withdrawal in chronic users, AWS reaches the proportions of the *delirium tremens* (DTs). The DTs are the most extreme expression of AWS, and even with the best of medical care, the DTs prove fatal in approximately 5% of the cases (Weaver, Jarvis, & Schnoll, 1999). The medical and behavioral symptoms of the DTs include delirium, hallucinations, delusional beliefs that one is being followed, fever, and tachycardia (Lieveld & Aruna, 1991). During the period when the individual is going through the DTs he or she is vulnerable to developing rhabdomyolsis[6] as a result of alcohol-induced muscle damage (Richards, 2000).

In some cases of DTs, the individual experiences a disruption of normal fluid levels in the brain (Trabert, Caspari, Bernhard, & Biro, 1992). This results when the mechanism in the drinker's body that regulates normal fluid levels is disrupted by the alcohol withdrawal process. Such individuals may become dehydrated, or they may retain *too much* fluid in the body. Some individuals become hypersensitive to the antidiuretic hormone (ADH). This hormone is normally secreted by the body to slow the rate of fluid loss through the kidneys when the person is somewhat dehydrated. This excess fluid may contribute to the damage that the alcohol has caused to the brain, possibly by bringing about a state of cerebral edema (Trabert, Caspari, Bernhard, & Biro, 1992). Researchers have found that only patients going through the DTs have the combination of higher levels of ADH and low body fluid levels. This finding suggests that a body fluid dysregulation process might somehow be involved in the development of the DTs (Trabert, Caspari, Bernhard, & Biro, 1992).

In the past, between 5% and 25% of those individuals who developed the DTs died from exhaustion (Lehman, Pilich, & Andrews, 1994; Schuckit, 2000). However, improved medical care has reduced the mortality from DTs to about 1% (Milzman & Soderstrom, 1994) to 5% (Yost, 1996). The main causes of death for persons going through the DTs include sepsis, cardiac and/or respiratory arrest, and cardiac and/or circulatory collapse (Lieveld & Aruna, 1991). Persons who are going through the DTs are also a high-risk group for suicide, as they struggle with the emotional pain and terror associated with this condition (Hirschfield & Davidson, 1988).

Although a number of different chemicals have been suggested as being of value in controlling the symptoms of alcohol withdrawal, the current medical practice is to use one of the benzodiazepines, usually chlordiazepoxide or diazepam. The use of pharmaceutical agents to control the alcohol withdrawal symptoms will be discussed in more detail in Chapter 32.

Other Complications from Chronic Alcohol Use

Either directly or indirectly, alcohol contributes to a large number of head injuries (Anderson, 1991; Sparadeo & Gill, 1989). For example, it is not uncommon for the intoxicated individual to fall and strike his or her head on coffee tables, magazine stands, or whatever happens to be in the way. Unfortunately, the chronic use of alcohol contributes to the development of three different bone disorders (Griffiths, Parantainen, & Olson, 1994):

1. *Osteoporosis* (loss of bone mass)
2. *Osteomalacia* (a condition where new bone tissue fails to absorb minerals appropriately)
3. *Secondary hyperparathyroidism* (a hormonal disorder that develops when alcohol interferes with the body's ability to regulate calcium levels in the blood for extended periods of time, resulting in the calcium in the bones being reabsorbed into the blood, and the bones becoming weakened through calcium loss)

These bone disorders in turn contribute to the higher-than-expected level of injury and death seen when alcoholics fall and when they are involved in automobile accidents.

Alcohol is also a factor in traumatic brain injury. Researchers believe that approximately half of the estimated one million people who suffer a traumatic head injury each year have alcohol in their blood at the time of the injury (Anderson, 1991; Sparadeo & Gill, 1989).

Chronic alcohol use is thought to cause 60–90% of all deaths from cirrhosis of the liver, 40–50% of deaths in motor vehicle accidents, up to 67% of home injuries, and 3–5% of cancer-related deaths (Miller, 1999). Chronic alcohol users are 10 times more likely to develop cancer than nondrinkers (Schuckit, 1998), and 4% of all cases of cancer in men and 1% of all cases of

[6]See the Glossary.

cancer in women are thought to be alcohol-related (Ordorica & Nace, 1998). Approximately 5% of the total number of deaths that occur each year in the United States are thought to be alcohol-related (Miller, 1999). In addition to this, women who drink while pregnant run the risk of causing alcohol-induced birth defects, a condition known as the *fetal alcohol syndrome* (to be discussed in Chapter 20).

Chronic alcoholism has been associated with a premature aging syndrome, in which the chronic use of alcohol contributes to a situation where the individual appears much older than she or he actually is (Brandt & Butters, 1986). In many cases, the overall physical and intellectual condition of the individual corresponds to that of a person between 15 and 20 years older than the individual's chronological age. One individual, a man in his 50s, was told by his physician that he was in good health—for a man about to turn 70!

Admittedly, not every alcohol-dependent person will suffer from every consequence reviewed in this chapter. Some chronic alcohol users will never suffer from stomach problems, for example, but may suffer from advanced heart disease as a result of their drinking. However, Schuckit (1989) noted that in one research study, 93% of alcohol-dependent individuals who were admitted to treatment had at least one important medical problem in addition to their alcohol use problem.

Research has demonstrated that in most cases, the first alcohol-related problems are experienced when the drinker is in his or her late 20s or early 30s. The team of Schuckit, Smith, Anthenelli, and Irwin (1993) outlined a progressive course for alcoholism, on the basis of their study of 636 male alcoholics. The authors admitted that their subjects experienced wide differences in the specific problems caused by their drinking, but as a group, these alcoholics began to experience severe alcohol-related problems in their late 20s. By the mid-30s, the individual was likely to recognize that he or she had a drinking problem and begin to experience more severe problems as a result of continued drinking. However, as the authors pointed out, there is a wide variation in this pattern, and not all alcoholics follow it.

Summary

This chapter explored the many facets of alcoholism. We reviewed the scope of alcohol abuse/addiction in this country, including the fact that alcoholism accounts for approximately 85% of the drug addiction problem in the United States. We discussed the different forms of tolerance and the ways in which the chronic use of alcohol can affect the body. The impact of chronic alcohol use on the central nervous system, the cardiopulmonary system, the digestive system, and the skeletal bone structure were reviewed. In addition, we examined the relationship between chronic alcohol use and physical injuries, and we saw how chronic alcohol use can lead to a decreased lifespan and premature aging. Finally, the process of alcohol withdrawal for the alcohol-dependent person was discussed.

CHAPTER NINE

Abuse of and Addiction to the Barbiturates and Barbiturate-like Drugs

Introduction

The anxiety disorders are, collectively, the most common form of mental illness found in the United States (Blair & Ramones, 1996). At any point in time, between 7% and 23% of the general population are thought to suffering from anxiety in one form or another (Baughan, 1995), and over the course of their lives, approximately one-third of all adults will experience at least transient periods of anxiety intense enough to interfere with their daily lives (Spiegel, 1996). Further, scientists believe that in a year's time, 35% or more of the adults in the United States experience some form of insomnia (Lacks & Morin, 1992).

For many thousands of years, alcohol was the only agent that could reduce the individual's anxiety level or help the individual fall asleep. However, as we saw in the last chapter, the effectiveness of alcohol as an anti-anxiety[1] agent (or "sedative") is quite limited. Thus, for many hundreds of years, there has been a very real demand for effective antianxiety or hypnotic[2] medications. In this chapter, we will review the various medications that were used to control anxiety or promote sleep before the benzodiazepines were introduced in the early 1960s. In the next chapter, we will focus on the benzodiazepine family of drugs and on medications that have been introduced since the benzodiazepines first appeared.

Early Pharmacological Therapy for Anxiety Disorders and Insomnia

In the year 1870,[3] *chloral hydrate* was introduced as a hypnotic. It was found that chloral hydrate was rapidly absorbed from the digestive tract and that an oral dose of 1–2 grams would cause the average person to fall asleep in less than an hour. The effects of chloral hydrate were found usually to last 8–11 hours, making it appear to be ideal for use as a hypnotic. However, physicians quickly discovered that chloral hydrate had several major drawbacks, not the least of which was that it was quite irritating to the stomach lining, and chronic use could result in significant damage to the lining of the stomach. Also, physicians discovered that chloral hydrate was addictive, and that at high doses it could exacerbate existing cardiac problems in patients with heart disease (Pagliaro & Pagliaro, 1998). Finally, it was discovered that withdrawal from chloral hydrate after extended periods of use was quite dangerous and that many patients developed life-threatening withdrawal seizures.

Technically, chloral hydrate is a *prodrug*.[4] After it is ingested, chloral hydrate is rapidly biotransformed into *trichloroethanol*, the active metabolite that causes the drug to be effective as a hypnotic. Surprisingly, in spite of its known dangers, chloral hydrate continues to have a limited role in modern medicine. Its relatively short

---

[1]Occasionally, mental health professionals will use the term "anxiolytic" rather than "antianxiety." For the purpose of this section, however, the term "antianxiety" will be utilized.

[2]A "hypnotic" is a medication designed to help the user fall asleep.

[3]Pagliaro and Pagliaro (1998) said that this happened in 1869, not 1870.

[4]See the Glossary.

biological half-life makes it of value in treating some elderly patients who suffer from insomnia.

Paraldehyde was isolated in 1829 and first used as a hypnotic in 1882. As a hypnotic, paraldehyde is quite effective. It produces little respiratory or cardiac depression, making it a relatively safe drug to use with patients who have some forms of pulmonary or cardiac disease. However, it tends to produce a very noxious taste, and users develop a strong breath odor. Paraldehyde is quite irritating to the mucous membranes of the mouth and throat and must be diluted in a liquid before use.

The half-life of paraldehyde ranges from 3.4 to 9.8 hours, and about 70–80% of a single dose is biotransformed by the liver prior to excretion. Between 11% and 28% of a single dose leaves the body unchanged, usually by being exhaled (causing the characteristic odor on the user's breath). Paraldehyde has an abuse/addiction potential similar to that of alcohol, and intoxication on paraldehyde resembles alcohol-induced intoxication. After the barbiturates were introduced, paraldehyde gradually fell into disfavor. However, it does have a very limited role in medicine, even today.

The *bromide salts* were first used for the treatment of insomnia in the mid-1800s. They were available without a prescription and were used well into the 20th century. Bromides are indeed capable of inducing sleep, but it was soon discovered that they tend to accumulate in the chronic user's body, causing a drug-induced depression after as little as a few days of continuous use. The bromide salts have been totally replaced by newer drugs, such as the barbiturates and the benzodiazepines.

Despite superficial differences in chemical structure, the compounds discussed above are all central nervous system (CNS) depressants. The normal dosage levels of the barbiturate-like drugs are reviewed in Table 9.1.

TABLE 9.1   Dosage Equivalency for Barbiturate-like Drugs

Generic name of drug of abuse	Dose equivalent to 30 mg of phenobarbital
Chloral hydrate	500 mg
Ethchlorvynol	350 mg
Meprobamate	400 mg
Methyprylon	300 mg
Glutethimide	250 mg

In spite of their superficial differences in chemical structure, these compounds share many characteristics, such as the ability to *potentiate* the effects of other CNS depressants. Another characteristic that these CNS depressants share is their significant potential for abuse. Still, in spite of these shortcomings, these agents were the treatment of choice for anxiety and insomnia until the barbiturates were introduced.

History and Current Medical Uses of the Barbiturates

Late in the last century, chemists discovered the barbiturates. Experimentation quickly revealed that the barbiturates were able to act either as a sedative or, at a higher dosage level, as a hypnotic. In addition to this, it was discovered that the barbiturates were safer and less noxious than the bromides, chloral hydrate, and paraldehyde (Greenberg, 1993). It was in 1903 that the first barbiturate—Veronal—was introduced for human use, and the barbiturates were soon marketed as over-the-counter medications (Nelson, 2000; Peluso & Peluso, 1988). Since the time of their introduction, some 2500 different barbiturates have been isolated by chemists. Most of these barbiturates were never marketed, and they have remained only laboratory curiosities. Perhaps 50 barbiturates were marketed at one point or another in the United States; about 20 are still in use (Nishino, Mignot, & Dement, 1995). The relative potency of the most common barbiturates are reviewed in Table 9.2.

In the United States, the barbiturates have been classified as Category II controlled substances[5] and are available only by a physician's prescription. After the introduction of the benzodiazepines in the 1960s, the barbiturates previously in use gradually fell into disfavor. At this time, the barbiturates have no role in the routine treatment of anxiety or insomnia (Uhde & Trancer, 1995).

In spite of the introduction of newer pharmaceuticals, however, there are still some areas of medicine (such as certain surgical procedures and the control of epilepsy) where certain barbiturates remain the pharmaceutical of choice. Surprisingly, in light of the fact that newer drugs have all but replaced the barbiturates in modern medicine, controversy still rages around the appropriate use of many of these chemicals. For ex-

[5]See Appendix 4.

TABLE 9.2   Normal Dosage Levels of
Commonly Used Barbiturates

Barbiturate	Sedative Dose*	Hypnotic Dose**
Amobarbital	50–150 mg/day	65–200 mg
Aprobarbital	120 mg/day	40–60 mg
Butabarbital	45–120 mg/day	50–100 mg
Mephobarbital	96–400 mg/day	Not used as hypnotic
Pentobarbital	60–80 mg/day	100 mg
Phenobarbital	30–120 mg/day	100–320 mg
Secobarbital	90–200 mg/day	50–200 mg
Talbutal	30–120 mg/day	120 mg

Source: Table based on information provided in Uhde & Trancer (1995).
*Administered in divided doses
**Administered as a single dose at bedtime.

ample, although the barbiturates were once thought to be effective in the control of pressure levels within the brain following trauma, physicians now question their effectiveness in the control of intracranial hypertension (Lund & Papadakos, 1995).

In some states, one form of the barbiturates is used to execute criminals by "lethal injection" (Truog, Berde, Mitchell, & Brier, 1992). Another, equally controversial use of the barbiturates is in the sedation of terminally ill cancer patients who are in extreme pain (Truog, Berde, Mitchell, & Brier, 1992). Thus, although the barbiturates have been in use for more than a century, they remain the agent of choice to treat certain medical conditions, and controversy surrounds the use of these pharmaceuticals.

The abuse potential of barbiturates. The barbiturates have a considerable abuse potential. Indeed, in the period between 1950 and 1970, the barbiturates were, as a group, second only to alcohol as drugs of abuse (Reinsch, Sanders, Mortensen, & Rubin, 1995). The barbiturates are still occasionally abused. For example, in years past, heroin addicts would use barbiturates to "boost" the effects of low-potency heroin. This is accomplished by mixing the barbiturate with the heroin prior to injection (Kaminski, 1992). However, in this era of high-potency heroin, the practice is rare.

In light of the fact that the barbiturates have not been extensively used since the late 1960s, it is quite

surprising to learn that 8.9% of the graduating seniors of the class of 1999 claim to have used barbiturates at least once (Johnston, O'Malley, & Bachman, 2000a). Just over 7% of the young adults between 19 and 32 who were surveyed admitted to having used a barbiturate at least once for recreational purposes (Johnston, O'Malley, & Bachman, 2000b). There are also a number of individuals over the age of 40 who became addicted to the barbiturates when they were younger. For people of this generation, the barbiturates were the most effective treatment for anxiety and insomnia, and many users became—and remain—addicted (Kaplan, Sadock, & Grebb, 1994). Finally, a small number of physicians have turned to the barbiturates as antianxiety and hypnotic agents in order to avoid extra paperwork imposed upon benzodiazepine prescriptions. Fortunately, the majority of physicians have not followed this practice.

Pharmacology of the Barbiturates

Chemically, the barbiturates are remarkably similar. The only major difference between the various members of the barbiturate family of drugs is the length of time it takes the individual's body to absorb, biotransform, and then excrete the specific form of barbiturate that has been used. One factor that influences the absorption of barbiturates is the drug's lipid solubility. Those barbiturates that are readily soluble in lipids are rapidly distributed to all blood-rich tissues such as the brain. Thus pentobarbital, which is very lipid-soluble, may begin to have an effect in 10–15 minutes. In contrast to this, phenobarbital is poorly lipid-soluble and does not begin to have an effect until 60 minutes or longer after the user has ingested the medication.

Although different barbiturates may differ in duration of effect and speed of action, the mechanisms by which all barbiturates work are similar. Barbiturates have been found to inhibit the ability of the $GABA_A$ chloride channel to close, thus slowing the rate at which the cell can "fire" (Olmedo & Hoffman, 2000). Using *duration of action* as the criteria, the barbiturates might be grouped into four different classes.[6] First,

[6]Other researchers might use different classification systems from the one that is used in this text. For example, some researchers use the chemical structures of the different forms of barbiturates as the defining criteria for classification. This text will follow the classification system suggested by Zevin & Benowitz (1998).

there are the *ultrashort*-acting barbiturates. The effects of the ultrashort-acting barbiturates begin in a matter of seconds after injection and last for less than half an hour. Examples include Pentothal and Brevital. The ultrashort-acting barbiturates are extremely lipid-soluble, pass through the blood-brain barrier quickly, and, when injected into a vein, have an effect on the brain in just a few seconds. These medications are often utilized in surgical procedures where a rapid onset of effects, and a short duration of action, are desirable.

Then there are the *short-acting* barbiturates. The effects of the short-acting barbiturates begin in a matter of minutes after injection and last for 3–4 hours (Zevin & Benowitz, 1998). Nembutal is an example (Kaplan, Sadock, & Grebb, 1994). In terms of lipid solubility, the short-acting barbiturates would fall between the ultrashort-acting barbiturates and the next group, the *intermediate-acting* barbiturates. The effects of the intermediate-acting barbiturates begin within an hour when the drug is ingested orally and last some 6–8 hours (Zevin & Benowitz, 1998). Included in this group are such drugs as Amytal (amobarbital) and Butisol (butabarbital) (Schuckit, 2000). Finally, there are the *long-acting* barbiturates. The long-acting barbiturates are absorbed slowly, and their effects last for 6–12 hours (Zevin & Benowitz, 1998). Phenobarbital is perhaps the most commonly encountered drug in this class.

Note that the short-acting barbiturates do *not* have extremely short half-lives. The biological half-life of a drug provides only a *rough* estimate of the period of time that a specific chemical will remain in the body. The shorter-acting barbiturates might have an effect on the user for only a few hours and still have a half-life of 8–12 hours or even longer. This is because their effects are limited not by the speed at which they are biotransformed by the liver, but by the speed with which they are removed from the blood and distributed to the various organs in the body. Significant levels of some shorter-acting barbiturates are stored in different body organs and are still present long after the drug stopped having its desired effect. The barbiturate molecules stored in the different body organs are slowly released back into the general circulation, possibly causing a barbiturate "hangover" (Uhde & Trancer, 1995).

Overall, the chemical structure of the various forms of barbiturates are quite similar, and, once in the user's body, they all tend to have similar effects. There are few significant differences in relative potency between various barbiturates. As a general rule, the shorter-term barbiturates are almost fully biotransformed by the liver before being excreted from the body (Nishino, Mignot, & Dement, 1995). In contrast, a significant proportion of the longer-term barbiturates are eliminated from the body essentially unchanged. Thus, for phenobarbital, which may have a half-life of 2–6 days, 25–50% of the drug will be excreted by the kidneys virtually unchanged. In contrast, the barbiturate methohexital has a half-life of only 3–6 hours, and virtually all of it is biotransformed by the liver before it is excreted from the body (American Society of Health-System Pharmacists, 1999). Another difference between the various barbiturates is the degree to which the drug molecules become protein-bound. As a general rule, the longer the drug's half-life, the stronger the protein binding.

When used on an outpatient basis, the barbiturates are typically administered orally. (On occasion, especially when used in a medical setting, an ultrashort-acting barbiturate might be administered intravenously, such as when it is used as an anesthetic in surgery or for seizure control. On rare occasions, the barbiturates are administered rectally, through suppositories.) When taken orally, the barbiturate molecule is rapidly and completely absorbed from the small intestine (Julien, 1992; Winchester, 1990). Once it reaches the blood, the barbiturate is distributed throughout the body, but the concentrations will be highest in the liver and the brain (American Society of Health-System Pharmacists, 1999). The barbiturates are all lipid-soluble, but they vary in their ability to form bonds with blood lipids. As a general rule, the more lipid-soluble a barbiturate, the more highly protein-bound that chemical (Winchester, 1990).

The behavioral effects of the barbiturates are very similar to those of alcohol (*Harvard Medical School Mental Health Letter*, 1988). Thus, like alcohol, once a barbiturate reaches the bloodstream, it is distributed throughout the body and affects all body tissues to some degree. At normal dosage levels, the barbiturates depress not only the activity of the brain but also to a lesser degree, the activity of the muscle tissues, the heart, and respiration (Matuschka, 1985). However, it is within the central nervous system (CNS) that the barbiturates have their strongest effect (Rall, 1990).

In the brain, the barbiturates are thought to simulate the effects of the neurotransmitter gamma-aminobutyric acid (GABA) (Carvey, 1998; Hobbs, Rall, & Verdoorn, 1995). At the same time, the barbiturates are thought to block the effects of another neurotransmitter, *glutamate*. GABA is thought to be the most important "inhibitory" neurotransmitter in the brain, whereas glutamate functions as a stimulating neurotransmitter (Nutt, 1996; Bohn, 1993; Tabakoff & Hoffman, 1992). Within the neuron, barbiturates reduce the frequency with which the $GABA_A$ receptor site is activated but also increases the time that it remains active, even in the absence of GABA itself (Carvey, 1998). This action reduces the electrochemical potential of the cell, reducing the frequency with which that neuron can fire (Cooper, Bloom, & Roth, 1996).

At the regional level within the brain, the barbiturates have their greatest impact on the cortex and the reticula activating system (RAS) (which is responsible for awareness), as well as the medulla oblongata (which controls respiration) (American Society of Health-System Pharmacists, 1999). At low dosage levels, the barbiturates reduce the function of the nerve cells in these regions of the brain, bringing on a state of relaxation and, at slightly higher doses, a drug-induced sleep. At extremely high dosage levels, the barbiturates interfere with the normal function of the neurons of the CNS to such a degree that death is possible. Indeed, barbiturate-induced death is not uncommon, for the therapeutic dose of the typical barbiturate is relatively close to the lethal dose. Some barbiturates have a ratio of therapeutic dosage level to lethal dosage level of only 1:3, reflecting the narrow therapeutic window of these agents. This low safety margin, combined with the significantly higher safety margin offered by the benzodiazepines, is one reason why the barbiturates have largely been replaced by newer medications in the treatment of anxiety and for inducing sleep.

Subjective Effects of Barbiturates at Normal Dosage Levels

At low doses, the barbiturates reduce feelings of anxiety or, possibly, bring on a sense of euphoria. Some users also report a feeling of sedation, or fatigue, perhaps to the point of drowsiness, and a decrease in motor activity. This results in an increase in the users' reaction time, and they might have trouble coordinating muscle movements, almost as though they were intoxicated by

alcohol (Peluso & Peluso, 1988; *The Harvard Medical School Mental Health Letter*, 1988). This is to be expected, because alcohol and the barbiturates affect the cortex of the brain through similar pharmacological mechanisms. The disinhibition effects of the barbiturates, like those of alcohol, may cause a state of "paradoxical" excitement or possibly even a paradoxical rage reaction. Patients who have received barbiturates for medical reasons have reported such unpleasant side effects as nausea, dizziness, and a feeling of mental slowness. Anxious patients report that their anxiety is no longer so intense, and patients who have been unable to sleep report that they can slip into a state of drug-induced sleep quickly.

Complications of the Barbiturates at Normal Dosage Levels

For almost 60 years, the barbiturates were the treatment of choice for insomnia. Given that the barbiturates were so extensively prescribed to help people sleep, it is surprising to learn that research has shown that tolerance rapidly develops to the hypnotic effects of barbiturates. Indeed, research suggests that they are not effective as hypnotics after just a few days of regular use (Ray & Ksir, 1993; Rall, 1990). In spite of their traditional use as a treatment for insomnia, the sleep that one achieves through the use of barbiturates is not the same as a normal state of sleep. The barbiturates suppress a portion of the sleep cycle known as the rapid eye movement (REM) state of sleep (Peluso & Peluso, 1988). Scientists who study sleep believe that people need to experience REM sleep for their emotional well-being, and about one-quarter of a young adult's total sleep time is normally spent in REM sleep (Kaplan, Sadock, & Grebb, 1994). Barbiturate-assisted sleep results in a reduction in the total amount of time that the individual spends in REM sleep (Rall, 1990). Thus, by interfering with the normal sleep pattern, barbiturate-induced sleep may adversely affect the emotional and physical health of the individual.

After a period of continuous use, the user experiences "REM rebound" when he or she discontinues a barbiturate. In this condition, the person dreams more intensely and more vividly for a while, as the body tries to catch up on lost REM sleep. These dreams have been described by some as nightmares strong enough to tempt them to return to the use of drugs in order to get a "good night's sleep again." This rebound effect might last for one to three weeks, although in rare cases it has been known to last for two months (Tyrer, 1993).

Barbiturates can cause a drug-induced "hangover" the day after the person used the drug (Shannon, Wilson, & Stang, 1995). Subjectively, the individual who is going through a barbiturate hangover simply feels that he or she is "unable to get going" the next day. This is because barbiturates often require an extended period of time for the body to completely biotransform and excrete the drug. As we noted in Chapter 3, it generally takes five half-life periods to eliminate a single dose of a chemical from the blood. Because many of the barbiturates have extended biological half-life periods, some small amounts of a barbiturate might remain in the person's bloodstream for hours, or even days, after a single dose. In some cases, the effects of the barbiturates on judgment, motor skills, and behavior last for several days (Kaminski, 1992).

If the person continually adds to this reservoir of unmetabolized drug by ingesting additional doses of the barbiturate, there is a greater chance that the individual will experience a drug "hangover." However, every barbiturate hangover is caused by the same mechanism: traces of unmetabolized barbiturates remaining in the individual's bloodstream for extended periods of time after the individual stops taking the medication. Subjectively, the individual might feel "not quite awake," or "drugged," the next day. The elderly and those with impaired liver function are especially likely to have difficulty with the barbiturates. This is because the liver's ability to metabolize many drugs, such as the barbiturates, declines with age. In light of this fact, Sheridan, Patterson, and Gustafson (1982) advised that older individuals who receive barbiturates be started at one-half the usual adult dosage, and that the dosage level gradually be increased until the patient reaches the point where the medication is having the desired effect.

One side effect of long-term phenobarbital use is a possible loss in intelligence. Researchers have documented a drop of approximately 8 IQ points on intelligence tests in patients who have been receiving phenobarbital for control of seizures for extended periods of time, although it is not clear whether this reflects a research artifact, a drug effect, or the cumulative impact of the seizure disorder (Breggin, 1998). It is also not clear whether this observed loss of IQ points might be reversed or whether a similar reduction in measured IQ develops as a result of the chronic use of other barbiturates. However, this observation does underscore the fact that the barbiturates are potential CNS agents that affect the normal function of the brain.

Even when the drug is used in a medical setting, barbiturate use can cause problems in sexual performance, such as decreased desire in either partner and both erectile problems and delayed ejaculation for the male (Finger, Lund, & Slagel, 1997). Hypersensitivity reactions have also been reported with the barbiturates. Such hypersensitivity reactions are most common in (but not limited to) individuals with asthma. Other complications occasionally seen at normal dosage levels include nausea, vomiting, diarrhea, and constipation. Some patients have developed skin rashes while receiving barbiturates, although the reason for this is not clear. Finally, some patients who take barbiturates develop an extreme sensitivity to sunlight known as *photosensitivity*. Thus patients who receive barbiturates must take special precautions to avoid sunburn, even limited exposure to the sun's rays. Because of these problems, and because medications are now available that do not pose these dangers, barbiturates are no longer considered to have any role in the treatment of anxiety or insomnia (Tyrer, 1993).

Children who suffer from attention deficit–hyperactivity disorder (ADHD) (what was once called hyperactivity) and who also receive phenobarbital are likely to experience a resurgence of their ADHD symptoms. This effect would seem to reflect the ability of the barbiturates to suppress the action of the reticula activating system (RAS) in the brain. Currently, it is thought that the RAS of children with ADHD is underactive, so any medication that further reduces the effectiveness of this neurological system will contribute to ADHD symptoms.

Drug Interactions Between the Barbiturates and Other Medications

Research has shown that the barbiturates are capable of interacting with numerous other chemicals, increasing or decreasing the amount of these drugs in the blood through various mechanisms. The mixture of barbiturates with any of the CNS depressants (such as alcohol, narcotic-based analgesics, phenothiazines, and the benzodiazepines) is especially dangerous and may result in death (Barnhill, Ciraulo, Ciraulo, & Greene, 1995). Each drug potentiates the effects of the other, by interfering with the biotransformation of the other chemical in the liver. This boosts the toxic effects of both drugs.

The antihistamines are another class of CNS depressants that might cause a potentiation effect in the patient using a barbiturate (Rall, 1990). Because many antihistamines are available without a prescription (in over-the-counter cold and allergy medicines, for example), there is a very real danger of unintentional potentiation effects.

Patients who are taking barbiturates should not use antidepressants known as monoamine oxidase inhibitors (MAOIs or MAO inhibitors), because the MAOI may inhibit the biotransformation of the barbiturates (Ciraulo, Creelman, Shader, & O'Sullivan, 1995). Patients using barbiturates should not take the antibiotic doxycycline, except under a physician's supervision. The barbiturates would reduce the effectiveness of this antibiotic, which might have serious consequences for the patient (Meyers, 1992). If the patient is using barbiturates and tricyclic antidepressants concurrently, the barbiturate causes the blood plasma levels of the tricyclic antidepressant to drop by as much as 60% (Barnhill, Ciraulo, Ciraulo, & Greene 1995). The barbiturates in such cases increase the speed with which the antidepressants are metabolized by activation of the liver's microsomal enzymes.

This is the same process through which the barbiturates speed up the metabolism of many oral contraceptives, corticosteroids, and the antibiotic Flagyl (metronidazole) (Kaminski, 1992). Thus, when used concurrently with these medications, barbiturates reduce their effectiveness. Women who are taking both oral contraceptives and barbiturates should be aware of the potential for barbiturates to reduce the effectiveness of oral contraceptives (Graedon & Graedon, 1996; Graedon & Graedon, 1995).

Individuals who are taking the anticoagulant medication warfarin should not use a barbiturate, except under a physician's supervision. Barbiturate use can interfere with the normal biotransformation of warfarin, resulting in abnormally low blood levels of this anticoagulant medication (Graedon & Graedon, 1995). Further, if the patient should stop taking barbiturates while on warfarin, the individual's warfarin levels can "re-bound" to dangerous levels. Thus, these two medications should not be mixed, except under a physician's supervision.

When the barbiturates are biotransformed by the liver, they activate a region of the liver that also is involved in biotransformation of the asthma drug theophylline (sold under a variety of brand names). Thus patients who use a barbiturate while taking theophylline might experience abnormally low blood levels of the latter drug, a condition that might result in less than optimal control of the asthma. These two medications should not be used by the same patient at the same time, except under a physician's supervision (Graedon & Graedon, 1995). Finally, in one research study, five of seven patients on pentobarbital who smoked marijuana began to hallucinate (Barnhill, Ciraulo, Ciraulo, & Greene, 1995). This would suggest that individuals who use barbiturates should not risk possible interactions between these medications and marijuana.

As is obvious from this list of potential interactions between barbiturates and other pharmaceuticals, the barbiturates are a powerful family of drugs. As always, a physician or pharmacist should be consulted before two different medications are utilized concurrently.

Effects of the Barbiturates at Above-normal Dosage Levels

Even when used above the normal dosage levels, barbiturates may cause a state of intoxication that is similar to alcohol intoxication. Patients who are intoxicated by barbiturates demonstrate such behaviors as slurred speech and unsteady gait, without the characteristic smell of alcohol (Jenike, 1991). Chronic abusers are at risk for the development of bronchitis and/or pneumonia, because these medications interfere with the normal cough reflex. Individuals under the influence of a barbiturate do not test positive for alcohol on blood or urine toxicology tests (unless they also have alcohol in their systems). Specific blood or urine toxicology screens must be carried out to detect barbiturate intoxication.

Unfortunately, because the barbiturates can cause a state of intoxication similar to that induced by alcohol, some barbiturate users ingest more than the normal dose of the drug. The small "therapeutic window" of the barbiturates gives these drugs a significant overdose potential. The barbiturates cause a dose-dependent

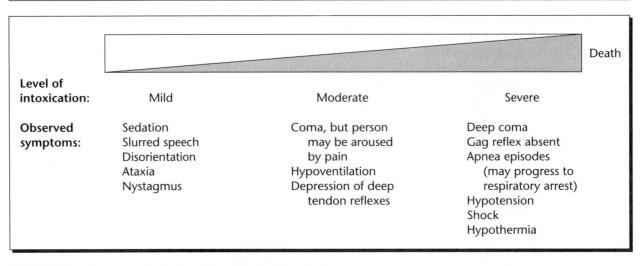

FIGURE 9.1   Symptoms observed at different levels of intoxication.

reduction in respiration as the increasing drug blood levels interfere with the normal function of the medulla oblongata (the part of the brain that maintains respiration and body temperature). Thus the barbiturates can cause both respiratory depression and hypothermia either when abused at larger-than-normal doses or when mixed with other CNS depressants (Pagliaro & Pagliaro, 1998). Other complications of larger-than-normal doses include a progressive loss of reflex activity and, if the dose was large enough, coma and ultimately death (Jenike, 1991).

In past decades, before the introduction of the benzodiazepines, the barbiturates accounted for more than three-quarters of all drug-related deaths in the United States (Peluso & Peluso, 1988). Even now, intentional or unintentional barbiturate overdoses are not unheard of. In their study of successful suicides in the San Diego, California, area, Mendelson and Rich (1993) found that approximately 10% of those individuals who committed suicide via a drug overdose used barbiturates either exclusively or as one of the chemicals ingested. Fortunately, the barbiturates do not directly damage the central nervous system. Overdose victims who reach medical support before they develop shock or hypoxia may recover completely from a barbiturate overdose (Sagar, 1991). It is for this reason that *any suspected barbiturate overdose should be treated by a physician immediately.*

Neuroadaptation to, Tolerance to, and Dependency on the Barbiturates

The primary use for barbiturates today is quite limited, because safer and more effective drugs have replaced the barbiturates for the most part. However, barbiturates continue to have a limited range of medical applications, including the control of epilepsy and the treatment of some forms of severe head injury (Julien, 1992).

One unfortunate characteristic of the barbiturates is that with regular use, even in a medical setting, neuroadaptation to many of their effects develops quite rapidly. The process of barbiturate-induced neuroadaptation is not uniform, however. For example, when the barbiturates are used for the control of seizures, tolerance may not be a significant problem. A patient who is taking phenobarbital for the control of seizures eventually becomes somewhat tolerant to the sedative effect of the medication but does not develop a significant tolerance to the anticonvulsant effect of the phenobarbital. If the patient were taking a barbiturate for its *sedating or hypnotic* effects, however, then she or he would become less responsive to this drug-induced effect with chronic use.

Patients have been known to try to overcome the process of neuroadaptation to the barbiturates by increasing their dosage of the drug without consulting with their physician. This attempt at self-medication has resulted in a large number of unintentional barbiturate overdoses, some of which have been fatal. This is because, although the individual might experience some degree of neuroadaptation and become less responsive to the original dose of a barbiturate, there is no concomitant increase in the lethal dose (Jenike, 1991).

Many barbiturate abusers report that the chemical can bring about a drug-induced feeling of euphoria. But as users become tolerant to the euphoric effects of barbiturates following a period of chronic use, they experience less and less euphoria from the drug. Here again, as the barbiturate abuser increases her or his daily dosage level in order to continue to experience the drug-induced euphoria, she or he comes closer and closer to the lethal dose.

In addition to the phenomenon of tolerance to the barbiturate family of drugs, *cross-tolerance* is also possible. Cross-tolerance is a condition whereby a person who has become tolerant to one family of chemicals also becomes tolerant to the effects of other, similar drugs. Cross-tolerance between alcohol and the barbiturates is common, as is some degree of cross tolerance between the barbiturates and the opiates and between barbiturates and the hallucinogen PCP (Kaplan, Sadock, & Grebb 1994).

The United States went through a wave of barbiturate abuse and addiction in the 1950s. Thus physicians have long been aware that *once the person is addicted, withdrawal from barbiturates is potentially life-threatening and should be attempted only under the supervision of a physician* (Jenike, 1991). The barbiturates should never be abruptly withdrawn; to do so could bring about an organic brain syndrome that might include confusion, seizures, brain damage, and even death. Approximately 80% of barbiturate addicts who abruptly discontinue the drug experience withdrawal seizures, according to the author.

There is no set formula to estimate the danger period for barbiturate withdrawal problems. The exact period during withdrawal when the barbiturate addict is most "at risk" for such problems as seizures depends on the specific barbiturate (Jenike, 1991). As a general rule, however, the longer-lasting forms of barbiturates tend to have longer withdrawal periods. When the individual abruptly stops taking a short- to intermediate-acting barbiturate, withdrawal seizures usually begin on the 2nd or 3rd day. Barbiturate-withdrawal seizures are rare after the 12th day following cessation of the drug. An individual who stops taking one of the longer-acting barbiturates might not have a withdrawal seizure until as late as the 7th day after the last dose of the drug (Tyrer, 1993).

The person who is physically dependent on the barbiturates experiences a number of symptoms during the withdrawal process. Virtually every barbiturate-dependent patient experiences a feeling of apprehension for the first 3–14 days of withdrawal ((Shader, Greenblatt, & Ciraulo, 1994). Other symptoms that the patient experiences during withdrawal include muscle weakness, tremors, anorexia, muscle twitches, and possibly delirium, according to the authors. All of these symptoms subside after 3–14 days, depending on the individual. Physicians can prescribe other medications to minimize these withdrawal symptoms, but there is no such thing as a symptom-free withdrawal.

Barbiturate-like Drugs

Because of the many adverse side effects of the barbiturates, pharmaceutical companies have long searched for substitutes that are effective yet safe to use. During the 1950s, a number of new drugs were introduced to treat anxiety and insomnia, including Miltown (meprobamate), Quaalude and Sopor (both brand names of methaqualone), Doriden (glutethimide), Placidyl (ethchlorvynol), and Noludar (methyprylon). (See Table 9.1.)

Although these drugs were thought to be "nonaddicting" when they were first introduced, research has shown that barbiturate-like drugs have an abuse potential very similar to that of barbiturates. This should not be surprising, because the chemical structure of some of the barbiturate-like drugs is very similar to that of the barbiturates themselves (Julien, 1992). Like the barbiturates, glutethimide and methyprylon are metabolized mainly in the liver.

Both Placidyl (ethchlorvynol) and Doriden (glutethimide) are considered especially dangerous, and neither drug should be used except in rare, special circumstances (Schuckit, 2000). The prolonged use of ethchlorvynol may result in a drug-induced loss of vision known as *amblyopia*. Fortunately, this drug-induced amblyopia gradually clears when the drug is discontinued (Michelson, Carroll, McLane, & Robin, 1988). Since its introduction, the drug glutethimide has become "notorious for its high mortality associated with overdose" (Sagar, 1991, p. 304). The lethal dose of glutethimide is only 10 grams, a dose that is only slightly above the normal dosage level (Sagar, 1991).

Meprobamate was a popular sedative in the 1950s, when it was sold under at least 32 different brand names, including Miltown and Equanil (Lingeman, 1974). Although it is considered obsolete by current standards (Rosenthal, 1992) and has generally not been used since the early 1970s, older physicians often continue to prescribe it. Quite a few older patients remain addicted to this medication as a result of their initial prescription(s) for meprobamate from the 1960s and 1970s (Rosenthal, 1992).

Surprisingly, despite its reputation and history, meprobamate still has a minor role in medicine, especially for patients who are unable to take benzodiazepines (Cole & Yonkers, 1995). The peak blood levels of meprobamate following an oral dose are seen in 1–3 hours, and the half-life is 6–17 hours following a single dose. The chronic use of meprobamate may result in the half-life being extended to 24–48 hours (Cole & Yonkers, 1995). The LD_{50} of meprobamate is estimated to be about 28,000 mg. However, some deaths have been noted following overdoses of 12,000 mg, according to the authors. Physical dependency on this drug is common when patients take 3200 mg/day or more.

Methaqualone achieved significant popularity among illicit drug abusers in the late 1960s and early 1970s. It was originally intended as a nonaddicting substitute for the barbiturates in the mid-1960s. Depending on the dosage level being used, physicians prescribed it both as a sedative and as a hypnotic (Lingeman, 1974). Illicit drug users quickly discovered that, when one resisted the sedative/hypnotic effects of methaqualone one experienced a sense of euphoria.

Methaqualone is rapidly absorbed from the gastrointestinal tract following an oral dose, and the individual begins to feel its effects in 15–20 minutes. The usual sedative dose was 75 mg, and the hypnotic dose was between 150 and 300 mg. Tolerance to the sedating and hypnotic effects of methaqualone developed rapidly, and many abusers gradually increased their daily dosage levels in an attempt to reachieve the initial effect. Some individuals who abused methaqualone were known to use more than 2000 mg in a single day (Mirin, Weiss, & Greenfield, 1991), a dosage level that was quite dangerous for the individual. Indeed, the lethal dose of methaqualone was estimated to be approximately 8000 mg for a typical 150-pound user (Lingeman, 1974).

Shortly after it was introduced, reports began to appear suggesting that methaqualone was being abused.

Indeed, methaqualone was purported to have aphrodisiac properties (this has never been proved), and was said to provide a mild sense of euphoria for the user (Mirin, Weiss, & Greenfield, 1991). Persons who have used methaqualone report feelings of euphoria, well-being, and behavioral disinhibition. As with the barbiturates, although tolerance to the drug's effects quickly develops, the lethal dosage of methaqualone remains the same. Death from methaqualone overdose was common, especially when the drug was taken with alcohol. The typical cause of death was heart failure, according to Lingeman (1974).

In the United States, methaqualone was withdrawn from the market in the mid-1980s, although it is still manufactured by pharmaceutical companies in other countries. It is often smuggled into this country or manufactured in illicit laboratories and sold on the street. Thus the substance abuse counselor must have a working knowledge of methaqualone and its effects.

Summary

For thousands of years, alcohol was the only chemical that was even marginally effective as an antianxiety or hypnotic agent. Although a number of chemicals with hypnotic action were introduced in the mid-1800s, all were of limited value in the fight against anxiety or insomnia. Then, in the early 1900s, the barbiturates were introduced. The barbiturates, which have a mechanism of action very similar to that of alcohol, were found to have an antianxiety and a hypnotic effect. The barbiturates rapidly became popular and were widely used both for the control of anxiety and to help people fall asleep.

Like alcohol, however, the barbiturates were found to also have a significant potential for addiction. This resulted in a search for nonaddictive medications that could replace the barbiturates. In the post–World War II era, a number of synthetic drugs with chemical structures very similar to those of barbiturates were introduced. Although the manufacturers often claimed that these drugs were "nonaddicting," they were ultimately found to have an addiction potential similar to that of the barbiturates. Since the introduction of the benzodiazepines, the barbiturates and similar drugs have fallen into disfavor. However, there is evidence to suggest that they might be making a comeback.

CHAPTER TEN

Abuse of and Addiction to Benzodiazepines and Similar Agents

Introduction

In 1960, the first of a new class of antianxiety[1] drugs, chlordiazepoxide, was introduced in the United States. Chlordiazepoxide is a member of a family of chemicals known as the *benzodiazepines*. Since the introduction of chlordiazepoxide, some 3000 different benzodiazepines have been developed, of which about 50 have been marketed around the world and about 12 are prescribed in the United States (Dupont & Dupont, 1998). Benzodiazepines have been found to be effective in the treatment of a wide range of disorders, such as the control of anxiety symptoms, insomnia, muscle strains, and seizures, without the risks inherent in the barbiturates. Since the first benzodiazepine was introduced, they have become *the* most frequently prescribed psychotropic medications in this country (Gonzales, Stern, Emmerich, & Rauch, 1992). Each year, approximately 10–20% of the adults in the Western world use a benzodiazepine at least once (Jenkins & Cone, 1998). Legally, the benzodiazepines are a Category II controlled substance.[2]

The benzodiazepines were initially introduced as nonaddicting substitutes for the barbiturates and barbiturate-like drugs. However, in the 40 years since their introduction, serious questions have been raised about the abuse potential of the benzodiazepines. Indeed, misuse and abuse of benzodiazepines result in hundreds of millions of dollars in unnecessary medical costs each year in the United States (Benzer, 1995). In this chapter, we will examine the history of the benzodiazepines, their medical applications, and the problem of the abuse of and addiction to the benzodiazepines and similar agents in the United States.

Medical Uses of the Benzodiazepines

The most common use of the benzodiazepines is the control of anxiety. Because the effects of the benzodiazepines are more selective than those of the barbiturates, they are able to reduce anxiety without causing the same degree of sedation and fatigue seen when barbiturates are used. The benzodiazepines that are utilized for the control of anxiety in the United States include diazepam (Valium), chlordiazepoxide (Librium), clorazepate (Tranxene), alprazolam (Xanax), and lorazepam (Ativan). In addition to this, some benzodiazepines have been found useful in the treatment of seizure disorders and muscle strains (Ashton, 1994; Shader & Greenblatt, 1993). The benzodiazepine clonazepam (Clonopin),[3] has been found to be especially effective in the long-term control of seizures and as an antianxiety agent (Shader & Greenblatt, 1993).

Chronic insomnia is a common complaint among adults. Some members of the benzodiazepine family of drugs have been found useful as a *short-term* treatment for insomnia; these include temazepam (Restoril),

[1]Some authors use the term "anxioyltic" in place of the term "antianxiety." In this text, the term "antianxiety" will be used.

[2]See Appendix 4.

[3]Some authors spell the name of this medication "Klonopin."

triazolam (Halcion), flurazepam (Dalmane), and quazepam (Doral) (Gillin, 1991; Hussar, 1990). Two different benzodiazepines, alprazolam (Xanax) and adinazolam (Deracyn), are reportedly of value in the treatment of depression.

Although it does not have antidepressant effects, alprazolam is frequently used to treat the anxiety that often accompanies depression. Researchers believe that adinazolam (Deracyn) works by increasing the sensitivity of certain neurons within the brain to serotonin (Cardoni, 1990). A deficit of, or insensitivity to, serotonin is thought to be the cause of at least some forms of depression. Thus, by increasing the sensitivity of the neurons of the brain to serotonin, Deracyn (adinazolam) seems to have a direct antidepressant effect that is lacking in most benzodiazepines.

Benzodiazepines and suicide attempts. The possibility of suicide through a drug overdose is a very real concern for the physician, especially when the patient is depressed. Because of their high therapeutic index (TI), the benzodiazepines have traditionally had the reputation of being "safe" drugs to use with patients who were potentially suicidal. The TI of the benzodiazepines has been estimated to be above 1:200 (Kaplan & Sadock, 1996) and possibly as high as 1:1000 (Carvey, 1998). In terms of overdose potential, animal research suggests that the LD_{50} for diazepam is around 720 mg per kilogram of body weight for mice, and 1240 mg/kg for rats (Medical Economics Company, 1999). The LD_{50} for humans is not known, but these figures do suggest that diazepam is an exceptionally safe drug. However, other benzodiazepines have smaller TIs than diazepam. Many physicians recommend that because of its greater margin of safety the benzodiazepine Serax (oxazepam) be used in cases where the patient is at risk for an overdose, (Buckley, Dawson, Whyte, & O'Connell, 1995).

It should be noted, however, that the benzodiazepine margin of safety is drastically reduced when an individual ingests one or more additional CNS depressants in an attempt to end his or her life. This is because of the synergistic[4] effect that develops when different CNS depressants are intermixed. This is one reason why *any* known or suspected overdose should be evaluated and treated by medical professionals. If the attending physician suspects that the individual has ingested a benzodiazepine in an attempt to end his or her life, that physician might consider using Mazicon (flumazenil) to counteract the effects of the benzodiazepine in the brain. Mazicon occupies the benzodiazepine receptor site without activating that site and thus helps protect the individual from the effects of a benzodiazepine overdose. Although this medication has provided physicians with a powerful new tool in treating the benzodiazepine overdose, it is effective only for 20–45 minutes and blocks only the effects of benzodiazepines (Brust, 1998).

Pharmacology of the Benzodiazepines

The benzodiazepines are very similar in their effects, differing mainly in their duration of action (*Harvard Medical School Mental Health Letter*, 1988). Table 10.1 reviews the relative potency and biological half-lives of some of the benzodiazepines currently in use in the United States.

Like many pharmaceuticals, the benzodiazepines can be classified on the basis of their pharmacological

TABLE 10.1   Selected Pharmacological Characteristics of Some Benzodiazepines

Generic name	Equivalent dose	Average half-life (hours)
Alprazolam	0.5 mg	6–20
Chlordiazepoxide	25 mg	30–100
Clonazepam	0.25 mg	20–40
Clorazepate	7.5 mg	30–100
Diazepam	5 mg	30–100
Flurazepam	30 mg	50–100
Halazepam	20 mg	30–100
Lorazepam	1 mg	10–20
Oxazepam	15 mg	5–21
Prazepam	10 mg	30–100
Temazepam	30 mg	9.5–12.4
Triazolam	0.25 mg	1.7–3.0

Sources: Based on Hyman (1988) and Reiman (1997).

[4]See the Glossary.

characteristics. Tyrer (1993), for example, adopted a classification system based not on the duration of the effects of the benzodiazepines, but on the basis of their elimination half-lives, separating the benzodiazepines into four groups:[5] *very short half-life* (4 hours or less), *short half-life* (4–12 hours), *intermediate half-life* (12–20 hours), and *long half-life* (20 or more hours).

The various benzodiazepines currently in use range from moderately to highly lipid-soluble (Ayd, 1994). Lipid solubility is important, because the more lipid-soluble a chemical is, the faster it is absorbed through the small intestine after being taken orally (Roberts & Tafure, 1990). Also, highly lipid-soluble drugs pass readily through the blood-brain barrier (Ballenger, 1995).

Once in the general circulation, the benzodiazepines are all protein-bound, but to varying degrees. Diazepam, for example, is more than 99% protein-bound (American Psychiatric Association, 1990), whereas 92–97% of chlordiazepoxide is protein-bound (Ayd, Janicak, Davis, & Preskorn, 1996) and alprazolam is only about 80% protein-bound (Medical Economics Company, 1999). This variability in protein binding is one factor that influences the duration of effect for each benzodiazepine after a single dose (American Medical Association, 1994).

The benzodiazepines are poorly absorbed from intramuscular or subcutaneous injection sites (American Medical Association, 1994). The limited absorption from injection sites makes it difficult to predict in advance the degree of drug bioavailability when a benzodiazepine is injected. For this reason, these medications are usually administered orally. One exception to this rule is when the patient is experiencing uncontrolled seizures. In such cases, intravenous injections of diazepam or a similar benzodiazepine might be used to help control the seizures.

Most benzodiazepines must be biotransformed before elimination can proceed, and in the process of biotransformation, some benzodiazepines produce metabolites that are biologically active. These biologically active metabolites may contribute to the duration of a drug's effects, and it may be a long time before they are eliminated from the body. Thus the *duration of effect* of many benzodiazepines is far different from the elimination half-life of the parent compound, a factor that physicians must keep in mind when prescribing these medications (Hobbs, Rall, & Verdoorn, 1995). For example, during the process of biotransformation, the benzodiazepine flurazepam produces five different metabolites, each of which has a psychoactive effect of its own. Because of normal variation in how long it takes the body to biotransform/eliminate flurazepam and its metabolites, this benzodiazepine might have an effect on the user for as long as 280 hours after a single dose. Fortunately, the benzodiazepines lorazepam, oxazepam, and temazepam either are eliminated without biotransformation or produce metabolites that have minimal physical effects on the user. As we shall see, these benzodiazepines are often preferred for older patients, who may experience oversedation as a result of the long half-lives of some benzodiazepine metabolites.

Although the benzodiazepines are often compared to the barbiturates, they actually are far different from the barbiturates in the way they function in the brain. The barbiturates simulate the action of the neurotransmitter gamma-aminobutyric acid (GABA), which is thought to be the most important "inhibitory" neurotransmitter in the brain (Nutt, 1996; Bohn, 1993; Tabakoff & Hoffman, 1992). This causes the barbiturates to depress nonselectively the activity of neurons in both the cortex and many other parts of the brain. Subjectively, this effect is interpreted as a reduction in anxiety levels and, possibly, the ability to fall asleep (although benzodiazepines actually interfere with normal sleep; see below).

In contrast to the barbiturates, the benzodiazepine molecule is thought to bind to one of the GABA receptor sites, and also to a chloride channel on the neuron surface, making the cell more sensitive to the GABA that already exists. This theory is supported by the fact that in the absence of GABA, the benzodiazepines have no apparent effect on the neuron (Pagliaro & Pagliaro, 1998; Hobbs, Rall, & Verdoorn, 1995). Neurons that utilize GABA are especially common in the *locus ceruleus* (Johnson & Lydiard, 1995; Cardoni, 1990). Nerve fibers from the locus ceruleus connect with other parts of the brain thought to be involved in fear and panic reactions. Animal research has suggested that stimulation of the locus ceruleus

---

[5]To complicate matters, the *distribution half-life* for benzodiazepines is often far different from the *elimination half-life*, or the *therapeutic half-life*. For a discussion of these concepts, see Chapter 6.

causes behaviors similar to those seen in humans who are having a "panic attack" (Johnson & Lydiard, 1995). It is thought that by enhancing the effects of GABA, the benzodiazepines reduce the level of neurological activity in the locus ceruleus, reducing the individual's anxiety level. Unfortunately, this theory does not provide any insight into the ability of the benzodiazepines to help muscle tissue to relax or to stop seizures (Hobbs, Rall, & Verdoorn, 1995). Much remains to be discovered about how these drugs work.

Surprisingly, we have little information about the long-term effectiveness of these compounds as antianxiety agents (Ayd, 1994). Some researchers believe that the antianxiety effects of the benzodiazepines last about 1–2 months and that these drugs are not useful in treating anxiety continuously over a long period of time (Ayd, Janicak, Davis, & Preskorn, 1996; Ashton, 1994). For example, one study (which the manufacturer did not share with physicians) found that after 8 weeks of continuous use, the patients who received Xanax had just as many panic attacks as the patients who received only a placebo (Walker, 1996).

Other researchers, however, believe that the benzodiazepines are an effective agent in the long-term control of anxiety. For example, the *Harvard Medical School Mental Health Letter* (1988) suggested that although patients might develop some tolerance to the sedative effects of benzodiazepines, they did not become tolerant to the antianxiety effects of these medications. Thus there is some degree of uncertainty about the long-term effectiveness of benzodiazepines in the control of anxiety symptoms.

Side Effects of the Benzodiazepines at Normal Dosage Levels

Some degree of sedation is common following the ingestion of a benzodiazepine (Ballenger, 1995), but excessive sedation is uncommon unless the patient ingested a dose that was too large (Ayd, Janicak, Davis, & Preskorn, 1996). Advancing age is one factor that may make the individual more susceptible to benzodiazepine-induced oversedation (Ayd, 1994; Ashton, 1994). Because of an age-related decline in blood flow to the liver and kidneys, elderly patients often require more time than younger adults to biotransform and/or excrete

many drugs (Bleidt & Moss, 1989). This contributes to oversedation, or, in some cases, to paradoxical excitement, as the bodies of older patients struggle to adjust to the effects of a benzodiazepine. To illustrate this process, consider the fact that an elderly patient might require three times as long as a young adult to fully metabolize a dose of diazepam or chlordiazepoxide (Cohen, 1989). When a benzodiazepine is required in an older individual, physicians tend to rely on lorazepam or oxazepam (Ashton, 1994; Graedon & Graedon, 1991), because these compounds have a shorter half-life and are more easily biotransformed than diazepam and similar benzodiazepines.

Both Deracyn (adinazolam) and Doral (quazepam) are exceptions to the rule that the older patient is more likely to experience excessive sedation than a younger patient. It is not uncommon for any patient to experience sedation from adinazolam. As many as two-thirds of those who receive this medication experience some degree of drowsiness, at least until their bodies adapt to the drug's effects (Cardoni, 1990). Further, because the active metabolites of Doral (quazepam) have a half-life of 72 hours or more, there is a strong possibility that the user will experience a drug-induced "hangover" the next day (Hartmann, 1995).

Drug-induced hangovers are possible with benzodiazepine use, especially with some of the longer-lasting benzodiazepines (Ashton, 1994, 1992). The data in Table 10.1 suggest that for some individuals, the half-life of some benzodiazepines may be as long as 100 hours. Remember that it usually requires 5 half-life periods before virtually all of a drug is biotransformed/ eliminated from the body. If that patient were to take a second or even a third dose of the medication before the first dose was fully biotransformed, he or she would begin to accumulate unmetabolized medication in body tissues. The unmetabolized medication would continue to have an effect on the individual's function well past the time that he or she thought the drug's effects had ended.

For reasons that are not yet clear, younger adults who use a benzodiazepine seem to be at increased risk for motor vehicle accidents (Barbone, McMahon, Davey, Morris, Reid, McDevitt, & MacDonald, 1998). It is possible that even therapeutic doses of benzodiazepines contribute to prolonged reaction times in users.

Neuroadaptation to Benzodiazepines, and Their Abuse/Addiction

Within a few years of the time they were introduced, reports of benzodiazepine abuse/addiction began to surface. Even patients who were taking the benzodiazepines only at recommended dosage levels appeared to experience what is known as a *discontinuance syndrome* after using these medications for just a few months. These observations fueled reports in the media that suggested the benzodiazepines had a significant abuse potential. In reality, physicians remain undecided as to the actual abuse potential of the benzodiazepines.

It is known that when a person takes a benzodiazepine for an extended period, his or her brain goes through a process of "neuroadaptation" (Sellers, Ciraulo, DuPont, Griffiths, Kosten, Romach, & Woody, 1993, p. 65), during which the CNS becomes tolerant to the drug's effects. If that person were to discontinue the medication suddenly, he or she would experience "rebound" or "discontinuance" symptoms, as his or her brain began to adapt to the absence of the benzodiazepine. Some researchers believe that this state of pharmacological tolerance to the benzodiazepines is evidence that the patient has become addicted to the medication.

Remember that two signs of addiction are a state of physical dependence and tolerance to the drug's effects. Some physicians believe that the discontinuance syndrome is clear evidence that the user will become tolerant to benzodiazepines and also physically dependent on them "within a few weeks, perhaps days" (Miller & Gold, 1991b, p. 28). Other researchers view the "rebound" or "discontinuance" symptoms as a natural consequence of benzodiazepine use. For example, Sellers *et al.* (1993) argued that "[evidence] of neuroadaptation is not sufficient to define drug-taking behavior as dependent" (p. 65). Thus, although the patient might experience a discontinuance syndrome after using a benzodiazepine at recommended doses for an extended period of time, this is seen as a natural process. Advocates of this position point to the fact that the body must go through a period of adjustment whenever *any* medication is discontinued.

Researchers disagree as to the percentage of patients who will develop a discontinuance syndrome after using the benzodiazepines for an extended time. Ashton (1994) suggested that approximately 35% of those patients who take a benzodiazepine continuously for 4 or more weeks become physically dependent on the medication. These individuals experience withdrawal symptoms when they stop taking the medication, according to the author. But in rare cases, pharmacological dependency on the benzodiazepines might develop in just days or weeks (Miller & Gold, 1991b; American Psychiatric Association, 1990; *Harvard Medical School Mental Health Letter*, 1988).

On the other hand, Blair and Ramones (1996) suggested that in most cases where the benzodiazepines are used at normal dosage levels for less than 4 months, the risk of a patient becoming dependent is virtually nonexistent. After 4 months of continuous use, the picture is even more confusing. The *Harvard Medical School Mental Health Letter* (1988) suggested that after 4–6 months of daily use, the majority of patients become physically dependent on benzodiazepines. After 8 months of daily use, "most" (p. 3) patients experience benzodiazepine withdrawal symptoms when they discontinue the drug, and "after a year almost all" (p. 3) patients experience symptoms suggestive of physical dependency on benzodiazepines.

In contrast to this estimate, Blair and Ramones (1996) suggested that only 25–45% of those patients who had used a benzodiazepine continuously for 2 years would be dependent on these drugs. Even after 6–8 years of continuous use at normal dosage levels, only 75% of the patients who used a benzodiazepine would be dependent on the drug, according to the authors. Although researchers disagree about what percentage of patients become addicted to a benzodiazepine after an extended use, they do not suggest that these drugs might be used for longer than 4 months without causing physical dependency in at least some patients.

Surprisingly, in light of their low "reward potential," the benzodiazepines are popular substances of abuse. In some cases, benzodiazepines are intermixed with opiates such as heroin or methadone to enhance the euphoric effect of these compounds (Longo & Johnson, 2000). Illicit users of benzodiazepines also use these substances to self-medicate drug withdrawal symptoms, (Longo & Johnson, 2000). Still others abuse the benzodiazepines to self-medicate the drug-induced anxiety brought on by cocaine or the amphetamines. Finally, a small percentage of abusers utilize the benzodiazepines to escape the feelings of dysphoria or anxiety that they face on a daily basis (Wesson & Ling, 1996; Cole & Kando, 1993).

Thus, although the benzodiazepines do not bring about a state of euphoria such as that induced by many of the other drugs of abuse, they retain a significant abuse potential (Walker, 1996; Spiegel, 1996). Abusers seem to prefer the shorter-acting benzodiazepines such as lorazepam or alprazolam (Longo & Johnson, 2000; Walker, 1996; Sellers, *et. al.*, 1993; Juergens & Morse, 1988), but evidence suggests that the long-acting benzodiazepine clonazepam is also frequently abused (Longo & Johnson, 2000).

Although in most cases the benzodiazepines are both appropriately prescribed and used according to the physician's instructions (Appelbaum, 1992; Woods, Katz, & Winger 1988), in a number of cases the user becomes physically dependent on one or more of these agents. In such cases, withdrawal from the benzodiazepine can be quite difficult. Individuals who have been using/abusing benzodiazepines for months, or years, might require a gradual "taper" in daily dosage levels over periods as long as 8–12 weeks (Miller & Gold, 1998). To complicate the withdrawal process, patients tend to experience an upsurge in anxiety symptoms when their daily dosage levels reach 10–25% of their original daily dose (Prater, Miller, & Zylstra, 1999). To combat these anxiety symptoms and increase the individual's chances of success, the authors recommended the use of a "mood-stabilizing" agent such as carbamazepin, or valproic acid during the withdrawal process.

Factors influencing the benzodiazepine withdrawal process. Rickels, Schweizer, Case, and Greenblatt (1990) examined the phenomenon of withdrawal from benzodiazepines to identify factors that might influence the withdrawal process. The authors concluded that the severity of benzodiazepine withdrawal depended on five different "drug treatment" factors, plus several "patient factors." According to the authors, the drug treatment factors included (1) the total daily dose of benzodiazepines being used, (2) the total time during which benzodiazepines had been used, (3) the half-life of the benzodiazepine being used, (short half-life benzodiazepines tend to produce more withdrawal symptoms than long half-life benzodiazepines), (4) the potency of the benzo-

diazepine being used, and (5) the rate of withdrawal (gradual, tapered withdrawal or abrupt withdrawal).

The patient factors that influenced the withdrawal from benzodiazepines included (1) the patient's premorbid personality structure, (2) expectations for the withdrawal process, and (3) individual differences in the neurobiological structures within the brain thought to be involved in the withdrawal process. Interactions between these two sets of factors were thought to determine the severity of the withdrawal process, according to Rickels *et al.* (1990). Thus, for the person who is addicted to these medications, withdrawal can be a complex, difficult process.

Complications Caused by Benzodiazepine Use at Normal Dosage Levels

The benzodiazepines are not perfect drugs. As a group, they have a number of drawbacks. For example, because tolerance develops to the anticonvulsant effects of benzodiazepines, they are of only limited value in the long-term control of epilepsy (Morton & Santos, 1989). Another shortcoming of the benzodiazepines is that excessive sedation is still occasionally reported even at normal dosage levels. This effect is most often noted in older patients, and patients with significant liver damage. The fact that the elderly are most likely to experience excessive sedation is unfortunate, in light of the fact that two-thirds of those who receive prescriptions for benzodiazepines are above the age of 60 years (Ayd, 1994).

Some of the side effects attributed to benzodiazepines include hallucinations, a feeling of euphoria, irritability, tachycardia, sweating, and disinhibition (Hobbs, Rall, & Verdoorn, 1995). One benzodiazepine, Dalmane (flurazepam), tends to cause confusion and oversedation, especially in the elderly. This medication is often used as a treatment for insomnia. One of the metabolites of flurazepam is desalkyflurazepam, which may have a half-life of between 40 and 280 hours (Gillin, 1991). Thus the effects of a single dose can last up to 12 days in some patients.

With such an extended half-life, using flurazepam for even a few days might cause a person to experience significant levels of CNS depression for some time after the last dose of the drug. Further, if a person should ingest alcohol, or even an over-the-counter cold remedy before the flurazepam is fully metabolized, the unmetabolized drug could combine with the depressant effects of the alcohol or cold remedy to produce serious levels of CNS depression.

Cross-tolerance among the benzodiazepines, alcohol, the barbiturates, and meprobamate is possible (Sands, Creelman, Ciraulo, Greenblatt, & Shader, 1995; Snyder, 1986). The benzodiazepines may also potentiate the effects of other CNS depressants, such as antihistamines, alcohol, and narcotic analgesics, presenting a danger of oversedation, or even death.[6,7] (Barnhill, Ciraulo, Ciraulo, & Greene, 1995). Many of the benzodiazepines have been found to interfere with normal sexual function, even when used at normal dosage levels (Finger, Lund, & Slagel, 1997). When the benzodiazepines are used for extended periods of time and then discontinued, the withdrawal symptoms may mimic the anxiety or sleep disorder for which the user originally started to use the medication (Miller & Gold, 1991b). The danger is that the patient might begin to take benzodiazepines again, in the mistaken belief that the withdrawal symptoms indicated that the original problem still existed.

Even when used at normal dosage levels, the benzodiazepines occasionally cause irritability, hostility, rage, or outright aggression (Walker, 1996; Hobbs, Rall, & Verdoorn, 1995; Ashton, 1994; Juergens, 1993). This *paradoxical rage reaction* in a person who has used a benzodiazepine is thought to result from the disinhibition effects of this family of drugs. As the benzodiazepine lowers social inhibitions, the person is more likely to engage in behavior that was successfully controlled before. A similar disinhibition effect is often seen in persons who drink alcohol. This is why the combination of alcohol and benzodiazepines occasionally results in a paradoxical rage reaction (Beasley, 1987).

Another complication common to benzodiazepines is that even at normal dosage levels, they seem to interfere with the formation of memory patterns (Ayd, 1994; Plasky, Marcus, & Salzman, 1988). Although in many cases the memory disturbance is so subtle as to escape

the individual's notice (O'Donovan & McGuffin, 1993; Juergens, 1993), every benzodiazepine in use can result in some degree of memory loss. Halcion (triazolam) has acquired a reputation for causing memory disturbance when used at therapeutic dosage levels; this effect would seem to be common to *all* the benzodiazepines (Hobbs, Rall, & Verdoorn, 1995; O'Donovan & McGuffin, 1993; Juergens, 1993). This effect is known as *anterograde amnesia*, a form of amnesia that involves the formation of memories after a specific event (Plasky, Marcus, & Salzman, 1988). In this case, the person might be unable to remember information presented to them after they ingested the drug. The process seems to be similar to that of the alcohol-induced "blackout" (Juergens, 1993).

Even at normal dosage levels, the benzodiazepines may disrupt the psychomotor skills necessary to operate mechanical devices, such as power tools. Problems with psychomotor coordination may persist for several days following the initial use of benzodiazepines (Woods *et al.*, 1988). Further, the benzodiazepines occasionally produce mild respiratory depression, even at normal therapeutic dosage levels, especially in persons with pulmonary disease. Because of this, the benzodiazepines should be avoided in patients who suffer from sleep apnea, chronic lung disease, or other sleep-related breathing disorders (Hobbs, Rall, & Verdoorn, 1995; Ashton, 1994). Also, benzodiazepines should not be used with patients who suffer from Alzheimer's disease, in whom they might potentiate preexisting sleep apnea problems (Doghramji, 1989).

In rare cases, therapeutic doses of a benzodiazepine have induced a depressive reaction in the patient (Ashton, 1994; Juergens, 1993; Ashton, 1992; Smith & Salzman, 1991). The exact mechanism by which the benzodiazepines cause—or at least contribute to—depressive episodes is not clear at this time. To further complicate matters, there is evidence that benzodiazepine use contributes to thoughts of suicide (Ashton, 1994; Juergens, 1993; Ashton, 1992). Although it is not possible to list every reported side effect of the benzodiazepines, this account should clearly illustrate that these medications are extremely potent and have a significant potential to harm the user.

The trials of Halcion. Ever since the benzodiazepine Halcion (triazolam) was introduced as a hypnotic, it has been a controversial drug. Numerous reports of adverse

---

[6]When in doubt about whether two or more medications should be used together *always* consult a physician, pharmacist, or the local poison control center.

[7]For example, the movie star Judy Garland reportedly died as a result of the combined effects of alcohol and the benzodiazepine diazepam (Snyder, 1986).

reactions, as well as admission by the manufacturer that there were "errors" in the original supporting research, have resulted in triazolam's being banned in the United Kingdom, Brazil, Argentina, Norway, and Denmark (Institute of Medicine Committee on the Efficacy and Safety of Halcion, 1999). In 1996, the U.S. Food and Drug Administration (FDA) carried out a year-long review of the drug. It was concluded that triazolam was safe when used as prescribed, but the FDA recommended that the manufacturer issue stronger warnings about potential side effects of the drug (Report of the Institute of Medicine Committee on the Efficacy and Safety of Halcion, 1999).

Some of the side effects of therapeutic doses of Halcion (triazolam) include periods of confusion and disorientation (Gillin, 1991; Salzman, 1990), behavioral disinhibition, hyperexcitabiity, daytime anxiety, amnesia, and confusion (O'Donovan & McGiffin, 1993; Gillin, 1991). As this list of side effects suggests, some view Halcion as ". . . a very, very dangerous drug" (Kayles, quoted in *60 Minutes*, 1994, p. 2). It has even been suggested that

> compared with other benzodiazepines, triazolam causes more agitation, confusion, amnesia, hallucinations, and bizarre or abnormal behavior. Suicides, attempted suicides, deaths, and violent crimes have been associated with triazolam administration. In most of the adverse reaction reports, the drug was taken as recommended. (Hand, 1989, p. 3)

Recently, evidence has come to light that, for reasons still unclear, the manufacturer underreported some of the side effects associated with Halcion during at least one early study into the drug's safety (*60 Minutes*, 1994; Cowley, 1992). This study, known as "Protocol 321," was presented to the FDA as evidence that the drug was safe (*60 Minutes*, 1994), but the true findings of this study were apparently not provided to the FDA review panel. The study actually found that 70% of the subjects experienced major side effects from the drug (*60 Minutes*, 1994). But this information was "either missing or minimized when Upjohn sent this official summary of the test to the FDA" (*60 Minutes*, 1994, p. 3).

For this reason, the FDA requested that an independent organization review the safety of Halcion (triazolam). This independent review was carried out by the Institute of Medicine, located in Washington, DC, and the results were summarized in a report issued in April of 1999. The authors concluded that Halcion (triazolam) was

> effective in achieving the defined end points in the general adult population with insomnia when used as directed (in the current labeling) at doses of 0.25 mg for as long as 7 to 10 days. (Institute of Medicine Committee on the Efficacy and Safety of Halcion, 1999, p. 350)

However, this committee also suggested that further research be conducted into the long-term effects of current hypnotic agents, including triazolam. Thus it would appear that triazolam will be a controversial drug for many years to come.

Drug interactions involving the benzodiazepines. There have been a "few anecdotal case reports" (Sarid-Segal, Creelman, & Shader, 1995, p. 193) of patients who have suffered adverse effects from the use of benzodiazepines while taking lithium. The authors reviewed a single case report of "profound hypothermia resulting from the combined use of lithium and diazepam" (p. 194). In this case, lithium was implicated as the agent that caused the individual to suffer a progressive loss of body temperature. Further, the authors noted that diazepam and oxazepam appear to cause increased levels of depression in patients who are also taking lithium. The reason for this increased level of depression in patients who are using both lithium and one of these benzodiazepines is not known at this time.

Patients who are on Antabuse (disulfiram) should use benzodiazepines with caution, because disulfiram reduces the speed at which the body can metabolize benzodiazepines such as diazepam and chlordiazepoxide (Zito, 1994). The author recommended that when a patient must use both medications concurrently, she or he use a benzodiazepine such as oxazepam or lorazepam, which do not produce any biologically active metabolites.

There is evidence that blood levels of Halcion (triazolam) might be as high as double when the patient also takes the antibiotic erythromycin (sold under a variety of brand names) (Graedon & Graedon, 1995). Further, there is evidence that probenecid might slow the biotransformation of the benzodiazepine lorazepam, thus causing excess sedation in some patients (Sands, Creelman, Ciraulo, Greenblatt, & Shader, 1995).

Patients who are taking a benzodiazepine should not use the antipsychotic medication clozapine (Zito, 1994). There have been reports of severe respiratory depression caused by the combination of these two medications, possibly resulting in several deaths. Patients with heart conditions who are taking the medication digoxin as well as a benzodiazepine should have frequent tests to check the digoxin level in their blood (Graedon & Graedon, 1995). There is some evidence that benzodiazepine use might cause the blood levels of digoxin to rise, possibly to the level of digoxin toxicity, according to the authors.

Further, the use of benzodiazepines with anticonvulsant medications such as phenytoin, mephenytoin, and ethotoin, with the antidepressant fluoxetine, or with medications for the control of blood pressure such as propranolol and metoprolol might cause higher-than-normal blood levels of such benzodiazepines as diazepam (Graedon & Graedon, 1995). Thus, it is unwise for a patient to use these medications at the same time.

Women who are using oral contraceptives should discuss their use of a benzodiazepines with a physician before taking one of these medications. Zito (1994) noted that oral contraceptives reduce the rate at which the body is able to metabolize some benzodiazepines, thus making it necessary to reduce the dose of these medications. Patients who are taking antitubercular medications such as isoniazid might need to adjust their benzodiazepine dosage (Zito, 1994). Further, there is evidence that patients who take antacids have trouble absorbing chlordiazepoxide as quickly as they might if they had taken the chlordiazepoxide without an antacid (Ciraulo, Shader, Greenblatt, & Barnhill, 1995).

Because of the possibility of excessive sedation, the benzodiazepines should *never* be intermixed with medications that are classified as CNS depressants, except under the supervision of a physician. Such medications include alcohol, narcotic analgesics, and the antihistamines (Graedon & Graedon, 1995). Another CNS depressant that should never be mixed with benzodiazepines is the herbal medicine Kava (Cupp, 1999). The combined effects of these two classes of compounds may result in excessive—if not dangerous—levels of sedation. This list is not exhaustive, but it illustrates that there is a potential for an interaction between the ben-

zodiazepines and a number of other medications. One should always consult a physician or pharmacist before taking two or more medications at the same time, to rule out the possibility of an adverse interaction.

Subjective Experience of Benzodiazepine Use

When used as antianxiety agents at normal dosage levels, benzodiazepines induce a gentle state of relaxation in the user. In addition to their effects on the cortex, the benzodiazepines have an effect on the spinal cord, which contributes to muscle relaxation through some unknown mechanism (Ballenger, 1995). When used in the treatment of insomnia, the benzodiazepines initially reduce the sleep latency period, and users report a sense of deep and refreshing sleep. However, the benzodiazepines interfere with the normal sleep cycle, almost suppressing stage III and IV (REM) sleep for reasons that are not clear (Ballenger, 1995). Those who use benzodiazepines for extended periods of time as hypnotics are likely to experience "REM rebound" (Hobbs, Rall, & Verdoorn, 1995; Ashton, 1994).[8] There are cases on record where an individual who had used a benzodiazepine as a hypnotic for only 1–2 weeks still experienced significant "rebound" symptoms when upon trying to discontinue the medication (Tyrer, 1993; *Harvard Medical School Mental Health Letter*, 1988). To help the individual return to normal sleep, the hormone melatonin is often used during the period of benzodiazepine withdrawal (Pettit, 2000; Garfinkel, Zisapel, Wainstein, & Laudon, 1999).

In addition to REM rebound, patients who have used a benzodiazepine for daytime relief from anxiety have reported symptoms such as anxiety, agitation, tremor, fatigue, difficulty concentrating, headache, nausea, gastrointestinal upset, a sense of paranoia, depersonalization, and impaired memory after stopping the drug (Graedon & Graedon, 1991). There have been reports of people experiencing rebound insomnia for as long as 3–21 days after their last benzodiazepine use (Graedon & Graedon, 1991). The benzodiazepines with shorter half-lives are most likely to cause rebound symptoms (Ayd, 1994; O'Donovan & McGuffin, 1993; Rosenbaum, 1990). Such rebound symptoms may be

[8]See the Glossary.

common when the patient experiences an abrupt drop in medication blood levels. For example, alprazolam has a short half-life, and the blood levels drop rather rapidly just before it is time for the next dose. This is when the individual is most likely to experience an increase in anxiety levels, a phenomenon known as "clock watching" (Rosenbaum, 1990, p. 1302), as the patient waits with increasing anxiety until it is time for his or her next dose.

To combat rebound anxiety, it has been suggested that a long-acting benzodiazepine such as clonazepam be substituted for the shorter-acting drug (Rosenbaum, 1990). The transition between alprazolam and clonazepam takes about a week, after which time the patient should be taking only clonazepam. This medication may then be gradually withdrawn, resulting in a slower decline in blood levels. However, there will still be some rebound anxiety symptoms. Although the patient might believe otherwise, these symptoms are not a sign that the original anxiety remains. Rather, these anxiety-like symptoms simply mean that the body is adjusting to the gradual reduction in clonazepam blood levels.

Long-term Consequences of Chronic Benzodiazepine Use

Although they were introduced as safe and nonaddicting substitutes for the barbiturates, the benzodiazepines do indeed have a significant abuse potential. Some of the signs of benzodiazepine abuse include (Dietch, 1983) (1) taking the drug after the medical/psychiatric need for its use has passed, (2) symptoms of physical or psychological dependency on one of the benzodiazepines, (3) taking the drug in greater than the prescribed amount, (4) taking the drug to obtain an euphoriant effect, and (5) using the drug in order to decrease self-awareness or the possibility of change.

During withdrawal, the benzodiazepine-dependent individual may experience anxiety, insomnia, dizziness, nausea and vomiting, muscle weakness, tremor, confusion, convulsions (seizures), irritability, sweating, and a drug-induced withdrawal psychosis (Juergens, 1993). There have also been rare reports of depression, manic reactions, and obsessive-compulsive symptoms (Juergens, 1993). In extreme cases, patients have been known to experience transient feelings of depersonalization, muscle pain, and a hypersensitivity to light

and noise during the benzodiazepine withdrawal process (Spiegel, 1996).

In addition to the problems of physical dependency, Dietch (1983) noted that it is possible to become *psychologically* dependent on benzodiazepines. Indeed, "Psychological dependence on benzodiazepines appears to be more common than physical dependence" (p. 1140). Such persons might take the drug either continuously or intermittently merely because they *believe* that they need benzodiazepines.

When used as hypnotics, the benzodiazepines are useful for short periods of time. However, researchers believe that the process of neuroadaptation limits the effectiveness of the benzodiazepines as sleep-inducing (hypnotic) medications to just a few days (Ashton, 1994) or to a week (Carvey, 1998) or to 2–4 weeks (Ayd, 1994; American Psychiatric Association, 1990) of continuous use. Given this fact, it is recommended that the benzodiazepines be used only for the *short-term* treatment of insomnia (Taylor, McCracken, Wilson, & Copeland, 1998). Even so, many people continue to use these benzodiazepines as a sleep aid for months or even years. This might reflect the fact that these medications have become part of the psychological ritual that the individual follows to ensure proper sleep (Carvey, 1998).

There is a tendency, at least among some users of the benzodiazepines, to increase their dosage level above that prescribed by their physician. This phenomenon is not well understood. Although the benzodiazepines do cause tolerance (Snyder, 1986), "the magnitude of such increases appears to be small" (Dietch, 1983, p. 1141), and in general, "subjects tended to titrate their dose according to the level of environmental stress." The limited information on this phenomenon is based on patients who were prescribed one of the benzodiazepines for medical/psychiatric reasons.

All of the CNS depressants, including the benzodiazepines, are capable of producing a *toxic psychosis*, especially in overdose situations. Some professionals call this condition an *organic brain syndrome*. The symptoms seen with a benzodiazepine-related toxic psychosis include visual and auditory hallucinations and/or paranoid delusions, as well as hyperthermia, delirium, convulsions, a drug-induced psychosis, and even death (Jenike, 1991). With proper treatment, this drug-induced psychosis usually clears in 2–14 days

(Miller & Gold, 1991b), but *withdrawal from benzodiazepines should be attempted only under the supervision of a physician.*

Benzodiazepines as a substitute for other drugs of abuse. There is little factual information available on the phenomenon of benzodiazepine abuse/addiction. It is estimated that 80% of the benzodiazepine abusers are polydrug addicts, who intermix benzodiazepines with other drugs to enhance their effects, to control some of the unwanted side effects of the primary drug of abuse, or to help them withdraw from the primary drug of abuse (Longo, Parran, Johnson, & Kinsey, 2000).

Because of the similarity between the effects of alcohol and those of the benzodiazepines, alcohol-dependent persons often substitute a benzodiazepine for alcohol in situations where they cannot drink. The author of this text has met a number of recovering alcoholics who reported that 10 mg of diazepam had the same subjective effect as 3–4 "stiff" drinks. Further, the long half-life of diazepam often is sufficient to allow the individual to work the entire day, without starting to go into alcohol withdrawal, thus enabling the user to avoid the smell of alcohol on his or her breath while at work.

Finally, opiate addicts who are in methadone maintenance programs often take a single, massive dose of a benzodiazepine (the equivalent of 100–300 mg of diazepam) to "boost" the effect of their daily methadone dose (American Psychiatric Association, 1990). There is evidence to suggest that the experimental narcotic buprenorphine may, when mixed with benzodiazepines, offer the user less of a "high," thus reducing the incentive for the narcotics user to mix his or her medications (Sellers *et al.*, 1993).

Buspirone

In 1986, a new medication by the name of *BuSpar* (buspirone) was introduced. Buspirone is a member of a new class of medications known as the *azapirones*, which are chemically different from the benzodiazepines. Buspirone was found as a result of a search by pharmaceutical companies for antipsychotic drugs that did not have the harsh side effects of the phenothiazines and similar chemicals (Sussman, 1994). The antipsychotic effect of buspirone was quite limited, but researchers found that it had an antianxiety effect "comparable with that of both diazepam and clorazepate"

(Feighner, 1987, p. 15; Manfredi, Kales, Vgontzas, Bixler, Isaac, & Falcone, 1991). As an additional advantage, it was found that buspirone only rarely causes sedation or fatigue (Sussman, 1994; Rosenbaum & Gelenberg, 1991), and there was no evidence of potentiation between buspirone and select benzodiazepines or between alcohol and buspirone (Manfredi *et al.*, 1991; Feighner, 1987).[9]

The side effects of buspirone at normal doses include gastrointestinal problems, drowsiness, decreased concentration, dizziness, agitation, headache, feelings of lightheadedness, nervousness, diarrhea, excitement, sweating/clamminess, nausea, depression, nasal congestion, and some feelings of fatigue (Pagliaro & Pagliaro, 1998; Cadieuz, 1996; Cole & Yonkers, 1995; Manfredi *et al.*, 1991; Graedon &Graedon, 1991; Feighner, 1987; Newton, Marunycz, Alderdice, & Napoliello, 1986). Buspirone has also been found to reduce sexual desire in some users and to cause sexual performance problems in some men (Finger, Lund, & Slagel, 1997).

In contrast to the benzodiazepine family of drugs, buspirone has no significant anticonvulsant action. It also lacks the muscle relaxant effects of the benzodiazepines (Cadieuz, 1996; Eison & Temple, 1987). Buspirone has been found to be of little value in those cases of anxiety that involve insomnia, which are a significant proportion of anxiety cases (Manfredi *et al.*, 1991). It has been found to be of value in controlling the symptoms of general anxiety disorder but does not seem to control the discomfort of anxiety/panic attacks.

On the positive side, buspirone was found to be effective in the treatment of many patients who suffered from an anxiety disorder with a depressive component (Cadieuz, 1996; Cohn, Wilcox, Bowden, Fisher, & Rodos, 1992). Indeed, there is evidence that buspirone might be of value in the treatment of some forms of depression, both as the primary form of treatment and as an agent to potentiate the effects of other antidepressants (Sussman, 1994). In addition to this, buspirone has been found to be of value in the treatment of obsessive-compulsive disorder, social phobias, post-traumatic stress disorder, and possibly alcohol withdrawal symptoms (Sussman, 1994). Physicians who treat geriatric

---

[9]This is *not* a suggestion that the user try to use alcohol and buspirone at the same time. The author does *not* recommend the use of alcohol with *any* prescription medication.

patients have found that buspirone is effective in controlling aggression in anxious, confused older adults, without adding to the psychomotor instability that can contribute to the patient's falling (Ayd, Janicak, Davis, & Preskorn, 1996). It has also been found to reduce the frequency of self-abusive behaviors (SAB) in mentally retarded subjects, according to the authors.

Researchers have found that adding buspirone to antidepressant medications seems to bring many resistant or nonresponsive cases of depression under control (Cadieuz, 1996). There also is limited evidence buspirone might be useful as an adjunct to cigarette cessation for those smokers who have some form of anxiety disorder (Covey, Sullivan, Johnston, Glassman, Robinson, & Adams, 2000).

The Pharmacology of Buspirone

The mechanism of action of buspirone is different from that of the benzodiazepines (Eison & Temple, 1987). Whereas the benzodiazepines tend to bind to receptor sites that utilize the neurotransmitter GABA, buspirone tends to bind to one of the many serotonin receptor sites known as the $5-HT_{1A}$ site (Ayd, Janicak, Davis, & Preskorn, 1996; Cadieuz, 1996; Sussman, 1994). Further, researchers have found that buspirone binds to dopamine and serotonin type 1 receptors in the hippocampus, a different portion of the brain from where the benzodiazepines exert their effect (Manfredi et al., 1991).

Within the brain, buspirone appears to function in a manner that moderates the level of serotonin (Cadieuz, 1996). If there is a deficit of serotonin, as there is in depressive disorders, buspirone seems to stimulate the production of more of this neurotransmitter (Anton, 1994; Sussman, 1994). If there is an excess of serotonin, as there appears to be in many forms of anxiety states, buspirone seems to lower the serotonin level (Cadieuz, 1996). Unfortunately, whereas the benzodiazepines are effective almost immediately, buspirone must be used for up to 2–4 weeks before its greatest effects are seen (Sussman, 1994; Graedon & Graedon, 1991; Thornton, 1990). The half-life of buspirone is only 1–10 hours (Cole & Yonkers, 1995). This short half-life requires that the individual take 3–4 divided doses of buspirone each day, whereas the half-life of benzodiazepines like diazepam makes it possible to use that drug only 1–2 times a day (Schweizer & Rickels, 1994). Finally, unlike many

other sedating chemicals, there does not appear to be any cross-tolerance between buspirone and the benzodiazepines, alcohol, the barbiturates, or meprobamate (Sussman, 1994).

The results of research into the abuse potential of buspirone are mixed at this time. Lader (1987) concluded that buspirone "failed to demonstrate any abuse liability in either animal or human studies" (p. 25), a conclusion supported by a number of other researchers (Anton, 1994; Rosenbaum & Gelenberg, 1991; Thornton, 1990). Certainly, there is no evidence of a withdrawal syndrome from buspirone such as that seen in chronic benzodiazepine abuse, and according to Sussman (1994), drug abusers rated this compound as rewarding to use as a placebo. In contrast to these conclusions, Murphy, Owen, and Tyrer (1989) found evidence of both an addictive effect of buspirone and a characteristic withdrawal syndrome. Thus, the potential for buspirone abuse/addiction remains unclear at this time.

Unlike the benzodiazepines, buspirone does not seem to have an adverse impact on memory (Rickels, Giesecke, & Geller, 1987). Unfortunately, buspirone has not been shown to lessen the intensity of withdrawal symptoms experienced by patients who were addicted to benzodiazepines (Rickels, Schweizer, Csanalosi, Case, & Chung, 1988). Indeed, there is evidence that patients currently taking a benzodiazepine might be slightly *less* responsive to buspirone while they are taking both medications (Cadieuz, 1996). But unlike the benzodiazepines, there is no evidence of tolerance to buspirone's effects, of physical dependence, or of a withdrawal syndrome from buspirone when the medication is used as directed for short periods of time (Cadieuz, 1996; Rickels, Schweizer, Csanalosi, Case, & Chung, 1988).

One very rare complication of buspirone use is the development of a drug-induced neurological condition known as *serotonin syndrome* (Mills, 1995). Although it is quite rare, approximately 11% of those patients who do develop serotonin syndrome will die, in spite of the best of medical care. Some of the symptoms of serotonin syndrome are irritability, confusion, an increase in anxiety, drowsiness, hyperthermia (increased body temperature), sinus tachycardia, dilation of the pupils, nausea, muscle rigidity, and seizures. Although serotonin syndrome might develop as long as 24 hours after the patient ingested a medication that affects the serotonin neurotransmitter system, 50% of the patients developed the syndrome within two hours of starting the medication (Mills, 1995).

There have been a limited number of cases in which patients who were taking buspirone and an antidepressant that was a monoamine oxidase inhibitor (MAOI, or MAO inhibitor) developed abnormally high blood pressure (Ciraulo, Creelman, Shader, & O'Sullivan, 1995). However there are countless other cases where patients have taken these two medications at the same time without apparent ill effect. It is not known what role either medication plays in the development of the observed hypertension.

The manufacturer's claim that buspirone offers many advantages over the benzodiazepines in the treatment of anxiety states has not been totally fulfilled. Indeed, Rosenbaum and Gelenberg (1991) cautioned that "many clinicians and patients have found buspirone to be a generally disappointing alternative to benzodiazepines" (p. 200). Nevertheless, the authors recommended a trial of buspirone for "persistently anxious patients" (p. 200). Further, buspirone would seem to be the drug of choice in the treatment of anxiety states in the addiction-prone individual.

Zolpidem

The drug zolpidem was used as a sleep-inducing (hypnotic) drug in Europe for 5 years before it was introduced to the United States in 1993 (Hobbs, Rall, & Verdoorn, 1995). In the United States., it is sold as an orally administered hypnotic by the brand name of *Ambien*, which is available only by a physician's prescription, and is marketed as a short-term (less than 4 weeks) treatment of insomnia.

Pharmacology of Zolpidem

Technically, zolpidem is not a member of the benzodiazepine family. Rather, it is the first of a new family of sleep-inducing chemicals known as *imidazopryidines*. Zopidem binds to just one of the receptor sites in the brain used by the benzodiazepines and thus is more selective. This selectiveness is why zolpidem has only a minor anticonvulstant effect and has minimal to no effect on muscle injuries.

The biological half-life of a single dose of zolpidem is about 1.5–2.4 hours in the healthy adult and approximately 2.5 hours in geriatric patients (Folks & Burke, 1998; Kryger, Steljes, Pouliot, Neufeld, & Odynski, 1991). Most of a single dose of zolpidem is biotransformed by the liver into inactive metabolites before excretion by the kidneys. There is little evidence of neuro-adaptation to zolpidem's hypnotic effects when the drug is used at normal dosage levels, even after it has been used as long as a year (Holm & Goa, 2000; Folks & Burke, 1998). There are, however, rare reports of patients who have become tolerant to the hypnotic effects of zolpidem after using this medication at very high dosage levels for a period of several years (Holm & Goa, 2000).

Unlike the benzodiazepines and the barbiturates, zolpidem causes only a minor reduction in REM sleep patterns at normal dosage levels (Hobbs, Rall, & Verdoorn, 1995). Further, it does not interfere with the other stages of sleep and hence allows the patient to get a more natural and restful night's sleep (Hartmann, 1995). When zolpidem is used as prescribed, its most common adverse effects are nightmares, headaches, gastrointestinal upset, agitation, and some daytime drowsiness (Hartmann, 1995). There have also been a few isolated cases of a zolpidem-induced psychosis (Ayd, Janicak, Davis, & Preskorn, 1996; Ayd, 1994). Side effects are more often encountered at higher dosage levels, and the dosage level of zolpidem should not exceed 10 mg/day (Hold & Goa, 2000; Merlotti, Roehrs, Koshorek, Zorick, Lamphere, & Roth, 1989).

Zolpidem has been found to cause some problems in cognitive performance similar to those seen with the benzodiazepines, although this medication appears less likely than the older hypnotics to cause memory impairment (Ayd, Janicak, Davis, & Preskorn, 1996). Further, alcohol enhances the effects of zolpidem and thus should not be used by patients on this medication because of the potentiation effect (Folks & Burke, 1998). Zolpidem is contraindicated in patients with obstructive sleep apnea because it increases the duration and frequency of apnea (Holm & Goa, 2000).

Effects of zolpidem at above-normal dosage levels. At dosage levels of 20 mg/day or above, zolpidem has been found to reduce REM sleep significantly and to cause rebound insomnia when the drug is discontinued. At dosage levels of 50 mg/day, volunteers who received zolpidem reported such symptoms as visual perceptual disturbances, ataxia, dizziness, nausea, and vomiting.

Patients who have ingested up to 40 times the maximum recommended dosage have recovered without significant aftereffects. It should be noted, however, that the effects of zolpidem will combine with those of other CNS depressants if the patient has ingested more than one medication in an overdose attempt, and such multiple-drug overdoses might prove fatal. As with all medications, *any suspected overdose of zolpidem, either by itself or in combination with other medications, should be treated by a physician.*

Abuse potential of zolpidem. There are few reports of zolpidem abuse, and such reports appear to be limited to individuals who have histories of sedative/hypnotic abuse (Holm & Goa, 2000). Thus the prescribing physician must balance the potential for abuse against the potential benefit of this medication to the patient.

Zaleplon

The drug Sonata (zaleplon), a member of the *pyrazolpyrimidine* class of chemicals, was introduced as the first of a new class of hypnotic agents intended for short-term symptomatic treatment of insomnia. Animal research suggests that zaleplon has some sedative and anticonvulsant effects, although it is approved only for use as a hypnotic in the United States (Danjou, Paty, Fruncillo, Worthington, Unruh, Cevallos, & Martin 1999). When used to induce sleep, it is administered orally in capsules containing 5 mg, 10 mg, or 20 mg of the drug. In most cases, the 10-mg dose is sufficient to induce sleep, although in the case of individuals with low body weight, 5 mg might be more appropriate (Danjou, Paty, Fruncillo, Worthington, Unruh, Cevallos, & Martin, 1999).

Once in the body, approximately 30% of the dose of zaleplon is biotransformed by the liver, through the "first-pass metabolism" process. Less than 1% of the total dose is excreted in the urine unchanged, the majority of the medication being biotransformed by the liver into less active compounds that are eventually eliminated from the body in either the urine or the feces. The half-life of zaleplon is approximately 1 hour. In the brain, zaleplon binds at the same receptor site as zolpidem (Walsh, Pollak, Scharf, Schweitzer, & Vogel, 2000; Danjou, Paty, Fruncillo, Worthington, Unruh, Cevallos, & Martin, 1999). There is little evidence of a drug "hangover" effect, although it is recommended

that the patient not attempt to operate machinery for 4 hours after taking the last dose (Walsh, Pollak, Scharf, Schweitzer, & Vogel, 2000; Danjou, Paty, Fruncillo, Worthington, Unruh, Cevallos, & Martin, 1999).

As noted earlier, this medication is intended for the *short-term* treatment of insomnia, in part because of the rapid development of tolerance to the effects of this (or similar) medication. Individuals who have used zaleplon nightly for extended periods of time have reported *rebound insomnia* upon discontinuation of this medication, especially when the drug is used at higher dosage levels than 5 mg/night. Because of the rapid onset of sleep, users are advised to take this medication just before going to sleep or after finding that they are unable to go to sleep naturally. The abuse potential of zaleplon is similar to that of the benzodiazepines, and patients have reported similar side effects from zaleplon, including headache, rhinitis, nausea, myalgia, periods of amnesia while under the effects of this medication, dizziness, depersonalization, drug-induced hangover, constipation, dry mouth, gout, bronchitis, asthma attacks, nervousness, depression, problems in concentration, ataxia, and insomnia.

When used for extended periods of time (which means periods that may be as short as two weeks of regular use), zaleplon has caused withdrawal symptoms such as muscle cramps, tremor, vomiting, and (on rare occasions) seizures.

Rohypnol

Rohypnol (flunitrazepam) first appeared in the United States in the mid 1990s. It is a member of the benzodiazepine family of pharmaceuticals and is used in more than 60 countries as a presurgical medication, a muscle relaxant, and a hypnotic. Each day, more than 2.3 million doses of flunitrazepam are sold around the world (Saum & Inciardi, 1997).

Because it is not manufactured as a pharmaceutical in the United States, there was little abuse of flunitrazepam by U.S. citizens before the mid 1990s, and substance abuse rehabilitation professionals in this country had virtually no experience with Rohypnol (flunitrazepam) when people began to bring it into this country. Possession of flunitrazepam in the United States was legal, until it was classified as an illegal substance by the U.S. government in October of 1996. Now that it is illegal, individuals convicted of trafficking in or distributing this drug may be incarcerated for up to 20 years (*Forensic Drug Abuse Advisor*, 1997a).

Flunitrazepam rapidly gained a reputation as a "date rape" drug (Saum & Inciardi, 1997). This is because the pharmacological characteristics of flunitrazepam, especially when it is mixed with alcohol, can cause a drug-induced amnesia that might last 8–24 hours. This, and the fact that it is a colorless, odorless, tasteless substance that is easily mixed with an alcoholic beverage, reportedly attracted the interest of predators who might use a drug to force themselves on others sexually (Saum & Inciardi, 1997). There are also reports of cocaine abusers ingesting flunitrazepam to counteract the effects of a cocaine run, and of heroin abusers mixing flunitrazepam with low-quality heroin to enhance its effect (Saum & Inciardi, 1997).

Chemically, flunitrazepam is a derivative of the benzodiazepine chlordiazepoxide (Eidelberg, Neer, & Miller, 1965) and is said to be 10 times as powerful as diazepam (*Substance Abuse Letter*, 1995). When it is used as a medication, the usual method of administration is by mouth, in doses of 0.5–2 mg. Flunitrazepam is well absorbed from the gastrointestinal tract, between 80–90% of a single 2-mg dose being absorbed by the user's body (Mattila & Larni, 1980). Following a single oral dose, the peak blood levels are reached after 1–2 hours (Saum & Inciardi, 1997). Once in the blood, 80–90% of the flunitrazepam is briefly bound to plasma proteins, but the drug is rapidly transferred from the plasma to body tissues. Because of this characteristic, flunitrazepam has an elimination half-life significantly longer than its duration of effect. Indeed, depending on the individual's metabolism, the elimination half-life can range from 15 to 66 hours (Woods & Winger, 1997).

During the process of biotransformation, flurintrazepam produces a number of different metabolites, some of which are themselves biologically active (Mattila & Larni, 1980). Less than 1% of the drug is excreted unchanged. About 90% of a single dose is eliminated by the kidneys after biotransformation; about 10% is eliminated in the feces. Because of this characteristic elimination pattern, patients who live in countries where flurintrazepam is legal and who have kidney disease require modification of their dosage level, because the main route of elimination is through the kidneys.

Although the usual pharmaceutical dose of flunitrazepam is less than 2 mg, illicit users often take 4 mg of the drug in one dose, which begins to produce sedation in 20–30 minutes. The drug's effects normally last for 8–12 hours. Some users mix flunitrazepam with ketamine (discussed in Chapter 35), nitrous oxide (discussed in Chapter 16), or fentanyl (discussed in Chapter 14) in order to enhance the effect (*Substance Abuse Letter*, 1995). Illicit users may also use flunitrazepam while smoking marijuana and while using alcohol (Lively, 1996). The combination of flunitrazepam and marijuana is said to produce a "floating" effect. There are reports of abusers inhaling flunitrazepam powder and of physical addiction developing to this substance following periods of continuous use. There are also reports of children as young as 8 years old using flunitrazepam, especially because of its low price (50¢ to $8.00 a tablet).

Although the drug is used as a sedative, flunitrazepam is, like the other benzodiazepines, capable of bringing about a state of paradoxical excitement or aggression. Flunitrazepam has an anticonvulsant effect (Eidelberg, Neer, & Miller, 1965) and can bring about a state of pharmacological dependency. Chronic users report that flunitrazepam can cause excessive sedation, headaches, tremor, and drug-induced amnesia (Office of National Drug Control Policy, 1996). Although flunitrazepam has a wide safety margin, concurrent use with alcohol or other CNS depressants may increase the danger of overdose. Withdrawal from flunitrazepam is potentially serious for the chronic abuser, and there have been reports of withdrawal seizures taking place as long as 7 days after the last use of flunitrazepam (*Substance Abuse Letter*, 1995). For this reason, patients should be withdrawn from flunitrazepam only under the supervision of a physician.

Summary

In the time since their introduction in the 1960s, the benzodiazepines have become one of the most frequently prescribed medications. As a class, the benzodiazepines are the treatment of choice for the control of anxiety and insomnia, as well as many other conditions. They have also become a significant part of the drug abuse problem. In spite of the fact that many of the benzodiazepines were first introduced as "nonaddicting and safe" substitutes for the barbiturates, there is evidence to suggest that they have an abuse potential similar to that of the barbiturate family of drugs.

A new series of pharmaceuticals, including buspirone (which is sold under the brand name BuSpar) and zolpidem, have been introduced in the past decade. Buspirone is the first of a new class of antianxiety agents that work through a different mechanism than the benzodiazepines. Buspirone was introduced as nonaddicting, but this claim has been challenged by at least one team of researchers. Zolpidem has an admitted potential for abuse; however, research at this time suggests that this abuse potential is less than that of the benzodiazepine most commonly used as a hypnotic, triazolam. Researchers are actively discussing the potential benefits and liabilities of these new medications.

CHAPTER ELEVEN

Abuse of and Addiction to Amphetamines and CNS Stimulants

Introduction

It is interesting to note that the use of central nervous system (CNS) stimulants dates back several thousand years. There is historical evidence that gladiators in ancient Rome used CNS stimulants at least 2000 years ago to help them overcome the effects of fatigue so that they could fight longer (Wadler, 1994). Not surprisingly, people still use chemicals that act as CNS stimulants to counter the effects of fatigue so that they can work, or, in times of conflict, fight, longer.

There are several different families of chemicals that might be classified as CNS stimulants, including cocaine, the amphetamines, amphetamine-like drugs such as Ritalin (methylphenidate), and ephedrine. The behavioral effects of these drugs are remarkably similar (Gawin & Ellinwood, 1988). For this reason, the amphetamine-like drugs will be discussed only briefly, whereas the amphetamines are reviewed in greater detail. Cocaine will be discussed in the next chapter. However, because the CNS stimulants are controversial and the source of much confusion, we will take an unusual approach in this chapter. First we will discuss the medical uses of the CNS stimulants, their effects, and complications arising from their use. Then we will explore CNS stimulant abuse.

I. THE CNS STIMULANTS AS USED IN MEDICAL PRACTICE

The Amphetamine-like Drugs

Ephedrine

More than 5000 years ago, Chinese physicians had identified plants of the genus *Ephedra* as having medicinal value (Ross & Chappel, 1998). The active agent of these plants, ephedrine, was not isolated by chemists until 1897 (Mann, 1992), and it remained nothing more than a curiosity until 1930. Then a report appeared in a medical journal suggesting that ephedrine was useful in treating asthma (Karch, 1996), and it quickly became the treatment of choice for this condition. The intense demand for ephedrine soon raised concern that the demand would exceed the supply of plants. (The importance of this fear will be discussed in a later section of this chapter.) In the United States, ephedrine has remained an over-the-counter agent that is marketed as a treatment for asthma and headaches.

Medical uses of ephedrine. Ephedrine is used to treat bronchial asthma and respiratory problems associated with bronchitis, emphysema, or chronic obstructive pulmonary disease (American Society of Health-System Pharmacists, 1999). Although ephedrine was once considered a valid treatment for nasal congestion, it is no longer used for this purpose. In hospitals it may also be used to control the symptoms of shock and in some surgical procedures where low blood pressure is a problem (Karch, 1996). Ephedrine might modify the cardiac rate, but with the introduction of newer, more effective medications, it is rarely used in cardiac emergencies now (American Society of Health-System Pharmacists, 1999). Ephedrine may, in some situations, be used as an adjunct to the treatment of myasthenia gravis (Shannon, Wilson, & Stang, 1995).

Pharmacology of ephedrine. In the human body, ephedrine's primary effects are strongest in the peripheral regions of the body rather than the central nervous system (CNS), and it is known that ephedrine stimulates the sympathetic nervous system in a manner similar to adrenaline (Laurence & Bennett, 1992; Mann, 1992). Ephedrine's ability to relax the smooth muscles surrounding the bronchial passages, thus reducing bronchial constriction and allowing for improved air flow into and out of the lungs, was what made it so useful in the treatment of asthma (American Society of Health-System Pharmacists, 1999).

Depending on the patient's condition, ephedrine might be taken orally or injected. Oral, intramuscular, and subcutaneous doses are completely absorbed. Peak blood levels from a single oral dose are achieved in 15 minutes to 1 hour (Shannon, Wilson, & Stang, 1995). Surprisingly, given the fact that it has been in use for more than three-quarters of a century, there is very little research into the way that ephedrine is distributed within the body. It is known that the biological half-life of a single dose of ephedrine is about 4–6 hours (Karch, 1996). Only a small percentage of the drug is biotransformed before ephedrine is eliminated from the body by the kidneys, virtually unchanged. The more acidic the urine, the greater the percentage that is eliminated without biotransformation (American Society of Health-System Pharmacists, 1999).

Tolerance to its bronchodilator action develops rapidly, so physicians recommend that ephedrine be used as a treatment of asthma only for short periods of time. And because the chronic use of ephedrine may contribute to cardiac or respiratory problems, it should always be used under a physician's supervision.

Side effects of ephedrine at normal dosage levels. These include anxiety, feelings of apprehension, insom-

nia, urinary retention, and heart palpitations (Graedon & Graedon, 1991). The drug may also cause a throbbing headache, confusion, hallucinations, tremor, seizures, arrhythmias, stroke, euphoria, hypertension, coronary artery spasm, angina, intracranial hemorrhage (American Society of Health-System Pharmacists, 1999; Karch, 1996; Cupp, 1999) and even death.

Ritalin (Methylphenidate)

Ritalin (methylphenidate) is a controversial pharmaceutical agent frequently prescribed for children who have been diagnosed as having Attention Deficit–Hyperactivity Disorder (ADHD) (Breggin, 1998). The global production of methylphenidate in 1997 was 10 tons, of which the United States consumed 90% (Breggin, 1998; Diller, 1998). Although there are many advocates for the use of methylphenidate in the control of ADHD, there are also critics of this practice. Indeed, there are serious questions about whether children are being turned into chemical "zombies" through the use of methylphenidate or similar agents, in the name of behavioral control. Clearly, the use of methylphenidate does not represent the best possible control of ADHD symptoms, as evidenced by the fact that about half of the prescriptions for this medication are never renewed (Breggin, 1998). Given the strident arguments for and against the use of methylphenidate, it is safe to say that this compound will remain controversial for many decades to come.

Medical uses of methylphenidate. Methylphenidate has been found to function as a CNS stimulant and is of value in the treatment of a rare neurological condition known as *narcolepsy.*

Pharmacology of methylphenidate. Methylphenidate was originally developed by pharmaceutical companies in the hope that it would prove to be a nonaddicting substitute for the amphetamines (Diller, 1998). Chemically, it is a close cousin to the amphetamines, and some pharmacologists classify methyphenidate as a true amphetamine. In this text, it will be considered an amphetamine-like drug.

When methylphenidate is used in the treatment of attention deficit–hyperactivity disorder, patients take between 15 and 90 mg per day, in divided doses (Wender, 1995). Oral doses of methylphenidate are rapidly absorbed from the gastrointestinal tract, and the drug is thought to be approximately half as potent as D-amphetamine (Wender, 1995). Peak blood levels are achieved in 1.9 hours following a single dose, although extended-release forms of the drug may not reach peak blood levels until 4–7 hours after the medication was ingested (Shannon, Wilson, & Stang, 1995). The half-life of methylphenidate is from 1 to 3 hours, and the effects of a single oral dose last for between 3 and 6 hours, according to the authors. The effects of a single dose of an extended-release form of methylphenidate might continue for 8 hours. About 80% of a single oral dose is biotransformed to ritanic acid, which is then excreted by the kidneys.

Within the brain, methylphenidate blocks the reuptake of dopamine after it has been released by a neuron, allowing it to remain in the synapse longer and thus enhancing its effect (Volkow, Wang, Fowler, Gatley, Logan, Ding, Hitzemann, & Pappas, 1998). Methylphenidate blocks, in a dose-dependent manner, the action of the molecular "transporter" system by which free dopamine molecules are absorbed back into the neuron. This means that the higher the dosage level, the greater the blockage of dopamine transporter molecules (Volkow *et al.*, 1998). At normal therapeutic doses, methylphenidate is able to block 50% or more of the dopamine transporters within 60–90 minutes of the time the drug is administered (Volkow *et al.*, 1998).

Side effects of methylphenidate. In spite of the fact that methylphenidate is the treatment of choice for ADHD, very little is known about the long-term effects of this medication. Further, the long-term effectiveness of methylphenidate as a treatment for ADHD, and its safety, have not been established (Breggin, 1998; Diller, 1998). Researchers do know that even when it is used at therapeutic dosage levels, methylphenidate can cause anorexia, insomnia, weight loss, failure to gain weight, nausea, heart palpitations, angina, anxiety, liver problems, dry mouth, hypertension, headache, upset stomach, enuresis, skin rashes, dizziness, and exacerbation of the symptoms of Tourette's syndrome (Fuller & Sajatovic, 1999). Other side effects of methylphenidate include stomach pain, blurred vision, leukopenia, possible cerebral hemorrhages, hypersensitivity reactions, anemia, and preseveration, a condition wherein the individual continues to engage in the same task long after it ceases to be a useful activity (Breggin, 1998).

Methylphenidate has been implicated as a cause of liver damage in some patients (Karch, 1996). Meth-

ylphenidate has the potential to lower the seizure threshold in patients with a seizure disorder, and the manufacturer recommends that the drug be discontinued immediately if the patient has a seizure. There are reports that suggest the possibility of methylphenidate-induced damage to the tissue of the heart—a frightening prospect in light of the frequency with which it is prescribed to children.

When used at recommended dosage levels, methylphenidate can, through rarely, cause a drug-induced psychosis (Breggin, 1998). There are reports that methylphenidate can cause a reduction in cerebral blood flow patterns when used at therapeutic doses, an effect that may have long-term consequences (Breggin, 1998). Animal research has also suggested the possibility of methylphenidate-induced cardiac muscle damage, although the exact relevance of these data to humans is not yet clear (Henderson & Fischer, 1994). These findings suggest a need for further research into the long-term consequences of methylphenidate use/abuse.

Children who are taking methylphenidate at recommended dosage levels have experienced a "zombie" effect, where the drug dampens personal initiative (Breggin, 1998; Diller, 1998). This seems to be a common effect of methylphenidate, even when it is used by normal individuals, although in the case of students with ADHD, this effect is claimed to be beneficial (Diller, 1998). Whether methylphenidate causes a "zombie" effect in children has yet to be determined.

On rare occasions, methylphenidate has been implicated in the development of a drug-induced depression, which might reach the level of suicide attempts (Breggin, 1998). Further, a long-term follow-up study of 5000 adolescents with ADHD who were treated with methylphenidate found that in adulthood, those adolescents who had received methylphenidate were three times as likely to have abused cocaine as were adolescents whose ADHD was treated by other methods (*Alcoholism & Drug Abuse Week*, 1998). However, the results of this study have been challenged (Stocker, 1999b), and the relationship among ADHD, pharmacological treatment of this disorder, and possible predisposition toward substance use disorders has not been clearly identified.

Challenges to the use of methylphenidate as a treatment for ADHD. Breggin (1998) and Diller (1998) are vocal critics of the use of CNS stimulants such as methylphenidate to treat ADHD. Indeed, in spite of what physicians tell children or their parents, Briggin (1998) noted that the professional literature is filled with research studies that failed to demonstrate any significant positive effect from methylphenidate on ADHD. In contrast to this pattern of reports in the clinical literature, parents (and teachers) are often assured that methylphenidate is *the* treatment of choice for ADHD, mainly because "[the] material on [methylphenidate's] lack of efficacy, while readily available in the professional literature, is not presented to the public" (Breggin, 1998, p. 111).

Breggin (1999) is a strong critic of the diagnosis of attention deficit–hyperactivity disorder (ADHD), and although many clinicians dismiss his comments as too extreme, some of his observations appear to have merit. For example, although the long-term benefits of methylphenidate use have never been demonstrated, the American Medical Association supports the long-term use of this medication to control the manifestations of ADHD. Research has also demonstrated that the child's ability to learn new material improves at a significantly lower dose of methylphenidate than is necessary to eliminate behaviors that are not accepted in the classroom (Pagliaro & Pagliaro, 1998). When the student is drugged to the point at which these behaviors are eliminated or controlled, learning suffers, according to the authors. These arguments present thought-provoking challenges to the current forms of pharmacological treatment of ADHD and suggest a need for further research in this area.

The Amphetamines

History of the amphetamines. Chemically, the amphetamines are *analogs*[1] of ephedrine (Lit, Wiviott-Tishler, Wong, & Hyman 1996). The amphetamines were first discovered in 1887, but it was not until 1927 that one of these compounds was found to have medicinal value (Kaplan & Sadock, 1996; Lingeman, 1974). Following the introduction of ephedrine for the treatment of asthma, concern arose that the demand might exceed the supply. Pharmaceutical companies began to search for synthetic alternatives to ephedrine and found that the amphetamines had a similar effect on asthma pa-

tients. In 1932 an amphetamine product called Benzedrine was introduced for use in the treatment of asthma and rhinitis (Karch, 1996; Derlet & Heischober, 1990). The drug was contained in an inhaler similar to "smelling salts." This ampule, which could be purchased over the counter, would be broken, releasing the concentrated amphetamine liquid into the surrounding cloth. The Benzedrine ampule would then be held under the nose, and the fumes inhaled, to reduce the symptoms of asthma.

It was not long, however, before it was discovered that the Benzedrine ampules could be unwrapped, carefully broken open, and the concentrated Benzedrine injected,[2] causing effects similar to that of cocaine. The dangers of cocaine were well known to drug abusers/addicts of the era, but because the long-term effects of the amphetamines were not known, they were viewed as a safe substitute for cocaine. Shortly afterwards, the world was plunged into World War II, and amphetamines were used by personnel in the American, British, German, and Japanese armed forces to counteract fatigue and heighten endurance (Brecher, 1972). United States Army Air Corps crew members stationed in England alone took an estimated 180,000,000 Benzedrine pills to help them stay awake and work longer during the war (Lovett, 1994). It is rumored that Adolf Hitler was addicted to amphetamines (Witkin, 1995).

It is possible to understand the use of amphetamines during World War II as being necessary to meet the demands of combat. But for reasons that are not clear, there were waves of amphetamine abuse in both Sweden and Japan immediately following World War II (Snyder, 1986). The amphetamines were frequently prescribed to patients in the United States in the 1950s and 1960s, and no less a person than President John F. Kennedy is rumored to have used methamphetamine during his term in office in the early 1960's (Witkin, 1995). The amphetamines continued to gain popularity as drugs of abuse, and by 1970 their use had reached "epidemic proportions" (Kaplan & Sadock, 1996, p. 305) in the United States. Physicians would prescribe amphetamines for patients who wished to lose weight or who were depressed, and illicit amphetamine users

---

[1]See the Glossary and Chapter 35.

[2]Needless to say, amphetamines are no longer sold over the counter (that is, without a prescription).

would take the drug because it helped them to feel good. Many of the pills prescribed by physicians for patients were "diverted" to illicit markets, and there is no way of knowing how many of the 10 billion amphetamine tablets manufactured in the United States in the year 1970 were actually used as prescribed.

The amphetamines occupy a unique position in history, for medical historians now believe that the arrival of large amounts of amphetamines, especially the form known as methamphetamine, contributed to the outbreak of drug-related violence that put an end to San Francisco's "summer of love" of 1967 (Smith, 1997). Amphetamine abusers had also discovered that when used at high dosage levels, the amphetamines caused agitation and could induce death from cardiovascular collapse. They had also discovered that these compounds could induce a severe depressive state that might reach suicidal proportions and that might last for days, or weeks, after the drug was discontinued. By the mid-1970s, amphetamine abusers had come to understand that chronic amphetamine use would come to dominate and undermine the individual's life. In San Francisco, physicians at the Haight-Ashbury "free clinic" coined the slogan "Speed kills" to warn the general public of the dangers of amphetamine abuse (Smith, 1997).

By this time, physicians had discovered that the amphetamines were not so effective as was once thought in the treatment of depressive states or obesity. This fact, along with the development of new medications for the treatment of depression, reduced the frequency with which physicians prescribed amphetamines. The amphetamines were classified as Schedule II substances by the U.S. government, which also limited their legitimate use. However, as we shall see, they continue to have a limited role in the control of human suffering. Further, although the dangers of amphetamine use are well known, during the "Operation Desert Storm" campaign of 1991, some 65% of U. S. pilots in the combat theatre admitted to having used an amphetamine compound at least once during combat operations (Emonson & Vanderbeek, 1995). Thus the amphetamines have never entirely disappeared from either the illicit drug world or the physician's handbag.

Medical uses of the amphetamines. The amphetamines improve the action of the smooth muscles of the body (Hoffman & Lefkowitz, 1990) and thus have the potential of improving athletic performance at least to some degree. However, these effects are not uniform, and regulatory agencies for different sports routinely test for evidence of amphetamine use among athletes. For these reasons, amphetamine abuse among athletes is limited.

The amphetamines have an *anorexic* side effect,[3] and at one time this side effect of the amphetamines was thought to be useful in the treatment of obesity. Unfortunately, subsequent research has demonstrated that the amphetamines are only minimally effective in weight control. Tolerance to the appetite-suppressing side effect of the amphetamines develops in only 4 weeks (Snyder, 1986). Thereafter, it is not uncommon for the user to regain all the weight initially lost. Indeed, research has demonstrated that after a 6-month period, there is no significant difference between the amount of weight lost by patients using amphetamines and by patients who simply dieted to lose weight (Maxmen & Ward, 1995).

Prior to the 1970s, the amphetamines were thought to be antidepressants and were widely prescribed for the treatment of depression. However, research revealed that the antidepressant effect of the amphetamines was short-lived. With the introduction of more effective antidepressant agents, the amphetamines fell into disfavor as a treatment for depression, and these are now only rarely used as an adjunct to the treatment of this disorder (Potter, Rudorfer, & Goodwin, 1987). However, the amphetamines have been found to be the treatment of choice for a rare neurological condition known as *narcolepsy*.[4] Researchers believe that narcolepsy is caused by a chemical imbalance within the brain in which the neurotransmitted dopamine is not released in sufficient amounts to maintain wakefulness. By forcing the neurons in the brain to release their stores of dopamine, the amphetamines are thought to at least partially correct the dopamine imbalance that causes narcolepsy (Doghramji, 1989).

The first recorded use of an amphetamine, Benzedrine, for the control of hyperactive children occurred in 1938 (Pliszka, 1998). Surprisingly, although the amphetamines are CNS *stimulants*, they appear to have a calming effect on individuals who have Attention

[3]See the Glossary.
[4]See the Glossary.

Deficit–Hyperactivity Disorder (ADHD). However, the use of amphetamines to treat ADHD is quite controversial, and although they are recognized as being of value in the control of ADHD symptoms, there are those who suggest that these medications may do more harm than good (Breggin, 1998).

Pharmacology of the Amphetamines

The amphetamine family of chemicals consists of several different variations of the parent compound. Each of these variations yields a molecule that is similar to the others, except for minor variations in potency and pharmacological characteristics. The most common forms of amphetamine are dextroamphetamine (*d*-amphetamine sulfate), which is considered twice as potent as the other common form of amphetamine (Lingeman, 1974), and methamphetamine (or, *d*-desoxyephedrine hydrochloride). Because of its longer half-life and its ability to cross the blood-brain barrier, illicit amphetamine abusers seem to prefer methamphetamine over dextroamphetamine (Albertson, Derlet, & Van Hoozen, 1999).

Methods of administration in medical practice. There are several methods by which physicians might administer an amphetamine to a patient. The drug molecule tends to be basic and, when taken orally, is easily absorbed through the lining of the small intestine (Laurence & Bennett, 1992). However, in spite of the fact that the amphetamines have been used in medical practice for generations, very little else is known about their absorption from the gastronintestinal tract in humans (Jenkins & Cone, 1998). It is known that a single oral dose of amphetamine will begin to have an effect on the user in 20 (Siegel, 1991) to 30 minutes (Mirin, Weiss, & Greenfield, 1991). The amphetamine molecule is also easily absorbed into the body when injected either into muscle tissue or into a vein.

In the normal patient who has received a single oral dose of an amphetamine, the peak plasma levels are achieved in 1–3 hours. The biological half-lives of the different forms of amphetamine vary, as a result of their different chemical structures. For example, the biological half-life of a single oral dose of dextroamphetamine is between 10–34 hours, whereas that of a single oral dose of methamphetamine is only 4–5 hours (Fuller & Sajatovic, 1999; Shannon, Wilson, & Stang, 1995; Medical Economics Company, 1999; Derlet & Heischober, 1990).

The basic amphetamine molecule closely resembles that of two different neurotransmitters: norepinephrine and dopamine, so amphetamines might be classified as agonists of these neurotransmitters (King & Ellinwood, 1997). The effects of amphetamines in the peripheral regions of the body are caused by its ability to stimulate norepinephrine release, whereas its CNS effects are the result of its impact on the dopamine-using regions of the brain (Lit, Wiviott-Tishler, Wong, & Hyman, 1996). Once in the brain, the amphetamine molecule is absorbed into those neurons that use dopamine as a neurotransmitter and stimulates those neurons to release their dopamine stores (Hyman & Nestler, 1996). The mesolimbic region of the brain is rich in dopamine-containing neurons and is thought to be part of the "pleasure center" of the brain. This fact seems to account for the ability of the amphetamines to cause a sense of euphoria in the user. Another region in the brain where the amphetamines have an effect is the medulla (which is involved in the control of respiration); here, the drug causes the individual to breathe more deeply and more rapidly. At normal dosage levels, the cortex is also stimulated, resulting in reduced feelings of fatigue and possibly increased concentration (Kaplan & Sadock, 1996).

There is considerable variation in the level of individual sensitivity to the effects of the amphetamines. For example, there have been rare reports of toxic reactions to amphetamines at dosage levels as low as 2 mg (Hoffman & Lefkowitz, 1990). Although the estimated lethal dose of amphetamines for a nontolerant individual is 20–25 mg/kg (Chan, Chen, Lee, & Deng, 1994), there is one clinical report of a case where a dose of only 1.5 mg/kg was fatal. There are also case reports where amphetamine-naive individuals (people who have not developed tolerance to the amphetamines) have survived a total single dose of 400–500 mg (or 7.5 mg/kg of body weight for a 160-pound person). However, the patients who ingested these dosage levels required medical support to overcome the toxic effects of the amphetamines. Individuals who are tolerant to the effects of the amphetamines may use massive doses "without apparent ill effect" (Hoffman & Lefkowitz, 1990, p. 212).

Some of the amphetamine in the body is biotransformed by the liver, and during this process a number of metabolites are formed. The exact number of metabolites varies with amphetamine. During the process of methamphetamine biotransformation, seven different metabolites are formed before the drug is finally eliminated from the body.

Although some of the amphetamines are biotransformed by the liver, a significant percentage of the amphetamines are excreted from the body essentially unchanged. Researchers have found that in the first several days following a single oral dose of an amphetamine, between 35% and 45% is excreted unchanged by the kidneys (Karch, 1996). If the individual's urine is quite acidic, up to 60% of a dose of amphetamine will be filtered from the blood and excreted unchanged (Shields, 1990). However, if the individual's urine is extremely alkaline, as little as 5% of a dose of amphetamine will be filtered out of the blood by the kidneys and excreted unchanged. This is because the drug molecules tend to be reabsorbed by the kidneys when the urine is more alkaline. Thus, the speed at which a dose of amphetamines is excreted from the body varies in response to how acidic the individual's urine is when the drug passes through the kidneys.

At one point, physicians were trained to try to make a patient's urine more acidic in order to speed up the excretion of the amphetamine molecules following an overdose. In recent years, however, it has been found that this treatment method increases the chances that the patient will develop cardiac arrhythmias and/or seizures, and physicians are less likely to utilize urine acidification as a treatment method for amphetamine overdose than they were 30 years ago (Albertson, Derlet, & Van Hoozen, 1999; Carvey, 1998).

Neuroadaptation/tolerance to amphetamines. The steady use of an amphetamine by a patient will result in an incomplete state of neuroadaptation. For example, when a physician prescribes an amphetamine to treat narcolepsy, it is possible for the patient to be maintained on the same dose for years without any loss of efficacy (Jaffe, 2000a). However, patients become tolerant to the anorexic effects of the amphetamines after only a few weeks, and the initial drug-induced sense of well-being does not last beyond the first few doses at therapeutic levels.

Interactions between the amphetamines and other medications. Patients should avoid taking amphetamines with fruit juices or ascorbic acid, because these substances decrease the absorption of amphetamines

(Maxmen & Ward, 1995). Patients should avoid mixing amphetamines with opiates; these drugs increase the anorexic and analgesic effects of narcotic analgesics. Further, patients who are taking a class of antidepressants known as monoamine oxidase inhibitors (MAOIs or MAO inhibitors) should avoid amphetamines, because combining these drugs can result in dangerous elevations in blood pressure (Barnhill, Ciraulo, Ciraulo, & Greene, 1995). *Always consult with a physician or pharmacist before taking two or more medications at the same time, to make sure that there is no danger of a harmful interaction between the chemicals being used.*

Subjective Experience of Amphetamine Use

The effects of the amphetamines on any given individual depend on that individual's mental state, the dosage level utilized, the relative potency of the specific form of amphetamine, and the manner in which the drug is used. The subjective effects of a single dose of amphetamines are very similar to those of cocaine or adrenaline (Kaminski, 1992). However, there are some major differences: (1) Whereas the effects of cocaine might last from a few minutes to an hour at most, the effects of the amphetamines last many hours. (2) Unlike cocaine, the amphetamines are effective when used orally. (3) Unlike cocaine, the amphetamines have only a very small anesthetic effect (Ritz, 1999).

When amphetamines are used in medical practice, the usual oral dosage level is between 15 and 30 mg per day (Lingeman, 1974). However, this depends on the potency of the amphetamine or amphetamine-like drug being used (Julien, 1992). At low to moderate oral dosage levels, the individual will experience feelings of increased alertness, an elevation of mood, mild euphoria, less mental fatigue, and an improved level of concentration (Kaplan & Sadock, 1996). Like many drugs of abuse, the amphetamines stimulate the "pleasure center" in the brain. Thus, when initially used, both the amphetamines and cocaine produce "a neurochemical magnification of the pleasure experienced in most activities" (Gawin & Ellinwood, 1988; p. 1174). The authors go on to note that the initial use of amphetamines or cocaine will

produce alertness and a sense of well-being, lower anxiety and social inhibitions, and heighten energy, self-esteem, and the emotions aroused by interpersonal experiences. Although they magnify pleasure, they do not distort it; hallucinations are usually absent. (p. 1174)

Side Effects of Amphetamine Use at Normal Dosage Levels

Patients who are taking amphetamines under a physician's supervision may experience such side effects as dryness of the mouth, nausea, anorexia, headache, insomnia, and periods of confusion (Fawcett & Busch, 1995). The patient's systolic and diastolic blood pressure will both increase, and the heart rate may reflexively slow down. More than 10% of the patients who take an amphetamine as prescribed experience an amphetamine-induced tachycardia (Fuller & Sajatovic, 1999; Breggin, 1998). Amphetamine use, even at therapeutic dosage levels, has been known to cause/exacerbate the symptoms of Tourette's syndrome (Fuller & Sajatovic, 1999; Breggin, 1998). Other potential side effects at normal dosage levels include dizziness, agitation, a feeling of apprehension, flushing, pallor, muscle pains, excessive sweating, and delirium (Fawcett & Busch, 1995). Rarely, a patient experiences a drug-induced psychotic reaction when taking an amphetamine at recommended dosage levels (Fuller & Sajatovic, 1999; Breggin, 1998).

Surprisingly, in light of the fact that the amphetamines are CNS stimulants, almost 40% of patients on amphetamines experience drug-induced feelings of depression, which may become so severe that the individual attempts suicide (Breggin, 1998). Feelings of depression and a sense of fatigue, or lethargy, which may last for a few hours or for days, are common when amphetamine use is discontinued.

II. CNS STIMULANT ABUSE

Scope of the Problem of Stimulant Abuse and Addiction

In the United States, amphetamine abuse peaked in the late 1960s or early 1970s, reached its lowest point in the late 1980s or early 1990s, and has been gradually increasing in the past few years as methamphetamine has replaced cocaine as the stimulant of choice (Graves, 1998). Currently, the peak age of amphet-

amine abuse is the early 20s (Albertson, Derlet, & Van Hoozen, 1999).

Nationally, methamphetamine appears to be the most popular *intravenously administered* drug currently in use by illicit drug abusers (Norton, Burton, & McGirr, 1996). It is estimated that about 800,000 people in the United States have abused some form of amphetamine at least once a month (Nash & Park, 1997), and 5 million people in the United States have abused methamphetamine at least once in their lives (Office of National Drug Control Policy, 1996). Users typically use amphetamines manufactured in clandestine laboratories, the majority of which are in California. It is estimated that a single ounce of methamphetamine manufactured in an illicit laboratory can provide about 110 doses of the drug. Another major source of illicit amphetamines is Mexican drug dealers, who manufacture the drug in that country and then smuggle it into the United States (Witkin, 1995; Lovett, 1994).

Effects of the CNS Stimulants When Abused

Ephedrine

Ephedrine was once available over the counter without restriction as a treatment for asthma and nasal congestion. The drug was often abused by cross-country truckers and college students, who used it to ward off the effects of fatigue. Ephedrine is also used by many "street" chemists to manufacture illicit amphetamines (*The Addiction Letter*, 1995b). Ephedrine is often sold in combination with other herbs under the guise of "herbal ecstasy" (Schwartz & Miller, 1997). Because of its potential for abuse, and because newer, more effective pharmaceuticals are available for the control of asthma symptoms, the federal government imposed restrictions on the over-the-counter sale of ephedrine in 1994. However, ephedrine is still available without a prescription, and it is still abused.

Effects of ephedrine when abused. Ephedrine is usually abused for its ability to stimulate the CNS. Alcohol abusers often ingest ephedrine to counteract the sedative effects of alcohol so that they can drink longer. At very high doses, ephedrine can evoke a sense of euphoria.

Methods of ephedrine abuse. The most common method of ephedrine abuse is for the user to ingest ephedrine pills purchased over the counter. On rare occasions, the pills are crushed and the powder either "snorted" or (even more infrequently) injected.

Consequences of ephedrine abuse. Abuse results in an exaggeration of the side effects of ephedrine seen at normal dosage levels. Although adverse effects *are* possible at very low doses, the higher the dosage level, the more likely the user is to experience an adverse effect from ephedrine (Antonio, 1997). At high dosage levels, ephedrine can increase the work-load of the cardiac muscle and cause the muscle tissue to use more oxygen—potentially dangerous effects if the user has some form of coronary artery disease that limits the amount of blood that can reach the muscle tissue. Other complications from ephedrine abuse may include necrosis (death) of the tissues of the intestinal tract, potentially fatal arrhythmias, urinary retention, irritation of heart muscle tissue (especially in patients with damaged hearts), nausea, vomiting, stroke, and exacerbation of preexisting psychopathology (American Society of Health-System Pharmacists, 1999; Antonio, 1997).

Ritalin (Methylphenidate)

Abusers report that the drug causes them to experience a feeling of euphoria. Abusers ingest this medication orally, which reportedly causes the user to experience a sense of mild euphoria (Diller, 1998). On occasion the tablet is crushed and the resulting power inhaled ("snorting") (Diller, 1998). The strongest effects of methylphenidate abuse are achieved when users inject the drug intravenously after crushing methylphenidate tablets and mixing the powder with water (Volkow *et al.*, 1998). These investigators theorized that intravenous methylphenidate brings about the rapid blockage of the dopamine transporter system that seems to cause the user to feel "high," whereas the slower absorption of the drug from oral or intranasal doses fails to accomplish this effect.

The Amphetamines

Effects of the amphetamines when abused. When the amphetamines are abused, their effects vary, depending on the route by which the drug was administered. At low doses, such as a single oral dose of amphetamines, the user experiences a sense of well-being, energy, and gentle euphoria. Some abusers claim that the amphet-

amines function as an aphrodisiac, but there is little scientific evidence to support this claim.

When methamphetamine is either injected into a vein or smoked, users experience an intense sense of euphoria, which has been called a rush or a flash. This sensation was described as "instant euphoria" by the author Truman Capote (quoted in Siegel, 1991, p. 72). Other users have compared the flash to sexual orgasm. Researchers have not studied the rush in depth, but it appears to last for only a short time and is limited to the initial period of amphetamine abuse (Jaffe, 2000a). Subsequent doses of amphetamine do not bring about the same intense euphoria, because the individual becomes tolerant to the euphoric effects of the amphetamines. Following the initial rush, the user may experience a warm glow, or gentle euphoria, that may last for several hours.

The chronic use of amphetamines at high dosage levels has been implicated as the cause of violent outbursts, which have even resulted in the death of bystanders (King & Ellinwood, 1997). Animal research suggests that following periods of chronic abuse at high dosage levels, norepinephrine levels are depleted throughout the brain and that the brain's norepinephrine may not return to normal even after six months of abstinence (King & Ellinwood, 1997). The effects of chronic amphetamine abuse on dopamine levels in the brain appears to be limited to the region known as the *caudate putamen*, but here again, animal research suggests that the dopamine levels in the caudate putamen may not return to normal even after 6 months of abstinence (King & Ellinwood, 1997). Animal research also suggests that the chronic use of amphetamines at high dosage levels may be toxic to those neurons in the brain that use serotonin (King & Ellinwood, 1997). Finally, although the mechanism by which this is accomplished is not clear, changes in the vasculature of the brain have been documented in chronic amphetamine abusers. It is also not clear whether these changes are permanent (Breggin, 1997).

Methods of amphetamine abuse. As we noted earlier in this chapter, the amphetamines are well absorbed when taken orally. The amphetamines are also well absorbed when injected into muscle tissue or into a vein. In the 1950s, illicit drug chemists developed a smokable form of methamphetamine that is sold under the name of "ice." When smoked, the amphetamine molecule is absorbed into the circulation through the lining of the lungs and reaches the brain in just a matter of seconds. In the U.S., the most common methods of methamphetamine abuse are the oral ingestion of tablets, smoking, or injection of methamphetamine powder (Karch, 1996). Less often, amphetamine powder is "snorted," the amphetamine molecule being absorbed through the tissues of the naso-pharynx.

Subjective effects of amphetamine abuse. The subjective effects of the amphetamines depend on whether tolerance to the drug has developed and on the method by which the drug was used. Amphetamine abusers who are not tolerant to the drug's effects and who either use oral forms of the drug or "snort" it report a sense of euphoria that may last several hours. Individuals who are not tolerant to the drug's effects and who inject amphetamines report an intense feeling of euphoria, followed by a less intense feeling of well-being that may last several hours.

Tolerance to the amphetamines. Amphetamine abusers quickly become tolerant to amphetamine-induced euphoric feelings. In an effort to recapture the initial drug-induced euphoria, amphetamine abusers try to overcome their tolerance to the drug in one of three ways: First, amphetamine *abusers* may try to limit their exposure to the drug to isolated periods of time, allowing their bodies to return to normal before the next exposure. The development of tolerance requires *constant* exposure to the compound, so some individuals are able to abuse amphetamines for years by following this pattern.

Other amphetamine abusers attempt to recapture the initial feeling of euphoria by using higher and higher doses (Peluso & Peluso, 1988). Some chronic amphetamine users, for example, have reached the point where they repeatedly inject small doses of amphetamines over the course of the day, ultimately injecting as much as 5,000–15,000 mg in a 24-hour period (Chan, Chen, Lee, & Deng, 1994; Derlet & Heischober, 1990). Such dosage levels would be fatal to the "naive" (inexperienced) drug user and are well within the dosage range found to be neurotoxic in animal studies. This pattern of amphetamine use is called a "speed run." Speed runs, which may last for hours or days, are a sign that the individual has progressed from amphetamine abuse to addiction to these compounds.

The third method by which amphetamine abusers try to overcome their tolerance to the drug is to substitute intravenously administered amphetamines for the oral or the intranasal doses. The intravenous form of drug administration rapidly delivers a large amount of concentrated drug. This process of "graduating" from oral or intranasal doses to intravenous doses is usually a sign of amphetamine addiction.

Consequences of Amphetamine Abuse

There is wide variation in what might be considered a toxic dose of amphetamine (Julien, 1992). However, a general rule is that the higher the concentration of amphetamines in the blood, the more likely the individual is to experience one or more of the adverse effects. Whereas adverse effects are rarely encountered when the drugs are used at therapeutic doses under the supervision of a physician, *abusers* are more likely to experience one or more amphetamine-induced side effects as their dosage level increases to overcome their tolerance to the drug.

Central nervous system. Researchers have discovered that amphetamine abuse can cause damage both on a cellular level and in large regions of the brain. At the cellular level, it has been discovered that up to 50% of the dopamine-producing cells in the brain may be damaged after prolonged exposure to even low levels of methamphetamine (Community Anti-Drug Coalitions of America, 1997). In addition, methamphetamine seems to be especially toxic to serotonin-producing neurons (King & Ellinwood, 1997; Jaffe, 2000a). There is evidence that methamphetamine-induced cellular damage reflects the ability of this compound to stimulate glutamate release within the brain and that higher levels of methamphetamine result in toxic levels of glutamate being released (Fischman & Haney, 1999). Animal research suggests that methamphetamine-induced brain damage on the cellular level might persist for more than 3 years (Fischman & Haney, 1999).

Amphetamine-induced regional brain damage is caused by the ability of these compounds, when abused, to bring about both temporary and permanent changes in the blood flow patterns within the brain. Some of the more dangerous temporary changes in cerebral blood flow caused by amphetamine abuse are the development of hypertensive episodes, cerebral vasculitis, and vasospasm in the blood vessels in the brain. All of these amphetamine-induced changes in cerebral blood flow can result in a cerebral vascular hemorrhage (CVA, or stroke) that may or may not be fatal (Albertson, Derlet, & van Hoozen, 1999; King & Ellinwood, 1997; Brust, 1997). Further, reductions in cerebral blood flow were found in 76% of amphetamine abusers, and these changes were found to persist for years after the individual had discontinued use of the drugs (Buffenstein, Heaster, & Ko, 1999).

Chronic amphetamine abusers might experience sleep disturbances for up to 4 weeks after their last use of the drug (Satel, Kosten, Schuckit, & Fischman, 1993). The authors also cited evidence that chronic amphetamine users might have abnormal EEG tracings (a measure of the electrical activity in the brain) for up to 3 months after their last drug use. Another very rare complication of amphetamine use/abuse is the development of the neurological condition known as *serotonin syndrome* (Mills, 1995).[5]

The emotions. The amphetamines can boost anxiety in both new and chronic users (Satel, Kosten, Schuckit, & Fischman, 1993). Up to 75% of amphetamine abusers report significant degrees of anxiety when they start using amphetamines (Breggin, 1998). Amphetamine-related anxiety episodes may reach the proportions of actual panic attacks, which have been known to persist for months, or even years, after the last use of amphetamines (Satel, Kosten, Schuckit, & Fischman, 1993).

It is not uncommon for illicit amphetamine users to try to counteract the drug-induced anxiety and tension with alcohol (a CNS depressant), marijuana, or benzodiazepines.[6] For example, Peluso and Peluso (1988) estimated that half of all regular amphetamine users may also be classified as heavy drinkers. Amphetamine users also might experience periods of drug-induced confusion, irritability, fear, suspicion, hallucinations, and/or delusions(King & Ellinwood, 1997; Julien, 1992). Other possible consequences of amphetamine abuse include assaultiveness, tremor, headache, weakness, insomnia, panic states, impotence, tachycardia, diarrhea or constipation, nausea, vomiting, suicidal tendencies, and homicidal tendencies (Albertson, Derlet, & van Hoozen, 1999; Derlet & Heischober, 1990). Physicians have

found that the compounds haloperidol and diazepam are effective in helping the individual calm down from an amphetamine-related period of agitation (Albertson, Derlet, & Van Hoozen, 1999).

The first clinical description of an amphetamine-induced psychotic reaction appeared in 1938 (Karch, 1996). In its early stages, this drug-induced psychosis is often indistinguishable from schizophrenia and may include confusion, suspiciousness, paranoia, hallucinations, delusional thinking, and periods of aggression (King & Ellinwood, 1997; Beebe & Walley, 1995; Kaplan & Sadock, 1996). The ability of the amphetamines to induce a psychotic state is reflected in the fact that 46% of amphetamine abusers report hallucinations and that 52% experience significant degrees of paranoia when they first begin to abuse amphetamines (Breggin, 1998). But the amphetamine-induced hallucinations tend to be mainly visual, which is not typical of a true schizophrenic condition (Kaplan & Sadock, 1996). Further, the amphetamine-induced hyperactivity and absence of a thought disorder help to distinguish an amphetamine psychosis from actual schizophrenia, according to the authors.

Under normal conditions, this drug-induced psychosis clears up within days after the drug is discontinued (Kaplan & Sadock, 1996) but, in some cases, it may require weeks or months to clear up. Researchers in Japan following World War II noted that in 15% of the cases of amphetamine-induced psychosis, it took up to 5 years following the last amphetamine use before the drug-induced psychotic condition eased (Flaum & Schultz, 1996). On occasion, the amphetamine-induced psychosis seems to become permanent. It was once thought that the amphetamine-induced psychosis reflected activation of a latent schizophrenia, but the amphetamines are now known to be able to cause a drug-induced psychosis even in essentially normal people (Kaplan & Sadock, 1996). The ability of chronic amphetamine abuse to alter the normal function of the brain seems to make the user vulnerable to the development of a drug-induced paranoid psychosis (Community Anti-Drug Coalitions of America, 1997; Flaum & Schultz, 1996).

Prolonged use of the amphetamines may also result in the individual experiencing a condition known as *formication*, the sensation of bugs crawling either on or just under the skin (*The Harvard Medical School Mental Health Letter*, 1990; Siegel, 1991). Victims have

---

[5]See the Glossary.

[6]The reverse is also true: Alcohol abusers may ingest an amphetamine, or other CNS stimulant, in an attempt to counteract the sedation that results from heavy drinking.

been known to scratch or burn the skin in an attempt to rid themselves of these unseen bugs. Many individuals also become fatigued and/or depressed following prolonged amphetamine abuse. It is not uncommon for the individual's depression to reach suicidal proportions (Fawcett & Busch, 1995). The post-amphetamine depressive reaction may last for *months* following cessation of amphetamine use.

The digestive system. There have been a few reports of liver damage associated with amphetamine abuse (Jones, Jarvie, McDermid, & Proudfoot, 1994). However, it is not clear by what mechanism(s) illicit amphetamines damage the liver. The consequences of prolonged amphetamine use, like that of cocaine, include the various complications seen in individuals who have neglected their dietary requirements. Vitamin deficiencies are a common consequence of chronic amphetamine abuse (Gold & Verebey, 1984). Prolonged use of the amphetamines may result in the user's vomiting, becoming anorexic, or developing diarrhea (Kaplan & Sadock, 1996).

The cardiovascular system. Overall, the amphetamines appear to have less potential than cocaine for causing cardiovascular damage (Karch, 1996). However, this does not mean that amphetamine abuse carries no risk of cardiovascular damage. For example, abuse of amphetamines can result in hypertensive reactions, tachycardia, or arrhythmias, especially when they are used at high dosage levels (Wender, 1995).

Amphetamine abusers have been known to suffer a number of cardiac problems, including chest pain (angina), atrial and ventricular arrhythmias, congestive heart failure (Derlet & Horowitz, 1995), myocardial ischemia (Derlet & Heischober, 1990), cardiomyopathy (Brent, 1995; Fawcett & Busch, 1995), and myocardial infarction (Fawcett & Busch, 1995; Packe, Garton, & Jennings, 1990). The amphetamines appear to induce a series of spasms in the coronary arteries at the same time as the heart's workload is increased by the drug's effects on the rest of the body (Hong, Matsuyama, & Nur, 1991; Packe, Garton, & Jennings, 1990). Also, through an unknown mechanism, amphetamine abuse can cause rhabodmyolysis in some users (Richards, 2000).

The pulmonary system. There has been little research on the impact of amphetamine abuse and lung function (Albertson, Walby, & Derlet, 1995). Because amphetamine smoking is a common method by which the drug is abused, it might be reasonable to expect side effects similar to those found when the user smokes cocaine. Thus amphetamine abuse might result in sinusitis, pulmonary infiltrates, pulmonary edema, exacerbation of asthma, pulmonary hypertension, and pulmonary hemorrhage/infarct (Albertson, Walby, & Derlet, 1995).

Other consequences of amphetamine abuse. There is evidence that amphetamine use/abuse exacerbates the symptoms of some medical disorders, such as Tourette's syndrome and tardive dyskinesia (Lopez & Jeste, 1997). In both men and women, amphetamine abuse may result in sexual performance problems (Finger, Lund, & Slagel, 1997). High doses of amphetamines or their chronic use can cause an inhibition of orgasm in the user, according to the authors, as well as delayed or inhibited ejaculation in men. Smoking methamphetamine has resulted in the formation of ulcers on the cornea of the eyes of some users (Chuck, Williams, Goldberg, & Lubniewski, 1996).

The addictive potential of amphetamines. Although most amphetamine users will not become addicted, some abusers do become either emotionally or physically addicted to these chemicals (Gawin & Ellinwood, 1988). At present, there is no test to identify those most "at risk" for amphetamine addiction—in itself enough reason not to abuse of these chemicals!

One effect of the amphetamines that contributes to their addictive potential is that the drugs create "vivid, long-term memories" (Gawin & Ellinwood, 1988, p. 1175) of the drug experience. These memories form part of the foundation of the craving that many amphetamine users report when they stop using the drug. The recovery process from prolonged amphetamine use follows the same pattern seen for cocaine, and this "euphoric recall" is a very real problem for recovering abusers.

"Ice"

In the late 1970s, a new form of methamphetamine known as "ice" was reported as having been abused on the mainland United States for the first time. Historical evidence suggests that ice was brought to Hawaii from Japan by U.S. Army troops following World War II, where its use remained endemic to Hawaii for many years (*Health News*, 1990). Police and drug abuse professionals now believe that ice reached the mainland

United States in the late 1970s or early 1980s (*The Economist*, 1989). However, this form of methamphetamine did not gain much notoriety until the news media on the West Coast began reporting its effects and dangers. Potential users on the mainland began to ask about the drug, creating a market for ice, and its use began to spread from a few isolated areas on the West Coast to other regions of this country.

Nobody can predict what the future of ice will be in this country. It has not spread as quickly as had once been anticipated, and by 1999 only 4.8% of the high school seniors surveyed, and 3.3% of the young adults between 19 and 32, admitted to having used ice at least once (Johnston, O'Malley, & Bachman, 2000b). The feared "ice storm," or epidemic of ice use, that was expected in the early 1990s never materialized (Brent, 1995; *Brown University Digest of Addiction Theory and Application*, 1994; *Forensic Drug Abuse Advisor*, 1994d). But ice does appear to be slowly spreading across the country.

Ice is a colorless, odorless form of concentrated crystal methamphetamine that resembles a chip of ice or clear rock candy. Some samples of ice sold on the street have been up to 98–100% pure amphetamine (Kaminski, 1992). Since its introduction, Ice has become quite popular in some places (Kaminski, 1992; *Playboy*, 1990). It is often sold on the street as a "safe" alternative to crack cocaine (*Mayo Clinic Health Letter*, 1989), and there are many different "street" names for ice.

How ice is used. Ice is smoked in a manner similar to crack. Like crack, the drug crosses into the blood through the lungs and reaches the brain in a matter of seconds. However, whereas the high from crack lasts perhaps 20 minutes, the high from ice lasts significantly longer; estimates range from 8 hours (*Playboy*, 1990) to 12 (*Minneapolis Star Tribune*, 1989; *Health News*, 1990), 14 (*The Economist*, 1989), 18 (McEnroe, 1990), 24 (Evanko, 1991), and even 30 hours (Kaminski, 1992). The long duration of its effect, while obviously in some dispute, is consistent with the pharmacological properties of the amphetamines as compared with those of cocaine.

How ice is produced. Like crack, this form of methamphetamine is manufactured in clandestine laboratories. However, unlike crack, which must be processed from cocaine that is smuggled into the country, ice can be manufactured from chemicals legally purchased from any chemical supply store (Siegel, 1991).

The effects of ice. In addition to the physical effects of the amphetamines, users have found that ice has several advantages over crack. First, although it is more expensive than crack, ice is actually cheaper dose for dose. Second, because of its duration of effect, it *seems* to be more potent than crack. Third, because ice melts at a lower temperature than crack, it does not require as much heat to use. This means that ice can be smoked without elaborate equipment.

Fourth, because it is odorless, ice may be smoked in public without any characteristic smell alerting passersby that it is being used. Finally, if the user decides to stop smoking ice for a moment or two, it cools and reforms as a crystal. This makes it highly transportable and also offers another advantage over crack: The user can use only a piece of the drug at any given time, rather than having to use it all at once.

Complications of ice abuse. Essentially, the complications of ice use are the same as those seen with other amphetamines. This is understandable; it is simply a different form of methamphetamine than the powder or pills sold on the street for intravenous or oral use. However, the typical amount of methamphetamine admitted into the body when the user smokes ice is *between 150 and 1000 times the maximum recommended therapeutic dosage* for methamphetamine (Hong, Matsuyama, & Nur, 1991). At such high dosage levels, it is common for the abuser to experience one or more adverse effects.

In addition to the adverse effects of amphetamine abuse, which ice users also experience, there are many problems specifically associated with the use of ice. Methamphetamine is a vasoconstrictor, which might be why some ice users develop potentially dangerous elevations in body temperature (Beebe & Walley, 1995). When the body temperature passes above 104°F, the prognosis for recovery is quite poor. There have also been reports that female patients who have had anesthesia to prepare them for caesarian sections have suffered cardiovascular collapse because of the interaction between the anesthesia and ice. Methamphetamine abuse has been known to cause kidney and/or lung damage, permanent damage to the structure of the brain, pulmonary edema, vascular spasm, cardiomyopathy, drug-induced psychotic reactions, acute myocardial infarctions (heart attacks), and cerebral arteritis (Albertson,

Walby, & Derlet, 1995; Hong, Matsuyama, & Nur, 1991; *Health News*, 1990). As these findings suggest, ice is hardly a safe drug.

It now appears that the addiction potential of ice is as great as that of crack, if not greater (*Health News*, 1990). But ice is not the last word in CNS stimulants. Indeed, a new CNS stimulant has been gaining in popularity in this country even as ice spreads from the West Coast to the rest of the United States. In the section that follows, we will discuss this latest arrival, methcathinone.

"Kat"

A recent arrival here in the United States is a CNS stimulant known as methcathinone, or "Kat" (sometimes spelled "Cat," "qat," "Khat," or "miraa"). Kat is a member of the cathinone family of chemicals, which are found naturally in several species of evergreen plants that normally grow 10–20 feet tall and are found in east Africa and southern Arabia (Community Anti-Drug Coalitions of America, 1997; Monroe, 1994; Goldstone, 1993). The plant produces the alkaloids cathinone and cathine, which cause a CNS stimulant effect. Illicit producers have been producing an analog of cathinone known as methcathinone, which has a chemical structure similar to that of the amphetamines and ephedrine (Karch, 1996).

The legal status of Kat. Kat was classified as a Category I[7] controlled substance in 1992, so its manufacture and distribution are illegal (Monroe, 1994).

How Kat is produced. Kat is easily synthesized by illicit laboratories, which use such compounds as drain cleaner, epsom salts, battery acid, acetone, toluene, various dyes, and hydrochloric acid to alter the basic ephedrine molecule. All the components from which Kat is produced are legally available in the United States (Monroe, 1994). These chemicals are mixed in such a way as to add an oxygen molecule to the original ephedrine molecule (*Forensic Drug Abuse Advisor*, 1995c) to produce a compound with the chemical structure (2-methylamino-1-phenylpropan-1-one).

The scope of Kat use. The use of Kat was limited to the former Soviet Union for many years. In the early 1990s, however, the drug surfaced in parts of the United States, and illicit laboratories have been found producing Kat in Michigan, Wisconsin, Illinois, Missouri, Texas, and Ohio (*Forensic Drug Abuse Advisor*, 1995c). It is now possible to purchase Kat in every major U.S. city (Finkelstein, 1997). In contrast to the other drugs of abuse, the evidence suggests that most of those who are addicted to Kat make their own drug (*Alcoholism and Drug Abuse Week*, 1993b).

The effects of Kat. Users typically either inhale or smoke Kat, although it can be injected (Monroe, 1994). The drug's effects are similar to those of the amphetamines. Users report that the drug can cause a sense of euphoria (Community Anti-Drug Coalitions of America, 1997), as well as a more intense high than cocaine (*Alcoholism and Drug Abuse Week*, 1993b). In contrast to cocaine, the effects of Kat can last for between 24 hours (Community Anti-Drug Coalitions of America, 1997) and up to 6 days (Monroe, 1994; Goldstone, 1993).

Once in the body, Kat is biotransformed into ephedrine (*Forensic Drug Abuse Advisor*, 1995c). Thus its effects on the user are very similar to those seen with high dosage levels of ephedrine. Following the period of drug use, it is not uncommon for Kat users to fall into a deep sleep that can last as long as several days (Monroe, 1994). Chronic users also have reported experiencing periods of depression following the use of Kat (*Alcoholism and Drug Abuse Week*, 1993b).

Adverse effects of Kat abuse. Because Kat is a new drug, much remains to be discovered about its effects on the user. The reported adverse effects include drug-induced psychotic reactions, agitation, hyperactivity, a strong, offensive body odor, sores in the mouth and on the tongue, and depression. Death has been known to occur as a result of Kat use, although the exact mechanism of death has not been identified. Monroe (1994) suggested that Kat users are at increased risk for heart attack and stroke. Brent (1995) suggested that an overdose of Kat produces many of the same effects, and responds to the same treatment, as an overdose of amphetamine.

It is still too early to tell how significant a role Kat will play in the world of drug abuse trends of the 21st century. At this time, Kat seems to have attracted not so much the casual user of chemicals as the hard-core stimulant abuser (*Alcoholism and Drug Abuse Week*, 1993b). However, in the 1990s, Kat slowly became more popular among illicit stimulant abusers.

---

[7]See Appendix 4.

Summary

Although they had been discovered in the 1880s the amphetamines were introduced as a treatment for asthma some 50 years later, in the 1930s. The early forms of amphetamine were sold over the counter in cloth-covered ampules that were used in much the same way as smelling salts. Within a short time, however, it was discovered that the ampules were a source of concentrated amphetamine, which could be injected. The resulting "high" was similar to that of cocaine, which had gained a reputation as being a dangerous drug to use and had the added "benefit" of lasting much longer.

The amphetamines were used extensively both during and after World War II. Following the war, American physicians prescribed amphetamines for the treatment of depression and as an aid in weight loss. By the year 1970, amphetamines accounted for eight percent of all prescriptions written. Since then, physicians have come to understand that the amphetamines present a serious potential for abuse. The amphetamines have come under increasingly strict controls that limit the amount of amphetamine manufactured and the reasons for prescribing it.

Because the amphetamines are easily manufactured, there has always been an underground manufacturing and distribution system for these drugs. In the late 1970s and early 1980s, street drug users drifted away from the amphetamines to the supposedly safe stimulant of the early 1900s, cocaine. In the late 1990s, the pendulum started to swing the other way, and illicit drug users began to use the amphetamines, especially methamphetamine, more and more frequently. This new generation of amphetamine addicts has not yet learned what was so painfully discovered by amphetamine users of the late 1960s: "Speed kills."

CHAPTER TWELVE

Cocaine

Introduction

The United States experienced a resurgence of interest in, and abuse of, cocaine in the early to mid-1980s. This wave of cocaine abuse peaked around 1986 and gradually declined in the mid to late 1990s. By the early years of the 21st century, cocaine abuse levels in the United States were significantly lower than those seen 15 years earlier. However, cocaine abuse never entirely disappeared, and it remains a serious problem in this country.

A Brief Overview of Cocaine

At some point in the distant past, a member of the plant species *Erythroxylon coca* began to produce a neurotoxin that would destroy the nervous systems of bugs that tried to ingest its leaves (Breiter, 1999). This neurotoxin, cocaine, was able to ward off most of the insects that would otherwise strip the coca plant of its leaves, allowing the coca plant to thrive in the higher elevations of Peru, Bolivia, and Java (DiGregorio, 1990). When the first settlers arrived in the high mountain regions, they discovered that chewing the leaves of the coca plant helped to ease the feelings of fatigue, thirst, and hunger that they experienced when they worked in the thin mountain air and this enabled them to be able to work for longer periods of time (White, 1989). By the time the first European explorers arrived, the Inca empire was at its height, and the coca plant was being used by the Incas not only in their religious ceremonies but

also as a medium of exchange (Ray & Ksir, 1993), and as part of the burial ritual (Byck, 1987).

Prior to the arrival of the first European explorers, the coca plant's use was generally reserved for the upper classes (Mann, 1992). However, European explorers soon found that by giving native workers coca leaves to chew on, made them more productive. The coca plant became associated with the exploitation of South America by European settlers, who encouraged its widespread use. Even today, the practice of chewing coca leaves, or drinking a form of "tea" brewed from the leaves, has continued. Modern natives of the mountain regions of Peru chew coca leaves mixed with lime, which is obtained from sea shells (White, 1989). The lime works with saliva to release the cocaine from the leaves and to reduce the bitter taste of the coca leaf. Chewing coca leaves is also thought to help the chewer absorb some of the phosphorus, vitamins, and calcium contained in the mixture (White, 1989). Thus, although its primary use is to help the natives work more efficiently at high altitudes, some small nutritional benefit may be obtained from the practice of chewing coca leaves.

As European scientists began to explore the biosphere of South America, they took a passing interest in the coca plant and attempted to isolate the compound(s) that made it so effective in warding off hunger and fatigue. In 1859,[1] a chemist named Albert

---

[1]Schuckit (2000) reported that cocaine was isolated in 1857, rather than 1859.

Neiman isolated the compound that was later named cocaine (Scaros, Westra, & Barone, 1990). This accomplishment enabled researchers to produce large amounts of relatively pure cocaine for research. One of these experiments involved the injection of concentrated cocaine directly into the bloodstream with another new invention: the hypodermic needle.

It was not long before researchers discovered that even orally administered cocaine made the user feel good. Extracts from the coca leaf were used to make a wide range of popular drinks, wines, and elixirs (Martensen, 1996). Physicians of the era, lacking effective pharmaceuticals for most human ills, experimented with cocaine concentrate as a possible agent to treat disease. No less a figure than Sigmund Freud experimented with cocaine, at first thinking it a cure for depression (Rome, 1984)[2] and later investigating it as a possible cure for narcotic withdrawal symptoms (Byck, 1987; Lingeman, 1974). When Freud discovered the drug's previously unsuspected addictive potential, he discontinued his research on cocaine, as did many other scientists of the era.

Cocaine in Recent U.S. History

In response to the decision by the city of Atlanta to prohibit the use of alcohol, John Stith-Pemberton developed a "temperance drink" (Martensen, 1996, p. 1615) that up until 1903 contained 60 mg of cocaine per 8-ounce serving (Gold, 1997). In time, the world would come to know Stith-Pemberton's product by the name "Coca-Cola." Although this is surprising to modern readers, one must remember that consumer protection laws were virtually nonexistent in the 1870s and 1880s, and chemicals such as cocaine and morphine were readily available without a prescription. These compounds were widely used in a wide variety of products and medicines, usually as a hidden ingredient. This practice contributed to the epidemics of cocaine abuse in developed Europe between the years 1886 and 1891, in both Europe and the United States between 1894 and 1899, and again in the United States between 1921 and 1929.

These waves of cocaine abuse/addiction, the use of cocaine in so many patent medicines, with fears over its supposed "narcotic" qualities, and the fear that cocaine was corrupting Southern blacks prompted both passage of the Pure Food and Drug Act of 1906 (Mann, 1992) and the classification of cocaine as a narcotic in 1914 (Martensen, 1996). The Pure Food and Drug Act of 1906 required makers to list the ingredients of a patent medicine or elixir on the label. As a result, cocaine was removed from many patent medicines. With the passage of the Harrison Narcotics Act of 1914, nonmedical cocaine use in the United States was prohibited (Derlet, 1989).

These regulations, the isolation of the United States during the First and Second World Wars, and the introduction of the amphetamines in the 1930s helped to virtually eliminate cocaine abuse in this country. It did not resurface as a major drug of abuse until the late 1960s. By then, cocaine had the reputation in this country of being the "champagne of drugs" (White, 1989, p. 34) for those who could afford it. It again became popular as a drug of abuse in the United States in the 1970s and early 1980s. There are many reasons for this resurgence in cocaine's popularity. First, cocaine had been all but forgotten since the Harrison Narcotics Act of 1914. The bitter lessons about the dangers of cocaine use that had been learned in the late 1800s and early 1900s were either forgotten or dismissed by physicians of the era as "moralistic exaggerations" (Gawin & Ellinwood, 1988, p. 1173).

Also, disillusionment with the amphetamines as drugs of abuse had been growing since the mid-1960s. The amphetamines had acquired a reputation as known killers. Drug users would warn each other that "Speed kills," a reference to the fact that the amphetmines could kill the user in any of a number of different ways. For better or worse, cocaine had the reputation of being able to bring about many of the same sensations as amphetamines without the dangers associated with the abuse of other CNS stimulants. Cocaine's reputation as a special, glamorous drug, combined with increasing government-sanctioned restrictions on amphetamine production by legitimate pharmaceutical companies, all helped focus drug abusers' attention on cocaine.

In the 1970s and the first half of the 1980s cocaine had once again become a popular drug of abuse in a number of countries around the world. For example, by the mid-1970s, the practice of smoking coca paste was

---

[2]Surprisingly, recent research (Post, Weiss, Pert, and Uhde, 1987) has cast doubt on the antidepressant properties of cocaine.

popular in parts of South America but had only started to gain popularity in the United States.

As cocaine became more popular, it attracted the attention of crime organizations who were eager to find new sources of revenue beyond their traditional involvement in narcotics trafficking. At the same time, cocaine dealers were eager to find new markets for their "product" in the United States, where the primary method of cocaine abuse was intranasal inhalation of the cocaine powder. Cocaine "freebase" (discussed below) was known to induce an intense feeling of euphoria when smoked but the user needed elaborate equipment to separate the cocaine base from the powder then being sold on the street (*U.S. News & World Report*, 1991). After a period of experimentation, illicit drug manufacturers developed "crack," a form of cocaine that could be smoked without elaborate preparations or equipment, and crack became the preferred form of cocaine in this country in the early 1980s.

The epidemic of cocaine use/abuse that swept the United States in the 1980s and 1990s will not be discussed here; this topic is worthy of a book in its own right. But by the start of the 21st century, drug abusers had come full circle: The dangers of cocaine abuse were well known, and drug users were eager for an alternative to cocaine. Just as the then-new amphetamines replaced cocaine as the preferred stimulant of choice in the 1930s, the amphetamines, especially methamphetamine, seem again to be replacing cocaine as the CNS stimulant of choice for drug abusers. Cocaine use/abuse appears to have peaked sometime around 1986 in the United States, and casual cocaine use has been on the decline since then (Kleber, 1991). However, cocaine has by no means disappeared. Recreational cocaine use has leveled off and it remains a significant part of the drug abuse problem in the United States (Gold, 1997).

Cocaine Today

At the start of the 21st century, *Erythroxylon coca* continues to thrive in the high mountain regions of South America, and the majority of the coca plants grown there are harvested for the international cocaine trade, not for local use (Mann, 1994). Virtually 98% of the world's cocaine is produced by Peru, Bolivia, and Co-

lombia. Peru produces 50% of the total, Bolivia and Colombia about 25% each.

A small proportion of the coca plant crop is used by the native people of South America, where people in the high mountain plateaus continue to chew coca leaves to help them live and work. Some researchers have pointed to this practice as evidence that cocaine is not as addictive as drug enforcement officials claim. For example, Jaffe (2000b) noted that although the natives of Peru chew cocaine on a regular basis, "few progress to excessive use or toxicity" (2000b, p. 1003). Jaffe thought this was possible because chewing the leaves is a rather inefficient method of abusing cocaine, and much of the cocaine that is released by this method is destroyed by the acids of the digestive tract. As a result, the native who chewed coca leaves was not thought to obtain a significant blood level of cocaine

Other researchers have suggested that the natives of South America who chew coca leaves do indeed become addicted to the stimulant effect of the cocaine. Studies have revealed that the blood level of cocaine achieved when coca leaves are chewed is in the lower range of blood levels achieved by those who "snort" cocaine in the United States and that although this is barely enough to have a psychoactive effect, in the opinion of some scientists it is still a large enough dose to be addicting (Karch, 1996). Thus the question of whether natives who chew coca leaves are addicted to the cocaine that they absorb has not been answered.

Current Medical Uses of Cocaine

Cocaine was once a popular pharmaceutical agent that was used in the treatment of a wide range of conditions. By the 1880s, physicians had discovered that cocaine was an effective local anesthetic (Mann, 1992; Byck, 1987). Cocaine was found to block the nerve signals, or impulses, of the peripheral nerves, changing the electrical potential of these nerves and thus preventing them from passing on pain impulses to the brain. Because of this effect, cocaine was once commonly used by physicians as a topical analgesic for procedures involving the ear, nose, throat, rectum, and vagina. The onset of cocaine's action as a local analgesic is approximately 1 minute, and its duration of effect can be as long as 2 hours (Shannon, Wilson, & Stang, 1995). Cocaine was also included in a mixture called Brompton's cocktail, which was used to control the pain of cancer. However, this mixture has fallen out of favor and is rarely if ever used today (Scaros, Westra, & Barone, 1990).

Cocaine's usefulness as a pharmaceutical was limited by its often undesirable side effects. Physicians have found a number of other chemicals that offer the advantages of cocaine without its side effects or potential for abuse. Today, cocaine "has virtually no clinical use" (House, 1990, p. 41), although on rare occasions it is still used by physicians to control pain.

Scope of the Problem of Cocaine Abuse and Addiction

Globally, an estimated 13 million people have used cocaine at least once (United Nations, 1997). The United States is still the world's largest consumer of cocaine (Sabbag, 1994), where more than 30% of the men and 20% of the women between the ages of 26 and 34 have used cocaine at least once (Warner, Greene, Buchsbaum, Cooper, & Robinson, 1998). An estimated 1.75 million people in the United States use cocaine at least once a month, and 652,000 people began using cocaine in 1996 alone (Department of Health and Human Services, 1997).

Estimates of the amount of cocaine used each year in the United States vary. The White House's drug control policy director Barry McCaffrey estimated that in 1998 (the latest year for which data are available) 454 *metric tons*[3] of cocaine were shipped into the country ("Despite War on Drugs, Prices for Cocaine, Heroin, Decrease," 2000). In contrast to this estimate, the Drug Enforcement Administration (DEA), reported that 1000–1200 tons of cocaine are smuggled into the country each year (*60 Minutes*, 1997a). This estimate is hard to accept, in light of the estimate by the United Nations' International Drug Control Program that the *total* global production of cocaine for 1996 was only about 1000 tons (United Nations, 1997).

Before it is sold in the United States illicit cocaine is usually "cut" with any of a number of foreign chemicals.[4] The compounds used to adulterate cocaine include talc, flour, cornstarch, lactose, sucrose, maltose, manitol, procaine, lidocaine, tetracaine, benzocaine, amphetamines, caffeine, methylphenidate, quinine, strychnine, thiamin, magnesium silicate, magnesium sulfate, and arsenic (Karan, Haller, & Schnoll, 1998). To purchase cocaine contaminated with these substances, U.S users spend an estimated $90 billion (Abt Associates, Inc., 1995a) to $100 billion each year (Will, 1993). Although casual cocaine abuse in the United States peaked in the mid-1980s, the amount of cocaine consumed each year in this country has remained at about the mid-1980 level (Abt Associates, Inc., 1995a). This apparent contradiction is explained by the fact that although there are fewer casual cocaine users, there has been no significant decrease in the number of *heavy* abusers since 1985 (Department of Health and Human Services, 1997).

Only a minority of those who use cocaine do so with any frequency. For example, two-thirds of the cocaine consumed in the United States is thought to be consumed by just 25% of users (Office of National Drug Abuse Policy, 1996). It is estimated that 23–24 million people in the United States have used cocaine at least once (Hollander, Hoffman, Burnstein, Shih, & Thode, 1995). Of these, however, only between 1.5 million (Nash & Park, 1997) and 5 million people are thought to use cocaine as often as once a month (Hollander, Shih, Hoffman, Harchelroad, Phillips, Brent, Kulig, & Thode, 1997). The team of Haverkos and Stein (1995) suggested that 2 million people use cocaine in the United States, that 600,000 of them use the drug at least once a week, and that 300,000 use it daily. The team of Warner, Kosten, and O'Connor (1997) concluded that there were 2.1 million cocaine-dependent individuals in this country. The amount of cocaine consumed by each user varies. For example, hard-core cocaine users in the United States are thought to have spent $23.3 billion on cocaine in 1993, whereas occasional users spent only $7.5 billion (Abt Associates, Inc., 1995a).

Thus there is no clear picture of the true scope of cocaine abuse either around the world or in this country. About all that researchers agree on is that its casual use peaked in the mid-1980s and has been declining ever since. But, as these figures suggest, cocaine remains a significant part of the drug abuse problem both globally and in the United States.

---

[3]A metric ton is equal to 1000 kilograms, or 2204.6 pounds. The figure of 340 metric tons would equal 374.78 standard tons, or 749,560 pounds, of pure cocaine.

[4]See Chapter 35.

Pharmacology of Cocaine

Cocaine is best absorbed into the body when it is administered as cocaine hydrochloride, which is a water-soluble compound. After cocaine enters the body, it quickly diffuses into the general circulation and is rapidly transported to the brain and other blood-rich organs such as the heart. It spite of its rapid distribution, the level of cocaine varies from one organ to another. Because it easily crosses the blood-brain barrier, the level of cocaine is usually higher in the brain than in the blood plasma, especially in the first two hours following use of the drug (*Forensic Drug Abuse Advisor*, 1994e).

The effects of cocaine on the central nervous system (CNS) are not well understood (Hollander, 1995). At one time, it was thought that cocaine's effects were the result of a drug-induced release of the neurotransmitter *dopamine* in the CNS. However, researchers now believe that cocaine does not cause the *release* of dopamine in the CNS. Rather, cocaine's effects seem to be caused by the ability of this compound to block the reuptake of the dopamine that has already been released by the CNS (Ritz, 1999). Further, researchers have found at least five different subtypes of dopamine receptors in the brain, and the reinforcing effects of cocaine seem to reflect its ability to stimulate some of these receptor subtypes more strongly than others. For example, Romach, Glue, Kampman, Kaplan, Somer, Poole, Clarke, Coffin, Cornish, O'Brien, and Sellers (1999) found that when the dopamine D_1 receptor was blocked, their volunteers failed to experience the pleasure that cocaine usually induces when it is injected into the circulation. On the basis of this finding, the authors concluded that the dopamine D_1 receptor site was involved in the experience of euphoria reported by cocaine abusers.

In the human brain, the dopamine D_1 receptors are concentrated in the so called "mesolimbic" system, which includes structures such as the nucleus accumbens and the amygdala that are known to be involved in the pleasure response induced by the drugs of abuse. Some researchers believe that cocaine causes a massive discharge of the neurotransmitter dopamine along the nerve pathways that connect the ventral tegmentum region of the brain to the nucleus accumbens (Restak, 1994; Beitner-Johnson & Nestler, 1992). But cocaine does not just cause the release of dopamine. It also

blocks the process of *reabsorption/reuptake* of the neurotransmitters dopamine, noradrenaline, and serotonin (Stocker, 1999a; Hoffman & Hollander, 1997; Henry, 1996). The effects of cocaine-induced blockage of the noradrenaline and serotonin reuptake systems is not known at this time, although the noradrenaline system is known to be involved in cardiac function, among other things, and thus might account for cocaine's impact on the cardiovascular system.

After periods of prolonged abuse, the neurons within the brain will have released all of their stores of the neurotransmitter dopamine, without being able to reabsorb virtually any of the dopamine, norepinephrine, or serotonin that was released. Low levels of these neurotransmitters are thought to be involved in the development of depression. This pharmacological effect of cocaine might explain the observed relationship between cocaine abuse and depression, which has been known to reach suicidal proportions in some cocaine abusers.

Tolerance to cocaine's euphoric effect may develop within "hours or days" (Schuckit, 2000, p. 124). As tolerance develops, the individual needs more and more cocaine to produce a euphoric effect. This urge to increase the dosage and continue using the drug can reach the point where it "may become a way of life and users become totally preoccupied with drug-seeking and drug-taking behaviors" (Seigel, 1982, p. 731).

Another of the brain subunits affected by cocaine is the diencephalon, which is the region of the brain responsible for temperature regulation. This will result in a higher-than-normal body temperature. At the same time that cocaine is altering the brain's temperature regulation system, it causes the constriction of surface blood vessels. This combination of effects results in hyperthermia: excess body heat. The individual's body will conserve body heat at just the time when it needs to release the excess thermal energy caused by the cocaine-induced dysregulation of body temperature. This is the mechanism through which cocaine-induced hyperthermia can prove dangerous or even fatal (Hall, Talbert, & Ereshefsky, 1990).

When it is used as a pharmaceutical, cocaine's effects are very short-lived. This is also true when cocaine is abused. For example, when cocaine is injected intravenously, the peak plasma levels are reached in just 5 minutes, and the effects begin to diminish after 20–40 minutes (Weddington, 1993). One reason why the effects of intravenously administered cocaine are so short-lived is that the half-life of a single dose of intravenously administered cocaine is only between 30–90 minutes (Mendelson & Mello, 1996; Jaffe, 2000b; Marzuk, Tardiff, Leon, Hirsch, Stajic, Portera, Hartwell, & Iqbal, 1995; Julien, 1992).

Cocaine is biotransformed in the liver, and there are about a dozen known metabolites produced (Karch, 1996). About 90–95% of a dose of intravenously administered cocaine is biotransformed into one of two primary metabolites: *benzoylecgonine* (BEG) and *ecgonine methyl ester* (Kerfoot, Sakoulas, & Hyman, 1996; Cone, 1993). The other metabolites are of minor importance, and we will not consider them further. Only about 5–10% of a single dose of cocaine is excreted from the body unchanged. Neither of the major metabolites of cocaine has any known biological activity in the body. BEG has a half-life of 7.5 hours (Marzuk, Tardiff, Leon, Hirsch, Stajic, Portera, Hartwell, & Iqbal, 1995). Because the half-life of BEG is longer than that of the parent compound, and because it is stable in frozen urine, this is the chemical that laboratories usually test for when they test a urine sample for evidence of cocaine use. Surprisingly, cocaine "autometabolizes" following the user's death. That is, the body continues to biotransform the cocaine in the blood even after the user has died. Thus a post-mortem blood sample might not reveal any measurable amount of cocaine in the blood, even in cases where the decedent was known to have used cocaine before his or her death.

Drug interactions involving cocaine. Cocaine is a potent chemical and thus has the potential to interact with a wide range of both pharmaceuticals and illicit drugs. Cross-addiction is a common complication of chronic cocaine use. For example, between 20% and 50% of alcohol-and-heroin dependent individuals are also dependent on cocaine (Gold & Miller, 1997a), and more than 75% of cocaine abusers are also dependent on alcohol (Zealberg & Brady, 1999).

The combination of alcohol and cocaine is especially dangerous, because when a person uses both cocaine and alcohol, some of the cocaine is biotransformed into *cocaethylene* (Gold & Miller, 1997a; Karch, 1996). Cocaethylene is so toxic to the user's body that it is estimated to be 25–30 times as likely to induce death as cocaine itself (Karan, Haller, & Schnoll, 1998). Its half-life is longer than that of cocaine itself, and because it func-

tions as a powerful calcium channel blocker, coca-ethylene may exacerbate the cardiovascular side effects of cocaine, increasing the risk of premature death (Karch, 1996; Mendelson & Mello, 1996; Barnhill, Ciraulo, Ciraulo, & Greene, 1995). There also is a possible relationship between the mixture of cocaine and alcohol, and death from *pulmonary edema* (Barnhill, Ciraulo, Ciraulo, & Greene, 1995). Unfortunately, cocaethylene may lengthen the period of cocaine-induced euphoria, making it more likely that the person will continue to use alcohol with cocaine in spite of the dangers associated with this practice.

Some abusers inject a combination of cocaine and an opiate, a process known as "speedballing." However, for reasons that are not well understood, cocaine enhances the respiratory depressive effect of the opiates, possibly resulting in episodes of respiratory arrest in extreme cases (Kerfoot, Sakoulas, & Hyman, 1996). As we will see later in this chapter, cocaine abuse often results in a feeling of irritation, or anxiety. In order to control cocaine-induced agitation and anxiety, users often ingest alcohol, tranquilizers, or marijuana. The combination of marijuana and cocaine appears capable of increasing heart rate by almost 50 beats per minute in individuals who are using both substances (Barnhill, Ciraulo, Ciraulo, & Greene, 1995).

There is one case report of a patient who was abusing cocaine and took an over-the-counter cold medication that contained phenylpropanolamine. This person developed what seems to have been a drug-induced psychosis that included homicidal thoughts (Barnhill, Ciraulo, Ciraulo, & Greene, 1995). It is not clear whether this was an isolated incident, or the interaction between cocaine and phenylpropanolamine precipitated a psychotic reaction, but the concurrent use of these chemicals is clearly not recommended.

How Illicit Cocaine Is Produced

The process of cocaine production has changed little in the past generation. First, the cocaine leaves are harvested. In some parts of Bolivia, this is done as often as once every three months, because the climate is well suited for the plant to grow. Second, the leaves are dried, usually by letting them sit in the sunlight for a few hours or days, and although this process is illegal in many parts of South America, the local authorities are quite tolerant and do little to interfere with the drying of coca leaves.

In the third step of cocaine production, the dried leaves are put in a plastic-lined pit and mixed with water and sulfuric acid (White, 1989). The mixture is crushed by workers who wade into the pit in their bare feet. After the mixture has been crushed, diesel fuel and bicarbonate are added to it. After a period of time, during which workers reenter the pit several times to continue to stomp through the mixture, the liquids are drained off. Lime is then mixed with the residue, forming a paste (Byrne, 1989b) known as cocaine *base*. It takes 500 kilograms of leaves to produce 1 kilogram of cocaine base (White, 1989).

The fourth step involves adding water, gasoline, acid, potassium permanganate, and ammonia to the cocaine paste. This forms a reddish brown liquid, which is then filtered. Adding a few drops of ammonia produces a milky solid that is filtered and dried. Then the dried cocaine base is dissolved in a solution of hydrochloric acid and acetone. A white solid forms and settles to the bottom of the tank (Byrne, 1989b; White, 1989). This solid material is the compound cocaine hydrochloride. Eventually, the cocaine hydrochloride is filtered and dried under heating lights. This causes the mixture to form a white, crystalline powder, which is gathered up, packed, and shipped, usually in kilogram packages. Before sale to the individual cocaine user, each kilogram is adulterated and the resulting compound packaged in 1-gram units.

How Cocaine Is Abused

Cocaine is used in several ways. First, cocaine hydrochloride powder may be inhaled through the nose (intranasal use or "snorting"). Second, it may be injected directly into a vein (an intravenous injection). Cocaine hydrochloride is a water-soluble form of cocaine and thus is well suited to either intranasal or intravenous use (Sbriglio & Millman, 1987). Third, cocaine may be used orally (sublingual use). Fourth, cocaine "base" may be smoked. We will examine each of these methods of cocaine abuse in detail.

Intranasal cocaine abuse. Historical evidence suggests that the practice of "snorting" cocaine began around 1903, which is the year that case reports of septal perforation began to appear in medical journals (Karch, 1996). Snorting cocaine powder is a common method of cocaine abuse. In the mid-1990s, 77–95% of cocaine abusers snorted it (Hatsukami & Fischman, 1996; Boyd, 1995). To snort cocaine powder, the user generally arranges it on a piece of glass in thin lines 3–5 cm long. Each of these "lines" contains between 25 and 100 mg of cocaine (Karch, 1996; Strang, Johns, & Caan, 1993). The powder is diced up, usually with a razor blade on a piece of glass or a mirror, to make the particles as small as possible, thus enhancing absorption. A gram of cocaine prepared in this manner might yield 25–30 "lines" (Karan, Haller, & Schnoll, 1998). The powder is then inhaled through a drinking straw or rolled paper.

When it reaches the nasal passages, which are richly supplied with blood vessels, the cocaine is quickly absorbed. This allows some of the cocaine to gain access to the blood stream rapidly, usually in 30–90 seconds (House, 1990), where it is carried to the brain. The peak effects of cocaine when it is snorted are reached within 10 minutes, and the effects wear off in about 45–60 minutes after a single dose (Weiss, Greenfield, & Mirin, 1994; Strang, Johns, & Caan, 1993), and in 2–3 hours for chronic users (Hoffman & Hollander, 1997).

Researchers disagree as to how much of the cocaine that is snorted is ultimately absorbed into the user's body. Because cocaine functions as a vasoconstrictor, it may limit its own absorption when it is snorted. Estimates of the amount of cocaine absorbed through the nasal passages range from 5% (Strang, Johns, & Caan, 1993) to 25–94% (Hatsukami & Fischman, 1996). Karch (1996) took a middle-of-the-road position on this issue, suggesting that because of its vasoconstrictive effect, it takes longer for cocaine to be absorbed when it is snorted but that virtually all of it is eventually absorbed. Thus the question of whether intranasally administered cocaine limits its own absorption has not been fully answered.

Intravenous cocaine abuse. It is possible to introduce cocaine directly into the body via intravenous injection. Cocaine hydrochloride powder is mixed with water and then injected into a vein. This actually is the least common method by which cocaine is used; only 7% of those individuals who use cocaine inject it (Hatsukami & Fischman, 1996). It has been claimed that intravenously administered cocaine reaches the brain in 3–5 seconds (Restak, 1994) and 15-20 seconds (Jones,

1987). Intravenous administration results in 20 times as much cocaine reaching the brain as intranasal cocaine use (Strang, Johns, & Caan, 1993).

Intravenous cocaine abusers often report a rapid, intense feeling of euphoria called the "rush" or "flash," which is similar to sexual orgasm but feels different from the rush reported by opiate abusers (Brust, 1998). Following the rush, the user experiences a feeling of euphoria that lasts 10–15 minutes. Researchers believe that the rush is the subjective experience of cocaine-induced changes in the ventral tegmentum in the midbrain, and the basal forebrain. As we have noted, intravenously administered cocaine is biotransformed quite quickly, which is one reason why its effects last only about 15 minutes (Weiss, Mirin, & Greenfield, 1994).

Sublingual cocaine use. This form of cocaine abuse, is becoming increasingly popular, especially when the hydrochloride salt of cocaine is utilized (Jones, 1987). The tissues in the mouth, especially under the tongue, are richly supplied with blood, allowing large amounts of the drug to enter the bloodstream quickly. The cocaine is then transported to the brain, with results similar to those seen in the intranasal administration of cocaine.

Cocaine smoking. Historically, the practice of burning or smoking different parts of the coca plant dates back to at least 3000 B.C., when the Incas burned coca leaves at religious festivals (Siegel, 1982). The practice of smoking cocaine resurfaced in the late 1800s, when coca cigarettes were used to treat hay fever and opiate addiction. By the year 1890, cocaine smoke was being used in the United States for the treatment of whooping cough, bronchitis, asthma, and a range of other conditions (Siegel, 1982). But in spite of this history of cocaine smoking for medicinal reasons, *recreational* cocaine smoking did not become popular in the United States until the early to mid-1980s.

This is because the medicinal uses of cocaine have gradually been reduced as other, more effective agents have been introduced for the control of various illnesses. When cocaine hydrochloride became a popular drug of abuse in the 1970's, users quickly discovered that it is not easily smoked. The high temperatures needed to vaporize cocaine hydrochloride also destroy it, making it of limited value to those who wished to smoke it. Dedicated cocaine abusers of the 1970s and 1980s knew that it was possible to smoke the alkaloid

base of cocaine; they also knew that transforming cocaine hydrochloride into an alkaloid base was a long, dangerous process. This made the practice of smoking cocaine unpopular before around 1985.

To transform cocaine hydrochloride into an alkaloid base, cocaine powder had to be mixed with a solvent such as ether and then a base such as ammonia (Warner, 1995). The cocaine then forms an alkaloid base that can be smoked. This form of cocaine is called "freebase" (or simply "base"). Next the precipitated cocaine freebase is passed through a filter, which effectively removes some of the impurities and increases the concentration of the obtained powder. Unfortunately, many of the impurities still remain in the alkaloid base (Siegel, 1982). Thus transforming cocaine hydrochloride into a form that can be smoked is quite difficult. Further, the chemicals used to separate cocaine freebase from its hydrochloride salt are quite volatile, and there is a very real danger of fire — or even an explosion — from these compounds. As a result, smoking cocaine freebase never became popular in the United States. But when cocaine freebase *was* smoked, the fumes would reach the brain in just 7 *seconds* (Beebe & Walley, 1991), with between 60% and 90% of the cocaine crossing into the general circulation from the lungs (Hatsukami & Fischman, 1996; Beebe & Walley, 1991). So potent are the effects of smoked cocaine that Gold and Verebey (1984) called it "tantamount to intravenous administration without the need for a syringe" (p. 714). Indeed, there is evidence that cocaine reaches the brain more quickly when it is smoked than when it is injected (Hatsukami & Fischman, 1996). Note also that cocaine has been called "the most addictive substance used by humankind" (Wright, 1999, p. 47).

This suggested to illicit drug producers that there would be a strong market for a form of cocaine that could easily be smoked, and by the mid 1980s such a product had reached U.S. streets. "Crack" is essentially a solid chunk of cocaine base that was prepared for smoking before it was delivered for sale at the local level. This is done in illicit "factories" or "laboratories" where cocaine hydrochloride is mixed with baking soda and water and then heated until the cocaine crystals begin to precipitate at the bottom of the container (Warner, 1995). Breslin (1988) described how one crack "factory" worked:

Curtis and his girlfriend dropped the cocaine and baking soda into the water, then hit the bottle with the blowtorch. The cocaine powder boiled down to its oily base. The baking soda soaked up the impurities in the cocaine. When cold water was added to the bottle, the cocaine base hardened into white balls. Curtis and Iris spooned them out, placed them on a table covered with paper, and began to measure the hard white cocaine. (p. 212)

The crack produced in such illicit factories is sold in small, ready-to-use pellets packaged in containers that allow the user one or two inhalations for a relatively low price (Beebe & Walley, 1991; Gawin, Allen, & Humblestone, 1989). In some parts of the country, the price of one piece of crack, known as a "rock," is as low as two dollars (*Forensic Drug Abuse Advisor*, 1994c). The low cost of crack is one reason why it is so attractive to the under-18 crowd and in low-income neighborhoods (Taylor & Gold, 1990; Bales, 1988). Since the introduction of crack, the practice of smoking cocaine has probably become the most widely recognized method of cocaine abuse. However, researchers believe that only about 36% of cocaine abusers in the United States smoke the drug (Hatsukami & Fischman, 1996).

In 1996, substance abuse rehabilitation professionals noted a new trend among some crack users both in England and in isolated U. S. cities. In these areas, limited numbers of users would dissolve the pellets of crack in alcohol, lemon juice, vinegar, or water and then inject it into their bodies through large-bore needles (*Forensic Drug Abuse Advisor*, 1996i). Apparently, intravenous cocaine abusers were resorting to this practice when their traditional sources of cocaine hydrochloride were unable to provide them with the powder used for injection. It is not known how popular this practice will become, but it does represent a disturbing new twist in the ongoing saga of cocaine abuse/addiction.

Subjective Effects of Cocaine When It Is Abused

Two factors influence the individual's subjective experience from cocaine. First, the individual's *expectations* play a role in how the user interprets the drug's effects. Second, there are the actual *physiological effects* of the

drug. These two factors interact to shape the individual's experience from cocaine and how it is abused.

Experienced cocaine users tend to experience both positive effects (e.g., euphoria) and negative effects (e.g., depression) from the drug (Schafer & Brown, 1991). The experienced cocaine abuser expects a generalized feeling of arousal, some anxiety, and feelings of relaxation and a reduction in the individual's level of tension.

Both intravenous injection and cocaine smoking can cause the user to experience a feeling of intense euphoria within seconds of using the drug (Jaffe, 2000b). This "rush" has been compared to sexual orgasm in intensity and pleasure and is so intense for some users that "it alone can replace the sex partner of either sex" (Gold & Verebey, 1984; p. 719). Some male abusers have reported having a spontaneous ejaculation without direct genital stimulation after either injecting or smoking cocaine. There also appears to be a link between chronic cocaine use and compulsive "acting out" behavior for both men and women (Washton, 1995). Within seconds, the initial rush is replaced by a period of excitation or euphoria that lasts for between 10 (Strang, Johns, & Caan, 1993) and 20 minutes (Weiss, Greenfield, & Mirin, 1994). During this period, the individual feels an increased sense of competence, energy (Gold & Verebey, 1984), or extreme self-confidence (Taylor & Gold, 1990). Some abusers report feeling powerful or "energized" while under the influence of cocaine, and the drug makes the individual feel decreased senses of fatigue and hunger and an increased awareness of sexual stimuli (Schuckit, 2000).

"Snorting" cocaine powder yields less intense effects than smoking or injecting it. Still, intranasal use of cocaine produces a sense of euphoria, as well as many of the effects noted in the last paragraph. This sense of cocaine-induced euphoria may last only a few minutes for the individual who smokes cocaine (Byck, 1987) and an estimated 20 minutes to an hour for the individual who snorts cocaine powder. Then the effects begin to wane, and to regain the cocaine-induced pleasurable feelings, the user must use cocaine again.

Tolerance to the euphoric effects of cocaine develops quickly. To overcome their tolerance, many users engage in a cycle of continuous cocaine use known as "coke runs." The usual cocaine run lasts about 12 hours, although there have been cases where they have lasted up to 7 days (Gawin, Khalsa, & Ellinwood, 1994). During this time, the user is smoking or injecting additional cocaine every few minutes, until the total cumulative dose reaches levels that would kill the inexperienced ("cocaine-naive") user. The "coke run" phenomenon is similar to the pattern seen when animals are given unlimited access to cocaine. Rats that can obtain intravenous cocaine by pushing a bar set in the wall of their cage will do so repeatedly, ignoring food and sex, until they die from convulsions or infection (Hall, Talbert, & Ereshefsky, 1990).

Complications of Cocaine Abuse/Addiction

Cocaine has the distinction of being the illicit drug that occasions the most visits to hospital emergency rooms (Shih & Hollander, 1996). Unfortunately, cocaine abuse is potentially fatal, and in some cases death from a cocaine overdose occurs so rapidly that "the victim never receives medical attention other than from the coroner" (Estroff, 1987, p. 25). In addition, cocaine abuse can cause a wide range of other problems:

Addiction. In the 1960s and early 1970s, there were those who believed that cocaine was not addictive. This belief probably arose because few users in the late 1960s could afford to use cocaine long enough to become addicted to it. The truth is that cocaine has a very real potential to cause physical and psychological addiction.[5] About 20% of those who try cocaine become regular users, and 5% become addicted to it (Karan, Haller, & Schnoll, 1998).

Physical dependence on cocaine does not develop instantly. Individuals who snort cocaine might take as long as 3–4 years to become fully addicted to the drug (Lamar, Riley, & Smghabadi, 1986), whereas those who smoke crack might be fully addicted in only 6–10 *weeks*. There also appears to be a progression in the methods by which cocaine abusers utilize the drug. As the users' need for the drug becomes more intense, they switch from the intranasal method of cocaine use to those methods that introduce greater concentrations of the drug into the body. For example, 79–90% of those who

admitted using crack started to use the drug intranasally (Hatsukami & Fischman, 1996).

Respiratory system dysfunctions. The cocaine smoker may experience chest pain, cough, and damage to the bronchioles of the lungs (O'Connor, Chang, & Shi, 1992). There have been reports that the alveoli of some users' lungs have ruptured, allowing air (and bacteria) to escape into the surrounding tissues. This will establish the potential for infection to develop, while the escaping gas may contribute to the inability of the lung to inflate fully (a condition called pneumothorax). Approximately one-third of chronic crack users develop wheezing sounds when they breathe (Tashkin, Kleerup, Koyal, Marques, & Goldman, 1996). Other potential complications of cocaine smoking include the development of an asthma-like condition known as chronic bronchiolitis ("crack lung"), hemorrhage, pneumonia, and chronic inflammation of the throat (Albertson, Walby, & Derlet, 1995; House, 1990; Taylor & Gold, 1990). There is evidence that cocaine-induced lung damage may be irreversible.

There is also evidence that at least some of the observed increase in the incidence of fatal asthma cases may be caused by unsuspected cocaine abuse (*Forensic Drug Abuse Advisor*, 1997b). Cocaine abuse may not be the cause of *all* asthma-induced deaths, but smoking crack can irritate the air passages in the lungs, contributing to both fatal and nonfatal asthma attacks (Tashkin *et al.*, 1996). The chronic intranasal use of cocaine can also cause sore throats, inflamed sinuses, hoarseness, and (on occasion) a breakdown of the cartilage of the nose. Damage to the cartilage of the nose may develop after as little as three weeks of intranasal cocaine use (O'Connor, Chang, & Shi, 1992). According to theses investigators, intranasal cocaine use may also cause bleeding from the nasal passages and the formation of ulcers there.

Cardiovascular system damage. Cocaine abuse can result in damage to the cardiovascular system. Indeed, the most common reason why cocaine-abusing patients seek medical treatment is cocaine-induced chest pain (Hoffman & Hollander, 1997). Cocaine abuse is also associated with such cardiovascular problems as severe hypertension, sudden dissection of the coronary arteries, sudden death, tachycardia, cardiac ischemia, and myocarditis (Brent, 1995; Albertson, Walby, & Derlet, 1995; Hollander, 1995; Derlet & Horowitz,

---

[5]Not everybody who uses cocaine becomes addicted, but at this time it is not possible to determine *who* will become addicted if they try this drug. This alone should discourage cocaine use.

1995; O'Connor, Chang, & Shi, 1992; Jaffe, 2000b; Derlet, 1989).

In addition to the foregoing complications of cocaine use/abuse, it can cause, or at least speed up, the development of atherosclerotic plaques in the coronary arteries of the user (Hollander, Shih, Hoffman, Harchelroad, Phillips, Brent, Kulig, & Thode, 1997; Hoffman & Hollander, 1997). Researchers still do not understand the exact mechanism by which cocaine abuse causes the development of these plaques, but animal research has revealed that cocaine abuse can trick the body's immune system into attacking the tissue of the heart and endothelial cells that line the coronary arteries (Tanhehco, Yasojima, McGeer, & Lucchesi, 2000). Cocaine accomplishes this feat by triggering what is known as the complement cascade, which is part of the immune system's response to invading microorganisms. This process makes protein molecules form on the cell walls of invading microorganisms, eventually causing them to burst from internal pressure. The damaged cells are then attacked by the body's "scavenger" cells, the microphages. Some researchers believe that the microphages are also involved in the process of atherosclerotic plaque formation and have suggested that atherosclerotic plaque is formed when the microphages mistakenly attack cholesterol molecules circulating in the blood and attach these molecules to the endothelial cells of the coronary arteries.

At one time, researchers believed that cocaine abuse could cause increased platelet aggregation—in other words, that cocaine somehow caused the user's blood cells to form blood clots more easily. This possible side effect of cocaine seemed to account for clinical reports in which cocaine abusers were found to be at risk for many of the cardiovascular problems noted in the last paragraphs. However, research has failed to support this hypothesis (Heesch, Negus, Steiner, Snyder, McIntire, Grayburn, Ashcraft, Hernandez, & Eichorn, 1996).

Researchers have found that cocaine can increase the heart rate while reducing the blood flow to the heart (Moliterno, Willard, Lange, Negus, Boehrer, Glamann, Landau, Rossen, Winniford, & Hollis, 1994). This effect is strongest in the cigarette-smoking cocaine abuser with coronary artery disease, whose coronary arteries were found to constrict by 19% compared to that of nonsmoking cocaine abusers. Cocaine smokers who did not smoke cigarettes experienced an average 7% decrease in coronary artery diameter after smoking cocaine, and smokers with no known coronary artery disease experienced a temporary 9% reduction in coronary blood flow, according to the authors. This process might account for cocaine's ability to induce *myocardial ischemia* in the heart of the cocaine abuser.

Cocaine-induced myocardial ischemia might develop up to 18 hours after the individual's last use of cocaine, leading to some confusion about the cause of this condition (Kerfoot, Sakoulas, & Hyman, 1996). It is important for the physicians treating the patient who has developed myocardial ischemia to be aware of possible cocaine abuse by the patient, because in hospitals, drugs known as beta-adrenergic antagonists are often used to treat myocardial ischemia. These drugs can contribute to cocaine-induced constriction of blood vessels, placing the patient's life at added risk if she or he had been abusing cocaine in the hours prior to hospitalization (Shih & Hollander, 1996). Thus it is imperative that the physician be informed whether the patient being treated for a possible myocardial ischemia has recently used cocaine.

Cocaine abuse has been associated with a number of other cardiac problems, including atrial fibrillation (Chandramouli & Kotler, 1998). However, researchers have not identified the exact mechanism by which cocaine causes cardiac arrhythmias. One theory is that cocaine affects cardiac function through its ability to alter the release of one or more members of the *catecholamine* family of chemicals. The catecholamines include epinephrine, a chemical that normally is produced in the adrenal glands, and the neurotransmitters norepinephrine and dopamine. In the body, epinephrine functions as a vasoconstrictor. There is evidence that the chronic use of cocaine interferes with the normal production and utilization of the catecholamines in the body (Beitner-Johnson & Nestler, 1992). Norepinephrine, in addition to its role as a neurotransmitter in the brain, is found in the heart tissue. Beitner-Johnson and Nestler (1992) suggested that cocaine may block the normal function of norepinephrine in the heart, causing the individual's death.

A variation of the catecholamine hypothesis suggested by Beitner-Johnson and Nestler (1992) was advanced by the *Forensic Drug Abuse Advisor* (1994f). In theory, the chronic use of cocaine increases levels of norepinephrine in the blood. Over time, the above-normal norepinephrine levels impose an increased workload on the heart, especially the left ventricle. Eventually, the heart weakens, becomes enlarged, and puts the individual at risk for sudden death.

Some scientists believe that cocaine abuse also causes microinfarcts, or microscopic areas of damage to the heart muscle (Gawin, Khalsa, & Ellinwood, 1994). These microinfarcts ultimately reduce the heart's ability to function effectively and may lead to further heart problems later on. There is also evidence that cocaine abuse may cause "silent" episodes of cardiac ischemia while the individual is withdrawing from cocaine, leaving him or her at risk for sudden death (Kerfoot, Sakoulas, & Hyman, 1996).

Researchers have since found that in some settings, fully 17% of the patients under the age of 60 seen in hospital emergency rooms for chest pain had cocaine metabolites in their urine (Hollander, Todd, Green, Heilpern, Karras, Singer, Brogan, Funk, & Strahan, 1995). There does not seem to be any pattern to cocaine-induced cardiovascular problems, and both first-time users and long-term cocaine users have suffered cocaine-related cardiovascular problems. In a hospital setting, between 56% an 84% of patients with cocaine-induced chest pain are found to have abnormal electrocardiograms (Hollander, 1995).

Another rare but potentially fatal complication of cocaine abuse is a condition known as *acute aortic dissection* (Brent, 1995). This condition is occasionally seen in individuals other than cocaine users, and it develops when a weak spot suddenly develops in the wall of the main artery of the body, the aorta. The exact mechanism by which cocaine causes an acute aortic dissection is not known, but it is a medical emergency that may require surgical intervention to save the patient's life.

Male cocaine abusers run the risk of developing erectile dysfunctions, including a painful, potentially dangerous condition known as priapism (Finger, Lund, & Slagel, 1997). In contrast to the intravenous injection of opiates, however, it is not common for intravenous cocaine abusers to develop scar tissue at the injection site. This is because the adulterants commonly found in powdered cocaine are mainly water-soluble and thus less irritating to the body than the adulterants found in opiates (Karch, 1996).

Cocaine abuse as a cause of liver damage. There is evidence that cocaine metabolites, especially coca-ethylene, are toxic to the liver (Karch, 1996). Medical research has also discovered that a small percentage of the population simply cannot biotransform cocaine, no matter how small the dosage level. In this *pseudo-cholinesterase deficiency*, the liver is unable to produce an essential enzyme necessary to break down the cocaine (Gold, 1989). For people with this condition, the use of even a small amount of cocaine could be fatal.

Cocaine abuse as a cause of central nervous system damage. Virtually nothing is known about the effects of either intentional or accidental cocaine abuse by children (Mott, Packer, & Soldin, 1994). The authors did find evidence that cocaine abuse by children might cause seizures, possibly by lowering the seizure threshold. They also found evidence of neurological damage in almost half of the children studied. The relationship between cocaine abuse and seizures in children was so strong that the authors recommended that *all* children and adolescents brought to the hospital for a previously undiagnosed seizure disorder be tested for cocaine abuse.

Neuropsychological testing has suggested that chronic use of cocaine might cause "moderate to severe" (Kaufman *et al.*, 1998, p. 376) brain damage in adults. O'Malley, Adamse, Heaton, and Gawin (1992) found, for example, that 50% of the subjects who abused cocaine on a regular basis showed evidence of cognitive impairment on the neuropsychological tests used in this study, compared to only 15% of the control subjects. This cognitive dysfunction is thought to be another consequence of cocaine's *vasoconstrictive* effects on the blood vessels in the brain (Brust, 1997; Pearlson, Jeffery, Harris, Ross, Fischman, & Camargo, 1993). If the cocaine-induced reduction in blood flow is prolonged, the neurons supplied by that blood vessel begin to die (Kaufman *et al.*, 1998).

There is increasing evidence that cocaine abuse can contribute to the formation of microscopic areas of damage in the brain, or what are known as microstrokes. Cocaine abuse is also a known cause of more traditional strokes. Indeed, for reasons that are not entirely clear, the frequency of cocaine-induced strokes has been increasing in recent years, reaching "epidemic proportions" among cocaine abusers (Kaufman *et al.*, 1998, p. 376). Perhaps the risk for a cocaine-induced CVA is cumulative, with long-term users being at greater risk than newer users. However, a cocaine-induced CVA is possible even in a first time-user.

One mechanism by which cocaine might cause CVAs, especially in users without preexisting vascular disease, is through drug-induced periods of hypertension (Brust, 1997). The periods of cocaine-induced hypertension are thought to cause otherwise normal blood vessels in the brain to rupture, inducing a CVA. Although the specific cause of cocaine-induced CVAs remains to be positively identified, these events have been documented to occur in the brain, retina, and spinal cord of individuals abusing this drug (Brust, 1997; Derlet & Horowitz, 1995; Mendoza & Miller, 1992; Jaffe, 2000b; Derlet, 1989). Depending on where the stroke occurs, it may kill the victim, result in blindness, or simply cause permanent neurological impairment. Cocaine abusers may also experience transient ischemic attacks (TIAs), which could very well be caused by the cocaine-induced vasoconstriction identified by Kafuman *et al.* (1998).

Another very rare complication of cocaine use is the development of a drug-induced neurological condition known as *serotonin syndrome* (Mills, 1995).[6] Further, cocaine has induced seizures in some users (O'Connor, Chang, & Shi, 1992; Derlet, 1989). For reasons that are still not clear, cocaine-induced seizures may not occur until up to 12 hours after the last use of the drug, according to the authors. There is no way to predict whether a cocaine-induced seizure will develop with the first episode of use or after repeated exposures to cocaine (Gold, 1997). It is theorized that through the process of "pharmacological kindling" (Post *et al.*, 1987), cocaine-induced seizures might develop at a dose that previously had not brought on such convulsions in the user.

Although cocaine itself has a short half-life, "the sensitization effects are long lasting" (Post *et al.*, 1987, p. 113). The authors believe that the sensitizing effects of cocaine might thus lower the seizure threshold, at least in some individuals; they went on to observe that

> Repeated administration of a given dose of cocaine without resulting seizures *would in no way assure the continued safety of this drug even for that given individual.* . . . (p. 159; italics added)

[6]See the Glossary.

The *amygdala* is part of the temporal lobe of the brain and is known to be vulnerable to kindling (Taylor, 1993). Thus cocaine's effects on the amygdala can make this region of the brain hypersensitive, causing the user to experience cocaine-induced seizures even at a dose that once was easily tolerated by the individual.

Cocaine's effects on the user's emotional state and perceptions. It has been suggested (Hamner, 1993) that cocaine abuse exacerbates the symptoms of post-traumatic stress disorders (PTSD). The exact mechanism by which cocaine adds to the emotional distress of PTSD is not clear at this time. However, there is evidence that PTSD is made worse by the psychobiological interaction between the effects of the drug, and the victim's traumatic experiences.

Cocaine use may exacerbate the symptoms of some medical disorders, such as Tourette's syndrome and tardive dyskinesia (Lopez & Jeste, 1997). Further, after periods of extended use, some people get the so-called "cocaine bugs," a hallucinatory experience wherein the person feels as though bugs were crawling on or under the skin of their bodies. The technical term for this is *formication* (*The Harard Medical School Mental Health Letter*, 1990). Patients have been known to burn their arms or legs with matches or cigarettes, or to scratch themselves repeatedly, in an effort to rid themselves of these unseen bugs (Lingeman, 1974).

Cocaine has also been implicated as one cause of drug-induced anxiety, or panic reactions (DiGregorio, 1990). One study found that in the early 1990s *one-quarter* of the patients seen at one panic disorder clinic eventually admitted to using cocaine (Louie, 1990). Further, up to 64% of cocaine users experience some degree of anxiety as a side effect of the drug, according to the author. As we noted earlier, there is a tendency for cocaine users to try to self-medicate this side effect with marijuana. Other chemicals that cocaine abusers often use in an attempt to control their drug-induced anxiety are the benzodiazepines, narcotics, barbiturates and alcohol. Cocaine-induced anxiety and panic attacks can continue for months (Gold & Miller, 1997a) or even years (Satel, Kosten, Schuckit, & Fischman, 1993) after the individual's last use of cocaine.

Between 53% (Decker & Reis, 1993) and 65% (Beebe & Walley, 1991) of chronic cocaine abusers develop a drug-induced psychosis very similar in appearance to paranoid schizophrenia. Although this "coke paranoia" is very similar to paranoid schizophrenia, the symptoms of a cocaine-induced psychosis tend to include more suspiciousness, and a strong fear of being discovered or harmed, while under the influence of cocaine (Rosse, Collins, Fay-McCarthy, Alim, Wyatt, & Deutsch, 1994). Further, the cocaine-induced psychosis is usually of relatively short duration, on the order of a few hours (Davis & Bresnahan, 1987) to a few days (Kerfoot, Sakoulas, & Hyman, 1996; Schuckit, 2000) after the person stops using cocaine. Gawin, Khalsa and Ellinwood (1994) suggested that the delusions that characterize a cocaine-induced psychotic reaction usually clear after the individual's sleep pattern has returned to normal.

The mechanism by which chronic cocaine abuse contributes to the development of a drug-induced psychosis remains unknown. One possibility is that those individuals who develop a cocaine-induced paranoid state possess a biological vulnerability for schizophrenia, which is then activated by chronic cocaine abuse (Satel & Edell, 1991). Another possibility is that the chronic use of cocaine simply results in a short-lived paranoid state, as an unwanted drug side effect, in certain susceptible individuals (Satel, 1992).

Approximately 20% of the chronic users of crack in one study reported drug-induced periods of rage or outbursts of anger and violent assaultive behavior (Beebe & Walley, 1991). Finally, a few hours after snorting the drug, or within 15 minutes of injecting it, the person slides into a state of depression. Cocaine-induced depression is thought to occur because cocaine depletes the nerve cells in the brain of the neurotransmitters norepinephrine and dopamine. After a period of abstinence, the neurotransmitter levels usually recover, and the individual's emotions return to normal. But there is a very real danger that the chronic cocaine abuser will attempt suicide as a result of a drug-induced depressive episode (Maranto, 1985). One recent study in New York City found that *one fifth* of all suicides involving a victim under the age of 60 were cocaine-related (Marzuk, Tardiff, Leon, Stajic, Morgan, & Mann, 1992).

Cocaine use as an indirect cause of death. In addition to its potential to cause death by a variety of mechanisms and to create depression that may lead to suicide, cocaine use may *indirectly* cause, or at least contribute to, premature death. Marzuk, Tardiff, Leon, Hirsch, Stajic, Portera, Hartwell, and Iqbal (1995) tested body fluids for

14,843 residents of New York City between the ages of 15 and 44 who died as a result of trauma from 1990 to 1993. They found either cocaine itself or the metabolite benzoylecgonine in 26.7% of these individuals.

This is not an indication that cocaine use *caused* these individuals to suffer some form of traumatic injury that resulted in their death, but the authors concluded that cocaine use, like alcohol use, increased the risk that the individual would participate in aggressive or risky behaviors that might result in death. Cocaine abuse is a known cause of rhabdomyolysis as a result of its toxic effects on muscle tissue and its vasoconstrictive effects, which can cause muscle ischemia (Richards, 2000).

Summary

Although people have used cocaine for hundreds if not thousands of years, the active agent of the coca bush was isolated and identified only 150 years ago. By coincidence, it became possible to concentrate large amounts of cocaine at about the same time when the intravenous needle was developed. This allowed users to inject large amounts of relatively pure cocaine directly into the circulatory system, where it was rapidly transported to the brain. Users quickly discovered that intravenously administered cocaine brought on a sense of euphoria, which immediately made it a rather popular drug of abuse.

At the turn of the century, government regulations limited the availability of cocaine, which was mistakenly classified as a narcotic at that time. The development of the amphetamine family of drugs in the 1930s, along with increasingly strict enforcement of the laws against cocaine use, allowed drug-addicted individuals to substitute legally purchased amphetamines for the increasingly rare cocaine. In time, the dangers of cocaine use were forgotten by all but a few medical historians.

As we saw in the last chapter, in the late 1960s and early 1970s, government regulations began to limit the availability of amphetamines. Cocaine emerged as a substitute in the late 1970s and early 1980s. To entice users, new forms of cocaine were introduced, including concentrated "rocks" of cocaine known as crack. To the cocaine user of the 1980s, cocaine seemed to be a harmless drug, although historical evidence suggested otherwise.

In the 1980s, users rediscovered the dangers associated with cocaine abuse, and the drug gradually fell into disfavor. The most recent wave of cocaine addiction in the United States peaked around the year 1986, and fewer people are now becoming addicted to cocaine. However, because of the threat of HIV infection and the increased popularity of heroin in the United States, many cocaine abusers are smoking a combination of crack cocaine and heroin. (Smoking avoids the danger of HIV transmission, because intravenous needles are not involved.) As a consequence, the reported numbers of cocaine- and heroin-related emergency room visits have significantly increased. Thus, cocaine will probably remain a part of the drug abuse problem well into the 21st century.

CHAPTER THIRTEEN

Marijuana Abuse and Addiction

Introduction

For many generations, marijuana has been a most controversial substance of abuse and the subject of many misunderandings. For example, people talk about marijuana as though it were a chemical in its own right, when in reality marijuana is not a chemical or a drug; it is a plant, a member of the *Cannabis sativa* family of plants. Some strains of *Cannabis sativa* are cultivated for the hemp fiber they produce, which is then used to manufacture a number of substances.[1] Other strains of the *Cannabis sativa* family contain high levels of certain compounds that can be abused, and some may even have medicinal properties. Through experimentation, it was discovered that smoking certain parts of some strains of the *Cannabis sativa* plant has a pleasant effect. (Smoking other strains yields only frustration, because these plants contain only trace amounts of the same compounds.)

Unfortunately, in the United States, the hysteria surrounding the use/abuse of *Cannabis sativa* has reached the point where *any* member of this plant family is automatically assumed to have an abuse potential (Williams, 2000). To differentiate between those forms of *Cannabis sativa* that produce compounds that might be abused from those forms that have low levels of these same compounds and are potentially useful plants for manufacturing and industry, Williams (2000) suggested

[1]The Gutenberg and King James bibles were first printed on paper manufactured from hemp, and Rembrandt and van Gogh both painted on "canvas" made from hemp (Williams, 2000).

that the term *hemp* be used for the latter. *Marijuana*, he suggested, should be used only to refer to those strains of *Cannabis sativa* that have an abuse potential. This is the pattern we will follow in this text.

Unlike alcohol, cocaine, and the amphetamines, then, marijuana is not in itself a drug of abuse. In a sense, it is similar to the tobacco plant: Both contain compounds that, when introduced into the body, cause the user to experience certain effects that the individual deems desirable. In this chapter, the uses and abuses of marijuana will be discussed.

History of Marijuana Use in the United States

Marijuana has undergone many transformations in its history. For thousands of years, physicians regarded marijuana as a useful pharmaceutical agent that could be used treat a number of different disorders. The first historical references to marijuana date back to the reign of the Chinese Emperor Shen Nung (2737 B.C.), when it was used as a medicine (Scaros, Westra, & Barone, 1990). As recently as the 19th century, physicians in the United States and Europe used marijuana as an analgesic, as a hypnotic, as a treatment for migraine headaches, and as an anticonvulsant (Grinspoon & Bakalar, 1993, 1995). An example of how marijuana was used in the treatment of disease is an 1838 case wherein physicians were able to use hashish to control completely the terror and "excitement" (Elliott, 1992, p. 600) of a patient who had contracted rabies.

During the first half of the 20th century, researchers found that the chemicals in the marijuana plant either were ineffective or at least were less effective than pharmaceuticals being introduced to combat disease. This, along with increasingly strict federal regulations against the use of marijuana, caused it to fall into disfavor as a pharmaceutical (Grinspoon & Bakalar, 1995, 1993). By the 1930s, marijuana was removed from the doctor's pharmacopoeia. By a historical coincidence, it was just at this time that recreational marijuana smoking was being introduced into the United States by immigrants and itinerant workers from Mexico, who had come north to find work in the 1920s (Mann, 1992). Recreational marijuana smoking was quickly adopted by others, especially jazz musicians (Musto, 1991). With the advent of Prohibition in 1920, many members of the working class turned to growing or importing marijuana as a substitute for alcohol (Gazzaniga, 1988). Its use declined with the end of Prohibition, when alcohol use once more became legal, but a small minority of the U.S. population continued to smoke marijuana.

Government officials became alarmed at this practice and attempted to eliminate the marijuana "problem" through such means as the Marijuana Tax Act of 1937.[2] But marijuana abuse never entirely disappeared, and in the 1960s it again became popular. Currently, marijuana is the most frequently used illicit substance in the world (Macfadden & Woody, 2000), in the United States (Nahas, 1986, p. 82), and in Canada (Russell, Newman, & Bland, 1994).

Medicinal marijuana. Since the 1970s, a small number of U.S physicians have again started to wonder whether some of the chemicals found in the marijuana plant might continue to be of value in the fight against disease and suffering. A number of physicians have used the marijuana plant, or selected chemicals found in that plant, to control the nausea sometimes caused by cancer chemotherapy. The drug Marinol (dronabinol)

was introduced as a synthetic version of THC, one of the chemicals found in marijuana. Marinol has met with mixed success, possibly because marijuana's antinausea effects are caused by a chemical other than THC (Smith, 1997).

Preliminary research conducted in the 1980s suggested that smoking marijuana might help control certain forms of otherwise unmanageable glaucoma (Voelker, 1994; Grinspoon & Bakalar, 1993; Jaffe, 1990). Unfortunately, the initial promise of marijuana in the control of glaucoma was not supported by follow-up studies (Watson, Benson, & Joy, 2000). Although marijuana smoking *does* cause a temporary reduction in the fluid pressure within the eye, only 60–65% of those patients who smoke marijuana experience this effect (Green, 1998). Further, it was found that in order to achieve and maintain an adequate reduction in eye pressure levels, the individual would have to smoke between 2990 and 3700 marijuana cigarettes per year—that is, one cigarette as often as every 2–3 hours (Green, 1998).

Although marijuana no longer is considered a possible therapeutic agent in the control of glaucoma, there continues to be strong support for its use in the treatment of multiple sclerosis and rheumatoid arthritis. It is also believed to be of possible value in treating chronic pain conditions (Watson, Benson, & Joy, 2000; Grinspoon & Bakalar, 1997), and it may help control the weight loss often seen in patients with late-stage AIDS or cancer (Watson, Benson, & Joy, 2000). Although accounts are often dismissed on the grounds that they are only anecodotal in nature (Marmor, 1998), the Institute of Medicine concluded that there was enough evidence to warrant an in-depth study of these and other claims that marijuana has medicinal value (Watson, Benson, & Joy, 2000). Unfortunately, the U.S. government does not seem to be at all motivated to follow these recommendations. In 1996, the United States Drug Enforcement Administration (DEA) began a series of administrative hearings to determine the status of marijuana as a possible medicinal agent. An administrative law judge ruled in 1988 that marijuana should be reclassified as a Schedule II substance (see Appendix 3). The DEA then overruled its own judge and ruled that marijuana would remain a Schedule I substance (Kassirer, 1997). In spite of evidence that at least some of the chemicals in marijuana

---

[2]Contrary to popular belief, the Marijuana Stamp Act of 1937 did not make *possession* of marijuana illegal but *did* impose a small tax on it. People who pay the tax receive a stamp, which shows that they have complied with this regulation. Obviously, because the stamp also alerts authorities to the fact that the applicants have marijuana in their possession, illegal users of marijuana do not apply for the proper forms to pay the tax. The stamps are of interest to stamp collectors, however, and a few collectors have actually paid the tax in order to obtain the stamp for their collections!

have medicinal value, all attempts at careful, systematic research into this issue have been prevented (Stimmel, 1997).

By 1996, the state legislature of different states had begun to debate the medicinal use of marijuana and put the matter to a vote. Several states, such as California, adopted measures approving the medicinal use of marijuana, often after a popular referendum on the subject had been approved by the voters. Unfortunately, the federal government continues to use bureaucratic mechanisms to block these efforts. For example, even if a person *does* use marijuana strictly for its medicinal value, the journal *Accounting Today* (1997) warned its readers that deduction of this expense would not be allowed under existing Internal Revenue Service (IRS) tax rules. Thus it would appear that marijuana will continue to remain a controversial recreational substance for many years to come.

The Potency of Marijuana Currently Being Used

Ever since the 1960s, marijuana abusers have sought ways to enhance the effects of the chemical(s) in the plant by adding other substances to the marijuana before smoking it or by using strains with the highest possible concentrations of the compounds thought to cause marijuana's effects. To this end, users have taken to growing strains of marijuana that have high concentrations of the compounds most often associated with pleasurable effects, and marijuana has become the biggest cash crop in the United States (Lewis, 1997; Guttman, 1996).[3]

There is strong evidence that much of the marijuana sold in the United States at this time is more potent than the marijuana commonly used in the 1960s and 1970s. Given that the potency of THC (to be discussed later in this chapter) in marijuana samples in storage declines by 5% per month, this is difficult to assess (Macfadden & Woody, 2000), but there are reports that some of the marijuana being sold today is up to *10 times as potent* as the marijuana sold just a few decades ago (Segal & Duffy, 1999). To further complicate the issue

of assessing these claims, the potency of marijuana purchased from illicit sources varies from sample to sample. As a general rule, however, "high-quality" marijuana has a THC content[4] of about 15% (Segal & Duffy, 1999), although some samples of the Sinsemilla and Netherwood strains of the plant have a THC level of up to 20% (Hall & Solowij, 1998; Weiss & Millman, 1998) and one strain developed in British Columbia, Canada, reportedly has up to a 30% THC content (Shannon, 2000).

A technical point. THC is found throughout the marijuana plant, but the highest concentrations of THC are found in the small upper leaves and flowering tops of the plant (Hall & Solowij, 1998). Historically, the term *marijuana* is used to identify preparations of the cannabis plant that are used for smoking or eating. The term *hashish* is used to identify the thick resin that is obtained from the flowers of the marijuana plant. This resin is dried, forming a brown or black substance that has a high concentration of THC. This is subsequently either ingested orally (often mixed with some sweet substance) or smoked. *Hash oil*, a liquid extracted from the plant with 25–60% THC, is added to marijuana or hashish to enhance its effect. However, in this chapter, the generic term *marijuana* is used for any part of the plant that is to be smoked or ingested.

Scope of the Problem of Marijuana Abuse

Globally, an estimated 200–300 million people are regular users of marijuana (Macfadden & Woody, 2000). In the United States, an estimated 70 million people have used marijuana at least once (Petersen, 2000), and an estimated 37.5 million people are regular users of marijuana (Johnson, Heriza, & St. Dennis, 1999). Each year an estimated 1,476 metric tons of marijuana are consumed, 75% of this amount being imported through illicit channels, and the rest produced locally (*Forensic Drug Abuse Advisor*, 1995b).

The average age at which marijuana users begin to use it is estimated to be approximately 18 years (Hubbard, Franco, & Onaivi, 1999). Marijuana use peaks in early adulthood, usually by the mid to late 20s, and most people use it only occasionally (Hall &

---

[3]It is the estimated value of the marijuana being raised in the United States, not the amount being cultivated, that makes it the most valuable cash crop in the country at this time.

[4]As we will see later in this chapter, THC is the active agent of marijuana.

Solowij, 1998). Of those who begin to use marijuana, only 10% become daily users, and 20–30% become weekly users (Hall & Solowij, 1998). Approximately 100,000 people seek treatment for marijuana addiction each year in the United States (Hubbard, Franco, & Onaivi, 1999).

Almost a generation ago, Peluso and Peluso (1998) suggested that a "few puffs on a joint is this generation's social martini" (p. 110). The truth of this is apparent in the fact that 54% of the adults between 19–32 who were surveyed admitted to having used marijuana at least once (Johnston, O'Malley, & Bachman, 1999b). Because of marijuana's popularity, the legal and the social sanctions against its use have repeatedly changed in the past 30 years. In some states, possession of a small amount of marijuana was decriminalized, only to be recriminalized a few years later (Macfadden & Woody, 2000). Currently, the legal status of marijuana varies from one state to another.

Pharmacology of Marijuana

The *Cannabis sativa* plant contains over 400 different identified compounds, of which an estimated 61 have some psychoactive effect (Weiss & Millman, 1998; Restak, 1994). The majority of marijuana's psychoactive effects in humans are apparently the result of a single compound, Δ-9-tetrahydro-cannabinol[5] (THC), which was first identified as the main active ingredient of marijuana in 1964 (Restak, 1994; Mirin, Weiss, & Greenfield, 1991; Schwartz, 1987; Bloodworth, 1987). A second compound, *cannabidiol* (CBD) is also inhaled when marijuana is smoked, but researchers are not sure this compound has a psychoactive effect on humans (Nelson, 2000).

THC, a lipid-soluble chemical, is also strongly protein-bound, with the result that only about 1% of the THC absorbed into the body passes the blood-brain barrier and reaches the brain (Macfadden & Woody, 2000; Jenkins & Cone, 1998). Researchers have found that THC binds to receptor sites in the hippocampus, cerebral cortex, basal ganglia, and cerebellum—findings that account for marijuana's observed effects on the user (Watson, Benson, & Joy, 2000; Hubbard, Franco, & Onaivi, 1999). Researchers have also discovered that THC inhibits the function of the enzyme *adenylate cy-*

clase, which is involved in the transmission of pain messages. This would seem to account for the analgesic effect of marijuana. Scientists have also identified a pair of molecules within the brain that bind to the same receptor sites that THC occupies when the individual smokes marijuana. The first of these molecules is called *anandamide* (Nutt, 1996; Restak, 1993), and the second is called *sn-2 arachidonyglycerol* (2-AG). This latter compound is manufactured in the hippocampus, a region of the brain known to be involved in the formation of memories, and this may account for marijuana's ability to interfere with memory formation while the person is under its influence. Neuroscientists are now attempting to isolate anandamide and 2-AG to better understand their function as neurotransmitters.

Marijuana has been found to affect the synthesis and turnover of the neurotransmitter acetylcholine in the limbic region of the brain (Hartman, 1995) and in the cerebellum (Fortgang, 1999). Acetylcholine is a neurotransmitter that is involved in the process of alertness, and this may be one reason why marijuana users tend to feel somewhat sedated and relaxed while under the influence of the drug. It is not known whether this effect is caused by THC or by one of the other psychoactive compounds found in marijuana (Watson, Benson, & Joy, 2000).

Once in the circulation, THC is rapidly distributed to blood-rich organs such as the heart, lungs, and brain. It then slowly works its way into tissues that receive less blood, such as the fat tissues of the body, where unmetabolized THC is stored. Repeated episodes of marijuana use over a short period of time allow significant amounts of THC to be stored in the body's fat reserves. In between periods of active marijuana use, the fat-bound THC is slowly released back into the blood (Schwartz, 1987). In rare cases, this process results in very heavy marijuana users' testing positive for THC in urine toxicology screens for weeks after their last use of marijuana (Schwartz, 1987). In the casual user, however urine toxicology tests will usually detect metabolites of THC for only about 3 days after the last use.[6]

The primary site of THC biotransformation is the liver, and more than 100 metabolites are produced dur-

---

[5] Δ is the Greek letter delta.

[6] Some individuals have claimed that their urine samples tested "positive" for THC because they had used a form of beer made from the hemp plant. Unfortunately, test data fail to support the claim that one can ingest THC from this beer.

ing the process of THC biotransformation (Hart, 1997). The half-life of THC appears to depend on whether metabolic tolerance has developed. However, the liver is not able to biotransform THC very quickly, and in experienced users, THC has a half-life of about 3 days (Schwartz, 1987) to a week (Bloodworth, 1987). About 65 percent of the metabolites of THC are excreted in the feces, the rest in the urine (Hubbard, Franco, & Onaivi, 1999; Schwartz, 1987).

Tolerance to the subjective effects of THC develops rapidly, and once tolerance has developed, users must either wait a few days until their tolerance for marijuana begins to diminish or alter the way they use it. For example, the chronic marijuana smoker must use "more potent cannabis, deeper, more sustained inhalations, or larger amounts of the crude drug" (Schwartz, 1987, p. 307) in order to overcome his or her tolerance to marijuana.

Interactions between marijuana and other chemicals. There has been relatively little research into the interaction of marijuana and other chemicals. It has been suggested that when patients who are taking lithium use marijuana, it causes their blood lithium levels to increase (Ciraulo, Shader, Greenblatt, & Barnhill, 1995). The reason for this increase in blood lithium level is not clear. However, given that lithium is quite toxic and has only a narrow "therapeutic window" between the optimal level of lithium and toxicity, this interaction between marijuana and lithium is potentially dangerous to the person who uses both substances.

There also has been one case report of a patient who smoked marijuana while taking Antabuse (disulfiram). The patient developed a hypomanic episode that subsided when the marijuana use was stopped (Barnhill, Ciraulo, Ciraulo, & Greene, 1995). Upon resuming the use of marijuana while taking Antabuse, the patient became hypomanic again, according to the authors. This suggests that the mania was due to some unknown interaction between these two chemicals. For reasons that are not clear, adolescents who use marijuana while taking an antidepressant medication such as *Elavil* (amitriptyline) run the risk of developing a drug-induced delirium; thus, individuals who are taking antidepressants should not use marijuana.

Cocaine users often smoke marijuana concurrently with their use of cocaine, because they believe that the sedating effects of marijuana will counteract the excessive stimulation caused by the cocaine. Unfortunately, the abuse of cocaine is known to have a negative impact on cardiac function. There has been no research into the combined effects of marijuana and cocaine on cardiac function in either healthy volunteers or patients with some form of preexisting cardiovascular disease.

Methods of Administration

Occasionally, users ingest marijuana by mouth, usually after it has been baked into a product such as cookies or brownies. But, for the most part, users in the United States smoke homemade cigarettes made out of marijuana either alone or mixed with other substances. Most commonly, the marijuana is smoked by itself, in the form of cigarettes. These "joints" usually contain 500–750 mg of marijuana and provide an effective dose of approximately 2.5–20 mg of THC. The marijuana in the average joint weighs about 0.014 ounce, and the typical user consumes about 18 joints a month (Abt Associates, Inc., 1995a).

A variation on the marijuana cigarette is the "blunt." Blunts are made by removing one of the outer leaves of a cigar, unrolling it, filling it with high-potency marijuana mixed with chopped cigar tobacco, and then rerolling the mixture into what is essentially a marijuana "cigar" (*The Addiction Letter*, 1993a). Users report some degree of stimulation, possibly from the nicotine in the cigar tobacco entering the lungs along with the marijuana smoke.

The technique by which marijuana is smoked is somewhat different from the smoking technique used for cigarettes or cigars (Schwartz, 1987). Users must inhale the smoke deeply into their lungs and then hold their breath for 20–30 seconds to get as much THC into the blood as possible (Schwartz, 1987). Researchers disagree as to the amount of THC that will be absorbed by the marijuana smoker. Scaros, Westra, and Barone (1990) suggested that about 18% of the available THC is absorbed through the lungs into the blood. Hall and Solowij (1998) suggested that between 20% and 70% of the THC in the marijuana cigarette might reach the lungs and that 5–24% of the total amount of THC might reach the circulation. In contrast to these estimates, Macfadden and Woody (2000) suggested that 75% of the available THC in the cigarette is destroyed by the process of smoking, leaving only 25% of the original dose to reach the lungs. Between 2% and 50% of this 25% will actually be absorbed through the lungs of the marijuana smoker, depending on the individual and the exact method of smoking.

When marijuana is smoked, the effects begin within seconds (Weiss & Mirin, 1988) to perhaps 10 minutes (Bloodworth, 1987). It has been estimated that in order to produce a sense of euphoria, the user must inhale approximately 25–50 micrograms per kilogram of body weight when marijuana is smoked and between 50 and 200 micrograms per kilogram of body weight when the marijuana was ingested orally (Mann, 1992). Doses of 200–250 micrograms per kilogram when marijuana is smoked, or 300–500 micrograms per kilogram when it is taken orally, may cause the user to hallucinate, according to the author.

As these figures suggest, it takes an extremely large dose of THC before the individual will begin to hallucinate. Marijuana users in other countries often have access to high-potency sources of THC and thus may achieve hallucinatory doses. But it is extremely rare for marijuana users in this country to have access to such potent forms of the plant. Thus, for the most part, the marijuana being smoked in this country will not cause the individual to hallucinate. Even so, in many parts of the country, law enforcement officials, classify marijuana as a hallucinogenic.

The effects of smoked marijuana reach peak intensity within 30 minutes and begin to decline in an hour (Nelson, 2000). Estimates of the duration of the subjective effects of smoked marijuana range from 2–3 hours (Brophy, 1993) to 4 hours (Grinspoon & Bakalar, 1997b; Bloodworth, 1987). When it is ingested orally, the user will not experience THC's effects until 30–60 minutes (Mirin, Weiss, & Greenfield, 1991) to perhaps 2 hours (Schwartz, 1987) after eating the compound. Oral use does not result in the same intensity of effects, because much of the THC is destroyed by the chemicals of the digestive tract when this compound is ingested orally. Oral users will absorb only a 4–12% of the available THC (Stimmel, 1997a; Jaffe, 1990). Estimates of the duration of marijuana's effects when ingested orally range from 3 to 5 hours (Mirin, Weiss, & Greenfield, 1991; Weiss & Mirin, 1988) upwards to 5 to 12 hours (Kaplan, Sadock, & Grebb, 1994).

Proponents of the legalization of marijuana point out that in terms of *immediate* lethality, marijuana appears to be a "safe" drug. Animal research suggests that the LD_{50} of THC is about 125 mg/kg (Nahas, 1986). A 160-pound person weighs about 72.59 kilograms. If the typical marijuana cigarette contains 20 mg of THC, then to reach the estimated LD_{50}, this person would have to smoke 453 marijuana cigarettes at once. And this estimate assumes that 100% of the available THC in the marijuana cigarette would be absorbed. If we take the high estimate of 50% of the THC in the average marijuana cigarette being absorbed, then the estimated number of marijuana cigarettes that a typical 160-pound person would have to smoke to reach the LD_{50} is just over 900 marijuana cigarettes at once. Annas (1997) suggested that a person would have to smoke 1500 *pounds* of marijuana in a 15-minute span of time to die as a result of a marijuana overdose.

In contrast to the estimated 434,000 deaths each year in this country from tobacco use, and the total of 125,000 yearly fatalities from alcohol use, there are only an estimated 75 marijuana-related deaths each year. Most marijuana-related deaths result from accidents that occur while the individual is under the influence of this substance, rather than as a direct result of any toxic effects of THC (Crowley, 1988). As these data suggest, there has never been a documented case of a marijuana overdose (Grinspoon & Bakalar, 1997a, 1995, 1993; Nahas, 1986). Indeed, in terms of its immediate toxicity, THC appears to be "among the least toxic drugs known to modern medicine" (Weil, 1986, p. 47). The effective dose of THC is estimated to be between 1/20,000 and 1/40,000 the lethal dose (Grinspoon & Bakalar, 1995, 1993; Kaplan, Sadock, & Grebb, 1994).

Subjective Effects of Marijuana

At moderate dosage levels, marijuana brings about a two-phase reaction (Brophy, 1993). The first phase begins shortly after the drug enters the bloodstream, when the individual experiences a period of mild anxiety, followed by a sense of well-being, or euphoria, as well as a sense of relaxation and friendliness (Kaplan, Sadock, & Grebb, 1994). These subjective effects are consistent with the known physical effects of marijuana. Research has found that marijuana causes "a transient increase in the release of the neurotransmitter dopamine" (Friedman, 1987, p. 47), a neurochemical thought to be involved in the experience of euphoria. For reasons that are not known, marijuana also causes the blood vessels in the eye to dilate, making the user's eyes appear red (Monroe, 1998).

As with many drugs of abuse, the individual's *expectations* influence how he or she interprets the effects of marijuana. Marijuana users tend to anticipate that the drug will (1) impair cognitive function, as well as the user's behavior, (2) help the user to relax, (3) help the user to interact socially and enhance sexual function, (4) enhance creative abilities and alter perception, (5) have some negative effects, and (6) bring about a sense of "craving" (Schafer & Brown, 1991). Individuals who are intoxicated on marijuana frequently report an altered sense of time, mood swings (Kaplan, Sadock, & Grebb, 1994), and feelings of well-being and happiness (Abood & Martin, 1992). Marijuana also seems to bring about a splitting of consciousness, in which the users may experience the sensation of observing themselves while under the influence of the drug (Kaplan, Sadock, & Grebb, 1994; Grinspoon & Bakalar, 1985).

Marijuana users have often reported a sense of being on the threshold of a significant personal insight but being unable to put this insight into words. These reported drug-related insights seem to come about during the first phase of the marijuana reaction. The second phase of the marijuana experience begins when the individual becomes sleepy, which occurs after the acute intoxication caused by marijuana (Brophy, 1993).

Adverse Effects of Occasional Marijuana Use

More than 2000 separate metabolites of the 400 chemicals found in the marijuana plant may be found in the body after the individual has smoked marijuana (Jenike, 1991). Many of these metabolites may remain present in the body for weeks after a single episode of marijuana smoking. Unfortunately, the long-term effects of these chemicals on the human body have not been studied in detail (University of California, Berkeley, 1990b). In addition, if the marijuana is adulterated (as it frequently is), the various adulterants make their own contribution to the flood of chemicals being admitted to the body when the person uses marijuana. Again, there is little research on the long-term effects of these adulterants or their metabolites on the user.

Because so much remains to be discovered about marijuana's effects on the user, researchers differ as to whether there are many immediate adverse reactions to marijuana when used by itself. Mirin, Weiss, and Greenfield (1991) concluded that marijuana has relatively few adverse effects. Whereas Hubbard, Franco, and Onaivi (1999) suggested that 40–60% of those who use marijuana experience at least one adverse effect. This difference may reflect the fact that the marijuana currently in use has a higher THC content that the marijuana sold a decade ago. Another possible explanation is that the different teams defined "adverse effects" differently.

It is known that when marijuana is smoked, some of the smaller blood vessels in the body dilate, although it is not clear whether this effect is caused by THC itself or by one of the other chemicals found in the cannabis plant. This is the mechanism that causes marijuana smokers to have "bloodshot" eyes.

Another common adverse reaction to marijuana use is the development of drug-induced anxiety or even full-blown panic attacks (Millman & Beeder, 1994; Kaplan, Sadock, & Grebb, 1994). Factors that seem to influence whether marijuana-related panic reactions occur are the individual's prior experience with marijuana, her or his expectations for the drug, the dosage level being used, and the setting in which the drug is used. Such panic reactions are most often seen in the inexperienced marijuana user (Mirin, Weiss, & Greenfield, 1991; Bloodworth, 1987). Usually the only treatment needed is reassurance that the drug-induced effects will soon pass (Millman & Beeder, 1994; Kaplan, Sadock, & Grebb, 1994).

Marijuana use also contributes to impaired reflexes for at least 24 hours after the individual last used this substance (Hubbard, Franco, & Onaivi, 1999). Schwartz (1987) reported that marijuana use may impair coordination and reaction time for 12–24 hours after the euphoria from the last marijuana use ended. Schwartz also noted that teenagers who smoked marijuana as often as six times a month "were 2.4 times more likely to be involved in traffic accidents" (p. 309) as were nonusers, and Meer (1986) demonstrated performance impairment on a flight simulator 24 hours after each 10 private airplane pilots had smoked one marijuana cigarette. Hubbard, Franco, and Onaivi (1999) suggested that marijuana users might be at increased risk for accidental injuries while using motor vehicles for extended periods after their last use of this substance.

Marijuana users experience a 30–50% increase in heart rate that begins within a few minutes of the time of use and can last up to 3 hours (Hall & Solowij, 1998). For unknown reasons, marijuana reduces the strength of the heart contractions and hence the amount of oxygen reaching the heart muscle—changes that are potentially serious for patients with heart disease (Schuckit, 2000; Barnhill, Ciraulo, Ciraulo, & Greene, 1995).

A more serious, but quite rare, adverse reaction is the development of a marijuana-induced psychotic reaction, often called a *toxic* or *drug-induced psychosis*. The effects of a marijuana-induced toxic psychosis are usually short-lived and clear up in a few days to a few weeks (Millman & Beeder, 1994). However, research has also demonstrated that marijuana use can exacerbate pre-existing psychotic disorders and can initiate a psychotic reaction in an individual predisposed to this form of psychiatric dysfunction (Linszen, Dingemans, & Lenior, 1994; Mathers & Ghodse, 1992; Nahas, 1986). Fortunately, researchers currently think that marijuana-induced psychotic reactions result only from extremely heavy marijuana use (Kaplan, Sadock, & Grebb, 1994; Mathers & Ghodse, 1992). Thus the danger of a marijuana-induced psychosis is thought to be quite low for the casual user.

One mechanism through which marijuana might contribute to the emergence of schizophrenia was suggested by Linszen, Dingemans, and Lenior (1994). These authors noted that THC functions as a dopamine agonist in the nerve pathways of the region of the brain known as the *medial forebrain bundles*, which use dopamine as the primary neurotransmitter. Dysregulation of normal dopamine activity has been suggested as one possible cause of schizophrenia, so this might be one mechanism through which marijuana might contribute to the emergence of psychotic symptoms in patients with schizophrenia.

Marijuana is known to reduce sexual desire in the user and, for male users, may contribute to erectile problems and delayed ejaculation (Finger, Lund, & Slagel, 1997). Finally, an extremely rare consequence of marijuana use is the development of an acute depressive reaction (Grinspoon & Bakalar, 1997b). This marijuana-related depression is most common in the inexperienced user and may reflect the activation of an undetected depression on the part of the user. The depressive episode is usually mild and does not require professional intervention except in rare cases, according to the authors. It usually clears up in less than 24 hours (Millman & Beeder, 1994).

Consequences of Chronic Marijuana Abuse

The active agent of marijuana, THC, has been demonstrated to cause lung damage and to reduce the effectiveness of the respiratory system's defenses against infection with chronic use (Hubbard, Franco, & Onaivi, 1999). Animal research also suggests the possibility of a drug-induced suppression of the immune system as a whole, although there "is no conclusive evidence that consumption of cannabinoids impairs human immune function" (Hall & Solowij, 1998, p. 1612).

Marijuana smokers typically expose themselves to many compounds found in regular tobacco cigarettes, but at concentrations far higher than in the latter. For example, marijuana has between 10 and 20 times as much "tar" as tobacco cigarettes (Nelson, 2000), and marijuana smokers are thought to absorb *four times* as much "tar" as cigarette smokers (Tashkin, 1993). In addition to this, the marijuana smoker absorbs *five times* as much carbon monoxide (Polen, Sidney, Tekawa, Sadler, & Friedman, 1993; University of California, Berkeley, 1990b; Oliwenstein, 1988). Smoking just 4 marijuana "joints" appears to have the same negative impact on lung function as smoking 20 regular cigarettes (Tashkin, 1990).

Chronic marijuana smokers develop the same type of damage to the cells lining the airways as do cigarette smokers who go on to develop lung cancer (Tashkin, 1993; University of California, Berkeley, 1990b; Oliwenstein, 1988). Research has shown that marijuana smoke contains 5–15 times as much benzopyrene (a known carcinogen) as does tobacco smoke (Tashkin, 1993; Bloodworth, 1987) Indeed, the heavy use of marijuana has been suggested as a cause of cancer of the respiratory tract and the mouth (tongue, tonsils, etc.) in a number of younger individuals who would not be expected to have cancer (Hall & Solowij, 1998; Tashkin, 1993).

There are several reasons for the observed relationship between heavy marijuana use and lung disease. In terms of absolute numbers, marijuana smokers tend to smoke fewer joints than cigarette smokers do cigarettes. However, they also smoke unfiltered joints, which allows more of the particles from smoked marijuana into the lungs. Marijuana smokers also smoke more of the joint than cigarette smokers do cigarettes. This increases the smoker's exposure to microscopic contaminants in the marijuana. Finally, marijuana smokers inhale more deeply than cigarette smokers and retain the smoke longer in the lungs (Polen, Sidney, Tekawa, Sadler, & Friedman, 1993). Again, this increases the individual's exposure to the potential carcinogenic agents in marijuana smoke. These facts may explain why, like tobacco smokers, marijuana users have an increased frequency of bronchitis and other upper respiratory infections (Hall & Solowij, 1998). The chronic use of marijuana also may contribute to the development of obstructive pulmonary diseases, similar to those seen in cigarette smokers (University of California, Berkeley, 1990b).

Marijuana use has been implicated as the cause of a number of reproductive system dysfunctions. For example, there is evidence that marijuana use contributes to reduced sperm counts (Brophy, 1993) and a reduction in testicular size (Hubbard, Franco, & Onaivi, 1999) in men. Further, male chronic marijuana users have been found to have 50 percent lower blood testosterone levels than men who do not use marijuana (Bloodworth, 1987).

Women who are chronic marijuana users have been found to experience menstrual abnormalities and/or a failure to ovulate (Hubbard, Franco, & Onaivi, 1999; Brophy, 1993). However, on the basis of the limited data available at this time, there is no evidence that chronic marijuana use results in fertility problems (Grinspoon & Bakalar, 1997b). It is difficult to isolate the effects of marijuana on fertility, or on fetal growth and development, because individuals who use marijuana tend to abuse other chemicals also (Grinspoon & Bakalar, 1997b).

People who have previously used hallucinogenics may have marijuana-related "flashback" experiences (Jenike, 1991). Such flashbacks are usually limited to the six-month period following the last marijuana use (Jeinke, 1991) and will eventually stop if the person does not use any further mood-altering chemicals (Weiss & Mirin, 1988). The flashback experience will be discussed in more detail in the chapter on the hallucinogenic drugs.

For years, researchers believed that marijuana did not cause any physical damage to the brain. Recently, however, researchers have uncovered evidence that the chronic use of marijuana "damages and destroys nerve cells and causes other pathological changes in the hippocampus" (Friedman, 1987 p. 47; Losken, Maviglia, & Friedman, 1996; Kaufman & McNaul; 1992; Schuster, 1990).

This would make sense, because there is evidence that chronic marijuana use causes problems with the retrieval mechanisms of memory (American Academy of Family Physicians, 1990a). Chronic marijuana use may also interfere with the function of other regions of the brain. Pope and Yurgelun-Todd (1996) found that heavy marijuana abusers had lower performance on psychological tests that tapped the "attentional/executive system" (p. 526) of the brain. They concluded that marijuana affects a number of different regions in the brain, including those involved in sustained attention (a brain stem function) and the capacity to shift attention (which is controlled by prefrontal cortical areas of the brain). Although the results of this investigation were suggestive, the authors cautioned that they were not conclusive and that further research into the effects of marijuana is needed.

Fletcher, Page, Francis, Copeland, Naus, Davis, Morris, Krauskopf, and Satz (1996) compared the test performance of two groups of marijuana users, a young-adult group and a middle-aged group, with that of nonusers of the same age. They found that the older marijuana-using subgroup performed significantly worse than did their nonusing counterparts on two tests of short-term memory, a finding that the authors interpreted as evidence that chronic marijuana use may interfere with memory function. However, these effects may only be temporary. Neuropsychological testing of chronic marijuana users in countries such as Greece, Jamaica, and Costa Rica has failed to yield evidence of permanent brain damage (Grinspoon & Bakalar, 1997b). Thus, it appears that chronic marijuana use can cause at least temporary brain dysfunction, although it is not clear whether this reflects permanent marijuana-induced brain damage.

Researchers have found, via electroencephalographic (EEG) studies, that chronic marijuana users have changes in the electrical activity of the brain that last for at least 3 months after their last use of this substance (Schuckit, 2000). Marijuana has been implicated in short-term memory impairment, and animal studies offer evidence of physical damage to the brain as a result of marijuana use.

There is conflicting evidence on whether chronic marijuana use can bring about an "amotivational syndrome." Some researchers have described a marijuana-related amotivational syndrome consisting of a decreased drive and ambition, short attention span, easy distractibility, and a tendency not to make plans beyond the present day (Mirin, Weiss, & Greenfield, 1991). However, there are also many researchers who do not believe that marijuana can have this effect (Abood & Martin, 1992). Weiss and Millman (1998) pointed out that chronic marijuana abusers often demonstrate "remarkable energy and enthusiasm in the pursuit of their goals" (p. 211) and suggested the alternative term *aberrant motivational syndrome* for this condition.

It has been suggested that the amotivational syndrome is only a research artifact. Individuals who tend to use marijuana on a regular basis are also likely to be people who are bored, depressed, listless, alienated from society, and cynical. These are some of the very same characteristics thought to be a result of the marijuana-induced amotivational syndrome (Grinspoon & Bakalar, 1997b). Thus, Mendelson and Mello (1998) concluded that marijuana use does not cause "a specific and unique 'amotivational syndrome'" (p. 2514).

Although in terms of immediate lethality, marijuana is quite safe, there is significant evidence that chronic marijuana use can either contribute to or cause a number of potentially serious medical problems. For example, there is evidence that some of the chemicals in marijuana might function as "dysregulators of cellular regulation" (Hart, 1997, p. 60) by slowing the process of cellular renewal within the body. Thus it would appear that marijuana use is not as benign as advocates of this substance would have us believe.

The myth of marijuana-induced violence. In the 1930s and 1940s, it was widely believed that marijuana would cause the user to become violent. Researchers no longer believe that marijuana is likely to induce violence. Indeed, the sedating and euphoric effects of marijuana are more likely to *reduce* the tendency towards violence while the user is intoxicated.[7]

---

[7] However, if the marijuana is adulterated with any other chemical, then the effects of that chemical must be considered as a possible cause of drug-induced violent behaviors. For example, the hallucinogen PCP is known to trigger violent behavior in some users, and it is a common adulterant in marijuana.

The Addiction Potential of Marijuana

As we noted in earlier chapters, two of the cardinal symptoms of addiction to any chemical are the development of tolerance to that chemical and the experiencing of a withdrawal syndrome when that drug is discontinued. By these criteria, marijuana is a potential addictive substance, because smoking as few as three marijuana cigarettes a week may result in tolerance to the effects of marijuana (Bloodworth, 1987). Perhaps 1 of every 11 people who smoke marijuana will become a heavy user for at least a period of time, although it is not clear what percentage of heavy users are actually addicted (Fortgang, 1999).

Chronic marijuana use may also result in a withdrawal syndrome that is, in a sense, self-limiting. Because of THC long half-life in the human body, the symptoms of withdrawal from it are not so severe as those seen in withdrawal from narcotics or barbiturates (Bloodworth, 1987). However, heavy, chronic marijuana use can result in a withdrawal syndrome that includes irritability, aggressive behaviors, anxiety, insomnia, nausea, and loss of appetite (Kouri, Pope, & Lukas, 1999; Abood & Martin, 1992; Group for the Advancement of Psychiatry, 1990; Bloodworth, 1987). Other symptoms of withdrawal may include sweating and vomiting (Nahas, 1986). Despite claims to the contrary, marijuana seems to meet the criteria for classification as an addictive compound.

Summary

Marijuana has been the subject of controversy for several generations. In spite of its popularity as a drug of abuse, surprisingly little is actually known about marijuana. However, after a 25-year search, researchers have identified what appears to be the specific receptor site at which the THC molecule exerts at least some of its effects on perception and memory.

In spite of the fact that very little is known about this drug, some groups have called for its complete decriminalization. Other groups maintain that marijuana is a serious drug of abuse with a high potential for harm. Even the experts differ on marijuana's potential to cause harm. For example, in contrast to Weil's (1986) assertion that marijuana is one of the safest drugs known, Oliwenstein (1988) classified it as a dangerous drug. At this time, the available evidence suggests that marijuana is not so benign as was once thought. Either alone or in combination with cocaine, marijuana increases heart rate, a matter of some significance to those with cardiac disease. There is evidence that chronic use of marijuana causes physical changes in the brain, and the smoke from marijuana cigarettes has been found to be even more harmful than tobacco smoke. Marijuana remains such a controversial drug that the U. S. government refuses to sanction research into its effects, because officials do not want to run the risk that researchers might find something about marijuana that proponents of its legalization would use to justify their demands (Smith, 1997).

CHAPTER FOURTEEN

Opiate Abuse and Addiction

Introduction

The opiates are a source of endless confusion not only for health care professionals but for the general public. The narcotic analgesics are derived from the opioid family of chemicals, but because of the history of opiates as drugs of abuse, the general public and physicians alike view them with distrust (Vourakis, 1998; Herrera, 1997). One reason for this is that over the years, myths and mistaken beliefs about opioids and pain management have been repeated from one health care professional to the next so often that they have been incorporated into professional journals and textbooks as medical "fact" (Vourakis, 1998). Physicians and nurses sometimes base clinical decisions for patient care on these half-truths and myths.

For example, research has found that more than 50% of physicians hesitate to prescribe narcotic analgesics in the mistaken belief that doing so might cause the patient to become "addicted" to these medications (60 Minutes, 1996a). Further, physicians often underprescribe narcotic analgesics, causing patients to suffer needless pain (Carvey, 1998). One study found that only slightly more than half of the 300 physicians surveyed were able to estimate correctly the dose of morphine needed to control cancer-related pain (Herrera, 1997). As many as 73% of patients in moderate to severe distress are thought to suffer needless pain because their physicians do not prescribe adequate doses of the appropriate analgesics (Stimmel, 1997).

In addition to this, regulatory policies of the Drug Enforcement Administration (DEA) aimed at discouraging the diversion of prescribed narcotic analgesics[1] often intimidate or confuse physicians who wish to prescribe these medications for patients in pain. As a result of irrational fear of causing the individual to become addicted, and of federal supervisory edicts, only a minority of patients are thought to receive adequate doses of a narcotic analgesic to control pain (Herrera, 1997; Paris, 1996).

This is unfortunate, for although the narcotic analgesics do have a significant abuse potential, they are potent and extremely useful medications. Thus, in order to clear up some of the confusion that surrounds the legitimate use of narcotic analgesics, this chapter is divided into two sections. In the first section, we will examine the use of narcotic analgesics as pharmaceutical agents. In the second section, the narcotic analgesics as drugs of abuse are discussed.

I. THE MEDICAL USES OF NARCOTIC ANALGESICS

A Short History of the Narcotic Analgesics

At some point in what has been called the "Stone Age," early humans discovered that if an incision is made at the top of the *Papaver somniferum* plant during a brief period in its life cycle, the plant extrudes a thick resin.

---

[1]Although it has never been shown that prescription drug diversion is a major problem, this has not prevented the DEA from placing a number of restrictions on physicians, thus eliminating a problem that has never been proved to exist.

This resin is "an elaborate cocktail containing sugars, proteins, ammonia, latex, gums, plant wax, tats, sulphuric and lactic acids, water, meconic acid, and a wide range of alkaloids" (Booth, 1996, p. 4). In the early 1800s, one of these alkaloids was identified as morphine, and this agent was found to possess a strong analgesic potential that proved useful in the control of pain.

Early humans did not have access to the resources of modern biochemical research, but they quickly discovered that the dried resin could be ingested by mouth to control pain. Eventually, this resin came to be called *opium*. Much of the early history of opium took place before the invention of written records. However, researchers have found the residue of the opium poppy plant in Stone Age dwellings in northern Italy and Switzerland (Restak, 1994). There is also archaeological evidence that the opium poppy was being cultivated as a crop in certain regions of Europe by the later part of the Neolithic period (Spindler, 1994; Booth, 1996).

The English word "opium" is derived from the Greek word *opion*, which means "poppy juice" (Stimmel, 1997). In a document known as the Ebers Papyri, which dates back to approximately 7000 B.C., there is a reference to the use of opium as a treatment for children who suffer from colic (Darton & Dilts, 1998). In an era when physicians had few effective treatments to offer the sick, opium came to be used in the treatment of virtually every ailment (Reisine & Pasternak, 1995; Ray & Ksir, 1993; Melzack, 1990). Opium was found to be useful in the mastery of mild to severe levels of pain, and it could control diarrhea, especially massive diarrhea such as that of dysentery.[2] Opium could also control anxiety, and its limited antipsychotic potential made it marginally effective in controlling the symptoms of psychotic disorders (Beeder & Millman, 1995; Woody, McLellan, & Bedrick 1995).

Although opium had been used for thousands of years, it was not until 1803 that Friedrich W. A. Serturner first isolated from opium a pure alkaloid base that was recognized as being the active agent of opium.[3] This chemical was later called *morphine* after the Greek god of dreams, Morphius. This "nitrogenous waste product" (Hart, 1997, p. 59) of the opium poppy happens to control many of the manifestations of pain in humans. As chemists explored the various chemical compounds found in the sap of the opium poppy, they discovered that 20 distinct alkaloids in addition to morphine could be obtained from that plant (Reisine & Pasternak, 1995; Gold, 1993). Medical science has found a use for many of these chemicals, but many of these alkaloids can also be abused. An example is the compound codeine, which is also obtained from the opium poppy. It is occasionally abused because of its ability to induce a sense of euphoria in some people.

In 1857, about half a century after morphine was first isolated from opium, Alexander Wood invented the hypodermic needle. This device made it possible to inject drugs into the body quickly and quite painlessly. Thus, by the middle of the 19th century, chemists were able to produce large amounts of relatively pure morphine from raw opium, and a means was available to introduce this chemical directly into the body. The mistaken belief that injected morphine was not addicting, the tendency for many people to treat their own ailments through the use of "patent" medicines, and the liberal use of morphine and opium in battlefield hospitals in the latter half of the 1800s resulted in a massive outbreak of opiate addiction in the United States.

It is important to remember that at this time, the average person placed little confidence in medical science. It was not unusual for people to rely on time-honored folk remedies and patent medicines, rather than seeking a physician's advice (Norris, 1994). In an era before government regulation, both cocaine and morphine were common ingredients in many of the "patent" medicines sold throughout the United States. Even if the users of a patent medicine were aware of the contents of the bottle they purchased, they were unlikely to believe the "medicine" in the bottle could harm them. The concept of an addictive medication was totally foreign to the average person, who distrusted medical professionals to begin with, and large numbers of people unknowingly became addicted to one or more chemicals in the patent medicines they had come to rely on. In other cases, the individual had started to use either opium or morphine for the control of pain or to treat diarrhea, only to become physically dependent on that chemical. When the user tried to stop, he or she would begin to experience withdrawal symptoms. Like magic, the patent medicine also was effective in treating

[2]See the Glossary.

[3]Restak (1994) gave the year in which morphine was first isolated as 1805, not 1803.

this new disorder! As a result of this process, *more than 1% of the entire population of the United States* was addicted to opium or to narcotics by the year 1900 (Restak, 1994).

During this period, the practice of smoking opium had been introduced to the United States by Chinese immigrants, many of whom came to work on the railroad in the era following the Civil War. Opium smoking became somewhat popular, especially on the Pacific coast, and many opium smokers became addicted to it. By the year 1900 fully a quarter of the opium imported into this country was used not for medicine but for smoking (Jonnes, 1995; Ray & Ksir, 1993). Faced with an epidemic of unrestrained opiate use, the U. S. Congress passed the Pure Food and Drug Act of 1906. This law required manufacturers to list the ingredients of their products on the label, revealing for the first time that many a trusted remedy contained narcotics. Other legislation, especially the Harrison Narcotics Act of 1914, prohibited the use of narcotics without a prescription signed by a physician. Since then, the battle against narcotic abuse/addiction has waxed and waned, but it has never entirely disappeared.

The Classification of Analgesics

Since morphine was first isolated, medical researchers have either isolated or developed a wide variety of compounds that in spite of differences in their chemical structure, have pharmacological effects similar to those of morphine. Segal and Duffy (1999) classified these compounds as falling into one of three groups:

1. *Natural opiates* are obtained directly from the opium; morphine and codeine are examples.
2. *Semisynthetic opiates* are chemically altered derivatives of natural opiates. Dihydromorphine and heroin are examples.
3. *Synthetic opiates* are synthesized in laboratories and are not derived from natural opiates at all. Methadone and propoxyphene are examples.

Admittedly, natural, semisynthetic, and synthetic opiates differ significantly in chemical structure. But all these compounds have similar pharmacological effects, so in this chapter they will be grouped together under the generic terms "opiates" or "narcotic analgesics."

To understand the role that the narcotic analgesics play in modern medicine, it is necessary to understand something about the nature of pain. Pain is the most common, and least understood, complaint encountered by physicians (Fishman & Carr, 1992). Indeed, the very word "pain" comes from the Latin *poena*, which means "a punishment or penalty" (Stimmel, 1997a). Because the experience of pain is so uncomfortable, there is a very real demand for medications that will control the individual's suffering.

To meet this demand, researchers have developed a group of medications that are known as *analgesics*. An analgesic is a chemical that is able to bring about the "relief of pain without producing general anesthesia" (Abel, 1982, p. 192). There are two different groups of analgesics. The first consists of those agents that cause *local anesthesia*. Cocaine was once the prototype local anesthetic. When used properly, cocaine (or any of the other local anesthetics developed after cocaine) blocks the transmission of nerve impulses from the site of the injury to the brain, which thus never receives the pain message.

The second group of analgesics are more global in nature. These drugs alter the individual's perception of pain within the central nervous system (CNS) itself. This group of analgesics was further divided into two subgroups by Abel (1982). The first subgroup consists of the *narcotics*, which have both a CNS-depressant capability and an analgesic effect. The second subgroup of global analgesics is made up of drugs such as aspirin, and acetaminophen, which will be discussed in Chapter 18.

Where Opium Is Produced

Surprisingly, the laboratory synthesis of morphine is extremely difficult, and most of the morphine used by physicians is still obtained from the opium poppy (Reisine & Pasternak, 1995). Crops of opium poppies are raised in Afghanistan, Iran, Pakistan, China, Burma, Laos, Thailand, Turkey, Colombia, and Mexico (Karch, 1996; Sabbag, 1994), and in India (Sabbag, 1994). Unfortunately, virtually all of the legitimate demand for opium around the world is satisfied by that produced by India alone. Nearly all of the excess opium finds its way to the illicit narcotics market, which is a thriving, multinational industry.

TABLE 14.1 Some Common Narcotic Analgesics*

Generic name	Brand name	Approximate equianalgesic parenteral dose
Morphine	—	10 mg every 3–4 hours
Hydromorphone	Dilaudid	1.5 mg every 3–4 hours
Meperidine	Demerol	100 mg every 3 hours
Methadone	Dolophine	10 mg every 6–8 hours
Oxymorphone	Numorphan	1 mg every 3–4 hours
Fentanyl	Sublimaze	0.1 mg every 1–2 hours
Pentazocine	Talwin	60 mg every 3–4 hours
Buprenorphine	Buprenex	0.3–0.4 mg every 6–8 hours
Codeine	—	75–130 mg every 3–4 hours**
Oxycodone	Perdocet, Tylox	Not available in parenteral dosage forms

Source: Based on information contained in Medical Economics Company (2000) and Cherny & Foley (1996).

*This chart is for purposes of comparison only. It is not intended to serve as, nor should it be used for, a guide to patient care.

**It is not recommended that doses of codeine above 65 mg be used, because doses above this level do not result in significantly increased analgesia and may result in increased risk of unwanted side effects.

Current Medical Uses of the Narcotic Analgesics

Since the introduction of aspirin, narcotics have not been utilized to control the milder levels of pain. As a general rule, the opiates are most commonly utilized to control severe, acute pain (Bushnell & Justins, 1993) and some forms of chronic pain (Belgrade, 1999; Savage, 1999). They are also of value in controlling severe diarrhea and in controlling the cough reflex in some forms of disease. A number of different opiate-based analgesics have been developed over the years, and they have minor variations in potency, absorption characteristics, and duration of effects. The generic and brand names of some of the more commonly used narcotic analgesics are given in Table 14.1.

Pharmacology of the Narcotic Analgesics

The resin collected from the *Papaver somniferum* plant contains 10–17% morphine (Jenkins & Cone, 1998). Chemists isolated the compound morphine from this resin almost 200 years ago and quickly discovered that it was the active agent of opium. In spite of the time that has passed since then, morphine is still the standard against which other analgesics are measured (Nelson, 2000). And only since the 1970s, have researchers been able to unravel some of the mystery of how the experience of pain is formed.

In the brain, the narcotic analgesics mimic the actions of a family of closely related chemicals known as the *opioid peptides* (Simon, 1997). There are at least 18 opioid peptides, which function as neurotransmitters in the brain and spinal cord (Hirsch, Paley, & Renner, 1996). The known opioid peptides are grouped into three families: the *beta endorphins*, the *enkephalins*, and the *dynorphins* (Carvey, 1998; Stimmel, 1997). Researchers are still trying to understand the many functions of these opioid peptides in the CNS. Already neuroscientists have discovered that opioid peptides are involved in such diverse functions in the CNS as the perception of pain, the moderation of emotions, the perception of anxiety, the feeling of sedation, appetite suppression, anticonvulsant activity within the brain, smooth muscle motility, the regulation of a number of body functions (such as temperature, heart rate, respiration, and blood pressure), and perhaps even the perception of pleasure (Simon, 1997; Restak, 1994; Hawkes,

1992). In the body, opioid peptides help to regulate the movement of food and fluid through the intestines (Pasternak, 1998).

As this list suggests, the opioid peptides are powerful chemicals. Morphine and its chemical cousins pale by comparison. For example, the opioid peptide known as *beta endorphin* (ß-endorphin) is thought to be 200 times as potent an analgesic as morphine. Currently, researchers believe that the narcotic analgesics function as opioid peptide agonists, occupying the receptor sites in the CNS that are normally utilized by the opioid peptides to simulate the action of these naturally occurring neurotransmitters.

In the past decade, researchers have identified a number of receptor sites within the brain that are utilized by the opioid peptides (Carvey, 1998). There is some disagreement about the exact number of receptor sites. However, the different receptor sites are identified by letters of the Greek alphabet. Table 14.2 summarizes what we know about the different receptor sites in the brain utilized by narcotic analgesics and the function controlled by each receptor subtype.

There is strong evidence that opioids alter the blood flow pattern within the human brain. Using single-photon-emission computed tomography (SPECT) scans to examine the cerebral blood flow in the brains of nine nondependent volunteers, Schlaepfer, Strain, Greenberg, Preston, Lancaster, Bigelow, Barta, and Pearlson (1998) studied changes in the blood flow patterns of various regions in the brains of their subjects. The authors found statistically significant changes in the regional blood flow pattern, with significantly more blood being sent to the anterior cingulate cortex, the thalamus, and the amygdalae when a drug known to occupy the mu receptor was administered. Although it was not clear whether the observed increase in blood flow was associated with the analgesic effect of the drug, it is known these areas of the brain have high concentrations of the mu receptor, which suggests that they play a role in pain perception in humans.

Research has demonstrated that the region of the brain involved in pain perception is different from the area of the brain involved in the experience of euphoria. The thalamus seems to be involved in the perception of pain (Restak, 1994), whereas the euphoria often reported by narcotics abusers seems to be caused by the effects of the opioids on the ventral tegmental region of

TABLE 14.2 Brain Receptor Sites Utilized by Narcotic Analgesics

Opioid receptor	Biological activity associated with opioid receptor
Mu	Analgesia, euphoria, respiratory depression, suppression of cough reflex
Delta	Analgesia, euphoria, endocrine effects, psychomotor functions
Kappa	Analgesia in spinal cord, sedation, miosis
Sigma	Dysphoria, hallucinations, increased psychomotor activity, respiratory activity
Epsilon	?
Lambda	?

Source: Based on information provided in Ashton (1992), Jaffe (1989), and Zevin & Benowitz (1998).

the brain (Kaplan, Sadock, & Grebb, 1994). This area of the brain uses dopamine as its major neurotransmitter, and connects the cortex of the brain with the limbic system. It is interesting to note that Sklair-Tavron, Ski, Lane, Harris, Bunny, and Nestler (1996) found that the chronic administration of morphine to rats caused these same dopamine-utilizing neurons to shrink approximately 25% in volume, which suggests that the morphine is causing these neurons to alter their function in an as-yet-undetermined manner.

The *amygdalae* (singular: amygdala) of the brain are also rich in opioid peptide receptors (Reeves & Wedding, 1994). These regions of the brain function as a halfway point between the senses and the hypothalamus, which is the "emotion center" of the brain, according to the authors. It is thought that the amygdala releases opioid peptides in response to sensory data. By releasing opioid peptides in response to various sensory inputs, the amygdala influences the formation of memory. For example, the sense of pleasure that one feels upon solving an intricate mathematics problem is caused by the amygdalae's release of opioid peptides. This pleasure, in turn, makes it more likely that the student will remember the solution to that problem if he or she encounters it again.

Clincially, narcotic analgesics are thought to mimic the action of opioid peptides in the brain. Stimulation of the mu receptor produces a sense of well-being, thereby reducing the individual's awareness of his or her pain with no significant loss of consciousness (Giannini, 2000). At first, narcotic analgesics also produce a sense of drowsiness, allowing a degree of sedation in spite of the individual's pain (American Medical Association, 1994; Jaffe, 1992). Through these effects, narcotic analgesics reduce the individual's anxiety level, promote drowsiness, and enable the individual to sleep in spite of severe pain (Jaffe, Knapp, & Ciraulo, 1997; Shannon, Wilson, & Stang, 1995). These latter effects seem to reflect the impact of the morphine molecule on the locus ceruleus region of the brain (Jaffe, Knapp, & Ciraulo, 1997; Gold, 1993).

Codeine. Codeine is an alkaloid contained in the milky sap from the same plant, *Papaver somnifeum,* from which opium is obtained. It was first isolated in 1832 (Jaffe, 2000c; Melzack, 1990). It has a mild analgesic effect, and like its chemical cousin morphine, it is able to suppress the cough reflex. Because of these properties, physicians frequently prescribe codeine to help control coughing and for the control of mild to moderate levels of pain. When used as an analgesic, codeine is generally administered in combination with aspirin or acetaminophen (Cherny & Foley, 1996).

Codeine has a number of applications in medicine. It has a mild analgesic potential and is often used in the control of mild to moderate levels of pain. About 10% of a dose of codeine is biotransformed into morphine, and it is this fraction of the total dose of codeine that reduces the individual's perception of pain (Reisine & Pasternak, 1995). Further, codeine, like many narcotic analgesics, is quite effective in the control of cough. This is accomplished through codeine's ability to suppress the action of the *medulla,* a portion of the brain that helps maintain the body's internal state (Jaffe, Knaff, & Ciraulo, 1997; Jaffe & Martin, 1990). Except in extreme cases, codeine is the drug of choice for cough control (American Medical Association, 1994).

Morphine. Morphine is well absorbed from the gastrointestinal tract, but for reasons that will be discussed later in this chapter, orally administered morphine is of limited value in the control of pain. Morphine is also readily absorbed from injection sites and thus is often administered through intramuscular or intravenous injection. Finally, morphine is easily absorbed through the mucous membranes of the body and is occasionally administered in the form of rectal suppositories.

The peak effects of a single dose of morphine are seen about 60 minutes after an oral dose and after 30–60 minutes when the drug is administered via intravenous injection (Shannon, Wilson, & Stang, 1995). After absorption into the circulation, morphine goes through a two-phase process of distribution throughout the body (Karch, 1996). In the first phase, which lasts only a few minutes, the morphine is distributed to various blood-rich tissues, including muscle tissue, the kidneys, liver, lungs, and spleen, and the brain. In the second phase, which proceeds quite rapidly, the majority of the morphine is biotransformed into a metabolite known as *morphine*-3-*glucuronide* (M3G). A smaller amount is biotransformed into the metabolite *morphine*-6-*glucuronide* (M6G) or into one of a small number of additional metabolites (Karch, 1996).

Morphine biotransformation takes place in the liver, and within six minutes of an intravenous injection, the majority of a single dose of morphine has been biotransformed into one of the two metabolites discussed in the last paragraph. Scientists have only recently discovered that M6G has biologically active properties, and this metabolite may even be more potent than the parent compound, morphine (Karch, 1996). About 90% of morphine metabolites are eventually eliminated from the body by the kidneys (Shannon, Wilson, & Stang, 1995); the other 10% are excreted as unchanged morphine (Karch, 1996).

Morphine has a biological half-life of 2–3 hours. Following a single dose, approximately one-third of the morphine becomes protein-bound (Karch, 1996). The analgesic effects of a single dose of morphine last for approximately 4 hours (American Medical Association, 1994). Although it is well absorbed when administered through intramuscular or intravenous injection, morphine takes 20–30 minutes to cross the blood-brain barrier to reach the areas in the brain where it has its primary effect (Angier, 1990). Thus there is a delay between injection of the narcotic analgesic and the time when the patient begins to experience some relief from his or her pain.

Neuroadaptation to narcotic analgesics. A number of reasons why a given patient might suddenly require more medication for pain control include disease progression, an increase in physical activity, lack of compliance in taking analgesics, and medication interaction effects (Pappagallo, 1998). None of these reasons reflects an addictive process. Another reason why a patient might require a larger amount of a narcotic analgesic, however, is that after an extended period of time neuroadaptation within a patient's brain will make him or her less responsive to the drug's effects.

The development of neuroadaptation is incomplete and uneven. For example, some patients develop a "craving" for opiates when the medication is discontinued after having received intravenous injections of morphine every 2 hours for just a single day (Nelson, 2000). Other patients become tolerant to the analgesic effect of a given dose of a narcotic analgesic in as little as 1–2 weeks of continual use (Tyler, 1994; McCaffery & Ferrell, 1994; Fulton & Johnson, 1993). However, in contrast, the patient may never become fully tolerant to the effect of narcotics on the size of the pupils of the eyes.

As the patient gradually becomes tolerant to the analgesic effects of lower doses of a narcotic, his or her daily dosage level might be raised to levels that would kill a patient who had not had time to complete the process of neuroadaptation. For example, a single intravenous dose of 60 mg of morphine is potentially fatal to the opiate-naive person (Kaplan, Sadock, & Grebb, 1994). In contrast to this, however, Fulton and Johnson (1993) gave an example of a patient whose daily morphine levels gradually increased from 60 mg/day to 3200 mg/day before that patient died of cancer.

When narcotics are used in the control of pain, most dosage increases are made necessary by progression of the disorder that is causing the patient to experience the pain (Savage, 1999). Only a minority of cases involve neuroadaptation to the analgesic effects of the opiate. Unfortunately, many physicians misinterpret the development of tolerance to the analgesic effects of an opiate as evidence of addiction rather than of neuroadaptation, a mistake that results in the underutilization of opiates in patients experiencing severe pain (Herrera, 1997). Cherny (1996) termed the patient's repeated requests for additional narcotic analgesics in such cases *pseudoaddiction*, noting that in contrast to true addiction, the patient ceases to request additional drugs once his or her pain is controlled.

Drug interactions involving narcotic analgesics.[4] Even a partial list of potential medication interactions clearly underscores the potential for narcotic analgesics to cause harm to the individual who mixes them with the wrong medication(s). The synthetic narcotic analgesic meperidine should not be used in patients who are taking, or have recently used, *monoamine oxidase inhibitors* (MAOIs or MAO inhibitors) (Peterson, 1997). The combined effects of these two classes of medications might prove fatal to the patient even if she or he stopped using MAOIs within the last 14 days (Peterson, 1997). Patients who are taking narcotic analgesics should not use any other chemical classified as a CNS depressant, except under a physician's supervision, because there is a danger of excessive sedation from the combination of two or more CNS depressants (Ciraulo, Shader, Greenblatt, & Barnhill, 1995).

Of 30 methadone maintenance patients who started a course of antibiotic therapy with Rifampin, 21 experienced opiate withdrawal symptoms that were apparently caused by an unknown interaction between the methadone and the antibiotic, according to Barnhill, Ciraulo, Ciraulo, and Greene (1995). The authors noted that the withdrawal symptoms did not manifest themselves until approximately the fifth day of Rifampin therapy, so the interaction between these two medications may require some time before symptoms are noted by the patient.

Patients who are taking narcotic analgesics should not use other CNS depressants (antihistamines, benzodiazepines, barbiturates, etc.) except under a physician's supervision. The combination of opiates with other CNS depressants can result in a potentially fatal drug-induced reaction if certain medications are used at the same time. This list does not include every possible interaction between opiates and other chemical agents, but it underscores the potential for harm that might result if narcotic analgesics are mixed with certain medication(s).

Subjective Effects of Narcotic Analgesics When Used in Medical Practice

As we have noted, the primary use of narcotic analgesics is to reduce the distress caused by pain (Darton &

---

[4] The reader is advised always to consult a physician or pharmacist before taking two different medications at the same time.

Dilts, 1998). In order to understand how this is achieved, one must understand that pain is a multifaceted phenomenon. For example, Melzack (1990) reported that there are actually two forms of pain. The first form of pain, which the author termed *phasic* pain, is a sharp expression of discomfort experienced at the instant of injury.

Following the injury, the individual begins to experience a steady, less intense, but more enduring form of pain known as *tonic* pain (Melzack, 1990). Not surprisingly, given the complexity of the central nervous system, there appear to be different neurological pathways for each form of pain. The neuropathways for phasic pain are naturally dampened quickly (Melzack, 1990), serving to warn the organism that injury has occurred without overwhelming it with needless pain messages. Tonic pain, on the other hand, seems to warn the organism to rest until recovery can take place. Morphine is of little value in the control of phasic pain, but it seems to be well suited for the enduring tonic form of pain (Fulton & Johnson, 1993; Melzack, 1990).

When therapeutic doses of morphine are given to a patient in pain, she or he usually reports that the pain becomes less intense or perhaps disappears entirely (Jaffe, Knapp, & Ciraulo, 1997; Reisine & Pasternak, 1995). Many factors affect the degree of analgesia achieved through the use of morphine, including the route by which the medication was administered, the interval between doses, the dosage level, and the half-life of the specific medication being used (Fishman & Carr, 1992).

Other factors that influence people's experience of pain include their anxiety level, their expectations for the narcotic, how long they have been receiving narcotic analgesics, and by their general state of tension. The more tense, frightened, and anxious a person is, the more likely he or she is to experience pain in response to a given stimulus. As we saw earlier in this chapter, one effect of narcotic analgesics is to moderate some of the fear, anxiety, and tension that normally accompany pain states (Gold, 1993).

Complications Caused by Narcotic Analgesics When Used in Medical Practice

Constriction of the pupils. When used at therapeutic dosage levels, the opiates cause some degree of constric-

tion of the pupils; some patients experience constriction of the pupils even in total darkness (Shannon, Wilson, & Stang, 1995). Although this is a diagnostic sign that physicians often use to identify the opioid abuser, it is not necessarily an indication that the patient is abusing his or her medication. Rather, this is a side-effect of opioids that the physician expects in the patient who is using a narcotic analgesic for legitimate medical reasons but is unexpected in the patient who is not receiving such a medication.

Respiratory depression. Another side effect seen at therapeutic dosage levels is some degree of respiratory depression. Although the degree of respiratory depression is not so significant when narcotics are given to a patient in pain (Bushnell & Justins, 1993), even following a therapeutic dose of morphine (or a similar agent), respiration may be affected for 4–5 hours. For this reason, many experts advise that narcotic analgesics be used with caution in individuals who suffer from respiratory problems such as asthma, emphysema, chronic bronchitis, and pulmonary heart disease.

Some experts in the field have challenged the belief that morphine has a significant effect on respiration when used properly (Peterson, 1997; Supernaw, 1991). For example, Peterson (1997) concluded that severe respiratory depression is uncommon in patients with no previous history of breathing problems. Thus, until there is a definitive answer to the question of whether narcotic analgesics cause respiratory depression, health care workers should anticipate that the narcotics will cause the respiratory center of the brain to become less sensitive to rising blood levels of carbon dioxide—and thus will cause some degree of respiratory depression (Bushnell & Justins, 1993; Darton & Dilts, 1998).

Gastrointestinal side effects. One common side effect of the narcotic analgesics at therapeutic dosage levels is some degree of nausea and vomiting (Fishman & Carr, 1992). At normal dosage levels, approximately 10–40% of ambulatory patients will experience some degree of nausea, and approximately 15% will actually vomit as a result of having received a narcotic analgesic (Cherny & Foley, 1996; Jaffe & Martin, 1990). Ambulatory patients seem to be most likely to experience nausea or vomiting as a result of having received a narcotic analgesic. Thus patients should not walk around immediately after taking a narcotic analgesic but, rather, should rest for a period of time.

These side effects are dose-related; that is, as the dosage level increases, these side effects occur in a greater percentage of the population. Some individuals, who are quite sensitive to the opiates, experience adverse reactions to narcotics at even low dosage levels. Melzack (1990) advanced the theory that the individual's response to the narcotics might be genetically mediated and went on to hypothesize that a genetic mechanism might also account for the phenomenon of narcotics addiction.

At therapeutic dosage levels, morphine and similar drugs have been found to affect the gastrointestinal tract. One side-effect of narcotic analgesics is that they can decrease the secretion of hydrochloric acid in the stomach. The muscle contractions of peristalsis (which push food along the intestines) are also restricted (Shannon, Wilson, & Stang, 1995). Narcotic analgesics may actually cause spasm in the muscles involved in the process of peristalsis (Reisine & Pasternak, 1995). This is the side effect that makes morphine so useful in the treatment of dysentery and severe diarrhea. But for the patient who is not suffering from diarrhea, this side effect of narcotic analgesics may cause the individual to experience some degree of constipation. Indeed, constipation is the adverse side effect most commonly encountered when narcotic analgesics are used for extended periods of time at therapeutic levels (Herrera, 1997; Cherny & Foley, 1996). This problem usually can be corrected by over-the-counter laxatives, according to Herrera (1997).

Effects on blood pressure. Under normal conditions, narcotic analgesics cause the patient to experience a mild degree of respiratory depression. In those patients who have experienced some form of head trauma, this might contribute to an increase in intracranial blood pressure, as the body attempts to compensate for the increased levels of carbon dioxide in the blood by pumping more blood to the brain (Pagliaro & Pagliaro, 1998). Thus narcotic analgesics should be used with caution in patients with head injuries, to avoid the potential complications caused by a drug-induced intracranial blood pressure increase.

Other side effects. Another troublesome side effect of the narcotic analgesics is stimulation of the smooth muscle tissue surrounding the bladder. This, along with a tendency for narcotic analgesics to reduce the voiding reflex, may result in a tendency for the patient to experience some degree of urinary retention (Jaffe, Knapp, & Ciraulo, 1997; Tyler, 1994). Some patients who receive narcotic analgesics complain of excessive sedation and (in the case of morphine) nightmares.

The danger of addiction. Many health care workers admit to being afraid that they will cause the patient to become addicted to narcotic analgesics by giving the patient too much medication.[5] In reality, the odds that a patient with no prior history of alcohol/drug addiction will become addicted to narcotic analgesics when these medications are used for the short-term control of severe pain have been estimated as only 1 in 12,000–14,000 (Roberts & Bush, 1996). Most patients who develop a psychological dependence on opiates after receiving them for the control of pain seem to have a preexisting addictive disorder (Paris, 1996). Further, as noted earlier in this chapter, neuroadaptation to the analgesic effects of opioids over time is a normal phenomenon and should not automatically be interpreted as a sign that the patient is becoming addicted to these medications (Hirsch, Paley, & Renner, 1996; McCaffery & Ferrell, 1994).

Unfortunately, in large part because of the individual's high state of tolerance to opioids, physicians tend to *under*medicate opiate-tolerant patients both before and after surgery (Imhof, 1995). Few physicians realize that those patients who have developed tolerance to the analgesic effects of opiates, through either the legitimate use of narcotic analgesics or the abuse of opioids, need higher-than-normal doses of opiates to control the pain of surgery. Fearing that they will bring about an overdose, or fearing that they are contributing to the patient's abuse of medications, physicians often undermedicate the patient, leaving him or her in needless pain.

Routes of administration for narcotic analgesics in medical practice. Although the narcotic analgesics are well absorbed from the gastrointestinal tract, orally administered narcotic analgesics are useful only in the control of mild to moderate levels of pain (Shannon, Wilson, & Stang, 1995). This is because the "first-pass metabolism" effect severely limits the amount of the drug that is able to reach the brain. For example, the liver biotransforms at least 80% of the morphine that is

---

[5] Technically, this would be an *iatrogenic* addiction, as opposed to the usual form of addiction to narcotics that is discussed later in this chapter.

absorbed through the gastrointestinal tract *before* it reaches the brain (Tyler, 1994). In order to achieve the same degree of analgesia that can be accomplished by a single intramuscular injection of 10 mg of morphine, Cherny and Foley (1996) recommend that the patient receive 60 mg of morphine when it is administered by mouth.

The intravenous administration of narcotics actually allows for the greatest degree of control over the amount of drug that actually reaches the brain. This is why the primary method of administration for narcotic analgesics is intravenous injection (Jaffe & Martin, 1990). However, there are exceptions, such as the new transdermal patch developed for the narcotic fentanyl

Withdrawal from narcotic analgesics in medical practice. Most patients who receive narcotic analgesics for the control of pain, even for extended periods of time, are able to discontinue the medication without problems. A small number of patients develop a "discontinuance syndrome" similar to that seen in patients who receive benzodiazepines for an extended period of time. This "discontinuance syndrome" is usually mild, but the patient may have to reduce his or her daily intake of narcotic analgesics gradually rather than stop using the medication all at once. Thus narcotic analgesics are relatively benign medications when used properly.

Fentanyl

In 1968, a new synthetic narcotic known as fentanyl (Sublimaze) was introduced. Because of its short duration of action, fentanyl has become an especially popular analgesic during and immediately after surgery (Shannon, Wilson, & Stang, 1995). It is well absorbed from muscle tissue, and a common method of administration is intramuscular injection. Because fentanyl can also be absorbed through the skin, a transdermal patch has been developed on the theory that by slowly absorbing small amounts of fentanyl through the skin, the patient might experience some relief from pain without requiring repeated injections of the medication. Unfortunately, the medication is only slowly absorbed through the skin, and therapeutic blood levels of fentanyl are not achieved for up to 12 hours after the individual first starts to use the "patch" (Tyler, 1994).

Recently, a new dosage form of fentanyl was introduced: fentanyl-laced candy for use as a premedication

for children about to undergo surgery (*Forensic Drug Abuse Advisor*, 1994b). It is interesting to note that opium was once used in Rome to calm infants who were crying (Ray & Ksir, 1993). After thousands of years of medical progress, we have come full circle and are again using opiates to calm the fears of children about to undergo surgery.

The Pharmacology and Subjective Effects of Fentanyl

Fentanyl is extremely potent, but there is some controversy over exactly how potent. For example, the journal *Forensic Drug Abuse Advisor* (1994b) suggested that fentanyl was 50 times as powerful as morphine. However, Karch (1996) suggested that it was between 50 and 100 times as powerful as morphine, and Ashton (1992) suggested that it was 1000 times as potent as morphine. Kirsch (1986) concluded that fentanyl is "approximately 3000 times stronger than morphine [and] 1000 times stronger than heroin" (p. 18). According to Kirsch (1986), the active dose of fentanyl in the human is 1 microgram. As a basis of comparison, the author noted that the average postage stamp weighs 60,000 micrograms. Thus the average effective dose of fentanyl is 1/60,000 the weight of the typical postage stamp!

Fentanyl is highly lipid-soluble and thus reaches the brain quickly after it is administered. This characteristic is of value when the drug is used in surgical procedures. The biological half-life of a single intravenous dose of fentanyl is rather short, perhaps 3 hours (Laurence & Bennett, 1992). Further, fentanyl's analgesic effect persists only for 30–120 minutes. The drug is rapidly biotransformed by the liver and excreted from the body in the urine (Karch, 1996).

The effects of fentanyl on the individual's respiration may last longer than the analgesia produced by the drug (Shannon, Wilson, & Stang, 1995), a possibility that must be kept in mind when the patient requires long-term analgesia. The major reason why fentanyl is so useful is that in a medical setting, fentanyl produces a more rapid analgesic response than morphine. The analgesic effects of fentanyl are often seen just minutes after it is injected. This is a decided advantage when the physician seeks to control pain during or immediately after surgery.

The *side effects of fentanyl* may include blurred vision, a sense of euphoria, nausea, vomiting, dizziness, delirium, lowered blood pressure, constipation, respiratory depression, and (in extreme cases) respiratory arrest and cardiac arrest (Shannon, Wilson, & Stang, 1995). At high dosage levels, muscle rigidity is possible (Foley, 1993). Physicians have noted that when fentanyl is administered, the patient's blood pressure may drop by as much as 20% and her or his heart rate by as much as 25% (Beebe & Walley, 1991). Thus, the physician must balance the potential benefits to be gained by using fentanyl against the drug's potential to cause adverse effects. Unfortunately, although fentanyl is an extremely useful pharmaceutical, it is also a popular drug of abuse. This aspect of fentanyl will be discussed in the next section.

Buprenorphine

Buprenorphine is a synthetic analgesic that was introduced in the 1960s and is estimated to be 25–40 times as potent as morphine (Singh, Mattoo, Malhotra, & Varma, 1992). Medical researchers quickly discovered that orally administered doses of buprenorphine are extremely useful in treating postoperative and cancer pain. Further, researchers have discovered that, administered orally, buprenorphine appears to be at least as effective as methadone in blocking the effects of illicit narcotics.

Buprenorphine has a rather unique absorption pattern. The drug is well absorbed from intravenous and intramuscular injection sites, as well as when administered sublingually (Lewis, 1995). These methods of drug administration offer the advantage of rapid access to the general circulation, without the danger of first-pass metabolism. When administered orally, buprenorphine suffers extensive first-pass metabolism, a characteristic that makes it difficult to use oral doses of buprenorphine for analgesia.

Upon reaching the general circulation, approximately 95% of buprenorphine becomes protein-bound (Walter & Inturrisi, 1995). The drug is biotransformed by the liver, with 79% of the metabolites being excreted in the feces and only 3.9% in the urine (Walter & Inturrise, 1995). Surprisingly, animal research suggests that the various drug metabolites are unable to cross the blood-brain barrier. This suggests that the drug's analgesic effects are achieved by the buprenorphine molecules that reach the brain rather than by any drug metabolites produced during the biotransformation process.

Once in the brain, buprenorphine binds to three of the same receptor sites in the brain that are utilized by morphine. Buprenorphine binds most strongly to the mu and kappa receptor sites, which is where narcotic analgesics tend to act to reduce the individual's perception of pain. However, buprenorphine does not cause the same degree of activation at the mu receptor site that morphine does. For reasons that are still not clear, buprenorphine is nevertheless able to cause clinically significant levels of analgesia (Negus & Woods, 1995).

Buprenorphine also tends to form weak bonds with the sigma receptor site (Lewis, 1995). However, just because a drug is able to *bind* at a receptor site does not mean that it is always able to *activate* the receptor site. Buprenorphine is an excellent example of a drug that binds to different receptor sites in the brain without having the same potential to activate these different receptor sites. In the human brain, buprenorphine easily binds to both the mu and the kappa receptor sites. However, the drug has relatively little effect on the kappa receptor site, while more strongly affecting the activity of the mu receptor site (Negus & Woods, 1995).

Virtually all of the drug's effects are achieved by buprenorphine's ability to bind at, and activate, the mu opiate receptors in the brain (Lewis, 1995). Indeed, the drug functions effectively as a kappa receptor site antagonist at the same dosage level at which it activates the *mu* opiate receptor sites to cause analgesia (Negus & Woods, 1995). Finally, buprenorphine molecules only slowly "disconnect" from their receptor sites, thus blocking large numbers of other buprenorphine molecules from reaching those same receptor sites. Thus, at high dosage levels, buprenorphine seems to act as its own antagonist, limiting its own effects.

As is obvious from this brief review of buprenorphine's pharmacology, it is a unique narcotic analgesic, more selective than morphine and more powerful than morphine. As we shall see in the following section, however, it is slowly becoming more popular as a drug of abuse.

II. OPIATES AS DRUGS OF ABUSE

Many of the opiates are popular as drugs of abuse. In this section of Chapter 14, we will discuss opiate abuse/addiction.

Why Do People Abuse Opiates?

Simply put, opiate-based analgesics are popular with illicit drug users because they make the user feel good. When they are used by people who are *not* experiencing any significant degree of pain, opioids reportedly cause the user to experience euphoria. When injected directly into the circulation, some opiates may cause the user to experience a "rush" or "flash" that is said to be similar to sexual orgasm (Jaffe, 2000c; Bushnell & Justins, 1993; Hawkes, 1992; Jaffe, 1992; Jaffe & Martin, 1990) but is different from the rush reported by CNS stimulant abusers (Brust, 1998). Following the rush, the user experiences a sense of euphoria, which usually lasts 1–2 minutes (Jaffe, 2000c). Finally, the user may experience a prolonged period of blissful drowsiness that may last several hours (Scarlos, Westra, & Barone, 1990). These are characteristics that appeal to some drug users.

Neuropsychopharmacologists believe that they have identified the reasons why narcotic analgesics are able to bring about these effects. As we noted in the first section of this chapter, narcotic analgesics seem to mimic the action of naturally occurring neurotransmitters. Two different regions of the limbic system of the brain, the *nucleus accumbens* and the *ventral tegmentum*, seem to be associated with the pleasurable response that many users report when they use opioids (Restak, 1994). Researchers believe that following a dose of opiates, the brain reacts as though massive amounts of endorphins were released.

Heroin

The mystique of heroin. Globally, the most serious form of illicit drug abuse revolves around the use of heroin, or *diacetylmorphine* (United Nations, 1997). It is estimated that 8 million people around the world use heroin, and global production is an estimated 300 tons/year (United Nations, 1997). Estimates of the scope of heroin abuse/addiction in the United States range from between 600,000 and 1 million people dependent on heroin, with an even greater (but unknown) number of abusers (Kranzler, Amin, Modesto-Lowe, & Oncken, 1999), up to the 1.5 million chronic heroin users suggested by Olmedo and Hoffman (2000). Each year, heroin-related deaths account for about half of all deaths attributed to illicit drug use in the United States (Epstein & Gfroerer, 1997; Karch, 1996).

A short history of heroin. Heroin was first developed by chemists at the Bayer pharmaceutical company of Germany (as was aspirin) in 1898. Like its chemical cousin morphine, heroin is obtained from raw opium. One ton of raw opium will, after processing, produce approximately 100 kilograms of heroin (*Forensic Drug Abuse Advisor*, 1997c). When the chemists who developed diacetylmorphine first tried it, they reported that the drug made them feel heroic. Thus the drug was given the brand name Heroin (Mann & Plummer, 1991, p. 26).

Following the Civil War in the United States, there were large numbers of men who had become addicted to morphine. Because heroin was found to suppress the withdrawal symptoms of morphine addicts at low doses, physicians at the turn of the century thought it was nonaddicting, and it was initially sold as a cure for morphine addiction. The true addictive potential of heroin was not recognized until 12 years later, long after many morphine addicts had become addicted to heroin and heroin abuse/addiction had become a fixture in the United States. During the 1920s, the term "junkie" was coined for the heroin addict who supported his other drug use by collecting scrap metal from industrial dumps, for resale to junk collectors (Scott, 1998).

Pharmacology of heroin. The heroin molecule is best visualized as a pair of morphine molecules that have been joined chemically. The result is an analgesic that is more potent than morphine: A standard conversion formula is that 4 milligrams (mg) of heroin is as powerful as 10 mg of morphine (Brent, 1995; Lingeman, 1974). The half-life of heroin is 3 minutes, although one of the primary metabolites also has an analgesic potential and has a half-life of 30 minutes (Kreek, 1997). Surprisingly, research has shown that the heroin molecule does not bind to known opiate receptor sites in the brain, and researchers have suggested that it might more accurately be described as a *prodrug*[6] than as a biologically active compound it its own right (Jenkins & Cone, 1998).

When the drug is used intranasally, about 25% of the available heroin is absorbed by the user's body. However, virtually 100% of intravenously administered heroin is absorbed. Because of differences in its chemical structure, heroin is much more lipid-soluble than

[6]See the Glossary.

morphine. This feature allows heroin to cross the blood-brain barrier 100 times faster than morphine (Angier, 1990). The speed with which it reaches the brain makes it an especially attractive drug of abuse.

The user's expectations help to shape his or her experience from heroin. Physically, the actions of heroin are quite similar to those of morphine. This makes sense, because morphine is a metabolite of heroin (Jaffe, 1992; Scaros, Westra, & Barone, 1990). It is not the heroin that functions as an analgesic but the morphine that emerges from the process of heroin biotransformation in the liver (Reisine & Pasternak, 1995). The main advantage of heroin for addicts is that it has only half the bulk of morphine, allowing for it to be transported more easily (Lingeman, 1974).

Subjective effects of heroin when abused. Users report that intravenous heroin produces a "rush" or a "flash" that is very similar to a sexual orgasm and lasts about 1 minute. Other sensations include a feeling of warmth under the skin, dry mouth, nausea, and a feeling of heaviness in the extremities. Users also report nasal congestion and itchy skin, both the result of heroin's ability to stimulate the release of histamine in the user's body. After this, the user experiences a sense of floating, or light sleep, that lasts for about 2 hours, and is accompanied by clouded mental function.

Heroin in the United States today. Heroin is *not* a recognized pharmaceutical in the United States, and its possession or manufacture is illegal. In spite of this, the sale of heroin is estimated to be a $12-billion-per-year industry in the United States (Abt Associates, Inc., 1995). In spite of the introduction of new synthetic and semisynthetic opiates in the past century, heroin still accounts for approximately 90% of opiate abuse/addiction in this country (Dygert & Minelli, 1993).

In the late 1990s, heroin became increasingly popular with younger drug abusers. The average age of the individual's first use of heroin dropped from 27 in 1988 to 19 by the middle of the 1990s (Hopfer, Mikulich, & Crowley, 2000; Cohen, Fleming, Glatter, Haghigi, Halberstadt, McHigh, & Woolf 1996). Adolescents—individuals from 12 to 17 years of age—made up just under 22% of those who admitted to using heroin in the United States (Hopfer, Mikulich, & Crowley, 2000). One major reason for this increase in popularity among younger drug abusers in the late 1990s was the availability of increasingly high-potency heroin for relatively low prices. In the mid-1980s the average sample of heroin from "the street" was about 5–6% pure (Sabbag, 1994). By the middle of the 1990s, heroin was being sold that was 65% (Gabriel, 1994) to 80% pure (Office of National Drug Control Policy, 1995). These figures reflect the glut of heroin available to illicit users in this country. The high purity of heroin being sold, combined with its relatively low cost and the misperception that intranasal heroin was nonaddicting, all contributed to an increase in heroin use in the United States (Ehrman, 1995).

Buprenorphine

Another drug that is growing in popularity as an opiate of abuse is buprenorphine. As we noted earlier in this chapter, buprenorphine has been found to be a useful narcotic analgesic. Researchers are also considering oral doses of buprenorphine as an alternative to methadone (see Chapter 32). Unfortunately, street addicts have discovered that *intravenously administered* buprenorphine has a significant abuse potential (Moore, 1995; Horgan, 1989). Indeed, buprenorphine is the most commonly abused opiate in Australia and New Zealand (Stimmel, 1997b), and there have been reports of its abuse from countries such as Ireland and India (Singh, Mattoo, Malhotra, & Varma, 1992), as well as here in the United States (Torrens, San, & Cami, 1993).

Researchers actually know very little about the abuse of buprenorphine (Fudala & Johnson, 1995). Apparently, the user injects either buprenorphine alone, or a mixture of buprenorphine and diazepam, cyclizine, or temazepam. Although it is not clear how significant buprenorphine will be as a drug of abuse, the reader should be aware that there have been reports of intravenous buprenorphine abuse in this country.

Methods of Opiate Abuse

When opiates are abused, they might be injected under the skin (a subcutaneous injection, or "skin popping"), injected directly into a vein ("mainlining"), smoked, or used intranasally. Opiates such as heroin are well absorbed through the lungs (as when smoked). The smoking of opium has not been common in the United States since the start of the 20th century. Supplies of opium are quite limited in the United States, and opium smoking wastes a great deal of the chemical.

However, in parts of the world where supplies of opium are more plentiful, the practice of smoking opium remains quite common.

"Snorting" heroin powder and smoking heroin have become popular ways of abusing this chemical in the United States. In some parts of this country, 60% of new heroin users snort the drug (Office of National Drug Control Policy, 1995), in part because of a fear of HIV-contaminated needles and in part because of the mistaken belief that intranasally administered heroin is not addictive (Smolowe, 1993). Heroin is snorted in a manner quite similar to the way cocaine powder is inhaled. The user employs a razor blade or knife to "dice" the powder until it is a fine, talcum-like consistency. The powder is then arranged in a small pile, or line, and inhaled through a straw.

Heroin can also be smoked. Heroin smoking is not very effective, however, and approximately 80% of the heroin is destroyed by the process of smoking (*Forensic Drug Abuse Advisor,* 1996k). Thus heroin smoking is possible only when the heroin is both potent and plentiful, as is the heroin available on the streets at this time. One method by which heroin may be smoked is known as "chasing the dragon" (Strang, Griffiths, Powis, & Gossop, 1992). In this process, the user heats heroin powder in a piece of aluminum foil, using a cigarette lighter or match as the heat source. The resulting fumes are then inhaled, allowing the individual to get high without exposing himself or herself to contaminated needles (*Alcoholism & Drug Abuse Week,* 1991c; Pinkney, 1990; Scaros, Westra, & Barone, 1990).

Another way that heroin is abused via smoking is the practice of smoking a combination of heroin and crack cocaine pellets called "speedball rock," "moon rock," or "parachute rock" (Dygert & Minelli, 1993). This combination of chemicals reportedly results in a longer high, and a less severe depression after use is suspended(Levy & Rutter, 1992). However, as we have seen, there is evidence that cocaine may exacerbate the respiratory depression produced by opiates.

The most common method of heroin abuse is intravenous injection. In this process,

[the] addict mixes heroin in the spoon with water, or glucose and water, in order to dissolve it. Lemon juice, citric acid or vitamin C may be added to aid dissolving. This cocktail is heated until it boils, drawn into the syringe through a piece of cotton wool or cigarette filter to remove solid impurities, and injected whilst still warm. (Booth, 1996, p.14)

Where do opioid addicts obtain their drugs? Opiate abusers obtain their daily supply of the drug from many sources. The usual practice for the street addict is to buy street opiates, unless she or he has access to a "pharmaceutical." Most opiates abused by illicit users are obtained from supplies of drugs smuggled into the United States from other regions, especially Southeast Asia, Mexico, and South American countries such as Colombia (DEA Press Release, 1995). These drugs are mixed with adulterants then distributed for sale on the local level. The opiates are usually sold in a powder form, in small individual packets. The powder is mixed with water, heated in a small container (usually a spoon) over a flame from a cigarette lighter and candle and then injected.

If abusers are health care professionals, with access to pharmaceutical supplies, they may divert medications to themselves. This is difficult, however, because of the rigid controls on supplies of narcotics. Other users might purchase "pharmaceuticals"[7] that have been diverted to the illicit drug market. For example, some opioid addicts have been known to befriend a person with a terminal illness, such as cancer, in order to steal narcotic analgesics from the suffering patient for their own use.

The user often injects the pharmaceutical, although some abusers ingest opioids. The user who injects a pharmaceutical, generally either crushes the tablet until it is a fine powder or will take the capsule apart and mix the powder with water. The mixture is then heated in a small container (usually a spoon or bottle cap) over a small fire, which helps mix the powder with the water. The resulting mixture is then injected, although intravenous opiate abusers inject the drug in a different manner from a physician or nurse injecting medication into a vein. The process has changed little in the past 50 years, and Lingeman's (1974) description of this technique, called "booting," remains as valid today as when it was first set to paper a quarter of a century ago. As the individual "boots" the drug, he or she injects it

[7]See the Glossary.

a little at a time, letting it back up into the eye dropper, injecting a little more, letting the blood-heroin mixture back up, and so on. The addict believes that this technique prolongs the initial pleasurable sensation of the heroin as it first takes effect—a feeling of warmth in the abdomen, euphoria, and sometimes a sensation similar to an orgasm. (p. 32)

In the process, however, the hypodermic needle and the syringe (or the eye dropper attached to a hypodermic needle, a common substitute for a hypodermic needle) become contaminated with the individual's blood. When other intravenous drug abusers share the same needle, which is a common practice, contaminated blood from one individual is passed to the next, and the next, and the next. . . .

Sometimes, the opiate abuser will attempt to inject a pharmaceutical tablet or capsule originally intended for oral ingestion. Unfortunately, this practice inserts starch or other fillers not intended for intravenous use directly into the bloodstream (Wetli, 1987). Normally, "fillers" are mixed with oral medication to give it body and form. When the medication is taken orally, these fillers are usually either destroyed by stomach acid or at least prevented from being absorbed into the body. In the latter case, the filler harmlessly passes through the body and ultimately is excreted. But when tablets or capsules are used for intravenous use, the fillers cannot be inactivated by the body's defenses. Further, repeated exposure to pharmaceutical fillers, or the adulterants often found in street drugs, can cause extensive scarring at the point of injection. These scars form the famous "tracks" caused by repeated injections of illicit opiates.

The development of tolerance. Over time, opiate abusers become tolerant to the euphoric effects of narcotics. As a result of their growing tolerance, they no longer experience the "rush" or "flash" from opiates with the same intensity. It is thought that the chronic use of narcotic analgesics causes the brain to reduce the amount of endorphins that it produces (Klein & Miller, 1986). In other words, over time, the brain substitutes the chemical opiates for natural endorphins, and the effect of the narcotics on the person becomes less intense.

Eventually, the user ceases to experience much euphoria at all from narcotic analgesics. There appears to be a "threshold effect" (Parry, 1992, p. 350), or a level after which the user experiences a "stable genial

state" (p. 350) without becoming "high" on the opiate she or he is using. The chronic opioid abuser who reaches this state is no longer using the drug to get high. Rather, he or she is taking narcotics just to function in a normal state.

Just as when narcotic analgesics are used in a medical setting, the illicit user develops tolerance to the various effects of the opiates at different rates (Jaffe, 1989). For example, the opiate abuser can develop "remarkable tolerance" (Jaffe, 1989, p. 649) to the respiratory depressant effect of opiates but never becomes tolerant to the constipating side-effect of this class of drugs (Zevin & Benowitz, 1998), which often causes significant problems for the illicit user (Reisine & Pasternak, 1995). Also, the user of illicit opiates experiences the same constriction of the pupils that patients on narcotic analgesics exhibit.

Scope of the Problem of Opiate Abuse and Addiction in the United States

The Abuse of Prescribed Narcotic Analgesics

The abuse of, and addiction to, narcotic analgesics has been a problem in the United States for more than a century. In spite of this, however, very little is known about whether large numbers of people are abusing narcotic analgesics obtained with a physician's prescription. There are many reasons for this lack of information. For one thing, people may not recognize that they are abusing a prescribed medication. For example, a man who had received a prescription for a narcotic analgesic after breaking a bone might share a leftover pill or two with a family member who had sprained an ankle and was in severe pain. This well-intentioned person has provided another with medications that are, technically, being abused, because the second person did not receive a prescription for the narcotic analgesic that she or he ingested. Nationally, an estimated 11 million people have abused opioid medications not prescribed for them (Kreek, 2000).

Further, most people who engage in the abuse of narcotic analgesics on a regular basis go to great lengths to avoid being identified as a medication abuser or as "drug seeking." It is not uncommon for patients to visit different physicians, or different hospital emergency rooms, with the same complaint in order to obtain multiple prescriptions for the same disorder. Patients have also been known to manufacture symptoms (after doing a bit of research) in order to simulate the signs of a disorder virtually guaranteed to result in a prescription for a narcotic analgesic. Finally, patients with actual disorders have been known to exaggerate their distress, in hopes of being able to obtain a prescription for a narcotic analgesic from an overworked physician. Yet such people would adamantly deny that they were abusing the medication; after all, it was prescribed by a *physician* who certainly would know whether such a potent medication was needed for pain control. Often overlooked in this neat rationalization is the fact that the patient had to see five, or perhaps even ten different doctors before finding one who would provide a prescription for narcotic analgesics without too much argument.

Thus, although the misuse of narcotic analgesics is acknowledged to be a problem, there is very little information about the actual percentage of such medications that are misused, and scientists know virtually nothing about the natural history of such medication misuse, how it compares to heroin abuse/addiction, and whether the abuse of prescribed narcotic analgesics carries with it a significant risk of premature death.

Heroin Abuse/Addiction

When the average person reflects about the problem of narcotics abuse/addiction, she or he probably thinks only of the abuse of or addiction to heroin. This substance has garnered a reputation as a dangerous drug that will enslave those who abuse it. For example, in the late 1960s it was widely believed that "the majority [of heroin abusers] go on to mainlining" (Lingeman, 1974, p. 106). Forty years later, researchers have concluded that only a fraction of those who *briefly* abuse opiates will become addicted (Jaffe, 1989).[8] To illustrate this point, consider that an estimated 3 million people in the United States are thought to have used heroin at least once (O'Connor, 2000), yet there are only an estimated 980,000 "long-term users of heroin in the United States" at this time (Johnson, Chutuape, Strain, Walsh, Stizer, & Bigelow, 2000, p. 1290). These figures suggest that the addictive potential of heroin may not be as high as has been hinted in the mass media. Even so, heroin

is a potentially addictive substance, and approximately half of those who *repeatedly* abuse an opioid such as heroin go on to become addicted (Jeinke, 1991).

Unfortunately, scientists know very little about the natural history of heroin abuse/addiction. It is presumed that it takes approximately 2 years between the initiation of heroin abuse and the development of physical dependency on this chemical (Hoegerman & Schnoll, 1991). Wide variations in individual opiate use patterns are also possible. For example, researchers have long been aware that some people are apparently able to abuse opiates occasionally without becoming addicted (Shiffman, Fischer, Zettler-Segal, & Benowitz, 1990). These "chippers" may constitute 40–50% of the people who abuse heroin (Sabbag, 1994). Chippers seem to use opiates more in response to social stimuli than for pharmacological reasons. In other words, they seem to use narcotics because of the social context or because of transient states of internal distress, rather than because they are addicted to one of these compounds, and they seem to have no trouble abstaining from opiates when they want to. But because research in this area is prohibited, scientists do not know what percentage of those who start out as chippers progress to a more addictive pattern of heroin use.

Researchers estimate that 10–15 metric tons of heroin are consumed each year in this country (Leland, Katel, & Hager, 1996). Heroin is an illegal substance in the United States, so all of this heroin is consumed by illicit users. Estimates of the number of heroin abusers/addicts in the United States vary. Nash and Park (1997) provided what may be the lowest estimate, that some 200,000 people in the United States use heroin at least once a month. This figure was only slightly lower than that offered by the Department of Health and Human Services (1997), which suggested that 216,000 people used heroin at least once a month.

In contrast to these low (some would say unrealistic) estimates, Eissenberg, Bigelow, Strain, Walsh, Brooner, Stitzer, and Johnson (1997), asserted that 586,000 people in the United States used illicit narcotics at least once per week. Dygert and Minelli (1993) estimated that 3.5 million individuals in this country abuse heroin by intravenous injection without being addicted to this drug. Clearly, scientists actually know very little about the true scope of heroin abuse/addiction.

---

[8]Of course, because it is not possible to predict in advance who will become addicted, and who will not, the abuse of narcotic analgesics is *not* recommended.

The most common estimate of the number of heroin-dependent people in the United States is between 977,000 (Roane, 2000; Warner, Kosten, & O'Connor, 1997) and 1 million persons (Kreek, 2000; Leinwand, 2000). Researchers generally agree that the typical heroin addict must spend about $250 per week to buy drugs necessary to support his or her habit (Abt Associates, Inc., 1995a). It also appears that about three-fourths of those who are addicted to heroin are males (Kaplan & Sadock, 1996). Thus, of the estimated 900,000 heroin addicts in this country, perhaps 675,000 are males and 225,000 are females. If the higher estimate of 1 million active heroin addicts is used, then some 250,000 women are addicted to heroin in this country. Geographically, heroin-addicted persons are thought to be concentrated on the coasts. It is estimated that between 200,000 (Eisenhandler & Drucker, 1993; Ross, 1991) and 300,000 (Kaplan, Sadock, & Grebb, 1994) heroin addicts live in New York City (Sabbag, 1994). Another 275,000 are thought to live in California (Pinkney, 1990; Leland, Katel, & Hager, 1996).

Do Some Factors Predispose One to Become Addicted to Opiates?

Psychoanalysts believe that there is a dynamic interaction between the psychological distress that a person experiences, and that person's vulnerability to developing an addiction to chemicals. In the case of opiates, the drugs may help the user control powerful feelings of rage and anger.

At this time, clinical research data do not fully support the psychological vulnerability hypothesis central to the psychoanalytic model of narcotics addiction. Research *does* suggest that as many as 50% of those who abuse narcotics have suffered from periods of depression (Melzac, 1990). Further, it appears that those individuals who use narcotics daily are significantly more depressed than those who occasionally abuse opioids and that both groups are more depressed than those who do not use narcotics (Maddux, Desmond, & Costello, 1987). However, it would appear that the dysphoria so often seen in chronic opioid users is a "pharmacological consequence" (Handelsman, Aronson, Ness, Cochrane, & Kanof, 1992, p. 284) of the prolonged use of narcotics, not a result of their abuse. Support for this theory was provided by Kanof, Aronson, and Ness (1993). The found that addicted persons who

were gradually withdrawn from methadone after being part of a methadone maintenance program for extended periods of time experienced episodes of depression that might last for several weeks after the withdrawal process was completed. They attributed this finding to the individual's prior use of narcotics, rather than to the process of withdrawal or to a preexisting depressive state.

One consequence of the drug-related depression seen in narcotics addiction is that for the recovering addict, feelings of dysphoria may serve as a cue that triggers further opiate use/abuse. Unless the individual is aware that dysphoric feelings are a consequence of prolonged heroin use, he or she may confuse the withdrawal-related dysphoria with "unhappy feelings that might have prompted experimentation with heroin in the first place" (Handelsman, Aronson, Ness, Cochrane, & Kanof, 1992, p. 285). It has yet to be determined whether opiate-dependent individuals use these drugs because they are attempting to self-medicate emotional pain or experience emotional pain as a pharmacological consequence of their chronic chemical use.

Withdrawal from Opioids for the Addicted Person

The hallmark of an addiction to opiates is the classic pattern of opioid withdrawal symptoms. The symptoms of withdrawal from narcotics vary in intensity, depending on three different factors: (1) the dose of the opiate that was abused, (2) how long the person has used the drug,[9] and, (3) how rapidly withdrawal is attempted (Jaffe, 1989). An opiate addict who has been using the equivalent of 50 mg of morphine a day for 3 weeks will have an easier detoxification than another individual who has been using the equivalent of 50 mg of morphine a day for 3 years. Also, an opiate addict who is withdrawn from opiates gradually (at the rate, say, of 10 mg of morphine a day) will have an easier detoxification than an opiate-dependent person who stops using the drug suddenly ("cold turkey").

The individual's perception of, and response to, the withdrawal process is influenced to a large degree by his or her cognitive "set." This "set" is, in turn, influenced by such factors as the individual's knowledge, attention, motivation, and degree of suggestibility. In the final

[9]However, after 2–3 months of continuous use, there is generally no increase in the severity of the withdrawal symptoms.

analysis, the level of discomfort experienced by an individual during opiate withdrawal is a learned phenomenon. This phenomenon might be confirmed in real-life settings, where narcotics addicts are forced to go through the withdrawal process "cold turkey." For example, when the individual is in a therapeutic community that actively discourages reports of withdrawal discomfort, opiate-dependent individuals do not go through the dramatic withdrawal displays so often noted in methadone detoxification programs (Peele, 1985). Further, when the narcotics addict is incarcerated and denied further access to the drug, the individual is often able to go through withdrawal without the dramatic withdrawal seen at a detoxification center.

Acute withdrawal. In general, opiate withdrawal symptoms begin 6–12 hours after the last dose of heroin (Weiss, Greenfield, & Mirin, 1994; Gold, 1993; Jaffe, 1989). To avoid these withdrawal symptoms, the addict must either inject the drug again or substitute another drug. Withdrawal symptoms include a craving for more narcotics, tearing of the eyes, running nose, repeated yawning, sweating, restless sleep, dilated pupils, anxiety, anorexia, irritability, insomnia, weakness, abdominal pain, nausea, vomiting, gastrointestinal upset, chills, diarrhea, muscle spasms and muscle aches, irritability, and, in male addicts, possible ejaculation (Gold, 1993; Hoegerman & Schnoll, 1991; Scaros, Westra, & Barone, 1990). Constipation is a potential complication of narcotics withdrawal and can, in rare cases, result in fecal impaction and intestinal obstruction (Jaffe, 1989, 1990).

Some researchers believe that the withdrawal symptoms might make the person so uncomfortable as to encourage continued drug use (Bauman, 1988). This is true even if the initial "rush" is no longer experienced because of drug tolerance (Jaffe, 1986, 1989). Indeed, research has suggested that perhaps 22–35% of opiate addicts have a fear of detoxification that is almost phobic in intensity (Milby, Hohmann, Gentile, Huggins, Sims, McLellan, Woody, & Haas, 1994). In other words, there is evidence that many opiate addicts continue to use these drugs, after developing tolerance to the chemical's euphoric effects, because they are afraid of the discomfort of withdrawal.

In a medical setting, opiate-dependent individuals often emphasize their physical distress during withdrawal, in an attempt to obtain additional drugs. Although such displays are often quite dramatic, they are hardly a reflection of reality. Withdrawal from narcotics may be uncomfortable, but it is not fatal (O'Brien, 1998; Henry, 1996; Mattick & Hall, 1996). The opiate withdrawal process is rarely a medical emergency (Kaplan & Sadock, 1996)[10] and usually involves about as much distress as what an adult experiences in a bad case of influenza (Weaver, Jarvis, & Schnoll, 1999; Brust, 1998; Mattick & Hall, 1996). The only possible exception to this rule is for the newborn addicted infant (Washton, 1995; Group for the Advancement of Psychiatry, 1990). Even in the absence of treatment, the acute symptoms of the opiate withdrawal syndrome eventually subside in the healthy individual.

Extended withdrawal symptoms. There is evidence, of a second phase of withdrawal from narcotics, which lasts beyond the period of acute withdrawal. During this extended phase of withdrawal, which may last for several months, the individual may experience fatigue, heart palpitations, and a general feeling of restlessness (Satel, Kosten, Schuckit, & Fischman, 1993). There is evidence that this phase of protracted abstinence may last for up to 30 weeks after acute withdrawal (O'Brien, 1996; Satel, Kosten, Schuckit, & Fischman, 1993).

During this stage of protracted abstinence, the physical functioning of the individual slowly returns to normal. Satel *et al.* support this hypothetical phase of protracted abstinence by citing research studies that have found significant changes in respiration rate, size of the pupils, blood pressure, and body temperature in recovering narcotics addicts for more than 17 weeks after the last dose of narcotics. However, Mattick and Hall (1996) suggested that the case for the existence of a protracted phase of withdrawal was quite weak and that this phenomenon is not an expected part of recovery from opiate addiction.

A rarely studied aspect of narcotics abuse is the tendency for opiate-dependent individuals to attempt withdrawal on their own. Gossop, Battersby, and Strang (1991) examined a group of 47 narcotics addicts in England and found that their sample had had a total of 212 "informal" detoxification episodes. The most common method for self-detoxification was simply going

---

[10]This assumes that the patient is using *only* opioids, and has no concurrent medical problems such as a seizure disorder or cardiac disease. A physician should supervise *any* drug withdrawal program in order to reduce potential danger to life that exists if the patient is a polydrug user.

"cold turkey," although a significant number of these attempts used either benzodiazepines or other narcotics to control the withdrawal symptoms. The authors concluded that very little is known about the self-detoxification and suggested that written guidelines for the addicted individuals who want to quit on their own might be of value.

Complications Caused by Chronic Opiate Abuse

Surprisingly, in light of the reputation that narcotics have for wrecking lives, there is relatively little evidence to suggest permanent organ damage from the chronic administration of pharmaceutical opiates (Jaffe, 1992). Indeed, patients in extreme pain (such as occurs in some forms of cancer, for example) receive massive doses of narcotic analgesics for extended periods of time without showing evidence of opiate-induced damage to any of the body's organ systems.

This is consistent with historical evidence from earlier in this century, where cases would come to light where a physician (or, less often, a nurse) had been addicted to morphine for years or even decades. These incidents were not uncommon in the era before strict government guidelines requiring physicians and health care facilities to account for each dose of narcotic analgesic they purchased. Apart from his or her opiate addiction, the addicted physician or nurse would appear to be in good health. For example, the famed surgeon William Halsted was addicted to morphine for 50 years without suffering any apparent physical problems (Smith, 1994).

However, health care professionals have access to pharmaceutical-quality narcotic analgesics, not street drugs. The typical opiate addict must inject drugs of questionable purity purchased from illicit sources. In addition, opioid addiction carries serious health risks. For example, morphine abuse has been implicated as a cause of decreased sexual desire for both men and women and of erectile problems in men (Finger, Lung, & Slagel, 1997). Other common health complications found in heroin abusers include cerebral vascular accidents (CVA, or "stroke"), cerebral vasospasms, infectious endocarditis, liver failure, disorders of blood clot formation, malignant hypertension, heroin-related nephropathy, and uremia (Brust, 1997, 1993).

It is not clear whether these effects are due directly to the abuse of heroin or to the "fillers" added to illicit opiates (for more information on drug fillers, see Chapter 35). However, one complication of intravenous heroin abuse/addiction that occasionally develops in some users is *cotton fever* (Brent, 1995). The heroin abuser/addict tries to "purify" the heroin by using wads of cotton as a crude filter. When heroin supplies are scarce, some users attempt to use the residual heroin found in old cotton filters. When they do so, they inject microscopic cotton particles, as well as the impurities filtered out by the cotton, and this often causes pulmonary arteritis (a serious medical condition wherein the pulmonary artery becomes inflamed).

Medical researchers are still not sure whether prolonged exposure to narcotic analgesics is entirely harmless. Studies involving rats, have found that the chronic use of heroin seems to cause dopamine-utilizing neurons in the brain's "reward system" to shrink (Nestler, 1997). Further, there appears to be an associational learning process at work, through which specific sights, sounds, smells, and/or activities are associated with the impending use of opiates (Schroeder, Holahan, Landry, & Kelly, 2000). These microscopic neurological changes then contribute to relapse in patients who are exposed to the stimuli that were formerly associated with the use of the desired substance. These findings are consistent with the theory that chronic exposure to opiates can result in physical changes within the brain (Dole, 1988, 1989; Dole & Nyswander, 1965).

This theory has been challenged, however. Hartman (1995) stated that opiates, including heroin, do not appear to have neurotoxic effects on human cognition. There is also evidence that the heroin-induced shrinkage in the dopamine-using neurons of the rat brain reverses itself with abstinence (Nestler, 1997). These findings raise questions about whether the observed opiate-induced neurological changes are permanent.

It should be noted that, when abused at high dosage levels, narcotics are capable of causing seizures (Foley, 1993). This rare complication of narcotics use is apparently caused by the high dosage level of the opioid being administered, and it usually responds to the effects of a narcotics blocker such as Narcan (naloxone), according to the author. One exception is seizures caused by the drug meperidine. Naloxone may actually reduce the patient's seizure threshold, making it more likely that he or she will continue to experience meperidine-induced seizures (Foley, 1993). Thus the physician must identify the specific narcotic(s) being abused in order to initiate the proper intervention for opioid-induced seizures.

Another consequence of heroin abuse is found in cases where the individual engaged in the act of "chasing the dragon" (inhalation of heroin fumes). In rare cases, this practice has resulted in a progressive spongiform leukoencephalopathy, a condition similar to the "mad cow" disease seen in English cattle in the mid-1990s (Kriegstein, Shungu, Millar, Armitage, Brust, Chillrud, Goldman, & Lynch, 1999). Very little is known about how inhaling heroin fumes leads to progressive spongiform leukoencephalopathy, and there is a chance that it is caused by one or more chemicals added to the heroin to dilute ("cut") it, according to Kriegstein *et al.*, (1999). There was an outbreak of heroin-induced progressive spongiform leukoencephalopathy in the Netherlands in the 1990s, and the first U.S. cases were identified in 1996, suggesting that while the practice of "chasing the dragon" avoids exposure to HIV infection, it is not entirely without its own unique dangers.

Opiate Overdose

There are a number of reasons why a given opiate abuser might overdose on narcotics. For example, it is difficult to estimate the potency of illicit narcotics, and abusers might miscalculate how much of the heroin that they had purchased could be safely injected. Some of these individuals die before they reach the hospital, but others survive long enough for health care professionals to intervene and rescue them from the effects of the drug overdose.

An overdose of narcotics produces a characteristic pattern of reduced consciousness, pinpoint pupils, and respiratory depression (Henry, 1996). Indeed, Carvey (1998) stated that the most common cause of death in an overdose of the prototypical opiate, morphine, is respiratory depression. Without medical intervention, death usually occurs 5–10 minutes after intravenous injection of an opiate overdose and 30–90 minutes after an intramuscular injection of an overdose of narcotic analgesics (Hirsch, Paley, & Renner, 1996). However, these data apply only for cases of overdose with pharma-

ceutical opiates. Medical experts are still not sure whether deaths from illicit narcotics are caused by the drugs themselves or by the multitude of other chemicals commonly added to street narcotics to dilute them.

For example, Scaros, Westra, and Barone (1990) reported that a typical sample of "street" heroin also contains between 68 and 314 mg of quinine, which is a common adulterant. The addict who slowly injects the drug over a 10-second period injects between 10 and 131 mg of quinine per second—a rate of injection *up to 182 times the maximum recommended rate of injection of quinine*. This rate of quinine injection is itself capable of causing a fatal reaction in many individuals.

Street myths and narcotics overdose. There are several "street" myths about the treatment of opiate overdose. First, there is the myth that cocaine (or another CNS stimulant) will help in the control of an opiate overdose. Another myth is that it is possible to control the symptoms of an overdose by putting ice packs under the arms and on the groin of the overdose victim. A third myth concerning the narcotics overdose is that the person who had the overdose should be kept awake, and be kept walking around, until the drug wears off.

Treating an opiate overdose is a complicated matter, which does not lend itself to such easy solutions. Even in the best-equipped hospital, a narcotics overdose may result in death. The current treatment of choice for a narcotics overdose is a combination of respiratory and cardiac support, as well as a trial dose of *Narcan* (naloxone hydrochloride) (Henry, 1996). Naloxone hydrochloride is thought to bind at the receptor sites within the brain occupied by opiate molecules, displacing the latter, from the receptors and reversing the effects of the opiate overdose.

Unfortunately, naloxone has a therapeutic half-life of only 60–90 minutes. Its effects are thus quite short-lived, and the patient may need several doses before he or she has fully recovered from the opiate overdose (Roberts, 1995). Although naloxone-induced complications are rare, they occasionally develop when this drug is used to treat opiate overdoses (Henry, 1996). Finally, the patient might have ingested or injected a number of different chemicals, each of which has its own toxicological profile. For these reasons, remember that *known or suspected opiate overdoses are life threatening emergencies that always require immediate medical support and treatment.*

Summary

The narcotic family of drugs has been effectively utilized by physicians for several thousand years. Indeed, after alcohol, the narcotics might be thought of as the oldest drugs. Various members of the narcotic family of drugs are effective in the control of severe pain, severe cough, and severe diarrhea. The only factor that limits their application in the control of less grave conditions is their addiction potential. The addiction potential of narcotics has been known for hundreds, if not thousands, of years. For example, opiate addiction was a common complication of military service in the last century and was even called "the soldier's disease."

Not until the advent of the chemical revolution, however, when synthetic narcotics were first developed, did new forms of narcotic analgesics become available to drug users. Fentanyl and its chemical cousins are products of the pharmacological revolution that began in the late 1800s and continues to this day. This chemical is estimated to be several hundred to several thousand times as powerful as morphine and promises to remain a part of the drug abuse problem for generations to come.

CHAPTER FIFTEEN

Hallucinogen Abuse and Addiction

Introduction

It has been estimated that about 6000 different species of plants might be used for their psychoactive properties (Brophy, 1993), including several species of mushrooms that will, when ingested, produce hallucinations (Rold, 1993). Many of these plants and mushrooms have been used for centuries in religious ceremonies, in healing rituals, for predicting the future (Berger & Dunn, 1982), and to prepare warriors for battle (Rold, 1993). Even today, certain religious groups use mushrooms with hallucinogenic properties as part of their worship, although their use is illegal in the United States (Rold, 1993). Chemicals with hallucinogenic properties are also popular drugs of abuse. In this chapter, the hallucinogens will be examined.

History of Hallucinogens in the United States

Over the years, researchers have identified approximately 100 different hallucinogenic compounds that are found in various plants or mushrooms. Many of these compounds have been extensively studied by scientists. Indeed, it was during a clinical research project that the effects of one hallucinogenic, lysergic acid diethylamide-25 (LSD-25, or simply LSD) were accidently discovered and recorded in 1938. LSD is a substance obtained from the rye fungus ergot, *Claviceps purpurea* (Lingeman, 1974). LSD was first isolated in 1938 by chemists looking for a cure for headaches

(Monroe, 1994). In 1943, a scientist accidentally ingested a small amount of LSD-25 while conducting an experiment, and later that day he experienced LSD-induced hallucinations. After he recovered, the scientist correctly concluded that the source of the hallucinations was the specimen of *Claviceps purpurea* on which he had been working. He again ingested a small amount of the fungus, and again experienced hallucination, thus confirming his original conclusion.

Following World War II, there was a great deal of scientific interest in the various hallucinogenics, especially in light of the similarities between the subjective effects of these chemicals and various forms of mental illness. Further, because they were so potent, certain agencies of the United States Government, such as the Department of Defense and the Central Intelligence Agency, experimented with various chemical agents, including LSD, as possible chemical warfare weapons (Budiansky, Goode & Gest, 1994). In the 1950s, the term "psychedelic" was coined to identify this class of compounds (Callaway & McKenna, 1998).

The hallucinogens were hardly a well kept secret after they were discovered, and in the 1960s these chemicals moved from the laboratory into the streets (Brown & Braden, 1987). The popularity and widespread abuse of LSD in the 1960s prompted the classification of this chemical as a controlled substance in 1970 (Jaffe, 1990). Over the years, LSD abuse has waxed and waned, reaching a low point in the late 1970s and then increasing until it was again popular in the early 1990s. The abuse of LSD in the United States peaked in 1996

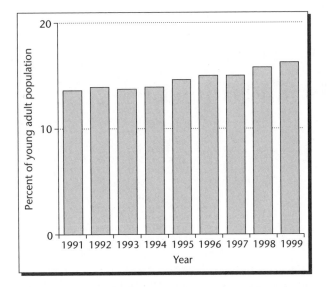

FIGURE 15.1   Lifetime LSD use by young adults: 1991–1999.

and has gradually been declining since then (Markel, 2000). However, 12% of high school seniors admit to having used LSD once, and 8% reported that they had used it within the past year (Markel, 2000). The incidence of reported LSD abuse by young adults is reviewed in Figure 15.1.

The hallucinogen *phencyclidine* (PCP) deserves special mention. Because of its toxicity, PCP fell into disfavor in the early 1970s (Jaffe, 1989). But in the 1980s, a form of PCP that could be smoked was introduced, and it again became popular with illicit drug users, in part because the smoker could more closely control how much of the drug she or he used. PCP remained a common drug of abuse until the mid-to late 1990s, when it declined in popularity. Currently, LSD is the hallucinogen ingested in 99% of the cases (Weaver, Jarvis, & Schnoll, 1999, but PCP is still being sold on the illicit drug market and is often sold to unsuspecting users in the guise of other, more desired substances. Another drug, N, alpha-dimethyl-1,3-benzodioxole-t-ethanamine (MDMA), became quite popular as a chemical of abuse in the late 1970s and early 1980s; it continued to be a popular drug of abuse in the 1990's and the first part of the 21st century. Both PCP and MDMA will be discussed in later sections of this chapter.

Scope of the Problem

Unfortunately, it is difficult to estimate the number of casual hallucinogen users. Monroe (1994) reported that each year in the United States, at least 2.8 million people use LSD at least once. Some 12% of the high school seniors of the class of 1999 admitted to having used LSD at least once, whereas 12.7% of the college students surveyed and 16% of the young adults aged 19–32 who were not in college admitted to having used LSD at least once (Johnston, O'Malley, & Bachman 2000a). In years past, the majority of those who used the hallucinogens such as LSD were those who experimented with the drug and then either totally avoided further hallucinogen use or went on to use hallucinogens only on an episodic basis (Jaffe, 1989). This, along with evidence that LSD users are using it more often than in the 1960s, suggests that much of what was discovered about the effects of LSD on the user in the 1960s and 1970s might not apply to the user of the early 21st century.

Pharmacology of the Hallucinogens

The commonly abused hallucinogenics can be divided into two major groups, on the basis of their chemical structure (Jaffe, 1989). First, there are the hallucinogens that bear a structural resemblance to the neurotransmitter serotonin: LSD, psilocybin, and the chemical dimethyl-tryptamine (DMT). DMT is often abused in combination with monoamine oxidase inhibitors (MAOIs), to enhance its effect (Community Anti-Drug Coalitions of America, 1997). The second group of hallucinogenics is chemically related to the neurotransmitters dopamine and norepinephrine and resembles the amphetamine family of drugs (Jaffe, 1989). These hallucinogenics include mescaline, MDMA, and DOM (also known as STP).

In spite of the chemical differences between hallucinogens and their differences in potency, illicit drug users tend to adjust their intake of the drug(s) to produce similar effects (Schuckit, 1995a). Indeed, there is evidence that the hallucinogens essentially function as serotonin agonists, causing some neurons in the brain to become hyperactive for several hours afterwards. One exception to this rule is DMT. The effects of DMT last only about 20 minutes, and it is for this reason that

DMT is often called a "businessman's high." The drug experience may fit into a typical half hour lunch break. In other ways, DMT is very similar to the other hallucinogens to be discussed in this chapter.

It is common for a person under the influence of one of the hallucinogens to believe that he or she has a new insight into reality. But these drugs do not generate new thoughts so much as alter one's perception of existing sensory stimuli (Snyder, 1986). These chemicals also produce hallucinations, or hallucinatory-like experiences, which the user generally recognizes as being drug-induced (Lingeman, 1974). Thus, the terms "hallucinogen" and "hallucinogenic" are usually applied to this class of drugs. Because LSD accounts for 99% of all hallucinogen abuse, this chapter will focus on LSD as the prototypical hallucinogenic; other drugs in this class will be discussed only as needed.

The Pharmacology of LSD

LSD is one of the most potent chemicals known. Researchers have found that LSD is 100–1000 times as powerful as the hallucinogenic chemicals naturally found in plants, such as psilocybin and peyote (Schwartz, 1995). However, it is weaker than synthetic chemicals such as the hallucinogenic DOM/STP (Schuckit, 2000).

For the casual user, LSD might be effective at doses as low as 50 micrograms, although the classic LSD "trip" usually requires that the user ingest twice that amount of the drug (Schwartz, 1995). Unfortunately, where users in the 1960s might ingest a single 100–200-microgram dose, current LSD doses on the street seem to fall in the 20- to 80-microgram range, possibly to make the drug more appealing to first-time users (Gold & Miller, 1997c). Although it is possible to inject LSD directly into a vein, it is most commonly taken orally (Henderson, 1994a).

The LSD molecule is water-soluble. In spite of the claims of some users whose chemical use was detected via urine toxicology testing, it is not possible to absorb LSD through the skin (Henderson, 1994a). When it is taken by mouth, LSD is rapidly absorbed from the gastrointestinal tract and distributed to all body tissues (Mirin, Weiss, & Greenfield, 1991). Because it is distributed throughout the body, only about 0.01% of the original dose actually reaches the brain (Lingeman,

1974). Thus, if the user were to ingest a 50-microgram dose of LSD, only half a microgram would actually reach the brain. The chemical structure of the LSD molecule is very similar to that of the neurotransmitter serotonin, which enables it to function as a serotonin agonist. Indeed, so similar is the LSD molecule to serotonin that physicians need to inquire about possible LSD use before starting the patient on a class of antidepressants known as *selective serotonin reuptake inhibitors* (SSRIs); there is evidence that SSRI use by a patient who has recently abused LSD can contribute to "flashback" experiences (Markel, 2000). Research suggests that the LSD molecule will bind to one of the 15 known subtypes of serotonin receptor sites in the brain called the $5-HT_2$ receptor site (Callaway & McKenna, 1998; Schwartz, 1995).[1]

The majority of the serotonin-based neurons in the brain are located in the *midbrain raphe nuclei*, a region also known as the dorsal midbrain raphe (Mirin, Weiss, & Greenfield, 1991). This part of the brain is interconnected with virtually every other, so any compound that interferes with the normal activity of the midbrain raphe nuclei would be expected to have widespread effects. This is exactly what is observed in the person who has ingested a dose of LSD, which suggests that this is the region of the brain where the compound exerts its major effect.

Scientists believe that the midbrain raphe nuclei regions functions as a modulator system, controlling the rate at which other regions of the brain function by inhibiting excessive nervous activity. LSD is thought to interfere with the inhibitory function of the midbrain raphe nuclei and thus to cause perceptual and mood distortions by allowing excessive neural activity in those regions of the brain involved in perception and the regulation of affect (Lemonick, Lafferty, Nash, Park, & Thompson, 1997; Henderson, 1994a). This is only a theory, however, and after more than 50 years of research, the exact mechanism of action for LSD is still not entirely clear (Henderson, 1994a).

Tolerance to the effects of LSD develops quickly, often within 2–4 days of continual use (Schwartz, 1995; Henderson, 1994a; Mirin, Weiss, & Greenfield, 1991). If the user has become tolerant to the effects of LSD,

---

[1]It is possible that LSD also binds to other receptor sites yet to be discovered.

then increasing the dosage level will have little or no effect (Henderson, 1994a). However, the individual's tolerance to LSD will abate after 2–4 days of abstinence (Henderson, 1994a; Jaffe, 1989; Lingeman, 1974). Cross-tolerance between the different hallucinogens is also quite common (Callaway & McKenna, 1998). Thus, most abusers alternate between active hallucinogen use and periods during which they abstain.

In terms of direct physical mortality, LSD is perhaps the safest drug known to modern medicine (Brown & Braden, 1987; Weil, 1986). There are only two reported human deaths from suspected LSD overdoses (Schwartz, 1995). In another incident reported by Lingeman (1974), an elephant that received a massive dose of LSD (297,000 micrograms, or 5940 doses at 50 micrograms each) died.[2] These reports suggest that LSD might prove toxic to the user, but the approximate lethal dose of LSD in humans is simply not known.[3] Indeed, Henderson (1994a) stated that "the risk of death from an overdose of LSD is virtually nonexistent" (p. 43). But LSD has been implicated as the indirect cause of death in some users, generally as a result of accidents.

The biological half-life of LSD is not known with any certainty. The drug is rapidly biotransformed by the liver, and thus it is rapidly eliminated from the body. Indeed, so rapid is the process of LSD biotransformation and elimination that traces of the major metabolite of LSD, 2-oxy-LSD, remain in the user's urine only for 12–36 hours after the last use of the drug (Schwartz, 1995). The estimates of the biological half-life of LSD range from 2–3 hours (Karch, 1996; Weiss, Mirin, & Greenfield, 1994; Shepherd & Jagoda, 1990; Jaffe, 1990, 1989) to 5 hours (Henderson, 1994a).

The effects of a single dose of LSD appear to last between 8 and 12 hours (Monroe, 1994; Kaplan & Sadock, 1996), although Mendelson and Mello (1998) suggested that the drug's effects might last 18 hours. Only about 1% of a single dose of LSD is excreted unchanged, the rest being biotransformed by the liver and excreted in the bile (Henderson, 1994a). LSD continues to challenge researchers, who struggle with such

questions as how, when the person ingests such a small dose of the original compound, and when such a small portion of the total ingested dose actually reaches the brain, LSD can have such a profound impact on the user's state of mind. Obviously, there is much to learn about the hallucinogens.

Subjective Effects of Hallucinogens

Subjectively, the user begins to feel the first effects of a dose of LSD in about 5–10 minutes. These initial effects include such symptoms as anxiety, gastric distress, and tachycardia (Schwartz, 1995). In addition, the user may experience: increased blood pressure, increased body temperature, dilation of the pupils, nausea, and muscle weakness (Jaffe, 1989). Other side effects of LSD include an exaggeration of normal reflexes (a condition known as hyperreflexia), dizziness, and some degree of muscle tremor (Jaffe, 1989). Lingeman (1974) characterized these changes as "relatively minor" (p. 133), although they might cause the inexperienced user anxiety.

The hallucinogenic effects of LSD usually begin anywhere between 30 minutes and an hour after the user ingests the drug (Henderson, 1994a). Scientists believe that the effects of a hallucinogen such as LSD vary with the individual's personality, her or his expectations for the drug, the environment in which the drug is used, and the dose of the compound (Callaway & McKenna, 1998).

Users often refer to the effects of LSD as a "trip," during which they may experience such effects as a loss of psychological boundaries, a feeling of enhanced insight, a heightened awareness of sensory data, enhanced recall of past events, a feeling of contentment and a sense of being at one with the universe (Callaway & McKenna, 1998). The LSD trip is made up of several distinct phases (Brophy, 1993). First, within a few minutes of taking LSD, there is a release of inner tension. This stage, which lasts 1–2 hours (Brophy, 1993) is characterized by either laughing or crying, as well as a feeling of euphoria (Jaffe, 1989). The second stage usually begins between 30–90 minutes (Brown & Braden, 1987) and 2–3 hours (Brophy, 1993), after ingestion of the drug. During this period, the individual experiences the perceptual distortions (such as visual illusions and hallucinations) that are the hallmark of the hallucinogenic experience. Mirin, Weiss, and Greenfield (1991)

---

[2] Lingeman (1974) did not explain how the elephant happened to ingest the LSD.

[3] This margin of safety does *not* extend to the other hallucinogens. It is possible to overdose on and die from some of the other, less popular hallucinogens.

described this phase as being marked by "wavelike perceptual changes" (p. 290) and noted that synesthesia is often experienced. Synesthesia is a phenomenon whereby information from one sense may "slip over" into another sensory system. Thus people who are experiencing synesthesia may report that they are able to taste colors or see music.

The third phase of the hallucinogenic experience begins 3–4 hours after the drug is ingested (Brophy, 1993). During this phase of the LSD trip, the person will experiences a distortion of the sense of time, and may also experience marked mood swings, and a feeling of ego disintegration. Panic occurs often, depression occasionally (Lingeman, 1974). These LSD-related anxiety reactions will be discussed in the next section. During this third stage of the LSD trip, some individuals believe that they possess quasi-magical powers or that they are magically in control of events around them (Jaffe, 1989). This loss of contact with reality is potentially fatal, and individuals have been known to jump from windows, or attempt to drive motor vehicles, during this phase of the LSD trip.

The effects of LSD start to wane 4–6 hours after it is ingested. As the individual begins to recover, he or she experiences "waves of normalcy" (Schwartz, 1995; Mirin, Weiss, & Greenfield, 1991, p. 290), which gradually blend into the normal state of awareness. Within 12 hours, the acute effects of LSD have cleared, although the user might experience a "sense of psychic numbness, [that] may last for days" (Mirin, Weiss, & Greenfield, 1991, p. 290).

The LSD "bad trips." As noted earlier, it is not uncommon for the individual who has ingested LSD to experience a great deal of anxiety, which may reach the level of panic. This is known as a "bad trip." The likelihood of a bad trip seems to be determined by three factors: (1) the individual's expectations for the drug (which is known as the "set"), (2) the setting in which the drug is used, and (3) the psychological health of the user (Mirin, Weiss, & Greenfield, 1991). The LSD "bad trip" is most likely to occur with inexperienced LSD users, who are most prone to LSD-induced feelings of anxiety or panic (Mirin, Weiss, & Greenfield, 1991). Users who do develop a panic reaction to the LSD experience often respond to calm, gentle reminders from others that these feelings are caused by the drug, and will pass. This is known as "talking down" the LSD user.

In extreme cases, the individual may require pharmacological intervention for the LSD-induced panic attack. There is some disagreement among physicians about which medications offer the greatest potential for relief during an LSD-related panic reaction. Kaplan and Sadock (1996) recommended that diazepam be used to treat anxiety. However, Jenike (1991) warned *against* the use of benzodiazepines such as diazepam in aborting an LSD-related panic reaction because of benzodiazepine-induced sensory distortion. Normally, this distortion is so slight as to be unnoticed by the typical patient who receives benzodiazepines. But when combined with the effects of LSD, the benzodiazepine-induced sensory distortion may cause the patient to have even more anxiety than before, according to Jenike (1991).

The antipsychotic medication haloperidol was suggested as the drug of choice for use by medical personnel to abort the LSD-related panic attack (Jenike, 1991). Schwartz (1995) recommended that 2–4 mg of haloperidol be administered by intramuscular injection every hour, until the patient's anxiety was under control.

Many samples of hallucinogens sold on the street are adulterated with belladonna or other anticholinergics (Henderson, 1994a). When mixed with phenothiazines, these substances may bring about coma and death through cardiorespiratory failure. Thus it is imperative that the physician treating a bad trip know what drug(s) have been used and, if possible, be provided with a sample of the drug(s) ingested, to determine what medication is best in treating each patient.

The LSD-induced bad trip normally lasts only a few hours, and it typically resolves itself as the drug's effects wear off (Henderson, 1994b). However, in rare cases, LSD is capable of activating a latent psychosis (Henderson, 1994b). Support for this position is offered by Carvey (1998), who noted that various Indian tribes who have used the hallucinogen *mescaline* for centuries fail to have significantly higher rates of psychosis than the general population. Although this suggests that the psychosis seen in the occasional LSD user is not a drug effect, no conclusive answer to this question has been found.

One reason why it is so difficult to identify LSD's relationship to the development of psychiatric disorders such as a psychosis is that the LSD experience "is so exceptional that there is a tendency for observers to attribute *any* later psychiatric illness to the use of LSD" (Henderson, 1994b, p. 65, italics added). Thus psychotic reactions that develop weeks, months, or even years after the last use of LSD have been attributed to the individual's use of this hallucinogen, rather than to nondrug factors. Accordingly, it has been suggested that LSD is capable of causing long-term complications such as a drug induced psychosis, but this theory has also been challenged by other researchers.

One extremely rare complication of LSD use is the overdose (Schuckit, 1995a). The symptoms of an LSD overdose include convulsions and hyperthermia. Medical care is necessary in any suspected drug overdose, in order to reduce the risk of death. In a hospital setting, the physician can take appropriate steps to monitor the patient's cardiac status and to counter drug-induced elevation in body temperature, seizures, and the like.

The LSD flashback. The "flashback" is a common, long-term consequence of LSD use that is not well understood. The flashback is a "spontaneous recurrence" (Mirin, Weiss, & Greenfield, 1991, p. 292) of the drug experience that might take place days, weeks, or even months after the last time LSD was used. Weiss and Millman (1998) have classified flashbacks as perceptual, somatic, or emotional. They maintain that the majority of flashbacks involve visual sensory distortion. Somatic flashbacks consist of feelings of depersonalization, and emotional "flashbacks" involve again experiencing distressing emotions felt during the period of active LSD use (Weiss & Millman, 1998).

The majority (Schwartz, 1995, p. 409) of those who use LSD at least ten times can expect to experience at least one flashback. There have been reports of LSD-induced flashbacks after the individual had used LSD only once, however (Batzer, Ditzler, & Brown, 1999). Flashbacks may be triggered by such things as stress, fatigue, marijuana use, emerging from a dark room, illness, the use of certain forms of antidepressant medications, and (occasionally) by intentional effort on the part of the individual. Sedating agents such as alcohol may also trigger LSD-induced flashbacks, although the reasons for this are not understood (Batzer, Ditzler, & Brown, 1999). Flashbacks usually last a few seconds to a few minutes, although they may last up to 24–48 hours or even longer (Kaplan & Sadock, 1996). Approximately 50% of those people who develop flash-

backs do so in the first 6 months following their last use of LSD. In about 50% of the cases, the individual continues to experience flashbacks longer than 6 months, and in some cases, they have recurred for 5 years (Schwartz, 1995; Weiss, Greenfield, & Mirin, 1994).

Although flashbacks are occasionally frightening to the inexperienced user, they seem to be accepted by seasoned LSD users in much the same way that chronic alcohol users accept some physical discomfort as being part of the price they must pay for their chemical use. LSD abusers may not even report flashbacks unless specifically questioned about these experiences (Batzer, Ditzler, & Brown, 1999). LSD users seem to enjoy the visual hallucinations, the flashes of color, the halos around different objects, the perception that things are growing smaller, the perception that things are growing larger, and the feelings of depersonalization that are common in an LSD flashback (Mirin, Weiss, & Green field, 1991). In spite of this general tendency toward acceptance of the LSD-related flashback, some individuals have been known to become depressed, to develop a panic disorder, or even to become suicidal after having had an LSD-related flashback (Kaplan & Sadock, 1996). Fortunately, the only treatment needed for the typical patient is reassurance that the flashback will end. On rare occasions a benzodiazepine may be used to control flashback-induced anxiety.

Posthallucinogen perceptual disorder. This is a rare, poorly understood complication of LSD use/abuse (Hartman, 1995). It has been reported that, for reasons that are poorly understood, some chronic users of LSD experience a disturbance in their visual perceptual system that may or may not become permanent. Victims of this disorder report seeing afterimages, or distorted "trails" following behind objects in the environment, for extended periods after their last use of LSD (Hartman, 1995). The exact mechanism by which LSD causes these effects is not known.

Although LSD has been studied by researchers for 50 years, much remains to be discovered about this elusive chemical. For example, there is one case report of a patient who developed grand mal seizures after taking LSD while taking the antidepressant fluoxetine (Ciraulo, Creelman, Shader, & O'Sullivan, 1995). The reason for this interaction between these two chemicals is not known. And even before scientists were able to learn all that there was to learn about LSD, another popular hallucinogen appeared. This hallucinogen is called PCP.

Phencyclidine (PCP)

The drug *phencyclidine* (PCP) was first introduced in 1957 as an experimental, intravenously administered surgical anesthetic (Milhorn, 1991). By the mid-1960's, researchers had discovered that 10–20% of the patients who had received PCP experienced a drug-induced delirium, and use of the drug with humans was discontinued (Milhorn, 1991; Brown & Braden, 1987). However, phencyclidine continued to be used in veterinary medicine in the United States until the mid-1970s. In 1978, all legal U.S. production of PCP was discontinued, and the drug was declared a controlled substance under the Comprehensive Drug Abuse Prevention and Control Act of 1970 (Slaby, Lieb, & Tancredi, 1981). However, it continues to be used as a veterinary anesthetic in other parts of the world and is legally manufactured by pharmaceutical companies outside this country (Kaplan, Sadock, & Grebb, 1994). In years past PCP was a major part of the drug abuse problem in the United States, and even though it has largely disappeared, it has the potential to become a popular drug of abuse once again (Richards, 2000).

PCP continues to be a potential problem for two reasons. First, in spite of its harsh effects (discussed below), PCP is easily manufactured in illicit laboratories (Slaby, Lieb, & Tancredi, 1981). And because PCP can be produced with minimal training in chemistry, it was often mixed into other "street" drugs to enhance the effects of low-quality illicit substances. In years past, dealers commonly mixed PCP with low-potency marijuana to make the latter seem more potent. PCP was also frequently sold in the guise of other chemicals more difficult to manufacture such as LSD or concentrated THC (*The Addiction Letter*, 1994b; Brophy, 1993).

Another reason why PCP became so popular as a drug of abuse is that users in the 1980s discovered that by smoking PCP, they could adjust the dose to suit their individual taste or needs. Users who found the drug experience too harsh and aversive, could simply stop smoking the PCP-laced cigarette for a while. This abil-ity to tailor the drug-induced effects cannot be achieved through the other methods of PCP abuse.

Methods of PCP administration. PCP can be smoked, used intranasally, taken by mouth, injected into the muscle tissue, or injected intravenously (Weaver, Jarvis, & Schnoll, 1999; Brown & Braden, 1987). The most common method of PCP administration is for the user to smoke a cigarette that contains PCP (Grinspoon & Bakalar, 1990). As noted above, this gives users a great deal of control over the drug's effects, because they can stop smoking when they reach a desired state of intoxication.

Subjective experience of PCP abuse. Phencyclidine's effects may last for several days, during which time the user experiences rapid fluctuations in his or her level of consciousness (Weaver, Jarvis & Schnoll, 1999). The main experience for the user is a sense of dissociation, in which reality appears distorted or distant. Parts of the user's body may feel numb or as if they were no longer attached. These experiences may frighten the inexperienced user, resulting in panic reactions. The desired effects of PCP intoxication include a sense of euphoria, decreased inhibitions, a feeling of immense power, a reduction in the level of pain, and an altered perception of time, space, and the user's body image (Milhorn, 1991).

Not all of the drug's effects are desired by the user. Indeed, "most regular users report unwanted effects" (Mirin, Weiss, & Greenfield, 1991, p. 295). Some of the more common negative effects are feelings of anxiety, restlessness, and disorientation. Sometimes the user retains no memory of the period of intoxication, a reflection of the anesthetic action of the drug (Ashton, 1992). Other negative effects of PCP include disorientation, mental confusion, assaultiveness, anxiety, irritability, and paranoia (Weiss & Mirin, 1988). Indeed, so many people have experienced so many different undesired effects from PCP that researchers are at a loss to explain why the drug is so popular (Newell & Cosgrove, 1988).

A PCP-induced depressive state is common among users (Berger & Dunn, 1982). In extreme cases, the individual's level of depression may reach suicidal proportions (Jenike, 1991; Weiss & Mirin, 1988). This is consistent with the observations of Berger and Dunn (1982), who, in describing the wave of PCP abuse that occurred in the 1970s reported that the drug would bring the user to either "the heights, or the depths" (p. 100) of emotional experience.

Scope of PCP use/abuse. Researchers have found that approximately 3% of the high school seniors who graduated in 1999 admitted to having used PCP at least once (Johnston, O'Malley, & Bachman, 2000a) and that 2.3% of adults aged 19–32 who were surveyed reported having used PCP at least once in their lives (Johnston, O'Malley, & Bachman, 2000b).

Pharmacology of PCP

Chemically, phencyclidine is a weak base, soluble in both water and lipids. When ingested orally, because it is a weak base it will be absorbed mainly through the small intestine rather than through the stomach lining (Zukin & Zukin, 1992). This will slow the absorption of the drug into the body, for the drug molecules must pass through the stomach to reach the small intestine. But the effects of an oral dose of PCP are still generally seen in just 20–30 minute, and last for 3–8 hours (*The Addiction Letter,* 1994b).

When smoked, PCP is rapidly absorbed through the lungs. The user begins to experience symptoms of PCP intoxication within 2–3 minutes after smoking the drug (Milhorn, 1991; Shepherd & Jagoda, 1990). However, much of the PCP in the cigarette is converted into the chemical *phenylcyclohexene* by the heat of the cigarette (Shepherd & Jagoda, 1990), and only about 30–50% of the PCP in the cigarette is actually absorbed (Crowley, 1995b). When the drug is injected or ingested orally, 70–75% of the available PCP reaches the circulation (Crowley, 1995b). The effects of injected PCP last for about 3–5 hours. PCP is very lipid-soluble, so it tends to accumulate in fatty tissues and in the tissues of the brain. Indeed, the level of PCP in the brain might be 31–113 times as high as blood plasma levels (Shepherd & Jagoda, 1990). Further, animal research data suggest that PCP remains in the brain for up to 48 hours after it is no longer detectable in the blood (Hartman, 1995). Once in the brain, PCP tends to act at a number of different receptor sites, including blocking those utilized by a neurotransmitter known as N-methyl-D-aspartic acid (NMDA) (Zukin, Sloboda, & Javitt, 1997). PCP functions as an NMDA channel blocker, preventing NMDA from carrying out its normal function (Zukin, Sloboda, & Javitt, 1997). It has also been suggested that PCP binds to one of the numerous opioid receptor sites

known as the sigma opioid receptor site (Daghestani & Schnoll, 1994), although Crowley (1995b) disputed this theory. Thus the issue of whether PCP binds to any of the opioid receptor sites has yet to be resolved.

Phencyclidine is an unusual drug. Depending on the dosage level and the route of administration, PCP might function as an anesthetic, a stimulant, a depressant, or a hallucinogenic (Weiss & Mirin, 1988; Brown & Braden, 1987). This is partly due to the fact that PCP affects several different neurotransmitters within the brain rather than just one (Roberts, 1995). Because of this, "few drugs seem to induce so wide a range of subjective effects" (Jaffe, 1990, p. 557).

PCP is biotransformed by the liver into a number of inactive metabolites, which are then excreted mainly by the kidneys (Zukin, Sloboda, & Javitt, 1997; Zukin & Zukin, 1992). Following a single dose of PCP, only about 10% (Shepherd & Jagoda, 1990) to 20% (Crowley, 1995b) of the drug is excreted unchanged. Unfortunately it takes the body a long time to biotransform/excrete PCP. The half-life of PCP following an overdose may be as long as 20 (Kaplan, Sadock, & Grebb, 1994) to 72 hours (Jaffe, 1989) up to a period of weeks (Grinspoon & Bakalar, 1990).

One reason for the extended half-life of PCP is that it tends to accumulate in the body's adipose (fat) tissues. In chronic users, PCP molecules can remain in the user's fat cells for days, or even weeks, following the last dose of the drug. There have even been cases where a chronic PCP user has lost weight (either as a result of the person's attempts to lose weight, or because of trauma) and unmetabolized PCP still in the person's adipose tissue has been released back into the general circulation, causing the user to have "flashback"-type experiences long after his or her last use of the drug (Zunkin & Zunkin, 1992).

Some physicians believe that it is possible to reduce the half-life of PCP in the body by making the urine more acidic. This is done by having the patient ingest large amounts of ascorbic acid or cranberry juice (Kaplan & Sadock, 1996; Grinspoon & Bakalar, 1990). However, one potentially dangerous complication of this technique is the possible development of a condition known as myoglobinuria, which may cause the kidneys to fail (Brust, 1993). For this reason, many physicians do not recommend acidification of the patient's urine.

There is virtually no research data on the possibility of users becoming tolerant to the effects of PCP. However, clinical evidence with burn patients who have received repeated doses of the anesthetic agent ketamine, which is similar in chemical structure to PCP, suggest that some degree of tolerance to its effects can develop (Zukin, Sloboda, & Javitt, 1997). There is no evidence of physical dependence on PCP (Zevin & Benowitz, 1998; Weiss, Greenfield, & Mirin, 1994).

Symptoms of mild PCP intoxication. Small doses of PCP, usually less than 1 mg, do not seem to have an effect on the user (Crowley, 1995b). At dosage levels of about 5 mg, the individual experiences a state resembling alcohol intoxication (Crowley, 1995b; Mirin, Weiss, & Greenfield, 1991), including faulty muscle coordination, staggering gait, slurred speech, and numbness of the extremities (Jaffe, 1989). Other effects of mild doses of PCP are agitation, some feelings of anxiety, flushing of the skin, visual hallucinations, irritability, possible sudden outbursts of rage, feelings of euphoria, nystagmus, changes in body image, and depression (Crowley, 1995b; Milhorn, 1991; Beebe & Walley, 1991).

The acute effects of a dose of about 5 mg of PCP last 4–6 hours. Following the period of acute effects is a post-PCP recovery period that can last 24–48 hours (Milhorn, 1991; Beebe & Walley, 1991). During the post-PCP recovery period, the user gradually "comes down," or returns to normal.

Symptoms of moderate PCP intoxication. As the dosage level increases to 5–10 mg, many users experience a range of symptoms, including a disturbance of body image, wherein different parts of their bodies no longer seem real (Brophy, 1993). The user may also experience slurred speech, nystagmus, dizziness, ataxia, tachycardia, and an increase in muscle tone (Brophy, 1993; Weiss & Mirin, 1988). Other symptoms of moderate levels of PCP intoxication include paranoia, severe anxiety, belligerence, and assaultiveness (Grinspoon & Bakalar, 1990) as well as unusual feats of strength (Brophy, 1993; Jaffe, 1989) and extreme salivation (Brendel, West, & Hyman, 1996). Some people exhibit drug-induced fever, drug-induced psychosis, and violence.

Symptoms of severe PCP intoxication. As the dosage level reaches 10–25 mg or higher, the individual's life is in grave danger. At this dosage level the PCP user may experience vomiting and seizures. Even if the user were still conscious, his or her reaction time would be seriously impaired. The user who has ingested more than 10 mg of PCP may experience hypertension and severe psychotic reactions similar to schizophrenia (Kaplan & Sadock, 1996; Grinspoon & Bakalar, 1990; Weiss & Mirin, 1988). Estimates of how long the PCP-induced coma might last range from up to 10 days (Mirin, Weiss, & Greenfield, 1991) to several weeks (Zevin & Benowitz, 1998). Further, because of the absorption/distribution characteristics of the drug, the individual might slip into, and apparently recover from, a PCP-induced coma several times before the drug is eliminated from the body (Carvey, 1998). Other symptoms of severe PCP intoxication might include cardiac arrhythmias, encopresis, visual and tactile hallucinations, and a drug-induced paranoid state. PCP overdoses have caused death from respiratory arrest, convulsions, and hypertension (Brophy, 1993).

Complications of PCP Abuse

As we noted earlier, PCP has been implicated as causing a drug-induced psychosis that may last for days, weeks (Jenike, 1991; Jaffe, 1989; Weiss & Mirin, 1988), or months (Ashton, 1992) after the last use of the drug. This PCP psychosis seems to be most likely in those persons who either have suffered a previous schizophrenic episode (Mirin, Weiss, & Greenfield, 1991) or are vulnerable to such an episode (Weiss & Millman, 1998).

Unfortunately, there is no way to predict in advance who might develop a PCP-induced psychosis. Grinspoon and Bakalar (1990) reported that 6 out of 10 patients who had developed a PCP psychosis went on to develop chronic schizophrenia. This may suggest a predisposition to schizophrenia in at least some of those who experienced a PCP psychosis. Ashton (1992), on the other hand, suggested that the apparent PCP-induced psychosis might result from organic brain damage induced by chronic PCP use. It is known that the chronic use of PCP can result in

> a long-lasting syndrome marked by neuropsychological deficits, social withdrawal, and affective blunting as well as hallucinations, formal thought disorder, paranoia and delusions. (Jentsch, Redmond, Elsworth, Taylor, Youngren, & Roth, 1997)

Thus it is clear that the chronic use of PCP can cause many of the behavioral manifestations of the condition known as schizophrenia, although it is not known whether this reflects the activation of latent schizophrenia within certain individuals or a drug-induced state that simulates actual schizophrenia.

It *is* known that the PCP psychosis generally progresses through three different stages, each of which lasts approximately five days (Mirin, Weiss, & Greenfield, 1991; Weiss & Mirin, 1988). The first stage of the PCP psychosis is usually the most severe and is characterized by paranoid delusions, anorexia, insomnia, and unpredictable assaultiveness. During this phase, the individual is extremely sensitive to external stimuli (Mirin, Weiss, & Greenfield, 1991; Jaffe, 1989), and the "talking down" techniques that might work with an LSD bad trip do not often work (Brust, 1993; Jaffe, 1990).

The middle phase is marked by continued paranoia and restlessness, but the individual is usually calmer and in intermittent control of his or her behavior (Mirin, Weiss, & Greenfield, 1991; Weiss & Mirin, 1988). This phase may also last 5 days and then gradually blends into the final phase of the PCP psychosis recovery process. This final phase is marked by a gradual recovery over 7 to 14 days, although in some patients the PCP psychosis may last for months (Mirin, Weiss, and Greenfield, 1991; Weiss and Mirin, 1988; Slaby, Lieb, & Tancredi, 1981). Social withdrawal and severe depression are also common following chronic use of PCP (Jaffe, 1990).

There would appear to be some minor withdrawal symptoms following prolonged hallucinogen use. Chronic PCP users have reported memory problems, which seem to clear when they stop using the drug (Jaffe, 1990; Newell and Cosgrove, 1988). There is evidence that chronic PCP users demonstrate the same pattern of neuropsychological deficits found in other forms of chronic drug use, which suggests that PCP may cause chronic brain damage (Jentsch *et al.*, 1997; Grinspoon & Bakalar, 1990; Newell & Cosgrove, 1988).

Research has also revealed that at high dosage levels, PCP can cause hypertensive episodes (Lange, White, & Robinson, 1992), that in extreme cases might last three days after the drug was ingested (Weiss & Millman, 1998). These periods of unusually high blood pressure may then cause the individual to experience a cerebral vascular accident (CVA, or stroke) (Daghestani & Schnoll, 1994; Brust, 1993). Although research into this area is lacking, it is possible that this is the mechanism through which PCP causes brain damage.

The majority of PCP users who die do so because of traumatic injuries that they suffer while under the drug's influence (*The Addiction Letter*, 1994b). For example, because of the assaultiveness frequently induced by PCP, many users end up as the victim or perpetrator of a homicide (Ashton, 1992). Given its effects on the user, researchers are mystified as to why anybody would wish to use PCP. Still, all of the available evidence suggests that PCP has been a popular drug of abuse for the last quarter of the 20th century and that its use remains fashionable at the start of the 21st century.

Ecstasy: Evolution of a New Drug of Abuse

In the mid-1970s, substance abuse professionals began dealing with patients who were using a "new" hallucinogenic: N, alpha-dimethyl-1,3-benzodioxole-t-ethanamine. On the streets, this drug is called by such names as "Ecstasy," "XTC," "M&M" or "Adam" (Beebe & Walley, 1991), and "rave" or simply by the letter "E" (Henry, Jeffreys, & Dawling, 1992), Clinicians and chemists simply refer to the drug by the initials MDMA. Although classified by some as a new "designer" drug, MDMA actually was first synthesized by scientists in 1914.[4] But a medical use for MDMA was never identified, and the chemical remained little more than a curiosity until the 1970s (Cook, 1995; Sternbach & Varon, 1992; Mirin, Weiss, & Greenfield, 1991; Climko, Roehrich, Sweeney, & Al-Razi, 1987). One exception to this was the U.S. Army, which briefly considered MDMA as a possible chemical warfare agent in the 1950s before moving on to other compounds (Abbott & Concar, 1992). Because nobody really seemed interested in MDMA, it was not classified as a controlled substance when the drug classification system currently in use was set up in the early 1970s. The British government banned MDMA in 1977 (Abbott & Concar, 1992), whereas the U.S. Drug Enforcement

---

[4]Cook (1995) said that MDMA was patented in 1913, and Rochester & Kirchner (1999) suggested that the patent was issued in 1912 in Germany. Schuckit (2000) said that MDMA was first synthesized in 1912 and that the patent for this compound was issued in 1914.

Administration did not classify MDMA as a controlled substance until July 1, 1985 (Climko *et al.*, 1987).

The chemical structure of MDMA is very similar to that of the amphetamines, and it is for this reason that MDMA is occasionally referred to as a "psychedelic amphetamine" (Cook, 1995). The chemical structure of MDMA is also similar to that of another hallucinogen, MDA (Schuckit, 2000; Creighton, Black, & Hyde, 1991; Kirsch, 1986).

MDMA briefly surfaced as a drug of abuse during the 1960s. But because LSD was more potent and did not cause the nausea or vomiting often experienced by MDMA users, LSD became the more popular hallucinogenic and MDMA remained only a footnote in history until the mid-1970s. Then illicit drug chemists "decided to resurrect, christen, package, market, distribute, and advertise" (Kirsch, 1986, p. 76) MDMA. One reason for the decision to focus on MDMA was the fact that it was not then classified as a controlled substance in the United States and thus could be legally manufactured and distributed.

Within the drug underworld, marketing plans and possible product names were discussed (Kirsch, 1986).The name "Empathy" was considered for a while, but "Ecstasy" was finally selected. The drug world had appropriated the techniques of big business. The unknown drug manufacturers first created a demand for a "product," which was then conveniently met by the very people who had first manipulated users into clamoring for MDMA. The original samples of ecstasy contained a "package insert" (Kirsch, 1986, p. 81) that "included unverified scientific research and an abundance of 1960s mumbo-jumbo" (p. 81). The package inserts also warned the user not to mix ecstasy with other alcohol or chemicals, to use it only occasionally, and to take care to ensure a proper "set" (surroundings) in which to use MDMA.

Within a few years, MDMA had become a popular drug of abuse both in the United States and in Europe. The official response in this country was swift: the Drug Enforcement Administration (DEA) classified MDMA as a controlled substance effective July 1, 1985 (Climko *et al.*, 1987). As of that date, "trafficking in MDMA (was) punishable by fifteen years in prison and a $125,000 fine" (Kirsch, 1986, p. 84). Immediately after this, several "labs" known to be involved in the production of MDMA were shut down by the DEA. Unfortu-nately, MDMA's popularity has continued to increase, and it is now one of the two or three most frequently abused hallucinogenic compounds in the United States (Schuckit, 2000).

Scope of the Problem of MDMA Abuse

The scope of MDMA abuse can be gauged only vicariously through such indirect measures as police reports of drug seizures, annual summaries of drug-related hospital emergency room visits, and anonymous surveys that include questions about drug use. Nevertheless, these indirect measures of MDMA use suggest that the drug is growing in popularity. One law enforcement operation completed in December of 1999, for example, discovered a package of 100 pounds of MDMA that was being shipped from France to the United States, and another 1.2 million tablets being seized at the package's destination (Cloud, Barnes, Graft, Reaves, & Shannon, 2000). In the first three months of the year 2000, authorities seized an estimated 3.3 million doses of MDMA—more than were seized in the entire preceding year (Cloud *et al.*, 2000).

One reason why MDMA has remained a popular drug of abuse, is that it is reportedly harmless (Ramcharan, Meenhorst, Otten, Koks, de Boer, Maes, & Beijnen,1998). It has found wide acceptance in a subculture devoted to loud music; and parties that revolves around the use of MDMA and dancing—a pattern similar to that of the LSD parties of the 1960s—are common (Randell, 1992). Further, the drug is viewed by many as a "dance-making drug," because users tend to dance for extended periods of time (*Medical Update*, 1994). These parties, known as "raves," may involve thousands of participants (Rochester & Kirchner, 1999) and are usually held in abandoned farms, factories, and the like.

Early demand for MDMA in the United States was fueled by news stories in the popular press about Ecstasy's supposed value in psychotherapy (Rochester & Kirchner, 1999). One indication of its early popularity is the fact that 10–40% of older adolescents and young adults admit to having used MDMA at least once (Schuckit, 2000). In spite of the fact that MDMA use is illegal in England, an estimated 500,000 (Williams, Dratcu, Taylor, Roberts, & Oyefeso, 1998) to 750,000 (Cook, 1995) doses of it are consumed in that country each weekend. Researchers have found that approximately 8% of the high school seniors who graduated in 1999 admitted to having used MDMA at least once (Johnston, O'Malley, & Bachman, 2000a) and that 7.1%% of adults aged 19–32 and 8.4% of the college students who were sampled reported having used MDMA at least once (Johnston, O'Malley, & Bachman, 2000b).

MDMA users tend to have different drug use patterns than those who abuse other chemicals. The typical MDMA abuser ingests 1–2 tablets, each of which contains 100–140 mg of the drug, during the weekend and then abstains from further MDMA use for the rest of the week (Gouzoulis-Mayfrank, Daumann, Tuchtenhagen, Pelz, Becker, Kunert, Fimm, & Sass, 2000). This rather unusual drug use pattern reflects the fact that MDMA users quickly become tolerant to the drug's effects, and the desired effects of the drug become weaker as tolerance develops. During the mid-1980s, it was reported that the *median* number of MDMA doses ingested by students who had used this drug was 4.0 (Peroutka, 1989). The dosage levels ingested in the mid-1980s were reportedly between 60 mg and 250 mg, a pattern that seems consistent with those reported by Gouzoulis-Mayfrank *et al.* (2000).

As the individual becomes tolerant to MDMA, she or he is more likely to experience the negative side effects associated with its use. Surprisingly, taking a double dose of the drug does not increase the desired effects of MDMA but, rather, makes it more likely that the individual will experience unpleasant side effects (Peroutka, 1989) and increases the chances of MDMA-induced brain damage (McGuire & Fahy, 1991). A disturbing trend is for some users to "stack" compounds, ingesting MDMA along with LSD, alcohol, marijuana, and/or other drugs of abuse (Schwartz & Miller, 1997).

Subjective and Objective Effects of MDMA Abuse

Currently, at least six different methods of making MDMA are known to exist, and specific instructions on how to make MDMA can be found on the Internet (Rochester & Kirchner, 1999). Specialized equipment and training in organic chemistry are required to avoid the danger of contamination of the MDMA by toxins, but apart from this, the drug is easily synthesized. Virtually everything that is known about MDMA's effects is based on observations made of illicit drug users; there

has been little objective research into the pharmacological or toxicological effects of MDMA (Karch, 1996)

After it is ingested, MDMA is well absorbed from the gastrointestinal tract (Ramcharan *et al.*, 1998). The effects of a dose of MDMA usually begin in about 20 minutes, and peak within an hour (Cook, 1995) to an hour and a half (Schwartz & Miller, 1997). Peak blood levels are usually seen in 1–3 hours after a single dose is ingested (Ramcharan *et al.*, 1998). MDMA is highly lipid-soluble and is able to cross the blood-brain barrier without significant delay. Within the brain, MDMA is thought to work by first forcing the release, and then by inhibiting the reabsorption, of the neurotransmitter serotonin.

Estimates of the duration of MDMA's effects range from 4–6 hours (Karch, 1996) to 8 hours or more (Schwartz & Miller, 1997). The elimination half-life of MDMA[5] is estimated to be approximately 8 hours. The major metabolite for MDMA is a compound that is itself a hallucinogen: MDA. However, one study, which used a single volunteer subject, found that almost three-quarters of the MDMA ingested was excreted unchanged in the urine within 72 hours of the time that the drug was ingested.

At dosage levels of 75–100 mg, users report experiencing a sense of euphoria and improved self-esteem (Beebe & Walley, 1991). At this dosage level, the user might also experience mild visual hallucinations (Evanko, 1991). Following the period of acute drug intoxication, some users experience confusion, anxiety, and depression (Buia, Gulton, Park, Shannon, & Thompson, 2000; Weiss, Greenfield, & Mirin, 1994). These feelings reportedly lasted anywhere from several hours to several days.

At one point, some psychiatrists advocated the use of MDMA as an aid to psychotherapy (Price, Ricaurte, Krystal, & Heninger, 1989, 1990). Climko *et al.*, (1987) reported that one "uncontrolled study" (p. 365) found that MDMA brought about a positive change in mood. But the authors also pointed out that MDMA has also been reported to cause

tachycardia, an occasional "wired" feeling, jaw clenching, nystagmus, a nervous desire to be in mo-

[5]See the Glossary..

tion, transient anorexia, panic attacks, nausea and vomiting, ataxia, urinary urgency, insomnia, tremors, inhibition of ejaculation, and rarely, transient hallucinations. (p. 365)

The user's tendency to clench his or her teeth while under the influence of MDMA is also known as bruxism (grinding of teeth) and has been linked to excessive wear on the teeth (Redfearn, Agrawl, & Mair, 1998). Other effects of a "typical" dose of MDMA include increase in heart rate, muscle tremor, tightness in jaw muscles, nausea, insomnia, headache, and sweating. People who are sensitive to the effects of MDMA might experience numbness and tingling in extremities of the body, vomiting, increased sensitivity to cold, visual hallucinations, ataxia, crying, blurred vision, nystagmus, and the sense that the floor is shaking. MDMA has been implicated as the cause of decreased sexual desire and, in men, erectile problems and inhibition of the ejaculatory reflex (Finger, Lund, & Slagel, 1997). However, males are often sexually aroused when the effects of MDMA begin to wear off (Buia, Gulton, Park, Shannon, & Thompson, 2000).

Complications of MDMA Use

Because it is an illegal substance, there is little information about the toxic dosage level of MDMA (Ramcharan *et al.*, 1998). Research using animals suggests that the LD_{50} following a single intravenous dose of MDMA is approximately 8–23 mg/kg in dogs and 17–28 mg/kg in Rhesus monkeys (Karch, 1996). In the early 1950s, the U. S. Army conducted a series of secret research projects to explore MDMA's possible military applications, and the data from these studies suggest that just 14 of the more potent MDMA pills being produced in illicit laboratories might prove fatal to the user (Buia, Gulton, Park, Shannon, & Thompson, 2000).

MDMA-related fatalities usually are the result of cardiac arrhythmias (Schwartz & Miller, 1997; Beebe & Walley, 1991). The mechanism by which MDMA causes death is not clear at this time, but it is thought that MDMA, like its chemical cousins, the amphetamines, is able to alter cardiac function (Karch, 1996). This altered cardiac function is clearly seen in the hospital records of 48 patients admitted to a hospital Accident and Trauma Center following the ingestion of MDMA; two-thirds were found to have heart rates above 100 beats per minute (Williams *et al.*, 1998). It was recommended that MDMA overdoses be treated with the same protocols used to treat amphetamine overdoses, with special emphasis on assessing and protecting cardiac function (Rochester & Kirchner, 1999).

MDMA also affects blood vessels that serve the brain. There have been reports of intracranial hemorrhage in some people who had used MDMA (Sternbach & Varon, 1992), and there is one case report of a young woman who developed a condition known as cerebral venous sinus thrombosis (a blood clot) after ingesting MDMA at a "rave" party (Rothwell & Grant, 1993). The authors speculated that dehydration was a factor in the development of this cerebral venous sinus thrombosis and warned of the need to maintain adequate fluid intake while exercising under the influence of MDMA.

Some MDMA abusers have developed an extreme elevation of the body temperature, a condition known as hyperthermia. As the individual's body temperature rises to dangerous levels, he or she may experience seizures, which may be fatal without proper treatment (Henry, 1996). At one point it was thought that this temperature elevation was most common in those who engaged in heavy exercise (such as prolonged, vigorous dancing) after taking the drug (Cook, 1995; Ames, Wirshing, & Friedman, 1993; Randall, 1992; Beebe & Walley, 1991). Another theory is that the elevation in body temperature is a side effect of the forced release of large amounts of serotonin in the brain (Buia, Gulton, Park, Shannon, & Thompson, 2000). However, this is only a theory, and researchers have not determined exactly what brings about hyperthermia in MDMA abusers (Bodenham & Mallick, 1996).

There are isolated reports of liver toxicity in people who have ingested MDMA, although it is not clear whether the observed toxic reactions were the result of the drug itself or of one or more contaminants in the dose consumed by the user (Cook, 1995; Jones, Jarvie, McDermid, & Proudfoot, 1994; Henry, Jeffreys, & Dawling, 1992). It has been suggested that the MDMA user might experience flash-backs very similar to those seen with LSD use (Creighton, Black, & Hyde, 1991). These MDMA flashbacks usually develop in the first few days following the use of the drug (Cook, 1995).

Another interesting drug effect is seen at normal dosage levels, where the user occasionally "relives" past memories. The memories that are experienced anew are often those suppressed because of the pain associated with the earlier events (Hayner & McKinney, 1986). Such individuals might find themselves reliving experiences they did not want to remember. This effect, which many psychotherapists had hoped might prove of benefit in the confines of the therapeutic relationship, may be so frightening to the user as to be "detrimental to the individual's mental health" (p. 343). Long-time use has contributed to episodes of violence and also to suicide (*Medical Update*, (1994).

The therapeutic index of MDMA is quite small, with a significant overlap between the usual dose of the drug and the amount necessary to cause a toxic reaction (Karch, 1996). Symptoms of an MDMA overdose include restlessness, agitation, sweating, tachycardia, hypertension, hypotension, heart palpitations, renal failure, muscle rigidity, and visual hallucinations (Williams *et al.*, 1998; Jaffe, 2000a), and there have been rare reports of fatalities as a result of MDMA abuse. Many experienced MDMA users eventually exhibit one or more of these complications, which suggests that the possibility of an adverse reaction continues throughout the period of MDMA use (Williams *et al.*, 1998). *The Economist* (1996) estimated that MDMA causes one death for each 3 million doses, possibly "at doses that were previously tolerated in susceptible individuals" (Hayner & McKinney, 1986, p. 342). Although the use of ß-blocking agents (Beta blockers, or beta-adrenergic blockers) was recommended early in the 1990s (Ames, Wirshing, & Friedman, 1993), Rochester & Kirchner (1999) advised against the use of these agents on the grounds that this might make controlling blood pressure more difficult because the alpha-adrenergic system would be unaffected.

MDMA abuse might also result in such residual effects as anxiety attacks, persistent insomnia, rage reactions and a drug-induced psychosis (Karch, 1996; McGuire & Fahy, 1991; Hayner & McKinney, 1986). The MDMA-induced psychosis is most commonly seen in chronic users of MDMA and resembles paranoid schizophrenia (Cook, 1995; Sternbach & Varon, 1992). Researchers are still not sure exactly how MDMA might cause a drug-induced psychosis. In theory, MDMA is thought to be able to activate a psychotic re-

action in a person who is predisposed to this disorder (McGuire & Fahy, 1991).

There is strong evidence based on animal and human research studies that once it reaches the brain, MDMA and its chemical cousins MDA and MDEA function as selective neurotoxins,[6] causing damage to those neurons that use serotonin as a neurotransmitter (Gouzoulis-Mayfrank *et al.*, 2000; Marston, Reid, Lawrence, Olverman, & Butcher, 1999; Morgan, 1999; McCann, Szabo, Scheffel, Dannals, & Ricaurte, 1998). Evidence is mounting that MDMA's neurotoxic effects involve the serotonin transporter system, which carries out serotonin reuptake (Ritz, 1999). This drug-induced brain damage would seem to be permanent, although improvement is possible in the first few months after the person stops using MDMA (Gouzoulis-Mayfrank *et al.*, 2000; Ritz, 1999).

Although at one point it was suspected that the neurotoxic effects of MDMA were due to contaminants in the MDMA rather than to the drug itself (Rochester & Kirchner, 1999), evidence continues to accumulate that at dosage levels often utilized by MDMA users, this compound is capable of causing permanent damage to the brain (McCann, Szabo, Scheffel, Dannals, & Ricaurte, 1998; Wareing, Risk, & Murphy, 2000; Reneman, Booij, Schmand, van den Brink, & Gunning, 2000). Positive emission tomographic studies have uncovered significant evidence of global, dose-related decreases in brain 5-HT transporter, a structural element of those neurons that utilize serotonin (McCann, Szabo, Scheffel, Dannals, & Ricaurte, 1998). Even limited MDMA use has been found to be associated with a 35% reduction in 5-HT metabolism (an indirect measure of serotonin activity in the brain) for men, and with an almost 50% reduction in 5-HT metabolism in women (Hartman, 1995). These findings strongly suggest organic brain damage at a cellular level.

Drug interactions involving MDMA. There is little research into the important topic of possible interactions between illicit drugs such as MDMA and pharmaceuticals (Concar, 1997). There have been case reports of interactions between the anti-HIV agent Ritonavir and MDMA (Harrington, Woodward, Hooton, & Horn, 1999; Concar, 1997; *Forensic Drug Abuse Advisor*, 1997f). Each agent affects the serotonin level in the

[6]See the Glossary.

blood, and the combination of these two chemicals results in a threefold higher level of MDMA than normal. Some fatalities have been reported in users who have mixed these compounds (Concar, 1997).

Summary

Weil (1986) suggested that people initially use chemicals in order to alter the normal state of consciousness. Hallucinogen use in this country, at least in the last generation, has occurred in a series of waves, as first one drug and then another became the current drug of choice for achieving this altered state of consciousness. In the 1960s, LSD was the major hallucinogen, and in the 1970s and early 1980s, it was PCP. Currently, MDMA seems to be gaining in popularity, even though research suggests that MDMA may cause permanent brain damage, especially to those portions of the brain that utilize serotonin as a primary neurotransmitter.

If we accept Weil's (1986) hypothesis as correct, then it is logical to expect that other hallucinogens will emerge over the years, as people look for a more effective way to alter their state of consciousness. One might expect that these drugs will, in turn, slowly fade as they are replaced by newer hallucinogenics. Just as cocaine faded from the drug scene in the 1930s, and was replaced for a period of time by the amphetamines, so one might expect wave after wave of hallucinogen abuse, as new drugs become available. Thus, chemical dependency counselors will have to maintain a working knowledge of an ever growing range of hallucinogens in the years to come.

CHAPTER SIXTEEN

Abuse of and Addiction to the Inhalants and Aerosols

Introduction

The inhalants are unlike the other chemicals of abuse. They are a group of toxic substances that include various cleaning agents, herbicides, pesticides, gasoline, kerosene, certain forms of glue, lacquer thinner, and chemicals in felt-tipped pens. These agents are not primarily intended to function as recreational substances, but when inhaled, many of the chemicals in these compounds alter the manner in which the brain functions. In part because of this characteristic, and in part because they are so easily accessible to children and adolescents, inhalant abuse has become the most rapidly growing form of chemical abuse in the United States (Heath, 1994).

At low doses, inhalants may cause the user to experience a sense of euphoria. It is often possible for adolescents—and even children—to purchase many agents that can be abused by inhalation. Because these chemicals are inhaled, they are often called *inhalants*, although Esmail, Meyer, Pottier, and Wright (1993) made a case for calling this class of chemicals "volatile substances." In this text, we will use the term "inhalants."

The History of Inhalant Abuse

The first recent historical episodes of inhalant abuse involved anesthetic abuse, which dates dating back to the 19th century. Indeed, the earliest use of the anesthetic gases appears to have been for recreation, and historical records from the 1800s document the use of such agents

as nitrous oxide for "parties." The use of gasoline fumes to get high is thought to have started before World War II (Morton, 1987); the practice was first documented in the early 1950s (Blum, 1984). By the mid-1950s and early 1960s, "glue sniffing" was described in the popular press (Morton, 1987; Westermeyer, 1987). This is the use of model airplane glue as an inhalent. The active agent of model glue in the 1950s was often toluene. Nobody knows how glue sniffing started, but there is evidence that it began in California, when teenagers accidentally discovered the intoxicating powers of toluene-containing model glue (Berger & Dunn, 1982).

The first known reference to this practice appeared in 1959, in the magazine section of a Denver newspaper (Brecher, 1972). Local newspapers soon began to carry stories on the dangers of inhalant abuse—in the process explaining just how to use airplane glue to become intoxicated and what effects to expect. Within a short time, a "Nationwide Drug Menace" (Brecher, 1972, p. 321) emerged in the United States. Currently, inhalant abuse is thought to be a worldwide problem (Brust, 1993) and is especially common in Japan and Europe (Karch, 1996).

Brecher (1972) suggested that the inhalant abuse "problem" was essentially manufactured through distorted media reports. The author went on to point out that in response to media reports of deaths due to glue sniffing, one newspaper tracked down several stories and found only nine deaths that could be attributed to glue sniffing. Of this number, six were due to asphyxiation: Each victim had used an airtight plastic bag and had suffocated. In one other case, there was evidence that asphyxiation was also the cause of death, and in the eighth case, there was no evidence that the victim had been using inhalants. In the ninth case, the individual was indeed found to have been using gasoline as an inhalant but was reported to have been in poor health prior to this incident. Furthermore, Brecher (1972) notes that "among tens of thousands of glue-sniffers prior to 1964, no death due unequivocally to glue vapor had as yet been reported. The lifesaving advice children needed was not to sniff glue with their heads in plastic bags" (p. 331).

Since these words were written, research has found that using inhalants may introduce potentially toxic chemicals into the user's body (Brunswick, 1989; Jaffe, 1989). Some of the consequences of inhalant abuse include cardiac arrhythmias, anoxia, damage to the visual perceptual system, and neuropathies (Hansen & Rose, 1995). Thus, although the media may have played a role in the development of this crisis back in the late 1950s and early 1960s, by the 1990s it had become a legitimate health concern.

The Pharmacology of the Inhalants

As we noted in Chapter 6, many chemical agents reach the brain more rapidly and efficiently when they are inhaled rather than ingested by mouth or injected. When a chemical is inhaled, it is able to enter the bloodstream without its chemical structure being altered in any way by the liver. Once a drug is in the blood, one factor that influences how fast it reaches the brain is whether the molecules are able to form chemical bonds with the lipids in the blood. As a general rule, inhalants are quite lipid-soluble (Henretig, 1996) and thus reach the brain in an extremely short period of time, usually within seconds (Hartman, 1995; Heath, 1994; Watson, 1984; Blum, 1984).

Cone (1993) grouped all of the inhalants into two broad categories: anesthetic gases and volatile hydrocarbons. In contrast to this classification scheme, Monroe (1995) suggested three classes of volatile substances:

1. The *solvents*, such as glues, paint, paint thinner, gasoline, kerosene, lighter fluid, fingernail polish, fingernail polish remover, correction fluids for use in the office, felt-tip markers, etc.

2. Various *gases*, such as the butane in cigarette lighters, propane gas, the propellant in whipping cream cans, cooking sprays, etc.

3. The *nitrites*, such as butyl nitrite and amyl nitrite

However, Espeland (1997)[1] suggested four classes of inhalants:

1. Volatile organic solvents such as those found in paint and fuel[2]

2. Aerosols, such as hair sprays, spray paints, and deodorants

3. Volatile nitrites (such as amyl nitrite and its close chemical cousin, butyl nitrite)

4. General anesthetic agents such as nitrous oxide

As these different classification systems suggest, a wide variety of chemicals can be used to produce fumes that will alter the user's sense of reality. Children and adolescents most often abuse the first two classes of these chemicals. Children and adolescents have limited access to the third category of inhalants and extremely limited access to general anesthetics, the final class of inhalants.

The chemistry of inhalants is so complex that it is difficult to talk about the "pharmacology" of inhalants. First, many different agents may be used as inhalants, and each has a unique chemical structure. Also, many of the chemicals used as inhalants are designed for industrial or household use, not inhalation. Thus there is little research into their specific effects on the human body.

Another problem that makes it difficult to speak of the "pharmacology" of inhalants is that multiple chemical agents are often combined to achieve the purpose for which these materials are designed—that is, to meet the needs of industry. The exact combination of chemicals included in any mixture depends on the purpose for which that mixture of chemicals is to be used and

[1]Children and adolescents have only limited access to volatile nitrites, although butyl nitrite is sometimes sold without a prescription in some states. Except in rare cases, the abuse of surgical anesthetics is limited to a small percentage of health care workers, because access to anesthetic gases is carefully controlled in the health care industry.

[2]Technically, alcohol might be classified as a solvent, but because the most common method of alcohol use/abuse is through oral ingestion, ethyl alcohol will not be discussed in this chapter.

the conditions under which it is to be used. This makes it hard to determine what agent(s) might cause the user to feel a sense of euphoria or initiate a potentially fatal arrhythmia (Jaffe, 1989; Morton, 1987).

Once in the brain, the inhalants are thought to alter the normal function of the membranes of the neurons. The exact mechanism by which each inhalant achieves this effect is not known (Henretig, 1996). There is no standard formula by which to estimate the biological half-life of an inhalant, because so many different chemicals are abused. It should be noted, however, that the half-life of most solvents is longer in obese users than in people who tend to be thin (Hartman, 1995). As a general rule, the half-life of the various compounds commonly abused through inhalation ranges from hours to days, depending on the exact chemicals being abused (Brooks, Leung, & Shannon, 1996). The process of removing the inhalants from the body usually involves a combination of pulmonary exhalation, excretion of the inhalant and/or metabolites in the urine, and biotransformation by the user's liver of the chemicals inhaled (Brooks, Leung, & Shannon, 1996).

Either directly or indirectly, the compounds that are inhaled for recreational purposes are *all* toxic to the human body to one degree or another (Fornazzazri, 1988; Morton, 1987; Blum, 1984). But there is little research into the effects of various industrial chemical compounds at the concentrations used by inhalant abusers (Blum, 1984; Morton, 1987; Fornazzazri, 1988). For example, the maximum permitted exposure to toluene fumes in the workplace is 50–100 parts per million (ppm) (Crowley, 2000). When toluene is used as an inhalant, it is not uncommon for individuals willingly to expose themselves to levels 100 times as high as the maximum permitted industrial exposure. Further, most of what is known about the effects of these chemicals is based on the short-term impact on the individual. There is very little research into the effects of chronic exposure to many of the compounds abused by inhalant users.

Thus, it is difficult to talk about the pharmacology of the inhalants.[3] Coverage of this topic would be many tens of thousands of pages long, because thousands of compounds might be abused by inhalation. However, behavioral observations of animals that have been exposed to inhalants suggest that many inhalants act like alcohol or barbiturates on the brain. Indeed, alcohol and the benzodiazepines have been found to potentiate the effects of many inhalants such as toluene. Ultimately, the pharmacology of a given inhalant depends on the various chemicals found in the specific compound being abused. Such compounds often contain dozens or even scores of different chemicals.

Scope of the Problem

Although the mass media most often focus on inhalant abuse in the United States, it is a worldwide problem (Spiller & Krenzelok, 1997). In this country, there is evidence to suggest that inhalants are often the first mood-altering agents to be used by the individual and that abuse of these compounds often begins in childhood (Spiller & Krenzelok, 1997; Newcomb & Bentler, 1989). The inhalants tend to be most popular among boys in their early teens, especially in poor or rural areas where more expensive drugs of abuse are not easily available (Spiller & Krenzelok, 1997; Henretig, 1996; Jaffe, 1989).

Fully 19.7% of eighth graders surveyed admitted to having abused an inhalant at least once, while only 15.4% of the seniors of the class of 1999 claimed to have abused an inhalant (Johnston, O'Malley, & Bachman, 2000a). This pattern of abuse is consistent with the theory that inhalants are increasingly popular with younger teens (Hansen & Rose, 1995). Behaviorally, most adolescents who abuse inhalants do so only a few times and then stop without going on to develop other drug use problems (Crowley, 2000). Spiller and Krenzelok (1997) found that the mean age of inhalant abusers identified in their study was 16.6 years, with a standard deviation of 7.3 years. Brooks, Leung, and Shannon (1996) found that inhalant abuse peaked between the ages of 11 and 13 years, after which it declined in popularity and frequency. However, although inhalant abuse tends to be most common in adolescence, there are reports of children as young as 5 abusing these agents (Beauvais & Oetting, 1988), and regular use has been reported in children as young as 7 or 8 years of age (Henretig, 1996).

[3]Hartman (1995) provides an excellent technical summary of the neuropsychological effects of chronic exposure to some of the more common industrial solvents.

Current evidence suggests that inhalant abuse begins somewhere in middle to late childhood and continues through middle adolescence. Brooks, Leung, and Shannon (1996) reported that approximately 1 in 5 students in the eighth grade admitted to having used an inhalant at least once. Although these figures are frightening, there is a positive note: More than a decade ago, Morton (1987) found that of those adolescents who abuse inhalants, 30–40% do so only on a few occasions. Another 40–50% abuse inhalants over a period of a few weeks to a few months and then discontinue the use of inhalants, according to the author. Only about 10% of those who try inhalants are thought to become "habitual abusers" (Morton, 1987, p. 454). But of those who continue to abuse inhalants, many do so for periods as long as 15 years or more (Schuckit, 1995a; Westermeyer, 1987).

The actual percentage of people who are using solvents remains unknown (Miller & Gold, 1991a). However, it has been suggested that for children and adolescents, inhalants are the most commonly abused substance after alcohol and tobacco (Wilson-Tucker & Dash, 1995). The practice of abusing inhalants appears to involve boys more often than girls by a ratio of about 3:1 (Crowley, 2000). Inhalant users are generally between 10 and 15 years of age (Miller & Gold, 1991a). In England 3–10% of the adolescents who were asked admitted to the use of inhalants at least once, and about 1% were thought to be current users (Esmail, Meyer, Pottier, & Wright, 1993). The most commonly abused compounds appear to be spray paint and gasoline, which collectively accounted for 61% of the compounds abused by subjects in a study by Spiller and Krenzelok (1997).

Unfortunately, for a minority of those who abuse them, the inhalants appear to function as a "gateway" chemical: The use sets the stage for further drug use in later years. Approximately one-third of the children and adolescents who abuse inhalants go on to abuse one or more of the traditional drugs of abuse within four years (Brunswick, 1989). Crowley (2000) reported, for example, that persons who admitted using inhalants were 45 times as likely to have used self-injected drugs, whereas those who admitted using inhalants and marijuana were 89 times as likely as the general population to have injected drugs.

There are several reasons why the inhalants are utilized by children and adolescents. First, these chemicals have a rapid onset of action, usually just a few seconds. Second, inhalant users report pleasurable effects, including a sense of euphoria, when they use these chemicals. Third, and perhaps most important, the inhalants are relatively inexpensive and are readily available to teenagers (Cohen (1977. Indeed, they are so easily obtained by adolescents that they have been called a "household drug" (Wisneiwski, 1994, p. 8E-x).

Virtually all of the commonly used inhalants can be easily purchased, for no legal restrictions are placed on their sale to teenagers. An additional advantage for the user is that the inhalants are usually available in small, easily hidden packages. Brunswick (1989) identified some of the more popular inhalants as being

> accessible and cheap. They are found at the corner drug store, in the garage, or under the kitchen sink. They take the form of magic markers, glue and fingernail polish. They produce a short but intense high that some have likened to the rush from rock cocaine, or "crack." (p. 6A)

Unfortunately, as we will see in the next section, many of the inhalants are capable of seriously harming the user or actually causing death. The inhalant abuser thus runs a great risk whenever he or she begins to "huff."[4]

Method of Administration

McHugh (1987) noted that inhalant abuse is "a group activity" (p. 334), as opposed to a solitary habit. There are a number of ways in which inhalants can be abused, depending on the specific chemical involved. Glue and adhesives may be poured into a plastic bag or milk carton, which is then placed over the mouth and nose (Esmail, Meyer, Pottier, & Wright, 1993). The individual then inhales the fumes. This practice is called "huffing" (Nelson, 2000). Liquids such as cleaning fluids may be dripped onto a cloth or into a small container (such as an empty plastic bottle), and the fumes inhaled from the container or cloth. This practice is called "bagging" (Nelson, 2000).

Fumes from aerosol cans may also be directly inhaled or sprayed directly into the mouth, according

[4] See the Glossary.

Esmail, Meyer, Pottier, and Wright (1993). This practice is called "sniffing" (Nelson, 2000). To inhale the fumes of glue, the user squirts the glue into a paper bag, covers his or her face with the bag, and inhales the fumes (Mirin, Weiss, & Greenfield, 1991). Another technique that children often use is simply to squirt the chemical into a rag and inhale the fumes from the rag (Brunswick, 1989). Finally, there have been reports of users trying to boil the substance to be abused so that they could inhale the fumes (Nelson, 2000). Obviously, if the substance being boiled is flammable, a significant risk of fire is associated with this practice.

Subjective Effects of Inhalants

The initial effects of the fumes on the individual may include a feeling of hazy euphoria, somewhat like the feeling of intoxication caused by alcohol (Henretig, 1996; Crowley, 2000; Blum, 1984). Other reported effects include a floating sensation, decreased inhibitions, and possible amnesia, slurred speech, excitement, double vision, ringing in the ears, and hallucinations (Schuckit, 1995a; Kaminski, 1992; Blum, 1984; Morton, 1987). Occasionally, the individual may believe he or she is omnipotent, and episodes of violence have been reported (Morton, 1987). In most cases, the effects of a single exposure to an inhalant last up to 45 minutes (Mirin, Weiss, & Greenfield, 1991).

One of the initial experiences of inhalant abuse is a feeling of euphoria, although nausea and vomiting may also occur (McHugh, 1987). The inhalant-induced euphoria lasts less than 30 minutes, in most cases. After the initial euphoria, depression of the central nervous system (CNS) develops. The individual may become confused, anxious, or disoriented and may develop a headache and experience a loss of inhibitions (Hartman, 1995; Kaminski, 1992; McHugh, 1987). Individuals who continue to inhale the fumes beyond this stage may experience stupor, seizures, and cardiorespiratory arrest leading to death (McHugh, 1987). The stages of inhalant abuse are summarized in Figure 16.1

In cases where the individual has used a solvent only once or twice, the effects usually disappear "fairly quickly, and, with the exception of headache, serious hangovers are usually not seen" (Schuckit, 1995a, p. 217). Where there might be some degree of inhalant "hangover," it generally clears "in minutes to a few

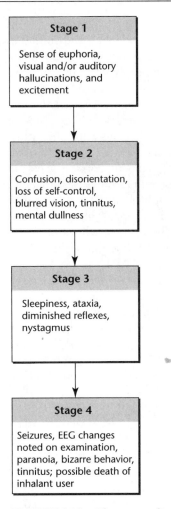

FIGURE 16.1　The stages of inhalant abuse.

hours" (Westermeyer, 1987, p. 903). However, in some cases, the user may experience a residual sense of drowsiness and/or stupor for several hours after the last use of inhalants (Kaplan, Sadock, & Grebb, 1994; Miller & Gold, 1991a). Further, there have been cases where the inhalant-induced headache has lasted for several days after the last use of the inhalant (Heath, 1994).

Complications from Inhalant Abuse

When the practice of abusing the inhalants first surfaced, most health care professionals did not think many serious complications could result from this practice. However, in the past quarter-century, researchers have found that inhalant abuse can cause a wide range of physical problems. Depending on the concentration of the solvent being abused, even a single episode of use may result in symptoms of solvent toxicity (Hartman, 1995).

Here is a partial list of the possible consequences of inhalant abuse (Weaver, Jarvis, & Schnoll, 1999; Henretig, 1996; Karch, 1996; Hansen & Rose, 1995; Monroe, 1995; Hartman, 1995; Brunswick, 1989; Morton, 1987):

Liver damage
Cardiac arrhythmias (irregularities in the heart beat that may be fatal if not corrected)
Kidney damage/failure, which may become permanent
Transient changes in lung function
Respiratory depression, possibly to the point of respiratory arrest
Reduction in blood cell production, possibly to the point of aplastic anemia
Possible permanent organic brain damage (including dementia)
Permanent muscle damage secondary to the development of rhabdomyolysis
Vomiting, with the possibility of the user aspirating some of the material being vomited, resulting in his or her death

Inhalant abuse may also cause damage to the bone marrow, sinusitis (irritation of the sinus membranes), erosion of the nasal mucosal tissues, and laryngitis (Henretig, 1996; Westermeyer, 1987). These complications of inhalant abuse "usually resolve after some weeks of abstinence" (Westermeyer, 1987, p. 903).

The effects of the inhalants on the central nervous system (CNS) are perhaps the most profound, if only because inhalant abusers are usually so young. Many of the inhalants have been shown to damage the central nervous system, causing such problems as cerebellar ataxia,[5] tremor, peripheral neuropathies, and deafness (Brooks, Leung, & Shannon, 1996; Maas, Ashe, Spiegel, Zee, & Leigh, 1991; Fornazzazri, 1988). Inhalant abuse may also result in such problems as coma, convulsions, cirrhosis, and even death (Henretig, 1996;

Mirin, Weiss, & Greenfield, 1991; McHugh, 1987). Indeed, inhalant abuse is "one of the leading causes of death in those under 18" (Esmail, Meyer, Pottier, & Wright, 1993, p. 359). Each year, between 100 and 1000 deaths in the United States are directly attributable to inhalant abuse (Hartman, 1995; Wisniewski, 1994).

Depending on the compound being used, there is a very real danger that the user will be exposed to toxic levels of various "heavy metals" such as copper or lead (Crowley, 2000). For example, gasoline "sniffing" by children is a major cause of lead poisoning (Henretig, 1996; Monroe, 1995; Parras, Patier, & Ezpeleta, 1988). Exposure to lead is a serious condition, which may have long-term consequences for the child's physical and emotional growth.

Although in the 1970s it was not thought that inhalant abuse could result in physical damage to the body, it is now known that this is not true. There is significant evidence that inhalant abuse may permanently damage the central nervous system (CNS). For example, chronic exposure to solvents has been found to have caused organic brain damage in European workers (Hartman, 1995). Further, although the standard neurological examination is often unable to detect signs of solvent-induced organic brain damage until it is quite advanced, sensitive neuropsychological tests often find signs of significant neurological dysfunction in workers who are exposed to solvent fumes on a regular basis (Hartman, 1995).

Toluene is found in many forms of glue and is the most commonly abused solvent (Hartman, 1995). Researchers have found that chronic toluene exposure can result in intellectual impairment, deafness, and a loss of the sense of smell (Maas, Ashe, Spiegel, Zee, & Leigh, 1991; Rosenberg, 1989). Chronic exposure to toluene may result in such extensive injury to the brain that it is detected via the magnetic resonance imaging (MRI) procedures physicians use to visualize the physical structure of the brain.

Finally, researchers have identified what appears to be a withdrawal syndrome that develops following extended periods of inhalant abuse (Mirin, Weiss, & Greenfield, 1991; Blum, 1984). This withdrawal syndrome appears very similar to that of alcohol-induced delirium tremens (DTs), according to the authors. The exact withdrawal syndrome that develops after episodes of inhalant abuse depends on the specific chemicals

---

[5] A loss of coordination caused by physical damage to the region of the brain that is responsible for coordinating muscle movements.

being abused, the duration of inhalant abuse, and the dosage levels being utilized (Miller & Gold, 1991). The symptoms that may be seen when a chronic inhalant user stops abusing inhalants are muscle tremors, irritability, anxiety, insomnia, muscle cramps, hallucinations, sweating, nausea, and perhaps seizures (Crowley, 2000). Thus it seems that when they are used on a chronic basis, the inhalants may be physically addictive.

Inhalant abuse and suicide. Espeland (1997) suggested a disturbing relationship between inhalant abuse and adolescent suicide. The author suggested that some suicidal adolescents might actually put some inhalant into a plastic bag and insert their head. The plastic bag is then closed about the head/neck area, allowing the inhalant to cause the individual to lose consciousness. She or he will quickly suffocate, as the oxygen in the bag is used up and will die unless found.

Misuse of Anesthetics

Berger and Dunn (1982) reported that nitrous oxide and ether, the first two anesthetic gases to be used, were introduced as recreational drugs prior to their introduction as surgical anesthetics. Indeed, these gases were routinely utilized as intoxicants for quite some time before they were used pharmacologically. Horace Wells, who introduced nitrous oxide to medicine, noted the pain killing properties of this gas when he observed a person under its influence trip and gash his leg, without any apparent pain (Brecher, 1972). As medical historians know, the first planned demonstration of nitrous oxide as an anesthetic was something less than a success. Because nitrous oxide has a duration of effect of about 2 minutes following a single dose and thus must be continuously administered, the patient regained consciousness in the middle of the operation and started to scream in pain. However, in spite of this rather frightening beginning, physicians soon learned how to use nitrous oxide properly to bring about surgical anesthesia, and it is now an important anesthetic agent (Brecher, 1972).

Julien (1992) noted that the pharmacological effects observed with the general anesthetics are the same as those observed with the barbiturates. There is a dose-related range of effects from the anesthetic, ranging from an initial period of sedation and relief from anxi-

ety on through sleep and analgesia. At extremely high dosage levels, the anesthetic gases can cause death.

Nitrous oxide presents a special danger in that special precautions must be taken to maintain a proper oxygen supply to the individual's brain. Room air alone does not provide sufficient oxygen when nitrous oxide is used (Julien, 1992), and oxygen must be supplied under pressure to avoid the danger of hypoxia (a decreased oxygen level in the blood that can result in permanent brain damage if not corrected immediately). In surgery, the anesthesiologist takes special precautions to ensure that the patient has an adequate oxygen supply. Few nitrous oxide abusers have access to supplemental oxygen sources, however, and thus they run the risk of serious injury, or even death, when they use this compound.

It is possible to achieve a state of hypoxia by abusing virtually any of the inhalants, including nitrous oxide (McHugh, 1987). In spite of this danger, nitrous oxide is a popular drug of abuse in some circles (Schwartz, 1989). Nitrous oxide abusers report that the gas brings about euphoria, giddiness, hallucinations, and a loss of inhibitions (Lingeman, 1974). Dental students, dentists, medical school students, and anesthesiologists, all of whom have access to surgical anesthetics through their professions, occasionally abuse agents such as nitrous oxide, as well as ether, chloroform, trichlorothylene, and halothane. Also, children and adolescents occasionally abuse the nitrous oxide used as a propellant in certain commercial products by finding ways to release the gas from the container. In rare cases, the nitrous oxide abuser even makes his or her own nitrous oxide, risking possible death from impurities in the compound produced (Brooks, Leung, & Shannon, 1996).

The volatile anesthetics are not biotransformed by the body to any significant degree but rather, enter and leave the body essentially unchanged (Glowa, 1986). Once the source of the gas is removed, the concentration of the gas in the brain begins to drop, and normal circulation brings the brain to a normal state of consciousness within moments. While the person is under the influence of the anesthetic gas, however, the ability of the brain cells to react to painful stimuli seems to be reduced.

The medicinal use of nitrous oxide, chloroform, and ether is largely confined to dental and general surgery. Very rarely, however, one encounters a person who has abused, or is currently abusing, these agents. There is little information available about the dangers of this practice, nor do we know much about the side effects of prolonged use.

Abuse of Nitrites

Two different forms of nitrites are commonly abused: *amyl nitrite* and its close chemical cousins *butyl nitrite* and *isobutyl nitrite*. When inhaled, these substances function as coronary vasodilators, allowing more blood to flow to the heart. This effect made amyl nitrite useful in the control of angina pectoris. The drug was administered in small glass containers embedded in cloth layers. The user would "snap" or "pop" the container with his or her fingers and inhale the fumes in order to control the chest pain of angina pectoris.[6]

With the introduction of nitroglycerine preparations, which are as effective as amyl nitrite but lack many of its disadvantages, amyl nitrite fell into disfavor and few people now use amyl nitrite for medical purposes (Schwartz, 1989). It does continue to have a limited role in diagnostic medicine and in the medical treatment of cyanide poisoning.

Whereas amyl nitrite is available only by prescription, butyl nitrite and isobutyl nitrite are often sold legally by mail-order houses or in specialty stores, depending on specific state regulations. In many areas, butyl nitrite is sold as a room deodorizer, being packaged in small bottles that can be purchased for under ten dollars. Both chemicals are thought to cause the user to experience a prolonged, more intense orgasm when they are inhaled just before the individual reaches orgasm. However, amyl nitrite is also known to be a cause of delayed orgasm and ejaculation in the male user (Finger, Lund, & Slagel, 1997). Aftereffects include an intense, sudden headache, increased pres-

---

[6]From the distinctive sound of the glass breaking within the cloth ampule, both amyl nitrite and butyl nitrite have come to be known as "poppers" or "snappers" by those who abuse these chemicals.

sure of the fluid in the eyes (a danger for those with glaucoma) possible weakness, nausea, and possible cerebral hemorrhage (Schwartz, 1989).

When abused, both amyl nitrite and butyl nitrite will cause a brief (90-second) "rush" that includes dizziness, giddiness, and rapid dilation of blood vessels in the head (Schwartz, 1989), which in turn causes an increase in intracranial pressure (*AIDS Alert*, 1989). This increase in intracranial pressure may contribute to the rupture of unsuspected aneurysms, causing the individual to suffer a cerebral hemorrhage (CVA, or stroke).

The use of nitrites is common among male homosexuals and may contribute to the spread of the virus that causes AIDS (Schwartz, 1989; *AIDS Alert*, 1989). It has been suggested that, by causing the dilation of blood vessels in the body, including the anus, the use of either amyl or butyl nitrite during anal intercourse (a common practice for male homosexuals) may actually facilitate the transmission of the HIV from the active to the passive member of the couple (*AIDS Alert*, 1989). Given the multitude of adverse effects, it is puzzling why use of the nitrates is popular during sexual intercourse.

Summary

For many individuals, the inhalants are the first chemicals abused. For the most part, inhalant abuse involves mainly teenagers, although children occasionally abuse an inhalant. The abuse of these chemicals appears to be a phase, during which the individual engages in the abuse of inhalants on an episodic basis.

Individuals who use these inhalants do not generally do so for more than a year or two. But there are a few individuals who continue to inhale the fumes of gasoline, solvents, or certain forms of glue for many years. The effects of these chemicals on the individual seem to be rather short-lived. There is evidence, however, that prolonged use of certain agents can result in permanent damage to the kidneys, brain, and liver. Death, either through hypoxia or through prolonged exposure to inhalants, is possible. Very little is known about the effects of prolonged use of this class of chemicals.

CHAPTER SEVENTEEN

The Unrecognized Problem of Steroid Abuse and Addiction

Introduction

Unlike alcohol, marijuana, and virtually every other drug of abuse, the anabolic steroids (or simply steroids) are not primarily abused for their ability to bring about a sense of euphoria. Rather, the anabolic steroids are abused because of persistent rumors that these chemicals enhance athletic performance. Indeed, so common has the use of steroids become in certain athletic training programs that more than a decade ago, athletes began to look upon these drugs as a "nutritional supplement" (Breo, 1990, p. 1697) rather than as potent chemical agents.

In 1991 Bower observed that very little was known about the problem of anabolic steroid abuse, and the same is true today. This is unfortunate, because in spite of their considerable potential to harm the user, a large number of teenagers and young adults are abusing one or more steroids. Recognition of the problem of anabolic steroid abuse is growing, however, and mental health and chemical dependency professionals should have a working knowledge of the effects of this class of medications.

An Introduction to the Anabolic Steroids

The term "anabolic" refers to the action of this family of drugs to increase the speed of growth of body tissues (Redman, 1990) or to the ability of this group of chemicals to force body cells to retain nitrogen (and thus indirectly enhance tissue growth) (Bagatell & Bremner,

1996). The term "steroids" refers to the chemical structure of these compounds (Redman, 1990). The steroids are chemically similar to testosterone, the male sex hormone, and because of this have a masculinizing (androgenic) effect on the user (Landry & Primos, 1990). There are more than 1000 known derivatives of the testosterone molecule (Sturmi & Diorio, 1998). At times, the anabolic steroids are referred to as the *anabolic-androgenic* steroids.

It has been suggested that when steroids are abused, they can cause the user to experience euphoria (Schrof, 1992; Kashkin, 1992; Johnson, 1990; Lipkin, 1989). However, this is not the primary reason why most people abuse the anabolic steroids. Rather, steroids are mainly abused either to stimulate the growth of muscle tissue or simply to slow the process of muscle tissue breakdown. Repeated, heavy physical exercise can actually result in damage to muscle tissues. The anabolic steroids have been found to stimulate protein synthesis, a process that users believe will indirectly help muscle tissue development, increase muscle strength, and limit the amount of damage done to muscle tissues through heavy physical exercise (Gottesman, 1992; Pettine, 1991; Pope & Katz, 1990).

In addition to the athlete who abuses steroids, many nonathlete users believe that using steroids will help them look more attractive (Corrigan, 1996; Brower, 1993; Schrof, 1992; Pettine, 1991; Johnson, 1990; Bahrke, 1990; Pope, Katz, & Champoux, 1986). Indeed, between 25% (Fultz, 1991) and 40% (Whitehead, Chillag, & Elliott, 1992) of adolescent steroid abusers take the drug because they believe it will give them a better physical appearance. In addition to this, there is a subgroup of people, especially some law enforcement/security officers, who abuse steroids in the belief that these drugs will increase their strength and aggressiveness (Galloway, 1997; Corrigan, 1996; Schrof, 1992).

Medical Uses of Anabolic Steroids

Although the anabolic steroids have been in use since the mid-1950s, there still is no clear consensus on how they work (Wadler, 1994); this is partly because there are few approved uses for these compounds (Dobs, 1999; Sturmi & Diorio, 1998). It is thought that the steroids force the body to increase protein synthesis and that they inhibit the action of chemicals known as the glucocorticoids, which cause tissue break down. In a medical setting, the anabolic steroids might be used to promote tissue growth and help damaged tissue recover from injury (Shannon, Wilson, & Stang, 1992).

Physicians may also use a steroid to treat certain forms of anemia, to help patients regain weight after periods of severe illness, to treat endometriosis, to treat delayed puberty in adolescents, and as an adjunct to the treatment of certain forms of breast cancer in women (Bagatell & Bremner, 1996). The steroids may also promote the growth of bone tissue following injuries to the bone, and they may be useful in the treatment of certain forms of osteoporosis (Council on Scientific Affairs, 1990b). There is evidence that the steroids might be of value in treating AIDS-related weight loss (the so-called "wasting" syndrome) and in certain forms of chronic kidney failure (Dobs, 1999).

The anabolic steroids be broken down into two classes: those that are active when used orally and those that are active only when injected into muscle tissue. Anabolic steroids taken orally tend to be more easily administered, but they have a shorter half-life and are also more toxic to the liver than parenteral forms of steroids (Bagatell & Bremner, 1996; Tanner, 1995).

The Legal Status of Anabolic Steroids

Since 1990 the anabolic steroids have been listed under the Controlled Substances Act of 1970 as a Category III controlled substance: available, with a doctor's prescription, for certain medical purposes. The law also identi-fied 28 different anabolic steroids as being illegal for nonmedical purposes, and it made their sale by individuals who are not licensed to sell medications a crime punishable by a prison term of up to 5 years (10 years if the steroids are sold to minors) (Fultz, 1991).

Scope of the Problem of Steroid Abuse

It is estimated that more than 1 million people in the United States either are abusing steroids or have done so at some time in their lives, and in Canada some 83,000 people between the ages of 11–18 admitted to having used a steroid at least once in the past year (Peters, Copeland, & Dillon, 1999). Other estimates of the scope of steroid abuse in the United States range from a low estimate of 300,000 current and 1 million former anabolic steroid abusers (Galloway, 1997; Karch, 1996; Bagatell & Bremner, 1996; Franklin, 1994), to a middle estimate of 1 million current abusers (Middleman & DuRant, 1996; Schrof, 1992; Porterfield, 1991) to a high estimate of 3 million current and at least 1 million former steroid abusers (Corrigan, 1996).

Adolescents of high school age, although known to abuse anabolic steroids, do not seem to make up the majority of steroid abusers. Compared to the approximately 20% of college athletes who are thought to have used steroids on at least one occasion (Hough & Kovan, 1990), only 2.9% of the high school seniors of the class of 1999 who were surveyed admitted having used steroids (Johnston, O'Malley, & Bachman, 2000a). In terms of actual numbers, it is thought that between 250,000 (DuRant, Rickert, Ashworth, Newman, & Slavens, 1993) and 500,000 (Wadler, 1994; Schrof, 1992) high school students are either current or former users of anabolic steroids. It appears that most steroid abusers of college age started to use these compounds just before or just after they entered college (Brower, 1993).

Sources and Methods of Steroid Abuse

Because of their illegality and the strict controls on their prescription by physicians, most anabolic steroids are obtained from illicit sources (Galloway, 1997). These sources include drugs smuggled into the United States and legitimate pharmaceuticals that are diverted to the black market. Another common source of steroids is veterinary products, which are then sold on the street for use by humans. These compounds are distributed through an informal network that frequently revolves around health clubs or gyms (Schrof, 1992; Johnson, 1990).

If a physician suspects that a patient has been abusing anabolic steroids, she or he might confront the individual and elicit a confession. Some physicians try to limit such a patient's use of anabolic steroids, promising to prescribe medications for the individual if he or she will promise to use *only* the medications prescribed (Breo, 1990) so that the physician can monitor and control the individual's steroid use. However, in most cases the user supplements the prescribed medications with steroids from other sources. Thus, this method of "harm reduction"[1] is not recommended for physicians (Breo, 1990).

Rarely, users obtain their steroids by "diverting"[2] prescribed medications or obtaining multiple prescriptions for steroids from different physicians. But between 80% (Bahrke, 1990) and 90% (Tanner, 1995) of the steroids used by athletes come from the "black market,"[3] and many of these steroids are smuggled in from Mexico or Europe (Johnson, 1990). Estimates of the scope of the illicit steroid market in the United States range from $100 million (Middleman & DuRant, 1996; DuRant, Rickert, Ashworth, Newman, & Slavens, 1993) to $300–500 million (Wadler, 1994; Council on Scientific Affairs, 1990b; Fultz, 1991) to $1 billion (Hoberman & Yesalis, 1995)!

Anabolic steroids may be injected into muscle tissue, they may be taken orally, or both intramuscular and oral doses may be used at once. Anabolic steroid abusers have developed a vocabulary of their own to describe many aspects of steroid abuse. Table 17.1 lists some of the terms they use.

Many of the practices described in Table 17.1 are quite common among steroid abusers. For example, fully 61% of steroid-abusing weight lifters were found to have engaged in the practice of "stacking" steroids (Porcerelli & Sandler, 1998; Brower, Blow, Young, & Hill, 1991). Some steroid abusers who engage in

---

[1]See the Glossary.

[2]See the Glossary.

[3]As used here, "black market" is a term that is applied to any steroid obtained from illicit sources and then sold for human consumption.

TABLE 17.1   Some Terms Associated with Steroid Abuse

Term	Definition
Blending	Mixing different compounds for use at the same time.
Bulking up	Increasing muscle mass through steroid use. Nonusers also use the term to refer to the process of eating special diets and exercising in order to add muscle mass before a sporting event such as a football game or race.
Cycling	Taking multiple doses of a steroid(s) over a period of time, according to a schedule, with drug holidays built into the schedule.
Doping	Using drugs to improve performance.
Injectables	Steroids that are designed for injection.
Megadosing	Taking massive amounts of steroids, usually by injection or a combination of injection and oral administration.
Orals	Steroids designed for oral use.
Pyramiding	Taking anabolic steroids according to a schedule that calls for larger and larger doses each day for a period of time, followed by a pattern of smaller doses each day.
Shotgunning	Taking steroids on an inconsistent basis.
Tapering	Slowly decreasing the dosage level of a steroid being abused.

"pyramiding" are, at the midpoint of the cycle, using massive amounts of steroids. Episodes of pyramiding are interspaced with periods of abstinence from anabolic steroid use that may last several weeks or months (Landry & Primos, 1990) or even as long as a year (Kashkin, 1992). Unfortunately, during the periods of abstinence, much of the muscle mass gained via the use of steroids is lost, sometimes quite rapidly. When this happens, anabolic steroid abusers often start another cycle of steroid abuse prematurely, in order to recapture the muscle mass that has disappeared (Corrigan, 1996; Tanner, 1995; Schrof, 1992).

Problems Associated with Anabolic Steroid Abuse

Much of what is known about the anabolic steroids is based on clinical experience from patients who are taking steroids under a physician's care, using specific recommended dosage levels to achieve a specific goal (Medical Economics Company, 1989). Numerous adverse effects have been documented at relatively low doses (Hough & Kovan, 1990). The potential consequences of long-term steroid abuse are not known (Porcerelli & Sandler, 1998; Wadler, 1994; Kashkin, 1992; Schrof, 1992).

For example, many adolescents and young adults who abuse steroids do so at dosage levels that are often 10 (Hough & Kovan, 1990), 40 (Johnson, 1990), 100 (Brower, Catlin, Blow, Eliopulos, & Beresford, 1991) or even 1000 times the maximum recommended therapeutic dosage level for these compounds (Wadler, 1994; Council on Scientific Affairs, 1990b). Brower, Blow, Young, and Hill (1991) found that the dosage range of steroids being used by their sample of weight lifters was between 2 and 26 times the recommended dosage level for these agents.

Another study found that the *lowest* dose of anabolic steroids being used by a group of weight lifters was still 350% above the usual therapeutic dose when the same drug was used by physicians (Landry & Primos, 1990). There is very little information available on the effects of the anabolic steroids on the user at these dosage levels (Kashkin, 1992; Johnson, 1990). It is known that the effects of the anabolic steroids on muscle tissue last for several weeks after the drugs are discontinued (Pope & Katz, 1991). This characteristic is known to muscle builders, who often discontinue their use of steroids before competition in order to avoid detection of their steroid use via urine toxicological screens.

Another reason why so little is known about the effects of anabolic steroid abuse is that, for the most part, research on steroid *abusers* has been limited to studies involving males. This bias in the research reflects the fact that steroid abusers are usually male. In one study, for example, fully 7% of high school boys, but only 1% of high school girls, in the survey admitted to the use of anabolic steroids (Karch, 1996). As a result of this male bias, virtually nothing is known about the long-term effects of anabolic steroid abuse on women (Gottesman, 1992).

It is known that the adverse effects of anabolic steroids depend on (1) the route of administration, (2) the specific drugs, (3) the dose, (4) the frequency of use, (5) the health of the individual, and (6) the individual's age (Johnson, 1990). However, even at recommended dosage levels, steroids are capable of causing sore throat or fever, vomiting (with or without blood being mixed into the vomit), dark-colored urine, bone pain, nausea, unusual weight gain or headache, and a range of other side effects (United States Pharmacopeial Convention, 1990b).

Often, illicit steroid users will abuse specific forms of anabolic steroids that are hard to detect or are thought to be undetectable by current laboratory tests (Sturmi & Diorio, 1998). Thus a "clean" urine sample thus does not rule out steroid use in modern sporting events, nor does it rule out the possibility that the individual is at risk for any of a wide range of complications.

Complications of Steroid Abuse

The reproductive system. Males who utilize steroids at the recommended dosage levels may experience enlargement of breasts (to the point where breast formation similar to that seen in adolescent girls takes place). The male steroid abuser might also experience increased frequency of erections or continual erection (a condition known as priapism, which is a medical emergency), unnatural hair growth or hair loss, reduced sperm production, and a frequent urge to urinate. In men, steroid abuse may cause degeneration of the testicles, enlargement of the prostate gland, difficulty in urination, impotence, and sterility (Sturmi & Diorio, 1998; Galloway, 1997; Pope & Katz, 1994; Kashkin, 1992). On rare occasions, steroid abuse has resulted in carcinoma (cancer) of the prostate (Tanner, 1995; Johnson, 1990; Landry & Primos, 1990) and urinary obstruction (Council on Scientific Affairs, 1990b). Both men and women may experience infertility and changes in libido as a result of steroid abuse (Sturmi & Diorio, 1998).

Women who use steroids at recommended dosage levels may experience an abnormal enlargement of the clitoris, irregular menstrual periods, unnatural hair growth and/or unusual hair loss, a deepening of the voice, and a possible reduction in the size of the breasts (Galloway, 1997; Tanner, 1995; Redman, 1990; Pope & Katz, 1988). The menstrual irregularities caused by steroid use often disappear after the steroids are discontinued (Johnson, 1990). The Council on Scientific Affairs (1990b) suggested that women who use steroids may experience beard growth, which is one example of the unnatural hair growth patterns that anabolic steroids can cause. Another possible outcome is for the woman who is using anabolic steroids to develop "male pattern" baldness. Often, steroid-induced baldness in a woman is irreversible (Tanner, 1995).

The liver, kidneys, and digestive system. Steroid abusers may experience altered liver function, which can be detected through blood tests such as the serum glautamic-oxaloacetic transaminase (SGOT) test and the serum glautamic-pyruvic transaminase (SGPT) test (Sturmi & Diorio, 1998; Johnson, 1990). As we have noted, oral forms of anabolic steroids are more likely to result in liver problems than injected forms (Tanner, 1995). Anabolic steroid abuse has been implicated as a cause of hepatoxicity (liver failure). There is also evidence that when steroids are used for periods of time at excessive doses, they may contribute to the formation of both cancerous and benign liver tumors (Sturmi & Diorio, 1998; Karch, 1996; Tanner, 1995; Council on Scientific Affairs, 1990b).

The cardiovascular system. Anabolic steroid abuse may result in the user developing high blood pressure, cardiomyopathy, and heart disease as a result of a steroid-induced reduction in high density lipoprotein levels and increase in low-density lipoprotein levels (Tanner, 1995; Fultz, 1991; Johnson, 1990; Council on Scientific Affairs, 1990b). In effect, the anabolic steroids may contribute to accelerated atherosclerosis of the heart and its surrounding blood vessels.

Anabolic steroid abuse may also result in the user experiencing a thrombotic stroke—that is, a stroke caused by a blood clot in the brain (Karch, 1996; Tanner, 1995). Such strokes are a side effect of high doses of the anabolic steroids, which cause blood platelets to clump together, forming clots. Researchers have also found evidence that steroids have a direct, dose-related, cardiotoxic effect (Slovut, 1992). Indeed, there is evidence of physical changes in the structure of the heart of some steroid users, although the mechanism by which steroids cause such changes are not known (Milddleman & DuRant, 1996).

The central nervous system. The anabolic steroid family of drugs has been suspected of causing behavioral changes in the user. To explore this belief, Wolkowitz, Rubinow, Doran, Breier, Berrettini, Kling, and Pickar (1990) administered 80 mg of a pharmaceutical steroid known as prednisone daily for 5 days, to a sample of healthy volunteers. The authors found that "prednisone administration was associated with decreases in levels of several biologically and behaviorally active neuropeptides or neurotransmitters" (p. 966). However, in spite of these measured changes in biochemical levels, the authors found "no significant prednisone-associated changes in group mean behavioral ratings" (p. 967).

Although the team of Wolkowitz *et al.* (1990) utilized only a 5-day drug administration period to explore whether prednisone might cause behavioral changes, steroid abusers often take these drugs for much longer than 5 days, and they commonly use dosage levels far above 80 mg of prednisone each day. As noted earlier, individuals who abuse steroids often do so at dosage levels between 40 (Johnson, 1990) and 1000 times the maximum recommended dosage level (Wadler, 1994; Council on Scientific Affairs, 1990b). Although 80 mg/day of prednisone is a moderately high dosage level, it is still within the range commonly utilized by physicians in the treatment of disease.

At the grossly inflated dosage levels commonly used by steroid abusers, there is a possibility of a drug-induced psychosis (Pope & Katz, 1994; Kashkin, 1992; Johnson, 1990; Pope, Katz, & Champoux, 1986). At the very least, the unpleasant side effects of anabolic steroids may be an incentive for people to use recreational drugs in an attempt to self-medicate their discomfort (Schrof, 1992). Kashkin (1992) reported that about 50% of steroid abusers will abuse other substances in an effort to control the side effects of the anabolic steroids. Some of the drugs that the author noted might be abused are diuretics (to counteract steroid-induced "bloating") and antibiotics (to control steroid-induced acne).

Although most abusers reported minimal impact on measured aggression levels, Pope, Kouri, and Hudson (2000) found that 2–10% of male abusers became manic and/or developed other neuropsychiatric problems after abusing steroids. The authors found no significant premorbid sign that might pinpoint those steroid abusers who would develop such problems as a result of their steroid use. It is not known why they responded so strongly to the chemicals they injected. Other responses noted in steroid abusers have included depressive reactions or drug-induced psychotic reactions (Pope & Katz, 1988; Pope & Katz, 1987).

Sometimes the individual becomes violent after using steroids, a condition known as " 'roid rage" by illicit steroid users (Galloway, 1997; Fultz, 1991; Johnson, 1990). In rare cases, steroid-induced violence has resulted in the death of the user or of someone who became the target of the abuser's anger (Pope, Phillips, & Olivardia, 2000).

In 1994, Pope and Katz investigated the psychiatric side effects of anabolic steroid abuse. Their research sample was made up of 88 steroid-abusing athletes and 68 individuals who were not abusing steroids. Twenty-three percent of the steroid-abusing athletes were found to have experienced a major mood disturbance, such as mania or depression, and an increased level of aggressiveness that was attributed to their steroid use. One member of the sample of steroid abusers reportedly started to smash three different automobiles out of frustration over a traffic delay (Pope & Katz, 1994). Another individual was implicated in a murder plot, and a third beat his dog to death. Still another individual in the research sample rammed his head through a wooden door, and several others were expelled from their homes because of their threatening behavior (*The Back Letter*, 1994). Other psychiatric effects of anabolic steroid abuse include loss of inhibition, lack of judgment, irritability, a "strange edgy feeling" (Corrigan, 1996, p. 222), impulsiveness, and antisocial behavior (Corrigan, 1996).

In the early 1990s a number of researchers challenged the suspected relationship between anabolic steroid abuse and increased violent tendencies. Yesalis, Kennedy, Kopstein, and Bahrke (1993) suggested that for some unknown reason, anabolic steroid abusers might have exaggerated the self-reports of violent behavior noted in earlier studies. A second possibility, according to the authors, was that violent individuals are prone to abuse steroids for some unknown reason, giv-

ing the illusion of a causal relationship. However, by the start of the 21st century, the existence of a causal relationship between aggressive behavior and steroid abuse for at least a minority of steroid abusers, is clear (Pope, Kouri, & Hudson, 2000; Pope, Phillips, & Olivardia, 2000).

Steroids may cause depression in both men and women, even when used at recommended dosage levels. Both depression and periods of mania are common side effects (Sturmi & Diorio, 1998; Porcerelli, & Sandler, 1998; Galloway, 1997; Pope & Katz; 1994). These drugs may also produce a toxic reaction if the individual is using too high a dose for his or her individual body chemistry. Symptoms of a toxic reaction to steroids include a drug-induced psychotic reaction, manic episodes, delirium, dementia, and a drug-induced depressive reaction that may reach suicidal proportions (Lederberg & Holland, 1989).

Other complications. Patients with medical conditions such as certain forms of breast cancer, diabetes mellitus, diseases of the blood vessels, kidney, and liver or heart disease, and males who suffer from prostate problems, should not utilize steroids unless the prescribing physician was aware that the patient had these problems (United States Pharmacopeial Convention, 1990). The anabolic steroids are thought to be possible carcinogens (Johnson, 1990), and their use is not recommended for patients with either active tumors or a history of tumors, except under a physician's supervision.

Other side effects of steroid use include severe acne (especially across the back) and a foul odor on the breath (Redman, 1990). There has been one isolated case of unnatural bone degeneration that was attributed to the long term use of steroids by a weight lifter (Pettine, 1991). Animal research suggests that anabolic steroids may contribute to the degeneration of tendons, a finding that is consistent with clinical case reports of athletes who are using anabolic steroids having tendons rupture under stress (Karch, 1996).

Surprisingly, although anabolic steroids are often abused in an effort to improve athletic performance, the evidence on this issue is mixed (Tanner, 1995). One factor that complicates research into athletic performance is the individual's belief that these drugs will improve his or her abilities. The authors suggested that the athlete's expectation of improved performance may contribute to the observed performance on the part of the user.

Growth patterns in the adolescent. Adolescents who use steroids run the risk of stunted growth, because these drugs may permanently stop bone growth (Schrof, 1992; Johnson, 1990; Council on Scientific Affairs, 1990b). A further complication of steroid abuse by adolescents is that the tendons do not grow at the same accelerated rate as the bone tissues, which causes increased strain on the tendons and a higher risk of injury to these tissues (Galloway, 1997; Johnson, 1990).

Anabolic steroid abuse and blood infections. Individuals who abuse steroids through intramuscular or intravenous injection often share needles. These individuals run the same risk of infections being transmitted by contaminated needles as heroin and cocaine addicts. Indeed, there have been cases of athletes contracting AIDS when they used a needle that had been used by another infected athlete (Kashkin, 1992).

Drug interactions between steroids and other chemicals. The anabolic steroids interact with a wide range of medications, including several drugs of abuse. Potentially serious drug interactions have been noted in cases where the individual has used acetaminophen in high doses while on steroids. The combination of steroids and acetaminophen should be avoided except when the individual is being supervised by a physician. Patients who utilize Antabuse (disulfiram) should not take steroids, nor should individuals who are taking Trexan (naltrexone), anticonvulsant medications such as Dilantin (phenytoin), Depakene (valproic acid), or any of the phenothiazines (United States Pharmacopeial Convention, 1990b).

Are Anabolic Steroids Addictive?

Surprisingly, when used for periods of time at high dosage levels, the anabolic steroids have an addictive potential. Some users have reported preoccupation with the use of these chemicals and "craving" when they were not using steroids (Middleman & DuRant, 1996). Further, anabolic steroids have been known to bring about a sense of euphoria both when used for medical purposes and when abused (Middleman & DuRant, 1996; Fultz, 1991). This may explain why steroid use is so attractive to at least some of those who abuse this family of drugs.

There also is evidence that the user can become either physically or psychologically dependent on the anabolic steroids (Johnson, 1990). Bower (1991), found that up to 57% of weight lifters who use steroids ultimately became addicted to these drugs. One hallmark of physical dependence on a chemical is a characteristic withdrawal syndrome. In the case of anabolic steroid addiction, the withdrawal syndrome is very similar to that seen with cocaine withdrawal. Symptoms of withdrawal from steroids include depressive reactions, possibly to the point of suicide attempts (Kashkin, 1992; Kashkin & Kleber, 1989). Other symptoms often reported during or after withdrawal from steroids include sleep and appetite disturbances, which seem to be part of the poststeroid depressive syndrome (Bower, 1991), fatigue, restlessness, anorexia, insomnia, and decreased libido (Brower, Blow, Young, and Hill, 1991).

Like their drug-using counterparts, many steroid abusers require gradual detoxification from the drugs over time, as well as intensive psychiatric support, to both limit the impact of withdrawal on the individual's life and to try to prevent a return to steroid use (Kashkin & Kleber, 1989; Hough & Kovan, 1990; Bower, 1991). According to Robert Dimeff, Donald Malone, and John Lombardo (cited in Bower, 1991) some of the symptoms of steroid addiction are

1. The use of higher doses than originally intended
2. A loss of control over the amount of steroids used
3. A preoccupation with further steroid use
4. The continued use of steroids in spite of the individual's awareness of the problems caused by their use
5. The development of tolerance to steroids, and the need for larger doses to achieve the effects once brought on by lower doses
6. The disruption of normal daily activities by steroid use
7. The continued use of steroids to control or avoid withdrawal symptoms

The authors suggested that exhibiting three or more of these symptoms would identify those individuals who were dependent on steroids. Kashkin (1992) suggested that those individuals who had gone through five or more "cycles" of steroid use were very likely to be "heavy" steroid users.

Summary

The anabolic steroids emerged as drugs of abuse in the mid-1980s. In spite of their popularity, the steroids are different from the chemicals abused for recreational purposes. Adolescents and young adults abuse steroids because of a belief that these substances will increase aggressiveness, boost athletic ability, and improve personal appearance. Little is known about the effects of these drugs at the dosage levels utilized by individuals who abuse steroids. The identification and treatment of steroid abusers are primarily a medical issue, but substance abuse counselors should have a working knowledge of the effects of steroid abuse and the complications of this practice.

CHAPTER EIGHTEEN

The Over-the-Counter Analgesics

Unexpected Agents of Abuse

Introduction

As we noted earlier, the narcotic analgesics are not the only class of pharmaceuticals available to physicians for pain control. Other medications with analgesic potential are available without a physician's prescription; these are known as the over-the-counter (OTC) analgesics.[1] The OTC analgesics have a different mechanism of action than narcotic analgesics and unique side-effect profiles. Examples of non-narcotic analgesics include aspirin,[2] ibuprofen, ketoprofen, naproxen,[3] and acetaminophen. Although they are not considered drugs of abuse in the traditional sense, the OTC analgesics still have a significant potential for harm to the user. In this chapter we will focus on the OCT analgesics.

A Short History of the OTC Analgesics

Plants that contain chemical cousins of aspirin have long been used to control pain and fever. For example, willow bark, which contains salicin (from *Salix*, the Latin name for "willow") has been used for the relief of pain and fever for 2000 years (Stimmel, 1997b). Around

the year 400 B.C., the Greek physician Hippocrates recommended that patients chew the bark of the willow tree for such conditions as headache, fever, and labor pain. Although willow bark was recognized as an herbal remedy for pain, its bitter taste, limited availability, and inconsistent effect forced physicians to utilize narcotic analgesics for even mild levels of pain. But because narcotic analgesics are addictive and have a depressant effect on the central nervous system, they are a poor choice for the control of anything less than severe pain (Giacona, Dahl, & Hare, 1987).

Then, in the 1880s, the active agent of willow bark was isolated, and ways were found to synthesize large amounts of this compound for commercial use. Aspirin, or *acetylsalicylic acid*, was first developed from the salicin found in the bark of certain willow trees. Chemists learned to produce a chemical cousin of salicin known as salicylic acid, which had the same properties as salicin but was easier to produce. Like salicin, however, salicylic acid was found to cause a great deal of gastric distress, so chemists continued to search for a compound that offered the advantages of salicin but which produced less intense side effects. Chemists in Germany introduced the compound acetylsalicylic acid in the year 1898, and Bayer pharmaceuticals marketed this compound under the brand name Aspirin.

The term "aspirin" is a historical accident. The word "Aspirin" (with a capital "A") was introduced by the Bayer pharmaceutical company as the brand name for its form of acetylsalicylic acid. Over time, however, the term "aspirin" (with a small "a") has come to mean *any*

---

[1]See the Glossary.

[2]Aspirin is one of a family of related compounds, many of which have some analgesic, anti-inflammatory, antipyretic (antifever) action. None of these aspirin-like chemical compounds is as powerful as aspirin, so they will not be discussed.

[3]These agents were available only by prescription until the 1990s, when they were approved by the Food and Drug Administration for use, in modified dosage levels, as over-the-counter drugs.

preparation of acetylsalicylic acid sold for human use.[4] Like its chemical cousin salicin, aspirin is effective in controlling mild to moderate levels of pain, without posing the danger of addiction found with the narcotic family of analgesics. It also produces less gastric distress than its chemical cousins salicylic acid and salicin. Further, aspirin has been found to control inflammation and reduce fever. Because of its multiple uses, aspirin has become the most frequently used drug in the world (Mann & Plummer, 1991). Each year, an estimated 50 billion doses of aspirin are consumed (Begley, 1997). In the United States alone, 80 million aspirin tablets are consumed each day (Graedon & Graedon, 1996; Stolberg, 1994; Graedon & Ferguson, 1993).

Although aspirin's side effects are less intense than those of salicylic acid and salicin, it still has a significant potential to cause harm. This was one of the reasons why pharmaceutical companies embarked on a search for pharmaceuticals that offered the analgesic, antipyretic[5] and anti-inflammatory actions of aspirin but were safer to use. This search resulted in the discovery of a class of chemicals known as the *propionic acids,* from which the pharmaceutical agents now known as naproxen, ketoprofen, and ibuprofen were developed (Yost & Morgan, 1994). These agents were initially available in the United States only by prescription, but in the past two decades, all three were approved for over-the-counter use in modified dosage form.

Acetaminophen was introduced as an OTC analgesic in this country in the 1950s. The true name of this chemical is *N-acetyl-para-aminophenol,* from which the term "acetaminophen" is derived. The drug was actually first isolated in 1878, and its ability to reduce fever was identified shortly thereafter. But at the time it was thought that acetaminophen would share the dangerous side effects found in a close chemical cousin, para-aminophenol. Thus it was set aside, and chemists did not pay much attention to this chemical until the early 1950s (Mann & Plummer, 1991).

By the early 1950s, sufficient evidence had accumulated to show that acetaminophen was much safer than para-aminophenol and that it did not have the same

potential for harm as aspirin. A massive advertising campaign followed the introduction of acetaminophen, playing on the fact that aspirin might irritate the stomach, whereas acetaminophen does not. By the early 1970s, acetaminophen had carved a small but respectable niche for itself in the OTC analgesic market. Since that time, these aspirin-like OTC analgesics have collectively captured the lion's share of the $2.7-billion OTC analgesic market in the United States. However, aspirin still remains a popular OTC analgesic, and it still accounts for 28% of the OTC analgesic sales in this country (*U.S. News & World Report,* 1994).

Aspirin has been called "the most cost-effective drug available today" (Elwood, Hughes, & O'Brien, 1998, p. 587). It is such a potent drug that if it had been discovered today rather than a century ago, its use would be closely regulated and it would be available only by prescription (Graedon & Ferguson, 1993). Indeed, since the early 1990s, physicians have discovered that all of the OTC analgesics are far more toxic to the user, even at normal dosage levels, than had been thought (*Harvard Health Letter,* 1995).

The origin of the term NSAID. As we shall see, aspirin and the propionic acid derivatives have an anti-inflammatory effect. Another class of chemicals that have an anti-inflammatory effect consists of the adrenocortical steroids, potent agents whose function lies beyond the scope of this text. However, because aspirin and the propionic acid derivatives differ in structure from the adrenocortical steroids, they are often called non-steroidal anti-inflammatory drugs (NSAIDs). Approximately 20 NSAIDs are currently in use in the United States, although most are available only by prescription. The exceptions to this rule are aspirin and the propionic acid derivatives ibuprofen, ketoprofen, and naproxen. The new COX-2 inhibitors, which are available only by prescription, have been classified as NSAID by Jackson and Hawkey (2000).

Medical Uses of the OTC Analgesics

Aspirin. Aspirin was first introduced in 1897, but scientists are still discovering new uses for it. The most common application for aspirin is in the control of mild to moderate levels of pain from such conditions as common headaches, neuralgia, the pain associated with oral surgery, toothache, dysmenorrhea, and various forms of

---

[4] The manner in which this came about is beyond the scope of this chapter but is reviewed in excellent detail by Mann and Plummer (1991).

[5] See the Glossary.

musculoskeletal pain (Supernaw, 1991; Giacona, Dahl, & Hare, 1987). Further, just one aspirin tablet every other day has been found to reduce the frequency of migraines by 20% in a small subgroup of patients who suffer migraine headaches (Graedon & Ferguson, 1993; Gilman, 1992; Graedon & Graedon, 1991).

Aspirin continues to be the most effective drug available for reducing fever (Payan & Katzung, 1995). This latter effect is brought on, in part, by aspirin's ability to cause peripheral vasodilation and sweating in the patient, as well as its ability to interfere with prostaglandin production in the hypothalamus[6] (Shannon, Wilson, & Stang, 1995; Laurence & Bennett, 1992). These effects help to reduce fever but do not lower the body temperature below normal. It has also been discovered that the daily use of aspirin can reduce the potential for a nonfatal myocardial infarction (heart attack) by 34% and the risk of a fatal myocardial infarction by 16% (Elwood, Hughes, & O'Brien, 1998) through its ability to interfere with the ability of human blood to form clots. This effect has also made aspirin a valuable adjunct to the treatment of an evolving myocardial infarction (Graedon & Graedon, 1996; Stolberg, 1994; Hennekens, Jonas, & Buring, 1994; Patrono, 1994).

There are several mechanisms by which aspirin is able to reduce the risk of myocardial infarction. Aspirin reduces the level of a compound found in the blood known as the *C-reactive protein* (Ridker, Cushman, Stampfer, Tracy, & Hennekens, 1997). The higher the level of C-reactive protein in the individual's blood, the greater his or her chances of a myocardial infarction; a stroke (CVA), in which a blood vessel becomes obstructed; or a blood clot that might block another vessel (a *venous thrombosis*). However, this beneficial effect of aspirin was noted only for individuals older than 50 years of age and was strongest for those individuals with lower blood cholesterol levels.

Another mechanism by which aspirin reduces the individual's risk of a myocardial infarction, a CVA brought on by a blood clot, or a venous thrombosis is its ability to inhibit the formation of blood clots by blood platelets. Aspirin permanently destroys the compound *thromboxane* A_2 in blood platelets, thus making it more difficult for blood clots to form (Patrono, 1994). But because blood platelets have a normal lifetime of 8–10

days, the body is constantly replacing old blood platelets with new ones. These new blood platelets will have unaltered thromboxane A_2 incrementally restoring the platelets' clot-forming proficiency. It is thus necessary for the patient to take a new dose of aspirin every day, or at least every other day, to achieve optimal inhibition of blood clot formation.

Aspirin's effects are not limited to the cardiovascular system. Researchers have found that aspirin is of value in the treatment of a rare neurological disorder known as *transient ischemic attacks* (TIAs). It has also been found to be an effective anti-inflammatory agent, making it valuable in controlling the inflammation caused by such disorders as rheumatoid arthritis and osteoarthritis (Graedon & Graedon, 1991; McGuire, 1990; Giacona *et al.*, 1987). There have even been reports suggesting that aspirin might be of value in the fight against colon cancer (Elwood, Hughes, & O'Brien, 1998). Researchers have determined that regular aspirin use may bring about a 40–50% reduction in the risk of death from colon cancer by blocking the production of a compound known as cyclooxygenase in the body. As will be discussed later in this chapter, there are two known subforms of cyclooxygenase in the human body. The subform known as COX-2 is thought to be involved in the inflammatory response and to be involved in the formation of tumors in the colon through an unknown mechanism (DuBois, Sheng, Shao, Williams, & Beauchamp, 1998).

Researchers are actively exploring possible new applications for aspirin. Preliminary evidence suggests that aspirin might slow the development of cataracts (Payan & Katzung, 1995), and there is mixed evidence that aspirin might help to control a form of hypertension that occasionally complicates pregnancy (Patrono, 1994; Graedon & Ferguson, 1993; Graedon & Graedon, 1991). Scientists have found evidence that aspirin use might prevent the formation of gallstones (Elwood, Hughes, & O'Brien, 1998), and there are even data suggesting that aspirin might interfere with the ability of the virus that causes AIDS to replicate (Stolberg, 1994).

Acetaminophen. Because acetaminophen has no significant anti-inflammatory effect, it is not usually classified as an NSAID (Supernaw, 1991). But it has been found to be as effective as aspirin in the control of fever (American Society of Health System Pharmacists, 1999). Further, acetaminophen is as potent an OTC

[6]See the Glossary.

analgesic as aspirin and might be used for pain control in virtually the same situations.

The propionic acids. As a class, the propionic acids are used to control fever, inflammation, and mild to moderate levels of pain. The anti-inflammatory effect of these compounds makes them useful in treating such conditions as rheumatoid arthritis, dysmenorrhea, gout, tendinitis, and bursitis, as well as headaches, the aches of the common cold, backache and muscle aches, arthritis, the discomfort of menstrual cramps, and fever (Gannon, 1994). Physicians have found that when they are used in combination with narcotic analgesics, some NSAID are of value in controlling the pain associated with some forms of cancer. In addition to such general applications, researchers have identified specific applications for each of these compounds.

Ibuprofen. In addition to its use as an OTC analgesic and anti-inflammatory agent, ibuprofen may help slow the progression of Alzheimer's disease (Stewart, Kawas, Corrada, & Metter, 1997). Another application of ibuprofen's anti-inflammatory action has been control of the tissue inflammation caused by cystic fibrosis (CF) (Konstan, Hoppel, Chai, & Davis, 1991; Konstan, Byard, Hoppel, & Davis, 1995).

Naproxen. In addition to its uses as an anti-inflammatory and analgesic, physicians have discovered that when it is used in combination with the antibiotic ampicillin, naproxen seems to reduce the distress felt by children with respiratory infections caused by bacteria.

Pharmacology of the OTC Analgesics

Aspirin. Aspirin is usually administered by mouth. In the body, acetylsalicylic acid is biotransformed into salicylic acid, the active agent for aspirin's effects (Peterson, 1997). The drug is rapidly absorbed, and when it is taken on an empty stomach, aspirin begins to reach the bloodstream in as little as 1 minute (Rose, 1988). However, its primary site of absorption is the small intestine, so it usually takes somewhat longer to achieve therapeutic blood levels.

After a single dose, peak blood levels of aspirin are achieved in between 15 (Shannon, Wilson, & Stang, 1995) and 60–120 minutes (Stimmel, 1997a; McGuire, 1990). It usually takes about an hour before aspirin brings about any significant degree of analgesia (Stimmel, 1997a). Once in the blood, between 80–90%

of aspirin is bound to plasma proteins (Stimmel, 1997a). Aspirin is rapidly biotransformed by the liver into water-soluble metabolites, which are then promptly removed from the blood by the kidneys (Payan & Katzung, 1995). Only about 1% of a single dose of aspirin is excreted unchanged from the body. Aspirin normally has a biological half-life of 2 hours, but when it is used at high dosage levels for longer than a week, its half-life might be extended to between 8 (Kacso & Terezhalmy, 1994) and 15 (Payan & Katzung, 1995) hours. It is rare for tolerance to the analgesic effects of aspirin to develop (Stimmel, 1997a).

Unlike the narcotic analgesics, which seem to work mainly within the cortex of the brain, aspirin has a different mechanism of action (Kacso & Terezhalmy, 1994). It appears to work at the site of the injury, in the hypothalamic region of the brain, and through unidentified sites in the spinal cord (Kacso & Terezhalmy, 1994; Graedon & Ferguson, 1993; Fishman & Carr, 1992).

To understand how aspirin works at the site of the injury, it is necessary to investigate the body's response to injury. Each cell in the human body contains several chemicals that are released, when that cell is damaged, to warn neighboring cells of the damage and activate the body's repair mechanisms. These chemicals include *histamine, bradykinin,* and a group of chemicals collectively known as the *prostaglandins.* The inflammation and pain that result when these chemicals are released serve both to warn the individual that he or she has been injured and to activate the body's repair mechanisms.

Aspirin's analgesic effect at the site of the injury may be attributed to its power to inhibit the production of the prostaglandins (American Society of Health System Pharmacists, 1999; Bushnell & Justins, 1993). Aspirin inhibits the production of both known subtypes of the enzyme *cyclooxygenase:* COX-1 and COX-2. COX-1 is predominantly involved in essential prostaglandin production in body organs, where the prostaglandins serve a protective function. Its chemical cousin, COX-2, is produced mainly by body tissues when they are damaged, contributing to the inflammation response (Rehman & Sack, 1999; Pairet, van Ryn, Manz, Schierok, Diederen, Turck, & Engelhardt, 1990). On a molecular level, COX-1 and COX-2 share about 60% of their chemical structure, and it is through the shared elements that NSAIDs interfere with the production of both COX-1 and COX-2 (Rehman & Sack, 1999). In other words, through their nonselective action on both COX-1 and COX-2, NSAIDs such as aspirin are able to block injury-induced prostaglandin production, lower pain levels, and reduce inflammation. One consequence of this nonselective inhibition of both forms of cyclooxygenase is the unwanted reduction of COX-1 levels in the body, which increases the risk of NSAID-induced tissue damage.

Acetaminophen. Acetaminophen is usually administered orally, although it may also be administered as a rectal suppository. Oral preparations include tablet, capsule, and liquid forms, and virtually 100% of the medication is absorbed through the gastrointestinal tract (Shannon, Wilson, & Stang, 1995). The peak effects are seen ½ to 2 hours after a single dose, and acetaminophen is metabolized in the liver. Virtually 100% of the drug is eliminated in the urine, although some acetaminophen might also be found in breast milk of nursing mothers.

In terms of its analgesic and fever-reducing potential, acetaminophen is thought to be as powerful as aspirin (Supernaw, 1991) and can be substituted for aspirin on a milligram-for-milligram basis. Exceeding the dosage levels recommended by the manufacturer raises the danger of acetaminophen toxicity. However, liver toxicity/damage from acetaminophen is rare, as long as the user does not ingest more than 4000 mg of acetaminophen per day (Cherny & Foley, 1996) or use the drug for more than 10 days (Peterson, 1997).

The exact manner in which acetaminophen reduces pain and fever remains unknown (Shannon, Wilson, & Stang, 1995). One theory suggests that, like aspirin, acetaminophen interferes with prostaglandin synthesis in the central nervous system. But acetaminophen-induced inhibition of prostaglandin is limited to the CNS, and does not extend to the peripheral regions of the body, which is why acetaminophen has no significant anti-inflammatory potential (Peterson, 1997). Unlike aspirin, acetaminophen does not interfere with the normal clotting mechanisms of the blood (Shannon, Wilson, & Stang, 1995). Finally, individuals who are allergic to aspirin do not usually suffer from adverse reactions when they take acetaminophen. These features often make acetaminophen an ideal substitute when the patient is allergic to aspirin, when she or he is prone to bleeding disorders, or when aspirin might interfere with another medication being used by the patient.

Ibuprofen. Ibuprofen is a member of the propionic acid family of chemicals, and it is most commonly administered orally. About 80% of a single dose of ibuprofen is absorbed from the gastrointestinal tract. The primary site of ibuprofen biotransformation is the liver, and its half-life is between 2 and 4 hours (Shannon, Wilson, & Stang, 1995). About 99% of the ibuprofen molecules become protein-bound following absorption into the general circulation (Olson, 1992). The therapeutic half-life of a single dose of ibuprofen is between 1.8 and 2.6 hours (American Medical Association, 1994). Peak plasma levels following a single oral dose are achieved in between 30 minutes and 1.5 hours. Ibuprofen and its metabolites are eliminated mainly by the kidneys, although a small amount of ibuprofen is eliminated through the bile.

Although ibuprofen inhibits the action of the enzyme cyclooxygenase, this does not mean that ibuprofen can automatically be substituted for aspirin to control inflammation. Payan and Katzung (1995) stated that when it is used at a dosage level of 2400 mg/day,[7] ibuprofen is as effective as aspirin in the control of inflammation in the average adult. When used at a dosage level lower than 2400 mg/day, however, ibuprofen is far less effective than aspirin as an anti-inflammatory agent (Payan & Katzung, 1995). Mann (1992), on the other hand, suggested that when it is used at effective dosage levels, ibuprofen is 30 times as effective as aspirin in fighting inflammation. As is obvious from these various reports, researchers still disagree about the anti-inflammatory potential of ibuprofen.

There is strong evidence that when ibuprofen is taken concurrently with aspirin, each of these chemicals interferes with the anti-inflammatory action of the other (Payan & Katzung, 1995). Thus ibuprofen should not be used by a patient taking aspirin, except under a physician's orders. Unfortunately, ibuprofen's anti-inflammatory effects are seen only after 2–4 weeks of continuous use (Fischer, 1989). Thus it would seem that it would be better to use aspirin for the control of inflammation, but one must remember that aspirin is quite irritating to the stomach. Ibuprofen is about one-fifth to one-half as irritating to the stomach as aspirin

---

[7]The 2400 mg is taken in divided doses, not all at once.

(Giacona *et al.*, 1987). Thus, ibuprofen is often utilized in cases where the individual is unable to tolerate the gastrointestinal irritation caused by aspirin. Even so, it has been estimated that 4–14% of those who use ibuprofen experience some degree of gastrointestinal irritation (Graedon & Graedon, 1996).

When ibuprofen is used for prolonged periods of time, approximately 3 of every 1000 users also experience some degree of drug-induced gastrointestinal bleeding (Carlson, Strom, Morse, West, Soper, Stolley, & Jones, 1987). Taha, Dahill, Sturrock, Lee, and Russell (1994) found that 27% of the members of their sample who had used ibuprofen for an extended period of time had evidence of ulcer formation in the gastrointestinal tract. However, the number of ibuprofen-using subjects in their sample was quite small, and it was not clear how representative these findings were of the ability of ibuprofen to contribute to gastrointestinal ulcers.

Naproxen is possibly more effective as an anti-inflammatory agent than aspirin (American Medical Association, 1994; American Society of Health-System Pharmacists, 1999; Graedon & Graedon, 1991). Like aspirin, naproxen has an antipyretic effect. Researchers are not sure of the exact mechanism through which naproxen reduces fever. However, it is thought that naproxen may suppress the synthesis of prostaglandins in the hypothalamus (American Society of Health-System Pharmacists, 1999).

When used as an analgesic, naproxen begins to have an effect in 1 hour, and its effects last for 7–8 hours (American Medical Association, 1994). The biological half-life of naproxen in the healthy adult is approximately 10–20 hours. About 30% of a given dose of naproxen is metabolized by the liver into the inactive metabolite *6-desmethylnaproxen* (American Society of Health-System Pharmacists, 1999), and only 5% (American Medical Association, 1994) to 10% (American Society of Health-System Pharmacists, 1999) of a standard dose of naproxen is excreted unchanged. The majority of the drug is excreted in the urine as either metabolized or unmetabolized drug.

As we have said, naproxen binds to proteins in the blood plasma, which can absorb only so much of the medication before reaching a saturation point. Research suggests that the concentration of naproxen reaches a plateau if the patient takes 500 mg twice daily for 2–3 days (American Society of Health-System Phar-

macists, 1999).[8] Thus, even under a physician's direction, the typical dosage level does not exceed 500 mg twice a day.

Ketoprofen. When it was sold as a prescription drug, patients were advised not to take more than 300 mg/day of ketoprofen, and they were usually advised to take their medication with food in order to minimize irritation to the gastrointestinal tract. Ketoprofen is well absorbed from the GI tract, and peak blood levels appear between 30 minutes and 2 hours after a single dose taken on an empty stomach (American Medical Association, 1994). It is more slowly absorbed when taken with food, but eventually, all of the ketoprofen is absorbed. Ketoprofen is extensively bound to plasma proteins, with 99% of the drug molecules being protein-bound. There are no known active metabolites of ketoprofen.

In young adults, the half-life of a single dose of ketoprofen is 3 hours; in the elderly, it might be 5 hours. Thus older patients and patients with impaired kidney function should consult their physicians before taking this medication.

Even though all of the OTC analgesics are useful in the control of mild to moderate levels of pain or fever, a common danger inherent in the use of these agents is that they might mask the development of a serious medical condition. For example, although the OTC analgesics are effective in controlling fever, the cause of the fever must still be identified and treated (Fishman & Carr, 1992).

Normal Dosage Levels of OTC Analgesics

Aspirin. McGuire (1990) reported that 650 mg of aspirin or acetaminophen—a standard dose of two regular-strength tablets of either medication—provided an analgesic effect equal to that of 50 mg of the narcotic painkiller meperidine (Demerol). Kaplan and Sadock (1990) suggested that 650 mg of aspirin has the same analgesic potential as 32 mg of codeine, 65 mg of Darvon (propoxyphene), or a 50-mg oral dose of Talwin (pentazocine). Thus, although it is an over-the-counter analgesic, aspirin would seem to be rather potent.

---

[8]It should be noted that a patient should not take 500 mg of naproxen twice a day except under a physician's supervision.

Even after more than a century of use, physicians still are not sure whether aspirin's analgesic effects are dose-related (Giacona *et al.*, 1987). It is also not clear whether there is any additional analgesic benefit from doses above 600 mg every 4 hours for an adult. Kacso and Terezhalmy (1994) reported that a single 1300-mg dose of aspirin provided a greater degree of relief from pain than a single 600-mg dose. However, dosage levels above 1300 mg in a single dose did not provide a greater degree of analgesia, and actually put the user at risk for a toxic reaction from the aspirin, according to the authors. These findings were consistent with the conclusions of Aronoff, Wagner, and Spangler (1986), who found a "ceiling effect" of "approximately 1000 mg every 4 hr" (p. 769) for aspirin. Dosage levels higher than this did not provide greater pain relief and would "only increase the threat of a toxic reaction" (McGuire, 1990, p. 30).

The American Society of Health-System Pharmacists (1994) recommends a normal adult oral dosage level of 325 to 650 mg of aspirin every 4 hours, as needed for the control of pain. Furthermore, this text warns that aspirin should not be used continuously for longer than 10 days by an adult or longer than 5 days for a child under the age of 12, except under a doctor's orders.[9]

When taken by mouth, aspirin is rapidly and completely absorbed from the gastrointestinal tract and is distributed by the blood to virtually every body tissue and fluid. The actual speed at which aspirin is absorbed by the user depends on the acidity of the stomach contents (Sheridan, Patterson, & Gustafson, 1982). When it is taken on an empty stomach, the rate at which aspirin is absorbed depends on how quickly the tablet crumbles after reaching the stomach (Rose, 1988). After the tablet crumbles, the individual aspirin molecules pass through the stomach lining into the general circulatory system.

When the individual takes aspirin with food, it may take 5–10 times longer to reach the individual's bloodstream (Pappas, 1990). Ultimately, however, *all* of the aspirin is absorbed from the gastrointestinal tract. Because this is so, Rodman (1993) suggested that the patient take aspirin with meals, or at least a snack, to limit aspirin-induced irritation to the stomach lining. However, in some cases, it is desirable to achieve as high a blood level of aspirin as possible. The patients should discuss with their physician or pharmacist whether they should take aspirin on an empty stomach or with a meal before using this technique to limit stomach irritation.

Aspirin is sold both alone and in combination with various agents designed to reduce the stomach irritation it might cause. In theory, timed-released and enteric coated tablets have the potential for reducing irritation to the gastrointestinal tract. However, both of these forms of aspirin have been known to have erratic absorption rates, making it harder to achieve the desired effect (Shannon, Wilson, & Stang, 1995). Some patients will take aspirin with antacids to reduce the irritation to the stomach caused by aspirin. When antacids are mixed with aspirin, the patient's blood level of aspirin will be 30–70% lower than when aspirin is used alone (Rodman, 1993; Graedon & Graedon, 1996). This is a matter of some concern for individuals who are taking the drug for the control of inflammation or pain.

Acetaminophen. The usual adult dose of acetaminophen is 325–650 mg every 4 hours, as needed for the control of pain (American Society of Health-System Pharmacists, 1999). In many ways, dosage recommendations for aspirin and acetaminophen are very similar. For example, Aronoff, Wagner, and Spangler (1986) observed that acetaminophen's antipyretic and analgesic effects are equal to those of aspirin and that these two drugs have the same ceiling level.

Peak blood concentrations were achieved in $\frac{1}{2}$ to 2 hours after an oral dose of acetaminophen (Shannon, Wilson, & Stang, 1995). The half-life of an oral dose of acetaminophen is normally from 1 to 4 hours. However, because this chemical is biotransformed in the liver, acetaminophen may have a longer half-life in people with significant liver damage. Such individuals should avoid using acetaminophen except under the supervision of a physician.

Ibuprofen. When ibuprofen is used as an OTC analgesic, the recommended dose is 200–400 mg every 4 hours (Dionne & Gordon, 1994). As a prescription

---

[9]When using aspirin in the treatment of arthritis, for example, a physician may have the patient take it at a higher than normal dosage levels for extended periods of time. This represents a special application of aspirin's anti-inflammatory effect, and the physician will weigh the advantages of using aspirin at such high dosage levels against the potential for harm to the patient. Since this is a special application of aspirin, however, it will not be discussed in this chapter.

medication, individual dosage levels of 400–800 mg of ibuprofen are often utilized, depending on the specific condition being treated. Shannon, Wilson, & Stang (1995) recommended that 400–800 mg of ibuprofen be used 3–4 times a day by adults who suffer from inflammatory diseases. The authors suggest that 400 mg every 4-6 hours be used in the control of mild to moderate pain. However, there is some disagreement about the analgesic potential of ibuprofen. Dionne and Gordon (1994) noted that the greatest degree of relief from pain is achieved with doses of 400–600 mg and that additional ibuprofen above this level is unlikely to result in greater levels of analgesia. In contrast to this, however, Rosenblum (1992) stated that 800 mg of ibuprofen provided greater control of postoperative pain than did therapeutic doses of the narcotic fentanyl, in a small sample of women who had laparoscopic surgery.

It is necessary to keep in mind the fact that the OTC dosage levels of ibuprofen are limited to 200–400 mg every 4 hours. A physician who prescribes this medication might elect to use a higher dosage level. However, even when ibuprofen is used as a prescription medication, the total daily dosage level should not exceed 3200 mg, in divided doses (Shannon, Wilson, & Stang, 1995; Dionne & Gordon, 1994). Ibuprofen is rapidly absorbed when used orally, and the drug is rapidly distributed throughout the body. About 80% of a single oral dose is absorbed from the intestinal tract. Following a single oral dose, peak blood plasma levels are achieved in 1–2 hours (American Society of Health-System Pharmacists, 1999). The drug's half-life is between 1.8 and 2.6 hours, and the effects of a single dose of ibuprofen last for about 6–8 hours following a single oral dose (Shannon, Wilson, & Stang, 1995).

Naproxen. When naproxen is used as an OTC analgesic, users are advised to take up to 3 tablets, twice a day. The medication is well absorbed from the intestinal tract, and 100% of a single dose is absorbed. Absorption is somewhat delayed when naproxen is ingested with food, but eventually all of the medication is absorbed. Peak blood concentrations are found 2–4 hours after a single dose, and 99% of the medication is bound to proteins in the blood after absorption. Although this compound will cross the placenta, it does so with difficulty, and fetal plasma levels are approximately 1% of those in the mother's blood (American Society of Health-System Pharmacists, 1999).

About 30% of a single dose of naproxen is biotransformed by the liver into the inactive metabolite 6-desmethylnaproxen (American Society of Health-System Pharmacists, 1999). The rest is biotransformed into other metabolites, and less than 1% is excreted unchanged by the kidneys. Only 5% of the drug is excreted in the feces, and 95% is excreted in the urine, mainly as one of the many metabolites formed when naproxen is biotransformed by the liver.

Ketoprofen. As a prescription medication, ketoprofen is available in 25-, 50-, and 75-mg capsules. Recommended dosage levels are 50–75 mg every 8 hours, up to a maximum of 300 mg/day. There is no evidence that dosage levels above 300 mg/day are more effective than lower doses, and the manufacturer does not recommend that ketoprofen be used in dosage levels above 300 mg per day (Medical Economics Company, 1999). In the modified OTC analgesic form, it is sold in 25 mg tablets.

Complications Caused by the Use of OTC Analgesics

The OTC analgesics are hardly "safe" medications. As a group, the NSAIDs account for nearly 25% of the adverse drug reactions reported to the Food and Drug Administration (FDA), and some 16,500 patients with osteoarthitis or rheumatoid arthritis die because of NSAID-related problems (Noble, King, & Olutade, 2000). Although these medications are available without a prescription, the OTC analgesics pose a significant potential for harm—a fact that many people tend to forget.

Aspirin. Aspirin is the most commonly used drug in this country. The popularity of aspirin is apparent in the statistics: Americans consume between 20 billion (Rapoport, 1993) and 40 billion (Talley, 1993) tablets of aspirin a year. Steele and Morton (1986) gave another measure of aspirin use in this country, stating that between 30 and 74 *million pounds* of aspirin are consumed in the United States each year.

Because aspirin is such a popular home remedy, many people underestimate both its usefulness and its potential for causing serious side effects (Jaffe & Martin, 1990). Even occasional use of aspirin at recommended doses will result in up to 15% of the users having at least one significant—potentially fatal—adverse side effect (Rapoport, 1993). For example, a single dose of aspirin can reduce the level of melatonin in the brain by as much as 75% (Pettit, 2000). At recommended dosage levels, aspirin causes minor bleeding in the gastrointestinal tract. The chronic use of aspirin can cause the patient to become anemic (Talley, 1993; Pappas, 1990), and 500–1000 people die each year in the United States from massive aspirin-induced hemorrhage (Grinspoon & Bakalar, 1993).

Up to 40% of the patients who use aspirin at recommended doses on a chronic basis experience an erosion in their stomach lining, and between 17% (Kitridou, 1993) and 30% (Taha, Dahill, Strurrock, Lee, & Russell, 1994) develop aspirin-induced stomach ulcers. Researchers also believe that the patient's use of aspirin is a factor in the formation of between 20% (Talley, 1993) and 41% (Wilcox, Shalek, & Cotsonis, 1994) of all cases of "bleeding" ulcers.[10] Even dosage levels as low as 75 mg/day have been found to increase significantly the individual's risk for damage to the lining of the gastrointestinal system (Guslandi, 1997).

In addition to its effects on the stomach lining, the regular use of aspirin can contribute to the formation of potentially life-threatening ulcers in the small intestine (Allison, Howatson, Torrance, Lee, & Russell, 1992). It is for these reasons that aspirin should not be used by persons with a history of ulcers, bleeding disorders, or other gastrointestinal disorders (American Society of Health-System Pharmacists, 1999). Further, it is suggested that people not take aspirin with acidic foods such as coffee, fruit juices, or alcohol, which might further irritate the gastrointestinal system (Pappas, 1990).

Many of the gastrointestinal ulcers that result from aspirin use fail to produce the major warning symptoms usually associated with ulcer formation (Taha, Dahill, Sturrock, Lee, & Russell, 1994). Aspirin's ability to cause gastric irritation is thought to be a side effect of its nonselective ability to interfere with production of both the COX-1 and the COX-2 subtypes of cyclooxygenase. This may also be why, when used at recommended dosage levels for extended periods of time, aspirin can cause breathing problems in up to 33% of users (Kitridou, 1993).

Aspirin can also cause allergic reactions in some users. Approximately 0.2% of the general population is al-

lergic to aspirin, and of those individuals with a history of *any* kind of allergic disorder, approximately 20% will be allergic to aspirin. Patients who are sensitive to aspirin are likely also to be sensitive to ibuprofen or naproxen; cross-sensitivity between these drugs is common (Shannon, Wilson, & Stang, 1995; Fischer, 1989). Symptoms of an allergic reaction to aspirin may include rash and breathing problems (Zuger, 1994). Patients with symptoms of the "aspirin triad"—that is, those individuals with a history of nasal polyps, asthma, and sensitivity to aspirin, should not use any NSAID except under the supervision of a physician (Craig, 1996).

Aspirin has been known to trigger fatal asthma attacks in patients with this disorder (Zuger, 1994). Indeed, all of the NSAIDs are capable of exacerbating the symptoms of asthma as a result of their ability to inhibit prostaglandin production (Craig, 1996; McFadden & Hejal, 2000). Persons with a history of chronic rhinitis should not use aspirin except under a physician's supervision (Shannon, Wilson, & Stang, 1995). These conditions are warning signals for individuals "at risk" for an allergic reaction to aspirin or similar agents. About 5–15% of those individuals who suffer from asthma will experience an adverse reaction if they use an NSAID (Craig, 1996). If the asthma patient also has a history of nasal polyps, the possibility of an adverse reaction to an NSAID may be as high as 40%, according to the authors.

Aspirin can cause a number of other side effects, including anorexia, nausea, and vomiting (Sheridan, Patterson, & Gustafson, 1982). Because of their effects on blood clotting, aspirin, naproxen, and ibuprofen should not be used by people with a bleeding disorder such as hemophilia (American Society of Health-System Pharmacists, 1999; Shannon, Wilson, & Stang, 1995). Persons who are undergoing anticoagulant therapy involving such drugs as heparin, or warfarin, should not use aspirin except when directed by a physician (Rodman, 1993). The combined effects of aspirin and the anticoagulant might result in significant, unintended blood loss for the patient, especially if he or she were to have an accident. Further, the anticoagulent effect of aspirin can contribute to the development of a hemorrhagic stroke (He, Whelton, Vu, & Klag, 1998). Thus the physician must weigh the advantages of using aspirin to treat heart disease against its potential to cause or contribute to a potentially fatal hemorrhagic stroke.

[10]See the Glossary.

As we noted earlier in this chapter, patients taking other NSAIDs such as ibuprofen or naproxen should not take aspirin, except under a physician's supervision. In addition to these medications' interfering with each other, their combined effects can cause significant gastrointestinal tract irritation (Rodman, 1993). Aspirin, naproxen, and ibuprofen may all cause a condition known as "tinnitus" (loss of hearing and a persistent ringing in the ears). The patient's hearing usually returns to normal when the offending medication is immediately discontinued. Aspirin use may also result in a very rare side effect known as *hepatotoxicity* (Gay, 1990). In such cases, aspirin prevents the liver from filtering the blood effectively (Gay, 1990). Another rare complication from aspirin use is a drug-induced depression (Mortensen & Rennebohm, 1989).

For reasons that are not entirely clear, the elderly are especially susceptible to toxicity from aspirin and similar agents. This may be because their bodies are unable to metabolize and excrete this family of drugs as effectively as younger adults. Bleidt and Moss (1989) suggested that this was due, at least in part, to the fact that as people grow older, there is a reduction in blood flow to the liver and kidneys. This results in the elderly having difficulty metabolizing and excreting many drugs, including aspirin. Another complication of aspirin use in the elderly is the development of drug-induced anxiety states (Sussman, 1988).

Neither aspirin nor related compounds should be used with children who are suffering from a viral infection, except when a physician so directs. Research strongly suggests that aspirin increases the possibility of the child developing Reye's syndrome as a complication to the viral infection (Stimmel, 1997a; Sagar, 1991; Graedon & Graedon, 1996; Sagar, 1991). Surprisingly, in light of the frequency with which aspirin is used to treat the symptoms of a common "cold" virus, it can actually suppress the body's immune response to the invading virus (Bartlett, 1999).

Surprisingly, aspirin has been implicated in the failure of the intrauterine device (IUD) to prevent pregnancy. The anti-inflammatory action of aspirin is thought to account for its ability to interfere with the effectiveness of intrauterine devices. Aspirin has also been implicated in fertility problems for couples who wish to have children. The use of aspirin at therapeutic dosage levels may reduce the ability of sperm to move (sperm motility) by up to 50%, a side effect that may reduce the chances of successful conception for some couples. Of course, this is not to say that aspirin might serve as a method of birth control, but the reduction in sperm motility might interfere with the couple's ability to conceive, when they wish to do so.

Medication interactions involving aspirin.[11] Patients being treated for hyperuricemia (a buildup of uric acid in the blood often found in gout and in other conditions) should not use aspirin. When used at normal dosage levels, aspirin reduces the body's ability to excrete uric acid, contributing to the problem of uric acid buildup. Further, if the individual is taking the prescription medication probenecid, one of the drugs used to treat hyperuricemia, he or she should not take aspirin. At therapeutic doses, aspirin inhibits the action of probenecid, allowing uric acid levels to build up in the blood. Acetaminophen has been proposed as a suitable substitute for patients who suffer from gout and who need a mild analgesic (Shannon, Wilson, & Stang, 1995).

Aspirin also should not be used in patients who are receiving medication for the control of their blood pressure or anticoagulants such as warfarin, except under a physician's supervision. It has been found that aspirin and the other NSAIDs may undermine the effectiveness of some antihypertensive medications (Fischer, 1989). The exact mechanism by which this happens is unclear, but it may reflect the impact of aspirin use on prostaglandin production within the kidneys, resulting in fluid retention (*Harvard Health Letter*, 1995).

It has been found that individuals who plan to consume alcohol should not use aspirin immediately before drinking or while they are drinking. Roine, Gentry, Hernandez-Munoz, Baraona, and Lieber (1990) found that taking aspirin prior to the ingestion of alcohol decreases the activity of gastric alcohol dehydrogenase, an enzyme produced by the stomach that starts to metabolize alcohol even before it reaches the bloodstream. This will result in a higher than normal blood alcohol level even in the infrequent social drinker who ingests aspirin shortly before drinking alcohol. Finally, patients

---

[11] It is not possible to list every interaction involving aspirin and other compounds. Readers should consult a physician or pharmacist if they have any questions about possible interactions between a given drug and aspirin.

who are using aspirin should not use the herbal medicine *Ginkgo biloba*, because this compound can contribute to excessive bleeding (Cupp, 1999).

Ibuprofen. Ibuprofen has been implicated as a cause of blurred vision (Nicastro, 1989). Graedon and Graedon (1996) suggested that persons who are using ibuprofen and experience some change in their vision discontinue the medication and consult their physician immediately. In addition to the 3–9% of patients on ibuprofen who experience skin rashes or hives as a side effect of this medication, ibuprofen has been implicated in the formation of cataracts (Graedon & Graedon, 1996) and as a cause of migraine headaches in both men and women (Nicastro, 1989).

When ibuprofen was first introduced as a prescription medication in 1974, it was manufactured by the Upjohn Company and sold under the brand name Motrin. The Upjohn Company warned that ibuprofen has been found to cause a number of side effects, including heartburn, nausea, diarrhea, vomiting, nervousness, hearing loss, congestive heart failure in persons who had marginal cardiac function, changes in vision, and elevation of blood pressure (Medical Economics Company, 1999).

Recent research also suggests that ibuprofen can cause or contribute to kidney failure in persons with high blood pressure, kidney disease, or other health problems (Squires, 1990). This may be a side effect of ibuprofen's ability to block the production of prostaglandin. By doing so, ibuprofen also reduces the blood flow throughout the body, especially to the kidneys. If the individual is already suffering from a reduction in blood flow to the kidneys for any reason, including "normal aging, liver or cardiovascular disease or simply dehydration from vomiting, diarrhea and fever accompanying the flu" (Squires, 1990, p. 4E), ibuprofen might either cause or at least contribute to acute kidney failure.

Patients who are suffering from systemic lupus erythematosus (lupus or SLE) should not use ibuprofen, except under a physician's supervision. Occasionally, ibuprofen has caused the development of a condition known as *aseptic meningitis* within hours of the time that a patient with SLE ingested the ibuprofen. Aseptic meningitis is also a complication in extremely rare cases in which a patient who does *not* have SLE has ingested ibuprofen (Zuger, 1994). However, there have been fewer than 40 reports of this side effect in patients who do not have SLE or some other autoimmune disorder.

When used by a client who is also taking lithium, ibuprofen may increase the blood levels of lithium by 25–60% (Rodman, 1993; Jenike, 1991). This effect is most pronounced in older people and may contribute to lithium toxicity in some individuals, according to the author. Close monitoring of blood lithium is necessary in patients who use both lithium and ibuprofen concurrently, to avoid the danger of lithium toxicity. Patients who are on lithium should report any use of ibuprofen, even OTC preparations, to the physician who is prescribing the lithium, so that appropriate steps may be taken.

Patients taking the prescription medication methotrexate should not use ibuprofen, because this drug reduces the rate at which methotrexate is excreted from the body (Rodman, 1993). Reduced excretion rates may result in toxic levels of methotrexate building up in the patient, according to the author. Rodman recommended acetaminophen if an OTC analgesic should be required. Also, ibuprofen should not be used in conjunction with other NSAIDs, including aspirin, except under a physician's supervision (Rodman, 1993). The combined effects of NSAIDs may result in excessive irritation to the gastrointestinal tract—and, possibly, severe bleeding.

Acetaminophen. Individuals with alcohol-related liver damage and individuals who are actively drinking should totally avoid the use of acetaminophen (Draganov, Durrence, Cox, & Reuben, 2000; Sands, Knapp, & Ciraulo, 1993; Johnston & Pelletier, 1997; Peterson, 1997). This is because the combined effects of alcohol and acetaminophen can produce toxic levels of the latter compound in the individual's body. When acetaminophen is ingested, about 4–5% of the drug is biotransformed into a toxic metabolite known as N-acetyl-p-benzoquinoneimine (Peterson, 1997). Normally, this metabolite of acetaminophen poses no danger to the user, and it is rapidly biotransformed into other substances by the liver enzyme glutathione. However, in cases where the user is actively drinking or has alcohol-induced liver damage, the body's supply of glutathione is rapidly depleted, even when the drug is used at recommended dosage levels; this sets the stage for acetaminophen toxicity.

Because of its cumulative toxic effects on the liver, acetaminophen should not be used longer than 10 days *at any dosage level* (Kacso & Terezhalmy, 1994). Another rare complication of acetaminophen use is the development of anaphylactic reactions on the part of the user. Acetaminophen has also been found to be *nephrotoxic*. That is, when used too often or at too high a dosage level, it may be toxic to the cells of the kidneys. To explore this possibility, Perneger, Whelton, and Klag (1994) examined the drug use patterns of 716 patients with what is known as end-stage renal disease (ESRD), and compared these data with the drug use patterns of 361 individuals of the same age who did not suffer from kidney disease. The authors found that patients who had taken as few as 1000 acetaminophen tablets during the course of their lifetime were twice as likely to develop ESRD as patients who did not use acetaminophen. Further, the authors found evidence to suggest a dose-related danger of ESRD when the patient consumed either more than 365 acetaminophen tablets in a year's time or a total of 1000 tablets in a lifetime. In other words, the authors suggest that beyond the cut-off limit, the greater the individual's use of acetaminophen, the greater the chances of that individual ultimately developing ESRD.

Whereas ESRD is a rare complication of OTC analgesic use, Perneger, Whelton, and Klag (1994) estimated that 8–10% of all cases of end-stage renal disease were caused by acetaminophen use. Their findings suggest that, as with all medications, acetaminophen should be utilized only when the benefits obtained through this OTC analgesic outweigh the dangers inherent in its use.

Naproxen. Much of the information available on naproxen and its effects is based on experience obtained with prescription forms of this chemical. Naproxen has been found to be a factor in potentially fatal allergic reactions, in some users. Patients with the "aspirin triad" (discussed earlier) should not use naproxen except under a physician's supervision. This medication may also contribute to the formation of peptic ulcers and to gastrointestinal bleeding. In rare cases, male users have experienced naproxen-induced problems achieving an erection and loss of the ability to ejaculate (Finger, Lund, & Slagel, 1997).

On occasion, naproxen has contributed to drowsiness, dizziness, feelings of depression, and vertigo. Patients have been known to experience diarrhea, heartburn, constipation, and vomiting while taking naproxen. Indeed, 3–9% of the patients who used prescription-strength naproxen experienced such side effects as constipation, heartburn, abdominal pain, and nausea. Taha, Dahill, Sturrock, Lee, and Russell (1994) found that 44% of their sample who had used naproxen for extended periods of time had evidence of gastrointestinal ulcers. It was not clear how representative these findings were of naproxen's ability to contribute to the formation of ulcers, but it is recommended that naproxen not be utilized by patients with a history of peptic ulcer disease (Dionne & Gordon, 1994).

As is true of acetaminophen, NSAIDs such as naproxen, but not aspirin itself, have been implicated as one cause of ESRD (Perneger, Whelton, & Klag, 1994). There have been rare reports of patients who developed side effects such as a skin rash, diarrhea, headache, insomnia, sleep problems, problems with their hearing, and/or tinnitus after using naproxen. There have also been reports of potentially fatal liver dysfunctions that seem to have been caused by naproxen. Thus, like all medications, naproxen should be used only when the benefits of this drug outweigh the potential dangers of using it.

Animal research has suggested the possibility of damage to the eyes as a result of naproxen use, although it is not clear at this time whether this medication may damage the visual system of a human being.

Ketoprofen. The side effects of ketoprofen are essentially the same as those seen with naproxen and other NSAID agents.

Overdose of OTC Analgesics

Acetaminophen. Acetaminophen is the drug most commonly ingested in an overdose attempt (Anker & Smilkstein, 1994; Lipscomb, 1989). Each year in the United States, there are an estimated 100,000 intentional cases of acetaminophen overdose (Sporer & Khayam-Bashi, 1996; Cetaruk, Dart, Horowitz, & Huribut, 1996). The fact that only 100 people died as a result of an acetaminophen overdose in 1994 is a tribute to the effectiveness of medical intervention in cases where an overdose of this drug was ingested, but it does not reflect the large number of people who are left with permanent organ damage as a result of their suicide attempt or who required a liver transplant in order to survive (Cetaruk, Dart, Horowitz, & Huribut, 1996).

Acetaminophen is often ingested by individuals, especially adolescents, who want to make a suicide gesture. Although the individual who makes this gesture rarely intends to commit suicide, the relatively low dose necessary to produce a toxic reaction to acetaminophen makes it a poor choice for an overdose. Because the first evidence of acetaminophen toxicity may not appear until 12–24 hours after the drug was ingested, the individual might falsely conclude that she or he is not at risk for adverse effects from the suicide gesture and not seek medical assistance until several hours, or even days, after the overdose was ingested.

The untreated acetaminophen overdose progresses through four different stages, if the patient lives. Within 30 minutes of the time the individual ingested the overdose, he or she will experience anorexia, nausea, and vomiting, in response to the effects of the acetaminophen on the GI tract (McDonough, 1998). In the second phase, which begins about 24 hours after the overdose was ingested, the individual will experience abdominal pain, oliguria[12] and pain over the liver (McDonough, 1998). During this phase, blood tests will reveal abnormal liver function. In the third phase, which begins 72–96 hours after the overdose was ingested, the individual will experience nausea, vomiting, jaundice, and symptoms of liver failure (McDonough, 1998). Other complications that might emerge during the third phase include hemorrhage, hypoglycemia, renal failure, and hypotensive episodes. It is during this phase that the individual might die if he or she ingested enough acetaminophen to be fatal.

However, if the person either did not ingest a fatal overdose or was treated for the overdose in time, she or he will proceed to the final phase: recovery. During the fourth phase, the liver gradually repairs itself, and recovery takes 2–4 weeks after the overdose was ingested (McDonough, 1998). It is unfortunate that the symptoms of an acetaminophen overdose can take so long to develop, because although an antidote to acetaminophen overdose is available, it must be administered *within twelve hours of when the overdose was ingested* to be fully effective. This antidote is a chemical known as *N-acetylcysteine* (NAC). When it is administered within several hours of the initial overdose, N-acetylcysteine is quite effective in the treatment of acetaminophen poisoning (American Medical Association, 1994). But if, as all too often happens, the individual waits until the symptoms of acetaminophen toxicity develop before seeking help, it may be too late to prevent permanent liver damage, or even death.

When taken in large doses, acetaminophen destroys the liver enzyme *glutathione*. Glutathione is a chemical that the liver produces to protect itself from various toxins (Anker & Smilkstein, 1994). Just 7.5–15 grams of acetaminophen (15–30 "extra-strength" tablets) in a single dose, or 5–8 grains (650–975 mg) per day for several weeks, is enough to cause a toxic reaction in the healthy adult (McDonough, 1998; Whitcomb & Block, 1994). For children, the toxic level is approximately 140 mg per kilogram of body weight.[13]

One factor that seems to contribute to liver damage in at least some cases is whether the individual ingested the acetaminophen on an empty stomach (Schiødt, Rochling, Casey, & Lee, 1997; Whitcomb & Block, 1994). Even otherwise normal patients who were attempting to control their weight through semi-starvation, or "fasting," seem to be especially at risk for an unintentional acetaminophen toxic reaction (Schiødt, Rochling, Casey, & Lee, 1997). The authors pointed out that the enzyme glutathione is depleted by starvation diets, placing the individual "at risk" for a toxic reaction to even normal dosage levels of acetaminophen. Thus the individual's diet is an important factor to consider when she or he is using acetaminophen for the control of mild to moderate levels of pain.

Supernaw (1991) also suggested that individuals who use acetaminophen at high dosage levels for extended periods of time (5000 mg/day for 2–3 weeks) were also at risk for drug-induced liver damage. However, Supernaw did not identify factors other than the chronic ingestion of above-normal acetaminophen doses that might contribute to hepatotoxicity. The results of these studies do suggest, however, that at least for certain individuals, acetaminophen has the potential to cause toxic reactions at dosage levels just above the normal therapeutic range.

---

[12] See the Glossary.

[13] *Any* suspected chemical overdose should be evaluated by a physician.

Aspirin is a drug that is commonly ingested in suicide gestures and attempts (Sporer & Khayam-Bashi, 1996). Unfortunately, although in the past 40 years scientists have learned a great deal about how an aspirin overdose affects the body (Yip, Dart, & Gabow, 1994), it remains a potentially dangerous chemical. For example, in 1990, aspirin caused approximately as many deaths in the United States as heroin overdoses (*Playboy*, 1991).

The average dosage level necessary to produce a toxic reaction to aspirin is about 10 grams for an adult and about 150 mg of aspirin for every kilogram of body weight for children. A dose of 500 mg of aspirin per kilogram of bodyweight is potentially fatal to the individual. Symptoms of aspirin toxicity include headache, dizziness, tinnitus, mental confusion, increased sweating, thirst, dimming of sight, and hearing impairment (Shannon, Wilson, & Stang, 1995). Some other possible effects of aspirin overdose are restlessness, excitement, apprehension, tremor, delirium, hallucinations, convulsions, stupor, coma, hypotension, and (at higher dosage levels) death (Sporer & Khayam-Bashi, 1996). Although these symptoms are most often seen in the person who has ingested a large dose of aspirin, even small doses can result in toxicity for the individual who is aspirin-sensitive.

Ibuprofen. Ibuprofen's popularity as an OTC analgesic has resulted in an increasing number of overdose attempts involving this drug (Lipscomb, 1989). Symptoms of overdose include seizures, acute renal failure, abdominal pain, nausea, vomiting, drowsiness, and metabolic acidosis (Lipscomb, 1989). There is no specific antidote for a toxic dose of ibuprofen, and medical care is often aimed at supportive treatment only.

Naproxen. The *Physician's Desk Reference* (Medical Economics Company, 1999) reported that the life-threatening dose of naproxen in humans is not known. Animal research involving dogs suggests that a dose of 1000 mg/kg is potentially fatal, although in hamsters the LD_{100} was estimated to be 4100 mg/kg. No specific antidote is known for an overdose of naproxen, and medical care is limited to supportive treatment. There are no symptoms specific to a naproxen overdose. Symptoms of an NSAID overdose include lethargy, drowsiness, nausea, vomiting, epigastric pain, respiratory depression, coma, and convulsions. The NSAIDs are capable of causing GI bleeding in overdose situa-

tions, and they may cause either hypotension or hypertension (Medical Economics Company, 1999). An overdose of naproxen is considered a medical emergency, and the overdose victim should be evaluated by a physician.

Ketoprofen. There is limited information about ketoprofen overdose. The 1999 *Physician's Desk Reference* identified 26 overdoses for the prescription form of ketoprofen known as Orudis (Medical Economics Company, 1999). There were no fatalities, although it should be noted that these overdoses reflect cases where the patient received immediate medical care. There are no symptoms specific to a ketoprofen overdose. Symptoms of NSAID overdose include lethargy, drowsiness, nausea, vomiting, epigastric pain, respiratory depression, coma, and convulsions. The NSAIDs are capable of causing GI bleeding in overdose situations and may cause either hypotension or hypertension (Medical Economics Company, 1999). An overdose of naproxen or ketoprofen is considered a medical emergency, and the overdose victim should be evaluated by a physician. The basic treatment procedures involve supportive treatment, as well as interventions designed to treat the individual's specific problems as they emerge (Medical Economics Company, 1999).

Summary

Over-the-counter analgesics are often discounted as not being "real" medications. But aspirin is America's most popular "drug." Each year, more than 20,000 tons of aspirin are manufactured and consumed in this country alone, and even so, aspirin accounts for only about 28% of the OTC analgesic sales.

Aspirin, acetaminophen, naproxen, and ibuprofen are all quite effective in the control of mild to moderate levels of pain, without exposing the patient to the side effects found with narcotic analgesics. Some of the OTC analgesics are also useful in controlling the inflammation of autoimmune disorders and in helping to control postsurgical pain. Researchers have discovered that the OTC analgesics are of value in controlling the pain associated with cancer, and in the case of aspirin, they may even contribute to the early detection of some forms of cancer. In spite of the fact that the oldest OTC analgesic, aspirin, was introduced more than a century ago, medical researchers are still discovering new applications for this potent medication and its chemical cousins.

In spite of the fact that they are available over the counter, the OTC analgesics do carry significant potential for harm. Acetaminophen at near-normal dosage levels has been implicated in toxic reactions in chronic alcohol users. It also has been implicated as the cause of death in people who have taken acetaminophen overdoses. Aspirin and ibuprofen have been implicated in fatal allergic reactions, especially in those who suffer from asthma. The use of aspirin in children with viral infections is not recommended.

CHAPTER NINETEEN

Tobacco Products and Nicotine Addiction

Introduction

Historians believe that the natives of the New World had used tobacco for many hundreds, if not thousands, of years before the arrival of the first European explorers. Tobacco was used in various religious ceremonies and for recreational purposes by the natives of North America. After the discovery of the "New World," the early explorers, many of whom had themselves adopted the habit of smoking tobacco during their time in the Americas, carried it back across the Atlantic to Europe.

In Europe, the use of tobacco for smoking was received with some skepticism, if not outright hostility. For example, in Germany, public smoking was once punishable by death, and in Russia, castration was the sentence for the same crime (Berger & Dunn, 1982). In Asia, the early Chinese rulers made the use or distribution of tobacco a crime punishable by death, and smokers were executed as infidels in Turkey. Despite these harsh measures, the practice of smoking became quite popular in Europe. Within a few decades of its introduction, the use of tobacco had spread across Europe and moved into Asia (Schuckit, 1995a).

In spite of a strong initial response against smoking in Europe, the practice soon became at least moderately acceptable in European society. Indeed, European physicians thought of tobacco as a medicine, and its use was encouraged as a cure for numerous conditions. Its use was interpreted as a mark of sophistication in both Europe and North America in the 19th and 20th centuries, but in the last half of the 20th century, tobacco use began to be criticized, especially after

medical research demonstrated an association between cigarette smoking and various diseases. In the first years of the 21st century, tobacco use is both widespread and the subject of much controversy. This chapter, reviews the history of tobacco use and the complications caused by using tobacco.

History of Tobacco Use in the United States

In reviewing tobacco use over the years, it is important to keep in mind that today's tobacco is much different from the tobacco used centuries ago. The tobacco that was used in the New World when the first European explorers arrived was probably "more potent and may have contained high concentrations of psychoactive substances" (Schuckit, 1995, p. 259) when compared to the tobacco of today. But European tobacco growers soon learned to substitute the milder, more acceptable *Nicotiana tabacum* for the more potent *Nicotina rustica* that the Native Americans used for their religious ceremonies (Hilts, 1996).

Several different forces combined in the mid-19th century to change the shape of tobacco use. First, new varieties of tobacco were planted, allowing for a greater yield than in previous years. Second, new methods of curing the leaf of the tobacco plant were found, speeding up the preparation of the leaf for use. Third, the manner in which tobacco was used changed. The advent of the industrial age brought with it machinery capable of manufacturing the cigarette, a smaller, less expensive, and neater way to smoke than cigars. Before then, cigars had been manufactured by hand—a slow, expensive process. However, just one machine, which was invented by James A. Bonsack, could produce 120,000 cigarettes a day. The development of such machines greatly increased the number of cigarettes that could be produced, increasing supply while reducing the price. This made it possible for the less affluent to afford tobacco products, and cigarettes soon became a favorite of the poor (Tate, 1989). For example, by the year 1890, the price of domestic cigarettes had fallen to a nickel for a pack of 20 (Tate, 1989), making them affordable to all but the poorest smoker. But the rapid acceptance of cigarettes was not always automatic. Indeed, by 1909, ten different states had laws that prohibited the use of cigarettes.

Prior to the introduction of the cigarette, the major method of tobacco use was chewing. The practice of chewing tobacco, and then spitting into the ever-present cuspidor, contributed to the spread of tuberculosis and other diseases (Brecher, 1972). Because of this, public health officials began to campaign against the practice of chewing tobacco after the year 1910. The new cigarette, manufactured in large numbers by the latest machines, provided a more sanitary and relatively inexpensive alternative to chewing tobacco. Cigarette smokers soon discovered that the smoke of the new cigarette was so mild that it could be inhaled (Burns, 1991). (The smoke from pipes or cigars is much more bitter, making it unlikely that the smoker will inhale deeply.) For many, cigarette smoking became the preferred method of servicing their nicotine addiction. The world has never been the same since.

Scope of the Problem

Cigarettes became popular after these changes took place in the tobacco industry. In the year 1900, the per capita cigarette consumption in the United States was just 54 cigarettes (United States Department of Health & Human Services, 1999). The use of cigarettes grew in popularity during and immediately after World War I, and this growth in cigarette smoking continued until its peak in the mid-1960s (Schuckit, 1995a). The social climate was one of "total social acceptance" (Jaffe, 1989, p. 680) of tobacco use, and "[until] quite recently, tobacco use was so common and socially acceptable

[that] almost everyone tried smoking" (p. 680). At the peak of its popularity, approximately 52 percent of adult American males and 32 percent of adult American females were cigarette smokers (Schuckit, 1995a).

Then, in 1964, the surgeon general of the United States released a report stating that cigarette smoking was a danger to the smoker's health and outlined the various problems that were thought to be caused by smoking. In doing so, the surgeon general joined a battle against smoking that had been going on since the late 1800s (Tate, 1989). The number of adults who continued to smoke in this country declined in the wake of the 1964 Report of the Surgeon General, and then leveled off in the mid-1990s. Currently, approximately 26% of the men and 22% of the women in the United States report that they smoke cigarettes (U.S. Department of Health and Human Services, 2000).

In the year 1960, approximately 4171 cigarettes were smoked for every person over the age of 18 (U.S. Department of Health and Human Services, 1994). This figure reached a peak in 1966, when 4287 cigarettes were smoked for every person over the age of 18 in this country. Since then, this figure has gradually been dropping. In 1998, the per capita consumption of cigarettes dropped to 2261 cigarettes for every person over the age of 18, as shown in Figure 19.1 (U.S. Department of Health and Human Services, 1999).

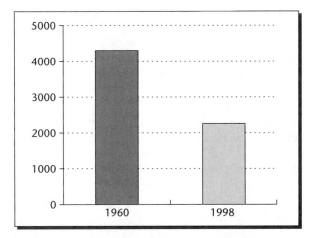

FIGURE 19.1 Comparison of 1960 per capita cigarette consumption with 1998 per capita cigarette consumption in the United States.

At the start of the 21st century, approximately three-quarters of those individuals between 15 and 54 have smoked at least 1 cigarette (Anthony, Arria, & Johnson, 1995). Most of those who smoke 1 cigarette do so out of curiosity. However, the authors also suggested that one in every three individuals who smoke that first cigarette will continue to smoke until they become addicted. For these individuals, the interval between experimental cigarette use and daily smoking is 2–3 years (Schwartz, 1996). Of the estimated 265 million people in the United States, approximately 46 million are thought to smoke cigarettes. Of this number, approximately 24 million are male and 22 million female. Unfortunately, in spite of the fact that the purchase of cigarettes by adolescents is illegal, 3.1 million of those who smoke are teenagers (Roberts & Watson, 1994).

Only a small minority of cigarette smokers abuse other chemicals, but it is not uncommon for substance abusers to be heavy smokers (Bobo, Slade, & Hoffman, 1995). Estimates of the prevalence of cigarette use suggests that cigarette smoking is two to three times higher in substance-abusing populations than in the general population, according to the authors. An estimated 74% of alcohol-dependent individuals, 77% of cocaine-dependent persons, and 85% of those who were dependent on heroin also smoked cigarettes (Bobo, Slade, & Hoffman, 1995). McIlvain, Bobo, Leed-Kelly, and Sitorius (1998) gave an even higher estimate, stating that 80–95% of all chemically dependent persons were cigarette smokers. These figures suggest that cigarette use is a significant problem for those who are addicted to chemicals in the United States.

Researchers have found that the average age at which the individual begins to experiment with cigarette smoking is about 12, and fully 90% of those individuals who begin to smoke will be regular smokers by the age of 14 (Hogan, 2000). But people's attitudes toward smoking are established even before they light that first cigarette—in childhood or, at the latest, by early adolescence. This is true even in those cases where the individual does not *begin* to smoke until late adolescence or early adulthood.

Pharmacology of Cigarette Smoking

The primary method by which tobacco is used is by smoking cigarettes (Schuckit, 1995a), although chewing tobacco and smoking cigars have again become popular in recent years. Chemically, cigar smoke is very similar to that of cigarette smoke, although it does contain a higher concentration of ammonia (Jacobs, Thun, & Apicella, 1999). For these reasons, the terms "smoking," "cigarette," and "tobacco" will be used interchangeably in this chapter, except when other forms of tobacco (such as tobacco prepared for chewing) are discussed.

Several variables that influence the composition of tobacco smoke (Jaffe, 1990): (1) the exact composition of the tobacco being used, (2) how densely the tobacco is packed in the cigarette, (3) the length of the column of tobacco (for cigarette and cigar smokers), (4) the characteristics of the filter being used (if any), (5) the paper being used (for cigarette smokers), and (6) the temperature at which the tobacco is burned. To complicate matters further, the cigarette of today is far different than the cigarette of 1900, or even that of 1950. According to Hilts (1996), up to 40% of today's typical cigarette is composed of "leftover stems, scraps and dust" (p. 44). Whereas in 1955 it took 2.6 pounds of tobacco leaves to produce a thousand cigarettes, the use of these fillers has reduced the amount of tobacco needed to produce a thousand cigarettes to 1.7 pounds (Hilts, 1996). It is easy to understand how today's profit margin on a cigarette is approximately 34% (Kadlec, Pascual, & Perman, 1997).

Cigarette tobacco smoke contains some 4000 different compounds, of which some 2550 come from the unprocessed tobacco itself (Burns, 1991). The remaining compounds come from additives, pesticides, and a range of other organic or metallic compounds that are incorporated into the cigarette tobacco either intentionally or unintentionally. Here is a partial list of the compounds found in tobacco smoke, or produced by the process of smoking tobacco:

> Carbon monoxide, carbon dioxide, nitrogen oxides, ammonia, volatile nitrosamines, hydrogen cyanide, volatile sulfur-containing compounds, nitrites and other nitrogen-containing compounds, volatile hydrocarbons, alcohols, and aldehydes and ketones (e.g., acetaldehyde, formaldehyde and acrolein). (Jaffe, 1990, p. 545)

In addition to all of these compounds, various perfumes are added to the tobacco leaves to give the cigarette a distinctive aroma (Hilts, 1996). Other compounds found in cigarettes or in the paper wrapper include various forms of sugar, insecticides, herbicides, fungicides, rodenticides, pesticides, and various manufacturing machine lubricants (which come into contact with the tobacco leaves or paper as these products move through machines used in the manufacturing process (Glantz, Slade, Bero, Hanauer, & Barnes, 1996). Although the smoker inhales these products when she or he smokes a cigarette, there has been virtually no research into the effects of these chemicals on the human body when they are smoked.

The concentrations of many of the chemicals found in cigarette smoke, such as carbon monoxide, are such that "uninterrupted exposure" (Burns, 1991, p. 633) would result in death. For example, the concentration of carbon monoxide found in cigarettes is "similar to that found in automobile exhaust" (p. 633), a known source of potentially dangerous concentrations of this chemical. Researchers have found that cigarette smoke also contains radioactive compounds, such as polonium-210 (Evans, 1993; Jaffe, 1990), and lead-210 (Brownson, Novotny, & Perry, 1993). These compounds for the most part are absorbed from the soil in which tobacco is grown. When the individual smokes, these radioactive compounds are carried into the lungs along with the smoke. Over a one-year period, the cumulative radiation exposure for a 2-pack/day smoker is equal to what a person would receive from 250–300 chest x-rays (Evans, 1993). Further, cigarette smoke is known to contain a small amount of arsenic (Banerjee, 1990).

Some of the chemicals found in tobacco smoke, such as benzene, are documented carcinogens.[1] At least 43 known or suspected carcinogens are found in cigarette smoke, and the smoker introduces these compounds into the body when he or she smokes (Hilts, 1996; Burns, 1991).

Nicotine. As a result of legal action against tobacco companies in the last years of the 20th century, it has come to light that these companies have long known that nicotine is the major psychoactive agent in cigarettes. Indeed, there is evidence that tobacco companies have long viewed cigarettes as little more than a single-dose container of nicotine that will quickly administer the chemical to the user (Hilts, 1996; Glantz, Slade, Bero, Hanauer, & Barnes, 1996; Glantz, Barnes, Bero, Hanauer, & Slade, 1995; Benowitz & Henningfield, 1994). There is strong evidence that tobacco companies selectively grew strains of tobacco plants with higher nicotine levels in the leaves, for use in producing cigarettes (*60 Minutes*, 1996b). In the settlement of a class-action lawsuit against the tobacco industry by 40 of the 50 states, the industry agreed to the Food and Drug Administration's gradually lowering the amount of nicotine permitted in cigarettes over the next 12 years (Smolowe, 1997).

Although nicotine is well absorbed through the gastrointestinal tract, much of orally administered nicotine is biotransformed by the liver as a result of the "first-pass metabolism" effect (see Chapter 3). To circumvent this process, tobacco companies encourage the use of cigarettes over the oral use of tobacco products. With each "puff" on a cigarettes, a small dose of nicotine gains admission to the circulation, and from there it reaches the brain in between 7 (Fiore, Jorenby, Baker, & Kenford, 1992) and 8 seconds (Hilts, 1996; Jaffe, 1990). The 1-pack/day smoker self-administers 60–80,000 doses of nicotine per day without the nicotine being subjected to "first-pass metabolism" (Parrott, 1999; Jorenby, 1997). Through this process, the smoker "overlearns" the nicotine self-administration process, receiving another dose of nicotine with each puff.

The lethal dose of nicotine for the average adult is estimated to be approximately 60 mg (Ashton, 1992). Although the average cigarette contains between 6 and 11 milligrams (mg) of nicotine (Henningfield, 1995), the bioavailability of nicotine from cigarette smoking is only 3–40% (Benowitz & Henningfield, 1994). This is because nicotine is not able to cross readily from the lungs to the blood. Thus the typical smoker absorbs only 1–3 mg of nicotine from each cigarette (Henningfield, 1995). In terms of absolute toxicity, the typical smoker receives between 1/60 and 1/24 of the estimated lethal dose of nicotine each time she or he smokes a cigarette. Over the course of the typical day, the average smoker absorbs a cumulative dose of 20–40 mg of nicotine, a dosage level that is quite toxic to the body (Henningfield, 1995).

Once in the body, nicotine is rapidly distributed to virtually every blood-rich tissue in the body, such as the lungs and the spleen, as well as the brain (Henningfield

[1]See the Glossary.

& Nemeth-Coslett, 1988). Nicotine is both water-soluble and lipid-soluble, so it crosses the blood–brain barrier very rapidly. Indeed, the measured levels of nicotine in the brain are twice as high as the level found in the blood (Fiore, Jorenby, Baker, & Kenford, 1992). Only between 0.05 and 2.5 mg of the nicotine from each cigarette actually reaches the brain (Lee & D'Alonzo, 1993; Ashton, 1992), where nicotine's effects are "similar to those of cocaine and amphetamine" (Rustin, 1988, p. 18). This accounts for the subjective reports that cigarette smoking causes the user to experience a nicotine-induced "high," a sense of release from stress, or possibly a sense of euphoria (Fiore, Jorenby, Baker, & Kenford, 1992). The reinforcement potential is one of the subjective effects of nicotine that we will discuss.

In the brain, nicotine stimulates the release of several different neurotransmitters, including the discharge of ß-endorphin from certain neurons in the limbic system. ß-endorphin is a neurotransmitter thought to be about 200 times as potent as morphine (Jorenby, 1997). Nicotine also causes the release of the neurotransmitter dopamine within the region of the limbic system known as the nucleus accumbens (Miller & Gold, 1993). These facts may account for the feeling of pleasure that many cigarette smokers report. Another region of the brain where nicotine exerts a major effect is the medulla, which is responsible for such functions as swallowing, vomiting, respiration, and the control of blood pressure (Restock, 1984). This is also why many first-time smokers experience both nausea and vomiting (Jaffe, 1990). However, with repeated exposure to tobacco chewing/smoking, the smoker becomes tolerant to this effect and no longer experiences nausea. Nicotine also stimulates the release of acetylcholine, a neurotransmitter involved in controlling many of the body's muscle functions. Nicotine-induced acetylcholine release seems to account, at least in part, for nicotine's immediate effects on the cardiovascular system, such as an increase in heart rate and blood pressure, as well as an increase in the strength of heart contractions (Jorenby, 1997). At the same time that the heart rate is increased, nicotine causes the blood vessels in the outer regions of the body to constrict, causing a reduction in peripheral blood flow (Schuckit, 1995a).

In addition to its effects on the brain, nicotine causes a decrease in the strength of stomach contractions

(Schuckit, 1995a), and cigarette smoke itself can irritate the tissues of the lungs and pulmonary system. Cigarette smoking deposits potentially harmful chemicals in the lungs and reduces the motion of the cilia[2] in the lungs. These features of cigarette smoking are thought to contribute to the development of pulmonary problems in long-term smokers.

Peak concentrations of nicotine are reached in the first minutes after the cigarette is smoked, and then the level of nicotine in the blood starts to drop. The biological half-life of nicotine is between 100 minutes (Rustin, 1992) and 2 hours, (Fiore, Jorenby, Baker, & Kenford, 1992). Because only 50% of the nicotine from one cigarette is biotransformed during the first half-life, over the course of a day a reservoir of unmetabolized nicotine is established in the smoker's body. A limited degree of tolerance to nicotine's effects develops each day, but this acquired tolerance is lost just as rapidly during the night hours when the typical smoker abstains from cigarette use (Bhandari, Sylvester, & Rigotti, 1996). This is why many smokers find that the first cigarette of the day has a strong effect.

Only 5–10% of the nicotine that enters the body is excreted unchanged. The rest is biotransformed by the liver. About 90% of the nicotine that is biotransformed is turned into *cotinine*, a metabolite of nicotine that has no known psychoactive properties. The other 10% of the nicotine is biotransformed into *nicotine-n-oxide*. These chemicals are then excreted from the body in the urine. Although it was once thought that cigarette smokers biotransformed nicotine more rapidly than nonsmokers, research has failed to support this belief (Benowitz & Jacob, 1993).

Acetaldehyde. In addition to nicotine, tobacco smoke includes a small amount of acetaldehyde. By coincidence, this is also the first metabolite produced by the liver when the body biotransforms alcohol. In terms of its psychoactive potential, acetaldehyde is thought to be more potent than alcohol. And like alcohol, acetaldehyde has a sedative effect on the user, which may be why cigarette smoking helps some smokers to relax (Rustin, 1988).

Cigarette smoking and Alzheimer's disease? In the early 1990s, researchers found a "negative association" (Brenner, Kukull, van Belle, Bowen, McCormick, Teri,

[2]See the Glossary.

& Larson, 1993, p. 293) between cigarette smoking and the later development of Alzheimer's disease. However, subsequent research failed to support this association (Riggs, 1996). Indeed, cigarette smokers were found to be at *increased* risk for developing some form of dementia in later life (Ott, Slooter, Hofman, van Harskamp, Witteman, Broeckhoven, & van Duijn, 1998).

Drug interactions between nicotine and other chemicals. Drug interactions between nicotine and various other therapeutic agents are well documented. Cigarette smokers, for example, require more morphine for the control of pain (Bond, 1989; Jaffe, 1990). Tobacco smokers may experience less sedation from benzodiazepines than do nonsmokers (Barnhill, Ciraulo, Ciraulo, & Greene, 1995). Thus the physician treating the patient who smokes might need to adjust the individual's daily benzodiazepine dose in order to achieve the desired level of sedation. Surprisingly, cigarette smokers seem to be able to biotransform THC faster than nonsmokers, so the effects of marijuana do not last quite as long in the cigarette smoker as in the nonsmoker (Nelson, 2000).

Cigarette smoking interacts with alcohol in a number of ways. First, cigarette smoking slows the process of gastric emptying—and thus the process of alcohol absorption (Nelson, 2000). Further, the nicotine absorbed by the smoker seems to counteract some of the sedation seen with alcohol use, which may explain why up to 95% of heavy drinkers also smoke.[3] Tobacco also interacts with many anticoagulants, as well as with the beta blocker propranol and with caffeine (Bond, 1989). Women who use oral contraceptives and who smoke are more likely to experience strokes, myocardial infarction, and thromboembolism than their nonsmoking counterparts, according to the author.

When cigarette smokers who use the medication theophylline stop smoking, they will experience a 36% rise in theophylline blood levels over the first week of abstinence. This seems to be due to the effects of such chemicals as benzopyrene, which are found in the tobacco smoke (Henningfield, 1995). Also, the concentration of caffeine in the blood may increase by as much as 250% following smoking cessation. Unfortunately, one of the effects of this high concentration of caffeine

is to cause substance-induced anxiety, which may convince the former smoker that she or he should have a cigarette.

Nicotine use has been found to decrease the blood levels of clozapine and of the antipsychotic medication haloperidol by as much as 30% (American Psychiatric Association, 1996). It has been found to increase the blood levels of medications such as clomipramine and of antidepressant medications such as desipramine, dozepin, and nortriptyline, according to the American Psychiatric Association. This list of potential interactions between nicotine and various pharmaceuticals is not exhaustive, but it highlights the fact that nicotine has a very strong effect on how other chemicals work in the human body.[4]

Subjective Effects of Nicotine Use

There is still much to be discovered about nicotine's effects on the central nervous system. It is thought that nicotine can bring about a dose-dependent, biphasic response at the level of the individual neurons of the brain, especially those that utilize the neurotransmitter acetylcholine (Ritz, 1999; Ashton, 1992; Restak, 1991; Benowitz, 1992). Initially, nicotine stimulates these neurons, perhaps contributing to the feeling of increased alertness on the part of the smoker. Over longer periods of time, however, the nicotine blocks the effects of acetylcholine, reducing the rate at which those neurons fire.

This theory would seem to account for the observed effects of cigarette smoking. Smokers are known to experience stimulation of the brain (Schuckit, 1995a), as well as decreased muscle tone (Jaffe, 1990). This is one reason why many smokers find that cigarette smoking helps them to relax when they are under pressure. About 90% of cigarette smokers report a sense of pleasure when they smoke (Ashton, 1992). This may, as animal research suggests, reflect the ability of nicotine to stimulate the release of the neurotransmitters norepinephrine and dopamine (Jaffe, 1990), chemicals known to be used by the brain's "pleasure system."

---

[3]The author of this text has met many alcohol abusers who report that they smoke *only* while they are drinking.

[4]In order to avoid potentially dangerous interaction effects between any pharmaceutical and a compound found in cigarettes, you should ask a physician or pharmacist whether there is any danger in taking that medicine while smoking.

The first-time smoker will report a sense of nausea and may even vomit (Restak, 1991). However, if the individual persists in his or her attempts to smoke, the stimulation of the neurotransmitter systems eventually results in an association between smoking and the nicotine-induced pleasurable sensations that occur as the neurotransmitters norepinephrine and dopamine are released within the brain.

Nicotine Addiction

Tobacco companies have understood that nicotine is addictive since at least the early 1960s, but this research was apparently suppressed by the tobacco industry for many years (Hurt & Robertson, 1998; Slade, Bero, Hanauer, Barnes, & Glantz, 1995). Indeed, one memo from 1963 illustrates how the tobacco industry knew that it was "in the business of selling nicotine, an addictive drug . . ." (p. 228) to smokers. However, it was not until 1997 that a major tobacco company in the United States, the Liggett Group, admitted in court that tobacco is addictive (Solomon, Rogers, Katel, & Lach 1997).

The addictive potential of cigarettes would seem to be significantly greater than that of cocaine, as illustrated by the observation that whereas only 3–20% of those who try cocaine once go on to become addicted to it (Musto, 1991), fully 33–50% of those who experiment with smoking will go on to become addicted (Henningfield, 1995; Pomerleau, Collins, Shiffman, & Pomerleau, 1993). Further, as with the other drugs of abuse, the greater the individual's level of exposure to cigarette smoking, the greater his or her chances of becoming addicted. Jaffe (1989) concluded that "a very high percentage" (p. 680) of those who smoke 100 cigarettes will go on to become daily smokers. Walker (1993) gave an even more frightening figure, noting that children who smoke just 4 cigarettes stand a 94% chance of continuing to smoke.

Even so, not everybody who begins to smoke will go on to become addicted to nicotine (Henningfield & Nemeth-Coslett, 1988). A small minority (perhaps 5–10%) of those who smoke cigarettes are not addicted to nicotine (Jarvik & Schneider, 1992; Shiffman, Fischer, Zettler-Segal, & Benowitz, 1990). These individuals, who demonstrate an episodic pattern of nicotine use, are classified as cigarette "chippers." As a group, chippers do not appear to smoke in response to social pressures, and they do not seem to smoke to avoid the symptoms of withdrawal (Shiffman, Fischer, Zettler-Segal, & Benowitz, 1990). Unfortunately, very little is known about the phenomenon of tobacco chipping, and researchers still do not understand what personality or biological characteristics separate those who chip from those who go on to become addicted to cigarette smoking.

It is known that 90–95% of those who smoke are addicted to nicotine. These individuals demonstrate all of the characteristics typically seen in drug addiction: tolerance, withdrawal symptoms, and drug-seeking behaviors (Rustin, 1992; 1988). Further, like drug abusers, tobacco users develop highly individual drug-using rituals that seem to provide the individual with a sense of security and contribute to the individual's tendency to smoke when she or he is anxious.

Unfortunately, for those individuals who are addicted to nicotine, their chemical addiction is a very real problem. Only 2–3% of those individuals who try to quit cigarette smoking each year are able to do so (Henningfield, 1995). To illustrate the addictive potential of cigarettes, one study of 1000 drug-addicted individuals found that 74% rated the task of quitting cigarette use at least as difficult as giving up their drug of choice (Kozlowski, Wilkinson, Skinner, Kent, Franklin, & Pope. 1989).

Cigarette smokers tend to smoke in such a way as to regulate the nicotine level in their blood (Djordjevic, Hoffmann, & Hoffmann, 1997). When given cigarettes of a high nicotine content, smokers use fewer cigarettes, whereas when given low-nicotine cigarettes, they smoke more of them (Djordjevic, Hoffmann, & Hoffmann, 1997; Benowitz, 1992; Jaffe, 1990). Smokers of "low-tar" brands also have been found to inhale more deeply, and to hold the smoke in their lungs longer, than smokers of cigarette brands with higher levels of "tar" (Djordjevic, Hoffmann, & Hoffmann, 1997). This difference in smoking pattern may account for the increase in the frequency with which certain forms of cancer develop in the lungs of some smokers. Obviously, there is a need for more research into how the "tar" content of a cigarette affects the manner in which the smoker engages in the habit of cigarette smoking.

Nicotine withdrawal. Withdrawal symptoms usually begin within 2 hours of the last use of tobacco, peak within 24 hours (Kaplan & Sadock, 1996), and then gradually decline over the next 10 days to several weeks (Hughes, 1992; Jaffe, 1989). The exact nature of the withdrawal symptoms varies from person to person. Surprisingly, in light of the numerous horror stories about the agony of giving up cigarette smoking, approximately one-quarter of those who quit smoking cigarettes report no significant withdrawal symptoms at all (Benowitz, 1992).

The symptoms of nicotine withdrawal include sleep disturbance, irritability, impatience, difficulty in concentrating, restlessness, a "craving" for tobacco, hunger, gastrointestinal upset, headache, and drowsiness (Fiore, Jorenby, Baker, & Kenford, 1992; Hughes, 1992). Other possible symptoms include depression, hostility, fatigue, lightheadedness, headaches, a tingling sensation in the limbs, constipation, and increased coughing (Jarvik & Schneider, 1992). Although smokers often report stress and anxiety during the early stages of cigarette withdrawal, some clinicians believe that these symptoms are caused by the process of smoking, not by the withdrawal process itself (Parrott, 1999; West & Hajek, 1997). The subjective distress caused by the cigarette withdrawal syndrome gradually decreases in frequency and intensity in the first two weeks after the individual's last cigarette. However, some withdrawal discomfort and "craving" for cigarettes may continue for more than six months after the last cigarette (Hughes, Gust, Skoog, Keenan, & Fenwick, 1991).

There is evidence that those individuals who smoke more tend to experience stronger withdrawal symptoms than "light" or "moderate" smokers (Jaffe, 1990). However, there has been little research into what smoking patterns or biochemical markers might be associated with more severe withdrawal symptoms. It *is* known that within two weeks of the last cigarette, the individual's heart rate and blood pressure begin to drop and there is an improvement in peripheral blood flow patterns (Jarvik & Schneider, 1992; Hughes, 1992). Although there is evidence that smoking cessation exacerbates preexisting depressive disorders in some people (Breslau, Kilbey, & Andreski, 1993; Jaffe, 1990), it is not clear whether this is a direct result of the withdrawal process from nicotine. Cigarette smoking and depression may be separate conditions that are influenced by the same genetic factors and thus tend to appear in the same people (Glassman, 1993; Breslau, Kilbey, & Andreski, 1993).

Another possible explanation for the observed relationship between cigarette smoking and depression is that cigarette smokers tend to use nicotine as a way to cope with negative emotional states such as anxiety, boredom, sadness, and depression (Sherman, 1994). Because nicotine quickly becomes an easily administered method for coping with these feelings, the smoker soon learns that he or she can control negative emotional states through the use of cigarettes. Thus people prone to depression might learn to "self-medicate" their depression through the use of cigarette smoking, rather than the depression being a consequence of smoking cessation.

Smoking cessation and weight gain. Smokers who stop smoking often report what is to them a distressing increase in weight during the first few weeks of abstinence. In spite of intense research efforts, the exact mechanism by which post-cessation weight gain comes about remains unknown (Eisen, Lyons, Goldberg, & True, 1993). One theory holds that cigarette smoking helps to suppress the individual's appetite (Jaffe, 1990). If this theory is accurate, then it would seem logical to assume that this smoking-related loss of appetite is reversed with the person stops smoking. But a smoker also tends to retain less fluid than a nonsmoker, and this may account for some of the weight gain noted after a person stops smoking.

Researchers have discovered that the average male smoker gains 2.8 kilograms (6.1 pounds)[5] and the average female smoker 3.8 kilograms (8.4 pounds) after they stop smoking (Williamson, Madans, Anda, Kleinman, Giovino, & Byers, 1991). For a minority of ex-smokers, some 10% of the men and 13% of the women who stop smoking, however, a larger weight gain of 13 kilograms (28.6 pounds) is observed in the weeks and months following the last cigarette. Surprisingly, research has suggested a relationship between *successful* smoking cessation and weight gain. Those individuals who gain weight following smoking cessation seem to be more likely to remain abstinent following their last cigarette (Hughes *et al.*, 1991). For example, Klesges, Winders, Meyers, Eck, Ward, Hultquist, Ray, and Shadish (1997) found that those former smokers who remained abstinent for an entire year averaged a 13-pound (5.90-kg) weight

---

[5] There are 2.2046 pounds per kilogram.

gain, whereas smokers who had "slipped" during the initial year had a smaller average weight gain of 6.7 pounds (3.04 kg). Although the initial weight gain is often distressing to the former smoker, there is strong evidence that the individual's weight will return "to precessation levels at 6 months" (Hughes *et al.*, 1991, p. 57).

As interesting twist to the problem of weight gain after cessation of smoking was suggested by Williamson, Madans, Anda, Kleinman, Giovino, and Byers (1991). As expected, the authors found that the average smoker in their sample weighed less than individuals who had never smoked. But "[by] the end of the study . . . the mean body weight of those who had quit had increased only to that of those who had never smoked" (p. 743). The implication of this study is that the weight gain following the decision to quit tobacco use might reflect the body's readjustment to appropriate weight levels, as opposed to smoking-induced anorexic-like weight levels (Williamson *et al.*, 1991).

Although obesity is a known risk factor for cardiovascular disease, the health benefits obtained by giving up cigarette use far outweigh the potential risks associated with any associated weight gain (Eisen, Lyons, Goldberg, & True, 1993). This is clearly seen in the fact that a former smoker would have to gain 50–100 pounds after giving up cigarettes before the health risks of the extra weight came close to those inherent in cigarette smoking (Brunton, Henningfield, & Solberg, 1994).

Complications of the Chronic Use of Tobacco

The impact of smoking on any given individual is quite difficult to determine. For example, consider the manner in which the exact amount of nicotine, "tar," and carbon monoxide obtained from a specific brand of cigarette is determined: The cigarette is "smoked" by a test machine, and the composition of the smoke is then analyzed (Hilts, 1994). Because this is a mechanical process, the test data obtained through this method bear little relationship to the chemicals the average smoker will inhale.[6] The machine does not hold the

cigarette with fingers that might block the microscopic holes in the filter of the cigarette, nor does it inhale the cigarette smoke deeply into the lungs in order to savor the flavor of the smoke. These smoker-specific behaviors all influence exactly which chemicals, and in what concentration, gain admission to the body when a person smokes a cigarette.

By the middle of the 20th century, researchers at the Mayo Clinic had found a relationship between smoking and coronary artery disease (Bartecchi, MacKenzie, & Schrier, 1994a). In the next half-century, thousands of research studies identified a relationship between cigarette smoking and other forms of illness. Scientists now believe that tobacco use causes of 19% of the annual deaths in the United States, resulting in an estimated 420,000 premature deaths in this country alone (Miller, 1999; Benson & Sacco, 2000). An additional 56,000 nonsmokers are injured, or die, from what is known as "passive smoking" environmental tobacco smoke (ETS), or "second-hand" smoke (this is discussed below).

It is difficult to put the problem of the risks associated with cigarette smoking into strong enough terms. Statistically, approximately half of all smokers will die a premature death from tobacco-related disease (Peto, Chen, & Boreham, 1996). This was illustrated by a research study by Phillips, Wannamethee, Thomson, and Smith (1996) who examined the data from the ongoing British Regional Heart Study. In this study, which has followed a sample of 7735 men since 1980, 44% of the lifelong smokers survived to age 73, whereas 78% of the nonsmokers reached that same age.

One of the mechanisms by which cigarette smoking is thought to cause death is by aiding—if not causing— the development of cancer in the smoker's body. Indeed, tobacco products are the only products sold in this country that are "unequivocally carcinogenic when used as directed" (MacKenzie, Bartecchi, & Schrier, 1994b, p. 977). Cigarette smokers are estimated to have a 1100–2400% greater chance of developing some form of cancer than nonsmokers of the same age (Pappas, 1995). Thirty percent of *all* cancer-deaths are caused by smoking (Bartecchi, MacKenzie, & Schrier, 1994a; Fiore, Epps, & Manley, 1994). Cigarette smoking is thought to cause more than 75% of all cases of esophageal cancer, 30–40% of all bladder cancers, and 30% of all cases of cancer of the pancreas (Sherman, 1991).

---

[6]According to Hilts (1994) and Cotton (1993), the Federal Trade Commission is aware of this fact but continues to rely on data provided by the tobacco industry itself to determine the content of cigarette smoke.

It is the single largest cause of preventable death in the United States (Bartecchi, MacKenzie, & Schrier, 1994a).

Each year in the United States, cigarette smoking is thought to cause (Miller, 1999)

- 17–30% of the deaths from cardiovascular disease
- 30% of the deaths from lung cancer
- 24% of the deaths from pneumonia and/or influenza
- 10% of infant deaths

The estimated total financial impact of smoking, in terms of lost productivity and health care costs for tobacco-related disease in the United States, is in excess of $130 billion/ year (Leistikow, 2000). Each pack of cigarettes has been estimated to cost society $2.59 in various direct and indirect problems (Bhandari, Sylvester, & Rigotti, 1996). One such indirect consequence of cigarette smoking is the relationship between smoking and accidental fires. Each year in this country there are an estimated 187,000 smoking-related fires, resulting in an additional loss of $550 million in property damage (Bhandari, Sylvester, & Rigotti, 1996).

There is hardly a body system that is not affected by cigarette smoking. What follows is just a short list of the various conditions known, or strongly suspected, to be a result of cigarette smoking.

The mouth, throat, and pulmonary system. Chronic cigarette smokers are known to suffer greater rates of respiratory problems during sleep than nonsmokers (Wetter, Young, Bidwell, Badr, & Palta, 1994). The authors reviewed data from 811 adults who were examined at the sleep disorders program at the University of Wisconsin-Madison medical center and found that current smokers were at greater risk than nonsmokers for such sleep-related breathing disorders as snoring and sleep apnea. The relationship between smoking and sleep disorders is so strong that Wetter, Young, Bidwell, Badr, and Palta (1994) recommended that smoking cessation be considered one of the treatment interventions for patients with a sleep-related breathing disorder.

Cigarette smokers are more likely than nonsmokers to develop cancer of the lung, the mouth, the pharynx, the larynx, and the esophagus. In addition to this increased risk for cancer, cigarette smokers have higher rates than nonsmokers for chronic bronchitis and for pneumonia and chronic obstructive pulmonary disease

(COPD) such as emphysema. Indeed, it has been estimated that 81% of all deaths from COPD can be traced to cigarette smoking (Sherman, 1991). Finally, although nonsmokers also develop respiratory disease, research has shown that smokers are more likely to die from a lung disorder, when one develops, than are nonsmokers (Lee & D'Alonzo, 1993; Burns, 1991; Jaffe, 1990; Schuckit, 1995a).

The digestive tract. Alcohol and cigarette smoking are both associated with an increased risk of cancer in the upper digestive and respiratory tracts (Garro, Espina, & Lieber, 1992). Heavy drinkers have an almost 6-fold greater chance of developing cancer in the mouth and pharynx than nondrinkers, and cigarette smokers have a 7-fold greater risk of mouth or pharynx cancer than nonsmokers. However, alcoholics who *also* smoke have a 38-fold greater risk for cancer of the mouth or pharynx than nonsmoking nondrinkers ("Alcohol and Tobacco," 1998).

There is even evidence to suggest that cigarette smoking is one risk factor for the development of diabetes. Rimm, Chan, Stampfer, Colditz, and Willett (1995) identified 41,810 men who were free of cancer, cardiovascular disease, and diabetes in 1986 and followed the members of this sample group for 6 years. Questionnaires were administered to identify the incidence of non-insulin dependent diabetes mellitus at the end of the 6-year period. After controlling for known risk factors, the authors found that cigarette smoking still emerged as a possible causal factor in the development of non-insulin-dependent diabetes.

The heart and cardiovascular system. Smoking is a known risk factor for the development of coronary heart disease, hypertension, the formation of aortic aneurysms, and atherosclerotic peripheral vascular disease. Cigarette smoking has been identified as "the single most important preventable risk factor for cardiovascular disease" (Tresch & Aronow, 1996, p. 24), causing 30% of the annual death toll from coronary heart disease in this country.

Cigarette smoking is also a known risk factor for the development of either a cerebral infarction or a cerebral hemorrhage (a "stroke," or CVA) (Robbins, Manson, Lee, Satterfield, & Hennekens, 1994; Sherman, 1991). Cigarette smoking is thought to be the cause of 60,000 strokes per year in the United States alone (Sacco, 1995). Cigarette smoking is also thought to cause approximately 14% of all cases of adult-onset leukemia in the United States (Brownson, Novotony, & Perry, 1993).

Another way in which cigarette smoking affects the cardiovascular system is by causing the coronary arteries to constrict briefly. Moliterno, Willard, Lange, Negus, Boehrer, Glamann, Landau, Rossen, Winniford, and Hillis (1994) measured the diameters of the coronary arteries of 42 cigarette smokers who were being evaluated for complaints of chest pain. The authors found a *7% decrease* in coronary artery diameter (as compared to presmoking diameters) for those individuals without coronary artery disease who had smoked a cigarette. The coronary arteries are the primary source of blood for the muscle tissues of the heart, so anything that reduces the blood flow through the coronary arteries, even for a short period of time, can damage the heart itself. Thus the short-term reduction in coronary artery diameter brought on by cigarette smoking may ultimately contribute to cardiovascular problems for the smoker.

In addition to causing a reduction in coronary artery diameter, cigarette smoking introduces large amounts of carbon monoxide into the circulation. The blood of a cigarette smoker might lose as much as 15% of its oxygen-carrying capacity, as the carbon monoxide binds to the hemoglobin in the blood and blocks the transportation of oxygen to the body's cells (Tresch & Aronow, 1996).

The visual system. Cigarette smoking appears to be associated with a higher risk of cataract formation in both men (Christensen, Manson, Seddon, Glynn, Buring, Rosner, & Hennekens, 1992) and women (Hankinson, Willett, Colditz, Seddon, Rosner, Speizer, & Stampfer, 1992). Although the exact mechanism for cataract formation was not clear, male smokers who used 20 or more cigarettes a day were thought to be twice as likely to form cataracts as were nonsmokers (Christensen *et al.*, 1992).

Research also revealed that women who had quit cigarette smoking, even if they had done so a decade earlier, were still at risk for cataract formation (Hankinson *et al.*, 1992). The findings from these two studies reveal that cigarette-induced disease is far more involved than had previously been thought and suggest that at least some of the physical damage caused by cigarette smoking does not reverse itself when the smoker quits.

Other complications caused by cigarette smoking. The use of tobacco products is thought to contribute to the formation of peptic ulcers (Lee & D'Alonzo, 1993; Jarvik & Schneider, 1992). For reasons that remain unclear, cigarette smoking seems to be a risk factor for the development of psoriasis (Baughman, 1993). Cigarette smokers are known to suffer from higher rates of cancer of the kidneys than nonsmokers, and there appears to be a relationship between cigarette smoking and a thyroid condition known as *Graves' disease.*

While the exact relationship between cigarette smoking and Graves' disease is not clear, researchers suspect that cigarette smoking "might be one of these environmental stimuli capable of inducing Graves' disease in genetically predisposed individuals" (Prummel & Wiersinga, 1993, p. 479).

As a group, older women who smoke were found to be physically weaker, and to have less coordination, than nonsmoking women of the same age (Nelson, Nevitt, Scott, Stone, & Cummings, 1994). The authors examined 9704 women who were at least 65 years of age and who were living independently, with a battery of physical and neuromuscular function tests. The results suggested that

> women who are current smokers, and to a lesser extent former smokers, are weaker, have poorer balance, and have impaired neuromuscular performance compared with those who have never smoked. (p. 1829)

However, the authors did not identify a mechanism by which cigarette smoking might interfere with neuromuscular performance in those women who did smoke cigarettes. Further, the authors admitted, their study was limited to volunteers who were able to come to the research center, and thus these women might, in some manner, be different from those women who were unable to participate in the research study because of ill health, lack of transportation, or the like.

Finally, there is evidence that smoking can cause changes in brain function that may persist for many years after the individual stops smoking (Sherman, 1994). There is a measurable decline in mental abilities that begins about 4 hours after the last cigarette. It is not known how long it takes for ex-smokers to return to their normal level of intellectual function. However, some former smokers report that they did not feel "right" for as long as *nine years* after their last cigarette. There has been no research into the long-term effects of cigarette abstinence on cognitive function (Sherman, 1994), but, these reports are quite suggestive.

Smoking and gender. An estimated 240,000 women are thought to die each year, in the United States alone, as a result of smoking-related illness (Peto, Lopez, Boreham, Thun, & Heath, 1992). Cigarette smoking was estimated to be the cause of between 20–25% (Simons, Phillips, & Coleman, 1993) and 30% (Bartecchi, MacKenzie, & Schrier, 1994a) of all cases of cervical cancer. Simons, Phillips, and Coleman (1993) examined a number of women and found damage to the DNA in the cells of the cervical epithelium to be significantly more common in women who smoked than in women who had never smoked. This damage is thought to be associated with the ultimate development of cervical cancer, and it may be the mechanism through which cigarette smoking contributes to the development of cervical cancer. Fortunately, evidence suggests that when a woman stops smoking, her risk of cervical cancer slowly declines; smoking cessation may even contribute to a reduction in the size of the cancerous growth (Szarewski, Jarvis, Sasieni, Anderson, Edwards, Steele, & Buillebaud, 1996).

Cigarette smoking is known to be a factor in the 56,000 annual deaths in women from lung cancer each year in the United States, as well as in the 46,000 deaths from cancer of the breast (Bartecchi, MacKenzie, & Schrier, 1994a). There is also significant evidence that cigarette smoking is associated with accelerated calcium loss in women after menopause (Hopper & Seeman, 1994).

The degrees of risk. There is a dose-related risk of premature death caused by cigarette smoking. For example, Robbins, Manson, Lee, Satterfield, and Hennekens (1994) found that male physicians who smoked less than a pack of cigarettes a day still had a significantly higher risk of both ischemic and hemorrhagic stroke than did nonsmokers. The authors found that male physicians who smoked more than a pack of cigarettes a day had an even higher risk of stroke, and they concluded that *any* cigarette use significantly increased the individual's risk of stroke.

The passive smoker. The danger of smoking-related death is not limited to the smoker alone, for a significant percentage of the population is exposed to tobacco smoke either at home or at work, in the spite of the fact that they are nonsmokers. Indeed, one study found that 87.9% of *nonsmokers* had cotinine in their blood, suggesting that passive exposure to cigarette smoke in the United States is quite common (Pirkle, Flegal, Bernert, Brody, Etzel, & Maurer, 1996).

This "passive smoking" (being around smokers and inhaling cigarette smoke even if you yourself do not smoke), which is also known as "second-hand" smoke, environmental tobacco smoke, or ETS, is thought to cause the death of 56,000 nonsmokers each year in the United States (Benson & Sacco, 2000). Children are especially affected by second-hand tobacco smoke, which causes an estimated 6100 childhood deaths and thousands of nonfatal bouts with such conditions as acute otitis media each year in this country alone (Aligne & Stoddard, 1997). In addition, ETS is thought to be a factor in 300,000 cases of various forms of respiratory disease each year in this country (Bartecchi, MacKenzie, & Schrier, 1994a). Pappas (1995) went even further, maintaining that secondhand smoke causes between 150,000 and 300,00 respiratory infections just in the 5.5 million children in this country who are under the age of 18 months. Further, second-hand smoke is thought to cause 150,000 heart attacks yearly (Associated Press, 1994b). ETS remains the third most common preventable cause of death in the United States, after active smoking and alcohol (Werner & Pearson, 1998).

The Environmental Protection Agency (EPA) has now classified second-hand tobacco smoke as a major carcinogen. Researchers have found many apparent precancerous changes in the lung tissue of nonsmokers who live with smokers (Trichopoulos, Mollo, Tomatis, Agapitos, Delsedime, Zavitsanos, Kalandidi, Katsouyanni, Riboli, & Saracci, 1992) and have concluded that nonsmoking women who were exposed to second-hand smoke had a 30% greater chance of developing lung cancer than did nonsmoking women who were not routinely exposed to tobacco smoke (Fontham, Correa, Reynolds, Wu-Williams, Buffler, Greenberg, Chen, Alterman, Boyd, Austin, & Liff, 1994). Nonsmoking women who are exposed to cigarette smoke have been found to have a higher incidence of breast cancer than those women who are not routinely exposed to cigarette smoke (Morabia, Bernstein, Heritier, & Khatchatrian, 1996), and there is evidence of a relationship between second-hand smoke and SIDS (Klonoff-Cohen, Edelstein, Lefkowitz, Srinivasan, Kaegl, Chang, & Wiley, 1995).

The most common cause of death for those who are exposed to environmental tobacco smoke is coronary artery disease (Kritz, Schmid, & Sinzinger, 1995). Each year, fully 70% of those people in the United States who die from second-hand smoke, or an estimated 62,000 individuals, do so from coronary heart disease caused by their passive smoking (Tresch & Aronow, 1996). Exposure to ETS is now thought to increase the speed at which atherosclerotic plaque forms by 20%, compared to 50% faster for the smoker (Howard, Wagenknecht, Burke, Diez-Roux, Evans, McGovern, Nieto, & Tell, 1998). These results underscore the fact that the passive smoker is exposed to virtually all of the same toxins as the smoker, and although the passive smoker is exposed to lower concentrations of these toxins, they are still sufficiently potent to cause an estimated 30,000–60,000 fatal heart attacks and three times this number of nonfatal heart attacks each year in the United States (Glantz & Parmley, 1995).

It is interesting to discover that in response to these studies, and to the EPA's decision to classify environmental smoke as a carcinogen, several scientists were paid by the tobacco industry to write letters or papers challenging these conclusions (Hanners, 1998). The tobacco industry paid 13 scientists some $156,000 to write letters or papers challenging the EPA's ruling and reviewed their work before it was submitted for editorial review for possible publication. In some cases, the letters or articles were actually written by the staff of law firms that represented the tobacco industry and then signed by the scientists in question (Hanners, 1998). These actions underscore the lengths to which the tobacco industry is willing to go to keep its product on the market with as few restrictions as possible.

Complications caused by chewing tobacco. There are three types of "smokeless" tobacco: moist snuff, dry snuff, and chewing tobacco (Westman, 1995). The latter is also known as "spit tobacco" (Bell, Spangler, & Quandt, 2000). It is thought that 5.6% of the men and 0.6% of the adult women in the United States use "smokeless" tobacco, although there are regional variations in the frequency with which people chew tobacco (Bell, Spangler, & Quandt, 2000).

Many of those who use chewing tobacco believe that oral tobacco is safer than cigarette smoking. But the practice of chewing tobacco is actually quite dangerous. A person who uses chewing tobacco achieves blood nicotine levels that approximate those achieved by smoking one cigarette (Gottlieb, Pope, Rickert, & Hardin, 1993). At least three compounds in smokeless tobacco—nicotine, sodium, and licorice— are capable of causing hypertension (Westman, 1995). Further, "smokeless" tobacco contains 28 different chemical compounds capable of causing the growth of tumors (Bartecchi, MacKenzie, & Schrier, 1994a).

Thus it would be natural to expect that individuals who use oral forms of tobacco would be at increased risk for cancer of the mouth and throat. Indeed, in one study cited by Spangler and Salisbury (1995), 93% of the patients with oral cancer reported using "snuff," and 6% admitted to the use of chewing tobacco. Other possible consequences of the use of "smokeless" tobacco include damage to the tissues of the gums, staining of the teeth, and damage to the teeth (Spangler & Salisbury, 1995).

It is not clear whether tobacco chewers have the same degree of risk for coronary artery disease as cigarette smokers, but they *do* have a greater incidence of coronary artery disease than individuals who neither chew nor smoke tobacco. Further, smokeless tobacco can contribute to problems with the control of the individual's blood pressure (Westman, 1995). Thus, although smokeless tobacco is often viewed as "the lesser of two evils," its use is certainly not without risk.

The cost of cigarette smoking around the world. The problem of cigarette-induced disease is not limited to this country. It has been estimated that tobacco use around the world is responsible for 3 million premature deaths each year (Peto, Chen, & Boreham, 1996). Further, it is estimated that if present trends continue, then by the year 2025, cigarette smoking will cause 10 million premature deaths each year, or 27,300 deaths each day from cigarette-related illness (Peto, Chen, & Boreham, 1996). Of these premature deaths, 70% will take place in the so-called Third World or "developing" world (Phillips, Savigny, & Law, 1995). It has been estimated that on a global basis, 1 in every 10 deaths will be caused by tobacco-related illness by the year 2020 (*Wisconsin State Journal*, 1996). As these figures suggest, cigarette smoking is a most dangerous pastime.

Recovery from risk. When a cigarette smoker stops, his or her body begins the process of recovery from the damage caused by smoking. Over time, the former smoker's risk for many of the complications caused by cigarette smoking drops, often to the same level as that of the nonsmoker. Over time, the former smoker's risk of developing lung cancer decreases, until, by 10–15 years after the last use of cigarettes, it is about the same as that of nonsmokers (Lee & D'Alonzo, 1993). The rate of coronary artery disease for former smokers reaches the same levels as for nonsmokers in 2–3 years for women and 5 years for men, according to the authors.

Wannamethee, Shaper, Whincup, and Walker (1995) conducted a prospective study of cardiovascular disease in 7735 men between the ages of 40 and 59. The names of these men were drawn at random from the health records of a number of towns in England. Smokers were found to have a fourfold greater risk of stroke than nonsmokers. When the authors examined the effects of giving up tobacco smoking (including pipes and cigars), they found that there was a reduction in the individual's risk of stroke over the first 5 years following the last use of tobacco. However, heavy smokers who stopped still had a twofold greater risk of stroke than nonsmokers. Thus, for the heavier smoker, giving up the use of tobacco products will reduce the risk of stroke, but not to the level of a nonsmoker.

Other improvements in the ex-smoker's health status include a slowing of peripheral vascular disease and an improved sense of taste and smell, according to Lee and D'Alonzo (1993). In addition to this, Grover, Gray-Donald, Joseph, Abrahamowicz, and Coupal (1994) found that former cigarette smokers as a group added between 2.5 and 4.5 years to their life expectancy when they stopped smoking. The authors found that cessation of cigarette use was several times as powerful a force in prolonging life as was changing one's dietary habits. Finally, as a group, former smokers show less cardiac impairment and lower rates of reinfarction than do smokers who continue to smoke after having a heart attack. As these findings suggest, there are very real benefits to giving up cigarette smoking.

Summary

Tobacco use, once limited to the New World, was first introduced to Europe by Columbus's men. Once the practice of smoking or chewing tobacco reached Europe, tobacco use spread rapidly. Following the introduction of the cigarette around the turn of the century, smoking became more common, and it quickly replaced tobacco chewing as the accepted method of tobacco use.

The psychoactive agent of tobacco, nicotine, has been found to have an addiction potential similar to that of cocaine or narcotics. A significant percentage of those who are currently addicted to nicotine will attempt to stop smoking cigarettes but will initially be unsuccessful in doing so. Current treatment methods have been unable to achieve a significant cessation rate, and more comprehensive treatment programs have been suggested for nicotine addiction. These comprehensive programs, which are patterned after alcohol addiction treatment programs, have not demonstrated a significantly improved cure rate for cigarette smoking. It has been suggested that such formal treatment programs might be of value for those individuals whose tobacco use has placed them at risk for tobacco-related illness.

CHAPTER TWENTY

Chemicals and the Neonate

The Consequences of Drug Abuse During Pregnancy

Introduction

The problem of intrauterine exposure to recreational drugs has received scant attention from health care researchers (Kandall, 1999). This is especially tragic because virtually every drug of abuse is able to cross the placenta and enter the fetal circulation (Behnke & Eyler, 1993). In those cases where the infant was exposed to recreational chemicals as a result of maternal drug abuse, society has tended to view the drug-exposed child as "damaged goods, with limited potential" (Johnson, Nusbaum, Bejarano, & Rosen, 1999). In reality, very little is known about the impact of maternal chemical use on fetal development or about which biological or environmental forces might intervene to mitigate against this potential damage. In this chapter, the topic of prenatal exposure to the drugs of abuse will be explored.

A period of special vulnerability. The very nature of prenatal growth makes the period of pregnancy, especially the first trimester, one of special vulnerability for the rapidly developing fetus (Barki, Kravitz, & Berki, 1998). There are many reasons for this enhanced vulnerability on the part of the fetus. For example, the process of organ differentiation takes place during the third to eighth weeks following conception, often before the mother-to-be is aware that she should take special precautions because she is pregnant. If the mother-to-be should ingest a chemical, or be exposed to an infectious agent, that interferes with normal fetal development during this period, the consequences could prove disastrous for the unborn child and possibly the mother.

Another reason why exposure to toxic compounds is potentially so devastating to the developing fetus is that only 60% of the blood that the fetus receives from the umbilical cord is processed by the liver before it proceeds to the rest of the body. The other 40% of the fetal venus blood, and any toxins found in that blood, directly enter the general circulation (Barki, Kravitz, & Berki, 1998). Further, because the fetal liver and excretory systems are still quite immature, even compounds that *are routed* to the liver by the fetal circulation may not be biotransformed into less toxic compounds at the same rate as in the mother's body. This contributes to the build-up of potential toxins within the fetal circulatory system. To further compound the problem, the fetus's immature blood-brain barrier permits many compounds to enter the fetal central nervous system more easily than they could do later in life (Barki, Kravitz, & Berki, 1998). Finally, the fetal circulatory system has lower blood protein levels than an adult's blood, and this allows a greater concentration of "unbound" drug molecules to circulate in fetal blood system than would be possible in an adult's blood system. All of these factors combine to magnify the effects of a toxin on the body of the fetus, possibly with lifelong consequences.

Scope of the Problem

Nationally, researchers believe that there are 4.1 million women between the ages of 15 and 44, the prime childbearing years, who use illicit drugs (Department of

Health and Human Services, 1997). It is estimated that 19% of pregnant women use alcohol, 20% smoke cigarettes, and 5.5% use an illicit drug at least once (Raut, Stephen, & Kosopsky 1996; Mathias, 1995). In terms of absolute numbers, it has been estimated that 140,000 pregnant women drink potentially dangerous levels of alcohol each year in the United States (Cohen, 2000) and that 221,000 infants are born each year in this country who were exposed to an illicit drug at least once during gestation (Kandall, 1999; Chasnoff, Anson, Hatcher, Stenson, Iaukea, & Randolph, 1998).

The medical care of children who were exposed to recreational drugs is a significant expense for society. Chasnoff (1991a) estimated that the median cost of care for children born to mothers who had used illicit chemicals during pregnancy was $1100–$4100 higher than for children whose mothers who did not use illicit chemicals while pregnant. Based on the figure of 221,000 infants born each year who were exposed to an illicit drug(s) during gestation, this figure translates into a potential expenditure of between $243 million and $906 million dollars in additional medical costs each year for treatment of drug-related neonatal health problems (Chasnoff, Anson, Hatcher, Stenson, Iaukea, & Randolph, 1998).

When these children reach school age, they may very well require further specialized services. Barden (1991) noted, for example, that whereas the average educational cost for the normal child is approximately $3,000 a year, the cost of the special-education classes often required by children who were born addicted to drugs might be as high as $15,000 a year per child. This is in addition to the extra medical costs, cost for social services, and so on, that such children often require.

A note of caution. Even in the best of circumstances, it is extremely difficult to identify the effects of a given chemical, infectious agent, or aspect of the prenatal environment on fetal growth and development. Numerous factors that can influence both fetal growth and maternal health include possible maternal illness during pregnancy, polychemical exposure, genetic predisposition toward various medical problems, the woman's state of health prior to pregnancy, stressors, adverse social conditions, acquired trauma to both mother and fetus, the mother's diet preceding and during of pregnancy.

To illustrate how one set of adverse social conditions might affect the course of pregnancy, one need only consider how social attitudes toward maternal drug and alcohol use during pregnancy can interfere with a woman's access to, and utilization of, prenatal medical care (Irwin, 1995). The negative stereotypes that some substance-abusing pregnant women encounter during their prenatal care—exacerbated by the fact that in some regions there have been strident calls for the incarceration of drug-abusing pregnant women and by the fear that county or state authorities will intervene to take the infant should their substance use problems become known—make some women hesitate to seek prenatal care (Irwin, 1995). Other adverse social conditions, such as poverty, inadequate social support for the parents (especially the single mother), potential victimization, and a lack of safety, can all affect prenatal development and the mother's ability to care for her newborn.

The effects of the drugs of abuse on neonatal growth are not limited to the prenatal period. Maternal preoccupation with drug use, the effects of poverty, the impact of maternal depression on the parent–child relationship, and/or competing demands for the mother's attention by siblings, combined with the intense needs of the drug-exposed infant, can result in a "serious mismatch between the mother's limited emotional resources and the infant's intense caregiving needs" (Johnson, Nusbaum, Bejarano, & Rosen, 1999, p. 450). Indeed, Werner (1989b) concluded that the impact of such adverse social factors were ten times as likely as perinatal complications to cause poor development in childhood, adolescence, and young adulthood.

Because all of these forces affect fetal growth and development, scientists have consistently failed to find a pattern, or syndrome, unique to prenatal drug exposure. Many of the consequences attributed to maternal drug use are similar to those reported in the literature for such conditions as maternal depression, stress, poverty, and limited social support—all conditions commonly found in the drug-abusing home (Johnson, Nusbaum, Bejarano, & Rosen, 1999). Yet scientists have been able to determine that the drugs of abuse have the potential to deflect normal development in a number of ways. The definitive example of this is the impact of maternal alcohol use on prenatal growth and development.

Fetal Alchohol Syndrome

For many decades, doctors were unaware of the damage that prenatal alcohol exposure might cause, and it was not until the 1970s that researchers began to understand that women who drink while pregnant run the risk of causing alcohol-induced birth defects in their children. The longer and the more severe the intrauterine exposure to alcohol might be, the more acute the diagnosis for the child following birth, and the greater the chance that she or he will require special support as a child and adolescent (Autti-Ramo, 2000). The most severe condition is known as *fetal alcohol syndrome* (or FAS). FAS has been found to be both the third most common cause of birth defects in the United States (North, 1996) and the only cause of birth defects in this country that is totally preventable (Beasley, 1987).

When an expectant mother drinks, the alcohol quickly crosses the placenta into the fetal bloodstream, reaching *the same level as the mother's bloodstream in only 15 minutes* (Rose, 1988). Thus the fetus is an unwilling participant in the mother's alcohol use, and an estimated 757,000 babies are born in the United States each year who were exposed to alcohol at least once before birth (Kandall, 1999). Each year in the United States, 140,000 pregnant women are thought to consume enough alcohol to present a danger to the health of the fetus (Cohen, 2000). If the mother has been drinking shortly prior to childbirth, the smell of alcohol can be detected on the breath of the infant following birth (Rose, 1988). If the mother is alcohol-dependent, the infant will also be alcohol-dependent, and he or she will begin to go through alcohol withdrawal 3–12 hours after delivery (American Academy of Pediatrics, 1998).

Fetal alcohol syndrome was found to be the most severe of a continuum of disabilities brought on by maternal alcohol use during pregnancy (Streissguth, Aase, Clarren, Randels, LaDue, & Smith, 1991). Some infants were found to demonstrate only some of the symptoms of FAS, a condition known as *fetal alcohol effects* (FAE) (Streissguth, *et al.*, 1991; Charness, Simon, & Greenberg, 1989).

Scope of the problem. The full prevalence of alcohol-related birth defects is not known (Cordero, 1990). Youngstrom (1992) estimated that one infant in 700–750 suffers from FAS, whereas Spohr, Williams, and Steinhausen (1993) estimated that 1–2 cases of FAS

occur for every 1000 children. Bell and Lau (1995) gave a slightly higher estimate of 2.2 cases for every 1000 live births in this country. But these statistics only reflect the ratio of children with FAS to the total number of live births. Perhaps between 2.5% (Gottlieb, 1994) and 6% (Charness, Simon, & Greenberg, 1989) of the children of alcoholic mothers will be born with FAS. In some communities where maternal alcohol use is exceptionally common, this figure may be as high as 19% (Hartman, 1995). In addition to these numbers are the 3 to 5 of every 1000 children who are thought to suffer from FAE (Spohr, Williams, & Steinhausen, 1993).

How maternal alcohol use affects fetal development. Maternal alcohol use during pregnancy is thought to inhibit the production (biosynthesis) of chemicals known as *gangliosides* within the developing fetal brain (Rosenberg, 1996). These chemicals play a role in the formation of the brain in the earliest stages of development. Those mothers who ingest the greatest amount of alcohol are thought to put the fetus at greatest risk, because the more frequent the exposure to alcohol, the greater the effects of this chemical on fetal ganglioside biosynthesis.

Characteristics of fetal alcohol syndrome children. Infants who suffer from fetal alcohol syndrome usually have a lower than normal birth weight, a characteristic pattern of facial abnormalities, and (often) a smaller brain size at birth. Noninvasive neurodiagnostic imaging examination of the brains of children who were exposed to alcohol before birth reveals damage to such structures of the infant's brain as the cerebral cortex, cerebellum, basal ganglia, hippocampus, and corpus callosum (Mattson & Riley, 1995). In later life, children with FAS often demonstrate behavioral problems such as hyperactivity, a short attention span, impulsiveness, poor coordination, and numerous other developmental delays (Committee on Substance Abuse and Committee on Children with Disabilities, 1993; Gilbertson & Weinberg, 1992; Charness, Simon, & Greenberg, 1989). Children with FAS also exhibit slower growth patterns following birth, and are more likely to be retarded. Maternal alcohol use during pregnancy is thought to be the leading cause of mental retardation in the United States (Bell & Lau, 1995; Strissguth *et al.*, 1991; Charness, Simon, & Greenberg, 1989).

As a group, children with FAS usually fall in the mild to moderately retarded range following birth, with an average IQ of 68 (Chasnoff, 1988).[1] However, some 40% of children with FAS will have IQs above 70 (Strissguth *et al.*, 1991). This is not to say that these children have not suffered from the mother's use of alcohol during pregnancy. Rather, these children do not qualify for special support services, because their measured IQ happens to be higher than the cut-off score of 70 used by most school districts to determine who qualifies for remedial services.

At present, research suggests that there is no "safe" dose of alcohol during pregnancy (Committee on Substance Abuse and Committee on Children with Disabilities, 1993). Although few heavy drinkers would consider 4–6 drinks/day a significant amount of alcohol, research has shown that 4-6 drinks/day for the typical woman during pregnancy will result in 33% of the children having FAS and 33% having FAE (Raut, Stephen, & Kosopsky, 1996). The gangliosides that shape neuronal growth in the fetal brain are thought to be most active during the first trimester, and alcohol's effects can be especially disruptive of fetal neurological growth during this period (Pirozzolo & Bonnefil, 1995). However, alcohol use at any point in pregnancy should be avoided (Gottlieb, 1994).

Unfortunately, even when children who suffer from FAS are identified at birth and enrolled in special rehabilitative programs, they still fail to achieve normal growth or intelligence (Spohr, Williams, & Steinhausen, 1993; Mirin, Weiss, & Greenfield, 1991). Children with FAS have been found to grow at only 60% the normal rate for height and at 33% of the normal rate for weight gain (Aase, 1994). Only 6% of those students with FAS were found to be able to function in regular school classes without special help (Strissguth *et al.*, 1991). Further, "major psychosocial problems and lifelong adjustment problems were characteristic of most of these patients" (Strissguth *et al.*, 1991, pp. 1965–1966). Surprisingly, the low birth weight that was characteristic of FAS seemed at least partially to resolve itself by adolescence, according to the authors. Even so,

[1]An IQ of 68 falls in the mildly retarded range of intellectual function. The average IQ is 100, with a standard deviation of 15 points. An IQ of 68 is thus more than 2 standard deviations below the mean.

"none of these (adolescent or young adult) patients were known to be independent in terms of both housing and income" (p. 1966) at the time of the study. These findings again underscore the lifelong impact, on the child of maternal alcohol use during pregnancy.

Breast-feeding and alcohol use. Alcohol in the mother's circulation passes freely into her breast milk in concentrations similar to her blood alcohol level (BAL) (Heil & Subramanian, 1998). Fortunately, even if the infant were to nurse while the mother was quite intoxicated, the amount of alcohol ingested along with the mother's milk would be diluted throughout his or her system, resulting in a lower BAL for the infant (Heil & Subramanian, 1998).

Unfortunately, even this limited exposure to alcohol has been shown to cause abnormal gross motor development for the infant, with higher levels of maternal alcohol consumption resulting in greater developmental delays (Little, Anderson, Ervin, Worthington-Roberts, & Clarren, 1989). In addition to this direct effect on infant growth, maternal alcohol use may interfere with the development of the child's immune system (Gilbertson & Weinberg, 1992). These results strongly suggest that alcohol use by the mother who is breast-feeding is indeed a risk factor for the infant and should be avoided.

Cocaine Use During Pregnancy

As recently as 1982, some medical textbooks claimed that maternal cocaine use did not have a harmful effect on the fetus (Revkin, 1989). Then, when the last wave of cocaine abuse in the United States began in the late 1970s and early 1980s, questions were raised about the possibility that maternal cocaine abuse might affect the growth and development of the fetus. A series of research studies warned of impaired children born to cocaine-abusing mothers. The mass media, either by accident or design, seized upon this first generation of studies and, on the basis of this research, provided the general public with ever-larger estimates of the number of infants whose lives were supposedly forever damaged by maternal cocaine abuse during pregnancy.

A wave of near hysteria followed, as states passed laws allowing the legal prosecution of pregnant women for child abuse if evidence of maternal cocaine abuse was found during prenatal testing. Women were prosecuted for child abuse under these new laws and, in many cases were incarcerated at least until the birth of the child who was supposedly put "at risk" by the mother's cocaine abuse. This resulted in some pregnant cocaine-abusing women failing to seek medical care until the onset of labor, to avoid possible prosecution under the new laws designed to protect unborn infants from cocaine's effects (Irwin, 1995).

Then a strange thing happened: The anticipated wave of brain-damaged "crack [cocaine] babies" simply failed to materialize (Garrett, 2000; Gray, 1998). Second- and third-generation research studies began to discover that the supposed effects of maternal cocaine use might more easily be explained by a lack of prenatal care, maternal use of toxic compounds such as tobacco and/or alcohol during pregnancy, and poor nutrition, etc. For example, research has consistently revealed that fully 50% of the women who abuse cocaine during pregnancy also drink alcohol, a known toxin, during their pregnancy (Sexson, 1994). Researchers also discovered that many cocaine-abusing women failed to obtain adequate prenatal care because of poverty and that in many cases, a cocaine-abusing pregnant woman received her first medical "care" when she arrived at a hospital emergency room in labor (Sexson, 1994). Yet even limited prenatal care was found to reduce significantly the possibility of abnormal fetal growth (Racine, Joyce, & Anderson, 1993).

Problems in the identification of infants exposed to cocaine in utero. In adults, blood or urine toxicology tests will detect cocaine for only 24–48 hours following the use of this compound. But the liver of the newborn infant is quite immature at birth, and it is unable to produce the concentrations of the enzyme *pseudocholinesterase*[2] found in an adult's blood. Thus, the newborn infant will require longer to biotransform and excrete any cocaine that might be in his or her body as a result of maternal cocaine use. In theory, this provides a larger "window of opportunity" during which it is possible to detect evidence of maternal cocaine use. But even in a newborn infant, the mebabolites of cocaine can be detected in the urine for only 4–6 days after the infant has been exposed to the drug (Levy & Rutter, 1992). Thus toxicology tests conducted at birth will detect only *recent* maternal cocaine use, even when the

infant's urine is tested rather than the mother's (Volpe, 1995).[3]

Another problem is that even if toxicology testing on samples of hair or urine from the infant *do* reveal evidence of cocaine use, this cannot automatically be interpreted as evidence of maternal cocaine abuse. It has been found that "side-stream" smoke from cocaine smokers can cause others in the room to absorb significant amounts of cocaine passively (Karch, 1996). Researchers have not ruled out the possibility that a person might test "positive" for cocaine through passive inhalation of the fumes, and until such research is conducted, the "presence of the drug [in a woman's urine] just proves that there is [cocaine] in the environment" (Karch, 1996, p. 29), not that she intentionally used the cocaine. Thus urine toxicology testing is of limited value in detecting infants who have been exposed to cocaine in utero.

What do we really know about the effects of maternal cocaine use? In spite of the expectations of many, the "great majority of cocaine-exposed pregnancies did not result in fetal structural abnormalities" (Behnke & Eyler, 1993, p. 1366). Maternal cocaine abuse during pregnancy may have resulted in significant levels of damage for a small number of infants, but researchers now believe that the effects of maternal cocaine abuse are subtle and are seen more often in developmental delays than in dramatic cases of impairment (Leshner, 1999). Further, most of the observed problems disappear in the first weeks to months of life, and there have been few cocaine-induced effects observed in two- and 3-year-old children exposed to cocaine *in utero* (Keller & Snyder-Keller, 2000).

Thus, in spite of sensationalist reports in the popular media about a wave of drug-impaired "crack" babies about to descend upon society,

> few effects of prenatal cocaine exposure on children's cognitive, motor, play, language and socio-emotional development during early childhood have been found. (Tronick & Beeghly, 1999, p. 152)

---

[3]Volpe (1995) suggested that it might be possible to detect evidence of maternal cocaine use through traces of cocaine found in the infant's *hair*, if the mother had used cocaine in the last two trimesters of pregnancy. However, this procedure is not in general use and remains controversial.

---

[2]See Chapter 12.

Where researchers *have* found differences between infants who were and those who were not exposed to cocaine prenatally, such findings have been small in magnitude. For example, researchers at Brown University have concluded that the IQ of infants exposed to cocaine in utero average 3.3 points lower than those of nonexposed infants from the same socioeconomic level (Tronick & Beeghly, 1999; Leshner, 1999). There also is evidence that prenatal cocaine use can result in developmental delays for the infant in such areas as psychomotor skills (Zickler, 1999).

What is the scope of the problem of prenatal cocaine exposure? There is a great deal of disagreement about the extent of maternal cocaine abuse during pregnancy. In the early to mid-1980s, researchers found that in some communities, as many as 17% of the women who experienced preterm labor had measurable amounts of cocaine in their urine (Ney, Dooley, Keith, Chasnoff, & Socol, 1990; Cordero, 1990). It was theorized that because cocaine can cause strong contractions in the uterus and might even initiate labor, there was a chance that maternal cocaine abuse could cause a late-stage abortion (Burkett, Yasin, Palow, LaVoie, & Martinez, 1994; Sexson, 1994). For this reason, some physicians advocated routine urine toxicology testing for women who experienced preterm labor (Peters & Theorell, 1991). However, this recommendation did not result in a formal treatment guideline to that effect, so researchers still do not know what percentage of premature births are initiated by maternal cocaine use.

There is a great deal of debate about the true scope of maternal cocaine abuse during pregnancy. Scafidi, Field, Wheeden, Schanberg, Kuhn, Symanski, Zimmerman, and Bandstra (1996) concluded that 10–15% of all expectant mothers used cocaine, either alone or in combination with other drugs, during the course of their pregnancy. The National Institute on Drug Abuse (NIDA) reached a different conclusion, however. In the 1990s the NIDA conducted a National Pregnancy and Health Survey, which was the first *national* survey of drug use during pregnancy, and found that only about 1.1% of the 4 million pregnant women, or just 45,000 women across the United States, used cocaine in *any* form during pregnancy (Kandall, 1999; Chasnoff, Anson, Hatcher, Stenson, Iaukea, & Randolph, 1998). Thus, after more than 30 years of research, scientists still do not have a coherent overview of the prevalence of maternal cocaine use during pregnancy or of the impact of such drug use on fetal growth and development.

The current theories. In spite of all of the rhetoric, there has been little empirical research into the long-term effects of prenatal cocaine exposure on the infant (Tronick & Beeghly, 1999). Researchers have failed to identify a specific pattern of deficits that might be attributed to maternal cocaine use during pregnancy. Biologists have found that the concentration of cocaine in the amniotic fluid may be higher than that in the maternal bloodstream (Woods, 1998). This finding is sobering when one considers that the skin of the fetus does not become able to block passive absorption of cocaine from the amniotic fluid until the 24th week of pregnancy (Woods, 1998) and that the long-term consequences of fetal cocaine exposure are simply not known (Keller & Snyder-Keller, 2000).

The most common consequences of maternal cocaine abuse on the fetus are lower birth weight, premature birth, increased frequency of respiratory distress syndrome following birth, malformations of genitourinary tract, infarctions of the bowels, cerebral infarctions, reduced head circumference, and increased chance of cerebral infarctions (Keller & Keller-Snyder, 2000; Scafidi *et al.*, 1996). Some researchers have suggested an association between maternal cocaine abuse during pregnancy and the later development of sudden infant death syndrome (SIDS) (Bell & Lau, 1995; Peters & Theorell, 1991). However, this possibility has been challenged by other researchers (Plessinger & Woods, 1993; Weathers, Crane, Sauvian, & Blackhurst, 1993). In a recent study, the team of Ostrea, Ostrea, and Simpson (1997) failed to find a significant relationship between prenatal drug exposure (as measured by toxicology testing of fetal meconium at birth) and SIDS. The authors based their conclusion on the records of a sample of 2964 infants in the first two years following birth and found that low birth weight, rather than prenatal cocaine exposure, seemed to be associated with a higher incidence of SIDS. Thus the relationship between SIDS and prenatal cocaine exposure remains unproved.

Unanswered questions. Animal research has revealed that at least some of the cocaine in the mother's blood crosses the placenta and enters the fetal circulation. However, it is still not clear whether the fetal cocaine levels are the same as, or significantly different from, those of the mother's blood. In some animal species, the placenta appears to be able to biotransform limited amounts of cocaine before it enters the fetal circulatory system. But it is not known whether humans also have this ability (Plessinger & Woods, 1993).

Animal research has demonstrated that maternal cocaine use during pregnancy can cause constriction of the blood vessels in the placenta and uterine bed, reducing the blood flow to the fetus for a period of time. This cocaine-induced reduction in uterine blood flow may cause poor intrauterine growth for the infant exposed to cocaine prenatally. The same mechanism has been suggested as the cause of premature labor and birth in pregnant cocaine-abusing women (Behnke & Eyler, 1993; Plessinger & Woods, 1993; Glantz & Woods, 1993; Chasnoff, 1991b). However, there has been no research to determine whether this is indeed the case.

Cocaine's vasoconstrictive effects may also be the mechanism by which maternal cocaine abuse results in injury to the developing bowel of the fetus (Cotton, 1994; Plessinger & Woods, 1993). Animal research suggests that maternal cocaine use causes damage to the mesenteric artery, which provides blood to the intestines, according to the authors. An alternative hypothesis is that cocaine causes a reduction in blood flow to nonvital organ systems of the developing fetus, including the bowel and kidneys. This would explain why Mitra, Ganesh, and Apuzzio (1994) found evidence that the renal artery in the fetus did not function normally, reducing the blood flow to the kidneys for extended periods of time.

There is also evidence that infants born to mothers who use cocaine during pregnancy suffer from small strokes prior to birth (Kandall, 1999; Volpe, 1995). One research study found that 6% of cocaine-exposed infants appeared have had at least one cerebral infarction (stroke, or CVA) (Volpe, 1995). Another study found evidence of CVAs in 35% of infants exposed to cocaine or the amphetamines in utero (Kandall, 1999). These strokes are thought to be a result of the rapid changes in the mother's blood pressure brought on by maternal cocaine use. Chasnoff (1988) postulated that such strokes are similar in nature to those occasionally seen in adults who use cocaine, adding that there is evidence that cocaine use during pregnancy may result in cardiac and central nervous system abnormalities in the fetus.

Cocaine and breast-feeding. Cocaine, because it is highly lipid-soluble, may be stored in breast milk. Thus some of the drug may be passed on to the infant by the mother through breast-feeding (Peters & Theorell, 1991; Revkin, 1989). But the level of cocaine exposure for the child might be far higher than it was for the mother. Research has shown that cocaine levels in a mother's milk can be *eight times* as high as the level of cocaine in her blood (Revkin, 1989). If the cocaine-using mother were to breast-feed her infant, that child might be exposed to extremely high levels of cocaine through the mother's milk. For this reason, maternal cocaine use during the time when the mother breast-feeds her infant should be discouraged.

Amphetamine Use During Pregnancy

Women who abuse amphetamines, especially methamphetamine, during pregnancy often deny abusing these chemicals, even when confronted with urine toxicology test results to the contrary (Catanzarite & Stein, 1995). This is unfortunate, because the effects of amphetamines on the developing human fetus, and on the mother, have not been studied in detail (Bell & Lau, 1995).

The effects of the amphetamines are so similar to those of cocaine that it might be assumed that the impact of maternal use of amphetamines during pregnancy might produce the same effects as maternal cocaine use during pregnancy (Pirozzolo & Bonnefil, 1995). Researchers have found that infants who were exposed to amphetamines during pregnancy tend to be born with a decreased head circumference, length, and body weight (Bell & Lau, 1995). The authors also suggested that maternal amphetamine use during pregnancy was associated with a higher rate of premature births and congenital brain lesions. It is possible that maternal amphetamine abuse during pregnancy increases the mother's risk for fatal complications of the pregnancy, although there is no definitive research in this area (Catanzarite & Stein, 1995).

There is virtually no research into the long-term effects of maternal amphetamine use on the growth patterns of the infant following birth (Catanzarite & Stein, 1995; Bell & Lau, 1995). There *is* evidence to suggest that maternal use of methamphetamine may result in premature birth, poor intrauterine growth, and a tendency for the placenta to separate from the wall of the uterus (Catanzarite & Stein, 1995). Other possible complications of maternal amphetamine use during pregnancy include meconium aspiration, placental hemorrhage, and neonatal anemia (Beebe & Walley, 1995).

There is evidence that children born to mothers who abused amphetamines during pregnancy experience abnormal psychosocial development (Bell & Lau, 1995) or frontal lobe dysfunction (Beebe & Walley, 1995). However, most normal developmental milestones are achieved on time, and there is little firm evidence of long-term damage to the fetus or neonate (Pirozzolo & Bonnefil, 1995).[4] Thus it is difficult to predict what long-term effects maternal amphetamine use during pregnancy will have on the child.

Opiate Abuse During Pregnancy

Because of the ability of narcotic analgesics to cross from the mother's circulation to that of the fetus, it is estimated that each year in this country, approximately 300,000 children are exposed to narcotics in utero (Glantz & Woods, 1993). Not all of these children are exposed to illicit narcotics. It is estimated that each year, 1–21% of expectant mothers use a narcotic analgesic at least once during pregnancy (Behnke & Eyler, 1993). Most of these women are using narcotic pharmaceuticals under a physician's supervision, for medical reasons, and their use of the narcotic analgesic is limited to periods of medical necessity. But an estimated 650,000 women have used heroin at least once, and approximately 88,000 women use heroin regularly (Bell & Lau, 1995). Some of these women are of childbearing age, and a significant percentage of those women who use heroin on a regular basis do so while they are pregnant. In the United States, maternal heroin abuse accounts for almost a quarter of all cases of fetal exposure to illegal drugs (American Academy of Family Physicians, 1990b). Each year in this country, some 9000 (Bell & Lau, 1995; Glantz & Woods, 1993) to 10,000 (Zuckerman & Bresnahan, 1991) children are born to women who are addicted to narcotics.

Unfortunately, many of the early symptoms of pregnancy—feelings of fatigue, nausea, vomiting, pelvic cramps, and hot sweats—might be interpreted by the narcotics-addicted woman as early withdrawal symptoms rather than signs of possible pregnancy (Levy & Rutter, 1992). According to the authors, even physicians experienced in the treatment of narcotics addiction find it quite difficult to diagnose pregnancy in narcotics-addicted women. All too often, rather than seeking prenatal care for her unborn child, the woman herself will initially try to self-medicate what she believes is withdrawal, by using even higher doses of narcotics. This results in the fetus being exposed to significant levels of narcotic analgesics (and the chemicals that are used to "cut" street narcotics) by a woman who is not yet aware that she is pregnant.

Maternal narcotics abuse during pregnancy carries with it a number of serious consequences for both the mother and the developing fetus. In addition to the dangers associated with narcotics abuse, the pregnant woman who abuses opioids runs the risk of septic thrombophlebitis, postpartum hemorrhage, depression, gestational diabetes, eclampsia, and death.

The physical complications associated with narcotics abuse during pregnancy include stillbirth, breech presentation during childbirth, placental insufficiency, spontaneous abortion, premature delivery, neonatal meconium aspiration syndrome (which may be fatal), neonatal infections acquired through the mother, lower birth weight, and neonatal narcotic addiction (Glantz & Woods, 1993; Levy & Rutter, 1992; Hoegerman & Schnoll, 1991; Chasnoff, 1988).

It has also been found that children born to women who are addicted to narcotics have a two to three times greater risk of SIDS than children whose mothers had never used illicit chemicals (Pirozzolo, & Bonnefil, 1995; Kandall, Gaines, Habel, Davidson, & Jessop, 1993). Volpe (1995) suggested that the risk of SIDS increased with the severity of the infant's withdrawal from narcotics.

Chronic use of narcotics during pregnancy results in the fetus's chronic exposure to opiates. Because of their passive exposure to the drug, such infants are physically dependent on narcotics at birth. Following birth, the infant is no longer able to absorb drugs from the mother's blood and begins going through drug withdrawal within 24–72 hours of birth. Depending on the specific narcotic(s) being abused by the mother, the withdrawal process may last for weeks, or even months, in the newborn (Volpe, 1995; Levy & Rutter, 1992;

---

[4]Of course, there also is no evidence that amphetamine use during pregnancy is safe. If only for this reason, amphetamine abuse by the pregnant woman should be discouraged.

Hoegerman & Schnoll, 1991). Pirozzolo and Bonnefil (1995) suggested that the *acute* stage of the neonatal withdrawal syndrome subsides in 3–6 weeks but that a *subacute* stage, marked by such symptoms as restlessness, agitation, tremors, and sleep disturbance, may continue for another 4–6 months.

Some of the most immediate symptoms of neonatal narcotic withdrawal are muscle tremors, hyperactivity, hyperirritability, a unique, high-pitched cry, frantic efforts to find comfort, sleep problems, vomiting, loose stools, increased deep-muscle reflexes, frequent yawning, sneezing, seizures, increased sweating, dehydration, constant sucking movements, fever, and rapid breathing (American Academy of Pediatrics, 1998). In years past, neonatal narcotics withdrawal resulted in an almost 90% mortality rate (Mirin, Weiss, & Greenfield, 1991). The mortality rate has dropped significantly in recent years, in response to increased medical awareness of the special needs of the addicted infant (Mirin, Weiss, & Greenfield, 1991).

Surprisingly, in light of the dangers that maternal narcotics abuse pose to the fetus, it is not recommended that the addicted mother be withdrawn from opioids during pregnancy. Hoegerman and Schnoll (1991) warned that, except in extreme circumstances, the dangers associated with maternal narcotics withdrawal during pregnancy outweigh the potential for harm to the developing fetus. The authors recognize that infants born to mothers who are addicted to narcotics present special needs and that they require special care to survive the first few days of life and beyond. But they cite evidence suggesting that maternal narcotics withdrawal during pregnancy can result in extreme stress for the fetus, possibly resulting in fetal death.

Further, there is evidence that children born to mothers whose opiate addiction has been stabilized on methadone tend to benefit from longer gestation periods, and to weigh more at birth, than children whose mothers were not using methadone (Kaltenbach, 1997). Research also suggests that it is better for the fetus if the mother's methadone dose is administered in two smaller units, one in the morning and the other in the late afternoon or early evening (Kandall, Doberczak, Jantunen, & Stein, 1999). This "split dosing" schedule has been found to result in lower daily dosage levels of methadone for the mother, and it seems to reduce the danger of drug-induced suppression of fetal activity (Kandall,

Doberczak, Jantunen, & Stein, 1999). Following delivery, both mother and child can then be detoxified from narcotics via methadone (Miller, 1994; Hoegerman & Schnoll, 1991).

There are many factors other than drugs that can contribute to later developmental problems for the child, including poverty and indifferent caregivers (Hawley, Halle, Drasin, & Thomas, 1995). Indeed, after following a sample of 330 children, 120 of whom were raised by heroin-dependent parents, researchers at the Hebrew University Medical School in Israel concluded that except for a small percentage of infants with neurological problems, the developmental delays noted in children born to heroin-dependent mothers resulted more from environmental deprivation than from the effects of prenatal heroin exposure (Fishman, 1996). Thus it appears that with the proper childhood environment, the child may outgrow most, if not all, of the negative effects of prenatal exposure to narcotic analgesics.

Narcotics and breast-feeding. The woman who is using narcotics and breast-feeding her child will pass some of the drug on to the infant (Lourwood & Riedlinger, 1989). Although the effects of a single dose of narcotics have only a minimal impact on the child, prolonged use of narcotics may cause the child to become sleepy, eat poorly, and develop respiratory depression. Because of the infant's "immature liver metabolizing functions" (Lourwood & Riedlinger, 1989, p. 85), there is a danger that narcotics will accumulate in the child's body if the mother is using a narcotic analgesic during breast-feeding. Indeed, the baby who is breast-fed by an opiate-abusing mother might actually obtain enough narcotics through breast milk to remain addicted to narcotics (Zuckerman & Bresnahan, 1991). In spite of that fact, Kaltenbach (1997) did not recommend that a woman on methadone not breast-feed her child unless she was also using medications other than methadone.

Marijuana Use During Pregnancy

Some researchers believe that marijuana is the illicit substance most commonly abused by women of childbearing age (Kandall, 1999). Nationally, it has been estimated that between 2.9% (Kandall, 1999) and 12% (Pirozzolo & Bonnefil, 1995) of the women who are pregnant in non-ghetto urban areas use marijuana at least once during their pregnancy. The estimate of 2.9%

of pregnant women would translate into approximately 119,000 women (Mathias, 1995).

Scientists have discovered that the placenta is able to provide the fetus with some protection from marijuana smoke; fetal blood levels of THC reach only one sixth those of the mother (Nelson, 2000). But there remains a great deal to discover about the effects of marijuana use on the pregnant woman and the fetus (Dreher, Nugent, & Hudgins, 1994). One confounding factor is that it is not possible to isolate the effects of maternal marijuana use from the effects of poor nutrition, the use of other drugs, poor prenatal care, or maternal health. Other variables that would affect such research include the frequency of marijuana use, the potency of the marijuana being used, and the amount of marijuana smoke the user inhaled. It is thus not surprising that research into the possible effects of maternal marijuana use on fetal growth and development has resulted in conflicting or inconclusive results.

In an early attempt to examine this problem, Nahas (1986) concluded that marijuana use during pregnancy might contribute to "intrauterine growth retardation, poor weight gain, prolonged labor, and behavioral abnormalities in the newborn" (p. 83). However, other researchers (Behnke & Eyler, 1993; Day & Richardson, 1991) found conflicting evidence about whether maternal marijuana use during pregnancy might result in poor intrauterine growth. Thus it is not clear at this time whether marijuana use during pregnancy has an effect on fetal growth.

A number of research studies, summarized by Eyler and Behnke (1999), have uncovered abnormal tremors, startle reflexes, and eye problems in children exposed to marijuana in utero. Women who used marijuana at least once a month during pregnancy were also found to have a higher risk of premature delivery and of delivering children who were lighter in weight and/or smaller than normal for their gestational age (Bays, 1992).

In contrast to the studies that identified a clear effect of maternal marijuana use on fetal growth and development is the study conducted by Dreher, Nugent, and Hudgins (1994). The authors examined 24 babies born in rural Jamaica, where heavy marijuana use is common, who were known to have been exposed to marijuana in utero. The development of these infants was contrasted with that of 20 other infants known not to have been exposed to marijuana. The authors failed to find *any* developmental differences between the two groups that could be attributed to maternal marijuana use. Where significant differences between the two groups of infants were found, the authors were able to attribute them to the mother's social status. Marijuana-using mothers were also found to have a greater number of adults living within the household and to have fewer children within the home. According to the authors, these factors allowed for more care to be given to the newborn than was the case in the homes where the mother did not use marijuana. Although these findings are suggestive, too little is known about either the short-term or the long-term effects of maternal marijuana use during pregnancy to allow researchers to reach any definite conclusions (Day & Richardson, 1991).

One possibility that has been overlooked in research efforts to date is that it might take several years for the effects of maternal marijuana use to be manifested in the child. Fried (1995) examined this possibility and found that in older children whose mothers used marijuana during pregnancy, subtle neuropsychological testing found deficits in the "executive functioning" regions of the brain (Fried, 1995, p. 2159). That is, the author found evidence of problems in prefrontal lobe brain function that were not exhibited until the child was 6–9 years of age.

Admittedly, there are many variables that might confound the conclusions reached by Fried (1995), including the quality of the child's environment, parental interactions with the child, and so on. However, given the lifelong consequences for the child if maternal marijuana use during pregnancy *does* have an effect on the fetus, marijuana use during pregnancy should be discouraged.

Marijuana and breast-feeding. THC, the active agent of marijuana, is concentrated in human milk and passed on to the infant during breast-feeding. The THC level in breast milk has been found to be six times (Nelson, 2000) to eight times (Hartman, 1995) as high as the mother's blood plasma level. This would suggest that maternal marijuana use might have some impact on the infant if the mother breast-feeds her child. Breast-feeding by mothers who smoke marijuana is thought to result in slower motor development for the child in the first year of life (Frank, Bauchner, Zuckerman, & Fried, 1992; Pediatrics for Parents, 1990). This causation is based on a preliminary study of the effects of the mother's use of marijuana on the infant's development, but it does suggest a potential hazard that should be avoided.

Benzodiazepine Use During Pregnancy

The question of whether pregnant women, especially those in their first trimester of pregnancy, should use any of the benzodiazepines remains controversial. Some studies have suggested that the use of benzodiazepines during the first trimester of pregnancy is associated with an increased risk of facial abnormalities, but other studies have failed to find such a relationship (Barki, Kravitz, & Berki, 1998). Currently, it is thought that the use of benzodiazepines during the first trimester is associated with a *slight* increase in cleft palate, inguinal hernia, and other minor craniofacial abnormalities (Barki, Kravitz, & Berki, 1998). Accordingly, these drugs should be used only when the anticipated benefits to the mother or fetus outweigh the potential danger to the fetus.

Animal research has also suggested the *possibility* of neurological changes in offspring who were exposed to benzodiazepines prenatally (Miller, 1994). Thus, until further research determines whether there is potential danger to the fetus, the benefits of benzodiazepine use during pregnancy should be weighed against the potential for harm.

Benzodiazepine use during breast-feeding. Because the benzodiazepines are found in the nursing mother's milk, Graedon and Graedon (1996) suggested that nursing mothers also not use benzodiazepines. Lourwood and Riedlinger (1989) concluded that, because these drugs are metabolized mainly by the liver, an organ that in the infant is not fully developed, nursing mothers should not use any of the benzodiazepines.

Hallucinogen Use During Pregnancy

There is only limited research into the effects of maternal hallucinogen abuse on fetal growth and development (Kandall, 1999).

PCP abuse during pregnancy. Tabor, Smith-Wallace, and Yonekura (1990) compared the birth records of 37 children born between 1982 and 1987 whose medical records indicated that the mothers had used PCP during pregnancy. The authors then compared these birth records with those of infants born to mothers who had abused cocaine during pregnancy. The majority of the

women in both groups had minimal prenatal care, a factor that might influence the growth and development of the fetus, and most of the women in the study were polydrug users. However, on the basis of their study, the authors concluded that exposure to PCP in utero was associated with intrauterine growth retardation and premature labor and that the infants often required extended hospitalization following birth. Infants born to women who had used PCP during pregnancy also seemed to experience abrupt changes in the level of consciousness, fine tremors, sweating, and irritability, according to Tabor, Smith-Wallace, and Yonekura (1990).

MDMA/Ecstasy use in pregnancy. Widespread abuse of ecstasy is a relatively recent phenomenon, so there has been little systematic research into the effects of this compound on fetal growth and development. However, McElhatton, Bateman, Evans, Pughe, and Thomas (1999) reported on the outcome of 136 pregnancies in the United Kingdom, 74 of which involved women who had abused only MDMA during their pregnancy. They found that 15% of the infants born to women who had abused MDMA at some point in their pregnancy had a congenital abnormality, a rate five times higher than the normal rate of 2–3%.

Three Substances Whose Effects During Pregnancy Are Not Clear

Buspirone. Buspirone has not been studied in sufficient detail to determine whether it has the potential to harm the human fetus (Barki, Kravitz, & Berki, 1998). Animal research involving rats found an increased risk for stillbirth when buspirone was used at high dosage levels, but there did not appear to be any effect on the speed with which newborn rats were able to learn, on their level of motor activity, or on their emotional development (Miller, 1994).

Bupropion. The effects of bupropion on the developing fetus have not been studied in detail (Miller, 1994).

Disulfiram. Disulfiram is not recommended for use in pregnant women (Miller, 1994). Animal research suggests that the combination of alcohol with disulfiram is potentially dangerous for the fetus, according to the author. Further, evidence based on animal research suggests that a metabolite of disulfiram, diethyldithiocarbamate, may bind to lead, allowing this metal to then cross the blood-brain barrier and reach the central nervous system. Lead is a known toxin, which can cause neurological disorders and mental retardation. There is a need for further research to determine whether disulfiram use contributes to higher lead levels in humans.

Cigarette Use During Pregnancy

Approximately 20% of the estimated 4 million women who give birth in this country each year, or approximately 820,000 women—smoke during their pregnancy (Mathias, 1995). Byrd and Howard (1995) give an even higher estimate, maintaining that 29% of the infants born in the United States each year—or 1 million infants each year—are exposed to cigarette smoke prenatally. An additional 22% of all infants are exposed to "second-hand" or environmental cigarette smoke after birth, even though their mothers did not themselves smoke cigarettes (Byrd & Howard, 1995).

Maternal cigarette smoking is a known risk factor for numerous fetal developmental problems, and in terms of fetal development, maternal cigarette use during pregnancy may be *worse than maternal cocaine use* (Cotton, 1994). Medical researchers have long known that children born to mothers who smoke cigarettes during pregnancy are likely to weigh an average of 200 grams less at birth than children born to nonsmoking mothers (Eyler & Behnke, 1999; Byrd & Howard, 1995; Bell & Lau, 1995). Indeed, the American Medical Association (AMA) (1993a) estimated that 20–30% of the problem of low-birth-weight children might be traced to maternal tobacco use. Further, nicotine use during pregnancy seems to be associated with such problems as premature labor and delivery and stillbirth.

Pregnant women who smoke have a 30% higher risk of stillbirth. Indeed, even after the child is born, there is a 26% higher risk of the infant dying within the first few days of life for the mother who smoked during pregnancy (Bell & Lau, 1995). Women who smoke (or who are exposed to cigarette smoke) during pregnancy are more likely to suffer spontaneous abortion, a decrease in the blood flow to the uterus, and an increased chance of vaginal bleeding (Lee & D'Alonzo, 1993). Women who smoke during pregnancy are also at risk for a premature rupture of membranes and for both delayed crying time and decreased fetal breathing time following birth (Graedon & Graedon, 1996).

There is also evidence that maternal cigarette smoking during pregnancy contributes to neurological prob-

lems for the developing fetus and, following birth, to cognitive developmental problems (Olds, Henderson, & Tatelbaum, 1994). The authors found in their study that children born to mothers who smoked 10 or more cigarettes a day during pregnancy scored an average of 4.35 points lower on a standardized intelligence test at ages 3–4 than did children born to nonsmoking mothers. The authors concluded that the observed effects were due to maternal cigarette use during pregnancy.

A growing body of literature that suggests maternal cigarette use during pregnancy is one risk factor for the development of attention deficit–hyperactivity disorder (ADHD) (Milberger, Biederman, Faraone, Chen, & Jones 1996). Maternal cigarette use during pregnancy has also been linked to such neurodevelopmental problems as impulsiveness, although it is not clear what role cigarette smoking plays in the development of these problems (Day & Richardson, 1994). Finally, after examining the records of some 1.57 million births in Hungary over a 10-year period, Czeizel, Kodaj, and Lenz (1994) concluded that maternal cigarette smoking was a risk factor for the condition known as *congenital limb deficiency* (a failure for the limbs of the fetus to develop properly). The authors hypothesized that nicotine's ability to disrupt blood flow patterns to the uterus might be the cause of this developmental abnormality.

Infants born to smoking mothers appear to suffer from reduced lung capacity, experiencing an average of a 10% reduction in lung function (Byrd & Howard, 1995). Finally, infants who are exposed to cigarette smoke suffer a significantly higher rate of SIDS than infants who are not exposed to this environmental hazard. Researchers in England have found that for each hour that a newborn infant is exposed to cigarette smoke, his or her risk for SIDS increases 100% (Los Angeles Times, 1996b). Thus, as these various studies suggest, maternal cigarette use during pregnancy carries with it a number of risks for the developing fetus.

Cigarette smoking during breast-feeding. Medical research reveals that the mother should abstain from cigarette use during the period that she is breast-feeding the infant. Nicotine tends to concentrate in breast milk, with a half-life of 1.5 hours (Byrd & Howard, 1995). The total concentration of nicotine in the woman's breast milk depends on the number of cigarettes she smokes and the time between the last cigarette and the time she breast-feeds the infant, according to the authors. Nicotine itself has been shown to interfere with the process of breast-feeding, reducing the amount of milk produced, and with the process of milk ejection (the "let down" reflex) (Byrd & Howard, 1995). Infants who are breast-fed by cigarette-smoking mothers tend to put on weight more slowly than breast-fed infants whose mothers do not smoke.

Use of Over-the-Counter Analgesics During Pregnancy

Aspirin. Women who are, or who suspect that they might be, pregnant should not use aspirin except under the supervision of a physician (Shannon, Wilson, & Stang, 1995). Aspirin has been implicated as a cause of decreased birth weight in children born to women who used it during pregnancy. There is also evidence that aspirin may be a cause of stillbirth and increased perinatal mortality (United States Pharmacopeial Convention, 1990a).

Briggs, Freeman, and Yaffe (1986) explored the impact of maternal aspirin use on the fetus and on the infant whose mother was breast-feeding. They reported that the use of aspirin by the mother during pregnancy might produce "anemia, antepartum and/or postpartum hemorrhage, prolonged gestation and prolonged labor" (p. 26a). Aspirin has also been implicated in significantly higher perinatal mortality and in retardation of intrauterine growth, when used at high doses by pregnant women (Briggs, Freeman, & Yaffe, 1986).

The authors noted that maternal use of aspirin in the week before delivery might interfere with the infant's ability to form blood clots following birth. The United States Pharmacopeial Convention (1990a) went further, warning that women should not use aspirin in the last two weeks of pregnancy. Aspirin has been found to cross the placenta, and research suggests that maternal use of aspirin during pregnancy might result in higher levels of aspirin in the fetus than in the mother (Briggs, Freeman, & Yaffe, 1986).

Acetaminophen. Acetaminophen was found to be "safe for short-term use" at recommended dosage levels by pregnant women (Briggs, Freeman, & Yaffe, 1986 p. 2a). There have been no reports of serious problems in women who have used acetaminophen during pregnancy. The authors noted, however, that the death of one infant from kidney disease shortly after birth was attributed to the mother's continuous use of acetamin-

ophen at high dosage levels during pregnancy. There is a need for further research into the effects of this analgesic during pregnancy.

Although acetaminophen is excreted in low concentrations in the mother's breast milk, Briggs, Freeman, and Yaffe (1986) found no evidence that this had adverse effects on the infant. Lourwood and Riedlinger (1989) suggested, however, that because acetaminophen is metabolized mainly by the liver, which is still quite immature in the newborn child, the mother who breast-feeds during the immediately postpartum period should not use this drug. However, the authors did not warn against the occasional use of acetaminophen in women who are breast-feeding their children after the postpartum period.

Ibuprofen. When used at therapeutic dosage levels, this drug was not reported to cause congenital birth defects (Briggs, Freeman, & Yaffe, 1986). However, similar drugs have been known to inhibit labor, prolong pregnancy, and cause other problems for the developing child. It is for this reason that ibuprofen use is not recommended during pregnancy (Briggs, Freeman, & Yaffe, 1986). Research suggests that ibuprofen does not enter human milk in significant quantities when used at normal dosage levels (Briggs, Freeman, and Yaffe, 1986) and that it is considered "compatible with breast feeding" (p. 217i). Indeed, Lourwood and Riedlinger (1989) reported that ibuprofen was "felt to be the safest" of the nonsteroidal anti-inflammatory drugs for the woman who is breast-feeding her child.

Inhalant Abuse During Pregnancy

Virtually nothing is known about the effects of the various inhalants on the developing fetus. Although only a small percentage of those who experiment with inhalants go on to abuse these chemicals on a chronic basis, more than 50% of those who do chronically abuse inhalants are women "in their prime childbearing years" (Pearson, Hoyme, Seaver, & Rimsza, 1994, p. 211). It is thus safe to assume that some children are being exposed to one or more of the inhalants during gestation.

Researchers have just started to study the effects of toluene inhalation on the developing fetus. Toluene is found in many forms of paint and solvents. It is known to cross the placenta into the fetal circulation when the mother inhales toluene fumes. In adults, about 50% of the toluene inhaled is biotransformed into hippuric acid, and the remainder is excreted unchanged (Pearson, Hoyme, Seaver, & Rimsza, 1994). But neither the fetus nor the newborn child has the ability to metabolize toluene. There is thus some question whether the effects of toluene exposure for the fetus or newborn would be the same as for the adult who inhaled toluene fumes.

To attempt to answer this question, Pearson, Hoyme, Seaver, and Rimsza (1994) examined 18 infants who were exposed to toluene through maternal paint sniffing during pregnancy. They found that there were several similarities between the effects of toluene on the developing fetus and those of alcohol. The authors found that like FAS, toluene exposure during pregnancy may cause a wide range of problems, including premature birth, cranofacial abnormalities (abnormal ears, thin upper lip, small nose, etc.), abnormal muscle tone, renal abnormalities, developmental delays, abnormal scalp hair patterns, and retarded physical growth.

To explain the similarity between the effects of toluene abuse and alcohol abuse on the developing fetus, the authors hypothesized that toluene and alcohol may both result in a state of maternal toxicity. This state of maternal toxicity would contribute to the fetal malformations seen in cases of toluene and alcohol exposure during pregnancy. Although the authors' work is only preliminary, it would appear that toluene exposure during pregnancy may have lifelong consequences for the developing fetus. Until proven otherwise, the only safe course is to assume that maternal abuse of the other inhalants would have similar destructive effects on the growing fetus.

Summary

When a substance-abusing woman is pregnant, the fetus that she carries becomes an unwilling participant in the mother's chemical use/abuse. However, the impact of the chemical use is often much greater on the growing fetus than on the mother. Thus infants born to women who have used chemicals of abuse during pregnancy represent a special subpopulation of alcohol/drug users.

An extreme example of the unwilling participation of infants in maternal alcohol or drug use occurs when the child is born already addicted to the chemicals that the mother used during pregnancy. Other fetal complications of maternal chemical abuse include stroke, retardation, lower weight at birth, and a number of other drug-specific complications. The over-the-counter analgesics present a special area of risk, for the effects of these medications on fetal growth and development are not well understood. However, available research suggests that the OTC analgesics should be used with caution by pregnant or nursing women.

The Hidden Faces of Chemical Dependency

Introduction

There are many faces to chemical dependency. Many of these images are familiar. For example, there is the stereotype of the "typical" "skid row" alcoholic, drinking a bottle of cheap wine wrapped in a brown paper bag. Another popular image is that of the young male heroin addict, with a belt wrapped around his arm, pushing a needle into a vein. A popular stereotype of the chemically addicted female is that of the "fallen" woman: immoral, a poor parent, and certainly nothing like "us." These popular stereotypes are both quite persistent and grossly inaccurate (Schneiderman, 1990), and few people recognize that they serve only to limit our vision. If the addicted person deviates from our expectations, we may not recognize the chemical dependency hiding behind the social façade. For example, how many of us would expect to meet a well-groomed, white, middle-class heroin addict at work? How many people would recognize the benzodiazepine dependency behind the smiling face of a day care worker?

It is the purpose of this chapter to explore some of the hidden faces of chemical dependency, so that the reader may become more sensitive to the many forms that substance abuse takes.

Women and Addiction: An Often Unrecognized Problem

All too often, the "lessons" of history are discovered through hindsight. Only rarely is a lesson from history acknowledged *before* a crisis develops, so that the problem might be circumvented. For example, during the epidemic of chemical abuse in the last years of the 19th century, the ratio of men to women who were addicted to chemicals was only 1:2 (Lawson, 1994). Significant numbers of women were addicted to various mail-order medicines that were freely available without prescription at the time. Then a series of laws were passed that limited the availability of compounds containing addictive substances, and the epidemic of drug addiction gradually waned.

Yet when the current epidemic of alcohol/drug abuse began in the second half of the 20th century, society tended to focus on *men* who had chemical use problems and virtually ignored the possibility that significant numbers of *women* might also be struggling with alcohol/drug abuse. A double standard evolved, in which the woman with a substance use problem was viewed as being "poor or sexually available or weak and stupid" (Lawson, 1994, p. 138)—in other words, as being defective in some ill-defined way—while the man was reluctantly viewed as having a "disease." Thus women substance abusers were stigmatized by society and were a barely recognized subgroup whose addiction to alcohol/drugs was somehow less important than that of men (Cohen, 2000; Ramlow, White, Watson, & Leukefeld, 1997).

As a group, substance-abusing women tend to be hidden, protected, and/or abandoned (Cohen, 2000). Possibly because of this social response to the problem of alcohol/drug misuse by women, it was not until the early 1980s that mental health professionals became aware of the fact that

Gender plays a role in differential use of various substances by men and women, in their physiological reactions to the substances, in familial and societal reactions to their problems, in their help-seeking behavior, and in their interactions with clinicians. (Lala & Straussner, 1997, p. 3)

Deplorably, we still have much to learn about the impact of chemical use/abuse on women. Although it is not possible to do full justice to the interplay between gender and chemical abuse, this section will attempt to provide an overview of some of the issues and controversies surrounding alcohol/drug abuse by women.

Statement of the problem. It is currently believed that fully 40% of those who are physically dependent on chemicals are women (Lawson, 1994; Anderson, 1993) and that one of every three alcohol-dependent individuals is a woman (North, 1996). Researchers believe that alcohol-dependent women are up to 23 times as likely as women who are not dependent on alcohol to commit suicide (Markarian & Franklin, 1998). Even so, there has been little systematic research into the need for, or the effectiveness of, gender-specific treatment programs (Brady & Randall, 1999). There is a "paucity of female-only support groups" (Coughey, Feighan, Cheney, & Klein, 1998, p. 929).

Obviously, there are inadequate resources to offer rehabilitation programs for all of the women who abuse chemicals. The situation is so dismal that *a decade ago* it was concluded that the treatment industry as a whole had failed to meet the needs of addicted women (Alexander, 1996; Levy & Rutter, 1992). Even now, in the first years of the 21st century, their needs are virtually ignored.

The "convergence" theory. As substance abuse rehabilitation professionals began to recognize that large numbers of women were abusing or addicted to recreational chemicals, they began to speak of a "convergence" in the incidence of substance abuse problems among men and women. It was thought that ever-growing numbers of women were becoming addicted to chemicals and that the time was rapidly drawing near when approximately equal numbers of men and women would struggle with substance use problems. Fortunately, however, there is little empirical evidence to support the concept of "convergence" in rates of alcohol/drug use (Anthony, Arria, & Johnson, 1995).

How Does Gender Affect the Rehabilitation Process?

Gender affects the process of rehabilitation in a number of ways. First, there are different pathways for men and women who become addicted to chemicals. Second, women present special needs in a rehabilitation setting (Kauffman, Dore, & Nelson-Zlupko, 1995). For example, women who are addicted to chemicals are also more likely than male substance abusers to present a history of having been exposed to some form of interpersonal violence, and many will have to come to terms with these victimization issues as part of their recovery program (Cohen, 2000; Byington, 1997; Del Boca & Hesselbrock, 1996; Miller & Downs, 1995; O'Connor, Samet, & Stein, 1994).

Another difference was found to exist in the way that the individual perceives the causes of his or her chemical addiction: Men tend to externalize the responsibility for their alcohol/drug use problem, whereas women tend to blame themselves (Lala & Straussner, 1997). It is for this reason that more alcohol-dependent women than men suffer from poor self-esteem (Cohen, 2000; Coughey, Feighan, Cheney, & Klein, 1998; Alexander, 1996; North, 1996). Indeed, there is some evidence that drug abuse represents an attempt on the part of the woman to medicate feelings of low self-worth (Alexander, 1996).

Women with alcohol/drug use problems tend to experience greater demands on their time than their male counterparts (O'Dell, Turner, & Weaver, 1998; Kauffman, Dore, & Nelson-Zlupko, 1995). For example, it is not uncommon for the woman to be granted custody of the children following divorce on the grounds that the children should live with their mother. If that mother has a substance use problem, she may find that few rehabilitation programs have provisions for taking care of the children while she is in treatment. In such cases, child custody often becomes an obstacle to the mother's participation in treatment for substance use problems (Kauffman, Dore, & Nelson-Zlupko, 1995; Beckman, 1994; Raskin, 1994).

Substance-abusing women tend to enter into the rehabilitation system in a far different manner than their male counterparts (Brady & Randall, 1999; Alexander, 1996; Weisner & Schmidt, 1992). Women tend to enter treatment programs through advertisements in the media, or upon the referral of a friend, whereas men are more likely to enter treatment as a result of a referral from a physician, employer, or court system (Beckman, 1994).

Research has also found that alcohol-addicted women are far more likely than alcohol-dependent men to suffer from a primary depression (Dixit & Crum, 2000). Further, the depressed alcohol-dependent woman usually has a better prognosis than a depressed male who is dependent on alcohol (Hill, 1995; Schutte, Moos, & Brennan, 1995). For women, the symptoms of depression are likely to serve as a drinking cue, triggering further alcohol use as the depressed woman attempts to self-medicate her depression. Men appear to be less likely to try to self-medicate a depressive disorder through alcohol use, and they may even reduce their alcohol use when they become depressed (Schutte, Moos, & Brennan, 1995).

This difference in the pathway that men and women typically follow toward alcohol dependency would seem to account for the observation that women initially tend to seek help from mental health providers rather than substance abuse rehabilitation professionals (Weisner & Schmidt, 1992). Men who are addicted to chemicals, on the other hand, tend to become involved with substance abuse treatment professionals immediately, according to the authors.

Women who enter treatment usually present a different constellation of problems than do men. As a general rule, men tend to sell drugs to support their addiction, whereas women are more likely to sell their bodies, although not every woman with a substance use problem engages in prostitution (Lala & Straussner, 1997). Women who enter treatment also have different interpersonal and intrapersonal resources than do men at the beginning of the rehabilitation process. For example, society places different expectations on men and women, and these behavioral expectations (social role, status, etc.) both help to shape the progression of substance use disorders in men and women and place barriers in the way of many women who seek to enter treatment (Del Boca & Hesselbrock, 1996).

The barriers that women face when they wish to enter substance abuse rehabilitation treatment include funding problems, child care/custody issues, transportation problems, lack of support from partners, and the stigmatization that often surrounds those who have a substance abuse problem. As a general rule, women

have smaller social support circles, and receive less emotional support from their friends, than do their male counterparts (O'Dell, Turner, & Weaver, 1998). As the individuals progressed along the road to recovery, there was a corresponding increase in the size, and in the level of support offered by, the social circles of the women studied (O'Dell, Turner, & Weaver, 1998).

Alcohol-dependent women have been found to be four times more likely to be living with a partner who also has an alcohol use problem than is the male alcoholic (Miller & Cervantes, 1997). Men faced with an alcoholic partner are more likely to turn to divorce as a way of resolving this marital problem than are women (Byington, 1997). For these reasons, many women report that they receive less support from their partner for their efforts to abstain from chemical use than do recovering men (O'Dell, Turner, & Weaver, 1998; Kauffman, Dore, & Nelson-Zlupko, 1995).

Work, gender, and chemical abuse. The relationship between employment and chemical abuse problems in women is quite complex. For some women, the social status, social support, and improved self-esteem that go along with full-time, paid employment seem to help reduce the chances that she will develop a substance use problem (Brady & Randall, 1999; Wilsnack & Wilsnack, 1995; Wilsnack, Wilsnack, & Hiller-Sturmhofel, 1994). Yet for reasons that are not well understood, employment can also facilitate the development of a chemical use problem in other women (Brady & Randall, 1999).

One employment variable that does seem to be associated with an increased risk of alcohol abuse is whether the woman is working in a traditionally male-dominated profession (Wilsnack & Wilsnack, 1995; Wilsnack, Wilsnack, & Hiller-Sturmhofel, 1994). Women employed in a profession where more than 50% of their co-workers are males tend to report higher levels of alcohol use problems, according to the authors. However, male alcohol use patterns do not seem to be affected by the gender of their co-workers, which again suggests that there are different pathways to alcohol use problems for men and women.

Unfortunately, many women in the work force are working below their potential, often in low-status high-frustration positions (Pape, 1988). Because they are underemployed, their chemical use is less likely to interfere with their job performance than it is for a man

(Kruzicki, 1987). This makes it more difficult to detect the woman whose job performance is impaired by drug or alcohol use. Also, the threat of loss of employment if the addicted woman does not seek treatment may not be so effective as it is for men. Many such women work only to supplement their husband's income, and it is often easier for them simply to quit the job than to confront their substance abuse (Pape, 1988).

Victimization histories and substance use patterns. Research has shown that women who are addicted to alcohol are 2.5 times as likely to report having been sexually abused in childhood than are nonalcoholic women (Byington, 1997; Miller & Downs, 1995). Further, up to 85% of the women in treatment for alcohol dependency give a history of having been an incest victim (Beckman, 1994). As these statistics suggest, there appears to be a tendency for those women who are treated for a substance use problem to have been the victim of some form of sexual violence (Blume, 1998; Alexander, 1996). However, as Holloway (1998) observed, alcohol/ drug misuse is not *necessarily* a result of having been abused by a significant other. The assumption that such an abuse history will result in a chemical use problem is "not only damaging but also antitherapeutic and disempowering" to women (p. 35). Thus staff must be careful in drawing conclusions about the role of victimization in the development of a substance use disorder.

Although the woman with a substance use problem is often referred to a mixed-sex group as part of her treatment program, research has found that many women fail to benefit from a mixed-group format (Lala & Straussner, 1997). Many women feel inhibited in mixed groups, especially if they have been victimized by a male at some time (Lala & Straussner, 1997; Alexander, 1996). The language used by men in the therapeutic setting is often intimidating to women, and may even revictimize them as memories of past abuse surface. This explains in part why women drop out of mixed groups more than out of unisex groups.

Gender and substance use patterns. Within the past generation, researchers have discovered that women usually obtain their drug of choice in different ways than men. Unlike male substance abusers, women drug abusers tend to obtain their drugs from their own physician. Indeed, a decade ago it was suggested that sedatives and "diet pills" had become "women's drugs" (Peluso & Peluso, 1988, p. 10). This trend could be seen in the fact that nearly 70% of all prescriptions for psychotropic medications are written for women (Cohen, Fleming, Glatter, Haghigi, Halberstadt, McHugh, & Woolf, 1996). But because these women obtain their drug of choice through a physician's prescription and the local pharmacy, their drug abuse problem is all too often "rendered invisible" (Peluso & Peluso, 1988, p. 9).

There is also another way in which substance use by women is rendered invisible. Many women were initially introduced to illicit drugs by their male partner, who then serves as a source of supply for that woman (Blume, 1998). In this manner, the woman's need for chemicals is met by a male partner, possibly in return for sexual favors, and she does not have to seek out illicit drugs actively on her own.

Differing Effects of Common Drugs of Abuse on Men and Women

As medical researchers learn more about the effects of various drugs on men and women, they are starting to uncover significant differences in how each gender responds to different chemicals. Not surprisingly, there are also differences in how men and women react when they use one or more of the popular drugs of abuse.

Narcotics abuse and gender. Griffin, Weiss, Mirin, and Lang (1989) found that the woman who was addicted to narcotics was likely to have started using opiates at a significantly older age than her male counterparts. But they also found that the typical narcotics-dependent woman has a history of heavier drug use than male addicts and that women addicted to narcotics tend to be approximately the same age as men at the time of their first admission into drug treatment.

At the same time, there appear to be differences in how opiate-dependent men and women use their drug of choice. In England, Gossop, Battersby, and Strang (1991) found that male narcotics addicts were more likely to inject their drug, female narcotics addicts to inhale narcotic powder. Female addicts were also found to be more likely to be involved in a sexual relationship with another drug user. Finally, just under half of the female narcotics addicts studied by the authors had received drugs as a present from a sexual partner, confirming that narcotics addiction follows a different course for women than for men.

Cocaine abuse and gender. Women make up approximately 50% of those addicted to cocaine (Lawson,

1994). However, research has revealed that cocaine use patterns differ between men and women. Female cocaine abusers tend to start their drug use at an earlier age and seem to reach the stage of addiction more rapidly (Kender & Prescott, 1998). The cocaine-addicted woman is likely to be significantly younger at the time of her first admission to a drug treatment program than her male counterpart, and to have followed a different pathway to cocaine addiction (Griffin, Weiss, Mirin, & Lang, 1989). Yet in spite of this growing awareness that men and women may become addicted to cocaine for different reasons, little research has been conducted into how the treatment program should be modified in order to be more effective with cocaine abusers of either sex.

Alcohol abuse and gender. As a general rule, women tend to require less alcohol to become intoxicated than do men. For example, the blood alcohol level (BAL) of a woman would be up to 40% higher than that of a man who had consumed the same amount of alcohol (Blume, 1998; North, 1996). Further, monthly variations in estrogen levels can affect the speed with which the woman's body absorbs alcohol, and oral contraceptive medications can slow the biotransformation of the alcohol already in her body (North, 1996).

There is significant evidence that women are more sensitive than men to the destructive effects of alcohol (Nixon, 1994). For example, one begins to see alcohol-related physical problems in female alcohol abusers at just one-third the level of alcohol intake necessary for the typical male alcohol abuser to experience similar problems (North, 1996). Further, women appear to be more sensitive than men to the toxic effects of alcohol on striated muscle tissues, such as the tissues of the heart (Urbano-Marquez, Estruch, Fernandez-Sola, Nicholas, Pare, & Rubin, 1995).

Researchers have also found that when women first enter treatment for alcoholism, their addiction—and the medical consequences of that addiction—are usually more severe than what one would expect for a man with the same drinking history (Weisner & Schmidt, 1992). Thus the typical alcoholic woman will develop cirrhosis of the liver after about 13 years of addictive drinking, whereas it might take the typical male alcoholic 22 years to develop the same disorder (Blume, 1994; Hennessey, 1992). In a sense, the woman's alcohol-related consequences are often "telescoped" into a shorter time frame than that found for the typical male

alcoholic (Schuckit, Daeppen, Tipp, Hellebrock, & Bucholz, 1998).

In addition to this, there is a known association between alcohol abuse and infertility, miscarriage, amenorrhea, uterine bleeding, dysmenorhea, osteoporosis, and possibly breast cancer (Cyr & Moulton, 1993; Hennessey, 1992). Unfortunately, in spite of this known association between alcohol abuse/addiction and illness, physicians are very poor at recognizing the signs of alcohol addiction in their female patients (North, 1996; Kitchens, 1994).

Gender is now considered one of the major variables that helps to define the developmental pathway of different subtypes of alcohol abuse/addiction (Del Boca & Hesselbrock, 1996). Research has uncovered at least two forms of alcohol dependency in women (Hill, 1995). The first group, which is composed only of a minority of women drinkers, appears to include those women whose alcoholism finds full expression between the ages of 18 and 24 years. These women might be said to have "early-onset" (Hill, 1995, p. 11) alcohol dependency, and their drinking pattern tends to be atypical. In contrast to this group is the larger group of alcohol-dependent women. These women are classified as the "later-onset" (Hill, 1995, p. 11) drinkers, and their drinking seems to reach its peak between the ages of 35 and 49 years. However, the relationship between the two subtypes of female alcoholics identified by Hill and the Type I/Type II typology of alcoholism in males (discussed elsewhere in this text) is still not clear.

In their examination of the subtypes of alcoholism, Del Boca and Hesselbrock (1996) concluded that at least two of the four subtypes of alcoholism that they identified were strongly influenced by the individual's gender. On the basis of their data, they concluded that there are a number of developmental pathways that can result in alcoholism for men and women. Although these authors do not explore possible etiologies of the different subforms of alcoholism, their data *do* suggest that the expression of alcoholism for men and women follows traditional gender role expectations in the United States.

However, Miller and Cervantes (1997) sound a positive note, having found that women with alcohol use problems were more likely to respond to minimal interventions. One reason for this is that women "are often first to recognize their drinking problem, while men are more likely to have confrontations, especially with authorities, that bring them involuntarily into contact with treatment caregivers" (Beckman, 1993, p. 236). Thus, according to the author, women are more accepting of the treatment process, and the need for treatment. One catalyst that seems to help bring the substance-abusing woman in for treatment is her responsibility for children (Kline, 1996).

Unfortunately, there are significant social barriers between the recovering woman and community resources such as AA. One such barrier is the sexism inherent in the AA program (Coker, 1997). The sexual bias in virtually all of the AA literature demonstrates a "subtle but significant form of sexism" (Coker, 1997, p. 268) that serves to make women who are addicted to alcohol/drugs feel unwelcome. Because of the differences in how men and women perceive the "self" when they are addicted to chemicals, and because of past victimization experiences, women tend to feel more shame than do men when they enter AA. It is for this reason that women are more likely than men with alcohol use problems to be solitary drinkers. AA's heavy emphasis on uncovering sources of shame might serve to make women feel unwanted, or unwelcome, in AA (Coker, 1997).

There is also evidence that the face of alcohol use problems in women is changing. Young women are apparently starting to drink alcohol at an earlier age, and in far greater quantities, than did their older counterparts (Weisner & Schmidt, 1992). But just at the time when society is starting to develop an awareness of the impact of alcohol/drug use problems, "there is evidence that the alcoholic beverage industry has targeted women as a "growth market," with advertising designed to make drinking more acceptable to women and to change their drinking patterns" (Blume, 1994, p. 9).

This is lamentable. It has been argued that because of the important role women play as primary caretakers of children, society has hesitated to recognize the problem of alcohol/drug addiction in women (Peluso & Peluso, 1988). And now that society has becomes able to accept that significant numbers of women have substance use problems, new forms of advertising are emerging, aimed at making alcohol use more attractive to women. We can only hope that society will learn to face the problem of drug addiction by offering both men and women compassion and unrestricted access to proven treatment methods.

Addiction and the Homeless

It is estimated that between 567,000 and 600,000 people are homeless in the United States (Smith, Meyers, & Delaney, 1998). Between 45% and 57% of these are thought to have an alcohol use disorder (Smith, Meyers, & Delaney, 1998).

Substance Use Problems and the Elderly

As the latest wave of cocaine abuse peaked in the mid-1980s, behavioral scientists began to explore the scope of recreational chemical use/abuse in the general population. They discovered that large numbers of adults of all ages were using one or more recreational chemicals in ways that could be defined as abusive. Researchers were surprised to find that recreational chemical use/abuse was not limited to young adults but was also a significant problem in old age. In this section, the problem of alcohol/drug abuse among the elderly will be examined.

Scope of the problem. The elderly make up approximately 12% of the population of the United States, and receive approximately one-third of all prescription medications (Reid & Anderson, 1997). Many of these prescriptions are for medications designed to control the symptoms of nonpsychiatric disorders, such as coronary artery disease, gout, and arthritis. As we saw in Chapter 7, even when ingested in an amount that by itself is not abusive, alcohol can interfere with virtually every class of medication, either reducing the effectiveness or enhancing the biotransformation of many pharmaceuticals (Rigler, 2000; Goldstein, Pataki, & Webb, 1996). The use of medications by an older person can also change the way his or her body responds to alcohol (Smith, 1997).

Research has also revealed that 13% of the men, and 2% of the women, who are over the age of 60 and live in the community have alcohol use problems (Rigler, 2000). Alcohol abuse is the third most common form of psychiatric dysfunction in the elderly, surpassed only by the various forms of dementia and by anxiety disorders (Abrams & Alexopoulos, 1998; Campbell, 1992). Other estimates of the scope of the problem of alcohol abuse range from 2% (Brennan & Moos, 1996) to 15% (Mosier, 1999; Prater, Miller, & Zylstra, 1999; Zimberg, 1996) of those individuals over the age of 65.

Nationally, 1.5 million individuals over the age of 65 are thought to be physically dependent on alcohol (Hyman & Cassem, 1995).

Elderly alcohol abusers are over-represented in the population of those who are seeking health care. Researchers estimate that between 5–15% (Dunne, 1994; Vandeputte, 1989) and 49% (Blake, 1990) of elderly patients seeking medical treatment for one reason or another have an alcohol/drug-related problem. These estimates are consistent with that of Dunlop, Manghelli, and Tolson (1989) who suggested that 25% of the elderly population are suffering from alcohol related problems. Zimberg (1995) suggested that 10% of the men and 20% of the women might be classified as "escape drinkers" (p. 413) who have an alcohol use problem.

Older adults also experience problems caused by the abuse of other chemicals besides alcohol. Abrams and Alexopoulos (1987) suggested that "more than 20% of patients over 65 years old admitted to a psychiatric hospital in one year could be considered drug dependent" (p. 1286). Up to 15% of older adults might be classified as having a drug abuse problem (Cohen, Fleming, Glatter, Haghigi, Halberstadt, McHugh, & Woolf, 1996). The vast majority of these individuals either abuse, or have become dependent on, prescribed medications. Yet illicit drug abuse continues to be a problem for older people, as evidenced by the fact that 2% of illicit drug abusers are older than 50 (Rosenberg, 1997). Rigler (2000) warned that about 15% of the elderly patients who are alcohol-dependent also abuse or are dependent on other psychoactive agents. In spite of this information, however, virtually nothing is known about the older drug abuser.

Researchers have found that older alcoholics take up a disproportionate part of the health care resources in the United States. For example, after examining discharge diagnosis statistics from across the United States, Adams, Yuan, Barboriak, and Rimm (1993) found that between 19 and 77 of every 10,000 elderly patients admitted to acute-care hospitals had an alcohol use disorder. The authors also found that the number of elderly patients being treated for myocardial infarction was between 17 and 44 per 10,000 patient admissions in the same age group. Their figures suggest that the rates of hospital admission for alcohol-related health problems in the elderly was "similar to those for myocardial infarction" (p. 1224) and may even have exceeded that for this form of heart disease in the elderly. This finding is consistent with the finding that families with an alcoholic member have health care costs 21 times as high as similar families without an alcoholic member. Nor is the problem of substance abuse in the older population limited to alcohol. If these figures are accurate, then chemical use problems are common in the elderly.

A definition of alcohol abuse in the elderly. Medical researchers now believe that one standard alcohol-containing beverage per day is the upper limit of "moderate" alcohol use for those over the age of 60 (Rigler, 2000). The consequences for older individuals who consume *more* than the recommended limit of one drink per day are all too evident. Fully 14% of the elderly patients seen in the Emergency Room, 23–44% of elderly patients seen in an inpatient psychiatric treatment center, 18% of the patients hospitalized for general medical problems, and 11% of the elderly patients admitted to a nursing home are thought to have an alcohol use problem (Goldstein, Pataki, & Webb, 1996).

Why is the detection of substance use disorders in the elderly so difficult? Alcohol/drug use problems are often unrecognized among older individuals (Dunne, 1994; Kitchens, 1994; Rains, 1990; Anderson, 1989b). This is unfortunate, because although older adults tend to have more medical problems than younger adults, physicians are ill prepared to recognize the signs of substance abuse/addiction in the elderly. First, as we noted in Chapter 1, few physicians are adequately trained in the area of addiction medicine. Furthermore, for reasons that are not well understood, older alcoholics seem less likely to visit their physician than are their nondrinking peers (Rice & Duncan, 1995).

There are many possible reasons why, as a group, older adults with alcohol use disorders are less likely to go to a physician on a regular basis. The older drinker may try to avoid seeing a physician in order to prevent his or her alcohol use disorder from being discovered. Also, older drinkers (like their physicians) tend to attribute physical complications caused by their drinking to the aging process instead. Thus older drinkers may not consult a physician because they do not understand the true cause of their medical problem(s).

Another reason why alcohol use disorders are so difficult to detect in the older drinker is that the traditional symptoms of excessive drinking, such as the number of drinks consumed, is a poor indicator of alcoholism in the elderly. As a result of the aging process, the bodies of older individuals contain lower levels of various body fluids than those of young adults. This contributes to a tendency for older drinkers to achieve higher blood alcohol levels than young adults after consuming a given amount of alcohol (Lieber, 1998; Zimberg, 1996). As a result of the normal aging process, just 3 beers or mixed drinks consumed by a 60-year-old may have the same effect on the drinker as 12 beers or mixed drinks consumed at the age of 21 (Anderson, 1989).

As a result of the aging process, the drinker's body does not respond to alcohol in the same way it did when the individual was a young adult (Blake, 1990; Rains, 1990). Because of age-related physical changes, the body of an older drinker contains about 9% less water than it did when he or she was in his or her early 20s, causing a higher BAL than in a younger adult who had consumed the same amount of alcohol (Baselt, 1996). The brain of an older drinker is more sensitive to the toxic effects of alcohol than it was decades earlier (Goldstein, Pataki, & Webb, 1996), and even social drinking can contribute to cognitive deterioration in the older drinker (Rains, 1990; Abrams & Alexopoulos, 1987). Given this fact, it should not be surprising to discover a "high association between alcoholism and dementia" (Goldstein, Pataki, & Webb, 1996, p. 941; Smith, 1997).

Although alcohol use/abuse is a known risk factor for the development of a wide range of psychosocial impairments, these problems are not so obvious in the older alcohol-abusing/dependent person as they are in the young adult (Abrams & Alexopoulos, 1998). All too often, alcohol-induced problems in the older individual, such as blackouts, financial problems, and job loss, are attributed to medical or age-related psychosocial problems, not to a possible abuse of alcohol (Szwabo, 1993). Many of alcohol's effects on the cognitive abilities of older adults mimic changes associated with normal aging. Even trained physicians find it difficult to differentiate between late-onset Korsakoff's syndrome and many forms of senile dementia, such as Alzheimer's disease, multiinfarct dementia, and the like (Blake, 1990; Rains, 1990).

Alcohol use in older persons is often hidden from family and friends (Peluso & Peluso, 1989; Vandeputte, 1989). To illustrate this point, just imagine the family's reaction if grandmother or grandfather were to announce at the dinner table, "I'm going out tonight to get wasted!" Shame also contributes to this process of avoidance; the individual's family and friends often feel guilty about the possibility that an older family member has an alcohol use problem. These feelings of shame prevent family and friends from reporting their suspicions to the individual's physician and from confronting the individual with their concerns (Goldstein, Pataki, & Webb, 1996; Peluso & Peluso, 1989; Vandeputte, 1989).

What are the consequences of alcohol/drug addiction in the elderly? Alcohol use/abuse may either directly or indirectly cause, or contribute to, accidental injuries in older adults. For example, in one study, 14% of the elderly patients seen for injuries suffered in motor vehicle accidents were found to have a positive blood alcohol screen (Higgins, Wright, & Wrenn, 1996). In addition, alcohol and/or drug misuse is considered a major factor in causing older adults to lose their balance, fall, and experience any of a number of bone fractures (Rigler, 2000; Council on Scientific Affairs, 1996). Thus one consequence of alcohol use/abuse is that the older drinker is at increased risk of accidental injury as a result of his or her drinking.

In addition to this, alcohol use may either complicate the treatment of other diseases or even cause the individual to develop various new medical problems that can become life-threatening (Vandeputte, 1989). Further, because they are more vulnerable to the negative effects of alcohol, older drinkers are more likely than younger adults to experience medical complications as a result of alcohol use (Dunne, 1994; Rains, 1990). Alcohol use in the elderly may either influence the development of, or actually cause, such medical problems as myopathy, cerebrovascular disease, gastritis, diarrhea, pancreatitis, cardiomyopathy, and various sleep disorders (Liberto, Oslin, & Ruskin, 1992). Other disorders that may be caused by alcohol use by older individuals include hypertension, diminished resistance to infections, peripheral muscle weakness, electrolyte and metabolic disturbances, and orthostatic hypotension (Szwabo, 1993).

Unfortunately, as we noted earlier, older drinkers are less likely to seek medical attention for their distress—at least until the complications caused by their drinking become severe enough to require hospitalization. And even when their drinking is identified, few elderly alcoholics receive treatment for their drug addiction (Vandeputte, 1989). This results in increased medical costs for the individual—and ultimately for society, to treat these alcohol-induced problems.

Although few people stop to consider the possible impact of alcohol/drug use problems on the mental health of older individuals, substance abuse takes a terrible toll on the older user's peace of mind. For example, depression is a common problem in old age. Depression is also a common consequence of alcohol/drug abuse, and it has been estimated that 25–50% of all elderly suicide victims have used alcohol prior to their suicide attempt (Abrams & Alexopoulos, 1998). For reasons that are not clear, there seems to be a relationship between alcohol abuse problems in early or middle adulthood and the development of depression in the elderly, even if the individual's alcohol use is not problematic in later adulthood (Abrams & Alexopoulos, 1998). Unrecognized substance-induced depressive episodes can result in both misdiagnosis and mistreatment of the individual's mental health problem (Council on Scientific Affairs, 1996), adding urgency to the need for an accurate diagnosis of the cause(s) of depression in the elderly.

Different patterns of alcohol/drug abuse in the elderly. Many older individuals develop alcohol use problems only in their later years (Zimberg, 1996). This phenomenon has been termed *late-onset alcoholism* (Rigler, 2000; Hurt, Finlayson, Morse, & Davis, 1988) and reactive alcoholism (Peluso & Peluso, 1989). Perhaps as many as 30–50% of the elderly alcoholic population actually began to have problems with alcohol in mid-life or later (Brennan & Moos, 1996; Liberto, Oslin, & Ruskin, 1992).

Zimberg (1995) suggested that there were three subgroups of older alcoholics. The first group was made up of those individuals who had no drinking problem in young or middle adulthood but who developed late-life alcoholism. These individuals could be said to have *late-onset alcoholism,* according to the author. The second subgroup of older alcoholics had a history of intermittent problem drinking over the years but developed a chronic alcohol problem only in late adulthood. This group of individuals could be said to have *late-onset exacerbation* drinking, according to Zimberg (1995). Finally, there were those individuals whose alcohol problems started in young adulthood and continued into the later part of the individual's life, a pattern known as *early-onset alcoholism* (Zimberg, 1995).

Misuse of medication by the elderly is another problem. Campbell (1992) estimated that 10% of the elderly misuse prescription medications. Drug misuse takes several forms, including (1) intentional overuse of a medication, (2) underuse of a medication, (3) erratic use of a prescribed medication, and (4) failure of the physician to obtain a complete drug history, including use of over-the-counter medications, resulting in dangerous combinations of medications (Abrams & Alexopoulos, 1998). The intentional misuse of prescribed medications is the largest category of drug abuse in the elderly. Surprisingly, however, the elderly are far more likely to underutilize than to overutilize prescription medications, mainly because of financial circumstances (Abrams & Alexopoulos, 1987, 1998).

The treatment of the older alcoholic. Unfortunately, only a minority of elderly people with a drug or alcohol problem are currently receiving help for that problem. Alcohol/drug addiction in the elderly is simply under-recognized and under-reported. Further, in an era of shrinking resources, public health agencies are often overwhelmed by the task of dealing with younger alcohol/drug abusers. One consequence is that substance use problems are undertreated in the elderly.

Even when the older alcoholic/drug-abusing patient is referred to treatment, she or he presents special treatment needs rarely found in younger addicts. Yet few treatment programs are geared to meet the needs of the older drug or alcohol abuser (Goldstein, Pataki, & Webb, 1996). To meet these special treatment needs, Dunlop, Manghelli, and Tolson (1989) recommended that treatment programs that work with the elderly include several different components:

1. A primary prevention program to warn about the dangers of using alcohol as a coping mechanism for life's problems
2. An outreach program to identify and serve older alcoholics who might be overlooked by more traditional treatment services
3. Detoxification services offered by people trained and experienced in working with the elderly, who frequently require longer detoxification periods than younger addicted persons

4. Protective environments for the elderly—that is, structured living environments that would allow the individual to take part in treatment while being protected from the temptation of further alcohol use
5. Primary treatment programs for those who could benefit from either inpatient or outpatient short-term primary treatment programs
6. Aftercare programs to help the older alcoholic with the transition between primary care and independent living
7. Long-term residential care for those individuals who suffer from severe medical and/or psychiatric complications from alcoholism
8. Access to social-work support services.

In working with the older alcoholic or drug-abusing patient, it is wise to keep in mind that he or she might require weeks, or even months, just to detoxify from alcohol or drugs (Anderson, 1989b). Rains (1990) suggested that older alcoholics might require up to 18 months of abstinence in order to recover fully from the effects of drinking. Thus the standard 21- to 28-day inpatient treatment program might fail to meet the needs of an elderly client, who would hardly have completed the detoxification process before being discharged as "cured." Older adults might also require more help than younger clients to build a nonalcoholic support structure (Anderson, 1989b). Further, the older client often moves at a slower physical and mental pace than younger individuals, presents a range of sensory deficits rarely found in younger clients, and very often dislikes the profanity commonly encountered with younger individuals in treatment (Dunlop, Manghelli, & Tolson, 1989).

Unless these special needs are addressed, the older individual is unlikely to be motivated to participate in treatment. In addition, treatment professionals must help the older addict deal with more than the direct effects of his or her chemical addiction. For example, health care professionals need to be aware of the possibility that the older alcoholic is experiencing age-specific stressors such as retirement, bereavement, loneliness, and the effects of physical illness (Zimberg, 1996; Dunlop, Manghelli, & Tolson, 1989). On a positive note, however, there is evidence that late-onset drinkers respond better to treatment than do younger alcoholics (Brennan & Moos, 1996). Group-therapy approaches that included a problem-solving and social-support component were thought to be useful in working with the older alcoholic, especially if such programs included exposure to the Alcoholics Anonymous Twelve-Step program (Rains, 1990; Dunlop, Manghelli, & Tolson, 1989; Zimberg, 1978).

The Homosexual and Substance Abuse

In spite of social changes in the 1980s and 1990s, the homosexual (gay) man or (lesbian) woman continues to be part of a "hidden minority" (Fassinger, 1991, p. 157) within this society. Estimates of the percentage of the population that is bisexual, gay, or lesbian vary. Seidman and Rieder (1994) estimated that 20% of the men in the United States have had at least one homosexual experience at some point in their lives and that between 1% and 6% of the male population have had a homosexual encounter in the last year. In spite of the fact that, statistically, homoerotic relationships appear to be common, society's response to individuals who engage in a nontraditional form of sexuality is less than supportive. Many gay/lesbian individuals feel ostracized by a culture that neither understands nor tolerates a homosexual lifestyle and go to great lengths to hide their sexual orientation.

Individuals who both are homosexual and have a substance use problem constitute a "special-needs" population for substance abuse rehabilitation professionals (Cabaj, 1997; Rathbone-McCuan & Stokke, 1997). It is estimated that 28–35% of gay men and lesbians have engaged in some form of recreational drug use that did not involve some form of injection, compared to 10–12% of the heterosexual population (Ungvarski & Grossman, 1999). Further, it has been hypothesized that gay/lesbian clients are at risk for alcohol use problems because of the central role that the "gay bar" plays in the homosexual lifestyle. To understand this special area of risk, it is necessary for the average person to understand that because gays live on the fringes of society, opportunities for socialization within the gay community are limited. It is for this reason that the "gay bar" assumes a role of central importance as a place to socialize without fear of ridicule, meet potential partners, or simply escape from society in general (Paul, Stall, & Bloomfield, 1991). The homosexual bar also continues to play a pivotal role for both gay men and lesbian women in the process of discovering one's sexuality.

There has been very little research into the frequency of alcohol use problems (Cabaj, 1997; Hughes & Wilsnack, 1997; Rathbone-McCuan & Stokke, 1997) or drug abuse problems (Warn, 1997) among gay/lesbian individuals. The limited data that are available suggest that there is a significantly higher alcoholism rate for gay/lesbian persons than for the general population. It has been estimated that 25–35% of the homosexual population meet the diagnostic criteria for a formal diagnosis of alcohol/drug dependency (Klinger & Cabaj, 1993). Indeed, there is evidence that more than half of all lesbians have alcohol use problems, a rate 5–7 times higher than that seen in nongay women (Blume, 1998; North, 1996).

There are a number of reasons for the apparent association between homosexuality and alcohol abuse. Some individuals, who are uncomfortable with their sexual orientation or anticipate rejection once their sexual preference becomes known, may use alcohol or drugs to self-medicate shame or guilt (Paul, Stall, & Bloomfield, 1991). The authors noted, for example, that individuals who experienced negative feelings surrounding their sexual orientation tended to use alcohol to reduce internal tension. Also, as noted above, the homosexual bar plays an important role within the gay community, often providing the only "safe" environment within which the individual can explore his or her sexuality.

The use of alcohol/drugs might also be involved with the process of exploring and coming to accept one's sexual identity in a society that rarely tolerates deviation from the self-proclaimed "norm" (Cabaj, 1997). This process would serve to strengthen the association between bisexuality/homosexuality and substance abuse. Finally, some researchers have suggested that alcohol/drugs might be abused by male homosexuals to deaden the pain of receptive anal intercourse (Ungvarski & Grossman, 1999).

Thus there is ample evidence that alcohol/drug use problems may be more common in the homosexual community than in the heterosexual population. However, to complicate matters, the practice of recruiting research subjects in "gay bars" has been challenged by researchers, who suggest that data from such samples might inflate estimates of alcohol and drug use disorders among the bisexual/gay/lesbian population (Cabaj, 1997; Friedman & Downey, 1994). Statistically, the people who frequent the bar are the very people who are most likely to have alcohol/drug use problems. As a result of this selection bias, individuals who are not alcohol/drug users tend to be under-represented in research samples drawn from homosexual bars. As a result, research samples drawn from such settings may overestimate the prevalence of alcohol/drug abuse among bisexual/gay/lesbian individuals.

In contrast to this theory, Hughes and Wilsnack (1997) concluded that lesbians may indeed have higher rates of alcohol use problems than their heterosexual counterparts. However, because of the lack of adequate research studies, and the fact that many of the estimates of alcohol use problems among lesbians are extrapolated from studies done on male homosexuals, the authors call for more research into alcohol/drug use patterns among homosexual women. At this time, it is virtually impossible to determine the actual prevalence of alcohol/drug use problems among the gay/lesbian population (Friedman & Downey, 1994). There also is little research into the special health care needs of the bisexual/gay/lesbian client and virtually no research into what treatment methods are effective for the substance-abusing gay/lesbian client (Cabaj, 1997). However, given that gay/lesbian individuals may make up 10–15% of the population (Fassinger, 1991), and that approximately one-third of gays and lesbians may abuse chemicals, it would appear that a significant percentage of those in treatment for substance abuse problems live a nontraditional lifestyle.

Unfortunately, the development of specialized treatment services for gay/lesbian clients has been "slow" (Hughes & Wilsnack, 1997, p. 31). There are few treatment programs dedicated to working with homosexual adults, and such programs are usually located in major cities where there is a significant homosexual population. There is no program known that is devoted entirely to the treatment of lesbians (Rathbone-McCuan & Stokke, 1997). A significant percentage of substance abuse professionals were deficient in their ability to work with the homosexual client, and in almost 40% of the cases, substance abuse counselors received no formal training in how to work effectively with the gays and lesbians (Hellman, Stanton, Lee, Tytun, & Vachon, 1989).

There has been a movement endorsing special AA groups oriented toward the needs of bisexual/gay/lesbian members (Paul, Raul, & Bloomfield, 1991), but these groups are usually located in major metropolitan areas. Needless to say, in spite of the progress that society has made toward accepting homosexual/lesbian persons, substance abuse counselors must become more aware of the unique needs of gay/lesbian clients and obtain the specialized training necessary to meet those needs effectively.

Substance Abuse and the Disabled

It is unfortunate that within this society, individuals who are physically challenged are often viewed as being "damaged" and different. These stereotypes may have contributed to limiting the research that has addressed the problem of substance abuse among the disabled (Tyas & Rush, 1993). Unfortunately, the limited research that has been done suggests that substance abuse is a significant problem among those who are physically challenged. For example, Nelipovich and Buss (1991) suggested that 15–30% of the 33–45 million Americans with disabilities abuse alcohol or drugs—a rate that is between one 1.5 and 3 times higher than for the physically able.

Although substance use problems are thus quite common for those who have a disability, the treatment resources are quite limited. Indeed, it is safe to conclude that as a group, "this is a highly underserved population" (Nelipovich & Buss, 1991, p. 344). For example, Cavaliere (1995) noted that although many treatment programs have videotapes of lectures with closed captioning, and utilize sign language interpreters for the hearing-impaired client during group-therapy sessions, few programs utilize sign language interpreters outside of group/individual therapy sessions. This prevents the hearing-impaired client from participating in the informal give-and-take discussions outside of group sessions that are so much a part of the rehabilitation program. Thus, even within the treatment setting, the hearing-impaired client continues to be isolated and treated as though she or he were "different."

In a very real sense, rather than being identified as a special-needs subgroup, the disabled are often "perceived as isolated occasional cases, only remembered because of the difficulty and frustration they present to the professionals trying to serve them" (Nelipovich & Buss, 1991, p. 344). The authors call for "creativity" (p. 345) on the part of rehabilitation staff who are attempting to meet the needs of the disabled substance-abusing client.

Unfortunately, only a minority of treatment programs have the special resources (wheelchair ramps and the like) necessary for working with the disabled. Indeed, many programs would rather not serve this subpopulation (Tyas & Rush, 1993). In contrast, drug *dealers* are only too happy to offer their services to the disabled. For example, there are hints that at least some drug dealers are specifically targeting hearing-impaired individuals, going so far as to learn sign language or recruit assistants who know sign language, in order to sell drugs to the hearing-impaired (*Associated Press*, 1993).

To complicate matters further, family members often come to believe that the disabled person is "entitled" to use recreational chemicals, even if he or she does so to excess. For example, a common attitude among family members is that a hearing-impaired person should be allowed to use chemicals because of his or her disability (Cavaliere, 1995). Family and friends often rationalize the substance abuse by the hearing-impaired individual ("I'd drink too, if I were deaf"). In this manner, the significant others of the hearing-impaired person may overlook signs that substance abuse is starting to interfere with the individual's life.

Thus the physically disabled form an invisible subgroup of those who abuse, or are addicted to, chemicals in the United States. As such, they are hidden victims of the world of drug abuse/addiction.

Substance Abuse and Ethnic Minorities

Native Americans. It is estimated that there are approximately 2 million individuals in the United States who might be classified as Native Americans (Beauvais, 1998). These individuals are members of the estimated 300 (Beauvais, 1998) and 500 (Caetano, Clark, & Tam, 1998) individual tribes in the United States, who possess more than 200 distinct languages. Only about one-third of these individuals live on identified "reservation" lands; the majority live in traditional residential areas of the country (Beauvais, 1998).

Native Americans are sometimes called Indians or American Indians, although these terms are objectionable to many. They are often viewed as a single group, although, as the statistics in the last paragraph demonstrate, Native Americans are a diverse group. Not surprisingly, drug/alcohol use patterns and recreational chemical use vary from tribe to tribe (Beauvais, 1998; Caetano, Clark, & Tam, 1998). This is clearly seen in the drinking patterns of the Navaho and Hopi tribes of the Southwest. Both the Navaho and Hopi tribes live in the same geographic region of Nevada, yet the Navaho tolerate alcohol use, whereas the Hopi view drinking a sign of irresponsibility (Caetano, Clark, & Tam, 1998). Thus it is not possible to speak of "Native American" drinking patterns, and research must be conducted into the specific expectations and beliefs about alcohol in each individual tribe.

Given that some tribes in the northern United States have diagnosed alcohol abuse addiction problems in 111 of every 1000 members, whereas some tribes in the Southwest have alcohol use problems diagnosed in only 11 people per 1000, there are obviously wide variations in alcohol use patterns from tribe to tribe (Beauvais, 1998). It has been suggested that alcohol use problems are about twice as common among the men as among the women of different tribes (Beauvais, 1998). And there is evidence of marked intergenerational differences in alcohol use rates, with the younger members of various tribes tending to use alcohol more often than their elders, according to Beauvais (1998).

Thus there are few specific facts to help clinicians work with clients from Native American cultures. Markarian and Franklin (1998) suggested that Native American clients in substance abuse rehabilitation programs might withdraw into themselves if exposed to high levels of confrontation similar to those found in many traditional treatment programs, reinforcing the observation that individuals working with these subpopulations must be sensitive to cultural differences and beliefs.

Garcia-Andrade, Wall, and Ehlers (1997) attempted to dispel the "firewater" myth that has persisted for almost 300 years. This theory suggested that the Native Americans were more sensitive to the effects of alcohol; its most recent manifestation was the theory that this sensitivity is genetically mediated. The authors examined the effects of alcohol on 40 healthy, nonalcoholic Native American males and found little evidence that these individuals reacted differently to alcohol than white males. Indeed, there is little evidence to suggest that Native Americans are especially vulnerable to alcohol's effects for either physical or psychological reasons (Caetano, Clark, & Tam, 1998).

Hispanics. Approximately 11% of the U. S. population is Hispanic American (Randolph, Stroup-Benham, Black, & Markides, 1998). Although sociologists tend to speak of the "Hispanic" subpopulation as a single entity, in reality a multitude of cultures fall under the heading of "Hispanic," each with different attitudes and expectations related to alcohol/drugs (Caetano, Clark, & Tam, 1998). About 60% of Hispanic Americans in the United States trace their national heritage through Mexico, another 15% originally were from Puerto Rico, 5% are Cuban Americans, and the remainder derive from one of the other Spanish-speaking nations in this hemisphere (Randolph, Stroup-Benham, Black, & Markides, 1998). As these statistics suggest, there is no standard model of drinking for the Hispanic population in the United States, because there is no single dominant "Hispanic culture" within this country.

In general, drinking—especially heavy drinking— tends to be a male activity. Women within Hispanic cultures in the United States tend either to be light drinkers or to abstain from alcohol use entirely (Randolph, Stroup-Benham, Black, & Markides, 1998). But there are significant variations within the Hispanic community, depending on the nation of origin. In one study, for example, 18% of Mexican American males emerged as heavy drinkers, whereas only 5% of Cuban American males met the criteria for heavy alcohol use. In each culture, 2% or less of the women met the criteria for heavy drinking, and 10–11% were light drinkers, compared with 4% of the Mexican American and 38% of the Cuban American males, (Randolph, Stroup-Benham, Black, & Markides, 1998). In each Hispanic subgroup, the largest percentage of women abstained from alcohol use.

Asian Americans. As with other cultures in the United States, there is no single "Asian American" model for recreational chemical use/abuse, because there is no dominant Asian-American culture. Rather, disparate cultural groups exhibit widely different patterns of alcohol/drug use, depending on the nation of origin for that specific culture (Caetano, Clark, & Tam, 1998). Individuals who came to this country from Viet Nam or from Cambodia must be considered separately from individuals whose national heritage can be traced back to Japan or Korea, although all four groups are classified as "Asian American."

In general, women from Asian American cultures are more likely to abstain, or to drink only on social occasions, than their male partners (Caetano, Clark, & Tam, 1998). But even this generalization must be tempered with the observation that women in different Asian American subgroups have widely disparate alcohol use patterns. For example, in one survey only 20% of Korean American women reported that they consumed alcohol, whereas 67% of Japanese American women reported using alcohol (Caetano, Clark, & Tam, 1998).

African Americans. Franklin (1989) found that of 16,000 articles on alcoholism published between 1934 and 1974, only 11 "were specifically studies of blacks" (p. 1120). In the decade since Franklin's original work, a small number of research studies have addressed the issue of alcohol use problems among African Americans. One such study was conducted by Markarian and Franklin (1998), who found that African American males are more likely to initiate heavy drinking later in life than European males and that their drinking rates peak at an age when those of European male alcoholics are declining. Further, the authors found that in comparison to alcoholics of European descent, blacks "have a higher incidence of medical complications from alcoholism" (Franklin, 1989, p. 1120)—possibly as much as ten times as high as would be seen in a similar group of white alcoholics.

National surveys designed to explore alcohol use patterns among different groups of people have found that, as a group, African Americans are more likely to abstain from alcohol use than are individuals of European descent (Jones-Webb, 1998). Fifty one percent of black women, and 35% of black men reported complete abstinence from alcohol at the time of their inclusion in the study, compared with 36% of white women and 28% of white men (Jones-Webb, 1998). In spite of this fact, African Americans were found to be as likely to engage in heavy, abusive drinking as were whites, possibly because of the tendency for blacks in the lower socioeconomic groups to abuse alcohol (Jones-Webb, 1998). Although it was founded by a group of mostly white, middle-class individuals, Alcoholics Anonymous (AA) has become a significant part of the treatment and recovery process within the black community (Franklin, 1989).

Summary

We all have, in our minds, an image of the "typical" addict. Some picture the "skid row" alcoholic, others the heroin addict injecting the drug in the ruins of an abandoned building. These images of addiction are accurate, yet each fails to reflect the many hidden faces of addiction.

Such stereotypical images ignore the grandfather who is quietly drinking himself to death and the mother who exposes her unborn child to staggering amounts of cocaine, heroin, or alcohol. And they render invisible the working woman whose chemical addiction is hidden behind a veil of productivity or sanctioned by unsuspecting physicians who are trying to help her cope with feelings of depression or anxiety. Their faces of addiction are so well hidden that even today, they are seldom recognized. As professionals, we must learn to look for, and recognize, the hidden forms of addiction.

CHAPTER TWENTY-TWO

The Dual-Diagnosis Client

Chemical Addiction and Mental Illness

Introduction

Mental health professionals know very little either about the forces that initiate a substance use disorder in patients with a form of mental illness or about the factors that maintain a substance abuse problem in this population (Sharp & Getz, 1998). Only in the early 1980s did substance abuse and mental health professionals begin to acknowledge that chemical abuse/addiction among the mentally ill is a serious problem. Since then, mental health professionals have slowly come to understand that patients in whom substance use problems and mental health issues coexist are not just a small minority of the mentally ill but, rather may constitute the majority of the individuals they see. This chapter explores the problem of substance abuse in people with some form of mental illness.

Definitions

Patients who suffer from a form of mental illness and who also abuse chemicals are often said to be dual-diagnosis clients. Unfortunately, the term "dual-diagnosis" has been applied to a wide range of coexisting problems, including combinations of substance abuse/addiction and anorexia, bulimia, gambling, spouse abuse, and AIDS. In this text, the terms "dual-diagnosis" and "MI/CD" (mentally ill/chemically dependent) will be used to denote individuals in whom a psychiatric disorder(s) and a substance abuse problem(s) *coexist* and *are equally important, independent disorders.* Admittedly, recreational chemical use can magnify preexisting psychiatric disorders or bring about a drug-induced disorder that simulates any of a wide range of psychiatric

problems (Washton, 1995; Cohen, 1995). These drug-induced complications usually diminish or entirely disappear shortly after the patient stops abusing recreational drug(s); thus they might be said to be "substance-induced" (Woody, McLellan, & Bedrick, 1995; Falls-Stewart & Lucente, 1994).

The concept of coexisting disorders really is not difficult to understand. Consider, for example, an alcohol-dependent person who also suffers from a concurrent medical problem. Perhaps the alcohol-dependent individual has a kidney dysfunction or a genetic disorder of some kind. The patient's medical condition did not *cause* him or her to become alcohol-dependent, nor did his or her alcohol dependency bring about the medical condition. Yet each disorder, once it develops, is intertwined with the other. The physician treating this hypothetical patient must take into account the impact of the patient's alcohol use problem on the treatment methods under consideration for his or her kidney disorder. This prudent approach acknowledges the fact that MI/CDs have separate disorders that are nevertheless intertwined, each condition able to influence the progression of the other (Woody, McLellan, & Bedrick, 1995; Carey, 1989).

Dual-Diagnosis Clients: A Diagnostic Challenge

For a number of reasons, dual-diagnosis clients present a special challenge to treatment professionals (Minkoff, 1997; Miller, 1994; Riley, 1994). As many as two-thirds of those patients admitted to substance abuse treatment programs have symptoms of psychiatric problems at the time of admission (Falls-Stewart & Lucente, 1994). But because many of these psychiatric problems remit after the individual is alcohol/drug-free for a period of time, the presenting symptoms are viewed as being alcohol/drug-induced rather than as an expression of mental illness. To identify those individuals with a dual diagnosis, treatment professionals must often wait as long as 6 *weeks* for the diagnostic picture to clear (Ziedonis & Brady, 1997; Director, 1995; Nathan, 1991; Evans & Sullivan, 1990; Carey, 1989; Wallen & Weiner, 1989; Rado, 1988).

The identification of MI/CD clients is frequently complicated by the fact that many individuals actively try to hide from their health care provider the fact that they engage in recreational chemical use (Shaner, Khalsa, Roberts, Wilkins, Anglin, & Hsieh, 1993).[1] Minimization is also a defense mechanism encountered in dual-diagnosis clients (Carey, Cocco, & Simons, 1996). In addition to the traditional reasons why substance-abusing clients use denial and minimization, dual-diagnosis clients often do so because of their on-going psychiatric problems (Kanwischer & Hundley, 1990). Other MI/CD patients hesitate to discuss their substance use problems with health care professionals because direct questions about alcohol or drug use evokes feelings of shame (Pristach & Smith, 1990). Some dual-diagnosis patients fear that, by admitting to a substance use problem, they will lose entitlements (such as Social Security payments), or they may be afraid of being denied access to psychiatric treatment (Mueser, Bellack, & Blanchard, 1992). Many MI/CD patients have little motivation to stop using a drug(s) of abuse because they view their situation as hopeless (Ziedonis & Brady, 1997). For these and a multitude of other reasons, collateral sources of information are imperative when a health care professional attempts to assess a patient's substance use pattern.

Why Worry About the Dual-Diagnosis Client?

The estimated economic loss caused by individuals with one or more forms of mental illness and a concurrent substance use disorder is approximately $300 billion per year, just in terms of lost productivity in the United States (Riley, 1994). In addition are the costs of psychiatric hospitalization, social services, and the like. For example, the cost of psychiatric care for individuals who have both a substance use disorder and some form of mental illness is 60% higher than the cost of psychiatric services for individuals with only a psychiatric problem (Sharp & Getz, 1998). Finally, there is the toll in human suffering endured by those who have both a substance abuse disorder and a concurrent mental illness.

This toll in individual suffering is illustrated by such research data as a study revealing that the alcohol-dependent individual's potential to commit suicide is increased 60–120-fold if he or she also has some form of mental illness (Nielson, Virkkunen, Lappalainen, Eggert, Brown, Long, Goldman, & Linnoila, 1998). As a group, dual-diagnosis clients are at increased risk of incarceration, are less likely to be able to handle their personal finances, and are more prone to depression and/or feelings of hopelessness (Drake, McHugo, Clark, Teague, Xie, Miles, & Ackerson, 1998). These feelings of hopelessness and the other symptoms of a psychiatric disorder can be exacerbated by the individual's abuse of recreational chemicals (Sharp & Getz, 1998; Cohen & Levy, 1992; Evans & Sullivan, 1990; Ries & Ellingson, 1990; Rubinstein, Campbell, & Daley, 1990; Pristach & Smith, 1990; Drake, Osher, & Wallach, 1989). Researchers have found, for example, that even drinking in amounts clearly not abusive by traditional standards, was one factor that predicted which of those clients who had schizophrenia would again require hospitalization within a year (RachBeisel, Scott, & Dixon, 1999; Drake, Osher, & Wallach, 1989). More than a decade ago, researchers discovered that psychiatric patients who abused chemicals on a regular basis had hospitalization rates 250% higher than psychiatric patients who rarely or never abused chemicals (Kanwischer & Hundley, 1990).

Alcohol/drug abuse is now viewed by mental health professionals as one reason why, as a group, MI/CD patients make less progress in therapy and suffer a greater number of problems while in treatment (Sharp & Getz, 1998; Osher & Drake, 1996; Drake, McHugo, Clark, Teague, Xie, Miles, & Ackerson, 1998; Woody, McLellan, & Bedrick, 1995; Osher, Drake, Noordsy, Teague, Hurlbut, Biesanz, & Beaudett, 1994; Kivlahan, Heiman, Wright, Mundt, & Shupe, 1991; Rubinstein,

---

[1]This is not a characteristic found only in MI/CD clients. Denial is often encountered in substance-abusing individuals. However, the impact of denial is often more pronounced in the dual-diagnosis client.

Campbell, & Daley, 1990). One such problem is that the individual's concurrent mental illness and chemical dependency place a financial strain on the family (Clark, 1994). When one stops to consider the emotional pain experienced by the mentally ill, the cost of lost productivity, the cost of hospitalization and treatment, and the added financial, social, and personal cost brought on by substance abuse on the part of mentally ill clients, the need to address this problem becomes undeniable.

The Scope of the Problem

What one takes to be the true scope of the problem of dual-diagnosis clients depends on which problems one takes as reflecting a "mental illness." For example, some researchers classify attention-deficit/hyperactivity disorder (ADHD) as a developmental disorder, rather than a form of mental illness. From this perspective, a substance-abusing individual with a coexisting ADHD diagnosis might be classified not as a dual-diagnosis client but as a substance abuser with a developmental disorder.

In the United States "mental illness" is usually defined in terms of the criteria established by the American Psychiatric Association in its *Diagnostic and Statistical Manual of Mental Disorders*, 4th edition (*DSM-IV-TR*) (American Psychiatric Association, 2000). A brief list of some of the infirmities included within the *DSM-IV* includes neurodegenerative disorders such as Alzheimer's disease, many forms of sleep disorders, conditions that reflect abnormal neurological function such as the schizophrenias, language acquisition and communication disorders, childhood behavioral disturbances such as the oppositional defiant disorder, various intensities of mental retardation, depression, mania, adjustment reactions to psychological trauma experienced at virtually any age in life, and developmental conditions such as the various personality disorders. Also included within the scope of "mental illness," as defined by the American Psychiatric Association, are various neurobehavioral disorders caused by physical injuries to the brain, adverse medication reactions, and a host of other conditions that might not be a focus of psychiatric intervention but should be noted by a competent physician treating a patient for some form of mental illness.

Researchers disagree about how many individuals suffer from both a mental illness and a coexisting substance use disorder. Svikis, Zarin, Tanielian, and Pincus (2000) found that only 12% of those patients under psychiatric care qualified for an alcohol abuse/addiction diagnosis. In contrast to this low estimate, Ries, Russo, Wingerson, Snowden, Comtois, Srebnik, and Roy-Byrne (2000) concluded that people with schizophrenia were three times as likely to abuse alcohol, and six times as likely to abuse drugs, as was the general population. Overall, it has been suggested that 40–75% of people with a severe mental illness have a separate substance use disorder (Appleby, Dyson, Luchins, & Cohen, 1997). Substance use problems are at least twice as common in the mentally ill as in the general population (Brown, Ridgely, Pepper, Levine, & Ryglewicz, 1989; Regier, Farmer, Rae, Locke, Keith, Judd, & Goodwin, 1990). At least 50% of those individuals with a psychiatric disorder also abuse alcohol/drugs (Leshner, 1997b).

Table 22.1 summarizes the overlap between substance use disorders and various psychiatric disorders.

A review of the professional literature reveals two different trends: First, a significant percentage of those with some form of mental illness have a concurrent

TABLE 22.1   The Overlap Between Substance Use Disorders and Various Psychiatric Disorders

Psychiatric Diagnosis	Lifetime Prevalence of Substance Use Disorder
Depression	32%
Bipolar affective disorder (or "manic-depression")	64%
Anxiety disorder	36%
Antisocial personality disorder	84%
Attention-deficit/hyperactivity disorder (ADHD)	23%
Eating disorders	28%
Schizophrenia	50%
Somatoform disorders	Unknown, but suspected to be related

Source: This chart is based on Ziedonis & Brady (1997).

substance use disorder. For example, RachBeisel, Scott, and Dixon (1999) found that about 50% of those individuals with a severe form of mental illness would develop a substance use disorder at some point in their lives. However, as the literature also demonstrates, mental health professionals are often ill equipped to detect substance abuse, especially in people with a psychiatric problem (Cohen & Levy, 1992). Lacking a pattern to look for, mental health professionals often fail to recognize the possibility that a mentally ill client might also have a substance abuse problem (Cohen & Levy, 1992; Peyser, 1989).

Characteristics of Dual-Problem Clients

Unfortunately, researchers speak of substance-abusing mentally ill clients as though they were all the same. In reality, because of the interplay between various combinations of mental illness and substance use disorders, the dual-diagnosis population is "not a uniform clinical entity, but a heterogeneous group who differ in psychiatric disorder, level of functioning, social support, and capacity for independent living" (Director, 1995, p. 377). In spite of this observation, different researchers have examined the MI/CD subpopulation and concluded that:

- As a group, dual-diagnosis patients are less impaired, but with more suicidal, homicidal, and impulsive behaviors than other psychiatric patients (Szuster, Schanbacher, & McCann, 1990; Kay, Kalathara, & Meinzer, 1989).
- As a group, dual-diagnosis patients are less severely psychotic, and more intelligent, than the typical psychiatric patient (Zisook, Heaton, Moranville, Kuck, Jernigan, & Braff, 1992; Mueser, Yarnold, & Bellack, 1992).
- Schizophrenic patients who abused alcohol are found to have poor social adjustment; to be more delusional, more disruptive, and more assaultive; to exhibit more treatment noncompliance; to have more housing instability and homelessness; to experience higher rates of rehospitalization; and to be more depressed (RachBeisel, Scott, & Dixon, 1999; Osher, Drake, Noordsy, Teague, Hurlbut, Biesanz, & Beaudett, 1994).

- MI/CD patients are at higher risk for suicide (Drake *et al.*, 1998; Osher & Drake, 1996; Osher, Drake, Noordsy, Teague, Hurlbut, Biesanz, & Beaudett, 1994).
- Psychiatric clients who also have substance use disorders seem to have more trouble staying sober (Osher & Drake, 1996).
- MI/CD clients are less likely to be able to use alcohol on a social/recreational basis for extended periods of time (Drake & Wallach, 1993).
- Dual-diagnosis clients tend to be "binge" users of recreational chemicals (Osher & Drake, 1996; Riley, 1994).
- MI/CD clients tend to be more manipulative than traditional psychiatric patients (Mueser, Bellack, & Blanchard, 1992).
- Although their risk factors for psychiatric complications are reduced when they abstain from chemicals, MI/CD clients as a group are less likely to work for total abstinence than traditional substance-abusing clients (Drake, Mueser, Clark, & Wallach, 1996).

The outcome of this process is that, while all of the characteristics reviewed above must be assumed to be true, *they are true only for certain subgroups of patients.* There is still a great deal to be discovered about the dual-diagnosis patient population. For example, although the severely depressed patient who drinks alcohol to excess and the patient with a severe form of schizophrenia who also drinks heavily might both be said to be dual-diagnosis patients, researchers are not at all sure to what degree they are similar.

Psychopathology and Drug of Choice

For many years, clinical lore has maintained that dual-diagnosis clients are attempting to "self-medicate" their emotional pain through chemical abuse (Rubinstein, Campbell, and Daley, 1990; Caton, Gralnick, Bender, and Simon, 1989). Because alcohol—and by extension the other drugs of abuse—offer an illusion of control over one's feelings (Brown, 1985), they furnish an avenue through which the individual might superimpose external structure and predictability on an internal environment marked by disorder and chaos. For example, although the drugs might cause a hypothetical patient with schizophrenia to experience additional hallucinations, she or he might at least have the illusion of controlling these hallucinations by deciding whether or not to take a recreational chemical at a given time.

Another example of the self-medication hypothesis might be seen in those patients who suffer from post-traumatic stress disorder (PTSD) (Chilcoat & Breslau, 1998; Volpicelli, Balaraman, Hahn, Wallace, & Bux, 1999). It has been suggested that individuals exposed to uncontrollable trauma turn to alcohol/drugs in an attempt to find a form of chemical anesthesia that will protect them from their psychiatric distress. Although this might be successful at first, over time the early symptoms of withdrawal become associated with the symptoms of PTSD, triggering additional distress on the part of the individual.

However, the theory that MI/CD clients are attempting to self-medicate their emotional pain has been challenged by Sharp and Getz (1998). It might be, the authors suggest, that at least some dual-diagnosis clients are drawn to recreational chemical use for the same reason that other people are: because it is considered "cool" (p. 642). Also the social stigma associated with substance use/abuse is far less severe than the stigma that continues to be associated with mental illness. Accordingly, some dual-diagnosis patients try to substitute the less severe stigma of alcohol/drug abuse for that associated with their mental illness.

One fact often overlooked by those who believe that dual-diagnosis clients are self-medicating their emotional distress is that the *availability* of alcohol/drugs shapes their substance use behavior (Mueser, Bellack, & Blanchard, 1992). For years, research studies have attempted to discover whether people with a certain diagnosis are prone to abuse one chemical over the others, without considering how the issue of availability influences the substance use behavior of their research sample. This might account for the observation that alcohol is one of the substances most commonly abused by dual-diagnosis clients: It is often available to those who wish to abuse a chemical.

At this time, there does not appear to be a strong relationship between the various forms of psychopathology and the individual's drug(s) of choice (Bellack & DiClemente, 1999). However, as we have noted, those individuals who suffer from some form of mental illness are not a uniform bloc, and people with different forms

of mental illness may not be equally likely to abuse recreational chemicals. In the sections that follow, we review the literature exploring some specific forms of mental illness and alcohol/drug abuse.

Attention-deficit/hyperactivity disorder (ADHD). Individuals with ADHD constitute approximately 25% of those adults in substance abuse treatment and an unknown percentage of those adolescents with substance use disorders (Diller, 1998; Milin, Loh, Chow, & Wilson, 1997). However, the apparent relationship between ADHD and substance use disorders might be an illusion. The team of Disney, Elkins, McGue, and Iacono (1999) examined 626 pairs of twins and their mothers and found that those adolescents with ADHD who had a concurrent diagnosis of *conduct disorder*[2] were the most likely to abuse alcohol/drugs. These authors also found a possible relationship between ADHD and nicotine dependency.

Unfortunately, researchers and clinicians lack standard guidelines for the assessment of ADHD in either children or adults (Diller, 1998; Milin, Loh, Chow, & Wilson, 1997). Further, as with other MI/CD disorders, it is necessary for the individual to be alcohol/drug-free before the ADHD can be assessed. However, researchers have yet to agree on how long the individual must be alcohol/drug-free before an evaluation for ADHD can be carried out. Indeed, the entire concept of attention-deficit/hyperactivity disorder has been questioned (Diller, 1998; Briggin, 1998).

Schizophrenia. Cuffel, Heithoff, and Lawson (1993) examined the drug use patterns of 231 individuals who were diagnosed as suffering from schizophrenia and found that the members of their sample tended to follow one of three different patterns. First, there were those individuals who did not abuse alcohol/drugs, a group that made up 54% of the total sample. The second group of individuals, who made up 31% of the research sample, were those with schizophrenia who tended to abuse alcohol, marijuana, or both. The last group that the authors found were those individuals who suffered from schizophrenia and were "poly-substance" abusers (14% of the overall sample). On the basis of their research, the authors concluded that there was no apparent relationship between drug of choice and psychiatric

[2]See the Glossary.

diagnosis, a conclusion that is supported by other, unrelated studies (Mueser, Yarnold, & Bellack, 1992; Kovasznay, Bromet, Schwartz, Ranganathan, Lavelle, & Brandon, 1993).

In contrast to other research that has found alcohol to be the most commonly abused substance, Kivlahan, Heiman, Wright, Mundt, and Shupe (1991) found that marijuana was the most frequently abused drug for their sample. The authors found that 88 percent of those individuals in their sample who abused alcohol/drugs used marijuana at least occasionally. The other drugs abused by their sample were amphetamines (used by 30% at some point), alcohol (by 22%), hallucinogenics (by 18%), cocaine and narcotics (both used by 13% of the total sample at some point). As these conflicting results suggest, there is much to be discovered about the relationship between substance abuse and schizophrenia.

Dissociative disorders. Dunn, Paolo, Ryan, and Van Fleet (1993) found evidence that *over 41% of the patients* in treatment settings for alcohol/drug use disorders might also experience some form of a dissociative disorder. The dissociative disorders are marked by episodes in which the individual loses touch with reality. At the most extreme, the individual can develop more than one personality, a condition known as *dissociative personality disorder* (DPD, once called multiple personality disorder, MPD). However, most patients who suffer from a dissociative disorder do not develop DPD, although they do have episodes in which they "disconnect" from reality.

Although diagnosing a dissociative disorder is quite complex, Kolodner and Frances (1993) found two diagnostic signs that might suggest that the patient being examined had a coexisting substance abuse and dissociative disorder. First, unlike "regular" patients who are addicted to chemicals, patients with dissociative disorders do not feel better after completing the detoxification stage of treatment but, rather, tend to experience significant levels of emotional pain. Second, patients who suffer from dissociative disorders tend to relapse at times of "relative comfort and clinical stability" (Kolodner & Frances, 1993, p. 1042), in contrast to "regular" substance-abusing patients, who are thought to relapse when under stress (see Chapter 27). The authors suggested that these situations might alert the clinician to the possibility that the patient suffered from a

dissociative disorder, which might then be addressed in treatment.

As was mentioned earlier, the most serious form of a dissociative disorder is the dissociative personality disorder. Perhaps one-third of those who suffer from DPD are thought also to abuse chemicals (Putnam, 1989). These individuals tend to utilize CNS depressants and/or alcohol, although stimulants are also frequently abused by DPD patients, according to the author. Perhaps because of the nature of DPD, hallucinogenics do not seem to be a popular drug of abuse for this subgroup (Putnam, 1989). It is not clear exactly why chemicals are so popular with those who suffer from DPD. However, clients who suffer from dissociative disorders, might be using chemicals in an attempt to medicate their internal distress (Putnam, 1989).

Obsessive-compulsive disorder. OCD is the fourth most common psychiatric disorder in the United States (Falls-Stewart & Lucente, 1994). The authors suggested that OCD is four to five times as common among substance abusers as in the general population, although the reason for this is not clear.

The bipolar affective disorders. What is now called a bipolar affective disorder (or simply a bipolar disorder) was once called Manic-Depression. As scientists have struggled to understand the etiology of the various subtypes of bipolar affective disorders, they have recognized symptom groups that are thought to reflect different, but related, subforms of the bipolar affective disorder.

It is estimated that 56% of those patients with a bipolar affective disorder will also have a substance use disorder at some point in their lives (Sonne & Brady, 1999; Jamison, 1999). The importance of this finding might be seen in the observation that although drug-induced mania usually resolves when the drug wears off, physicians must wait until 2–4 weeks after the patient's last use of a drug before attempting to determine whether his or her depressive symptoms were drug-induced or not (Sonne & Brady, 1999). A further reflection of the importance of accurate differentiation between those individuals with and those without a bipolar affective disorder is seen in the fact that substance abuse by patients with an affective disorder complicates the treatment of their psychiatric illness, contributing to the need for more frequent hospitalizations and reducing the individual's control of symptoms (Sonne & Brady, 1999). This process contributes to higher hospitalization costs for society and to needless emotional suffering.

There is even evidence that at least some patients with bipolar affective disorders actively abuse drugs in order to cause some of the symptoms of this disorder. Behavioral health professionals now believe that some individuals with manic-depression use cocaine to induce or prolong the sense of power and invulnerability often experienced in the earlier stages of mania (Jamison, 1999). Evidence also suggests that individuals with bipolar disorder are most prone to alcohol/drug use problems during the manic phase of their illness, although they might also drink alcohol to relieve their depression (Modesto-Lowe & Kranzler, 1999). Unfortunately, some of the symptoms of mania—elevated mood, grandiosity, irritability, and aggressiveness—are also found during alcohol intoxication. Thus the individual must be observed both during and after alcohol withdrawal before a definitive diagnosis is possible (Modesto-Lowe & Kranzler, 1999).

Depression. Depression can range in intensity from simply feeling "blue" through what is now called "dysthymia"[3] to the agony of a major depression with psychotic features. Substance abuse frequently complicates treatment of the different forms of depression. One study found, for example, that the amount of money spent for treating patients with comorbid dysthymia and substance use disorders was *almost five times as great* as the amount of money spent on patients with only a chemical abuse diagnosis (Westermeyer, Eames, & Nugent, 1998). The importance of this finding is underscored by the observation that 31% of those patients with dysthymia will also have a substance use disorder at some time in their lives (Sonne & Brady, 1999). And 27% of those patients with a major depressive disorder will also have a chemical use problem at some time (Sonne & Brady, 1999; Jamison, 1999).

Antisocial Personality Disorder

As a group, individuals with antisocial personality disorder (ASPD) tend to abuse alcohol/drugs more often than other personality types (Ziedonis & Brady, 1997). Therefore, researchers in the field of mental health have explored extensively the relationship between this developmental disorder and substance abuse.

There is evidence that the category ASPD, which includes only a small percentage of the general population, might itself be overly inclusive. Alterman, McDermott, Cacciola, Rutherford, Boardman, McKay, and Cook (1998) utilized the Psychopathy Checklist (revised) and the Socialization scale of the California Personality Inventory to examine the personalities of 252 individuals in a methadone maintenance program. The authors found *six* subgroups of individuals, all of whom met the criteria for ASPD:

1. *Early-onset/strong ASPD features.* This subgroup, which made up just over 10% of the total sample, had a history of, or met the criteria for a diagnosis of, conduct disorder as children and/or adolescents.
2. *Late-onset/strong ASPD features.* This subgroup constituted 12% of the sample group, but their history of having engaged in behaviors typical of conduct-disordered children or adolescents was not as strong as that of the first subgroup. Members of this group had histories of anti-social behaviors as adults and of substance use problems. As a group, they were found to suffer from anxiety and/or depressive disorders.
3. *"Emotionally unstable" ASPD.* This subgroup made up about 18% of the research sample. Individuals in this subgroup had moderately strong histories of conduct-disorder behaviors in childhood and/or adolescence and of drug/alcohol use disorders that were of intermediate severity. This subgroup was marked by symptoms of hostility, guilt, dependency and avoidant personality traits, according to the authors.
4. *Non-ASPD/drug-related behaviors.* This subgroup made up 17% of the sample, and their antisocial behaviors could be traced to their substance use problems. Members of this group usually did not have conduct-disorder problems in childhood or adolescence.
5. *Moderate substance use problems/moderate ASPD.* This group constituted 15% of the sample and was identified by a tendency to have high scores on the ASPD measures but low to moderate levels of distress in the areas of drug abuse, alcohol use, and family problems. This subgroup also suffered from very low levels of guilt or depression.
6. *Low ASPD.* This subgroup, which made up 28% of the total sample, demonstrated low levels of

---

[3]Depressive neurosis.

conduct-disorder behavior as children and adolescents, and also low levels of ASPD behavior as adults.

The results of this study by Alterman *et al.* (1998) open the door for further research into the problem of ASPD and substance use disorders, in order to develop diagnostic criteria with which to effectively differentiate between ASPD and substance-induced behaviors.

Although clinical lore suggests that individuals with ASPD and comorbid substance use disorders are unlikely to benefit from traditional rehabilitation programs, this might not be true. Modesto-Lowe and Kranzler (1999) noted that those individuals with ASPD and comorbid substance use disorders *who are able to experience psychiatric distress* in the form of anxiety and/or depression, may be able to benefit from treatment for their alcohol/drug use problem. However, the authors suggest that those ASPD individuals with histories of violence resulting in serious injury to a victim, those who tend to rationalize away antisocial behavior, those who tend to use fear to control others, and those who are unable to form deep emotional attachments to others are poor candidates for traditional rehabilitation programs.

A note on other forms of personality disorders and substance abuse. There has been virtually no research into the relationship between the majority of the *DSM-IV* personality disorder categories and substance abuse. Thus nothing is known about the relationship between, for example, the schizotypal personality pattern and substance abuse, or the dependent personality disorder and alcohol/drug abuse. This area remains to be examined in the future.

Problems in Working with Dual-Diagnosis Clients

The first step for the substance abuse specialist who works with MI/CD clients is to examine his or her own attitudes toward psychopharmacology. Some individuals in the recovering community are uncomfortable with a patient's use of *any* medication(s) to control a psychiatric disorder and view the use of prescribed medication as an indication that the patient is substituting one addiction for another (Riley, 1994; Fariello & Scheidt, 1989; Evans & Sullivan, 1990). Mental health

or substance abuse professionals should examine their attitudes toward the use of prescribed psychotropic medications by substance abusers, and if they are uncomfortable with the idea, they should not work with MI/CD clients.

The outlook for dual-diagnosis clients has traditionally been thought to be quite poor. One reason for this is that the treatment philosophies of substance abuse counselors and mental health professionals often conflict (Carey, 1989; Osher & Kofoed, 1989; Wallen & Weiner, 1989; Howland, 1990). In addition, dual-diagnosis clients have trouble (1) recognizing that substance abuse is a personal problem, (2) seeing the relationship between chemical use and their problems, and (3) accepting abstinence as a viable treatment goal. These factors may bring about a significant degree of confusion and frustration both for the client and for treatment professionals.

Denial is a common problem for people with substance use disorders, and this is even more true for dual-diagnosis patients with severe forms of mental illness, where "coexisting thought or affective disorders may exacerbate denial of substance abuse" (Kofoed, Kania, Walsh, & Atkinson, 1986, p. 1209). The added dimension of a psychiatric disorder means that the individual's denial will be expressed in different ways. Some clients, for example, focus almost exclusively on their psychiatric disorder when talking to a substance abuse rehabilitation professional—and entirely on their chemical abuse problem when talking to a mental health professional. This evasion might be conscious, or it might reflect unconscious defenses, but the goal is the same in either case: avoid recognizing part of the problem. Another expression of this denial is seen when, once the psychiatric condition is controlled, the client self-terminates (drops out of treatment).

In this "interchangeable" or "free-floating" denial, the client is using one disorder as a shield against intervention for the other disorder. One example occurs when individuals who suffer from multiple personality disorder attribute their loss of memory (experienced when one personality is forced out of consciousness and another takes over) to the use of chemicals rather than to the process of dissociation.

The mentally ill, chemically dependent client is often a "crisis user" (Rubinstein, Campbell, & Daley, 1990, p. 99) of medical and chemical dependency services. This makes it hard for treatment staff to invest a great deal of time and energy in working with MI/CD clients. To complicate this problem of treatment dropout, dual-diagnosis patients are often viewed by chemical dependency professionals as primarily psychiatric patients, while mental health professionals often see the MI/CD client as being primarily substance abusers. In the 1970s and early 1980s, federal drug treatment initiatives resulted in the establishment of a number of agencies devoted to the identification and rehabilitation of the substance user (Osher & Drake, 1996). At the same time, rehabilitation efforts for patients with psychiatric problems was assigned to a different series of federal agencies. Interdepartmental communication and cooperation were virtually nonexistent, and as a result of this "political" (Layne, 1990, p. 176) atmosphere, the treatment of substance abuse cases became separated from traditional psychiatric care.

Although mental health professionals have recognized for more than a generation that MI/CD clients exist, there continue to be ongoing battles over treatment methods and philosophies (Minkoff, 1997). When the MI/CD client does come into contact with a treatment center, the staff frequently views the patient as "not our problem" and refers her or him elsewhere. The deplorable outcome of this refusal-to-treat philosophy is that clients are bounced between psychiatric and chemical dependency treatment programs (Osher & Kofoed, 1989; Wallen & Weiner, 1989).

Unfortunately, staff psychiatrists in traditional psychiatric hospitals usually lack training and experience in working with the addicted (Riley, 1994; Howland, 1990). When such patients are admitted to a psychiatric facility, they may receive, as part of their psychiatric care, potentially addictive substances prescribed by a psychiatrist more experienced in working with the "traditional" client. This practice is often contraindicated for the MI/CD client (Drake, Mueser, Clark, & Wallach, 1996).

The MI/CD client and medication compliance. There appears to be a relationship between substance use/abuse and medication noncompliance for MI/CD clients (Bellack & DiClemente, 1999; Drake *et al.*, 1998; Owen, Fischer, Booth, & Cuffel, 1996). As a group, MI/CD patients are 8.1 times more likely than non–drug-abusing psychiatric patients not to take medications as prescribed (RachBeisel, Scott, & Dixon,

1999). Medication noncompliance might include not only refusing to take prescribed medications but also continuing to use drugs of abuse even after admission to inpatient psychiatric treatment (Alterman, Erdlen, La Porte, & Erdlen, 1982). Some MI/CD clients will even stop taking prescribed medication in anticipation of recreational drug use, in order to avoid potentially dangerous chemical interactions (Ryglewicz & Pepper, 1996). The most common reason for these behaviors is not to self-medicate psychiatric distress but simply a desire to get "high" (Bellack & DiClemente, 1999).

Remember that some psychiatric medications have a significant abuse potential of their own. For example, it is not uncommon for patients who receive anticholinergic medications, which are often prescribed to help control the side effects of antipsychotic agents, to abuse their anticholinergic medications (Buhrich, Weller, & Kevans, 2000). The anticholinergics may potentiate the effects of alcohol or of the amphetamines (Land, Pinsky, & Salzman, 1991). Even when they are used alone, the "buzz" that may be obtained from anticholinergic medications is often substituted for the effects of other chemicals, when supplies run short. Thus treatment center staff must keep in mind the fact that the MI/CD client might even resort to abusing his or her psychiatric medications.

Urine toxicology testing is a useful tool to help determine whether the patient is taking antipsychotic medications as prescribed. Urine toxicology testing is also valuable in detecting illicit chemical use, because MI/CD clients often test "positive" for recreational drugs even when they openly deny the use of such agents (Drake, Mueser, Clark, & Wallach, 1996). Another approach to the problem of noncompliance is the use of long-term injectable forms of some phenothiazines currently available, rather than the more traditional short-term preparations, for control of the thought disorder and agitation often found in dual-diagnosis clients (Fariello & Scheidt (1989).

Treatment Approaches

In the last two decades of the 20th century, mental health professionals slowly came to accept that dual-diagnosis clients require specialized treatment (Bellack & DiClemente, 1999). The traditional approach to dual-diagnosis clients has been to address the client's mental illness first, and then, after psychiatric stabilization has been achieved, to begin to explore the client's chemical use pattern (Rado, 1988). Usually, different professionals work with the client in turn, first to achieve a reduction in the patient's psychiatric symptoms and then to address his or her substance use problem. This approach is an example of the *serial treatment model* (Miller, 1994).

The decision whether to treat the psychiatric condition or the drug dependency first is often quite arbitrary (Howland, 1990; Kofoed *et al.*, 1986). Indeed, there are little research data to suggest which treatment format works best with the dual-diagnosis client (Evans & Sullivan, 1990; Osher & Kofoed, 1989). One alternative, suggested by Layne (1990), is to treat both disorders *concurrently*.

Miller (1994) identified two subtypes of concurrent treatment models. In the first, which he termed the *parallel treatment model*, the patient "shuttles" between treatment facilities, dealing with his or her mental health concerns on one unit and with substance use issues on another unit. Unfortunately, this treatment approach makes it imperative that the staff on each unit communicate freely with their counterparts on the other. But this is often a problem, especially if the psychiatric rehabilitation staff is not used to working with substance abuse rehabilitation professionals. Second, the need to move physically from one unit to another might be stressful to vulnerable patients, exacerbating their psychiatric problems. Finally, parallel treatment facilities tend to experience significant patient attrition (Drake, Mueser, Clark, & Wallach, 1996).

The second subtype of concurrent treatment, which Miller (1994) termed the *integrated treatment model*, is clearly the most efficient. In an integrated treatment setting, there are both mental health and substance abuse rehabilitation professionals on the same staff. By coordinating their treatment goals, they are able to address both psychiatric and chemical use issues at the same time, in the same treatment facility. In such a treatment model, interstaff communications and cooperation are essential. This treatment approach offers the advantage of dealing with the client's substance use and psychiatric issues simultaneously, while reducing the potential for conflict between different treatment professionals. Ries *et al.* (2000) found that the substance-abusing patients with schizophrenia in their sample

seemed to recover more quickly than patients with schizophrenia alone. They attributed this to the availability of an integrated treatment program for the dual-diagnosis patients.

In the concurrent treatment models discussed above, one basic requirement is the team approach. The rehabilitation "team" provides a forum where the different treatment philosophies of psychiatric and chemical dependency professionals can be synthesized into a unified approach for working with the substance-abusing mentally ill client (Riley, 1994; Osher & Kofoed, 1989; Evans & Sullivan, 1990). Chemical detoxification is a necessary first step in treating a dual-diagnosis client (Layne, 1990; Wallen & Weiner, 1989). This requires psychiatric support from professionals who are knowledgeable in both psychiatry and chemical dependency (Evans & Sullivan, 1990). Once detoxification has been achieved, the treatment team is in a position to identify which problems are a result of the client's chemical use, which problems are manifestations of the client's psychiatric disorder, and in what order the problems need to be addressed.

The treatment setting. The general psychiatric unit is usually not suited to meeting the needs of a dual-diagnosis client (Kofoed & Keys, 1988; Howland, 1990). Kofoed and Keys (1988) suggested that traditional psychiatric units might do best if treatment goals were limited to (1) detoxification from drugs of abuse, (2) psychiatric stabilization, and (3) persuasion of the client to enter chemical dependency treatment. The clinician must be patient, often waiting years until conditions are right to persuade a dual-diagnosis client to enter treatment. The ideal program for a dual-diagnosis client has facilities for working with both the psychiatric and the chemical use problems, which enables the staff to utilize whatever treatment resources the dual-diagnosis patient needs most at that moment. This is obviously easier in a facility that follows the integrated treatment model. Such a program might be offered on either an outpatient (Kofoed *et al.*, 1986) or an inpatient basis (Pursch, 1987), depending on the client's needs and the available resources. However, in more difficult cases, long-term inpatient treatment may be the only option for effectively working with the MI/CD client (Caton, Gralnick, Bender, & Simon, 1989).

The stages of treatment. The dual-diagnosis client usually comes to the attention of mental health or chemical dependency professionals as a result of a crisis situation such as repeated hospitalizations, legal problems, psychiatric decompensation, or eviction from his or her apartment (Fariello & Scheidt, 1989; Rubinstein, Campbell, & Daley, 1990). It is at this point that treatment might be initiated. Indeed, Durell, Lechtenberg, Corse, and Frances (1993) pointed out that a crisis "can provide the motivation for overcoming addiction" (p. 428). Director (1995) called this first phase of treatment that of *initial assessment/engagement*, whereas Lehman, Myers, and Corty (1989) refers to it as *acute treatment and stabilization* (p. 1020). Minkoff (1989) termed this part of treatment the phase of *acute stabilization*. The possibility that this stage might be subdivided into early and late phases has been suggested (Bellack & DiClemente, 1999). It is during this phase of treatment that the client's psychiatric condition is stabilized and detoxification is carried out. The possibility of a dual diagnosis is also considered by the clinician during this phase of evaluation and treatment. If the symptoms that suggest a psychiatric disorder completely clear during detoxification, then the possibility that the client is not a dual-diagnosis patient should be considered (Layne, 1990).

However, if the psychiatric symptoms persist after detoxification, then the diagnosis of a dual-diagnosis client becomes more likely (Lehman, Myers, & Corty, 1989). In either case, during this second phase of treatment, staff should focus on helping the individual understand the relationship between the crisis and his or her untreated psychiatric problem(s). Staff will try to break "the cycle of substance abuse, noncompliance, decompensation, and rehospitalization once the patient is sober and psychiatrically stable" (Fariello & Scheidt, 1989, p. 1066). This process might include the introduction of money management programs, psychoeducational materials or lectures, and social support.

It is during this phase of treatment that staff attempt to break through the denial that surrounds both the individual's mental illness and his or her addiction. Both Osher and Kofoed (1989) and Minkoff (1989) termed this phase of treatment that of *engagement*. Layne (1990) termed this phase of treatment that of *early engagement*, and Director (1995) called it the period of *primary care*. The goal during this phase of treatment is for the professional staff to establish a therapeutic relationship, arrive at an accurate diagnosis, and

convince the client that treatment has something to offer. Staff members should attempt to work with family members or legal representatives during this period, to bring the client into treatment on an involuntary basis if necessary.

Group therapy appears to offer "a more acceptable source of support and confrontation than is usually available . . . on a general psychiatric ward" for the dual-diagnosis client (Kofoed & Keys 1988, p. 1209). It is usually more effective for these groups to be held on the psychiatric unit than on the substance abuse unit (Kofoed & Keys, 1988; Layne, 1990). During the next phase, that of *maintenance and rehabilitation*, the clinician should work toward the goal of preventing a recurrence of both the chemical abuse and the psychiatric disorder (Lehman, Myers, & Corty, 1989). This is the same process that Fariello and Scheidt (1989) identified as *breaking the cycle of addiction*. Osher and Kofoed (1989) called this phase of treatment that of *persuasion*. The therapeutic goals of this phase of treatment are: (a) to persuade client to accept the reality of his/her drug dependency, and, (b) to persuade the clients to seek continued treatment for his/her substance abuse problem (Kofoed & Keys, 1988).

The third phase of treatment, that of *active treatment* (Osher & Kofoed, 1989), attempts to help the client learn "the attitudes and skills necessary to remain sober" (p. 1027). Director (1995) called this phase of treatment *continuing care*. Many of the same techniques utilized in general drug addiction treatment groups are useful in working with dual-diagnosis clients. Osher and Kofoed (1989) argued against lower treatment expectations, or the acceptance of relapse as being inevitable, for dual diagnosis clients. Layne (1990) suggested that treatment staff might need to teach her or him specific life skills in order to help the client learn how to function in society without abusable drugs and in spite of ongoing delusions.

However, the very nature of the client population offers unique challenges and requires modification of techniques used in traditional chemical dependency work. The confrontational model often used with traditional substance-abusing clients is often counterproductive with MI/CD clients, especially those with schizophrenia (Bellack & DiClemente, 1999). It has been suggested that when confrontation is utilized with dual-diagnosis clients who are in treatment, the confrontation should be less intense than the confrontation utilized with traditional personality-disordered clients (Riley, 1994; Penick *et al.*, 1990; Carey, 1989).

Unfortunately, once the patient's psychiatric condition is controlled, his or her drug-related defenses again begin to operate (Kofoed & Keys, 1988). Dual-diagnosis clients often express a belief that once their psychiatric symptoms are controlled, they are no longer in danger of being addicted to chemicals. These clients are unable to see the relationship between their chemical abuse and the psychiatric symptoms that they experience. This is a form of denial, but not one that is unique to the MI/CD client. For example, the patient who has financial problems and an addictive disorder may express a similar belief once his or her financial problem is resolved. A common form of denial that is frequently found in traditional clients is evident when the client informs the drug rehabilitation specialist that he or she has discontinued all drug/alcohol use. In effect, the client enters a period during which he or she will "tell the counselor what he wants to hear" in order to avoid confrontation. This is an evasion that is frequently exhibited by all clients, including those who suffer from mental illness.

MI/CD clients are often unable to utilize traditional support systems such as Alcoholics Anonymous or Narcotics Anonymous, because MI/CD clients tend to feel out of place in traditional self-help group meetings (Fariello & Scheidt, 1989; Wallen & Weiner, 1989). This is especially true in the earlier states of rehabilitation (Drake, Mueser, Clark, & Wallach, 1996). It is for this reason that a group of peers is most effective in working with the dual-diagnosis client; group members who have dropped out of treatment in the past can share their experiences with the group (Kofoed & Keys, 1988).

Therapy groups provide an avenue through which clients can share their experiences with even limited recreational drug use, discuss the need for the support of a Twelve-Step group, and explore problems in the use of Twelve-Step programs (Fariello & Scheidt, 1989; Kofoed & Keys, 1988; Rado, 1988). It was noted that, when the group is effective, dual-diagnosis clients tend to achieve a lower rehospitalization rate (Kofoed & Keys, 1988), and function better in society. However, the few limited follow-up studies suggest that MI/CD clients tend to continue to abuse alcohol and/or drugs in spite of the best efforts of staff (Drake, Mueser, Clark, & Wallach, 1996).

Summary

The dual-diagnosis client presents a difficult challenge to both mental health and chemical dependency professionals. Many of the syndromes that may result from the chronic use of chemicals are virtually indistinguishable from organic or psychiatric problems. This makes it hard to arrive at an accurate diagnosis. Further, MI/CD clients often use defenses, such as an interchangeable system of denial, that further complicate the diagnostic process.

Dual-diagnosis clients are also difficult to work with in the rehabilitation setting. When they are in treatment, dual-diagnosis clients will often talk only about their psychiatric problem with drug addiction counselors and only about their drug abuse or addiction with mental health professionals. Therefore, it has been found necessary to modify some of the traditional treatment methods when working with the chemically dependent client. For example, the degree of confrontation useful in working with a personality-disordered client is far too strong for working with a dual-diagnosis client who suffers from schizophrenia or any other form of mental illness. However, gentle confrontation is often effective with the mentally ill and drug-dependent client who does not have a personality disorder.

CHAPTER TWENTY-THREE

Chemical Abuse by Children and Adolescents

Introduction

For a number of reasons, childhood and adolescence are periods of special concern for substance abuse rehabilitation professionals. Research has demonstrated that midadolescence is the period in life when individuals most commonly begin to use recreational chemicals (Flanagan & Kokotailo, 1999). Even so, medical researchers do not understand how substance abuse during this critical period of growth might affect the various body systems, which are still maturing during childhood and adolescence. Finally, research has revealed that in the United States, recreational chemical use peaks in the early 20s, which is the end of adolescence in the opinion of many experts on human development, and for the majority of chemical abusers, the frequency and duration of substance use gradually decline thereafter.

Surprisingly, while the news media speak of the problem of substance use/abuse by children and adolescents as though it were a new phenomenon, this problem has been with us for a long time. During the early 1800s, for example, alcoholism was rampant among the youth of England (Wheeler & Malmquist, 1987). Indeed, child and adolescent alcohol use in the 19th century was one of the reasons behind the child welfare movement. The social reforms brought about by the child welfare movement in the 19th and 20th centuries helped to drive the problem of child and adolescent recreational chemical use underground. However, children and adolescents have always wondered about, and experimented with, recreational chemicals, as evi-

denced by the fact that 50 years ago, just under half of the adolescents entering high school had already used alcohol at least once (Takanishi, 1993).

Currently, the developmental periods of childhood and adolescence are of special importance to drug abuse rehabilitation professionals, if only because the use of alcohol/drugs by children/adolescents appears to be more widespread, and more widely accepted, than at any previous time. Further, researchers are only now starting to identify the consequences of child/adolescent substance use disorders on the individual's later growth and development. In this chapter, we shall focus on the problem of chemical use/abuse by children and adolescents.

The Importance of Childhood and Adolescence in the Evolution of Substance Use Problems

In the last two decades, researches have uncovered evidence that the period of greatest vulnerability for developing a substance use problem is between the ages of 15 and 19 years and that the median age for developing an alcohol use problem is approximately 21 years (Chatlos, 1996). Children or adolescents who begin to abuse alcohol/drugs at earlier ages are more likely to go on to develop substance use problems than are individuals who wait until later in life to experiment with recreational chemicals. For example, 16% of those children who begin to experiment with marijuana before the age of 12 will go on to use heroin, compared to only

8% of those individuals whose first marijuana exposure is after the age of 12 years (Kandel, 1997).

Researchers have discovered that one factor that motivates the child/adolescent either to abuse or to abstain from abusing alcohol or drugs is the quality of his or her *attachment bonds* with the parents (Bell, Forthun, & Sun, 2000; Hogan, 2000). Infants with positive attachment bonding experiences tend to become adolescents who have positive relationships with their parents, have more positive peer relationships, are more socially competent, and exhibit better coping skills. Thus at least some of the roots of child/adolescent substance abuse may stretch back to the period of infancy. This fact helps to explain why antidrug programs developed for students in grade school are not strong enough to help adolescents withstand the almost constant barrage of drug use messages that they receive starting at about the age of 12 or 13 (Shalala, 1997). These discoveries, combined with the awareness that significant numbers of children and adolescents are abusing recreational chemicals, have made the childhood and adolescent periods of life of special interest to substance abuse rehabilitation professionals.

Problems in the assessment of child and adolescent drug use patterns. Surprisingly, very little is actually *known* about the problem of substance use/abuse in childhood or adolescence (Bukstein, 1995; Kaminer, 1994; Evans & Sullivan, 1990). Indeed, many of the estimates of childhood/adolescent substance abuse are little more than watered-down versions of the assumptions made about chemical abuse in adults (Knight, 2000; Bukstein, 1995). This lack of research into diagnostic criteria has resulted in the distinctions among substance use, abuse, and dependence being blurred and arbitrary (Hogan, 2000).

More than a decade ago, Newcomb and Bentler (1989) observed that there was virtually no research into the chemical use patterns of children and that the research data on teenage drug use patterns was limited at best (Bukstein, 1995; Evans & Sullivan, 1990). At the start of the 21st century, there has been little change in this sad situation. This lack of research data means that virtually *all* chemical use during adolescence is interpreted by many people as a sign of a serious drug abuse problem (Bell, 1996; Newcomb & Bentler, 1989).

Much of what researchers believe is true about adolescent drug use patterns is based on studies that use school students as research subjects. Given the fact that 15–30% of adolescents drop out of school before graduation (Eccles, Midgley, Wigfield, Buchanan, Reuman, Flanagan, & MacIver, 1993), school-based studies are of limited value in helping us understand adolescent chemical use patterns, so it is quite difficult to determine current drug abuse trends. The lack of a comprehensive database also makes it difficult to identify forces that motivate the adolescent to begin to use chemicals or to differentiate between a normal phase of experimentation and problem use.

Finally, drug use patterns among children and adolescents may show rapid fluctuation and wide variation. The variables that influence adolescent drug use trends include the individual's geographic location, her or his peer group, and the current drug use "trends." The phenomenon of inhalant abuse is one such drug use "fad," which rapidly waxes and wanes in a given geographic area as individuals embrace and then discard the use of these substances.

Scope of the Problem

Childhood chemical abuse patterns. Surprisingly, alcohol use during childhood seems to be more common than most parents are willing to admit. This is clearly seen in the fact that 52% of the children/adolescents older than 12 years of age admit to having used alcohol at least once in the preceding 30 days (Hogan, 2000; Johnston, O'Malley, & Bachman, 2000a). In the United States, the average age of taking the first drink is between 12 and 13 years (Novello & Shosky, 1992). Boys tend to begin drinking earlier than girls; their average age for the first drink of alcohol is 11.9 years, as compared with 12.7 years for girls (Alexander & Gwyther, 1995; Morrison, Rogers, & Thomas, 1995). This observed age difference may reflect different patterns of alcohol *availability* (Van Etten, Neumark, & Anthony, 1999). The authors found evidence suggesting that boys and girls are equally likely to abuse chemicals if they have equal access to recreational substances. However, it would appear that boys are more likely than girls to have access to alcohol/drugs. By the time they reach adolescence, most children have had at least limited exposure to alcohol/drug use.

Unfortunately, this is the period in life when the region of the brain known as the *hippocampus* matures, and researchers have found evidence that alcohol use during this time can affect hippocampal development (DeBellis, Clark, Beers, Soloff, Boring, Hall, Kersh, & Keshavan, 2000). On the basis of animal research, developmental neurologists now believe that the still-developing adolescent brain might be four to five times as vulnerable to alcohol-induced brain damage as the adult brain (Wuethrich, 2001). This brain damage might not become evident until after the individual has stopped drinking, when a small (7–10%) but marked decline in psychological test performance is noted. This decline in cognitive abilities appears to be permanent, suggesting that adolescent binge drinking can have life long consequences.

However, alcohol is not the only recreational chemical that children or adolescents are likely to experiment with. Many children use inhalants as their first mood-altering chemical (Hogan, 2000). As we saw in Chapter 16, adolescent inhalant abuse is a serious problem that, although it may not be the norm for childhood, is still quite common. For example, 19.7% of the eighth graders surveyed in 1999 had used an inhalant at least once (Johnston, O'Malley, & Bachman, 2000a). Fortunately for most children and adolescents, inhalant abuse is usually only a transient process, and thus the potential for inhalant-induced brain damage is limited. Most adolescents will engage in rare, episodic inhalant abuse over a span of 1–2 years, after which they abandon this practice.

The "gateway" drug theory. Some researchers have suggested that certain drugs of abuse, such as the inhalants (Brunswick, 1989) and marijuana (Millman & Beeder, 1994), serve as an introduction to the abuse of more destructive compounds. One investigation of 1160 subjects from the ages 15 to 35 did find evidence of such a progression from the "gateway" chemicals to more serious forms of substance use (Kandel, Yamaguchi, & Chen, 1992). On the other hand, it has been suggested that marijuana's role as a "gateway" chemical is simply an illusion (Watson, Benson, & Joy, 2000). It has been observed that "most drug users begin with alcohol and nicotine before marijuana" (Watson, Benson, & Joy, 2000, p. 551) and that the illusion of marijuana as a gateway drug becomes apparent when drug dealers, not having any marijuana to sell, convince buyers to try something else (Phillips, 2001). Personality characteristics such as whether the individual has an antisocial per-

sonality disorder or conduct disorder in adolescence are more predictive of subsequent substance use disorders.

Kandel and Chen (2000) examined the marijuana use patterns of a community-based sample of 708 marijuana abusers (364 males and 344 females) who were followed from adolescence until the age of 34–35 years. The marijuana abusers fell into four groups: (1) early-onset, heavy-use group, (2) early-onset, light-use group, (3) midadolescence-onset, heavy-use group, and (4) midadolescence-onset, light-use group. By itself, the early use of marijuana was not found to be predictive of later problems or of a progression to the abuse of other chemicals. However, the authors found that the individual's *motivation* for using marijuana and the presence of other dysfunctional behaviors were associated with later drug abuse/dependency, a result that casts doubt on the "gateway" theory's application to marijuana abuse. Thus it has not been proved whether there are certain "gateway" substances that predispose the individual to the abuse of other compounds.

Adolescent Chemical Abuse Patterns

The available research would suggest that adolescent drug use peaked sometime around the year 1981 and then slowly declined for about a decade (see Figure 23.1). In the 1990s, adolescent chemical use was more or less stable or perhaps slowly increased (Johnston, O'Malley, & Bachman, 2000a; Edwards, 1993). Nationally, it is estimated that up to 3 million adolescents have serious alcohol/drug use problems (Tweed, 1998). Fully 10% of older adolescents in the United States meet the diagnostic criteria for an alcohol use disorder (De Bellis *et al.*, 2000).

Not surprisingly, adolescent drug use patterns tend to mirror those of society (Callahan, 1993). Thus, in a society where alcohol is the most popular recreational chemical, it should not be surprising to learn that alcohol is by far the most popular chemical of choice for adolescents (Hogan, 2000; Johnston, O'Malley, & Bachman, 2000a; Morrison, Rogers, & Thomas, 1995). The Department of Health and Human Services (1997) estimated that 9 million children and adolescents between the ages of 12 and 20 consume alcohol each year in the United States. The percentage of high school seniors who have experimented with alcohol has remained relatively stable over the past decade (Knight, 2000). For example, 80% of the class of 1999 had used

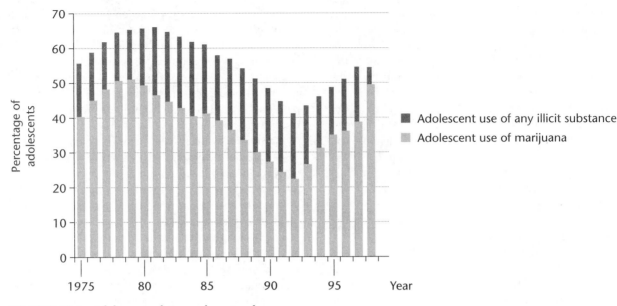

FIGURE 23.1 Adolescent substance abuse trends.

alcohol at least once (Johnston, O'Malley, & Bachman, 2000a). There also is evidence that the percentage of those high school seniors who drink heavily has remained stable over the past decade, with approximately 30–40% of adolescents being classified as heavy drinkers (Knight, 2000).

The most popular form of alcohol for the adolescents surveyed is beer, although wine "coolers" are increasing in popularity (Novello & Shosky, 1992). Adolescent use of "hard" liquor is so rare that even occasional experimentation with vodka, gin, whiskey, or bourbon should be considered a sign of an alcohol abuse problem (Rogers, Harris, & Jarmuskewicz, 1987). Surprisingly, although many parents worry about possible alcohol use by their adolescent children, they are poor sources of information about their teenagers' use of this chemical. It has been found that parents tend to underestimate their teenagers' alcohol consumption by a factor of at least 10 (Morrison, Rogers, & Thomas, 1995; Rogers, Harris, & Jarmuskewicz, 1987; Zarek, Hawkins, & Rogers, 1987). More distressing is the fact that 40% of parents surveyed think that they have no influence over their teenagers' decision whether to use alcohol/drugs (Comerci, Fuller, & Morrison, 1997).

In spite of its popularity, alcohol is not the only recreational chemical used by adolescents. By the time of graduation, 54% of the seniors in the class of 1999 admitted to having used an illicit chemical at least once (Johnston, O'Malley, & Bachman, 2000a). The most popular illicit drug for adolescents appears to be marijuana, which accounts for 75% of illicit drug use by teens (Hogan, 2000). Some 49% of the seniors in the class of 1999 admitted to having used marijuana at least once, according to the authors (Johnston, O'Malley, & Bachman, 2000a). For eighth graders, alcohol is the most commonly used mood-altering chemical; with 52% of the eighth-grade students surveyed in 1999 admitting to having used alcohol at least once (Johnston, O'Malley, & Bachman, 2000a). Inhalants have replaced marijuana as the most frequently used illicit mood-altering chemical; 20% of the eighth graders surveyed in 1998 admitting to having used inhalants at least once (Johnston, O'Malley, & Bachman, 2000a). Hallucinogenics are increasingly popular, with 12.2% of the high school seniors surveyed in 1999 admitting to the use of LSD, and 6.7% admitting to the use of some other hallucinogen (Johnston, O'Malley, & Bachman, 2000a).

It has been suggested that adolescents who develop substance use problems show a definite progression in their substance use (Kandel & Davies, 1996). In the first stage, the adolescent will engage in the use of a chemical normally reserved for adults (such as tobacco and/or alcohol). Most adolescents do not progress beyond this stage (Newcomb, 1996). But for those who do, the next step is the use of an illicit chemical. Kandel and Davies (1996) noted that this substance is usually marijuana. Again, of those adolescents who reach this stage, most do not proceed further. For some, however, the use of marijuana precedes the use of "hard" drugs such as cocaine, according to the authors. Thus the progression of substance abuse first identified in the 1970s seems still to apply to adolescent chemical use patterns at the start of the 21st century.

College students make up a unique subpopulation. Traditionally, college is viewed as spanning the period from late adolescence to early adulthood, a period in life when risk-taking behaviors reach their peak (Anrett, 2000). Legally, most college students are considered adults. At the same time, these individuals are still below the age of 21, which is the age at which an adult can purchase alcohol in most states. In spite of this inconvenience, college students "spend more on alcohol than they spend on books, soda, coffee, juice, and milk combined" (Jersild, 2001, p. 99). As a group, college students drink more heavily than their noncollege peers (Demers-Gendreau, 1998; Coombs, 1997).

It has been argued that the prohibition against underage drinking has caused adolescents to become obsessed with alcohol use and encouraged them to engage in a binge pattern of overuse when they do drink (Barr, 1999). Most certainly, the "binge" pattern of alcohol use appears to be the most common pattern on the college campus (Weingardt, Baer, Kivlahan, Roberts, Miller, & Marlatt, 1998). Fully 84% of the college students surveyed drink alcohol, and approximately half of this number, 44%, engage in binge drinking with the goal of getting drunk (Demers-Gendreau, 1998). A "binge" was defined as a period in which an individual consumed five or more drinks in an evening. Further, Wechsler *et al.* (1994) found that most of the students in their sample had followed the same drinking pattern in high school as they did in college.

Surprisingly, in spite of this pattern of alcohol consumption, the majority of those who consumed alcohol in college did not consider their drinking to indicate a problem. This is consistent with the observations of Weingardt, Baer, Kivlahan, Roberts, Miller, and Marlatt (1998), who found that only a minority (5–19% of those students surveyed) continued to drink abusively over extended periods of time. This would suggest that for the majority of college students who drink, excessive alcohol use reflects a stage of experimentation. One reason why many college students might abuse alcohol is their misperception of the amount of alcohol ingested by their peers. As a group, college students tend to overestimate both their peers' acceptance of drunken behavior and the number of their peers who are drinking heavily (DeAngelis, 1994b). This is unfortunate, because by the time that students arrive at college, the influence of their peer group is one of the strongest factors that helps to shape their drinking patterns (Weingardt, Baer, Roberts, Miller, & Marlatt, 1998).

Further, there is a tendency among heavy drug/alcohol users to equate substance use with fun (DeAngelis, 1994b). Fortunately, although the authors found that brief intervention programs might have a beneficial impact on alcohol use patterns of high-risk students, "most young heavy drinkers mature out of their risky behavior as they become more experienced as drinkers and are faced with greater life responsibilities" (Marlatt *et al.*, 1998, p. 614). Although this would suggest that alcohol/drug abuse by college students is only a phase, researchers still have not isolated the diagnostic signs that a given individual is "at risk" for a substance use disorder later in adulthood.

The 1997 Tobacco Lawsuit Settlement and Tobacco Use by Children and Adolescents

Cigarettes and other tobacco products occupy a unique place in our society: These substances are known to be addictive, are terribly destructive, and yet can be legally purchased by adults. Unfortunately, tobacco use problems are also a very real part of childhood and adolescence. In the United States, the *average* age at which a smoker begins smoking is about 12 years, and most of those who begin to smoke at this stage of life are regular smokers by the age of 14 (Hogan, 2000). More than one in every three adolescents smokes at least one cigarette a day (Dickinson, 2000).

In the late 1990s, evidence introduced in support of various lawsuits against cigarette manufacturers revealed that cigarette manufacturers used their knowledge that nicotine is addictive to try to manipulate adolescents into starting to smoke cigarettes. At least one major tobacco company conducted research into the phases of adolescent cigarette smoking, apparently in order to learn how best to encourage the transition to regular cigarette smoking (Hilts, 1996). In an internal memo, another major tobacco company referred to adolescents as a "up and coming new generation of smokers" (Phelps, 1996, p. 1A). The R.J. Reynolds Tobacco Co., a major cigarette producer, classified 12-year-old children as "younger adult" smokers (*Newsweek*, 1998).

In 1997, what has variously been called "Big Tobacco" or "The Tobacco Industry" offered to settle a lawsuit brought against it by representatives of 40 of the 50 states. Without admitting any wrongdoing, the major tobacco producers offered a financial settlement of $368.5 billion and agreed to discontinue a number of advertising tactics, especially the development of advertising aimed at children and adolescents (Smolowe, 1997). Included in this legal settlement was a provision that, if the number of underaged smokers was not reduced by 50% within 7 years of the settlement, that the tobacco industry would pay additional penalties. One of the forces that helped to bring about this settlement was an admission by one of the smaller tobacco companies that the industry had specifically targeted children and adolescents for years (Smolowe, 1997). These discoveries help to explain why an estimated 6000 children/adolescents *begin* to smoke each day in the United States, in spite of the health dangers known to be associated with this practice (Dickinson, 2000).

Adolescents tend to think of themselves as being immortal, and thus they tend to underestimate the long-term consequences of high-risk behaviors such as tobacco use. Further, the natural rebelliousness of adolescents makes them especially vulnerable to the image, encouraged by many tobacco companies' advertising, that cigarette smoking is a way to rebel against parental authority (Dickinson, 2000; Hilts, 1996). The same appears to be true of the estimated 1.5 million people under the age of 19 who use "smokeless tobacco" (Kessler, 1995). Just under three-quarters of

these tobacco users started to do so by the time they were in the ninth grade (Barker, 1994). Further, 90% of cigarette smokers are already *addicted* to nicotine by the age of 20 (Walker, 1993). These figures underscore the need to address the use of tobacco products during childhood or adolescence.

By the time of graduation from high school, 22.4% of the students surveyed admitted to the daily use of cigarettes, and an additional 3.2% used "smokeless" tobacco, at least once each day (Johnston, O'Malley, & Bachman, 1999a). The authors found that just over 65% of the seniors surveyed in 1998 had used cigarettes at least once. DiFranza and Tye (1990) found that 18.1% of high school seniors smoked cigarettes on a daily basis. The American Heart Association estimated that 2.2 million children between the ages of 12 and 17 smoke cigarettes (Associated Press, 1994), and Mead (1993) offered a figure of 3 million children and adolescents in this country who either smoke or use "smokeless" tobacco products. An estimated 100,000 of the adolescents who smoke are thought to be below the age of 13 (Bhandari, Sylvester, & Rigotti, 1996).

Although advertising by the tobacco industry aimed at children/adolescents is a major factor in the initiation of smoking, another force that shapes whether the child/adolescent will begin to smoke is whether her or his parents smoke. Males (1992), who observed that 75% of all teenagers who smoke had parents who also smoked, suggested that "teenage smoking is largely the active continuation of a childhood of passive smoking" (p. 3282). This theory is certainly consistent with research suggesting that the transition from nonsmoker to smoker in childhood or adolescence appears to pass through several stages (Holland & Fitzsimons, 1991):

1. *Preparatory phase.* Forming attitudes accepting of cigarette smoking.
2. *Initiation phase.* Smoking for the first time.
3. *Experimentation phase.* Learning how to smoke.
4. *Transition.* Smoking regularly.

Hints for successful intervention. Given the progression from forming attitudes accepting of smoking through the addictive use of tobacco, it would seem that attempts at intervention need to be aimed at children who have not yet started to form pro-smoking attitudes (Holland & Fitzsimons, 1991). Attempts at intervention should focus on helping children learn social skills that will enable them to resist smoking, according to the authors, on the grounds that if the adolescent reaches 16–18 years of age without having initiated smoking, he or she is unlikely to do so. Fully 90% of those who *begin* to smoke cigarettes after the age of 21 are unlikely to continue the habit, according to Hilts (1996).

However, successful intervention will require further investigation of the "refusal skills" utilized by boys and girls who are offered the opportunity to smoke or use alcohol/drugs (Moon, Hecht, Jackson, & Spellers, 1999). The authors have found that boys are less likely than girls to "just say no" and that they tend, rather, to explain why they do not want to use. This makes them vulnerable to counterexplanations and raises their risk of ultimately giving in and accepting tobacco/drugs when these are offered. A successful intervention program would need to enhance the refusal skills of both boys and girls who are offered the opportunity to smoke or abuse chemicals.

Why Do Adolescents Use Chemicals?

Hogan (2000) suggested that there are five basic reasons why adolescents use/abuse chemicals: (1) to feel grown up, (2) to take risks and rebel against authority, (3) to fit into a specific peer group, (4) to relax and feel good, and (5) to satisfy curiosity about the drug's effects. To this list might be added the fact that some adolescents self-medicate negative feelings such as depression or interpersonal stress through the use of alcohol/drugs (Joshi & Scott, 1988; Morrison, Rogers, & Thomas, 1995). For some adolescents, using alcohol/drugs is a way to prove sexual prowess (Barr, 1999; Morrison, Rogers, & Thomas, 1995), whereas others do so in response to peer pressure (Petraitis, Flay, Miller, Torpy, & Greiner, 1998). So pervasive is the influence of the mass media in defining what is expected of the individual socially that Hogan (2000) referred to the media as a "superpeer" (p. 937).

As this list of potential contributing factors illustrates, there is no simple reason why adolescents use recreational chemicals. One thing that seems to affect whether the individual uses recreational chemicals is his or her cognitive level. Because adolescents tend to view themselves as immortal, many have trouble seeing themselves as vulnerable to the negative effects of alcohol/drugs (Hogan, 2000). In the section that follows, the relationship between these factors and adolescent substance use/abuse will be examined in more detail.

Adolescent affective disorders. Depression, especially severe depression, has been found to be a risk factor for adolescent substance use/abuse (Kriechbaum & Sernig, 2000). Thus affective disorders such as anxiety and depression should be viewed as warning signs for adolescents at "high risk" (Burke, Burke, & Rae, 1994, p. 454) for substance abuse problems.

Extremes of behavior (such as total abstinence or serious drug abuse) were found in adolescents who were most maladjusted; the healthiest were those who experimented with chemicals occasionally (Shedler & Block, 1990). These findings, although surprising at first, do make clinical sense. The emotionally healthy adolescent might experiment with recreational drug use but ultimately would have the skills necessary to cope with life. However, as Shedler and Block (1990) reported, those adolescents who used drugs frequently demonstrated poor impulse control, a pattern of social alienation, and emotional distress—all signs that these individuals lack the emotional resources the first group exhibited. Further, those individuals who totally abstained from chemical use were found to be anxious, emotionally constricted, and lacking in social skills. These individuals seemed to lack the self-confidence to explore their environments. The authors concluded that the individual's chemical use pattern, (abstinence, experimental drug use, or frequent drug abuse) could be interpreted only in light of his or her level of emotional adjustment.

Peer group influences on adolescent substance use patterns. Intuitively, one would expect a relationship between the peer group membership and substance use patterns of the individual, and research confirms such a relationship (Petraitis *et al.*, 1998; Farrell & White, 1998; Kaminer & Bukstein, 1998; Bukstein, 1995; Adger & Werner, 1994). Indeed, exposure to alcohol-using social models, especially peers, was found to predict the development of positive expectations for alcohol in children/adolescents in the fifth through seventh grades (Cumsille, Sayer, & Graham, 2000).

Surprisingly, peer group selection is the *last step* in the chain of events that ultimately results in the adolescent's use of alcohol/drugs (Kumpfer, 1997). Adolescents actively seek out a peer group consistent with their values, expectations, and demands, including the area of substance use patterns (Oetting, Deffenbacher, & Donnermeyer, 1999). Thus peer group selection often precedes active chemical use, because the individual's perception of approval from peers precedes his or her first use of marijuana. The actual use of a chemical, then, is often the *last step* in a chain of events that began with the selection of a specific peer group, moved to anticipation that members of this group would approve of chemical use, and concluded with the actual use of the substance.

The peer group influence model has been challenged by other scientists, however (Bauman & Ennett, 1994; Novello & Shosky, 1992). Novello and Shosky (1992) noted, for example, that of the 10.6 million adolescents who consume alcohol, nearly one-third do so when alone, rather than in groups. The authors interpreted this finding as evidence that the theory that adolescents use chemicals in response to peer pressure does not hold in all cases.

Bauman and Ennett (1994) have even suggested that adolescent friend selection may reflect a congruence of substance use patterns. In other words, adolescents who are most prone to use chemicals will form friendships mainly with other drug abusers, a pattern that might cause researchers to overestimate the influence of peer groups on substance use.

Another factor that might undermine the apparent relationship between substance use patterns and peer group membership is the possibility of *projection* on the part of the research subjects. When asked about their friends' substance use, drug-using adolescents are more likely to respond on the basis of *their own* drug use behavior than on the basis of what they know about their friend's chemical use. In support of this theory, Bauman and Ennett (1994) pointed out that adolescents who do not use chemicals are more likely to be judged as using recreational drugs by their drug-using friends than by their non–drug-using friends. On the basis of their research, Bauman and Ennett (1994) suggested that the effect of adolescent peer use on substance abuse patterns was "overestimated" (p. 820).

Personal values and their influence on adolescent chemical use patterns. One factor that *does* seem to protect the child/adolescent from pressure to use alcohol/ drugs is his or her personal values. There is a negative correlation between the individual's substance use be-

haviors and such factors as scholastic performance, church attendance, and beliefs about the importance of academic achievement (Kaminer & Bukstein, 1998). However, because correlation does not imply causality, it is not clear whether these forces help to protect the adolescent from becoming ensnared in substance use problems.

The impact of parent–child relationships on adolescent chemical use patterns. Research has shown that parental influence on values development and subsequent drug use behavior, is strongest during the childhood years. Parental behaviors such as spending time with their children, parental substance use patterns, and the degree of parental emotional involvement have all been found to influence the individual's substance use in childhood and adolescence (Kaminer & Bukstein, 1998). This is seen in the fact that children who reported that their parents spent more time with them, and made greater efforts to communicate with them, have lower rates of alcohol/tobacco use (Griffin, Botvin, Scheier, Diaz, & Miller, 2000; Cohen, Richardson, & LaBree, 1994). Children/adolescents are also very aware of parental modeling behaviors (Shalala, 1997; Cohen, Richardson, & LaBree, 1994; Rogers, Harris, & Jarmuskewicz, 1987). Thus, what the parents *do* often has a stronger influence on the child than what they *say* about chemical abuse (Chassin, Curran, Hussong, & Colder, 1996; Alexander & Gwyther, 1995).

As the individual moves into adolescence, parental leverage on her or his behavior is muted by social and peer influences, but it does not entirely disappear. Parental impact on such emerging facets of the adolescent's personality as his or her values and the quality of the family's affectional interactions also help shape the individual's tendency to use or not use recreational chemicals (Cohen, Richardson, & LaBree, 1994). Children whose parents spent more time interacting with them were less likely to abuse chemicals, and those adolescents who felt that their parents were emotionally supportive, or who came from intact families, were also found to be less likely to engage in alcohol/drug abuse (Griffin, Botvin, Scheier, Diaz, & Miller, 2000; Farrell & White, 1998; Petraitis *et al.*, 1998).

Parental control seems to be another factor that shapes the individual's chemical use pattern (Chassin, Curran, Hussong, & Colder, 1996). Parents who made the time and the effort to monitor their child/

adolescent's behavior seemed to be associated with lower rates of delinquency and substance abuse (Griffin, Botvin, Scheier, Diaz, & Miller, 2000). In contrast to this, parents who abused recreational chemicals tended to engage in fewer "parental control practices" (Chassin, Curran, Hussong, & Colder, 1996 p. 70), allowing their adolescent more opportunities to join social groups likely to engage in recreational drug/alcohol use, according to the authors.[1]

Personal abuse history. Another factor that consistently seems to identify adolescents at risk for substance use problems is whether the individual has ever been the victim of some form of physical/sexual abuse (Fuller & Cabanaugh, 1995) or witnessed violence within the family (Kilpatrick, Acierno, Saunders, Resnick, Best, & Schnurr, 2000). It is thought that adolescents might turn to alcohol/drugs as a way of self-medicating their feelings of shame and fear as a result of having been victimized. Another group of adolescents who are vulnerable to the effects of recreational chemicals are those who become aware of homosexual urges within themselves. According to Fuller and Cavanaugh (1995), the homosexual adolescent might use alcohol and/or drugs in an attempt to self-medicate feelings of guilt, inadequacy, or self-depreciation.

Rebellion. A number of researchers have suggested that the very fact that their use of alcohol is prohibited makes drinking a goal for many adolescents (Barr, 1999). Indeed, because *any* use of alcohol by the adolescent is considered illegal by authorities, individuals who indulge in heavy alcohol use are viewed by peers as especially daring (Barr, 1999). As we shall see in Chapter 35, many other countries allow adolescents to drink alcoholic beverages *with their families*, and these countries do not seem to suffer from the problem of alcohol misuse by adolescents.

Section Summary

Ultimately, the research data do not support the simplistic, linear theory that the individual's peer group membership dictates his or her chemical use (Curran,

---

[1]An interesting question to consider is which came first: Do the parents fail to provide adequate supervision because they are using chemicals? Or do they use recreational chemicals because they are immature and poorly adjusted people, who are unable to fulfill their parental roles?

Stice, & Chassin, 1997). Rather, such factors as the quality of parent–child relationships, whether the adolescent is depressed, and his or her age-specific struggle for autonomy all play a role in the development of substance use/abstinence patterns in the teenager. The early adolescent years appear to be a time of special vulnerability for later drug use problems.

The Adolescent Abuse/Addiction Dilemma: How Much Is Too Much?

Adolescent substance use/abuse/addiction falls along a continuum with total abstinence at one end and severe dependency at the other. In between these two extremes are the conditions of experimental chemical use, occasional chemical use, and regular use of recreational chemicals (Tweed, 1998). Unfortunately, researchers still do not have a proven way to determine which adolescents are in need of professional help because of their chemical use/abuse (Knight, 2000), nor have they conducted much research into the question of how to measure the adolescent's motivation to participate in treatment (Melnick, DeLeon, Hawke, Jainchill, & Kressel, 1997). These may be some of the reasons why 50% of those adolescents who are admitted to substance abuse treatment programs return to the abuse of recreational chemicals within 90 days of their discharge (Latimer, Newcomb, Winters, & Stinchfield, 2000).

There is a very real need for diagnostic criteria by which to identify adolescents who are abusing alcohol/drugs. For example, chest pain is the third most common reason why adolescents seek medical care, and research has found that 17% of the adolescents tested in a hospital setting had evidence of ephedrine in their urine, in spite of their denial that they had used this compound (James, Farrar, Komoroski, Wood, Graham, & Bornemeier, 1998). Thus physicians need diagnostic tools to rule out *both* cocaine use and/or ephedrine abuse as a possible cause of chest pain in adolescents who are seen in the emergency room setting for this reason.

Tweed (1998) suggested several symptoms that might indicate an adolescent with an alcohol/substance use problem: unexplained weight loss, nasal irritation, frequent "colds" or "allergies" (brought on by intranasal use of drugs or inhalants), hoarseness, chronic cough, unexplained injuries, needle tracks, social withdrawal, promiscuity, fights (with family or individuals outside of the family), hiding bottles or drug paraphernalia, selling possessions, and legal problems. Another possible warning sign was a drastic change in the individual's sleep pattern, without apparent reason.

Most certainly, if an adolescent *is* abusing alcohol/drugs, that chemical abuse must be considered in terms of the his or her psychosocial development (Kriechbaum & Zernig, 2000; Cattarello, Clayton, & Leukefeld, 1995; Bukstein, 1995). Heavy use of alcohol/drugs to the point of intoxication in early adolescence appears to indicate adolescents who are at risk for later drug use problems (Bukstein, 1995). After the age of 15, the experimental use of alcohol or drugs might not be a reflection of serious problems so much as a reflection of society's more liberal attitude toward recreational substance use.

Problems in diagnosis and treatment of adolescent drug abuse. In spite of the attention that has been paid to adolescent substance use/abuse since the mid-1980s, "the standards guiding diagnosis and treatment decisions specifically related to adolescents are relatively primitive and often lack empirical support" (Bruner & Fishman, 1998, p. 598). For the most part, the diagnostic criteria used for adolescents are based on standards developed for use with adults (Kaminer, 1999; Pollock & Martin, 1999). It is possible that the adult standards are not valid when applied to adolescents.

One way to improve the accuracy of an assessment of an adolescent's chemical use pattern is to establish an extensive database about the individual and his or her substance use patterns (Evans & Sullivan, 1990). For example, the occasional use of alcohol or marijuana at a party—say, once every six months—is not necessarily a sign of a drug abuse problem; it may merely reflect curiosity about the effects of these chemicals (Hogan, 2000).

Referrals for a chemical dependency evaluation on an adolescent come from many sources. The juvenile court system, especially the emerging "drug courts," often refer an offender for an evaluation, especially when that individual was under the influence of chemicals at the time of his or her arrest. School officials may request an evaluation on a student suspected of abusing chemicals. Treatment center admissions officers frequently recommend an evaluation, although this referral is usually made to in-house staff rather than to an independent professional. Some parents, especially those with "religious, restrictive families" (Farrow, 1990, p. 1268), request an evaluation and/or treatment after the first known episode of alcohol or drug use.

As a group, adolescents tend to have a rather immature view of life and of the consequences of their decisions. Unfortunately, this simplistic outlook on life, and possible continued chemical use, may be mistakenly interpreted by treatment staff as a sign of denial or resistance. A multidisciplinary team approach to assessment in cases of suspected adolescent substance abuse will allow the treatment team to identify accurately the client's strengths, weaknesses, level of maturity, and adaptive style.

The stages of adolescent chemical use. For adolescents who abuse chemicals, there is a progression that ultimately leads, to more serious substance use problems. Jones (1990) viewed the individual's progression from experimental substance use to a substance use problem as passing through four different stages. Chatlos (1996), on the other hand, suggested a five-stage model of adolescent substance use/abuse. These two models are compared in Table 23.1.

It is interesting to note that each model suggests that the adolescent substance user must first be exposed to the chemical(s) she or he will abuse and learn what to expect from the use of that substance. Each model suggests that for those adolescents who continue to engage in recreational chemical use, a change in friendship patterns occurs as the adolescent begins to drift away from his or her former peer group, toward a new peer group that is more accepting of chemical use. Other behaviors that might develop during this stage include erratic school performance, unpredictable mood swings, and manipulative behaviors, all in the service of continued substance abuse.

When the individual becomes preoccupied "with the mood swing" (Jones, 1990, p. 680), non–drug-using friends are avoided, family fights and confrontations develop, and there may be a loss of employment, expulsion from school, consistent lying, and daily use of mood-altering chemicals. The individual's daily activities revolve around the use of chemicals (Tweed, 1998). Ultimately, some individuals will progress to the final stage of substance use, wherein they must use drugs just "to feel normal" (Jones, 1990, p. 680). Tweed (1998) refers to this as the "burnout" stage (p. 33) of adolescent chemical abuse. During this stage, the individual expe-

TABLE 23.1 Two Theories of the Stages of Adolescent Substance Abuse

Stages of Adolescent Substance Use/Abuse According to Jones (1990)	*Stages of Adolescent Substance Use/Abuse According to Chatlos (1996)*
Learning the mood swing: The adolescent is exposed to substance us and learns, from more experienced users, what to expect from the use of recreational substances.	*Initiation:* Individual begins the use of mood-altering chemicals.
Seeking the mood swing: The young substance user's life begins to revolve around chemical use, and his or her use of recreational chemicals increases.	*Learning the mood swing:* The new substance user learns what effects to expect from his or her chemical use and why these effects are to be desired.
Preoccupied with the mood swing: The young person ends relationships with non-using friends; may lose job or be expelled from school; uses mood-altering drugs daily; may lie to friends and family to protect his or her continued use of drugs.	*Regular use/seeking the mood swing:* The adolescent continues to seek what she or he has come to view as the positive effects of recreational chemical use.
Using just to feel normal: Drug/alcohol use has reached the point where the individual must use chemicals just to feel "normal" and to function. The person experiences some consequences of chronic chemical abuse; may become paranoid, have memory loss, or experience flashbacks.	*Abuse/harmful consequences:* The negative effects of recreational chemical use begin to make themselves felt on the user's life (poor academic performance, etc.), but the individual continues to use recreational chemicals.
	Substance dependency/compulsive use: The adolescent is now physically addicted to chemicals, or at least is trapped in a cycle of compulsive use, in spite of the serious consequences of this behavior.

riences physical complications from drug use, memory loss and/or flashback experiences, paranoia, anger, and drug/alcohol overdoses. Feelings of guilt, shame, depression, and remorse—and suicidal thinking—are all possible during this phase (Tweed, 1998).

Adolescence and addiction to chemicals. Whereas a history of alcohol withdrawal symptoms is one of the major landmarks used to identify an adult with an alcohol use disorder, only 23% of those adolescents diagnosed as being dependent on alcohol had ever experienced any symptoms of alcohol withdrawal (Martin & Winters, 1998). Partly for this reason, it was once thought that adolescents were unlikely to have had the opportunity to use a drug(s) long enough to develop physical dependency on that chemical (Kaminer & Frances, 1991). It is now known that this theory is incorrect.

Adolescents who *are* physically dependent on alcohol/drugs tend to exhibit fewer, and less severe, symptoms of their addiction than do adults (Kriechbaum & Zernig, 2000; Kaminer & Frances, 1991). The signs of adolescent alcohol/drug addiction are often less subtle than those seen in adults who are dependent on the same chemicals. One of the most frequently encountered symptoms of alcohol/drug dependency in adoles-

cents is the development of physical tolerance to the effects of their drug of choice (Martin & Winters, 1998). Hoffmann, Belille, and Harrison (1987) found, for example, that more than three-quarters of their sample of 1000 adolescents, all of whom were in treatment at the time, reported having developed tolerance to alcohol or other drugs.

Certainly, because adolescents usually lack the extensive history of substance abuse found in many adults, they are less likely to have experienced any major organ damage as a result of their alcohol/drug abuse (Kriechbaum & Zernig, 2000). Thus "physical health problems associated with substance abuse were found to be infrequent in adolescents" (Harrison, Fulkerson, & Beebe, 1998, p. 491). But it still is possible for blood studies of the adolescent alcohol/drug abuser to reveal evidence of organ damage in (Chassin & DeLucia, 1996).

The mental health professionals who question whether adolescents can become addicted to alcohol/drugs are in a distinct minority. Farrow (1990) was one researcher who challenged the concept of adolescent addiction, stating that "the number of teenagers who are truly chemically dependent is less than 1% of all users" (p. 1268). Another 10–15% might meet the diagnostic criteria for drug or alcohol abuse, and a full 10–15% of all teens have little or no experience with either alcohol or drugs. The remainder are occasional users of alcohol/drugs and will probably adjust "their use in non-problematic ways as they grow older" (p. 1268). However, even Farrow's (1990) conclusions support the possibility of adolescent addiction and alcohol/drug use disorders.

Adolescent substance use: A cause for optimism? On the bright side, there is significant evidence that the majority of those adolescents who engage in recreational chemical use will not go on to develop drug dependency (Larimer & Kilmer, 2000; Kriechbaum & Zernig, 2000; Kaminer, 1999; Kaminer, 1994). Heavy alcohol/drug use is often "adolescence limited" (Kaminer, 1999, p. 277), with only a small percentage of adolescents going on to develop a more serious drug abuse problem (Chatlos, 1996). For most adolescents, recreational substance use might be viewed as reflecting no more than a phase of experimentation (Miller, Westerberg, & Waldron, 1995). During this phase of experimentation, the individual is exploring new forms of behavior that are commonly found in the culture in which he or she lives. Only a small percentage of adolescents continue to have problems with chemicals later in life.

The financial incentive for overdiagnosis. The admissions officers of many treatment centers hold that the use of chemicals by adolescents automatically signals a drug abuse problem. Such treatment professionals, perhaps with an eye more on the balance sheet than on the individual's needs, frequently recommend treatment at the first sign of drug abuse by an adolescent. Harold Swift, president of the world-famous Hazelden Foundation, was quoted by Iggers (1990) as asking "What harm has been done?" when a teenager is mistakenly told that he or she was addicted to chemicals. This question ignores the fact that an unknown percentage of intervention programs actually harm the adolescent (Dishion, McCord, & Poulin, 1999) and assumes that *any* treatment exposure for the adolescent would be a positive experience for that individual.

Because it is against the law for adolescents to buy or use alcohol or recreational chemicals, in many treatment centers "the term substance 'use' has been largely abandoned in favor of substance 'abuse,' reflecting the ideology that *any* use among minors constitutes abuse, since it violates the law" (Harrison, Fulkerson, & Beebe, 1998, p. 486, italics added). One reason why

treatment program staff might unconsciously wish to blur the boundary between adolescent chemical use and abuse is financial gain. The adolescent chemical dependency treatment program concept grew into a "lucrative industry" (Bell, 1996 p. 12) in the 1980s, and in order to maximize profits, many treatment centers tended to blur the lines between use, abuse, and addiction for adolescents.

Forcing the individual—even if this person is "only" an adolescent—into treatment when he or she does not have a chemical addiction may have lifelong consequences (Peele, 1989). Such action may violate the rights of the individual, and in some states, it is illegal to force an adolescent into treatment against his or her will, even with parental permission (Evans & Sullivan, 1990). Further, in spite of the fact that diagnostic criteria to identify adolescents with substance use problems have not been developed, many drug rehabilitation programs continue to try to convince the patients that they are permanently impaired because of problem alcohol/drug use in their adolescent years and that they will never again be "whole" emotionally (Peele, 1989). Lamentably, there is no research into how this treatment approach itself affects the individual's subsequent emotional growth. Nor is there research to determine whether there is a negative consequence to telling the adolescent that he or she is forever an addict at such a young age, especially when the literature does not support this extreme view.

A possible solution to this dilemma is offered by Beeder and Millman (1995):

> After one year or more of abstinence and *appropriate social adjustment*, young people may be encouraged to think of themselves as similar to their peers, though with the recognition that they continue to be at increased risk. (p. 79, italics added)

Thus the authors neatly sidestep the issue of whether the adolescent is "addicted" to chemicals. From this perspective, the goal of treatment should be to help the individual develop appropriate social behaviors, including the ability to abstain from recreational chemicals on the grounds that the individual might be "at risk" for substance use problems.

Statistically, the peak period for substance use problems is between the ages of 18 and 22; after this, the average individual tends to return to a more appropriate pattern of chemical use (Bukstein, 1995). This means that although many adolescents will experience substance use problems at some point in their lives, the majority will adopt a more acceptable pattern of chemical use in young adulthood (Evans & Sullivan, 1990; Peele, 1989). For example, one recent study found that of those adolescents identified as heavy drinkers at age 18, half were not judged to be heavy drinkers 12 years later (Bukstein, 1994). Thus the adolescent who has abused chemicals on a regular basis may or may not go on to develop a problem with chemicals in young adulthood.

The risks of underdiagnosis. Diagnosing adolescent drug/alcohol abuse is quite complicated, and there are significant risks associated with failing to treat those adolescents for whom drug use is a serious problem (Evans & Sullivan, 1990). First, protracted chemical use may interfere with the adolescent's ability to develop age-specific coping mechanisms (Kaminer, 1994). Further, by the time the individual's drug use has resulted in serious physical changes, or she or he has contracted a blood infection from "dirty" needles, the individual is scarred not just for the rest of adolescence, but for life. Once a brain cell has died, it will never regenerate. AIDS is forever. Thus there are very real reasons to identify adolescents who have a chemical use problem, before it is too late to avoid lifelong damage.

Researchers have discovered that alcoholism or drug dependence is one of the factors associated with an increased risk of suicide in the adolescent population (Bukstein, 1995; Callahan, 1993). The exact nature of this relationship is not clear, but researchers do know that chemical abuse is a factor in 70% of all adolescent suicides (Bukstein, Brent, Perper, Moritz, Baugher, Schweers, Roth, & Balach, 1993; Group for the Advancement of Psychiatry, 1990).

Bukstein *et al.* (1993) attempted to identify the factors associated with successful adolescent suicides and uncovered several risk factors. No single risk factor emerged, but the factors associated with successful adolescent suicide included (1) active chemical abuse by the individual, (2) suffering from a major depression, (3) thoughts of suicide within the past week, (4) a family history of suicide and/or depression, (5) legal problems, and (6) access to a handgun within the home.

Substance abuse is commonly a factor in accidental injuries to adolescents (Chassin & DeLucia, 1996;

Loiselle, Baker, Templeton, Schwartz, & Drott, 1993). After receiving parental permission, Loiselle, Baker, Templeton, Schwartz, and Drott (1994) conduced urine toxicology tests on 65 adolescents admitted to a major hospital for the treatment of traumatic injuries, and 34% of these individuals tested positive for alcohol and/or drugs. Because alcohol/drug use was so common in the patients seen for traumatic injuries, the authors suggested that urine toxicology tests be a standard part of the treatment protocol for such cases. Along the same lines, Morrison (1990) observed that the first sign of an adolescent substance use problem might be his or her visit to a hospital emergency room for treatment of injuries or substance-induced physical problems.

Thus the chemical dependency treatment professional who works with adolescents must attempt to find the middle ground between underdiagnosis, with all of the dangers associated with teenage drug/alcohol abuse, and overdiagnosis, which may leave the individual with the lifelong scars of a false diagnosis of chemical dependency.

The D.A.R.E. program: A promise unfullfilled. Although supporters have appealed for ever-increasing levels of funding and larger amount of students' classroom time, there is minimal evidence that school-based programs such as Drug Abuse Resistance Education (D.A.R.E.) have any long-term impact on adolescent drug or alcohol use (Rowe, 1998). Lynam, Milich, Zimmerman, Novak, Logan, Martin, Leukefeld, and Clayton (1999) explored the possibility that the D.A.R.E. program might have effects apparent in early adulthood, though not in adolescence, but they failed to find any significant difference between the substance abuse levels of those young adults who participated in D.A.R.E. programs and those who did not. The authors speculated that this program continues to be popular in spite of its proven lack of effectiveness, because to the unsophisticated reviewer it *appears* to work.

Possible Diagnostic Criteria for Adolescent Drug/Alcohol Problems

A wide range of diagnostic criteria to help the clinician identify the child/adolescent with a substance use problem have been suggested over the years; they include low socioeconomic status, lack of religious commitment, low self-esteem, and coming from a disturbed family (Miller, Davies, & Greenwald, 2000; Newcomb & Bentler, 1989). Other possible predictors are the individual's peer group, the quality of familial relationships, the individual's personality pattern, experiencing withdrawal symptoms after periods of alcohol use, tolerance to the effects of alcohol, unsuccessful attempts to cut back on the amount of alcohol being used, unsuccessful attempts to stop using alcohol, alcohol-related blackouts, and continued alcohol use in spite of adverse social, educational, physical, or psychological consequences, and/or alcohol-related injuries (Committee of Substance Abuse, 1995).

Chung, Colby, Barnett, Rohsenow, Spirto, and Monti (2000) attempted to identify brief screening tools that would be effective in detecting alcohol abuse problems in adolescents. They administered modified versions of the CAGE, the TWEAK, and the AUDIT (see Chapter 26) to a sample of 415 adolescents who failed to have a detectable blood alcohol level (BAL) at the time of their admission to a hospital emergency room for treatment of an injury. Of these adolescents, 18% were found to have an alcohol use problem, according to the authors, who went on to recommend that a cut-off score of 4 points be used when the AUDIT is administered to an adolescent. The TWEAK performed best when the cut-off score was only 2 points, the CAGE when a cut-off score of 1 point was used (Chung *et al.*, 2000).

Some factors that might identify adolescents who are at risk for alcohol abuse problems are the following (Miller, Davies, & Greenwald, 2000; Kriechbaum & Zernig, 2000; Tweed, 1998; Fuller & Cabanaugh, 1995; Alexander & Gwyther, 1995; Adger & Werner, 1994; Wills, McNamara, Vaccaro, & Hirky, 1996; Jones, 1990; Johnson, Hoffmann, & Gerstein, 1996; Nunes & Parson, 1995):

- Family history of alcoholism or drug abuse
- Depression or other psychiatric illness
- A history of suicide attempt(s)
- Loss of loved one(s)
- Low self-esteem
- High levels of stress
- Poor social skills and maladaptive coping mechanisms
- Problems in relationships with parents (parents are either too permissive or too authoritarian) resulting in lower levels of parental support

- Coming from a single-parent or blended family
- Feelings of alienation or having run away from home
- School problems or limited commitment to school
- Low expectations for school
- Family tolerance for deviant behavior
- Peer tolerance for deviant behavior
- Attitude accepting of drug use
- Early cigarette use
- High levels of engagement with drug-using peers
- Antisocial behavior or poor self-control
- Early sexual experience
- Early experimental drug use
- Legal problems during adolescence
- Absence of strong religious beliefs
- Tendency to seek novel experiences or take risks

Nunes and Parson (1995) suggested that the adolescent who had five or more of these risk factors were virtually guaranteed to have a substance use problem.

Age at the onset of alcohol use was found to be one significant factor: The individual's risk of developing a lifelong alcohol use problem declined 8–14% for each year beyond the age of 12 that the individual delayed the start of alcohol abuse (Larimer & Kilmer, 2000). But even with this subgroup of alcohol abusers, only 40% of those who were abusing alcohol at age 12 would meet the diagnostic criteria for alcohol dependency for the rest of their lives, according to the authors. These conclusions were similar to those of DeWit, Adlaf, Offord, and Obgorne (2000), who found that 40% of those individuals with an alcohol use disorder began to drink before the age of 14, whereas only 10% of those who began to drink after the age of 20 went on to develop such a problem.

According to Martin and Winters (1998), the signs of an individual who is experiencing a substance use disorder are (1) use of alcohol/drugs under hazardous conditions (driving while under the influence of chemicals, for example), (2) use of alcohol/drugs in a manner that allows *tolerance* to the effects of that chemical to develop, (3) reduction of activities that are not alcohol/drug-related, (4) blackouts, (5) loss of consciousness due to chemical abuse, (6) engaging in risky sexual behavior while under the influence of chemicals, (7) development of "craving" for the drug(s) of choice between periods of active use, (8) unsuccessful attempts on the part of the individual to quit on his or her own, and, (9) a drop in academic performance due to substance use.

As adolescents become more and more preoccupied with chemical use or demonstrate an interest in an expanding variety of chemicals, they might be said to exhibit the adolescent equivalent of the progression of chemical use often seen in adults (Evans & Sullivan, 1990). They will also demonstrate poor academic performance, and a loss of control, expressed through violations of personal rules about drug use (such as "I will only drink on weekend parties"). Thus those adolescents who are preoccupied with substance use or who wish to experiment with a wide range of chemicals should be evaluated and referred to treatment, if indicated.

Even when a legitimate need for treatment is identified, there are several factors that may interfere with the treatment process. These include unrealistic parental expectations for treatment, hidden agendas for treatment by both the adolescent and the parents, parental psychopathology, and parental drug or alcohol abuse (Kaminer & Frances, 1991). Another factor is parental refusal to provide consent for treatment even for a teenager who has been identified as an alcohol or drug abuser (Kaminer, 1994).

The Special Needs of the Adolescent in a Substance Abuse Rehabilitation Program

The adolescent who has been found to be in need of rehabilitation because of a substance use problem presents special needs. First, treatment staff should be sufficiently aware of the developmental process that is taking place during adolescence to be able to understand the adolescent's cognitive abilities, strengths, and defensive style. Second, the treatment center should be able to offer a wide variety of services, taking into account the student's educational needs, recreational needs, and possible coexisting psychiatric disorders (Bukstein, 1994). The staff should also address issues peripheral to the adolescent's substance abuse, such as AIDS, birth control, and the individual's vocational needs, according to the author.

Treatment center staff must be sensitive to the adolescent's cultural heritage and to the social status of the adolescent and his or her family (Bukstein, 1994,

1995). Having a diverse staff helps to ensure that the adolescent is able to find at least one staff member to identify with during the treatment program. Rehabilitation center staff should attempt to engage family members in the treatment process (Bukstein, 1994). The goals that might be addressed with family members include improving communications between family members, developing problem resolution skills, resolving discipline problems, and identifying problems within the family unit that might undermine the efforts of the treatment center staff (such as undiagnosed substance use by one or both of the parents). The treatment process should be of sufficient duration to ensure a meaningful change in how the adolescent and his or her family cope with life's problems (Bukstein, 1995). Latimer, Newcomb, Winters, and Stinchfield (2000) found that adolescents who had a significant non-using peer, and who remained in treatment/aftercare for approximately a year, were less likely to relapse than adolescents who failed to meet these criteria. These findings make sense in that behavioral change takes time, and time is also necessary for the individual to change his or her attitudes. Thus the treatment process should be long enough. and intense enough, to allow for these necessary components of recovery to take place.

The adolescent treatment center staff should have access to a wide range of specialized social service agencies. In addition to their own work with the adolescent, treatment center staff might need to make referrals to juvenile justice, child welfare, and social support agencies (Bukstein, 1994, 1995). As part of the rehabilitation process, involvement in AA/NA might be useful for the adolescent, especially if there is a "young person's" group available. Al-Anon might prove to be valuable for family members who question their role in the adolescent's substance use. Finally, the goal of the rehabilitation effort should be for the adolescent to achieve a chemical-free lifestyle (Bukstein, 1995; 1994).

Adolescents offer treatment center staff unique challenges, but there are also special rewards to be earned through working effectively with a younger substance abuser. Adolescents are less entrenched in their pathology and thus, in many cases, more responsive to rehabilitation efforts. When substance abuse does become an issue for adolescents, rehabilitation professionals have an opportunity to help them turn their lives around.

Summary

Clearly, children and adolescents are often hidden victims of drug addiction. Yet there is a serious lack of research into the problem of child and adolescent drug use/abuse. Although mental health professionals acknowledge that peer pressure and family environment influence the adolescent's chemical use pattern, the exact role that these forces (or the media) play in shaping the adolescent's behavior is still not known. There are many unanswered questions surrounding the issue of child and adolescent drug use, and in the years to come, there may be significant breakthroughs in our understanding of the forces that shape beliefs about chemical use and patterns of use in the young. In the face of this dearth of clinical research, the treatment professional must steer a cautious path between underdiagnosis and overdiagnosis of chemical dependency in the younger client. Just as surgery performed on the individual during childhood or adolescence has lifelong consequences, so would the traumatic experience of being forced into treatment for a problem that may not exist. As with surgery, the treatment professional should carefully weigh the potential benefits from such a course of action against its potential to harm the individual.

During a phase of adolescent experimentation, a teenager might demonstrate repeated and regular use of one or more chemicals, only to settle down in young adulthood to a more acceptable pattern of chemical use (Evans & Sullivan, 1990; Peele, 1989). One recent study, for example, found that among individuals identified as "problem drinkers" during adolescence, fully 53% of the men and 70% of the women were not judged to be problem drinkers 7 years later (Zarek, Hawkins, & Rogers, 1987).

Although treatment professionals understand that chemical use during adolescence is a factor in a wide range of emotional and physical problems that develop during this phase of life, the diagnostic criteria needed to identify those adolescents who are at risk for subsequent problems as a result of their chemical use are still evolving. Thus treatment professionals have no firm guidelines with which to differentiate the adolescent who is passing through a phase of experimental chemical use from the adolescent whose chemical use reflects a more serious problem.

CHAPTER TWENTY-FOUR

Codependency and Enabling

Introduction

Scientists who specialize in the behavioral sciences are often faced with a bewildering array of behaviors that they must both categorize and try to understand. To help them express complex ideas to others more easily, behavioral scientists utilize *constructs*. An example of a construct is the symbol of a weather "front" on a meteorological map. In reality, there are no lines between different weather cells and no firm boundaries between different bodies of air. But by using the analogy of battle lines from World War I, meteorologists can quickly summarize data and communicate that information to others.

As substance abuse rehabilitation professionals began to explore with a substance abuser, the interpersonal dynamics within his or her family, they developed a number of new constructs to help them explain the impact of alcoholism or drug addiction on the family. Two of these constructs are *codependency* and *enabling*, concepts that were frequently invoked in the 1980s and early 1990s but have drifted out of the public spotlight in the past few years. In this chapter, we will examine the constructs of enabling and codependency

Enabling

Essentially, to *enable* someone means to behave *knowingly* in such a way as to make it possible for that person to continue to use chemicals without having to pay the natural consequences. The concept of enabling emerged in the early 1980s, when some therapists suggested that within some families there almost seemed to be a conspiracy in which at least some family members supported the continued use of chemicals by the individual with a substance use problem. In this manner, the behavior of some family members became part of the problem, not a part of the solution. The enabler came to be viewed as doing something that prevented the person with a chemical use problem from taking advantage of the many opportunities to discover firsthand the cost and consequences of his or her chemical abuse. The spouse, for example, might call the partner's workplace with the excuse that the substance-abusing partner was "sick," when he or she actually was under the influence of chemicals.

A popular misconception is that only family members can enable a substance abuser. The truth is that an "enabler" can be a parent, sibling, co-worker, neighbor, or even supervisor. Other potential enablers include a well-meaning friend, a trusted advisor, a teacher, a therapist, or even a drug rehabilitation worker. Any person who *knowingly* acts in such a way as to protect the alcohol/drug abuser from the natural consequences of his or her behavior might be said to be an enabler. For example, in speaking of alcoholism, the booklet *The Family Enablers* (Johnson Institute, 1987), defined an enabler as *any* person who "reacts to an alcohol-dependent person in such a way as to shield the alcoholic from experiencing the full impact of the harmful consequences of alcoholism" (p. 5). The same criteria can be applied to those who enable people who are addicted to other drugs of abuse.

One does not need to be involved in an ongoing relationship with a person who abuses chemicals, or is addicted to them, in order to enable him or her. A person who refuses to provide testimony about a crime that he or she witnessed out of reluctance to become involved, or out of fear, might be said to have enabled the perpetrator of that crime to escape. But the clinical theory suggests that the enabler is usually involved in an ongoing relationship with the person who has a substance use problem.

Styles of enabling. Over the years, a number of different patterns of enabling have been suggested. Ellis, McInerney, DiGiuseppe, and Yeager (1988) offered one a framework within which to understand the different styles of behavior that enabled another to continue to use chemicals. According to the authors, some people can be called *joiners* (p. 109). A joiner actively supports the use of chemicals by another person and may actually use alcohol/drugs with that person. A classic example of a joiner is the woman who seeks marital counseling because her husband will not limit his cocaine use to the $100 a week that she has set aside in the family budget for his drug use!

Another, all too common example of the joiner is the spouse who drinks or uses chemicals along with the addicted person in the hope of somehow controlling his or her chemical use. For example, substance abuse rehabilitation professionals know that it is quite common for a spouse to go to a bar with the alcohol-abusing/dependent partner in an effort to teach the partner how to drink in a "responsible" manner. Such efforts to join the spouse in substance use and change him or her from within usually are doomed to failure. After all, if the addicted spouse were capable of drinking or using chemicals in a responsible manner, she or he wouldn't be addicted in the first place.

A second type of enabler suggested by Ellis *et al.* is the *messiah* (p. 109). The messiah fights against the addict's chemical use but does so in such a way that the addict is never forced to experience the consequences of his or her behavior. Consider the father of one opiate-dependent young adult. In a mixed group of family members and other opiate-addicted patients, the father tearfully admitted that he had taken out a personal loan more than once to pay off his daughter's drug debts. The father offered this as an example of how much he loved his daughter. Another group member, who had been in recovery for some time, asked why the father would do this. After all, if the father pays off her debts, she will not have to worry about having to pay her drug debts herself. The father responded that if he did not, his daughter "might leave us!" Several group members then suggested to this parent that the daughter might need to suffer some consequences on her own, in order to "hit bottom" and come to terms with her addiction. The father was silent for a moment, and then said, "Oh, I couldn't do that! She's not ready to assume responsibility for herself yet!"

Ellis, McInerney, DiGiuseppe, and Yeager (1988) suggested a third form of enabler, whom they termed the *silent sufferer* (p. 109). The silent sufferer almost seems to live by the philosophy that "As long as I suffer, I *am* somebody!" In a very real sense, the silent sufferer lives the life of a martyr. She or he will live with an alcohol/drug-abusing family member, in spite of the pain this troubled environment inflicts. The silent sufferer is unwilling to leave, according to the authors. It is almost as though the silent sufferer believes she or he would not have a life if she or he left the substance-abusing partner.

With the best of intentions, the silent sufferer prevents the alcohol/drug abuser from suffering the consequences of his or her behavior by "always being there and pretending that nothing is wrong" (Ellis, McInerney, DiGiuseppe, & Yeager, 1988, p. 109). The authors viewed the goal of this relationship pattern as being that of *security*. Rather than losing what little emotional security the partner offers, the silent sufferer tries not to "rock the boat." Indeed, people who play this role may act as a lightning rod, drawing all of the pain and suffering away from the disturbed family members to themselves, in an attempt to defuse family conflict.

The relationship between enabling and codependency. The key concept to remember is that an enabler *knowingly* behaves in such a way as to protect the addicted person from the consequences of his or her behavior. We all behave in ways that, in retrospect, may have enabled someone to avoid some consequences of his or her drug use. This is a point that is often quite confusing to the student of addiction. Codependency and enabling may be—and often are—found in the

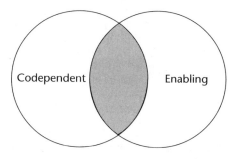

FIGURE 24.1   Relationship between codependency and enabling behaviors.

same person. Because he or she is in an ongoing relationship with the addict, the codependent individual also frequently enables the alcohol/drug-abusing person. However, one may enable an addicted person without being codependent on that person. A tourist who gives a street beggar money, knowing that the beggar is probably addicted and in need of drugs, might be said to have enabled the beggar. But the tourist is hardly in a meaningful relationship with the addicted person. Enabling refers to *specific behaviors*, whereas codependency refers to *a relationship pattern*. Figure 24.1 illustrates how these two forms of behavior may overlap. But it is important to remember that enabling and codependency are two different patterns of behavior that may or may not be found in the same person.

Codependency

The concept of "codependency" has emerged in the past two decades to become one of the cornerstones of rehabilitation. It is a theoretical construct, and there is no standard definition of *codependency* (Heimel, 1990; Tavris, 1990). Indeed, mental health professionals have yet to agree on such a basic issue as whether the word is hyphenated (*co-dependency*) or not (*codependency*) (Beattie, 1989). But even so, many families and friends of addicted persons believe that they have suffered, and often continue to suffer, as a result of having "a relationship with a dysfunctional person" (Beattie, 1989, p. 7).

Codependency defined. Codependency might be viewed as a condition

> that is characterized by preoccupation and extreme dependence (emotionally, socially, and sometimes

physically) on a person or object. Eventually, this dependence becomes a pathological condition that affects the co-dependent in all other relationships. (Wegscheider-Cruse, 1985, p. 2)

A different conceptualization of codependency suggests that it is a relationship in which

> the needs of two people are met in dysfunctional ways. The chemical dependent's need for a care taker, caused by an increasing inability to meet basic survival needs as the drug becomes increasingly intrusive is . . . met by the codependent's need to control the behavior of others who have difficulty caring for themselves. . . . (O'Brien & Gaborit, 1992. p. 129)

In contrast to this, Gorski (1992) explains "codependency" as a general term

> describing a cluster of symptoms or maladaptive behavior changes associated with living in a committed relationship with either a chemically dependent person or a chronically dysfunctional person either as children or adults. (p. 15)

Perhaps the most inclusive definition is offered by Zelvin (1997), who suggested that "codependency [is a] problematic or maladaptive seeking of identity, self worth, and fulfillment outside the self" (p. 50).

All of these definitions seek to identify different core aspects of codependency: (1) *overinvolvement* with the dysfunctional family member, (2) *obsessive* attempts on the part of the codependent person to control the dysfunctional family member's behavior, (3) the extreme tendency to use *external sources of self-worth* (i.e., approval from others, including the dysfunctional person in the relationship), and (4) the *tendency to make personal sacrifices* in an attempt to "cure" the dysfunctional family member of his or her problem behavior.

The dynamics of codependency. In an early work on the subject, Beattie (1987) spoke of codependency as being a process whereby the individual's life becomes unmanageable because she or he is involved in a committed relationship with a person who is addicted to chemicals (Beattie, 1987). The codependent person interprets the commitment as prohibiting him or her from leaving the addicted person. In many cases, the codependent individual also comes to believe that the addicted person's behavior is somehow a reflection on him or her. This process of extreme involvement in the life of another person is called *enmeshment*.

As a result of enmeshment, the codependent person believes that "*your* behavior is a reflection of *me*," and thus views inappropriate behavior on the part of the significant other as a threat to his or her own self-esteem. To avoid this threat to self-worth, the codependent person often becomes obsessed with the need to control the behavior of the person who is addicted to chemicals, assuming responsibility for decisions/events not normally under his or her control (Beattie, 1987). An extreme example of this process occurs when the codependent person assumes responsibility for the significant other's recreational chemical use. "It's my fault that he (or she) went out drinking" is a common belief of the codependent partner.

Thus the codependent person is often *preoccupied* (Wegscheider-Cruse, 1985), or *obsessed* (Beattie, 1989) with controlling the addict's drug use—or even all of the addict's life. An excellent example of this obsessive attempt to control the significant other's behavior took place several years ago. A staff psychologist at a maximum security penitentiary for men in the Midwest received a telephone call from the elderly mother of an inmate. She asked the psychologist to "make sure that the man who shares my son's cell is a good influence" on her son, because "there are a lot of bad men in that prison, and I don't want him falling in with a bad crowd!"

The woman in this case overlooked the grim reality that her son was not simply in prison for singing off-key in choir practice and that he had been to prison on several different occasions for various crimes. Rather than letting him live his life, and trying to get on with hers, she continued to treat him as a child, was overly involved in his life, and was quite upset at the suggestion that it might be time to let her son learn to suffer (and perhaps learn from) the consequences of his own behavior. This woman had yet to learn how to *detach* from her son's behavior. *Detachment* is one of the cornerstones of the recovery process (Brown & Lewis, 1995). By learning to detach and separate from her dysfunctional son, this woman could learn to "let go" and stop trying to control his life.

The rules of codependency. Although the codependent person often feels as though he or she is going crazy, an outside observer will notice that there are certain patterns, or "rules," to codependent behavior. Beattie (1989) identified several of these unspoken "rules" of codependency:

1. It's not okay for me to feel.
2. It's not okay for me to have problems.
3. It's not okay for me to have fun.
4. I'm not lovable.
5. I'm not good enough.
6. If people act bad or crazy, I'm responsible.

These rules are actively transmitted from one partner in the relationship to the other, setting the pattern for codependency. "If you weren't so unreasonable, I would never have gone out drinking last night!" is a common example of rule 6. "You shouldn't have tried in the first place!" might enforce rules 2, 3, 4, and 5.

Are codependents born or made? Proponents of the concept of codependency suggest that codependency is a *learned behavior*. In general, there are three routes to codependency (Zelvin, 1997): (1) being in a close relationship with an alcohol/drug abuser, (2) growing up in a dysfunctional family, or (3) being socialized into accepting a codependent role. All of these routes allow codependency to be passed from one generation to another. For example, a parent might confront a child who wants to go to college with the taunt "You're too dumb to go to college! The best you can hope for is that somebody will be stupid enough to marry you and take care of you!"

Clinicians have long recognized that people frequently tend to try to resolve "unfinished business" from their childhood by recreating, in their adult lives, significant early relationships (Scarf, 1980). Repeatedly, especially for individuals who struggle with feelings of low self-esteem as a result of having been raised in a dysfunctional home, the choice of a partner is often made in an effort to resolve their original parent-child conflicts. Depending on how healthy or unhealthy these surrogates may be, this process can be a positive one for the individual or one that traps him or her in unhealthy cycles.

As the dysfunctional elements in the relationship develop, the codependent person frequently comes to feel "imprisoned" in the relationship. Of course, all relationships have some dysfunctional elements, but in a healthy relationship, the partners confront these negative components and work on resolving them to the satisfaction of both partners. For example, one partner might express the opinion that their finances are getting a little tight and that perhaps they should cut back on unnecessary spending for a couple of weeks. In the codependent relationship, however, this "working through" process is stalled. If one partner expresses concern over a possible problem, the other partner moves to prevent the problem from being clearly identified or resolved.

As part of the effort not to displease the partner who has the substance use problem, the codependent person may avoid certain people or sensitive topics of conversation. Eventually, a self-fulfilling prophecy is thought to be established, where the codependent person is afraid to say "the wrong thing," afraid to talk to "the wrong people," and is afraid to assert self-hood. According to the theory of codependency, she or he also fears to leave, believing she or he has nobody but the alcohol/drug-abusing partner, and yet is not quite satisfied in the relationship, either.

Codependency and self-esteem. In an attempt to live up to the unspoken rules of codependency, the codependent experiences a great deal of emotional pain. The core of codependency, as viewed by Zerwekh and Michaels (1989) is "related to low self-esteem" (p. 111) on the part of the codependent person. The authors go on to conclude that

> Co-dependents frequently appear normal, which in our culture is associated with a healthy ego. Nevertheless, they also describe themselves as "dying on the inside," which is indicative of low self-worth or esteem. (p. 111).

Lacking enough self-esteem to withstand the demands of the addicted partner, the codependent person often comes to measure personal worth by how well he or she can take care of the dysfunctional partner. Codependent individuals also measure self-worth in terms of the sacrifices they make for significant others (Miller, 1988). In this way, codependent individuals substitute an external measure of personal worth for their inability to generate *self*-worth.

Drug rehabilitation workers are often surprised at the amount of pain that codependent family members suffer and confused about why they do not do something to end the pain. There is a reward for enduring this pain! Many people achieve a sense of moral victory through suffering at the hands of another (Shapiro, 1981). By suffering at the hands of a dysfunctional spouse, the codependent individual is able to accuse "the offender by pointing at his victim; it keeps alive in the mind's record an injustice committed, a score unsettled" (p. 115). For some people, such suffering is "a necessity, a principled act of will, from which he cannot release himself without losing his self-respect and feeling more deeply and finally defeated, humiliated, and powerless" (Shapiro, 1981, p. 115). Through this process, the trials and suffering imposed on the codependent person become almost a badge of honor, a defense against the admission of personal powerlessness or worthlessness. In such cases, it is not uncommon for the codependent person to affirm personal worth by being willing to "bear the cross" of another person's addiction or dysfunctional behavior.

The relationship between codependency and emotional health. There is a very real tendency for some to *overidentify* with the codependency concept. As Beattie (quoted in Tavris, 1992) has pointed out, there are those who believe that codependency is "anything, and [that] everyone is codependent" (p. 194). This extreme position overlooks the fact that many of the same characteristics that define codependency are also found in healthy human relationships. Only a few "saints and hermits" (Tavris, 1990, p. 21A) fail to demonstrate at least some of the characteristics of the so-called "codependent" individual.

Even Wegscheider-Cruse and Cruse (1990), strong advocates of the codependency construct, admitted that "co-dependency is an exaggeration of normal personality traits" (p. 28). But in some cases, these traits grow so pronounced that the individual "becomes disabled (disease of codependency)" (p. 28). To complicate matters further, in this society there is a strong relationship between love and codependency (Zelvin, 1997). This is because our society places much emphasis on the blending of identities, or the loss of ego boundaries, in love relationships, making the individual vulnerable to codependency (Zelvin, 1997). This is in sharp contrast to many personality patterns, where the individual's ego boundaries are so intensely defended that he or she is virtually isolated from interpersonal feedback. Between

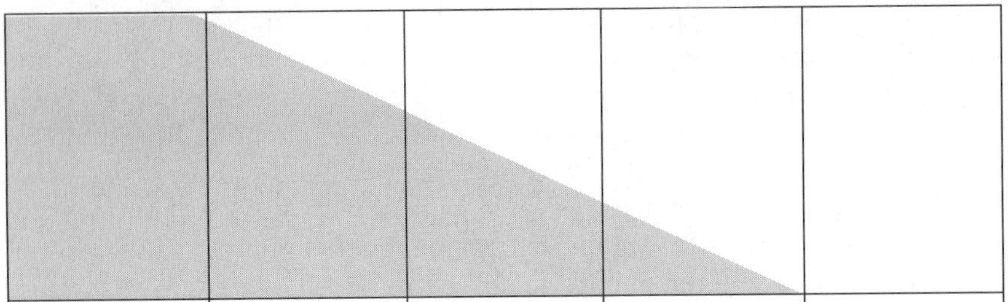

0	1	2	3	4
Codependent: Totally dependent on external feedback for self-worth	Strong codependent traits	Interdependent: Balances own feelings with external feedback	Strong tendency to isolate self from feedback from others	Totally discounts external feedback in favor of own desires

FIGURE 24.2   The continuum between isolation and dependency.

these two extremes is an *interdependency* that is the hallmark of healthy relationships. The continuum that includes codependency at one end and rigid affirmation of the ego's boundaries on the other end might resemble Figure 24.2.

The point to remember is that codependency is not an all-or-nothing phenomenon. *There are degrees of codependency*, just as there are degrees of ego affirmation and isolation from interpersonal feedback. Few of us are at either extreme, and the majority of people tend to fall somewhere in the middle, exhibiting both tendencies to behave in codependent ways and tendencies to be overly isolated from feedback from others.

The codependent person is so dependent on external affirmation, which is usually supplied by the alcohol/drug-dependent spouse, that he or she is extremely vulnerable to real or imagined threats of abandonment. And because the addicted partner is so heavily invested in control of his or her environment, she or he often learns to use the threat of abandonment to control the behavior of the partner or other family members.

How to build a codependent. Substance abuse professionals often speak of a "cycle" of codependency to express the fact that codependency takes on a life of its own. A graphical representation of the cycle of codependency appears in Figure 24.3. Note that on this model of the steps involved in the growth of codependency, there are two necessary components. First, one partner, the codependent, must suffer from low self-esteem. A part-

ner who did not suffer from low self-esteem would be able to affirm his or her "self" and back away from a dysfunctional partner or, at the very least, find a way to cope without depending on the dysfunctional partner's approval. In such a case, it is unlikely that a codependent relationship pattern would evolve.

Second, the "significant other" must be dysfunctional. If the partner were emotionally healthy, he or she would affirm the codependent. Such an atmosphere would enhance psychological growth on the part of the codependent partner, who would, in time, come to be able to affirm his or her "self" without the need for external supports. Thus codependency rests on an interaction between the "pathologies" (for want of a better word) of the two partners.

Reactions to the Concept of Codependency

Ever since the concept of codependency was first introduced, mental health professionals have struggled to determine whether it is indeed a legitimate form of psychopathology or simply a "fad." Given that it has been characterized as "an addiction, a personality disorder, a psychosocial condition, and an interpersonal style" (Hurcom, Copello, & Orford, 2000, p. 487), one could argue that it is hardly more than a "garbage can" diagnosis that communicates little useful information about the patient.

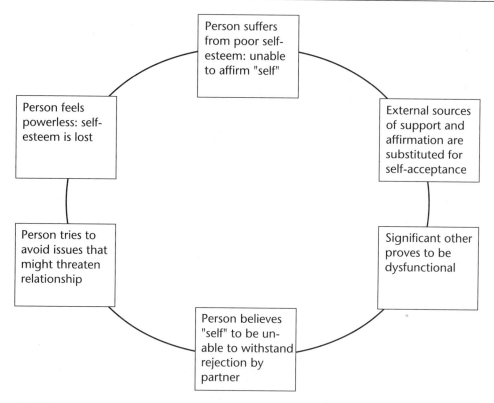

FIGURE 24.3 The circle of codependency.

Many professionals believe that codependency is a *pseudo*-problem more than a legitimate mental health concern, and research into codependency and enabling all but disappeared from the professional journals by the first few years of the 21st century. The concept of codependency was attacked by mental health professionals for its tendency to "disempower" the individual and for its medicalization of relationship problems (Hurcom, Copello, & Orford, 2000). In contrast to most effective forms of psychotherapy, the concept of codependency was found to *reduce* the individual's power base. The concept of codependency relies on traditional Twelve-Step program beliefs that the "disease" of codependency is progressive and that the individual can come to terms with his or her codependency only through the aid of the appropriate self-help group (Randle, Estes, & Cone, 1999).

Proponents of the concept of codependency point out that individuals diagnosed as having this disorder tend to have similar life experiences and similar person-

ality traits. However, such uniformity in patient histories and presenting symptoms might be an artifact introduced into the therapeutic relationship by therapist expectations, selective attention to symptoms that confirm rather than dispute the diagnosis, and vague, self-fulfilling diagnostic criteria that guarantee that virtually everybody will qualify for the condition of "codependency" (Randle, Estes, & Cone, 1999). The very nature of the defining characteristics of the "codependent" person virtually guarantees that any given individual will meet at least one of the defining "criteria" (Walker, 1996; Tarvis, 1992).

One reason for the uniformity of codependency is the assumption that up to 99% of all people are raised in a "dysfunctional" home. Much of the codependency literature strives to convince readers that they are "doomed to suffer as a result of the trauma of childhood travails" (Japenga, 1991, p. 174). They are "encouraged to see themselves as victims of family life rather than self-determining participants" (Kaminer, 1992, p. 13).

Those who challenge the concept of codependency point out that the family is viewed as nothing more than an "incubator of disease" (Kaminer, 1992, p.12). Within this incubator, the helpless child is infected with one or more dread conditions that he or she will have to struggle with forever, unless salvation is achieved through the appropriate Twelve-Step group.

Yet there is little research evidence that a child raised in a "dysfunctional" home is automatically doomed. Indeed, many—perhaps a majority—of those who are exposed even to extreme conditions in childhood find a way to adjust, survive, and fulfill their life goals (Garbarino, Dubrow, Kostelny, & Pardo, 1992). Of course, some children suffer deep emotional scars as a result of childhood trauma. But the evidence does not suggest children are *necessarily* doomed to suffer if their home life is less than perfect.

Researchers now believe that some children are able to develop a natural resilience and to withstand even extreme forms of psychological trauma (Wolin & Wolin, 1995, 1993; Werner, 1989a). This natural resilience seems to help them weather the emotional storms not only of childhood but also of adult life. Indeed, the very fact that the child's environment *is* dysfunctional may spur the development of positive emotional growth (Wolin & Wolin, 1995, 1993; Garbarino, Dubrow, Kostelny, & Pardo, 1992). However, proponents of codependency seem to reject this observation and to believe that *all* children raised in a dysfunctional environment have emotional scars that need to be addressed.

Another objection to the concept of codependency is that Twelve-Step groups tend to "promote dependency under the guise of recovery" (Katz & Liu, 1991, p. xii). Further, to maintain membership and their identify within the group, members are expected to produce material that is consistent with the expectations of the group—that is, to continue to behave (and think) in a "codependent" manner (Randle, Estes, & Cone, 1999). The codependency model subtly demands that the individual not grow and achieve a sense of autonomy but, rather, conform to a standard prescription for salvation and grace (Kaminer, 1992). According to the codependency model, no matter how trivial or serious the trauma, there is just one model for recovery. If the individual resists the various "insights" offered by different books on codependency, that person is auto-matically viewed as being in "denial" (Kaminer, 1992; Katz & Liu, 1991). There is no room for individuality in the codependency model, as it is applied to therapeutic situations.

Another challenge to the codependency movement was based on the theory that all suffering is relative and that it is virtually impossible to equate degrees of suffering (Kaminer, 1992). To illustrate this point, consider the case of two hypothetical children in two different families. Each was the oldest boy in a family of three children, with an alcoholic father. In the first family, the father was a "happy" drunk who would drink each evening after work, tell a few "funny" jokes, watch television, and fall asleep in his favorite chair. In the second family, the father would drink each evening after work and become violently angry. He physically abused his wife and children and occasionally fired a rifle at family members. Each of these fathers would certainly have a different impact on the family. Yet in the literature on codependency, both situations are treated as being of equal importance.

Critics of the codependency movement have pointed out that the theory of codependency seems to excuse the addicted individual from all responsibility for his or her behavior (Roehling, Koelbel, & Rutgers, 1994; Tavris, 1990). In effect, through the "disease" of codependency, blame is shifted from the individual with the substance use problem to his or her significant other, who is said to "enable" the unhealthy behaviors of the afflicted person to continue. Further, the codependency model pathologizes the spouse for engaging in behaviors that might very well be role-specific, simply because his or her partner is addicted to alcohol (Hurcom, Copello, & Orford, 2000). Thus the foundation of the codependency movement rests on the flawed assumptions that (1) responsibility for the alcoholic's behavior lies within the dysfunctional family and, (2) the members of the dysfunctional family are not responsible for their behavior because they have the disease of "codependency."

Within this model, family members are judged not in terms of their own accomplishments but on the basis of whether another family member is able to abstain from chemicals. In other words, they are guilty of "addiction by association" (Katz & Liu, 1991, p. 13). By this standard, entire communities, states, and even nations might be described as codependent (Hurcom, Copello, & Orford, 2000)! Through the application of the concept of codependency, the problem becomes not one parent's alcohol-dependence, her or his physical and/or sexual abuse of family members, or the fact that she or he is emotionally absent. Rather, the problem is that the *family* members suffer from the disease of codependency!

This contradiction might arise from the fact that "codependency" is actually an outgrowth of the theory (popular in the 1950s) that the spouse of the alcohol was a "co-alcoholic" (Simmons, 1991; Sher, 1991). This theory held that the co-alcoholic was as much in need of treatment as the alcoholic, on the assumption that he or she (1) helped to bring about the other's alcoholism, (2) currently continues to support it, and (3) must, accordingly, be quite disturbed. These beliefs reflect the historical fact that the spouses of alcoholics have "been blamed and pathologized for their partner's drinking" (Hurcom, Copello, & Orford, 2000, p. 473). Over the last 50 years, researchers have failed to find any evidence that the spouse of the alcoholic has any predictable form of psychopathology (Tavris, 1992). But according to some critics of codependency, the discredited theory of co-alcoholism has been resurrected in the guise of "codependency."

Nor is codependency limited to the world of addiction. It has even been suggested (O'Brien & Gaborit, 1992) that codependency is a separate condition that may, or may not, involve substance abuse within the marriage. In other words, the authors suggested that codependency is a clinical syndrome in its own right. From this perspective, if codependency does exist in a marriage wherein one or both partners are abusing chemicals, this is only a coincidence. The hypothetical "disease" of codependency might also be found in a variety of non–substance-abusing relationships, according to O'Brien and Gaborit.

Another challenge to the concept of codependency rests on its lack of firm parameters. The term appears to be vague, without foundation. Consider M. Scott Peck's definition of codependency as "a relationship in which the partners cater to—and thereby encourage—each other's weaknesses" (1997a, p. 180). This would certainly seem to be an apt definition of virtually all relationships, not just those that are "codependent," be-

cause we all encourage others to behave in unhealthy ways from time to time.

Many critics of the concept of codependency point out that it rests on little more than a foundation of "new age" rhetoric. For example, the husband-and-wife team of Wegscheider-Cruse and Cruse (1990) speak knowingly of how codependency results from

> [the] interaction between one's own manufactured "brain chemicals" (having to do with our reinforcement center) and one's behavior that stimulates the brain to establish compulsive and addictive behavior processes. (p. 12)

The authors go on to conclude that codependency is a disease of the brain, on the grounds that "we have a brain that gives us an excessive rush, [and] we get into self-defeating behaviors that keep the rush coming [codependency]" (pp. 12–13).

What the authors overlook is that there is no scientific evidence to support this theory. Science has so far failed to find evidence of "an excessive rush" (what would be a "sufficient rush"?). Nor have scientists found evidence that people tend to "get into self-defeating behaviors that keep the rush coming." Indeed if human beings, as a species engaged in self-defeating behaviors simply for the "rush," how would *Homo sapiens* ever have survived?

In considering the construct of codependency, we need a sense of balance. Admittedly, there are those people who experience significant hardship because of their relationship with an addict. But not every person who is in such a relationship is codependent. Indeed, there is little evidence to support the concept of codependency, according to its detractors. Further, according to the codependency model, the victim must somehow come to terms with his or her emotional pain *without* blaming the substance abuser for anything. In other words,

> according to adherents of this theory, families of alcoholics cannot . . . hold them responsible for the abuse. Somehow the victim must get well by dint of pure self-analysis, meditation and prayer, without reference to the social, economic, legal and psychological forces that create dysfunctional families in

the first place. (University of California, Berkeley, 1990a, p. 7)

For many people, this is an impossible task.

Summary

In the late 1970s, substance abuse professionals were introduced to a new way of viewing the substance-abusing person and his or her support system. The constructs of "codependency" and "enabling" were introduced as a way of explaining the way members of the substance abuser's support system behave. However, proponents seized upon these theoretical entities and suggested that they are real manifestations of a new "disease," that of "codependency." In the last decade, a battle has raged over whether such a disorder really exists and how best to address the problem of substance-related interpersonal dysfunctions.

A number of challenges to the constructs of codependency and enabling have been suggested over the years. For example, some researchers point out that "codependency" is only a reincarnation of the 1950s theory that the alcoholic's spouse was a "co-alcoholic"— a theory that was discredited in the 1960s. These constructs may still be evolving, and it remains to be seen what role, if any, they will play in the understanding, and rehabilitation, of substance abusers.

CHAPTER TWENTY-FIVE

Addiction and the Family

Introduction

There has been very little research into the impact of even the most common drug of abuse, alcohol, on the evolving marital unit (Leonard & Roberts, 1996). However, researchers are starting to discover that the effect of alcohol—and, by extension, the other recreational chemicals—on the young adult during the premarital years and the early years of marriage is far more complex than was once thought. For example, it has been discovered that during the courtship phase and the first year of marriage, alcohol abusers commonly reduce their alcohol intake (Leonard & Roberts, 1996). Following marriage, the individual often changes the context within which she or he drinks alcohol and the people with whom she or he drinks (Leonard & Roberts, 1996). But the drinker usually continues to abuse alcohol.

If there are children, they are also affected. In this chapter, the impact of parental alcohol/drug abuse on the marriage, and on the family unit, will be examined.

Scope of the Problem

The relationship between alcohol/drug abuse and the family is extremely complex. To illustrate the problem, consider a marriage wherein one partner drinks alcohol but the other does not. If, while intoxicated, the alcohol-using spouse were to lash out and strike his or her partner just once in 25 years of marriage, should this be cited as an example of alcohol affecting the marriage, as a momentary indiscretion that is unlikely to be repeated, or as an example of spousal abuse?

It is known that there is a reciprocal relationship between alcohol/drug use and marital problems (O'Farrell, 1995). Further, individuals who abuse chemicals often have children. It has been estimated that *one of every six individuals* in the United States was raised, or is being raised, in a home with at least one alcohol-dependent parent (Kelly & Myers, 1996). This translates into an estimated 28 million people (Kelly & Myers, 1996). Very little research has been conducted into the problem of parental abuse of substances other than alcohol (Merikangas, Dierker, & Szatmari, 1998). Still, it is safe to say that significant numbers of children have been raised in homes where there is some form of parental substance abuse/addiction.

Addiction and Marriage

The role that chemicals might play within a family, or marital unit, remains for the most part a mystery (Leonard & Roberts, 1996). The little information that is available deals almost exclusively with the impact of spousal alcohol use problems on the marital unit. Even when the research topic is limited to alcohol abuse and its impact on the marriage, the close interrelationship between the marriage and the substance misuse makes it difficult to identify specific areas that are affected *only* by the use of alcohol (McCrady & Epstein, 1995).

At one time, it was automatically assumed that alcohol abuse prior to marriage suggested that alcohol would prove to be a problem for the marital unit. Researchers have now discovered that for many individuals, marriage is followed by a change in their alcohol use pattern (Leonard & Roberts, 1996). It is not clear whether this change in alcohol use is a result of the marriage itself or a reflection of the changes that occur in the individual's life status at about the time when he or she marries (stable employment, independence, growing involvement in the world of adulthood, etc.). However, it is known that many adults modify their alcohol use into a more socially acceptable pattern following the decision to marry and in the first year of marriage (Leonard & Roberts, 1996).

For some individuals, their alcohol use pattern plays a role in their choice of a marital partner. That is, people tend to marry a partner whose alcohol use is very similar to their own. When there is a discrepancy between the alcohol use patterns of the partners, there are several possible adjustments. In the majority of cases, each individual adjusts his or her alcohol use until it is more consistent with that of the partner. However, in a minority of cases, a wider discrepancy evolves instead. The heavier drinker's alcohol abuse/addiction will have a negative impact on the marriage or the family. In such cases, family/marital therapy is often of value in the rehabilitation of the problem drinker.

The family systems perspective. As a general rule, people tend to marry those who have achieved similar levels of "differentiation of self" (Bowen, 1985, p. 263). The concept of differentiation is "roughly equivalent to the concept of emotional maturity" (Bowen, 1985, p. 263). A primary developmental task is for the individual to separate from his or her parents (*individuate*) and to resolve the various emotional attachments to the parents that evolved during childhood.

Over time, the relationship between the parent and the child should evolve, as the child becomes more and more independent. A primary force in this process of change within the family is the pattern of communication. For example, at birth and for the first few years, the child is almost totally dependent on his or her parents, but as he or she matures, the child becomes less and less dependent on them. By a variety of means children communicate their growing independence to their parents, who, in a healthy relationship, gradually withdraw their control as the child becomes more capable of independent living. This process of separating from one's parents is known as *individuation* (Bowen, 1985). The parents may either encourage the child's emotional

growth or they might inhibit it. Bowen (1985) believed that it was possible for the child to fail to learn to resolve the many conflicts encountered in childhood and adolescence—to fail to individuate. Family therapists who endorse the "family systems" model suggest that this often happens in the home where there is an alcohol-dependent parent.

Communication patterns within the home where alcohol is abused are often quite poor (McCrady & Epstein, 1995). One reason for this is parental psychopathology. Because of their own lack of emotional maturity, the parents are unable to provide the maturing child with the proper guidance and support. In some cases, the parents might even increase their control over the child as she or he grows. This lack of parental support makes it more difficult for the child to make the emotional break necessary to individuation. In such a case, he or she would remain emotionally dependent on the parents, viewing himself or herself as being weak and perhaps incompetent.

Such a person would remain dependent on external sources of feedback and support, which might be provided by continued dependency on the parents or on a parental substitute. We all tend to select, as a marital partner, a person whose level of emotional independence is similar to our own (Bowen, 1985). If neither partner has achieved a significant degree of individuation, each would look to his or her partner to meet his or her emotional needs, according to Bowen. The effort to achieve further emotional growth in such a marriage entails great risks. For some this risk is too great, and they turn away from the potential for growth to the pseudo-intimacy, and the illusion of control, offered by alcohol or chemicals.

The marriage characterized by alcohol abuse. Remember that the addicted individual's first priority is the service of his or her addiction. Within the marriage where one member is an alcohol abuser/addict, issues of control become important as each person struggles to achieve some sense of order within the unstable marital unit. Control often becomes a central theme within the marriage, and *conditional* love becomes one of the avenues through which each tries to control the other. Such conditional love finds expression in demands, such as these: You must behave in a certain way if you want to be (a) loved by me, (b) supported by me, and so on. If you don't meet my demands, I will (a) leave you,

(b) withdraw my love from you, (c) not give you money, (d) go out and get drunk, or (e) abuse you physically.

For the alcohol-dependent spouse, the goal of these control "games" is to make sure that family members do not stray too far from the alcoholic fold. Such manipulation often results in the nondrinking spouse withdrawing emotionally, and upwards of 50% of those married to an alcohol-abusing spouse use this tactic as a way to cope (Hurcom, Copello, & Orford, 2000). Such withdrawal, or *detachment,* may come to reflect the nondrinking spouse's acceptance of the fact that he or she is powerless over his or her partner's drinking (Hurcom, Copello, & Orford, 2000). Detachment also becomes both an expression of *unconditional* love and the vehicle that transports one away from the *emeshment* found in the dysfunctional family. However, in working with overly involved spouses of alcoholics, it is often necessary to teach them the difference between *concern* for another, and *responsibility* for that person. In effect, the individual must learn that it is possible to have feelings for another person but not be responsible for living that person's life.

Often it is also necessary to help the codependent person learn appropriate interpersonal *boundaries.* The alcoholic home, resting as it does on the shifting sands of addiction, is in constant danger of being washed away. Each family member develops an unnatural involvement in the lives of the other. As part of the natural growth process that results in individuation, the child must learn to establish boundaries between "self" and "other," but in the alcoholic home the child learns to become *emeshed* in the lives of others. Each person has been trained to believe that he or she is responsible for every other member of the family.

Addiction and the Family

From the family systems perspective, the treatment of an addictive disorder involves the identification, and ultimately the modification, of whatever dysfunctional family system allowed the development and maintenance of the addiction in the first place (Bowen, 1985). For example, it has long been known that in the alcoholic marriage, the alcoholism becomes a "secret partner" first of the marriage and ultimately of the family. Within the framework of this "family secret," the individual's addiction becomes the dominating issue around which the family's rules and rituals revolve (Brown, 1985). Parental injunctions then serve to transmit the "secret" to the children, allowing the dysfunctional communication system to be passed from one generation to the next. Such parental injunctions might include "There is no alcoholism in this home" and "Don't you dare talk about it!"

One of the developmental tasks facing a child is to learn to adapt to the environment into which she or he was born. If the child was born into a family where one or both parents were abusing alcohol, this task is more difficult. Indeed, the whole family must learn to meet the demands of the alcohol-dependent parent(s) (Ackerman, 1983). The family might come to terms with parental alcoholism by structuring itself in such a way that the alcoholic parent is allowed to continue drinking. Although this is often surprising to an outside observer, there are rewards for this behavior! For example, in some marital/family units, one partner's alcohol abuse could be viewed as a stabilizing influence within the family unit (Hurcom, Copello, & Orford, 2000). In such cases, the alcohol use of one parent might help the marital/family unit cope with other problems that exist (Heath & Stanton, 1998).

For the person with an alcohol use problem, the act of marriage offers a chance to form a "drinking partnership" (Leonard & Roberts, 1996, p. 194) with his or her partner. An interesting "role reversal" (Ackerman, 1983) may develop in such families. The alcohol-dependent member of the marital unit gives up some of the power and status that she or he would normally hold within the marital/family unit, in return for opportunities to drink. In time, this role reversal might span two, or even three, generations, as an unhealthy state of interlocking dependency patterns evolves within that marital/family unit. Often marital partners or family members find themselves holding unusually powerful positions within the new family constellation, as the family adapts to the individual's alcoholism

The process of adaptation to familial rules, values, and beliefs is a normal part of family life (Bradshaw, 1988b). However, when the family's rules, values, and beliefs are warped by a dysfunctional partner, the entire family must struggle to adapt to the resulting unhealthy family themes. This process of adjustment to the addiction of one member takes place without external guidance or support. Family members are left to their own devices as they struggle with the problems within the family, and they often come to use the very same defense mechanisms so characteristic of addicted individuals: denial, rationalization, and projection.[1]

As the other family members assume responsibilities formerly held by the addicted member of the family, the addicted individual becomes less and less responsible for his or her family duties and less and less involved in the family life. An older brother assumes responsibility for disciplining the children, or a daughter assumes responsibility for making sure that the children are fed each night before they go to bed. In each case, one of the children has assumed a parental responsibility left vacant, because of alcoholism.

Fear, either alone, or in combination with guilt and threats (both real and imagined), are commonly used by the alcoholic parent to force his or her will on the family: "If you don't do what I want, I will go out drinking again, and it will be *your* fault!" So effective are the threats and assaults of the addicted partner that in some families one finds "chaos (covert or overt), inconsistency, unpredictability, blurring of boundaries, unclear roles, arbitrariness, changing logic, and perhaps violence and incest" (Brown & Lewis, 1995, p. 285). It is in this atmosphere that the family as a unit, and each individual member, must attempt to achieve some degree of stability.

Within such a marital/family unit, a form of *pseudo-stability* might be unconsciously accepted by the family members. Although the family members are uncomfortable with the alcohol/drug addiction of one member, they might be quite happy with the current distribution of power and responsibility and with the temporary peace and quiet that result from this state of pseudo-stability. *Peace at any cost* becomes the central theme of the family, and in service of this goal, the family members turn a blind eye toward the continued use of alcohol/drugs by the dysfunctional member. If the members of the family lose sight of the origins of this state of pseudo-stability, or of the fact that it evolved out of an attempt by the family to accommodate itself to the dysfunctional behavior of one member, they may come to defend it as the status quo and thereby enable the individual's sick behavior to continue.

The state of familial pseudo-stability evolves in an atmosphere of real and unspoken fear and guilt that is passed from one generation to another (Stein, Newcomb, & Bentler, 1993; Beattie, 1989). For this reason, many professionals view addiction as a multi-generational, family-centered disorder in which parental alcohol/drug addiction becomes "a governing agent affecting the development of the family as a whole and the individuals within" (Brown & Lewis, 1995, p. 281). Without professional intervention, it is difficult for the individual members of the family to learn how to detach from the member who is addicted to chemicals, and family members are unlikely to learn how to let the addicted individual suffer the natural consequences of his or her behavior (Johnson Institute, 1987). Rather, the life of the entire family revolves around the pathology of a single member, and the other family members live their lives in an attempt to somehow "cure" his or her addiction.

The cost of parental addiction. Until recently, clinicians did not understand the impact of parental alcoholism on the development of children. Current theory suggests that parental alcoholism creates a disturbed home environment that negatively affects the child's physical, social, and psychological development (Hurcom, Copello, & Orford, 2000; Kelly & Myers, 1996). Researchers have found relationships between parental alcoholism and conduct disorders, poor academic performance, inattentiveness (Owings-West & Prinz, 1987), antisocial personality disorder (Silverman, 1989), and suicide attempts (Hurcom, Copello, & Orford, 2000).

One theory, advanced by Webb (1989), suggested that some children raised in an alcoholic home become "addicted" to excitement. Such children might engage in fire-setting behaviors or become "super-responsible" and assume roles far beyond their abilities or maturity, such as spending "an inordinate amount of time worrying about the safety of the whole (family) system" (Webb, 1989, p. 47). Further, the author suggests that as adolescents, these children may stay awake while the alcoholic parent is out drinking, check on the safety of sleeping siblings, and develop elaborate fire escape plans that might involve returning time and time again to the burning house to rescue siblings, pets, and valuables. In response to this distorted family system, Webb (1989) suggested that many adolescents become overly

---

[1]The Johnson Institute (1987) termed denial "avoiding."

mature, serious, and well organized—behaviors that develop in an attempt to maintain control of their home environment.

Adolescents who were raised in an alcoholic home had to spend so much time and energy meeting basic survival needs that they were unlikely to have the opportunity to establish a strong self-concept (Webb, 1989). Because of the atmosphere of "chronic trauma" (Brown & Lewis, 1995, p. 285), a significant percentage of the children raised in alcoholic homes were thought to have sustained long-lasting emotional injuries as a result. These observations are consistent with clinical experience, which suggested that children who were raised in an alcoholic home did indeed seem to have suffered some form of psychological harm.

Since the 1980s, however, researchers have discovered that parental alcohol/drug abuse does not inevitably result in problems for the growing child. There are a number of factors that shape the impact of parental alcoholism on the developing children in the family (Ackerman, 1983). For example, there is the sex of the substance-abusing parent. Given that each parent plays a different role within the family, an alcoholic mother will have a far different impact on the family than an alcoholic father.

A second factor that influences the impact of parental substance abuse on the family is how long the parent has actively been abusing or addicted to chemicals. For example, an alcoholic father who has used chemicals for "only" 3 years will have a far different impact on the family than an alcoholic father who has been physically dependent on alcohol for 15 or 16 years. A third factor that influences the impact of parental substance use problems on the individual child's growth and development is the sex of the child. For example, a daughter will be affected differently by an alcohol-dependent father than will a son (Ackerman, 1983). The specific family constellation also plays a role in how parental alcoholism affects each individual child.

This is a difficult point for many people to understand. Consider two different families. In the first family, the father has a 3-month relapse when the third boy in a family of six children is 9 years old. Contrast this child's experience with that of the oldest child in a family of six children whose father relapsed for 3 months when the child was 9 years old. Both of these children would experience a far different family constellation

than would the only child, a girl, whose father relapsed for 3 months when she was 9 years old. And all three of these children would have a far different experience than would the third boy in a family of six children whose mother was constantly drinking until he turned 14 years of age.

Finally, as Ackerman (1983) observed, it is possible for the child to blunt the blow of parental alcoholism if he or she is able to find a *parental surrogate*. Ackerman (1983) found that if the child has a parental substitute (an uncle, a neighbor, a real or imagined hero), it may be possible for that child to avoid the worst effects of his father's alcoholic parenting. For more information, see the section of this chapter entitled "Criticism of the ACOA Movement."

The Adult Children of Alcoholics (ACOA) Movement

As we have noted, many researchers believe that the effects of growing up in an alcoholic home often last beyond the individual's childhood years. Within the past generation, a large number of adults have stepped forward to claim that they were harmed by parental alcohol abuse/addiction. These individuals are known as adult children of alcoholics (ACOA). An entire treatment industry evolved to meet their perceived needs in the early to mid-1980s; then it quietly dissolved. However, treatment professionals and lay persons alike occasionally hear hints that the ACOA movement is still alive.

A decade ago, estimates of the number of "adult children of alcoholics" (ACOA) in this country ranged from between 22 million (Collette, 1990) and 34 million (Mathew, Wilson, Blazer, & George, 1993). adults. Proponents of the ACOA model suggested that the alcoholic home shared many characteristics with other forms of dysfunctional homes and, because of this, would scar the developing child. Woititz (1983), an early pioneer in the field of therapeutic intervention with ACOAs, reported that the adult children of alcoholic parents exhibit a number of characteristics including:

1. Having to "guess" what normal adult behavior is like, including a tendency to have trouble in intimate relationships

2. A tendency to have difficulty following a project through from beginning to end

3. A tendency to lie in situations where it is just as easy to tell the truth

4. A tendency not to be able to "relax," but always to judge themselves harshly, and to feel a need to keep busy all the time

5. A tendency not to feel comfortable with themselves but, rather, constantly to seek affirmation from significant others

Berkowitz and Perkins (1988) also suggested that ACOAs are more critical of themselves, and depreciate themselves more, than do adult children of nonalcoholic parents.

Hunter and Kellogg (1989) argued that the traditional view of the adult child of alcoholic parents was too narrow. In addition to the expected forms of psychopathology, the authors suggested that ACOAs might instead develop personality characteristics the *opposite of those expected of a child raised in a dysfunctional home*. For example, ACOAs are thought likely to have trouble following a project through from start to finish. Yet Hunter and Kellogg (1989) suggested that some ACOAs might actually be compulsive workaholics, who struggle to finish projects in spite of feedback that this work is no longer necessary, or is even counterproductive.

Sher, Walitzer, Wood, and Brent (1991) explored the differences between young adults who had been raised by alcoholic parents and young adults who had not. The authors used a volunteer sample of college students, whose parental drinking status was confirmed by extensive interviews. Here are some of their findings:

1. College freshmen with an alcoholic father tended to drink more, and to have more symptoms of alcoholism, than freshmen who were not raised by an alcoholic father.

2. Women who were raised by an alcoholic parent or parents reported a greater number of alcohol-related consequences than their nondrinking counterparts.

3. Children of alcoholic parents have an increased risk not only of using alcohol, but also of using other drugs of abuse.

4. Adolescent children of alcoholic parents had more positive expectancies for alcohol than did adolescent children of nonalcoholic parents.

5. As adults, children raised by alcoholic parents tended to have higher scores on test items suggesting "behavioral undercontrol" (p. 444) than did those individuals who were not raised by alcoholic parents.

6. As college students, children raised by alcoholic parents tended to score lower on academic achievement tests than did their non-ACOA counterparts.

The results of this research study failed to answer many questions about the assumed relationship between the parental drinking pattern and the student's academic performance. However, this study *did* suggest that parental alcoholism had a strong impact on the subsequent growth and adjustment of the children raised in that family, thus providing support for the ACOA model.

Drawing on data collected in a study of the prevalence of psychiatric disorders in a selected area, Mathew, Wilson, Blazer, and George (1993) examined the differences in mental health between adults raised by alcoholic parents and adults not raised by alcoholic parents. They concluded that, as a group,

adult children of alcoholics had higher rates of dysthymia, generalized anxiety disorder, panic disorder, simple phobia, agoraphobia and social phobia than did matched comparison subjects. (p. 795)

There are other ways in which adult children of alcoholic parents have suffered, beyond the development of psychiatric problems. During childhood, many children of alcoholic parents blame themselves for the parental drinking (Freiberg, 1991), and they may carry this self-blame well into adulthood. Collette (1990, 1988), for example, spoke of how she blamed herself for her father's pain and was close to suicide until she became involved in an ACOA self-help group. Sanders (1990) related how he felt responsible for his father's drinking, and of how he "paid the price" for his father's drinking with fear and dread, as his father threatened to leave time after time or argued with his mother night after night.

Thus several theoretical models have suggested that adult children of alcoholic parents will suffer from emotional distress. A number of research studies have revealed higher levels of psychiatric problems in samples of adult children of alcoholic parents, providing some support for the theoretical models advanced in the late 1970s and early 1980s. In response to this pain, many ACOA children banded together and formed self-help groups.

The growth of ACOA groups. Obviously, in a survey text such as this, it is not possible to examine the self-help movement for adult children of alcoholic parents in great detail. However, the reader should be aware that the historical growth, and later decline, of ACOA groups was phenomenal. At one point, it was estimated that 40% of the adults in this country belonged to some kind of a Twelve-Step self-help group, such as the groups for adult children of alcoholics (Garry, 1995). This number is a reflection, first, of how many people have been hurt by a parent's alcoholism and, second, of the desire of these hidden victims of parental addiction to find peace by working through the shame and guilt that was left over from their childhood years (Collette, 1990).

Criticism of the ACOA movement. The ultimate goal of the ACOA movement was to provide a self-help group format for those who believed that their emotional growth had been stunted by their having been raised in a dysfunctional environment. However, there were those who criticized the ACOA movement, and some researchers questioned whether being raised in a home with parental alcoholism automatically resulted in psychological distress for the child (Kaminer & Bukstein, 1998). Still others challenge the ACOA concept on philosophical grounds:

> We all want to feel like victims. [But] if you identify yourself as a survivor of incest or abuse, you are making an existential and self-hypnotic statement that defines you by the most destructive thing that ever happened to you. In the short term, it's important to say it, but you can get stuck there. (Elkin, quoted in Collette, 1990, p. 30)

Some critics of the ACOA movement pointed out that therapies that focus on traumatic events such as rape or childhood abuse tend to keep the focus on the trauma, not on the individual's strengths and potential for further growth (Walker, 1996). This seemed to account for the phenomenon in which the individuals became dependent on the ACOA program, almost as though they were "addicted" to being in an ACOA recovery group (May, 1991).

Other critics of the ACOA movement noted that the process of attaching a label to the "adult child" would merely "perpetuate the process of blaming in a new language" (Treadway, 1990, p. 40). In other words, the format of the ACOA movement encourages the "adult children" to continue to blame their parents for whatever problems they have encountered in life. Thus, although the ACOA group might help meet the ever-present need within our culture for "a sense of community, empowerment, and spiritual renewal" (Treadway, 1990, p. 40), one must ask at what cost this sense of belonging is achieved.

Further, critics argued, the concept of ACOA limited individual growth by keeping the focus on the previous generation (Peele, Brodsky, & Arnold, 1991). Admittedly, some children are raised in terrible, abusive environments. But the central thesis of the ACOA movement rests on the impact of *past* (often, years past!) parental behavior on the individual's *current* problems. In a very real sense, the ACOA movement tends to encourage the individual to define his or her "self" on the basis of his or her parents' problems and choices, according to Peele, Brodsky, and Arnold.

Unfortunately, one of the cornerstones of the ACOA movement was never even examined to determine whether it was valid: In spite of repeated statements about how being raised in a dysfunctional home hurt the child, nobody ever examined the possibility that "healthy," conflict-free families never really exist. Members of ACOA groups would frequently bemoan the fact that their families did not meet the stereotypical standard of the American family. In reality, however, historians "have been unable to identify a period in America's past when family life was untroubled" (Furstenberg, 1990, p. 148). In other words, familial conflict has been the norm within this culture, not the exception. But this fact was never understood by those who flocked to the ACOA banner.

Another criticism of the ACOA model is that it rests upon an assumption that Wolin and Wolin (1995, 1993) term the *damage model.* This model holds that children raised in a dysfunctional environment *inevitably* suffered psychological harm. "All children are affected" (Black, 1982, p. 27). Other proponents of this model included Brown and Lewis (1995) and Anderson (1995). Children raised by an alcoholic parent were viewed as never having had a chance to express their "anger or outrage in a healthy manner" (Anderson, 1995, p. 4E-x), to their everlasting emotional pain.

The damage model assumes that people are simply "passive vessels whose dysfunctional histories inhabit and control them like so many malignant spirits" (Garry, 1995, p. 10A). Yet the damage model has never been established as actually being applicable to situations where the child is raised in a disturbed home. Indeed, research studies have generally failed to support the damage model. For example, Tweed and Ryff (1991) found no clear differences between the emotional adjustment of the adults raised in homes with an alcoholic and the adjustment of those raised in nonalcoholic homes.

Senchak, Leonard, Greene, and Carroll (1995) examined a group of 82 adult children of alcoholic parents, 80 adult children of divorced parents, and 82 control subjects, whose parents were neither divorced nor alcoholic, in an attempt to determine what impact being raised in a dysfunctional home might have on later adjustment. The authors concluded that "negative outcomes among adult children of alcoholics are neither pervasive nor specific to paternal alcoholism" (p. 152). Indeed, after allowing for confounding variables such as parental depression and the effects of low socioeconomic status, a number of studies have failed to find *any* significant form of psychopathology specific to the adult children of alcoholic parents (D'Andrea, Fisher, & Harrison, 1994; Giunta & Compas, 1994).

Finally, Kelly and Myers (1996) administered the Beck Depression Inventory (BDI) to a sample of 20 volunteer ACOA female undergraduate college students and to a control group of 20 female undergraduate college students whose parents were not alcohol-dependent. Although there was a statistically significant difference in measured level of depression between these two groups, the average BDI score for both subgroups fell within the normal range. In other words, as a group, neither the ACOA sample nor the control sample seemed to be significantly depressed. These findings cast doubt on the damage model, which is the foundation of the ACOA movement. Indeed, it would appear that many individuals are able to avoid significant emotional scars, in spite of the fact that they were raised in a "dysfunctional" environment (Wolin & Wolin, 1995).

Perhaps a more appropriate model for how children respond to the problem of having an alcoholic parent might be called the *challenge model* (Wolin & Wolin, 1993). This model takes into account the possibility of individual resiliency, something the damage model fails

to do. *Resiliency* does *not* mean that the individual is invulnerable to the trials and tribulations of life (Blum, 1998). Rather, the individual who is resilient is able to learn from life's experiences, in spite of the emotional scar tissue that may have developed as a result of trauma (Blum, 1998). Children who are resilient seem to overcome environmental handicaps by being "particularly adept at recruiting . . . surrogate parents when a biological parent was unavailable . . . or incapacitated" (Werner, 1989a, p. 108D). Adults who are resilient form support systems, rather than coping with adversity alone (Blum, 1998). They are also able to look for things to change in the future and to set goals, as well as to recognize the personal strengths that they have developed in spite of adverse situations.

The damage model suggests that emotional trauma in childhood causes problems in later life. But research has found that "childhood adversity is *not* always associated with a poor outcome" (Parker, Barrett, & Hickie, 1992, p. 883, italics added). The quality of interpersonal relationships formed in later life may moderate, or even overcome, the impact of adverse life events such as poor parenting (Parker, Barrett, & Hickie, 1992; Werner, 1989b). These studies would seem to provide at least partial support for Ackerman's (1983) assertion that the child who finds a suitable parental substitute, can escape the full consequences of parental alcoholism. And they call into question the validity of the ACOA model.

There is "a danger in assuming . . . that growing up in an alcoholic home inevitably leads to dysfunction in adulthood" (D'Andrea, Fisher, & Harrison, 1994, p. 580), a warning that proponents of the damage model overlooked. The fact that being raised in a dysfunctional home does not automatically result in some lasting form of psychological distress was suggested by Garbarino, Dubrow, Kosteiny, and Pardo (1992). The authors examined the effects of extreme psychological trauma on children, especially children raised in the inner cities or in war zones. They found that perhaps as many as 80% had no permanent emotional scars caused by their childhood environments. The authors interpreted their findings as supporting the "challenge" model of growth, noting that one factor that was essential for the child not to be scarred by the childhood environment was a stable, mature relationship with at least one adult.

Domenico and Windle (1993), who examined the intrapersonal and interpersonal functioning of 616 middle-aged women, also failed to find evidence that supported the theory of ACOA psychopathology. The authors compared the adjustment of women who were adult children of an alcoholic parent with that of women who were not raised by an alcoholic parent. Although the ACOA women had higher levels of depression and lower levels of self-esteem, as a group the ACOA women scored in the normal range on the tests used in this study. These findings are consistent with those of Seilhamer, Jacob, and Dunn (1993), who failed to find any consistent impact, either positive or negative, of parental alcoholism on parent–child interactions.

One is left with the impression that in the absence of hard research data, the theory on which the ACOA movement is based rests on nothing more than "assertions, generalizations and anecdotes" (The University of California, Berkeley, 1990a, p. 7). Indeed, the ACOA literature is "long on rhetoric and short on empirical data" (Levy & Rutter, 1992, p. 12). This weakness is reflected in the fact that although research into characteristics of the ACOA population was popular for a few years, little research has been conducted in this area for almost a decade.

Another criticism of the ACOA movement is based on the observation that the clinical theories in terms of which parental alcoholism is thought to affect the emotional well-being of the child have been oversimplified (Zweig & Wolf, 1997). Proponents have ignored the impact of parental alcoholism (or parental abuse) on the development of the child's unconscious mind. Further, in the process of simplifying the basic theory, many less skilled proponents of the ACOA rehabilitation model have overlooked the fact that simply to name a process is not necessarily to understand it on all levels. Thus, according to the authors, the reconstructive model is often left unfinished because it did not procede to the deeper levels of the victim's personality.

In the United States, the self-help movement, of which the ACOA movement is a part, has been a growth industry ever since its inception (Blau, 1990; Boyd, 1992). It has even been suggested that the publishing industry, knowing that the majority of those who purchase self-help books are women, slant their titles and design their covers so that they attract the attention, and activate the insecurities, of women (Boyd, 1992). One could argue that the ACOA movement is the step-child of the publishing industry, which used the move-

ment to develop a market for a new line of self-help books. This could explain how the original ACOA movement, which focused on survivors of extreme abuse, has expanded to the point where virtually *all* parents are blamed for what they did (or did not) do. Blaming one's parents "has become a national obsession — and big business" (Blau, 1990, p. 61; Kaminer, 1992).

If the truth be told, in spite of the fact that psychology as a science is more than a century old, very little is known about what constitutes a "normal" family or about the limits to which unhealthy behaviors might be tolerated in an otherwise "normal" family. There has been even less valid scientific research into the psychodynamics of families of alcohol/drug-addicted individuals (D'Andrea, Fisher, & Harrison, 1994; The University of California, Berkeley, 1990a; Goodwin & Warnock, 1991; Sher, 1997, 1991). Yet on this nonexistent foundation, proponents of the ACOA model claim that 96 percent of the population was raised in a "dysfunctional" family (Garry, 1995; Peele, Brodsky, & Arnold, 1991).

Notwithstanding the fact that there has never been any research to suggest that this 96% figure is accurate (Hughes, 1993), proponents of the ACOA movement quote it as though it were gospel truth. They point to studies in which a high percentage of the ACOA adults questioned claim to have one or more of the characteristics often attributed to ACOAs. However such studies are flawed by the fact that the language used to describe the typical adult child of alcoholic parents is so vague that Sher (1997) suggested it has a P.T. Barnum quality to it: "a little something in it for everybody" (p. 252). Both ACOA and non-ACOA adults tend to agree that these descriptors apply to them (Sher, 1997). Given these findings, one must wonder to what degree the characteristics identified by the proponents of the ACOA movement reflect not some form of pathology but simply common problems that arise in living in today's society.

Blau (1990) challenged the ACOA concept on the grounds that the "adult child" is simply a reflection of the "baby-boomers'" reluctance to accept that they are now adults who are themselves entering middle adulthood. Developmentally, the adults of the "baby-boomer" generation are no longer the children of their parents, at least in the same sense that they were four decades ago. They are now middle-aged adults who are now discovering that they will not fulfill all of the dreams of young adulthood. Perhaps, as Blau (1990) suggested, the ACOA movement is simply a reaction by the "baby-boomer" generation against growing older. This possibility is certainly supported by the way the focus of "baby boomers" has shifted from ACOA issues to those of impending retirement and health care.

The ACOA movement places great emphasis on the so-called "inner child." However, the "inner child" concept is not a part of any single therapeutic theory. Rather, the theory behind the ACOA concept of the inner child is a complex blend of "[Carl] Jung, New Age mysticism, holy child mythology, pop psychology, and psychoanalytic theories about narcissism and the creation of a false self" (Kaminer, 1992, p. 17). However, "just at the moment when Americans ought to be figuring out where their Inner *Adult* is, and how that disregarded oldster got buried under the rubble of pop psychology and short-term gratification" (Hughes, 1993, p. 29, italics added), along comes the ACOA movement, to focus not on the problems of adulthood but on what should have happened one or more generations ago. Given that the "inner child" represents a phase of life when the individual was developmentally, socially, psychologically, and neurologically immature, one must wonder the degree it can help the individual meet the demands of adult life.

Finally, as Levy and Rutter (1992) point out, the ACOA movement is essentially a white, middle-class invention. It is not known whether this model applies to inner-city children, whose parents might be addicted to heroin or cocaine. As the authors note, children of heroin and cocaine addicts are "primarily nonwhite, minority members who live in poverty. They have no national movement . . . [and] do not write books and make the rounds of the talk shows" (p. 5). Thus virtually nothing is known about them. However, as the authors remind us, many children are raised by parents who are addicted to chemicals other than alcohol, in environments other than the white, middle-class world. There is no research on whether the ACOA model applies to these other children of addiction.

Summary

This chapter explored the family of the addicted individual and the impact that one individual's addiction to chemicals is thought to have on the rest of the family. Unfortunately few research studies have investigated the impact of one member's alcohol/drug addiction on the other members of the family. Much of what is assumed to be true about the family in which one or more persons is addicted to alcohol/drugs is based on theory, not established fact.

The theory of codependency assumes that the individual who is codependent is "trained" by a series of adverse life events to become dependent on the feedback and support of others. Further, it is assumed that family members come to take on new roles as the addicted person gives up the power and responsibility that he or she would normally exercise within the family. In this manner, the family comes to "accommodate," or adapt to, the individual's chemical addiction.

From the perspective of the codependency model, the individual's substance abuse is viewed as a family-centered disorder that is passed on from one generation to the next. The self-help group movement of "adult children" of alcoholics is viewed as a logical response to the pain and suffering that the family members experienced because of their participation in a "dysfunctional" family. However, the "adult child" concept has met with criticism. Some health care professionals stress that the theory behind the "adult children" movement places too much emphasis on past suffering, at the expense of resilience and future growth.

The "adult children" movement has also been criticized on the grounds that it assumes that the individual *must* experience some lasting psychological trauma as a result of parental alcoholism or drug addiction. This theory has never been tested, so a great deal of the ACOA self-help movement rests on a series of unproven assumptions.

Research is needed so that we may begin to understand how chemical addiction affects the growth and development of both individual family members and the family unit itself.

CHAPTER TWENTY-SIX

The Evaluation of Substance Abuse Problems

Introduction

In this era of managed care, program cutbacks, and increased accountability, health care professionals are being required to justify each procedure in advance, to ensure the maximum return for each dollar spent on health care. Thus, although the assessment process forms the "cornerstone" (Bukstein, 1995, p. 95) of the rehabilitation process, it is increasingly being viewed as fulfilling both a gatekeeping function and the more traditional role of identifying those who require some form of professional intervention to help them deal with their substance use problem(s). In this chapter, we will explore the process of evaluating a client's drug/alcohol use pattern and how assessment is related to the process of rehabilitation.

The Theory Behind Alcohol and Drug Use Evaluations

One of the most important decisions that a mental health or medical care provider makes is whether a given individual's recreational chemical use reflects social use, abuse of that substance, or an addictive disorder (Kidorf, Brooner, King, Stoller, & Wertz, 1998). Many substance abusers experience transient problems as a result of their chemical use. In such cases, it is often the task of the substance abuse professional to determine whether the individual requires some assistance for a substance abuse problem. This decision may have life-long implications. For example, a person's eligibility for health care insurance at age 50 may be affected by a di-

agnosis of alcohol dependency made 30 years earlier, when she or he was only 20 years of age.

The assessment process is quite complicated. For example, simply *screening* a patient (to determine whether indications of a specific condition are present) is not the same as making a formal *diagnosis* (Miller, Westerberg, & Waldron, 1995). Even after the appropriate diagnosis has been made, the criteria on which that diagnosis rests need to be indicated, and the appropriate form or level of care identified. Those individuals who merely wish to camouflage antisocial behavior with an "illness" label such as chemical dependency need to be screened out, so that the limited treatment resources can be utilized in treating those who are most in need of such intervention. Thus the assessor must determine whether there is evidence of a substance use disorder, the severity of any such disorder, and the most appropriate form of treatment for each individual.

Rustin (2000) has suggested using the "four C's" to help determine whether an individual exhibits a substance use disorder. Those criteria are

1. The individual has a *Compulsion* to use chemicals.
2. The individual has struggled to *Control* his or her chemical use (or can no longer control it).
3. The individual has tried to *Cut down* on his or her chemical use.
4. The individual has suffered *Consequences* of his or her alcohol or drug use.

If substance abusers were all alike, there would be no need for the assessment process to move beyond the step of determining whether the individual has a chemical use problem. However, all substance abusers are not alike. Each patient presents the clinician with a unique combination of hopes, strengths, needs, fears, and past experiences.

> [To] the extent that treatment is selected and individualized to address clients' differing needs and problems, comprehensive evaluation provides an information foundation upon which to plan treatment. (Miller, Westerberg, & Waldron, 1995, p. 64)

It is through the process of evaluation that the therapist can identify problem areas that need to be addressed (Lehman, 1996). On the basis of the information uncovered during a careful evaluation, the substance abuse rehabilitation professional can identify the appropriate goals and treatment strategies for each client. The opposite of this is also true: Without a careful evaluation of the client's strengths, experiences, and needs, it will be difficult to identify appropriate goals or to intervene effectively. The evaluation process itself consists of three interrelated phases: *screening*, *assessment*, and *diagnosis*.

Screening

The first step in the assessment process is to identify those individuals who might have a chemical abuse/ addiction problem and who might benefit from treatment. The screening process may be relatively simple and straightforward or quite complicated and time-consuming. For example, consider the individual who arrives in a hospital Emergency Room with alcohol-induced liver disease, alcohol-induced gastritis, a history of five prior admissions for alcohol-related disorders, and a blood alcohol level of 0.230 at the time of the current admission. It seems clear that this person has an alcohol use disorder. However, not every case is as simple and easy to screen as this hypothetical example.

To aid in the screening process, researchers have devised a number of paper-and-pencil tests, or questionnaires, to help detect those individuals who may have a substance use problem. These instruments are filled out either by the client (and thus are known as *self-report* instruments) or by the assessor as he or she asks questions of the person being evaluated. Self-report instruments are inexpensive, and they may be less threatening to the client than a face-to-face interview (Cooney, Zweben, & Fleming, 1995).

One of the most popular self-report instruments for alcohol use problems is the Michigan Alcoholism Screening Test (MAST) (Selzer, 1971). The MAST is composed of 24 questions that the respondent answers by either "yes" or "no." Test items are weighted with a value of 1, 2, or (in some cases) 5, points. A score of 8 points or more suggests an alcohol use problem. The effectiveness of this screening instrument has been demonstrated in clinical literature (Miller, 1976). But the MAST has some drawbacks: (1) It can be used only in cases of alcohol dependency (Lewis, Dana, & Blevins, 1988). (2) It provides only a "crude general screen" (Miller, Westerberg, & Waldron, 1995, p. 62) for alcohol use problems. (3) The MAST does not detect "binge" drinking. (4) It does not shed light on the individual's drinking pattern (Smith, Touquet, Wright, & Das Gupta 1996). (5) It does not differentiate between current and past drinking (Schorling & Buchsbaum, 1997). Thus, although the MAST is suited to the detection of individuals with severe alcohol dependency (Saunders, Aasland, Babor, de la Fuente, & Grant, 1993), it is of limited value in cases where the person abuses other chemicals or is a "problem drinker" who is not alcohol-dependent.

Another screening tool for alcoholism that is growing in popularity is the "CAGE" questionnaire (Ewing, 1984). CAGE is an acronym for the four questions that make up this test:

- Have you ever felt you ought to **CUT DOWN** on your drinking?
- Have people **ANNOYED** you by being critical your drinking?
- Have you ever felt bad or **GUILTY** about your drinking?
- Have you ever had a drink first thing in the morning to steady your nerves, or to get rid of a hangover (**EYE-OPENER**)?

A "yes" response to any one of these four questions indicates the need for a more detailed inquiry by the assessor. Giving an affirmative answer to two or more items suggests that the client has an alcohol use problem. The CAGE questionnaire has been found to have an accuracy of 80–90% in detecting alcoholism when the client answers "yes" to two or more of these questions. Like the MAST, however, the CAGE is most effective in detecting alcohol-*dependent* individuals rather than alcohol *abusers* (Saunders, Aasland, Babor, de la Fuente, & Grant, 1993). It is also relatively insensitive to binge drinking (Smith, Touquet, Wright, & Das Gupta, 1996) and may be relatively insensitive to alcohol use problems in white female populations (Bradley, Boyd-Wickizer, Powell, & Burman, 1998). For these reasons the CAGE might miss up to 50% of "at risk" drinkers (Fleming, 1997, p. 345).

Another paper-and-pencil screening tool that has grown in popularity in the past decade is the Alcohol Use Disorders Identification Test (AUDIT) (Saunders, Aasland, Babor, de la Fuente, & Grant, 1993). Research suggests that the AUDIT is over 90% effective in detecting alcohol use disorders (Brown, Leonard, Saunders, & Papasoulioutis, 1997). However, the AUDIT tends to miss active drinkers above the age of 65 (Isaacson & Schorling, 1999). Other instruments have been developed for the detection of other forms of chemical abuse. For example, Roffman and George (1988) developed a self-report instrument used in the evaluation of marijuana use patterns, and Washton, Stone, and Hendrickson (1988) introduced a "Cocaine Abuse Assessment Profile." Unfortunately, each of these tests, though useful, focuses on the use of only one chemical of abuse. Thus all are of limited value in the assessment of polydrug abusers

Brown, Leonard, Saunders, and Papasoulioutis (1997) suggested the use of a simple, two-item question set to detect possible substance use disorders. These items were

1. In the last year, have you ever drunk or used drugs more than you meant to?
2. Have you felt you wanted or needed to cut down on your drinking or drug use in the last year?

Despite this test's brevity, the authors claimed that a "yes" answer to one item indicated a 45% chance that the individual had a substance use disorder, whereas a "yes" response to both items indicated a 75% chance that the respondent had a chemical use problem (Brown, Leonard, Saunders, & Papasoulioutis 1997).

Although these results are promising, the authors also pointed out that their two-item test might result in false-positive results in some cases and that their initial findings needed to be replicated in follow-up studies. However, this two-item test shows promise as a screening tool for health care workers.

One instrument that is often mistakenly considered a screening/assessment tool is the Minnesota Multiphasic Personality Inventory (MMPI). The original MMPI was introduced almost 65 years ago. In 1965, the *MacAndrew Alcoholism Scale* (also known as the "Mac" scale) was added, after an item analysis suggested that alcohol-dependent individuals tended to answer 49 of the 566 items of the MMPI differently than nonalcoholics. A cut-off score of 24 items out of 49 answered in the "scorable" direction correctly identified 82% of the alcohol-dependent clients in a sample of 400 male psychiatric patients (Graham, 1990).

In 1989, when an updated version of the MMPI, the Minnesota Multiphasic Personality Inventory-2 (or MMPI-2) was introduced, the "Mac" scale was essentially retained in its original form. However, in the time since it was first introduced, research has revealed that the "Mac" scale has several inherent problems. First, it has been discovered that black clients tend to score higher on the "Mac" scale than do white clients. Further, research has suggested that rather than being specific for alcohol use problems, the "Mac" scale may measure a general tendency toward addictive behaviors (Graham, 1990). Also, clients who are extroverted, are exhibitionistic, experience "blackouts" for *any* reason, are assertive, or enjoy risk-taking behaviors tend to score higher on the "Mac" scale even if they are not addicted to chemicals (Graham, 1990).

Although the "Mac" scale was designed to detect alcoholics, in working with the original MMPI, Otto, Lang, Megargee, and Rosenblatt (1989) discovered that alcohol-dependent persons might be able to "conceal their drinking problems even when the relatively subtle special alcohol scales of the MMPI are applied" (p. 7). This is because personality inventories such as the MMPI/MMPI-2 are vulnerable to both conscious and unconscious attempts at denial, self-deception, and distortion (Isenhart & Silversmith, 1996). Thus, although the MMPI "Mac" scale was designed as a subtle test for alcoholism, it is possible for either "false-positive" or "false-negative" results to be obtained from the MMPI

"Mac" scale. Until it is proven otherwise, counselors should assume that the revised "Mac" scale on the MMPI-2 shares this same weakness with the original "Mac" scale.

Unlike many other assessment tools, the MMPI offers the advantage of having five "truth" scales built into it. These scales offer insight into how truthful the individual taking the test has been; they are discussed in more detail by Graham (1990). A major disadvantage of the MMPI is how long it takes the typical client to complete the MMPI/MMPI-2 test items. This makes the MMPI/MMPI-2 a test that might better be employed in the *diagnosis* phase of assessment (discussed later in this chapter).

Assessment

During the assessment phase of the evaluation process, the assessor attempts to measure the severity of the individual's substance use problem. One of the most useful tools of the assessment phase is the clinical interview, which forms the cornerstone of the drug/alcohol use evaluation. The information the client provides is an important source of data about his or her current and previous chemical use. It is important to keep in mind, however, the possibility that the client may either consciously or unconsciously distort the facts. Thus other sources of data should also be utilized in the evaluation of a person suspected to have a chemical use problem.

The first part of the interview process is an introduction by the assessor. It is explained that the assessor will be asking questions about the client's possible chemical use patterns and that *specific* responses are most helpful. It is explained that many of these questions may have been asked by others in the past but that this information is important. The client is asked whether he or she has any questions, after which the interview begins. The assessor should attempt to review the diagnostic criteria for chemical use problems outlined in the *Diagnostic and Statistical Manual of Mental Disorders*, 4th edition, Text Revision (*DSM-IV-TR*) (American Psychiatric Association, 2000). This manual provides a framework within which the diagnosis of chemical dependency can be made, and it uses terminology that is understood by most treatment professionals. The *DSM-IV* criteria for alcohol/drug use problems will be discussed in more detail in the next section.

Many of the questions asked in the clinical interview are designed to explore the same piece of information from different perspectives. For example, at one point in the interview process, the client might be asked, "In the average week, how many nights would you say that you use drugs/alcohol?" Then later in the interview, this same client might be asked, "How much would you say, on the average, that you spend for drugs/alcohol in a week?" The purpose of this redundancy is not to "trap" the client so much as provide different perspectives on the client's chemical use pattern. For example, it is often wise to consider the *percentage of the client's income spent on recreational chemicals* (Washton, 1995). For example, consider the case of a client who claimed to use alcohol one or two nights a week, spending $60 dollars a week on beer. This person's alcohol use would be seen as excessive in anybody's eyes. But if the client's only source of income is a weekly unemployment check for $120, this person is spending fully 50% of his or her income on alcohol. This information reveals more about the individual's chemical use pattern, helping the evaluator better understand the client.

There are a number of assessment instruments available to help the professional who is conducting an alcohol/drug use evaluation.[1] Perhaps the most popular for individuals over the age of 16 is the *Alcohol Use Inventory* (AUI). The AUI is a copyrighted instrument made up of 228 items and takes 30–60 minutes for the individual to complete. The answers to the test items provide data for 24 subscales that the assessor can use to understand the client's alcohol use pattern better. But the AUI is limited to alcohol use problems.

A popular research instrument that is gaining popularity as an assessment tool is the *Addiction Severity Index* (ASI). The ASI is administered to adults during a semistructured interview with the client. The 5th edition contains 161 items and requires approximately an hour to complete. The administrator asks the questions of the client and records his or her answers on the answer form. The ASI is "public domain"—that is, it is not copyrighted—and it provides a severity rating score based on the impressions of the person who administers

[1]There are many assessment instruments currently in use, and new tools are constantly being introduced. This section will discuss only some of the more popular instruments currently in use.

the test. Unlike the AUI, the ASI can be used for evaluating the severity of other forms of drug abuse such as that of cocaine and opiates.

Diagnosis

The final stage in the evaluation process is diagnosis. Abel (1982), identified four elements as being necessary to the diagnosis of alcohol/drug addiction: (1) a compulsion to continue use of the drug, (2) the development of tolerance, (3) major withdrawal symptoms following withdrawal from the drug, and (4) adverse effects from drug use both for the individual and for society. A more standardized conceptual model was presented by the American Psychiatric Association (2000). In its *Diagnostic and Statistical Manual of Mental Disorders*, 4th edition, Text Revision (*DSM-IV-TR*) the American Psychiatric Association suggested that the signs of alcohol/drug addiction include

1. *Preoccupation* with use of the chemical between periods of use.
2. *Using more of the chemical* than had been anticipated.
3. *The development of tolerance* to the chemical in question.
4. A *characteristic withdrawal syndrome* from the chemical.
5. *Use of the chemical to avoid or control withdrawal symptoms.*

6. *Repeated efforts to cut back or stop* the drug use.
7. *Intoxication at inappropriate times* (such as at work) or *withdrawal interfering with daily functioning* (hangover makes person too sick to go to work, for example).
8. *A reduction in social, occupational, or recreational activities* in favor of further substance use.
9. *Continuation of chemical use* in spite of the individual having suffered social, emotional, or physical problems related to drug use.

Any combination of three or more of these signs is taken to identify an individual who suffers from an addiction to one or more recreational chemicals.

As you may recall, the concept of a substance use continuum was introduced in Chapter 1. The chart shown in Figure 26.1 was utilized to illustrate the continuum of drug use/abuse, with the different points on the continuum ranging from total abstinence from chemicals to chronic addiction. The individual who meets four or more of the *DSM-IV* criteria might be viewed as falling in level 3 or 4 of the continuum of drug use shown in Figure 26.1.

In its *DSM-IV-TR* (2000), the American Psychiatric Association provides a standardized framework within which a professional might make a diagnosis of substance dependency. It is through the evaluation process that the professional gathers data on the basis of which to make such a diagnosis—that is, an opinion of where the individual being assessed falls on any of the

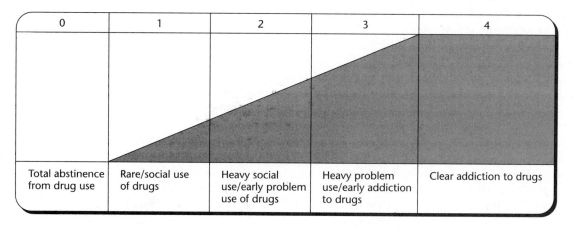

FIGURE 26.1 The continuum of recreational chemical use.

diagnostic continua we have examined. A second part of the evaluation process is determining, to whatever degree this is possible, the client's motivation. An all-too-common dilemma facing treatment center staff develops when an alleged drug "pusher" is arrested and, after being released on bail, enters "treatment" only to make a good impression on the judge. This type of client could be said to be in treatment for the purposes of *impression management* (Wild, Cunningham, and Hobdon (1998), not rehabilitation. Although it is true the vast majority of those individuals who are abusing or addicted to chemicals are unready or unwilling to pursue abstinence (Miller, Westerberg, & Waldron, 1995), the client who enters "treatment" for the sole purpose of trying to manipulate the courts wastes valuable treatment resources better used to treat other patients.

The Assessor and Data Privacy

The client *always* has a right to privacy, and this means that the assessor does not automatically have access to personal information about the client. The client may refuse to answer a specific question or refuse to give another person permission to reveal specific information to the assessor.

Both federal and state data privacy laws often apply when one is working with individuals who are thought to be addicted to drugs or alcohol. If the client agrees to the assessment, then he or she is willingly providing information about himself or herself during the assessment process. But the client still has the right to refuse to answer any question. If information is to be obtained from persons other than the client, *the professional should always first obtain written permission* from the client authorizing him or her to contact *specific* individuals in order to obtain information about the client's chemical use or any other aspect of his or her life. This written permission is recorded on a form known as a *release-of-information authorization form*.

Occasionally, the client will refuse such permission. The client retains this right and can refuse to allow the assessor to speak with *any* other person. This refusal in itself may say a great deal about how open and honest the client has been with the assessor, especially if the evaluator has explained to the client exactly what infor-

mation will be requested. One possible solution to this problem, which some professionals advocate, is to have the client sit in on the collateral interview. One drawback to this solution is that the client's presence may inhibit the source of collateral information from freely discussing her or his perception of the client. Thus, it is rarely productive to have the client, or the client's representative, sit in on collateral interviews.

When the client is being referred for an evaluation by the court system, the court will often provide information about the client's previous legal history. The courts may also include a detailed social history of the client, which was part of the pre-sentencing investigation. Clients occasionally ask to see the records provided by the court during the clinical interview. Frequently, these clients are checking to see what information has been provided by the courts, in order to decide how much and what they should admit to during the interview period. If asked, the evaluator should acknowledge having read this information but should not discuss it with the client, for two reasons. First, the purpose of the clinical interview is to assess the client's *chemical use patterns*, and discussion of what information the court provided does nothing to further that evaluation. Second, the client has access to this information through his or her attorney. Thus, if the client wishes to review the information provided by the court, he or she may do so at another time through established legal channels.

Those persistent clients who demand to see their court records on the grounds that "it is about me, anyway" should be reminded that the purpose of this interview is to explore the client's drug and alcohol use patterns, not to review court records. *Under no circumstances* should the chemical dependency/mental health professional let the client read her or his referral records. To do so would be a violation of the data privacy laws, because the referral information was released to the professional, *not* to the client.

When the final evaluation is written, the evaluator should identify the source of the information summarized in the final assessment. Collateral information sources should be advised that the client, or his or her attorney, has a right to request a copy of the final report before the interview. It is extremely rare for a client to request a copy of the final report, although technically the client does have the right to do so after the proper release-of-information authorization forms have been signed.

Diagnostic Rules

Many—perhaps most—clients will initially resist a diagnosis of chemical dependency (Washton, 1990). Because of this, two diagnostic rules should be followed as closely as possible in the evaluation and diagnosis of a possible drug addiction. Occasionally, it is not possible to adhere to both of these diagnostic rules, but even in special cases, one should always attempt to evaluate each individual case carefully in light of these guidelines. And when one of these rules is not followed, the professional making the diagnosis should explain why it could not be followed in the given situation.

Rule 1: Gather collateral information. Traditional belief holds that alcohol/drug-dependent individuals are deceptive. This belief is only a half-truth. Research has shown that *as a group*, alcohol-dependent individuals will, when sober, report the amount and frequency of their alcohol use reasonably accurately. But there are exceptions, such as when the individual is facing some kind of legal problem (McCrady, 1993; Donovan, 1992). Further, individuals who have both a mental illness problem and a substance use problem also tend to underreport the extent of their substance use problems (Carey, Cocco, & Simons, 1996).

Because of the importance of the diagnostic process, the professional attempting to determine whether a diagnosis of addiction is warranted should *utilize as many sources of information as possible* (McCrady, 1993). One should never "ever diagnose using information based only on the client's presentation at the time of assessment" (Evans & Sullivan, 1990, p.54). To illustrate the importance of collateral information, every chemical dependency professional has encountered cases where the individual being evaluated has claimed to drink "once a week . . . no more than a couple of beers after work." The spouse of the person being evaluated however, may report that the client was intoxicated "five to seven nights a week."

Collateral information sources might include (Slaby, Lieb, & Tancredi, 1981) patient's families, friends of the patient, the patient's employer or co-workers, clergy members, local law enforcement authorities, the patient's primary-care physician, and the patient's psychotherapist (if any).

Obviously, the time restrictions imposed on the assessment process may prevent the use of some of these collateral resources. If the assessment must be completed by the end of the week, and the professional is unable to contact the client's mother, it may be necessary to write the final report without the benefit of her input. Other people involved may simply refuse to provide any information. It is the assessor's responsibility, however, to *attempt* to contact as many of these individuals as possible and to include their views in the final evaluation report.

Rule 2: Always assume deception until proven otherwise. Even though alcoholics *as a group*, are quite accurate in their self-report of the amount of alcohol they consume, and the frequency of their alcohol use, clinicians still insist that the nature of addiction is deception. There is a reason for this belief! For example, Sierles (1984) found that substance abusers were one of the two sub-groups of patients most likely to attempt to deceive assessors (individuals with a history of sociopathic behaviors composed the other subgroup). Cunnien (1988) went so far as to state that the addict will be "persistent" (p. 25) in her or his attempts to deceive others.

It is not uncommon for people who are addicted to alcohol to admit only to drinking "once or twice a week" until they are reminded that their medical problems were unlikely to have been caused by such moderate drinking. Then these individuals sometimes admit to more frequent drinking episodes. However, even when confronted with evidence of their serious, continual use of alcohol, many alcoholics deny the reality of their alcoholism. Clients have been known to admit to "one" arrest for driving under the influence of alcohol or possession of a controlled substance. Records provided by the court at the time of the client's admission into treatment have often revealed that the person in question had been arrested in two or three different states for similar charges. When confronted, these clients might respond that they thought that the evaluator "only meant in *this* state!" or that "since that happened outside of this state, it doesn't apply." Thus, to avoid the danger of deception, the assessor must assume, until collateral information proves otherwise, that the client is underreporting his or her substance use.

The Assessment Format

The assessor's diagnosis is usually recorded on a standardized record form, which is often titled "Alcohol and Drug Use Evaluation Summary." This assessment format, which is modified as necessary to take into account the differences among individuals, provides a useful framework within which to evaluate the individual and his or her chemical use pattern. Let's look at the areas covered by this assessment format.

Area 1: Circumstances of Referral

The first step in the diagnostic process is to examine the circumstances under which the individual is seen. For example, the case of a patient who is seen in a hospital alcohol detoxification (or "detox") unit for the first time is far different the patient who has been in the detox unit ten times in the last three years. Thus the first item on the chemical dependency assessment is a review of the circumstances surrounding the individual's referral.

The manner in which the client responds to the question "What brings you here today?" can provide valuable information about how willing a participant the individual will be in the evaluation process. The individual who responds, "I don't know, they told me to come here" or "You should know, you've read the report" is obviously being less than fully cooperative. The rare client who responds, "I think I have a drug problem" is demonstrating some degree of cooperativeness with the assessor. Thus the manner in which the client identifies the circumstances surrounding her or his referral for evaluation is a valuable piece of information for the assessor.

Area 2: Drug and Alcohol Use Patterns

The next step is for the evaluator to explore the individual's drug and alcohol use patterns *both past and present*. All too often, clients will claim to drink "only once a week, now" or to have had "nothing to drink in the last six months." Treatment center staff are not surprised to find out that this drinking pattern has been the rule only since the person's last arrest for an alcohol-related offense.

From time to time, one will encounter a person who proudly claims not to have had a drink, or to have used chemicals, in the last 6–12 months or perhaps even longer. Such individuals may forget to add that they were locked up in the county jail awaiting trial during that time, or were under strict supervision after being released on bail, and had little or no access to chemicals. This is a far different situation from the client who reports that he or she has not had a drink or used chemicals in the last year, is not on probation or parole, and has no charges pending.

Thus the evaluator should explore the client's living situation to determine whether there were any environmental restrictions on the individual's drug use. (People who are incarcerated, who are in treatment, or whose probation officer requires frequent, unannounced, and supervised urine screens to detect drug/alcohol use obviously have environmental restrictions imposed on them.) Also, the individual's chemical use pattern and *beliefs about his or her drug use* should be compared with the circumstances surrounding referral. Consider, for example, the person who has expressed the belief that he or she does not have a problem with chemicals. Earlier in the interview, he or she may also have admitted to recently having been arrested on the charge of possession of a controlled substance for the second time in four years. In this situation, the client has provided two important—but quite discrepant—pieces of information to the evaluator.

Several important areas should be explored at this point in the evaluation process. The evaluator needs to consider whether the client has ever been in a treatment program for chemical dependency and whether the individual's drug or alcohol use has ever resulted in legal, family, financial, social, or medical problems. The assessor also needs to consider whether the client has ever exhibited any signs of either psychological dependency or physical addiction to drugs or alcohol.

To understand this point, one need only contrast the case of two hypothetical clients who were seen following their arrest for driving a motor vehicle while under the influence of alcohol/drugs. The first person might claim (and have collateral information sources to support the claim) that he or she drank only in moderation once every few weeks. Furthermore, a background check conducted by the court might reveal that this client never had any previous legal problems of any kind.

The evaluation might reveal that after receiving a long-awaited promotion, the client celebrated with some friends. The client was a rare drinker, who uncharacteristically drank heavily with friends to celebrate the promotion and apparently misjudged the amount of alcohol that he or she had consumed.

The other individual's collateral information sources seemed to suggest to the evaluator a more extensive chemical use pattern than the client had described during the interview. (The interview process will be discussed in more detail below.) A background check conducted by the police at the time of the individual's arrest revealed several prior arrests for the same offense.

In the first case, one might argue that the client simply made a mistake. Admittedly, the person in question was driving under the influence of alcohol. However, he or she had never done so in the past and does fit the criteria for a diagnosis of heavy social drinking. The report to the court would outline the sources of data examined and, in this case, would provide a firm basis for concluding that this individual made a mistake in driving after drinking.

In the second case, however, the individual's drunk driving arrest signals a larger problem, which would be outlined in the report to the court. The assessor would detail supporting information provided by family members, the individual's physician, the patient, the county sheriff's department, and friends of the client. The final report in this case would conclude that the client has a significant addiction problem that requires treatment in a chemical dependency treatment program.

Area 3: Legal History

The assessment process should include an examination of the client's legal history. This information might be based on the individual's self-report or on a review of the client's police record provided by the court, the probation/parole officer, or other source. *It is important to identify the source of the information on which the report is based.* Include in the assessment

- What charges have been brought against the client in the past by the local authorities, and what was their disposition.
- What charges have been brought against the client in the past by authorities in other localities, and what was their disposition.

- The nature of any current charges against the individual.

There are many cases on record where the individual was finally convicted of a misdemeanor charge for possession of less than an ounce of marijuana. However, all too often, a review of the client's police record reveals that this individual was *arrested* for a felony drug-possession charge and that the charges were reduced through plea-bargaining agreements. In some states, it is possible for an arrest for the charge of driving a motor vehicle under the influence of alcohol (a felony in many states) to be reduced to a misdemeanor charge, such as public intoxication, via plea negotiation. Thus the assessor needs to be aware of *both the initial charge, and the ultimate disposition* by the court of these charges. The assessor should also inquire whether the client has had charges brought against him or her in other states or by federal authorities. Individuals may admit to *one* charge for possession of a controlled substance, only for the staff later to learn that this same client has had several arrests, and several convictions, for the same charge in other states. Or the client may admit to having been *arrested* for possession charges in other states but may not mention that he or she left the state before the charges were brought to trial.

Many clients will reason that, because they were never *convicted* of the charges, they will not have to mention them during the assessment. That the charges were never proved in court because the client was a fugitive from justice (to say nothing of the fact that interstate flight to avoid prosecution may itself be a possible federal offense) may well be overlooked by the client.

Past military record. One important, and often overlooked, source of information is the client's *military history, if any.* Many clients with a military history will report only on their civilian legal history unless specifically asked about their military legal record. Clients who have denied any drug/alcohol legal charges whatsoever may, upon inquiry, admit to having been reprimanded or brought before a superior officer on charges because of their chemical use while in the military.

The assessor must specifically inquire about whether the individual has ever been in the service. If the client says no, it can be useful to inquire *why* the client has never been in the service. This question often elicits a response to the effect that "I wanted to join the Navy, but I had a felony arrest record" or "I had a DWI (driving while intoxicated) on my record and couldn't join." These responses provide valuable information and open new areas for investigation. If the client has been in the military, was the client's discharge status "Honorable," a "General" discharge under honorable conditions, a "General" discharge under dishonorable conditions, or a "Dishonorable" discharge? Was the client ever brought up on charges while in the service? If so, what was the disposition of these charges? Was the client ever referred for drug treatment while in the service? Was the client ever denied a transfer or promotion because of drug/alcohol use? Finally, was the client ever transferred because of his or her use of drugs or alcohol?

The client's legal history should be verified, if possible, by contacting the court or probation/parole officer, especially if the client was referred for evaluation for an alcohol/drug-related offense. The legal history often provides significant information about the client's lifestyle and about the extent to which her or his drug use has resulted in conflict with social rules and expectations.

Area 4: Educational/Vocational History

The next step in the assessment process is to determine the individual's educational and vocational history. This information, which might be based on the individual's self-report, school record, or employment record, provides information on the client's level of functioning and on whether chemical use has interfered with her or his education or vocation. As before, the evaluator should identify the source of this information. For example, the client who says that she dropped out of school in the tenth grade "because I was into drugs" presents a different picture than does the client who completed a Bachelor of Science degree. The individual who has had five jobs in the last two years presents a far different picture than the individual who has held a series of responsible positions, and has earned regular promotions, with the same company for the last ten years. Thus the assessor should assess clients' educational/vocational history to determine their educational level, their potential, and the degree to which their chemical use has started to interfere with their educational or work life.

Area 5: Developmental/Family History

The assessor can often uncover significant material through an examination of the client's developmental and family history. The client might reveal that his or her father was "a problem drinker" in response to the question "Was either of your parents chemically dependent?" but might hesitate to call that parent an alcoholic. How the client describes parents' or siblings' chemical use might also reveal how the client thinks about his or her own chemical use.

For example, the client who says that her mother "had a problem with alcohol" might be far different from the client who says, "My mother was an alcoholic." The client who hesitates to call a sibling alcoholic but is comfortable with the term "a problem drinker" may be hinting that he or she is also uncomfortable applying the term "alcoholic" to herself. Information about either parental or sibling chemical use is also important for another reason. There is significant evidence of a genetic predisposition toward alcoholism. Future research may uncover a genetic link for other forms of drug addiction, as well. Thus a sibling who is perceived as being addicted to alcohol/drugs *hints* at the possibility of a familial predisposition toward substance use disorders.

In addition to this, the reviewer will be able to explore the client's attitudes about parental alcohol/drug use in the home while he or she was growing up. Did the client view this chemical use as normal? Was the client angry or ashamed about his or her parents' chemical use? Does the client view chemical use as having been a problem for the family? Thus it is important for the assessor to examine the possibility of either parental or sibling chemical use either while the client was growing up, or at the present time. Such information will offer insights into whether the client may be "at risk" to develop an addiction. Furthermore, an overview of the family environment provides clues to how the client views drug or alcohol use.

As we saw in Chapter 25, family environments differ. The client whose parents were infrequent social drinkers would have been raised in a far different environment from the client whose parents where drug addicts. The client who reported never knowing his mother because she was a heroin addict who put the children up for adoption when they were little might view drugs far differently than the client who was raised to believe that hard work would see a person through troubled times, and whose parents never consumed alcohol.

Area 6: Psychiatric History

Chemical use often results in either outpatient or inpatient psychiatric treatment. A natural part of the assessment process should be to discuss with the client whether he or she has ever been treated for psychiatric problems on either an inpatient or an outpatient basis and whether his/her alcohol and drug use patterns contributed to the need for hospitalization (Beeder & Millman, 1995).

For example, clients have been known to admit to having been hospitalized for observation because they were hallucinating, had attempted suicide, were violent, or were depressed. Upon admission to chemical dependency treatment, perhaps months or years later, this same individual might reveal that she or he was using drugs at the time of this hospitalization for a "psychiatric" disorder and that she or he had failed to mention that substance abuse to the staff of the psychiatric hospital. This might happen because the client lied to the hospital staff or because the hospital staff simply never asked the appropriate questions.

It is for these reasons that the assessor should always inquire:

- Whether the client has ever been hospitalized for psychiatric treatment.
- Whether the client has ever had outpatient psychiatric treatment.
- If so, whether the client revealed to the mental health professional the truth about his or her drug use.

If possible, the assessor should obtain a release-of-information form from the client and send for the treatment records, and the discharge summary, from the treatment center where the client was previously hospitalized. The possibility that drugs contributed to the psychiatric hospitalization or outpatient treatment should be either confirmed or ruled out, if possible. This information then will enable the assessor to determine whether the client's drug use has resulted in psychiatric problems serious enough for professional help to be necessary.

Area 7: Medical History

The assessor needs to explore the client's medical history, especially as it is related to his or her chemical use history. Questions such as "Has the client ever been hospitalized, and, if so, for what reason(s)?" are of special relevance when working with alcohol/drug abusing clients. The client's hospitalization might have been for drug-related injuries (such as one client who reported having been hospitalized many times after rival drug dealers had tried to kill him) or for treatment of an infection acquired through the use of illicit chemicals. When in doubt, after getting the proper written authorization from the client, the assessor should try to obtain copies of admission/discharge summaries from the hospital(s) where the client was treated. The assessor should also inquire about *current* medical problems, the possibility that the client is taking one or more prescription medication(s), and any use of over-the-counter medication. An attempt should be made to identify the client's regular physician and to determine whether the client has been "doctor shopping" to try to obtain prescriptions.

Area 8: Previous Treatment History

In working with a person who may be addicted to chemicals, it is helpful for the evaluator to determine whether the client has ever been in a treatment program for chemical dependency. This information, which may be based on the client's self-report or on information provided by the court system, sheds light on the client's past and on her or his potential to benefit from treatment.

The person who has been hospitalized three times for a heart condition but continues to deny having any heart problems is failing to confront the reality of his or her condition. The same is true of the client who says that she does not think she has a problem with chemicals but has been in drug treatment three times. The problem then becomes one of making a recommendation for the client in light of his or her previous treatment history and current status.

The assessor should pay attention to the client's status at the time of discharge from previous treatment programs and to how long after treatment the person maintained abstinence. More than one client has bragged about being "alcohol-free" for a given time, only to admit to having used marijuana during that same period.

Further, clients may admit that they started to use drugs shortly after they were discharged, if not before. Deplorably, the tale of a client using chemicals on the way home from the treatment facility is well known to chemical dependency professionals. Of course a client who admits to using chemicals throughout the time that he or she was in treatment is providing valuable information about his or her possible attitude toward *this* treatment exposure, as well. This client would have a different prognosis than would a client who had maintained total sobriety for three years following his or her last treatment exposure and who then relapsed.

The evaluator should pay attention to the individual's past treatment history, to the discharge status from these treatment programs, and to the total period of time that the individual was sober *after* treatment ended. Specific questions should be asked as to *when they entered treatment, how long were they there, and when did they start to use chemicals following treatment?*

Other Sources of Information

Medical Test Data

Laboratory test data are of only limited value in the assessment of a person who is suspected of being addicted to chemicals. There are no blood/urine tests specific for alcohol/drug addiction. It has been suggested that elevated values on certain blood tests, such as tests of liver function, might serve as "alerting factors" (Hoeksema & de Bock, 1993, p. 268) for possible alcohol dependency. For example, if a patient being assessed admits that his or her personal physician warned him or her about alcohol-related liver damage three years ago, this would suggest that the problems caused by the patient's alcohol use date back at least that long, and it provides strong evidence that the client is alcohol-dependent.

Medical test data can often shed light on the client's chemical use pattern at the time of the evaluation by detecting actual traces of alcohol/illicit drugs in the patient's body. It is for this reason that Washton (1995) recommended that urine toxicology testing be a routine part of assessment for drug or alcohol use. Consider the case of the client who claimed never to have used marijuana, only to have a supervised blood or urine toxicology test be "positive" for THC. This would strongly suggest that the patient was using marijuana, in spite of what she or he had said.

Medical tests can often

- Confirm the presence of certain chemicals in the client's blood or urine samples.
- Identify the *amount* of certain chemicals present in a person's blood/urine sample (example, the BAL).
- Determine whether the drug levels in the blood or urine sample have increased (suggesting further drug use), remained the same (which also might suggest further drug use), or declined (suggesting no further drug use since the last test).
- Offer hints to how long the patient has been using chemicals.

The detection of chemical use by laboratory testing is a very technical and is affected by many different variables (Verebey, Buchan, & Turner, 1998). Furthermore, both blood and urine toxicology testing involve an element of intrusiveness (Cone, 1993). At the very least, urine toxicology testing involves an invasion of privacy, and the process of obtaining a blood sample for toxicology screening is physically invasive. However, medical test data are often quite useful to the assessor. It is not uncommon, for example, for a client who was involved in an automobile accident to claim to have "only had two beers" before starting to drive. A blood alcohol level (BAL) test conducted within an hour of the accident may reveal, however, that the client's BAL was far higher than what would result from two beers. This information would suggest some distortion on the client's part.

Clients who have tested negative for marijuana on one occasion may very well test positive for this same chemical only a few days later. Subsequent inquiry may reveal that they used drugs sometime after the first test, thinking that it was "safe." Such deception might be detected via *frequent* and *unannounced* urine tests that are *closely supervised.*[2] It is for these reasons that the assessor should always try to use medical test information to establish a foundation for the diagnosis of a chemical use problem.

Psychological Test Data

There are a number of psychological tests that may be of use, either directly or indirectly, in the diagnosis of chemical dependency. A major disadvantage of paper-

[2]The use of urine, hair, and saliva samples for toxicology testing is discussed in Chapter 30.

and-pencil tests is that they are best suited to situations where the client is unlikely to fake (the technical term is "positively dissimulate") his or her answers in order to appear less disturbed (Evans & Sullivan, 1990). As chemical dependency rehabilitation professionals know well, these instruments are subject to the same problems of denial, distortion, and outright misrepresentation that are often encountered in the clinical interview setting.

A technique that may be useful in detecting intentional dissimulation is to review the test results with not only the client present, but also the client's spouse or significant other. The assessor then reviews the test item by item, stating the client's response. Often, the spouse or significant other will contradict the client's response to one or more test items, providing valuable new data for the assessment process. For example, on the Michigan Alcoholism Screening Test (MAST), clients often answer "no" to the question that inquired whether the client had ever been involved in an alcohol-related accident. The client's wife, if present, may speak up at this point, asking about "that time when you drove off the road into the ditch a couple of years ago." When, in this hypothetical example, the client points out that the police ruled that the cause of the accident was ice on the road, the wife may respond, "But you told me that you had been drinking earlier that night."

Another way to detect dissimilation is to administer the same test, or ask the same questions, twice during the assessment process. The Michigan Alcoholism Screening Test may be administered during the initial interview and again at the follow-up interview a week or more later. If there are significant discrepancies, this is explored with the client in order to determine why there are so many differences between the two sets of test data. If a client scored 13 points when she or he first took the MAST but only 9 points a month later, an assessor might assume that the client was actively denying her or his alcohol use problem.

Psychological test data can often provide valuable insights into the client's personality pattern and chemical use. Many such tests require a trained professional to administer the test to the client and to interpret it. The value of psychological test data in the detection of alcohol/drug abusers has been disputed (*Forensic Drug Abuse Advisor*, 1997g). However, when used properly, psychological test data can add an important dimension to the diagnostic process.

The Outcome of the Evaluation Process

At the end of the assessment, the chemical dependency professional should be in a position to address four interrelated issues: (1) whether the client seems to have a substance use problem, (2) the *severity* of that individual's substance use problem, (3) the individual's *motivation to change*, and (4) the *factors that seem to contribute to further substance use* by the individual (McCrady, 1993). On the basis of his or her assessment, the professional should also be able to determine what level of care appears to be necessary to help the client and to make some recommendations about the disposition of the client's case. Figure 26.2 outlines the assessment process.

Obviously, if the client is found to be addicted to one or more chemicals, a recommendation that he or she enter treatment is appropriate. The detection of a substance use problem is of little value, if there is no recommendation for treatment (Appleby, Dyson, Luchins, & Cohen, 1997; Paton, 1996). The form of treatment recommended, however, depends on what the assessor believes is the *appropriate level of care*. Treatment programs are ranked by the *intensity* of the treatment program. For example, a medical inpatient treatment program is considered more intense than a day outpatient treatment program that meets five days a week, and both of these are considered more intense than an evening outpatient treatment program that meets once a week. The deciding factor is the client's need for treatment.

Summary

The evaluation process involves three phases: screening, assessment, and diagnosis. We discussed the application of various tools, such as the Addiction Severity Index, the Minnesota Multiphasic Personality Inventory (MMPI), and the Michigan Alcoholism Screening Test (MAST), as aids in the evaluation process. The goal of each phase of the evaluation process was discussed, as was the need for a wide data base to provide as comprehensive a picture of the client's chemical use pattern as possible. Data sources include the client, collateral sources of information, and medical test data.

Information from medical personnel, who would be in a position to evaluate the client's physical status, can

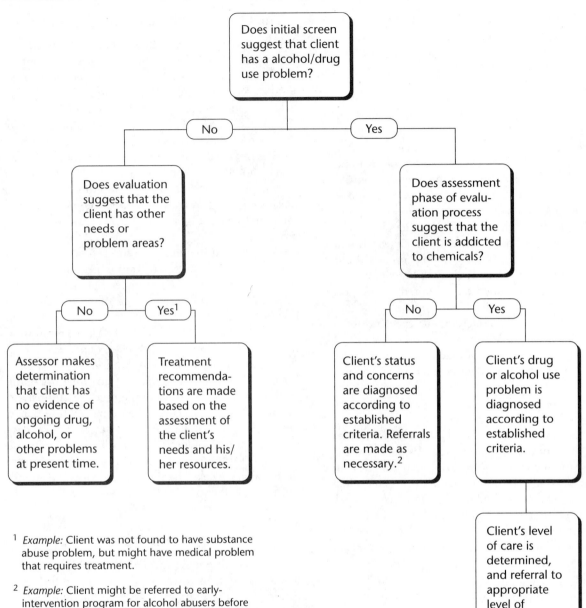

FIGURE 26.2   A flowchart of the assessment process.

[1] *Example:* Client was not found to have substance abuse problem, but might have medical problem that requires treatment.

[2] *Example:* Client might be referred to early-intervention program for alcohol abusers before demonstrating evidence of alcohol addiction.

[3] *Example:* On the basis of standardized criteria such as those proposed by the American Society of Addiction Medicine (ASAM), client might be referred to day outpatient treatment, inpatient program, or intensive evening program.

often prove valuable in understanding a client and the role that drugs have had in his or her life. Finally, psychological test data may reveal much about the client's personality profile and drug use pattern. However, psychological test data are easily manipulated by a client who wishes to dissimulate.

The outcome of the assessment process should be a formal report outlining the evidence that supports the assessor's conclusion about whether the client is or is not abusing chemicals, or is or is not dependent on them. The recommendations that result from the evaluation process may include suggestions for further treatment, even if the client is found not to be addicted to chemicals.

CHAPTER TWENTY-SEVEN

The Process of Intervention

Introduction

The benefits of treating individuals who are abusing or addicted to recreational chemicals are apparent in the finding that the average monthly medical cost for an individual who is still abusing chemicals is $750 (Rosenbloom, 2000). Following treatment, those same costs drop to $200 per month (the typical monthly cost of medical care for a person who has never abused recreational chemicals is $100 per month). These figures demonstrate that the effort to rehabilitate substance abusers/addicts is cost-effective and could bring about a marked reduction in the annual expenditure for health care in this country.

Surprisingly, in light of the fact that alcohol/drug use figures in so many accidents and diseases, the cost of insurance benefits for substance abuse rehabilitation was found to be only 13% of the total expenditure for behavioral health care, and to be less than 1% of the expenditure for overall health care (Schoenbaum, Zhang, & Strum, 1998). This suggests that substance abuse/addiction causes an inordinate drain on the health care resources of this country. Even so, substance abuse rehabilitation professionals encounter resistance from both the substance abuser and health insurance providers when they attempt to intervene in such cases. In this chapter, we will discuss the process of intervention in cases where the person is abusing chemicals.

A Definition of Intervention

It was once thought that, in order to accept the need for help, the addict had to "hit bottom," as it is called in AA. "Bottom" is the point where the alcohol/drug-dependent individual has to admit absolute, total defeat and has no question about the need to stop using chemicals. However, this passive approach to treatment meant that many alcohol/ drug abusers died before "hitting bottom," and many others never accepted the need to stop abusing chemicals.

Vernon Johnson (1980), a pioneer in the intervention process, challenged the belief that it was necessary for the addict to "hit bottom" before he or she could accept help. He suggested that the alcohol-dependent person can learn to comprehend the reality of his or her addiction, *if this information is presented in language that he or she could understand*. Even the substance-abusing client who is functioning poorly (McCrady, 1993) and the person who is "not in touch with reality" (Johnson, 1980, p. 49) because of his or her chemical abuse are "capable of accepting some useful portion of reality, *if that reality is presented in forms they can receive*" (p. 49). Further, because of the physical and emotional damage that uncontrolled addiction can cause, Johnson (1980) did not recommend that concerned family/ friends wait until the addicted person "hit bottom." Rather, he advocated *early intervention* in cases of alcohol/drug addiction.

In a later work, Johnson described intervention as

[a] process by which the harmful, progressive and destructive effects of chemical dependency are interrupted and the chemically dependent person is helped to stop using mood-altering chemicals, and to develop new, healthier ways of coping with his or her needs and problems. (1987, p. 61)

In the eyes of Twerski (1983), an early advocate of the intervention process, intervention is

> a collective, guided effort by the significant persons in the patient's environment to precipitate a crisis through confrontation, and thereby to remove the patient's defensive obstructions to recovery. . . . (p. 1028)

A final definition. Drawing on all these definitions, it is possible to define an intervention project as an *organized* effort on the part of *significant others* in the addict's environment to *break through the wall of denial, rationalization, and projection* by which the addict seeks to protect his or her addiction. The purpose of this collective effort, which is *usually supervised* by a chemical dependency professional, is to secure an agreement to seek treatment *immediately*.

A possible drawback of early intervention. One concern about early intervention is that the person abusing chemicals may not view his or her alcohol/drug use as problematic (McCrady, 1993). Not having "hit bottom," the individual might not have come to understand or accept the relationship between the problems he or she has encountered and his or her chemical use. Thus the individual may resist efforts by concerned others to intervene in an area where he or she does not see a need for corrective action.

Characteristics of the Intervention Process

The most important thing to remember about the intervention effort is that *there is no malice involved*. This is not a place for people to their vent pent-up frustration. The intervention process is a "profound act of caring" (Johnson Institute, 1987, p. 65) through which significant others in the addict's social circle break the rule of silence surrounding his or her addiction. Effective intervention sessions are *planned in advance* and are repeatedly *rehearsed* by the individual participants to ensure that the information presented is appropriate for an intervention session.

Further, participants must agree *in advance* about the goal of the intervention effort. This goal is to help the addicted person accept the need to enter treatment *immediately*. To do this, each person involved affirms

his or her concern for the addict but also confronts the addicted person with specific evidence that he or she has lost control of his or her drug use, in language that the individual can understand. The participants also express their desire for the addict to seek professional help (Williams, 1989). The collective hope is that those involved will be able to break through the addicted person's system of denial.

Although the intervention process has been an accepted tool for more than a generation, there has been little research into which types of families benefit most from intervention training or what type of client benefits most from the intervention process (Edwards & Steinglass, 1995). In a very real sense, intervention might be said to be based on a clinical theory that has not been subjected to research studies designed to assess its utility or identify the conditions under which it might best be utilized.

The Mechanics of Intervention

As we have noted, the intervention process is *planned* and should be rehearsed beforehand by the participants. Usually, three or four sessions are held prior to the formal intervention session so that participants can learn more about the process of intervention and practice what they are going to say (O'Farrell, 1995). The intervention process should involve *every* person in the addicted persons life who has something to add, including spouse, siblings, children, friends, supervisor or employer, minister, co-workers, and others. Johnson Institute (1987) suggested that the supervisor be included because the addicts often use their perception that job performance is adequate as an excuse not to listen to the others in the intervention. All participants are advised to bring up *specific incidents* when the addicted person's behavior, especially her or his chemical use, interfered with their lives in some way.

Individually confronting an addicted person is difficult at best and, in most cases, is an exercise in futility (Johnson Institute, 1987). Anyone who has tried to talk to an addicted person will attest to the fact that the addict will deny, rationalize, become enraged, or simply try to avoid any confrontation that threatens her or his continued drug use. If the spouse questions, individually, whether the alcoholic was physically able to drive the car home last night, he or she might meet with the response "No, but my friend Joe drove the car home for me and then walked home after he parked the car in the driveway." However, if Joe *also* is present, he might then confront the alcoholic with the fact that he did *not* drive the car home last night, or any other night for that matter! His wife might be surprised to hear this; the claim "Joe drove me home last night" could very well have been a common one. But nobody had ever asked Joe about it, just as nobody usually checks out isolated lies, rationalizations, or episodes of denial. The addicted individual's denial, projection, and rationalization often crumble when confronted with all of the significant people in his or her environment. This is why a collective intervention session is most powerful in working with the alcohol/drug-addicted person.

Twerski (1983) observed that it is common for people for whom intervention sessions are called to promise to change their behavior. These promises might be made in good faith, or, they might be made simply as a means of avoiding further confrontation. But the fact remains that because the disease of addiction "responds to treatment and not to manipulation, it is unlikely that any of these promises will work, and the counselor must recommend treatment as the optimum course" (Twerski, 1983, p. 1029).

If the person refuses to acknowledge addiction, or acknowledges that she or he is addicted to chemicals but refuses to enter treatment, each participant in the intervention session should be prepared to detach from the addict. This is *not* an attempt to manipulate the addict through empty threats, and each person should be willing to follow through. For example, if the individual's employer or supervisor has decided to participate he or she needs to clearly state that if the addicted individual does not seek treatment, his or her employment will be terminated. Then, if the addicted person refuses treatment, the employer or supervisor should follow through with this action.

Family members should also have thought about and discussed possible options through which they will begin to detach from the addict. This should be done prior to the start of the intervention session, and if the addicted person refuses treatment (perhaps by leaving the session before it ends), they should follow through with their plan. The options should be discussed with the other participants in the intervention process, and during the rehearsal, each participant should practice

informing the addicted person what she or he will do if the addicted person does not accept treatment.

Again, there is no malice in the intervention process. There is, however, a very real danger that without proper guidance, the intervention session might become little more than a weapon used by some family members to control the behavior of another (Claunch, 1994). The participants in the intervention process do not engage in threats to force the addicted person into treatment. Helping the addicted person see and accept the need for treatment is one goal of the intervention process, but an even more important goal is for participants to break the conspiracy of silence that surrounds the subject of the addicted person's behavior.

Each participant learns that he or she has the right to choose how he or she will respond, should the addict decide to continue to use chemicals. The addicted person is still able to exercise his or her own freedom of choice by either accepting the need for treatment or not. But, now the involuntary "support system" composed of friends and family members, will not be as secure: People will be talking to each other and drawing strength from each other. Here again, although having the addict either accept the need for treatment or clearly understand the consequences of not going into treatment is one goal of the intervention session, an equally important goal is that all participants be heard when they voice their concerns (Claunch, 1994).

Family intervention. Family intervention is a specialized intervention process in which *all* concerned family members, under the supervision of a trained professional, gather and plan a joint confrontation of the individual. The family intervention session, like all other forms of intervention, is carried out in order to break through the addict's denial, enable the family members to begin to voice their concerns, and possibly obtain a commitment from the addict to enter treatment. The focus is on the individual's drug-using behaviors and on the concern that the participants have for the addicted family member.

An advantage of the intervention session is that through confrontation, family members of the addicted person may begin to "detach" from the addict. The conspiracy of silence that existed within the family is broken, and family members may begin to communicate more openly and more effectively. Meyer (1988) identified the intervention process as an "opportunity for healing" (p. 7) for this reason. The participants in the intervention session can both express their love for the addicted person and reject her or his drug-induced behaviors.

It is often helpful for the participants in the intervention process to have written notes that they can refer to. These notes should include information about the specific episodes of drug use, dates, and the addict's response to these episodes of drug use. Sometimes, family members bring in a personal diary to use as a reference in the intervention session. These written notes help keep participants focused on the specific information they wish to bring to the intervention session.

During the rehearsal, the professional who will coordinate the intervention session decides who will present their information and in what order. As much as possible, this planned sequence is followed during the intervention session itself. The participants do not threaten the addict. Rather, they present specific concerns and information that highlights the need for the addicted person to enter treatment. Johnson's (1980; Johnson Institute, 1987) work provides a good overview of the intervention process.

An Example of a Family Intervention Session

In this hypothetical intervention session, the central character is a patient named "Jim." Also involved are his parents, his two sisters, and a chemical dependency counselor. The intervention session was held at Jim's parents' home, where he has been living. During the early part of the session, Jim asserted that he had never drunk to the point of passing out. He also claimed that he always drank at home so that he wouldn't be out on the roads while intoxicated. He maintained that his drinking was not as bad as everybody thought, and he said he couldn't understand why everybody was so concerned.

One of the Jim's siblings, a sister by the name of "Sara," also lives at home, with their parents. She promptly described how, just three weeks ago, Jim had run out of vodka early in the evening, after having four or five mixed drinks. She pointed out that Jim had hopped into the car to drive down to the liquor store to buy a new bottle or two. Sara concluded that she was not calling Jim a liar but that she *knew* that he had driven a car after drinking, at least on this one occasion. She was concerned that he could have had an accident

and still felt uncomfortable about this incident. She was afraid that he might do it again and that the next time, he might not be lucky enough to make it back home in one piece.

Jim's mother then spoke. She pointed out that she had found her son unconscious on the living room floor twice in the past month. She cited the exact dates that this had happened and observed that she felt uncomfortable with his sleeping on the floor, surrounded by empty beer bottles. Accordingly, she had picked up the empty bottles, to keep them from being broken by accident, and had covered Jim up with a blanket while he slept. She concluded by saying that she also was concerned and that she believed her son was drinking more than he thought.

As Jim's mother finished, his other sister, Gloria, began to present her information and concerns. She revealed that she had had to ask Jim to leave her house the previous week, which was news to the rest of the family. She took this step, she explained, because Jim was intoxicated, loud, and abusive toward his nephew. She pointed out that everybody who was present, including a friend of her son who happened to be visiting at the time, smelled the alcohol on his breath and was repulsed by his behavior. Gloria concluded by stating that Jim would no longer be welcome in her home unless he went through treatment and abstained from alcohol use in the future.

At this point, the chemical dependency counselor spoke, pointing out to Jim that his behavior was not so very different from that of many thousands of other addicts. The counselor noted that this was about the point in the intervention session where the addict begins to make promises to cut back or totally eliminate the drug use—a prediction that caught Jim by surprise because it was true. His protests and promises died in his throat before he even opened his mouth.

Before Jim could think of something else to say, the counselor went on to state that Jim gave every sign of having a significant alcohol problem. The counselor listed the symptoms of alcohol addiction one by one and reviewed how Jim's family had identified different symptoms of addiction in their presentations. "So now," the counselor concluded, "we have reached a point where you must make a decision. Will you accept help for your alcohol problem?" If Jim says "Yes," the family members will explain that they have contacted the admissions officers of two or three nearby treatment centers, which have agreed to hold a bed for him until after the intervention session. Jim will be given a choice of which treatment center to enter and will be told that travel arrangements have been taken care of. His luggage is packed and waiting in the car, and if Jim wishes, the family will escort him to the treatment center as a show of support.

If Jim says "No," the family members will confront him about the steps that they are prepared to take to separate from his addiction. His parents may inform him that they have arranged for a restraining order and present him with papers from the court informing Jim that if he comes within a quarter of a mile of his parents' home, he will be arrested. The other family members might then inform Jim that until he seeks professional assistance for his drinking, he is not welcome to live with them, either. (If his employer were present, Jim might be told that his job is no longer there for him if he does not enter treatment.[1])

Jim may be told that, no matter what he may think, these steps are not being taken as punishment. Each person will inform him that because of his drug addiction, they find it necessary to detach from Jim until such time as he chooses to get his life in order. Each person there will affirm his or her concern for Jim but will also begin the process of no longer protecting Jim from his addiction to chemicals. These decisions have all been made in advance of the intervention session. Which option the participants take depends in large part on Jim's response to the question "Will you accept help for your alcohol problem?" Through the process of intervention, the family members have been helped to identify boundaries—limits that they can enforce for their own well-being (Claunch, 1994).

Intervention with Other Forms of Chemical Addiction

The Johnson Institute (1987) addressed the issue of intervention when the person's drug of choice was not alcohol but any of a wide range of other chemicals. The same techniques used in alcoholism also apply when the individual is abusing cocaine, benzodiazepines,

marijuana, amphetamines, or virtually any other drug of abuse. Significant others gather, discuss the problem, and review their data about the addict's behavior. Practice intervention sessions are held, and the problems are addressed during the practice sessions as they are uncovered.

Finally, when everything is ready, the formal intervention session is held. The addicted person may have to be tricked into attending the intervention session, but there is no malice in the attempt to help the addict see how serious his or her drug addiction has become. Rather, there is a calm, caring review of the facts by person after person, until the addict is forced to realize that he or she is addicted to chemicals and in need of professional help.

The goal of the intervention session is, again, to secure the individual's agreement to enter treatment immediately. During the pre-intervention practice sessions, arrangements are made to find a time when the addicted person will be able to participate. A family reunion might provide the opportunity to carry out an intervention session, for example. At first glance, this might seem disruptive to a family holiday, but would the intervention session be any more painful than the family's unspoken anger and frustration at the addicted member's behavior? Indeed, the intervention process might serve as a catalyst for change within the family constellation, opening the door for improvement in other areas. In any case, the timing of the intervention process must be such that the person who is the focus of the effort can participate for as long as the intervention session lasts.

Arrangements are made in advance for the individual's admission into treatment. This can be accomplished by a simple telephone call to the admissions officer of the treatment center. The caller explains the situation and asks whether the facility would be willing to accept the target person as a client. Usually, the treatment center staff will want to follow up with its own chemical dependency evaluation, but most treatment centers are more than willing to consider a referral that results from a family intervention process.

The Ethics of Intervention

As humane as the goal of intervention is, questions have been raised about the ethics of this practice. Rothenberg (1988) noted that there is some question

[1]The employee has certain legal rights, and any employer who agrees to participate in an intervention session should consult an attorney to ensure that she or he does not violate the employee's rights. See Kermani and Castaneda (1996) for a discussion of this issue.

whether it is necessary to confirm the diagnosis of chemical dependency before an attempt at intervention is made. In other words, should there be an independent verification of the diagnosis of drug addiction before an attempt at intervention is carried out? If there is not, can legal sanctions be brought against a chemical dependency professional who, in good faith, supervises an attempt at intervention?

This question becomes very important in light of the fact that some families may try to use the intervention process as a weapon that they can employ to control the behavior of a wayward individual (Claunch, 1994). To avoid this danger, the wise treatment professional should independently confirm the diagnosis before allowing the intervention process to proceed. Furthermore, the question of whether chemical dependency professionals involved in an intervention process should tell the client that he or she is free to leave at any time has not been answered (Rothenberg, 1988). It is possible that some intervention processes have violated either state or federal law, because failing to inform the client that he or she is free to leave might be interpreted as kidnapping or unlawful detention.

Rothenberg's (1988) warning raises some interesting moral and legal questions for the chemical dependency professional. In future years, the courts may rule that the professional is legally obligated to inform the client that he or she is free to leave the intervention session at any time. Furthermore, the courts may rule that the professional can make no move to retain the client either by physical force or by threats, should he or she express a desire to leave. Alternatively, the courts may rule that intervention is a legitimate treatment technique when used by trained professionals. Legal precedents for this area have not been set at this time. Obviously, legal counsel is necessary to guide the chemical dependency professional through this quagmire, and chemical dependency professionals are advised to consult an attorney to discuss the specific laws that might apply.

Intervention via the Court System

Court-ordered treatment is a reflection of the theory that although internal motivation appears to be necessary for the individual to change his or her substance use behavior, *external* motivation can promote abstinence during the critical early stages of recovery while the individual, it is hoped, develops the internal moti-

vation to sustain a recovery program (Satel, 2000; DiClemente, Bellino, & Neavins, 1999). Individuals who participate in a rehabilitation program at the invitation of the court may do so after having been convicted of driving while under the influence of alcohol, of possessing chemicals, or of some other drug-related charge. In such court-ordered treatment, the judge offers the offender an alternative to incarceration: *Either* you successfully complete a drug treatment program, *or* you will be incarcerated.

The exact length of time that the individual spends in jail depends on the specific crime of which she or he was convicted. However, "either/or" treatment situations are unique in that such individuals are offered a choice. They may select incarceration in order to fulfill their obligation to the courts, or they may accept completion of a treatment program as an alternative to incarceration. In many ways, such "either/or" treatment admissions are easier to work with than voluntary admissions to treatment. Court-sponsored intervention is a powerful incentive for the individual to complete the treatment program, and research suggests that such individuals work harder on treatment goals than those who volunteer to enter treatment (Satel, 2000; Moylan, 1990).

The fact that there is a legal hold on the person means that he or she is not free to leave treatment when his or her denial system is confronted. Also, the individual's court-mandated admission can be used to confront the individual about the severity of his or her chemical use problem. After all, it is difficult for people who have just been arrested for a second or third substance-related offense to deny that they have a chemical use problem, although this has been known to happen!

The theory behind court-mandated treatment is that

proactive approaches involving persons with addictive behaviors, in contrast to the more traditional reactive approaches of waiting until motivation for treatment is fully developed, can be helpful in reaching individuals who are not currently interested in changing the addictive behavior. (DiClimente & Prochaska, 1998, p. 7)

This theory was put to the test by a pair of research studies in which individuals who were "legally induced to seek treatment" (Collins & Allison, 1983, p. 1145) were compared with those who entered treatment voluntarily. In both studies, there were no significant differences in outcome (Ouimette, Finney, & Moos, 1997; Collins & Allison, 1983). But those individuals who were in treatment at the court's invitation were likely to stay in treatment longer than were those who had no restrictions placed on them. On the basis of their research, Collins and Allison (1983) concluded that

> the use of legal threat to pressure individuals into drug treatment is a valid approach for dealing with drug abusers and their undesirable behaviors. Legal threat apparently helps keep these individuals constructively involved in treatment and does not adversely affect long-term treatment goals. (p. 1148)

In her review of the effectiveness of court-mandated treatment, Wells-Parker (1994) concluded that individuals who were mandated to treatment because of having been convicted of driving a motor vehicle while under the influence of alcohol/drugs were 8–9% less likely than were untreated offenders to have a subsequent such offense. Further, the author concluded that DWI (driving while intoxicated) offenders who were mandated to treatment had a 30% lower mortality rate than untreated offenders, although the exact mechanism through which treatment may reduce mortality is not yet clear.

Although a naive clinician might conclude that court-mandated treatment is the answer to the problem of substance abuse in this country, remember that individuals who are court-ordered into treatment do *only* about as well as those individuals who are self-referred for treatment (Kleber, 1997; Miller, 1995). For a number of reasons, court- mandated treatment is not a guarantee of success. Three of these reasons were identified by Howard and MaCaughrin (1996). The authors examined 330 treatment programs that accepted court-mandated treatment patients but did not utilize methadone. The authors found that (1) those treatment programs where staff did not view the fact that the client was court-ordered into treatment as a hindrance had better client outcomes, (2) those programs with more than 75% court-mandated referrals had poor client outcomes, and (3) those treatment programs that allowed court-mandated clients some input into the conditions of their treatment (the length of stay, whether or not the employer is to be notified that the individual is in treatment, the treatment goals, and the treatment methods) seem to have better client outcomes than programs that did not grant court-mandated clients these rights.

Although they are suggestive, these findings do not find universal support among clinicians. For example, Peele (1989) viewed such "either/or" referrals as intrusive and counterproductive. He pointed out that individuals convicted of driving a motor vehicle while under the influence of chemicals responded better to legal sanctions (i.e., jail, probation) than to being forced into treatment. In place of treatment, Peele (1989) argued that the individual be held responsible for his or her actions, *including the initial decision to use chemicals*, and that chemical use or abuse did not excuse the individual from responsibility for her or his behavior. Thus the issue of the use of such legal sanctions in the treatment of chemical abuse has not yet been settled.

Court-ordered involuntary commitment. In more than 30 states, it is possible for individuals to be committed to treatment against their will, if the courts have sufficient reason to believe that they are in imminent danger of harming themselves or others (Olson, Mylan, Fletcher, Nugent, Lynch, & Willenbring, 1997). The exact provisions of such court-ordered commitments vary from state to state, but they usually are imposed in cases where the individual has failed to respond to less intensive sanctions (Olson *et al.*, 1997). In spite of the frequency with which it occurs, there is little research into the effectiveness of this form of intervention (Olson *et al.*, 1997). Wild, Cunningham, and Hobdon (1998) suggested that clients who enter treatment because of such external motivation might comply with treatment expectations for a short period of time, without undergoing any permanent changes in attitude or behavior.

Occasionally, the individual will enter treatment on a voluntary basis—a client who demonstrates *autonomous motivation* (Wild, Cunningham, & Hobdon, 1998). As Johnson (1987) observed, this is unusual, although it does happen. It is more common, however, to learn that the substance-abusing person would continue to use chemicals if he or she could do so. This is why external pressure of some kind, whether it be family, legal, medical, or professional penalties, is often necessary to help the addicted person see the need to enter treatment.

Other Forms of Intervention

Another form of "either/or" situation comes about when the spouse, or even the alcoholic's employer, confronts the person who has an alcohol/drug use problem with the threat that "*Either* you stop drinking, *or* I will — — —." Clients who enter treatment under such circumstances are said to demonstrate *controlled motivation* (Wild, Cunningham, & Hobdon, 1998). A common source of such external motivation is when a physician threatens to file commitment papers on the individual with a substance use problem unless she or he enters treatment. Also, with the advent of worksite-mandated urine toxicology testing, it is not uncommon for the "suggestion" that a person enter treatment to come from an employer. External motivation is also frequently supplied by the spouse: "Either you stop using chemicals, or I will leave!"

Employer-mandated treatment With the advent of widespread urine toxicology testing at the job site, and with increasing sensitivity on the part of industry to the economic losses incurred as a result of employee substance abuse, employer-mandated treatment referrals are becoming more and more common. But there is relatively little research data to indicate which forms of intervention are most effective in the workplace (Roman & Blum, 1996).

It has been found that although employees who have to be coerced into treatment under threat of loss of employment tend to have more serious substance use problems, they also tend to benefit more from treatment (Lawental, McLellan, Grissom, Brill, & O'Brien, 1996; Adelman & Weiss, 1989). Employer-mandated treatment has been justified from an economic standpoint, on the grounds that employees with alcohol/drug use problems tend to be absent from work 16 times as often as nonabusing co-workers (Lawental, McLellan, Grissom, Brill, & O'Brien, 1996). On the basis of the evidence available to date, it would appear that employ-

ment settings that utilize such "constructive coercion" (Adelman & Weiss, 1989, p. 515) may actually do a valuable service to those employees with substance use problems. However, a great deal of research is needed to determine which forms of intervention are most effective in the workplace (Roman & Blum, 1996).

Summary

The intervention process is an organized effort on the part of significant others in the addicted person's social environment to break through the wall of defenses that protect the individual from realizing that his/her life is out of control. Intervention processes are usually supervised by a substance abuse rehabilitation professional and have the goal of securing an agreement for the individual to enter treatment immediately.

In this chapter, we discussed the mechanics of the intervention project and some of the more common forms that intervention takes. It was pointed out that the individual retains the right to choose whether to enter treatment or to refuse to do so. Participants in the intervention process must be prepared for either choice and must have a plan of how they will "detach" if the addicted individual does not accept the need for treatment.

Also in this chapter we discussed the fact that the individual retains certain rights, even during the intervention process. Indeed, the individual cannot be detained if he or she expresses the wish to leave the intervention session. Finally, we considered the question of when legal sanctions should be imposed and when treatment might be substituted for these legal sanctions.

CHAPTER TWENTY-EIGHT

The Treatment of Chemical Dependency

Introduction

Questions about the effectiveness of substance abuse treatment no longer spark fierce debate among health professionals. Overall, the success rate of substance abuse rehabilitation compares very well with that of the treatment of other chronic, relapsing diseases such as diabetes, hypertension, and multiple sclerosis (Frances & Miller, 1998; Smith, 1997; Morey, 1996). It has been estimated that the return for every dollar invested in rehabilitation efforts ranges from $4–12 (Frances & Miller, 1998) to as much as $50 (Garrett, 2000). Treatment for cocaine abuse/addiction has been found to be *seven times as effective* in reducing cocaine use as law enforcement activities (Lewis, 1997; Scheer, 1994b). Each dollar invested in the treatment of alcohol/drug use disorders results in a $4–12 savings in social, economic, and medical costs in the years following the individual's treatment exposure (Carroll, 1997). Further, treatment was found to enhance the health status not only of the drinker but his or her family. Rice and Duncan (1995) found, for example, that health care costs for families with at least one alcoholic member were *21 times higher* than for families without an alcoholic member. Thus treating the alcoholic member helped to reduce these costs to the individual, the family, and society at large.

Unfortunately, in the United States, treatment programs for individuals with substance use problems evolved in a haphazard manner largely without scientific feedback (Miller & Brown, 1997). As a result, those treatment methods that are least effective seem to be the most deeply entrenched (Miller, Andrews, Wilbourne, & Bennett, 1998; Miller & Brown, 1997). Fierce debates have raged in the professional literature about which form of treatment is most effective for individuals with chemical use problems. This chapter explores the basic elements of traditional substance abuse treatment in the United States. Some possible outcome measures of treatment effectiveness are reviewed in Table 28.1. The specific components of treatment vary from one program to another. For example, a treatment program that specializes in working with alcohol-dependent businessmen would have little use for a methadone maintenance component. Yet treatment programs also have many elements in common. These are the subject of this chapter.

The Substance Abuse Rehabilitation Professional

The relationship between the client and the counselor is central to the rehabilitation process (Bell, Montoya, & Atkinson, 1997). Indeed, the therapeutic relationship is of such critical importance that these investigators compare it to the individual's initial relationship with his or her parents.

In order to help people with substance use disorders effectively, the helper should have certain characteristics, one of the most important being the absence of any pressing personal issues. Individuals who are dealing with chemical dependency or psychological issues of their own should be discouraged from actively working with individuals in treatment, at least until they have

TABLE 28.1 Summary of Possible Treatment Outcomes

Domain	Possible Outcome
Substance use	• Abstinence • Reduced consumption of chemical(s) • Fewer days intoxicated by a chemical(s) • Substitution of illicit drug by authorized medication (as in methadone maintenance programs)
Medical/physical health	• Individual more likely to meet his or her basic food and shelter needs • Improved over-all health, resulting in reduced use of health care resources • Fewer medical problems • Reduced use of health care resources by spouse or significant other • Reduced incidence of "high-risk" sexual behavior • Reduced sharing of needles
Psychosocial functioning	• Individual introduced to substance-free lifestyle • Improved quality of interpersonal relationships • Reduced level of conflict within family • Reduced danger of neglect/abuse within family • Improved psychological function for individual • Emotional disorders identified and treated • Psychiatric disorders identified and treated • Parenting skills improved
Employment history	• Increased chances of finding suitable work • Increased job retention • Improved job performance in present position • Increased number of days worked without missing work • Reduced number of potential accidents • Reduced absenteeism
Criminal justice	• Reduced involvement with criminal justice system • Reduction in number of subsequent DWI or drug-related arrests • Reduced involvement in number of criminal activities • Reduced violent behavior
Relapse prevention	• Reduced possibility of subsequent substance use • Individual learns how to prepare for possibility of relapse • Individual learns how to minimize adverse effects of possible relapse for self/family.

Source: Chart based on information provided in Landry (1997).

resolved their own problems. This injunction makes sense: A counselor preoccupied with personal problems, including those of chemical addiction, is unlikely to be able to help the client advance further in terms of personal growth.

Rogers (1961) suggested a number of characteristics that he thought essential to the effective mental health counselor: warmth, dependability, consistency, and the ability to care for and respect the client, to be separate from the client (which is the ability not to try to "live through" a client), not to be perceived as a threat by the client, to resist the urge to judge or evaluate the client, and to see the client as a person capable of growth.

In a sense, the client who enters a rehabilitation program is admitting to being unable to change on his or her own (Bell, Montoya, & Atkinson 1997). Thus it makes sense that a therapist with strong interpersonal skills will be best equipped to help the client change.

The therapeutic alliance that evolves between the client and the therapist is one important factor in a positive outcome to the treatment process (Connors, Carroll, DiClemente, Longabaugh, & Donovan, 1997).

The client's acceptance of the therapist's efforts is another essential characteristic of a successful therapeutic relationship, according to Bell, Montoya, and Atkinson (1997). The other characteristics that most strongly influence the client's efforts to change include his or her ability to trust the therapist, to depend on the therapist, to be open with the professional, and to accept help. All of these findings underscore the importance of the therapeutic alliance that evolves between the client and the counselor.

One essential element of a good therapeutic alliance is the therapist's interpersonal skills. Adelman and Weiss (1989) found that those staff members who possessed the highest level of interpersonal skills were best equipped to help their clients. Clients of low-skill counselors were found to be twice as likely to relapse as patients of counselors with high interpersonal skills (Adelman & Weiss, 1989). Further, although the counselor should be able to establish a good therapeutic relationship, this *does not mean that he or she should be permissive!* Caring for a client does *not* mean protecting her or him from the consequences of her or his behavior.

Confrontation and other treatment techniques. For a number of years, substance abuse rehabilitation in the United States has used a "hard-hitting, directive, exhortational style" (Miller, Genefield, & Tonigan, 1993, p. 455) that serves to overwhelm the unconscious defense mechanisms that defend the client against acceptance and understanding of his or her disease. Confrontation has been a central feature of many rehabilitation programs. The theory is that it can help the client begin to understand the impact that substance use has had on his or her life, but there is actually little evidence to suggest that confrontation helps to bring about behavior change (Zoldan, 2000; Miller, 1995; Washton, 1995; Hester, 1994; Miller, Genefield, & Tonigan, 1993; Miller & Rollnick, 1991).

Indeed, research evidence suggests that harsh, confrontational approaches are counterproductive in substance abuse rehabilitation (Miller, Andrews, Wilbourne, & Bennett, 1998; Miller, Genefield, & Tonigan, 1993). It has been found, for example, that as the therapist's level of confrontation increases, the

client's level of resistance will increase proportionally (Miller, Genefield, & Tonigan, 1993). To counter this resistance, *empathy*, combined with a "supportive-reflective" (Miller, Genefield, & Tonigan, 1993, p. 455) style of therapy seems to be effective (Miller, 1998; Miller, Andrews, Wilbourne, & Bennett, 1998). Such a therapeutic style emphasizes the client's ability to change, his or her responsibility for change, therapist advice, the development of behavioral alternatives, and attempts to help the client achieve a sense of self-efficacy.

The Minnesota Model of Chemical Dependency Treatment

To say that what has come to be called the Minnesota Model of chemical dependency treatment has been a success is something of an understatement. First designed in the 1950s by Dr. Dan Anderson, the Minnesota Model has long served as one of the major treatment formats in the fight against alcoholism and drug abuse. Until managed-care companies began to exert their influence over the substance abuse rehabilitation industry, inpatient treatment programs, especially those that followed the Minnesota Model, were viewed as *the* treatment of choice for substance abuse problems (Washton & Rawson, 1999). Although such programs are now quite rare, it is still useful for medical/mental health professionals to understand the Minnesota Model. It is the foundation to rehabilitation programs in the United States.

In order to earn money to finish his college education, Dr. Anderson worked as an attendant at the State Hospital in Willmar, Minnesota (Larson, 1982). After graduation, Anderson returned to the State Hospital in Willmar to work as a recreational therapist. He was assigned to work with the alcoholics who were in treatment at the State Hospital—the least desirable position at that time. Anderson was himself influenced by the work of Mr. Ralph Rossen, who was later to become the Minnesota State Commissioner of Health. At the same time, Dan Anderson and a staff psychologist by the name of Dr. Jean Rossi drew on the growing influence of Alcoholics Anonymous as a means of understanding and working with the alcoholic. They were supported in this approach by the medical director of the Hospital, Dr. Nelson Bradley (Larson, 1982).

These individuals joined together in an effort to understand and treat the patients who were sent to the State Hospital for treatment of their alcoholism. They came from different professions, and each contributed a unique perspective on the patient's needs, and on addiction. To this team was added the Reverend John Keller, who had been sent to Willmar State Hospital to learn about alcoholism in 1955. The staff then had "knowledge of medicine, psychology, AA and theology together under one roof to develop a new and innovative alcohol treatment program" (Larson, 1982, p. 35).

This new treatment approach, now called the Minnesota Model of treatment, was designed to work with dependency on alcohol (*Alcoholism & Drug Abuse Week*, 1990a). In the time since its introduction, it has also been used as a model for the treatment of other forms of chemical addiction. The Minnesota Model utilizes a *treatment team* that consists of chemical dependency counselors familiar with AA, psychologists, physicians, nurses, recreational therapists, and members of clergy, all of whom will work with the client during her or his treatment program.

Stage 1 of the Minnesota Model treatment approach, the evaluation phase, involves each member of the treatment team meeting with the client to assess his or her needs from the professional's own perspective. Each professional then makes recommendations for the client's treatment. In Stage 2, goal setting, the professionals meet *as a team* to discuss the areas that they feel should be the focus of treatment. The treatment team meeting is chaired by the *case manager*. This individual, who is ultimately responsible for execution of the treatment process, is usually the chemical dependency counselor. All of the assessments, and the recommendations derived from them, are reviewed and discussed by the treatment team. The team then selects those recommendations that their training and experience suggest are most appropriate to help the client achieve and maintain recovery. All interested parties, such as the client, his or her parole/probation officer, and family members, are invited to participate in the treatment plan meeting.

On the basis of this meeting, the case manager and client enter Stage 3 of the treatment process. In this phase, the client and his or her case manager develop a formal *treatment plan*. The treatment plan that emerges as a result of this process is multimodal and offers a wide variety of potential treatment goals and recommendations. It identifies specific problem areas, behavioral objectives, methods by which one can measure progress toward these objectives, and a target date for each goal. The treatment plan will be discussed in more detail in the next section of this chapter. A flowchart of the treatment plan process is shown in Figure 28.1

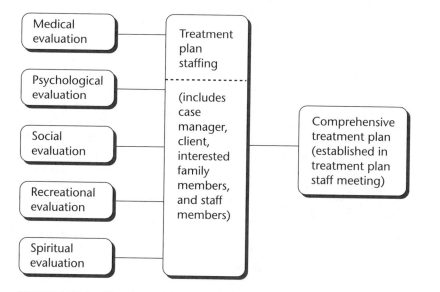

FIGURE 28.1 Flowchart of the evolution of a treatment plan.

The strength of the Minnesota Model of treatment lies in its redundancy and in its multimember concept. The information provided by the client is reviewed by many different professionals, each of whom may identify a potential treatment problem that others have overlooked. This allows for the most comprehensive evaluation of the client's needs, strengths, and priorities. The Minnesota Model also allows for different professionals to work together in the rehabilitation of the client, depending on that client's specific needs. Under such a system, the chemical dependency counselor does not need to try to be a "jack of all trades, master of none." This feature helped make the Minnesota Model one of the dominant treatment program models in the field of chemical dependency rehabilitation for more than 40 years, although under managed care it has largely been modified or replaced by other treatment formats.

The Treatment Plan

No matter what treatment approach the therapist chooses, he or she should develop a *treatment plan* with the client. The treatment plan is "the foundation for success" (Lewis, Dana, & Blevins, 1988, p. 118) of the treatment process. It is a highly specific form, which in some states might be viewed as a legal document. Different treatment centers tend to use different formats, depending on the specific licensure requirements in that state and the treatment methods being utilized.

However, all treatment plans share several features. First, the treatment plan should provide a brief summary of the problem(s) that brought the client into treatment. Another section might provide a brief summary of the client's physical and emotional health. A third section might contain the individual's own input into the treatment process—what she or he thinks should be included in the treatment plan. The fourth section is the heart of the treatment plan, where the specific goals of treatment are identified. Following this are discharge criteria—what must be accomplished in order for the client to be discharged from treatment. Finally, there is a brief summary of those steps that are to be made part of the client's *aftercare* program.

We have said that the treatment goals are the heart of the treatment plan. The treatment goals should include, for each problem the treatment plan addresses, (1) a brief statement of the *problem*, (2) *long-term goals*,

(3) *short-term objectives*, (4) *measurement criteria*, and (5) a *target date*. The problem statement is a short statement, usually a sentence or two in length, that identifies a *specific problem* to be addressed in treatment. The *long-term goal* is the ultimate objective and thus is a general statement of a hoped-for outcome. This statement is also usually only one or two sentences long. Following the long-term goal is a *short-term objective*. The objective is *a very specific behavior that can be measured*. The objective, which is usually between one and three sentences long, identifies the measurement criteria by which both client and staff will assess whether progress toward this objective is being made. Finally, there is the *target date* by which this goal will be achieved.

An example of a treatment goal for a 24-year-old male who is polydrug-addicted (cocaine, alcohol, marijuana, and occasionally benzodiazepines), who has abused chemicals daily for the last 27 months, might appear as follows:

Problem. Client has used chemicals daily for at least the past two years and has been unable to abstain from drug use on his own.
Long-term Goal. That the client abstain from further chemical abuse.
Short-term Objective. That the client not use mood-altering chemicals for 90 days.
Method of Measurement. Random, supervised urine toxicology screens to detect possible drug use. Patient self-report.
Target Date. Scheduled discharge date.

The typical treatment plan might identify as many as five or six different problem areas. Each of these goals might be modified as the treatment program progresses, and each provides a yardstick of the client's progress. Obviously, if the client is not making progress on *any* of the goals, it is time to questions whether the client is serious about treatment.

Although the Minnesota Model of treatment was long considered the gold standard against which other programs were compared, it was not without critics. In the next section, we will examine some of the criticism of the Minnesota Model.

Reaction to the Minnesota Model. The Minnesota Model has been challenged for a number of reasons.

First, this model was designed to work with cases of alcoholism. There has been no research into whether it is applicable to other forms of substance addiction. Yet the Minnesota Model has been utilized in the treatment of virtually every known form of substance abuse (*Alcoholism & Drug Abuse Week*, 1990a).

The Minnesota Model of treatment draws heavily on the philosophy of Alcoholics Anonymous (AA). Yet AA itself is not a form of treatment (Clark, 1995). Further, as we will see in Chapter 34, there is no clear evidence that AA is effective in cases where the individual is coerced into joining, and one of the central tenets of the Minnesota Model is mandatory participation in AA. Another challenge to the Minnesota Model involves its length. When it was developed, the client's stay at Willmar State Hospital was often arbitrarily set at 28 days. There is, however, little research data supporting a need for a 28-day inpatient treatment stay (Turbo 1989). Indeed, the optimal length of treatment for inpatient treatment programs has yet to be defined (McCusker, Stoddard, Frost, & Zorn, 1996). Unfortunately, the 28-day treatment program became something of an industry standard for Minnesota Model programs (Turbo, 1989) and at one time served as a guide for insurance reimbursement (Berg & Dubin, 1990). Further, there is little evidence that the Minnesota Model was actually effective in helping people deal with their chemical use problems (McCrady, 1993; Holder, Longabaugh, Miller, & Rubonis, 1991).

Other Treatment Formats for Chemical Dependency

In recent years, health care professionals and mental health care workers have developed a number of different treatment approaches to alcoholism rehabilitation that differ from the Minnesota Model. The guiding philosophy of these treatment programs is often quite different from that of the Minnesota Model. Although it is not possible to do full justice to each treatment philosophy, we will briefly examine some of the more promising treatment models that have emerged in the past two decades.

Before Treatment, Detoxification

Technically, the term "detoxification" refers to the process of removing toxins from the body. A second, re-

lated definition is the medical management of the patient's withdrawal from a drug(s) of abuse (Haack, 1998). Alcohol/drug detoxification is not in itself considered form of "treatment." The individual's addiction to chemical(s) does not end with successful detoxification from chemicals (Tinsley, Finlayson, & Morse, 1998; Mattick & Hall, 1996). But "detox" *is* often the first step in the process of rehabilitation for individuals with substance abuse problems.

The goal of detoxification is to offer the patient a safe, humane withdrawal from alcohol/drugs of abuse (Mattick & Hall, 1996). The patient's safety is assured, to the degree that this is possible, by the detoxification process being carried out under the supervision of a physician who has both training, and experience in this area of medicine (Miller, Frances, & Holmes, 1988). The physician evaluates the patient's needs and resources and then recommends that the process of detoxification be carried out either on an inpatient or an outpatient basis.

Although detoxification from alcohol/drugs has usually been carried out in a hospital setting, in recent years it has become clear that automatically admitting the alcohol-dependent person into a hospital for detoxification may not be cost-effective (Mattick & Hall, 1996; Berg & Dubin, 1990). Depending on the patient's drug of choice, the resources available to her or him, and the patient's medical status, the detoxification process may be carried out on an outpatient basis. For example, Abbott, Quinn, and Knox (1995) found that with careful screening, it was possible for more than 90% of the alcohol-dependent patients that they worked with to be detoxified on an outpatient basis. Indeed, one recent study from Australia found that less than 0.5% of the alcohol-dependent patients *required* hospitalization for detoxification (Mattick & Hall, 1996).

Patients who are selected for outpatient detoxification, which is called "ambulatory detox" (National Academy of Sciences, 1990, p. 175) or "social detox" (Mattick & Hall, 1996) first are evaluated by a physician. Then, depending on their medical status, they may be referred to a special detoxification setting or sent home with instructions on how to complete the detoxification process. In either case, the patient's progress is monitored by a physician, nurses, or other trained personnel. When the patient is sent home, a nurse may stop by to check on his or her progress once or twice a day, or the patient may be instructed to see his or her physician on a daily basis (Prater, Miller, & Zylstra, 1999). In the detoxification center, the patient's progress and vital signs are monitored as often as necessary.

As long as the patient's physical status does not indicate that she or he is in danger of experiencing severe withdrawal-related distress, the patient is not referred to a more staff-intensive setting such as a general hospital. If, on the other hand, the patient does experience significant withdrawal-related distress or is unable to complete detoxification on an outpatient basis, then he or she is transferred to a more suitable setting.

One of the factors to be considered when deciding whether to refer the patient to an inpatient or an outpatient detoxification program is his or her drug of choice. Some of the drugs of abuse can, when the patient is addicted to them, cause severe or even life-threatening problems during the detoxification process. For example, withdrawal from either the barbiturates or the benzodiazepines can result in life-threatening seizures for patients who are physically dependent on these drugs. In the case of opiate withdrawal, although detoxification is unlikely to pose any significant physical danger to the patient, there is strong evidence that those opiate-dependent patients who are detoxified on an inpatient basis are more likely to complete the detoxification process (Mattick & Hall, 1996).

There is some debate as to whether detoxification programs should function as a "funnel" for guiding patients into the rehabilitation process. When detoxification is carried out at an independent clinic, many patients fail to go on to participate in rehabilitation programs (Miller & Rollnick, 1991). On the other hand, the charge has been made that detoxification programs that are housed in treatment settings are often little more than recruitment centers for the treatment program. To counter this danger, the patient should be advised of his or her treatment options, including the possibility of seeking treatment elsewhere, in order to avoid a possible conflict of interest.

Whether detoxification is carried out on an inpatient or an outpatient basis, the patient being withdrawn from chemicals should be closely monitored by staff to detect signs of drug overdose or of seizures, to monitor medication compliance, and to ensure abstinence from recreational chemicals (Miller, Frances, & Holmes, 1988). Unfortunately, it is not uncommon for patients who are addicted to chemicals to "help out" the withdrawal process by taking additional drugs when they are supposedly being withdrawn from chemicals.

The process of detoxification is vulnerable to being abused in other ways besides the patient self-administering alcohol/drugs. For example, some individuals who are addicted to alcohol/drugs who will go through detoxification dozens—or perhaps even hundreds—of times to give themselves a place to live (Whitman, Friedman, & Thomas, 1990). Other individuals will "check into detox" to give themselves a safe haven from drug debts or to hide from the police. Individuals who are addicted to opiates have been known to enter into a "detox" program when they are unable to obtain drugs or when they want to lower their daily drug requirement to more affordable levels. At other times, the authorities may create a "panic" by arresting a major drug supplier or breaking up a major drug supply source. In such cases, it is not uncommon for large numbers of opiate-dependent patients to seek admission to "detox" in order to have a source of drugs while they wait for opiates to become available again through illicit sources. Thus, although detoxification programs provide a valuable service, they are also vulnerable to abuse.

After "Detox," Treatment

Videotape/self-confrontation. Many programs include videotaping clients while they are under the influence of chemicals, to let them see their own behavior while intoxicated. The goal of this procedure, according to Holder, Longabaugh, Miller, and Rubonis (1991), is to allow the drinker's own drunken behavior to illustrate the need for treatment. After the individual has recovered from the acute effects of drinking, he or she must watch a videotape of his or her behavior. The videotape is usually made in the Emergency Room of the local hospital. Unfortunately, there is no evidence that this brief treatment approach is effective.

Acupuncture is a form of "alternative medicine" that is occasionally applied in treating the addictive disorders. Treatment professionals are still divided on how acupuncture works. Small, sterile needles are inserted into specific locations on the individual's body. Acupuncture can be effective as an analgesic and in treating certain conditions, but at this time, there is little evidence that it is effective in the rehabilitation of substance abusers (Holder, Longabaugh, Miller, & Rubonis, 1991).

For example, Avants, Margolin, Chang, and Birch (1995) attempted to utilize acupuncture in the treatment of cocaine addiction. The authors used a treatment sample of 40 cocaine-dependent individuals who were split into a treatment group and a control group. All subjects had acupuncture needles inserted into their bodies. However, the control group had needles inserted approximately 2 mm away from the active sites at which, according to acupuncture theory, the needles must be placed. The authors concluded that there were no significant differences in treatment outcomes for these two groups; the benefits of acupuncture in the treatment of cocaine addiction have yet to be proven.

Family and marital therapy. It has been suggested that communications patterns within the marital unit or the family where there is an alcohol-dependent person tend to be unhealthy, which in turn helps support the individual's addiction (Alter, 2001). Marital/family therapy approaches that stress communications skills training have thus been found to be up to 4–5 times as effective as rehabilitation programs that focus on the individual (Alexander & Gwyther, 1995), and provisions for marital/family therapy are often made in the rehabilitation of the substance-abusing individual.

Such therapy is quite difficult. For example, it is not uncommon for the defense system of the addicted member, and those of the other family members, to be *inter*-reinforcing (Williams, 1989). As a result of this pattern of interlocking defense systems, the family will, *as a unit,* resist any change in the addicted person's behavior. Also, as was discussed in the section of codependency, boundaries are often fluid, or nonexistent, within the dysfunctional family. These and other issues can be addressed within the context of family/marital therapy.

In their review of the cost-effectiveness of various treatment methods for alcoholism, Edwards and Steinglass (1995) concluded that marital therapy was potentially useful and effective as a treatment approach at some points in the treatment process. The authors conducted a *meta*-analysis of research articles on marital therapy as a treatment modality for alcoholism rehabilitation. They found that there was clearcut evidence suggesting that family/marital therapy was effective during the intervention and aftercare phases of treatment for alcohol-dependent individuals.

Overall, Edwards, and Steinglass (1995) concluded that marital/family therapy is an effective treatment modality for working with the alcohol-dependent individual. However, the authors also note that there is a need for further research on the subject of which treatment methods might be most effective in working with the alcohol/drug-addicted client. Further, the field of family/marital therapy has become a specialized area of expertise, with a vast, evolving body of literature of its own (Bowen, 1985). It is beyond the scope of this chapter to provide a comprehensive overview of the application of marital therapy to the treatment of the addictions. The chemical dependency professional should be aware that these specialized approaches offer some promise in substance abuse rehabilitation programs.

Group therapy approaches. Group psychotherapy offers a number of advantages over individual therapy (Yalom, 1985). First, therapy groups allow one professional to work with a number of different individuals at once. Second, members of the therapy group are able to learn from each other and offer feedback to each other. Finally, because of the nature of the therapy group, each individual finds within the group a reflection of his or her family of origin, and this may enable him or her to work through problems from earlier stages of growth. These advantages are utilized in chemical dependency treatment programs, where therapy groups are frequently the primary treatment approach offered to the client. Individual sessions may be used for special problems too sensitive to discuss in a therapy group situation, but the client is usually encouraged to bring her or his concerns "to group," which may meet every other day, daily, or more often than once a day, depending on the pace of the program.

Unfortunately, there is limited evidence that group psychotherapy approaches are at all effective in the rehabilitation of substance abusers (Holder, Longabaugh, Miller, & Rubonis, 1991). However, group therapy formats that utilize cognitive-behavioral approaches to help the client learn how to deal with painful affective states that might contribute to the urge to use chemicals seem to be effective in working with personality-disordered substance abusers (Fisher & Bentley, 1996).

McCrady (1993) pointed out that women who have substance use problems seem to be somewhat inhibited in group settings. In such cases, the woman seems to do better in an individual therapy setting than in a group, possibly because of shame-based issues. Further, the author suggested, the elderly may feel overwhelmed by the complex pattern of interactions within the group setting. Again, the individual may respond more favorably to being seen on an individual basis. Thus, although group therapy approaches are a common treatment modality, there is limited evidence of their effectiveness, and they may be contraindicated for some clients.

Assertiveness/social skills training. Lewis, Dana, and Blevins (1988) identified special training groups for assertiveness as being useful in building self-esteem and self-confidence in interpersonal relationships. Individuals who are addicted to chemicals often lack the ability to assert themselves (Lewis *et al.*, 1988) and can benefit from training in this interpersonal skill. In addition to assertiveness, many other social skills may be taught to the recovering addict.

There is evidence that assertiveness/social skills training is quite effective in the rehabilitation of alcoholics (Holder, Longabaugh, Miller, & Rubonis, 1991). Thus programs that emphasize helping the alcohol-addicted individual learn how to assert himself or herself appropriately seem likely to enhance the individual's recovery.

Self-help groups. The topic of self-help, or Twelve-Step groups will be discussed in Chapter 34. However, the reader should be aware that participation in such groups is often required for individuals in substance abuse rehabilitation programs.

Biofeedback training. A number of treatment plans advocate the use of biofeedback training as an aid in the treatment of addictive disorders. The technique of biofeedback involves monitoring a selected physical parameter (such as skin temperature, brain wave patterns, or muscle tension) and giving the individual information about how his or her body is doing. Depending on the parameter selected and the training provided, the individual can often learn how to modify his or her body function in a desired direction, such as to relax without the use of drugs.

Peniston and Kulkosky (1990) attempted to teach a small number of patients in an alcoholic treatment program to change the frequency with which their brains produced alpha and theta waves. These patterns of electrical activity in the brain are thought to reflect the individual's relaxation and stress-coping responses. The

authors found that their sample exhibited significant changes on standard psychological tests used to measure the personality pattern of the respondent and that these changes continued over an extended follow-up period. The authors suggested that biofeedback training, especially alpha and theta brain wave training, may offer an effective treatment approach for working with the chronic alcoholic.

Ochs (1992) examined the application of biofeedback training techniques to the treatment of addictive disorders. The author concluded that the term "biofeedback training" for the addictions was a bit misleading because different clinicians employed a wide range of techniques and focused on a wide range of body functions. Even so, biofeedback training did seem to have value for the treatment of addictive disorders, especially when biofeedback was integrated into a larger treatment format designed to address social, economic, vocational, psychological, and family problems. Thus biofeedback training may play an increasing role in the treatment of addictive disorders.

Harm reduction model. The *harm reduction* (HR) model of substance abuse rehabilitation is quite different from the Minnesota Model and from the other models of treatment discussed in this chapter. It is based on the assumption that it is possible, over time, to change the behavior of alcohol/drug abusers, including the way(s) they use chemicals, so that they will gradually come to behave in ways that reduce the consequences of their substance abuse (MacCoun, 1998). This model is in sharp contrast to "zero tolerance" (Marlatt, 1994) and supply reduction (MacCoun, 1998) models of chemical use intervention.

The use of nicotine skin patches or nicotine gum is viewed by Marlatt (1994) as an example of the HR philosophy, in that both reduce the individual's risk of negative consequences from cigarette smoking. From this perspective, formal detoxification from chemicals in a medical setting might also be viewed as a form of harm reduction. Another example of the HR philosophy is the "needle exchange" programs that are in place in several cities around the country. Because the virus that causes AIDS is often transmitted through contaminated intravenous needles, some cities allow intravenous drug abusers to exchange "dirty" needles for new, uncontaminated ones. In Baltimore, Mayor Kurt

Schmoke authorized a needle exchange program in that city in order to limit the damage done by HIV, defending his decision on a cost/benefit basis:

> This program costs $160,000 a year. The cost to the state of Maryland of taking care of just one adult AIDS patient infected through the sharing of a syringe is $102,000 to $120,000. In other words, if just two addicts are protected from HIV through the city's needle exchange, the program will have paid for itself. (Schmoke, 1996, p. 40)

Needle exchange programs slow the transmission of the virus that causes AIDS. Further, although critics were afraid that this type of program would encourage intravenous drug use, there is little evidence of an increase in drug use in communities with needle exchange programs (MacCoun, 1998). Unfortunately, in spite of the apparent advantages, fewer than 100 U.S. communities had needle exchange programs as of 1998, and resistance to such programs is strong (MacCoun, 1998).

Although the HR model is somewhat controversial, it seems to offer an alternative to the less tolerant Minnesota Model.

Aftercare Programs

The goals of *aftercare* programs are to maintain gains made in the formal treatment process and to help prevent relapse to active chemical use/abuse (McKay, McLellan, Alterman, Cacciola, Rutherford, & O'Brian, 1998). Included in the concept of aftercare programs are identifying and correcting mistaken beliefs that might contribute to a relapse, as well as helping the client establish "the habit of sobriety" (Downing, 1990, p. 22).

The aftercare program often includes participation in self-help groups such as Alcoholics Anonymous and Narcotics Anonymous. This is especially true of those programs that are based on the Minnesota Model of treatment (Clark, 1995). Medical problems identified earlier in the rehabilitation process are also addressed in aftercare, as are such issues as transitional living facilities or special needs. The aftercare program is designed and carried out on the assumption that treatment does not end with the individual's discharge from a formal rehabilitation program. Rather, treatment is the first part of a recovery program that continues for the rest of the individual's life.

Summary

This chapter reviewed the Minnesota Model of treatment, which is one of the primary treatment models found in this country. The concept of a *comprehensive treatment plan*, which serves as the heart of the treatment process, was discussed. We also explored various pharmacological supports for people in the early stages of sobriety and for those going through detoxification from chemicals.

This chapter also examined the role of assertiveness training, biofeedback, and marital and family therapy in the substance abuse treatment program. The use of blood and urine samples for toxicology screening to detect medication compliance, and illicit drug use, was also reviewed.

CHAPTER TWENTY-NINE

Treatment Formats for Chemical Dependency Rehabilitation

Introduction

For the past 20 years, researchers and clinicians have vigorously debated the relative merits of *outpatient* versus *inpatient* substance abuse rehabilitation programs. To date, neither side has scored a decisive victory, and both inpatient and outpatient treatment programs have vocal proponents. In this chapter, we will discuss some of the characteristics of the typical outpatient treatment program, those of the typical inpatient program, and some of the claims that have been made about the relative advantages and disadvantages of each.

Outpatient Treatment

A *working definition of outpatient treatment.* Outpatient chemical dependency treatment may best be defined as follows: It is a formal treatment program involving one or more professionals who are trained to work with individuals addicted to a chemical(s). It is designed specifically to work with the addicted person to help him or her achieve and maintain recovery. To this end, it will utilize a number of different treatment modalities (such as psychoeducational approaches and family, marital, individual, and/ or group therapies) to help the addicted person come to terms with his or her chemical abuse problem. And it will do so on an outpatient basis. At the start of the 21st century, an estimated 85% of all patients in substance abuse treatment received their care in an outpatient rehabilitation program (Fuller & Hiller-Sturmhofel, 1999; Tinsley, Finlayson, & Morse, 1998).

Components of Outpatient Treatment Programs

Outpatient treatment programs incorporate many of the components of treatment that we discussed in the last chapter. Such programs include individual and group therapy, as well as marital and family therapy, in working with the addicted person. Most such programs follow a Twelve-Step philosophy and are associated with either Alcoholics Anonymous or Narcotics Anonymous; the individual is expected to attend regular self-help group meetings. The individual's treatment program is usually coordinated by a certified chemical dependency counselor (sometimes called an addictions, AODA, or substance abuse counselor).

During the rehabilitation process, a formal treatment plan is established, regular review sessions are scheduled, and the client's progress toward the agreed-upon goals is monitored. Individual and group therapy sessions are used to help the individual work through denial and face the problems of daily living *without* chemicals. Psycho-educational lectures may also present the client with factual information about the disease of chemical addiction and its treatment.

Referrals to vocational counseling centers, or to community mental health centers for individual, family, or marital counseling, are made as necessary. Some programs provide for a "family night," where family members are encouraged to participate once a week or once a month to discuss their concerns. Other programs feature a "family group" orientation, where couples participate together daily. In this format, the spouse of the addicted person sits in on the group sessions and participates as an equal with the addicted person in the group therapy.

Whatever the general approach, the goal of any outpatient treatment program is to enhance the addicted person's level of functioning, while providing support for her or his recovery from substance abuse. Some programs require that the detoxification phase of treatment, during which the individual is withdrawn from chemicals, be carried out either at a detoxification center or in a general hospital. However, the individual is usually expected to have stopped all chemical use before starting any treatment program. Abstinence from alcohol/drug use is expected. Many treatment programs require the use of Antabuse (disulfiram) or carry out random breath and urine tests to detect any alcohol/drug use by the patient. One advantage of urine testing is that it enables the staff to check on the individual's compliance in taking Antabuse.

Outpatient treatment programs allow the individual to live at home, continue to work, and take part in family activities while participating in a rehabilitation program designed to help him or her achieve and maintain abstinence (Youngstrom, 1990b). Unfortunately, in spite of these advantages, research suggests that outpatient treatment programs are plagued by high dropout rates.

Outpatient Treatment Programs for Substance Abuse Rehabilitation

The DWI school. Outpatient rehabilitation programs differ mainly in terms of the frequency with which the individual meets with treatment professionals and the specific methods that staff members use in working with the client. For example, the psycho-educational approach is often the mainstay of the "DWI school" or DWI class. The DWI school is usually limited to first-time offenders, who are assumed simply to have made a mistake by driving under the influence of chemicals. Participants in the DWI school are not, in the opinion of the assessor, addicted to alcohol/drugs. Participants in DWI school are exposed to 8–12 hours of educational lectures designed to help them better understand the dangers inherent in driving while under the influence of chemicals. This is done in the hope that they will learn from their mistake.

Short-term outpatient programs (STOP). STOP-level programs are usually time-limited programs. Some utilize only individual therapy sessions; others combine in-dividual and group therapy for individuals whose substance use problem is, in the opinion of the assessor, mild to moderate. The individual may be required to attend Alcoholics Anonymous (AA) or similar self-help group meetings and to meet with the therapist at least once a week. Clients in STOP-level programs are often assigned material to read between sessions with the therapist, and psycho-educational lectures may be used to give program participants factual information about the effects of the drugs of abuse. The individual client participates in program activities 1–2 nights a week for a period of time that is usually less than 2 months.

The goals of STOP-level programs are (1) to break through the individual's denial about his or her substance use, (2) to achieve a commitment to abstinence from the client, and (3) to make appropriate referrals for those individuals who appear to require more in-depth help. Such programs are generally utilized with patients whose substance use problems are of lesser severity. However, Shepard, Larson, and Hoffmann (1999) reported that short-term rehabilitation programs were the *least* effective method of intervention with individuals who do not have extensive substance abuse problems.

Intensive short-term outpatient programs (I-STOP). Programs at the I-STOP level are aimed at the patient with a moderate to severe substance use problem. Program participants are usually seen in both individual and group therapy sessions for up to 5 nights a week. Programs at the I-STOP level are time-limited, but in addition to providing more intensive treatment than STOP programs (1–2 times a week versus 4–5 times a week), programs at this level usually last longer (up to 6 months). Program participants are often required to attend self-help group meetings, such as AA, in addition to participating in scheduled treatment activities. Additional sessions for family/marital counseling are scheduled outside of scheduled treatment hours for those individuals whose recovery requires additional forms of intervention/support.

Patients assigned to I-STOP-level intervention programs are usually those with moderately-severe substance use problems. The goals of I-STOP level programs are (1) to break through the individual's denial about his or her substance use, (2) to achieve a commitment to abstinence from the client who is unlikely to respond to less intense forms of treatment, and (3) to make appropriate referrals for those individuals who appear to require more in-depth help. Shepard, Larson, and Hoffmann (1999) concluded that programs at this level of intensity were most effective, especially when applied to the target population of individuals with mid-severity substance use problems.

Intensive long-term outpatient treatment (ILTOT). ILTOT-level programs are usually open-ended outpatient treatment programs designed for the individual whose substance use problem is moderate to severe in intensity and for whom less radical treatment would hold little chance of success. ILTOT level programs usually last for a minimum of 6 months and often for as long as 12–18 months. Program participants are involved in a series of individual and group therapy sessions for a specified number of days each week; the exact timing and sequence of individual and group sessions are determined by the individual's treatment plan.

ILTOT-level programs are designed to be used with patients with moderate to severe substance use problems. The goals of ILTOT-level programs are (1) to break through the individual's denial about his or her substance use, (2) to achieve a commitment to abstinence from the client who either has not been able to benefit from less intense forms of treatment or whose substance use pattern suggests that less intense treatment is likely to fail, (3) to support the individual during the early stages of his or her recovery from drug/alcohol use problems, and (4) to make appropriate referrals for those individuals who appear to require more in-depth help. Surprisingly, such programs were found to be less effective than short-term intervention programs for people with moderate to severe substance use problems (Shepard, Larson, & Hoffmann, 1999).

Advantages of Outpatient Treatment Programs

Outpatient treatment programs are popular. For example, it has been reported that as many as 88% of those who are treated for alcohol abuse or addiction are treated on an outpatient basis (McCaul & Furst, 1994). Outpatient treatment enjoys an obvious cost advantage over inpatient treatment. A 28-day inpatient treatment program might cost between $7000 and $30,000 (*Alcoholism & Drug Abuse Week*, 1990; Turbo, 1989). In contrast to this, a 6-month outpatient treatment program might cost as little as $1000 (Turbo, 1989).

Another major advantage of the outpatient chemical dependency treatment format is that it avoids the need

to remove the patient from his or her environment, and no community reorientation period is needed after outpatient treatment (Youngstrom, 1990b). In addition, outpatient treatment programs tend to last longer than do inpatient rehabilitation programs. Nace (1987) suggested that the "ideal" outpatient treatment program would last a full year. A treatment program 1 year in duration would offer long-term follow-up for the crucial first year of recovery, the time when the client is most likely to relapse.

Berg and Dubin (1990) outlined an intensive outpatient treatment program that was divided into four phases. Each of the first three phases (intensive, intermediate, and moderate treatment) was designed to last for 2 weeks. The individual's placement was determined by "the severity of the patient's addiction, progress in treatment, financial resources, and ability to attend the program" (Berg & Dubin, 1990, p. 1175). The final phase of treatment, the extended phase, involved an aftercare meeting once a week for an indefinite period of time. Lewis, Dana, and Blevins (1988) note that because outpatient treatment programs tend to last longer than inpatient programs, this rehabilitation format offers the counselor a longer period of time to help the client achieve the goals outlined in his or her treatment plan. The client also has an extended period of time in which to practice—and perfect—new behaviors that will support his or her recovery from substance abuse/addiction.

Outpatient treatment programs offer yet another advantage over inpatient treatment programs: *flexibility* (Turbo, 1989). Clients may participate through an *outpatient day treatment* program, where treatment activities are scheduled during normal working hours, or through an *outpatient evening treatment* program. Finally, outpatient treatment programs offer the client the opportunity to practice sobriety while still living in the community. This is a significant advantage over traditional inpatient treatment programs, where the client is removed from his or her home community for the duration of treatment.

Disadvantages of Outpatient Treatment Programs

Inpatient treatment might cost more, but because of available insurance coverage, many clients actually pay *less* for inpatient treatment than they would for outpatient treatment. The costs of outpatient treatment programs traditionally are not reimbursed by health insurance carriers at the same rate as the (greater) costs of inpatient substance abuse programs. This factor often encourages health care providers to recommend inpatient over outpatient treatment programs (Berg & Dubin, 1990).

Although statistical research has found no significant difference between the percentages of outpatient and inpatient treatment program "graduates" who remain sober, this is not to say that outpatient treatment is as effective as inpatient treatment. Rather, inpatient treatment programs tend to deal more effectively with a different type of client than do outpatient treatment programs. This fact makes it hard to compare the inpatient and outpatient form of treatment.

Outpatient treatment programs typically do not offer the same degree of structure and support as inpatient treatment settings. Further, outpatient treatment programs offer less control over the client's environment and thus are of limited value for some patients who require a great deal of support during the early stages of recovery. Although outpatient treatment of substance abuse seems to work for many clients, it does not appear to be the ultimate answer to the problem of chemical dependency.

Inpatient Treatment

Definition of inpatient treatment. The inpatient treatment program might best be defined as a residential treatment facility where the client lives while he or she participates in treatment. Such programs usually deal with the hard-core, seriously ill, or "difficult" patient. These are individuals for whom outpatient treatment has not been successful or has been ruled out. Residential treatment program usually have a strong emphasis on a Twelve-Step philosophy and utilize individual and group therapy extensively. The client's length of stay in treatment depends on his or her motivation, his or her support system, and a range of other variables that the treatment team considers when working with any given individual.

Residential treatment programs provide the greatest degree of support and help in response to the challenge presented by the client. Inpatient treatment also is "the most restrictive, structured, and protective of treatment settings" (Klar, 1987, p. 340). It combines the greatest

potential for positive change with high financial cost and the possibility of branding the patient for life (Klar, 1987). The decision to utilize inpatient treatment should not be made lightly.

Many general hospitals offer inpatient rehabilitation programs for drug/alcohol use problems. For example, Bell (1995) estimated that 21% of the hospitals surveyed offered inpatient treatment for substance abuse. But other forms of inpatient treatment are not hospital-based. For example, there are *therapeutic communities* and *halfway houses*, as well as a number of inpatient rehabilitation programs that are not part of a hospital complex.

Inpatient Treatment Programs for Substance Abuse Rehabilitation

Hospital/center-based inpatient treatment. Traditional inpatient drug rehabilitation is often carried out either in a center that specializes in chemical dependency treatment or in a traditional hospital setting (as part of a specialized drug treatment unit). Some of these programs follow the "Minnesota Model," which was explored in detail in Chapter 28, although this is becoming less and less common as managed-care providers demand shorter treatment stays for their clients.

Inpatient rehabilitation programs, especially those in a hospital setting, often begin with detoxification, and in this case, the patient can begin treatment in the last stages of withdrawal from chemicals. This blending of withdrawal and treatment can enhance patient retention. Patients live on the treatment unit and participate in a program of daily lectures and individual and group therapy sessions. Each patient is assigned some sort of "homework," which may include reading certain material that rehabilitation staff believe will support the individual's recovery. In most programs, she or he is also expected to begin to follow the Twelve-Step program of AA or a similar self-help group, and attendance at self-help group meetings is required.

Therapeutic communities. One controversial form of inpatient treatment is the therapeutic community (TC). There are an estimated 10,000–12,000 patients in therapeutic communities in the United States (Kleber, 1997). In spite of this commitment to the TC approach, there is no generally recognized model for therapeutic communities (DeLeon, 1994; National Academy of Sciences, 1990). Rather, there are a multitude of different programs, all of which recommend different lengths of stay, have different client-to-staff ratios, treatment philosophies, and staff compositions. In general, however, the "traditional" TC might be viewed as a program that operates on the theory that drug abuse is

> a deviant behavior, reflecting impeded personality development or chronic deficits in social, educational, and economic skills. . . . The principal aim of the TC is a global change in life-style: abstinence from illicit substances, elimination of antisocial activity, development of employability, and prosocial attitudes. . . . (DeLeon, 1994, p. 392)

In terms of length of stay, the "traditional" TC programs usually require a commitment of between 1 and 3 years (DeLeon, 1994, 1989), although some programs have a minimal commitment of only 6 months. This extended length of stay is thought to be necessary to change the drug-using behavior. Such long-term residential treatment programs are thought to be quite effective with those individuals whose addiction is complicated by an antisocial personality disorder, or what *Alcoholism & Drug Abuse Week* (1990) called "social pathology" (p. 3).

When the TC movement began in the United States, it worked mainly with individuals addicted to opiates, but this is no longer true. The majority of the clients in today's TCs were using chemicals other than opiates before their admission to treatment (DeLeon, 1994). Most TC programs follow a single therapeutic model; that is, all members of the treatment staff have the same treatment philosophy. This adherence to a single vision seems to contribute to the effectiveness of TCs in working with the drug-dependent individual (Ellis, McInerney, DiGiuseppe, & Yeager, 1988). But the TC model has not been widely accepted in the United States. DeLeon (1989) found, for example, that of the estimated 500 drug-free residential treatment programs in the United States, less than a quarter follow the TC model.

One central tenet of the TC model is "its perspective of drug abuse as a *whole person* disorder" (DeLeon, 1989, p. 177; DeLeon, Melnick, & Kressel, 1997). Other characteristics of the TC include social and physical isolation, a structured living environment, a

firm system of rewards and punishments, and an emphasis on self-examination and the confession of past wrongdoing. Clients are expected to work, either outside of the TC in an approved job or within the TC itself as part of the housekeeping or kitchen staff. In many TCs, there is some potential mobility from the status of client to that of paraprofessional staff member (National Academy of Sciences, 1990).

Although many TCs utilize the services of mental health professionals, there is a tendency for much of the treatment to be carried out by paraprofessional staff members, who are often former residents of the TC. This is done on the theory that only someone "who has been there" can understand the addicted person. Such paraprofessional counselors are thought to be effective in breaking through the client's denial and manipulation.

The TC might offer an extended family for the individual—a "family" that the recovering addict may be encouraged never to leave. Indeed, the original members of Synanon (one of the early therapeutic communities) were expected to remain there permanently as part of the "family" (Lewis, Dana, & Blevins, 1988). But in spite of the "family" orientation, TCs have been found to suffer from significant dropout rates (DeLeon, Melnick, & Kressel, 1997; *The Addiction Letter*, 1989b). DeLeon (1994) suggested that 30–40% of those admitted to a TC will drop out in the first 30 days. Further, over the course of treatment, a significant percentage of those who do not leave on their own either are asked or are discharged from treatment for various infractions of the rules (Gelman, Underwood, King, Hager, & Gordon, 1990). Ultimately, only 15–25% of those admitted to TCs actually graduate (DeLeon, 1994; National Academy of Sciences, 1990). The recovery rates of those who drop out of TCs in the earliest phases of treatment "basically cannot be distinguished from those [of] individuals who did not enter any treatment modality" (National Academy of Sciences, 1990, p. 167). Thus, although the TC offers some hope for the addicted person, it does not appear to be for everyone.

There is a great deal of controversy surrounding therapeutic communities. Some (Ausabel, 1983) caution that joining a therapeutic community may not be a positive step for the individual. Many TCs use methods such as ego stripping and demand unquestioned submission to the rules of the program. Lewis, Dana, and Blevins (1988) pointed out that the social isolation inherent in the TC prevents the client from going out into the community to try new social skills. However, others (DeLeon, 1994; Peele, 1989; DeLeon, 1989; Yablonsky, 1967) note that the TC has been effective in some cases where traditional treatment methods have been of limited value. Peele (1989) observed that the TC functions best when it strives to help the individual learn social skills and values inconsistent with drug-using behaviors. Therapeutic communities have been found to be quite effective, with upwards of 80% *of those who complete the program* remaining drug-free following discharge (*Alcoholism & Drug Abuse Week*, 1990; National Academy of Sciences, 1990).

Is There a Legitimate Need for Inpatient Treatment?

A flurry of studies conducted in the mid-1980s reached the conclusion that "the relative merits of residential treatment are less than clear" (Miller & Hester, 1986, p. 794). In order to explore the possibility that certain types of patients might respond better than others to an inpatient or an outpatient setting, the Project MATCH Research Group carried out a research project in the mid-1990s to try and isolate what patient characteristics predicted a better response to inpatient versus outpatient treatment for alcoholism. The project failed to find evidence that matching patients to one form of treatment or another yielded any additional benefit or that there were specific patient characteristics that suggested that one treatment setting was more advantageous than the other (Rychtarik, Connors, Whitney, McGillicuddy, Fitterling, & Wirtz, 2000). As a result of such studies, the "advantages of inpatient versus outpatient care . . . have been difficult to show" (Chick, 1993, p. 1374).

Miller and Hester (1986) do not try to hide their criticism of inpatient treatment programs. At the same time they do not advocate the abolition of residential treatment:

> There may be subpopulations for whom more intensive treatment is justifiable. From the limited matching data available at present, it appears that intensive treatment may be better for severely addicted and socially unstable individuals. (p. 1246)

In response to Miller and Hester's original (1986) work, Adelman and Weiss (1989) conducted their own research into the merits of inpatient treatment. They reported that 77% of those alcoholics treated for their alcoholism eventually required some form of inpatient treatment. The authors also found that treatment programs in "medically oriented facilities" (p. 516) had lower dropout rates than treatment programs in nonmedical centers. The authors also concluded that patients discharged after short inpatient treatment programs tended to relapse more frequently than those who remained in treatment longer.

In 1991, Walsh *et al.* reported the results of a research project in which 227 workers at a large factory who were known to be abusing alcohol were randomly assigned to one of three treatment programs: compulsory attendance at Alcoholics Anonymous, compulsory inpatient treatment, or the patient's choice between these two alternatives. The authors were surprised to find that although the referral to compulsory AA meetings *initially* was more cost-effective, inpatient treatment resulted in higher abstinence rates in the long run.

The emerging consensus seems to be that the people most likely to benefit from inpatient treatment programs for substance use disorders are those who have the most severe alcohol/drug addiction problems and those with substance use and mental illness issues (Rychtarik *et al.*, 2000; Shepard, Larson, & Hoffmann, 1999; Moos, King, & Patterson, 1996). Some researchers have found evidence of a "threshold effect" for the treatment process, with stronger results being achieved after 14 days of inpatient treatment for those patients who require inpatient treatment (Moos, King, & Patterson, 1996). Other researchers have found that lower-functioning alcohol abusers/addicts appear to benefit more from inpatient than outpatient treatment (Rychtarik *et al.*, 2000).

The benefits of inpatient treatment do not appear to be limited to alcohol abusers alone, for inpatient treatment also appears to be a cost-effective approach to the rehabilitation of heroin addicts. Swan (1994) noted that the cost of a 6-month inpatient treatment program for a person addicted to heroin would be about $8250, whereas the cost to society of *not* treating the heroin-addicted person (in terms of criminal activity, social support services, and health care services) would be approximately $21,500 for the same period. Although a residential treatment program was four times as expensive as simply placing the heroin addict in a methadone maintenance program, it was still only 40% as expensive as not providing any form of treatment for the individual. Thus residential treatment programs appear to be a cost-effective way to deal with individuals who are addicted to heroin.

Advantages of Inpatient Treatment Programs

Although the case for outpatient treatment programs is a strong one, inpatient treatment programs offer certain advantages as well. For example, research conducted by Bell, Williams, Nelson, and Spence (1994) revealed that fully 76% of the clients who were assigned to inpatient treatment completed their program, as opposed to just under 64% of those subjects assigned to outpatient day treatment programs. What are some reasons for this significant difference in retention rates?

One reason why a greater percentage of patients who enter inpatient rehabilitation programs actually complete treatment is that such programs offer *more comprehensive treatment programming* than is possible in an outpatient treatment setting (Klar, 1987). This is a big plus in more advanced cases of drug dependency, because often the addicted individual's life has revolved around the chemical for such a long time that she or he will be unable to benefit from a less restrictive treatment approach. Further, because addicted clients frequently live alone or lack close interpersonal support, a medical emergency might go undetected for hours or days.

In the inpatient treatment setting, medical emergencies can be detected quickly, and the appropriate action taken by staff to help the client. Close supervision by staff members also helps discourage further drug use. Clients, especially those with a longstanding drug problem, often are tempted to "help out" with the detoxification process by taking a few additional drugs or drinks during withdrawal.

Another advantage of the almost total control over the client's environment offered by the inpatient rehabilitation setting is the opportunity that this structured environment offers the client to participate in individual and group therapy sessions, meals, recreational activities, self-help group meetings, and spiritual counseling (Berg & Dubin, 1990). For clients who have lived, at least recently, a drug-centered lifestyle, the concept of a drug-free way of life is often quite foreign. All too often, for example, clients report that they were not eating regularly before entering treatment. An inpatient rehabilitation setting allows staff to monitor and treat any dietary disorders that have been caused by the individual's addicted lifestyle. Supplementary vitamins and dietary supplements have often been found to be of value in such cases, and inpatient treatment allows the staff to monitor closely the client's recovery from the physical effects of his or her addiction.

Many clients will attend their first Alcoholics Anonymous or Narcotics Anonymous meeting while in an inpatient setting. In some cases, the client later admits that he or she would never have attended such a meeting if he or she had not been required to do so by treatment staff. Adelman and Weiss (1989) concluded that participation in Alcoholics Anonymous was an essential component of an effective inpatient treatment program.

Another advantage of inpatient treatment is that it can provide *around-the-clock support during the earliest stages of abstinence*. It is not unusual to find a client sitting up at 2 o'clock in the morning, talking about personal problems with the staff member on duty. Nor is it uncommon to find a client still up at 3 o'clock in the morning, struggling through the earliest stages of withdrawal. When such a client is asked what he or she would do if he or she were not in treatment, the most common answer is "I would go out and score some drugs!" But because the client is in inpatient treatment, the staff on duty can help him or her. This support might be in the form of a sympathetic ear when the client needs somebody to talk to or the administration of previously prescribed medications to help the client through the discomfort of withdrawal.

It has long been known that outpatient treatment can become a "revolving door" (Nace, 1987, p. 130). Inpatient treatment programs offer an alternative to the ineffective treatment–relapse–treatment cycles that can occur with outpatient placement.

Disadvantages of Inpatient Treatment Programs

Residential/inpatient treatment is quite disruptive to the individual's social, vocational, and family life (Morey, 1996). The individual is forced to leave her or his normal environment to participate in the rehabilitation program. The economic cost of inpatient treatment is also significantly higher than that of outpatient rehabilitation programs. Inpatient treatment programs tend to address severe and chronic substance use problems and may not be suitable for individuals with less intense chemical abuse (Larimer & Kilmer, 2000). Finally, the treatment center setting can be quite isolated, preventing easy contact with the client's friends and family. All of these factors are disadvantages of the inpatient rehabilitation program.

Inpatient or Outpatient Treatment?

Whether to utilize inpatient or outpatient treatment for a client is one of the most important decisions that treatment professionals make (Washton, Stone, & Hendrickson, 1988). Fortunately, in the last decade several organizations have published referral guidelines to assist in referring the substance abuser to the proper rehabilitation program. For example, the Group for the Advancement of Psychiatry (1990) identified several factors that can be used to determine whether a client would benefit more from an inpatient, or an outpatient, treatment program:

1. Whether the client's condition was associated with significant *medical* or *psychiatric* conditions or complications.
2. The *severity of actual or anticipated withdrawal* from the drug/(s) being used.
3. Whether *multiple failed attempts at outpatient treatment* have occurred.
4. The strength of the client's *social support systems.*
5. The *severity of the client's addiction* and the *possibility of polysubstance* abuse.

Another organization that has produced a list of placement criteria is the American Society of Addiction Medicine (ASAM). In it, the client's strengths and needs in each of six areas, or dimensions, are assessed. Depending on the client's requirements in each area, she or he is then be placed in one of four levels of care. The ASAM placement criteria can be thought of as forming a 4 × 6 grid on which each individual's needs are plotted (see Table 29.1). Patient placement criteria such as those suggested by ASAM help to guide the rehabilitation professional through an otherwise difficult

decision-making process. Both outpatient and inpatient treatment programs offer unique advantages and disadvantages. It is up to the assessor to determine the best "match" between the patient's needs and the available treatment options.

For example, in terms of total cost, outpatient treatment programs are usually less expensive than inpatient programs. Outpatient rehabilitation programs are also best suited to those clients who have not had an extensive prior treatment history (Nace, 1987). The individual's motivation for treatment and past treatment history offer hints as to whether inpatient or outpatient programs would be most effective in his or her recovery. Further, as noted in the ASAM criteria, whether the client needs inpatient detoxification from chemicals should be considered.

It is sad but true that financial considerations often affect which treatment options are available for the individual. The person whose insurance will pay only for inpatient chemical dependency treatment, for example, is subject to such financial restrictions. Availability of funding, then, is one factor that influences the decision whether to seek inpatient or outpatient treatment for substance abuse. Finally, the individual's psychiatric status and the availability of social support should be evaluated when considering outpatient treatment (Nace, 1987; Group for the Advancement of Psychiatry, 1990). Obviously, a deeply depressed individual who is recovering from an extended period of cocaine use might benefit more from the greater support offered by an inpatient treatment program, at least during the initial recovery period when the depression is most severe.

Turbo (1989) identified several criteria that suggest that an inpatient treatment program may be better for the client than the outpatient setting. These criteria included (1) repeated failure to maintain sobriety in outpatient treatment, (2) assessment of the client as acutely suicidal, (3) a seriously disturbed home environment, (4) serious medical problems, and (5) serious psychiatric problems. Allen and Phillips (1993) suggested that the client's legal status should also be considered in making the decision whether to refer her or him to inpatient or outpatient treatment. Those individuals who have been arrested for drug possession or for driving while under the influence of chemicals might do better in an outpatient treatment program, according to the

TABLE 29.1   The ASAM Placement Criteria*

Level of Care / Dimension	Level I	Level II	Level III	Level IV
	Outpatient treatment	Intensive outpatient treatment/partial hospitalization program	Medically monitored inpatient treatment (residential treatment)	Medically managed inpatient treatment (traditional medical treatment)
Acute intoxication/ withdrawal potential**	None	Minimal	Severe risk, but does not require hospitalization	Severe risk that requires hospitalization
Biomedical conditions or complications**	None/stable	Minimal: can be managed in outpatient setting	Serious: requires medical monitoring	Severe: requires inpatient hospitalization
Emotional/behavioral conditions or complications	None/stable	Mild: but can be managed in outpatient setting	Serious: requires patient to be monitored 24 hours/day	Severe: requires inpatient psychiatric care
Treatment acceptance or resistance	Cooperative: needs guidance and monitoring	Some resistance: intensive treatment needed	Resistance is severe: requires intensive treatment	N/A
Relapse potential	Minimal risk of relapse: needs monitoring and guidance only	High risk of relapse without close monitoring and support by staff	Patient is unable to control use without being in inpatient setting	N/A
Recovery environment	Patient has skills and support to abstain on own	Patient lacks environmental support but has skills to cope, given some structure	Environment is dangerous to patient, and she or he must be removed from it	N/A

*This table is designed to illustrate the ASAM placement criteria and should not be utilized as a guide to patient placement.
**As determined by a licensed physician.

authors. Patients who had achieved periods of sobriety but then relapsed might be treated briefly on an inpatient basis. But after a brief "stabilization" stay in the hospital, these patients might be switched to an outpatient treatment program, according to Allen and Phillips.

The final decision whether to suggest an inpatient or an outpatient treatment program ultimately comes down to this issue: Given the client's resources and needs, what is the *least restrictive treatment alternative?* (American Psychiatric Association, 1995). The treatment referral criteria advanced by ASAM (Morey, 1996) are useful guides to the selection of the least restrictive alternative that will meet the client's needs. Although there are those who argue that the inpatient treatment program is dehumanizing, one must recall that the dysfunction caused by drug addiction often requires drastic forms of intervention.

Partial-Hospitalization Options

In recent years, several new treatment formats have been explored that combine elements of inpatient and outpatient rehabilitation programs. In terms of effectiveness, partial-hospitalization programs offer success rates that are equal to, or even superior to, inpatient treatment, yet they are only one-third to one-half as expensive (Gastfriend & McLellan, 1997). Each of these rehabilitation formats offers advantages and disadvantages, yet each should be considered as a viable treatment option for clients who present themselves for treatment.

Depending on the client's needs, some of the new treatment formats might prove to be quite beneficial.

Two-by-four programs. One proposed solution to the dilemma of whether to utilize inpatient or outpatient treatment is the so-called two-by-four program (originally 2 weeks of inpatient care followed by 4 weeks of outpatient treatment). This program format borrows from both inpatient and outpatient treatment programs to establish a biphasic rehabilitation system that seems to have some promise. The patient is first hospitalized for a short period of time—usually 2 weeks—in order to achieve total detoxification from chemicals. Depending on the individual's needs, the initial period of hospitalization might be somewhat shorter or longer than this. However, the goal is to help the client reach, as soon as possible, the point where she or he can participate in outpatient treatment. If, as occasionally happens, the client is unable to function successfully in the less restrictive outpatient rehabilitation program, he or she may be returned to the inpatient treatment format. Later, when additional progress has been made, the client may again return to an outpatient setting to complete his or her treatment program.

Turbo (1989) discussed an interesting variation on the two-by-four program developed for the Schick Shadel chain of hospitals, which are located in California, Texas, and Washington. These programs admit the individual for 10 days of inpatient treatment, followed by 2 additional inpatient "reinforcement" days later. The first "reinforcement" day of hospitalization occurs 1 month after discharge, and another 2 days of inpatient treatment are scheduled for 2 months following the initial admission. One disadvantage of inpatient treatment is that admission to such a level of care, even if only for short periods of time, appeared to result in "a lower probability of complying with outpatient aftercare" (Berg & Dubin, 1990, p. 1177) by the client. The authors found a 60% dropout rate for those who were initially hospitalized for a brief period of time and then were referred to an intensive outpatient treatment program.

Day hospitalization. The day hospitalization format is also known as *partial-day hospitalization.* Such programs typically provide 3–12 hours of treatment each day, for 3–7 days a week. After detoxification has been accomplished, the client is allowed to live at home. But he or she comes to the treatment center during scheduled treatment hours to participate in the rehabilitation program.

Partial-hospital programs for substance abuse rehabilitation offer a number of advantages, including the fact that such programs provide

> an intensive and structured treatment experience for patients with substance dependence who require more services than those generally available in traditional outpatient settings. (American Psychiatric Association, 1995, p. 23)

Further, day hospitalization programs tend to be less expensive than traditional inpatient treatment programs, the cost of day treatment being approximately half that of inpatient treatment (French, 1995). Such programs are designed to provide for a greater intensity of therapeutic intervention than is available through traditional outpatient treatment, while still avoiding the need for inpatient treatment where possible (Guydish, Werdeger, Sorensen, Clark, & Acampora, 1998).

It is essential, for day hospitalization, that the client have a supportive, stable, family. Obviously, if the client's spouse (or other family member) also has a chemical abuse problem, day hospitalization may not be a viable treatment option. If the client's spouse is severely codependent and continues to enable the client's continued chemical use, day hospitalization should not be the treatment of choice. But if the client has a stable home environment, day hospitalization offers a way to combine intensive programming with the opportunities for growth afforded by having the client spend part of the day at home. Such programs are especially valuable for clients who need to rebuild family relationships after a protracted period of chemical use, and they have been found to be as effective as inpatient treatment programs in the rehabilitation of clients (Guydish, Werdeger, Sorensen, Clark, & Acampora, 1998).

Halfway houses. The halfway house concept emerged in the 1950s in response to the need for an intermediate step between inpatient treatment and independent living (Miller & Hester, 1980). For those clients who lack a stable social support system, the period of time following treatment is often the most difficult. Even if strongly motivated to remain sober, the client must struggle against the urge to return to chemical use. The halfway house provides a transitional living facility for such clients during the period of time immediately following treatment.

Miller and Hester (1980) identified several characteristics that halfway houses share: (1) small patient population (usually less than 25 individuals), (2) a brief patient stay (less than a few months), (3) an emphasis on Alcoholics Anonymous or a similar Twelve-Step philosophy, (4) minimal rules, and (5) a small number of professional staff members. Many halfway houses hold in-house self-help group meetings, such as Alcoholics Anonymous; others require attendance at a specified number of community self-help group meetings a week. Each individual is expected to find work within a specified period of time (usually 2–3 weeks) or is assigned a job within the halfway house.

The degree of structure found in the traditional halfway house setting is somewhere between what is found in an inpatient treatment program setting and what is found in a traditional household. The idea is to provide the client with enough support so that she or he can function during the transitional period between treatment and self-sufficiency but, at the same time, give the client a chance to make choices about his or her life. Halfway house participation is usually limited to 3–6 months, after which the client is ready to assume his or her responsibilities again.

Although Miller and Hester (1980) concluded that there was little evidence that the halfway house was a useful adjunct to treatment, a number of subsequent studies have failed to support this conclusion. For example, Moos and Moos (1995) followed a sample of 1070 subjects who had been treated for substance abuse problems at one of 77 Veterans Administration medical centers across the United States and had been referred to community residential living facilities following completion of their primary treatment program. The authors found that those patients who had remained in the community residential living facility were significantly less likely to have been readmitted for substance use in the 4 years following their discharge from the community living unit. In other words, those patients who remained in the halfway house longer were less likely to require additional treatment for substance use problems.

These findings are consistent with those of Hitchcock, Stainback, & Roque (1995), who compared the relapse rate of 82 patients who elected not to enter a halfway house setting with that of 42 patients who were admitted to a halfway house. The authors found that patients discharged to a community setting (i.e., to return home, to live in an apartment, or to live with friends/relatives) were significantly more likely to drop out of treatment in the first 60 days following discharge from an inpatient substance abuse rehabilitation program. On the basis of their findings, the authors concluded that halfway house placement can significantly enhance patient retention in aftercare programs, thus improving the treatment outcome.

Two variables that seem to affect patient outcome after placement in a halfway house were length of stay in the halfway house and whether the individual continues to be involved in a rehabilitation program. Moos, Moos, and Andrassy (1999) examined the outcome of 2376 cases of patients who were admitted to halfway house settings after completing primary treatment in Veterans Administration hospital units. The authors found that those patients who remained in the halfway house longer abstained from alcohol/drug use longer. Further, the authors found that those individuals assigned to halfway houses that emphasized continued rehabilitation by expecting clients to participate in programming designed to help them abstain from chemicals did better than those who were referred to "undifferentiated" halfway houses, where there was no attempt at continued treatment.

The findings of the team of Moos, Moos, and Andrassy (1999) would seem to explain the often contradictory findings of earlier researchers who examined the question of whether halfway house placement is useful for substance-abusing clients. That is, it is necessary to examine the treatment philosophies of the different halfway houses considered in previous research studies to determine whether they tried to involve the resident in some form of continued treatment. Thus, although early research failed to support the halfway house concept, subsequent investigations have revealed that halfway houses do indeed seem to be an effective adjunct to the rehabilitation of chemical abusers.

Summary

There is significant evidence that, at least for some addicted individuals, outpatient treatment is an option that treatment professionals should consider. For those with the proper social support, and for whom there is no coexisting psychiatric illness or physical need for in-patient hospitalization, outpatient therapy for drug addiction may enable the individual to participate in treatment while still living at home. This avoids the need for a reorientation period following treatment.

Outpatient treatment also allows for long-term therapeutic support that is often not available from shorter-term inpatient programs. Within an outpatient drug addiction program, random urine toxicology screening may be used to check on medication compliance and to identify those individuals who have engaged in illicit drug use. Research evidence suggests that for many patients, outpatient drug addiction treatment is as effective as inpatient chemical dependency programs. There is a significant dropout rate from outpatient treatment programs, however, and much remains to be learned about how to make outpatient addiction treatment more effective.

Inpatient treatment is often viewed as a drastic step. Yet for a minority of those who are addicted to chemicals, it is a drastic step that is necessary if the client is ever to regain control of his or her life. The inpatient rehabilitation program offers many advantages over less restrictive treatment options, including a depth of support services unavailable in outpatient treatment. For many of those in the advanced stages of addiction, inpatient treatment offers the only realistic hope of recovery.

In recent years, questions have been raised concerning the need for inpatient treatment programs or halfway house placement following treatment. It has been suggested that inpatient treatment does not offer any advantage over outpatient treatment and that a longer stay is no more effective than short-term treatment. However, others have concluded that length of stay is inversely related to the probability of relapse following treatment.

CHAPTER THIRTY

The Process of Recovery

Introduction

It is not uncommon for substance abuse rehabilitation professionals to speak of the process of recovering from a drug/alcohol use problem as though it were a single step. Even the language of recovery seems to imply that achieving abstinence is a single step. In reality, it is a *process*, that, like life itself, has a definite beginning but no definite end point. In this chapter, we will discuss the process of recovering from an alcohol/drug abuse problem.

The Stages of Recovery

It is regrettable, but even after more than a decade of the "war on drugs," there is little empirical research into the effect of the individual's motivation, his or her readiness to change, or the drug(s) being abused, on the process of helping the person recover from a substance use problem (DeLeon, Melnick, & Kressel, 1997). Virtually nothing is known about the process of change, and theoretical models of the recovery process are only now starting to emerge.

Lichtenstein and Glasgow (1992) presented a model for smoking cessation in which recovery was viewed as a multistage process. Their model was based on the work of Prochaska, DiClemente, and Norcross (1992), who suggested that recovery from drug abuse/addiction involves definite stages (see Table 30.1). The first stage of recovery is *precontemplation* (DiClemente, Bellino, & Neavins, 1999; Prochaska, 1998; Prochaska,

DiClemente, & Norcross, 1992; Lichtenstein & Glasgow, 1992). About 40% of the substance-abusing population is thought to be in this stage (DiClemente & Prochaska, 1998), during which the individual is actively abusing chemicals and it has not occurred to him or her to try to abstain from chemical use/abuse. This phase can continue for years or even decades, and it is during this phase of chemical use that *denial* is most prominent. The therapeutic challenge for the therapist who is faced with a client in the precontemplation phase is (1) to teach him or her the effects of the drugs of abuse, (2) to teach him or her the danger(s) associated with continued substance use/abuse, (3) to help awaken within the client a desire for a different lifestyle, (4) to help the client identify barriers to his or her recovery, and, (5) to help the client identify ways to enhance his/her self-esteem.

It is only during the *contemplation* phase that the client begins to entertain the idea of possibly stopping the alcohol/drug use "one of these days." About 40% of the population of alcohol/drug abusers are in the contemplation phase (DiClemente & Prochaska, 1998). During this phase, the individual remains ambivalent about the possibility of change but has a growing sense of dissatisfaction with her or his alcohol/drug-centered lifestyle. An individual might remain in this phase for months or even years, while continuing to engage in chemical use. For the therapist who is confronted with a client at this stage in the recovery process, the challenge is to:(1) enhance his or her motivation to change, (2) awaken within the client a desire for spiritual growth

TABLE 30.1 The Stages of Recovery

Stage	Behaviors	Therapeutic Challenge	
Precontemplation	Individual is still actively using chemicals and has not thought of stopping the use of recreational chemicals. Individual might not see use of chemicals as a problem.	Teach client about effects of drugs of abuse and risks associated with their use. Help client build self-esteem. Help client identify barriers to recovery.	*Relapse pathway*
Contemplation	Individual is still actively using chemicals but has ambivalence about whether she or he wants to continue.	Teach client about effects of drugs of abuse and risks associated with their use. Enhance motivation for change.	
Determination	Individual has decided to quit in the immediate future.	Enhance motivation for change. Help individual make behavioral plans to support impending change.	
Action	Individual has started to try to avoid further chemical use.	Identify relapse triggers. Help individual recognize symptoms of impending relapse.	
Maintenance	Individual has made behavior change and continues to work to learn behaviors that will support recovery from chemical use.	Ensure stability of change. Help individual identify and deal with any personal issues that might be a threat to his or her recovery program.	

Source: Chart based on Prochaska, DiClemente, & Norcross (1992); Prochaska (1998); and Brown (1997).

(see Chapter 34), and (3) help the client understand how the chemical use has affected his or her life.

Brown (1997) calls this next stage the *determination* phase. During this phase of recovery the individual begins to make the cognitive changes necessary to support his or her attempt at abstinence. It is the therapist's goal to nurture the change process, offering encouragement, support, feedback, gentle confrontation, humor, and external validation for the client's struggles and successes.

Only 20% of alcohol/drug abusers can be found in the last three stages of this model (DiClimente & Prochaska, 1998). The actual initiation of abstinence is known as the *action phase* of the recovery process (DiClemente, Bellino, & Neavins, 1999; Brown, 1997; Prochaska, DiClemente, & Norcross, 1992). It is during this phase that the individual becomes actively engaged in the process of change and takes the first steps towards his or her recovery. The therapist's goals during this phase include (1) optimizing opportunities for growth, (2) being alert to signs that the client is unable to handle the perceived level of stress, (3) encouraging the client to begin the process of building a substance-free support system, (4) helping the client handle the emotional "roller coaster" that she or he may experience, (5) help-

ing the client to be realistic about his or her progress (clients often overestimate their growth and progress), and (6) serving as a parent substitute, mentor, cheering squad, and guide.

Relapse is a very real danger during this phase of recovery, but it does not automatically signal a treatment "failure" (Burge & Schneider, 1999). Rather, one must view change as a dynamic process that will proceed through the various stages of change in a *cyclical* rather than a linear manner (DiClimente & Prochaska, 1998). Consider the struggle many people face in giving up cigarette smoking. In the first 3–4 weeks following cessation of cigarette smoking, the individual is especially vulnerable to smoking "cues" such as being around other smokers (Bliss, Garvey, Heinold, & Hitchcock, 1989). At such times, the individual is less likely to cope effectively with the urge to smoke and is in danger of relapsing into active cigarette smoking. This is one reason why smokers who want to quit typically require an average of 3–4 attempts (Prochaska, DiClemente, & Norcross, 1992) to perhaps as many as 5–7 "serious attempts" (Brunton, Henningfield, & Solberg, 1994, p. 105; Sherman, 1994) before they are finally able to stop smoking cigarettes. Thus one task that the client faces during the *action* phase of recovery is learning about his or her relapse "triggers" (discussed in the next chapter).

Finally, after the individual has abstained from recreational chemical use for at least 6 months, he or she enters the *maintenance* phase (Brown, 1997; Prochaska, DiClemente, & Norcross, 1992). During the maintenance phase, the individual works on learning the behaviors that will enable him or her to continue to abstain from chemical use. During the maintenance phase, the individual might have to confront personal issues that contributed to, or at least supported, his or her use of chemicals. It is during this phase of recovery that the individual must learn the skills necessary to support an alcohol/drug-free lifestyle, including the need to find or keep a job and to enter into relationships that will support recovery. The *maintenance* phase has no specific end point but rather, if all goes well, continues through the client's life. During this period, the therapist works to ensure the stability of change, to help the client identify issues that might threaten her or his recovery, and to address these issues.

One of the more frustrating aspects of substance abuse rehabilitation is that it *does* proceed in a cyclical rather than a linear manner. Because of this, relapse *must* be acknowledged as a possible outcome for any given attempt at abstinence. The process of quitting smoking provides an excellent example, because periods of abstinence are intermixed with periods of relapse. Indeed, "the return to smoking . . . occurs so frequently that it should be thought of as a part of the process of quitting and not as a failure in quitting" (Lee & D'Alonzo, 1993 p. 39). This is not to say that rehabilitation professionals should *accept* continued chemical use/abuse as unavoidable. Rather, they should recognize recovery from alcohol/drug addiction as a difficult, ongoing process in which relapse to active chemical use is a constant danger.

One interesting observation was offered by Cunningham, Sobell, Gavin, Sobell, and Breslin (1997), who suggested that the individual with a substance use problem subjectively evaluates the benefits and costs of quitting far differently at each of the discrete stages in the recovery process. In other words, a person in the precontemplation stage of recovery would view the benefits and costs of stopping the use of alcohol far differently than would a person in the maintenance stage of recovery. Thus the substance abuse rehabilitation pro-

fessional working with a client who wishes to stop using chemicals must help him or her to reassess the potential benefits of abstinence, and the discomfort associated with achieving abstinence, at each stage of recovery.

Surprisingly, the model suggested by Prochaska, DiClemente, and Norcross (1992) seems to apply both to those who recover from substance use problems with professional intervention and those who recover without it. This makes sense, because as a general rule, less than 25% of those individuals who have a substance use problem at some time in their lives ever seek professional help (DiClimente & Prochaska, 1998).

Another model of recovery was suggested by Nowinski (1996). The first stage of recovery from a chemical use problem, according to Nowinski's model, is the stage of *acceptance* (Nowinski, 1996). But there appear to be several pathways to recovery for the individual: (1) She or he could decide that the anticipated benefits of further use of the chemical are not worth the consequences and cut back on or discontinue the use of that chemical on her or his own. (2) The individual might turn to a self-help group such as Alcoholics Anonymous to help him or her learn how to abstain from chemical use. (3) The individual might seek outpatient therapy to help him or her learn how to abstain from chemical use. (4) The individual might seek inpatient treatment to help him or her learn how to abstain from further chemical use.

During this stage, the individual struggles to understand why will power alone is not sufficient to guarantee abstinence/recovery. It is only after the individual has reached the second stage, that of *surrender*, that she or he becomes willing to make the changes in lifestyle necessary to support recovery, according to Nowinski (1996). As we will see later in this chapter, the goal of the substance abuse rehabilitation professional is to facilitate the individual's movement through the different stages of recovery.

Reactions against stage models of recovery. It is often surprising to the student of substance abuse rehabilitation to learn that stage models of change are not universally accepted. However, few theoretical models of any kind are accepted without challenge, modification, or even extensive revision. In psychology, stage models tend to pass through several, well, stages, starting with the uncritical acceptance that follows the introduction of a new theoretical model (Davidson,

1998). After a period of time, the model is subjected to guarded and sympathetic commentary; soon, as exceptions to its predictions emerge, cautious criticism is offered suggesting that the model may not be totally accurate. This tide of criticism rises until the theoretical model is awash in a sea of downright hostility, and then it is relegated to the archives as being good only for illustrative purposes because not every person goes through every stage in the predicted order (Davidson, 1998).

In terms of recovery from substance abuse problems, it is not clear what percentage of clients do so by progressing in an orderly manner from one stage to the next (Davidson, 1998). Further, variation between individuals might result in one person progressing rapidly from one stage to the next, while another remains in the same stage for 2 years or more (Davidson, 1998). Davidson suggested that stage models of recovery such as those discussed in this text are "at best descriptive rather than explanatory" (p. 32). Thus such stage models illustrate a general process and are not an outline of specific stages that each individual must pass through.

Then what works in predicting substance abuse and recovery? There are a number of psychosocial, medical, and legal forces that can contribute to the individual's recovery from problematic alcohol/drug use. Humphreys, Moos, and Finney (1995) identified a number of these factors

- *Interpersonal relationships.* Those individuals who drink more have fewer interpersonal relationships to draw upon as sources of support. Those individuals who drink less seem to have stronger interpersonal support systems.
- *Cognitive reappraisals.* Many former drinkers describe reaching a point where they realized that their alcohol use was causing physical and emotional damage as being critical to their recovery.
- *Demographic variables.* There is a tendency for those who drink more to come from lower socioeconomic groups.
- *Severity of drinking problems.* Alcohol-related problems such as blackouts, job problems, and legal problems may serve as warning signs to some people that their drinking has started to reach problematic levels.

- *Health problems.* Health problems may serve as a warning to the individual that his or her alcohol use has started to reach problematic levels.
- *Involvement in AA and/or religious groups.* These may help the individual begin to realize that his or her drinking has started to cause problems.
- *Individual expectations and self-evaluation.* These serve to shape the individual's beliefs about his or her "self" and his or her behavior.

Although Humphreys, Moos, and Finney (1995) wrote primarily about alcohol, their comments apply to other drugs as well.

Humphreys, Moos, and Finney (1995) followed a sample of 135 individuals classified as "problem drinkers" who either went through an alcohol detoxification program or contacted an alcoholism information and referral center, to determine what steps these individuals went through in their recovery. Although their subjects did not enter formal treatment for their alcohol use problems, the authors discovered that there were two distinct "pathways" away from problem drinking. Further, the authors found that their subjects fell into 3 subgroups at the end of a 3-year period. The first subgroup was made up of individuals who reported that they had achieved stable abstinence and who were apparently able to abstain from further alcohol use during the 3-year follow-up period. The second subgroup was composed of those subjects who had achieved a moderate drinking pattern, consuming no more than five beers or mixed drinks within any given 24-hour time span during the 3-year follow-up period. The final group was composed of those who continued to use alcohol in a problematic manner.

Humphreys, Moos, and Finney (1995) then examined the histories of the individuals in these three groups to determine what factors seemed relevant to the observed outcome. The authors found that those problem drinkers who became *controlled drinkers* consumed less alcohol at the start of the study and tended to be members of higher socioeconomic groups. As a group, they also viewed their drinking as being less of a problem than did other drinkers, had higher self-esteem, and were more confident that they could resist the temptation to return to abusive drinking. Further, the authors found that those individuals who adopted an *alcohol-free lifestyle* tended to be from lower socioeconomic groups.

TABLE 30.2 Variables That Affect Rehabilitation

Variable	*Reason*
Age	Older clients are more likely to have a successful treatment outcome. Research suggests that clients younger than 30 are more likely to become readdicted to narcotics following treatment, for example.
Employment	Clients with a stable employment history seem to do better in treatment than those with a history of employment problems.
Motivation	Clients who acknowledge that their substance use is causing them problems, and who seek help on their own, seem to be more likely to benefit from treatment.
Consequences or sanctions brought on by substance use/abuse	Clients who understand that continued substance use will result in sanctions of some kind (health problems, loss of employment, legal problems) seem to do better in treatment and afterwards.
Physical/social environment	Clients who make a break with past associates and avoid going to places where they used to use alcohol/drugs (bars, homes of friends who use drugs, etc.) are less likely to resume using chemicals.
Legal status or peer criminal activity	Clients with fewer arrests have higher success rate than clients with a long legal history. Clients who restrict or avoid contact with friends who are still using alcohol/drugs have higher success rates.
Social support	If clients' interpersonal support systems are strained, they are more likely to relapse. For example, if there is a lot of family conflict, the family will be unable to provide much support for recovering individual.
History of drug use	Clients who use a greater variety of chemicals, who use chemicals more often, who began to use at a younger age, and who have been addicted for longer periods of time seem to relapse more often. Length of previous sobriety also seems to predict level of success; clients with long periods of sobriety in their past are more likely to benefit from treatment.
Past treatment history	Clients who are "treatment wise" as a result of having been enrolled in many treatment programs in the past are more likely to return to the use of chemicals than are those individuals who haven't been in treatment before.
Concurrent psychiatric problems	Clients with concurrent psychiatric diagnosis are more likely to return to the use of chemicals. (Dual-diagnosis clients are discussed in Chapter 22.)
Anger	Clients with a great deal of anger (a history of fighting, etc.) are more likely to have trouble handling stress—and thus more likely to use chemicals to help them deal with their frustration. They are less likely to be able to abstain, without help learning how to deal with their anger/frustration.
History of past victimization in interpersonal relationships	Clients who have been physically, sexually, and/or emotionally abused in past have trouble dealing with the intense feelings of anger/shame that surface during treatment and are a high risk for return to chemical use.
Chronic illness	Clients who have concurrent chronic illness (chronic back pain, cancer, arthritis, asthma, HIV infection, etc.) are at high risk for return to chemical use as a way of dealing with the pain of their disease and/or the emotional frustration caused by their disorder.

Source: Chart based on Alemi, Stephens, Llorens, & Orris (1995).

These individuals tended to suffer a greater number of lost jobs, and economic problems, related to their drinking. As a group, the alcohol-free subjects were less sure of their ability to control their drinking, and they tended to turn to social support groups, such as church and/or AA, in their quest for recovery.

Overall, the model that is emerging from clinical experience and research is that recovery from an alcohol/drug use problem is a dynamic process in which people proceed through a series of specific stages before they can make meaningful change(s) in their chemical use patterns. Some of the variables that affect whether rehabilitation is successful are reviewed in Table 30.2.

Should abstinence be the goal of treatment? One issue that substance abuse rehabilitation professionals fiercely debate is whether the goal of treatment should be to help the individual learn to *control* his or her chemical use or to *abstain* from all recreational alcohol/drug use. Although most treatment programs reflect the belief that abstinence is the only viable goal of rehabilitation, the truth is that following treatment, the majority of those with alcohol use disorders continue to use alcohol at least occasionally (Peele, Brodsky, & Arnold, 1991; Peele, 1985). In his follow-up studies of identified alcohol-dependent individuals, George Vaillant (1996, 1983) found that over the course of their alcohol use, they tended to alternate between periods of more, and periods of less, problematic drinking.

This raises an interesting question, in that treatment centers advocate that the individual abstain from *all* chemical use, an outcome that is achieved by only a very small minority of those who are "treated" for alcohol/drug use problems. For example, in the case of marijuana addiction, total abstinence from *all* psychoactive drugs is considered essential if treatment is to be effective (Bloodworth, 1987). We still have a great deal to learn about the natural history of alcohol/drug misuse and its treatment.

Specific Points to Address with Common Drugs of Abuse

Although the process of recovering from any substance use problem would tend to reflect the steps identified by Prochaska, DiClemente, and Norcross, (1992), there are specific issues that must be considered when working with individuals who have been abusing, or ad-

dicted to, the various chemicals of abuse. In this section, we will address some of the specific issues associated with abstinence from different drugs of abuse.

Opiate Addiction: Is Treatment Worthwhile?

"Once an opiate addict, always an addict" seems to be the belief of the average lay person, who is quite pessimistic about treatment for narcotic addiction. Indeed, there *does* seem to be some basis for this pessimism: Research has found that 90% of opiate-dependent individuals who successfully withdraw from narcotics will return to chemical use within 6 months (Schuckit, 1995a).

Another gloomy view of the evolution of narcotics addiction was provided by Hser, Anglin, and Powers (1993). In 1986 the authors found that, 24 years after being identified as opiate addicts by the criminal justice system, only 22% of the original sample of 581 narcotics addicts were opiate-free. Some 7% of the original sample was involved in a methadone maintenance program, and 10% reported engaging in only occasional narcotics use. Almost 28% of the original sample had died, the main causes of death being homicide, suicide, and accidents, in that order.

Surprisingly, a greater percentage of these opiate-dependent individuals had died than had achieved lasting abstinence (Hser, Anglin, & Powers, 1993). Furthermore, the authors found that if the opiate-addicted persons in their sample had not stopped using chemicals by their late 30s, they were unlikely to do so. This is indeed a rather grim view of the course of opiate addiction. However, there are also some studies that have concluded that more than one-third of all opiate-dependent persons will ultimately be able to stop using drugs. For those individuals who survive their addiction to opiates and establish a recovery program, abstinence from opiate use is finally achieved between 6 (Smith, 1994) and 9 (Jenike, 1991; Jaffe, 1989) years after their addiction to opiates first developed.

CNS Stimulant Abuse: Withdrawal and Recovery Issues

Although a great deal is known about the manifestations of CNS stimulant abuse/addiction, very little is known about the natural history of dependence on these agents (Jaffe, 1990). Much remains to be discovered about the abuse of and addiction to cocaine, the amphetamines, and similar drugs. For example, although cocaine has a reputation of being exceptionally addictive, not everybody who abuses cocaine becomes addicted. The National Institute on Drug Abuse (quoted in Kotulak, 1992) suggested that only about 10% of those who use cocaine actually go on to become heavy users. Restak (1994) gave a higher estimate, maintaining that 25–33% of those who use cocaine become addicted.

Unfortunately, there is virtually no research into the factors that contribute to the development of addiction to CNS stimulants. In contrast to the research into the genetics of alcoholism, "research on genetic factors in stimulant abuse has not been pursued" (Gawin & Ellinwood, 1988, p. 1177). Thus we know nothing about genetic "markers" that might identify the person who is vulnerable to cocaine or amphetamine addiction. This is important because not all CNS stimulant users are, or will become, addicted. It is only through the process of *assessment* (discussed in Chapter 25) that the individual's need for treatment for a cocaine use problem, and the appropriate level of care for that person, is determined. Fortunately, people whose abuse problems involve only CNS stimulants rarely require hospital-based detoxification (*The Harvard Medical School Mental Health Letter*, 1990). This is because physical withdrawal from the CNS stimulants is rarely life-threatening.

One major exception to this rule is the fact that CNS stimulant abuse/addiction can result in suicidal thinking. If the individual is suffering from a post-stimulant depression that has reached suicidal proportions, hospital-based observation and treatment may be necessary to protect the client from self-destructive impulses. The decision whether to hospitalize a CNS stimulant abuser should be made on a case-by-case basis by qualified physicians. The factors that must be considered in making this decision include the individual's current state of mind, his or her medical status, and whether he or she has adequate resources and social support to deal with the withdrawal process on an outpatient basis.

Although the physical withdrawal from CNS stimulants is achieved quite rapidly, researchers now believe that protracted cocaine abuse may result in an extended withdrawal syndrome (Satel, Price, Palumbo, McDougle, Krystal, Gawin, Charney, Heninger, & Kleber, 1991; Hazleton, 1984). Gawin and Ellinwood (1988) characterized the cocaine withdrawal syndrome as "comparable to the acute withdrawal of the alcohol hangover" (p. 1176). Although the cocaine withdrawal syndrome does not include the severe physical withdrawal distress such as that seen in opiate withdrawal, it may include paranoia, depression, fatigue, "craving" for cocaine, agitation, chills, insomnia, nausea, changes in sleep patterns, ravenous hunger, muscle tremors, headache, and vomiting (DiGregorio, 1990). According to the authors, these symptoms begin within 24–48 hours after the last dose of cocaine, and persist for 7–10 days. Amphetamine withdrawal would seem to involve similar symptoms.

Stages of recovery from CNS stimulant abuse/addiction. A triphasic model for the post-cocaine-binge recovery process has been proposed (Gawin, Khalsa, & Ellinwood, 1994; Gawin & Kleber, 1986). According to this model, in the early part of the first stage, which lasts from 1 to 4 days, the person experiences feelings of agitation, depression, and anorexia (loss of desire to eat), as well as a strong craving for cocaine. As the person progresses through the second half of the first phase, she or he loses the craving for cocaine but experiences insomnia and exhaustion, combined with a strong desire for sleep. The second half of the first phase lasts from the 4th until the 7th day of abstinence.

The second phase begins after the 7th day of abstinence. The person returns to a normal sleep pattern but gradually experiences stronger cravings for cocaine or stimulants and higher levels of anxiety. Conditioned cues exacerbate the individual's craving for stimulants, drawing the person back to chemical abuse. The person who withstands those environmental and intrapersonal cues moves into the "extinction" phase, where he or she gradually returns to a more normal level of functioning.

The extinction phase begins after 10 weeks of abstinence. If the person were to relapse, the cycle would repeat itself. But if she or he withstands the craving, there is a good chance of a lasting recovery. For example, Hall, Havassy, and Wasserman (1991) concluded that approximately 80% of those cocaine addicts who were able to abstain from cocaine use for 12 weeks after treatment were still drug-free after 6 months. However, this does not mean that the individual has fully recovered from CNS stimulant addiction. Cocaine and amphetamine addicts may suddenly experience craving for these drugs "months or years after [the craving's] last appearance" (Gawin & Ellinwood, 1988, p. 1176) and long after the last period of chemical use.

Satel, Price, Palumbo, McDougle, Krystal, Gawin, Charney, Heninger, and Kleber (1991) examined the cocaine withdrawal process and concluded that their data failed to support the model advanced by Gawin and Kleber (1986). For their sample, the cocaine withdrawal process was marked by mild withdrawal symptoms that declined over the first 3 weeks of inpatient treatment. However, the withdrawal symptoms that they noted were much milder than had been anticipated and failed to follow the triphasic model suggested by earlier research.

Although researchers have acknowledged that there appears to be a withdrawal syndrome following prolonged cocaine use, they have not reached agreement about its exact nature. A number of pharmacological agents are being investigated in the hope of finding a drug, or combination of drugs, that will control the craving that complicates the treatment of cocaine addiction for many of those who are recovering. These agents will be discussed in Chapter 32.

The treatment of stimulant addiction involves more than just helping the user discontinue drug use. For example, the individual has often forgotten what a drug-free life is like (Siegel, 1982). Further, prolonged stimulant abuse may have interfered with the user's dietary habits, resulting in vitamin deficiencies, especially of the B complex and C vitamins (Gold & Verebey, 1984). Because the stimulant effects of the amphetamines are so similar to those of cocaine, one would expect that the amphetamines would also lead to vitamin deficiencies in a pattern similar to that seen in chronic cocaine abuse. To test this hypothesis, the authors examined a number of cocaine abusers and found that 73% had at least one vitamin deficiency. Thus Gold and Verebey (1984) recommended that vitamin replacement therapy be a routine part of the treatment of cocaine abusers.

Total abstinence from recreational chemicals is thought to be essential if the individual wants to avoid further problems with CNS stimulant use. For example, Hall, Havassy, and Wasserman (1991) found that those cocaine-dependent people who made a commitment to full abstinence following treatment were more likely to avoid problems with cocaine use than were addicts who did not aspire to total abstinence. Follow-up treatment should include behavior modification and psycho-

therapy to help clients learn the skills they will need to continue to abstain from chemicals (Gold & Verebey, 1984). Social support and self-help group support, in the form of Alcoholics Anonymous (AA), Narcotics Anonymous (NA), or Cocaine Anonymous (CA), is often of great value. As with the other forms of drug addiction, the recovering individual is at risk for cross-addiction to other chemicals and must avoid other recreational drug use for the rest of his or her life.

Issues Surrounding Recovery from Marijuana Abuse

Although marijuana use has been popular in this country since the Prohibition era, and certainly after the "hippie" generation "discovered" marijuana in the 1960s, virtually nothing is known about the treatment of marijuana abuse/dependency (*The Addiction Letter*, 1995; Stevens, Roffman, & Simpson, 1994). It is known that the short-term, acute reaction to marijuana does not require any special intervention (Brophy, 1993). Thus marijuana-induced feelings of anxiety or panic usually respond to "firm reassurance in a nonthreatening environment" (Mirin, Weiss, & Greenfield, 1991, p. 304). However, the individual should be watched to ensure that no harm comes either to the marijuana user or to others.

There are a number of problems associated with working with marijuana abusers, First, it is rare for a person to be abusing *only* marijuana, so treatment usually must focus on the abuse of a number of chemicals. Second, marijuana users seldom present themselves for treatment unless there is some form of coercion. This is because, in spite of their chemical use, marijuana abusers rarely view themselves as being addicted to a recreational chemical (*The Addiction Letter*, 1995).

Unfortunately, specific therapeutic methods for working with the chronic marijuana user have not been well developed (Mirin, Weiss, & Greenfield, 1991). It is known that marijuana users often turn to it as a way to cope with negative feelings, especially anger (*The Addiction Letter*, 1995). Thus rehabilitation professionals must help the client to identify specific problem areas in his or her life and then to find non-drug-related ways to cope with these "trigger" situations.

A treatment program that identifies the individual's reason(s) for continued drug use, and that helps the individual find alternatives to further drug use, is thought to be most effective. Auxiliary groups that focus on vocational rehabilitation and socialization skills are also valuable in treating the chronic marijuana user (Mirin, Weiss, & Greenfield, 1991). Jenike (1991) reported that treatment efforts should focus on understanding the abuser's disturbed psychosocial relationships. Bloodworth (1987) concluded that "family therapy is almost a necessity" (p. 183). Group therapy is vital in helping the marijuana user deal with peer pressure to use chemicals, and the value of self-help support groups such as AA and NA[1] "cannot be overemphasized" (Bloodworth, 1987, p. 183).

Issues Surrounding the Treatment of Nicotine Addiction

When one asks a cigarette smoker why he or she continues to smoke in spite of the dangers associated with this habit, the response is often "I can't help myself. I'm addicted." Indeed, it is believed that the addictive power of nicotine explains why 90–98% of those who attempt to quit smoking in any given year ultimately fail (Henningfield, 1995; Benowitz & Henningfield, 1994; Sherman, 1994).

Although health care workers have tried for many years, they have been largely unable to determine what factors contribute to a person's success in quitting smoking (Kenford, Fiore, Jorenby, Smith, Wetter, & Baker, 1994). Thus cigarette cessation programs are something of a hit-or-miss affair, in which neither the leaders nor the participants know what *really* works. Smoking cessation training programs usually help 70–80% of the participants to stop smoking on a short-term basis. Of those who attempt to stop smoking, however, two-thirds may stop for a very few days, but only 2–3% will be tobacco-free a year later (Henningfield, 1995). Hughes *et al.* (1991) found that 65% of their experimental sample relapsed within the first month of quitting, which suggests that the first month is especially difficult for the ex-smoker.

There appears to be a relationship between the frequency with which a given individual smokes and his or her success in giving up tobacco. Cohen *et al.* (1989) reviewed data from ten different research projects that involved a total of 5000 subjects who were attempting to stop smoking cigarettes.

[1]Discussed in detail in Chapter 34.

The authors found that light smokers, who were defined as those who smoked fewer than 20 cigarettes each day, were significantly more likely than heavy smokers to be able to stop smoking on their own. Cohen *et al.* (1989) also found that the number of unsuccessful previous attempts was unrelated to whether the smoker would be able to quit this time. They concluded that "most people who fail a single attempt [to quit smoking] will try again and again and eventually quit" (p. 1361).

Another factor that seems to be associated with the difficulty a smoker experiences when he or she attempts to quit is his or her *expectancies* for the nicotine withdrawal process. Tate, Stanton, Green, Schmitz, Le, and Marshall (1994) formed four subgroups from their research sample of 62 cigarette smokers. Those former smokers who were led to believe that they would not experience any significant distress during the nicotine withdrawal process reported significantly fewer physical or emotional complaints than the other research groups. There is other evidence that the individual's expectations for recovery influence his or her experience of abstinence. Kviz, Clark, Crittenden, Warnecke, and Freels (1995) found that for smokers over the age of 50, the perceived degree of difficulty in quitting was negatively associated with the individual's actual attempts to quit smoking. In other words, the harder the individual expected the task of quitting to be, the less likely she or he was to do so. Thus the individual's expectations for the nicotine withdrawal were found to have a significant effect on whether the individual actually did quit smoking cigarettes.

Thus the smoker who wishes to quit should be warned that the struggle against cigarette smoking is a lifelong one and, that his or her "mindset" will play a major role in whether she or he is successful. Further, former smokers should realize that for the rest of their lives, they will be vulnerable to relapsing to cigarette smoking.

Although there has been a great deal of emphasis on formal cigarette cessation treatment programs, perhaps as many as 90% (Brunton, Henningfield, & Solberg, 1994; Fiore, Novotny, Pierce, Giovino, Hatziandreu, Newcomb, Surawicz, & Davis, 1990) to 95% (Hughes, 1992; Peele, 1989; Kozlowski *et al.*, 1989) of cigarette smokers who quit do so without participating in a formal treatment program. For those smokers who do quit, it would seem that their motivation to quit smoking is most "critical" (Jaffe, 1989, p. 682) to the success of their efforts. These conclusions raise serious questions about whether extensive treatment programs are necessary for tobacco dependency. But formal treatment programs may be of value to those who are heavy smokers or are at risk for tobacco-related illness.

Issues Surrounding the Treatment of Anabolic Steroid Abusers

The first step in the treatment of the steroid abuser is identification of those individuals who are indeed abusing anabolic steroids. The physician may, on the basis of clinical history, blood tests, and/or urine tests, be the first person to suspect that a patient is abusing steroids and may thus be in the best position to confront the user. At this early stage, the addictions counselor is not thought to have a significant role to play in the treatment of the anabolic steroid user.

Once the steroid abuser has been identified, close medical supervision of the patient is necessary to identify and treat potential complications of steroid abuse. The attending physician may want to consider a gradual detoxification program for the steroid abuser. Most medical complications of steroid abuse clear up after the individual stops using steroids (Hough & Kovan, 1990), However some of the damage caused by steroid abuse (such as heart tissue damage) may be permanent. It may be possible to correct some of the side effects of steroid use via surgical intervention (Hough & Kovan, 1990), but this is not always possible.

Following detoxification from anabolic steroids, staff members should work with the patient to determine why he or she started using steroids. Problems with self-concept should be identified, and therapy should be initiated to help the steroid user learn to accept himself or herself without leaning on an artificial underpinning such as chemicals. Proper nutritional counseling may be necessary to help the athlete learn how to enhance body strength without using potentially harmful substances such as anabolic steroids. Group and individual support programs should also be considered as possible treatment modalities, depending on the client's needs.

Summary

In this chapter, two different models of the recovery process were discussed. The most popular model was introduced by Prochaska, DiClemente, and Norcross (1992). This model suggests that clients who wish to make behavioral change(s) pass through stages: *pre-contemplation*, in which no specific change is being contemplated; *contemplation*, in which the individual is thinking about making some changes; *determination*, in which she or he actively considers the possibility of change; *action*, in which the client attempts to make the desired behavioral changes; and, if rehabilitation has been successful, *maintenance*, the phase in which the new behavior becomes entrenched. This chapter also discussed some specific points that should be addressed in treating clients who are abusing some of the more popular drugs of abuse.

CHAPTER THIRTY-ONE

Problems That Can Arise in Treating Chemical Dependency

Introduction

Research has consistently demonstrated that treatment is more effective than criminal justice sanctions as a way of dealing with the problem of drug abuse (Scheer, 1994b). But no matter which treatment approach the therapists utilizes, there are a number of potential problems that they might experience in working with the substance-abusing person. In this chapter, we will examine some of the more common, and more serious, problems that treatment professionals encounter in working with recovering addicts in different settings.

Limit Testing by Clients in Treatment

Clients in therapeutic relationships, including addicted clients in a treatment setting, often "test the limits," either consciously or unconsciously, to determine whether the professional will be consistent in his or her treatment of the client. This limit testing can take a number of different forms, from missing appointments to using chemicals while in treatment.

The chemical dependency professional should be aware that "consistency" also applies to enforcement of the rules of the program. For example, patients in a methadone maintenance program who were informed that if their urine toxicology tests detected evidence of illicit drug use four times in a year, they would be removed from the program did better than those who did not have this expectation (McCarthy & Borders, 1985).

The counselor and treatment "secrets." It is not uncommon for the client to ask for an individual conference with the staff member and then to confess to a rules infraction. Often, this admission of guilt is made to a student or intern at the agency, rather than to a regular staff member. The confession might be an admission of having used chemicals while in treatment or some other infraction of the rules. Then, for fear of being discharged from treatment, the client will ask that the staff member not bring this information to the group, to other staff members, or to the program director.

For the chemical dependency professional to honor such a request not to tell other staff members would be for that person to enter into a partnership with the addicted individual—a partnership that, because it was set up by the addicted person, will make the professional an "enabler." Not to report this violation might also make the professional vulnerable to later extortion by the client, who would be in a position to report the professional to his or her superiors for not passing on the information to staff as he or she should have done.

The proper response to this situation is *immediately* to document the material discussed, in writing, through proper channels. This might be a memo or an entry into the client's progress notes, as well as a discussion of the material revealed by the client with the professional's immediate supervisor. This is done without malice, both to ensure uniform enforcement of the rules for all clients, and to protect the professional's reputation.

Treatment Noncompliance

In no other sphere of medicine is the social stigma that surrounds substance use so apparent as in the arguments that because substance abuse rehabilitation programs suffer from high dropout and relapse rates, they are not effective. These assertions are not applied to the other specialties in medicine, where patient noncompliance is also a problem, but are directed exclusively at the field of addiction medicine. To illustrate this point, consider how a patient who is repeatedly hospitalized for diabetes-related problems might be termed a "brittle" diabetic by physicians, whereas the alcohol-dependent individual who is repeatedly hospitalized is called "a treatment failure." Both patients have a chronic, relapsing disorder, yet only in the field of substance abuse rehabilitation is rehospitalization referred to as a treatment failure.

Patient noncompliance is a problem for each specialty in medicine, not just substance abuse rehabilitation. For example, 14% of the patients who went to a physician, and who received a prescription, failed even to have it filled (Lacombe, Vicente, Pages, & Morselli, 1996). Even if the patient does have the prescription filled, up to 86% fail to take the medication as recommended (Pirisi & Sims, 1997). For example, only 40% of those patients being treated for depression take their antidepressant medication for a full year, which is the period of time recommended to limit the possibility of relapsing into a depressive state (Cramer & Rosenheck, 1998). Table 31.1 lists several types of medications conditions and shows, for each, the percentage of patients who do not follow treatment recommendations when such medications are prescribed.

Although treatment noncompliance is not limited to substance abuse rehabilitation programs, it *is* a common problem. For example, many patients request "detoxification" from alcohol/drugs, only to fail to complete the detoxification process initiated at their own request because of factors such as the severity of medical disease and the severity of drug use (Franken & Hendriks, 1999). Other studies have found that only 10–30% of those who are deemed to be "at risk" for an alcohol use disorder actually follow through with treatment recommendations (Cooney, Zweben, & Fleming, 1995).

People who are dependent on chemicals may openly admit their addiction not because they wish to abstain

TABLE 31.1 Approximate Rates of Treatment Noncompliance

Class of medications	Percentage of patients who fail to follow dosing instructions
Antiepileptics	30–50%
Antihypertensives	30–60
Blood-lipid-lowering agents	25–30
Antiarrhythmics	20
Antidepressants	30–40
Immunosuppressive agents	18
Antidiabetics	30–50
Anticoagulants	30
Antiasthmatics	20–60

Sources: Chart based on P. S. Lacombe, J. A. G. Bicente, J. C. Pages, & P. L. Morselli (1996). "Causes and Problems of Nonresponse or Poor Response to Drugs." *Drugs, 51,* 552–570; and A. T. McLellan, D. C. Lewis, C. P. O'Brien, & H. D. Kleber (2000). "Drug Dependence, a Chronic Medical Illness." *Journal of the American Medical Association, 284,* 1689–1695.

from chemicals but because making this admission seems to give them an excuse to *continue* to use chemicals. The word "addicted" comes to mean "hopelessly addicted," and thus they give themselves permission continue to use chemicals. This bizarre rationalization overlooks the fact that addiction is a treatable disease. The first part of the "treatment" is often spent convincing the person that he or she is indeed addicted, and needs help for the drug dependency that has come to dominate his or her life. This awareness and the commitment to enter into treatment are often achieved through the intervention process.

Unfortunately, substance abuse rehabilitation programs suffer significant levels of patient attrition. It has been found that up to 50% of those admitted to substance abuse rehabilitation programs drop out of treatment before the 90th day and that 66% drop out by the end of 6 months (McCusker, Stoddard, Frost, & Zorn, 1996). Thus, as is true for health care professionals in virtually every other field of medicine, noncompliance with treatment recommendations is a very real problem for substance abuse rehabilitation professionals.

Rabinowitz and Marjefsky (1998) examined the issue of premature termination from treatment at a treatment facility in Israel, through a retrospective analysis of the records of 764 male patients. The authors found that social isolation was a major predictor of patient dropout. Behaviors such as solitary drinking, not being married, having no children, and being unemployed were associated with a greater chance of treatment failure. These indicators would seem to serve as possible warning signals of male patients who are "at risk" for premature termination from treatment, possibly alerting staff as to the need for special efforts to help these individuals remain in treatment.

Relapse and Relapse Prevention

One of the more destructive forms of treatment noncompliance is for the individual to return to the active use of chemicals. Indeed, "the most common treatment outcome for alcoholics and addicts is relapse" (Dimeff & Marlatt, 1995, p. 176). Thus entry into treatment should not be seen as a guarantee that the person will actually stop using chemicals. Indeed, even patients who complete treatment are likely to return to the use of drugs/alcohol at least briefly, before finally undergoing an effective abstinence program.

In the last decades of the 20th century, it was discovered that total abstinence following treatment was the exception rather than the norm. Most graduates of treatment programs, it was found, still use chemicals occasionally "with alternating periods of abstinence and relapse" (DeJong, 1994, p. 682). Within this context, the first 90 days following discharge from treatment is a period of special vulnerability for the individual's potential relapse to drug use (Dimeff & Marlatt, 1995; DeJong, 1994). However, this does not mean that rehabilitation is a waste of effort. Rather, the grim frequency of relapse following efforts at treatment reinforces the basic message that the disease of addiction is one that can be *arrested* but can never be *cured*.

To combat this tendency for the former patient to return to the use of chemicals, treatment professionals began to place emphasis on *relapse prevention* skills that the patient might develop while in treatment and use after completing the rehabilitation program. It has been suggested that there are four elements common to those who relapse (Chiauzzi, 1990; 1991). First, those individuals who relapsed often demonstrated *personality traits* that interfered with continued sobriety. Such relapse-prone personality traits include a tendency toward compulsive behaviors, because such individuals do not adjust well to even minor changes in routine. Another personality trait that interfered with recovery was a tendency toward dependency; such individuals had trouble asserting their wish to maintain in a recovery program (Chiauzzi, 1990, 1991). Passive-aggressive personality traits also place the individual at risk for relapse, because a tendency to blame others for one's behavior is associated with this constellation of traits. The narcissistic traits often found in addicted persons prevent many from admitting to their need for help during a weak moment, and antisocial personality traits underscore a tendency toward impulsiveness and a desire not to follow the road taken by others (Chiauzzi, 1990, 1991).

A second factor is a tendency for the individual to *substitute addictions* for the chemicals that she or he once abused (Chiauzzi, 1990, 1991). Examples of such substitute addictions include compulsive work, relationships, or eating behaviors and switching from one drug of abuse to another. Third, the individual's *narrow view of recovery* often predicts relapse (Chiauzzi (1990, 1991). An example of this process might be found in the individual who equates abstinence with "recovery." Such a view of recovery places the individual at risk for relapse, because he or she is not working to change the personality structure, or work on the interpersonal problems, that contributed to the development of the addiction in the first place. Such individuals do not develop the self-awareness necessary to recognize that they are drifting toward relapse.

Finally, Chiauzzi (1990, 1991) found that what he termed *warning signals* of impending relapse were often overlooked by the individual. Chiauzzi's (1990, 1991) concept of warning signals is very similar to the concept of the mini-decisions first reported by Cummings, Gordon, and Marlatt (1980). A mini-decision can be either conscious or unconscious (Chiauzzi, 1991), but in either case, it does *not* involve a decision to use chemicals. Rather, the road to the ultimate relapse is paved with lesser decisions that will, when added together, "set the stage for a relapse to occur" (Cummings, Gordon, and Marlatt (1980, p. 297). For example, the recovering person might decide to continue a friendship with another individual who remains actively addicted, or the recovering alcoholic might decide to go over to the local bar to socialize or "just to play pool." A common mini-decision on the part of the recovering individual is the decision to attend support-group meetings less frequently. Often, there is what appears at the time to be a valid reason for the mini-decisions, and it is only after the individual relapses that their impact on his or her recovery program becomes apparent. One element of a mini-decision is that the recovering individual rarely sees in it any potential danger of a relapse. Indeed, recovering individuals often seem surprised at a subsequent relapse and may view it is a random event (Chiauzzi, 1991). However, neutral observers are often able to identify the step-by-step progression by which these seemingly innocent individual mini-decisions ultimately increased the odds that the recovering individual would relapse (Cummings, Gordon, & Marlatt, 1980).

Another potential threat to the individual's recovery program are *maladaptive thoughts* that may contribute to a return to active chemical use (Keller, 1996). The alcohol/drug-addicted individual may return to the old "using" environment "just to see if I could walk down the same street and not feel the urge to use anymore." Or the recovering individual may just "stop off to pay a friend some money that I owe him" and then find drugs all over the place, as though the drug-using behavior of this friend were a revelation. A third example of a maladaptive thought is the individual's conclusion that "I've been doing pretty good . . . one drink surely couldn't hurt me!"

When maladaptive thoughts put the individual "at risk" to use chemicals, the newly recovering individual is at a decision point and must either reaffirm his or her commitment to personal abstinence or start back on the path to the active use of chemicals. If the individual has adequate coping skills to support continued abstinence, he or she will reaffirm the commitment to recovery. However, individuals whose coping skills are inadequate are in danger of relapsing to active chemical use.

It is virtually guaranteed that every recovering person will encounter at least one "high-risk" situation where the possibility of drug use is high. Dimeff and Marlatt (1995) reported that fully 75% of all relapses involved the failure to deal successfully with a high-risk situation. Essentially, high-risk situations fall into two categories (Cummings, Gordon, & Marlatt, 1980). The first category consists of the acute period of drug withdrawal,

when the individual is likely to be motivated to avoid further withdrawal discomfort by ingesting chemicals.

The second group of high-risk situations includes the social, environmental, and emotional states that the individual perceives as stressful, for which she or he has used drugs as a coping mechanism in the past (Keller, 1996; Cummings, Gordon, & Marlatt, 1980). In this second group of high-risk situations, cognitive evaluations of the social, environmental, or emotional stimuli mediate whether the individual considers the possibility of drug use. Such cognitive evaluations may then be interpreted by the individual as an *urge* or *craving* to use a substance.

There are also a number of "stimulus factors" (Shiffman, 1992, p. 9) that can contribute to a relapse. Research evidence now suggests that conditioned learning takes place during the time the individual is using alcohol/drugs. When she or he is later exposed to sights, sounds, or emotions similar to those associated with the chemical use, the individual might again feel a "craving" for chemicals. For example, it has been found that recovering opiate-dependent individuals may suddenly experience craving for narcotics, even after being drug-free for months or years, if they return to the neighborhood where they once used chemicals (Galanter, 1993). The mechanism through which this takes place might be based in the unconscious, for

> most of a person's everyday life is determined not by . . . conscious intentions and deliberate choices but by mental processes that are put into motion by features of the environment and that operate outside of conscious awareness. (Bargh & Chartrand, 1999, p. 462)

To combat the influence of environmental triggers toward chemical use, Shiffman (1992) advocated the use of behavioral rehearsals that would help the client learn skills that would enable him or her to avoid relapse. A second area of emphasis is the identification of the client's feelings of demoralization and self-blame during the early phases of recovery, according to the author. Such "cognitive" intervention has been shown to be at least as effective as behavioral training for environmental triggers toward relapse.

One way to address this problem is to try to *anticipate* the high-risk situations that may arise for each individual

TABLE 31.2   Common Relapse Situations

Category of relapse	Description of situation that contributed to or caused relapse	Percentage of cases
Negative emotional states	Feelings of frustration, anger, anxiety, depression, or boredom	35%
Peer pressure	Pressure from either a single person (such as a close friend) or a group of people (co-workers, for example) to use chemicals	20
Interpersonal conflict	Conflict between patient and a friend, employer, employee, family member, or dating partner	16
"Craving" for drugs/alcohol	Person becoming preoccupied with use of alcohol and/or drugs, in spite of abstinence	9
Testing personal control	Person exposing self to "high risk" situation, in order to see whether he or she is able to resist urges to use chemicals	5
Negative physical states	Person experiencing a negative physical state such as illness, postsurgical distress, or injury	3

Source: Chart based on material provided by Dimeff and Marlatt (1995).

(Annis & Davis, 1991). To do this, it is necessary for the individual to engage in self-monitoring of internal states, supplemented by direct observation of the client by treatment center staff. The authors also advocated the use of such psychological tests as the Inventory of Drinking Situations (IDS-100).[1] The resulting test data yield a hierarchy of drinking situations, which staff use to help identify the client's strengths and resources and the environmental supports that she or he could call upon to deal with the potential relapse situation. The client then rehearses how she or he might deal with a high-risk situation. A reminder card may also be carried in the wallet or purse, so that the individual will have written instructions on the steps to take to avoid relapse. This process helps the client overcome the feelings of helplessness often experienced by clients who are attempting to stop using chemicals (Niaura, Rohsenow, Binkoff, Monti, Pedraza, & Abrams, 1988).

DeJong (1994) identified a number of "antecedents" of relapse: stress, negative emotional states, interpersonal conflict, social pressure, positive emotional states, use of other substances, and the presence of drug-related cues. Some of the more common triggers for relapse are summarized in Table 31.2.

Another factor that may contribute to relapse is for the patient to take a very short-term view of recovery.

Drawing on a 50-year longitudinal study of white males, Vaillant (1996) found that, in contrast to the high relapse rates in the first 5 years of abstinence, relatively few men who had been alcohol-free for 6 or more years returned to the use of this chemical. This study suggests that treatment staff must help recovering patients learn not to let down their guard before abstinence becomes a new "lifestyle"—a process that seems to take more than 5 years.

There is strong evidence that relapse prevention programs are effective (Irvin, Bowers, Dunn, & Wang, 1999). Such programs may very well combat the sense of demoralization, anger, and depression, that seem to characterize those individuals most prone to relapse, according to Miller and Harris (2000). Although relapse prevention programs are not 100% effective, they do seem to provide support for the individual in the earliest stages of recovery, when she or he is most vulnerable.

"Cravings" and "Urges"

Although the concepts of "urges" and "craving" are frequently encountered in the popular press, there has been little systematic research into the meaning of these terms (Anton, 1999; Merikle, 1999). Different researchers have used each term in widely disparate ways, resulting in confusion not only in the professional lit-

[1]See the Glossary.

erature, but also in the popular media and the general population.

For the purpose of this text, a *craving* is an intense, subjective emotional and physical experience that varies from one individual to another (Merikle, 1999). Symptoms of craving may include not only obsessive thoughts about obtaining the drug(s) of choice but also physical symptoms of arousal, such as sweating palms, rapid heartbeat, and salivation (Anton, 1999; Merikle; 1999). The individual may become fixated on his or her drug of choice and may feel compelled to obtain and use that chemical to satisfy an internal sensation of intense incompleteness that can be eased only through the use of that specific chemical. As part of the cognitive preoccupation with the chemical of choice, the individual might think about how he or she felt while under the influence of the substance and how nice it would be to feel that way again (Anton, 1999; Beck, Wright, Newman, & Liese, 1993).

Another component of craving is the cognitive process by which the individual reframes his or her chemical use in positive terms. The individual comes to view the drug-induced experience of euphoria as desirable, and the return to chemical use is interpreted as a positive step in the process of recreating this sense of chemical-induced euphoria. Vernon Johnson (1980) termed this process *euphoric recall*.

Urges are viewed by Merikle (1999) as being less intense than craving and as more of a cognitive experience. In contrast to this definition, Beck, Wright, Newman, and Liese (1993) suggested that urges were behavioral impulses to find and use one's drug of choice. As behavioral scientists come to understand better the forces that sustain human motivation, they are discovering that many of the triggers for decision making are based on unconscious perceptions and motivations that are only later rationalized by the conscious mind (Bargh & Chartrand, 1999). This insight opens up new avenues to investigating the sources of urges and craving for chemicals, and why people respond to these sensations the way they do.

Beck, Wright, Newman, and Liese (1993) identified four different situations that contributed to urges to use chemicals: The first was the individual's learned *response to the discomfort of withdrawal*. As we have seen, the use of many of the recreational chemicals can result in a characteristic pattern of withdrawal symptoms. To avoid this withdrawal syndrome, the individual will engage in additional substance use. For example, nicotine-dependent individuals will smoke a cigarette, and alcohol-dependent individuals will have another drink, when they experience the earliest symptoms of withdrawal.

Next, there was the individual's tendency to want to use chemicals when unhappy or uncomfortable (Beck, Wright, Newman, & Liese, 1993). These urges are triggered by some of the "antecedents" of relapse identified by DeJong (1994) (see the previous section). These antecedent situations then cause the individual to "crave" chemicals as a way of coping with the negative situation. Over time, the individual gives in to these cravings by beginning to make specific plans to use chemicals: the "urge" to use alcohol/drugs.

The third source of the urge to use drugs was external "cues," according to the authors. Such chemical use "cues" might include cleaning out one's apartment and finding a "stash" of alcohol or drugs, a chance (or intentional) encounter with a former using partner, the return to the same environment where the individual had once used chemicals, or a chance encounter with one of the many sights, sounds, and smells associated with chemical use. For example, some recovering heroin addicts will begin to think about using heroin again if they happen to smell the smoke of a burning match.

Finally, the fourth source of chemical use urges was the individual's desire to enhance positive experiences (Beck, Wright, Newman, & Liese, 1993). Many recovering alcohol/drug-dependent individuals associate chemical use with feelings of pleasure. When, especially in the earlier stages of recovery, they find themselves starting to feel good, they begin to fear losing this feeling. They are tempted to return to the use of chemicals in order to extend or enhance the positive experience. This type of urge was discussed by DeJong (1994) under the heading of "positive emotional states."

Although urges and periods of craving seem to be common following extended episodes of substance use, researchers have yet to identify the mechanism(s) by which they are generated. Further, it is not known whether urges and craving for chemicals are significant predictors of relapse (Anton, 1999). However, most individuals in the earliest stages of recovery experience "craving" and "urges" and must learn how to cope with them.

Controlled Drinking

In contrast to England, where 75% of all alcohol rehabilitation programs offer patients training to help them moderate their drinking (Barr, 1999), the theory that the alcoholic might return to "social" or "controlled" drinking has met with skepticism in the United States (Vaillant & Hiller-Sturmhofel, 1996; Hester, 1995; Helzer, Robins, Taylor, Carey, Miller, Combs-Orme, & Farmer, 1985). Unfortunately, ever since the first preliminary reports that it *might* be possible to help a small number of people with alcohol use problems return to a state of "controlled" drinking, many alcohol-dependent individuals have seized on the concept as a justification for their continued drinking.

Research has shown, however, that controlled drinking is a viable goal only for those individuals who clearly are not addicted and who have not experienced significant problems associated with alcoholism (Hester, 1995). Thus it may be possible to teach a large percentage of those who *abuse* alcohol to control their drinking. But less than 2% of individuals who are dependent on alcohol can return to a state of social drinking (Vaillant, 1996; Vaillant & Hiller-Sturmhofel, 1996; Helzer *et al.* 1985).

Researchers have found that individuals who are moderately to severely addicted to alcohol quickly return to abusive drinking if they attempt to learn how to drink on a "social" basis (Watson, Hancock, Malovrh, Gearhart, & Raden, 1996). The authors found that those who attempted controlled alcohol use following treatment were four times as likely to return to abusive drinking as were the control subjects. Indeed, the authors found that the majority of those who tried to drink moderately returned to total abstinence following their attempt at "limited" drinking. These findings lend support to the growing body of evidence that for alcohol-dependent individuals, "controlled" drinking is virtually impossible to achieve after physical dependency on alcohol has developed.

Self-control training appears to be effective only for those individuals with less severe alcohol use problems (Hester, 1995; Meyer, 1989a). For example, controlled drinking might be viewed as a viable treatment goal for those individuals who are capable of dealing with their alcohol use problems without professional assistance. Unfortunately, many alcohol-dependent individuals cling to the hope that they can somehow return to a "controlled" or "social" pattern of alcohol use. Given the fact that only 1–2% of the alcohol-dependent individuals who have been tested to date have been able to achieve a return to social drinking patterns, one must question whether controlled drinking should ever be a goal for the person who is suspected of having an alcohol-use problem.

Hester (1995) suggested that those alcohol-dependent individuals who wish to attempt to learn how to drink in a "social" manner be allowed to try to learn to do so. A failed attempt at "controlled drinking" may help the individual acknowledge the need for total abstinence (Hester, 1995) and accept the fact that alcoholism is a disease "that can be arrested with abstinence but never cured in a way that will permit the person to drink again" (Brown, 1995, p. 11). Further, many individuals who start out working to become social drinkers switch to total abstinence as they come fully to understand the consequences of continued alcohol use (Hester, 1995).

Of course, the mental health or substance abuse professional needs to weigh the potential benefits of this trial against the potential risks. Confirmed alcoholics who believe that they can learn social drinking behaviors once again, and maintain a pattern of social drinking for the rest of their lives, are taking a bet where the odds are at best 49:1, if not 99:1, against them. There are very few of us who would be willing to chance an operation where the odds were 50 to 1 against us. Few would be willing to consent to a surgical procedure from which there is only a 1% or 2% chance of recovery. Yet many an alcoholic has voiced the secret wish that he or she could win this bet and land in what more than one alcoholic has called "the lucky 2%."

Clients Who Appear for Their Appointment While Under the Influence of Chemicals

It is not uncommon for the substance abuse rehabilitation worker to suspect that his or her client is under the influence of chemicals because of the client's behavior. Perhaps it is the way the client slurs his or her words, the look in the individual's eyes, or the smell of alcohol or marijuana that surrounds him or her. In such cases, the treatment professional might (1) confront the client with his or her suspicion that the client is under the influence of chemicals and/or (2) request that the client provide, under appropriate supervision, a urine sample for toxicology testing.

The client's use of chemicals prior to a therapy session raises two issues: one a clinical issue and the second a matter of liability. The client's use of chemicals during his or her therapy can hardly be said to be a minor matter. It is impossible to conduct a therapy session when the client is under the influence of recreational chemicals (Washton, 1995). Thus, meeting with a client who is intoxicated is a waste of time, and the session should be rescheduled for a later date.

But the client's use of recreational chemicals prior to a therapy session also raises a number of liability issues for the client—and the therapist. Thus the health care worker's responsibility might not end with simply rescheduling the appointment. Depending on state law, the therapist might be required to intervene actively in order to protect the client and/or others. For example, if the client should have an accident on the way home, the therapist might be held liable for any injuries, on the grounds that she or he allowed the client to drive while under the influence of chemicals.

Here is another situation wherein the therapist might be held liable: The client arrives for a session obviously intoxicated, and the therapist recommends that the client go home to "sleep it off." If the client should then suffer an adverse reaction at home, the therapist might be held liable on the grounds that he or she knew that the client had used alcohol/drugs but did not take steps to ensure that the client had medical supervision while her or his body recovered from the effects of the chemical(s) ingested. Thus mental health workers might be required to intervene in cases of substance use, possibly to the point of initiating an involuntary commitment to a hospital for detoxification from chemicals. In order to limit their liability, substance abuse rehabilitation professionals must be aware of the specific state laws that govern professional responsibility in cases where they should know or suspect that the client is intoxicated during a session.

Toxicology Testing as a Measure of Treatment Compliance and Drug Use

The abuse of illicit drugs is thought to cost industry $60 billion a year in the United States, with just over half of this figure representing lost productivity (May, 1999). To combat this loss of revenue and to limit liability for workplace-related injuries, U.S. businesses spend approximately $250 million each year testing for drugs in the workplace (May, 1999). Although it is possible to detect some illicit drugs in blood plasma, the low concentrations at which many recreational chemicals are biologically active means that blood testing is not the most efficient way to detect them (Woolf & Shannon, 1995). In contrast to toxicology testing of blood samples, it is possible to detect metabolites of many recreational chemicals in urine samples for hours, days, or (in the case of some chemicals) weeks after the substance was used. When properly utilized, urine toxicology testing provides one of the most comprehensive means of monitoring recreational substance use. This is why urine toxicology testing is the most common method by which industry attempts to police its workforce and detect evidence of illicit drug use.

However, urine toxicology testing is quite controversial. Random toxicology testing in the workplace and in schools has been challenged, and many people have questioned the erosion of civil liberties inherent in this procedure. As a critic of the urine-testing movement, Petersen (2000) cited one situation where 38 different federal agencies tested 29,000 employees in 1990, at a cost of $12 million, with the result that 156 individuals were identified as having "positive" urine samples. This was accomplished at a cost of $77,000 per "positive" sample, according to Petersen (2000), who argued (convincingly!) that such urine testing was not cost-effective. In contrast to this conclusion, however, the National Institute on Drug Abuse (NIDA) estimated that if *every* worker in the United States were to be tested for alcohol/drug use at once, between 14% and 25% would test "positive" for a controlled substance (Vereby, Buchan, & Turner, 1998). The continued use of toxicology tests is justified by proponents of this procedure on the grounds that the tests are a useful way to break through the individual's denial, to help him or her accept the reality of his or her substance use problem, and to check compliance with rehabilitation programs (Verebey & Buchan, 1997).

Urine toxicology testing is not perfect. Routine urine toxicology testing must be conducted only after obtaining the patient's consent (Woolf & Shannon, 1995). Further, it is possible for the tests to mistakenly identify a patient as having abused one or more recreational chemicals when in fact that individual did not do so.

For example, some non-steroidal anti-inflammatory drugs (NSAIDS), such as aspirin, ibuprofen, and Tolmetin, may interfere with some of the tests conducted on urine samples to detect illicit drug use. The non-narcotic cough suppressant dextromethorphan may register as a metabolite of a narcotic or PCP on one popular urine toxicology test known as the EMIT, and a number of other over-the-counter or prescription drugs may register as a recreational substance on one or more of the urine toxicology tests currently in use.

It should also be noted that commercial drug tests may fail to detect the use of some semisynthetic narcotics such as Dilaudid (hydromophone) and fentanyl (*Forensic Drug Abuse Advisor*, 1995e). Another complication of the toxicology testing process is that it is not uncommon for individuals to try to manipulate the results of their urine toxicology tests. Indeed, at least two products sold over the counter purport to help remove "toxins" from the urine and correct any apparent urinary imbalances caused by "flushing" the body with massive amounts of water (Coleman & Baselt, 1997). In their examination of whether these products live up to these claims, the authors tested the urine of an adult male volunteer who had, after testing "negative" for illicit chemicals, ingested test doses of amphetamine and THC. They found that at 2, 4, 8, and 24 hours after the subject had ingested the trial doses of these chemicals, urine samples still tested "positive" for amphetamine and THC in spite of the subject's having used two products that purported to "flush" toxins (such as illicit chemicals and their metabolites) from the body. Coleman and Baselt (1997) concluded that these products seem to be effective *only* when the level of illicit chemicals in the user's body or urine is close to the cut-off level used by laboratories to detect drug abuse.

The authors also examined the effectiveness of "flushing" the body with large amounts of fluid in the hours or days before giving the urine sample for toxicology testing. Some illicit drug users, who believe that they can dilute their urine by "forcing" fluids into their body, may ingest up to a gallon of water at once. But according to Coleman and Baselt (1997), the urine sample obtained as a result of this process would have an abnormally low specific gravity, acidity level, and creatinine levels, alerting staff that the urine sample had been altered in some way. Thus forcing fluids is of limited value to the addict who wishes to avoid detection through urine toxicology testing. Many laboratories also discourage "forcing" by recommending that the urine sample submitted for testing be drawn from the client's first visit to the toilet in the morning, when urine is most concentrated.

There are a number of other methods commonly utilized by drug users to manipulate the results of a urine toxicology test. For example, individuals have been known to try either to substitute another person's urine sample for their own or to substitute a specimen of their own urine collected earlier. This is accomplished by having a "clean" (drug-free) urine sample in a balloon or small bottle. When asked for a urine sample, the client walks into the toilet stall and quietly empties the container into the sample bottle.

Another way in which clients attempt to tamper with the test results is to "accidentally" dip the bottle into the water in the toilet. This will dilute their urine so much that it is unlikely that the laboratory could detect any *urine*, let alone any chemical use! One way to avoid this danger is to test the specific gravity and level of acidity of the urine sample, because toilet water has a different specific gravity and acid level than urine. Another way to avoid this danger is to have the water in the toilet colored with a dye so that it cannot be substituted for urine.

Some clients attempt to defeat the urine toxicology screen by substituting another substance for the urine sample. The list of compounds submitted as "urine" by various individuals includes (but is not limited to) apple juice, citrus-flavored soda, dilute tea, ginger ale, lemonade, salt water, plain tap water, and white grape juice (Winecker & Goldberger, 1998). At one point in the early 1990s, two ounces of an unnamed diet soda would, after being held under the arm for an hour to simulate the body's warmth, be accepted as a valid urine sample "98% of the time" (*Playboy*, 1991, p. 56). Obviously, this false "urine" sample would not betray *any* drug/alcohol use. However, it would also lack the other characteristics of urine, which would soon be evident if laboratory staff were to test the sample for specific gravity, chemical composition, or acid level of the fluid.

Finally, some drug users try to "hide" evidence of chemical use in a urine sample by adding foreign substances that they believe will defeat the chemical tests conducted on the urine. There are various substances and some commercial products that supposedly will eliminate evidence of illicit drug use from urine samples. For example, depending on the procedure used, "Visine" eye drops might camouflage evidence of marijuana use (*Forensic Drug Abuse Advisor*, 1995a). A partial list of the compounds added to urine samples in an attempt to disguise illicit drug use includes (Winecker & Goldberger, 1998)

ammonia	blood	Drano
ethanol	gasoline	kerosene
lemon juice	liquid soap	peroxide
sodium bicarbonate	table salt	vinegar
bleach		

On some tests, bleach or table salt added to the urine sample might hide evidence of recent cocaine use, for example (Winecker & Goldberger, 1998; Warner, 1995). Small amounts of table salt, liquid soap, or Drano will, when added to the urine sample, alter the chemical properties of the fluid enough that evidence of chemical use might not be detected (Woolf & Shannon, 1995; *Forensic Drug Abuse Advisor*, 1995a). On some tests, each of these substances will prevent evidence of THC from being detected in a urine sample.

But the addition of one or more adulterants to a urine sample is not without risk. For example, when Drano was added to a "clean" urine sample, it tested "positive" for amphetamine abuse on one test commonly in use (*Forensic Drug Abuse Advisor*, 1995a). Although a small amount of the metal salt alum might hide evidence of methamphetamine use, it will also alter the acidity of the urine sample, a characteristic that can easily be detected by a simple test (*Forensic Drug Abuse Advisor*, 1995d). Thus there are few adulterants that can "safely" be added to a urine sample without actually increasing the risk of having that specimen testing "positive" for recreational chemicals. But the fact that such adulterants exist confirms the need for *extremely close supervision of both male and female clients who are giving a urine sample for detection of illicit drug use*. This means that the person supervising the collection of the urine sample *must actually see the urine enter the bottle*, not just stand outside of the men's room or lady's room, or the toilet stall, while the client is within.

If the staff person suspects that the client has substituted another person's urine for his or her own, there are several ways to try to determine whether this is true.

First, urine is within 1 or 2 degrees of the core body temperature if the temperature of the urine sample is measured within 4 minutes after the sample is produced. The client whose urine sample is at 70°F, for example, is likely to have substituted somebody else's urine sample for his or her own and should be confronted with this fact.

Another technique is for a staff person to wait, on an occasion when no urine test is scheduled, until the client is about to enter the lavatory and then say that he or she has been selected for another urine sample for drug testing. It is unlikely that the client will carry around a bottle of substitute urine all the time, on the off chance of being asked for a urine sample. This ruse is likely to force the client to give a sample of his or her own urine. Still another technique is for the counselor to announce, at the beginning of a group session or other supervised activity, that the client has 2 hours in which to provide a supervised urine sample for toxicology screen. The client will then be unable to leave the group to pick up a urine sample stored in his or her room without staff being aware that he or she has left the group. The client should have access to water, coffee, or soda to stimulate the production of urine, which can be collected for toxicology testing without the client leaving the group room until he or she is escorted to the bathroom for collection of the urine sample.

Note that even when a valid urine sample has been obtained under supervised conditions, most "routine" drug screens do not test for *every possible* drug of abuse (Verebey & Buchan, 1997). Indeed, substances such as LSD, Fentanyl, MDMA, and many of the "designer drugs" are not routinely included in standard drug screens (Verebey, Buchan, & Turner, 1998). A further disadvantage of urine toxicology screening is that the procedure involves an invasion of the patient's right to privacy (Cone, 1993). It is for this reason that written consent for urine toxicology testing is required. Such written consent states that staff may collect a urine sample at their discretion, as part of the treatment process, and specifies the conditions under which a urine toxicology sample is to be obtained.

Thus, although it is often a useful adjunct to assessment or treatment, urine toxicology testing is an imperfect procedure. Depending on the method used, laboratories can detect either the drugs, or metabolites produced by the body as the liver breaks down the drugs, for various periods of time. The chemical dependency professional should request a written summary from the laboratory of

- The *methods* by which the laboratory attempts to detect illicit chemical use
- The *accuracy* of this method
- *The specific chemicals that can be detected* by that laboratory
- *The period of time after the person has used chemicals when the urine test may reveal such drug use*
- *What other drugs* (including over-the-counter medications) might yield false positive results

Detection of marijuana. Surprisingly, there has been little research into the question of how long THC can be detected in the urine of a marijuana user (*Forensic Drug Abuse Advisor*, 1995i). Woolf and Shannon (1995) suggested that a urine sample from a person who is a moderate user of marijuana would be "positive" for THC for 5 days after the last use of this chemical, at a cut-off level of 20 ng/mL of urine. However, because the body stores THC and gradually releases it back into the blood, chronic marijuana users will test positive at the 20-ng/mL level for 10–20 days, according to the authors. Roberts (1995) suggested that THC might be detected in the daily user's urine for 3–6 weeks following the last use of marijuana, whereas the journal *Forensic Drug Abuse Advisor* (1996f) suggested that urine samples will test positive for THC for at least 4 days (p. 42) following the use of a single marijuana cigarette.

Ravel (1989) advocates the testing of new urine samples every 4–5 days for chronic users and maintains that if there has been no additional marijuana use, such serial urine samples should show "a progressive downward trend in the values" (p. 629). The journal *Forensic Drug Abuse Advisor* (1995k) suggested daily urine toxicology tests until the user has tested negative for three days in a row, to ensure that any residual THC has been eliminated from the user's body.

One potential problem for drug-testing companies and employers alike is that the synthetic THC compound Marinol has been classified as a Schedule III compound, making it possible for physicians to prescribe it for a wide range of conditions. Unfortunately, every urine toxicology test available today will detect Marinol and report that the user has used THC

(McWilliams, 1999). To avoid this problem, drug-testers have to determine whether the individual being tested has been placed on this medication by a physician and must confirm this claim by examination of the original prescription or a conversation with the prescribing physician.

Occasionally, people whose urine has tested positive for THC claim to have passively inhaled marijuana smoke because they were in a room where other people were smoking it. The journal *Forensic Drug Abuse Advisor* (1995i) did suggest that under special conditions, it is possible for nonusing individuals to be exposed to concentrations of second-hand marijuana smoke high enough to cause their urine to test positive for THC. However, in one study where this was attempted, the volunteers had to sit in a chamber filled with such dense smoke from the marijuana cigarettes that they had to wear special eye protection! Thus, under normal circumstances, it is unlikely for an individual to test positive for THC through exposure to second-hand smoke from marijuana cigarettes.

Detection of cocaine. Depending on the route of administration and the amount of cocaine utilized, it is possible to detect metabolites of cocaine in urine samples for about 24–48 hours after the last drug use (Woolf & Shannon, 1995; House, 1990). Some authors have suggested that it is possible to detect benzoylecgonine (the major metabolite of cocaine) for up to 96 hours after the person last used the drug (Roberts, 1995; Weddington, 1993). The journal *Forensic Drug Abuse Advisor* (1995g) has said there is strong evidence that in extremely heavy users, large amounts of cocaine might be stored in the body tissues, only to be released into the general circulation days, weeks, or even months after the person last used the drug. A more conservative estimate was offered by Nelson (2000), who suggested that individuals with liver damage might continue to test "positive" for cocaine for up to 8 days after their last use of this substance.

The implication of these findings is that a person might continue to test positive for cocaine on a urine toxicology test for many days or weeks after his or her last use of the drug (*Forensic Drug Abuse Advisor*, 1995g; 1995k). However, it is doubtful that a client who initially tested negative, or who tested "positive" at a low level, would suddenly show evidence of high levels of cocaine metabolites in his or her blood.

As a general rule of thumb, the casual user might show evidence of cocaine use in his or her urine for 2–3 days after the episode of drug use if enzyme immunoassay techniques were used, or up to 7 days if tested via the more sensitive radioimmunoassay technique. Researchers have found evidence suggesting the possibility of a nonuser absorbing some cocaine fumes from second-hand smoke. However, the blood levels of cocaine in nonusers was not high enough to cause any physiological reaction, and the concentration of cocaine metabolites in the nonuser's urine would not result in a "positive" toxicology test at the cut-off levels recommended by the National Institute on Drug Abuse (NIDA).

Detection of PCP abuse. The hallucinogen PCP or its metabolites might be detected for up to 1 week following use by a casual user and for 3 weeks after the chronic user last used this substance (Woolf & Shannon, 1995). As we saw in Chapter 15, the speed at which PCP is excreted from the body depends on the acidity of the urine. Cone (1993) suggested that PCP might be detected in body fluids for up to 5–8 days in the casual user and for as long as 30 days in the chronic user.

Detection of amphetamine abuse. The amphetamines, can be detected for only 24–48 hours after the last use of this class of drugs (Roberts, 1995; Cone, 1993).

Detection of opiates. The often-abused analgesic Darvon (propoxyphene) can be detected for just 8 hours following its use, although metabolites of propoxyphene may be detected for up to 48 hours (Woolf & Shannon, 1995; Roberts, 1995). The "window of detection" for Darvon thus depends on whether the laboratory is testing for the drug itself or for metabolites of the drug. Other narcotic analgesics such as heroin, morphine, codeine, and Dilaudid (hydromophone) might be detected for 1–2 days following the last use of this class of drugs (Roberts, 1995; Ravel, 1989). Methadone may be detected for a slightly longer period of time than other narcotic analgesics, according to Roberts (1995). However, even methadone can be detected for only 2–3 days following the last dose.

Detection of Rohypnol. Although it is possible to test for Rohypnol (flunitrazepam) in urine samples, the drug can be detected only within 60 hours of the time that it was ingested (Lively, 1996). Special testing procedures must be followed to detect flunitrazepam in urine

samples, and in most cases laboratories must be directed to test for traces of this drug separately from their standard drug screen.

False-positive test results and the need for retesting. Urine toxicology testing is an imprecise art, and a number of factors can occasion inaccurate test results. Poppy seeds, for example, are often used for baking certain kinds of bread. Depending on the method by which the urine sample was tested, a person who ingested some of this bread might then produce a urine sample that tested "positive" for opioids, even if the person had not used a narcotic (Ravel, 1989). The OTC medication pseudoephedrine hydrochloride (which is sold under a number of different brand names) may cause some urine toxicology tests to be positive for amphetamines (Woolf & Shannon, 1995).

Given these facts, it is unfortunate that "on site" testing is becoming increasingly popular in the workplace and in other settings where supervisory personnel want information about possible substance use by another person. On-site tests have a high "false-positive" rate; that is, the test results frequently indicate possible illicit drug use in cases where the individual has not used chemicals (*Forensic Drug Abuse Advisor*, 1997d). On-site test results should *always* be confirmed by independent toxicology testing in a certified laboratory, which will be able to confirm the on-site test results if there was evidence of illicit drug use. For example, Moyer and Ellefson (1987) reported that when a pure urine specimen is utilized, the enzyme-mediated immuno-technique (EMIT) detects marijuana use with better than 95% accuracy. Combining the EMIT with other tests, such as gas chromatography/mass spectrometry (GC/MS), makes it possible to obtain virtually 100% accuracy when testing urine specimens for evidence of marijuana use.

Given the fact that the EMIT procedure has a 3% false-positive rate, testing with another technique such as GC/MS is essential to rule out false-positive results. Ravel (1989) also advocated the use of additional testing, such as mass spectrometry or gas chromatography, to confirm or deny the original positive test results for all drugs of abuse. These are highly specialized test procedures that essentially separate the constituents of a urine sample for identification. Following up with multiple test procedures for all positive urine samples will help to identify those who have truly used illicit chemicals and greatly reduce the danger of false-positive test results (Woolf & Shannon, 1995).

Other uses of urine toxicology tests. Urine toxicology testing is also used to help determine whether the client is taking the medications that have been prescribed. Obviously, for a person being detoxified from narcotics through methadone withdrawal, urine toxicology testing should reveal evidence of methadone for up to 72 hours following the last use of the drug (Woolf & Shannon, 1995). If the individual does *not* test positive for this drug the day after he or she supposedly received a dose of methadone, the staff should consider the possibility that this person has substituted another urine sample for his or her own and should examine why the client might wish to do so.

Hair as a source of toxicology test samples. When a person uses a chemical, molecules of that substance are circulated throughout the body, where they may enter different types of cells in addition to the neurons of the central nervous system. If the cell were to die and be ejected from the body before the drug molecule was released back into the general circulation, then the drug molecule would remain attached to the cell wall. In theory, this characteristic might make it possible to detect evidence of illicit drug use in hair samples of patients. This is because the roots of hair remain alive, but the hair itself is composed of long strands of dead cells pushed outward from the root by the pressure of new hair cells forming at the root.[2] Scientists have developed the technology to detect metabolites of many illicit drugs in the hair of the user.

Advocates of hair follicle testing point out that this procedure is far less intrusive than urine toxicology testing, and although some people think that shaving their heads will defeat the process of hair follicle testing, *any* body hair can be used for such tests (Brady, 1997). Detractors of the process point out that it is virtually impossible to determine *when* the user indulged in illicit drug use by hair sample testing. They also caution that the hair sample might be contaminated by drug molecules in the air (such as marijuana smoke) (McPhillips, Strang, & Barnes, 1998).

The theory is that by measuring the distance of the drug molecules from the root, and then estimating the time that it would take for hair to grow that distance at a standard rate of growth of 1 centimeter (cm) per month, one could estimate how long it has been since that person used an illicit chemical(s). Unfortunately, this theory has not been borne out in practice (*Forensic Drug Abuse Advisor*, 1996b). It is possible that different ethnic groups absorb drug metabolites into hair follicles at differing rates and at any given point in time 15% of the hairs are either in resting phase or ready to fall out (McPhillips, Strang, & Barnes, 1998). Finally, "false-positive" results are possible, although researchers do not know all of the circumstances under which such inaccurate test results might be produced. Thus, although toxicological testing of hair samples is possible, its value in detecting illicit drug use remains uncertain at this time.

Saliva testing to detect illicit drug use. Another emerging technology is the use of saliva to test for residual traces of alcohol (Wilson & Kunsman, 1997). Although laboratories have been able to use saliva samples to test for alcohol traces since the 1950s, new techniques are making this procedure attractive for workplace screening programs, according to the authors. The individual places a cotton swab in his or her mouth, allowing it to become moistened by saliva. The cotton swab is then tested by exposing it to chemicals that will react to the presence of alcohol. The use of saliva allows for a simple, short (less than 20-minute) test that is just as accurate as breath testing but can be carried out in the workplace. As with any screening procedure, there is a need for follow-up testing to rule out false-positive results.

Insurance Reimbursement Policies

There are two different ways to view health care (Kluge, 2000). The first viewpoint is that health care is a right, and the second is that health care is a commodity. Unfortunately, the increasing effectiveness of medical care, along with the aging of the adult population in the United States, means that expenditures for health care must increase (Levant, 2000). For example, as treatment advances reduce the death rate from myocardial infarctions, a pool of heart attack survivors who require aggressive medical management is established, placing a drain on health care resources. Thus the increase in health care costs over the past decades appears to re-

---

[2]This is why it is possible to have your hair cut without feeling pain. The hair is dead and thus does not have functional nerve endings.

flect, in part, the impact of successful medical interventions in earlier decades, not evidence of inefficiency on the part of health care providers.

Insurance companies, however, have adopted the positions that (1) health care is a commodity and (2) increased costs reflect inefficiency, not increased effectiveness. Given this perception on the part of health care insurers, it was only natural that they institute programs designed to reduce costs. These programs have been called "managed care" (MC) initiatives. Although the proported goal of MC efforts was to control the rising cost of providing health care, the most aggressive efforts to impose such controls were in the areas of mental health and substance abuse—in spite of the fact that the cost of providing these services was increasing *more slowly* than the cost of health care in general (Teich, 2000).

In theory, MC is designed to provide the most appropriate care for the patient at the best possible price to the insurance company. But, in reality, the MC system "wasn't meant to care for sick people; it was meant to make and manage money" for the insurance company (Glasser, 1998, p. 36). The danger is that although many MC systems have a legitimate interest in helping people find the appropriate medical care at an affordable price,

> there are great potential profits for the unscrupulous managed care companies that will maximize their profits without concern for the well being of the patient. Ethics do not seem dependent on the size of the company and unethical companies appear from among the largest as well as the smallest companies. (Frances & Miller, 1998, p. 11)

Indeed, many health care providers have come to call managed care "managed profits" instead, because of the way this process often limits the amount of care that an insurance company is liable to pay for under its policy with the individual. For example, in the decade 1989–1999, the value of benefits paid out by managed care companies during this same period *fell* by 54%, which "translated into big money for these largely for-profit companies" (Magellan Slashes Fees . . ., 1999, p. 5). During this same period of time, the cost of health care increased approximately 8.3% per year (Teich, 2000).

A point that is often overlooked by health care providers is that insurance companies *do not exist to provide funding for health care procedures*. They exist to make money for the owners of the company (stockholders), and one way they do this is by selling health insurance. A health insurance policy is, in effect, a gamble by the insurance company that the policy holder will not become ill for the period of time that the policy is in effect. The company charges a "premium," which it keeps if the policy holder does not become ill with any of the conditions identified by the company as reflecting "illness." If the policy holder *does* become ill, the insurance company is then required to provide a certain level of care, as identified in the policy, if it is "medically necessary" (Ford, 2000).

Needless to say, the insurance company will try to control costs in order to maximize its profit. Up to half of the insurance fee charged each client in some managed-care companies goes for administrative fees and company profit (Gottlieb, 1997). The money an insurance company spends providing health care coverage for those who have purchased a policy from that company is considered a financial loss to the company. The insurance company thus attempts to maximize the inflow of money while reducing the need to pay money to policy holders. To this end, the company may exclude as many conditions as possible from the health insurance coverage and exclude individuals with known medical problems from participation in the policy on the grounds of a "preexisting condition."

A third way in which insurance companies try to limit their losses is to adopt a very conservative definition of disease. It has been charged that insurance companies have come to substitute *symptom reduction* for the "treatment" or "cure" of disease (Kaiser, 1996). In the area of alcohol/drug use problems, insurance companies commonly invoke a very conservative definition of "recovery" to determine when benefits should be terminated. Consider the effect this has on substance abuse rehabilitation programs. First, there is ample evidence that

> the minimum stay in residential treatment programs needed to yield improvement in long-term outcomes was several months and that improvements in outcomes continue to be manifested for full-time treatment of up to 1 year in length (McCusker, Stoddard, Frost, & Zorn, 1996, p. 482)

A large number of studies have found that the longer the individual is involved in rehabilitation programs, the better the chance of a successful outcome (Brochu, Landry, Bergeron, & Chiocchio, 1997). In the current climate, however, it is rare for a health care insurancer to fund even 2–3 weeks of inpatient substance abuse rehabilitation. All too often, funding is limited to 5–7 days of inpatient treatment. Although such programs are more cost-effective by some measures, one sad consequence is that many clients are referred to aftercare programs without having completed treatment (Coughey, Feighan, Cheney, & Klein, 1998).

This situation has come about because insurance companies are able to present *symptom resolution* as a substitute for long-term treatment. In other words, health insurance companies have come to view the stabilization of the immediate crisis, rather than long-term rehabilitation, as an acceptable goal for inpatient treatment. Unfortunately, symptom reduction does not *necessarily* mean that the condition that caused the symptoms has been resolved. (Patients who suffer a ruptured appendix frequently report a significant reduction in pain after the appendix has burst. Do we therefore consider their condition resolved?) The fact that a patient is no longer in imminent danger of acute alcohol withdrawal does not mean that his or her substance abuse/addiction has been adequately resolved. Adequate treatment of the addictive disorders requires time to effect meaningful change.

Few health care providers are willing to accept symptom resolution, which in this case means the immediate cessation of chemical use, as adequate "treatment." In contrast to this, the health care insurance companies interpret "adequate" treatment as stabilization of the immediate crisis. Managed-care companies often view substance abuse rehabilitation treatment as imperfect at best, an attitude that reflects their

deep suspicion of anything unquantifiable, unprovable, or lingering as probably being poor technique on the therapist's part, self-indulgence on the patient's, and a waste of money by both. (Gottlieb, 1997, p. 47)

This is clearly seen in the fact that in 1996 (the last year for which figures are available), the combined national expenditures for mental health and substance abuse treatment were estimated to be $79 billion. Of this figure, a little over $12.6 billion was for alcohol/drug rehabilitation programs (Teich, 2000). Further, private insurance companies paid for only 26% of the total expenditure for mental health and alcohol/drug treatment (Teich, 2000). To protect this $3 billion spent on alcohol/drug rehabilitation, many managed-care companies routinely ear-mark mental health claims in general, and substance abuse rehabilitation claims in particular, for administrative review.

Summary

Even after a client has been identified as being in need of substance abuse rehabilitation services, the course of treatment is often a difficult one. Some clients test the limits imposed by the therapist or the treatment center. Other clients challenge the accuracy of urine toxicology test results. Clients occasionally come to treatment sessions under the influence of chemicals. Virtually all clients experience "urges" and "craving" to use chemicals after they begin a recovery program. Some of these individuals will "relapse" and return to active chemical abuse, especially if they fail to respond appropriately to relapse "triggers" encountered in everyday life. Finally, insurance company policies often severely limit the length of time that a given client may remain in either an inpatient or an outpatient rehabilitation program.

CHAPTER THIRTY-TWO

Pharmacological Intervention Tactics and Substance Abuse[1]

Introduction

The pharmacological treatment of substance abuse is a logical extension of the medical model. It is based on the premise that the individual's substance use problem might be controlled, or totally eliminated, through the use of various biochemicals. Surprisingly, given the popularity of the medical model in the United States the role of pharmaceuticals in the treatment of the addictive disorders is rather limited (Kranzler, Amin, Modesto-Lowe, & Oncken, 1999). Further, there is no standard model to guide the use of pharmaceuticals in substance abuse rehabilitation programs. However, as a general rule, pharmacological interventions consist of the use of selected chemicals by trained medical personnel in support of substance abuse rehabilitation efforts.

Pharmacological Treatment of Alcohol Abuse and Dependency

Medications used in the treatment of the alcohol withdrawal syndrome. Traditionally, the benzodiazepines have been the treatment of choice for the alcohol withdrawal syndrome. The judicious use of a benzodiazepine such as chlordiazepoxide (20–100 mg either orally or intravenously every 6 hours) or diazepam (5–20 mg either orally or intravenously every 6 hours) has been found to control the tremor, hyperactivity, convulsions, and anxiety associated with alcohol withdrawal (Yost, 1996; Milhorn, 1992; Miller, Frances, & Holmes, 1989).

In spite of their acceptance as the treatment of choice for the alcohol withdrawal syndrome, physicians still disagree about the best way to use the benzodiazepines. Some physicians issue "standing orders" for the administration of benzodiazepines whenever a patient goes into alcohol withdrawal. Such a program might involve the patient receiving an oral dose of 50–100 mg of chlordiazepoxide every 6 hours, with an additional dose of 25–100 mg of chlordiazepoxide by mouth administered at 1-hour intervals, until the withdrawal symptoms are controlled (Saitz & O'Malley, 1997). Then the daily dosage level should be reduced by 10–20% each day, until the medication is finally discontinued (Miller, Frances, & Holmes, 1989).

Other physicians worn that this practice might result in extended hospital stays (Saitz, Mayo-Smith, Roberts, Redmond, Bernard, & Calkins, 1994) and recommend a "symptom-triggered" (p. 519) approach instead. Under such a program, the benzodiazepine chlordiazepoxide is administered only if the patient's physical status suggested that he or she were going into acute alcohol withdrawal. Such a program has been found to result in fewer doses of medication being administered—and a shorter hospital stay—than traditional methods of treating the alcohol withdrawal syndrome. In extreme cases,

[1]The pharmacological support of alcohol or drug withdrawal, or of the treatment of an ongoing substance abuse problem, should be supervised by a licensed physician who is skilled and experienced in working with substance abuse cases. This chapter is provided for information purposes only. It is not intended to encourage self-treatment of substance abuse problems, nor should it be interpreted as a standard of care for patients who are abusing or addicted to chemicals.

such as when the patient is experiencing alcohol hallucinosis, low doses of an antipsychotic medication, such as 1–2 mg of haloperidol every 4 hours, in addition to benzodiazepines, can be used to control the withdrawal symptoms (Milhorn, 1992).

Medications used in the treatment of alcohol dependency. Frances and Miller (1991) struck a rather pessimistic note when they observed that even after a century of searching for an antidipsotrophic[2] medication,

> at this writing there is no proven biological treatment for alcoholism. Each promising drug that has been tested in the hope it would reduce relapse by intervening in the basic disease process has failed. (p. 13)

However, the authors noted, Antabuse (disulfiram) continues to provide one avenue for the symptomatic treatment of alcoholism.

Antabuse (disulfiram). At the 1949 annual meeting of the American Psychiatric Association, Barrera, Osinski, and Davidoff (1949/1994) presented a paper in which they reported the outcome of their research into the possible use of Antabuse (disulfiram) as an antidipsotrophic medication. The original theory behind the use of disulfiram was a variation on aversive conditioning, according to the authors. The combination of alcohol and Antabuse would produce "unpleasant effects" for the drinker, thus reducing the reward value of the alcohol.

In the time since it was first suggested as a way to combat chronic alcoholism, researchers have discovered that disulfiram is a potentially dangerous drug that should not be used with patients who have serious medical disorders (Schuckit, 1996a). Some of the side effects of disulfiram include skin rash, fatigue, halitosis, a rare, potentially fatal form of hepatitis, peripheral neuropathies, potential optic nerve damage, severe depression, and psychosis (Schuckit, 1996a). Surprisingly, in spite of its popularity within the rehabilitation community, research studies have failed to demonstrate that the use of Antabuse results in higher abstinence rates, or longer periods of abstinence, than occur when this

medication is not used (Kick, 1999; Tinsley, Finlayson, & Morse, 1998). Although there is some evidence to suggest that those individuals who take disulfiram tend to drink less frequently than those who do not (Tinsley, Finlayson, & Morse, 1998), the patient must be motivated to use the medication as prescribed. Obviously, given the voluntary nature of medication use, compliance in taking Antabuse is an ongoing problem for substance abuse rehabilitation programs (Tinsley, Finlayson, & Morse, 1998). To avoid the problem of medication compliance, researchers have experimented with disulfiram implants designed to release a steady supply of the medication into the user's circulatory system. However, subsequent research has failed to demonstrate that the implants yield any significantly better abstinence rates than oral preparations of disulfiram (Tinsley, Finlayson, & Morse, 1998).

For those patients who *do* use Antabuse (disulfiram) appropriately, it can provide an additional source of support in a weak moment. Because these individuals know that they cannot drink alcohol until the medication is entirely out of their bodies, a process that can take as long as 10–14 days, disulfiram can provide time for "second thoughts." But this does not mean that Antabuse (disulfiram) will reduce the frequency or intensity of the individual's "craving" for alcohol. It can only interfere with the biotransformation of alcohol after the drug enters the individual's body, causing a number of unpleasant—*potentially fatal*—effects.

Clinically, disulfiram interferes with the body's ability to biotransform alcohol, by destroying the enzyme aldehyde dehydrogenase in the drinker's body. This allows the alcohol metabolite acetaldehyde to build up in the blood. Acetaldehyde is a toxin, and even small amounts of alcohol will cause the disulfiram-treated patient to experience such symptoms of acetaldehyde poisoning as facial flushing, heart palpitations, a rapid heart rate, difficulty in breathing, nausea, vomiting, and possibly a serious drop in blood pressure (Schuckit, 1995b).

Under normal conditions, it takes 3–12 hours after the first dose of disulfiram before it can begin to interfere with the metabolism of alcohol. But the individual who has been using disulfiram for several days and then ingests alcohol will experience the alcohol–disulfiram reaction within about 30 minutes. Typically, the disulfiram–alcohol interaction lasts for 30–180 minutes, although there are case reports of its lasting longer than

---

[2]This term derives from the 19th century, when alcoholics were said to suffer from "dipsomania." A medication that was antidipsotrophic would thus act against dipsomania.

this. The strength of these side effects depends on several factors: (1) how much alcohol has been ingested, (2) the amount of disulfiram being used each day, and (3) the period of time since the last dose of disulfiram was ingested. The period of time since the last dose of disulfiram is important because the body tends to metabolize the drug. Thus, over time, the effects of any given dose become less and less powerful.

In order to make sure that the user understands the consequences of mixing alcohol with disulfiram, patients are repeatedly warned about the danger of drinking while under the influence of disulfiram. Some treatment centers advocate a learning process wherein the patient takes disulfiram for a short time (usually a few days) and then is allowed to drink a small amount of alcohol under controlled conditions. This is done so that the individual can experience the negative consequences of mixing alcohol and dilsulfiram in a setting where there is rapid access to medical support services. The hope is that this experience will make the individual less likely to drink a large amount of alcohol later.

On occasion, the spouse of an alcohol abuser will inquire of a treatment professional about the possibility of obtaining disulfiram to "teach him (her) a lesson." The desperate spouse usually wants to slip disulfiram into the alcoholic's coffee so that the next time that the alcoholic drinks, he or she will experience the alcohol–disulfiram interaction, without expecting it. Needless to say, *disulfiram should never be given to an individual without the user's knowledge and consent* (American Psychiatric Association, 1995). The interaction between disulfiram and alcohol is *potentially serious and may be fatal.*

Disulfiram is not a perfect solution to the problem of alcohol dependency. For example, it is not an effective aversive-conditioning agent. Theoretically, an effective behavior modification program for alcohol dependency would involve an immediate negative consequence to shape the drinker's behavior. But the 30-minute delay between the ingestion of alcohol and the disulfiram–alcohol reaction is far too long for it to serve as an *immediate* consequence for the drinker. This makes it difficult for the person to associate the use of alcohol with the delayed discomfort caused by the alcohol–disulfiram reaction.

Another disadvantage of disulfiram is that its *full* effects last only about 24–48 hours. There have been rare reports of alcohol–disulfiram interactions up to 2 weeks after the last dose of disulfiram. But in most cases, the individual's body ceases to react to alcohol on the sixth or seventh day after his or her last dose of disulfiram. Because of the body's biotransformation of disulfiram, most patients take the drug every day, or perhaps every other day, for optimal effectiveness. Thus it is up to the individual to take the medication according to the schedule worked out with his or her physician, to ensure that there is an adequate supply of the drug in the body at all times.

Further, disulfiram often reacts to the small amounts of alcohol found in many over-the-counter cough syrups, as well as in aftershaves and in many other products. The individual using disulfiram should be warned by his or her physician to avoid certain products, in order to keep from having an unintentional reaction caused by the small amounts of alcohol found in these products. Most treatment centers and physicians who utilize disulfiram have lists of such products and foods.

Research has suggested that disulfiram interacts with the neurotransmitter serotonin to boost brain levels of a byproduct of serotonin known as 5-hydroxy-tryptophol (or 5-HTOL) (Cowen, 1990). Animal research suggests that increased levels of 5-HTOL result in greater alcohol consumption. Research with human subjects has yet to be completed, but preliminary data suggest a need for alcoholics not to eat "serotonin-rich" foods such as bananas and walnuts, to avoid increasing the craving for alcohol that many recovering alcoholics experience.

Disulfiram is *not* recommended for individuals who have a history of cardiovascular and cerebrovascular disease, kidney failure, depression, or liver disease or for women who might be pregnant (Fuller, 1995). It is not recommended for use in elderly patients, because of the potential danger that it might cause or contribute to hypotension, myocardial infarction, and stroke in the older individual (Goldstein, Pataki, & Webb, 1996). This medication has also been implicated as a possible cause of peripheral neuropathies and has been found to lower the seizure threshold for individuals with idiopathic seizure disorders (Schuckit, 1996a; Fuller, 1995). Further, there are reports that disulfiram has exacerbated the symptoms of schizophrenia in those patients with this disorder (Fuller, 1995).

Drug interactions between disulfiram and phenytoin (sold under the brand name of Dilantin), warfarin, isoniazid (used in the treatment of tuberculosis), diazepam (Valium), chlordiazepoxide (Librium), and several commonly used antidepressants have been reported (Fuller, 1989). Patients who are taking the antitubercular drug isoniazid (INH) should not take disulfiram. These drugs may, when used together, bring on a toxic psychosis or cause other neurological problems in the patient (Meyers, 1992).

There are reports that disulfiram may interfere with male sexual performance. Schiavi, Stimmel, Mandeli, and White (1995) noted that half of the chronic males in their sample who reported having trouble achieving an erection claimed that this problem began when they started to take disulfiram. This would be a frightening side effect for some users, especially if they are not warned of this possibility before starting the medication. Further, patients who use disulfiram should do so only under the supervision of a physician who has a *complete* history of the patient's medication use. Because of the danger of disulfiram–medication interactions, the use of multiple prescriptions from different doctors should be most strongly discouraged.

Admittedly, some individuals will drink in spite of the disulfiram in their system, which is known as trying to "drink through" the disulfiram. Other individuals will drink in spite of having ingested disulfiram in the recent past because they think they know how to neutralize the drug while it is in the body. Many alcohol abusers/addicts stop taking the drug several days before a "spontaneous" relapse, and only about 20% of those individuals who start the drug actually take it for a full year. Still, in spite of these disadvantages, for the majority of those who use disulfiram as intended, the drug gives the individual an extra bit of support during weak moments.

Lithium. In the late 1980s and early 1990s, there was a great deal of interest in the possible use of lithium in the treatment of alcoholism. Lithium is an element that has been found to be useful in controlling the mood swings of bipolar affective disorder (formerly called manic–depressive disorder). Early research suggested that lithium could also reduce the number of relapses that chronic alcoholics experienced, reduce the apparent level of intoxication, and reduce the desire of chronic alcohol users to drink (Miller, Frances, &

Holmes, 1989; Judd & Huey, 1984). Unfortunately, subsequent research failed to support these early findings. An obvious exception to this rule occurs when the patient has a bipolar affective disorder in addition to alcohol abuse/dependence.

Ondansetron. Ondansetron has been used with some success to treat early-onset alcoholism (Johnson, Roache, Javors, DiClemente, Cloninger, Prihoda, Bordnick, Ait-Daoud, & Hensler, 2000). Drawing on the knowledge that early-onset alcoholism might reflect a serotonergic system dysfunction, the authors utilized a serotonin-blocking agent that focuses its effects on the 5-HT_3 receptor subtype, which has been found to be involved in the subjective experience of alcohol-induced pleasure for the drinker. The use of ondansetron was found to reduce the individual's desire to drink and the subjective experience of pleasure if the individual did drink. However, this medication is still experimental, and research suggests that it works best when taken twice a day. Whether ondansetron has a role in the treatment of alcoholism remains to be seen.

Naltrexone hydrochloride. As we saw in Chapter 7, when an individual consumes alcohol, his or her brain is thought to release endogenous opioids. These are neurotransmitters thought to be involved in the "pleasure center" of the brain. In recent years, researchers have discovered that drugs that function as antagonists for one of the neurotransmitter binding sites for endogenous opioids (*mu* opioid receptor site) seem to reduce alcohol consumption in both animals and humans (Swift, Whelihan, Kuznetsov, Buongiorno, & Hsuing, 1994).

One such compound is naltrexone hydrochloride, which is sold under the brand name of ReVia. In January of 1995, naltrexone hydrochloride was approved by the Food and Drug Administration (FDA) for the treatment of alcohol dependency (*Minneapolis Star-Tribune*, 1995a). Researchers have found that individuals who take 50 mg/day of naltrexone seem to derive less pleasure from their use of alcohol, to "crave" it less, and to have a lower relapse rate following treatment (Mason, Salvato, Williams, Ritvo, & Cutler, 1999; Volpicelli, Rhines, Rhines, Volpicelli, Alterman, & O'Brien, 1997). However, medication noncompliance is a significant problem with alcohol-dependent patients who are prescribed naltrexone for relapse prevention.

Naltrexone hydrochloride is able to reduce alcohol's reward value as a drug of abuse and the "craving" for alcohol that so often complicates rehabilitation efforts (American Psychiatric Association, 1995; Swift, Whelihan, Kuznetsov, Buongiorno, & Hsuing, 1994; Holloway, 1991). In addition to its ability to reduce "craving" for alcohol, clinical evidence suggests that naltrexone is able to make the use of alcohol less rewarding for the individual who has relapsed, so that he or she is less likely to continue drinking (Meza & Kranzler, 1996). Unfortunately, this medication has a dose-dependent toxic effect on the liver, limiting its use to individuals who have not suffered significant levels of liver damage (Mason, Salvato, Williams, Ritvo, & Cutler, 1999). Thus, although naltrexone hydrochloride appears to have a role in the fight against alcoholism, it is not a "magic bullet" that will cure patients who are dependent on this recreational chemical.

Other pharmacological treatments for chronic alcohol dependency. Over the years, researchers have experimented with a number of compounds that seemed to be potential antidipsotrophic medications. In the 1970s, the antibiotic compound Flagyl (metronidazole) was examined as a possible adjunct to the treatment of alcoholism, because this medication causes discomfort when mixed with alcohol. But this research was discontinued when little evidence emerged that metronidazole was effective as an antidipsotrophic medication (Holder, Long-Oabaugh, Miller, & Rubonis, 1991).

One medication that is showing promise in the treatment of alcohol dependency is Acamprosate (calcium acetylhomotaurinate). This compound has been found to have no "rebound" effect, or abuse potential, and is not known to interact with other pharmaceutical agents (Sherman, 2000a). Calcium acetylhomotaurinate has a chemical structure similar to that of the neurotransmitter GABA. Rather than interacting with alcohol to cause unpleasant physical reactions, Acamprosate stimulates the production of GABA. This, in turn, inhibits the effects of neurotransmitters such as glutamate that stimulate the CNS (Whitworth *et al.*, 1996). The apparent effect is that the individual feels less *need* to ingest alcohol, although the exact mechanism of action for Acamprosate is still not known. The drug is not thought to be extensively biotransformed prior to excretion, and its primary route of excretion is thought to be through the kidneys (Sherman, 2000a). Although this medication has shown some promise in the treatment of chronic alcohol use/abuse and is used in Canada, it is still being studied as a possible agent for use with recently detoxified alcoholics in the United States (Mason, Salvato, Williams, Ritvo, & Cutler, 1999).

Another compound that is being examined for possible use with alcohol-dependent individuals is nalmefene, an opioid antagonist that is similar to naltrexone in chemical structure (Mason, Salvato, Williams, Ritvo, & Cutler, 1999). The medication has a longer half-life than naltrexone, and it binds more effectively than naltrexone at the mu, kappa, and sigma opioid receptor sites (which are thought to be most involved in the pleasurable effects caused by drinking).

Buspirone. Research studies have suggested that buspirone may be useful in controlling the anxiety and excessive worry associated with protracted abstinence (Meza & Kranzler, 1996; Schuckit, 1996a). Unfortunately, the first research studies to examine the effectiveness of buspirone in the treatment of alcohol dependency were poorly designed. Thus there is a need for further research into the possible effectiveness of buspirone.

Selective serotonin reuptake inhibitors (SSRIs). In the late 1980s, psychiatrists began to use a new class of medications known as *selective serotonin reuptake inhibitors (SSRIs)* in the treatment of depression. This class of antidepressants includes Prozac (fluoxetine). Subsequent research has failed to support the theory that the SSRIs should reduce alcohol abuse/addiction, except in those cases where the drinker has a concurrent depressive disorder.

Neurotransmitter precursor loading. In the 1980s, Blum and Trachtenberg (1988) suggested a different treatment approach to the problem of rehabilitation of the alcoholic. The authors theorized that alcohol craving might be influenced by the neurochemicals available in the brain and advocated the use of a "neurotransmitter precursor loading" system (Blum & Trachtenberg, 1988, p. 5) to aid in the treatment of alcoholism. Proper nutritional supplements were believed to help the brain naturally balance the neurotransmitter deficit thought to cause "craving" for alcohol/drugs. However, subsequent research has failed to find any positive effects from this approach, and it is no longer viewed as a viable treatment option for alcohol/drug dependency (Peele, 1991).

Pharmacological Treatment of Opiate Addiction

Naltrexone hydrochloride. Although it has been found to be of value in the treatment of alcohol dependency (discussed earlier in this chapter), naltrexone hydrochloride is used primarily in the treatment of opioid addiction. Naltrexone is an opioid antagonist with no significant agonist effect (Kranzler, Amin, Modesto-Lowe, & Oncken, 1999). The drug is well absorbed when taken orally, and peak blood levels are achieved within an hour of taking the drug, according to Kranzler *et al.* (1999). In spite of its elimination half-life of 3.9–10.3 hours, the drug has an extended action within the brain, and depending on the dosage level being used, it is possible for naltrexone to block the euphoric effects of injected opiates for up to 72 hours.

The theory behind the use of naltrexone hydrochloride is that if people taking this medication do not experience any feelings of euphoria from opiates, they are less likely to use opiates again. But there are a number of dangers associated with naltrexone. First, to avoid the danger of initiating an undesired opiate withdrawal syndrome, this medication *should be used only after the person is completely detoxified from opiates.* To avoid the danger of overdose, the patient must also be warned not to try to "shoot through" a narcotic antagonist such as naltrexone (injecting a large dose in an effort to overcome the antagonist) (Callahan, 1980). Further, when the individual stops using naltrexone, she or he will begin to reexperience a craving for narcotics. There is no extinction of the craving for the drug during the period of time that the narcotics addict is maintained on a narcotics blocker, and the patient must be warned about this to minimize the danger of relapse.

Jenike (1991) reported that a 50-mg dose of naltrexone hydrochloride will block the euphoria of an injection of narcotics for 24 hours, a 100-mg dose for about 48 hours, and a 150-mg for 72 hours. According to Jenike, the usual dosage schedule is three times a week, with 100 mg being administered on Monday and Wednesday and 150 mg on Friday to provide a longer-term dose for the weekend.

To date, there is no research that *unequivocally* demonstrates a benefit from this medication in the treatment of narcotics addiction (Medical Economics Company, 1999). Indeed, a major drawback of naltrexone hydrochloride is that the majority of opiate-dependent individuals discontinue the drug on their own (Youngstrom, 1990a). *Only* 2% of the one sample of opiate-dependent patients continued to take this drug for 9 months (Youngstrom, 1990a). Obviously, naltrexone hydrochloride is no "magic pill" for the treatment of opiate addiction.

Ibogaine. An experimental drug under consideration in the rehabilitation of narcotics addicts is an alkaloid obtained from the root bark of the shrub *Tabernanthe iboga*, which grows in some regions of Africa. Research has demonstrated that ibogaine is able to eliminate the individual's "craving" for narcotics such as heroin in the early phases of abstinence (Glick & Maisonneuve, 2000). However, the side effects of ibogaine, as well as animal studies, suggest that high doses can result in cellular damage to certain regions of the brain.

The major metabolite of ibogaine, *noribogaine*, has a biological half-life of several weeks, and the chemical structure of ibogaine lends itself to chemical manipulation by scientists, who hope to find a chemical cousin to ibogaine that is effective yet lacks the potentially destructive side effects of this compound (Glick & Maisonneuve, 2000). At least one such derivative of ibogaine, known as 18-methoxycoronaridine (18-MC), has demonstrated promise in this regard (Glick & Maisonneuve, 2000).

Methadone maintenance. Methadone is a synthetic narcotic analgesic developed by German chemists during World War II for use in treating wounded soldiers. Although the analgesic effect of a single oral dose of methadone usually lasts 4–6 hours, researchers discovered that orally administered methadone would block the narcotic withdrawal process and the "craving" for narcotics for 24 hours, when used in sufficient doses (Kreek, 2000). The use of methadone was first advocated by Dole and Nyswander (1965), and it has since become the treatment of choice for those individuals who are addicted to opiates (especially heroin).

In the United States, approximately 179,000 individuals are in a methadone maintenance program, and a similar number are on methadone maintenance programs elsewhere around the world (Kreek, 2000). Nationally, 23% of all the patients in methadone maintenance programs are in New York, and 17% are in California (Epstein & Gfroerer, 1997).

The theory behind methadone maintenance is that the use of opiates in certain individuals causes permanent changes in brain function at the cellular level (Dole, 1988; Dole & Nyswander, 1965). It has been suggested that *even a single dose* of a narcotic analgesic brings about a change in the structure of the brain of the addict-to-be, forever altering the way that his or her brain functions (Dole & Nyswander, 1965). According to this theory, when the narcotics are removed from the body, the individual "craves" narcotics for months or possibly even years afterward. This drug craving then makes it more likely that the individual will ultimately return to the use of narcotics in order to feel "normal" again.

The key to treating an addiction to narcotics was to eliminate the almost constant sense of "craving" for drugs, according to Dole and Nyswander (1965). Research had revealed that oral doses of the synthetic opioid methadone would block the majority of the euphoric effects of injected narcotics, control the individual's "craving" for opiates, and keep the patient from going into a state of opiate withdrawal. Surprisingly, research has shown that only 25–35% of the opiate receptor sites in the brain need be occupied by methadone to accomplish this effect (Kreek, 2000).

Dole (1988), one of the major proponents of the methadone maintenance concept, has observed that this treatment approach is "corrective, but not curative" (p. 3025) for the suspected, but as yet unproven, neurological dysfunction that brings about the compulsive use of narcotics. The usual dosage level is between 40–120 mg of methadone each day, the most effective dose for most patients being above 90 mg/day (Karch, 1996). Theoretically, one reason why higher dosage levels are more effective is that opiate-dependent persons who are placed at low doses of either methadone or buprenorphine might continue to experience a prolonged withdrawal syndrome after their acute withdrawal symptoms have been controlled (Stein & Kosten, 1994). Higher dosage levels of methadone are thought to block this hypothetical protracted withdrawal syndrome, making the use of other compounds less appealing.

When used in a maintenance program, methadone is administered in a single dose, usually in the morning.

It is adminstered as a liquid, which is often mixed with a fruit juice. Although some programs have been found that utilize daily doses of methadone as low as 20–35 mg, research has shown that the greatest benefit is obtained when the patient receives moderate (50–80 mg/day) to high (80 mg/day or more) doses of methadone (Strain, Bigelow, Liebson, & Stitzer, 1999).

Since the time of its inception, methadone maintenance has become *the* treatment of choice for opiate-dependent individuals in the United States, especially those addicted to heroin ("Effective Medical Treatment of Opiate Addiction," 1998). Unfortunately, in spite of the fact that the successful methadone maintenance program offers the patient access to psychosocial support/rehabilitation services, many methadone maintenance clinics have become little more than drug distribution centers where no effort is made at actual rehabilitation (Cohen & Levy, 1992). This approach is in sharp contrast to the original concept of methadone maintenance as advanced by Dole and Nyswander (1965), who held that when the suspected neurological dysfunction brought on by the use of narcotics "has been normalized, the ex-addict, supported by counseling and social services, can begin the long process of social rehabilitation" (Dole, 1988, p. 3025).

Research has consistently shown that when methadone maintenance is combined with a range of psychosocial support services (psychotherapy, vocational counseling, social services, etc.), significantly larger numbers of opiate-dependent individuals are able to remain drug-free for longer periods of time than when such services are lacking (McLellan, Arndt, Metzger, Woody, & O'Brien, 1993). Such approaches are clearly cost-effective for the severely impaired person (McLellan, Arndt, Metzger, Woody, & O'Brien, 1993). Yet in spite of the body of literature that supports this view, many methadone maintenance programs continue to provide little more than a steady supply of oral methadone.

Admittedly, there is a point where increased support services are no longer cost-effective. Kraft, Rothbard, Hadley, McLellan, and Asch (1997) examined the impact of increased/decreased spending for supplementary services on abstinence rates for methadone maintenance programs and found that program participants seemed to benefit most from intermediate levels of support. The authors found that methadone maintenance combined with three counseling sessions per week seemed to be most cost-effective in terms of the total number of clients who were able to abstain from heroin use.

Methadone maintenance is quite controversial. Some physicians challenge the concept on the grounds that it is only replacing one addictive substance with another, in effect substituting a legal drug for an illegal one (Cornish, McNicholas, & O'Brien, 1995; *Harvard Mental Health Letter*, 1995a). Many European physicians believe that through such "substitute treatment" (Seivewright & Greenwood, 1996, p. 374), substance abuse treatment professionals can try to engage the client in long-term rehabilitation programs. Critics also point out that the assumption that narcotics use results in permanent neurological changes has never been proved. For example, the *Harvard Mental Health Letter* (1995a) noted that patients might take methadone for years without any apparent toxic effects. This fact raises serious questions about whether opiate-addicted individuals *really* suffer neurological changes as postulated by Dole and Nyswander (1965).

Further, critics argue, between 50% and 90% of the patients in methadone maintenance programs will use other recreational drugs (Glantz & Woods, 1993). It has been found that many of the other recreational drugs, especially alcohol and cocaine, speed up the process of methadone biotransformation, resulting in the patient's experiencing earlier withdrawal symptoms and needing to use higher doses of methadone to avoid opiate withdrawal (Kreek, 2000; Karch, 1996). Other patients on methadone try to obtain the drug propoxyphene (Darvon, Darvocet-N), which will enhance the effects of the methadone to produce a sense of euphoria (DeMaria & Weinstein, 1995). In the eyes of some critics, these drug-seeking behaviors raise serious questions about the individual's motivation for using methadone.

Dole (1989) acknowledged that methadone is "highly specific for the treatment of opiate addiction" (p. 1880) and that it will not block the euphoric effects of other drugs of abuse. Further, methadone "diversion" is a significant problem (Dole, 1995), although the abuse potential of methadone is quite limited. The dropout rate from methadone maintenance programs is greater than 50% in the first year (Schottenfeld, Pakes, Oliveto, Ziedonis, & Kosten, 1997), which suggests that such programs are not the final answer to the problem of narcotics addiction.

However, there are a number of advantages to the methadone maintenance program concept, not the least of which is cost-effectiveness. For example, participants in methadone maintenance programs are less likely to engage in criminal activity than nonparticipants who are opiate-dependent ("Effective Medical Treatment of Opiate Addiction," 1998; National Academy of Science, 1990). Swan (1994) reported that the average cost to society—in terms of criminal activity, social support, legal costs, and medical expenses—for a single untreated drug abuser/addict for 6 months was $21,500. Yet the cost of methadone maintenance for that same individual for 6 months was only $1750.

Buprenorphine. This chemical cousin to morphine has both agonist and antagonist properties. Accordingly, buprenorphine tends to be self-limiting in the sense that doses above a certain level force the body to respond to the drug as though it were an antagonist (O'Connor, 2000). Researchers have discovered that low doses of orally administered buprenorphine (2–4 mg/day) can block the euphoric effects of intravenously administered narcotics (Weiss, Greenfield, & Mirin, 1994; Rosen & Kosten, 1991; Horgan, 1989). For this reason, buprenorphine has been considered as an alternative to methadone (O'Connor, 2000; Ling, Wesson, Charuvastra, & Klett, 1996).

Like methadone, buprenorphine only needs to be administered once a day. Oral buprenorphine doses of 2–8 mg/day are thought to be as effective as up to 65 mg of methadone in blocking the euphoric effects of illicit narcotics (Stine & Kosten, 1994; Strain, Stitzer, Liebson & Bigelow, 1994). Another advantage that buprenorphine offers is that, whereas withdrawal from methadone may last up to 2 weeks and is moderately uncomfortable, withdrawal from buprenorphine lasts only a few days and has fewer symptoms (O'Connor, 2000).

Unfortunately, researchers have found that even when used at high doses, buprenorphine is *only as effective* as methadone in the treatment of opiate addiction (Schottenfeld, Pakes, Oliveto, Ziedonis, & Kosten, 1997; Ling, Wesson, Charuvastra, & Klett, 1996). Further, *intravenously* administered buprenorphine has a significant abuse potential. To combat this, the pharmaceutical company that produces buprenorphine has applied for Food and Drug Administration (FDA) approval to market a combination of buprenorphine and naloxone for oral use, the latter compound being included to induce narcotic withdrawal should the user attempt to grind the pill into a powder and inject it (Leinwand, 2000). It has been suggested that dosage levels of buprenorphine above 8 mg/day might be necessary to suppress illicit opiate use (Fudala & Johnson, 1995). Thus, because of its abuse potential, and because of uncertainty about how it can be used most effectively, it is too soon to say how large a role buprenorphine will play in the fight against narcotics addiction.

LAAM. Another chemical that has been approved as a possible agent in treating opiate addicts is L-alpha-acetylmethadol (LAAM), which is sold in this country under the brand name Orlaam. Like methadone, orally administered LAAM prevents the opiate-addicted individual from going into withdrawal. But the fact that LAAM has a biological half-life of in excess of 48 hours (compared with methadone's half-life of 24 hours) means that the individual need take the drug only once every 2–3 days (Leinwand, 2000). This would virtually eliminate the need for the patient to take doses home, vastly reducing the problem of drug diversion to the illicit market.

Research has found that patients on the highest doses of LAAM have the lowest rates of opiate abuse, as measured by self-report and urine toxicology testing (Eissenberg, Bigelow, Strain, Walsh, Brooner, Stitzer, & Johnson, 1997). Further, research has suggested that LAAM withdrawal does not cause as much distress as withdrawal from methadone (*Alcoholism & Drug Abuse Week*, 1993). However, in spite of its many advantages over methadone, only about 5000 individuals across the country are currently using LAAM to control their opiate "craving" (Leinwand, 2000).

Narcotics withdrawal. Programs that specialize in the treatment of addiction to narcotics often offer controlled withdrawal from opiates. Occasionally, a hospital will offer narcotics withdrawal programs even though it does not attempt to provide long-term treatment for opiate-dependent persons. The detoxification component in each center is very much the same. In the United States, orally administered methadone is the traditional drug of choice for opiate withdrawal (Jenike, 1991).

On the first day, the individual going through opiate withdrawal will receive a dose of 10 mg of methadone each hour until the withdrawal symptoms are brought under control (Mirin, Weiss, & Greenfield, 1991). Once the withdrawal symptoms have been controlled,

the total dose of methadone administered becomes the starting dose for withdrawal. On day 2 of withdrawal, the narcotics addict receives the same dosage level that was found to terminate withdrawal symptoms on day 1, but the entire dose is to be administered in the morning, as a single dose. Starting on the third day, the daily dose of methadone is reduced by 5 mg/day until the patient is completely withdrawn from opiates (Mirin, Weiss, & Greenfield, 1991).

Researchers have found that between 15% and 30% of those individuals who begin the detoxification process will fail to complete it (Rabinowitz, Cohen, & Kotler, 1998). One reason may be the fact that as the daily dosage levels drop to 15 or 20 mg/day, the individual experiences a return of withdrawal symptoms (Mirin, Weiss, & Greenfield, 1991). Although it was hoped that extended (180-day) opiate withdrawal procedures might improve the rather dismal success rate of traditional opiate withdrawal programs, there has been scant evidence that such programs are more effective than traditional short-term opiate withdrawal programs (O'Connor, 2000).

Other programs, however, operate on the philosophy that methadone withdrawal is inappropriate. Some narcotics addicts have reported that methadone withdrawal is worse than going "cold turkey." As we noted in the chapter on narcotics, opiate withdrawal is not life-threatening, and many addicts have reported that withdrawal from narcotics is often no more uncomfortable than having a bad cold or the flu.

Clonidine. The antihypertensive clonidine has been found to be of value in controlling the symptoms of opiate withdrawal. As was noted in Chapter 14, narcotic analgesics suppress the action of the locus ceruleus region of the brain. During the withdrawal process, the locus ceruleus becomes hyperactive, contributing to the individual's subjective sense of discomfort. Clonidine, which is technically an alpha-2 adrenergic agonist, helps to suppress the activity of the locus ceruleus, easing the individual's withdrawal-related discomfort. However, it is not clear whether clonidine is effective with all opiate-dependent patients or just with those who use lower doses of narcotics (Stimmel, 1997a). Thus researchers must determine what patient population clonidine is best suited to help during the withdrawal process.

Although clonidine is often used as the primary agent in controlling withdrawal discomfort, some programs use a combination of clonidine and an opiate blocker, naltrexone hydrochloride, to bring about a 4–5 day opiate withdrawal (Stein & Kosten, 1992). The combination of naltrexone hydrochloride and clonidine is not a standard treatment for narcotics withdrawal (Weiss, Greenfield, & Mirin, 1994). However, the authors noted that this approach "holds promise" (p. 281) as a method of withdrawal from opiates. When used appropriately, the combination of clonidine and naltrexone hydrochloride appears to be as effective as a 20 day methadone withdrawal program for opiate addicts (Stein & Kosten, 1992). The combined effects of naltrexone hydrochloride (which blocks the opiate receptors in the brain) and clonidine (which serves to control the individual's craving for narcotics and the severity of the withdrawal symptoms), thus allows for rapid detoxification from opiates with minimal discomfort.

The authors found that over 95% of their sample were completely withdrawn from narcotics at the end of 5 days. There is some degree of discomfort for the addicted person, but Stein and Kosten (1992) suggested that individuals report about the same level of discomfort as they experienced during a methadone taper. Milhorn (1992) suggested that withdrawal discomfort might be further reduced via transdermal clonidine patches, which would provide a steady supply of the drug while the patch was in place. However, because of the delay in absorption, the author advocated the administration of an oral "loading" dose of 0.2 mg of clonidine at the beginning of the withdrawal cycle.

Although clonidine has been proved to be an effective tool in the control of withdrawal symptoms in opiate-dependent individuals, some individuals have learned to combine clonidine with methadone, alcohol, benzodiazepines, or other drugs to produce a sense of euphoria (Jenike, 1991). Health care professionals must carefully monitor the patient's medication use to avoid the danger of clonidine abuse by the patient.

Experimental methods of opiate withdrawal. One exciting, though unproven, method of opiate withdrawal has been advocated by at least some physicians in Israel (Sawicki, 1995). The Center for Investigation and Treatment of Addiction (CITA) in Israel has developed an "ultrarapid" program for opiate detoxification, wherein the detoxification process is carried out while the patient is in a state of general anesthesia. Both clonidine and opiate antagonists are administered to the

patient while she or he is unconscious, and the entire withdrawal process is completed within a single day (Rabinowitz, Cohen, & Kotler, 1998). After completion of this method of opiate withdrawal, the individual receives a 6-month follow-up course of naltrexone and individual counseling. The former is to block the euphoric effects of narcotics that the individual might attempt to use following detoxification; the latter is to help identify and resolve issues that might contribute to the individual's relapse. Proponents of this method of detoxification claim an 80% success rate after a 6-month period of time, although Rabinowitz, Cohen, and Kotler (1998) claimed that 57% of their sample of 113 male opiate-dependent males had not relapsed in the 6 months following ultrarapid detoxification from opiates.

Pharmacological Treatment of Cocaine Addiction

In spite of an extensive search, researchers have failed to identify a pharmacological agent that will effectively treat cocaine abuse/dependency (Fischman & Haney, 1999). In the early 1980s, scientists believed that antidepressant medications such as imipramine (Wilbur, 1986) and desipramine hydrochloride (Gawin, Kleber, Byck, Rounsaville, Kosten, Jatlow & Morgan, 1989) would be effective in curbing the postwithdrawal "craving" for cocaine. It was hoped that because these antidepressants alter the function of those regions of the brain where cocaine exerts its main effects, they would prove useful in controlling the individual's urge to return to the use of cocaine. This initial research was promising, but subsequent investigation into the possible use of antidepressants in the treatment of cocaine use problems failed to support the initial scientific optimistism.

For example, Meyer (1992) examined the results of the study by Gawin, Kleber, Byck, Rounsaville, Kosten, Jatlow, and Morgan (1989) and challenged their validity on methodological grounds. According to Meyer, the study by Gawin *et al.* was flawed in that the clients *reported* less cocaine use, but urine toxicology tests did not support these claims. Thus the conclusions of this early study are suspect.

In another study that challenged the use of pharmacological agents in the treatment of cocaine abuse/

addiction, Campbell, Thomas, Gabrielli, Lisdow, and Powell (1994) examined the effects of the antidepressant desipramine, the anticonvulsant medication carbamazepine (often used to control the symptoms of epilepsy), and a placebo on 65 cocaine-dependent patients. In the study, the subject pool was divided into three subgroups: 21 subjects received desipramine, 19 carbamazepine, and 25 a placebo. The authors failed to find that the medications utilized had any effect of patient retention or abuse of other chemicals by their subjects, a result that casts doubt on these medications being of value in the routine treatment of cocaine dependency.

At this time, desimipramine hydrochloride is thought to be useful only for the subset of cocaine users who either had symptoms of depression prior to their use of cocaine or became depressed immediately after starting to use cocaine (Mendelson & Mellow, 1996). But even in this limited number of cocaine users, there is a possibility that the desimipramine might cause cardiac problems (Decker, Fins, & Frances, 1987). In an effort to avoid these possible cardiac complications, Margolin, Kosten, Petrakis, Avants, and Kosten (1991) used the "second-generation" antidepressant *bupropion* (Wellbutrin) to try to control postwithdrawal cocaine craving. The authors reported that five of the subjects completed the experiment and one was dropped for medical reasons. Of these five individuals, four subjects had stopped using cocaine after a period of 4 weeks and were still cocaine-free after 3 months. However, the conclusions of this study were marred by the fact that the research sample was made up of only six subjects. Subsequent research failed to confirm that bupropion was effective in the treatment of cocaine use/abuse (Mendelson & Mello, 1996). Again, an agent that was initially thought to hold some promise in the pharmacological treatment of cocaine abuse/addiction has failed to live up to the expectations of researchers.

Another drug that initially demonstrated some efficacy in controlling cocaine craving, at least in experimental settings, was bromocriptine (sold in this country under the brand name *Parlodel*) (DiGregorio, 1990). When administered in a single dose of 1.25 mg, bromocriptine was found to decrease postwithdrawal cocaine craving, according to DiGregorio (1990), and 0.625 mg given by mouth four times a day was found to reduce psychiatric symptoms associated with cocaine withdrawal. Unfortunately, bromocriptine's side effects include headaches, sedation, muscle tremor, and dry mouth, which made some users so uncomfortable that they discontinued it. Further, the possibility that bromocriptine is itself addictive raised concern about its use. Early clinical trials with bromocriptine failed to yield any positive results, and it is now thought to be of little value in the treatment of cocaine addiction (Mendelson & Mello, 1996; Holloway, 1991).

Surprisingly, the drug *flupenthixol* not only demonstrated some initial promise in the treatment of cocaine use problems but has also continued to appear effective in controlling cocaine use/abuse (Mendelson & Mello, 1996). Flupenthixol is currently available in Europe, the Far East, and the Carribean, but not in the United States. This drug would seem to be quite effective in the control of postwithdrawal cocaine craving, according to the authors. Holloway (1991) found that some cocaine-addicted persons on flupenthixol report that their craving for cocaine is "manageable but is not eliminated" (p. 100). Thus flupenthixol appears to hold some promise as a possible pharmacological agent in the treatment of cocaine use problems. Whether that promise will be fulfilled remains to be seen.

A number of compounds are now under investigation as possible agents in the treatment of cocaine addiction, including compounds that block the action of the dopamine reuptake "pump" (Stocker, 1997). Such compounds include chemicals identified as GBR 12909, a long-acting form of GBR 12909 known as Compound 5, and another chemical known as PTT (Stocker, 1997). Another radical approach to the treatment of cocaine abuse/addiction involves teaching the body to use the immuse system against cocaine molecules (Wright, 1999). There is theoretical reason to believe it may be possible to mount an immune response against certain elements of the cocaine molecule. The body would then form "antibodies" designed to destroy any molecule that had the same chemical structure. In theory, a vaccine could be developed that would allow the body to develop an immune response to cocaine molecules introduced into it (Wright, 1999).

The anticocaine vaccine is now in experimental use (Wright, 1999). However, it is not the ultimate answer to the problem of chemical abuse/addiction, because it will be specific to cocaine and thus will not interfere with the use of other recreational drugs (Wright, 1999). Indeed, for this innovative approach to be totally effective, scientists would have to devise a vaccine that would activate the immune system against all the drugs of abuse—a goal that remains elusive. Finally, the individual would have to be motivated enough to be innoculated against cocaine, and few cocaine abusers/addicts would view this as desirable.

Although buprenorphine initially demonstrated some promise in the control of cocaine withdrawal "craving," subsequent research failed to support the early reports of effectiveness, and buprenorphine's apparent salutary potential in the control of cocaine "craving" has been questioned (Schottenfeld, Pakes, Oliveto, Ziedonis, & Kosten, 1997).

In the late 1980s, a different treatment approach for cocaine addiction was proposed. Trachtenberg and Blum (1988) theorized that cocaine addiction might be influenced by the neurochemicals available in the brain and suggested the use of a "nutritional neurochemical support" system (p. 326) to aid in the treatment of cocaine addiction. By using a combination of amino acids, selected minerals, and vitamins, the authors tried to boost the formation of the neurotransmitters depleted by chronic cocaine use and thus reduce the "craving" cocaine users report when they stop using the drug. In one research study, the authors presented claims of a ninefold reduction in dropout rates for patients in an experimental group who received a patented formulation of "nutritional neurochemical support" (p. 326), compared to those who did not receive such support. Subsequent research has failed to replicate these findings, however, and there has been little interest in the neuronutrient approach to the treatment of cocaine addiction since the early 1990s.

Researchers have found some evidence that carbamazepine, a medication used to control seizure, might also be useful not only during the withdrawal phase of cocaine addiction treatment but also afterwards, when the individual is most at risk for relapse (Sherman, 2000b). However, the need for pharmacological support following cocaine withdrawal has been challenged (Satel, Price, Palumbo, McDougle, Krystal, Gawin, Charney, Heninger, & Kleber, 1991). The authors concluded that their data "failed to demonstrate the emergence" (p. 1715) of severe withdrawal symptoms following the initiation of abstinence and that, although there were reports of craving for cocaine, their subjects experienced a marked decline in the strength and frequency of such craving over the first 3 weeks of abstinence. For these reasons, Satel *et al.* (1991) concluded that there did not seem to be a need for routine pharmacological support of cocaine addicts during the early stages of recovery.

Pharmacological Treatment of Nicotine Dependency

Nicotine replacement therapies. The most common approach to helping smokers quit has been some form of nicotine replacement therapy (Benowitz, 1997b). Unfortunately, nicotine replacement therapies have achieved only a "modest success rate" (Covey, Sullivan, Johnston, Glassman, Robinson, & Adams, 2000, p. 17) in helping people give up the habit of smoking cigarettes. The theory is that alternative methods of nicotine administration enable the individual to substitute the nicotine replacement system for the practice of smoking cigarettes. This would expose the individual to fewer potentially harmful chemicals, and after the individual had achieved a reduction in her or his level of nicotine ingestion, the nicotine substitution system would gradually be discontinued.

Nicotine-containing gum was first introduced to U.S. consumers in 1984. Originally, nicotine-containing gum was available only with a physician's prescription. However, in 1996 the Food and Drug Administration approved the sale of nicotine-containing gum without a prescription as an aid to smoking cessation. The nicotine in the gum is released when the gum is chewed, and it is slowly absorbed through the soft tissues in the mouth. However, the manner in which nicotine-containing gum is chewed differs from that normally used for traditional "chewing gum." With nicotine-containing gum, the individual must adopt a "chew-park-chew-park" (Fiore, Jorenby, Baker, & Kenford, 1992, p. 2691) system of chewing the gum. When this method is adopted, about 90% of the nicotine in the gum is released in the first 30 minutes that the gum is chewed.

Unfortunately, researchers soon discovered that the use of nicotine-containing gum resulted in a lower blood level of nicotine than that achieved by cigarette smoking. Nicotine-containing gum with 2 mg of nicotine was found to bring about a blood level of nicotine only about one-third as high as that achieved through cigarette use, and a piece of gum with 4 mg of nicotine brought about a blood level only about two-thirds of that achieved through smoking (American Psychiatric Association, 1996). Further, the use of nicotine-containing gum itself was found to cause side effects such as sore gums, excessive salivation, nausea, anorexia, headache, and the formation of ulcers on the gums (Lee & D'Alonzo, 1993). Beverages with a high acid content, such as orange juice and coffee, were found to block the absorption of the nicotine from the gum, making it necessary for the smoker to avoid such acidic compounds while using nicotine-containing gum.

Unfortunately, the initial enthusiasm for nicotine-containing gum soon gave way to disappointment, as later studies found that the success rate of nicotine-containing gum was about the same as that of a placebo. At this time, nicotine-containing gum is thought to have little value in smoking-cessation programs (Fiore, Jorenby, Baker, & Kenford, 1992).

Several factors were found to influence the effectiveness of nicotine-containing gum. First, smoking-cessation counseling was found to increase the individual's chances of successfully quitting when the individual used nicotine-containing gum (Fiore, Smith, Jorenby, & Baker, 1994). Another factor that affected the individual's chances of successfully quitting was his or her expectations for the nicotine-containing gum (Gottlieb, Killen, Marlatt, & Taylor, 1987).

By 1991, several companies had introduced transdermal nicotine patches designed to supply a constant blood level of nicotine to the user without the need for the user to smoke cigarettes. It was hypothesized that the smoker might find it easier to break the habit of smoking if he or she did not actually have to smoke to obtain a moderately high blood level of nicotine. Later, usually 2–8 weeks after the individual no longer engaged in the physical motions of smoking, the dosage levels of nicotine in the patches would be reduced, providing a gradual taper in blood nicotine levels.

Researchers found that transdermal nicotine patches were moderately effective adjuncts to smoking-cessation programs (Fiore, Smith, Jorenby, & Baker, 1994; Fiore, Jorenby, Baker, & Kenford, 1992). Of those individuals who had used the "patch," approximately 22–42% were still smoke-free 6 months after treatment, compared to only 5–28% of those individuals who used a placebo transdermal patch. Further, transdermal nicotine re-

placement systems reduce some of the more troublesome side effects, such as insomnia, that many people experience as they try to quit smoking (Wetter, Fiore, Baker, & Young, 1995).

But the transdermal nicotine patch was found to have several drawbacks. First, in contrast to the nearly instantaneous rise in blood nicotine levels achieved when a person smokes a cigarette, the transdermal nicotine patch requires approximately 1 hour for blood nicotine levels to reach their peak (Nelson, 2000). Another problem with transdermal nicotine patches is that individuals who smoke while using the nicotine transdermal patch, or within an hour of removing the patch, run the risk of nicotine toxicity and even cardiovascular problems. Further, although the transdermal nicotine patch reduces levels of nicotine craving, the nicotine blood levels achieved via transdermal patches often are lower than those achieved by cigarette smoking, so the user may experience some degree of "craving" for cigarettes (Henningfield, 1995).[3] Also, the transdermal patch was found to cause skin irritation in some users, as well as abnormal or disturbing dreams, insomnia, diarrhea, and a burning sensation near where the patch is resting on the skin.

Even with the use of the transdermal nicotine patch, a significant number of smokers were found to return to the practice of cigarette smoking. Kenford, Fiore, Jorenby, Smith, Wetter, and Baker (1994) attempted to identify factors that would predict which individuals would, and which would not, succeed in giving up cigarette smoking while using a transdermal nicotine patch. Study participants also received group counseling. The authors found that those individuals who were able to abstain from cigarette smoking during the first 2 weeks of treatment, especially during the second week of treatment, were most likely to give up their cigarette use. However, 90% of those individuals who smoked during the second week of treatment while using a transdermal nicotine patch were still smoking cigarettes 6 months later.

The results of Kenford *et al.* (1994) are consistent with earlier studies that suggest that the first month of

---

[3]To address this problem, the American Psychiatric Association (1996) recommended that the user try supplementary doses of nicotine-containing gum if he or she finds that the transdermal skin patch does not provide sufficiently high levels of nicotine to block this "craving."

smoking cessation is especially difficult for the ex-smoker. Further, the results of this study suggest that the transdermal nicotine patch, though useful as an adjunct to smoking-cessation programs, is not totally effective in helping smokers quit. Indeed, there is some evidence that some former smokers will require transdermal nicotine patches for years in order to abstain from cigarette use (Sherman, 1994). Of course, these individuals will still be obtaining nicotine in their systems, but at least they will not be exposing themselves to the multitude of known and suspected toxins in cigarette smoke.

A nicotine-containing nasal spray has been developed for use in the control of tobacco craving following smoking cessation and was approved by the Food and Drug Administration as an aid to smoking cessation in March 1996. This spray is sold in the United States under the brand name *Nicotrol NS*, and the user administers one spray in each nostril up to 40 times a day (Pagliaro & Pagliaro, 1998). Within 10 minutes of using the spray, the nicotine blood level approximates that achieved by smoking one tobacco cigarette, according to the authors. It is suggested that this spray be used for less than 6 months, because it carries considerable potential for physical addiction (Benowitz, 1992). Indeed, in their investigation into the effectiveness of a nasal spray as an aid to smoking cessation, Sutherland, Stapleton, Russell, Jarvis, Hajek, Belcher, and Feyerabend (1992) found that after 6 months, the nicotine concentrations were three-quarters of those found in active smokers. Although the authors concluded that the "systemic nicotine replacement" (p. 328) that the individuals in their research sample achieved by using the nasal spray was responsible for lower levels of nicotine craving, it is possible that their sample was simply replacing dependency on tobacco with dependency on the nasal spray.

Sutherland *et al.* (1992) found that the nasal spray utilized in their investigation was rapidly absorbed through the nasal membranes and that, with the exception of some sinus irritation, this method of nicotine administration has no serious side effects. According to the authors, only 2 subjects of the 116 in the treatment group had to discontinue use of the nicotine nasal spray because of adverse side effects, a result that suggests this method of nicotine replacement therapy is quite safe. Heavy smokers seemed to be the most likely to benefit from the nasal spray (Sutherland *et al.*, 1992). Smokers who used the spray had less weight gain than subjects who received a placebo nasal spray, and 26% of the smokers who had received the nicotine-containing nasal spray had remained smoke-free for a full year, whereas only 10% of the group that received the placebo was able to abstain from cigarette smoking.

In 1998, McNeil Pharmaceuticals introduced a nicotine inhalation system for use by smokers trying to quit. This device, which is used in place of cigarettes, delivers to the user about 4 mg out of the 10 mg of nicotine contained in the cartridge. (The remaining nicotine either evaporates during use or remains in the cartridge.) The device is designed for short-term use only, and the individual should not use more than 16 cartridges per day, but 20% of smokers who used this system in preliminary studies were able to abstain from smoking for 6 months.

Clonidine. A number of researchers have attempted to use the antihypertensive drug clonidine to control the craving for nicotine often reported by former cigarette smokers. Although the initial research studies were promising, subsequent research suggested that the side effects of clonidine were so severe that it was not useful as an initial approach to smoking cessation (Gourlay & Benowitz, 1995). At this time, scientists believe that clonidine might be most effective only in those smokers who experience high levels of agitation when they try to quit smoking (Covey *et al.*, 2000). The American Psychiatric Association (1996) recommended that clonidine be used only with those individuals who had attempted nicotine replacement therapy without success.

Silver acetate. When used by a cigarette smoker, silver acetate produces a disulfiram-like reaction (Hymowitz, Feuerman, Hollander, & Frances, 1993). Chewing gum and lozenges have been used in Europe for the purpose of smoking cessation for more than a decade now, although this medication is not available in the United States. When the individual has recently used the gum or lozenge and then attempts to smoke, a "noxious metallic taste" results (Hymowitz *et al.*, 1993, p. 113). This obnoxious taste then causes the smoker to discard the cigarette and replaces the nicotine-based pharmacological reward with an aversive experience.

Silver acetate is quite dangerous, and overuse may result in *permanent* discoloration of the skin and body organs (Hymowitz, Feuerman, Hollander, & Frances, 1993). However, the authors point out that this side effect of silver acetate is quite rare and is usually seen only after "massive overuse and abuse" (p. 113). Another drawback of silver acetate is that its effectiveness in smoking cessation has not been fully tested. However, preliminary research has suggested a possible role for silver acetate lozenges and gum as an aid in smoking cessation.

Buspar. Buspar (buspirone, discussed in Chapter 10) was initially thought to be potentially useful in smoking-cessation programs. Theoretically, the ability of buspirone to conteract the agitation and anxiety often experienced when the individual tries to quit smoking made this medication appear useful to researchers. However, subsequent research failed to support the use of buspirone unless the individual experienced high levels of anxiety when she or he tried to quit smoking (Covey et al., 2000).

Bupropion. Cigarette smoking causes the release of dopamine within the brain's "pleasure center," and for this reason, agents that stimulate the release of dopamine are potentially useful in controlling cigarette "craving" (Nelson, 2000). This is the theory behind the use of timed release forms of the antidepressant bupropion, which is sold under the brand name of Zyban. Bupropion has a weak ability to stimulate the release of dopamine within the brain, and up to 44% of cigarette smokers who used it at high dosage levels (150 mg/bid, for example) were able to stop smoking for short periods of time, compared with 19% of those individuals who received a placebo (Benowitz, 1997b).

Other agents. Other agents that have been utilized in the treatment of nicotine withdrawal over the years include the tricyclic antidepressants and lobeline (a drug derived from a variety of tobacco) (Lee & D'Alonzo, 1993). The *combination* of nicotine replacement therapies with bupropion has also been suggested but has not been tested (Benowitz, 1997b). In spite of extensive research, however, no single substance has yet proved effective beyond any reasonable doubt in treating the symptoms of nicotine withdrawal.

Summary

The pharmacological treatment of substance abuse involves the use of selected chemicals to aid the recovering addict in his or her attempt to maintain sobriety. To this end, a number of different chemicals have been utilized as experimental agents, in the hope that one or more would prove useful in controlling either the withdrawal symptoms experienced by a recovering addict in the early stages of sobriety or the "craving" that many addicts experience after they stop using chemicals.

CHAPTER THIRTY-THREE

Substance Abuse/Addiction and Infectious Disease[1]

Introduction

Infectious diseases are, collectively, one of the most serious medical complications of intravenous drug abuse (Passaro, Werner, McGee, MacKenzie, & Vugia, 1998; Mathew, Addai, Ashwin, Morrobel, Maheshwari, & Freels, 1995). These infectious agents gain admission into the individual's body in a variety of ways: by being "punched through" the skin by intravenous drug abusers, by being inhaled by individuals who smoke a drug of abuse, or via passive exposure in an environment that predisposes the individual to infection. The infections commonly found in intravenous drug addicts include peripheral cellulitis, skin abscesses, pneumonia, lung abscesses, and tetanus.

Why Is Infectious Disease Such a Common Complication of Alcohol/Drug Abuse?

Chronic substance abuse is a prime cause of malnutrition, which in turn lowers the individual's resistance to infection. For example, both alcohol-related malnutrition and vitamin malabsorption syndromes can compromise the effectiveness of the immune system. Finally, alcohol use by itself can impair the effectiveness of the body's immune system (Szabo, 1997). All of these factors contribute to the higher rate of infectious disease seen in alcohol abusers/addicts.

Sterile technique. The conditions under which intravenous drug abusers inject the chemicals also practically guarantees infection. This is because intravenous drug abusers rarely use proper "sterile technique" when injecting a chemical. In a hospital setting, staff will sterilize the injection site with either alcohol or an antiseptic solution and then inject a sterile solution containing the pharmaceutical into the patient's body. As a rule, however, drug addicts simply find a vein and then insert the needle directly into it without even attempting to wash the injection site with any kind of an antiseptic. This pushes microscopic organisms found on the surface of the skin directly into the intravenous drug addict's body, bypassing the protective layers of skin that usually keep such microorganisms from the blood-rich tissues within.

Another reason why IV drug users are prone to infections is that intravenous "street" drugs are often contaminated with various microscopic pathogens. Thus injecting the compound also injects whatever microscopic pathogens are in the mixture. Further, intravenous drug abusers often share needles. In some parts of this country, it is not uncommon for several people to use the same needle and syringe in turn, without stopping to sterilize it. This practice exposes each subsequent user of that needle to infectious agents in the blood of previous users (Garrett, 1994). When intravenous drug users try to clean the needle by licking it, they transfer microorganisms such as *Neisseria sicca* and *Streptococcus viridans*, (bacteria normally limited to the mouth) to the intravenous needle, contributing

[1]The author would like to thank John P. Doweiko, M.D., for his kindness in reviewing this chapter for technical accuracy.

further to infection (Dewitt & Paauw, 1996). Some IV drug abusers have been known to wash the "rig"[2] with water. But ordinary tap water may also contain microorganisms that are harmless to the individual when the water is ingested but can cause infection when injected into the user's circulation (Dewitt & Paauw, 1996).

The infections that can be transmitted from one person to another through contaminated needles include all the viruses that cause hepatitis (discussed later in this chapter). Occasionally, malaria is transmitted from one person to another through the use of contaminated intravenous needles (Garrett, 1994; Cherubin & Sapira, 1993). Bacterial infections such as syphilis can also be transmitted from one person to another via contaminated needles. Some of the more common forms of infection transmissible by this route are discussed below.

Endocarditis. Endocarditis is a condition that develops when bacteria infect the valves of the heart. Approximately 1 in every 20,000 people in the general population will develop this condition, which can be life-threatening. However, IV drug abusers are "at risk" for the development of endocarditis, and 1 in every 500 intravenous drug abusers will eventually develop this disorder (Robinson, Lazo, Davis, & Kufera, 2000). The chronic use of irritating chemicals such as those often used to adulterate illicit narcotics is one cause of endocarditis (Mathew, Addai, Anand, Morrobel, Meheshwari, & Freels, 1995). Another is thought to be the bacteria normally found on the skin, which are punched into the subdermal tissues when an intravenous drug abuser fails to use the proper technique to sterilize the injection site. Finally, shared needles allow bacterial infections to be transmitted rapidly from one individual to another.

Necrotizing fascitis. This is an infection in which subcutaneous tissues are attacked by bacteria normally found on the surface of the skin (Karch, 1996). There are clinical indications that cocaine users are especially vulnerable to necrotizing fascitis, but it can develop in any intravenous drug abuser who fails to use the proper antiseptic procedures to prepare the skin before injection, thus pushing bacteria found on the skin into the blood-rich tissues of the body. As the bacteria destroy the tissues under the skin, the infection might spread to deeper tissues or to internal organs.

[2]See the Glossary.

The surface of the skin appears normal until late in the course of the infection, making diagnosis difficult. This condition can be fatal.

Skin abscesses. These are a common complication of intravenous drug abuse. It is thought that adulterants mixed with heroin or cocaine cause or contribute to skin abscesses. Because the adulterants are usually not water-soluble, they cause the body to react to their presence at the injection site. Further, most I V drug abusers do not utilize proper antiseptic techniques, setting the stage for bacterial infection. The result of these factors is the formation of abscesses under the surface of the skin, which may develop into a life-threatening infection.

The Pneumonias

Technically, the term *pneumonia* refers to an acute infection of the lung tissue, usually caused by bacteria. Pneumonia is generally diagnosed by x-ray examination of the lungs. Numerous conditions contribute to the development of pneumonia, including alcohol dependency, immune system disorders, cigarette smoking, extreme age, vitamin malabsorption syndromes, and exposure to infective agents. Alcohol/drug abuse can predispose the individual to one or more forms of pneumonia. For example, as a group, alcoholics have at least twice the rate of bacterial pneumonia as nonalcoholics (Nace, 1987).

Fungal pneumonia. Fungal pneumonia is a common complication of HIV-1 infection (discussed below) and of heroin abuse/addiction (Karch, 1996). There are two primary reasons for this. First, chronic heroin abuse interferes with the effectiveness of the immune system. Second, many samples of "street" heroin are contaminated by fungi. When the user injects fungi-contaminated heroin, the fungi are able to evade the defensive barriers of the skin and respiratory tract. To complicate matters, the fungi are often deposited within the lungs by the circulatory system, resulting in fungal pneumonia.

Aspirative pneumonia. In addition to providing a holding site for undigested food, the stomach allows bacteria essential to the digestive process access to the food that has been ingested. Here they begin transforming essential nutrients into forms that are be absorbed by the body. By blocking the normal function of the upper digestive tract, especially the vomiting and gag reflexes, alcohol can cause the drinker to inhale (aspirate) some of the stomach contents being passed up the esophagus to the outside during the act of vomiting. As a result, (1) bacteria normally found only in the digestive tract gain access to the respiratory tract, which has few defenses specific to them, and (2) undigested food particles may also be aspirated into the respiratory tract, where they decay, fueling bacterial growth. The chronic use of alcohol also (3) alters the normal pattern of bacterial growth in the mouth and throat and (4) interferes with the normal cough reflex. These factors combine to make it more likely that the chronic drinker will aspirate, and in the course of vomiting be exposed to bacteria not normally found in the lungs, which then infect the lung tissues (Saitz, Ghali, & Moskowitz, 1997).

All these processes contribute to the development of what is known as *aspirative pneumonia*, which can be fatal. An additional danger is that if the individual is unconscious or only semiconscious during vomiting, she or he may choke on the material aspirated and suffocate. It is not known how many cases of aspirative pneumonia develop each year in the United States, partly because many such cases are misdiagnosed as community-acquired pneumonia (discussed below). Aspirative pneumonia is known to be a potentially fatal medical problem that will require drastic medical intervention(s) to save the individual's life.

Community-acquired pneumonia. Intravenous heroin abusers, cigarette smokers, and alcohol-dependent persons are all known to be at increased risk for a condition known as community-acquired pneumonia (CAP) (Karch, 1996).[3] CAP affects an estimated 2–4 million people in the United States each year. There are 10 different microorganisms that can cause a form of community-acquired pneumonia (Finch & Woodhead, 1998). Mild cases may be treated on an outpatient basis, but fully 20% of patients with CAP eventually require hospitalization (Rubins & Janoff, 1997; Campbell, 1994). Those individuals who are most likely to require hospitalization for CAP are persons with "co-morbid" conditions in addition to the lung infection, a term that includes alcohol/drug abusers. Unfortunately, depending on the patient's age and health status, between 5% and 50% of those who are hospitalized with CAP will die, in spite of the best medical care (Finch & Woodhead, 1998; Leeper & Torres, 1995; Campbell, 1994).

As early as the 1890s, pneumonia was recognized as a significant cause of death for alcohol-dependent individuals, although doctors did not know how alcohol contributed to the development of pneumonia (Leeper & Torres, 1995). Since then, researchers have found that chronic alcohol use interferes with the lung's ability to defend itself against infectious microorganisms. Researchers have also discovered that IV drug abuse can indirectly impair the effectiveness of the immune system. Finally, cigarette smoking both reduces the effectiveness of the lung's defenses and causes changes within the lungs, making smokers vulnerable to CAP, especially the form caused by the bacteria *H. influenzae* (Finch & Woodhead, 1998; Rubins & Janoff, 1997; Leeper & Torres, 1995).

Acquired Immune Deficiency Syndrome (AIDS)

In 1981 it became clear to medical researchers that a previously unknown disease had began to spread through the population of the United States. Initially, the disease seemed to be isolated to the homosexual male population. In certain individuals, the immune system would rapidly fail, leaving them vulnerable to "opportunistic infections" rarely if ever encountered in the patient with a normal immune system. Medical researchers termed this condition *acquired immune deficiency syndrome* (AIDS).

Shortly after it was identified, physicians began to uncover cases of AIDS in intravenous drug abusers and in individuals whose only apparent "risk factor" was that they had received a blood transfusion in the past. These facts suggested to researchers that some kind of blood-borne infection was involved in the development of AIDS. Within a short period of time, researchers had isolated a virus that has since come to be known as the *human immunodeficiency virus* (HIV) (McCutchan, 1990). As different members of the same virus family have been identified, it has become necessary to identify each by a number. The virus that is thought to cause AIDS is now known to medicine as HIV-1.

What is AIDS? Technically, AIDS is not a disease in its own right but a *constellation of symptoms*, the most

---

[3]As opposed to pneumonia acquired in a hospital setting, aspirative pneumonia, or pneumonia secondary to some form of lung trauma.

important of which is the destruction of the individual's immune system (Welsby, 1997). AIDS is the end stage of a viral infection caused by HIV-1. As the HIV-1 infection progresses, the patient eventually dies from an infection, or neoplasm, or from some other condition that the immune system was once able to control easily.

Where did HIV-1 come from? HIV-1 is now viewed by scientists as just one of the multitude of infections that have "jumped" from animals to humans as the causal microbe has adapted to human beings as a new host species (Fauci, 1999; Preston, 1999).[4] For a long time, scientists have known that viruses

> have an ability to move from one type of host to another in what is known as a trans-species jump. The virus changes during the course of a jump, adapting to its new host. The trans-species jump is the virus's most important means of long-term survival. Species go extinct; viruses move on. (Preston, 1999, p. 54)

It is thought that HIV-1 originally infected members of the chimpanzee species *Pan troglodytes troglodytes* and that it may have "jumped" to a human host when a person with an open cut on his or her hands butchered a chimpanzee for human consumption, possibly sometime in the 1930s (Park, 2000; Fauci, 1999). On the basis of genetic similarities between HIV-1 and similar viruses that infect primates, scientists believe that HIV-1 and those viruses that affect other primates shared a common viral ancestor as recently as 600–1200 years ago (Bowers, 2000; Barre-Sinoussi, 1996). However, until the advent of modern transportation systems, HIV-1 infection remained isolated in remote Africa and thus never was noticed by medical researchers. There is little if any creditable evidence that HIV-1 was intentionally released into the population to target homosexual males or other minority group members or that it represents divine retribution for past sins (Karlen, 1995).

How does AIDS kill? In brief, every bacterial species, every virus, and every fungus has a characteristic pattern of protein molecules in the wall of its cells. When the human body is invaded by one of these microorgan-

isms, the immune system learns to recognize the specific pattern of proteins that make up the cell wall of the invader. The body also learns how to tell the difference between the protein pattern of an invading organism and that of the body's own cells. The immune system learns to protect the body from invading organisms by building "antibodies," which recognize foreign cells, and attack them.

The first time that the body is exposed to a new organism, it must rely on more generalized disease-fighting cells known as *lymphocytes*. These generalists roam through the body, seeking out and attacking *any* invader with a foreign protein pattern in its cell wall. These antibodies are the ones that mount the initial attack against a new invader while the body "learns" to produce disease-specific antibodies. Unfortunately, producing the disease-specific cells necessary to fight off a specific bacterium or virus may take hours, days, weeks, or even years.

After it has been exposed to a virus, fungus, or bacterium, the body "tailor-makes" some immune cells (antibodies) for each different form of microorganism that it encounters. These pathogen-specific antibodies are designed to recognize the individual protein pattern on the surface of each invading species. These disease-specific antibodies then drift in the individual's blood, spending their entire lives patrolling for just one specific virus, fungus, or bacterium. This is the mechanism through which a person who has once had an infection becomes "immune" to that disease. After recovering from the infection, the individual will have in reserve a number of white blood cells from the previous exposure to the invader, patiently waiting until the next time that same microorganism tries to enter the individual's body. He or she is now "immune" to that disease.

In the body, viral particles often show a preference for certain organ systems. In humans, HIV-1 exhibits a preference for the cells of the immune system, especially the type of lymphocytes known as the CD4+ or "T-helper" cells (Lisanti & Zwolski, 1997). These cells serve to "activate" the body's immune response. Between 93% and 99% of the HIV-1 viral particles in a person's body might be found in the CD4+ cells (Pomerantz, 1998). Thus, in the infected individual, the greatest concentration of the virus lurks in the very cells of the individual's body designed to destroy HIV-1. Small concentrations of the virus invade other regions of the body, such as the cells of

---

[4]This is a common occurrence. For example, Karlen (1995) identified almost 300 different infectious diseases in humans that were acquired when, sometime in the past, the microbe that causes that specific disease "jumped" from the original host to human beings.

the retina, the brain, and the testes (Pomerantz, 1998), providing reservoirs of virus particles that can reinfect a person whose body has been otherwise cleansed of the virus (Pomerantz, 1998).

In the early 1980s, researchers believed that the virus passed through a period of latency, in which there was little viral activity (Weiner, 1997). This was because the bodies of individuals infected with HIV-1 might take up to 9 months to begin to manufacture lymphocytes specific to the AIDS virus (McCutchan, 1990). After the development of special HIV-1 "viral load" tests, however, scientists discovered that HIV-1 begins rapidly multiplying virtually the moment it enters the individual's body, but that it takes several months before the body's immune system is able to produce lymphocytes against HIV-1 (Henry, Stiffman, & Feldman, 1997).

Each time the HIV-1 virus replicates in a person's body, it produces slightly different copies of itself. The specific mechanism is quite technical, but in brief, HIV-1 tends to be "sloppy" during the process of replication, allowing subtle "mistakes" to slip into the genetic code of each new generation of viral particles. These HIV-1 variations are, in time, released into the general circulation. Because of the altered genetic code of each new generation of HIV-1, the body responds to them all as though they were "new" viral invaders (Terwilliger, 1995; Nowak & McMichael, 1995). As a result of this process, by the later stages of HIV-1 infection, a single individual might have as many as *a billion* different forms of the HIV-1 virus in his or her body (Richardson, 1995). Further, research suggests that up to *10 billion* new viral particles are produced each day in an infected person's body (Henry, Stiffman, & Feldman, 1997; Saag, 1997). Toward the end of the infectious process, the individual's body is host to a "swarm" of viruses (Barre-Sinoussi, 1996, p. 32; Terwilliger, 1995; Beardsley, 1994). As the immune system becomes weaker, various "opportunistic infections," caused by microorganisms that were once easily controlled by the immune system, begin to develop. Eventually, the body's weakened defenses are overwhelmed by these invading microbes, and the patient dies.

The chain of HIV-1 infection. HIV-1 is a fragile virus that is not easily transmitted (Langone, 1989); rather the virus must be passed *directly* from one individual to another. The apparent modes of HIV-1 transmission are the direct mixing of one's blood with infected body fluids (as occurs when one uses a contaminated intravenous needle), receiving a transfusion of a blood product contaminated with the virus, passage of the virus from mother to fetus, transmission via the mother's milk to a suckling baby (Kruger & Jerrells, 1992), and infection through sexual contact with an infected person. Each year in the United States 7000 infants are born already infected with HIV-1 (Klirsfeld, 1998). Globally, 75–85% of all cases of HIV are transmitted as a result of sexual contact between an infected and a noninfected individual (Klirsfeld, 1998; Royce, Sena, Cates, & Cohen, 1997).

By early 1983, researchers had concluded that HIV-1 could be passed from one person to another through blood donations if the donor had been infected with the virus (Goodnough, Brecher, Kanter, & AuBuchon, 1999). Since then, scientists have developed a number of tests to detect blood samples donated by persons infected with HIV-1. With the advent of these new tests, there has been a drastic reduction in the level of HIV-1 transfusion in the United States through contaminated blood. At this time, it is estimated that the patient who receives a blood transfusion consisting of one "unit" of blood[5] has approximately 1 chance in 2,000,000 of contracting HIV-1 (Goodnough, Brecher, Kanter, & AuBuchon, 1999).

In the United States, the most common means by which HIV-1 is transmitted from one person to another is by the sharing of contaminated drug paraphernalia. Between 3% and 9% of U.S. intravenous drug abusers become infected with HIV-1 each year (Darton & Dilts, 1998). This is in contrast to the rest of the world, where sexual contact with an infected partner is the most common means by which the disease is passed on to new victims. Because of this fact, many experts now classify HIV-1 as a sexually transmitted disease (STD). As with any other STD, the greater the number of sexual partners one individual has, the greater his or her chance of being exposed. To illustrate the danger of contracting HIV-1 through sexual relations, consider the fact that of those women in the United States who received their diagnosis between July 1997 and June 1998, fully 37% were infected via sexual relations with an infected partner, whereas only 30% contracted the infection from contaminated needles (Zelentz & Epstein, 1999).

---

[5]Usually 1000 cubic centimeters, or just under 1 pint of blood.

These differences in the mode of HIV-1 transmission in this country as compared with the rest of the world reflect the fact that there are at least 10 different subtypes of HIV-1, which are classified as types A, B, etc. (Barre-Sinoussi, 1996). The E subtype, which is found mainly in Asia and Africa, is more easily passed from an infected male to his female partner. This is why heterosexual transmission of HIV-1 is *the* most common means by which the virus is passed from one person to another in Asia and Africa. The B subtype of the HIV-1 virus, which is the prevalent strain in the United States, is not able to pass easily into the mucous membranes of the woman, thus making heterosexual transmission of the B subtype more difficult (Anderson, 1993). However, homosexual transmission of this subtype of HIV-1 occurs more readily, and approximately 6% of the gay males contract HIV-1 each year (Garrett, 2000).

The scope of the problem. At the start of the 21st century, HIV-1 is estimated to have infected 34.3 million people globally, with another 15,000 persons becoming infected with each passing day (Schrof-Fisher, 2000; Dowell, 2000). It is estimated that by the year 2020, 500 million people may be infected with HIV-1 (Garrett, 2000). The continent of Africa has been hit especially hard; 23.3 million people on that continent are estimated to be infected with HIV-1 (Dowell, 2000). The rate of infection varies from country to country: 25% of the adults in Zimbabwe are infected with the virus (Ezzell, 2000), whereas in other certain countries in Africa, 70% of the women of reproductive age are HIV-1-positive (Sowell, Moneyham, & Aranda-Naranjo, 1999). In some regions of Africa, 80% of the adults between 20 and 49 years of age are thought to be infected with HIV-1 (Bowers, 2000). Just under 90% of those infected with HIV live in the "Third World."

In the United States, approximately 2 million people are believed to be infected with HIV-1, with 40,000–70,000 more people being infected each year ("Addiction Treatment in the Age of HIV/AIDS," 1999). Approximately a quarter of those infected with HIV-1 in this country are women (Klirsfeld, 1998). Researchers have found that there are differences in how men and women typically are exposed to the virus in the United States. Only 3% of the men infected with HIV-1 acquired the infection through heterosexual contacts, whereas approximately 50% of HIV-1-infected women contracted the virus as a result of sexual contact with an infected male (Klirsfeld, 1998; Amaro, 1995). This difference in transmission rate reflects the fact that it is estimated to be 12 times as difficult for a woman with HIV-1 to infect the male as it is for the male to infect his female partner (Klirsfeld, 1998; Amaro, 1995). The other half of the U.S. women infected with HIV-1 acquired the infection through the use of contaminated intravenous needles (Klirsfeld, 1998; Amaro, 1995).

Women are advised to have a Papanicolaou ("Pap") smear immediately after being diagnosed as having been infected (Kocurek, 1996). If no abnormalities are found at the time of the first test, a second test should be carried out 6 months later. The physician should also perform tests to rule out the possibility that the woman has contracted either gonorrhea or chlamydia. Because a pregnant woman who is infected with HIV-1 may pass the virus on to her unborn child, appropriate testing to confirm or rule out pregnancy should also be conducted.

How HIV-1 infection is diagnosed. Simply stated, the standard method of screening for HIV-1 infection is through one or more blood tests designed to detect the body's immune response to the virus. These cells are known as the $CD4^+$ lymphocyte cells[6] or the $CD4^+$ T-helper cells (Hollander & Katz, 1993). However, one characteristic of HIV-1 infection is that the immune system often requires 6 months to begin to produce $CD4^+$ T-helper cells against the AIDS virus. As we have said, this interval was once called the "latency" period of HIV-1 infection.

Most cases of HIV-1 infection are detected by routine blood testing well before the stage of AIDS. A person whose blood indicates that she or he is infected with HIV-1 is said to be seropositive. As of 1998, the Centers for Disease Control (CDC) recommended a two-stage process for detecting HIV-1 antibodies in human blood. First, a screening enzyme immunoassay (EIA) is performed on a sample of blood from the individual (Kleinman, Busch, Hall, Thomson, Glynn, Gallahan, Ownby, Williams, 1998). A second test, usually the Western blot assay, is then conducted to screen for three specific genetic markers indicative of HIV-1 infection. Once the person is known to be infected, a more detailed procedure known as the "viral load" test

---

[6]The name of this cell is based on a pattern of proteins found in the cell wall.

can be performed; it measures the approximate number of HIV-1 virus particles per cubic millimeter of the individual's blood (Henry, Stiffman, & Feldman, 1997).

The stages of HIV-1 infection. In humans, the HIV-1 infection progresses through three distinct stages (Atkinson & Grant, 1994):

1. Seroconversion (the point where antibodies to HIV-1 are detected in the individual's blood for the first time, indicating that he or she has been infected with the virus).
2. A period of time in which the individual is infected but essentially asymptomatic. (During this stage, the virus is slowly destroying the individual's immune system, a process that can take many years.)
3. The period during which symptomatic disease begins and the progression to AIDS is started.

In years past, the CD4[+] lymphocyte cell count was the only test available to physicians that provided any data as to the progression of the HIV-1 infection. However in the mid-1990s scientists developed the "viral load" test, which provides an estimate of the number of viral particles per unit of blood (Saag, 1997). Currently, many physicians use *both* the CD4[+] lymphocyte cell count and the "viral load" test to provide more information about whether treatment efforts are at all effective and to ascertain the current stage of the HIV-1 infectious process.

The individual who, upon testing, does not have any HIV-1-specific CD4[+] lymphocyte cells in his or her blood is classified as seronegative. There are two possible explanations for a "negative" finding: (1) The individual in question has never been exposed to the HIV-1 or (2) he or she has been exposed to the virus but has not had sufficient time to develop HIV-1-specific CD4[+] lymphocyte cells. In either case, the individual should be tested again at a later date, usually 6–10 months after the initial blood test or last "high-risk" behavior, to rule out the second possibility.[7]

When a person contracts HIV-1, the infectious process progresses through several distinct stages.[8] Between

40% and 90% of those who contract HIV-1 experience a flu-like syndrome in the first weeks after infection. Unfortunately, HIV-1 infection is often misdiagnosed at this stage, because the symptoms seen are not specific to the HIV-1 syndrome (Yu & Daar, 2000; Khan & Walker, 1998). If the physician is suspicious, she or he can order special tests that *might* detect the presence of HIV-1 in the patient's blood a few days after infection, although in most cases it takes 2–6 weeks before blood tests can detect evidence of HIV-1 infection (Yu & Daar, 2000).

When HIV-1-specific CD4[+] lymphocyte cells are first detected, the individual is said to have become seropositive. An infected person infected might remain seropositive, but essentially asymptomatic, for a number of years after the HIV-1 virus is first detected. During this phase of the HIV-1 infection process, the virus can be detected only through blood tests. In the mid 1980s, the Centers for Disease Control (CDC) suggested an elaborate classification system for HIV infection, which was reviewed in earlier editions of this text (see Table A4.2). However, physicians are increasingly using the *viral load*[9] test to determine the individual's status, and the CDC classification system is being slowly replaced by this new measure.

Normally, there are 1000–1200 CD4[+] T cells for every cubic millimeter of blood (Lisanti & Zwolski, 1997). When the number of CD4[+] T cells falls below 200 per cubic millimeter (mm^3) of blood, the individual usually becomes vulnerable to "opportunistic infections" rarely seen except in patients whose immune systems have been compromised in some manner. Such disorders include *Pneumocystis carinii pneumonia* (*P. carinii,* or "*PCP*"), various tumors, bacterial and fungal infections, and tuberculosis (TB). Tuberculosis is 100 times more common in those individuals infected with HIV-1 than in the general population (Bartlett, 1999). Thus whenever a physician encounters a patient who has developed TB, he or she automatically considers the possibility that the patient has AIDS.

AIDS and suicide. The relationship between the possibility of being infected with HIV-1 and suicide is quite complex. However, the current evidence suggests that individuals who carry the virus are at higher risk for suicide than those who are uninfected (Kalichman, Heckman, Kochman, Sikkema, & Bergholte, 2000). The period of greatest risk appears to be right after the

---

[7] It should be noted that screening tests to detect exposure to HIV-1 are not perfect. Kleinman, Busch, Hall, Thomson, Glynn, Gallahan, Ownby, & Williams, (1998) found a "false-positive" rate of 1 in every 379,000 samples of blood tested at one of five blood banks. An initial "positive" screen should be verified through further testing.

[8] This is known as the "natural history" of the viral infectious process.

[9] See the Glossary.

individual learns that she or he is infected with HIV-1. For example, Kalichman *et al.* (2000) cite one study that found that 29% of those individuals who were infected contemplated suicide in the week before being tested to see whether they carried the virus, 27% contemplated suicide after confirmation that they were infected, and 16% reported suicidal thoughts 2 months after learning that they were infected with HIV-1. However, suicide risk must be assessed on a case-by-case basis.

AIDS and Kaposi's sarcoma. When AIDS was first identified in the early 1980s, physicians thought that a rare form of cancer known as *Kaposi's sarcoma* was a manifestation of AIDS. This misconception arose because 40% of those individuals who had AIDS in 1981 also developed Kaposi's sarcoma—and because doctors still had not isolated the cause of AIDS itself (Antman & Chang, 2000). However, by the early 1990s researchers had identified the causes of AIDS and Kaposi's sarcoma. AIDS was found to result from infection with HIV-1, whereas Kaposi's sarcoma is caused by a member of the herpes virus family known as the Kaposi's sarcoma-associated herpes virus (KSHV, or human herpes virus 8) (Antman & Chang, 2000).

As researchers came to understand KSHV better, they realized that Kaposi's sarcoma was usually found in patients whose immune systems were either compromised by HIV-1 infection or suppressed by physicians after organ transplant procedures (Antman & Chang, 2000), or exposure to radiation (Miles, 1996). The virus was also found to be endemic in certain regions of Africa, according to Antman and Chang (2000). Physicians have continued to explore the relationship between HIV-1 infection and Kaposi's sarcoma and have concluded that although Kaposi's sarcoma is the most common AIDS-related cancer in the United States, it is a separate disorder from HIV-1 (Antman & Chang, 2000; Miles, 1996).

The progression of HIV-1 infection. At one time, it was thought that 42–62% of those individuals who were infected with HIV-1 would progress to AIDS within 10 years of the time of infection (Lisanti & Zwolski, 1997). However, the introduction of highly effective chemotherapy programs has altered this progression (Collaborative Group on AIDS Incubation and HIV Survival, 2000). Before these antiviral drugs were introduced, it was estimated that 5–10% of those people infected with HIV-1 would progress to the stage of AIDS each year (Searight & McLaren, 1997). But following the intro-

duction of the protease inhibitors, AIDS-related deaths dropped from 29.4 per 100 patient-years[10] in 1995 to just 8.8 per 100 patient-years in 1997 (Palella, Delaney, Moorman, Loveless, Fuhrer, Satten, Aschman, & Holmberg, 1998). Although these figures are impressive, they still mean that almost 9 of every 100 patients whose HIV-1 infection has progressed to the stage of AIDS die each year, in spite of the most aggressive treatment with the most advanced medications available.

Current treatment methods offer some hope to those who are infected with HIV-1. In the mid-1980s, researchers developed a class of medications known as *nucleoside analogues*— compounds that include agents such as AZT, ddI, ddC, d4T and 3TC. These are chemicals that block the action of the enzyme *reverse transcriptase*, which is essential for reproduction of the virus (Freiberg, 1996). These agents were found to be of limited effectiveness in slowing the reproduction of HIV-1. Some strains of HIV-1 were found to be resistant to the action of nucleoside analogues, and they would quickly reproduce in the victim's body after these medications eliminated the susceptible strains of the virus.

In the mid-1990s, a new class of medications known as *protease inhibitors* were introduced. The protease inhibitors interfere with the viral reproduction process by blocking the action of the protease enzyme, which is essential to the replication of HIV-1 (Freiberg, 1996). The first of these agents, Saquinavir, was approved for use in the treatment of HIV-1 in 1996, and a number of similar agents have been introduced since that time. Unfortunately, the HIV-1 virus is able to develop resistance to the protease inhibitors, so the standard practice is for multiple antiviral compounds with different mechanisms of action to be used in the hope of slowing progression of the HIV-1 infection (Goldschmidt & Moy, 1996)[11,12]

These antiviral agents seem to slow the process of the HIV-1 infection, but they do not prevent the ultimate progression to AIDS (Garrett, 2000). Before the

---

[10] See the Glossary.

[11] Note that it is entirely possible for a person being treated for HIV-1 infection to pass the infection on to others, in spite of the fact that he or she is taking antiviral drugs.

[12] Another group of agents that have shown promise as a potential treatment for HIV-1 infection are known as the *integrase inhibitors*. Researchers are exploring the possibility that one or more of these drugs will prove useful in the fight against AIDS by helping to stop HIV-1 replication in the host's body.

introduction of the protease inhibitors and nucleoside analogues, the average survival period was only about 12 years after "seroconversion" in young adults (Collaborative Group on AIDS Incubation and HIV Survival, 2000) and only 2–4 years after the infection had progressed to AIDS (Hellinger, 1993). Although the introduction of new drugs that are effective against HIV-1 makes it difficult to estimate long-term survival for those who are infected, thus far there has not been a single proven "cure" of an HIV-1-infected person (Flexner, 1998). The virus is known to persist in areas of the body that are not affected by the current generation of antiviral agents, which makes eradication of the virus in the individual's body virtually impossible (Fauci, 1999). Further, it has been estimated that current drug therapies cost up to $60,000 per year per individual, and thus they are too expensive for use in the "developing" world (Ezzell, 2000; Garrett, 2000). Further, the side effects of the current antiviral medications are often quite debilitating for many individuals, making it difficult for them to continue to take these medications (Farber, 2000).

As the 21st century begins, researchers are hopeful that they can eventually develop a treatment program that will completely arrest the progression of HIV-1. However, to cure the individual, it will be necessary to eliminate *every last viral particle* from the person's body. To understand this task, remember that up to one trillion copies of the HIV-1 virus might nestle in the body of an infected person and that the virus might "hide" in the body for up to 2 years after antiviral treatment was initiated (Flexner, 1998). A treatment that was 99.99% effective would still leave 10 billion viral particles in the body of an infected person—particles that would begin to reproduce when the opportunity presented itself. Science has no idea how to eliminate every viral particle from the body of a living person, and the cost of antiviral therapy is such that without government assistance, many infected persons cannot afford the medications currently available. Given these facts, it is clear that the ultimate treatment for AIDS at this time lies in prevention. To paraphrase the old saying, "What's an ounce of prevention worth when there isn't any cure?"

Tuberculosis (TB)

The return of tuberculosis (TB) may offer an example of how chronic substance abuse might indirectly contribute to the spread of disease (Cherubin & Sapira, 1993). It is estimated that 50% of the world's population has been or will be exposed to TB at some time in their lives (Garrett, 1994). However, for the most part, the individual's immune system is able to fight off the danger of infection, and only about 10% of those who are exposed will develop TB (Szabo, 1997).

For those who are unfortunate enough to become infected with tuberculosis, however, the outlook is quite grim. There are an estimated 7–8 million new cases of TB around the globe each year, and 2–3 million people die annually from it (Seymour, 1997; Hopewell, 1996). This makes TB the leading cause of death from infectious disease (Wilkinson, Liewelyn, Toossi, Patel, Pasvol, Lalvani, Wright, Latif, & Davidson, 2000; Szabo, 1997), with 500 million new cases expected globally in the next 50 years (Savitch, 1998).

Tuberculosis itself is an opportunistic disease: It preys mainly on those whose immune systems have been weakened by illness or malnutrition. There is preliminary evidence that either dietary or metabolic conditions that limit the body's absorption of vitamin D place the individual at increased risk for contracting tuberculosis (Wilkinson *et al.*, 2000). Because individuals who abuse drugs or alcohol on a chronic basis tend to also be malnourished, the vitamin D hypothesis might help to explain why this sub-group of people tends to be at risk for developing TB. So strong is the relationship between chronic alcohol use and TB that Cunha (1998) recommended that the attending physician specifically rule out tuberculosis in alcohol-abusing patients who exhibit symptoms of pneumonia. Individuals whose immune systems are compromised by infection, such as HIV-1, are also at high risk for contracting TB (Garrett, 1994). Indeed, the first outward sign that an individual is infected with HIV-1 is often development of tuberculosis (Karlen, 1995). This is why alcohol/drug rehabilitation counselors must be aware of the relationship between substance misuse and tuberculosis infections.

What is tuberculosis? Tuberculosis (TB) is an infectious disease caused by the bacteria *Mycobacterium tuberculosis* (Karlen, 1995). Physicians have struggled against TB for hundreds of generations, but until recently, the treatment of TB was a long, complicated affair that did not guarantee success. Then, in the 1950s, antibiotic medications were introduced that offered the hope of completely curing the patient of the disease in just a few months. In the 1970s, medical school students were taught that TB would be eliminated by the year 2000, and physicians became complacent about the disease (Savitch, 1998).

To achieve a cure, it is necessary for the infected individual to take 3–4 different medications several times a day, for months. Unfortunately, the life-style of the typical alcohol/drug abuser often makes compliance with treatment for TB difficult. This factor, combined with professional complacency and the rise of AIDS, contributed to the rise of the antibiotic-resistant strains of TB that began to be identified in the early 1990s. The mortality rate from antibiotic-resistant TB is 80–90%, and it is a growing threat to some segments of the population in the United States and abroad. For example, 90% of antibiotic-resistant TB infections occur in those individuals who are already infected with HIV-1 (Telenti & Iseman, 2000; Savitch, 1998). Also at risk for antibiotic-resistant TB infections are people who are impoverished (and thus likely to be malnourished, infected with HIV-1 or both). For example, alcohol/drug-abusing welfare recipients in New York City were found to have rates of TB infection 70 times as high as those found across the United States as a whole (Friedman, Williams, Singh, & Frieden, 1996).

How does TB kill? TB most often invades the pulmonary system, although it is possible for TB to infect virtually any organ system in the body. The bacteria seem to prefer oxygen-rich body tissues, such as those found in the lungs, the central nervous system, and the kidneys (Boutotte, 1993).

Whenever a person sings, talks, coughs, or sneezes, he or she releases microscopic droplets of moisture from the lungs, and these remain suspended in the air for extended periods of time. If that person has active TB in the respiratory system, then these moisture droplets will carry bacteria into the surrounding air, where another person might inhale them (Boutotte, 1993). Once TB gains admission to the body, the individual's immune system attacks the invading bacteria. The initial response by a part of the immune system is to send *macrophages* to engulf the invading bacteria, surround them, and wall them inside little pockets known as granulomas. This prevents the infection from proceeding further. However, *Mycobacterium tuberculosis* is difficult for the body to destroy, and the bacteria may survive, in a dormant stage within the granulomas, for years or decades.

If the individual's immune system becomes weakened by another infection, or by disease or malnutri-

tion, the body loses its ability to isolate the TB bacteria in the granulomas. Eventually, the TB bacteria may burst out and again invade the surrounding body tissue. Such "reactivation TB" accounts for about 85% of all cases of TB in the United States (Boutotte, 1993). It is at this point that the body mounts a different sort of attack on the invading bacteria. Another part of the immune system, the lymphocytes, attempt to destroy the bacteria that cause TB. Unfortunately, during this process they release a toxin that destroys surrounding lung tissue. Eventually, as less and less of the lung is able to function properly, the patient dies of pulmonary failure.

The treatment of TB. Although a great deal has been written about "treatment-resistant" TB in the past few years, physicians still have a wide range of medications that they can call upon to treat this infection. Even so, the treatment process might take as long as 6–12 months, and the patient would need to take the proper medications on a daily basis for that period of time (Boutotte, 1993). Failure to follow the established treatment program will result in the patient retaining, in his or her body, some active TB germs that (because they have survived the patient's initial use of the medication) will be more resistant to these same medications in the future. Over time, new TB strains emerge that are totally resistant to medications once able to eradicate the infection.

Viral Hepatitis

There are at least seven different viruses that can infect the liver. Each form of viral infection results in inflammation of the liver, a condition known as *hepatitis*. Physicians often refer to each virus simply by a letter, such as hepatitis A, B, and so on. At least four different forms of viral hepatitis are known to affect alcohol/drug users.

Hepatitis A (HVA) infections are the most common, accounting for 200,000 new cases each year in the United States (Shute, Licking, & Schultz, 1998). The causal agent of HVA was identified as a virus most often transmitted through food or water that has become contaminated with fecal matter. But for many years, physicians were aware that some patients who had received blood transfusions developed symptoms of liver disease suggestive of a viral infection other than HVA. These patients were said to have developed "serum hepatitis."

In 1966 a virus that was later classified as hepatitis B (HVB) was first isolated (Lee, 1997). Unfortunately, scientists soon realized that the virus that causes HVB was responsible for only between 28% (Bondesson & Saperston, 1996) and 43% (Vail, 1997) of all new cases of viral hepatitis in this country (Hoffnagle & Di Bisceglie, 1997). There was evidence of at least one other virus capable of causing hepatitis, and for many years it was classified simply as "non-A, non-B" hepatitis. Only in the past decade has it become clear that "non-A, non-B" hepatitis results from an infection by one of five separate viral agents, which have since been classified as hepatitis virus type C (HVC), type D (HVD), type E (HVE), type F (HVF), and type G (HVG) (Sjogren, 1996). Surprisingly, there is genetic evidence to suggest that HVG is a distant cousin to HVC.

Relationship between viral hepatitis and IV drug abuse. Although the most common route of HVA infection is through exposure to food or water that has been contaminated by feces, the reuse of intravenous needles by drug abusers does account for about 2% of the new cases of HVA (Bondesson & Saperston, 1996). But because HVA infection is only rarely passed on via intravenous drug abuse, we will not discuss it further.

Unlike HVA, the viruses that cause HVB, HVC, HVD, HVF, and HVG are all transmitted from one person to another only through exposure to body fluids, including the small amount of fluid that remains in intravenous needles shared by IV drug abusers (Vail, 1997; Becherer, 1995). The use of contaminated needles is the most common way that HVC is spread in the United States (Rose, 1999).

Prevalence of HVB. Globally, 5% of the world's population, or about 350 million (Lee, 1997) to 400–500 million people (Bondesson & Saperston, 1996), are thought to be infected with HVB. HVB infection is the most common cause of liver disease on the face of the earth (Vail, 1997). In the United States, there are 300,000 new cases of HVB each year (Vail, 1997; Karlen, 1995). Of this number, approximately 10% will become chronic carriers of the virus, and 15–20% of these people will die as a result of their infection with HVB (Vail, 1997).

Prevalence of HVC. Since the virus that causes HVC was first isolated in 1988 (Kirchner, 1999), researchers have discovered that HVC is the most common chronic blood-borne infection in the United States (Dieperink, Willenbring, & Ho, 2000). Globally, some 3% of the population is thought to be infected with one of the six subtypes of HVC (Seymour, 1997; Flynn, 1996), but the prevalence of HVC infection varies. About 9–14.6% of the population of north Africa have been exposed to the virus, whereas other regions have much lower rates of infection (Dieperink, Willenbring, & Ho, 2000). In the United States, an estimated 4 million people (1.8% of the population) are thought to be infected with HVC (DiBisceglie & Bacon, 1999; Kirchner, 1999), and there are approximately 30,000 new cases of HVC infection each year in this country (Dieperink, Willenbring, & Ho, 2000).

Prevalence of HVD and HVE. Fortunately, these viruses are only rarely found in the United States. There are an estimated 5000 new cases of HVD each year, while HVE is not commonly found in this country (Shute, Licking, & Schultz, 1998).

Routes of transmission for HVB. HVB is *extremely* contagious. By comparison, HVB is perhaps on the order of 100 times as contagious as HIV-1. There have been cases where people have contracted HVB by sharing either a toothbrush or a razor or even simply by kissing an infected person (Brody, 1991).

The HVB virus may be transmitted through blood transfusions. In the early 1970s, the rate of infection with the hepatitis B virus was 1 per 100 units of blood transfused (Edelson, 1993). However, new blood tests for screening potential blood donors (and new ways of storing blood prior to use) have reduced the rate of HVB infection to about 1 in 250,000 units of blood used for transfusion in the United States (Goodnough, Brecher, Kanter, & AuBuchon, 1999).

Blood tests of intravenous drug abusers in the United States reveal that 75–98% of these individuals have been exposed to HVB virus at some time in their lives (Michelson, Carroll, McLane, & Robin, 1988). It is assumed, given the mode of HVB transmission via contaminated intravenous needles, that the majority of these individuals contracted this viral infection as an unintended consequence of their chemical abuse. However, another common route of HVB infection is passage of the virus from an infected individual to a noninfected partner through sexual contact. HVB is also found in the semen of most infected men. Up to 70% of homosexual males have antibodies in their blood, suggesting that they have been exposed to HVB (Vail, 1997). Thus, like HIV-1, HVB may be passed on to another person through semen, and it is now classified as a *sexually transmitted disease* (STD). In some communities in the United States, HVB accounts for 30% of all new STD cases (Garrett, 1994). This is a major reason why people should avoid sexual relationships with partners who are likely to have been exposed to HVB (a list that includes, but is not limited to, sexually promiscuous persons, prostitutes, and bisexual and/or homosexual males).

Routes of transmission for HVC. With the advent of new blood tests designed to detect HVC infection, the risk of transmitting the virus during blood transfusion is estimated to be 1 case for each 103,000 units of blood transfused (Dieperink, Willenbring, & Ho, 2000; Goodnough, Brecher, Kanter, & AuBuchon, 1999). New blood tests being developed promise to reduce the number of transfusion-related HVC infections to near 0 (Hughes, 1999). The greatest number of infected individuals are thought to have acquired HVC infection by sharing intravenous needles (Najm, 1997). Indeed, so common is needle-borne HVC transmission that 50–80% of new intravenous drug abusers will have evidence of HVC infection in their blood in their first year of IV drug abuse (Dieperink, Willenbring, & Ho, 2000; Moyer, Mast, & Alter, 1999; Hughes, 1999).

Because of the similarity between the modes of infection for HVC and HIV-1, it is not uncommon for the individual to be infected with both viruses. In some communities, upwards of 94% of HIV-1-positive intravenous drug abusers are also infected with HVC (Thomas, 1997). Further, like HIV-1, HVC infection has an extended "latency" period during which there are no outward manifestations of the disease, in spite of the infection within the body. For example, a person might be infected with HVC for 20–30 years without showing any outward signs of liver damage (Kirchner, 1999). Finally, as is true of HIV-1 infection, it may not be possible to cure HVC without killing every viral particle in the patient's body; both viruses are able to "hide" in various cells in the body of the host (Kirchner, 1999).

The evidence about whether HVC can be transmitted sexually is mixed. Some researchers have suggested that as many as 15% of the cases of HVC infection are sexually transmitted (Hughes, 1999; Bondesson & Saperston, 1996; Sharara, Hunt, & Hamilton, 1996). Other researchers point out that the sexual partners of infected individuals who are in monogamous relationships rarely contract HVC and that the infection rate of

homosexual males is no higher than that of the general population; both observations suggest that HVC is not usually sexually transmitted (DiBisceglie & Bacon, 1999). Other known routes of HVC transmission include contaminated needles used in tattooing, organ transplant procedures where the donor had been infected with HVC, sharing straws used to inhale drugs through the nose, and hemodialysis (DiBisceglie & Bacon, 1999; Hager & Reibstein, 1998; Sharara, Hunt, & Hamilton, 1996). But in 40–50% of the cases, the patient has no history of having engaged in known high-risk behaviors, and this implies that there are other, as yet unidentified, routes of HVC transmission.

Routes of transmission for HVD. HVD is a blood-borne virus, and researchers have discovered that 20–80% of intravenous drug abusers have antibodies in their blood for HVD (Vail, 1997). Surprisingly, the virus that causes HVD is an "incomplete" or "defective" (Sjogren, 1996, p. 948) virus, and infects only individuals who have previously been exposed to HVB. Approximately 10% of those individuals with chronic HVB infections also test positive for exposure to HVD (DiBisceglie, 1995). In the United States, only some 70,000 individuals are thought to have the HVD virus in their bodies (Najm, 1997).

Routes of transmission for HVE. Although HVE might be transmitted by exposure to body fluids, the most common method of transmission is exposure to water contaminated by humans who were infected (Shute, Licking, & Schultz, 1998).

What are the consequences of HVB infection? HVB is potentially fatal. There are several mechanisms through which HVB might kill the infected person. First, as the virus infects the liver, it damages that organ. The body's immune response to HVB infection may cause even more damage to the liver (Lee, 1997). If the HVB-induced liver damage is great enough, cirrhosis of the liver develops. It is estimated that between 3500 (Lee, 1997) and 5000 (Karlen, 1995) people die each year, in this country alone, as a result of HVB-induced cirrhosis.

Hepatitis B may also kill in another way. For reasons that are not known at this time, the person who has been infected with the hepatitis B virus is *10–390 times* as likely as a noninfected person to develop liver cancer (Gordon, 2000; Bondesson & Saperston, 1996). Liver cancer is quite difficult to detect or treat, and it is usually fatal. Each year, there are an estimated 1200 cases of

HVB-related liver cancer in the United States (Karlen, 1995).

What are the consequences of HVC infection? Approximately 15% of those who are infected are able to fight off HVC infection without serious complications (Dieperink, Willenbring, & Ho, 2000; Sharara, Hunt, & Hamilton, 1996). Of the remainder, approximately 75% of the cases of HVC remain asymptomatic until the disease is quite advanced. During this "latency" period, the HVC infection can be detected only via blood tests (Najm, 1997). HVC exposure results in a chronic liver infection in about 80% of those who are exposed to the virus. Approximately 60–80% of those who are infected with HVC eventually develop chronic hepatitis, and 20–30% of these cases progress to cirrhosis of the liver (Dieperink, Willenbring, & Ho, 2000; Najm, 1997; Flynn, 1996). It usually requires 20–30 years after the individual was infected for cirrhosis to develop (Najm, 1997). Cancer of the liver might develop in 1–4% of those infected with HVC (Kirchner, 1999). Researchers believe that this cancer is a possible consequence of HVC-induced chronic liver inflammation and necrosis of liver tissue (Thomas, 1997).

Hepatitis C-induced liver failure is now the most common reason for liver transplants in the United States (Hager & Reibstein, 1998). Researchers believe that HVC infection kills 10,000 people each year in this country, a number that is expected to triple by the year 2020 (Hager & Reibstein, 1998; Thomas, 1997).

What are the consequences of HVD infection? Early evidence suggests that the combination of HVB and HBD infections results in a more severe syndrome than seen in HVB alone (Najm, 1997). Approximately 60–70% of those individuals who are infected with HVD will develop cirrhosis of the liver, usually in between 2–15 years after being infected (Najm, 1997).

What are the consequences of HVE infection? Scientists are still exploring the impact of HVE infection on the individual. The virus can cause loss of appetite, nausea, and vomiting as a result of liver inflammation, as well as fever, fatigue, and abdominal pain (Shute, Licking, & Schultz, 1998). Up to 20% of the pregnant women who contract HVE die as a result of the infection (Gorbach, Mensa, & Gatell, 1997).

The treatment of HVB. The most effective "treatment" for HVB is prevention. A vaccine against HVB was developed in the early 1980s, and individuals who are likely to be exposed to the body fluids of an infected individual should be vaccinated against possible HVB infection (Vail, 1997). In some states, vaccination against HVB is required before a child is admitted to public school (Vail, 1997). Other people who should be immunized against HVB include health care workers and the spouses and children of infected individuals.

The pharmacological treatment options for HVB infection are quite limited. Daily injections of the medication Interferon Alfa for 4–6 months have been shown to be effective 25–40% of the time (Gordon, 2000; Hoffnagle & Di Bisceglie, 1997). Another medication, lamivudine, has been found to suppress replication of the HVB virus for a short time, although long-term suppression of the virus has proved difficult (Gordon, 2000). Doctors have yet to determine the optimal period of time that a patient should take lamivudine even in cases where the medication has proved effective. The search for more effective medications to treat HVB infection is ongoing.

The treatment of HVC. Injections of interferon are the treatment of choice for HVC infection (Flynn, 1996). After an appropriate course of treatment, approximately half of the patients who are treated with interferon do not show further evidence of ongoing liver damage when their blood is tested. However, research now suggests that 90% of those individuals treated with interferon-alpha will show evidence of renewed viral activity after they discontinue treatment (Dieperink, Willenbring, & Ho, 2000). To improve this dismal performance, doctors have developed a combination of interferon injections three times a week and daily oral doses of ribavirin, which has proved capable of suppressing HVC replication in up to 68% of cases (Gordon, 2000). Researchers are attempting to develop drug treatments of HVC infection that will prove even more effective (Gordon, 2000). But as with HVB, the most effective treatment for HVC infection is prevention.

The treatment of HVD. Preliminary evidence suggests that because co-infection with HVB is necessary for HVD infection to develop, immunization against HVB will provide protection against HVD (Vail, 1997). Immunization against HVB blocks the chain of infection, preventing HVD co-infection if an individual should be exposed to this virus (Najm, 1997).

The treatment of HVE, HVF, and HVG. Very little is know about how these viral infections might be treated.

Thus the most effective "treatment" for these viral infections is prevention—by avoiding exposure to the body fluids of people who are known or suspected to have a form of viral hepatitis.

Summary

It is impossible to identify every infectious disease that substance abusers are exposed to as a result of their chemical use. In this chapter, a few of the more common forms of infection that might arise as a result of alcohol/drug abuse have been reviewed. Although this chapter is not intended to serve as a guide for the treatment of these infections, it is important that substance abuse rehabilitation professionals understand some of the risk factors associated with infectious diseases commonly found in alcohol/drug-abusing individuals. These include the hepatitis family of viral infections, HIV-1, and tuberculosis (TB). This knowledge will make substance abuse treatment professionals better able to understand both the needs of their clients and their own potential for being exposed to these disorders as a result of their work with infected individuals.

CHAPTER THIRTY-FOUR

Self-Help Groups

The Twelve Steps of Alcoholics Anonymous[1]

Step One: We admitted that we were powerless over alcohol—that our lives had become unmanageable.

Step Two: Came to believe that a Power greater than ourselves could restore us to sanity.

Step Three: Made a decision to turn our will and our lives over to the care of God *as we understood Him.*

Step Four: Made a searching and fearless moral inventory of ourselves.

Step Five: Admitted to God, to ourselves, and to another human being the exact nature of our wrongs.

Step Six: Were entirely ready to have God remove all these defects of character.

Step Seven: Humbly asked Him to remove our shortcomings.

Step Eight: Made a list of all persons we had harmed, and became willing to make amends to them all.

Step Nine: Made direct amends to such people wherever possible, except when to do so would injure them or others.

---

[1] The Twelve Steps are reprinted by permission of Alcoholics Anonymous World Services, Inc. Permission to reprint this material does not mean that AA has reviewed or approved the contents of this publication, nor that AA agrees with the views expressed herein. AA is a program of recovery from alcoholism—use of the Twelve Steps in connection with programs and activities that are patterned after AA, but which address other problems, does not imply otherwise.

Step Ten: Continued to take personal inventory and when we were wrong, promptly admitted it.

Step Eleven: Sought through prayer and meditation to improve our conscious contact with God *as we understood Him,* praying only for knowledge of His will for us, and the power to carry that out.

Step Twelve: Having had a spiritual awakening as the result of these steps, we tried to carry this message to alcoholics, and to practice these principles in all our affairs.

Introduction

Alcoholics Anonymous (AA) is the "most frequently consulted source of help for drinking problems" (Miller & McCrady, 1993, p. 3). Approximately 1 in every 10 adults in the United States has attended an AA meeting at least once (Tonigan & Toscova, 1998; Zweben, 1995; Miller & McCrady, 1993). Not all of these people had alcohol use problems of their own. Perhaps two-thirds of those who have attended at least one AA meeting have done so out of concern for another person's drinking (Zweben, 1995). However, one-third of those who have attended AA, or 3.1% of the adults in the United States, have done so because they thought that they might have an alcohol use problem (Godlaski, Leukefeld, & Cloud, 1997).

In spite of its popularity, AA is perhaps the least rigorously studied element in the spectrum of rehabilitation programs (Meza & Kranzler, 1996). And even

418

though it has existed for over 60 years, "the empirical research on the efficacy of Alcoholics Anonymous is sparse and inconclusive" (Watson, Hancock, Gearhart, Mendez, Malovrh, & Raden, 1997, p. 209). AA remains something of a mystery not only to nonmembers but also, all too often, to active members as well, a fact that makes AA and similar self-help groups rather controversial. Supporters claim that AA is the most effective means of treating alcoholism. Critics of AA and of similar programs challenge this claim. In this chapter, we will examine the self-help group phenomenon patterned after the Alcoholics Anonymous program.

The History of AA

The diverse forces that were to blend together to form Alcoholics Anonymous (AA) include the American temperance movement of the late 1800s (Peele, 1984; 1989); a nondenominational religious group known as the Oxford Group, which was popular in the 1930s (Bufe, 1998; Nace, 1987); and the psychoanalysis of an American alcoholic by Carl Jung in the year 1931 (Edmeades, 1987). Over the years, many early members of Alcoholics Anonymous were hospitalized, mistakes were made, questions were asked, and the early pioneers of AA embarked on a struggle for sobriety that transcended individual members.

Historically, AA was thought to have been founded on June 10, 1935, the day an alcoholic physician had his last drink (Nace, 1997). Earlier, following a meeting between a stock broker, William Griffith Wilson, and the surgeon, Dr. Robert Holbrook Smith, the foundation to AA was set down. William "Bill" Wilson was struggling to protect his newfound sobriety while on a business trip in a strange city. After making several telephone calls to try and find support in his struggle, Wilson was asked to talk to Dr. Smith, who was drinking at the time Wilson called.

Rather than looking out for his own needs, Wilson carried a message of sobriety to another alcoholic, and the self-help philosophy of AA was born. Since then, it has grown to a fellowship of 97,000 "clubs" or AA groups, that include chapters in 150 countries, with a total membership estimated at more than 2 million persons (Emrick, 1999; Humphreys, 1997). Of this number, 1.2 million members are from either the United States or Canada (Marvel, 1995). Thus 68% of the entire world membership of AA is found in North America alone.

During its early years, AA struggled to find a method that would support its members in their struggle to both achieve and maintain sobriety. Within three years of its founding, three different AA groups were in existence, but even with three groups, "it was hard to find two score of sure recoveries . . ." (*Twelve Steps and Twelve Traditions*, 1981, p. 17). Nevertheless, the fledgling group continued to grow, until, by the fourth year following its inception, there were about 100 members in isolated AA groups (Nace, 1997). In spite of this rather limited beginning, the early members decided to write of their struggle to achieve sobriety and share their discoveries with others. The book that was published as a result of this process was the first edition of the book *Alcoholics Anonymous* in 1939. The organization took its name from the title of this book, which has since come to be known as the "Big Book" of AA (*Twelve Steps and Twelve Traditions*, 1981).

Elements of AA

There are several factors that help to shape an effective self-help group (Rootes & Aanes, 1992):

1. Members have *shared experience* — in this case, their inability to control their drug or alcohol use.
2. *Education*, not psychotherapy, is the primary goal of AA membership.
3. Self-help groups are *self-governing*.
4. The group places emphasis on *accepting responsibility for one's behavior*.
5. There is but a *single purpose* to the group.
6. Membership is *voluntary*.
7. The individual member must make a *commitment to personal change*.
8. The group places emphasis on *anonymity and confidentiality*.

George Vaillant (2000) identified four factors that were common to programs for recovery from substance use disorders: (1) compulsory supervision, (2) introduction of and use of competing behavior to replace the chemical use pattern, (3) new love relationships, and (4) increased spirituality and religiosity. Many of these are elements of the AA program.

Most researchers accept that the core characteristics of AA are very much a product of society in the United States in the late 1930s, especially the Oxford Group movement (Bufe, 1998). Americans have always had a strong belief in the process of public confession, contrition, and salvation through spirituality. Further, as *Twelve Steps and Twelve Traditions* (1981) acknowledged, the early members of AA also freely borrowed from the fields of medicine and religion to establish a program that worked for them. The program that emerged consists of the famous "Twelve Steps" of AA.

A breakdown of the Twelve Step. The core of the recovery program that AA advocates is the Twelve Steps, which are suggested not as the *only* way to recovery but as *a* way that may work for the individual (Beazley, 1998). The Twelve Steps might be viewed as falling into three groups. The first three steps are necessary for the acceptance of one's limitations. Through these steps, the individual acknowledges that his or her own resources are insufficient for dealing with the problems of life, especially his or her addiction to alcohol.

Steps Four through Nine are a series of change-oriented activities. These steps are designed to help the individual identify, confront, and ultimately overcome character shortcomings that were so much a part of the individual's addicted lifestyle. Through these steps, one may work through the guilt associated with past behaviors and learn to recognize the limits of personal responsibility. These steps allow the person to learn the tools of non-drug-centered living, something that at first is often alien to both the alcohol-dependent person and his or her family.

Finally, Steps Ten through Twelve challenge the individual to continue to build on the foundation established in Steps Four through Nine. The individual is asked to continue to search out personal shortcomings and confront them. The person also is challenged to continue the spiritual growth initiated during the earlier steps and to carry the message of hope to others.

In a sense, AA might be viewed as functioning as a form of psychotherapy that aids personal growth (Peck, 1993; Tobin, 1992; Alibrandi, 1978). The guiding philosophy behind AA is that it is through a lifelong commitment to the group that the individual is able to achieve some measure of control over the incurable disease of addiction (Davison, Pennebaker, & Dicker-

son, 2000). As a self-help growth program, the AA program might be viewed as being composed of five different phases (Alibrandi, 1978). The *first stage* starts on the first day of membership in AA and lasts for the next week. During this phase, the individual's goal is simply to stay away from his or her first drink (or episode of chemical use).

The *second stage* of recovery starts at the end of the first week and lasts until the end of the second month of AA membership (Alibrandi, 1978). Major steps during this part of the recovery process include the recovering addict's accepting the disease concept of addiction and learning the willingness to accept help with his or her addiction. During this phase, the individual struggles to replace old drug-centered habits with new, sobriety-oriented habits. The *third stage* of recovery spans the interval from the second to the sixth month of recovery, according to Alibrandi (1978). During this stage, the individual is to use the Twelve Steps as a guide and to try to let go of old ideas. Guilt feelings about past chemical use are to be replaced with gratitude for sobriety, wherever possible, and the member is to stand available for service to other individuals who are addicted to alcohol.

The *fourth stage* begins at around the sixth month of recovery, and lasts until after the first year of abstinence (Alibrandi, 1978). During this stage, the individual is encouraged to take a searching and fearless moral inventory of "self" and to share this with another person. At the same time, if the individual is still "shaky," he or she is encouraged to work with another member. Emphasis during this phase of recovery is on acceptance of responsibility and on resolution of the anger and resentments on which the basis of addiction is so often established. Finally, after the first year of recovery, the rehabilitation process has reached what Brown (1985) termed "ongoing sobriety." Alibrandi (1978) identified the goal during this *fifth stage* of recovery as being the maintenance of a "spiritual condition." The person is warned not to dwell on the shortcomings of others, to suspend judgment of self and others, and to beware of the false pride that could lead to chemical use again.

Although the AA program is designed to aid spiritual growth, this process is not rapid. It takes many years to correct the spiritual defects upon which alcoholism rests. Beazley (1998), for example, suggested that the member must be actively involved in AA for at least 5 years before the process of spiritual growth begins. But, once this process of spiritual renewal is initiated,

> there is no going back. You develop a knowledge that is so powerful that you will wonder how you could have lived any other way. The awakened life begins to own you, and then you simply know within that you are on the right path. (Dyer, 1989, p. 17).

Whether the Twelve Steps are effective and, if so, why they are effective are often disputed. But, within the AA community, there are those who believe that the Twelve Steps offer a program within which personality transformation can be accomplished (DiClemente, 1993). Others believe that the Twelve Steps might be viewed as a series of successive approximations toward the goal of abstinence (McCrady & Delaney, 1995). Surprisingly, the Steps are not required for AA membership. But they are viewed within AA as a proven method of behavioral change that offers the addicted individual a chance to rebuild her or his life. There are many who believe that these Steps were instrumental in saving their lives.

AA and Religion

The discussion of spiritual matters in the United States is frequently complicated by the fact that the words *faith, religion,* and *spirituality* are commonly—but incorrectly—used interchangeably. To illustrate the difference, McDargh (2000) observed that "Religion is for those who are afraid of going to hell ... spirituality is for those who have already been there [as a result of their substance use problems]." Within this context, it is possible to understand how AA might present itself as being a program for *spiritual* growth, but not as a religious movement (Vaillant, 2000; McGowan, 1998; Wallace, 1996; Berenson, 1987). To understand better the distinction between spirituality and belief, it is helpful to view religion as the *form,* and spirituality as the *content,* of belief (McGowan, 1998). This distinction makes it possible to understand how AA might identify with no single religious group or doctrine, while still claiming to be a program for spiritual growth (*Twelve Steps and Twelve Traditions,* 1981).

This is often a difficult point for the new member of AA to grasp. However,

> having faith is not a question of clinging to a particular set of beliefs, a particular set of ... practices or psychotherapeutic techniques. Having faith ... requires that we let go of what we are clinging to. (Rosenbaum, 1999, p. xii)

Within this context, the spirituality component of AA requires that the individual *be receptive to the possibility that there is more than "self"* and to learn how to stop carrying the doubts, resentments, and demands that so often set the stage for alcoholism.

The emphasis on spiritual growth in the AA program rests on the dual assumptions that (1) each individual seems to desire a relationship with the infinite [higher power] and (2) the individual's distorted perception of "self" as the center of the universe helps to make him or her vulnerable to alcoholism (McDargh, 2000; McCrady, 1994). The AA Twelve-Step program counters this rather narcissistic stance by placing strong emphasis on the individual establishing a relationship with a Higher Power without endorsing a specific religious doctrine for its members. An example of this process is Step Three of the AA Twelve-Step program. This step "doesn't demand an immediate conversion experience ... but ... does call for a decision" (Jensen, 1987b, p. 22) as the alcohol-dependent person resolves to turn his or her will over to their God.

The concept of a Higher Power that nevertheless is not incorporated into formal religious doctrine is perhaps best reflected by the Lakota Wisdomkeeper Matthew King:

> You can call Wakan-Tanka by any name you like. In English I call Him God or the Great Spirit.
> He's the Great Mystery, the Great Mysterious. That's what Wakan-Tanka really means—the Great Mysterious.
> You can't define Him. He's not actually a "He" or a "She," a "Him" or a "Her." We have to use those kinds of words because you can't just say "It." God's never an "It." (Arden, 1994, pp. 4–5)

The Third Step of the AA program "simply assumes that there is a God to understand and that we each have a God of our own understanding" (Jensen, 1987b, p. 23). In this manner, AA sidesteps the question of religion, while still addressing the spiritual disease that it views as forming the foundation for the addiction. In turning her or his will over to a Higher Power, the individual comes to accept that her or his own will is not enough to maintain recovery. The individual learns how resentments from the past contribute to the spiritual sickness that is so essential to alcohol addiction, and learns how to resolve or renounce these resentments. In order to further the process of spiritual growth, the individual is encouraged to carry out a daily self-examination similar to that of the *Examen* or *Consciousness Examen* proposed by Ignatius as one of the rules of the Jesuit order. This is done in order to understand better the will of one's Higher Power and how it applies to one's life. Thus AA offers a spiritual program that ties the individual's will to that of a "higher power" without offering a specific religious dogma that might offend members.

One "A" Is for Anonymous

Anonymity is central to the AA program (*Understanding Anonymity*, 1981), and this is one major reason why most meetings are closed. There are three types of "closed" meetings. In the first, where there is a designated speaker, one individual speaks at length about his or her life and substance use and how he or she came to join AA and benefit from the program (Nowinski, 1996). In the second form of closed AA meeting, the discussion meeting, a theme or problem of interest to the members of the AA group is identified, and each member of the group is offered a chance to talk about how this problem affects her or him. Finally, in the last type of closed meeting, the "Step" meeting, the group focuses on one of the Twelve-Steps for a month at a time. Each member is offered a chance to talk about his or her understanding of the step and, how he or she attempts to put that step into practice. Closed meetings are limited to members of AA. There are also "open" AA meetings that any interested person may attend. One or two volunteers speak in such gatherings, and visitors are encouraged to ask questions about AA and how it works.

Anonymity is a central concept of AA, and many AA members believe that court-ordered or employer-mandated attendance of AA runs counter to the central philosophy of anonymity: The individual must ask a member of AA to break anonymity in order to confirm that the person indeed did attend the meeting(s) she or he was ordered to attend. The AA program places emphasis on anonymity to protect the identities of members *and* to ensure that no identified spokesperson emerges who claims to speak for AA (*Understanding Anonymity*, 1981). Through this policy, the members of AA strive for humility; each knows that he or she is equal to the other members. The concept of anonymity is so important that it is said to serve as "the spiritual foundation of the Fellowship" of AA (*Understanding Anonymity*, 1981, p. 5).

The concept of equality of the members underlies the AA tradition that no "directors" are nominated or voted on. Rather, "service boards" or special committees are created from the membership as needed. These boards always remain responsible to the group *as a whole* and must answer to the entire AA group. As is noted in Tradition Two of AA "our leaders are but trusted servants; they do not govern" (*Twelve Steps and Twelve Traditions*, 1981, p. 10). Because of this emphasis on equality, the structure of AA has evolved into one where the "interpersonal conflicts and the petty jealousy, greed, or self-importance that could create havoc among fellowship members" (DiClemente, 1993, p. 85) is minimized, if not almost totally avoided.

AA and Outside Organizations

Each Alcoholics Anonymous group is both self-supporting and not-for-profit. Individual groups are autonomous and support themselves only through the contributions of the members. Further, each individual member is prohibited from contributing more than $1000 per year to AA. Outside donations are discouraged, as are outside commitments for AA groups. As *Twelve Steps and Twelve Traditions* (1981) puts it, AA groups will not "endorse, finance, or lend the AA name to any related facility or outside enterprise, lest problems of money, property and prestige divert us from our primary purpose" (p. 11).

The relationships between different autonomous AA groups, and between different AA groups and other organizations, are governed by the Twelve Traditions of AA. The Traditions are a set of guidelines or a framework within which different groups may interact, and through which AA as a whole may work together. They will not be reviewed in this chapter; interested readers are referred to *The Twelve Steps and Twelve Traditions* (1981).

The Primary Purpose of AA

This "primary purpose" of AA is twofold. First, the members of AA strive to "carry the message to the addict who still suffers" (*The Group*, 1976, p. 1). Second, AA seeks to provide for its members a program for living without chemicals. This is done not by preaching at the alcohol/drug-addicted individual. Rather, it is accomplished by presenting a simple, truthful, realistic picture of the disease of addiction in language that the alcohol/drug-addicted person can understand. In AA, speakers share their own life stories, telling of the lies, the distortions, the self-deceptions, and the denial that supported their own chemical use. Thus they hope to break through the defensiveness of the alcohol-addicted person by showing that others have walked the same road and yet have found a way to recovery.

Helping others is a central theme of AA, in part because

> Even the newest of newcomers finds undreamed rewards as he tries to help his brother alcoholic, the one who is even blinder than he. . . . And then he discovers that by the divine paradox of this kind of giving he has found his own reward, whether his brother has yet received anything or not. (*Twelve Steps and Twelve Traditions*, 1981, p. 109)

In this, one finds a therapeutic paradox (not the only one!) in AA. For the speaker seeks first of all to help himself or herself through the public admission of powerlessness over chemicals. Through the public admission of weakness, the speaker seeks to gain strength from the group. It is almost as though, by his or her own addiction, the speaker says, "This is what *my* life was like, and sharing it with you reminds me of the reason why I will not to return alcohol again."

This is the method pioneered by Bill Wilson in his first meeting with Bob Smith. In that meeting, Bill Wilson spoke at length of his own addiction to alcohol, of the pain and suffering that he had caused others, and that he had suffered, in the service of his addiction. He did not preach but simply shared with Dr. Smith the history of his own alcoholism. Bill Wilson concluded with the following statement: "So thanks a lot for hearing me out. I know now that I'm not going to take a drink, and I'm grateful to you" (Kurtz, 1979, p. 29).

Thus the methods of AA present a paradox: It is by helping others that the speaker comes to receive help for his or her own addiction to alcohol/drugs. At the same time, she or he confronts the defenses of the new member by saying, in effect, "I am a mirror of yourself, and just as you cannot look into a mirror without seeing your own image, you cannot look at me without seeing a part of yourself."

As we have noted, Alcoholics Anonymous is a spiritual program that is at the same time not religious. Within the AA program, alcoholism is viewed as a

> spiritual illness, and drinking as a symptom of that illness. The central spiritual "defect" of alcoholics is described as an excessive preoccupation with self. . . . Treatment of the preoccupation with self is at the core of AA's approach. (McCrady & Irvine, 1989, p. 153)

From the theoretical model of AA, alcoholism is viewed as the end product of a process that begins when the individual loses his or her spirituality (Miller & Hester, 1995; McCrady, 1994). To combat the excessive preoccupation with "self," AA offers the Twelve-Steps as a guide for spiritual growth and for living. But the individual is not *required* to follow the Twelve Steps to participate in AA. Rather, "*the program* does not issue orders; it merely *suggests* Twelve Steps to recovery" (Jensen, 1987a; p. 15). Thus the individual is offered a choice: the way of life that preceded AA or acceptance of a program that others have used to achieve and maintain their sobriety. But the individual does not just *passively* accept the Twelve-Steps. Rather, the emphasis is on *working* the Twelve Steps, a process that requires "the active participation and intentional engagement of each individual who desires to change their drinking and become sober" (DiClemente, 1993, p. 80).

The Twelve Steps offer the tools necessary for daily abstinence. One of these tools is that the member of AA is not encouraged to look for the "cause" of his or her addiction to alcohol. Rather, the individual's alcoholism is accepted as a given fact. "It is not so much *how* you came to this place as what you are going to do now that you are here," one member said to a newcomer. Neither is the member admonished for being unable to live without chemicals. Members of AA know from bitter experience that relapse is possible and common (McCrady & Irvine, 1989). Chemical addiction is assumed in membership: "If chemicals were not a problem for you, you would not be here!" In place of the chemical-centered lifestyle, the new member is offered a step-by-step program for living that makes it possible to achieve and maintain recovery.

To take advantage of this program, the member need only accept *the program*. Admittedly, in doing so, the individual is asked to accept yet another therapeutic paradox. Step One, which is the only step that specifically mentions alcohol by name, asks that the individual accept, on the deepest level of being, that she or he is powerless over this chemical. Thus the individual is forced to embrace humility and acknowledge inability to face life alone (Norris, 1998). This is a difficult Step. The individual must learn that he or she is not God—a lesson that must be learned time and time again (Yancey, 2000). The essence of the Step One is acceptance, in the deepest level of the individual's soul, that he or she is *addicted to and totally powerless over* alcohol.

It is not uncommon for new members to continue to believe that alcohol alone is the problem. Confronting the rationalization that they are helpless victims of the disease of addiction forces them to accept that

> it is we ourselves, not the pills or alcohol, who cause most of our problems. Chemicals will not bring destruction upon a person until that person learns how to justify continual use and abuse of those chemicals. (Springborn, 1987, p. 8)

In other words, the individual is helped to see that although she or he is not responsible for having the biological/psychological/spiritual/genetic predisposition to alcoholism, she or he *is* responsible for working toward recovery (Wallace, 1996).

Hitting bottom. The process of learning how completely alcohol/drugs have come to dominate a person's life is often called "hitting bottom." This is a moment of painful self-discovery, when the person accepts the bitter, frightening reality that his or her life is being spent in the service of the addiction. At this moment, addicts come to understand that *nothing* they can do will enable them to control their chemical use, for they are *addicted*. This is a moment of extreme despair, when the addicted person might turn to another and say, "I need help." According to the AA model, it is at this moment that the alcohol/drug dependent individual takes the First Step (the ultimate admission of powerlessness), and becomes receptive to learning how to face problems without the continued use of alcohol or other chemicals.

Of AA and Recovery

Alcoholics Anonymous does not speak of a "cure" for the disease of alcoholism. The members of AA do not speak of themselves as having "recovered." For although the members of AA believe that addiction is a disease whose progress may be arrested, they also acknowledge that alcoholism can never be cured. Thus members may speak of themselves as *recovering*, but never as *having recovered*. An excellent example of this is the fact that several months often elapse between the time when a new member begins to attend AA and the time she or he when stops drinking. Indeed, new members might attend AA for 20 months before they even admit to being members of AA and for 8 more months before they stops drinking (Zweben, 1995). Thus the average person is an AA member for slightly over two years before he or she stops drinking.

Alcoholics Anonymous also does not speak of itself as an ultimate "cure" for alcoholism because it views the recovering person as being only a moment away from the next "slip." The 25-year veteran might, in a weak moment, relapse into active drinking. Simple affiliation with AA does not guarantee abstinence from alcohol/drugs (McCrady & Irvine, 1989). Each member faces a personal struggle to abstain from alcohol/drugs—a struggle that members are famously advised to face "one day at a time." If "today" is too long a period to think about, the individual is encouraged to think about abstaining for the next hour, or the next minute, or just the next second.

Once the addicted person accepts *the program*, he or she finds a way of living that provides support for recovery 24 hours a day, for the rest of his or her life (DiClemente, 1993). In accepting the program, the addicted may discover a second chance that they thought was forever lost.

Sponsorship

To help each person on the spiritual odyssey that it is hoped will result in their sobriety, new members of AA are encouraged to find a "sponsor." Indeed, sponsorship is seen as a key element of the AA program (McCrady & Delaney, 1995; Zweben, 1995). Sponsors are people who have worked their way through the step program and who have achieved a basic understanding of their own addiction. Sponsors act as spiritual (but not religious) guides, offering the new member equal amounts of confrontation, insight, and support.

It is the duty of the sponsor to take an interest in the newcomer's progress, but *not to take responsibility for it* (McCrady & Irvine, 1989; Alibrandi, 1978). Each new AA member is expected to have daily contact with his or her sponsor either by telephone or in person, at least at first (Nowinski, 1996). Even so, the responsibility for recovery remains with the individual. In a sense, the sponsor says to the client, "I can be concerned for you, but I am not responsible for you." In today's terminology, the sponsor is a living example of what might be called "tough love." In a sense, the sponsor's role is similar to that of a skilled folk psychotherapist (Peck, 1993).

The sponsor should not try to control the newcomer's life, ideally should recognize his or her own personal limitations, and should be the same sex as the new AA member being sponsored (McCrady & Delaney, 1995). The sponsor should also possess many—if not all—of the characteristics of the healthy human services professional identified by Rogers (1974).

The sponsor, acting as an extension of AA, is a tool. But it is up to the newcomer to grasp and use this tool to achieve sobriety. There are no guarantees, and the sponsor often struggles with many of the same issues the newcomer faces. The newcomer must assume the responsibility for reaching out and using the tools that are offered. Sponsorship is, in essence, an expression of the second mission of AA, which is to "carry the message" to other addicts who are still actively using chemicals. This is a reflection of Step Twelve, and sponsors often speak of having participated in a Twelfth-Step visit or of being involved in Twelfth-Step work. The sponsor is a guide, friend, peer counselor, fellow traveler, conscience, and devil's advocate, all rolled into one.

AA and Psychological Theory

The psychiatrist and popular writer M. Scott Peck (1993) advanced the theory that AA offers a form of folk psychology. The AA/NA step programs are different from other therapeutic programs that the addict may have been exposed to in that the Steps are "reports of action taken rather than rules not to be broken" (Alibrandi, 1978, p. 166). Each Step then is a public (or private) demonstration of action taken in the struggle to achieve and maintain sobriety, rather than a rule that might be broken.

Brown (1985) speaks of the AA steps as serving another purpose as well. For Brown (1985), the Twelve Steps serve to keep the recovering addict focused on his or her addiction. Just as the alcohol was an "axis" around which the individual's life revolved, through the Twelve Steps the addict continues to center his or her life on alcohol in a different way: a way without chemicals. During the period of active chemical use, the individual was constantly preoccupied with his or her drug of choice (Brown, 1985). The individual needs to learn how to relate openly to his or her addiction in a way that enables him or her to achieve and maintain sobriety. According to Brown (1985), the Twelve Steps accomplish this by providing a structured program by which the individual continues to relate to his or her addiction, while still being able to draw on the group for support and strength.

How Does AA Work?

In light of the fact that AA has been a social force in the United States for more than half a century, there has been surprisingly little research into what elements of the program are effective (Emrick, Tonigan, Montgomery, & Little, 1993). Charles Bufe (1988) offered three reasons why he thought AA was effective "at least for some people" (p. 55). First, AA provides a social outlet for its members. "Loneliness," Bufe (1988) observed, "is a terrible problem in our society, and people will flock to almost *anything* that relieves it—even AA meetings" (p. 55).

Second, AA allows its members to recognize that their problems are not unique (Bufe, 1988; Alibrandi, 1978). AA participation restores identity and self-esteem through the unconditional acceptance of its members, all of whom suffer from the same disease (Nace, 1997). Through this, each member of AA is able to discover a relatedness to others. Finally, AA can offer a proven path to follow that can "look awfully attractive when your world has turned upside down and you no longer have your best friend—alcohol—to lean on" (Bufe, 1988, p. 55). Thus the AA program is able to offer people *hope* at a time when they feel there is nobody to turn to (Nace, 1997; Bean-Bayog, 1993). Hope is an essential part of recovery, but one must wonder whether, as Bufe (1988) concluded, "These things, especially the first two, are all that is really needed" (p. 55). Bufe's (1988) view would also appear to be rather limited, however. For AA seems to offer more than just a way to deal with loneliness and a way of relating to others.

Herman (1988) observed that Twelve-Step programs such as AA also offer at least one more thing to the recovering addict: *predictability*. Consistency was one of the characteristics identified by Rogers (1974) as being of value in the helping relationship, and the predictability of AA may be one of the therapeutic aspects of this self-help group. However, this remains only a hypothesis.

The AA Twelve-Step program provides a format for "a planned spontaneous remission" (Berenson, 1987, p. 29) that is "designed so that a person can stop drinking by either education, therapeutic change, or transformation" (p. 30). As part of the therapeutic transformation inherent in AA participation, Berenson (1987) speculated that people would "bond to the group and use it as a social support and as a refuge to explore and release their suppressed and repressed feelings" (p. 30). Most certainly, these things are possible in the typical AA meeting, which is "generally characterized by warmth, openness, honesty, and humor" (Nace, 1987, p. 242)—attributes that may promote personal growth. AA is thought to be "the treatment of choice" (Berenson, 1987, p. 27) for active alcoholics, although Brodsky (1993) challenged this claim. Brodsky's challenge to the AA Twelve-Step recovery model is discussed later in this chapter.

Outcome Studies: The Effectiveness of AA

Many substance abuse rehabilitation professionals view AA as the single most important component of a person's recovery program. Indeed, at least one study found that AA participation was the *only* significant predictor of long-term recovery (McCaul & Furst, 1994). But AA is not without its critics (Marvel, 1995; Brodsky, 1993; Uva, 1991; Ogborne & Glaser, 1985). Indeed, virtually everything about AA has been challenged and debated. For example, there are those who suggest that AA "should be used only as a supportive adjunct to treatment" (Lewis, Dana, & Blevins, 1988; p. 151) and not considered a "treatment" of alcoholism by itself. At the same time, there are those who argue that AA has many similarities to a therapeutic program of change and thus should be viewed as a form of treatment in its own right (Tobin, 1992).

It is surprising, in light of the controversy that surrounds AA, that there has been very little empirical research into its effectiveness (Watson *et al.*, 1997) or for what types of people it might be most useful (George & Tucker, 1996; Tonigan & Hiller-Sturmhofel, 1994; McCaul & Furst, 1994; Galanter, Castaneda, & Franco, 1991). Indeed, many question whether AA is necessary for every individual with an alcohol/drug use problem (Peele, Brodsky, & Arnold, 1991; Peele, 1989). However, even critics of AA seem to accept the fact that it might be helpful at least to some who have a problem with chemicals (Brodsky, 1993; Ogborne & Glaser, 1985).

It has been pointed out that those people who join and remain in AA are *not* a representative sample of those who are dependent on alcohol (Galanter, Castaneda, & Franco, 1991). Thus the membership of AA is different from those alcohol-dependent individuals who choose not to join AA or who join but do not remain active members.[2] Further, *at least half* of newcomers to AA stop going to meetings within 3 months, and at the end of 1 year, 95% of the new members will have dropped out (Dorsman, 1996). Even among those who remain in AA, there is a significant relapse rate.

[2]Yet it was on data obtained from members of AA that Jellinek (1960) based his model of alcoholism.

Only 70% of those who abstain from alcohol for 1 year will still be alcohol-free at the end of their second year, and just 90% of those who abstain from alcohol for 2 full years will still be alcohol-free at the end of their third year of AA participation. Statistically, then, only 2% of those individuals who initially join AA will be alcohol-free at the end of 2 years (Dorsman, 1996). Abstinence rates for those individuals who maintained their involvement in AA over an 8-year period were found to be very similar to those achieved by a sample of alcohol-dependent individuals who entered formal treatment programs (Timko, Moos, Finney, & Lesar, 2000).

One factor that seems to predict abstinence is not just *attending* Twelve-Step program meetings but also *participating* in the meetings (Chappel & DuPont, 1999). This variable might explain why Humphreys and Moos (1996) obtained the results they did in their research study. The authors followed a sample of 201 alcohol-dependent individuals, of whom 135 elected to join AA and the remainder chose professional outpatient counseling for their alcoholism. There were no significant differences between these two subgroups in terms of age, sex, or socioeconomic status. The subjects were interviewed at the start of the research project and at the end of 1 and 3 years. The authors found that after 3 years, the group that had entered into outpatient counseling had the same percentage of abstinent members as did those subjects who elected to join AA. However, the authors did not assess how active the AA members were at meetings. They cautioned that their sample was self-selected in that the clients selected the form of treatment (AA versus professional outpatient counseling) for their alcohol use problems. In spite of the limitations of their study, Humphreys and Moos (1996) concluded that "alcohol self-help organizations may promote positive outcomes in alcohol-dependent individuals and may also take a significant burden off the public and private health care sectors" (p. 712).

A factor closely related to the need for active involvement in AA is the *frequency* with which a person attends AA meetings (Watson, Hancock, Gearhart, Mendez, Malovrh, & Raden, 1997). There is a positive relationship between the number of AA meetings attended in the time following discharge from inpatient treatment and the rate of abstinence from chemicals (Watson,

Hancock, Gearhart, Mendez, Malovrh, & Raden, 1997; Morgenstern, Labouvie, McCrady, Kahler, & Frey, 1997). AA involvement appears to reflect some of the same forces that predicted the individual's efforts to make meaningful personality change(s), such as his or her attempting to learn more effective ways to cope with stress (Morgenstern, Labouvie, McCrady, Kahler, & Frey, 1997).

One popular belief is that life stressors trigger increased alcohol use, but this theory actually is misleading. The team of Miller and Harris (2000) found that a sense of general depression and demoralization seemed to be predictive of relapse in those individuals who had successfully completed treatment. People who feel overwhelmed by the stressors they face are more likely to engage in increased alcohol use/abuse. Further, it has been found that increased alcohol use seems to *predate the development of many stressors*, which then set the stage for even more alcohol use by the individual (Humphreys, Moos, & Finney, 1996). Active involvement in AA seems to allow the individual to begin to develop a support system that both is nondrinking and seeks to help the individual cope with his/her problems without encouraging him or her to drink, thus breaking the cycle of drinking and ineffectual coping, according to the authors.

Although the results of these studies are suggestive, there still is not enough evidence to conclude that AA is effective in the treatment of alcoholism (Hester, 1994; Holder, Longabaugh, Miller, & Rubonis, 1991). And even if AA *is* an effective tool in the rehabilitation of the problem drinker, the majority of alcohol-dependent individuals never join an AA group (Bean-Bayog, 1993). This may be because AA "is not effective for *all* kinds of persons with alcohol problems" (Ogborne & Glaser, 1985, p. 188). In any case, it would appear that AA is most effective with a subset of problem drinkers: socially stable white males, over 40 years of age, who are physically dependent on alcohol, are prone to guilt, and are the first-born or only child.

This picture of the person who is most likely to benefit from AA membership was only the result of the first effort to identify the "typical" AA member. Other research suggests that those individuals who have strong religious beliefs and those who are severely addicted to alcohol are more likely to attend AA meetings (Weiss,

Griffin, Gallop, Luborsky, Siqueland, Frank, Onken, Daley, & Gastfriend, 2000). Research also suggests that approximately 35% of the members of AA are women, a figure that increases to 43% for those under the age of 30 (Coker, 1997).

Surprisingly, in light of how often individuals are required by the courts to attend AA meetings, there is little evidence that this approach is effective (Miller, Andrews, Wilbourne, & Bennett, 1998; Humphreys & Moos, 1996; Clark, 1995; Peele, Brodsky, & Arnold, 1991; Peele, 1989; Glaser & Ogborne, 1982). The practice of requiring the individual to attend AA meetings has been cited as one factor that has changed the AA movement itself (Humphreys & Moos, 1996). Further, there is evidence that those individuals who face legal consequences (jail or probation) as a result of driving while intoxicated have better subsequent driving records (fewer accidents and fewer further arrests) than those "sentenced" to treatment (Bufe, 1998; Peele, Brodsky, & Arnold, 1991). These findings raise questions about the effectiveness of court-ordered participation in AA or similar Twelve-Step groups.

Ultimately, the issue of whether AA is effective is far too complex to be measured by a single research study (Ogborne, 1993; Glaser & Ogborne, 1982). The very nature of AA ensures that there will be vast differences among AA groups, in spite of the fact that they all share the same name (Ogborne, 1993). There continues to be a need for a series of well-controlled research studies designed to identify all the variables that might influence the outcome of AA participation (McCrady & Irvine, 1989). In the absence of such studies, the very nature of the question "Is AA effective?" makes it unanswerable. For example, would the chronic alcoholic who, as a result of participation in AA, stopped drinking on a daily basis, but then began a pattern of binge drinking, be measured as a successful outcome or as a failure? Would the chronic alcohol user who entered AA, stopped drinking, but died of alcohol-induced liver disease six weeks later, represent a successful or an unsuccessful outcome? These examples illustrate why the question "Is AA effective?" is unlikely to generate a meaningful answer (Ogborne & Glaser, 1985). A more meaningful approach would be to try to identify which types of people are most likely to benefit from Twelve-Step programs such as AA.

Narcotics Anonymous

In 1953, another self-help group patterned after AA was founded. Although Narcotics Anonymous (NA) acknowledges its debt to Alcoholics Anonymous, the members of Narcotics Anonymous feel that

> We follow the same path with only a single exception. Our identification as addicts is all-inclusive in respect to any mood-changing, mind-altering substance. "Alcoholism" is too limited a term for us; our problem is not a specific substance, it is a disease called "addiction." . . . (*Narcotics Anonymous*, 1982, p. x)

To the members of NA, the problem is the disease of addiction. This self-help group emerged for those whose only common denominator is that "we failed to come to terms with our addiction" (*Narcotics Anonymous*, 1982, p. x). Whereas Alcoholics Anonymous addresses only alcoholism, NA addresses addiction to chemicals in addition to alcohol.

The growth of NA has been phenomenal: There was a 600% increase in the number of NA groups from 1983 to 1988 (Coleman, 1989), and there are more than 25,000 chapters of NA meetings in the United States (Humphreys, 1997). Alcoholics Anonymous and Narcotics Anonymous are not affiliated with each other, although there is an element of cooperation between them (Jordan, M. personal communication, 27 February 1989). Each follows a Twelve-Step program that offers the addicted person a day-by-day program for recovery. This is understandable, given that NA is essentially an outgrowth of AA.

Neither program has any inherent advantages over the other. Some people feel quite comfortable going to AA for their addiction to alcohol. Other people feel that NA offers them what they need to deal with their addiction. In the final analysis, the name of the group does not matter so much as whether it offers the recovering person the support and understanding that he or she needs to abstain for today.

Al-Anon and Alateen

The book *Al-Anon's Twelve Steps and Twelve Traditions* provides a short history of Al-Anon in its introduction.

According to this history, wives would often meet while their husbands were at the early AA meetings. As they waited, they would often talk over their problems. At some point, they decided to try to apply to their own lives the same Twelve Steps that their husbands had found so helpful. The group known as *Al-Anon* was born.

In the beginning, each independent group made whatever changes it felt necessary in the Twelve Steps. However, by 1948 the wife of one of the cofounders of AA became involved in the growing organization, and in time, a uniform family support program emerged. This program, known as the Al-Anon Family Group, borrowed and modified the AA Twelve Steps and Twelve Traditions to make them applicable to the needs of *families of alcoholics*. However, although joining Al-Anon is the most common recommendation for spouses of alcohol-abusing individuals, there is limited research into its effectiveness (O'Farrell, 1995). Little is known about the characteristics of an effective Al-Anon group or the successful Al-Anon member. Although Al-Anon is viewed as a resource for the spouse of the alcohol-abusing individual, its effectiveness has not been proven.

By 1957, in response to the recognition that teenagers in families with an alcoholic member have special needs and concerns, Al-Anon itself organized a modified Al-Anon group for teens known as *Alateen*. Alateen members follow the same Twelve Steps outlined in the Al-Anon program. The goal of the Alateen program, however, is to give teenagers an opportunity to share their experiences, discuss current problems, learn how to cope more effectively with their various concerns, and offer each other encouragement (*Facts About Alateen*, 1969).

Through Alateen, teenagers come to understand that alcoholism is a disease and learn to detach emotionally from the alcoholic's behavior, while still loving the individual. The goal of Alateen is also to help each member to learn that he or she did not cause the alcoholic to drink and to see that he or she can build a rewarding life in spite of the alcoholic's continued drinking (*Facts About Alateen*, 1969).

Support Groups Other Than AA

The AA program has been criticized for its emphasis on spiritual growth, its failure to empower women, and its basic philosophy. Several new self-help groups that have emerged since 1986 offer alternatives to AA.

Self-Management and Recovery Training. SMART was founded in 1985. Initially part of the "Rational Recovery" movement, it broke away from this group in 1994 (Chappel & DuPont, 1999; Horvath, 2000). Currently, SMART has more than 300 groups around the United States. It also offers a 24-hour "online" support group for members with access to the Internet (Horvath, 2000). The program draws heavily on the cognitive-behavioral school of psychotherapy and stresses four points: (1) enhancing and maintaining the individual's commitment to abstain, (2) coping with thoughts/cravings about chemicals, (3) solving old problem behaviors through cognitive-behavioral techniques, and (4) developing a balance in one's lifestyle (Horvath, 2000). Within this perspective, alcoholism (or other drug abuse) is viewed as reflecting the impact of negative, self-defeating thought patterns (Tonigan & Toscova, 1998; Ouimette, Finney, & Moos, 1997). For example, members are encouraged to stop drinking as a sign of self-respect, as opposed to drinking in order to feel good about themselves. Groups are advised by mental health professionals, and they strive to help the individual addict identify and correct self-defeating ways of viewing "self" and the world.

Gorski (1993) identified two general types of irrational thinking that contribute to the individual's substance use. The first of these was termed *addictive thinking* (p. 26) and defined as the individual's use of irrational thoughts to support her or his "right" to use chemicals and the claim that chemical use is not the cause of her or his problems. The second type of irrational thinking used to support substance use consists of *relapse justifications* (p. 26): specific thoughts marshaled to justify the individual's return to chemical use. "I can't cope with the stress without having a drink!" is one example of this kind of thinking.

SMART groups assume that virtually any approach to rehabilitation will be of some value to the individual, and thus they encourage participation in traditional Twelve-Step groups (Horvath, 2000). In a comparison of the effectiveness of traditional Twelve-Step programs and cognitive-behavioral (CB) treatment approaches, Ouimette, Finney, and Moos (1997) discussed the results of a multicenter experiment involving 3018 patients who were being treated for substance use problems at one of 15 selected Veterans Administration Hospitals in the United States. The subjects in this study were assigned to one of three treatment conditions: "pure" Twelve-Step treatment, "pure" CB treatment, or a mixed CB/Twelve-Step format. Participants in this study were interviewed after one year's time to determine their employment and substance use status. The authors concluded that "pure" cognitive-behavioral and "pure" Twelve-Step programs were equally effective in helping people address substance use problems (with no significant difference using the mixed format). This study thus supported treatment approaches such as the SMART program for persons with substance use problems.

Secular Organizations of Sobriety. SOS was founded in 1986, and currently it is estimated that there are about 2000 SOS groups meeting each week (Chappel & DuPont, 1999), with more than of 100,000 members around the world (Marvel, 1995). SOS is a self-help group that emerged as a reaction to the heavy emphasis on spirituality in AA and NA (*Alcoholism & Drug Abuse Week,* 1991). The guiding philosophy of SOS stresses personal responsibility, the role of critical thinking in recovery, and identification of the individual's specific "cycle of addiction" (Tonigan & Toscova, 1998).

Women for Sobriety. WFS was founded in 1976 (Chappel & DuPont, 1999). Approximately 325 WFS groups meet in the United States (McCrady & Delaney, 1995). This organization for women was founded on the theory that the AA program failed to address the very real differences between the meanings of alcoholism for men and women. WFS has 13 core statements, or beliefs, which are aimed at providing the member with a new perspective on herself. There is a great deal of emphasis on building the member's self-esteem. Research has revealed that about one-third of the members of WFS continue their involvement in AA and that approximately the same percentage of members of WFS groups as of AA groups learn to abstain from chemicals (Chappel & DuPont, 1999).

Alcoholics Anonymous for Atheists and Agnostics. Quad A is a Twelve-Step program that draws heavily on traditional AA (Rand, 1995). However, it tends to downplay the emphasis on religion inherent in traditional AA, and thus tends to be attractive to those individuals whose beliefs do not include the possibility of a

supreme being. The Quad A format tends to place less emphasis on "letting go" of one's personal will and ego—features that make it attractive to many women (Rand, 1995). Further, in place of the emphasis on the "power greater than ourselves" found in traditional AA meetings, Quad A tends to the forces in the individual's life that support recovery (Rand, 1995).

Quad A is found mainly in the Chicago area. There are an estimated 400–500 members at this time (Rand, 1995). Whereas traditional AA meetings usually last about an hour, Quad A meetings might last for several hours, especially when members become involved in a heated discussion of a topic of interest to a number of those present. Only time will tell whether the Quad A format will spread across the country or remain a local phenomenon. However, for those in the Chicago area, it offers an interesting alternative to traditional AA meetings.

Moderation Management. MM was founded in 1993 (Chappel & DuPont, 1999) and has been quite controversial ever since. MM evolved out of the frustration of its founder, Shirley Kishline, with traditional alcohol rehabilitation programs. Kishline felt that although she was referred to a traditional inpatient treatment program that placed great emphasis on involvement with Alcoholics Anonymous, her addiction to alcohol was never firmly established. In time, Kishline came to accept *moderation* as a more appropriate goal for her than abstinence, on the grounds that she was a "problem drinker" (Kishline, 1996, p. 53) but not an alcoholic. Ms. Kishline defined a problem drinker as a person who consumes no more than 35 drinks per week and who has experienced only mild to moderate alcohol-related problems (Kishline, 1996). In contrast, chronic drinkers are physically dependent on alcohol, and most experience severe withdrawal symptoms when they stop drinking (Shute & Tangley, 1997).

The goal of MM was to "provide a supportive environment in which people who have made the decision to reduce their drinking can come together to help each other change" (p. 55).

MM drew heavily upon behavior modification principles used by professionals to help individuals learn how to change their behavior. The MM movement initially gained some acceptance, and eventually meetings were held in 25 states. Critics of the MM movement, however, suggested that members with actual alcohol dependency problems would use the group as an excuse to continue to try to achieve "controlled" drinking. The founder of MM later renounced her objections to traditional Twelve-Step groups and accepted total abstinence as the treatment methods of choice for her alcohol use disorder (Vaillant, 2000). Then, shortly after taking this step, Kishline was involved in an alcohol-related motor vehicle accident in which a man and his 12-year-old daughter were killed when her truck struck theirs on an interstate highway (DeMillo, 2000). Kishline's measured blood alcohol level was 0.260, more than three times the legal limit for the State of Washington, and she was charged with and convicted of the crime of vehicular homicide. What this will mean for the future of MM remains to be seen.

Criticism of the AA/Twelve-Step Movement

Although the Twelve-Step movement has achieved an almost irreproachable status in the addictions recovery community, it is not without a small, vocal group of critics. For example, Brodsky (1993) noted that the Twelve-Step program advocated by AA is potentially "damaging, violative and ineffective" (p. 21) for many individuals. The author bases his criticism on the assumption that although it might be a useful tool for some, the Twelve-Step program is based on "a 19th-century fundamentalist tradition" (p. 21) that is essentially conservative Protestant in nature. Such a program might, when forced upon many people, prove more destructive than helpful, according to Brodsky.

Another vocal critic of the AA/Twelve-Step model is Marianne Gilliam (1998), who suggested that the AA program is based on fear, demands conformity, and fails to affirm the individual. Gilliam admits that AA has helped thousands of people but points out that this program was established in the 1930s. It might not meet the needs of addicted people of the next century, because AA "was founded on the experiences of one hundred men and one token woman. All these men were white, privileged, and in Bill Wilson's own words, suffered from 'self-will run riot'" (p. 29). Originally, the AA program was designed to "completely deflate the [individual's] ego," on the assumption that an inflated ego was a common characteristic of those who were addicted to alcohol. But this assumption might make AA

inappropriate for many of those who struggle with chemical use disorders at the start of the 21st century, according to the author, because it is not clear that this core assumption continues to be valid for many of those who have chemical use disorders.

Other critics of the Twelve-Step movement note that the spiritual "awakening" of one of the founders of AA, William ("Bill") Griffith Wilson, may have been based on his having received belladonna, under his physician's supervision, to help him recover from the acute effects of alcohol intoxication (Bufe, 1998; Lemanski, 1997; Peck, 1993). Others object to the heavy emphasis of such programs on a "higher power" (Wallace, 1996; Marvel, 1995). Because it was an outgrowth of an early-20th-century religious movement, the Twelve-Step model posits the necessity of the individual "surrendering" to an external, supernatural "higher power" if she or he is to learn how to abstain from drugs/alcohol.

It is interesting to note that what might be viewed as one of the more destructive elements of the Twelve-Step program, the need for spiritual desperation, is only rarely acknowledged as a possible problem (Gilliam, 1998; Lemanski, 1997). Yet any other form of psychological/psychiatric treatment that required the individual to experience the depths of despair and defeat, as the experience of "hitting bottom," would be branded as abusive by the mental health community.

Stanton Peele (1998, 1989) has pointed out a number of problems with the AA/Twelve-Step model as it is currently used in the United States. For example, the program is based on an unproven theory of the cause of alcoholism that was first suggested by the physician Benjamin Rush in the 17th century. Another problem with the AA/Twelve-Step model, according to Peele, is that it points to those individuals who were *least* successful in dealing with their addiction—the members who were able to recover only through the Twelve-Step program, as role models for new members. Yet these role models often are people who had extended periods of failure and relapse before their ultimate recovery—behaviors that are hardly acceptable in most role models. It should also be noted that the goal of AA/Twelve-Step programs, total abstinence, is only rarely achieved: Most alcohol-dependent individuals merely cut back on the amount of their alcohol use, and very few achieve total abstinence (Peele, 1998).

Critics point out that many of the basic tenets of AA, such as the twin beliefs that alcoholism will *always* grow worse without treatment, and that people cannot cut back or quit drinking on their own, are not supported by research data. Alcohol-dependent persons rarely follow the downward spiral thought by AA to be inescapable. Further, the majority of those individuals with alcohol use problems learn to control or discontinue drinking without formal intervention (Peele, 1989; Vaillant, 1983). The manner in which the AA program is implemented has been characterized as a form of "indoctrination" (Bufe, 1998, p. 6).

Finally, many critics of AA have observed that the AA/Twelve-Step model does not embrace the possibility of a "cure" (Gilliam, 1998; Lemanski, 1997). Indeed, does not even incorporate the concept of *health*, according to Gilliam (1998). Critics also note that the only way for the AA/Twelve-Step program to be effective is for the individual to continue to attend meetings forever, although few people actually maintain their involvement in AA/Twelve-Step programs for extended periods of time.

Summary

The self-help group Alcoholics Anonymous (AA) has emerged as one of the predominant forces in the field of drug abuse treatment. Drawing on the experience and knowledge of its members, AA has developed a program for living that is spiritual without being religious, that is confrontive without using confrontation in the traditional sense of the word, that relies on no outside support, and that many of its members believe is effective in helping them stay sober on a daily basis.

The program for living established by AA is based on principles that early members believed were important to their own sobriety. This program for living is known as the Twelve Steps. The Steps are suggested as a guide to new members. Emphasis is placed on the equality of all members, and there is no board of directors within the AA group.

Questions continue to exist about whether AA is effective. Researchers agree that it seems to be effective for some people, but not for all of those who join. The question of how to measure the effectiveness of AA is quite complex. A series of well-designed research projects is needed to identify the multitude of variables involved in AA's effectiveness for some people.

In spite of these unanswered questions, AA has served as a model for many other self-help groups, including Narcotics Anonymous (NA). One of the central tenets of Narcotics Anonymous is that AA's focus on alcohol is too narrow for persons who have become addicted to other chemicals, either alone or in combination with alcohol. Narcotics Anonymous maintains that addiction is a common disease that may express itself through many different forms of drug dependency. NA has established a Twelve-Step program that is based on the Twelve Steps of Alcoholics Anonymous. But NA also seeks to reach out to those whose addiction involves chemicals other than alcohol.

Other self-help groups that have emerged as a result of the AA experience include Al-Anon and Alateen. Al-Anon, which emerged from informal encounters among the spouses of early AA members, strives to help the families of those who are addicted to alcohol. Alateen emerged from Al-Anon, in response to the recognition that adolescents have special needs. Both groups try to help members learn how to be supportive of, without being dependent on, the alcoholic and learn how to detach from the alcoholic and his or her behavior.

CHAPTER THIRTY-FIVE

Crime and Drug Use

Introduction

The "war" on drugs is almost 100 years old (Shenk, 1999). It has been a most curious war: The face of the "enemy" is shaped by religious, social, and political forces that are only poorly understood, and the war has been fought with weapons that have proved to be ineffective. Further, the rights of the majority have been compromised in order for society to impose its will upon a small minority of the population. The most destructive chemicals, alcohol and tobacco, are largely exempt from attack, whereas relatively benign chemicals with high social disapproval ratings are subjected to multipronged assaults. Entire books have been devoted to the subject of the war on drugs and how it has manufactured "criminals" in this country. In this chapter, we will discuss the "war" on drugs and drug-related criminal activity.

Drug Abuse and Criminal Behavior

It is exceptionally difficult to assess the true relationship between drug abuse and criminal behavior. For one thing, much of the research in this area is biased by the researcher's preexisting assumptions. There are those researchers who assume that *any* crime committed by a person under the influence of chemicals is drug-related. Take the often repeated example of heroin addicts resorting to crime to support their habit. The criminal activity of the heroin-addicted person is thus assumed to be caused by his or her addiction to heroin, rather than by such social forces as poverty and lack of education.

A different perspective is that individuals who are predisposed to crime might also be predisposed to use of alcohol and/or drugs (Moore, 1991). From this perspective, it is possible to argue that people who engage in the abusive use of chemicals simply tend to be the kinds of people who also engage in criminal activity. This position is supported by research revealing that *more than 50% of heroin-dependent individuals in the United States have a legal history prior to their first use of narcotics* (Jaffe, 1995, 1989).

Yet another perspective on the relationship between criminal activity and chemical abuse was offered by Elliott (1992). The author suggested that chemical abuse and criminal activity both reflect the "decline in the power of cultural restraints" (p. 599) taking place in this country. The author supported his argument with the observation that Europe has experienced "tidal waves of crime" (Elliott, 1992, p. 599) every few decades since the 14th century. A similar pattern has emerged here in the United States over the past 200 years. A common thread connecting these waves of crime, according to the author, is that in each successive period of social unrest, one could observe

> an erosion of personal integrity, widespread dehumanization, a contempt for life, material greed, corruption in high places, sexual promiscuity, *and increased recourse to drugs and alcohol.* (p. 599, italics added)

But the initial question remains: What is the relationship between recreational substance use and criminal activity? It is known that 54% of those incarcerated in state prisons had a diagnosable substance use disorder at the time that they committed their crime (Evans, 1998). It is also known that fully a quarter of all property crimes (car theft, burglary, and so on) can be traced to recreational drug use (National Academy of Sciences, 1990). These figures are suggestive, and chemical use and crime do appear to be related. But whether the substance use causes criminal behavior, is one of a number of factors associated with a crime, or is totally unrelated to the crime must be determined on a case-by-case basis.

Criminal activity and personal responsibility. The issue of personal responsibility in cases where the individual might have been under the influence of chemicals at the time of the offense is a difficult one. In many cases, this issue is neatly sidestepped through the use of the social fiction that the drugs somehow interfered with the individual's ability to think coherently. Thus, as was observed a quarter-century ago, any

> perceived correlation between the use of a drug and the unwanted consequences is attributed to the drug, removing the individual from any and all responsibility. (National Commission on Marihuana and Drug Abuse, 1973, p. 4)

The view that crimes committed under the influence of chemicals were caused by the drugs is an extension of the "demon rum" philosophy of the late 1800s (Peele, 1989). According to this interpretation, once the person ingests even one drink, the alcohol totally overwhelms his or her self-control. From that point on, the person has no control over his or her behavior: It is controlled by the demon hidden within the bottle of alcohol. The modern version of this belief is that when a crime is committed by a person who is under the influence of chemicals, the responsibility for that crime is attributed not to the person but to the chemical. The individual's role in the commission of that crime is overlooked, or at least minimized, and the person is viewed as a helpless victim of the drug's effects. The outcome of this process is that although drug use in itself is not an excuse for criminal behavior, *extreme* drug use often derails the legal system.

This is not to say that substance abuse/addiction can be used to justify criminal activity. The courts have ruled that the use of recreational chemicals involves

some element of choice (Kermani & Castaneda, 1996), so the individual is still held responsible for the acts committed while under the influence of chemicals. Unfortunately, however, the criminal justice system is often unable to determine whether or not the individual actually *intended* to commit a crime while under the influence of chemicals. In such cases, the criminal justice system often simply accepts the compromise that the individual suffered "diminished capacity" as a result of his or her use of chemicals; many difficult cases are cleared from the court schedule in this manner. As a result of this social and legal fiction, it is not unusual for defense attorneys to negotiate a reduced sentence on the basis of the claim that the defendant was under the influence of chemicals at the time of the offense (Graham, 1989).

The "War on Drugs": The Making of a National Disaster

The lessons of history. In the 1930s, the United States carried out an experiment in social reform known as "Prohibition" in which the nonmedicinal use of alcohol was prohibited by law. As a result of this "noble experiment," a black market quickly emerged to manufacture alcohol and distribute it to those who desired to use it (Gray, 1998). Criminal elements, sensing a huge profit, moved in to take control of the emerging supply/distribution network, killing those who resisted, bribing officials to look the other way or to leave them alone, and fighting among themselves for control of the criminal enterprise.

Another change brought on by national Prohibition was that it forced people to switch from drinking beer to hard liquor (Gray, 1998). In contrast to the bulk, low alcohol content, and short shelf life of beer, hard liquor offered a high alcohol content, had less bulk, and did not spoil. Before the start of Prohibition, alcohol users would "sip" alcoholic beverages throughout the day, or drink beer, without evidence of widespread intoxication (Barr, 1999; Gray, 1998). Following the start of Prohibition, drinkers shifted to a "binge" pattern of drinking: Periods of heavy alcohol use were interspaced with periods of abstinence, intoxication being the goal of drinking (Barr, 1999; Gray, 1998). At the same time, alcohol users switched from beer to hard liquor, which resulted in the highest levels of intoxication in the least time

(Gray, 1998). In this manner, the "nobel experiment" of Prohibition helped to shape the drinking habits of people for generations to come.

Something similar took place in the 1970s, although the parallels with the Prohibition era were not recognized until much later. Researchers now believe that the interdiction efforts against marijuana may have caused drug smugglers to switch from transporting marijuana to trafficking in cocaine (Scheer, 1994a). This theory is based on the fact that, pound for pound, cocaine is "less bulky, less smelly, more compact, and more lucrative" (Nadelmann, Kleinman, & Earls, 1990, p. 45) than is marijuana. The prohibition against recreational cocaine use also contributed to the wave of violence that spread across the United States in the late 1980s, as drug pushers fought over potential markets much as gang members during the Prohibition era fought for the right to distribute alcohol in city after city (Hatsukami & Fischman, 1996).

The modern era. In spite of the lessons from Prohibition, the process of drug interdiction has become one of the most enduring features of the "war on drugs" in the United States. The belief that drug interdiction could be an effective response to the problem of drug abuse/addiction overlooks the fact that on a worldwide level, the production/distribution of illicit drugs is a $400 billion/year industry, most of which is controlled by criminal groups interested only in making a profit (United Nations, 1997). These criminal groups will use both bribery and violence to make sure that their drugs reach those who are willing to pay for them (Gray, 1998).

As was true of the efforts of law enforcement agencies to stop the flow of alcohol during Prohibition, only a small percentage of the illicit drugs sent to this country are ever confiscated by law enforcement officials. These efforts at interdiction result only in short-term, local reductions in the supply of certain chemicals. Also, in a pattern that is similar to that seen when law enforcement agencies tried to stop the flow of alcohol during Prohibition,

> the more "effective" police activity is, the more [drug] prices rise, increasing the profits of smuggling, and the more likely it will be that drug purity and concentration will also increase, to make importation more cost-effective and detection more difficult. (Manderson, 1998, p. 589)

One reason why the illicit drug distribution system is so resistant to the efforts of law enforcement officials is simple: There is a *lot* of money involved in the drug trade. As a result of the prohibition against recreational drugs, their production, distribution, and sale are for the most part carried out by those who are, by definition, criminals. As was the case with alcohol during the Prohibition era, a black market has evolved that makes drugs available to potential users—for a price (Buckley, 1996; Nadelmann & Wenner, 1994; Nadelmann, 1989; McWilliams, 1993). In a process quite similar to that of alcohol distribution in the Prohibition era, the price for drugs is rigidly controlled by those who operate the supply/distribution network. In return for running the risk of criminal prosecution for bringing the drugs into this country, the modern drug supplier demands a significant profit margin. The supply/distribution network generates an estimated $50–$60 billion in *profits* each year for those who supply drugs to users in this country (Nadelmann & Wenner, 1994).

An example of how suppliers control the profit margin of their business, consider that the cost to manufacture a single tablet of illicit MDMA in an established illicit drug laboratory is approximately 10¢, and yet this same tablet will sell for $30 on the streets of New York City (Cloud, Barnes, Graft, Reaves, & Shannon, 2000). Another example of the potential profits created by the prohibition against illicit drugs is the fact that with just $75 worth of chemicals, a street "chemist" can manufacture PCP that will ultimately sell for as much as $20,000 on the illicit market (Shepherd & Jagoda, 1990). Heroin or cocaine that might be worth $500 in the country of origin will sell for upwards of $100,000 on the streets in the United States, (McNamara, 1996). The same chemicals purchased legally at any chemical supply store for $1000 might produce a supply of methamphetamine powder that could sell for as much as $40,000 on the street (*Playboy*, 1990a; Peluso & Peluso, 1988).

Nor are these profits limited to chemical compounds that are produced here. A native farmer on an illicit opium farm in Mexico is paid approximately $100 for the opium gum he obtains from the poppies in his fields. For each 7 kilograms of opium gum, illicit laboratories can manufacture 1 kilogram of heroin. Later, when shipped to the United States by various means, this single kilogram of heroin will sell for as much as $500,000 (Shoumatoff, 1995). Such profits have helped the drug distribution and sales infrastructure become quite resilient in the face of law enforcement attempts to prohibit trafficking in illegal drugs (*The Lancet*, 1991b). We now realize that there is always somebody willing to risk arrest for the chance to participate in such a highly profitable trade. This fact would have been clear from the nobel experiment of Prohibition, if anybody had bothered to examine the history books.

Manufacturing criminals. Unlike law enforcement agencies during the Prohibition era, in the modern "war on drugs," federal and state authorities have instituted legal sanctions against those who would engage in recreational drug use, effectively turning what had been a medical problem into a legal issue. When the use of these compounds is illegal, individuals who indulge in their use are by definition, criminals, and thus they are subject to attack with the full ferocity of the legal system. This general policy, in effect since the 1930s, has proved to be ineffective in the battle against recreational chemical use (Gray, 1998), yet it remains a centerpost of the government's efforts to eliminate drug use/abuse in the United States.

Some political observers have suggested that personal, recreational drug use (as opposed to distribution of illicit chemicals to others) is simply a consensual crime: The individual who is using a recreational chemical has made the choice to do so in a manner that does not hurt others (McWilliams, 1993; Royko, 1990). Indeed, many individuals have demonstrated a remarkable persistence in obtaining illicit chemicals, in spite of society's efforts to block their use. By classifying individual drug use as a consensual crime, it might be possible to avoid the "gun battles, the corruption and the wasted money and effort trying to save the brains and noses of those who don't want them saved" (Royko, 1990, p. 46).

It has been suggested that recreational drug use be legalized, possibly with restrictions on who may dispense the compounds now deemed illegal by the authorities. This would allow some measure of control over who has access to drugs, and at what age they are allowed to use them, in much the manner that access to alcohol is restricted by law. Another benefit of this approach to the problem is that the compounds would at least be available to each person who wished to "sniff away his nose or addle his brain" (Royko, 1990, p. 46),

without the classification of large numbers of citizens who engage in this consensual act as "criminals."

The prohibition against recreational drug use has also contributed to the development of criminal activity in another way: by forcing some individuals to engage in criminal activity to support their drug use. As we shall see later in this chapter, the national prohibition against drug use has served mainly to increase the price of the forbidden chemicals, because they are under the control of criminals rather than sold in a free market. To obtain the money necessary to buy the drugs needed to feed their addiction, many people are forced to engage in burglary, armed robbery, prostitution (heterosexual and homosexual), car theft, forgery, or a range of other crimes. Another common means of obtaining money to buy drugs for personal use is by engaging in drug sales (itself a criminal act).

The person who supports his or her drug use through theft will receive only a fraction of the stolen material's worth. The result of this process is that the individual must steal more and more so that the pittance he or she receives for the stolen property will meet his or her drug needs. It has been estimated that the typical heroin addict in an average city would need to steal some $200,000 worth of goods annually to support a drug "habit" (Kreek, 1997). In this way, the national prohibition against the drugs of abuse might be said to have contributed to the wave of crime that developed in the United States in the 1970s.

Frustrated with the failure of the "war on drugs" to curb the abuse of illegal drugs, the United States government initiated a "zero tolerance" program in the early 1980s. Legal sanctions and incarceration were immediately imposed on those who were convicted of a drug-related criminal offense, even if the crime was only the possession of a single seed of a marijuana plant. Mandatory-sentencing provisions were also applied in cases where the individual had used a controlled substance. Although political support for mandatory sentencing was almost universal, its success has recently been criticized by many social scientists and physicians. Again, the mandatory sentencing of drug offenders provides an abject example of how the lessons of history are ignored in order to continue the "war on drugs."

In the 21st century, it is all too easy to forget the fact that in the 1950s, Congress passed a series of mandatory minimum-sentence laws in the fight against narcotics use/abuse in this country (Schlosser, 1994). These laws were loosely termed the "Boggs Act," which imposed minimum prison sentences for the illicit use of narcotics. Although support for the Boggs Act was almost universal, James V. Bennett, then director of the United States Bureau of Prisons, expressed strong reservations about its effectiveness. Although he had not personally broken any laws in doing so, Mr. Bennett, himself a federal employee, was subsequently followed by agents of the Federal Bureau of Narcotics, who submitted to their superiors regular reports on the content of speeches that he gave (Schlosser, 1994).

By the late 1960s, it was clear that Mr. Bennett was right: Mandatory sentencing did little to reduce the scope of narcotics use/abuse in this country. In 1970, the Boggs Act was replaced by a more flexible series of sentencing guidelines, through which a judge could assess the merits of each individual case and sentence defendants on that basis. Just 14 years later, however, Congress again imposed mandatory prison sentences for drug-related offenses. The lessons of past decades were forgotten. Through the Sentencing Reform Act of 1984, Congress took away the judge's power to determine appropriate prison sentences by reinstituting the application of mandated minimum prison terms. Even first-time offenders were sent to prison for extended periods, without hope of parole.

One result of the Sentencing Reform Act of 1984 was that the prison system soon became filled with individuals serving lengthy mandatory sentences. Whereas, in 1970, only 16% of all federal prisoners were incarcerated because of drug-related convictions, by 1994 62% of those incarcerated in federal penitentiaries were there because of drug-related convictions (*Playboy*, 1995a; Nadelmann & Wenner, 1994; Schlosser, 1994). By the year 2001, it was estimated that *more than three-quarters* of all federal inmates might be incarcerated for drug-related mandatory minimum prison terms.

In retrospect, like the Boggs Act, the Sentencing Reform Act of 1984 has been a dismal failure. Many of those incarcerated for drug-related crimes are "first-time" offenders who have never had a prior conviction for *any* offense and who are sentenced to serve terms out of all proportion to the offense. Consider, for example, the fact that although the offender who is convicted of intentional homicide is usually *sentenced* to life in prison,

> the average sentence *served* for murder in the U.S. is six and a half years, while eight years with no possibility of parole is *mandatory* for the possession of 700 marijuana plants. (Potterton, 1992, p. 47, italics added)

Another example of the unfair nature of the sentences imposed on first-time drug offenders is the fact that an employee caught embezzling between $10 million and $20 million from a bank where he or she was employed would be sentenced to prison for 5 years. This is the same sentence that a person would receive for possession of 5 grams of "Crack" cocaine (Bovard, 1997).

The impact of mandatory prison sentences for those convicted of drug-related offenses has reached the point where habitual and violent prisoners are being released from prison in order to make room for *first-time* offenders convicted and sentenced under mandatory drug enforcement laws (Asseo, 1993; Potterton, 1992). In 1996, the number of people sentenced to prison for drug-related offenses exceeded the number of people incarcerated for violent crimes (Bovard, 1997). If the existing federal laws against drug possession/use were to be fully implemented, it would be necessary for the United States government to build a new 650-bed prison *every month* to house those convicted of violating just the federal antidrug laws (*Forensic Drug Abuse Advisor*, 1994g).

Other critics of the mandatory sentencing laws for possession of illegal substances point out that small-time users are generally the ones subjected to lengthy mandatory prison terms (Steinberg, 1994).[1] In spite of the intent of the law (which was to punish those involved in drug distribution), midlevel and upper-level suppliers are frequently able to use their knowledge of who is buying drugs from them to bargain for lighter prison sentences. Thus,

> [the] former hippie with 1000 marijuana plants growing in his basement and no drug ring to rat on

---

[1]This is not always the case, however. When the son of Indiana Congressman Dan Burton was arrested, and was found to have 8 pounds of marijuana in the trunk of his car and 30 marijuana plants in his apartment, he was simply placed on probation.

gets the full decade in prison, while the savvy dealer bringing in boatloads of pot from south of the border can finger a few friends and be out in half the time. (Steinberg, 1994, p. 33)

As a result of this process, fully 52% of those individuals incarcerated in the United States under mandatory sentencing provisions are drug users or those who "deal" on the streets, whereas only 11% might be classified as major suppliers (Dwyer, 2000; Petersen, 1999).

The Sentencing Reform Act of 1984 has also been found to be quite discriminatory. Researchers have noted that cocaine hydrochloride, which is most often sold as a *powder*, is abused mainly by middle-class users, whereas *Crack* is found most often in the ghetto areas. Federal sentencing guidelines require that a first-time offender with 5 grams of Crack be sentenced to prison for 5 years, but a first-time offender would need to have 500 grams of cocaine hydrochloride in her or his possession to receive a similar sentence (Hatsukami & Fischman, 1996). This distinction has contributed to inequities in prosecution and sentencing. For example, fully 90% of all those incarcerated for drug-related crimes in state and federal prisons during the George Bush administration were either African-American or Latino (Garrett, 2000).

To underscore the cost of incarcerating individuals who are convicted of drug-use related offenses, consider the following statistics: In 1972, there were an estimated 200,000 jail and prison cells in the entire United States. By the year 1998, 400,000 individuals were in various state and federal prisons just for violating antidrug laws, and there were 1.7 million people incarcerated in various local jails and state and federal prisons (MacCoun & Reuter, 1998). Just one state, California, was projected to have the same number of cells in its prison system as were found in the entire country just two generations earlier (Ryglewicz & Pepper, 1996). The vast majority of these new jail and prison cells are necessary to house individuals convicted of drug-related crimes.

It is expensive to keep a person in prison. For example, in 1997 there were 800,000 individuals incarcerated for drug-related convictions (McCaffrey, 1997). The cost of keeping one individual incarcerated for one year has been estimated as falling between $35,000 and $70,000, depending on the inmate's status and the location of the prison (Kree, 1997). If a median figure of $60,000/year is used, then $48 *billion* is being spent every year just to keep convicted drug offenders incarcerated. And although treatment programs must demonstrate their effectiveness in order to obtain funding, prisons are not required to do so (MacCoun & Reuter, 1998).

The "war on drugs" initiated by President Ronald Reagan, and reaffirmed by every president elected since then, has been estimated to cost each man, woman, and child in the United States $133 every year (Buckley, 1997). What have we gotten for our money? The past 20 years have seen an erosion of traditional constitutional rights, but we have yet to become drug-free (Elders, 1997).

Perhaps the war on drugs continues

> because it suits politicians to blame drug abusers for many of the social problems that currently beset America; by sounding tough on drugs they can sound tough on crime without having to address the real problems confronting the urban poor. (Barr, 1999, p. 304)

In other words, the "war on drugs" is a convenient smoke screen that diverts attention from the real social problems facing this nation (Barr, 1999; Gray, 1998).

The twin policies of prohibition and interdiction of illicit chemicals have been the watchword in this country for almost a century. An estimated $150 billion has been spent "fighting" the war on drugs at the federal level in the past decade, and an estimated $17.8 billion was devoted to this "war" in the year 2000 (Dwyer, 2000). Yet in spite of all of the time, energy, and money that has been invested in the "war" on drugs, it has been a dismal failure (Finkelstein, 1997; Gray, 1998). The situation has deteriorated to the point where "[in the] current moral–judicial system, *talking* about drugs disapproved of by politicians is a worse crime than killing citizens" (Bovard, 1997, p. 55, italics added).

As should be obvious by now, the government's effort to solve the drug abuse problem through law enforcement/interdiction has been a failure. Of course this does not stop law enforcement officials from trumpeting the successes of the past year or from hinting that, for just a few billion dollars more, it may be possible to eliminate the problem of recreational drug use in the United States. However, there is a small group of people who are openly calling the war on drugs a failure and are looking for alternatives to this social policy.

The debate over legalization. It is impossible to enter into the debate over the legalization of some or all of the drugs of abuse without becoming ensnared in the minefield of political agendas. Gray (1998) suggested, for example, that federal and state drug enforcement agencies *need* to keep marijuana classified as an illicit substance, because marijuana abusers make up the bulk of those classified as "drug abusers" in the United States. If this group of people were to be reclassified as nonoffenders via the legalization of marijuana, then the number of illegal drug abusers in this country would instantly drop from 13 million to 3–4 million, a number that would make it difficult to justify the expenditure of so many billions of dollars on enforcement/interdiction (Dwyer, 2000; Gray, 1998).

To justify the continued existence of federal and state drug enforcement agencies, authorities have often simply manufactured data (Gray, 1998). Further support for the continued efforts of antidrug agencies is obtained through the use of questionable statistical methods. In 1994, for example, "the Center on Addiction and Substance Abuse at Columbia University made the shocking announcement that marijuana smokers were eighty-five times more likely to go on to cocaine than nonsmokers" (Gray, 1998, p. 177). This figure has since been frequently cited as evidence that marijuana is a "gateway" drug, the use of which will result in further drug abuse. Yet few people understand that this "fact" was uncovered by "taking the estimated number of cocaine users who had smoked reefer first and dividing it by the estimated number who hadn't (almost nobody)" (Gray, 1998, p. 177). Using such quasi-statistical methods, the author pointed out, it would be possible to "prove" that coffee, alcohol, tobacco, and apple pie were also gateway chemicals leading to drug abuse.

Advocates of drug legalization point out that legalization would remove an important source of revenue for what is loosely termed "organized crime." (The manufacture and transport of illicit drugs are a key source of income for criminal groups). Further, there is a chance that drugs would lose their appeal to adolescents and young adults, many of whom are drawn to substance use as a form of rebellion (Barr, 1999). An example of what might happen if drugs were legalized is the situation in New Zealand, where no laws prohibit minors from buying or consuming alcohol in public if they are with their parents. There is no minimum age requirement for the purchase of alcohol in Portugal and Belgium, and in France, Spain, England, Austria, and Italy, an adolescent may legally purchase alcohol at the age of 16 (Barr, 1999; Peele, 1996). In these countries, it is felt that adolescents should learn to drink within the context of their families in order to learn moderate, social drinking. In spite of this rather liberal pattern of alcohol use, these countries have rates of child/adolescent alcohol abuse similar to those in the United States.

One alternative to the free-market legalization program so fearfully envisioned by Frances (1991) is making recreational drugs available through a physician's prescription (Schmoke, 1997; Lessard, 1989). This is a very similar approach to that adopted in England, where physicians who hold a special license may prescribe heroin to individuals proven to be addicts (*60 Minutes*, 1992). On another front, the medical journal *The Lancet* (1995) went so far as to call for the legalization of marijuana, with controls similar to those imposed on the sale of tobacco, on the grounds that the criminal sanctions currently in place against marijuana only add a degree of glamour to its use.

Admittedly, chemical users might experience health problems. However, Curley (1995) suggested that insurance companies be permitted to charge higher health insurance premiums for drug users, as they do now for cigarette smokers. These higher health care premiums would cover the expense of providing health care to people who engage in such "high-risk" behaviors as abusing recreational chemicals. In this way, access to the drugs could be limited, and the profit incentive for organized crime would be removed. What Lessard (1989) suggested, in other words, is that the problem of drug abuse be approached from a health perspective, as it is in Holland and England.

Adulterants. An unintended consequence of the prohibition against the recreational chemicals is that most illicit drugs are rarely sold to the user in pure form. Rather, in order to increase their profits, mid- and upper-level drug suppliers frequently "cut" (adulterate) the drug before selling it (Coomber, 1997). Through this process, an ounce of pure cocaine will become two ounces of 50% pure cocaine. The buyer who does not like paying for adulterated chemicals can't very well appeal to the Better Business Bureau!

In an effort to scare those who might abuse chemicals, the mass media often report that illicit chemicals are mixed with dangerous substances such as ground up glass, dust from bricks, and the like. There is little evidence that this is a common practice (Coomber, 1997). Intuitively, it does not make much sense for a drug dealer to kill his customers . . . at least not immediately. More commonly, the adulterants added at each stage of the drug manufacturing distribution process are substances that merely increase bulk and thus inflate the price of the compound at each stage in the distribution process.

For example, the farmer in Pakistan who raises opium poppies might be paid $90 for a kilogram of raw opium. The illicit heroin produced from this opium is then "cut" (adulterated) at each stage of the production process. When it is finally sold on the street, a single kilogram of heroin has a final retail potency of about 40%. The powder is sold in small packets (perhaps a small balloon or a condom) for between $5.00 (a "nickel bag") and $10 (a "dime bag") each, and the retail price would be $290,000 per kilogram (United Nations, 1997). Heroin sold in the United States averages around 73% (Sabbag, 1994) "pure" heroin. The rest of the contents of the "bag" consists of various adulterants that have been added along the way, usually by the "high-end" or mid-level suppliers rather than the "street-level" dealer (Coomber, 1997).

In the case of cocaine, say raw cocaine leaves were sold by the farmer in South America for $610 a kilogram (2.4 pounds).[2] From these leaves, a small amount of coca paste is obtained, which is eventually sold for about $860 a kilogram. This coca paste yields an even smaller amount of cocaine hydrochloride, which will be sold for up to $1500 a kilogram. Following transportation to the United States, the cocaine hydrochloride might be refined into "Crack," which sells for about $50,000 a kilogram, or it might be sold as cocaine powder, which might sell for about $110,000 a kilogram (United Nations, 1997). Chemical analysis of the cocaine being sold on the streets of the United States in 1995 revealed that the purity averaged about 61%. This means that on average, approximately 40% of each gram of cocaine purchased on the street is actually something other than cocaine. These adulterants were found to fall into one of five categories: (1) various forms of sugar, (2) stimulants, (3) local anesthetics, (4) toxins, and (5) any of a number of inert compounds added to give the product bulk. The various forms of sugar were the most common adulterants (Scaros, Westra, & Barone, 1990; Schauben, 1990).

The adulterants that have been found in illicit narcotics include food coloring, talc powder, starch, powdered milk, baking soda, brown sugar, and, even dog manure (Scaros, Westra, & Barone, 1990). Aspirin, amphetamine compounds, belladonna, caffeine, instant coffee, lactose, LSD, magnesium sulfate, meprobamate, pentobarbital, pepper, powdered milk, secobarbital, starch, and warfarin have also been used to "cut" illicit opiates sold in the United States (Scaros, Westra, & Barone, 1990; Schauben, 1990).

Marijuana is also frequently adulterated. It is not uncommon for up to half of the "marijuana" purchased on the street to be seeds and woody stems, which must be removed before the marijuana can be smoked. Further, the marijuana may be laced with other compounds ranging from PCP, cocaine paste, and opium to toxic compounds such as "Raid" insect spray (Scaros, Westra, & Barone, 1990). Marijuana samples have also been found to have been adulterated with dried shredded cow manure (which may expose the user to salmonella bacteria), as well as herbicide sprays such as paraquat (Jenike, 1991). Other substances reported to have been found in marijuana samples include alfalfa, apple leaves, catnip, cigarette tobacco, hay, licorice, mescaline, methamphetamine, opium, pipe tobacco, straw, wax, and wood shavings (Schauben, 1990).

When drug abusers use a compound that has been adulterated, some or all of the adulterants are introduced into their bodies increasing the health risks associated with chemical abuse. This is the primary reason why "pharmaceuticals" (drugs produced by legal pharmaceutical manufacturers that have been diverted to the streets) are so highly prized among illicit drug users. "Pharmaceuticals" are of a known quality and potency and are also unlikely to be contaminated.

Other consequences of the prohibition against drug abuse. Medical sociologists have observed that because of the prohibition against drugs, individuals must use their limited supply of drugs under hazardous conditions. It has been estimated, for example, that 2–4% of

---

[2]It takes about 300 tonnes of coca leaves to produce 1 ton of pure cocaine (United Nations, 1997).

all active heroin-addicted persons die each year; the higher level of mortality reflects the impact of HIV on the population of intravenous heroin abusers (Anthony, Arria, & Johnson, 1995). Other causes of death in opiate-addicted persons include drug overdose, infections other than AIDS, malnutrition, accidents, and violence.

Section summary. Although legalization might not be the answer to the problem of alcohol/drug abuse in this country, it is clear that the current U.S. policy of interdiction and punishment of those who violate the substance use laws has failed. It is not clear how policy makers should proceed to address this problem, but it is abundantly clear that new social policies on substance use and abuse should be developed with the lessons of the past firmly in mind.

Drug Use and Violence: The Unseen Connection

Researchers have recently discovered what police officers have long known: that there is a relationship between substance abuse and violence. Indeed, recent research has found that as a group, substance abusers are 12–16 times as likely as the general population to resort to violence (Marzuk, 1996).

For a number of reasons, the amphetamines and cocaine tend to predispose the user to violence. One study found that 31% of homicide victims in New York City had cocaine in their bodies at the time of death (Swan, 1995a). Overall, cocaine users are 10–50 times as likely to be murdered as are nonusers, according to the author. There are a number of reasons for this: Cocaine users tend to associate with people who are more likely to respond with violence, and they are less likely to avoid situations where violence may occur. Further, individuals under the influence of cocaine might behave in ways that trigger others to respond violently to them, resulting in what is known as a "victim-precipitated homicide."

The disinhibition effects of many recreational drugs may also account for some of the observed tendency toward violence among alcohol/drug abusers. As in Chapter 4, alcohol commonly figures in violent behavior. For example, "more than half" (Kermani & Castaneda, 1996, p. 2) of those who committed homicide were actively using chemicals at the time of the murder. But this does not automatically mean that alcohol caused the homicide. A significant percentage of homicides were planned in advance, and the murderer then drank in order to bolster his or her resolve. In other cases, the murder was an unplanned act brought on, at least in part, by the disinhibiting effect of alcohol. Thus the relationship between alcohol and interpersonal violence is more complex than a simple cause and effect.

The world of illicit drug use/abuse is a violent one. Jaffe (1989) reported that one study in St. Louis found that 35% of the addicts surveyed reported having been shot or wounded with a knife, at some point during their drug-using careers. Drug pushers have been known to attack customers in order to steal their money, secure in the knowledge that the drug user is unlikely to press charges. After all, when one engages in illegal acts (such as the use of illicit chemicals) or has obtained money through illegal channels (such as burglary), one is unlikely to report being victimized by another criminal.

Drug pushers have been known to kill their customers in retaliation for unpaid drug debts and as a warning to others who might be behind in their payments. One study found that 18% of all the homicides committed in New York state in 1986 were the result of drug-related debts (Goldstein, 1990). On occasion, drug pushers themselves are shot and then dropped in front of the hospital emergency room or simply left to die where they fall. Sometimes this is done by other drug pushers, in order to scare off competition over "territory" or because of unpaid drug debts.

At this time, there does not appear to be any end to the drug-related violence. It has been suggested that if drug use were legalized, there would be a significant *decrease* in the level of violence in this country. However, this is only a theory.

Unseen Victims of Street-Drug Chemistry

As we noted earlier in this chapter, many of the illicit chemicals used in this country are produced in illicit laboratories. Product reliability is hardly a strong component of clandestine and illegal drug laboratories. Again, the problems familiar from the Prohibition era have returned to haunt us today. During the Prohibition era, a very real danger was that "bathtub gin" or "home brew" might contain methanol (a form of alcohol that can blind or even kill people) rather than the desired ethanol. Indeed, the victims of methanol poisoning during prohibition were thought to number in the "tens of thousands" (Nadelmann, Kleiman, & Earls, 1990, p. 46). This is one reason why the smuggling of legitimate alcoholic beverages was so popular during Prohibition.

Nor were the problems associated with illegally manufactured alcohol limited to the Prohibition era. Even today, whiskey produced by illegal "stills"—known in many parts of the country as "moonshine" (or "shine")—is frequently contaminated with high levels of lead (Pegues, Hughes, & Woernie, 1993). The lead contamination is caused by the tendency of many producers to filter the brew through old automobile radiators, where it comes into contact with lead from soldered joints. So common is this problem that the authors concluded that illegal whiskey is "an important and unappreciated source of lead poisoning" (p. 1501) in some parts of this country.

In today's world, contaminants are commonly found in the drugs sold on the street. If the drug was manufactured in an illegal laboratory, a simple mistake in the production process might produce a dangerous or even lethal chemical combination. For example, the illicit production of methamphetamine requires only a few common chemicals and only a basic knowledge of chemistry. But the use of lead acetate in one of the production processes most commonly used to make illicit methamphetamine can contaminate the drug with high levels of lead if the "chemist" makes a mistake (Norton, Burton, & McGirr, 1996).

In the mid-1970s heroin addicts in California were sold a compound that was, they were told, "synthetic heroin." These addicts injected the drug and quickly developed a drug-induced condition very similar to advanced cases of Parkinson's disease (Kirsch, 1986). Chemists discovered that as a result of a mistake in the production process, what had been produced was not 1-methyl-4-4-phenyl-4-pro-pionoxy-piperidine (a synthetic narcotic known as MPPP) but the chemical 1-methyl-4-phenyl-1,2,3,6-tetrahydropyridine (known as MPTP).[3] Once MPTP is in the body, the enzyme monoamine oxidase biotransforms it into a neurotoxin known as 1-methyl-4-phenylpyridinium (MPP+), which kills the dopamine-producing cells in the nigrostriatal region of the brain (Lopez & Jeste, 1997; Langston & Palfreman, 1995). Subsequent research revealed that the loss of these same neurons is implicated in the development of Parkinson's disease. Unfortunately, because MPTP was sold on the street, many opiate abusers died as a result of this mistake in the manufacture of "synthetic heroin." Others developed a lifelong drug-induced disorder very similar to Parkinson's disease.

There is no way to determine how many people have suffered or died because of other impurities in illicit drugs. But, it is known that addicts have been, and still are being, poisoned because of mistakes made in the production of street drugs. There have been cases, for example, where heroin contaminated with lead has been sold to abusers (Parras, Patier, & Ezpeleta, 1988). The users of amphetamines have also been exposed to toxic levels of lead, or to any of a number of possible carcinogenic compounds, as a result of using impure street drugs (Evanko, 1991; Centers for Disease Control, 1990). In France, some samples of heroin were found to be contaminated with the heavy metal thallium, which killed at least one individual (*Forensic Drug Abuse Advisor*, 1996e). In the United States, there are cases where cocaine has been contaminated with arsenic as a result of a mistake made in the manufacturing process (Lombard, Levin, & Weiner, 1989).

Nor is the problem of contaminated drugs limited to narcotics or cocaine alone. Most of the drugs

> intended for popular recreational use are most often produced in clandestine laboratories with little or no quality control, so generally speaking users cannot be sure of the purity of what they are ingesting. (Hayner and McKinney, 1986 p. 341)

Where illicit drugs are concerned, "Misrepresentation is the rule" (Brown & Braden, 1987, p. 341). A capsule sold on the street as THC might actually contain PCP, a far different chemical. The buyer cannot, without a detailed chemical analysis, be sure what the substance purchased actually is, whether it is contaminated, or how potent it is. Thus one should never assume that any illicit drug actually is what it is purported to be. Indeed, without a chemical analysis, one should not even assume that the chemical is safe for human consumption. In the world of illicit drug use, it is indeed a case of "let the buyer beware."

---

[3] The very names of these chemicals gives the reader some idea as to how easy it would be for chemists to make a mistake in their manufacture.

Drug Analogues: The "Designer" Drugs

When a pharmaceutical company develops a new compound for use in the fight against disease, that drug is patented. To apply for a patent, the pharmaceutical company must identify and record the exact location of each atom in relation to every other atom in the chemical chain of that drug molecule. After review by the Food and Drug Administration, the pharmaceutical company may then be granted a patent on that drug molecule for a specific period of time.

When law enforcement agencies wish to classify a drug as an illicit substance, they must go through much the same process. Chemists must identify the chemical structure of the new drug molecule and specify the exact location of each atom in relation to every other atom in the chemical chain of that drug molecule. This process can take several months, but it yields a chemical formula that can then used to identify that specific compound as an illicit substance.

Because drug molecules are very complex, it is often possible to add, rearrange, or remove some atoms from the "parent" drug molecule without having much of an impact on the original drug's psychoactive effect. Depending on the exact chemical structure of the "parent" drug, it is possible to develop dozens—or even hundreds—of variations on the original drug molecule. For example, there are 184 known potential variations on the parent drug from which the hallucinogen MDMA is developed (*The Economist*, 1993b). These variations on the original drug molecule are called analogue drugs, or analogues. Many of the drug analogues have no psychoactive effect and thus are of little interest to the illicit chemists who produce chemicals for sale on the street. But some drug analogues will be abusable and may even, in some cases, be more potent than the original chemical. For example, as we will see in the next section, some of the analogues of the pharmaceutical fentanyl are more powerful than the original drug.

The main point to keep in mind is that even if the difference is just one atom that has been added, or moved around on the chemical chain, the chemical structure of the drug analogue will be different from that of the parent drug. If the parent drug has been classified as an illegal substance, it may be possible, by removing just one atom from the chemical chain of the original drug, to create a "new" drug that has not been

outlawed yet. For the sake of discussion, assume that the following simplified drug "molecule" has been outlawed as an illegal hallucinogen.[4]

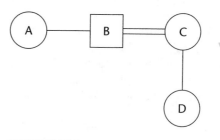

FIGURE 35-1

Note that this parent drug molecule has only four atoms, not the thousands of atoms found in some actual chemical molecules. However, a drug with the following chemical structure would technically be a different drug, because its molecular structure is not *exactly* the same as that of the first chemical.

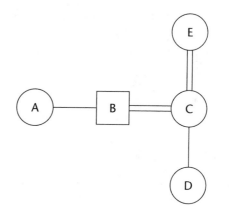

FIGURE 35.2

This chemical would thus be a drug analogue of the parent drug. The new atom that was added to the chemical structure (atom E) might not make the analogue more potent than the parent compound. But, it differs from that drug just enough so that it is not covered by the law that made the original drug illegal. For this analogue to be declared illegal, researchers would have to identify the location of every atom in the second

[4] I have not used real drug molecules for this illustration.

compound and the nature of the chemical bonds that hold that atom in place (in these diagrams, one line between atoms represents a single bond, two times a double bond). Then law enforcement officials would have to present their findings to the appropriate agency. This process might take months or even longer. And as soon as this *did* happen, it would be a simple matter to change the chemical structure once more, build a new analogue, and start the whole cycle over again. For example, the new analogue might look like this:

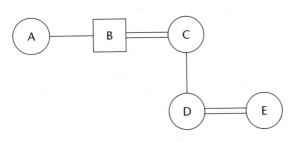

FIGURE 35.3

And if *this* drug molecule is later outlawed, the street chemist might again change the drug into something like this:

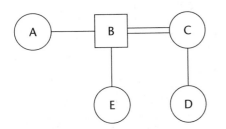

FIGURE 35.4

The drug "molecule" used in this example was a very simple one, with only five "atoms." When you stop to consider that many of the psychoactive drug molecules contain many hundreds, or even thousands, of atoms, the number of potential combinations is daunting.

Some Existing Drug Analogues

Some of the following drug analogues have been outlawed by government agencies; action against some of the other compounds discussed below is still pending.

Analogues of the amphetamines. The amphetamine molecule lends itself to manipulation, and several analogues of the original amphetamine molecule have been identified by law enforcement agencies. The known analogues of the amphetamines include 2,5-dimethoxy-4-methylamphetamine, or the hallucinogenic DOM (Scaros, Westra, & Barone, 1990). MDMA, also known as "ecstacy," is itself one of 184 known analogues of its parent amphetamine, some of which are known to have a psychoactive effect on the user.

The drug 3,4-methylenedioxyamphetamine, or MDEA, is another drug analogue of the amphetamine family. When the hallucinogen "ecstacy" (MDMA) was classified as a controlled substance in 1985, many "street" chemists simply started to produce MDEA. The chemical structure of MDEA is very similar to that of MDMA, and its effects are reported to be very similar as well (Mirin, Weiss, & Greenfield, 1991). This substance is often sold under the name of "Eve." There have been isolated reports of death associated with MDEA use, and it is not known what role, if any, MDEA had in these deaths. Further, the long-term effects of this MDEA are still unknown.

A recent addition to the list of illicit stimulants being produced by street chemists in this country is methcathinone, or "Kat." This compound was discussed in Chapter 11. However, the reader should be aware that Kat is also a "designer" drug.

Another derivative of the amphetamines is a compound known as "Ya ba," used in southeast Asia and especially in Thailand (Hilditch, 2000). This compound, which includes ephedrine, methamphetamine, lithium (obtained from extended-use batteries) and some chemicals from household cleaning products, provides an extended (8- to 12-hour) "high." The compound can be inhaled, smoked, or used transdermally in the form of a skin patch, but it is usually taken orally. Long-term use seems to contribute to suicidal/homicidal impulses, so most abusers follow a pattern of taking the drug for 2–3 days, followed by a day or two of sleep. Very little is known about the toxicology of Ya ba, which has not been subjected to controlled research by physicians.

Analogues of PCP. PCP is a popular "parent" drug molecule for illicit chemists to experiment with. To date, at least 30 drug analogues of PCP have been identified, many of which are actually more potent than PCP itself (Crowley, 1995b; Weiss, Greenfield, &

Mirin, 1994). These include the drugs N-ethyl-1-phenylcyclohexylamine (also known as PCE); (1-(1-2-thienylcyclohexyl) piperidine) or TCP; (1-(1-phenyl-cyclohexyl)-pyrrolidine), or PHP; (1-piperidinocyclo-hexanecarbonitrile), or PCC; and Eu4ia (pronounced "euphoria"), an amphetamine-like drug synthesized from legally purchased, over-the-counter chemicals (Scaros, Westra, & Barone, 1990).

Ketamine. The compound (2-(o-chlorophenyl-2-methylamino cyclohexanone) is a chemical cousin to PCP, which is a legitimate pharmaceutical agent. Ketamine is a surgical anesthetic used for both humans and animals (Bushnell & Justins, 1993). When used as a surgical anesthetic, Ketamine may be introduced into the body by way of intravenous injection, by intramuscular injection, or in oral form. Further, because Ketamine does not cause respiratory or cardiac depression, it is of value in situations where opioid-based anesthetics cannot be used.

When it is abused, Ketamine is said to have effects similar to those of heroin (*The Economist*, 1989). The drug causes a short-lived sense of euphoria, and the side effects of Ketamine abuse include a sense of psychological dissociation, panic states, and hallucinations (Jansen, 1993). The half-life of Ketamine is between 3 and 4 hours. The drug is extensively biotransformed before excretion from the body, and only 3% of a single dose is excreted unchanged in the urine. Long-term use, especially at high doses, may result in drug-induced memory problems (Jansen, 1993). This and the fact that it is effective at doses lower than those necessary to produce anesthesia have reportedly made Ketamine popular as a "date rape" drug.

Aminorex. For a number of years, the drug analogue 2-amino-4-methyl-5-phenyl-2-oxazoline has appeared on the streets from time to time. This compound is derived from a diet pill sold in Europe under the brand name of Aminorex in the 1980s, and it is easily synthesized (Karch, 1996). The effects of this drug, which is often sold on the street as "U-4-E-UH" or "EU4EA," are not well known at this time, but available evidence suggests that it is a CNS stimulant with effects similar to those of the amphetamines (Karch, 1996). There are reports that the drug has been sold on both the East and the West coast.

Following a single oral dose of the pharmaceutical compound Aminorex, peak blood levels are seen in about 2 hours, and the half-life of Aminorex is approximately 7.7 hours (Karch, 1996). There is no clinical research into the effect of illicit forms of 2-amino-4-methyl-5-phenyl-2-oxazoline on the human body, and the potential for harm from Aminorex-like compounds available on the street remains unknown.

Gamma hydroxybutyric acid (GHB). Although neurochemists first synthesized gamma hydroxybutyric acid (GHB) in 1960, there was little abuse of this compound until the 1990s, when body builders began to use it as a legal alternative to anabolic steroids after preliminary evidence emerged that GHB might possibly stimulate the production of growth hormones. Because it was legally manufactured, it was possible for GHB to be sold in health food stores as a natural sleep aid.

GHB is normally found in the human kidney, heart, muscle tissue, and brain, where it is thought to function as a neurotransmitter (Marwick, 1997). Following the receipt of a number of complaints, the Food and Drug Administration outlawed the manufacture and sale of GHB in 1992 (Ingels, Rangan, Bellezzo, & Clark, 2000). In response to this ban, users simply switched to any of a number of legal precursors of GHB, allowing their bodies to biotransform the precursors into GHB itself. Instructions on how to manufacture GHB are also available over the Internet, which enables amateur chemists to produce their own stockpiles of the drug if they are unwise enough to do so (Moore & Ginsberg, 1999; (Li, Stokes, & Woechener, 1998).

When used at low doses, GHB can induce a sense of euphoria and can lower inhibitions. When the drug is mixed with alcohol, GHB's effects are enhanced, and it quickly gained a reputation as a "date rape" drug. Persons who had ingested a mixture of GHB and alcohol quickly become relaxed and sleepy. At one point physicians experimented with GHB as a possible preanesthetic agent, but they found that it had a very narrow therapeutic window and could cause seizures (*Forensic Drug Abuse Advisor*, 1997e). Interest in it as a pharmaceutical agent quickly waned.

Technically, GHB is a metabolite of gamma aminobutryric acid (GABA). Clinical research suggests that GHB alters the normal activity of the neurotransmitter dopamine in the brain (Tunnicliff, 1997). At doses of 0.1–1.5 mg/kg, GHB is able to induce a sleep like state characterized by both delta sleep and REM sleep (Li, Stokes, & Woechener, 1998). Side effects of a low dose of GHB include low blood pressure, bradycardia, nausea, vomiting, diarrhea, urinary incontinence, increased libido, dizziness, tremor, and headache. At doses of 10 mg/kg, GHB can produce euphoria—an effect consistent with its ability to alter the release of dopamine within the brain. Oral doses are well absorbed, with effects beginning within 15 minutes and lasting about 3 hours following a single dose (Li, Stokes, & Woechener, 1998).

GHB easily crosses the blood-brain barrier, and its elimination half-life is only 27 minutes (Li, Stokes, & Woechener, 1998). Because of this short elimination half-life, urine toxicology tests can detect GHB in the user's urine only for about 12 hours after ingestion of a single dose (Moore & Ginsberg, 1999). Doses of 50 mg/kg of body weight can produce tunnel vision, ataxia, confusion, agitation, hallucinations, seizures, coma, and respiratory arrest. A withdrawal syndrome consisting of tremor, insomnia, and anxiety has been identified in chronic GHB abusers. These symptoms usually start about 12 hours after the last dose and continue for about 12 days (Olmedo & Hoffman, 2000). Symptoms of a GHB overdose include (but are not limited to) bradycardia, low blood pressure, nausea, vomiting, diarrhea, ataxia, tunnel vision, confusion, agitation, hallucinations, seizures, and respiratory arrest and coma that may progress to the user's death. Conservative medical care is the best treatment for a GHB overdose, although intubation is occasionally necessary (Chin, Sporer, Cullison, Dyer, & Wu, 1998).

GHB will interact with many other compounds, and its effects are intensified by the concurrent use of other CNS depressants, such as alcohol, hydrocodone, the benzodiazepines. Patients taking any of the antiviral drugs known as protease inhibitors should not use GHB, for these antiviral compounds alter the liver's ability to biotransform many drugs, including GHB (Harrington, Woodward, Hooton, & Horn, 1999).

NEXUS. This illicit compound has been found in isolated parts of the United States. The active agent has been identified as 2,5DimethoxyPhenethylamine, a synthetic hallucinogen. A single oral dose of 10–20 mg of 2,5DimethoxyPhenethylamine will cause the user to experience intoxication, euphoria, and visual distortions/hallucinations for 6–8 hours. Because this compound is not intended for human use and is illegal in the United States, virtually nothing is known about its toxicology at this time.

Fentanyl. The fentanyl molecule is easy to manipulate and can be synthesized from a few ordinary industrial chemicals (Langston & Palfreman, 1995). By making just a minor change in the molecule of the parent drug, it is possible to produce a fentanyl analogue that will extend the drug's effects from the normal 30–90 minutes up to 4–5 hours or, with the right modifications to the parent drug, even 4–5 *days*, according to the authors. Thus it is a popular drug for illicit drug manufacturers to produce.

In the early 1980s, a series of fatal narcotics overdoses occurred in California, as street chemists started to produce various "designer drugs" that were similar to the analgesic fentanyl (discussed Chapter 14) (Hibbs, Perper, & Winek, 1991). Kirsch (1986) identified nine different drug analogues to fentanyl that are known or suspected to have been sold on the streets. These drug analogues range in potency from 1/10 that of morphine for the fentanyl analogue benzyl fentanyl to between 1000 times (Hibbs, Perper, & Winek, 1991) and 3000 times (Kirsch, 1986) more potent than morphine for 3-methyl fentanyl.

The drug 3-methyl fentanyl is also known to chemists as TMF. A decade ago, this analogue of fentanyl was identified as the cause of numerous narcotics overdoses (Hibbs, Perper, & Winek, 1991; *Newsweek*, 1991). The chemical structure of fentanyl makes it possible for the drug molecule to be "snorted" much like cocaine. When it is used intranasally, the drug is deposited on the blood-rich tissues of the sinuses, where it is absorbed into the general circulation. Fentanyl can also be smoked. As is true of cocaine, when fentanyl is smoked, the molecules easily cross into the general circulation through the lungs. Indeed, so rapidly is fentanyl absorbed through the lungs that it is possible for the user to overdose on the medication after just one inhalation (*Forensic Drug Abuse Advisor*, 1994b).

Given the characteristics of fentanyl, it is safe to assume that analogues of this chemical will present similar abuse profiles. Law enforcement officials have struggled to deal with the problem of diversion of fentanyl products to illicit users almost from the moment the drug was introduced. But the drug is so powerful that even small amounts have a value to illicit drug users. For example, some opiate abusers will scrape the residual medication from transdermal fentanyl patches to obtain small amounts of fentanyl, which may then be smoked.

Fentanyl is so potent a drug that extremely small doses are effective in humans. To detect it, a special test of a blood or urine sample must be carried out (Evanko, 1991). Routine drug toxicology screens often fail to detect the presence of such small amounts of fentanyl in the blood or urine of a suspected drug user (*Forensic Drug Abuse Advisor*, 1994b). Thus even a "clean" urine or blood drug toxicology test may not rule out fentanyl use on the part of an addict.

Some opiate abusers have been known to die so rapidly after using fentanyl that they were found with the needle still in their arms (Evanko, 1991). This phenomenon is well documented in cases of narcotics overdoses, but is not fully understood. Some researchers attribute the rapid death to the narcotic itself; others have suggested that the user's death is caused by the various chemicals added to the drug to "cut," or dilute, it on the street. Fentanyl is so potent that some samples of the drug sold on the street are made up of 0.01% fentanyl and 99.9% "filler" (Langston & Palfreman, 1995).

It is difficult to understand the addictive potential of fentanyl. Dr. William Spiegelman (quoted in Gallagher, 1986) observed that "it can take years to become addicted to alcohol, months for cocaine, and one shot for fentanyl" (p. 26). To complicate matters further, "street chemists" are manipulating the chemical structure of fentanyl, adding a few atoms to the basic fentanyl chain here, snipping a few atoms there, to produce drug analogues. Unfortunately, fentanyl and its analogues continue to be a significant part of the drug abuse problem in the United States, and no end to their use is in sight.

Summary

The relationship between criminal activity and substance use/abuse is exceptionally complex, and in this chapter we briefly explored the relationship between alcohol/drug use and crime. Although some criminal activity does seem to result from the use/abuse of recreational chemicals, it also has been suggested that many of those who engage in criminal activity and substance use are simply people who are prone to engage in illegal activities. In such cases, the apparent relationship between substance use and criminal behavior is not a causal one but, rather, a complex interaction between the individual's personality, his or her use of chemicals, and his or her tendency to engage in illegal behavior.

There is strong evidence that at least some of the harm associated with chemical use/abuse is a direct result of society's efforts to reduce supply (MacCaun, 1998), and some have used this information to call for the legalization of recreational drugs. The sanctions against chemical use have resulted in overburdened courts, overcrowded jails and prisons, and no apparent reduction in the level of illicit drug use in the United States. In this chapter, we reviewed alternatives to the prohibition and interdiction used in this country, including the public health approach utilized in England and Holland.

We noted that illicit drug producers are motivated to find new "designer" drugs by the way that drugs are identified and regulated in the United States and by the rewards for finding unregulated drug molecules for sale to consumers of recreational drugs. The role that adulterants play in the production and distribution of illicit drugs was discussed, and many of the more common adulterants were identified. We discussed the fact that many drug distributors bargain their knowledge about who is involved in the drug trade for reduced sentences, whereas the first-time user may have no such ploy to use to avoid a lengthy mandatory sentence. And we reviewed the evidence that the current "war on drugs" has largely been lost.

Sample Assessment: Alcohol Abuse Situation[1]

HISTORY AND IDENTIFYING INFORMATION

Mr. John D— is a 35-year-old married white male, from —— county, Missouri. He is employed as an electrical engineer for the XXXXX company, where he has worked for the last three years. Prior to this, Mr. D— was in the United States Navy, where he served for four years. He was discharged under Honorable conditions and reported that he had only "a few" minor rules infractions. He was never brought before a court-martial, according to Mr. D—.

CIRCUMSTANCES OF REFERRAL

Mr. D— was seen after having been arrested on a charge of driving while under the influence of alcohol. Mr. D— reported that he had been drinking with co-workers to celebrate a promotion at work. His measured blood alcohol level (BAL) was .150, well above the legal limit—hence the charge of driving while under the influence. Mr. D— reported that he had "seven or eight" mixed drinks in an approximately 2-hour time span. By his report, he was arrested within a quarter-hour of the time he left the bar. After his initial court appearance, Mr. D— was referred to this evaluator by the court to determine whether Mr. D— has a chemical dependency problem.

DRUG AND ALCOHOL USE HISTORY

Mr. D— reports that he began to drink at the age of 15, when he and a friend would steal beer from his father's supply in the basement. He would drink an occasional beer from time to time after that, and he first became intoxicated when he was 17, by Mr. D—'s report.

1

When he was 18, Mr. D— enlisted in the United States Navy, and after basic training he was stationed in the San Diego area. Mr. D— reported that he was first exposed to chemicals while he was stationed in San Diego and that he tried both marijuana and cocaine while on weekend liberty. Mr. D— reported that he did not like the effects of cocaine and that he used this chemical only once or twice. He did like the effects of marijuana and reported that he would smoke one or two marijuana cigarettes, obtained from friends, perhaps once a month.

During this portion of his life, Mr. D— reports that he would drink about twice a weekend, when on liberty. The amount that he would drink ranged from "one or two beers" to twelve or eighteen beers. Mr. D— reported that he first had an alcohol-related blackout while he was in the Navy and that he "should" have been arrested for driving on base while under the influence of alcohol on several different occasions but was never stopped by the Shore Patrol.

Following his discharge from the Navy under Honorable conditions at the age of 22, Mr. D— enrolled in college. His chemical use declined to the weekend use of alcohol, generally in moderation, but Mr. D— reported that he did drink to the point of an alcohol-related blackout "once or twice" in the four years he spent in college. There was no other chemical use following his discharge from the Navy, and Mr. D— reports that he has not used other chemicals since the age of 20 or 21.

Upon graduation, at the age of 26, Mr. D— began to work for the XXXXX Company, where he is employed now. He met his wife shortly after he began working for the XXXXX Company, and they were married after a courtship of one year. Mr. D—'s wife, Pat, does not use chemicals other than an "occasional" social drink. Exploration of this revealed that Mrs. D— will drink a glass of wine with a meal about twice a month. She denied other chemical use.

Mrs. D— reported that her husband does not usually drink more than one or two beers and that he will drink only on weekends. She reported that the night when he was arrested was "unusual" for him in the sense that he is not a drinker. His employer was not contacted, but court records failed to reveal any other arrest records for Mr. D—.

Mr. D— admitted to several alcohol-related blackouts, but none since he was in college. He denied seizures, D.T.'s, or alcohol-related tremor. No evidence of ulcers, gastritis, or cardiac problems was noted. His last physical was "normal," according to information provided by his personal physician. There were no abnormal blood chemistry findings, nor did his physician find any evidence suggesting alcoholism. Mr. D— denied ever having been hospitalized for an alcohol-related injury, and there was no evidence that he has been involved in fights.

On the Michigan Alcoholism Screening Test (MAST), Mr. D—'s score of 4 points would not suggest alcoholism. This information was reviewed in the presence of his wife, who did not suggest that there was any misrepresentation on his test scores. On this administration of the MMPI-2, there was no evidence of psychopathology. Mr. D—'s MacAndrew Alcoholism Scale score fell in the normal range, failing to suggest an addictive disorder at this time.

PSYCHIATRIC HISTORY
Mr. D— denied psychiatric treatment of any kind. He did admit to having seen a marriage counselor "once" shortly after he married but reported that overall, he and his wife are happy together. Apparently, they had a question about a marital communications issue that was cleared up after one visit, which took place after three or four years of marriage.

SUMMARY AND CONCLUSIONS
There is little evidence to suggest an ongoing alcohol problem. Mr. D— would seem to be a well-adjusted young man who drank to excess after having been offered a long-desired promotion at work. This would seem to be an unusual occurrence for Mr. D—, who usually limits his drinking to one or two beers on the weekends. There was no evidence of alcohol-related injuries, accidents, or legal problems noted.

RECOMMENDATIONS
Recommend light sentence, possibly a fine and limited probation, with no restrictions on license. It is also recommended that Mr. D— attend "DWI School" for 8 weeks to learn more about the effects of alcohol on driving.

3

Sample Assessment:
Chemical Dependency Situation[1]

HISTORY AND IDENTIFYING FEATURES

Mr. Michael S— is a 35-year-old divorced white male who is self-employed. He has been a resident of —— County, Kansas, for the last three months. Prior to this, he apparently was living in —— County, New York, according to information provided by Mr. S—. On the night of June 6 of this year, Mr. S— was arrested on a charge of possession of a controlled substance. Specifically, Mr. S— was found to be in possession of two grams of cocaine, according to police records. This is his first arrest for a drug-related charge in Kansas, although he has been arrested on two other occasions, for similar charges, in New York state. A copy of his police record is attached to this report.

CIRCUMSTANCES OF REFERRAL

Mr. Michael S— was referred to the undersigned for a chemical dependency evaluation, which will be part of his pre-sentence investigation (PSI) on the charge of felony possession of a controlled substance and the charge of sale of a controlled substance.

DRUG AND ALCOHOL USE HISTORY

Mr. S— reported that he began to use alcohol when he was 13 years of age and that by the age of 14 he was drinking on a regular basis. Exploration of this revealed that just before his 15th birthday, Mr. S— was drinking "on weekends," with friends. He reported that he first became intoxicated on his 15th birthday but projected responsibility for this onto his friends, who by his report "kept on pouring more and more into the glass until I was drunk."

1

By the age of 16, Mr. S— was using alcohol "four or five nights a week" and was also using marijuana and hallucinogenics perhaps two or three times a week. He projected responsibility for his expanded chemical use onto his environment, noting that "everybody was selling the stuff. You couldn't walk down the street without people stopping you to ask if you wanted to buy some."

Also by the age of 16, Mr. S— was supporting his chemical use through burglaries, which he committed with his friends. He was never caught but volunteered this information, informing the undersigned that because the statute of limitations has expired, he no longer has to fear being charged for these crimes.

By the age of 21, Mr. S— was using cocaine "once or twice a week." He was arrested for the first time when he was about 22, for possession of cocaine. This was when he was living in the state of —. After being tried in court, he was convicted of felony possession of cocaine and placed on probation for five years. When asked whether he used chemicals while he was on probation, Mr. S— responded, "I don't have to answer that."

Mr. S— reported that he first entered treatment for chemical dependency when he was 27 years of age. At that time, he was found to be addicted to a number of drugs, including alcohol, cocaine, and "downers." Although in treatment for two months, at the chemical dependency unit of — Hospital, Mr. S— reported that "I left as addicted as when I arrived" and added with some degree of apparent pride that he had found a way to use chemicals even while in treatment. His chemical use apparently was the reason for his ultimate discharge from this program. Although Mr. S— was somewhat vague about the reasons why he was discharged, he did report that "they did not like how I was doing" while he was in treatment.

Since that time, Mr. S— has been using cocaine, alcohol, various drugs obtained from a series of physicians, and opiates. Mr. S— was quite vague as to how he would support his chemical use but noted that "there are ways of getting money if you really want some."

Mr. S— reported that in the last year, he has been using cocaine "four or five times a week," although he did admit to occasionally having used cocaine "for a whole week straight." He has been sharing needles with other cocaine users from time to time but reported that "I am careful." In spite of this, however, he was diagnosed as having hepatitis B in the last year, according to Mr. S——. He also reported that he has overdosed on cocaine "once or twice" but that he treated this overdose himself with benzodiazepines and alcohol.

In addition to the possible cocaine overdoses noted above, Mr. S— admitted to having experienced chest pain while using cocaine on at least two occasions, and he has used alcohol or tranquilizers to combat the side effects of cocaine on a regular basis. He has admitted to using tranquilizers or alcohol frequently to help him sleep after using cocaine for extended periods of time. He also admits to having spent on drugs money that was meant for other expenses (loan payments, etc.) and, by his report, has had at least one automobile repossessed for failure to make payments on the loan.

Mr. S— has been unemployed for at least the last 2 years but is rather vague about how he supports himself. He apparently was engaged in selling cocaine at the time of his arrest, this being one of the charges brought against him by the police.

Mr. S— had not seen a physician for several years prior to this arrest. During this interview, however, it was noted that he had scars strongly suggestive of intravenous needle use on both arms. When asked about these marks, he referred to them as "tracks," a street term for drug needle scars. This would suggest long-term intravenous drug use on Mr. S—'s part. He denied the intravenous use of opiates, but a urine toxicology screen detected narcotics. This would suggest that Mr. S— has not been very open about his narcotic drug use.

On this administration of the Michigan Alcoholism Screening Test (MAST), Mr. S— received a score of 17 points, a score that is strongly suggestive of alcoholism. He reported that the longest period that he has been able to go without using chemicals in the last 5 years was only "hours." His profile on this administration of the Minnesota Multiphasic Personality Inventory (MMPI) was suggestive of a very impulsive, immature individual who is likely to have a chemical dependency problem.

PSYCHIATRIC HISTORY

Mr. S— reported that he has been hospitalized for psychiatric reasons only "once." This hospitalization took place several years ago, while Mr. S— was living in the state of ——. Apparently, he was hospitalized for observation following a suicide attempt in which he slit his wrists with a razor blade. Mr. S— was unable to recall whether he had been using cocaine prior to this suicide attempt, but he thought it was "quite possible" that he had experienced a cocaine-induced depression.

MEDICAL HISTORY

As noted above, Mr. S— had not seen a physician for several years before his arrest. Since his arrest, however, he has been examined by a physician for a cough that he has had for some time. The physician (report enclosed) concluded that Mr. S— is "seropositive" for HIV and classified Mr. S— as falling into level C-1 on the CDC classification schedule. Although it is not possible to determine whether Mr. S— contracted HIV through sharing needles, this is at least a possibility.

SUMMARY AND CONCLUSIONS

Overall, it is apparent that Mr. S— has a long-standing chemical dependency problem. In spite of his evasiveness and denial, there was strong evidence of significant chemical dependency problems. Mr. S— seems to support his drug and alcohol use through criminal activity, although he is rather vague about this. He has been convicted of drug-related charges in the state of —— and was on probation following this conviction. One might suspect that Mr. S—'s motivation for treatment is quite low at this time; he has expressed the belief that his attorney will "make a deal for me" whereby he will not have to spend time in prison.

RECOMMENDATIONS

1. Given the fact that Mr. S— has contracted HIV, and hepatitis B from infected needles, it is strongly recommended that he be referred to the appropriate medical facility for treatment.
2. It is the opinion of this reviewer that Mr. S—'s motivation for treatment is low at this time. If he is referred to treatment, it is recommended that this be made part of his sentencing agreement with the court. If he is incarcerated, chemical dependency treatment might be made part of his treatment plan in prison.
3. Referral to a therapeutic community for long-term residential treatment should be considered for Mr. S—.

Signed ——

4

The "Jellinek" Chart for Alcoholism

Following the publication of earlier editions of *Concepts of Chemical Dependency*, questions were raised about my decision not to mention the so-called "Jellinek" chart in the text. This chart, which is viewed as gospel within the alcohol/drug rehabilitation industry, proports to show the progression from social drinking to alcoholism and then on to recovery (see Figure A 3.1). Ever since it was introduced, this chart has been used to illustrate the "unalterable" progression of alcoholism to countless patients who were in the earlier stages of alcohol use problems, as well as to browbeat reluctant individuals into accepting the need for help with their supposed drinking problem. Variations on this chart have been developed for compulsive gambling, steroid abuse, compulsive spending, and both heroin and cocaine addiction, as well as countless other disorders.

The problem is that Jellinek did *not* devise this chart! In spite of the fact that it is often attributed to

him, this chart is actually the work of Dr. Maxwell Glatt, a British physician who was so taken by Jellinek's work that he operationalized the *Gamma* subtype of alcoholism in chart form. This chart, which addresses *only* the Gamma subtype of alcoholism as suggested by Jellinek (1960), has mistakenly been accepted by countless alcohol/drug rehabilitation professionals as *the* chart that traces the progression of *all* forms of alcoholism. As a result of this mistake, many patients in rehabilitation programs whose symptoms of alcohol use problems did not "fit" the symptoms suggested in this chart have been subjected to countless hours of confrontation because they were judged to be "in denial."

Rather than perpetuate this misunderstanding, I decided not to refer to this chart in *Concepts of Chemical Dependency*.

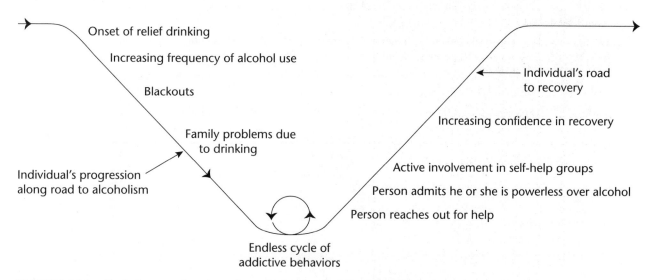

FIGURE A3.1   Alcohol progression chart often mistakenly called the "Jellinek" chart.

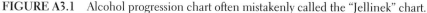

Drug Classification Schedules

One of the most confusing aspects of drug rehabilitation work for both physicians and mental health professionals is that the legal classification of many of the drugs of abuse is carried out not on the basis of the pharmacological properties of the compound in question but on the basis of its perceived abuse potential. Thus compounds that are perceived to have no accepted medical use in the United States, such as the narcotic analgesic heroin and the hallucinogen MDMA, are lumped together by the Drug Enforcement Administration. The following tables should help you to understand the drug classification schedule now in use in the United States.

TABLE A4.1   Drug Classification Schedule

Schedule	Definition	Examples
Schedule I	Compounds with no accepted medical use	Marijuana, LSD, MDMA, heroin
Schedule II	Compounds with recognized medical use, but with severe abuse potential	Morphine, methadone, amphetamines
Schedule III	Compounds with recognized medical use, but with moderate abuse potential	Acetaminophen with codeine compounds
Schedule IV	Compounds with recognized medical use, but with mild abuse potential	Phenobarbital, benzodiazepines
Schedule V	Compounds with recognized medical use, but with low abuse potential	Buprenorphine

TABLE A4.2   Modified Centers for Disease Control HIV/AIDS Classification Chart*

Number of CD4+ T-helper cells per cubic millimeter of blood	*Asymptomatic*	*Symptomatic but not full-blown AIDS*	*Patient has full-blown AIDS*
Greater than or equal to 500 cells	A 1	B 1	C 1
Between 499 and 200 T-helper cells	A 2	B 2	C 2
Fewer than 200 T-helper cells	A 3	B 3	C 3
		Patients in this column would have developed infections not specific to AIDS patients alone, such as bacterial endocarditis, meningitis, pneumonia, or sepsis. For example, it is not uncommon for individuals with normal immune systems to develop bacterial pneumonia. Contrast this with the defining criteria for the last column.	Patients in this column have developed one or more infection(s) rarely seen except in patients who have AIDS. For example, the patient might have a candidiasis infection of the esophagus, or AIDS-induced diarrhea that lasts longer than one month.

Source: Chart based on Rubin (1993).
*The normal person has between 800 and 1200 CD4+ T-helper cells per cubic millimeter of blood.

Glossary

Abruptio placentae: A condition in which bleeding starts between the placenta and the wall of the uterus. As the blood accumulates, it gradually separates the placenta from the wall of the uterus, cutting the fetus off from its supply of oxygen. The result may be fatal for both the mother and the infant.

Absorption: The movement of drug molecules from the site of entry, through various cell boundaries, to the site of action.

Acetaldehyde: Acetaldehyde is the first intermediate chemical, or *metabolite*, formed when the alcohol molecule is biotransformed. This occurs through the process known as *oxidation*, and acetaldehyde is quite toxic to the body. In low levels, it is also found in cigarette smoke.

Acetylcholine: One of the major *neurotransmitters* in the body. Acetylcholine is found mainly in the outer regions of the body, where the *central nervous system* interacts with the tissues of the body. Acetylcholine has a calming effect on the body and might be viewed as telling the body tissues to relax after facing a stressor.

Addiction: A progressive, chronic, primary, relapsing disorder that involves features such as a compulsion to use a chemical(s), loss of control over the use of a substance(s), and continued use of a drug(s) in spite of adverse consequences of its use.

Affinity: The strength with which drug molecules bind to the *receptor site* in the cell wall.

Agonist: A chemical molecule that has the ability, because of its unique structure, to bind with a *receptor* molecule located in the cell wall. The degree of the "match" between the *agonist* and the *receptor* is called the *affinity* of the agonist molecule. An *agonist* can be a natural substance or an artificial compound.

Albumin: One of the primary protein molecules found in the general circulation.

Allee: One of the variants of a gene.

Amino acids: Chemical molecules that the body uses to form proteins, which have a variety of functions in the body.

Amygdala: A region of the brain that is shaped like an almond, is found in the *temporal lobe* of the brain, and is part of the brain's *limbic system*.

Analogue of a drug: A compound that is a variation on the chemical structure of a different drug, producing a "new" drug. The original compound is known as the parent drug.

Anandamide: A compound that is produced in the brain and functions as a neurotransmitter in certain regions of the brain, especially those regions involved in pain perception.

Anorectic: Causing loss of appetite.

Anorexia: Loss of desire to eat.

Antagonist: A compound that blocks, or reverses, the effect of an *agonist*.

Antisocial personality disorder (ASPD): A personality pattern marked by a pervasive disregard for the rights of others, repeated violations of the rights of others, impulsiveness, risk taking, disregard for the truth, and self-centeredness. Individuals with ASPD may be very articulate and convincing, but they tend to be most interested in their own gratification even at the expense of other people.

Anxiety: An emotional state that can range from mild to severe in intensity, wherein the individual feels that she or he is in some form of imminent danger, although there is no identified threat.

Anxiogenic: A compound or experience that increases the individual's level of anxiety.

Apnea: Cessation of normal respiration.

Atherosclerosis: A condition in which fatty plaques accumulate in the inner walls of the arteries of the circulatory system. If too much of the artery is obstructed, the blood flow through that artery is curtailed.

Basal ganglia: A region of the brain involved in the exertion of the individual's will on conscious movement. This is the area of the brain where spontaneous movement is initiated. The basal ganglia have indirect connections to the reticular activating system and extensive connections to the cortex of the brain.

Bioavailability: Concentration of the unchanged chemical at the *site of action.*

Biotransformation: The process, usually carried out in the *liver,* by which the body alters the chemical structure of a foreign molecule to a form that enables it to be eliminated from the body, usually by *excretion.* The process of changing a foreign molecule into a form that can be excreted yields intermediate *metabolites,* some of which may be biologically active.

Blind research study: A study in which the data are examined without the researcher knowing whether any given result or measurement is from the research sample or the control sample. For example, tissue samples from subjects might be examined by a researcher who did not know whether the tissue sample came from an alcoholic or a nonalcoholic person.

Botulism: A form of paralysis usually seen when the victim ingests food contaminated by a toxin produced by the microscopic organism *Clostridium botulinum.* The toxin is one of the most potent neurotoxins known, and exposure to this agent is potentially fatal.

Carcinogen: A chemical that is known, or strongly suspected, to cause cancer in humans.

Cardiomyopathy: A disease of the heart muscle, in which the muscle becomes flabby and weaker than usual. One or more of the ventricles of the heart might enlarge, and this condition might progress to *congestive heart failure.*

Catecholamines: Any of a family of related chemicals that are involved in the function of the nervous system.

Central nervous system (CNS): The brain and spinal cord.

Cerebellum: A part of the central nervous system located at the base of the brain. This region of the brain is involved in coordination of muscle activity, balance, and some sensorimotor activity.

Cerebrum: The largest region of the brain, including the *cortex.*

Cilia A microscopic hair-like projection from the cell wall. Cilia are found in many regions of the human body. In the lungs, the motion of the cilia helps to push mucus to the top of the lungs, where it is expelled. This helps to keep the lungs clean.

Conduct disorder: A condition, seen in childhood or adolescence, marked by behaviors that repeatedly violate the rights of others or age-appropriate norms and rules. Usually, the violation of rules is quite serious, such as running away from home two or more times where there is no physical/sexual abuse situation, violation of parental curfews before the age of 13, vandalism, arson, theft, or the like. Deceitfulness is commonly seen in conduct-disordered children/adolescents, and the child has little empathy for others, including those that he or she has hurt. By definition, this condition is not due to any other form of mental illness, such as intellectual impairment or schizophrenia.

Congestive heart failure: Inadequate heart function, resulting in shortness of breath, fluid accumulation in the extremities, and possible arrhythmias, formation of emboli, and sudden death.

Conjugation: One of the four primary methods of *biotransformation* carried out by the liver.

Cortex: The outermost layer of the human brain, which is where the "higher functions" of thought are generated. This region of the brain is intricately folded in upon itself in the adult human brain and contains specialized neurons devoted to motor coordination, speech, language interpretation, and processing of sensory information.

COX-1: A subtype of cyclooxygenase found in the human body. Researchers think that COX-1 is normally produced by the body to help regulate the activity of different organs.

COX-2: A subtype of cyclooxygenase found in the human body. Researchers think that COX-2 is produced mainly when body tissues are damaged and that it helps to trigger the inflammatory response at the site of injury.

Cross-tolerance: A phenomenon in which an individual becomes tolerant to the effects of one substance, such as alcohol, and the tolerance then transfers to other, similar compounds. In the case of alcohol, for example, the alcohol-tolerant individual would also become tolerant to the benzodiazepines and barbiturates.

Cyclooxygenase: An enzyme involved in the production of prostaglandins in the human body.

Date rape: Experience in which one partner in a dating relationship forces sexual activity onto the partner. The use of drugs by the aggressor, to overcome the victim's resistance to sexual advances, is often a part of date rape.

Dependency: A state wherein the body requires the regular use of a compound in order to continue to function. See also *Neuroadaptation.*

Depression: An emotional state that is marked by pervasive and intense sadness and may include disturbance of sleep pattern and blunting of the individual's sex drive, appetite, ability to concentrate, and enthusiasm for daily activities. The depressed individual may experience feelings of worthlessness, may feel guilt about real or imagined past mistakes, and may actively seek to terminate his or her life through the act of *suicide.*

Distribution: How the chemical molecules are moved about in the body. This is usually accomplished by the circulatory system.

Diversion of drugs: A process through which compounds originally prescribed by a physician(s) are used by people for whom those drugs were not prescribed. Sometimes, the medications are stolen from drug stores or someone's medicine cabinet. On other occasions, an individual with a legitimate need for a desired medication(s) will (for a fee) visit several different doctors in a short period of time, to obtain prescriptions from each physician for the same medication. The medications obtained in this manner are then sold to other drug abusers.

Dopamine: One of the major *neurotransmitters* in the body. Dopamine is used as a neurotransmitter in many different regions of the CNS. There are five known subtypes of *dopamine* found in the CNS.

Downregulation: A process in which the number of neurotransmitter receptors in a neuron is reduced, thus lowering the sensitivity of the cell to a certain form of stimulation.

Dysentery: A painful infection of the lower intestinal tract caused by ingesting contaminated water. The person with dysentery develops massive diarrhea that is often mixed with blood and mucus. Unless the fluid loss caused by the diarrhea is rapidly controlled, dysentery can be fatal. Dysentery was common in the crowded army camps of the 1700 and 1800s, as well as in many cities of that era.

Effective dose: A calculation performed by pharmacologists to estimate what percentage of a population will respond to a given dose of a chemical. For example, the dose to which 95% of the population will respond is indicated by pharmacologists as the ED_{95}.

Elimination half-life: The period of time that the body requires to eliminate 50% of a single dose of a drug. Contrast this to the *therapeutic* half-life of a drug.

Embolism: The process by which a blood vessel is blocked by a foreign substance (a blood clot, fat droplet, talc, etc.) known as an *embolus.* The embolus is transported by the blood from another part of the body, and it might lodge in any number of different blood vessels. If it lodges in a blood vessel in the lung, it is called a pulmonary embolism; if in the brain, it is said to cause an *ischemic event, ischemic stroke,* or *cerebral vascular accident* (CVA).

Embolus: A fat droplet, or a blood clot, or possibly a foreign substance such as talc introduced into the body when a drug abuser injects a drug contaminated with this substance. The embolus travels through the blood stream, propelled by the action of the heart, until it lodges in a blood vessel too small to allow it to move any farther. A cork or a plug would be a good analogy.

Enkephalins: Small molecules that belong to the neuropeptide family of chemicals. The enkephalins bind to the opioid receptor sites in the CNS, contributing to the control of mood, movement, and behavior and to pain perception.

Excretion: A process by which the body removes waste products or foreign chemicals from the general circulation. This is usually accomplished by the kidneys, although some drugs are excreted from the body in the feces or through the lungs.

First-order biotransformation process: A subform of biotransformation in which a set percentage of the medication is biotransformed each hour.

First-pass metabolism: A process through which substances absorbed into the body from the small intestine are routed through the liver, allowing that organ to begin to neutralize poisons before they reach the general circulation. As a result of first-pass metabolism, the liver is often able to biotransform many medications that are administered orally before they have had a chance to reach the site of action.

GABA: Shorthand for gamma-amino-butyric acid. GABA is the main inhibitatory neurotransmitter in the brain. Neurons that utilize GABA are found in the cortex, the cerebellum, the hippocampus, the superior and inferior colliculi regions of the brain, the amygdala, and the nucleus accumbens.

Gastritis: Inflammation of the lining of the stomach,

Glossitis: A very painful inflammation of the tongue

Glutamate: A chemical that functions as an excitatory neurotransmitter in certain regions of the brain. Excessive amounts of glutamate can be toxic to the neurons with which it comes into contact.

Half-life: The period of time that it takes for the concentration of a drug in the blood plasma to be reduced by 50% following a single dose. This process depends in part on the health of the individual's liver and kidneys.

Harm reduction: An approach to drug abuse that attempts to limit the damage the drug(s) might cause to the individual's body. This approach is based on the theory that limiting the amount of damage to the individual reduces the ultimate cost of that person's chemical abuse to society.

Hippocampus: A portion of the brain that is thought to be involved in the processing of sensory information and in memory formation.

Huff: A slang term for inhaling an inhalant.

Hydrolysis: One of the four primary methods of drug biotransformation used by the liver.

Hypertension: Abnormally high blood pressure, usually defined as blood pressure in excess of 140/90.

Hypertensive: Related to hypertension.

Hypothalamus: A region of the brain that helps to regulate body temperature.

Iatrogenic disease: A disorder that arises as a complication of the medical treatment of a separate disorder.

IDS-100 See *Inventory of Drinking Situations.*

Intramuscular: Within muscle tissue.

Intranasal method of drug administration: Depositing a compound on the blood-rich tissues of the sinuses, where it can be absorbed into the circulation.

Intravenous: Within the veins of the circulatory system.

Inventory of Drinking Situations A 100-item questionnaire, the results of which shed light on situations in which a person is most likely to drink.

Ischemia: Local oxygen deprivation within tissue, usually caused by a reduction in the amount of blood reaching that region of the body, which may result in the destruction of the tissue.

Ischemic stroke: Blockage of a blood vessel in the brain, leading to ischemia in that region of the brain. If this condition is not corrected immediately, those brain cells may be damaged or even die.

Lethal dose level: A calculation performed by scientists to determine what percentage of the general population will die from exposure to a toxin/chemical. For example, the *lethal dose* (LD) at which 95% of the population will die without medical intervention is written as LD_{95}.

Limbic system: Region of the brain thought to be involved in the development and expression of emotions.

Lipids: Fat molecules within the blood, used by the body for various purposes, including formation of cell walls.

Locus ceruleus: A region of the brain thought to be involved in the perception of pain and the sensation of anxiety.

Mean corpuscular volume (MCV): A measure of the average size of a sample of an individual's red blood cells.

Metabolite: One of the compounds that is formed, usually by the liver, during drug *biotransformation*. Each of the me-tabolites is a variation on the original *parent molecule* that has been chemically altered so that the body can remove it from the circulation via the process of *elimination*.

Myocardial infarction: Commonly called a heart attack. A process in which the blood supply to a region of the heart is disrupted, possibly by coronary artery disease or by an embolus that blocks a blood vessel leading to the heart. Those heart muscle cells that are deprived of blood may be damaged or may even die. This condition can kill the individual if enough cardiac tissue is destroyed, and it results in scar tissue formation in those patients who do survive. If the patient survives, his or her cardiac function may be impaired to the point where he or she becomes "at risk" for later myocardial infarctions, congestive heart failure, the formation of emboli, and arrhythmias.

N-methyl-D-aspartate: An amino acid that functions as an excitatory *neurotransmitter* within some regions of the brain.

Narcolepsy: A very rare, lifelong neurological condition, in which the patient experiences sudden attacks of sleep.

Neuroadaptation: A process whereby the *neurons* within the CNS make basic changes in how they perform, in an attempt to continue normal function in spite of chronic exposure to a chemical that affects the CNS. This process is called neuro-adaption when the individual is using a prescribed medication. This same process was once called tolerance, although this term is now used primarily to describe the process of neuroadaptation to drugs of abuse.

Neuron: A nerve cell. Neurons are actually microscopic chemical–electrical generators that produce a small electrical "message" by actively moving sodium and calcium ions back and forth across the cell boundary. Sodium and calcium ions pass through the cell wall via special "channels" formed by protein molecules. The concentration of sodium ions inside the cell establishes a small electric potential. When the neuron fires, calcium ions rush into the cell, replacing the sodium ions, and the cell loses the electric charge it had built up. The cell then repeats the cycle, pumping calcium ions out and sodium ions back in, to build up another electric charge so that it can "fire" again. Any chemical that interacts with the protein molecules that form sodium/calcium ion channels in the cell wall of the body's tissues will affect how those cells function.

Neurotoxin: A chemical that destroys nerve cells (neurons).

Neurotransmitter: Any molecule released by a neuron to cause a change in the function of a designated *target cell*. After being released, the neurotransmitter molecules cross the *synapse* to bind at a *receptor site* on the *target cell*. This then causes the target cell to respond to the chemical message transmitted by the first cell's *neurotransmitter* molecules.

NMDA: See *N-methyl-D-aspartate.*

Nucleus accumbens: A region of the brain thought to be involved in the pleasure response. Because of this, the nucleus accumbens is also thought to be one region of the brain where drugs are able to cause the sensation of pleasure.

Oliguria: Significant reduction in the amount of urine produced by the kidneys.

Over-the-counter medication: A medication that can be purchased without a prescription. It thus might be sold in various outlets besides a pharmacy, such as a grocery store. Over 600 medications that were once available in the United States only by prescription have now been classified as OTC medications by the Food and Drug Administration (Scheller, 1998).

Oxidation: One of the four primary methods of drug biotransformation exhibited by the liver. In this process, a hydrogen atom is removed from the molecule being biotransformed, changing its chemical structure in a minor way. Ultimately, the atom in question is changed in such a way that the kidneys can eliminate the compound from the blood.

Panic attack: The experience of intense feelings of anxiety, often with symptoms such as shortness of breath, rapid heartbeat, and a feeling that something terrible is about to happen. Panic attacks are usually very brief (10–20 minutes).

Parent compound: The original drug molecule, usually a molecule before it is altered by the process of *biotransformation.*

Patient year: A statistical concept. For example, 100 patient years means 100 patients, all of whom have a certain condition, who are followed for 1 year.

Pharmaceuticals: In the study of chemical dependency, compounds produced for use with humans that have been diverted to illicit markets. For example, narcotic analgesics stolen from a pharmacy during a burglary and then sold on the street are called pharmaceuticals to distinguish them from the drugs produced in illegal laboratories.

Platelets: Disk-shaped bodies that circulate in the blood until there is an injury, at which time they help to form a blood clot to stop bleeding.

Polydrug abuse: The abuse of more than one substance at once. Prior to the mid-1970s, individuals with substance use problems tended to abuse just one chemical, such as alcohol or heroin. This pattern of substance abuse is rarely seen today, except in older individuals whose substance use pattern was established in the mid-1970s or early 1980s. Currently, it is more common for the individual who has a substance use problem to be abusing more than one chemical at a time.

Polypharmacology: See *Polydrug abuse.*

Potentiate: Intensify. Often, when similar compounds are ingested, the effects of one drug intensify those of the other(s),

possibly producing lethal results. See also *Synergistic response.*

Prime effect of a drug: The intended effect of a drug. For example, a person with a fever might take some aspirin to lower his or her fever. This reduction in fever is thus the *prime effect* of the aspirin. Compare with *Side effects of a drug.*

Prodrug: A compound that is administered to a patient and then biotransformed by her or his liver into a compound that is biologically active. Technically, this compound is a *metabolite* of the parent drug. The parent drug may or may not have a biological action of its own, but the metabolite has a stronger biological action than the parent compound, and it is for this action that the patient is using the parent drug.

Prostaglandins: Any of a family of compounds found in the body that help to mediate the inflammatory response following an injury and also help to control body functions.

Receptor: A protein molecule or group of molecules, anchored in the cell wall, that allows the cell to receive chemicals from the outside wall. If the chemical molecule transmits information between cells, it is called a *transmitter* molecule. Examples of these include hormones, antigens, and peptides. If the transmitter molecule derives from one of the neurons of the CNS, it is referred to as a neurotransmitter. Neurotransmitters pass information between neurons.

Receptor site: The region in the cell wall of a neuron where a receptor is located.

Reduction: One of the four primary methods of drug biotransformation used by the liver.

REM rebound: The individual's experiencing an *increase* in the amount of sleep time spent in REM sleep after stopping the use of a CNS depressant, apparently so that the body can "catch up" on lost REM sleep. This period is characterized by vivid dreams, which may be quite frightening to the dreamer. In some cases, the nightmares are so disturbing that the patient begins to use alcohol/drugs again just to "get a good night's sleep."

Reye's syndrome: A serious medical condition generally seen in children between the ages of 2 and 12. The condition usually follows a viral infection such as influenza or chickenpox. Symptoms include swelling of the brain, seizures, disturbance of consciousness, a fatty degeneration of the liver, and coma. About 30% of the cases result in death.

Rhabdomyolysis: Destruction of skeletal muscle tissue on a massive scale. When muscle cells die, they release a chemical known as myoglobin, which helps to store oxygen in the muscle cell. In rhabdomyolsis, massive amounts of myoglobin are released at once. The accumulated myoglobin interferes with kidney function and in extreme cases can result in kidney failure.

Rhinitis: Inflammation of the nasal passages.

Rig: Intravenous needle.

Schizophrenia: A psychiatric disorder characterized by delusional thinking, hallucinations, and disorganized behavior.

Serotonin: One of the major *neurotransmitters* in the body. There are 15 known subtypes of serotonin found in the CNS, each of which is assumed to control one or more subfunctions within the CNS.

Serotonin syndrome: A rare, drug-induced neurological disorder that can be life-threatening. In spite of the best medical care, some 11% of those afflicted with this condition will die. Symptoms of serotonin syndrome include irritability, confusion, increased anxiety, drowsiness, hyperthermia (increased body temperature), sinus tachycardia, dilation of the pupils, nausea, muscle rigidity, and seizures. Although serotonin syndrome may develop as long as 24 hours after the patient has ingested a medication that affects the serotonin neurotransmitter system, in 50% of the cases, the patient develops the syndrome within just 2 hours of starting the medication/illicit drug (Mills, 1995). This condition constitutes a medical emergency that should be treated by a physician.

Side effects of a drug: The unintended effects of a chemical in the body. For example, if a person takes some aspirin to control his or her fever, this is the *prime effect* of the aspirin. The ability of aspirin to contribute to gastrointestinal bleeding is an undesired *side effect* of that compound.

"Silent" cardiac ischemia: An episode of cardiac ischemia that is not accompanied by pain or shortness of breath, symptoms that usually occur when the heart muscle is deprived of oxygen. See *Ischemia*.

Single-photon emission computed tomography: A scanning device that allows scientists to study blood flow patterns in living tissues.

Site of action: The place where a drug has its *prime effect*.

Sleep apnea: A breathing disorder in which the individual's ability to breathe is disrupted during sleep. Complications of sleep apnea can include high blood pressure, a disruption of the normal heart rate, and even death.

Sleep latency: The period of time between when the individual first goes to bed and when he or she finally falls asleep.

Subdural hematoma: Hemorrhage in the skull, leading to the collection of blood in the space between the membranes surrounding the brain or spinal cord, and the skull bones. This condition usually develops as a result of trauma. It puts pressure on the surrounding tissues of the CNS and can lead to paralysis or even death.

Sublingual method of drug administration: Method of drug administration in which a tablet, capsule, or liquid is placed under the tongue. Some medications, and a small number of the drugs of abuse, can be absorbed through the blood-rich tissues under the tongue.

Suicide: The intentional taking of one's own life.

Synapse: A microscopic gap between two neurons, across which one neuron releases *neurotransmitter* molecules to *receptor sites* in order to transmit a message to the next *neuron* in that nerve pathway.

Synergistic response: The process by which two or more compounds with the same, or similar, actions multiply each other's effects.

T-helper cell: A type of cell, found in the body's immune system, that helps to activate the body's immune response to a foreign cell.

Temporal lobe: A region of the brain's *cortex* involved in sensory function, language use, and some aspects of emotions.

Therapeutic half-life: The period of time that the body requires to reduce the effectiveness of a single dose of a drug by 50%.

Therapeutic Index (TI): The ratio between the ED_{50} and the LD_{50}.

Therapeutic threshold: The point at which the concentration of a specific chemical begins to have the desired effect on the user.

Therapeutic window: The dosage range at which the person is taking enough of a pharmaceutical agent to benefit from it, without taking so much as to experience toxic effects from an overdose of that compound.

Thiamine: Also known as vitamin B-1. One of the B family of vitamins, which helps to maintain the health and appropriate function of cells in the cardiovascular and nervous systems.

Tolerance: The development of resistance to a drug's effects over time, as the body adapts to the repeated administration of a chemical compound.

Transdermal: Literally, "across the skin."

Ulcer, "bleeding" See also *Ulcer, gastric*. If a stomach ulcer forms over a blood vessel, the acid will destroy the walls of the blood vessel, allowing blood to escape into the stomach. This is a "bleeding" ulcer. Such bleeding ulcers are a life-threatening emergency.

Ulcer, gastric: Stomach acid is brought into contact with the tissues of the stomach, and gradually an area of stomach lining is destroyed by the stomach's acid. This is an ulcer. The condition is usually quite painful.

Upregulation: The process by which a neuron increases the number of receptors in the cell wall, thus increasing the sensitivity of that neuron to a certain *neurotransmitter*. This is usually done to compensate for a decrease in the availability of a certain neurotransmitter molecule over time.

Vasospasm: A blood vessel's going into spasms, which interferes with the ability of that vessel to control blood flow. If the vasospasm continues long enough, blood clots may form, which can then cause an occlusion by blocking the blood flow through either an artery or a vein.

Ventricular fibrillation: A pattern of rapid and essentially uncoordinated contractions of the lower two chambers of the heart (the "ventricles"), disrupting the pumping action of the heart.

Viral load test: A procedure that uses DNA technology to provide an estimate of the number of virus particles in a given unit of blood (usually a cubic millimeter). This test is used to estimate the progression of viral infections such as HIV/AIDS and the various hepatitis viruses.

Withdrawal: The characteristic process of reverse adaptation, which occurs when a drug that has been repeatedly used over a short period of time is suddenly discontinued. See also *Tolerance.*

Wound botulism: A form of *botulism* that develops when spores of the microscopic organism *Clostridium botulinum* infect a wound and begin to produce the neurotoxin *botulinum.*

Zero-order biotransformation process: A type of biotransformation in which a foreign chemical is metabolized at a set rate, no matter how high the concentration of that chemical in the blood.

References

Aanavi, M. P., Taube, D. O., Ja, D. Y., & Duran, E. F. (2000). The status of psychologists' training about and treatment of substance-abusing clients. *Journal of Psychoactive Drugs, 31*, 441–444.

Aase, J. M. (1994). Clinical recognition of FAS. *Alcohol Health & Research World, 18* (1), 5–9.

Aase, J. M., Jones, K. L., & Clarren, S. K. (1995). Do we need the term "FAE"? *Pediatrics, 95*, 428–430.

Abbott, A., & Concar, D. (1992). A trip into the unknown. *New Scientist, 135*, 30–34.

Abbott, P. J., Quinn, D., & Knox, L. (1995). Ambulatory medical detoxification for alcohol. *American Journal of Drug and Alcohol Abuse, 21*, 549–564.

Abel, E. L. (1982). *Drugs and behavior: A primer in neuro-psychopharmacology.* Malabar, FL: Robert E. Krieger Publishing Co.

Abrams, R. C., & Alexopoulos, G. (1987). Substance abuse in the elderly: Alcohol and prescription drugs. *Hospital and Community Psychiatry, 38*, 1285–1288.

Abrams, R. C., & Alexopoulos, G. S. (1998). Geriatric addictions. In *Clinical textbook of addictive disorders* (2nd ed.) (Frances, R. J., & Miller, S. I., eds.). New York: Guilford.

Abt Associates, Inc. (1995a). *What America's users spend on illegal drugs, 1988–1993.* Washington, DC: Office of National Drug Control Policy.

Abt Associates, Inc. (1995b). *Pulse check.* Washington, DC: Office of National Drug Control Policy.

Accounting Today. (1997). Then I suppose my crack habit is out of the question. *11* (17), 32.

Achord, J. L. (1995). Alcohol and the liver. *Scientific American Science & Medicine, 2* (2), 16–27.

Ackerman, R. J. (1983). *Children of alcoholics: A guidebook for educators, therapists, and parents.* Holmes Beach, FL: Learning Publications, Inc.

Adams, J. K. (1988). Setting free chemical dependency. *Alcoholism & Addiction, 8* (4), 20–21.

Adams, W. L., Yuan, Z., Barboriak, J. J., & Rimm, A. A. (1993). Alcohol-related hospitalizations of elderly people. *Journal of the American Medical Association, 270,* 1222–1225.

Addiction Letter, The. (1989). Therapeutic community research yields interesting results. *5* (1), 2.

Addiction Letter, The. (1993a). Blunts and crude: Two new marijuana products are on the streets. *9* (11), 1, 7.

Addiction Letter, The. (1994a). Heroin is back, with younger users. *10* (11), 1–3.

Addiction Letter, The. (1993b). Dangerous inhalants are increasingly popular among adolescents. *9* (8), 1, 7.

Addiction Letter, The. (1994b). Consequences of PCP abuse are up. *10* (3), 3.

Addiction Letter, The. (1995a). Treatment protocols for marijuana dependence are starting to emerge. *11* (8), 1–2.

Addiction Letter, The. (1995b). Ephedrine is used illegally as a precursor to street drugs. *11* (2), 5.

Addiction Treatment Forum, VIII. (1999). Addiction treatment in the age of HIV/AIDS. (4), 1, 5.

Adelman, S. A., & Weiss, R. D. (1989). What is therapeutic about inpatient alcoholism treatment? *Hospital and Community Psychiatry, 40* (5), 515–519.

Adger, H., & Werner, M. J. (1994). The pediatrician. *Alcohol Health & Research World, 18*, 121–126.

AIDS Alert. (1989). Research on nitrites suggests drug plays role in AIDS epidemic. *4* (9), 153–156.

Al-Anon's Twelve Steps & Twelve Traditions. (1985). New York: Al-Anon Family Group Headquarters, Inc.

Albertson, T. E., Derlet, R. W., & van Hoozen, B. E. (1999). Methamphetamine and the expanding complications of amphetamines. *Western Journal of Medicine, 170,* 214–219.

Albertson, T. E., Walby, W. F., & Derlet, R. (1995). Stimulant-induced pulmonary toxicity. *Chest, 108,* 1140–1150.

Alcohol Alert. (1993). Alcohol and nutrition. Washington, DC: National Institute on Alcohol Abuse and Alcoholism.

Alcohol Alert. (1994). Alcohol and hormones. Washington, DC: National Institute on Alcohol Abuse and Alcoholism.

Alcohol Alert. (1995). Alcohol-medication interactions. Washington, DC: National Institute on Alcohol Abuse and Alcoholism.

Alcohol Alert. (1996). Drinking and driving. Washington, DC: National Institute on Alcohol Abuse and Alcoholism.

Alcohol Alert. (1998). Alcohol and tobacco. Washington, DC: National Institute on Alcohol Abuse and Alcoholism.

Alcoholics Anonymous. (1976). New York: Alcoholics Anonymous World Services,

Alcoholism & Drug Abuse Week. (1990). ONDCP gives rundown on treatment approaches. 2 (26), 3–5.

Alcoholism & Drug Abuse Week. (1991a). DAWN: Emergency rooms seeing fewer drug cases. 3 (6), 1.

Alcoholism & Drug Abuse Week. (1991b). Groups offer self-help alternatives to AA. 3 (37), 6.

Alcoholism & Drug Abuse Week. (1991c). Mixed signals on possible upsurge in heroin use. 3 (24), 4–5.

Alcoholism & Drug Abuse Week. (1993a). Methadone alternative nears approval. 5 (22), 4.

Alcoholism & Drug Abuse Week. (1993b). 'Cat' poses national threat, experts say (methcathinone). 5 (47), 5–6.

Alcoholism & Drug Abuse Week. (1997). Residential or outpatient, early 90's treatment reduced use (addiction treatment). 9 (48), 1–2.

Alcoholism & Drug Abuse Week: (1998). Ritalin may increase risk of cocaine use later. *10* (17), 8.

Alcoholism Report, The. (1991). AA survey findings released. *19* (7), 8–10.

Alemi, F., Stephens, R. C., Llorens, S., & Orris, B. (1995). A review of factors affecting treatment outcomes: Expected treatment outcome scale. *American Journal of Drug and Alcohol Abuse, 21,* 483–510.

Alexander, D. E., & Gwyther, R. E. (1995). Alcoholism in adolescents and their families. *Pediatric Clinics of North America, 42,* 217–234.

Alexander, M. J. (1996). Women with co-occuring addictive and mental disorders. *American Journal of Orthopsychiatry, 66,* 61–70.

Alibrandi, L. A. (1978). The folk psychotherapy of Alcoholics Anonymous. In *Practical approaches to alcoholism psychotherapy* (Zimberg, S., Wallace, J., & Blume, S., eds.). New York: Plenum Press.

Aligne, C. A., & Stoddard, J. J. (1997). Tobacco and children. *Archives of Pediatric and Adolescent Medicine, 151,* 648–653.

Allen, M. G., & Phillips, K. L. (1993). Utilization review of treatment for chemical dependence. *Hospital and Community Psychiatry, 44,* 752–756.

Allison, M. C., Howatson, A. G., Torrance, C. J., Lee, F. D., & Russell, R. I. (1992). Gastrointestinal damage associated with the use of nonsteroidal antiinflammatory drugs. *The New England Journal of Medicine, 327,* 749–754.

Alper, J., & Natowics, M. R. (1992). The allure of genetic explanations. *British Medical Journal, 305,* 666.

Alter, J. (2001). Making marriage work: Communications in recovery. Symposium presented to the Dept. of Psychiatry of The Cambridge Hospital, Boston, MA, March 2, 2001.

Alterman, A. I., Erdlen, D. I., LaPorte, D. J., & Erdlen, F. R. (1982). Effects of illicit drug use in an inpatient psychiatric population. *Addictive Behaviors, 7,* 231–242.

Alterman, A. I., McDermott, P. A., Cacciola, J. S., Rutherford, M. I., Boardman, C. R., McKay, J. R., & Cook, T. G. (1998). A typology of antisociality in methadone patients. *Journal of Abnormal Psychology, 107,* 412–422.

Amaro, H. (1995). Love, sex and power. *American Psychologist, 50,* 437–447.

American Academy of Family Physicians. (1989). Screening for alcohol and other drug abuse. *American Family Physician, 40* (1), 137–147.

American Academy of Family Physicians. (1990a). Effects of fetal exposure to cocaine and heroin. *American Family Physician, 41* (5), 1595–1597.

American Academy of Family Physicians. (1990b). Marijuana use and memory loss. *American Family Physician, 41* (3), 930–932.

American Academy of Pediatrics. (1998). Neonatal drug withdrawal. *Pediatrics, 101,* 1079–1089.

American Association of Practicing Psychologists (1999). Magellan slashes fees: An outrage or opportunity? 2 (1), 5, 7.

American Medical Association. (1992). Costs from drug abuse doubled since 1986. *American Medical News, 35* (30), 37.

American Medical Association. (1993a). *Factors contributing to the health care cost problem.* Chicago: American Medical Association.

American Medical Association. (1993b). Injury prevention must be part of nation's plan to reduce health costs, say control experts. *Journal of the American Medical Association, 270,* 19–20.

American Medical Association. (1994). *Drug evaluations annual 1994.* Washington, DC: American Medical Association.

American Psychiatric Association. (1990). *Benzodiazepine dependence, toxicity, and abuse.* Washington, DC: American Psychiatric Association.

American Psychiatric Association. (1995). Practice guidelines for the treatment of patients with substance use disorders: alcohol, cocaine, opioids. *American Journal of Psychiatry, 152* (11) (supplement).

American Psychiatric Association. (1996). Practice guidelines for the treatment of patients with nicotine dependence. *American Journal of Psychiatry, 153* (10) (supplement).

American Psychiatric Association. (2000). *Diagnostic and statistical manual of mental disorders* (4th ed., Text Revision). Washington, DC: American Psychiatric Association.

American Society of Health-System Pharmacists. (1999). *AHFS drug information.* Bethesda, MD: American Society of Health-System Pharmacists.

Ames, D., Wirshing, W. C., & Friedman, R. (1993). Ecstasy, the serotonin syndrome, and neuroleptic malignant syndrome—a possible link? *Journal of the American Medical Association, 269,* 869–870.

Anderson, D. J. (1989). An alcoholic is never too old for treatment. *Minneapolis Star-Tribune, VIII* (200), 7 ex.

Anderson, D. J. (1991). Alcohol abuse takes a toll in head injuries. *Minneapolis Star-Tribune, X* (152), 7E.

Anderson, D. J. (1993). Chemically dependent women still face barriers. *Minneapolis Star Tribune, XII* (65), 8E.

Anderson, D. J. (1995). Adult children of alcoholics must deal with anger. *Minneapolis Star Tribune, XIII* (274), 4Ex.

Anderson, R. (1993). AIDS: trends, predictions, controversy. *Nature, 363,* 393–394.

Angell, M., & Kassirer, J. P. (1994). Alcohol and other drugs—toward a more rational and consistent policy. *The New England Journal of Medicine, 331,* 537–539.

Angier, N. (1990). Storming the wall. *Discover, 11* (5), 67–72.

Anker, A. L., & Smilkstein, M. J. (1994). Acetaminophen. *Emergency Medical Clinics of North America, 12,* 335–349.

Annas, G. J. (1997). Reefer madness—the federal response to California's medical-marijuana law. *The New England Journal of Medicine, 337,* 435–439.

Annis, H. M., & Davis, C. S. (1991). Relapse prevention. *Alcohol Health & Research World, 15* (3), 204–212.

Anrett, J. J. (2000). Emerging adulthood. *American Psychologist, 55,* 469–480.

Anthony, J. C., Arria, A. M., & Johnson, E. O. (1995). Epidemiological and public health issues for tobacco, alcohol, and other drugs. In *Review of psychiatry (Vol 14)* (Oldham, J. M., & Riba, M. B., eds.). Washington, DC: American Psychiatric Press.

Antman, K., & Chang, Y. (2000). Kaposi's sarcoma. *New England Journal of Medicine, 342,* 1027–1038.

Anton, R. F. (1994). Medications for treating alcoholism. *Alcohol Health & Research World, 18,* 265–271.

Anton, R. F. (1999). What is craving? Models and implications for treatment. *Alcohol Research & Health, 23,* 165–173.

Antonio, R. (1997). The use & abuse of ephedrine. *Muscle & Fitness, 58* (10), 178–180.

Appelbaum, P. S. (1992). Controlling prescription of benzodiazepines. *Hospital & Community Psychiatry, 43,* 12–13.

Appleby, L., Dyson, V., Luchins, D. J., & Cohen, L. S. (1997). The impact of substance abuse screening on a public psychiatric inpatient population. *Psychiatric Services, 48,* 1311–1316.

Arden, H. (1994). *Noble red man.* Hillsboro, OR: Beyond Words Publishing, Inc.

Aronoff, G. M., Wagner, J. M., & Spangler, A. S. (1986). Chemical interventions for pain. *Journal of Consulting and Clinical Psychology, 54,* 769–775.

Ashton, H. (1992). *Brain function and psychotropic drugs.* New York: Oxford.

Ashton, H. (1994). Guidelines for the rational use of benzodiazepines. *Drugs, 48* (1), 25–40.

Asseo, L. (1993). Drug war clogs system, ABA says. *St. Paul Pioneer Press, 144* (287), 2A.

Associated Press. (1993). Drug dealers find new prey—the deaf. *San Francisco Examiner, 128* (21), B-7.

Associated Press. (1994a). About 2.2 million children smoke, heart group says. *Minneapolis Star-Tribune XII* (212), 2A.

Associated Press. (1994b). Spraying away the cigarette craving? *Minneapolis Star-Tribune, XIII* (120), 5A, 6A.

Astrachan, B. M., & Tischler, G. L. (1984). Normality from a health systems perspective. In *Normality and the life cycle* (Offer, D., & Sabshin, M., eds.). New York: Basic Books.

Atkinson, I. H., & Grant, I. (1994). Natural history of neuropsychiatric manifestations of HIV disease. *Psychiatric Clinics of North America, 17,* 17–33.

Ausabel, D. P. (1983). Methadone maintenance treatment: The other side of the coin. *International Journal of the Addictions, 18,* 851–862.

Autti-Ramo, I. (2000). Twelve-year follow-up of children exposed to alcohol in utero. *Developmental Medicine & Child Neurology, 42,* 406–411.

Avants, S. K., Margolin, P., Chang, T. R., & Birch, S. (1995). Acupuncture for the treatment of cocaine addiction: Investigation of a needle puncture control. *Journal of Substance Abuse Treatment, 12,* 195–205.

Ayd, F. J. (1994). Prescribing anxiolytics and hypnotics for the elderly. *Psychiatric Annals, 24* (2), 91–97.

Ayd, F. J., Janicak, P. G., Davis, J. M., & Preskorn, S. H. (1996). Advances in the pharmacotherapy of anxiety and sleep disorders. *Principles and Practice of Psychopharmacotherapy, 1* (4), 1–22.

Baber, A. (1998). Addiction's poster child. *Playboy, 45* (5), 29.

Back Letter, The. (1994). Steroid-abusing patients: Handle with care. *Archives of General Psychiatry, 51,* 83.

Bagatell, C. J., & Bremner, W. J. (1996). Androgens in men—uses and abuses. *New England Journal of Medicine, 334,* 707–714.

Bahrke, M. S. (1990). *Psychological research, methodological problems, and relevant issues.* Paper presented at the 1990 meeting of the American Psychological Association, Boston, MA.

Bales, J. (1988). Legalized drugs: Idea flawed, debate healthy. *APA Monitor, 19* (8), 22.

Ballenger, J. C. (1995). Benzodiazepines. In *Textbook of psychopharmacology* (Schatzberg, A. F., & Nemeroff, C. B., eds.). Washington, DC: American Psychiatric Association.

Banerjee, S. (1990). Newest wrinkle for smokers is on their faces. *Minneapolis Star-Tribune, VIII* (341). 1ex, 5ex.

Barbone, F., McMahon, A. D., Davey, P. G., Morris, A. D., Reid, C., McDevitt, D. G., & MacDonald, T. (1998). Association of road-traffic accidents with benzodiazepine use. *The Lancet, 352,* 1331–1336.

Barden, J. C. (1991). In depth. *Minneapolis Star-Tribune, X* (153). 4A, 6A.

Bargh, J. A., & Chartrand, T. L. (1999). The unbearable automaticity of being. *American Psychologist, 54,* 462–479.

Barker, D. (1994). Reasons for tobacco use and symptoms of nicotine withdrawal among adolescent and young adult tobacco users—United States, 1993. *Journal of the American Medical Association, 272,* 1648–1649.

Barki, Z. H. K., Kravitz, H. M., & Berki, T. M. (1998). Psychotropic medications in pregnancy. *Psychiatric Annals, 28,* 486–500.

Barnhill, J. G., Ciraulo, A. M., Ciraulo, D. A., & Greene, J. A. (1995). Interactions of importance in chemical dependence. In *Drug interactions in psychiatry* (2nd ed.) (Ciraulo, D. A., Shader, R. I., Greenblatt, D. J., & Creelman, W., eds.). New York: Williams & Wilkins.

Barondes, S. H. (1999). An agenda for psychiatric genetics. *Archives of General Psychiatry, 56,* 549–552.

Barr, A. (1999). *Drink: A social history of America.* New York: Carroll & Graf Publishers, Inc.

Barrera, S. E., Osinski, W. A., & Davidoff, E. (1949/1994). The use of antabuse (tetra-ethylthiuramdisulphide) in chronic alcoholics. *American Journal of Psychiatry, 151,* 263–267.

Barre-Sinoussi, F. (1996). HIV as the cause of AIDS. *The Lancet, 348,* 31–35.

Bartecchi, C. E., MacKenzie, T. D., & Schrier, R. W. (1994). The human costs of tobacco use. *The New England Journal of Medicine, 330,* 907–912.

Bartlett, J. G. (1999). *Management of respiratory tract infections* (2nd ed.). New York: Lippincott Williams & Wilkins.

Baselt, R. C. (1996). Disposition of alcohol in man. In *Medicolegal aspects of alcohol* (3rd ed.) (Garriott, J. C., ed.). Tuscon, AZ: Lawyers & Judges Publishing Co.

Batzer, W., Ditzler, T., & Brown, C. (1999). LSD use and flashbacks in alcoholic patients. *Journal of Addictive Diseases, 18* (2), 57–63.

Baughan, D. M. (1995). Barriers to diagnosing anxiety disorder in family practice. *American Family Physician, 52* (2), 447–450.

Baughman, R. D. (1993). Psoriasis and cigarettes. *Archives of Dermatology, 129,* 1329–1330.

Bauman, J. L. (1988). Acute heroin withdrawal. *Hospital Therapy, 13,* 60–66.

Bauman, K. E., & Ennett, S. T. (1994). Peer influence on adolescent drug use. *American Psychologist, 63,* 820–822.

Bays, J. (1992). The care of alcohol and drug-affected infants. *Pediatric Annals, 21* (8), 485–495.

Bean-Bayog, M. (1988). Alcohol and drug abuse: Alcoholism as a cause of psychopathology. *Hospital and Community Psychiatry, 39,* 352–354.

Bean-Bayog, M. (1993). AA processes and change: How does it work? In *Research on Alcoholics Anonymous* (McCrady, B. S., & Miller, W. R., eds.). New Brunswick, NJ: Rutgers Center of Alcohol Studies.

Beardsley, T. (1994). The lucky ones. *Scientific American, 270* (5), 20, 24, 28.

Beasley, J. D. (1987). *Wrong diagnosis, wrong treatment: The plight of the alcoholic in America.* New York: Creative Infomatics, Inc.

Beattie, M. (1987). *Codependent no more.* New York: Harper & Row.

Beattie, M. (1989). *Beyond codependency.* New York: Harper & Row.

Beauvais, F. (1998). American Indians and alcohol. *Alcohol Health & Research World, 22,* 253–259.

Beauvais, F., & Oetting, E. R. (1988). Inhalant abuse by young children. In *Epidemiology of inhalant abuse: An update.* Washington, DC: National Institute on Drug Abuse.

Beazley, H. (1998). The integration of AA and clinical practice. Symposium presented to the Dept. of Psychiatry at The Cambridge Hospital, Boston, MA.

Becherer, P. R. (1995). Viral hepatitis. *Postgraduate Medicine, 98,* 65–74.

Beck, A. T., Wright, F. D., Newman, C. F., & Liese, B. S. (1993). *Cognitive therapy of substance abuse.* New York: Guilford.

Beckman, L. J. (1993). Alcoholics Anonymous and gender issues. In *Research on Alcoholics Anonymous* (McCrady, B. S., & Miller, W. R., eds.). New Brunswick, NJ: Rutgers Center of Alcohol Studies.

Beckman, L. J. (1994). Treatment needs of women with alcohol problems. *Alcohol Health & Research World, 18,* 206–211.

Beebe, D. K., & Walley, E. (1991). Substance abuse: The designer drugs. *American Family Physician, 43,* 1689–1698.

Beebe, D. K., & Walley, E. (1995). Smokable methamphetamine ("Ice"): An old drug in a different form. *American Family Physician, 51,* 449–454.

Beeder, A. B., & Millman, R. B. (1995). Treatment strategies for comorbid disorders: psychopathology and substance abuse. In *Psychotherapy and substance abuse* (Washton, A. M., ed.). New York: Guilford.

Begley, S. (1997). Jagged little pill. *Newsweek, CXXX* (7), 66.

Behnke, M., & Eyler, F. D. (1993). The consequences of prenatal substance use for the developing fetus, newborn and young child. *International Journal of the Addictions, 28,* 1341–1391.

Beitner-Johnson, D., & Nestler, E. J. (1992). Basic neurobiology of cocaine: Actions within the mesolimbic dopamine system. In *Clinician's guide to cocaine addiction.* (Kosten, T. R., & Kleber, H. D., eds.). New York: Guilford.

Belgrade, M. J. (1999). Opioids for chronic nonmalignant pain. *Postgraduate Medicine, 106* (6), 115–124.

Bell, D. C., Montoya, I. D., & Atkinson, J. S. (1997). Therapeutic connection and client progress in drug abuse treatment. *Journal of Clinical Psychology, 53,* 215–224.

Bell, D. C., Williams, M. L., Nelson, R., & Spence, R. T. (1994) An experimental test on retention in residential and outpatient program. *American Journal of Drug and Alcohol Abuse, 20* (3), 331–341.

Bell, G. L., & Lau, K. (1995). Perinatal and neonatal issues of substance abuse. *Pediatric Clinics of North America, 42,* 261–281.

Bell, N. J., Forthun, L. F., & Sun, S. W. (2000). Attachment, adolescent competencies, and substance use: Developmental considerations in the study of risk behaviors. *Substance Use & Misuse, 35,* 1177–1206.

Bell, R. (1995). Determinants of hospital-based substance abuse treatment programs. *Hospital & Health Services Administration, 39* (1), 93–102.

Bell, R. A., Spangler, J. G., & Quandt, S. A. (2000). Smokeless tobacco use among adults in the southeast. *Southern Medical Journal, 93,* 456–462.

Bell, T. (1996). Abuse or addiction? *Professional Counselor, 11* (5), 12.

Bellack, A. S., & DiClemente, C. C. (1999). Treating substance abuse among patients with schizophrenia. *Psychiatric Services, 50,* 75–80.

Benet, L. Z., Kroetz, D. L., & Sheiner, L. B. (1995). Pharmacokinetics: The dynamics of drug absorption, distribution and elimination. In *The pharmacological basis of therapeutics* (9th ed.). (Hardman, J. G., & Limbird, L. E., editors-in-chief). New York: McGraw-Hill.

Benowitz, N. L. (1992). Cigarette smoking and nicotine addiction. *Medical Clinics of North America, 76,* 415–437.

Benowitz, N. L. (1997a). The role of nicotine in smoking-related cardiovascular disease. *Preventive Medicine, 26,* 412–417.

Benowitz, N. L. (1997b). Treating tobacco addiction—nicotine or no nicotine? *The New England Journal of Medicine. 337,* 1230–1231.

Benowitz, N. L., & Henningfield, J. E. (1994). Establishing a nicotine threshold for addiction. *New England Journal of Medicine, 331,* 123–126.

Benowitz, N. L., & Jacob, P. (1993). Nicotine and cotinine elimination pharmacokinetics in smokers and nonsmokers. *Clincial Pharmacology & Therapeutics, 53,* 316–323.

Benson, R. T., & Sacco, R. L. (2000). Stroke prevention. *Neurologic Clinics of North America. 19,* 309–320.

Benzer, D. G. (1995). *Use and abuse of benzodiazepines.* Paper presented at the 1995 annual Frank P. Furlano, M.D. memorial lecture, Gunderson-Lutheran Medical Center, La Crosse, Wisconsin.

Berenson, D. (1987). Alcoholics Anonymous: From surrender to transformation. *The Family Therapy Networker, 11* (4), 25–31.

Berg, B. J., & Dubin, W. R. (1990). Economic grand rounds: Why 28 days? An alternative approach to alcoholism treatment. *Hospital and Community Psychiatry, 41,* 1175–1178.

Berg, I. K., & Miller, S. D. (1992). *Working with the problem drinker.* New York: Norton.

Berg, R., Franzen, M. M., & Wedding, D. (1994). *Screening for brain impairment: A manual for mental health practice* (2nd ed.). New York: Springer Publishing.

Berger, P. A., & Dunn, M. J. (1982). Substance induced and substance use disorders. In *Treatment of mental disorders* (Griest, J. H., Jefferson, J. W., & Spitzer, R. L., eds.). New York: Oxford University Press.

Berger, T. (2000). Nervous system. In *Handbook of alcoholism* (Zernig, G., Saria, A., Kurz, M., & O'Malley, S. S., eds.). New York: CRC Press.

Berkowitz, A., & Perkins, H. W. (1988). Personality characteristics of children of alcoholics. *Journal of Consulting and Clinical Psychology, 56,* 206–209.

Bernstein, E., Tracey, A., Bernstein, J., & Williams, C. (1996). Emergency department detection and referral rates for patients with problem drinking. *Substance Abuse, 17,* 69–76.

Bhandari, M., Sylvester, S. L., & Rigotti, N. A. (1996). Nicotine and cigarette smoking. In *Source book of substance abuse and addiction* (Friedman, L., Fleming, N. F., Roberts, D. H., & Hyman, S. E., eds.). New York: Williams & Wilkins.

Bierut, L. J., Dinwiddie, S. H., Begleiter, H., Crowe, R. R., Hesselbrock, V., Nurnberger, J. I., Porjesz, B., Schuckit, M. A., & Reich, T. (1998). Familial transmission of substance dependence: alcohol, marijuana, cocaine and habitual smoking. *Archives of General Psychiatry, 55,* 982–988.

Black, C. (1982). *It will never happen to me.* Denver, CO: M.A.C. Printing and Publications.

Blair, D. T., & Ramones, V. A. (1996). The undertreatment of anxiety: Overcoming the confusion and stigma. *Journal of Psychosocial Nursing, 34* (6), 9–17.

Blake, R. (1990). Mental health counseling and older problem drinkers. *Journal of Mental Health Counseling, 12* (3), 354–367.

Blansjaar, B. A., & Zwinderman, A. H. (1992). The course of alcohol amnesic disorder: A three-year follow up study of clinical signs. *Acta Psychiatricia Scandinavica, 86,* 240–246.

Blau, M. (1990). Toxic parents, perennial kids: Is it time for adult children to grow up? *Utne Reader, 42,* 60–65.

Bleidt, B. A., & Moss, J. T. (1989). Age-related changes in drug distribution. *U.S. Pharmacist, 14* (8), 24–32.

Bliss, R. E., Garvey, A. J., Heinold, J. W., & Hitchcock, J. L. (1989). The influence of situation and coping on relapse crisis outcomes after smoking cessation. *Journal of Consulting and Clinical Psychology, 57,* 443–449.

Blondell, R. D., Frierson, R. L., & Lippmann, S. B. (1996). Alcoholism. *Postgraduate Medicine, 100,* 69–72, 78–80.

Bloodworth, R. C. (1987). Major problems associated with marijuana abuse. *Psychiatric Medicine, 3* (3), 173–184.

Blue, J. G., & Lombardo, J. A. (1999). Steroids and steroid-like compounds. *Clinics in Sports Medicine, 18,* 667–687.

Blum, D. (1998). Finding strength. *Psychology Today, 31* (3), 32–38, 66–67, 69, 72–73.

Blum, K. (1984). *Handbook of abusable drugs.* New York: Gardner Press, Inc.

Blum, K. (1988). The disease process in alcoholism. *Alcoholism & Addiction, 8* (5), 5–8.

Blum, K., Cull, J. G., Braverman, E. R., & Comings, D. E. (1996). Reward deficiency syndrome. *American Scientist, 84* (2), 132–144.

Blum, K., Noble, E. P., Sheridan, P. J., Montgomery, A., Ritchie, T., Jagadeeswaran, P., Nogami, H., Briggs, A. H., & Cohn, J. B. (1990). Allelic association of human dopamine D_2 receptor gene in alcoholism. *Journal of the American Medical Association, 263* (15), 2055–2060.

Blum, K., & Payne, J. E. (1991). *Alcohol and the addictive brain.* New York: The Free Press.

Blum, K., & Trachtenberg, M. C. (1988). Neurochemistry and alcohol craving. *California Society for the Treatment of Alcoholism and Other Drug Dependencies News, 13* (2), 1–7.

Blume, S. B. (1994). Gender differences in alcohol-related disorders. *Harvard Review of Psychiatry, 2,* 7–14.

Blume, S. B. (1998). Addictive disorders in women. In *Clinical textbook of addictive disorders* (2nd ed.) (Frances, R. J., & Miller, S. I., eds.). New York: Guilford.

Bobo, J. K., Slade, J., & Hoffman, A. L. (1995). Nicotine addiction counseling for chemically dependent patients. *Psychiatric Services, 46,* 945–947.

Bode, C., Maute, G., & Bode, J. C. (1996). Prostaglandin E_2 and prostaglandin F_{2a} biosynthesis in human gastric mucosa: Effect of chronic alcohol misuse. *Gut, 39,* 348–352.

Bodenham, A. R., & Mallick, A. (1996). New dimensions in toxicology: Hyperthermic syndrome following amphetamine derivatives. *Intensive Care Medicine, 22,* 622–624.

Bohn, M. J. (1993). Alcoholism. *Psychiatric Clinics of North America, 16,* 679–692.

Bond, W. S. (1989). Smoking's effects on medications. *American Druggist, 200* (1), 24–25.

Bondesson, J. D., & Saperston, A. R. (1996). Hepatitis. *Emergency Medical Clinics of North America, 14,* 695–718.

Bongar, B. (1997). *Suicide: What therapists need to know.* Seminar presented at the 1997 meeting of the American Psychological Association, Chicago, Illinois.

Booth, M. (1996). *Opium: A history.* New York: St. Martin's Griffin.

Boutotte, J. (1993). T.B. The second time around.... *Nursing 93, 23* (5), 42–49.

Bovard, J. (1997). Time out for justice. *Playboy, 44* (12), 54–55.

Bowden, S. J. (1994). Neuropsychology of alcohol and drug dependence. In *Neuropsychology in clinical practice* (Touyz, S., Byrne, D., & Gilandas, A., eds.). New York: Academic Press.

Bowen, M. (1985). *Family therapy in clinical practice.* Northvale, N. J.: Jason Aronson.

Bower, B. (1991). Pumped up and strung out. *Science News, 140* (2), 30–31.

Bowers, D. H. (2000). HIV: Past, present and future. *Postgraduate Medicine, 107,* 109–113.

Bovard, J. (2001). Wanted: drug czar. *Playboy,48* (3), 50.

Boyd, C. (1992). Self-help sickness? *St. Paul Pioneer Press, 143* (346), 1C, 4C.

Boyd, L. M. (1995). Moved by the spirit. *San Francisco Chronicle, 130* (16), 10.

Bradley, K. A., Boyd-Wickizer, J., Powell, S., & Burman, M. L. (1998). Alcohol screening questionnaires in women. *Journal of the American Medical Association, 280,* 166–171.

Bradshaw, J. (1988a). Compulsivity: The black plague of our day. *Lear's Magazine, 42,* 89–90.

Bradshaw, J. (1988b). *Bradshaw on: The family.* Deerfield Beach, FL: Health Communications, Inc.

Brady, K. T., & Randall, C. L. (1999). Gender differences in substance use disorders. *Psychiatric Clinics of North America, 22,* 241–252.

Brady, T. (1997). Bad hair days: Hair follicle testing offers an alternative to traditional drug tests. *Management Review, 86* (2), 59–62.

Brandt, J., & Butters, N. (1986). The alcoholic Wernicke-Korsakoff syndrome and its relationship to long term alcohol use. In *Neuropsychological assessment of neuropsychiatric disorders.* (Grant, I., & Adams, K. M., eds.). New York: Oxford University Press.

Brecher, E. M. (1972). *Licit and illicit drugs.* Boston: Little, Brown & Co.

Breggin, P. R. (1998). *Talking back to Ritalin.* Monroe, MI: Common Courage Press.

Breggin, P. R. (1999). Letter to the editor. *Journal of the American Medical Association, 281,* 1490–1491.

Breiter, H. C. (1999). *The biology of addiction.* Symposium presented to the Dept. of Psychiatry of The Cambridge Hospital, Boston, MA, March 6.

Brendel, D., West, H., & Hyman, S. E. (1996). Hallucinogens and phencyclidine. In *Source book of substance abuse and addiction* (Friedman, L., Fleming, N. F., Roberts, D. H., & Hyman, S. E., eds.). New York: Williams & Wilkins.

Brennan, D. F., Betzelos, S., Reed, R., & Falk, J. L. (1995). Ethanol elimination rates in an ED population. *American Journal of Emergency Medicine, 13,* 276–280.

Brennan, P. L., & Moos, R. H. (1996). Late-life drinking behavior: The influence of personal characteristics, life context, and treatment. *Alcohol Health & Research World, 20,* 197–204.

Brenner, D. E., Kukull, W. A., van Belle, G., Bowen, J. D., McCormick, W. C., Teri, L., & Larson, E. B. (1993). Relationship between cigarette smoking and Alzheimer's disease in a population-based case-control study. *Neurology, 43,* 293–300.

Brent, D. A., Kupfer, D. J., Bromet, E. J., & Dew, M. A. (1988). The assessment and treatment of patients at risk for suicide. In *American Psychiatric Association annual review (Vol 7).* (Frances, A. J., & Hales, R. E., eds.). Washington, DC: American Psychiatric Association Press, Inc.

Brent, J. A. (1995). Drugs of abuse: An update. *Emergency Medicine, 27* (7), 56–70.

Breo, D. L. (1990). Of MD's and muscles—lessons from two "retired steroid doctors." *Journal of the American Medical Association, 263,* 1697–1705.

Breslau, N., Kilbey, M., & Andreski, P. (1993). Vulnerability to psychopathology in nicotine-dependent smokers: An epidemiologic study of young adults. *American Journal of Psychiatry, 150,* 941–946.

Breslin, J. (1988). Crack. *Playboy, 35* (12), 109–110, 210, 212–213, 215.

Briggs, G. G., Freeman, R. K., & Yaffe, S. J. (1986). *Drugs in pregnancy and lactation* (2nd ed.). Baltimore, MD: Williams and Wilkins.

Brochu, S., Landry, M., Bergeron, J., & Chiocchio, F. (1997). The impact of a treatment process for substance users as a function of their degree of exposure to treatment. *Substance Use & Misuse, 32,* 1993–2011.

Brodsky, A. (1993). The 12 steps are not for everyone—or even for most. *Addiction & Recovery, 13* (2), 21.

Brody, J. (1991). Hepatitis B still spreading. *Minneapolis Star-Tribune, X* (269), 4E.

Brody, J. (1993). To drink or not to drink? For women its benefit to heart vs. cancer risk. *Minneapolis Star-Tribune, XII* (168), 12Ex.

Brooks, J. T., Leung, G., & Shannon, M. (1996). Inhalants. In *Source book of substance abuse and addiction* (Friedman,

L., Fleming, N. F., Roberts, D. H., & Hyman, S. E., eds.). New York: Williams & Wilkins.

Brophy, J. J. (1993). Psychiatric disorders. In *Current medical diagnosis and treatment* (Tierney, L. M., McPhee, S. J., Papadakis, M. A., & Schroeder, S. A., eds.). Norwalk, CT: Appleton & Lange.

Brower, K. J. (1993). Anabolic steroids. *Psychiatric Clinics of North America, 16,* 97– 103.

Brower, K. J., Blow, F. C., Young, J. P., & Hill, E. M. (1991). Symptoms and correlates of anabolic-androgenic steroid dependence. *British Journal of Addiction, 86,* 759– 768.

Brower, K. J., Catlin, D. H., Blow, F. C., Eliopulos, G. A., & Beresford, T. P. (1991). Clinical assessment and urine testing for anabolic-androgenic steroid abuse and dependence. *American Journal of Drug and Alcohol Abuse, 17,* (2), 161–172.

Brown, R. L. (1997). *Stages of change.* Paper presented at symposium: Still getting high—a 30 year perspective on drug abuse. Gundersen-Lutheran Medical Center, La Crosse, Wisconsin, May 2.

Brown, R. L., Leonard, T., Saunders, L. A., Papasoulioutis, O. (1997). A two-item screening test for alcohol and other drug problems. *The Journal of Family Practice, 44,* 151–160.

Brown, R. T., & Braden, N. J. (1987). Hallucinogens. *Pediatric Clinics of North America, 34* (2), 341–347.

Brown, S. (1985). *Treating the alcoholic: A developmental model of recovery.* New York: John Wiley & Sons, Inc.

Brown, S., & Lewis, V. (1995). The alcoholic family: A developmental model of recovery. In *Treating alcoholism* (S. Brown, ed.). New York: Jossey-Bass.

Brown, S. A. (1990). Adolescent alcohol expectancies and risk for alcohol abuse. *Addiction & Recovery, 10* (5/6), 16–19.

Brown, S. A. (1995). Introduction. In *Treating alcoholism* (Brown, S. A., ed.). New York: Jossey-Bass.

Brown, S. A., Creamer, V. A., & Stetson, B. A. (1987). Adolescent alcohol expectancies in relation to personal and parental drinking patterns. *Journal of Abnormal Psychology, 96,* 117–121.

Brown University Digest of Addiction Theory and Application. (1994). Whatever happened to Ice? *13* (3), 6–8.

Brown, V. B., Ridgely, M. S., Pepper, B., Levine, I. S., & Ryglewicz, H. (1989). The dual crisis: Mental illness and substance abuse. *American Psychologist, 44,* 565– 569.

Browning, M., Hoffer, B. J., & Dunwiddie, T. V. (1993). Alcohol, memory and molecules. *Alcohol Health & Research World, 16* (4), 280–284.

Brownlee, S., Roberts, S. V., Cooper, M., Goode, E., Hetter, K., & Wright, A. (1994). Should cigarettes be outlawed? *U.S. News & World Report, 116* (15), 32–36, 38.

Brownson, R. C., Novotny, T. E., & Perry, M. C. (1993). Cigarette smoking and adult leukemia. *Archives of Internal Medicine, 153,* 469–475.

Bruner, A. B., & Fishman, M. (1998). Adolescents and illicit drug use. *Journal of the American Medical Association, 280,* 597–598.

Brunswick, M. (1989). More kids turning to inhalant abuse. *Minneapolis Tribune, VII* (356), 1 A, 6 A.

Brunton, S. A., Henningfield, J. E., & Solberg, L. I. (1994). Smoking cessation: What works best? *Patient Care, 25* (11), 89–115.

Brust, J. C. M., (1993). Other agents: Phencyclidine, marijuana, hallucinogens, inhalants, and anticholinergics. *Neurologic Clinics, 11,* 555–561.

Brust, J. C. M. (1997). Vasculitis owing to substance abuse. *Neurologic Clinics of North American 15,* 945–957.

Brust, J. C. M. (1998). Acute neurologic complications of drug and alcohol abuse. *Neurologic Clinics of North American 16,* 503–519.

Buber, M. (1970). *I and thou.* New York: Charles Scribner's Sons.

Buckley, N. A., Dawson, A. H., Whyte, I. M., & O'Connell, D. L. (1995). Relative toxicity of benzodiazepines in overdose. *British Medical Journal, 310* (6974), 219–222.

Buckley, W. F. (1996). The war on drugs is lost. *National Review, XLVIII* (2), 35–38.

Buckley, W. F. (1997). Save money, cut crime, get real. *Playboy, 44* (1), 129, 192–193.

Budiansky, S., Goode, E. E., & Gest, T. (1994). The cold war experiments. *U.S. News & World Report, 116* (3), 32–38.

Bufe, C. (1988). A. A.: Guilt and god for the gullible. *Utne Reader, 30,* 54–55.

Bufe, C. (1998). *Alcoholics Anonymous: Cult or cure?* (2nd ed.). Tuscon, AZ: See Sharp Press.

Buffenstein, A., Heaster, J., & Ko, P. (1999). Chronic psychotic illness from methamphetamine. *American Journal of Psychiatry, 156,* 662.

Buhrich, N., Weller, A., & Kevans, P. (2000). Misuse of anticholinergic drugs by people with serious mental illness. *Psychiatric Services, 51,* 928–929.

Buia, C., Fulton, G., Park, A., Shannon, E., & Thompson, D. (2000). The lure of ecstasy. *Time, 155* (23), 62–68.

Bukstein, O. G. (1994). Treatment of adolescent alcohol abuse and dependence. *Alcohol Health and Research World, 18,* 297–301.

Bukstein, O. G. (1995). *Adolescent substance abuse.* New York: Wiley Interscience.

Bukstein, O. G., Brent, D. A., Perper, J. A., Moritz, G., Baugher, M., Schweers, J., Roth, C., & Balach, L. (1993). Risk factors for completed suicide among adolescents with a lifetime history of substance abuse: A case controlled study. *Acta Psychiatrica Scandinavica, 88,* 403–408.

Burge, S. K., & Schneider, F. D. (1999). Alcohol-related problems: Recognition and intervention. *American Family Physician, 59,* 361–370.

Burke, J. D., Burke, K. C., & Rae, D. S. (1994). Increased rates of drug abuse and dependence after onset of mood or anxiety disorders in adolescence. *Hospital and Community Psychiatry, 45,* 451–455.

Burkett, G., Yasin, S. Y., Palow, D., LaVoie L., & Martinez, M. (1994). Patterns of cocaine binging: Effects on pregnancy. *American Journal of Obstetrics and Gynecology, 171* (2), 372–379.

Burns, D. M. (1991). Cigarettes and cigarette smoking. *Clinics in Chest Medicine, 12*, 631–642.

Bushnell, T. G., & Justins, D. M. (1993). Chosing the right analgesic. *Drugs, 46*, 394–408.

Butcher, J. N. (1988). Introduction to the special series. *Journal of Consulting and Clinical Psychology, 56*, 171.

Butterworth, R. F. (1995). The role of liver disease in alcohol-induced cognitive defects. *Alcohol Health & Research World, 19*, 123–129.

Byck, R. (1987). Cocaine use and research: Three histories. In *Cocaine: Clinical and behavioral aspects* (Fisher, S., Rashkin, A., & Unlenhuth, E. H., eds.). New York: Oxford University Press.

Byington, D. B. (1997). Applying relational theory to addictions treatment. In *Gender and addictions* (Straussner, S. L. A., & Zelvin, E., eds.). Northvale, NJ: Jason-Aronson.

Byrd, R. C., & Howard, C. R. (1995). Children's passive and prenatal exposure to cigarette smoke. *Pediatric Annals, 24*, 640–645.

Byrne, C. (1989). Cocaine alley. *Minneapolis Star Tribune, VIII* (215), 29a–32a.

Cabaj, R. P. (1997). Gays, lesbians and bisexuals. In *Substance abuse: A comprehensive textbook* (3rd ed.) (Lowinson, J. H., Ruiz, P., Millman, R. B., & Langrod, J. G., eds.). New York: Williams & Wilkins.

Caetano, R., Clark, C. L., & Tam, T. (1998). Alcohol consumption among racial/ethnic minorities: Theory and research. *Alcohol Health & Research World, 22*, 229–242.

Cahill, T. (1998). *The gifts of the Jews.* New York: Doubleday.

Callahan, E. J. (1980). Alternative strategies in the treatment of narcotic addiction: A review. In *The addictive behaviors* (Miller, W. R., ed.). New York: Pergamon Press.

Callahan, J. (1993). Blueprint for an adolescent suicidal crisis. *Psychiatric Annals, 23* (5), 263–270.

Callaway, J. C., & McKenna, D. J. (1998). Neurochemistry of psychodelic drugs. In *Drug abuse handbook* (Karch, S. B., editor-in-chief). New York: CRC Press.

Campbell, G. D. (1994). Overview of community-acquired pneumonia. *Medical Clinics of North America, 78*, 1035–1048.

Campbell, J. L., Thomas, H. M., Gabrielli, W., Lisdow, B. I., & Powell, B. J. (1995). Impact of desipramine or carbamazepine on patient retention in outpatient cocaine treatment: Preliminary findings. *Journal of Addictive Diseases, 13* (4), 191–199.

Campbell, J. W. (1992). Alcoholism. In *Primary care geriatrics* (2nd ed.) (Ham, R. J., & Sloane, P. D., eds.) Boston: Mosby.

Cantor, N. F. (2001). *In the wake of the plague.* New York: The Free Press.

Cardoni, A. A. (1990). Focus on *adinazolam:* a benzodiazepine with antidepressant activity. *Hospital Formulary, 25*, 155–158.

Carey, K. B. (1989). Emerging treatment guidelines for mentally ill chemical abusers. *Hospital and Community Psychiatry, 40*, 341–342, 349.

Carey, K. B., Cocco, K. M., & Simons, J. S. (1996). Concurrent validity of clinicians' ratings of substance abuse among psychiatric outpatients. *Psychiatric Services, 47*, 842–847.

Carlson, J. L., Strom, B. L., Morse, L., West, S. L., Soper, K. A., Stolley, P. D., & Jones, J. K. (1987). The relative gastrointestinal toxicity of the nonsteroidal anti-inflammatory drugs. *Archives of Internal Medicine, 147*, 1054–1059.

Carroll, K. M. (1997). New methods of treatment efficacy research. *Alcohol Health & Research World, 21*, 352–359.

Carroll, K. M., & Rounsaville, B. J. (1992). Contrast of treatment-seeking and untreated cocaine abusers. *Archives of General Psychiatry, 49*, 464–471.

Carvey, P. M. (1998). *Drug action in the central nervous system.* New York: Oxford University Press.

Castro, F. G., Barrington, E. H., Walton, M. A., & Rawson, R. A. (2000). Cocaine and methamphetamine: Differential addiction rates. *Psychology of Addictive Behaviors, 14*, 390–396.

Catanzarite, V. A., & Stein, D. A. (1995). "Crystal" and pregnancy methamphetamine-associated maternal deaths. *The Western Journal of Medicine, 162*, 545–547.

Caton, C. L. M., Gralnick, A., Bender, S., & Simon, R. (1989). Young chronic patients and substance abuse. *Hospitial and Community Psychiatry, 40*, 1037–1040.

Cattarello, A. M., Clayton, R. R., & Leukefeld, C. G. (1995). Adolescent alcohol and drug abuse. In *Review of psychiatry* (Vol 14) (Oldham, J. M., & Riba, M. B., eds.). Washington, DC: American Psychiatric Press, Inc.

Cavaliere, F. (1995). Substance abuse in the deaf community. *APA Monitor, 26* (10), 49.

Centers for Disease Control. (1990). Lead poisoning associated with intravenous methamphetamine use—Oregon, 1988. *Journal of the American Medical Association, 263*, 797.

Cetaruk, E. W., Dart, E. C., Horowitz, R. S., & Huribut, K. M. (1996). Extended-release acetaminophen overdose. *Journal of the American Medical Association, 275*, 686.

Chan, P., Chen, J. H., Lee, M. H., & Deng, J. F. (1994). Fatal and nonfatal methamphetamine intoxication in the intensive care unit. *Journal of Toxicology: Clinical Toxicology, 32*, 147–156.

Chandramouli, B. V., & Kotler, M. N. (1998). A trial fibulation: Drug therapies for ventricular rate control and restoration of sinus rhythm. *Geriatrics, 53* (6), 46–60.

Chang, G. (2001). Gender and addictions. Symposium presented to the Dept. of Psychiatry of The Cambridge Hospital, Boston, MA, March 2, 2001.

Chappel, J. N., & DuPont, R. L. (1999). Twelve-step and mutual help programs for addictive disorders. *Psychiatric Clinics of North America, 22*, 425–446.

Charness, M. E., Simon, R. P., & Greenberg, D. A. (1989). Ethanol and the nervous system. *The New England Journal of Medicine, 321* (7), 442–454.

Chasnoff, I. J. (1988). Drug use in pregnancy: Parameters of risk. *Pediatric Clinics of North America, 35* (6), 1403–1412.

Chasnoff, I. J. (1991a). Drugs, alcohol, pregnancy, and the neonate. *Journal of the American Medical Association, 266*, 1567–1568.

Chasnoff, I. J. (1991b). Cocaine and pregnancy: Clinical and methadologic issues. *Clinics in Perinatology, 18,* 113–123.

Chasnoff, I. J., Anson, A., Hatcher, R., Stenson, H., Iaukea, K., & Randolph, L. A. (1998). Prenatal exposure to cocaine and other drugs. *Annals of the New York Academy of Sciences, 846,* 314–328.

Chasnoff, I. J., & Schnoll, S. H. (1987). Consequences of cocaine and other drug use in pregnancy. In *Cocaine: A clinician's handbook* (Washton, A. M., & Gold, M. S., eds.). New York: The Guilford Press.

Chassin, L., Curran, P. J., Hussong, A. M., & Colder, C. R. (1996). The relation of parent alcoholism to adolescent substance use: A longitudinal follow-up study. *Journal of Abnormal Psychology, 105,* 70–80.

Chassin, L., & DeLucia, C. (1996). Drinking during adolescence. *Alcohol Health & Research World, 20,* 175–180.

Chatlos, J. C. (1996). Recent developments and a developmental approach to substance abuse in adolescents. *Child and Adolescent Psychiatric Clinics of North America, 5,* 1–27.

Cherny, N. I. (1996). Opioid analgesics: Comparative features and prescribing guidelines. *Drugs, 51,* 713–737.

Cherny, N. I., & Foley, K. M. (1996). Nonopioid and opioid analgesic pharmacology of cancer pain. *Hematology/Oncology Clinics of North America, 10,* 79–102.

Cherubin, C. E., & Sapira, J. D. (1993). The medical complications of drug addiction and the medical assessment of the intravenous drug user: 25 years later. *Annals of Internal Medicine, 119,* 1017–1028.

Chiauzzi, E. (1990). Breaking the patterns that lead to relapse. *Psychology Today, 23* (12), 18–19.

Chiauzzi, E. (1991). *Preventing relapse in the addictions.* New York: Pergamon.

Chick, J. (1993). Brief interventions for alcohol misuse. *British Medical Journal, 307,* 1374.

Chilcoat, H. D., & Breslau, N. (1998). Posttraumatic stress disorder and drug misuse. *Archives of General Psychiatry, 55,* 913–917.

Chin, R. L., Sporer, K. A., Cullison, B., Dyer, J. E., & Wu, T. D. (1998). Clinical course of gamma hydroxybutyrate overdose. *Annals of Emergency Medicine, 31,* 716–722.

Chopra, D. (1997). *Overcoming addictions.* New York: Three Rivers Press.

Christensen, W. G., Manson, J. E., Seddon, J. M., Glynn, R. J., Buring, J. E., Rosner, B., & Hennekens, C. H. (1992). A prospective study of cigeratte smoking and risk of cataract in men. *Journal of the American Medical Association, 268,* 989–993.

Chuck, R. S., Williams, J. M., Goldberg, M. A., & Lubniewski, A. J. (1996). Recurrent corneal ulcerations associated with smokable methamphetamine abuse. *American Journal of Ophthalmology, 121,* 571–573.

Chung, T., Colby, S. M., Barnett, N. P., Rohsenow, D. J., Spirto, A., & Monti, P. M. (2000). Screening adolescents for problem drinking: Performance of brief screens against DSM-IV alcohol diagnoses. *Journal of Studies on Alcohol, 61,* 579–587.

Ciancio, S. G., & Bourgault, P. C. (1989). *Clinical pharmacology for dental professionals* (3rd ed.). Chicago: Year Book Medical Publishers, Inc.

Ciraulo, D. A., Creelman, W., Shader, R. I., & O'Sullivan, R. O. (1995). Antidepressants. In *Drug interactions in psychiatry* (2nd ed.) (Ciraulo, D. A., Shader, R. I., Greenblatt, D. J., & Creelman, W., eds.). Baltimore: Williams & Wilkins.

Ciraulo, D. A., Sarid-Segal, O., Knapp, C., Ciraulo, A. M., Greenblatt, D. J., & Shader, R. I. (1996). Liability to alprazolam abuse in daughters of alcoholics. *American Journal of Psychiatry, 153,* 956–958.

Ciraulo, D. A., Shader, R. I., Ciraulo, A., Greenblatt, D. J., & von Moltke, L. L. (1994a). Alcoholism and its treatment. In *Manual of psychiatric therapeutics* (2nd ed.) (Shader, R. I., ed.). Boston: Little, Brown & Co.

Ciraulo, D. A., Shader, R. I., Ciraulo, A., Greenblatt, D. J., & von Moltke, L. L. (1994b). Treatment of alcohol withdrawal. In *Manual of psychiatric therapeutics* (2nd ed.) (Shader, R. I., ed.). Boston: Little, Brown & Co.

Ciraulo, D. A., Shader, R. I., Greenblatt, D. J., & Barnhill, J. G. (1995). Basic concepts. In *Drug interactions in psychiatry* (2nd ed.) (Ciraulo, D. A., Shader, R. I., Greenblatt, D. J., & Creelman, W., eds.). Baltimore: Williams & Wilkins.

Clark, C. M. (1995). Alcoholics Anonymous. *The Addictions Newsletter, 2* (3), 9, 22.

Clark, R. E. (1994). Family costs associated with severe mental illness and substance abuse. *Hospital and Community Psychiatry, 45,* 808–813.

Clark, W. G., Bratler, D. C., & Johnson, A. R. (1991). *Goth's medical pharmacology* (13th ed.). Boston: Mosby.

Clark, W. R. (1995). *At war within.* New York: Oxford.

Claunch, L. (1994). Intervention can be used as a tool—or as a weapon against clients. *The Addiction Letter, 10* (4), 1–2.

Climko, R. P., Roehrich, H., Sweeney, D. R., & Al-Razi, J. (1987). Ecstacy: A review of MDMA and MDA. *International Journal of Psychiatry in Medicine, 16* (4), 359–372.

Cloninger, C. R., Bohman, M., & Sigvardsson, S. (1981). Inheritance of alcohol abuse: Cross fostering analysis of adopted men. *Archives of General Psychiatry, 38,* 861–868.

Cloninger, C. R., Sigvardsson, S. Bohman, M. (1996). Type I and Type II alcoholism: An update. *Alcohol Health & Research World, 20* (1), 18–23.

Cloud, J., Barnes, E., Graft, J. L., Reaves, J. A., & Shannon, E. (2000). It's all the rave. *Time, 155* (10), 64–66.

Cocaine link to heart attack bolstered. (2001). *Science News, 159,* 24.

Cohen, D. A., Richardson, J., & LaBree, L. (1994). Parenting behaviors and the onset of smoking and alcohol use: A longitudinal study. *Pediatrics, 94,* 368–375.

Cohen, G., Fleming, N. S., Glatter, K. A., Haghigi, D. B., Halberstadt, J., McHigh, K. M., & Woolf, A. (1996). Epidemiology of substance use. In *Source book of substance abuse and addiction* (Friedman, L., Fleming, N. F., Roberts, D. H., & Hyman, S. E., eds.). New York: Williams & Wilkins.

Cohen, J., & Levy, S. J. (1992). *The mentally ill chemical abuser: Whose client?* New York: Lexington Books.

Cohen, L. S. (1989). Psychotropic drug use in pregnancy. *Hospital and Community Psychiatry, 40* (6), 566–567.

Cohen, M. (2000). *Counseling addicted women.* Thousand Oaks, CA: Sage.

Cohen, M. S. (1995). HIV and sexually transmitted diseases. *Postgraduate Medicine, 98* (3), 52–64.

Cohen, R. S. (1998). *The love drug.* New York: Haworth Medical Press.

Cohen, S. (1977). Inhalant abuse: An overview of the problem. In *Review of inhalants: Euphoria to dysfunction* (Sharp, C. W., & Brehm, M. L., eds.). Washington, DC: U.S. Government Printing Office.

Cohen, S. I. (1995). Overdiagnosis of schizophrenia: Role of alcohol and drug misuse. *The Lancet, 346,* 1541–1542.

Cohen, S., Lichtenstein, E., Prochaska, J. O., Rossi, J. S., Gritz, E. R., Carr, C. R., Orleans, C.T., Schoenbach, V. J., Biener, L., Abrams, D., DiClemente, C., Curry, S., Marlatt, G.A., Cummings, K. M., Emont, S. L., Giovino, G., & Ossip-Klein, D. (1989). Debunking myths about self-quitting. *American Psychologist, 44,* 1355–1365.

Cohn, J. B., Wilcox, C. S., Bowden, C. L., Fisher, J. G., & Rodos, J. J. (1992). Double-blind clorazepate in anxious outpatients with and without depressive symptoms. *Psychopathology, 25* (Supplement 1), 10–21.

Coker, M. (1997). Overcoming sexism in A.A.: How women cope. In *Gender and addictions* (Straussner, S.L.A., & Zelvin, E., eds.). Northvale, NJ: Jason-Aronson.

Colburn, N., Meyer, R. D., Wrigley, M., & Bradley, E. L. (1993). Should motorcycles be operated within the legal alcohol limits for automobiles? *The Journal of Trauma, 34* (1), 183–186.

Cole, J. O., & Kando, J. C. (1993). Adverse behavioral events reported in patients taking alprazolam and other benzodiazepines. *Journal of Clinical Psychiatry, 54* (10) (Supplement), 49–61.

Cole, J. O., & Younkers, K. A. (1995). Nonbenzodiazepine anxiolytics. In *Textbook of psychopharmacology* (Schatzberg, A. F., & Nemeroff, C. B., eds.). Washington, DC: American Psychiatric Association Press, Inc.

Coleman, D. E., & Baselt, R. C. (1997). Efficacy of two commercial products for altering urine drug test results. *Journal of Toxicology: Clinical Toxicology, 35* (6), 637–642.

Coleman, E. (1988). Chemical dependency and intimacy dysfunction: Inextricably bound. In *Chemical dependency and intimacy dysfunction* (Coleman, E., ed.). New York: The Haworth Press.

Coleman, P. (1989). Letter to the editor. *Journal of the American Medical Association, 261* (13), 1879–1880.

Collaborative Group on AIDS Incubation and HIV Survival. (2000). Time from HIV-1 seroconversion to AIDS and death before widespread use of highly-active antiretroviral therapy: A collaborative re-analysis. *The Lancet, 355,* 1131–1137.

Collette, L. (1988). Step by step: A skeptic's encounter. *Utne Reader, 30,* 69–76.

Collette, L. (1990). After the anger, what then? *Networker, 14* (1), 22–31.

Collins, J. J., & Allison, M. (1983). Legal coercion and retention in drug abuse treatment. *Hospital and Community Psychiatry, 34,* 1145–1150.

Comerci, G. D., Fuller, P., & Morrison, S. F. (1997). Cigarettes, drugs, alcohol & teens. *Patient Care, 31* (4), 57–83.

Committee on Substance Abuse. (1995). Alcohol use and abuse: A pediatric concern. *Pediatrics, 95,* 439–442.

Committee on Substance Abuse and Committee on Children with Disabilities. (1993). Fetal alcohol syndrome and fetal alcohol effects. *Pediatrics, 91,* 1004–1006.

Community Anti-Drug Coalitions of America. (1997). *The meth challenge: Threatening communities coast to coast.* Interactive live national teleconference, June 19.

Concar, D. (1997). Deadly combination. *New Scientist, 155,* 2090–2091.

Cone, E. J. (1993). Saliva testing for drugs of abuse. In *Saliva as a diagnostic fluid.* (Malamud, D., & Tabak, L., eds.). New York: New York Academy of Sciences.

Connors, G. J., Carroll, K. M., DiClemente, C. C., Longabaugh, R., & Donovan, D. M. (1997). The therapeutic alliance and its relationship to alcoholism treatment participation and outcome. *Journal of Consulting and Clinical Psychology, 65,* 588–598.

Cook, A. (1995). Ecstasy (MDMA): Alerting users to the dangers. *Nursing Times, 91,* (16), 32–33.

Coomber, R. (1997). The adulteration of illicit drugs with dangerous substitutes—the discovery of a "myth." *Contemporary Drug Problems, 24* (2), 239–271.

Coombs, R. H. (1997). *Drug-impaired professionals.* Cambridge, MA: Harvard University Press.

Cooney, N. L., Zweben, A., & Fleming, M. F. (1995). Screening for alcohol problems and at-risk drinking in health-care settings. In *Handbook of alcoholism treatment approaches* (2nd ed.). (Hester, R. K., & Miller, W. R., eds.). New York: Allyn & Bacon.

Cooper, J. R., Bloom, F. E., & Roth, R. H. (1986). *The biochemical basis of neuropharmacology* (5th ed.). New York: Oxford University Press.

Cooper, J. R., Bloom, F. E., & Roth, R. H. (1996). *The biochemical basis of neuropharmacology* (7th ed.). New York: Oxford University Press.

Cordero, J. F. (1990). Effect of environmental agents on pregnancy outcomes: Disturbances of prenatal growth and development. *Medical Clinics of North America, 72* (2), 279–290.

Cornell, W. F. (1996). Capitalism in the consulting room. *Readings, 11* (1), 12–17.

Cornish, J. W., McNicholas, L. F., & O'Brien, C. P. (1995). Treatment of substance-related disorders. In *Textbook of psychopharmacology* (Schatzberg, A. F., & Nemeroff, C. B., eds.). Washington, DC: American Psychiatric Association.

Cornwell, E. E., Blezberg, H., Velmahos, G., Chan, L. S., Demetriades, D., Stewart, B. M., Oder, D. B., Kahuku, D., Chan, D., Asensio, J. A., & Berne, T. V. (1998). The prevalence and effect of alcohol and drug abuse on cohort-matched critically injured patients. *The American Surgeon, 64*, 461–465.

Corrigan, B. (1996). Anabolic steroids and the mind. *Medical Journal of Australia, 165*, 222–226.

Corwin, J. (1994). Outlook. *U.S. News & World Report, 116*, (23), 15–16.

Cotton, P. (1993). Low-tar cigarettes come under fire. *Journal of the American Medical Association, 270*, 1399.

Cotton, P. (1994). Smoking cigarettes may do developing fetus more harm than ingesting cocaine, some experts say. *Journal of the American Medical Association, 271*, 576–577.

Coughey, K., Feighan, K., Cheney, R., & Klein, G. (1998). Retention in an aftercare program for recovering women. *Substance Use & Misuse 33*, 917–932.

Council on Scientific Affairs. (1990a). The worldwide smoking epidemic. *Journal of the American Medical Association, 263*, 3312–3318.

Council on Scientific Affairs. (1990b). Medical and nonmedical uses of anabolicandrogenic steroids. *Journal of the American Medical Association, 264*, 2923–2927.

Council on Scientific Affairs. (1996). Alcoholism in the elderly. *Journal of the American Medical Association, 275*, 797–801.

Cousins, N. (1989). *Head first: The biology of hope.* New York: E. P. Dutton.

Covey, L. W., Sullivan, M. A., Johnston, A., Glassman, A. H., Robinson, M. D., & Adams, D. P. (2000). Advances in non-nicotine pharmacotherapy for smoking cessation. *Drugs, 59*, 17–31.

Cowen, R. (1990). Alcoholism treatment under scrutiny. *Science News, 137*, 254.

Cowley, G. (1992). Halcion takes another hit. *Newsweek, CXIX* (7), 58.

Cox, B. J., & Taylor, S. (1999). Anxiety disorders. In *Oxford textbook of psychopathology.* (Million, T., Blaney, P. H., & Davis, R. D., eds.). New York: Oxford University Press.

Crabbe, J. C., & Goldman, D. (1993). Alcoholism. *Alcohol Health & Research World, 16* (4), 297–303.

Craft, N. (1994). WHO denounces health benefits of alcohol. *British Medical Journal, 309*, 1249.

Craig, T. J. (1996). Drugs to be used with caution in patients with asthma. *American Family Physician, 54*, 947–953.

Cramer, J. A., & Rosenheck, R. (1998). Compliance with medication regimens for mental and physical disorders. *Psychiatric Services, 49*, 196–201.

Creighton, F. J., Black, D. L., & Hyde, C. E. (1991). "Ecstacy" psychosis and flashbacks. *British Journal of Psychiatry, 159*, 713–715.

Crowley, T. J. (1988). *Substance abuse treatment and policy: Contributions of behavioral pharmacology.* Paper presented at the 1988 meeting of the American Psychological Association, Atlanta, Georgia.

Crowley, T. J. (1995). Phencyclidine (or phencyclidine-like) related disorders. In *Comprehensive textbook of psychiatry* (6th ed.) (Kaplan, H. I., & Sadock, B. J., eds.). Baltimore: Williams & Wilkins.

Crowley, T. J. (2000). Inhalant-related disorders. In *Comprehensive textbook of psychiatry* (7th ed.). (Kaplan, H. I., & Sadock, B. J., eds.). Baltimore: Lippincott, Williams & Wilkins.

Cuffel, B. J., Heithoff, K. A., & Lawson, W. (1993). Correlates of patterns of substance abuse among patients with schizophrenia. *Hospital and Community Psychiatry, 44*, 247–251.

Cummings, C., Gordon, J. R., & Marlatt, G. A. (1980). Relapse: Prevention and prediction. In *The addictive behaviors* (Miller, W. R., ed.). New York: Pergamon Press.

Cumsille, P. E., Sayer, A. G., & Graham, J. W. (2000). Perceived exposure to peer and adult drinking as predictors of growth in positive alcohol expectancies during adolescence. *Journal of Consulting & Clinical Psychology, 68*, 531–536.

Cunha, B. A. (1998). TB pneumonia. *Emergency Medicine, 30* (6), 102, 107, 111.

Cunnien, A. J. (1988). Psychiatric and medical syndromes associated with deception. In *Clinical assessment of malingering and deception* (Rogers, R., ed.). New York: Guilford.

Cunningham, J. A., Sobell, L. C., Gavin, D. R., Sobell, M. B., & Breslin, F. C. (1997). Assessing motivation for change: Preliminary development and evaluation of a scale measuring the benefits and costs of changing alcohol or drug use. *Psychology of Addictive Behaviors, 11*, 107–114.

Cupp, M. J. (1999). Herbal remedies: Adverse effects and drug interactions. *American Family Physician, 59*, 1239–1244.

Curley, B. (1995). Drugs demand distinction between rights and responsibilities. *Alcoholism & Drug Abuse Week, 7* (19), 5.

Curran, P. J., Stice, E., & Chassin, L. (1997). The relation between adolescent alcohol use and peer alcohol use: A longitudinal random coefficients model. *Journal of Consulting and Clinical Psychology, 65*, 130–140.

Cyr, M. G., & Moulton, A. W. (1993). The physician's role in prevention, detection, and treatment of alcohol abuse in women. *Psychiatric Annals, 23*, 454–462.

Czeizel, A. E., Kodaj, I., & Lenz, W. (1994). Smoking during pregnancy and congenital limb deficiency. *British Medical Journal, 308*, 1473–1476.

Daghestani, A. N., & Schnoll, S. H. (1994). Phencyclidine. In *Textbook of substance abuse treatment* (Galanter, M., & Kleber, H. D., eds.). Washington, DC: American Psychiatric Press, Inc.

Dance safe. (2001). *Playboy, 48* (1), 157.

D'Andrea, L. M., Fisher, G. L., & Harrison, T. C. (1994). Cluster analysis of adult children of alcoholics. *International Journal of the Addictions, 29*, 565–582.

Dangerous habits. (1998). *The Lancet, 352* (9140), 1565.

Danjou, P., Paty, I., Fruncillo, R., Worthington, P., Unruh, M., Cevallos, W., & Martin, P. (1999). A comparison of the residual effects of zaleplon and zolpidem following administration 5 to 2 h before awakening. *British Journal of Clinical Pharmacology, 48* (3), 367–374.

Darton, L. A., & Dilts, S. L. (1998). Opioids. In *Clinical textbook of addictive disorders* (2nd ed.) (Frances, R. J., & Miller, S. I., eds.). New York: Guilford.

Davidson, R. (1998). The transtheoretical model. In *Treating addictive behaviors* (2nd ed.) (Miller, W. R., & Heather, N., eds.). New York: Plenum.

Davis, J. M., & Bresnahan, D. B. (1987). Psychopharmacology in clinical psychiatry. In *American Psychiatric Association annual review* (Vol. 6). Washington, DC: American Psychiatric Association Press, Inc.

Davison, K. P., Pennebaker, J. W., & Dickerson, S. S. (2000). Who talks? *American Psychologist, 55,* 205–217.

Day, N. L., & Richardson, G. A. (1991). Prenatal marijuana use: Epidemiology, methodologic issues, and infant outcome. *Clinics in Perinatology, 18,* 77–91.

Day, N. L., & Richardson, G. A. (1994). Comparative tetragenicity of alcohol and other drugs. *Alcohol Health & Research World, 18,* 42–48.

DEA. (1995). *Press release: 21 June, 1995.* Washington, DC: Drug Enforcement Administration.

DeAngelis, T. (1994). Perceptions influence student drinking. *APA Monitor, 25* (12), 35.

DeBellis, M. D., Clark, D. B., Beers, S. R., Soloff, P. H., Boring, A. M., Hall, J., Kersh, A., & Keshavan, M. S. (2000). Hippocampal volume in adolescent-onset alcohol use disorders. *American Journal of Psychiatry, 157,* 737–744.

Decker, S., Fins, J., & Frances, R. (1987). Cocaine and chest pain. *Hospital & Community Psychiatry, 38,* 464–466.

Decker, S., & Reis, R. K. (1993). Differential diagnosis and psychopharmacology of dual disorders. *Psychiatric Clinics of North America, 16,* 703–718.

DeJong, W. (1994). Relapse prevention: An emerging technology for promoting long-term abstinence. *International Journal of the Addictions, 29,* 681–785.

Del Boca, F. K., & Hesselbrock, M. N. (1996). Gender and alcoholic subtypes. *Alcohol Health & Research World, 20,* 56–62.

DeLeon, G. (1989). Psychopathology and substance abuse: What is being learned from research in therapeutic communities. *Journal of Psychoactive Drugs, 21* (2), 177–188.

DeLeon, G. (1994). Therapeutic communities. In *Textbook of substance abuse treatment* (Galanter, M., & Kleber, H. D. eds.). Washington, DC: American Psychiatric Press, Inc.

DeLeon, G., Melnick, G., & Kressel, D. (1997). Motivation and readiness for therapeutic community treatment among cocaine and other drug abusers. *American Journal of Drug and Alcohol Abuse, 23,* 169–190.

DeMaria, P. A., & Weinstein, S. P. (1995). Methadone maintenance treatment. *Postgraduate Medicine, 97* (3), 83–92.

Demers-Gendreau, C. (1998). *Diagnosing and treating addictions in college students.* Symposium presented to the Dept. of Psychiatry of The Cambridge Hospital, Boston, MA, March 6.

DeMillo, A. (2000). "Moderate Drinking" author pleads guilty. *Seattle Times,* June 30.

Department of Health and Human Services (1997). *Preliminary Results from the 1996 National Household Survey on Drug Abuse.* Rockville, MD: National Clearinghouse for Alcohol and Drug Information.

Derlet, R. W. (1989). Cocaine intoxication. *Postgraduate Medicine, 86* (5), 245–248, 253.

Derlet, R. W., & Heischober, B. (1990). Methamphetamine: stumulant of the 1990's? *The Western Journal of Medicine, 153,* 625–629.

Derlet, R. W., & Horowitz, B. Z. (1995). Cardiotoxic drugs. *Emergency Medicine Clinics of North American, 13,* 771–791.

Dewit, D. J., Adlaf, E. M., Offord, D. R., Obgorne, A. C. (2000). Age at first alcohol use: A risk factor for the development of alcohol disorders. *American Journal of Psychiatry, 157,* 745–750.

Dewitt, D. E., & Paauw, D. S. (1996). Endocarditis in injection drug users. *American Family Physician, 53,* 2045–2049.

DiBisceglie, A. M. (1995). Chronic hepatitis B. *Postgraduate Medicine, 98,* 99–103.

DiBisceglie, A. M., & Bacon, B. R. (1999). The unmet challenges of hepatitis C. *Scientific American, 281* (4), 80–85.

Dickinson, A. (2000). Smoke screen. *Time, 155* (11), 92.

DiClemente, C. C. (1993). Alcoholics Anonymous and the structure of change. In *Research on alcoholics anonymous* (McCrady, B. S., & Miller, W. R., eds.). New Brunswick, NJ: Rutgers Center of Alcohol Studies.

DiClemente, C. C., & Prochaska, J. O. (1998). Toward a comprehensive, transtheoretical model of change. In *Treating addictive behaviors* (2nd ed.) (Miller, W. R., & Heather, N., eds.). New York: Plenum.

DiClemente, C. C., Bellino, L. E., & Neavins, T. M. (1999). Motivation for change and alcoholism treatment. *Alcohol Health & Research World, 23* (2), 86–92.

Dieperink, E., Willenbring, M., & Ho, S. B. (2000). Neuropsychiatric symptoms associated with hepatitis C and interferon alpha: A review. *American Journal of Psychiatry, 157,* 867–876.

Dietch, J. (1983). The nature and extent of benzodiazepine abuse: An overview of recent literature. *Hospital and Community Psychiatry, 34,* 1139–1144.

DiFranza, J. R., & Tye, J. B. (1990). Who profits from tobacco sales to children? *Journal of the American Medical Association, 263,* 2784–2787.

DiGregorio, G. J. (1990). Cocaine update: Abuse and therapy. *American Family Physician, 41* (1), 247–251.

Diller, L. H. (1998). *Running on Ritalin.* New York: Bantam Books.

Dimeff, L. A., & Marlatt, G. A. (1995). Relapse prevention. In *Handbook of alcoholism treatment approaches* (2nd ed.) (Hester, R. K., & Miller, W. R., eds.). New York: Allyn & Bacon.

Dionne, R. A., & Gordon, S. M. (1994). Nonsteroidal antiinflammatory drugs for acute pain control. *Dental Clinics of North America, 38,* 645–667.

Director, L. (1995). Dual diagnosis: outpatient treatment of substance abusers with coexisting psychiatric disorders. In

Psychotherapy and substance abuse (Washton, A. M., ed.). New York: Guilford.

Discover. (1994). Gallic hearts. *15,* (9), 14–15.

Dishion, T. J., McCord, J., & Poulin, F. (1999). When interventions harm. *American Psychologist, 54,* 755–764.

Disney, E. R., Elkins, I. J., McGue, M., & Iacono, W. G. (1999). Effects of ADHD, conduct disorder, and gender on substance use and abuse in adolescence. *American Journal of Psychiatry, 156,* 1515–1521.

Dixit, A. R., & Crum, R. M. (2000). Prospective study of depression and risk of heavy alcohol use in women. *American Journal of Psychiatry, 157,* 751–758.

Djordjevic, M. V., Hoffmann, D., & Hoffmann, I. (1997). Nicotine regulates smoking patterns. *Preventive Medicine, 26,* 435–440.

Dobkin, P. L., Tremblay, R. E., & Sacchitelle, C. (1997). Predicting boys' early-onset substance abuse from father's alcoholism, son's disruptiveness, and mother's parenting behavior. *Journal of Consulting and Clinical Psychology, 65,* 86–92.

Dobs, A. S. (1999). Is there a role for androgenic anabolic steroids in medical practice? *Journal of the American Medical Association, 281,* 1326–1327.

Doghramji, K. (1989). Sleep disorders: A selective update. *Hospital and Community Psychiatry, 40,* 29–40.

Dole, V. P. (1988). Implications of methadone maintenance for theories of narcotic addiction. *Journal of the American Medical Association, 260,* 3025–3029.

Dole, V. P. (1989). Letter to the editor. *Journal of the American Medical Association, 261* (13), 1880.

Dole, V. P. (1995). On federal regulation of methadone treatment. *Journal of the American Medical Association, 274* (16), 1307.

Dole, V. P., & Nyswander, M. A. (1965). Medical treatment for diacetylmorphine (heroin) addiction. *Journal of the American Medical Association, 193,* 645–656.

Domenico, D., & Windle, M. (1993). Intrapersonal and interpersonal functioning among middle-aged female adult children of alcoholics. *Journal of Consulting and Clinical Psychology, 61,* 659–666.

D'Onofrio, G., Rathlev, N. K., Ulrich, A. S., Fish, S. S., & Freedland, E. S. (1999). Lorazepam for the prevention of recurrent seizures related to alcohol. *The New England Journal of Medicine, 340,* 915–919.

Donovan, D. M. (1992). The assessment process in addictive behaviors. *The Behavior Therapist, 15* (1), 18.

Doria, J. (1990). Alcohol, women and heart disease. *Alcohol Health & Research World, 14* (4), 349–351.

Dorsman, J. (1996). Improving alcoholism treatment: an overview. *Behavioral Health Management, 16* (1), 26–29.

Dowell, W. (2000). Addressing Africa's agony. *Time, 155* (3), 36.

Downing, C. (1990). The wounded healers. *Addiction & Recovery, 10* (3), 21–24.

Draganov, P., Durrence, H., Cox, C., & Reuben, A. (2000). Alcohol-acetaminophen syndrome. *Postgraduate Medicine, 107,* 189–195.

Drake, R. E., McHugo, G. J., Clark, R. E., Teague, G. B., Xie, H., Miles, K., & Ackerson, T. H. (1998). Assertive community treatment for patients with co-occurring severe mental illness and substance use disorder: A clinical trial. *American Journal of Orthopsychiatry, 68,* 201–215.

Drake, R. E., Osher, F. C., & Wallach, M. A. (1989). Alcohol use and abuse in schizophrenia. *The Journal of Nervous and Mental Disease, 177,* 408–414.

Drake, R. E., & Wallach, M. A. (1993). Moderate drinking among people with severe mental illness. *Hospital and Community Psychiatry, 44,* 780–781.

Dreher, M. C., Nugent, K., & Hudgins, R. (1994). Prenatal marijuana exposure and neonatal outcomes in Jamaica: An ethnographic study. *Pediatrics, 93,* 254–260.

DuBois, R. N., Sheng, H., Shao, J., Williams, C., & Beauchamp, R. D. (1998). Inhibition of intestinal tumorigenesis via selective inhibition of COX-2. In *Selective COX-2 inhibitors* (Vane, J., & Botting, J., eds.). Hingham, MA: Kluwer Academic Publishers.

Duke, S. B. (1996). The war on drugs is lost. *National Review, XLVIII* (2), 47–48.

Dunlop, J., Manghelli, D., & Tolson, R. (1989). Senior alcohol and drug coalition statement of treatment philosophy for the elderly. *Professional Counselor, 4* (2), 39–42.

Dunn, G. E., Paolo, A. M., Ryan, J. J., & Van Fleet, J. (1993). Dissociative symptoms in a substance abuse population. *American Journal of Psychiatry, 150,* 1043–1047.

Dunne, F. J. (1994). Misuse of alcohol or drugs by elderly people. *British Medical Journal, 308,* 608–609.

Dupont, R. L., & Dupont, C. M. (1998). Sedative/hypnotics and benzodiazepines. In *Clinical textbook of addictive disorders* (2nd ed.) (Frances, R. J., & Miller, S. I., eds.). New York: Guilford.

DuRant, R. H., Rickert, V. I., Ashworth, C. S., Newman, C., & Slavens, G. (1993). Use of multiple drugs among adolescents who use anabolic steroids. *The New England Journal of Medicine, 328,* 922–926.

Durell, J., Lechtenberg, B., Corse, S., & Frances, R. J. (1993). Intensive case management of persons with chronic mental illness who abuse substances. *Hospital and Community Psychiatry, 44,* 415–416, 428.

Duvour, M. C. (1999). What is moderate drinking. *Alcohol Health & Research World, 23* (1), 5–14.

Dwyer, J. (2000). Casualty in the war on drugs. *Playboy, 47* (10), 78–80, 175–176.

Dyehouse, J. M., & Sommers, M. S. (1998). Brief intervention after alcohol-related injuries. *Nursing Clinics of North America, 33,* 93–104.

Dyer, W. W. (1989). *You'll see it when you believe it.* New York: William Morrow and Company, Inc.

Dygert, S. L., & Minelli, M. J. (1993). Heroin abuse progression chart. *Addiction & Recovery, 13* (1), 27–31.

Eccles, J. S., Midgley, C., Wigfield, A., Buchanan, C. M., Reuman, D., Flanagan, C., & MacIver, D. (1993). Development during adolescence. *American Psychologist, 48,* 90–101.

Economic analysis aids alcohol research. (2000). *Alcohol Research & Health, 24*, 62–71

Economist, The. (1989). Ice overdose. *313* (7631). 29–31.

Economist, The. (1993). Market update. *329* (7830), 68.

Economist, The. (1996). Better than well: Society's moral confusion over drugs is neatly illustrated by its differing reactions to Prozac and ecstacy. *339* (7960), 87–89.

Edelson, E. (1993). Fear of blood. *Popular Science, 242* (6), 108–111, 122.

Edmeades, B. (1987). Alcoholics Anonymous celebrates its 50th year. In *Drugs, society and behavior* (Rucker, W. B., & Rucker, M. E. eds.). Guilford, CT: Dashkin Publishing Group, Inc.

Edwards, M. E., & Steinglass, P. (1995). Family therapy treatment outcomes for alcoholism. *Journal of Marital and Family Therapy, 21*, 475–509.

Edwards, R. W. (1993). Drug use among 8th grade students is increasing. *International Journal of the Addictions, 28*, 1621–1623.

Ehrenreich, B. (1992). Stamping out a dread scourge. *Time, 139* (7), 88.

Ehrman, M. (1995). Heroin chic. *Playboy, 42* (5), 66–68, 144–147.

Eidelberg, E., Neer, H. M., & Miller, M. K. (1965). Anticonvulsant properties of some benzodiazepine derivatives. *Neurology, 15*, 223–230.

Eisen, S. A., Lyons, M. J., Goldberg, J., & True, W. R. (1993). The impact of cigarette and alcohol consumption on weight and obesity. *Archives of Internal Medicine, 153*, 2457–2463.

Eisenhandler, J., & Drucker, E. (1993). Opiate dependence among the subscribers of a New York area private insurance plan. *Journal of the American Medical Association, 269*, 2890–2891.

Eison, A. S., & Temple, D. L. (1987). Buspirone: Review of its pharmacology and current perspectives on its mechanism of action. *The American Journal of Medicine, 80* (Supplement 3 B), 1–9.

Eissenberg, T., Bigelow, G. E., Strain, E. C., Walsh, S. L., Brooner, R. K., Stitzer, M. L., & Johnson, R. E. (1997). Dose-related efficacy of Levomethadyl acetate for treatment of opioid dependence. *Journal of the American Medical Association, 277*, 1945–1951.

Elders, M. J. (1997). Save money, cut crime, get real. *Playboy, 44* (1), 129, 191–192.

Elliott, F. A. (1992). Violence. *Archives of Neurology, 49*, 595–603.

Ellis, A., McInerney, J. F., DiGiuseppe, R., & Yeager, R. J. (1988). *Rational emotive therapy with alcoholics and substance abusers.* New York: Pergamon Press.

Elwood, P. C., Hughes, C., & O'Brien, J. R. (1998). Platelets, aspirin, and cardiovascular disease. *Postgraduate Medical Journal, 74*, 587–591.

Emonson, D. L., & Vanderbeek, R. D. (1995). The use of amphetamines in the U.S. Air Force tactical operations during Desert Shield and Storm. *Aviation, Space and Environmental Medicine, 66*, (3), 260–263.

Emrick, C. D. (1999). Alcoholics Anonymous and other twelve-step groups. In *Textbook of substance abuse treatment* (2nd ed.) (Galanter, M., & Kleber, H. D., eds.). Washington, DC: American Psychiatric Association, Inc.

Emrick, C. D., Tonigan, S., Montgomery, H., & Little, L. (1993). Alcoholics Anonymous: What is currently known? In *Research on alcoholics anonymous* (McCrady, B. S., & Miller, W. R., eds.). New Brunswick, NJ: Rutgers Center of Alcohol Studies.

Epstein, J. F., & Gfroerer, J. C. (1997). *Heroin abuse in the United States.* Rockville, MD: Substance Abuse and Mental Health Services Administration.

Esmail, A., Meyer, L., Pottier, A., & Wright, S. (1993). Deaths from volatile substance abuse in those under 18 years: Results from a national epidemiological study. *Archives of Disease in Childhood, 69*, 356–360.

Espeland, K. E. (1997). Inhalants: The instant, but deadly high. *Pediatric Nursing, 23* (1), 82–86.

Estroff, T. W. (1987). Medical and biological consequences of cocaine abuse. In *Cocaine: A clinician's handbook* (Washton, A. M., & Gold, M. S., eds.). New York: The Guilford Press.

Evanko, D. (1991). Designer drugs. *Postgraduate Medicine, 89* (6), 67–71.

Evans, G. D. (1993). Cigarette smoke = radiation hazard. *Pediatrics, 92*, 464.

Evans, K., & Sullivan, J. M. (1990). *Dual diagnosis.* New York: The Guilford Press.

Evans, W. N. (1998). Assessment and diagnosis of the substance use disorders (SUDs). *Journal of Counseling & Development, 76*, 325–333.

Ewing, J. A. (1984). Detecting alcoholism: The CAGE questionnaire. *Journal of the American Medical Association, 252*, 1905–1907.

Eyler, F. D., & Behnke, M. (1999). Early development of infants exposed to drugs prenatally. *Clinics in Perinatology, 26*, 107–150.

Ezzell, C. (2000). Care for a dying continent. *Scientific American, 282* (5), 96–105.

Facts about Alateen. (1969). New York: Al-Anon Family Group Headquarters.

Falls-Stewart, W., & Lucente, S. (1994). Treating obsessive-compulsive disorder among substance abusers: A guide. *Psychology of Addictive Behaviors, 8*, 14–23.

Farber, C. (2000). Science fiction. *Gear, 2* (6), 86–97.

Fariello, D., & Scheidt, S. (1989). Clinical case management of the dually diagnosed patient. *Hospital & Community Psychiatry, 40*, 1065–1067.

Farrell, A. D., & White, K. S. (1998). Peer influences and drug use among urban adolescents: Family structure and parent-adolescent relationship as protective factors. *Journal of Consulting and Clinical Psychology, 66*, 248–258.

Farrow, J. A. (1990). Adolescent chemical dependency. *Medical Clinics of North America, 74*, 1265–1274.

Fassinger, R. E. (1991). The hidden minority: Issues and challenges in working with lesbian women and gay men. *The Counseling Psychologist, 19*, 157–176.

Fauci, A. S. (1999). The AIDS epidemic. *New England Journal of Medicine, 341*, 1046–1050.

Fawcett, J., & Busch, K. A. (1995). Stimulants in psychiatry. In *Textbook of psychopharmacology* (Schatzberg, A. F., & Nemeroff, C. B., eds.). Washington, DC: American Psychiatric Association Press, Inc.

Feighner, J. P. (1987). Impact of anxiety therapy on patients' quality of life. *The American Journal of Medicine, 82* (Supplement A), 14–19.

Fernandez-Sola, J., Estruch, R., Grau, J. M., Pare, J. C., Rubin, E., & Urbano-Marquez, A. (1994). The relation of alcoholic myopathy to cardiomyopathy. *Annals of Internal Medicine, 120*, 529–536.

Fetro J. V., Coyle K. K., & Pham P. (2001) Health-risk behaviors among middle school students in a large majority-minority school district. *Journal of School Health, 71*(1), 30–37.

Figueredo, V. M. (1997). The effects of alcohol on the heart. *Postgraduate Medicine, 101*, 165–176.

Finch, R. G., & Woodhead, M. A. (1998). Practical considerations and guidelines for the management of community-acquired pneumonia. *Drugs. 56* (1), 31–45.

Fingarette, H. (1988). Alcoholism: The mythical disease. *Utne Reader, 30*, 64–69.

Finger, W. W., Lund, M., & Slagel, M. A. (1997). Medications that may contribute to sexual disorders: A guide to assessment and treatment in family practice. *Journal of Family Practice, 44*, 33–44.

Finkelstein, K. E. (1997). Deadly morals. *Playboy, 44* (8), 80–82, 112–114, 165.

Fiore, M. C., Epps, R. P., & Manley, M. W. (1994). A missed opportunity. *Journal of American Medical Association, 271*, 624–626.

Fiore, M. C., Jorenby, D. E., Baker, T. B., & Kenford, S. L. (1992). Tobacco dependence and the nicotine patch. *Journal of the American Medical Association, 268*, 2687–2694.

Fiore, M. C., Novotny, T. E., Pierce, J. P., Giovino, G. A., Hatziandreu, E. J., Newcomb, P. A., Surawicz, T. S., & Davis, R. M. (1990). Methods used to quit smoking in the United States. *Journal of the American Medical Association, 263*, 2760–2765.

Fiore, M. C., Smith, S. S., Jorenby, D. E., & Baker, T. B. (1994). The effectiveness of the nicotine patch for smoking cessation. *Journal of the American Medical Association, 271*, 1940–1947.

Fischer, R. G. (1989). Clinical use of nonsteroidal anti-inflammatory drugs. *Pharmacy Times, 55*, (8), 31–35.

Fischman, M. W., & Haney, M. (1999). Neurobiology of stimulants. In *Textbook of substance abuse treatment* (2nd ed.). Washington, DC: American Psychiatric Association Press, Inc.

Fisher, M. S., & Bentley, K. J. (1996). Two group therapy models for clients with a dual diagnosis of substance abuse and personality disorder. *Psychiatric Services, 47*, 1244–1250.

Fishman, R. H. B. (1996). Normal development after prenatal heroin. *The Lancet, 347*, 1397.

Fishman, S. M., & Carr, D. B. (1992). Clinical issues in pain management. *Contemporary Medicine, 4* (10), 92–103.

Flanagan, P., & Kokotailo, P. (1999). Adolescent pregnancy and substance use. *Clinics in Perinatology, 26*, 185–200.

Flaum, M., & Schultz, S. K. (1996). When does amphetamine-induced psychosis become schizophrenia? *American Journal of Psychiatry, 153*, 812–815.

Fleming, M. F. (1997). Strategies to increase alcohol screening in health care settings. *Alcohol Health & Research World, 21*, 340–347.

Fleming, N. F., Potter, D., & Kettyle, C. (1996). What are substance abuse and addiction? In *Source book of substance abuse and addiction* (Friedman, L., Fleming, N. F., Roberts, D. H., & Hyman, S. E., eds.). New York: Williams & Wilkins.

Fletcher, J. M., Page, J. B., Francis, D. J., Copeland, K., Naus, M. J., Davis, C. M., Morris, R., Krauskopf, D., & Satz, P. (1996). Cognitive correlates of long-term cannabis use in Costa Rican men. *Archives of General Psychiatry, 53*, 1051–1057.

Flexner, C. (1998). HIV-protease inhibitors. *New England Journal of Medicine, 338*, 1281–1292.

Flynn, P. M. (1996). Hepatitis C infections. *Pediatric Annals, 25*, 496–500.

Foley, K. M. (1993). Opioids. *Neurologic Clinics, 11*, 503–522.

Folks, D. G., & Burke, W. J. (1998). Sedative hypnotics and sleep. *Clinics in Geriatric Medicine, 14*, 67–86.

Fontham, E. T. H., Correa, P., Reynolds, P., Wu-Williams, A., Buffler, P. A., Greenberg, R. S. Chen, V., Alterman, T., Boyd, P., Austin, D. F., & Liff, J. (1994). Environmental tobacco smoke and lung cancer in nonsmoking women. *Journal of the American Medical Association, 271*, 1752–1759.

Ford, W. E. (2000). Medical necessity and psychiatric managed care. *Psychiatric Clinics of North America, 23*, 309–317.

Forensic Drug Abuse Advisor. (1994b). Take time to smell the fentanyl. *6* (5), 34–35.

Forensic Drug Abuse Advisor. (1994c). Feds say heroin use up, cocaine and heroin prices down, and cocaine snorting back in fashion. *6* (6), 41–43.

Forensic Drug Abuse Advisor. (1994d). Asiatic amphetamine abuse: Strokes, infarcts, agitated delirium, and postmortem levels. *6* (8), 60–62.

Forensic Drug Abuse Advisor. (1994e). Cocaine in the brain. *6* (9), 67.

Forensic Drug Abuse Advisor. (1994f). How cocaine causes sudden death. *6* (10), 76–77.

Forensic Drug Abuse Advisor. (1994g). Ibogaine and minimum sentencing hot topics at DPF meeting. *6* (10), 78–79.

Forensic Drug Abuse Advisor. (1994h). European drug dealings. *6* (10), 79.

Forensic Drug Abuse Advisor. (1995a). Cheaters advised to avoid using Drano. *7* (1), 3–4.

Forensic Drug Abuse Advisor. (1995b). How much marijuana do Americans really smoke? *7* (1), 7–8.

Forensic Drug Abuse Advisor. (1995c). Other AAFS highlights. 7 (3), 18.

Forensic Drug Abuse Advisor. (1995d). Tolmetin foils EMIT assay. 7 (3), 23.

Forensic Drug Abuse Advisor. (1995e). Dilaudid users may be escaping detection. 7 (3), 26–27.

Forensic Drug Abuse Advisor. (1995f). DAWN Survey: Surge in heroin-related deaths, cocaine deaths rise. 7 (5), 33–34.

Forensic Drug Abuse Advisor. (1995g). The sauna defense. 7 (6), 42.

Forensic Drug Abuse Advisor. (1995h). Cocaine use dangerous for mothers, too. 7 (6), 44.

Forensic Drug Abuse Advisor. (1995i). Not enough data on how long marijuana users test positive. 7 (9), 66–68.

Forensic Drug Abuse Advisor. (1995j). Secondhand crack smoke is not an acceptable excuse. 7 (10), 75–76.

Forensic Drug Abuse Advisor. (1996b). Researchers claim hair testing unreliable for quantitating drug use; racial bias also questioned. 8 (3), 17–19.

Forensic Drug Abuse Advisor. (1996c). New law nets mostly marijuana users. 8 (3), 29.

Forensic Drug Abuse Advisor. (1996d). Alum may mask methamphetamine abuse. 8 (3), 27.

Forensic Drug Abuse Advisor. (1996e). Bald is not beautiful, thallium found in French heroin. 8 (5), 35–36.

Forensic Drug Abuse Advisor. (1996f). CPPD in Puerto Rico, meeting highlights, French heroin. 8 (6), 41–44.

Forensic Drug Abuse Advisor. (1996g). Marijuana initiative makes California ballot. 8 (6), 44–45.

Forensic Drug Abuse Advisor. (1996h). Federal drug plans and statistics. 8 (6), 46–47.

Forensic Drug Abuse Advisor. (1996i). Crack injecting in Chicago—first U.S. reports of dangerous new practice. 8 (8), 60.

Forensic Drug Abuse Advisor. (1996j). Politicians discover the drug war. 8 (9), 70–72.

Forensic Drug Abuse Advisor. (1996k). Heroin smoking analyzed by Swiss researchers. 8 (10), 78–79.

Forensic Drug Abuse Advisor. (1997a). Rohypnol and date rape. 9 (1), 1–2.

Forensic Drug Abuse Advisor. (1997b). Asthma deaths blamed on cocaine use. 9 (2), 14.

Forensic Drug Abuse Advisor. (1997c). South American drug production increases. 9 (3), 18.

Forensic Drug Abuse Advisor. (1997d). Why confirmatory testing is always a necessity. 9 (4), 25.

Forensic Drug Abuse Advisor. (1997e). Introduction to GHB. 9 (5), 37–38.

Forensic Drug Abuse Advisor. (1997f). Ecstasy-using HIV patients at risk of death? 9 (7), 49.

Forensic Drug Abuse Advisor. (1997g). California judges get tougher on science. 9 (8), 61.

Fornazzari, L. (1988). Clinical recognition and management of solvent abusers. *Internal Medicine for the Specialist*, 9 (6), 99–108.

Fortgang, E. (1999). Is pot bad for you? *Rolling Stone*, 87, 53, 101.

Foulks, E. F., & Pena, J. M. (1995). Ethnicity and psychotherapy. *The Psychiatric Clinics of North America*, 18, 607–620.

Frances, R. J. (1991). Should drugs be legalized? Implications of the debate for the mental health field. *Hospital and Community Psychiatry*, 42, 119–120, 125.

Frances, R. J., & Miller, S. I. (1991). Addiction treatment: The widening scope. In *Clinical Textbook of Addictive Disorders* (Frances, R. J., & Miller, S. I. eds.). New York: The Guilford Press.

Frances, R. J., & Miller, S. I. (1998). Addiction treatment. In *Clinical textbook of addictive disorders* (2nd ed.) (Frances, R. J., & Miller, S. I., eds.). New York: Guilford.

Frank, D. A., Bauchner, H., Zuckerman, B. S., & Fried, L. (1992). Cocaine and marijuana use during pregnancy by women intending and not intending to breast feed. *Journal of the American Dietetic Association*, 92, 215–217.

Franken, I. H. A., & Hendriks, V. M. (1999). Predicting outcome of inpatient detoxification of substance abusers. *Psychiatric Services*, 50, 813–817.

Franklin, J. (1987). *Molecules of the mind.* New York: Dell Publishing Co.

Franklin, J. E. (1989). Alcoholism among blacks. *Hospital and Community Psychiatry*, 40, 1120–1122, 1127.

Franklin, J. E. (1994). Addiction medicine. *Journal of the American Medical Association*, 271, 1650–1651.

Frederickson, P. A., Richardson, J. W., Esther, M. S., & Lin, S. (1990). Sleep disorders in psychiatric practice. *Mayo Clinic Procedures*, 65, 861–868.

Freeborn, D. (1996). By the numbers. *Minneapolis Star-Tribune*, XV (94), D2.

Freiberg, P. (1991). Panel hears of families victimized by alcoholism. *APA Monitor*, 22 (4), 30.

Freiberg, P. (1996). New drugs give hope to AIDS patients. *APA Monitor*, 27 (6), 28.

French, M. T. (1995). Economic evaluation of drug abuse treatment programs: Methodology and findings. *American Journal of Drug and Alcohol Abuse*, 21 (1), 111–135.

Frezza, M., Di Padova, C., Pozzato, G., Terpin, M., Baraona, E., & Lieber, C. S. (1990). High blood alcohol levels in women. *The New England Journal of Medicine*, 322 95–99.

Fried, P. A. (1995). The Ottawa prenatal prospective study (OPPS): Methodological issues and findings—it's easy to throw the baby out with the bath water. *Live Sciences*, 56, 2159–2168.

Friedman, D. (1987) Toxic effects of marijuana. *Alcoholism & Addiction*, 7 (6), 47.

Friedman, L. N., Williams, W. T., Singh, T. P., & Frieden, T. R. (1996). Tuberculosis, AIDS, and death among substance abusers on welfare in New York City. *The New England Journal of Medicine*, 334, 828–833.

Friedman, R. C., & Downey, J. I. (1994). Homosexuality. *The New England Journal of Medicine*, 331, 923–930.

Friend, T. (1998). Drug errors kill outpatients at a rising rate. *USA Today*, 16 (119), 1D.

Fromm, E. (1956). *The art of loving.* New York: Harper & Row.

Fromm, E. (1968). *The revolution of hope*. New York: Harper & Row.

Fudala, P. J., & Johnson, R. E. (1995). Clinical efficacy studies of buprenorphine for the treatment of opioid dependence. In *Buprenorphine* (Cowan, A., & Lewis, J. W., eds.). New York: Wiley-Liss.

Fuller, M. A., & Sajatovic, M. (1999). *Drug information handbook for psychiatry*. Cleveland, OH: Lexi-Comp, Inc.

Fuller, P. G., & Cabanaugh, R. M. (1995). Basic assessment and screening for substance abuse in the pediatrician's office. *Pediatric Clinics of North America, 42*, 295–307.

Fuller, R. K. (1995). Antidipsotropic medications. In *Handbook of alcoholism treatment approaches* (2nd ed.) (Hester, R. K., & Miller, W. R., eds.). New York: Allyn & Bacon.

Fuller, R. K., & Hiller-Sturmhofel, S. (1999). Alcoholism treatment in the United States. *Alcohol Health & Research World, 23* (2), 69–77.

Fulton, J. S., & Johnson, G. B. (1993). Using high-dose morphine to relieve cancer pain. *Nursing '93, 23* (2), 35–39.

Fultz, O. (1991). 'Roid rage. *American Health, X* (4), 60–64.

Furstenberg, F. F. (1990). Coming of age in a changing family system. In *At the threshold* (Feldman, S. S., & Elliott, G. R., eds.). Cambridge, MA: Harvard University Press.

Gabriel, T. (1994). Heroin finds a new market along cutting edge of style. *The New York Times, CXLIII* (49,690), 1, 17.

Galanter, M. (1993). Network therapy for addiction: A model for office practice. *American Journal of Psychiatry, 150*, 28–36.

Galanter, M., Castaneda, R., & Franco, H. (1991). Group therapy and self-help groups. In *Clinical textbook of addictive disorders* (Frances, R. J., & Miller, S. I., eds.). New York: Guilford.

Gallagher, W. (1986). The looming menace of designer drugs. *Designer, 7* (8), 24–35.

Galloway, G. P. (1997). Anabolic-androgenic steroids. In *Substance abuse: A comprehensive textbook* (3rd ed.) (Lowinson, J. H., Ruiz, P., Millman, R. B., & Langrod, J. G., eds.). New York: Williams & Wilkins.

Gannon, K. (1994). OTC naproxen sodium set to shake OTC analgesics. *Drug Topics, 138* (3), 34.

Garbarino, J., Dubrow, N., Kostelny, K., & Pardo, C. (1992). *Children in danger*. New York: Jossey-Bass.

Garcia-Andrade, C., Wall, T. L., & Ehlers, C. L. (1997). The firewater myth and response to alcohol in mission Indians. *American Journal of Psychiatry, 154*, 983–988.

Gardner, E. L. (1997). Brain reward mechanisms. In *Substance abuse: A comprehensive textbook* (3rd ed.) (Lowinson, J. H., Ruiz, P., Millman, R. B., & Langrod, J. G., eds.). New York: Williams & Wilkins.

Garfinkel, D., Zisapel, N., Wainstein, J., & Laudon, M. (1999). Facilitation of benzodiazepine discontinuation by melatonin. *Archives of Internal Medicine, 159*, 2456–2460.

Garrett, L. (1994). *The coming plague*. New York: Farrar, Straus & Giroux.

Garrett, L. (2000). *Betrayal of trust*. New York: Hyperion.

Garriott, J. C. (1996). Pharmacology and toxicology of ethyl alcohol. In *Medicolegal aspects of alcohol* (3rd ed.) (Garriott, J. C., ed.). Tucson, AZ: Lawyers and Judges Publishing Co.

Garro, A. J., Espina, N., & Lieber, C. S. (1992). Alcohol and cancer. *Alcohol Health & Research World, 16* (1), 81–85.

Garry, P. (1995). Oh, judge, can't you make them stop picking on me? *Minneapolis Star-Tribune, XIV* (106), 10A.

Gastfriend, D. R., & McLellan, A. T. (1997). Treatment matching. *Medical Clinics of North America, 81*, 945–966.

Gawin, F. H., Allen, D., & Humblestone, B. (1989). Outpatient treatment of "crack" cocaine smoking with flupenthixol deconate: A preliminary report. *Archives of General Psychiatry, 46*, 122–126.

Gawin, F. H., & Ellinwood, E. H. (1988). Cocaine and other stimulants: Actions, abuse, and treatment. *New England Journal of Medicine, 318*, 1173–1182.

Gawin, F. H., Khalsa, M. E., & Ellinwood, E. (1994). Stimulants. In *Textbook of substance abuse treatment* (Galanter, M., & Kleber, H. D., eds.). Washington, DC: American Psychiatric Press, Inc.

Gawin, F. H., & Kleber, H. D. (1986). Abstinence symptomology and psychiatric diagnosis in cocaine abusers. *Archives of General Psychiatry, 43*, 107–113.

Gawin, F. H., Kleber, H. D., Byck, R., Rounsaville, B. J., Kosten, T. R., Jatlow, P. I., & Morgan, C. (1989). Desipramine facilitation of initial cocaine abstinence. *Archives of General Psychiatry, 46*, 117–121.

Gay, G. R. (1990). Another side effects of NSAIDs. *Journal of the American Medical Association, 164*, 2677–2678.

Gazzaniga, M. S. (1988). *Mind matters*. Boston: Houghton-Mifflin.

Gelman, D., Underwood, A., King, P., Hager, M., & Gordon, J. (1990). Some things work! *Newsweek, CXVI* (13), 78–81.

Gentilello, L. M., Donovan, D. M., Dunn, C. W., & Rivara, F. P. (1995). Alcohol interventions in trauma centers: Current practice and future directions. *Journal of the American Medical Center, 274*, 1043–1048.

George, A. A., & Tucker, J. A. (1996). Help-seeking for alcohol-related problems: Social contexts surrounding entry into alcoholism treatment or Alcoholics Anonymous. *Journal of Studies on Alcohol, 57*, 449–457.

George, F. R. (1999). Genetic factors in addiction. In *Drugs of abuse and addiction: Neurobehavioral toxicology* (Niesink, R.J.M., Jaspers, R. M. A., Korney, L. M. W., & van Ree, J. M., eds.). New York: CRC Press.

Giacchino, S., & Houdek, D. (1998). Ruptured varicies! *RN, 61* (5), 33–36.

Giacona, N. S., Dahl, S. L., & Hare, B. D. (1987). The role of nonsteroidal anti-inflammatory drugs and non-narcotics in analgesia. *Hospital Formulary, 22*, 723–733.

Giannini, A. J. (2000). An approach to drug abuse, intoxication and withdrawal. *American Family Physician, 61*, 2763–2774.

Gilbertson, P. K., & Weinberg, J. (1992). Fetal alcohol syndrome and functioning of the immune system. *Alcohol Health & Research World, 16* (1), 29–38.

Gilliam, M. (1998). *How Alcoholics Anonymous failed me*. New York: William Morrow & Co., Inc.

Gillin, J. C. (1991). The long and the short of sleeping pills. *The New England Journal of Medicine, 324,* 1735–1736.

Gilman, S. (1992). Advances in neurology. *The New England Journal of Medicine, 326,* 1608–1616.

Giunta, C. T., & Compas, B. E. (1994). Adult daughters of alcoholics: Are they unique? *Journal of Studies on Alcohol, 55,* 600–606.

Glantz, J. C., & Woods, J. R. (1993). Cocaine, heroin, and phencyclidine: Obstetric perspectives. *Clinical Obstetrics and Gynecology, 36,* 279–301.

Glantz, S., & Parmley, W. W. (1995). Passive smoking and heart disease. *Journal of the American Medical Association, 273,* 1047–1053.

Glantz, S. A., Barnes, D. E., Bero, L., Hanauer, P., & Slade, J. (1995). Looking through a keyhole at the tobacco industry. *Journal of the American Medical Association, 274,* 219–224.

Glantz, S. A., Slade, J., Bereo, L. A., Hanauer, P., & Barnes, D. E. (1996). *The cigarette papers.* Los Angeles: University of California Press.

Glaser, F. B., & Ogborne, A. C. (1982). Does A. A. really work? *British Journal of the Addictions, 77,* 88–92.

Glasser, R. J. (1998). The doctor is not in. *Harper's Magzine, 296* (1774), 35–42.

Glassman, A. H. (1993). Cigarette smoking: Implications for psychiatric illness. *American Journal of Psychiatry, 150,* 546–553.

Glick, S. D., & Maisonneuve, I. M. (2000). Development of novel medications for drug addiction. In *New medications for drug abuse* (Glick, S. D.., & Maisonneuve, I. B., eds.). New York: New York Academy of Sciences.

Global TB. (2001). *Minneapolis Star-Tibune, XIX* (353), A18.

Glowa, J. R. (1986). *Inhalants: The toxic fumes.* New York: Chelsea House.

Godlaski, T. M., Leukefeld, C., & Cloud, R. (1997). Recovery: With and without self-help. *Substance Use & Misuse, 32,* 621–627.

Gold, M. S. (1993). Opiate addiction and the locus coeruleus. *Psychiatric Clinics of North America, 16,* 61–73.

Gold, M. S. (1997). Cocaine (and crack): Clinical aspects. In *Substance abuse: A comprehensive textbook* (3rd ed.) (Lowinson, J. H., Ruiz, P., Millman, R. B., & Langrod, J. G., eds.). New York: Williams & Wilkins.

Gold, M. S., & Miller, N. S. (1997a). Cocaine (and crack): Neurobiology. In *Substance abuse: A comprehensive textbook* (3rd ed.) (Lowinson, J. H., Ruiz, P., Millman, R. B., & Langrod, J. G., eds.). New York: Williams & Wilkins.

Gold, M. S., & Miller, N. S. (1997b). Intoxication and withdrawal from alcohol. In *Manual of therapeutics of addictions* (Miller, N. S., Gold, M. S., & Smith, D. E., eds.). New York: Wiley-Liss.

Gold, M. S., & Miller, N. S. (1997c). Intoxication and withdrawal from marijuana, LSD, and MDMA. In *Manual of therapeutics of addictions* (Miller, N. S., Gold, M. S., & Smith, D. E., eds.). New York: Wiley-Liss.

Gold, M. S., & Verebey, K. (1984). The psychopharmacology of cocaine. *Psychiatric Annuals, 14,* 714–723.

Goldman, B. (1991). How to thwart a drug seeker. *Emergency Medicine, 23* (6), 48–61.

Goldschmidt, R. D., & Moy, A. (1996). Antiretroviral drug treatment for HIV/AIDS. *American Family Physician, 54,* 574–580.

Goldstein, P. (1990). *Drugs and violence.* Paper presented at the 1990 meeting of the American Psychological Association, Boston, MA.

Goldstein, M. Z., Pataki, A., & Webb, M. T. (1996). Alcoholism among elderly persons. *Psychiatric Services, 47,* 941–943.

Goldstone, M. S. (1993). "Cat": Methcathinone, a new drug of abuse. *Journal of the American Medical Association, 269,* 2508.

Gonzales, J. J., Stern, T. A., Emmerich, A. D., & Rauch, S. L. (1992). Recognition and management of benzodiazepine dependence. *American Family Physician, 45,* 2269–2276.

Goodman, E., & Capitman, J. (2000). Depressive symptoms and cigarette smoking among teens. *Pediatrics, 106,* 748–755.

Goodnough, L. T., Brecher, M. E., Kanter, M. H., & AuBuchon, J. P. (1999). Transfusion medicine. *The New England Journal of Medicine, 340,* 438–447.

Goodwin, D. W. (1989). Alcoholism. In *Comprehensive textbook of psychiatry/V.* (Kaplan, H. I., & Sadock, B. J., eds.). Baltimore: Williams & Wilkins.

Goodwin, D. W., & Warnock, J. K. (1991). Alcoholism: A family disease. In *Clinical textbook of addictive disorders* (Frances, R. J., & Miller, S. I., eds.). New York: The Guilford Press.

Gorbach, S. L., Mensa, J., & Gatell, J. M. (1997). *Pocket book of antimicrobial therapy & prevention.* Baltimore, MD: Williams & Wilkins.

Gordis, E. (1995). The national institute on alcohol abuse and alcoholism. *Alcohol Health & Research World, 19,* 5–11.

Gordis, E. (1996a). Alcohol research. *Archives of General Psychiatry, 53,* 199–201.

Gordis, E. (1996b). Drinking and driving—a commentary by NIAAA director Enoch Gordis, M.D. *Alcohol Alert, 31,* 3.

Gordon, S. C. (2000). Antiviral therapy for chronic hepatitis B and C. *Postgraduate Medicine, 107,* 135–144.

Gorski, T. T. (1992). Diagnosing codependence. *Addiction & Recovery, 12* (7), 14–16.

Gorski, T. T. (1993). Relapse prevention. *Addiction & Recovery, 13* (2), 25–27.

Gortner, E. T., Gollan, J. K., & Jacobson, N. S. (1997). Psychological aspects of perpetrators of domestic violence and their relationships with the victims. *The Psychiatric Clinics of North America, 20,* 337–351.

Gossop, M., Battersby, M., & Strang, J. (1991). Self-detoxification by opiate addicts. *British Journal of Psychiatry, 159,* 208–212.

Gottesman, J. (1992). Little is known about effects of steroids on women. *Minneapolis Star-Tribune, XI* (211), 7C.

Gottlieb, A. M. (1997). Crisis of consciousness. *Utne Reader, 79,* 45–48.

Gottlieb, A. M., Killen, J. D., Marlatt, G. A., & Taylor, C. B. (1987). Psychological and pharmacological influences in cigarette smoking withdrawal: Effects of nicotine gum and expectancy on smoking withdrawal symptoms and relapse. *Journal of Clinical and Consulting Psychology, 55,* 606–608.

Gottlieb, A., Pope, S., Rickert, V. I., & Hardin, B. H. (1993). Patterns of smokeless tobacco use by young adolescents. *Pediatrics, 91,* 75–78.

Gottlieb, M. I. (1994). Alcohol and pregnancy: A potential for disaster. *Emergency Medicine, 26* (1), 73–79.

Gourlay, S. G., & Benowitz, N. L. (1995). Is clonidine an effective smoking cessation therapy? *Drugs, 50,* 197–207.

Gouzoulis-Mayfrank, E., Daumann, J., Tuchtenhagen, F., Pelz, S., Becker, S., Kunert, H. J., Fimm, B., & Sass, H. (2000). Impaired cognitive performance in drug free users of recreational ecstasy (MDMA). *Journal of Neurology, Neurosurgery and Psychiatry, 68,* 719–725.

Graedon, J., & Ferguson, T. (1993). *The aspirin handbook.* New York: Bantam.

Graedon, J., & Graedon, T. (1991). *Graedons' best medicine.* New York: Bantam Books.

Graedon, J., & Graedon, T. (1995). *The people's guide to deadly drug interactions.* New York: St. Martin's Press.

Graedon, J., & Graedon, T. (1996). *The people's pharmacy— revised.* New York: St. Martin's Griffin.

Graham, B. (1988). The abuse of alcohol: Disease or disgrace? *Alcoholism & Addiction, 8* (4), 14–15.

Graham, J. R. (1990). *MMPI-2 assessing personality and psychopathology.* New York: Oxford University Press.

Graham, M. (1989). One toke over the line. *The New Republic, 200* (16), 20–22.

Grant, I. (1987). Alcohol and the brain: Neuropsychological correlates. *Journal of Clinical and Consulting Psychology, 55,* 310–324.

Graves, C. (1998). Meth is new drug of choice. *Minneapolis Star-Tribune, XVII* (176), 1A, 10A.

Gray, M. (1998). *Drug crazy.* New York: Routledge.

Green, K. (1998). Marijuana smoking vs cannabinoids for glaucoma therapy. *Archives of Ophthalmology, 116,* 1433–1437.

Greenberg, D. A. (1993). Ethanol and sedatives. *Neurologic Clinics, 11,* 523–534.

Greene, M. A., & Gordon, D. E. (1998). Lessons of the new genetics. *Family Therapy Networker, 22* (2), 26–41.

Griffin, K. W., Botvin, G. J., Scheier, L. M., Diaz, T., & Miller, N. L. (2000). Parenting practices as predictors of substance use, delinquency, and aggression among urban minority youth: Moderating effects of family structure and gender. *Psychology of Addictive Behaviors, 14,* 174–184.

Griffin, M. L., Weiss, R. D., Mirin, S. M., & Lange, U. (1989). A comparison of male and female cocaine abusers. *Archives of General Psychiatry, 46,* 122–126.

Griffiths, H. J., Parantainen, H., & Olson, P. (1994). Alcohol and bone disorders. *Alcohol Health & Research World, 17,* 299–304.

Grinfeld, M. J. (2001). Decriminalizing addiction. *Psychiatric Times, XVIII* (3), 1, 5, 6.

Grinspoon, L., & Bakalar, J. B. (1990). What is phencyclidine? *The Harvard Medical School Mental Health Letter, 6* (7), 8.

Grinspoon, L., & Bakalar, J. B. (1993). *Marijuana: The forgotten medicine.* New Haven, CT: Yale University Press.

Grinspoon, L., & Bakalar, J. B. (1995). Marijuana as medicine. *Journal of the American Medical Association, 273,* 1875–1876.

Grinspoon, L., & Bakalar, J. (1997a). Smoke screen. *Playboy, 44* (6), 49–53.

Grinspoon, L., & Bakalar, J. B. (1997b). Marijuana. In *Substance abuse: A comprehensive textbook* (3rd ed.) (Lowinson, J. H., Ruiz, P., Millman, R. B., & Langrod, J. G., eds.). New York: Williams & Wilkins.

Grover, S. A., Gray-Donald, K., Joseph, L., Abrahamowicz, M., & Coupal, L. (1994). Life expectancy following dietary modification or smoking cessation. *Archives of Internal Medicine, 154,* 1697–1704.

Group for the Advancement of Psychiatry. (1990). Substance abuse disorders: A psychiatric priority. *American Journal of Psychiatry, 148,* 1291–1300.

Group, The. (1976). Van Nuys, CA: Narcotics Anonymous World Service Office, Inc.

Guslandi, M. (1997). Gastric toxicity of antiplatelet therapy with low-dose aspirin. *Drugs, 53,* 1–5.

Guydish, J., Werdeger, D., Sorensen, J. L., Clark, W., & Acampora, A. (1998). Drug abuse day treatment: A randomized clinical trial comparing day and residential treatment programs. *Journal of Consulting and Clinical Psychology, 66,* 280–289.

Haack, M. R. (1998). Treating acute withdrawal from alcohol and other drugs. *Nursing Clinics of North America, 33,* 75–92.

Hager, M., & Reibstein, L. (1998). Do you have hepatitis C? *Newsweek, CXXXI* (18), 83.

Hall, S. M., Havassy, B. E., & Wasserman, D. A. (1991). Effects of commitment to abstinence, positive moods, stress and coping on relapse to cocaine use. *Journal of Consulting and Clinical Psychology, 59,* 526–532.

Hall, W., & Sannibale, C. (1996). Are there two types of alcoholism? *The Lancet, 348,* 1258.

Hall, W., & Solowij, N. (1998). Adverse effects of cannabis. *The Lancet, 352,* 1611–1616.

Hall, W. C., Talbert, R. L., & Ereshefsky, L. (1990). Cocaine abuse and its treatment. *Pharmacotherapy, 10* (1), 47–65.

Hamner, M. B. (1993). PTSD and cocaine abuse. *Hospital and Community Psychiatry, 44,* 591–592.

Hand, R. P. (1989). Taking another look at triazolam—is this drug safe? *Focus on Pharmacology: Theory and Practice, 11* (6), 1–3.

Handelsman, L., Aronson, M. J., Ness. R., Cochrane, K. J., & Kanof, P. D. (1992). The dysphoria of heroin addiction. *American Journal of Drug and Alcohol Abuse, 18* (3), 275–287.

Hankinson, S. E., Willett, W. C., Colditz, G. A., Seddon, J. M., Rosner, B., Speizer, F. E., & Stampfer, M. J. (1992). A prospective study of cigarette smoking and risk of cataract surgery in women. *Journal of the American Medical Association, 268*, 994–998.

Hanners, D. (1998). Scientists paid to write on tobacco. *St. Paul Pioneer Press, 150* (100), 1A, 5A.

Hansen, W. B., & Rose, L. A. (1995). Recreational use of inhalant drugs by adolescents: a challenge for family physicians. *Family Medicine, 27*, 383–387.

Harrington, R. D., Woodward, J. A., Hooton, T. M., & Horn, J. R. (1999). Life-threatening interactions between HIV-1 protease inhibitors and the illicit drugs MDMA and gamma-hydroxybutyrate. *Archives of Internal Medicine, 159*, 2221–2224.

Harrison, P. A., Fulkerson, J. A., & Beebe, T. J. (1998). DSM-IV substance use disorder criteria for adolescents: A critical examination based on a statewide school survey. *American Journal of Psychiatry, 155*, 486–492.

Hart, R. H. (1997). On the cannabinoid receptor: A study in molecular psychiatry. *Psychiatric Times, XIV* (7), 59–60.

Hartman, D. E. (1995). *Neuropsychological toxicology* (2nd ed.). New York: Plenum.

Hartmann, P. M. (1995). Drug treatment of insomnia: indications and newer agents. *American Family Physician, 51* (1), 191–194.

Harvard Health Letter (1995). Strong medicine. 20 (6), 4–6.

Harvard Medical School Mental Health Letter, The. (1988). Sleeping pills and antianxiety drugs. 5 (6), 1–4.

Harvard Medical School Mental Health Letter, The. (1990). Amphetamines. 6 (10), 1–4.

Harvard Mental Health Letter, The. (1992a). Addiction—Part I. 9 (4), 1–4.

Harvard Mental Health Letter, The. (1992b). Addiction—Part II. 9 (5), 1–4.

Harvard Mental Health Letter, The. (1995). Treatment of drug abuse and addiction—Part I. 12 (2), 1–4.

Harwitz, D., & Ravizza, L. (2000). Suicide and depression. *Emergency Medicine Clinics of North America, 18*, 263–271.

Hatsukami, D. K., & Fischman, M. W. (1996). Crack cocaine and cocaine hydrochloride. *Journal of the American Medical Association, 276*, 1580–1588.

Haverkos, H. W., & Stein, M. D. (1995). Identifying substance abuse in primary care. *American Family Physician, 52*, 2029–2035.

Hawkes, C. H. (1992). Endorphins: The basis of pleasure? *Journal of Neurology, Neurosurgery and Psychiatry, 55*, 247–250.

Hawley. T. L., Halle, T. G., Drasin, R. E., & Thomas, N. G. (1995). Children of addicted mothers' effects of the "crack epidemic" on the caregiving environment and the development of preschoolers. *American Journal of Orthopsychiatry, 65* (3), 364–379.

Hayner, G. N., & McKinney, H. (1986). MDMA: The dark side of ecstasy. *Journal of Psychoactive Drugs, 18* (4), 341–347.

He, J., Whelton, P. K., Vu, B., & Klag, M. J. (1998). Aspirin and risk of hemorrhagic stroke. *Journal of the American Medical Association, 280*, 1930–1935.

Health News. (1990). Drug problems in perspective. 8 (3), 1–10.

Heath, A. W., & Stanton, M. D. (1998). Family-based treatment. In *Clinical textbook of addictive disorders* (2nd ed.) (Frances, R. J., & Miller, S. I., eds.). New York: Guilford.

Heath, D. B. (1994). Inhalant abuse. *Behavioral Health Management, 14* (3), 47–48.

Heerema, D. L. (1990). Drug use in the 1990's. *Business Horizons, 33* (1), 127–132.

Heesch, C. M., Negus, B. H., Steiner, M., Snyder, R. W., McIntire, D. D., Grayburn, P. A., Ashcraft, J., Hernandez, J. A., & Eichorn, E. J. (1996). Effects of in vivo cocaine administration on human platelet aggregation. *The American Journal of Cardiology 78*, 237–239.

Heil, S. H., & Subramanian, M. G. (1998). Alcohol and the hormonal control of lactation. *Alcohol Health & Research World, 22* (3), 178–184.

Heimel, C. (1990). It's now, it's trendy, it's codependency. *Playboy, 37* (5), 43.

Heinz, A., Dufeu, P., Kuhn, S., Dettling, M., Graf, K., Kurten, I., Rommelspacher, H., & Schmidt, L. G. (1996). Psychopathological and behavioral correlates of dopaminergic sensitivity in alcohol-dependent patients. *Archives of General Psychiatry, 53*, 1123–1128.

Heinz, A., Ragan, P., Jones, D. W., Hommer, D., Williams, W., Knable, M. B., Gorey, J. G., Doty, L., Geyer, C., Lee, K. S., Coppola, R., Weinberger, D. R., & Linnoila, M. (1998). Reduced central serotonin transporters in alcoholism. *American Journal of Psychiatry, 155*, 1544–1549.

Hellinger, F. J. (1993). The lifetime cost of treating a person with HIV. *Journal of the American Medical Association, 270*, 474–478.

Hellman, R. E., Stanton, M., Lee, J., Tytun, A., & Vachon, R. (1989). Treatment of homosexual alcoholics in government-funded agencies: Provider training and attitudes. *Hospital and Community Psychiatry, 40*, 1163–1168.

Helzer, J. E., Robins, L. N., Taylor, J. R., Carey, K., Miller, R. H., Combs-Orme, T., & Farmer, A. (1985). The extent of long-term moderate drinking among alcoholics discharged from medical and psychiatric treatment facilities. *The New England Journal of Medicine, 312*, 1678–1682.

Henderson, L. A. (1994a). About LSD. In *LSD: Still with us after all these years.* (Henderson, L. A., & Glass, W. J., eds.). New York: Lexington Books.

Henderson, L. A. (1994b). Adverse reactions. In *LSD: Still with us after all these years* (Henderson, L. A., & Glass, W. J., eds.). New York: Lexington Books.

Henderson, T. A., & Fischer, V. W. (1994). Effects of methylphenidate (Ritalin) on mammalian myocardial ultrastructure. *American Journal of Cardiovascular Pathology, 5* (1), 68–78.

Hennekens, C. H., Jonas, M. A., & Buring, J. E. (1994). The benefits of aspirin in acute myocardial infarction. *Archives of Internal Medicine, 154*, 37–39.

Hennessey, M. B. (1992). Identifying the woman with alcohol problems. *Nursing Clinics of North America, 27*, 917–924.

Henningfield, J. E. (1995). Nicotine medications for smoking cessation. *New England Journal of Medicine, 333,* 1196–1203.

Henningfield, J. E., & Nemeth-Coslett, R. (1988). Nicotine dependence. *Chest, 93* (2), 37s-55s.

Henretig, F. (1996). Inhalant abuse in children and adolescents. *Pediatric Annals, 25* (1), 47–52.

Henry, J. A. (1996). Management of drug abuse emergencies. *Journal of Accident & Emergency Medicine, 13,* 370–372.

Henry, J. A., Jeffreys, J. A., & Dawling, S. (1992). Toxicity and deaths from 3,4–methylenedioxymethamphetamine ("ecstacy"). *The Lancet, 340,* 384–387.

Henry, K., Stiffman, M., & Feldman, J. (1997). Antiretroviral therapy for HIV infection. *Postgraduate Medicine, 102* (4), 100–120.

Herman, E. (1988). The twelve step program: Cure or cover? *Utne Reader, 30,* 52–53.

Herman, R. (1993). Alcohol debate may drive you to drink. *St. Paul Pioneer Press, 144* (356), 11G.

Herrera, S. (1997). The morphine myth. *Forbes, 159,* 258–260.

Hester, R. K. (1994). Outcome research: Alcoholism. In *Textbook of substance abuse treatment* (Galanter, M., & Kleber, H. D., eds.). Washington, DC: American Psychiatric Press, Inc.

Hester, R. K., (1995). Self-control training. In *Handbook of alcoholism treatment approaches* (Hester, R. K., & Miller, W. R., eds.). New York: Allyn & Bacon.

Hibbs, J., Perper, J., & Winek, C. L. (1991). An outbreak of designer drug-related deaths in *Pennsylvania Journal of the American Medical Association, 265,* 1011–1013.

Higgins, J. P., Wright, S. W., & Wrenn, K. D. (1996). Alcohol, the elderly, and motor vehicle crashes. *American Journal of Emergency Medicine, 14,* 265–267.

Hilditch, T. (2000). Ya ba. *Gear, 2* (11), 86–88.

Hill, D. B., & Kugelmas, M. (1998). Alcoholic liver disease. *Postgraduate Medicine, 103,* 261–275.

Hill, S. Y., (1995). Vulnerability to alcoholism in women. In *Recent developments in alcoholism* (Vol. 12) (Galanter, M., ed.). New York: Plenum Press.

Hilts, P. J. (1994). Labeling on cigarettes called a smoke screen. *St. Paul Pioneer Press, 146* (5), 1A, 6A.

Hilts, P. J. (1996). *Smoke screen.* New York: Addison-Wesley Publishing Co.

Hingson, R. (1996). Prevention of drinking and driving. *Alcohol Health & Research World, 20,* 219–226.

Hirsch, D., Paley, J. E., & Renner, J. A. (1996). Opiates. In *Source book of substance abuse and addiction* (Friedman, L., Fleming, N. F., Roberts, D. H., & Hyman, S. E., eds.). New York: Williams & Wilkins.

Hirschfeld, R. M. A., & Davidson, L. (1988). Risk factors for suicide. In *Review of psychiatry* (Vol. 7) (Frances, A. J., & Hales, R. E., eds.). Washington, DC: American Psychiatric Association Press, Inc.

Hitchcock, H. C., Stainback, R. D., & Roque, G. M. (1995). Effects of halfway house placement on retention of patients in substance abuse aftercare. *American Journal of Drug and Alcohol Abuse, 21,* 379–391.

Hobbs, W. R., Rall, T. W., & Verdoorn, T. A. (1995). Hypnotics and sedatives; ethanol. In *The pharmacological basis of therapeutics* (9th ed.). (Hardman, J. G., & Limbird, L. E., editors-in-chief). New York: McGraw-Hill.

Hoberman, J. M., & Yesalis, C. E. (1995). The history of synthetic testosterone. *Scientific American, 272* (2), 76–81.

Hoegerman, G., & Schnoll, S. (1991). Narcotic use in pregnancy. *Clinics in Perinatology, 18,* 52–76.

Hoeksema, H. L., & de Bock, G. H. (1993). The value of laboratory tests for the screening and recognition of alcohol abuse in primary care patients. *The Journal of Family Practice, 37,* 268–276.

Hoffman, B. B., & Lefkowitz, R. J. (1990). Catecholamines and sympathomimetic drugs. In *The pharmacological basis of therapeutics* (8th ed.) (Gilman, A. G., Rall, T. W., Nies, A. S., & Taylor, P., eds.). New York: Pergamon Press.

Hoffmann, N. G., Belille, C. A., & Harrison, P. A. (1987). Adequate resources for a complex population? *Alcoholism & Addiction, 7* (5), 17.

Hoffman, R. S., & Hollander, J. E. (!997). Evaluation of patients with chest pain after cocaine use. *Critical Care Clinics of North America, 13,* 809–828.

Hoffnagle, J. H., & DiBisceglie, A. M. (1997). The treatment of chronic viral hepatitis. *The New England Journal of Medicine, 336,* 347–356.

Hogan, M. J. (2000). Diagnosis and treatment of teen drug use. *Medical Clinics of North America, 84,* 927–966.

Holden, C. (1998). New clues to alcoholism risk. *Science, 280,* 1348–1349.

Holder, H., Longabaugh, R., Miller, W. R., & Rubonis, A. V. (1991). The cost effectiveness of treatment for alcoholism: A first approximation. *Journal of Studies on Alcohol, 52,* 517–540.

Holland, W. W., & Fitzsimons, B. (1991). Smoking in children. *Archives of Disease in Childhood, 66,* 1269–1270.

Hollander, H., & Katz, M. H. (1993). HIV infection. In *Current medical diagnosis & treatment* (Tierney, L. M., McPhee, S. J., Papadakis, M. A., & Schroeder, S. A., eds.). Norwalk, CT: Appleton & Lange.

Hollander, J. E. (1995). The management of cocaine-associated myocardial ischemia. *New England Journal of Medicine, 333,* 1267–1271.

Hollander, J. E., Hoffman, R. S., Burnstein, J. L., Shih, R. D., & Thode, H. C. (1995). Cocaine-associated myocardial infarction. *Archives of Internal Medicine, 155,* 1081–1086.

Hollander, J. E., Shih, R. D., Hoffman, R. S., Harchelroad, F. P., Phillips, S., Brent, J., Kulig, K., & Thode, H. C. (1997). Predictors of coronary artery disease in patients with cocaine-associated myocardial infarction. *American Journal of Medicine, 102,* 159–163.

Hollander, J. E., Todd, K. H., Green, G., Heilpern, K. L., Karras, D. J., Singer, A. J., Brogan, G. X., Funk, J. P., & Strahan, J. B. (1995). Chest pain associated with cocaine: An assessment of prevalence in suburban and urban emergency departments. *Annals of Emergency Medicine, 26,* 671–676.

Holloway, M. (1991). Rx for addiction. *Scientific American, 264* (3), 94–103.

Holloway, R. (1998). Doubtful demons. *Nursing Times, 94* (21), 34–36.

Holm, K. J., & Goa, K. L. (2000). Zolpidem. *Drugs, 59,* 865–889.

Hong, R., Matsuyama, E., & Nur, K. (1991) Cardiomyopathy associated with smoking of crystal methamphetamine. *Journal of the American Medical Association, 265,* 1152–1154.

Hopewell, P. C. (1996). Mycobacterium tuberculosis an emerging pathogen? *Western Journal of Medicine, 164,* 33–35.

Hopfer, C. J., Mikulich, S. K., & Crowley, T. J. (2000). Heroin use among adolescents in treatment for substance use disorders. *Journal of the American Academy of Child and Adolescent Psychiatry, 39.* 1316–1323.

Hopkins, G. L. (1998). Why people abuse drugs. *Vibrant Life, 14* (1), 4–6.

Hopper, J. L., & Seeman, E. (1994). The bone density of female twins discordant for tobacco use. *The New England Journal of Medicine, 330,* 387–392.

Horgan, J. (1989). Lukewarm turkey; Drug firms balk at pursuing a heroin-addiction treatment. *Scientific American, 260* (3), 32.

Horney, K. (1964). *The neurotic personality of our time.* New York: W. W. Norton & Co.

Horvath, A. T. (2000). SMART recovery. *The Addictions Newsletter, 7* (2), 11.

Hough, D. O., & Kovan, J. R. (1990). Is your patient a steroid abuser? *Medical Aspects of Human Sexuality, 24* (11), 24–32.

House, M. A. (1990). Cocaine. *American Journal of Nursing, 90* (4), 40–45.

Howard, D. L., & McCaughrin, W. C. (1996). The treatment effectiveness of outpatient substance misuse treatment organizations between court-mandated and voluntary clients. *Substance Use & Misuse, 31,* 895–925.

Howard, G., Wagenknecht, L. E., Burke, G. L., Diez-Roux, A., Evans, G. W., McGovern, P., Nieto, J., & Tell, G. S. (1998). Cigarette smoking and the progression of atherosclerosis. *Journal of the American Medical Association, 279,* 119–124.

Howard, M. O., Kivlahan, D., & Walker, R. D. (1997). Cloninger's tridimensional theory of personality and psychopathology: Applications to substance use disorders. *Journal of Studies on Alcohol, 58,* 48–67.

Howland, R. H. (1990). Barriers to community treatment of patients with dual diagnoses. *Hospital & Community Psychiatry, 41,* 1136–1138.

Hser, Y., Anglin, D., & Powers, K. (1993). A 24 year follow-up of California narcotics addicts. *Archives of General Psychiatry, 50,* 577–584.

Hubbard, J. B., Franco, S. E., & Onaivi, E. S. (1999). Marijuana: Medical implications. *American Family Physician, 60,* 2583–2593.

Hughes, C. (1999). Living with hepatitis C. *Saturday Evening Post, 271* (5), 28–31.

Hughes, J. R. (1992). Tobacco withdrawal in self-quitters. *Journal of Consulting and Clinical Psychology, 60,* 689–697.

Hughes, J. R., Gust, S. W., Skoog, K., Keenan, R. M., & Fenwick, J. W. (1991). Symptoms of tobacco withdrawal. *Archives of General Psychiatry, 48,* 52–59.

Hughes, R. (1993). Bitch, bitch, bitch... *Psychology Today, 26* (5), 28–30.

Hughes, T. L., & Wilsnack, S. C. (1997). Use of alcohol among lesbians: Research and clinical implications. *American Journal of Orthopsychiatry, 67,* 20–36.

Humphreys, K. (1997). Clinicians' referral and matching of substance abuse patients to self-help groups after treatment. *Psychiatric Services, 48,* 1445–1449.

Humphreys, K., & Moos, R. H. (1996). Reduced substance-abuse-related health care costs among voluntary participants in Alcoholics Anonymous. *Psychiatric Services, 47,* 709–713.

Humphreys, K., Moos, R. H., & Finney, J. W. (1995). Two pathways out of drinking problems without professional treatment. *Addictive Behaviors, 20,* 427–441.

Humphreys, K., Moos, R. H., & Finney, J. (1996). Life domains, Alcoholics Anonymous, and tole incumbency in the 3 year course of problem drinking. *The Journal of Nervous and Mental Disease, 184,* 475–481.

Humphreys, K., & Rappaport, J. (1993). From the community mental health movement to the war on drugs. *American Psychologist, 48,* 892–901.

Hunter, M., & Kellogg, T. (1989). Redefining ACA characteristics. *Alcoholism & Addiction, 9* (3), 28–29.

Hurcom, C., Copello, A., & Orford, J. (2000). The family and alcohol: Effects of excessive drinking and conceptualizations of spouses over recent decades. *Substance Use & Misuse, 35,* 473–502.

Hurt, R. D., Finlayson, R. E., Morse, R. M., & Davis, L. J. (1988). Alcoholism in elderly persons: Medical aspects and prognosis of 216 inpatients. *Mayo Clinic Proceedings, 63,* 753–760.

Hurt, R. D., Offord, K. P., Croghan, I. T., Gomez-Dahl, L., Kottke, T. E., Morse, R. M., & Melton, J. (1996). Mortality following inpatient addictions treatment. *Journal of the American Medical Association, 275,* 1097–1103.

Hurt, R. D., & Robertson, C. R. (1998). Prying open the door to the tobacco industry's secrets about nicotine. *Journal of the American Medical Association, 280,* 1173–1181.

Hussar, D. A. (1990). Update 90: New drugs. *Nursing 90, 20* (12), 41–51.

Hyman, S. E. (1988). *Manual of psychiatric emergencies* (2nd ed.). Boston: Little, Brown.

Hyman, S. E. (1996). Drug abuse and addiction. In *Scientific American medicine.* (Rubenstein, E., & Federman, D. D., eds.). New York: Scientific American Press.

Hyman, S. E., & Cassem, N. H. (1995). Alcoholism. In *Scientific American medicine.* (Rubenstein, E., & Federman, D. D., eds.). New York: Scientific American Press.

Hyman, S. E., & Nestler, E. J. (1996). Initiation and adaption: A paradigm for understanding psychotropic drug action. *American Journal of Psychiatry, 153,* 151–162.

Hymowitz, N., Feuerman, M., Hollander, M., & Frances, R. J. (1993). Smoking deterence using silver acetate. *Hospital and Community Psychiatry, 44*, 113–114, 116.

Iggers, J. (1990). The addiction industry. *Minneapolis Star-Tribune, IX* (102), 1E, 4E, 10EX.

Imhof, J. E. (1995). Overcoming countertransference. In *Psychotherapy and subtance abuse* (Washton, A.M. ed.). New York: Guilford.

Ingels, M., Rangan, C., Bellezzo, J., & Clark, R. F. (2000). Coma and respiratory depression following the ingestion of GHN and its precursors: Three cases. *Journal of Emergency Medicine, 19*, 47–50.

Irvin, J. E., Bowers, C. A., Dunn, M. E., & Wang, M. C. (1999). Efficacy of relapse prevention: A meta-analytic review. *Journal of Consulting and Clinical Psychology, 67*, 563–570.

Irwin, K. (1995). Ideology, pregnancy and drugs: Differences between crack-cocaine, heroin and methamphetamine users. *Contemporary Drug Problems, 22* (4), 613–638.

Isaacson, J. H., & Schorling, J. B. (1999). Screening for alcohol problems in primary care. *Medical Clinics of North America, 83*, 1547–1563.

Isenhart, C. E., & Silversmith, D. J. (1996). MMPI-2 response styles: Generalization to alcoholism assessment. *Psychology of Addictive Behaviors, 10*, 115–123.

Jackson, L. M., & Hawkey, C. J. (2000). COX-2 selective non-steroidal anti-inflammatory drugs. *Drugs, 59* (6), 1207–1216.

Jacob, T., & Windle, M. (2000). Young adult children of alcoholic, depressed and nondistressed parents. *Journal of Studies on Alcohol, 61*, 836–844.

Jacobs, E. J., Thun, M. J., & Apicella, L. F. (1999). Cigar smoking and death from coronary heart disease in a prospective study of U.S. men. *Archives of Internal Medicine, 159*, 2413–2418.

Jaffe, J. H. (1992). Opiates: Clinical aspects. In *Substance abuse: A comprehensive textbook* (2nd ed.) (Lowinson, J. H., Ruiz, P., Millman, R. B., & Langrod, J. G., eds.). New York: Williams & Wilkins.

Jaffe, J. H. (1986). Opioids. In *American Psychiatric Association annual review* (Vol. 5). Washington, DC: American Psychiatric Association.

Jaffe, J. H. (1989). Drug dependence: Opioids, nonnarcotics, nicotine (tobacco) and caffeine. In *Comprehensive textbook of psychiatry/ V.* (Kaplan, H. I., & Sadock, B. J., eds.). Baltimore: Williams & Wilkins.

Jaffe, J. H. (1990). Drug addiction and drug abuse. In *The pharmacological basis of therapeutics* (8th ed.). (Gilman, A. G., Rall, T. W., Nies, A. S., & Taylor, P., eds.). New York: Macmillan Publishing Co.

Jaffe, J. H., & Martin, W. R. (1990). Opioid analgesics and antagonists. In *The pharmacological basis of therapeutics* (8th ed.). (Gilman, A. G., Rall, T. W., Nies, A. S., & Taylor, P., eds.). New York: Macmillan Publishing Co.

Jaffe, J. H., (2000a). Amphetamine (or amphetaminelike) disorders. In *Comprehensive textbook of psychiatry* (7th ed.). (Kaplan, H. I., & Sadock, B. J., eds.). Baltimore: Lippincott, Williams & Wilkins.

Jaffe, J. H., (2000b). Cocaine-related disorders. In *Comprehensive textbook of psychiatry* (7th ed.). (Kaplan, H. I., & Sadock, B. J., eds.). Baltimore: Lippincott, Williams & Wilkins.

Jaffe, J. H., (2000c). Opioid-related disorders. In *Comprehensive textbook of psychiatry* (7th ed.). (Kaplan, H. I., & Sadock, B. J., eds.). Baltimore: Lippincott, Williams & Wilkins.

James, L. P., Farrar, H. C., Komoroski, E. M., Wood, W. R., Graham, C. J., & Bornemeier, R. A. (1998). Sympathomimetic drug use in adolescents presenting to a pediatric emergency department with chest pain. *Journal of Toxicology: Clinical Toxicology, 36*, 321–329.

Jamison, K. R. (1999). *Night falls fast.* New York: Knopf.

Jansen, K. L. R. (1993). Non-medical use of ketamine. *The Lancet, 306*, 601–602.

Japenga, A. (1991). You're tougher than you think! *Self, 13* (4), 174–175, 187.

Jarvik, M. E., & Schneider, N. G. (1992). Nicotine. In *Substance abuse: A comprehensive textbook* (2nd ed.) (Lowinson, J. H., Ruiz, P., Millman, R. b., & Langrod, J. G., eds.). New York: Williams & Wilkins.

Jellinek, E. M. (1952). Phases of alcohol addiction. *Quarterly Journal of Studies on Alcohol, 13*, 673–674.

Jellinek, E. M. (1960). *The disease concept of alcoholism.* New Haven, CT: College and University Press.

Jenkins, A. J., & Cone, E. J. (1998). Pharmacokinetics: Drug absorption, distribution, and elimination. In *Drug abuse handbook* (Karch, S. B., editor-in-chief). New York: CRC Press.

Jenike, M. A. (1991). Drug abuse. In *Scientific American medicine* (Rubenstein, E., & Federman, D. D., eds.). New York: Scientific American Press, Inc.

Jensen, G. B., & Pakkenberg, B. (1993). Do alcoholics drink their neurons away? *The Lancet, 342*, 1201–1204.

Jensen, J. G. (1987a). Step two: A promise of hope. In *The twelve steps of Alcoholics Anonymous.* New York: Harper & Row.

Jensen, J. G. (1987b). Step three: Turning it over. In *The twelve steps of Alcoholics Anonymous.* New York: Harper & Row.

Jentsch, J. D., Redmond, D. E., Elsworth, J. D., Taylor, J. R., Youngren, K. D., & Roth, R. H. (1997). Enduring cognitive deficits and cortical dopamine dysfunction in monkeys after long-term administration of phencyclidine. *Science, 277*, 953–955.

Jersild, D. (2001). *Happy hours.* New York: HarperCollins.

Johns, A. (2001). Psychiatric effects of cannabis. *British Journal of Psychiatry, 178*, 116–122.

Johnson, B. A., Roache, J. D., Javors, M. A., DiClemente, C. C., Cloninger, C. R., Prihoda, T. J., Bordnick, P. S., Ait-Daoud, N., & Hensler, J. (2000). Ondansetron for reduction of drinking among biologically predisposed alcoholic patients. *Journal of the American Medical Association, 284*, 963–970.

Johnson, G. (2001). Playboy interview. *Playboy 48* (1), 79–86, 197–198.

Johnson, H. L., Nusbaum, B. J., Bejarano, A., & Rosen, T. S. (1999). An ecological approach to development in children with prenatal drug exposure. *American Journal of Orthopsychiatry, 69,* 448–456.

Johnson Institute. (1987). *The family enablers.* Minneapolis: The Johnson Institute.

Johnson, M. D. (1990). Anabolic steroid use in adolescent athletes. *The Pediatric Clinics of North America, 37,* 1111–1123.

Johnson, M. D., Heriza, T. J., & St. Dennis, C. (1999). How to spot illicit drug abuse in your patients. *Postgraduate Medicine, 106* (4), 199–216.

Johnson, M. R., & Lydiard, R. B. (1995). The neurobiology of anxiety disorders. *The Psychiatric Clinics of North America, 18,* 681–725.

Johnson, R. A., Hoffmann, J. P., & Gerstein, D. R. (1996). *The relationship between family structure and adolescent substance use.* Rockville, MD: U.S. Department of Health and Human Services.

Johnson, R. E., Chutuape, M. A., Strain, E. C., Walsh, S. L., Stitzer, M. L., & Bigelow, G. E. (2000). A comparison of levomethadyl acetate, buprenorphine, and methadone for opioid dependence. *New England Journal of Medicine, 343,* 1290–1297.

Johnson, V. E. (1980). *I'll quit tomorrow.* San Francisco: Harper & Row.

Johnston, L. D., O'Malley, P. M., & Bachman, J. G. (2000a). *National survey results on drug use from the monitoring the future study, 1975–1999.* Rockville, MD: U.S. Department of Health and Human Services.

Johnston, L. D., O'Malley, P. M., & Bachman, J. G. (2000b). *National survey results on drug use from the monitoring the future study, 1975–1999* (Vol. II). Rockville, MD: U.S. Department of Health and Human Services.

Johnston, S. C., & Pelletier, L. L. (1997). Enhanced hepatoxicity of acetaminophen in the alcoholic patient. *Medicine, 76* (3), 185–191.

Jones, A. L., Jarvie, D. R., McDermid, G., & Proudfoot, A. T. (1994). Hepatocellular damage following amphetamine intoxication. *Journal of Toxicology, 32* (4), 435–445.

Jones, A. W. (1996). Biochemistry and physiology of alcohol: Applications to forensic sciences and toxicology. In *Medicolegal aspects of alcohol* (3rd ed.) (Garriott, J. C., ed.). Tuscon, AZ: Lawyers & Judges Publishing Co.

Jones, R. L. (1990). Evaluation of drug use in the adolescent. In *Clinical management of poisoning and drug overdoses* (2nd ed.) (Haddad, L. M., & Winchester, J. F., eds.). New York: W. B. Saunders.

Jones, R. T. (1987). Psychopharmacology of cocaine. In *Cocaine: A clinician's handbook* (Washton, A. G., & Gold, M. S., eds.). New York: The Guilford Press.

Jones, R. T., & McMahon, J. (1998). Alcohol motivations as outcome expectancies. In *Treating addictive behaviors* (2nd ed.) (Miller, W. R., & Heather, N., eds.). New York: Plenum.

Jones-Webb, R. (1998). Drinking patterns and problems among African-Americans: Recent findings. *Alcohol Health & Research World, 22,* 260–264.

Jonnes, J. (1995). The rise of the modern addict. *The American Journal of Public Health, 85* (8), 1157–1162.

Jorenby, D. E. (1997). Effects of nicotine on the central nervous system. *Hospital Practice * A Special Report, 38* (4), 17–20.

Jorgensen, E. D. (2001). Dual diagnosis in treatment resistent adolescents. Symposium presented to the Dept. of Psychiatry at The Cambridge Hospital, Boston, MA, March 3, 2001.

Joshi, N. P., & Scott, M. (1988). Drug use, depression, and adolescents. *The Pediatric Clinics of North America, 35* (6), 1349–1364.

Journal of the American Medical Association, (1998). Effective medical treatment of opiate addiction. *280,* 1936–1943.

Judd, L. L., & Huey, L. Y. (1984). Lithium antagonizes ethanol intoxication in alcoholics. *The American Journal of Psychiatry, 141,* 1517–1521.

Juergens, S. M. (1993). Benzodiazepines and addiction. *Psychiatric Clinics of North America, 16,* 75–86.

Juergens, S. M., & Morse, R. M. (1988). Alprazolam dependence in seven patients. *The American Journal of Psychiatry, 145,* 625–627.

Julien, R. M. (1992). *A primer of drug action* (6th ed.). New York: W. H. Freeman & Co.

Kacso, G., & Terezhalmy, G. T. (1994). Acetylsalicylic acid and acetaminophen. *Dental Clinics of North America, 38,* 633–644.

Kadlec, D., Pascual, A. M., & Perman, S. (1997). How tobacco firms will manage. *Time, 149* (26).

Kadushin, C., Reber, E., Saxe, L., & Livert, D. (1998). The substance use system: Social and neighborhood environments associated with substance use and misuse. *Substance Use & Misuse, 33,* 1681–1710.

Kaiser, D. (1996). Not by chemicals alone: A hard look at "psychiatric medicine." *Psychiatric Times, XIII* (12), 41–44.

Kales, J. P., Barone, M. A., Bixler, E. O., Miljkovic, M. M., & Kales, J. D. (1995). Mental illness and substance use among sheltered homeless persons in lower-density population areas. *Psychiatric Services, 46,* 592–596.

Kalichman, S. C., Heckman, T., Kochman, A., Sikkema, K., & Bergholte, J. (2000). Depression and thoughts of suicide among middle-aged and older persons living with HIV-AIDS. *Psychiatric Services, 51,* 903–907.

Kaltenbach, K. (1997). *Maternal and fetal effects.* Paper presented at NIDA conference: Heroin Use and Addiction. Washington, DC, September 29–30.

Kaminer, W. (1992). *I'm dysfunctional, you're dysfunctional.* New York: Addison-Wesley Publishing Co., Inc.

Kaminer, Y, (1991). Adolescent substance abuse. In *Clinical textbook of addictive disorders* (Frances, R. J., & Miller, S. I., eds.). New York: The Guilford Press.

Kaminer, Y. (1994). Adolescent substance abuse. In *Textbook of substance abuse treatment* (Galanter, M., & Kleber, H. D., eds.). Washington, DC: American Psychiatric Press, Inc.

Kaminer, Y. (1999). Addictive disorders in adolescents. *Psychiatric Clinics of North America, 22,* 275–288.

Kminer, Y. (2001). Adolescent substance abuse treatment: where do we go from here? *Psychiatric Services, 52,* 147–149.

Kaminer, Y., & Bukstein, O. G. (1998). Adolescent substance abuse. In *Clinical textbook of addictive disorders* (2nd ed.) (Frances, R. J., & Miller, S. I., eds.). New York: Guilford.

Kaminer, Y., & Frances, R. J. (1991). Inpatient treatment of adolescents with psychiatric and substance abuse disorders. *Hospital and Community Psychiatry, 42,* 894–896.

Kaminski, A. (1992). *Mind-altering drugs.* Madison, WI: Wisconsin Clearinghouse, Board of Regents, University of Wisconsin System.

Kandall, S. R. (1999). Treatment strategies for drug-exposed neonates. *Clinics in Perinatology, 26,* 231–243.

Kandall, S. R., Gaines, J., Habel, L., Davidson, G., & Jessop, D. (1993). The relationship of maternal substance abuse to subsequent sudden infant death syndrome in offspring. *The Journal of Pediatrics, 123,* 120–126.

Kandel, D. (1997). *Sequencing of drug involvement: Marijuana and heroin.* Paper presented at NIDA conference: Heroin Use and Addiction. Washington, DC, September 29–30.

Kandel, D. B., & Chen, K. (2000). Types of marijuana users by longitudinal course. *Journal of Studies on Alcohol, 61,* 367–378.

Kandel, D. B., & Davies, M. (1996). High school students who use crack and other drugs. *Archives of General Psychiatry, 53,* 71–80.

Kandel, D. B., & Raveis, V. H. (1989). Cessation of illicit drug use in young adulthood. *Archives of General Psychiatry, 46,* 109–116.

Kandel, D. B., Yamaguchi, K., & Chen, K. (1992). Stages of progression in drug involvement from adolescence to adulthood: Further evidence for the gateway theory. *Journal of Studies on Alcohol, 53* (5), 447–458.

Kanof, P. D., Aronson, M. J., & Ness, R. (1993). Organic mood syndrome associated with detoxification from methadone maintenance. *American Journal of Psychiatry, 150,* 423–428.

Kantall, S. R., Doberczak, T. M., Jantunen, M., & Stein, J. (1999). The methadone maintained pregnancy. *Clinics in Perinatology, 26,* 173–181.

Kanwischer, R. W., & Hundley, J. (1990). Screening for substance abuse in hospitalized psychiatric patients. *Hospital & Community Psychiatry, 41,* 795–797.

Kaplan, H. I., & Sadock, B. J. (1996). *Concise textbook of clinical psychiatry.* Baltimore: Williams & Wilkins.

Kaplan, H. I., Sadock, B. J., & Grebb, J. A. (1994). *Synopsis of psychiatry* (7th ed.). Baltimore: Williams & Wilkins.

Karan, L. D., Haller, D. L., & Schnoll, S. H. (1998). Cocaine and stimulants. In *Clinical textbook of addictive disorders* (2nd ed.) (Frances, R. J., & Miller, S. I., eds.). New York: Guilford.

Karch, S. (1999). The problem of methamphetamine today. *Western Journal of Medicine, 170,* 232.

Karch, S. B. (1996). *The pathology of drug abuse* (2nd ed.). New York: CRC Press.

Karhunen, P. J., Erkinjuntti, T., & Laippala, P. (1994). Moderate alcohol consumption and loss of cerebellar Purkinje cells. *British Medical Journal, 308,* 1663–1667.

Karlen, A. (1995). *Man and microbes.* New York: G. P. Putnam's Sons.

Kashkin, K. B. (1992). Anabolic steroids. In *Substance abuse: A comprehensive textbook* (2nd ed.) (Lowinson, J. H., Ruiz, P., Millman, R. B., & Langrod, J. G., eds.). New York: Williams & Wilkins.

Kashkin, K. B., & Kleber, H. D. (1989). Hooked on hormones? An anabolic steroid addiction hypothesis. *Journal of the American Medical Association, 262,* 3166–3173.

Kassirer, J. P. (1997). Federal foolishness and marijuana. *New England Journal of Medicine, 336,* 366–367.

Katz, S. J., & Liu, A. E. (1991). *The codependency conspiracy.* New York: Warner Books.

Kauffman, E., Dore, M. M., & Nelson-Zlupko, L. (1995). The role of women's therapy groups in the treatment of chemical dependence. *American Journal of Orthopsychiatry, 65,* 355–363.

Kaufman, E., & McNaul, J. P. (1992). Recent developments in understanding and treating drug abuse and dependence. *Hospital and Community Psychiatry, 43,* 223–236.

Kaufman, G. (1989). *The psychology of shame.* New York: Springer.

Kaufman, M. J., Levin, J. M., Ross, M. H., Lange, N., Rose, S. L., Kukes, T. J., Mendelson, J. H., Lukas, S. E., Cohen, B. M., & Renshaw, P. F. (1998). Cocaine-induced vasoconstriction detected in humans with magnetic resonance angiography. *Journal of the American Medical Association, 279,* 376–380.

Kay, S. R., Kalathara, M., & Meinzer, A. E. (1989). Diagnostic and behavioral characteristics of psychiatric patients who abuse substances. *Hospital and Community Psychiatry, 40,* 1062–1065.

Keller, D. S. (1996). Exploration in the service of relapse prevention: A psychoanalytic contribution to substance abuse treatment. In *Treating substance abuse* (Rotgers, F., Keller, D. S., & Morgenstern, J. eds.). New York: Guilford.

Keller, R. W., & Snyder-Keller, A. (2000). Prenatal cocaine exposure. In *New medications for drug abuse* ((Glick, S. D., & Maisonneuve, I. B., eds.). New York: New York Adacemy of Sciences.

Kelly, V. A., & Myers, J. E. (1996). Parental alcoholism and coping: A comparison of female children of alcoholics with female children of nonalcoholics. *Journal of Counseling & Development, 74,* 501–504.

Kemm, J. (1993). Alcohol and heart disease: The implications of the U-shaped curve. *British Medical Journal, 307,* 1373–1374.

Kender, K. S., Heath, A. C., Neale, M. C., Kessler, R. C., & Eves, J. (1992). A population-based twin study of alcoholism in women. *Journal of the American Medical Association, 268,* 1877–1882.

Kender, K. S., & Prescott, C. A. (1998). Cocaine use, abuse and dependence in a population-based sample of female twins. *British Journal of Psychiatry, 173,* 345–350.

Kendler, K. S., Thornton, L. M., & Pedersen, N. L. (2000). Tobacco consumption in Swedish twins reared apart and reared together. *Archives of General Psychiatry, 57,* 886–892.

Kenford, S. L., Fiore, M. C., Jorenby, D. E., Smith, S. S., Wetter, D., & Baker, T. B. (1994). Predicting smoking cessation. *Journal of the American Medical Association, 271,* 589–594.

Kerfoot, B. P., Sakoulas, G., & Hyman, S. E. (1996). Cocaine. In *Source book of substance abuse and addiction* (Friedman, L., Fleming, N. F., Roberts, D. H., & Hyman, S. E., eds.). New York: Williams & Wilkins.

Kermani, E. J., & Castaneda, R. (1996). Psychoactive substance use in forensic psychiatry. *American Journal of Drug and Alcohol Abuse, 22,* 1–28.

Kessler, D. A. (1995). Nicotine addiction in young people. *The New England Journal of Medicine, 333,* 186–189.

Kessler, R. C., Crum, R. M., Warner, L. A., Nelson, C. B., Schulenberg, J., & Anthony, J. C. (1997). Lifetime co-occurence of DSM-III-R alcohol abuse and dependence with other psychiatric disorders in the National Comorbidity Survey. *Archives of General Psychiatry, 54,* 313–321.

Kessler, R. C., McGonagle, K. A., Zhao, S., Nelson, C. B., Hughes, M., Eshleman, S., Hans-Ulrich, W., & Kendler, K. S. (1994). Lifetime and 12 month prevalence of DSM-III-R psychiatric disorders in the United States. *Archives of General Psychiatry, 51,* 8–19.

Khan, J. O., & Walker, B. D. (1998). Acute Human Immunodeficiency Virus Type 1 infection. *The New England Journal of Medicine, 339,* 33–39.

Khantzian, E. J., Mack, J. E., & Schatzberg, A. F. (1999). Heroin use as an attempt to cope. In *Treating addiction as a human process* (Khantzian, E. J., ed.). New York: Aronson.

Kick, S. D. (1999). Evluation and management of chronic alcohol abuse. *Hospital Practice, 34* (4), 95–106.

Kidorf, M., Brooner, R. K., King, V. L., Stroller, K. B., & Wertz, J. (1998). Predictive validity of cocaine, sedative, and alcohol dependence diagnoses. *Journal of Consulting and Clinical Psychology, 66,* 168–173.

Kilpatrick, D. G., Acierno, R., Saunders, B., Resnick, H. S., Best, C. L., & Schnurr, P. P. (2000). Risk factors for adolescent substance abuse and dependence: Data from a national sample. *Journal of Consulting and Clinical Psychology, 2000,* 19–30.

King, G. R., & Ellinwood, E. H. (1997). Amphetamines and other stimulants. In *Substance abuse: A comprehensive textbook* (3rd ed.) (Lowinson, J. H., Ruiz, P., Millman, R. B., & Langrod, J. G., eds.). New York: Williams & Wilkins.

Kirchner, J. T. (1999). Hepatitis C: Who should we be treating? *American Family Physician, 59* (2), 273–275.

Kirsch, M. M. (1986). *Designer drugs.* Minneapolis: CompCare Publications.

Kishline, A. (1996). A toast to moderation. *Psychology Today, 29* (1), 53–56.

Kitchens, J. M. (1994). Does this patient have an alcohol problem? *Journal of the American Medical Association, 272,* 1782–1787.

Kitridou, R. C. (1993). The efficacy and safety of oxaproxzin versus aspirin: Pooled results of double-blind trials in rheumatoid arthritis. *Drug Therapy, 23,* supplement, 21–25.

Kivlahan, D. R., Heiman, J. R., Wright, R. C., Mundt, J. W., & Shupe, J. A. (1991). Treatment cost and rehospitalization rate in schizophrenic outpatients with a history of substance abuse. *Hospital and Community Psychiatry, 42,* 609–614.

Klar, H. (1987). The setting for psychiatric treatment. In *American Psychiatric Association annual review* (Vol. 6). Washington, DC: American Psychiatric Association Press, Inc.

Klass, P. (1989). Vital signs. *Discover, 10* (1), 12–14.

Klatsky, A. L. (1990). Alcohol and coronary artery disease. *Alcohol Health & Research World, 14* (4), 289–300.

Kleber, H. D. (1991). Tracking the cocaine epidemic. *Journal of the American Medical Association, 266,* 2272–2273.

Kleber, H. D. (1997). *Overview of treatment and psychiatric comorbidity.* Paper presented at NIDA conference: Heroin Use and Addiction. Washington, DC, September 29–30.

Klesges, R. C., Winders, S. E., Meyers, A. W., Eck, L. H., Ward, K. D., Hultquist, C. M., Ray, J. W., & Shadish, W. R. (1997). How much weight gain occurs following smoking cessation? A comparison of weight gain using both continuous and point prevalence abstinence. *Journal of Consulting and Clinical Psychology, 65,* 286–291.

Klein, J. M., & Miller, S. I. (1986). Three approaches to the treatment of drug addiction. *Hospital and Community Psychiatry, 37,* 1083–1085.

Kleinman, S., Busch, M. P., Hall, L., Thomson, R., Glynn, S., Gallahan, D., Ownby, H. E., & Williams, A. E. (1998). False-positive HIV-1 test results in a low-risk screening setting of voluntary blood donation. *Journal of the American Medical Association, 280,* 1080–1085.

Kline, A. (1996). Pathways into drug user treatment: The influence of gender and racial/ethnic identity. *Substance Use & Misuse, 31,* 323–342.

Klinger, R. L., & Cabaj, R. P. (1993). Characteristics of gay and lesbian relationships. In *Review of psychiatry* (Vol. 12) (Oldham, J. M., Riba, M. B., & Tasman, A., eds.). Washington, DC: American Psychiatric Association.

Klirsfeld, D. (1998). HIV disease and women. *Medical Clinics of North America, 82,* 335–357.

Klonoff-Cohen, H. S., Edelstein, S. L., Lefkowitz, E. S., Srinivasen, I. P., Kaegl, D., Chang J. C., & Wiley, K. J. (1995). The effect of passive smoking and tobacco exposure through breast milk on Sudden Infant Death Syndrome. *Journal of the American Medical Association, 173,* 795–798.

Kluge, E. H. W. (2000). Social values, socioeconomic resources, and effectiveness coefficients. *Annals of the New York Academy of Sciences, 913,* 23–31.

Knapp, C. (1996). *Drinking: A love story.* New York: The Dial Press.

Knight, J. R. (2000). *Screening for adolescent substance abuse.* Symposium presented to the Dept. of Psychiatry at The Cambridge Hospital, Boston, MA. March 3.

Kocurek, K. (1996). Primary care of the HIV patient. *Medical Clinics of North America, 80,* 375–410.

Kofoed, L., Kania, J., Walsh, T., & Atkinson, R. M. (1986). Outpatient treatment of patients with substance abuse and coexisting psychiatric disorders. *The American Journal of Psychiatry, 143*, 867–872.

Kofoed, L., & Keys, A. (1988). Using grup therapy to persuade dual-diagnosis patients to seek substance abuse treatment. *Hospital & Community Psychiatry, 39*, 1209–1211.

Kolodner, G., & Frances, R. (1993). Recognizing dissociative disorders in patients with chemical dependency. *Hospital and Community Psychiatry, 44*, 1041–1044.

Kolodny, R. C. (1985). The clinical management of sexual problems in substance abusers. In *Alcoholism and substance abuse: Strategies for clinical intervention* (Bratter, T. E., & Forrest, G. G., eds.). New York: The Free Press.

Konstan, M. W., Byard, P. J., Hoppel, C. L., & Davis, P. B. (1995). Effect of high-dose ibuprofen in patients with cystic fibrosis. *The New England Journal of Medicine, 332*, 848–854.

Konstan, M. W., Hoppel, C. L., Chai, B., Davis, P. B. (1991). Ibuprofen in children with cystic fibrosis: Pharmacokinetics and adverse effects. *Journal of Pediatrics, 118*, 956–965.

Kotulak, R. (1992). Recent discoveries about cocaine may help unlock secrets of brain. *St. Paul Pioneer Press, 143* (345), 4C.

Kotulak, R. (1997). Unlocking secrets of alcohol's grip. *Chicago Tribune, 151* (267), 1, 16.

Kotz, M., & Covington, E. C. (1995). Alcoholism. In *Conn's current therapy* (Rakel, R. E., ed.). Philadelphia: W. B. Saunders Co.

Kouri, E. M., Pope, H. G., & Lukas, S. E. (1999). Changes in aggressive behavior during withdrawal from long-term marijuana use. *Psychopharmacology, 143*, 302–308.

Kovasznay, B., Bromet, E., Schwartz, J. E., Ranganathan, R., Lavelle, J., & Brandon, L. (1993). Substance abuse and onset of psychotic illness. *Hospital and Community Psychiatry, 44*, 567–571.

Kozlowski, L. T., Wilkinson, A., Skinner, W., Kent, W., Franklin, T., & Pope, M. (1989). Comparing tobacco cigarette dependence with other drug dependencies. *Journal of the American Medical Association, 261*, 898–901.

Kraft, M. K., Rothbard, A. B., Hadley, T. R., McLellan, A. T., & Asch, D. A. (1997). Are supplementary services provided during methadone maintenance really cost effective? *American Journal of Psychiatry, 154*, 1214–1219.

Kranzler, H. R., Amin, H., Modesto-Lowe, V., & Oncken, C. (1999). Pharmacologic treatments for drug and alcohol dependence. *Psychiatric Clinics of North America, 22*, 401–423.

Kranzler, H. R., Burleson, J. A., Del Boca, F. K., Babor, T. F., Korner, P., Brown, J., & Bohn, T. F. (1994). Buspirone treatment of anxious alcoholics. *Archives of General Psychiatry, 51*, 720–731.

Kreek, M. J. (1997). *History and effectiveness of methadone treatment.* Paper presented at NIDA conference: Heroin Use and Addiction. Washington, DC, September 29–30.

Kreek, M. J. (2000). Methadone-related opioid agonist pharmacotherapy for heroin addiction. In *New medications for drug abuse* (Glick, S. D., & Maisonneuve, I. B., eds.). New York: New York Adacemy of Sciences.

Kriechbaum, N., & Zernig, G. (2000). Adolescent patients. In *Handbook of alcoholism* (Zernig, G., Saria, A., Kurz, M., & O'Malley, S. S., eds.). New York: CRC Press.

Kriegstein, A. R., Shungu, D. C., Miller, W. S., Armitage, B. A., Brust, J. C., Chillrud, S., Goldman, J., & Lynch, T. (1999). Leukoencephalopathy and raised brain lactate from heroin vapor inhalation ("chasing the dragon"). *Neurology, 53*, 1765–1773.

Krishnan-Sarin, S. (2000). Heritability. In *Handbook of alcoholism* (Zernig, G., Saria, A., Kurz, M., & O'Malley, S. S., eds.). New York: CRC Press.

Kritz, H., Schmid, P., & Sinzinger, H. (1995). Passive smoking and cardiovascular risk. *Archives of Internal Medicine, 155*, 1942–1948.

Kruger, T. E., & Jerrells, T. R. (1992). Potential role of alcohol in human immunodeficiency virus infection. *Alcohol Health & Research World, 16* (1), 57–63.

Kruzicki, J. (1987). Dispelling a myth: The facts about female alcoholics. *Corrections Today, 49*, 110–115.

Kryger, M. H., Steljes, D., Pouliot, Z., Neufeld, H., & Odynski, T. (1991). Subjective versus objective evaluation of hypnotic efficacy: Experience with Zolpidem. *Sleep, 14* (5), 399–407.

Kuiken, C., Thakallapalli, R., Eskild, A., & de Ronde, A. (2000). Genetic analysis reveals epidemiologic patterns in the spread of Human Immunodeficiency Virus. *American Journal of Epidemiology, 152*, 814–822.

Kumpfer, K. L. (1997). *Focus on families: Prevention in action.* Paper presented at NIDA conference: Heroin Use and Addiction. Washington, DC, September 29–30.

Kunitz, S. J., & Levy J. E. (1974). Changing ideas of alcohol use among Navaho Indians. *Quarterly Journal of Studies on Alcohol, 46*, 953–960.

Kurtz, E. (1979). *Not God: A history of Alcoholics Anonymous.* Center City, MN: Hazelden.

Kushner, M. G., Sher, K. J., & Beitman, B. D. (1990). The relation between alcohol problems and the anxiety disorders. *American Journal of Psychiatry, 147*, 685–695.

Kviz, F. J., Clark, M. A., Crittenden, K. S., Wernecke, R. B., & Freels, S. (1995). Age and smoking cessation behaviors. *Preventative Medicine, 24*, 297–307.

Lacks, P., & Morin, C. M. (1992). Recent advances in the assessment and treatment of insomnia. *Journal of Consulting and Clinical Psychology, 60*, 586–594.

Lacombe, P. S., Vicente, J. A. G., Pages, J. C., & Morselli, P. L. (1996). Causes and problems of nonresponse or poor response to drugs. *Drugs, 51*, 552–570.

La Crosse Tribune (1999). Typical drug user not poor. 96, (142), A-3.

La Crosse Tribune (2000). Despite war on drugs, prices for cocaine, heroin decrease. 96 (336), A-3.

Lader, M. (1987). Assessing the potential for buspirone dependence or abuse and effects of its withdrawal. *The American Journal of Medicine, 82* (Supplement 5A), 20–26.

Lala, S., & Straussner, A. (1997). Gender and substance abuse. In *Gender and addictions* (Straussner, S.L.A., & Zelvin, E., eds.). Northvale, NJ: Jason-Aronson.

Lamar, J. V., Riley, M., Smghabadi, R. (1986). Crack: A cheap and deadly cocaine is spreading menace. *Time, 128*, 16–18.

The Lancet. (1991a). The smoking epidemic. 338, 1387.

The Lancet. (1991b). Your heroin, sir. 337, 402.

The Lancet. (1995). Deglamorising cannabis. 346, 1241.

Land, W., Pinsky, D., & Salzman, C. (1991). Abuse and misuse of anticholinergic medications. *Hospital and Community Psychiatry, 42*, 580–581.

Landry, G. L., & Primos, W. A. (1990). Anabolic steroid abuse. *Advances in Pediatrics, 7*, 185–205.

Landry, M. J. (1997). *Overview of addiction treatment effectiveness*. Rockville, MD: U.S. Department of Health and Human Services.

Lange, W. R., White, N., & Robinson, N. (1992). Medical complications of substance abuse. *Postgraduate Medicine, 92*, 205–214.

Langone, J. (1989). Hot to block a killer's path. *Time, 133* (5), 60–62.

Langston, J. W., & Palfreman, J. (1995). *The case of the frozen addicts*. New York: Pantheon Books.

Larimer, M. E., & Kilmer, J. R. (2000). Natural History. In *Handbook of alcoholism* (Zernig, G., Saria, A., Kurz, M., & O'Malley, S. O., eds.). New York: CRC Press.

Larson, K. K. (1982). Birthplace of "The Minnesota Model." *Alcoholism, 3* (2), 34–35.

Latimer, W. W., Newcomb, M., Winters, K. C., & Stinchfield, R. D. (2000). Adolescent substance abuse treatment outcome: the role of substance abuse problem severity, psychosocial, and treatment factors. *Journal of Consulting and Clinical Psychology, 68*, 684–696.

Laurence, D. R., & Bennett, P. N. (1992). *Clinical pharmacology* (7th ed.). New York: Churchill Livingstone.

Lawental, E., McLellan, A. T., Grissom, G. R., Brill, P., & O'Brien, C. (1996). Coerced treatment for substance abuse problems detected through workplace urine surveillance: Is it effective? *Journal of Substance Abuse, 8*, 115–128.

Lawson, C. (1994). Flirting with tragedy: Women who say yes to drugs. *Cosmopolitan, 217* (1), 138–141.

Layne, G. S. (1990). Schizophrenia and substance abuse. In *Managing the dually diagnosed patient* (O'Connell, D. F., ed.). New York: The Haworth Press.

Lazarou, J., Pomeranz, B. H., & Corey, P. N. (1998). Incidence of adverse drug reactions in hospitalized patients. *Journal of the American Medical Association, 279*, 1200–1205.

Le Bon, O., Verbanck, P., Hoffmann, G., Murphy, J. R., Staner, L., De Groote, D., Mampuza, S., Den Dulk, A., Vacher, C., Kornreich, C. Pelc, I. (1997). Sleep in detoxified alcoholics: Impairment of most standard sleep parameters and increased risk for sleep apnea, but not myoclonias—a controlled study. *Journal of Studies on Alcohol, 58*, 30–36.

Lederberg, M. S., & Holland, J. C. (1989). Psycho-oncology. In *Comprehensive textbook of psychiatry/ V* (Kaplan, H. I., & Sadock, B. J., eds.). Baltimore: Williams & Wilkins.

Lee, E. W., & D'Alonzo, G. E. (1993). Cigarette smoking, nicotine addiction, and its pharmacologic treatment. *Archives of Internal Medicine, 153*, 34–48.

Lee, W. M. (1997). Hepatitis B virus infection. *The New England Journal of Medicine, 337*, 1733–1745.

Leeper, K. V., & Torres, A. (1995). Community-acquired pneumonia in the intensive care unit. *Clinics in Chest Medicine, 16*, 155–171.

Lehman, A. F. (1996). Heterogeneity of person and place: Assessing co-occuring addictive and mental disorders. *American Journal of Orthopsychiatry, 66*, 32–41.

Lehman, A. F., Myers, C. P., & Corty, E. (1989) Assessment and classification of patients with psychiatric and substance abuse syndromes. *Hospital and Community Psychiatry, 40*, 1019–1025.

Lehman, L. B., Pilich, A., & Andrews, N. (1994). Neurological disorders resulting from alcoholism. *Alcohol Health & Research World, 17*, 305–309.

Leinwand, D. (2000). New drugs, younger addicts fuel push to shift treatment from methadone clinics. *USA Today 18* (179), 1, 2.

Leistikow, B. N. (2000). The human and financial cost of smoking. *Clinics in Chest Medicine, 21*, 189–197.

Leland, J., Katel, P., & Hager, M. (1996). The fear of heroin is shooting up. *Newsweek, CXXVIII* (9), 55–56.

Lemanski, M. J. (1997). The tenacity of error in the treatment of addiction. *The Humanist, 57* (3), 18–24.

Lemonick, M. D., Lafferty, E., Nash, J. M., Park, A., & Thompson, D. (1997). The mood molecule. *Time, 150* (13), 74–82.

Lender, M. E. (1981). The disease concept of alcoholism in the United States: Was Jellinek first? *Digest of Alcoholism Theory and Application, 1* (1), 25–31.

Leo, J. (1990). The it's-not-my-fault syndrome. *U.S. News & World Report. 109* (12), 16.

Leonard, K. E., & Roberts, R. J. (1996). Alcohol in the early years of marriage. *Alcohol Health & Research World, 20*, 192–196.

Leshner, A. I. (1997a). Drug abuse and addiction treatment research—the next generation. *Archives of General Psychiatry, 54*, 691–694.

Leshner, A. I. (1997b). Drug abuse and addiction are biomedical problems. *Hospital Practice * A Special Report. 38* (4), 2–4.

Leshner, A. I. (1998). Addiction is a brain disease, and it matters. *Science, 278*, 45–47.

Leshner, A. I. (1999). Research shows effects of prenatal cocaine exposure are subtle but significant. *NIDA Notes, 14* (3), 3–4.

Leshner, A. I. (2001). Addiction and the brain. Symposium presented to the Dept. of Psychiatry of The Cambridge Hospital, Boston, MA, March 2, 2001.

Lessard, S. (1989). Busting our mental blocks on drugs and crime. *Washington Monthly, 21* (1), 70.

Lester, D. (2000). Alcoholism, substance abuse, and suicide. In *Comprehensive textbook of suicidology* (Maris, R. W., Berman, A. L., & Silverman, M. M., eds.). New York: Guilford.

Levant, R. F. (2000). Rethinking healthcare costs. *The Independent Practitioner, 20*, 246–248.

Levy, S. J., & Rutter, E. (1992). *Children of drug abusers.* New York: Lexington Books.

Lewis, D. C. (1997). The role of the generalist in the care of the substance-abusing client. *Medical Clinics of North America, 81*, 831–843.

Lewis, J. A., Dana, R. Q., & Blevins, G. A. (1988). *Substance abuse counseling.* Pacific Grove, CA: Brooks/Cole.

Lewis, J. W. (1995). Buprenorphine—medicinal chemistry. In *Buprenorphine* (Cowan, A., & Lewis, J. W., eds.). New York: Wiley Interscience.

Li, G., Baker, S. P., Smialek, J. E., & Soderstrom, C. A. (2001). Use of alcohol as a risk factor for bicycling injury. *Journal of the American Medical Association, 285*, 893–896.

Li, J., Stokes, S. A., & Woeckener, A. (1998). A tale of novel intoxication: A review of the effects of gamma hydroxybutyric acid with recommendations for management. *Annals of Emergency Medicine*, 729–744.

Li, T. (2000). Pharmacogenetics of responses to alcohol and genes that influence alcohol drinking. *Journal of Studies on Alcohol, 61*, 5–12.

Liberto, J. G., Oslin, D. W., & Ruskin, P. E. (1992). Alcoholism in older persons: A review of the literature. *Hospital and Community Psychiatry, 43*, 975–984.

Lichtenstein, E., & Glasgow, R. E. (1992). Smoking cessation: What we have learned over the past decade. *Journal of Consulting and Clinical Psychology, 60*, 518–526.

Lieber, C. S. (1995). Medical disorders of alcoholism. *The New England Journal of Medicine, 333*, 1058–1065.

Lieber, C. S. (1996). *Metabolic basis of alcoholic liver disease.* Paper presented at the 1996 annual Frank P. Furlano, M.D. memorial lecture, Gunderson-Lutheran Medical Center, La Crosse, Wisconsin.

Lieber, C. S. (1998). Hepatic and other medical disorders of alcoholism: From pathogenesis to treatment. *Journal of Studies on Alcohol, 59* (1), 9–25.

Liebschutz, J. M., Mulvey, K. P., & Samet, J. H. (1997). Victimization among substance-abusing women. *Archives of Internal Medicine, 157*, 1093–1097.

Lieveld, P. E., & Aruna, A. (1991). Diagnosis and management of the alcohol withdrawal syndrome. *U.S. Pharmacist, 16* (1), H 1–H 11.

Lindman, R. E., Sjoholm, B. A., & Lang, A. R. (2000). Expectations of alcohol-induced positive affect: A cross-cultural comparison. *Journal of Studies on Alcohol, 61*, 681–687.

Ling, W., Wesson, D. R., Charuvastra, C., & Klett, C. J. (1996). A controlled trial comparing buprenorphine and methadone maintenance in opioid dependence. *Archives of General Psychiatry, 53*, 401–407.

Lingeman, R. R. (1974). *Drugs from A to Z: A dictionary.* New York: McGraw Hill.

Linszen, D. H., Dingemans, P. M., & Lenior, M. E. (1994). Cannabis abuse and the course of recent-onset schizophrenic disorders. *Archives of General Psychiatry, 51*, 273–279.

Lipkin, M. (1989). Psychiatry and medicine. In *Comprehensive textbook of psychiatry/ V.* (Kaplan, H. I., & Sadock, B. J., eds.) Baltimore: Williams & Wilkins.

Lipman, J. L. (2001). Personality, drug abuse and murder. *The Forensic Examiner, 10* (1), 20–26.

Lipscomb, J. W. (1989). What pharmacists should know about home poisonings. *Drug Topics, 133* (15), 72–80.

Lisanti, P., & Zwolski, K. (1997). Understanding the devastation of AIDS. *American Journal of Nursing, 97* (7), 26–34.

Lit, E., Wiviott-Tishler, W., Wong, S., & Hyman, S. (1996). Stimulants: Amphetamines and caffeine. In *Source book of substance abuse and addiction* (Friedman, L., Fleming, N. F., Roberts, D. H., & Hyman, S. H., eds.). New York: Williams & Wilkins.

Little, R. E., Anderson, K. W., Ervin, C. H., Worthington-Roberts, B., & Clarren, S. K. (1989). Maternal alcohol use during breast-feeding and infant mental and motor development at one year. *The New England Journal of Medicine, 321*, 425–430.

Littleton, J. (1998). Neurochemical mechanisms underlying alcohol withdrawal. *Alcohol Health & Research World, 22* (1), 13–24.

Liu, S., Siegel, P. Z., Brewer, R. D., Mokdad, A. H., Sleet, D. A., & Serdula, M. (1997). Prevalence of alcohol-impaired driving. *Journal of the American Medical Association, 277*, 122–125.

Lively, K. (1996). The "date rape drug": Colleges worry about reports of use of Rohypnol, a sedative. *The Chronicle of Higher Education, 42*, (42), A29.

Løberg, T. (1986). Neuropsychological findings in the early and middle phases of alcoholism. In *Neuropsychological assessment of neuropsychiatric disorders.* (Grant, I., & Adams, K. M., eds.). New York: Oxford University Press.

Loebl, S., Spratto, G. R., & Woods, A. L. (1994). *The nurse's drug handbook* (7th ed.). New York: Delmar Publishers, Inc.

Loiselle, J. M., Baker, M. D., Templeton, J. M., Schwartz, G., & Drott, H. (1993). Substance abuse in adolescent trauma. *Annals of Emergency Medicine, 22*, 1530–1534.

Longo, L. P., & Johnson, B. (2000). Addiction: Part I. *American Family Physician, 61*, 2121–2128.

Longo, L. P., Parran, T., Johnson, B., & Kinsey, W. (2000). Addiction: Part II. *American Family Physician, 61*, 2401–2408.

Lopez, W., & Jeste, D. V. (1997). Movement disorders and substance abuse. *Psychiatric Services, 48*, 634–636.

Los Angeles Times. (1996a). A very venerable vintage. *Minneapolis Star-Tribune, XV* (63), A16.

Los Angeles Times. (1996b). Tobacco smoke greatly increases SIDS risk, study finds. *Minneapolis Star-Tribune, XV* (113), A1, A16.

Louie, A. K. (1990). Panic attacks—when cocaine is the cause. *Medical Aspects of Human Sexuality, 24* (12), 44–46.

Lourwood, D. L., & Riedlinger, J. E. (1989). The use of drugs in the breast feeding mother. *Drug Topics, 133* (21), 77–85.

Lovett, A. R. (1994, May 5). Wired in California. *Rolling Stone,* 39–40.

Lund, N., & Papadakos, P. J. (1995). Barbiturates, neuroleptics, and propofol for sedation. *Critical Care Clinics, 11,* 875–885.

Lynam, D. R., Milich, R., Zimmerman, R., Novak, S. P., Logan, T. K., Martin, C., Leukefeld, C., & Clayton, R. (1999). Project DARE: No effects at 10–year follow-up. *Journal of Consulting and Clinical Psychology, 67,* 590–593.

Maas, E. F., Ashe, J., Spiegel, P., Zee, D. S., & Leigh, R. J. (1991). Acquired pendular nystagmus in toluene addiction. *Neurology, 41,* 282–286.

MacCoun, R. J. (1998). Towards a psychology of harm reduction. *American Psychologist, 53* (11), 1199–1208.

MacCoun, R., & Reuter, P. (1998). Interpreting Dutch cannabis policy: Reasoning by analogy in the legalization debate. *Science, 278,* 47–52.

MacCoun, R., & Reuter, P. (2001). Evaluating alternative cannabis regimes. *British Journal of Psychiatry, 178,* 123–128.

Macfadden, W., & Woody, G. E. (2000). Cannabis-related disorders. In *Comprehensive textbook of psychiatry* (7th ed.). (Sadock, B. J., & Sadock, V. A., eds.). New York: Lippincott Williams & Wilkins.

MacKenzie, T. D., Bartecchi, C. E., & Schrier, R. W. (1994). The human costs of tobacco use (first of two parts). *The New England Journal of Medicine, 330,* 907–912.

Maddux, J. F., Desmond, D. P., & Costello, R. (1987). Depression in opioid users varies with substance use status. *American Journal of Drug & Alcohol Abuse, 13* (4), 375–378.

Maguire, J. (1990). *Care and feeding of the brain.* New York: Doubleday.

Maisto, S. A., & Connors, G. J. (1988). Assessment of treatment outcome. In *Assessment of addictive disorders* (Donovan, D. M., & Marlatt, G. A., eds.). New York: Guilford.

Males, M. (1992). Tobacco: Promotion and smoking. *Journal of the American Medical Association, 267,* 3282.

Mandell, L. A., & Niederman, M. S. (1999). *Guide to prognosis and management of community-acquired pneumonia (CAP) & hospital-acquired pneumonia (HAP).* Greenwood Lake, NY: Sheffield Dawson Publishers, LTD.

Manderson, D. R. A. (1998). Drug abuse and illicit drug trafficking. *Medical Journal of Australia, 12,* 588–589.

Manfredi, R. L., Kales, A., Vgontzas, A. N., Bixler, E. 0., Isaac, M. A., & Falcone, C. M. (1991). Buspirone: Sedative or stimulant effect? *American Journal of Psychiatry, 148,* 1213–1217.

Mann, C. C., & Plummer, M. L. (1991). *The aspirin wars.* New York: Knopf.

Mann, J. (1992). *Murder, magic and medicine.* New York: Oxford.

Mannino, D. M., Moorman, J. E., Kingsley, B., Rose, D., & Repace, J. (2001). Health effects related to environmental tobacco smoke exposure in children in the United States. *Archives of Pediatric and Adolescent Medicine, 155,* 36–41.

Maranto, G. (1985). Coke: The random killer. *Discover, 12* (3), 16–21.

Margolin, A., Kosten, T., Petrakis, I., Avants, S. K., & Kosten, T. (1991). Bupropion reduces cocaine abuse in methadone-maintained patients. *Archives of General Psychiatry, 48,* 87.

Markarian, M., & Franklin, J. (1998). Substance abuse in minority populations. In *Clinical textbook of addictive disorders* (2nd ed.) (Frances, R. J., & Miller, S. I., eds.). New York: Guilford.

Markel, H. (2000). Easy answer might not be the right one. *The New York Times, CL* (51551), D8.

Marlatt, G. A. (1994). Harm reduction: A public health approach to addictive behavior. *Division on Addictions Newsletter, 2* (1), 1, 3.

Marlatt, G. A., Baer, J. S., Kivlahan, D. R., Dimeff, L. A., Larimer, M. E., Quigley, L. A., Somers, J. M., & Williams, E. (1998). Screening and brief intervention for high-risk college student drinkers: Results from a 2-year follow-up assessment. *Journal of Consulting and Clinical Psychology, 66,* 604–615.

Marmor, J. B. (1998). Medical marijuana. *Western Journal of Medicine, 168,* 540–543.

Marsano, L. (1994). Alcohol and malnutrition. *Alcohol Health & Research World, 17,* 284–291.

Marshall, J. R. (1994). The diagnosis and treatment of social phobia and alcohol abuse. *Bulletin of the Menninger Clinic, 58,* A58–A66.

Marston, H. M., Reid, M. E., Lawrence, J. A., Olverman, H. J., & Butcher, S. P. (1999). Behavioral analysis of the acute and chronic effects of MDMA treatment in the rat. *Psychopharmacology, 144,* 67–76.

Martensen, R. L. (1996). From papal endorsement to southern vice. *Journal of the American Medical Association, 276,* 1615.

Martin, C. S., & Winters, K. C. (1998). Diagnosis and assessment of alcohol use disorders among adolescents. *Alcohol Health & Research World, 22,* 95–101, 104.

Martin, P. J., Enevoldson, T. P., & Humphrey, P. R. D. (1997). Causes of ischaemic stroke in the young. *Postgraduate Medical Journal, 73,* 8–16.

Marvel, B. (1995). AA's "higher power" challenged. *St. Paul Pioneer Press, 147* (44), 4A.

Marwick, C. (1997). Coma-inducing drug GBH may be relcassified. *Journal of the American Medical Association, 277,* 1505–1506.

Marzuk, M. M. (1996). Violence, crime and mental illness. *Archives of General Psychiatry, 53,* 481–486.

Marzuk, P. M., Tardiff, K., Leon, A. C., Hirsch, C. S., Stajic, M., Portera, L., Hartwell, N., & Iqbal, M. I. (1995). Fatal injuries after cocaine use as a leading cause of death among young adults in New York City. *The New England Journal of Medicine, 332,* 1753–1757.

Marzuk, P. M., Tardiff, K., Leon, A. C., Stajic, M., Morgan, E. B., & Mann, J. J. (1992). Prevalence of cocaine use among residents of New York City who committed suicide during a one-year period. *American Journal of Psychiatry, 149,* 371–375.

Mason, B. J., Salvato, F. R., Williams, L. D., Ritvo, E. C., & Cutler, R. B. (1999). A double-blind, placebo-controlled study of oral nalmefene for alcohol dependence. *Archives of General Psychiatry, 56,* 719–724.

Masse, L. C., & Tremblay, R. E. (1997). Behavior of boys in kindergarten and onset of substance use during adolescence. *Archives of General Psychiatry, 52,* 62–68.

Mathers, D. C., & Ghodse, A. D. (1992). Cannabis and psychotic illness. *British Journal of Psychiatry, 161,* 648–653.

Mathew, J., Addai, T., Ashwin, A., Morrobel, A., Maheshwari, P., & Freels, S. (1995). Clinical features, site of involvement, bacteriologic findings and outcome of infection endocarditis in intravenous drug users. *Archives of Internal Medicine, 155,* 1641–1649.

Mathew, R. D., Wilson, W. H., Blazer, D. G., & George, L. K. (1993). Psychiatric disorders in adult children of alcoholics: Data from the epidemiologic catchment area project. *American Journal of Psychiatry, 150,* 793–800.

Mathias, R. (1995). NIDA survey provides first national data on drug use during pregnancy. *NIDA Notes 10* (1), 6–7.

Mattick, R. P., & Hall, W. (1996). Are detoxification programs effective? *The Lancet, 347,* 97–100.

Mattila, M. A. K., & Larni, H. M. (1980). Flunitrazepam: A review of its pharmacological properties and therapeutic use. *Drugs, 20,* 353–374.

Mattson, S. N., & Riley, E. P. (1995). Prenatal exposure to alcohol. *Alcohol Health & Research World, 19,* 273–278.

Matuschka, P. R. (1985). The psychopharmacology of addiction. In *Alcoholism and substance abuse: Strategies for clinical intervention* (Bratter, T. E., & Forrest, G. G., eds.). New York: The Free Press.

Maxmen, J. S., & Ward, N. G. (1995). *Psychotropic drugs fast facts* (2nd ed.). New York: W. W. Norton & Co.

May, D. (1999). Testing by necessity. *Occupational Health & Safety, 68* (4), 48, 50–51.

May, G. G. (1988). *Addiction & grace.* New York: Harper & Row.

May, G. G. (1991). *The awakened heart.* New York: Harper & Row.

Mayo Clinic Health Letter. (1989). *America's drug crisis.* Rochester, MN: Mayo Foundation for Medical Education and Research.

McAnalley, B. H. (1996). Chemistry of alcoholic beverages. In *Medicolegal aspects of alcohol* (3rd ed.) (Garriott, J. C., ed.). Tucson, AZ: Lawyers and Judges Publishing Co.

McCaffrey, B. (1997). Kreek, M. J. (1997). *The national drug control strategy: 1997.* Paper presented at NIDA conference: Heroin use and addiction. Washington, DC, September 29–30.

McCaffery, M., & Ferrell, B. R. (1994). Understanding opioids and addiction. *Nursing 94,* 24 (8), 56–59.

McCann, U. D., Szabo, Z., Scheffel, U., Dannals, R. F., & Ricaurte, G. A. (1998). Positron emission tomographic evidence of toxic effect of MDMA ("Ecstasy") on brain sero-tonin neurons in human beings. *The Lancet, 352,* 1433–1437.

McCarthy, J. J., & Borders, O. T. (1985). Limit setting on drug abuse in methadone maintenance patients. *American Journal of Psychiatry, 142,* 1419–1423.

McCaul, M. D., & Furst, J. (1994). Alcoholism treatment in the United States. *Alcohol Health & Research World, 18,* 253–260.

McCrady, B. S. (1993). Alcoholism. In *Clinical handbook of psychological disorders* (2nd ed.). (Barlow, D. H., ed.). New York: Guilford.

McCrady, B. S. (1994). Alcoholics Anonymous and behavior therapy: Can habits be treated as diseases? Can diseases be treated as habits? *Journal of Consulting and Clinical Psychology, 62,* 1159–1166.

McCrady, B. S., & Epstein, E. E. (1995). Marital therapy in the treatment of alcoholism. In *Clinical handbook of couple therapy* (Jacobson, N. S., & Gurman, A. S., eds.). New York: Guilford.

McCrady, B. S., & Delaney, S. I. (1995). Self-help groups. In *Handbook of alcoholism treatment approaches* (2nd ed.) (Hester, R. K., & Miller, W. R., eds.). New York: Allyn & Bacon.

McCrady, B. S., & Irvine, S. (1989). Self-help groups. In *Handbook of alcoholism treatment approaches* (Hester, R. K., & Miller, W. R., eds.). New York: Pergamon Press.

McCrady, B. S., & Langenbucher, J. W. (1996). Alcohol treatment and health care system reform. *Archives of General Psychiatry, 53,* 737–746.

McCusker, J., Stoddard, A., Frost, R., & Zorn, M. (1996). Planned versus actual duration of drug abuse treatment. *Journal of Nervous and Mental Disease, 184,* 482–489.

McCutchan, J. A. (1990). Virology, immunology, and clinical course of HIV infection. *Journal of Clinical and Consulting Psychology, 58,* 5–12.

McDargh, J. (2000). *The role of spirituality in the recovery process.* Symposium presented to the Dept. of Psychiatry of The Cambridge Hospital, Boston, MA, March 4.

McDonough, J. (1998). Acetaminophen overdose. *American Journal of Nursing, 98* (3), 52.

McElhatton, P. R., Bateman, D. N., Evans, C., Pughe, K. R., & Thomas, S. H. L. (1999). Congenital anomalies after prenatal ecstasy exposure. *The Lancet, 354,* 1441.

McEnroe, P. (1990). Hawaii is fighting losing battle against the popularity of drug "ice." *Minneapolis Star-Tribune, IX* (44), 1, 20A.

McFadden, E. R., & Hejal, R. B. (2000). The pathobiology of acute asthma. *Clinics in Chest Medicine, 21,* 213–224.

McGowan, R. (1998). *Finding God in all things: Ministering to those suffering from addictions.* Symposium presented to the Dept. of Psychiatry of The Cambridge Hospital, Boston, MA, March 7.

McGrath, P. J., Nunes, E. V., & Quitkin, F. M. (2000). Current concepts in the treatment of depression in alcohol-dependent patients. *The Psychiatric Clinics of North America, 23,* 695–711.

McGuire, L. (1990). The power of non-narcotic pain relievers. *RN, 53* (4), 28–35.

McGuire, P., & Fahy, T. (1991). Chronic paranoid psychosis after misuse of MDMA ("ecstacy"). *British Medical Journal, 302,* 697.

McHugh, M. J. (1987). The abuse of volatile substances. *The Pediatric Clinics of North America, 34* (2), 333–340.

McIlvain, H. E., Bobo, J. K., Leed-Kelly, A., & Sitorius, M. A. (1998). Practical steps to smoking cessation for recovering alcoholics. *American Family Physician, 57,* 1869–1876.

McKay, J. R., McLellan, T., Alterman, A. I., Cacciola, J. S., Rutherford, M. J., & O'Brian, C. P. (1998). Predictors of participation in aftercare sessions and self-help groups following completion of intensive outpatient treatment for substance abuse. *Journal of Studies on Alcohol, 59,* 152–162.

McLellan, A. T. (2001). Is addiction treatment effective: Compared to what? Symposium presented to the Dept. of Psychiatry of The Cambridge Hospital, Boston, MA, March 2, 2001.

McLellan, A. T., Arndt, I. O., Metzger, D. S., Woody, G. E., & O'Brien, C. P. (1993). The effects of psychosocial services in substance abuse treatment. *Journal of the American Medical Association, 269,* 1953–1959.

McLellan, A. T., Lewis, D. C., O'Brien, C. P., & Kleber, H. D. (2000). Drug dependence, a chronic medical illness. *Journal of the American Medical Association, 284,* 1689–1695.

McNamara, J. D. (1996). The war on drugs is lost. *National Review, XLVIII* (2), 42–44.

McPhillips, M. A., Strang, J., & Barnes, T. R. E. (1998). Hair analysis. *British Journal of Psychiatry, 173,* 287–290.

McWilliams, P. (1993). Ain't nobody's business. *Playboy, 40* (9), 49–52.

McWilliams, P. (1999). The general's loophole. *Playboy, 46* (12), 61.

Mead, R. (1993). Teen access to cigarettes in Green Bay, Wisconsin. *Wisconsin Medical Journal, 92,* 23–25.

Medical Economics Company. (1989). Anabolic steroid abuse and primary care. *Patient Care, 23* (8), 12.

Medical Economics Company. (2000). *2000 Physician's Desk Reference* (54th ed.). Oradell, NJ: Medical Economics Company.

Medical Update. (1994). The agony of "ecstasy." 17 (11), 5–6.

Meer, J. (1986). Marijuana in the air: Delayed buzz bomb. *Psychology Today, 20,* 68.

Melnick, G., De Leon, G., Hawke, J., Jainchill, N., & Kressel, D. (1997). Motivation and readiness for therapeutic community treatment among adolescents and adult substance abusers. *American Journal of Alcohol Abuse, 24,* 485–506.

Melzack, R. (1990). The tragedy of needless pain. *Scientific American, 262* (2), 27–33.

Mendelson, J. H., & Mello, N. K. (1996). Management of cocaine abuse and dependence. *The New England Journal of Medicine,334,* 965–972.

Mendelson, J. H., & Mello, N. K. (1998). Cocaine and other commonly abused drugs. In *Harrison's principles of internal medicine* (14th ed.) (Fauci, A. S., Martin, J. B., Braunwald, E., Kasper, D. L., Isselbacher, K. J. Hauser, S. L., Wilson, J. D., & Longo, D. L., eds.). New York: McGraw-Hill.

Mendelson, W. B., & Rich, C. L. (1993). Sedatives and suicide: The San Diego study. *Acta Psychiatrica Scandinavica, 88,* 337–341.

Mendoza, R., & Miller, B. L. (1992). Neuropsychiatric disorders associated with cocaine use. *Hospital and Community Psychiatry, 43,* 677–678.

Merikangas, K. R., Dierker, L. C., & Szatmari, P. (1998). Psychopathology among offspring of parents with substance abuse and/or anxiety disorders: A high risk study. *Journal of Child Psychology & Psychiatry, 39,* 711–720.

Merikangas, K. R., Stolar, M., Stevens, D. E., Goulet, J., Preisig, M. A., Fenton, B., Zhang, H., O'Malley, S. S., & Rounsaville, B. J. (1998). Familial transmission of substance use disorders. *Archives of General Psychiatry, 55,* 973–979.

Merikle, E. P. (1999). The subjective experience of craving: An exploratory analysis. *Substance Use & Misuse, 34,* 1011–1015.

Merlotti, L., Roehrs, T., Koshorek, G., Zorick, F., Lamphere, J., & Roth, T. (1989). The dose effects of zolpidem on the sleep of healthy normals. *Journal of Clinical Psychopharmacology, 9* (1), 9–14.

Merton, T. (1961). *New seeds of contemplation.* New York: New Directions Publishing.

Merton, T. (1978). *No man is an island.* New York: New Directions Publishing.

Meyer, R. (1988). Intervention: Opportunity for healing. *Alcoholism & Addiction, 9* (1), 7.

Meyer, R. E. (1989a). Who can say no to illicit drug use. *Archives of General Psychiatry, 46,* 189–190.

Meyer, R. E. (1989b). What characterizes addiction? *Alcohol Health & Research World, 13* (4), 316–321.

Meyer, R. E. (1992). New pharmacotherapies for cocaine dependence…revisited. *Archives of General Psychiatry, 49,* 900–904.

Meyer, R. E. (1994). What for, alcohol research? *American Journal of Psychiatry, 151,* 165–168.

Meyer, R. E. (1996). The disease called addiction: Emerging evidence is a 200 year debate. *The Lancet, 347,* 162–166.

Meyers, B. R. (1992). *Antimicrobial therapy guide.* Newtown, PA: Antimicrobial Prescribing, Inc.

Meza, E., & Kranzler, H. R. (1996). Closing the gap between alcoholism research and practice: the case for pharmacotherapy. *Psychiatric Services, 47,* 917–920.

Michelson, J. B., Carroll, D., McLane, N. J., & Robin, H. S. (1988). Drug abuse and ocular disease. In *Surgical treatment of ocular inflammatory disease* (Michelson, J. B., & Nozik, R. A., eds.). New York: J. B. Lippincott Co.

Middleman, A. B., & DuRant, R. H. (1996). Anabolic steroid use and associated health risk behaviors. *Sports Medicine, 21,* 251–255.

Milberger, S., Biederman, J., Faraone, S. V., Chen, L., & Jones, J. (1996). Is maternal smoking during pregnancy a risk factor for Attention Deficit Hyperactivity Disorder in children? *American Journal of Psychiatry, 153,* 1138–1142.

Milby, J. B., Hohmann, A. A., Gentile, M., Huggins, N., Sims, M. K., McLellan, T., Woody, G., & Haas, N. (1994). Methadone maintenance outcome as a function of detoxification phobia. *American Journal of Psychiatry, 151,* 1031–1037.

Miles, S. A. (1996). Pathogenesis of AIDS-related Kaposi's sarcoma. *Hematology/Oncology Clinics of North America, 10,* 1011–1021.

Milhorn, H. T. (1991). Diagnosis and management of phenocyclidine intoxication. *American Family Physician, 43,* 1293–1302.

Milhorn, H. T. (1992). Pharmacologic management of acute abstinence syndromes. *American Family Physician, 45,* 231–239.

Milin, R., Loh, E., Chow, J., & Wilson, A. (1997). Assessment of symptoms of Attention-Deficit Hyperactivity Disorder in adults with substance use disorders. *Psychiatric Services, 48,* 1378–1380.

Miller, A. (1988). *The enabler.* Claremont, CA: Hunter House.

Miller, B. A., & Downs, W. R. (1995). Violent victimization among women with alcohol problems. In *Recent developments in alcoholism* (Vol. 12) (Galanter, M., ed.). New York: Plenum Press.

Miller, L. J., (1994). Psychiatric medication during pregnancy: Understanding and minimizing risks. *Psychiatric Annals, 24* (2), 69–75.

Miller, L., Davies, M., & Greenwald, S. (2000). Religiosity and substance use and abuse among adolescents in the National Comorbidity Survey. *Journal of the American Adademy of Child and Adolescent Psychiatry, 39,* 1190–1197.

Miller, N. S. (1994). Psychiatric comorbidity: Occurrence and treatment. *Alcohol Health & Research World, 18,* 261–264.

Mller, N. S. (1999). Mortality risks in alcoholism and effects of abstinence and addiction treatment. *Psychiatric Clinics of North America, 22,* 371–383.

Miller, N. S., & Gold, M. S. (1991a). Organic solvent and aerosol abuse. *American Family Physician, 44,* 183–190.

Miller, N. S., & Gold, M. S. (1991b). Abuse, addiction, tolerance, and dependence to benzodiazepines in medical and nonmedical populations. *American Journal of Drug and Alcohol Abuse, 17* (1), 27–37.

Miller, N. S., & Gold, M. S. (1991c). Dual diagnosis: Psychiatric syndromes in alcoholism and drug addiction. *American Family Physician, 43,* 2071–2076.

Miller, N. S., & Gold, M. S. (1993). A hypothesis for a common neurochemical basis for alcohol and drug disorders. *Psychiatric Clinics of North America, 16,* 105–117.

Miller, N. S., & Gold, M. S. (1998). Management of withdrawal syndromes and relapse prevention in drug and alcohol dependence. *American Family Physician, 58* (1), 139–146.

Miller, S. I., Frances, R. J., & Holmes, D. J. (1988). Use of psychotropic drugs in alcoholism treatment: A summary. *Hospital & Community Psychiatry, 39,* 1251–1252.

Miller, S. I., Frances, R. J., & Holmes, D. J. (1989). Psychotropic medications. In *Handbook of alcoholism treatment approaches* (Hester, R. K., & Miller, W. R., eds.). New York: Pergamon Press.

Miller, W. R. (1976). Alcoholism scales and objective measures. *Psychological Bulletin, 83,* 649–674.

Miller, W. R. (1995). Increasing motivation for change. In *Handbook of alcoholism treatment approaches* (2nd ed.) (Hester, R. K., & Miller, W. R., eds.). New York: Allyn & Bacon.

Miller, W. R. (1998). Enhancing motivation for change. In *Treating addictive behaviors* (2nd ed.) (Miller, W. R., & Heather, N., eds.). New York: Plenum.

Miller, W. R., Andrews, N. R., Wilbourne, P., & Bennett, M. E. (1998). A wealth of alternatives. In *Handbook of alcoholism treatment approaches* (2nd ed.) (Hester, R. K., & Miller, W. R., eds.). New York: Allyn & Bacon.

Miller, W. R., & Brown, S. A. (1997). Why psychologists should treat alcohol and drug problems. *American Psychologist, 52,* 1269–1279.

Miller, W. R., & Cervantes, E. A. (1997). Gender and patterns of alcohol problems: Pre-treatment responses of women and men to the comprehensive drinker profile. *Journal of Clinical Psychology, 53,* 263–277.

Miller, W. R., Genefield, G., & Tonigan, J. S. (1993). Enhancing motivation for change in problem drinking: A controlled comparison of two therapist styles. *Journal of Consulting and Clinical Psychology, 61,* 455–462.

Miller, W. R., & Harris, R. J. (2000). A simple scale of Gorski's warning signs for relapse. *Journal of Studies on Alcohol, 61,* 759–765.

Miller, W. R., & Hester, R. K. (1980). Treating the problem drinker: Modern approaches. In *The addictive behaviors* (Miller, W. R., ed.). New York: Pergamon Press.

Miller, W. R., & Hester, R. K. (1986). Inpatient alcoholism treatment. *American Psychologist, 41* (7), 794–806.

Miller, W. R., & Hester, R. K. (1995). Treating alcohol problems: Toward an informed eclectism. In *Handbook of alcoholism treatment approaches* (2nd ed.) (Hester, R. K., & Miller, W. R., eds.). New York: Allyn & Bacon.

Miller, W. R., & Kurtz, E. (1994). Models of alcoholism used in treatment: Contrasting AA and other perspectives with which it is often confused. *Journal of Studies on Alcohol, 55,* 159–166.

Miller, W. R., & McCrady, B. S. (1993). The importance of research on Alcoholics Anonymous. In *Research on Alcoholics Anonymous* (McCrady, B. S., & Miller, W. R., eds.). New Brunswick, NJ: Rutgers Center of Alcohol Studies.

Miller, W. R., & Rollnick, S. (1991). *Motivational interviewing.* New York: Guilford.

Miller, W. R., Westerberg, V. S., & Waldron, H. B. (1995). Evaluating alcohol problems in adults and adolescents. In *Handbook of alcoholism treatment approaches* (2nd ed.)

(Hester, R. K., & Miller, W. R., eds.). New York: Allyn & Bacon.

Millman, R. B., & Beeder, A. B. (1994). Cannabis. In *Textbook of substance abuse treatment* (Galanter, M., & Kleber, H. D., eds.). Washington, DC: American Psychiatric Press, Inc.

Millon, T. (1981). *Disorders of personality.* New York: John Wiley.

Mills, K. C. (1995). Serotonin syndrome. *American Family Physician, 52,* 1475–1482.

Milzman, D. P., & Soderstrom, C. A. (1994). Substance use disorders in trauma patients. *Critical Care Clinics, 10,* 595–612.

Minkoff, K. (1989). An integrated treatment model for dual diagnosis of psychosis and addiction. *Hospital and Community Psychiatry, 40,* 1031–1036.

Minkoff, K. (1997). Substance abuse versus substance dependence. *Psychiatric Services, 48,* 867.

Minneapolis Star Tribune. (1989). New drug "ice" grips Hawaii, threatens mainland. VIII (150), 12A.

Minneapolis Star Tribune. (1995a). FDA approves new alcoholism treatment. XIII (288), 7A.

Minneapolis Star Tribune. (1995b). High court weighs school drug testing. XIII (359), 7A.

Minneapolis Star Tribune. (1995c). Do-it-yourself drug detector. XIII (359), 1A.

Minneapolis Star Tribune. (1997). A grim report on AIDS' reach. XVI (237), 1A.

Mirin, S. M., Weiss, R. D., & Greenfield, S. F. (1991). Psychoactive substance use disorders. In *The practitioner's guide to psychoactive drugs* (3rd ed.) (Galenberg, A. J., Bassuk, E. L., & Schoonover, S. C., eds.). New York: Plenum Medical Book Co.

Mitra, S. C., Ganesh, V., & Apuzzio, J. J. (1994). Effect of maternal cocaine abuse on renal arterial flow and urine output in the fetus. *American Journal of Obstetrics and Gynecology, 171,* 1556–1560.

Modesto-Lowe, V., & Kranzler, H. R. (1999). Diagnosis and treatment of alcohol-dependent patients with comorbid psychiatric disorders. *Alcohol Research & Health, 23* (2), 144–149.

Moliterno, D. J., Willard, J. E., Lange, R. A., Negus, B. H., Boehrer, J. D., Glamann, B., Landau, C., Rossen, J. D., Winniford, M. D., & Hollis, L. D. (1994). Coronary-artery vasoconstriction induced by cocaine, cigarette smoking, or both. *The New England Journal of Medicine, 330,* 454–459.

Monforte, R., Estruch, R., Valls-Sole, J., Nicolas, J., Villalta, J., & Urbano-Marquez, A. (1995). Autonomic and peripheral neuropathies in patients with chronic alcoholism. *Archives of Neurology, 51,* 45–51.

Monroe, J. (1994). Designer drugs: CAT & LSD. *Current Health, 20* (1), 13–16.

Monroe, J. (1995). Inhalants: Dangerous highs. *Current Health, 22* (1), 16–20.

Monroe, J. (1998). Marijuana: A mind-altering drug. *Current Health, 24* (7), 16–20.

Moon, D. B., Hecht, M. L., Jackson, K. M., & Spellers, R. E. (1999) Ethnic and gender differences and similarities in adolescent drug use and refusals of drug offers. *Substance Use & Misuse, 34,* 1059–1083.

Moore, M. H. (1991) Drugs, the criminal law, and the administration of justice. *The Milbank Quarterly, 69* (4), 529–560.

Moore, M. K., & Ginsberg, L. (1999). The date rapist's scary new weapon. *Cosmopolitan, 226* (2), 202.

Moore, R. A. (1995). Analysis. In *Buprenorphine* (Cowan, A., & Lewis, J. W., eds.). New York: Wiley Interscience.

Moos, R. H., King, M. J., & Patterson, M. A. (1996). Outcomes of residential treatment of substance abuse in hospital and community-based programs. *Psychiatric Services, 47,* 68–74.

Moos, R. H., & Moos, B. S. (1995). Stay in residential facilities and mental health care as predictors of readmission for patients with substance use disorders. *Psychiatric Services, 46,* 66–72.

Moos, R. H., Moos, B. S., & Andrassy, J. M. (1999). Outcomes of four treatment approaches in community residential programs for patients with substance use disorders. *Psychiatric Services, 50,* 1577–1583.

Morabia, A., Bernstein, M., Heritier, S., & Khatchatrian, N. (1996). Relation of breast cancer with passive and active exposure to tobacco. *American Journal of Epidemiology, 143,* 918–928.

Morey, L. C. (1996). Patient placement criteria. *Alcohol Health & Research World, 20,* 36–44.

Morgan, M. J. (1999). Memory deficits associated with recreational "ecstasy" (MDMA). *Psychopharmacology, 141,* 30–36.

Morgenstern, J., Labouvie, E., McCrady, B. S., Kahler, C. W., & Frey, R. M. (1997). Affiliation with Alcoholics Anonymous after treatment: A study of its therapeutic effects and mechanisms of actions. *Journal of Consulting and Clinical Psychology, 65,* 768–777.

Morrison, M. A. (1990). Addiction in adolescents. *The Western Journal of Medicine, 152,* 543–547.

Morrison, S. F., Rogers, P. D., & Thomas, M. H. (1995). Alcohol and adolescents. *Pediatric Clinics of North America, 42,* 371–387.

Morse, R. M., & Flavin, D. K. (1992). The definition of alcoholism. *Journal of the American Medical Association, 268,* 1012–1014.

Mortensen, M. E., & Rennebohm, R. M. (1989). Clinical pharmacology and use of non-steroidal anti-inflammatory drugs. *Pediatric Clinics of North America, 36,* 1113–1139.

Morton, H. G. (1987). Occurrence and treatment of solvent abuse in children and adolescents. *Pharmacological Therapy, 33,* 449–469.

Morton, W. A., & Santos, A. (1989). New indications for benzodiazepines in the treatment of major psychiatric disorders. *Hospital Formulary, 24,* 274–278.

Mosier, W. A. (1999). Alcohol addiction: Identifying the patient who drinks. *Journal of the American Academy of Physician's Assistants, 12* (5), 25–26, 28–29, 35–36, 38, 40.

Mott, S. H., Packer, R. J., & Soldin, S. J. (1994). Neurologic manifestations of cocaine exposure in childhood. *Pediatrics*, 93, 557–560.

Moyer, L. A., Mast, E. E., & Alter, M. J. (1999). Hepatitis C: Part I. Routine serologic testing and diagnosis. *American Family Physician*, 59, 79–88.

Moyer, T. P., & Ellefson, P. J. (1987). Marijuana testing—how good is it? *Mayo Clinic Procedures*, 62, 413–417.

Moylan, D. W. (1990). Court intervention. *Adolescent Counselor*, 2 (5), 23–27.

Mueller, T. I., Lavori, P. W., Keller, M. B., Swartz, A., Warshaw, M., Hasin, D., Coryell, W., Endicott, J., Rice, J., & Akiskall, H. (1994). Prognostic effect of the variable course of alcoholism on the 10 year course of depression. *American Journal of Psychiatry*, 151, 701–706.

Mueser, K. T., Bellack, A. S., & Blanchard, J. J. (1992). Comorbidity of schizophrenia and substance abuse: Implications for treatment. *Journal of Counseling and Clinical Psychology*, 60, 845–856.

Mueser, K. T., Yarnold, P. R., & Bellack, A. S. (1992). Diagnostic and demographic correlates of substance abuse in schizophrenia and major affective disorder. *Acta Psychiatrica Scandinavica* 85, 48–55.

Mundle, G. (2000). Geriatric patients. In *Handbook of alcoholism* (Zernig, G., Saria, A., Kurz, M., & O'Malley, S. S., eds.). New York: CRC Press.

Murphy, G. E., Wetzel, R. D., Robins, E., & McEvoy, L. (1992). Multiple risk factors predict suicide in alcoholism. *Archives of General Psychiatry*, 49, 459–463.

Murphy, S. L., & Khantzian, E. J. (1995). Addiction as a self-medication disorder: application of ego psychology to the treatment of substance abuse. In *Psychotherapy and substance abuse* (Washton, A. M., ed.). New York: Guilford.

Murphy, S. M., Owen, R., Tyrer, P. (1989). Comparative assessment of efficacy and withdrawal symptoms after 6 and 12 weeks' treatment with diazepam or buspirone. *British Journal of Psychiatry*, 154, 529–534.

Musto, D. F. (1991). Opium, cocaine and marijuana in American history. *Scientific American*, 265 (1), 40–47.

Musto, D. F. (1996). Alcohol in American history. *Scientific American*, 274 (4), 78–83.

Mylonakis, E., Paliou, M., & Rich, J. D. (2001). Plasma viral load testing in the management of HIV infection. *American Family Physician*, 63, 483–490.

Nace, E. P. (1987). *The treatment of alcoholism*. New York: Brunner/Mazel.

Nace, E. P. (1997). Alcoholics Anonymous. In *Substance abuse: A comprehensive textbook* (3rd ed.) (Lowinson, J. H., Ruiz, P., Millman, R. B., & Langrod, J. G., eds.). New York: Williams & Wilkins.

Nace, E. P., & Isbell, P. G. (1991). Alcohol. In *Clinical textbook of addictive disorders* (Frances, R. J., & Miller, S. I., eds.). New York: Guilford.

Nadelmann, E. A. (1989). Drug prohibition in the United States: Costs, consequences, and alternatives. *Science*, 245, 939–946.

Nadelmann, E. A., Kleiman, M. A. R., & Earls, F. J. (1990). Should some illegal drugs be legalized? *Issues in Science and Technology*, VI (4), 43–49.

Nadelmann, E., & Wenner, J. S. (1994, May 5). Towards a sane national drug policy. *Rolling Stone*, 24–26.

Nahas, G. G. (1986). Cannabis: Toxicological properties and epidemiological aspects. *The Medical Journal of Australia*, 145, 82–87.

Najm, W. (1997). Viral hepatitis: How to manage type C and D infections. *Geriatrics*, 52 (5), 28–37.

Narcotics Anonymous. (1982). Van Nuys, CA: Narcotics Anonymous World Service Office, Inc.

Nash, J. M., & Park, A. (1997). Addicted. *Time*, 149 (18), 68–76.

Nathan, P. E. (1988). The addictive personality is the behavior of the addict. *Journal of Consulting and Clinical Psychology*, 56, 183–188.

Nathan, P. E. (1991). Substance use disorders in the DSM-IV. *Journal of Abnormal Psychology*, 100, 356–361.

National Academy of Sciences. (1990). *Treating drug problems* (Vol. 1). Washington, DC: National Academy Press.

National Center on Addiction and Substance Abuse at Columbia University. (2000). *CASA releases physician survey*. Press release, May 10.

National Commission on Marihuana and Drug Abuse. (1973). *Drug use in America: Problem in perspective*. Washington, DC: U.S. Government Printing Office.

National Foundation for Brain Research. (1992). *The cost of disorders of the brain*. Washington, DC: National Foundation for Brain Research.

Neeleman, J., & Farrell, M. (1997). Suicide and substance misuse. *British Journal of Psychiatry*, 171, 303–304.

Negus, S. S., & Woods, J. H. (1995). Reinforcing effects, discriminative stimulus effects, and physical dependence liability of buprenorphine. In *Buprenorphine* (Cowan, A., & Lewis, J. W., eds.). New York: Wiley Interscience.

Nelipovich, M., & Buss, E. (1991). Investigating alcohol abuse among persons who are blind. *Journal of Visual Impairment & Blindness*, 85, 343–345.

Nelson, H. D., Nevitt, M. C., Scott, J. C., Stone, K. L., & Cummings, S. R. (1994). Smoking, alcohol, and neuromuscular and physical function in older women. *Journal of the American Medical Association*, 272, 1825–1831.

Nelson, T. (2000). Pharmacology of drugs of abuse. Seminar presented by the Division of Continuing Studies, University of Wisconsin—Madison, Madison, WI, March 29–31.

Nesse, R. M., & Berridge, K. C. (1998) Psychoactive drug use in evolutionary perspective. *Science*, 278, 63–66.

Nestler, E. J. (1997). Basic neurobiology of heroin addiction. Paper presented at NIDA conference: Heroin Use and Addiction. Washington, DC, September 29–30.

Nestler, E. J., Fitzgerald, L. W., & Self, D. W. (1995). Neurobiology. In *Review of psychiatry* (Vol. 14) (Oldham, J. M., & Riba, M. B., eds.). Washington, DC: American Psychiatric Press.

Newcomb, M. D. (1996). Adolescence: Pathologizing a normal process. *The Counseling Psychologist*, 24, 482–490.

Newcomb, M. D., & Bentler, P. M. (1989). Substance use and abuse among children and teen agers. *American Psychologist, 44*, 242–248.

Newell, T., & Cosgrove, J. (1988). *Recovery of neuropsychological functions during reduction of PCP use.* Paper presented at the 1988 annual meeting of the American Psychological Association, Atlanta, GA.

Newsweek. (1991). A new market for a lethal drug. *CXVII* (7), 58.

Newsweek. (1998) Big tobacco's secret kiddie campaign. *CXXXI* (4), 29.

Newton, R. E., Marunycz, J. D., Alderdice, M. C., & Napoliello, M. J. (1986). Review of the side effects of buspirone. *The American Journal of Medicine, 80* (Supplement 3B).

Ney, J. A., Dooley, S. L., Keith, L. G., Chasnoff, I. J., & Socol, M. L. (1990). The prevalence of substance abuse in patients with suspected preterm labor. *American Journal of Obsterics and Gynecology, 162*, 1562–1568.

Niaura, R. S., Rohsenow, D. J., Binkoff, J. A., Monti, P. M., Pedraza, M., & Abrams, D. B. (1988). Relevance of cue reactivity to understanding alcohol and smoking relapse. *Journal of Abnormal Psychology, 97* (2), 133–153.

Nicastro, N. (1989). Visual disturbances associated with over-the-counter ibuprofen in three patients. *Annuals of Ophthalmology, 21*, 447–450.

Nielson, D. A., Virkkunen, M., Lappalainen, J., Eggert, M., Brown, G. L., Long, J. C., Goldman, D., & Linnoila, M. (1998). A tryptophan hydroxylase gene marker for suicidality and alcoholism. *Archives of General Psychiatry, 55*, 593–602.

Nisbet, P. A. (2000). Age and the lifespan. In *Comprehensive textbook of suicidology.* (Maris, R. W., Berman, A. L., & Silverman, M. M., eds). New York: Guilford.

Nishino, S., Mignot, E., & Dement, W. C. (1995). Sedative-hypnotics. In *Textbook of psychopharmacology* (Schatzberg, A. F., & Nemeroff, C. B., eds.). Washington, DC: American Psychiatric Association Press, Inc.

Nixon, S. J. (1994). Cognitive deficits in alcoholic women. *Alcohol Health & Research World, 18*, 228–231.

Nobel, E. P., Blum, K., Ritchie, T., Montgomery, A., & Sheridan, P. F. (1991). Allelic association of the D2 dopamine receptor gene with receptor-binding characteristics in alcoholism. *Archives of General Psychiatry, 48*, 648–654.

Nobel, S. L., King, D. S., & Olutade, J. I. (2000). Cyclooxygenase-2 enzyme inhibitors: place in therapy. *American Family Physician, 61*, 3669–3676.

Norris, D. (1994). War's 'wonder' drugs. *America's Civil War, 7* (2), 50–57.

Norris, K. (1998). *Amazing grace.* New York: Riverhead Books.

North, C. S. (1996). Alcoholism in women. *Postgraduate Medicine, 100*, 221–224, 230–232.

Norton, R. L., Burton, B. T., & McGirr, J. (1996). Blood lead of intravenous drug users. *Journal of Toxicology: Clinical Toxicology, 34* (4), 425–431.

Novello, A. C., & Shosky, J. (1992). From the Surgeon General, US Public Health Service. *Journal of the American Medical Association, 268*, 961.

Nowak, M. A., & McMichael, A. J. (1995). How HIV defeats the immune system. *Scientific American, 273* (2), 58–65.

Nowinski, J. (1996). Facilitating 12-step recovery from substance abuse and addiction. In *Treating substance abuse* (Rotgers, F., Keller, D. S., & Morgenstern, J., eds.). New York: Guilford.

Nunes, J. V., & Parson, E. B. (1995). Patterns of psychoactive substance use among adolescents. *American Family Physician, 52*, 1693–1697.

Nutt, D. J. (1996). Addiction: Brain mechanisms and their treatment implications. *The Lancet, 347*, 31–36.

O'Brien, C. P. (1997). Progress in the science of addiction. *American Journal of Psychiatry, 154*, 1195–1197.

O'Brien, C. P. (1998). A range of research-based pharmacotherapies for addiction. *Science, 278*, 66–70.

O'Brien, C. P., & McLellan, A. T. (1996). Myths about the treatment of addiction. *The Lancet, 347*, 237–240.

O'Brien, C. P., & McLellan, A. T. (1997). Addiction medicine. *Journal of the American Medical Association, 277*, 1840–1841.

O'Brien, P. E., & Gaborit, M. (1992). Codependency: A disorder separate from chemical dependency. *Journal of Clinical Psychology, 48* (1), 129–136.

O'Connor, P. G. (2000). Treating opioid dependence—new data and new opportunities. *New England Journal of Medicine, 343*, 1332–1333.

O'Connor, P. G., Chang, G., & Shi, J. (1992). Medical complications of cocaine use. In *Clinician's guide to cocaine addiction* (Kosten, T. R., & Kleber, H. D., eds.). New York: Guilford.

O'Connor, P. G., Samet, J. H., & Stein, M. D. (1994). Management of hospitalized intravenous drug users: Role of the internist. *American Journal of Medicine, 96*, 551–558.

Ochs, L. (1992). EEG treatment of addictions. *Biofeedback, 20* (1), 8–16.

O'Dell, K. J., Turner, N. H., & Weaver, G. D. (1998). Women in recovery from drug misuse: An exploratory study of their social networks and social support. *Substance Use & Misuse, 33*, 1721–1734.

O'Donnell, M. (1986). The executive ailment: "Curable only by death." *International Management, 41* (7), 64.

O'Donovan, M. C., & McGuffin, P. (1993). Short acting benzodiazepines. *British Medical Journal, 306*, 182–183.

Oetting, E. R., Deffenbacher, J. L., & Donnermeyer, J. F. (1999). Primary socialization theory. The role played by personal traits in the etiology of drug use and deviance. II. *Substance Use & Misuse, 33*, 1337–1366.

O'Farrell, T. J. (1995). Marital and family therapy. In *Handbook of alcoholism treatment approaches* (2nd ed.) (Hester, R. K., & Miller, W. R., eds.). New York: Allyn & Bacon.

Office of National Drug Control Policy. (1995). *Pulse check.* Washington, DC: U.S. Government Printing Office.

Office of National Drug Control Policy. (1996). *The national drug control strategy: 1996.* Washington, DC: U.S. Government Printing Office.

Ogborne, A. C. (1993). Assessing the effectiveness of Alcoholics Anonymous in the community: Meeting the challenges. In *Research on Alcoholics Anonymous* (McCrady, B. S., & Miller, W. R., eds.). New Brunswick, NJ: Rutgers Center of Alcohol Studies.

Ogborne, A. C., & Glaser, F. B. (1985). *Evaluating Alcoholics Anonymous in alcoholism and substance abuse: Strategies for clinical intervention* (Bratter, T. E., & Forrest, G. G., eds.). New York: The Free Press.

Olds, D. L., Henderson, C. R., & Tatelbaum, R. (1994). Intellectual impairment in children of women who smoke cigarettes during pregnancy. *Pediatrics, 93,* 221–227.

Oliwenstein, L. (1988). The perils of pot. *Discover, 9* (6), 18.

Olmedo, R., & Hoffman, R. S. (2000). Withdrawal syndromes. *Emergency Medical Clinics of North America, 18,* 273–288.

Olson, D. H., Mylan, M. M., Fletcher, L. A., Nugent, S. M., Lynch, J. W., & Willenbring, M. L. (1997). A clinical tool for rating response to civil commitment for substance abuse treatment. *Psychiatric Services, 48,* 1317–1322.

Olson, J. (1992). *Clinical pharmacology made ridiculously simple.* Miami, FL: MedMaster, Inc.

O'Malley, S., Adamse, M., Heaton, R. K., Gawin, F. G. (1992). Neuropsychological impairment in chronic cocaine abusers. *American Journal of Drug and Alcohol Abuse, 18* (2), 131–144.

Ordorica, P. I., & Nace, P. E. (1998). Alcohol. In *Clinical textbook of addictive disorders* (2nd ed.) (Frances, R. J., & Miller, S. I., eds.). New York: Guilford.

Osher, F. C., Drake, R. E., Noordsy, D. L., Teague, G. B., Hurlbut, S. C., Biesanz, J. C., & Beaudett, M. S. (1994). Correlates and outcomes of alcohol use disorder among rural outpatients with schizophrenia. *Journal of Clinical Psychiatry, 55,* 109–113.

Osher, F. C., & Drake, R. E. (1996). Reversing a history of unmet needs: Approaches to care for persons with co-occuring addictive and mental disorders. *American Journal of Orthopsychiatry, 66,* 4–11.

Osher, F. C., & Kofoed, L. L. (1989). Treating patients with psychiatric and psychoactive substance abuse disorders. *Hospital and Community Psychiatry, 40,* 1025–1030.

Ostrea, E. M., Ostrea, A. R., & Simpson, P. M. (1997). Mortality within the first 2 years in infants exposed to cocaine, opiate or cannabinoid during gestation. *Pediatrics, 100,* 79–84.

Ott, A., Slooter, A. J. C., Hofman, A., van Harskamp, F., Witteman, J. C. M., Broeckhoven, C. V., & van Duijn, C. M. (1998). Smoking and risk of dementia and Alzheimer's disease in a population-based cohort study: The Rotterdam study. *The Lancet, 351,* 1840–1843.

Otto, R. K., Lang, A. R., Megargee, E. I., & Rosenblatt, A. I. (1989). Ability of alcoholics to escape detection by the MMPI. *Critical Items, 4* (2), 2, 7–8.

Ouimette, P. C., Finney, J. W., & Moos, R. H. (1997). Twelve-step and cognitive-behavioral treatment for substance abuse: A comparison of treatment effectiveness. *Journal of Consulting and Clinical Psychology, 65,* 230–240.

Owen, R. R., Fischer, E. P., Booth, B. M., & Cuffel, B. J. (1996). Medication noncompliance and substance abuse among patients with schizophrenia. *Psychiatric Services, 47,* 853–858.

Owings-West, M., & Prinz, R. J. (1987). Parental alcoholism and child psychopathology. *Psychological Bulletin, 102* (2), 204–281.

Packe, G. E., Garton, M. J., & Jennings, K. (1990). Acute myocardial infarction caused by intraveneous amphetamine abuse. *British Heart Journal, 64,* 23–24.

Pagliaro, L. A., & Pagliaro, A. M. (1998). *The pharmacologic basis of therapeutics.* New York: Brunner-Mazel.

Pairet, M., van Ryn, J., Mauz, A., Schierok, H., Diederen, W., Turck, D., & Engelhardt, G. (1998). Differential inhibition of COX-1 and COX-2 by NSAIDS: A summary of results obtained using various test systems. In *Selective COX-2 inhibitors* (Vane, J., & Botting, J., eds.). Hingham, MA: Kluwer Academic Publishers.

Palella, F. J., Delaney, K. M., Moorman, A. C., Loveless, M. O., Fuhrer, J., Satten, G. A., Aschman, D. J., & Holmberg, S. D. (1998). Declining morbidity and mortality among patients with advanced human immunodeficiency virus infection. *The New England Journal of Medicine, 338,* 853–860.

Pape, P. A. (1988). EAP's and chemically dependent women. *Alcoholism & Addiction, 8* (6), 43–44.

Pappagallo, M. (1998). The concept of pseudotolerance to opioids. *Journal of Pharmacological Care and Symptom Control, 6,* 95–98.

Pappas, N. (1990). Dangerous liaisons: When food and drugs don't mix. *Health, 4* (4), 22–24.

Pappas, N. (1995). Secondhand smoke: Is it a hazard? *Consumer Reports, 60* (1), 27–33.

Paris, P. M. (1996). Treating the patient in pain. *Emergency Medicine, 28* (9), 66–76, 78–79, 83–86, 90.

Park, A. (2000). When did AIDS begin? *Time, 155* (6), 66.

Parker, G. B., Barrett, E. A., & Hickie, I. B. (1992). From nurture to network: Examining links between perceptions of parenting received in childhood and social bonds in adulthood. *American Journal of Psychiatry, 149,* 877–885.

Parker, R. N. (1993). The effects of context on alcohol and violence. *Alcohol Health & Research World, 17* (2), 117–122.

Parras, F., Patier, J. L., & Ezpeleta, C. (1988). Lead contaminated heroin as a source of inorganic lead intoxication. *The Staff, 316,* 755.

Parrott, A. C. (1999). Does cigarette smoking cause stress? *American Psychologist, 54,* 817–820.

Parry, A. (1992). Taking heroin maintenance seriously: The politics of tolerance. *The Lancet, 339,* 350–351.

Parsons, O. A., & Nixon, S. J. (1993). Neurobehavioral sequelae of alcoholism. *Behavioral Neurology, 11,* 205–218.

Passaro, D. J., Werner, S. B., McGee, J., Mac Kenzie, W. R., & Vugia, D. J. (1998). Wound botulism associated with black tar heroin among injecting drug users. *Journal of the American Medical Association, 279*, 859–863.

Pasterna, C. A. (1998). *The molecules within us.* New York: Plenum.

Paton, A. (1996). The detection of alcohol misuse in accident and emergency departments grasping the opportunity. *Journal of Accident & Emergency Medicine, 13*, 306–308.

Patrono, C. (1994). Aspirin as an antiplatelet drug. *New England Journal of Medicine, 330*, 1287–1294.

Paul, J. P., Stall, R., & Bloomfield, K. A. (1991). Gay and alcoholic. *Alcoholic Health & Research World, 15*, 151–160.

Payan, D. G., & Katzung, B. G. (1995). Nonsteroidal anti-inflammatory drugs: Nonopioid analgesics; drugs used in gout. In *Basic & clinical pharmacology* (Katzung, B. G., ed.). Norwalk, CT: Appleton & Lange.

Pearlson, G. D., Jeffery, P. J., Harris, G. J., Ross, C. A., Fischman, M. W., & Camargo, E. E. (1993). Correlation of acute cocaine-induced changes in local cerebral blood flow with subjective effects. *American Journal of Psychiatry, 150*, 495–497.

Pearson, M. A., Hoyme, E., Seaver, L. H., & Rimsza, M. E. (1994). Toluene embryopathy: Delineation of the phenotype and comparison with fetal alcohol syndrome. *Pediatrics, 93*, 211–215.

Peck, M. S. (1978). *The road less traveled.* New York: Simon & Schuster.

Peck, M. S. (1993). *Further along the road less traveled.* New York: Simon & Schuster.

Peck, M. S. (1997a). *The road less traveled & beyond.* New York: Simon & Schuster.

Peck, M. S. (1997b). *Denial of the soul.* New York: Harmony Books.

Pediatrics for Parents. (1990). Marijuana and breast feeding. *11* (10), 1.

Peele, S. (1984). The cultural context of psychological approaches to alcoholism. *American Psychologist, 39*, 1337–1351.

Peele, S. (1985). *The meaning of addiction.* Lexington, MA: D. C. Heath & Co.

Peele, S. (1989). *Diseasing of America.* Lexington, MA: D. C. Heath & Co.

Peele, S. (1991). What we now know about treating alcoholism and other addictions. *The Harvard Mental Health Letter, 8* (6), 5–7.

Peele, S. (1994). Hype overdose: Why does the press automatically accept reports of heroin overdoses, no matter how thin the evidence? *National Review, 46* (21), 59–61.

Peele, S. (1998). All wet. *The Sciences, 38* (2), 17–21.

Peele, S. (1996). Recovering from an all-of-nothing approach to alcohol. *Psychology Today, 29* (5), 35, 37, 39, 41, 43, 70.

Peele, S., Brodsky, A., & Arnold, M. (1991). *The truth about addiction and recovery.* New York: Simon & Schuster.

Pegues, D. A., Hughes, B. J., & Woernie, C. H. (1993). Elevated blood lead levels associated with illegally distilled alcohol. *Archives of Internal Medicine, 153*, 1501–1504.

Peluso, E., & Peluso, L. S. (1988). *Women & drugs.* Minneapolis, MN: CompCare Publishers.

Peluso, E., & Peluso, L. S. (1989). Alcohol and the elderly. *Professional Counselor, 4* (2), 44–46.

Penick, E. C., Nickel, E. J., Cantrell, P. F., Powell, B. J., Read, M. R., & Thomas, M. M. (1990). The emerging concept of dual diagnosis: An overview and implications. In *Managing the dually diagnosed patient* (O'Connell, D. F., ed.). New York: The Halworth Press.

Peniston, E. G., & Kulkosky, P. J. (1990). Alcoholic personality and alpha-theta brainwave training. *Medical Psychotherapy, 3*, 37–55.

Perneger, T. V., Whelton, P. K., Klag, M. J. (1994). Risk of kidney failure associated with the use of acetaminophen, aspirin, and nonsteroidal antiinflammatory drugs. *The New England Journal of Medicine, 331*, 1675–1679.

Peroutka, S. J. (1989). "Ecstacy": A human neurotoxin? *Archives of General Psychiatry, 46*, 191.

Perry, J. C., & Cooper, S. H. (1989). An empirical study of defense mechanisms. *Archives of General Psychiatry, 46*, 444–452.

Peters, H., & Theorell, C. J. (1991). Fetal and neonatal effects of maternal cocaine use. *Journal of Obstetric, Gynecologic, and Neonatal Nursing, 20* (2), 121–126.

Peters, R., Copeland, J., & Dillon, P. (1999). Anabolic-androgenic steroids user characteristics, motivations and deterrents. *Psychology of Addictive Behaviors, 13* (3), 232–242.

Petersen, J. R. (1999). Snitch culture. *Playboy, 46* (6), 51.

Petersen, J. R. (2000). My millennium fix. *Playboy, 47* (1), 53–54.

Peterson, A. M. (1997). Analgesics. *RN, 60* (4), 45–50.

Peto, R., Chen, Z., & Boreham, J., (1996). Tobacco—the growing epidemic in China. *Journal of the American Medical Association, 275*, 1683–1684.

Peto, R., Lopez, A. D., Boreham, J., Thun, M., & Heath, C. (1992). Mortality from tobacco in developed countries: Indirect estimation from national vital statistics. *The Lancet, 339*, 1268–1278.

Petraitis, J., Flay, B. R., Miller, T. Q., Torpy, E. J., & Greiner, B. (1998). Illicit substance use among adolescents: A matrix of prospective predictors. *Substance Use & Misuse, 33*, 2561–2604.

Pettine, K. A. (1991). Association of anabolic steroids and avascular necrosis of femoral heads. *The American Journal of Sports Medicine, 19* (1), 96–98.

Pettit, J. L. (2000). Melatonin. *Clinician Reviews, 10* (6), 87–88, 91.

Peyser, H. S. (1989). Alcohol and drug abuse: Under-recognized and untreated. *Hospital and Community Psychiatry, 40* (3), 221.

Pferrerbaum, P., Sullivan, E. V., Rosenbloom, M. J., Mathalon, D. H., & Lim, K. O. (1998). A controlled study of cortical gray matter and ventricular changes in alcoholic men over a 5 year interval. *Archives of General Psychiatry, 55*, 905–912.

Phelps, D. (1996). Records suggest nicotine enhanced. *Minneapolis Star-Tribune, XV* (5), 1A, 22A.

Phillips, A., Savigny, D., & Law, M. M. (1995). As Canadians butt out, the developing world lights up. *Canadian Medical Journal, 153,* 1111–1114.

Phillips, A. N., Wannamethee, M. W., Thomson, A., & Smith, G. D. (1996). Life expectancy in men who have never smoked and those who have smoked continuously: 15 year follow up of large cohort of middle aged British men. *British Medical Journal, 313,* 907–908.

Pickens, R. W., Svikis, D. S., McGue, M., Lykken, D. T., Heston, L. L., & Clayton, P. J. (1991). Heterogeneity in the inheritance of alcoholism: A study of male and female twins. *Archives of General Psychiatry, 48,* 19–28.

Pihl, R. O. (1999). Substance abuse: Etiological considerations. In *Oxford textbook of psychopathology* (Millon, T., Blaney, P. H., & Davis, R. D., eds.). New York: Oxford University Press.

Pinkney, D. S. (1990). Substance abusers seen shifting to "kitchen lab" drugs. *American Medical News, 33* (16), 5–7.

Pirisi, A., & Sims, S. (1997). Why we're so paranoid about pills. *Remedy, IV* (5), 20–25.

Pirkle, J., Flegal, K. M., Bernert, J. T., Brody, D. J., Etzel, R. A., & Maurer, K. R. (1996). Exposure of the U.S. population to environmental tobacco smoke. *Journal of the American Medical Association, 275,* 1233–1240.

Pirozzolo, F. J., & Bonnefil, V. (1995). Disorders appearing in the perinatal and neonatal period. In *Pediatric neuropsychology* (Batchelor, E. S., & Dean, R. S., eds.). New York: Allyn & Bacon.

Plasky, P., Marcus, L., & Salzman, C. (1988). Effects of psychotropic drugs on memory: Part 2. *Hospital & Community Psychiatry, 39,* 501–502.

Playboy. (1990). Raw data. 37 (1), 16.

Playboy. (1991). Forum. 38 (1), 52.

Playboy. (1995a). Raw data. 42 (1), 16.

Playboy. (1995b). The drug index. 42 (9), 47.

Plessinger, M. A., & Woods, J. R. (1993). Maternal, placental, and fetal pathophysiology of cocaine exposure during pregnancy. *Clinical Obstetrics and Gynecology, 36,* 267–278.

Pliszka, S. R. (1998). The use of psychostimulants in the pediatric patient. *Pediatric Clinics of North America, 45,* 1085–1098.

Polen, M. R., Sidney, S., Tekawa, I. S., Sadler, M., & Friedman, G. D. (1993). Health care use by frequent marijuana smokers who do not smoke tobacco. *Western Journal of Medicine, 158,* 596–601.

Pollock, N. K., & Martin, C. S. (1999). Diagnostic orphans: Adolescents with alcohol symptoms who do not qualify for a DSM-IV abuse or dependence diagnosis. *American Journal of Psychiatry, 156,* 897–901.

Pomerantz, R. J. (1998). How HIV resists eradication. *Hospital Practice, 33* (9), 87–90, 93–95, 99–101.

Pomerleau, O. D., Collins, A. C., Shiffman, S., & Pomerleau, C. S. (1993). Why some people smoke and others do not: New perspectives. *Journal of Clinical and Consulting Psychology, 61,* 723–731.

Ponnappa, B. C., & Rubin, E. (2000). Modeling alcohol's effects on organs in animal models. *Alcohol Research & Health, 24* (2), 93–104.

Pope, H. G., & Katz, D. L. (1987). Bodybuilder's psychosis. *The Lancet. 334,* 863.

Pope, H. G., & Katz, D. L. (1988). Affective and psychotic symptoms associated with anabolic steroid use. *American Journal of Psychiatry, 145,* 487–490.

Pope, H. G., & Katz, D. L. (1990). Homicide and near-homicide by anabolic steroid users. *Journal of Clinical Psychiatry, 51* (1), 28–31.

Pope, H. G., & Katz, D. L. (1991). What are the psychiatric risks of anabolic steroids? *The Harvard Mental Health Letter, 7* (10), 8.

Pope, H. G., & Katz, D. L. (1994). Psychiatric and medical effects of anabolic-androgenic steroid use. *Archives of General Psychiatry, 51,* 375–382.

Pope, H. G., Katz, D. L., & Champoux, R. (1986). Anabolic-androgenic steroid use among 1,010 college men. *The Physician and Sports Medicine, 17* (7), 75–81.

Pope, H. G., Kouri, E. M., & Hudson, J. I. (2000). Effects of supraphysiologic doses of testosterone on mood and aggression. *Archives of General Psychiatry, 57,* 133–140.

Pope, H. G., Phillips, K. A., & Olivardia, R. (2000). *The Adonis complex: The secret crisis of male body obsession.* New York: The Free Press.

Pope, H. G., & Yurgelun-Todd, D. (1996). The residual cognitive effects of heavy marijuana use in college students. *Journal of the American Medical Association, 275,* 521–527.

Porcerelli, J. H., & Sandler, B. A. (1998). Anabolic-pandrogenic steroid abuse and psychopathology. *The Psychiatric Clinics of North America, 21,* 829–833.

Porterfield, L. M. (1991). Steroid abuse. *Advancing Clinical Care, 6* (2), 44.

Post, R. M., Weiss, S. R. B., Pert, A., & Uhde, T. W. (1987). Chronic cocaine administration: Sensitization and kindling effects. In *Cocaine: Clinical and behavioral aspects* (Fisher, S., Rashkin, A., & Unlenhuth, E. H., eds.). New York: Oxford University Press.

Potter, J. D. (1997). Hazards and benefits of alcohol. *The New England Journal of Medicine, 337,* 1763–1764.

Potter, W. Z., Rudorfer, M. V., & Goodwin, F. K. (1987). Biological findings in bipolar disorders. In *American Psychiatric Association annual review* (Vol. 6). Washington, DC: American Psychiatric Association Press, Inc.

Potterton, R. (1992). A criminal system of justice. *Playboy, 39* (9), 46–47.

Powell, B. J., Read, M. R., Penick, E. C., Miller, N. S., & Bingham, S. F. (1987). Primary and secondary depression in alcoholic men: An important distinction. *Journal of Clinical Psychiatry, 48,* 98–101.

Prater, C. D., Miller, K. E., & Zylstra, R. G. (1999). Outpatient detoxification of the addicted or alcoholic patient. *American Family Physician, 60,* 1175–1183.

Pratt, C. T. (1990). Addiction treatment for health care professionals. *Addiction & Recovery, 10* (3), 17–19, 38–41.

Prescott, C. A., & Kendler, K. S. (1999). Genetic and environmental contributions to alcohol abuse and dependence in a population-based sample of male twins. *American Journal of Psychiatry, 156,* 34–40.

Preston, R. (1999). The demon in the freezer. *The New Yorker, LXXV* (18), 44–61.

Preuss, U. W., & Wong, W. M. (2000). Comorbidity. In *Handbook of alcoholism* (Zernig, G., Saria, A., Kurz, M., & O'Malley, S. S., eds.). New York: CRC Press.

Price, L. H., Ricaurte, G. A., Krystal, J. H., & Heninger, G. R. (1989). Neuroendocrine and mood responses to intravenous L-tryptophan in 3, 4–Methylenedioxymethamphetamine (MDMA) users. *Archieves of General Psychiatry, 46,* 20–22.

Price, L. H., Ricaurte, G. A., Krystal, J. H., & Heninger, G. R. (1990). In reply. *Archives of General Psychiatry, 47,* 289.

Pristach, C. A., & Smith, C. M. (1990). Medication compliance and substance abuse among schizophrenic patients. *Hospital and Community Psychiatry, 41,* 1345–1348.

Prochaska, J. (1998). *Stage model of change.* Paper presented at symposium. La Crosse, Wisconsin Gundersen-Lutheran Medical Center, September 17.

Prochaska, J. O., DiClemente, C. C., & Norcross, J. C. (1992). In search of how people change. *American Psychologist, 47,* 1102–1114.

Prummel, M. F., & Wiersinga, W. M. (1993). Smoking and the risk of Graves' disease. *Journal of the American Medical Association, 269,* 479–482.

Pursch, J. A. (1987). Mental illness and addiction. *Alcoholism & Addiction, 7* (6), 42.

Putnam, F. W. (1989). *Diagnosis and treatment of multiple personality disorder.* New York: The Guilford Press.

Rabinowitz, J., Cohen, H., & Kotler, M. (1998). Outcomes of ultrarapid opiate detoxification combined with naltrexone maintenance and counseling. *Psychiatric Services, 49,* 831–834.

Rabinowitz, J., & Marjefsky, S. (1998). Predictors of being expelled from and dropping out of alcohol treatment. *Psychiatric Services, 49,* 187–189.

RachBeisel, J., Scott, J., & Dixon, L. (1999). Co-occurring severe mental illness and substance use disorders: A review of recent research. *Psychiatric Services, 50,* 1427–1434.

Racine, A., Joyce, T., & Anderson, R. (1993). The association between prenatal care and birth weight among women exposed to cocaine in New York City. *Journal of the American Medical Association, 270,* 1581–1586.

Rado, T. (1988). The client with a dual diagnosis—a personal perspective. *The Alcohol Quarterly, 1* (1), 5–7.

Rains, V. S. (1990). Alcoholism in the elderly—the hidden addiction. *Medical Aspects of Human Sexuality, 24* (10), 40–42, 43.

Rall, T. W. (1990). Hypnotics and sedatives. In *The pharmacological basis of therapeutics* (8th ed.) (Gilman, A. G., Rall, T. W., Nies, A. S., & Taylor, P, eds.). New York: Pergamon Press.

Ramcharan, S., Meenhorst, P. L., Otten, J. M. M. B., Koks, C. H. W., de Boer, D., Maes, R. A. A., & Beijnen, J. H. (1998). Survival after massive ecstasy overdose. *Journal of Toxicology: Clinical Toxicology, 36,* 727.

Ramlow, B. E., White, A. L., Watson, D. D., & Leukefeld, C. G. (1997). The needs of women with substance use problems: An expanded vision for treatment. *Substance Use & Misuse, 32,* 1395–1404.

Rand, L. (1995). A different road. *Chicago Tribune, 148* (53), Tempo section: 1,7.

Randall, T. (1992). Medical news & perspectives. *Journal of the American Medical Association, 268,* 1505–1506.

Randle, K. D., Estes, R., & Cone, W. P. (1999). *The abduction enigma.* New York: Forge.

Randolph, W. M., Stroup-Benham, C., Black, S. A., Markides, K. S. (1998). Alcohol use among Cuban-Americans, Mexican-Americans, and Puerto-Ricans. *Alcohol Health & Research World, 22,* 265–269.

Rapoport, R. J. (1993). The efficacy and safety of oxaproxzin versus aspirin: Pooled results of double-blind trials in osteoarthritis. *Drug Therapy, 23,* supplement, 3–8.

Raskin, V. D. (1994). Psychiatric aspects of substance use disorders in childbearing populations. *Psychiatric Clinics of North America, 16,* 157–165.

Rasymas, A. (1992). Basic pharmacology and pharmacokinetics. *Clinics in Podiatric Medicine and Surgery, 9,* 211–221.

Rathbone-McCuan, E., & Stokke, D. (1997). Lesbian women and substance abuse. In *Gender and addictions* (Straussner, S. L. A., & Zelvin, E., eds.). Northvale, NJ: Jason-Aronson.

Raut, C. P., Stephen, A., & Kosopsky, B. (1996). Intrauterine effects of substance abuse. In *Source book of substance abuse and addiction* (Friedman, L., Fleming, N. F., Roberts, D. H., & Hyman, S. E., eds.). New York: Williams & Wilkins.

Ravel, R. (1989). *Clinical laboratory medicine: Clinical application of laboratory data* (5th ed.). Chicago: Year Book Medical Publishers, Inc.

Ray, O. S., & Ksir, C. (1993). *Drugs, society and human behavior* (6th ed.). St. Louis: C. V. Mosby.

Redfearn, P. J., Agrawal, N., & Mair, L. H. (1998). An association between the regular use of 3,4 methylendioxy-methamphetamine (Ecstasy) and excessive wear of the teeth. *Addiction, 93* (5), 745–748.

Redman, G. L. (1990). Adolescents and anabolics. *American Fitness, 8* (3), 30–33.

Reeves, D., & Wedding, D. (1994). *The clinical assessment of memory.* New York: Springer Publishing Co.

Regier, D. A., Farmer, M. E., Rae, D. S., Locke, B. Z., Kieth, S. J., Judd, L. L., & Goodwin, F. K. (1990). Comorbidity of mental disorders with alcohol and other drug abuse. *Journal of the American Medical Association, 264,* 2511–2518.

Rehman, Q., & Sack, K. E. (1999). When to try COX-2 specific inhibitors. *Postgraduate Medicine, 106,* 95–105.

Reid, M. C., & Anderson, P. A. (1997). Geriatric substance use disorders. *Medical Clinics of North America, 81,* 999–1016.

Reiman, E. M. (1997). Anxiety. In *The practitioner's guide to psychoactive drugs* (4th ed.) (Gelenberg, A. J., & Bassuk, E. L., eds.). New York: Plenum.

Reinsch, J. M., Sanders, S. A., Mortensen, E. L., & Rubin, D. B. (1995). In utero exposure to phenobarbital and intelligence deficits in adult men. *Journal of the American Medical Association, 174*, 1518–1525.

Reiser, M. F. (1984). *Mind, brain, body*. New York: Basic Books, Inc.

Reisine, T., & Pasternak, G. (1995). Opioid analgesics and antagonists. In *The pharmacological basis of therapeutics* (9th ed.) (Hardman, J. G., & Limbird, L. E., editors-in-chief). New York: McGraw-Hill.

Renaud, S., & DeLorgeril, M. (1992). Wine, alcohol, and the French paradox for coronary heart disease. *The Lancet, 339*, 1523–1526.

Reneman, L., Booij, J., Schmand, B., van den Brink, W., & Gunning, B. (2000). Memory disturbances in "Ecstasy" users are correlated with an altered brain serotonin neurotransmission. *Psychopharmacology, 148*, 322–324.

Renner, J. A. (2001). Dual diagnosis in treatment resistant adults. Symposium presented to the Dept. of Psychiatry at The Cambridge Hospital, Boston, MA, March 3, 2001.

Report of the Institute of Medicine committee on the efficacy and safety of Halcion. (1999). *Archives of General Psychiatry, 56*, 349–352.

Restak, R. (1984). *The brain*. New York: Bantam Books.

Restak, R. (1991). *The brain has a mind of its own*. New York: Harmony Books.

Restak, R. (1993). Brain by design. *The Sciences, 33* (5), 27–33.

Restak, R. (1994). *Receptors*. New York: Bantam.

Restak, R. (1995). *Brainscapes*. New York: Hyperion Press.

Revkin, A. C. (1989). Crack in the cradle. *Discover, 10* (9), 63–69.

Rice, C., & Duncan, D. F. (1995). Alcohol use and reported physician visits in older adults. *Preventive Medicine, 24*, 229–234.

Rice, D. P. (1993). The economic cost of alcohol abuse and alcohol dependence: 1990. *Alcohol Health & Research World, 17* (1), 10–11.

Richards, J. R. (2000). Rhabdomyolsis and drugs of abuse. *Journal of Emergency Medicine, 19*, 51–56.

Richardson, S. (1995). The race against AIDS. *Discover, 16* (5), 28–32.

Rickels, K., Schweizer, E., Csanalosi, I., Case, W. G., & Chung, H. (1988). Long-term treatment of anxiety and risk of withdrawal. *Archives of General Psychiatry, 45*, 444–450.

Rickels, K., Schweizer, E., Case, W. G., Greenblatt, D. J. (1990). Long-term therapeutic use of benzodiazepines: I. Effects of abrupt discontinuation. *Archives of General Psychiatry, 47*, 899–907.

Rickels, L. K., Giesecke, M. A., & Geller, A. (1987). Differential effects of the anxiolytic drugs, diazepam and buspirone on memory function. *British Journal of Clinical Pharmacology, 23*, 207–211.

Ridker, P. M., Cushman, M., Stampfer, M. J., Tracy, R. P., & Hennekens, C. H. (1997). Inflammation, aspirin, and the risk of cardiovascular disease in apparently healthy men. *The New England Journal of Medicine, 336*, 973–979.

Ries, R. K., & Ellingson, T. (1990). A pilot assessment at one month of 17 dual diagnosis patients. *Hospital and Community Psychiatry, 41*, 1230–1233.

Ries, R. K., Russo, J., Wingerson, D., Snowden, M., Comtois, K. A., Srebnik, D., & Roy-Byrne, P. (2000). Shorter hospital stays and more rapid improvement among patients with schizophrenia and substance disorders. *Psychiatric Services, 51*, 210–215.

Rigler, S. K. (2000). Alcoholism in the elderly. *American Family Physician, 61*, 1710–1716.

Riggs, J. E. (1996). The "protective" influence of cigarette smoking on Alzheimer's and Parkinson's diseases. *Neurologic Clinics, 14*, 353–358.

Riley, J. A. (1994). Dual diagnosis. *Nursing Clinics of North America, 29*, 29–34.

Rimm, E. B., Chan, J., Stampfer, M. J., Colditz, G. A., & Willett, W. C. (1995). Prospective study of cigarette smoking, alcohol use, and the risk of diabetes in men. *British Medical Journal, 310*, 555–559.

Ritz, M. C. (1999). Molecular mechanisms of addictive substances. In *Drugs of abuse and addiction: Neurobehavioral toxicology* (Niesink, R. J. M., Jaspers, R. M. A., Korney, L. M. W., & van Ree, J. M., eds.). New York: CRC Press.

Rivara, F. P., Mueller, B. A., Somes, G., Mendoza, C. T., Rushforth, N. B., & Kellerman, A. L. (1997). Alcohol and illicit drug use and the risk of violent death in the home. *Journal of the American Medical Association, 278*, 569–575.

Rivera, E. (2000). License to drink. *Time, 156* (5), 46.

Roane, K. R. (2000). A scourge of drugs strikes a pious place. *U.S. News & World Report, 128* (9), 26–28.

Robbins, A. S., Manson, J. E., Lee, I., Satterfield, S., & Hennekens, C. H. (1994). Cigarette smoking and stroke in a cohort of U.S. male physicians. *Annals of Internal Medicine, 120*, 458–462.

Roberts, D. H., & Bush, B. (1996). Inpatient management issues and pain management. In *Source book of substance abuse and addiction* (Friedman, L., Fleming, N. F., Roberts, D. H., & Hyman, S. E., eds.). New York: Williams & Wilkins.

Roberts, D. J. (1995). Drug abuse. In *Conn's current therapy* (Rakel, R. E., ed.) Philadelphia: W. B. Saunders Co.

Roberts, J. R., & Tafure, J. A. (1990). Benzodiazepines. In *Clinical management of poisoning and drug overdose* (2nd ed.) (Haddad, L., & Winchester, J. F., eds.). Philadelphia: W. B. Saunders Co.

Roberts, M. (1986). MDMA: "Madness, not ecstasy." *Psychology Today, 20*, 14–16.

Roberts, S. V., & Watson, T. (1994). Teens on tobacco. *U.S. News & World Report, 116* (15), 38, 43.

Robinson, D. J., Lazo, M. C., Davis, T., & Kufera, J. A. (2000). Infective endocarditis in intravenous drug users:

Does HIV status alter the presenting temperature and white cell count? *Journal of Emergency Medicine, 19,* 5–11.

Robinson, P. (2001). Therapeutic aspects of cannabis and cannabinoids. *British Journal of Psychiatry, 178,* 107–115.

Rochester, J. A., & Kirchner, J. T. (1999). Ecstasy (3,4–Methylenedioxymethamphetamine): History, neurochemistry and toxicity. *Journal of the American Board of Family Practice, 12,* 137–142.

Rodgers, J. E. (1994). Addiction—a whole new view. *Psychology Today, 27* (5), 32–38, 72, 74, 76, 79.

Rodman, M. J. (1993). OCT interactions. *RN, 56* (1), 54–60.

Roehling, P., Koelbel, N., & Rutgers, C. (1994). *Codependence—pathologizing feminity?* Paper presented at the 1994 annual meeting of the American Psychological Association, Los Angeles, CA.

Roehrs, T., & Roth, T. (1995). Alcohol-induced sleepiness and memory function. *Alcohol Health & Research World, 19* (2), 130–135.

Roffman, R. A., & George, W. H. (1988). Cannabis abuse. In *Assessment of addictive behaviors* (Donovan, D. M., & Marlatt, G. A., eds.). New York: Guilford.

Rogers, C. R. (1961). *On becoming a person.* Boston: Houghton-Mifflin Co.

Rogers, P. D., Harris, J., & Jarmuskewicz, J. (1987). Alcohol and adolescence. *The Pediatric Clinics of North America, 34* (2), 289–303.

Rohde, P., Lewinsohn, P. M., Kahle, C. W., Seeley, J. R., & Brown, R. A. (2001). Natural course of alcohol use disorders from adolescence to young adulthood. *Journal of the American Academy of Child and Adolescent Psychiatry, 40,* 83–90.

Roine, R., Gentry, T., Hernandez-Munoz, R., Baraona, E., & Lieber, C. S. (1990). Aspirin increases blood alcohol concentrations in humans after ingestion of alcohol. *Journal of the American Medical Association, 264,* 2406–2408.

Rold, J. F. (1993). Mushroom madness. *Postgraduate Medicine, 78* (5), 217–218.

Romach, M. K., Glue, P., Kampman, K., Kaplan, H. L., Somer, G. R., Poole, S., Clarke, L., Coffin, V., Cornish, J., O'Brien, C. P., & Sellers, E. M. (1999). Attenuation of the euphoric effects of cocaine by the Dopamine D1/D5 antagonist Ecopipam (SCH 39166). *Archives of General Psychiatry, 56,* 1101–1106.

Roman, P. M., & Blum, T. C. (1996). *American Journal of Health Promotion, 11* (2), 136–149.

Rome, H. P. (1984). Psychobotanica revisited. *Psychiatric Annuals, 14,* 711–712.

Rootes, L. E., & Aanes, D. L. (1992). A conceptual framework for understanding self-help groups. *Hospital and Community Psychiatry, 43,* 379–381.

Rose, G. S. (2001). Motivational interviewing. Symposium presented to the Dept. of Psychiatry of The Cambridge Hospital, Boston, MA, March 2, 2001.

Rose, K. J., (1988). *The body in time.* New York: John Wiley & Sons, Inc.

Rose, V. L. (1999). CDC issues new recommendations for the prevention and control of Hepatitis C virus infection. *American Family Physician, 59,* 1321–1323.

Rosen, M. I., & Kosten, T. R. (1991). Buprenorphine: Beyond methadone? *Hospital and Community Psychiatry, 42,* 347–349.

Rosenbaum, J. F. (1990). Switching patients from alprazolam to clonazepam. *Hospital and Community Psychiatry, 41,* 1302.

Rosenbaum, J. F., & Gelenberg, A. J. (1991). Anxiety. In *The practitioner's guide to psychoactive drugs* (3rd ed.) (Gelenberg, A. J., Bassuk, E. L., & Schoonover, S. C., eds.). New York: Plenum.

Rosenbaum, R. (1999). *Zen and the heart of psychotherapy.* New York: Brunner/ Mazel.

Rosenberg, A. (1996). Brain damage caused by prenatal alcohol exposure. *Scientific American Medicine, 3* (4), 42–51.

Rosenberg, H. (1997). Use and abuse of illicit drugs among older people. In *Older adults misuse of alcohol, medicines and other drugs* (Gurnack, A. M., ed.). New York: Springer Publishing Co.

Rosenbloom, D. L. (2000). *The community perspective on addictions: Joining together.* Symposium presented to the Dept. of Psychiatry at The Cambridge Hospital, Boston, MA, March 3.

Rosenblum, M. (1992). Ibuprofen provides longer lasting analgesia than fentanyl after laparoscopic surgery. *Journal of the American Medical Association, 267,* 219.

Rosenthal, E. (1992). Bad fix. *Discover, 13* (2), 82–84.

Ross, A. (1991). Poland's dark harvest. *In Health, 5* (4), 66–70.

Ross, S. M., & Chappel, J. N. (1998). Substance use disorders. *The Psychiatric Clinics of North America, 21,* 803–828.

Rosse, R. B., Collins, J. P., Fay-McCarthy, M., Alim, T. N., Wyatt, R. J., & Deutsch, S. I. (1994). Phenomenologic comparison of the idiopathic psychosis of schizophrenia and drug-induced cocaine and phencyclidine psychosis: A retrospective study. *Clinical Neuropharmacology, 17,* 359–369.

Rothenberg, L. (1988). The ethics of intervention. *Alcoholism & Addiction, 9* (1), 22–24.

Rothwell, P. M., & Grant, R. (1993). Cerebral venous sinus thrombosis induced by "ecstacy." *Journal of Neurology, Neurosurgery and Psychiatry, 56,* 1035.

Rouse, S. V., Butcher, J. N., & Miller, K. B. (1999). Assessment of substance abuse in psychotherapy clients: the effective of the MMPI-2 substance abuse scales. *Psychological Assessment 11* (1), 101–107.

Rowe, C. (1998). Just say no. *Playboy, 45* (10), 44–45.

Roy, A. (1993). Risk factors for suicide among adult alcoholics. *Alcohol Health & Research World, 17,* 133–136.

Royce, R. A., Sena, A., Cates, W., & Cohen, M. S. (1997). Sexual transmission of HIV. *The New England Journal of Medicine, 336,* 1072–1078.

Royko, M. (1990). Drug war's over: Guess who won. *Playboy. 37* (1), 46.

Rubin, E., & Doria, J. (1990). Alcoholic cardiomyopathy. *Alcohol Health & Research World, 14* (4), 277–284.

Rubin, R. H. (1993). Acquired immunodeficiency syndrome. In *Scientific American medicine* (Rubenstein, E., & Federman, D. D., eds.). New York: Scientific American Press, Inc.

Rubino, F. A. (1992). Neurologic complications of alcoholism. *Psychiatric Clinics of North America, 15,* 359–372.

Rubins, J. B., & Janoff, E. N. Community-acquired pneumonia. (1997). *Postgraduate Medicine, 102* (6), 45–60.

Rubinstein, L., Campbell, F., & Daley, D. (1990). Four perspectives on dual diagnosis: Overview of treatment issues. In *Managing the dually diagnosed patient* (O'Connell, D. F., ed.). New York: The Halworth Press.

Russell, J. M., Newman, S. C., & Bland, R. C. (1994). Drug abuse and dependence. *Acta Psychiatrica Scandinavica, Supplement 376,* 54–62.

Rustin, T. (1988). Treating nicotine addiction. *Alcoholism & Addiction, 9* (2), 18–19.

Rustin, T. (1992, August). *Review of nicotine dependence and its treatment.* Consultation to La Crosse addiction treatment programs, Lutheran Hospital and St. Francis Hospital. Symposium conducted for staff, Lutheran Hospital, La Crosse, WI.

Rustin, T. (2000). Assessing nicotine dependence. *American Family Physician, 62,* 579–584.

Rychtarik, R. G., Connors, G. J., Whitney, R. B., McGillicuddy, N. B., Fitterling, J. M., & Wirtz, P. W. (2000). Treatment settings for persons with alcoholism: Evidence for matching clients to inpatient versus outpatient care. *Journal of Consulting and Clinical Psychology, 68,* 277–289.

Ryglewicz, H., & Pepper, B. (1996). *Lives at risk.* New York: The Free Press.

Saag, M. S. (1997). Use of HIV viral load in clinical practice: Back to the future. *Annals of Internal Medicine, 126,* 983–986.

Sabbag, R. (1994, May 5). The cartels would like a second chance. *Rolling Stone,* 35–37, 43.

Sacco, R. L. (1995). Risk factors and outcomes for ischemic stroke. *Neurology, 45* (Supplement 1), S10–S14.

Sacks, O. (1970). *The man who mistook his wife for a hat.* New York: Harper & Row.

Sagar, S. M. (1991). Toxic and metabolic disorders. In *Manual of neurology* (Samuels, M. A., ed.). Boston: Little, Brown & Co.

Saitz, R. (1998). Introduction to alcohol withdrawal. *Alcohol Health & Research World, 22* (1), 5–12.

Saitz, R., Ghali, W. A., & Moskowitz, M. A. (1997). The impact of alcohol-related diagnoses on pneumonia outcomes. *Archives of Internal Medicine, 157,* 1446–1452.

Saitz, R., Mayo-Smith, M. F., Roberts, M. S., Redmond, H. A., Bernard, D. R., & Calkins, D. R. (1994). Individualized treatment for alcohol withdrawal. *Journal of the American Medical Association, 272,* 519–523.

Saitz, R., & O'Malley, S. S. (1997). Pharmacotherapies for alcohol abuse. *Medical Clinics of North America, 81,* 881–907.

Salloway, S. (1998). The nucleus accumbens: A key structure mediating substance abuse and reward. *Psychiatric Times, XV* (4), 62–64.

Salloway, S., Southwick, S., & Sadowsky, M. (1990). Opiate withdrawal presenting as posttraumatic stress disorder. *Hospital & Community Psychiatry, 41,* 666–667.

Salzman, C. (1990). What are the uses and dangers of the controversial drug Halcion? *The Harvard Medical School Mental Health Letter, 6* (9), 8.

Sanders, S. R. (1990). Under the influence. *The Family Therapy Networker, 14* (1), 32–37.

Sands, B. F., Creelman, W. L., Ciraulo, D. A., Greenblatt, D. J., & Shader, R. I. (1995). Benzodiazepines. In *Drug interactions in psychiatry* (2nd ed.) (Ciraulo, D. A., Shader, R. I., Greenblatt, D. J., & Creelman, W., eds.). Baltimore: Williams & Wilkins.

Sands, B. F., Knapp, C. M., & Ciraulo, D. A. (1993). Medical consequences of alcohol-drug interactions. *Alcohol Health & Research World, 17,* 316–320.

Sapolsky, R. (1997). A gene for nothing. *Discover, 18* (10), 40–46.

Sapolsky, R. (1998). Is biology destiny? *Family Therapy Networker, 22* (2), 33–35.

Sarid-Segal, O., Creelman, W. L., & Shader, R. I. (1995). Lithium. In *Drug interactions in psychiatry* (2nd ed.) (Ciraulo, D. A., Shader, R. I., Greenblatt, D. J., & Creelman, W., eds.). Baltimore: Williams & Wilkins.

Satel, S. L. (1992). Craving for and fear of cocaine: A phenomenologic update on cocaine craving and paranoia. In *Clinician's guide to cocaine addiction* (Kosten, T. R., & Kleber, H. D., eds.). New York: Guilford.

Satel, S. L. (2000). *The limits of drug treatment and the case for coercion.* Symposium presented to the Dept. of Psychiatry at The Cambridge Hospital, Boston, MA, March 3.

Satel, S. L., & Edell, W. S. (1991). Cocaine-induced paranoia and psychosis proneness. *American Journal of Psychiatry, 148,* 1708–1711.

Satel, S. L., Kosten, T. R., Schuckit, M. A., & Fischman, M. W. (1993). Should protracted withdrawal from drugs be included in DSM-IV? *American Journal of Psychiatry, 150,* 695–704.

Satel, S. L., Price, L. H., Palumbo, J. M., McDougle, C. J., Krystal, J. H., Gawin, F., Charney, D. S., Heninger, G. R., & Kleber, H. D. (1991). Clinical phenomenology and neurobiology of cocaine abstinence: A prospective inpatient study. *American Journal of Psychiatry, 148,* 1712–1716.

Saum, C. A., & Inciardi, J. A. (1997). Rohypnol misuse in the United States. *Substance Use & Misuse, 32,* 723–731.

Saunders, J. B., Aasland, O. G., Babor, T. F., de la Fuente, J. R., & Grant, M. (1993). Development of the alcohol use disorders identification test (AUDIT): WHO collaborative project on early detection of persons with harmful alcohol consumption—II. *Addiction, 88,* 791–804.

Savage, S. R. (1993). Opium: The gift and its shadow. *Addiction & Recovery, 13* (1), 38–39.

Savage, S. R. (1999). Opioid use in the management of chronic pain. *Medical Clinics of North America, 83,* 761–786.

Savitch, C. (1998). Planes, trains and tuberculaids. *The Saturday Evening Post, 270* (4), 50–51.

Sawicki, T. (1995). Tel Aviv's miracle cure for addicts. *World Press Review, 42* (9), 37–39.

Sbriglio, R., & Millman, R. B. (1987). Emergency treatment of acute cocaine reactions. In *Cocaine: A clinician's handbook* (Washton, A. M., & Gold, M. S., eds.). New York: The Guilford Press.

Scafidi, F. A., Field, T. M., Wheeden, A., Schanberg, S., Kuhn, C., Symanski, R., Zimmerman, E., & Bandstra, E. S. (1996). Cocaine-exposed preterm neonates show behavioral and hormonal differences. *Pediatrics, 97,* 851–856.

Scarf, M. (1980). *Unfinished business.* New York: Ballantine Books.

Scaros, L. P., Westra, S., & Barone, J. A. (1990). Illegal use of drugs: A current review. *U.S. Pharmacist, 15* (5), 17–39.

Schafer, J., & Brown, S. A. (1991). Marijuana and cocaine effect expectancies and drug use patterns. *Journal of Consulting and Clinical Psychology, 59,* 558–565.

Schauben, J. L. (1990). Adulterants and substitutes. *Emergency Medicine Clinics of North America, 8,* 595–611.

Scheer, R. (1994a). The drug war's a bust. *Playboy, 41* (2), 49.

Scheer, R. (1994b). Fighting the wrong war. *Playboy, 41* (10), 49.

Scheer, R. (1995). Cracked obsession. *Playboy, 42* (4), 49.

Scheller, M. (1998). The ABC's of OTC's. *Current Health 2, 24* (4), 19–22.

Schenker, S., & Speeg, K. V. (1990). The risk of alcohol intake in men and women. *The New England Journal of Medicine, 322,* 127–129.

Schiavi, R. C., Stimmel, B. B., Mandeli, J., & White, D. (1995). Chronic alcoholism and male sexual function. *American Journal of Psychiatry, 152,* 1045–1051.

Schiødt, F. V., Rochling, F. A., Casey, D. L., & Lee, W. M. (1997). Acetaminophen toxicity in an urban county hospital. *The New England Journal of Medicine, 337,* 1112–1117.

Schirmer, M., Wiedermann, C., & Konwalinka, G. (2000). Immune system. In *Handbook of alcoholism* (Zernig, G., Saria, A., Kurz, M., & O'Malley, S. S., eds.). New York: CRC Press.

Schlaepfer, T. E., Strain, E. C., Greenberg, B. D., Preston, K. L., Lancaster, E., Bigelow, G. E., Barta, P. E., & Pearlson, G. D. (1998). Site of opioid action in the human brain: Mu and kappa agonists subjective and cerebral blood flow effects. *American Journal of Psychiatry, 155,* 470–473.

Schlosser, E. (1994). Marijuana and the law. *The Atlantic Monthly, 274* (3), 84–86, 89–90, 92–94.

Schmoke, K. (1996). The war on drugs is lost. *National Review, XLVIII* (2), 40–42.

Schmoke, K. (1997). Save money, cut crime, get real. *Playboy, 44* (1), 129, 190–191.

Schoenbaum, M., Zhang, W., & Strum, R. (1998). Costs and utilization of substance abuse care in a privately insured population under managed care. *Psychiatric Services, 49,* 1573–1578.

Schottenfeld, R. S., Pakes, J. R., Oliveto, A., Ziedonis, D., & Kosten, T. R. (1997). Buprenorphine vs. methadone maintenance treatment for concurrent opioid dependence and cocaine abuse. *Archives of General Psychiatry, 54,* 713–720.

Schneiderman, H. (1990). What's your diagnosis? *Consultant, 30* (7), 61–65.

Schorling, J. B., & Buchsbaum, D. G. (1997). Screening for alcohol and drug abuse. *Medical Clinics of North America, 81,* 845–865.

Schroeder, B. E., Holahan, M. R., Landry, C. F., & Kelley, A. E. (2000). Morphine—associated environmental cues elicit condition gene expression. *Synapse, 37* (2), 1–13.

Schrof, J. M. (1992). Pumped up. *U.S. News & World Report, 112* (21), 54–63.

Schrof-Fisher, J. (2000). Searching for that ounce of prevention. *U.S. News & World Report, 129* (3), 45–46.

Schuckit, M. A. (1994). Low level of response to alcohol as a predictor of future alcoholism. *American Journal of Psychiatry, 151,* 184–189.

Schuckit, M. A. (1995a). *Drug and alcohol abuse: A clinical guide to diagnosis and treatment* (4th ed.). New York: Plenum Press.

Schuckit, M.A. (1995b). Alcohol related disorders. In *Comprehensive textbook of psychiatry* (6th ed.) (Kaplan, H. I., & Sadock, B. J., eds.). Baltimore, MD: Williams & Wilkins.

Schuckit, M. A. (1996a). Alcohol, anxiety and depressive disorders. *Alcohol Health & Research World, 20,* 81–86.

Schuckit, M. A. (1996b). Recent developments in the pharmacology of alcohol dependence. *Journal of Consulting and Clinical Psychology, 64,* 669–676.

Schuckit, M. A. (1998). Alcohol and alcoholism. In *Harrison's principles of internal medicine* (14th ed.) (Fauci, A. S., Martin, J. B., Braunwald, E., Kasper, D. L., Isselbacher, K. J. Hauser, S. L., Wilson, J. D., & Longo, D. L., eds.). New York: McGraw-Hill.

Schuckit, M. A. (2000). *Drug and alcohol abuse: A clinical guide to diagnosis and treatment* (5th ed.). New York: Plenum Press.

Schuckit, M. A., Daeppen, J. B., Tipp, J. E., Hellebrock, M., & Bucholz, K. K. (1998). The clinical course of alcohol-related problems in alcohol dependent and non-alcohol dependent drinking women and men. *Journal of Studies on Alcohol, 59,* 581–590.

Schuckit, M. A., Klein, J., Twitchell, G., & Smith, T. (1994). Personality test scores as predictors of alcoholism almost a decade later. *American Journal of Psychiatry, 151,* 1038–1042.

Schuckit, M. A., & Smith, T. L. (1996). An 8-year follow-up of 450 sons of alcoholic and control subjects. *Archives of General Psychiatry, 53,* 202–210.

Schuckit, M. A., Smith, T. L., Anthenelli, R., & Irwin, M. (1993). Clinical course of alcoholism in 636 male inpatients. *American Journal of Psychiatry, 150,* 786–792.

Schuckit, M. A., Zisook, S., & Mortola, J. (1985). Clinical implications of DSM-III diagnoses of alcohol abuse and alcohol dependence. *American Journal of Psychiatry, 142*, 1403–1408.

Schuster, C. R. (1990). The National Institute on Drug Abuse in the decade of the brain. *Neuropsychopharmacology, 3*, 315–318.

Schutte, K. K., Moos, R. H., & Brennan, P. L. (1995). Depression and drinking behavior among women and men: A three-wave longitudinal study of older adults. *Journal of Consulting and Clinical Psychology, 63*, 810–822.

Schwartz, R. H. (1987). Marijuana: An overview. *The Pediatric Clinics of North America, 34* (2), 305–317.

Schwartz, R. H. (1989). When to suspect inhalant abuse. *Patient Care, 23* (10), 39–50.

Schwartz, R. H. (1994). Letter to the editor. *New England Journal of Medicine, 331*, 126–127.

Schwartz, R. H. (1995). LSD. *Pediatric Clinics of North America, 42*, 403–413.

Schwartz, R. H. (1996). Let's help young smokers quit. *Patient Care, 30* (8), 45–51.

Schwartz, R. H., & Miller, N. S. (1997). MDMA (ecstasy) and the rave: A review. *Pediatrics, 100*, 705–708.

Schweizer, E., & Rickels, K. (1994). New and emerging clinical uses of buspirone. *Journal of Clinical Psychiatry, 55* (5) (Supplement), 46–54.

Schwertz, D. W. (1991). Basic principles of pharmacologic action. *Nursing Clinics of North America, 26*, 245–262.

Science Digest. (1989). Nightcap dangers. 2 (5), 90.

Scott, I. (1998). A hundred-year habit. *History Today, 48* (6), 6–8.

Searight, H. R., & McLaren, L. (1997). Behavioral and psychiatric aspects of HIV infection. *American Family Physician, 55*, 1227–1237.

Segal, B., & Duffy, L. K. (1999). Biobehavioral effects of psychoactive drugs. In *Drugs of abuse and addiction: Neurobehavioral toxicology* (Niesink, R. J. M., Jaspers, R. M. A., Korney, L. M. W., & van Ree, J. M., eds.). New York: CRC Press.

Segal, R., & Sisson, B. V. (1985). Medical complications associated with alcohol use and the assessment of risk of physical damage. In *Alcoholism and substance abuse: Strategies for clinical intervention* (Bratter, T. E., & Forrest, G. G., eds.). New York: The Free Press.

Seidman, S. N., & Rieder, R. O. (1994). A review of sexual behavior in the United States. *American Journal of Psychiatry, 151*, 330–341.

Seilhamer, R. A., Jacob, T., & Dunn, N. J. (1993). The impact of alcohol consumption on parent-child relationships in families of alcoholics. *Journal of Studies on Alcohol, 54* (2), 189–198.

Seivewright, N., & Greenwood, J. (1996). What is important in drug misuse treatment? *The Lancet, 347*, 373–376.

Sellers, E. M., Ciraulo, D. A., DuPont, R. L., Griffiths, R. R., Kosten, T. R., Romach, M. K., & Woody, G. E. (1993). Alprazolam and benzodiazepine dependence. *Journal of Clinical Psychiatry, 54* (10) (Supplement), 64–74.

Selwyn, P. A. (1993). Illicit drug use revisited: What a long, strange trip it's been. *Annals of Internal Medicine, 119*, 1044–1046.

Selzer, M. (1971). The Michigan Alcoholism Screening Test: The quest for a new diagnostic instrument. *American Journal of Psychiatry, 127*, 1653–1658.

Senchak, M., Leonard, K. E., Greene, B. W., & Carroll, A. (1995). Comparisons of adult children of alcoholic, divorced and control parents in four outcome domains. *Psychology of Addictive Behaviors, 9* (3), 147–156.

Sexson, W. R. (1994). Cocaine: A neonatal perspective. *International Journal of the Addictions, 28*, 585–598.

Seymour, J. (1997). Old diseases, new danger. *Nursing Times, 93* (14), 22–24.

Shader, R. I. (1994). A perspective on contemporary psychiatry. In *Manual of psychiatric therapeutics* (2nd ed.). Boston: Little Brown & Co.

Shader, R. I., & Greenblatt, D. J. (1993). Use of benzodiazepines in anxiety disorders. *The New England Journal of Medicine, 328*, 1398–1405.

Shader, R. I., Greenblatt, D. J., & Ciraulo, D. A. (1994). Treatment of physical dependence on barbiturates, benzodiazepines, and other sedative-hypnotics. In *Manual of psychiatric therapeutics* (2nd ed.). Boston: Little Brown & Co.

Shaffer, H. J. (2001). What is addiction and does it matter? Symposium presented to the Dept. of Psychiatry of The Cambridge Hospital, Boston, MA, March 2, 2001.

Shaffer, H. J., & Robbins, M. (1995). Psychotherapy for addictive behavior: A stage-change approach to meaning making. In *Psychotherapy and substance abuse* (Washton, A. M., ed.). New York: Guilford.

Shalala, D. E. (1997). *Introductory remarks.* Paper presented at NIDA conference: Heroin use and addiction. Washington, DC, September 29–30.

Shaner, A., Khalsa, E., Roberts, L., Wilkins, J., Anglin, D., & Hsiech, S. C. (1993). Unrecognized cocaine use among schizophrenic patients. *American Journal of Psychiatry, 150*, 758–762.

Shannon, E. (2000). The world's best pot now comes from Vancouver. *Time, 155* (10), 66.

Shannon, M. T., Wilson, B. A., & Stang, C. L. (1995). *Drugs and nursing implications* (8th ed.). Norwalk, CT: Appleton & Lange.

Shapiro, D. (1981). *Autonomy and rigid character.* New York: Basic Books.

Sharara, A. I., Hunt, C. M., & Hamilton, J. D. (1996). Hepatitis C. *Annual of Internal Medicine, 125*, 658–668.

Sharp, M. J., & Getz, J. G. (1998). Self-process in comorbid mental illness and drug abuse. *American Journal of Orthopsychiatry, 68*, 639–644.

Shedler, J., & Block, J. (1990). Adolescent drug use and psychological health. *American Psychologist, 45*, 612–630.

Shenk, J. W. (1999). America's altered states. *Harper's Magazine, 298* (1788), 38–52.

Shepard, D. S., Larson, M. J., & Hoffmann, N. G. (1999). Cost-effectiveness of substance abuse services. *Psychiatric Clinics of North America, 22*, 385–400.

Shepherd, S. M., & Jagoda, A. S. (1990). PCP. In *Clinical management of poisoning and drug overdose* (2nd ed.)

(Haddad, L.D., & Winchester, J. F., eds.). Philadelphia: W.B. Saunders Co.

Sher, K. J. (1991). *Children of alcoholics.* Chicago: University of Chicago Press.

Sher, K. J. (1997). Psychological characteristics of children of alcoholics. *Alcohol Health & Research World, 21* (3), 247–254.

Sher, K. J., Walitzer, K. S., Wood, P. K., & Brent, E. E. (1991). Characteristics of children of alcoholics: Putative risk factors, substance use and abuse, and psychopathology. *Journal of Abnormal Psychology, 100,* 427–448.

Sheridan, E., Patterson, H. R., & Gustafson, E. A. (1982). *Falconer's the drug, the nurse, the patient* (7th ed.). Philadelphia: W. B. Saunders.

Sherman, C. (1994). Kicking butts. *Psychology Today, 27* (5), 40–45.

Sherman, C. (2000a). Acamprosate proven effective for alcohol tx. *Clinical Psychiatry News, 28* (7), 14.

Sherman, C. (2000b). Anticonvulsants may help treat benzodiazepine, cocaine withdrawal. *Clinical Psychiatry News, 28* (7), 14.

Sherman, C. B. (1991). Health effects of cigarette smoking. *Clinics in Chest Medicine, 12,* 643–658.

Shields, R. O. (1990). Amphetamines. In *Clinical management of poisoning and drug overdose* (2nd ed.). (Haddad, L. M., & Winchester, J. F., eds.). Philadelphia: W. B. Saunders.

Shiffman, L. B., Fischer, L. B., Zettler-Segal, M., & Benowitz, N. L. (1990). Nicotine exposure among nondependent smokers. *Archives of General Psychiatry, 47,* 333–340.

Shiffman, S. (1992). Relapse process and relapse prevention in addictive behaviors. *The Behavior Therapist, 15* (1), 99–11.

Shih, R. D., & Hollander, J. E. (1996). Management of cocaine-associated chest pain. *Hospital Physician, 32* (11), 11–20, 45.

Shoumatoff, A. (1995). Trouble in the land of muy verde. *Outside, XX* (3), 56–63, 149– 154.

Shute, N., Licking, E. F., & Schultz, S. (1998). Hepatitis C: A silent killer. *U.S. News & World Report, 124* (24), 60–66.

Shute, N., & Tangley, L. (1997). The drinking dilemma. *U.S. News & World Report, 123* (9), 54–65.

Siebert, C. (1996). Are we more than ever at the mercy of our genes? *Minneapolis Star-Tribune, XIV* (286), A13.

Siegel, B. S. (1986). *Love, medicine & miracles.* New York: Harper & Row.

Siegel, B. S. (1989). *Peace, love & healing.* New York: Harper & Row.

Siegel, L. (1989). Want to take the risks? It should be your choice. *Playboy, 36,* (1), 59.

Siegel, R. K. (1982). Cocaine smoking disorders: Diagnosis and treatment. *Psychiatric Annals, 14,* 728–732.

Siegel, R. K. (1991). Crystal meth or speed or crank. *Lear's, 3* (1), 72–73.

Siegel, R. L. (1986). Jungle revelers: When beasts take drugs to race or relax, things get zooey. *Omni, 8* (6), 70–74, 100.

Sierles, F. S. (1984). Correlates of malingering. *Behavioral Sciences and the Law, 2* (1), 113–118.

Sigvardsson, S., Bohman, M., & Cloninger, R. (1996). Replication of the Stockholm adoption study. *Archives of General Psychiatry, 53,* 681–687.

Silverman, M. M. (1989). Children of psychiatrically ill parents: A prevention perspective. *Hospital & Community Psychiatry, 40,* 1257–1265.

Simmons, A. L. (1991). A peculiar dialect in the land of 10,000 treatment centers. *Minneapolis Star-Tribune, X* (24), 23A.

Simons, A. M., Phillips, D. H., & Coleman, D. V. (1993). Damage to DNA in cervical epithelium related to smoking tobacco. *British Medical Journal, 306,* 1444–1448.

Sims, A. (1994). "Psyche"—spirit as well as mind? *British Journal of Psychiatry, 165,* 441–446.

Singh, R. A., Mattoo, S. K., Malhotra, A., & Varma, V. K. (1992). Cases of buprenorphine abuse in India. *Acta Psychiatrica Scandinavica, 86,* 46–48.

Sinha, R. (2000). Women. In *Handbook of alcoholism* (Zernig, G., Saria, A., Kurz, M., & O'Malley, S. S., eds.). New York: CRC Press.

60 Minutes. (1992). XXV (15). Rx drugs. Livingston, NJ: Burrelle's Information Services.

60 Minutes. (1994). XXVI (42). Halcion. Livingston, NJ: Burrelle's Information Services.

60 Minutes. (1996a). XXVIX (13). Pain killer. Livingston, NJ: Burrelle's Information Services.

60 Minutes. (1996b). XXVIX (13). How he won the war. Livingston, NJ: Burrelle's Information Services.

60 Minutes. (1997a). XXIX (31). North of the border. Livingston, NJ: Burrelle's Information Services.

60 Minutes. (1997b). XXIX (33). The tobacco tapes. Livingston, NJ: Burrelle's Information Services.

Sjogren, M. H. (1996). Serologic diagnosis of viral hepatitis. *Medical Clinics of North America, 80,* 929–956.

Sklair-Tavron, L., Ski, W. X., Lane, S. B., Harris, H. W., Bunny, B. S., & Nestler, E. J. (1996). Chronic morphine induces visable changes in the morphology of mesolimbic dopamine neurons. *Proceedings of the National Academy of Sciences, 93,* 11202–11207.

Skog, O. J., & Duckert, F. (1993). The development of alcoholics' and heavy drinkers' consumption: A longitudinal study. *Journal of Studies on Alcohol, 54,* 178–188.

Slaby, A. E., Lieb, J., & Tancredi, L. R. (1981). *Handbook of psychiatric emergencies* (2nd ed.). Garden City, NY: Medical Examination Publishing Co., Inc.

Slade, J., Bero, L. A., Hanauer, P., Barnes, D. E., & Glantz, S. A. (1995). Nicotine and addiction. *Journal of the American Medical Association, 274,* 225–233.

Slovut, G. (1992). Sports medicine. *Minneapolis Star-Tribune, X* (353), 20C.

Smith, B. D., & Salzman, C. (1991). Do benzodiazepines cause depression? *Hospital and Community Psychiatry, 42,* 1101–1102.

Smith, D. (1997). *Prescription drug abuse.* Paper presented at the May, 1997 WisSAM Symposium: "Still Getting High: A 30 year perspective on drug abuse," Gundersen-Lutheran Medical Center, La Crosse, Wisconsin.

Smith, G. T. (1994). Psychological expectancy as mediator of vulnerability to alcoholism. In *Types of alcoholics* (Babor, T. F., Hesselbrock, V., Meyer, R. E., & Shoemaker, W., eds.). New York: New York Academy of Sciences.

Smith, G. T., Goldman, M. S., Greenbaum, P. E., & Christiansen, B. A. (1995). Expectancy for social facilitation from drinking: The divergent paths of high-expectancy and low-expectancy adolescents. *Journal of Abnormal Psychology, 104,* 32–40.

Smith, J. E., Meyers, R. J., & Delaney, H. D. (1998). The community reinforcement approach with homeless alcohol-dependent individuals. *Journal of Consulting and Clinical Psychology, 66,* 541–548.

Smith, J. W. (1997). Medical manifestations of alcoholism in the elderly. In *Older adults' misues of alcohol, medicines and other drugs* (Gurnack, A.M., ed.). New York: Springer.

Smith, S. G. T., Touquet, R., Wright, S., & Das Gupta, N. (1996). Detection of alcohol misusing patients in accident and emergency departments: The Paddington alcohol test (PAT). *Journal of Accident & Emergency Medicine, 13,* 308–312.

Smith, T. (1994). How dangerous is heroin? *British Medical Journal, 307,* 807.

Smolowe, J. (1993). Choose your poison. *Time, 142* (4), 56–57.

Smolowe, J. (1997). Sorry, pardner. *Time, 146* (26),

Snyder, S. H. (1986). *Drugs and the brain.* New York: Scientific American Books, Inc.

Sobell, M. B., & Sobell, L. C. (1993). *Problem drinkers.* New York: Guilford Press.

Solomon, J., Rogers, A., Katel, P., & Lach, J. (1997). Turning a new leaf. *Newsweek, CXXIX* (13), 50.

Sonne, S. C., & Brady, K. T. (1999). Substance abuse and bipolar comorbidity. *Psychiatric Clinics of North America, 22,* 609–627.

Sowell, R. L., Moneyham, L., & Aranda-Naranjo, A. (1999). The care of women with AIDS. *Nursing Clinics of North America, 34,* 179–199.

Soyka, M. (2000). Alcohol-induced psychotic disorders. In *Handbook of alcoholism* (Zernig, G., Saria, A., Kurz, M., & O'Malley, S. S., eds.). New York: CRC Press.

Spanagel, R., & Hoelter, S. M. (2000). Controversial research areas. In *Handbook of alcoholism* (Zernig, G., Saria, A., Kurz, M., & O'Malley, S. S., eds.). New York: CRC Press.

Spangler, J. G., & Salisbury, P. L. (1995). Smokeless tobacco: Epidemiology, health effects and cessation strategies. *American Family Physician, 52,* 1421–1430.

Sparadeo, F. R., & Gill, D. (1989). Effects of prior alcohol use on head injury recovery. *Journal of Head Trauma Rehabilitation, 4* (1), 75–82.

Spiegel, R. (1996). *Psychopharmacology: An introduction* (3rd ed.). New York: John Wiley & Sons.

Spiller, H. A., & Krenzelok, E. P. (1997). Epidemiology of inhalant abuse reported to two regional poison centers. *Journal of Toxicology: Clinical Toxicology, 35,* 167–174.

Spindler, K. (1994). *The man in the ice.* New York: Harmony Books.

Spohr, H. L., Williams, J., & Steinhausen, H. C. (1993). Prenatal alcohol exposure and long-term consequences. *The Lancet, 341,* 907–910.

Sporer, K. A., & Khayam-Bashi, H. (1996). Acetaminophen and salicylate serum levels in patients with suicidal ingestion or altered mental states. *American Journal of Emergency Medicine, 14,* 443–446.

Springborn, W. (1987). Step one: The foundation of recovery. In *The twelve steps of Alcoholics Anonymous.* New York: Harper & Row.

Steele, T. E., & Morton, W. A. (1986). Salicylate-induced delirium. *Psychosomatics, 27* (6), 455–456.

Stein, B., Orlando, M., & Sturm, R. (2000). The effect of copayments on drug and alcohol treatment following inpatient detoxification under managed care. *Psychiatric Services, 51,* 195–198.

Stein, J. A., Newcomb, M. D., & Bentler, P. M. (1993). Differential effects of parent and grandparent drug use on behavior problems of male and female children. *Developmental Psychology, 29,* 31–43.

Stein, M. D., Freedberg, K. A., Sullivan, L. S., Savetsky, J., Levenson, S. M., Hingson, R., & Samet, J. H. (1998). Sexual ethics. *Archives of Internal Medicine, 158,* 253–257.

Stein, S. M., & Kosten, T. R. (1992). Use of drug combinations in treatment of opioid withdrawal. *Journal of Clinical Psychopharmacology, 12* (3), 203–209.

Stein, S. M., & Kosten, T. R. (1994). Reduction of opiate withdrawal-like symptoms by cocaine abuse during methadone and buprenorphine maintenance. *American Journal of Drug and Alcohol Abuse, 20* (4), 445–459.

Steinberg, N. (1994, May 5). The cartels would like a second chance. *Rolling Stone,* 33–34.

Steinberg, W., & Tenner, S. (1994). Acute pancreatitis. *New England Journal of Medicine, 330,* 1198–1210.

Steinglass, P., Bennett, L. A., Wolin, S. J., & Reiss, D. (1987). *The alcoholic family.* New York: Basic Books.

Sternbach, G. L., & Varon, J. (1992). Designer drugs. *Postgraduate Medicine, 91,* 169–176.

Stetter, F. (2000). Psychotherapy. In *Handbook of alcoholism* (Zernig, G., Saria, A., Kurz, M., & O'Malley, S. S., eds.). New York: CRC Press.

Stevens, R. S., Roffman, R. A., & Simpson, E. E. (1994). Treating adult marijuana dependence: A test of the relapse prevention model. *Journal of Consulting and Clinical Psychology, 62,* 92–99.

Stewart, W. F., Kawas, C., Corrada, M., & Metter, E. J. (1997). Risk of Alzheimer's disease and duration of NSAID use. *Neurology, 48,* 626–632.

Stimmel, B. (1997a). *Pain and its relief without addiction.* New York: The Harworth Medical Press.

Stimmel, B. (1997b). *Drug abuse and social policy in America: The war that must be won.* Paper presented at the 1997 annual Frank P. Furlano, M.D., memorial lecture, Gunderson-Lutheran Medical Center, La Crosse, Wisconsin.

Stocker, S. (1997). Compounds show strong promise for treating cocaine addiction. *NIDA Notes, 12* (3), 12–13.

Stocker, S. (1999a). Cocaine's pleasurable effects may involve multiple chemical sites in the brain. *NIDA Notes, 14* (2), 5–7.

Stocker, S. (1999b). Medications reduce incidence of substance abuse among ADHD patients. *NIDA Notes, 14* (4), 6–8.

Stockwell, T., & Town, C. (1989). Anxiety and stress management. In *Handbook of alcoholism treatment approaches* (Hester, H. K., & Miller, W. R., eds.). New York: Pergamon Press.

Stolberg, S. (1994). Aspirin isn't just for headaches. *Minneapolis Star-Tribune, XIII* (179), 4A.

Stone, J. (1991). Light elements. *Discover, 12* (1), 12–16.

Stoschitzky, K. (2000). Cardiovascular system. In *Handbook of alcoholism* (Zernig, G., Saria, A., Kurz, M., & O'Malley, S. S., eds.). New York: CRC Press.

Strain, E. C., Bigelow, G. E., Liebson, I. A., & Stitzer, M. L. (1999). Moderate vs. high-dose methadone in the treatment of opioid dependence. *Journal of the American Medical Association, 281*, 1000–1005.

Strain, E. C., Stritzer, M. L., Liebson, I. A., & Bigelow, G. E. (1994). Comparison of buprenorphine and methadone in the treatment of opioid dependence. *American Journal of Psychiatry, 151*, 1025–1030.

Strang, J., Griffiths, P., Powis, B., & Gossop, M. (1992) First use of heroin: Changes in route of administration over time. *British Medical Journal, 304*, 1222–1223.

Strang, J., Johns, A., & Caan, W. (1993). Cocaine in the UK—1991. *British Journal of Psychiatry, 162*, 1–13.

Streissguth, A. P., Aase, J. M., Clarren, S. K., Randels, S. P., LaDue, R. A., & Smith, D. F. (1991). Fetal alcohol syndrome in adolescents and adults. *Journal of the American Medical Association, 265*, 1961–1967.

Sturmi, J. E., & Diorio, D. J. (1998). Anabolic agents. *Clinics in Sports Medicine, 17*, 261–282.

Substance Abuse Letter. (1995). Rohypnol use spreading throughout southern U.S. 2 (1), 1, 6.

Supernaw, R. B. (1991). Pharmacotherapeutic management of acute pain. *U.S. Pharmacist, 16* (2), H 1–H 14.

Sussman, N. (1988). Diagnosis and drug treatment of anxiety in the elderly. *Geriatric Medicine Today, 7* (10), 1–8.

Sussman, N. (1994). The uses of buspirone in psychiatry. *Journal of Clinical Psychiatry, 55* (5) (Supplement), 3–19.

Suter, P. M., Schultz, Y., & Jequier, E. (1992). The effect of ethanol on fat storage in healthy subjects. *The New England Journal of Medicine, 326*, 983–987.

Sutherland, G., Stapleton, J. A., Russell, M. A. H., Jarvis, M. J., Hajek, P., Belcher, M., & Feyerabend, C. (1992). Randomised controlled trial of nasal nicotine spray in smoking cessation. *The Lancet, 340*, 324–329.

Svikis, D. S., Zarin, D. A., Tanielian, T., & Pincus, H. A. (2000). Alcohol abuse and dependence in a national sample of psychiatric patients. *Journal of Studies on Alcohol, 61*, 427–430.

Swan, N. (1994). Research demonstrates long-term benefits of methadone treatment. *NIDA Notes, 9* (4), 1, 4–5.

Swan, N. (1995). 31% of New York murder victims had cocaine in their bodies. *NIDA Notes, 10* (2), 1, 4.

Swan, N. (1998). Drug abuse cost to society set at $97.7 billion, continuing steady increase since 1975. *NIDA Notes, 13* (4), 1, 12.

Swift, R., & Davidson, D. (1998). Alcohol hangover. *Alcohol Health & Research World, 22*, 54–60.

Swift, R. M., Whelihan, W., Kuznetsov, O., Buongiorno, G., & Hsuing, H. (1994). Naltrexone-induced alterations in human ethanol intoxication. *American Journal of Psychiatry, 151*, 1463–1467.

Szabo, G. (1997). Alcohol's contribution to compromised immunity. *Alcohol Health & Research World, 21* 30–41.

Szarewski, A., Jarvis, M. J., Sasieni, P., Anderson, M., Edwards, R., Steele, S. J., & Buillebaud, J. C. (1996). Effect of smoking cessation on cervical lesion size. *The Lancet, 347*, 941–943.

Szasz, T. (1997). Save money, cut crime, get real. *Playboy, 44* (1), 129, 190.

Szasz, T. S. (1972). Bad habits are not diseases: A refutation of the claim that alcoholism is a disease. *The Lancet, 319*, 83–84.

Szasz, T. S. (1988). A plea for the cessation of the longest war of the twentieth century—the war on drugs. *The Humanistic Psychologist, 16* (2), 314–322.

Szasz, T. S. (1996). The war on drugs is lost. *National Review, XLVIII* (2), 45–47.

Szuster, R. R., Schanbacher, B. L., & McCann, S. C. (1990). Characteristics of psychiatric emergency room patients with alcohol- or drug-induced disorders. *Hospital and Community Psychiatry, 41*, 1342–1345.

Szwabo, P. A. (1993). Substance abuse in older women. *Clinics in Geriatric Medicine, 9*, 197–208.

Tabakoff, B., & Hoffman, P. L. (1992). Alcohol: neurobiology. In *Substance abuse: A comprehensive textbook* (2nd ed.) (Lowinson, J. H., Ruiz, P., Millman, R. B., & Langrod, J. G., eds.). New York: Williams & Wilkins.

Tabor, B. L., Smith-Wallace, T., & Yonekura, M. L. (1990). Perinatal outcome associated with PCP versus cocaine use. *American Journal of Drug and Alcohol Abuse, 16*, 337–349.

Taha, A. S., Dahill, S., Sturrock, R. D., Lee, F. D., & Russell, R. I. (1994). Predicting NSAID related ulcers—assessment of clinical and pathological risk factors and importance of differences in NSAID. *Gut, 35*, 891–895.

Takanishi, R. (1993). The opportunities of adolescence—research, interventions, and policy. *American Psychologist, 48*, 85–87.

Talley, N. J. (1993). The effects of NSAIDs on the gut. *Contemporary Internal Medicine, 5* (2), 14–28.

Tanhehco, E. J., Yasojima, K., McGeer, P. L., & Lucchesi, B. R. (2000). Acute cocaine exposure up-regulates complement expression in rabbit heart. *Journal of Pharmacology and Experimental Therapeutics, 292*, 201–208.

Tanner, S. (1995). Steroids: A breakfast of champions. *Orthopaedic Nursing, 14* (6), 26–30.

Tarter, R. E., Ott, P. J., & Mezzich, A. C. (1991). Psychometric assessment. In *Clinical textbook of addictive disorders* (Frances, R. J., & Miller, S. I., eds.). New York: The Guilford Press.

Tashkin, D. P. (1990). Pulmonary complications of smoked substance abuse. *The Western Journal of Medicine, 152,* 525–531.

Tashkin, D. P. (1993). Is frequent marijuana smoking harmful to health? *The Western Journal of Medicine, 158,* 635–637.

Tashkin, D. P., Kleerup, E. P., Koyal, S. N., Marques, J. A., & Goldman, M. D. (1996). Acute effects of inhaled and IV cocaine on airway dynamics. *Chest, 110,* 907–914.

Tate, C. (1989). In the 1800's, antismoking was a burning issue. *Smithsonian, 20* (4), 107–117.

Tate, J. C., Stanton, A. L., Green, S. B., Schmitz, J. M., Le, T., & Marshall, B. (1994). Experimental analysis of the role of expectancy in nicotine withdrawal. *Psychology of Addictive Behaviors, 8,* 169–178.

Tavris, C. (1990). One more guilt trip for women. *Minneapolis Star-Tribune, VIII,* (341), 21A.

Tavris, C. (1992). *The mismeasure of woman.* New York: Simon & Schuster.

Tavris, C. (1998). A grain of salt. *Family Therapy Networker, 22* (2), 42–43, 109.

Taylor, D. (1993). Addicts' abuse of sleeping pills brings call for tough curbs. *The Observer,* # 10531, 6.

Taylor, M. A. (1993). *The neuropsychiatric guide to modern everyday psychiatry.* New York: The Free Press.

Taylor, S., McCracken, C. F. M., Wilson, K. C. M., & Copeland, J. R. M. (1998). Extent and appropriateness of benzodiazepine use. *British Journal of Psychiatry, 173,* 433–438.

Taylor, W. A., & Gold, M. S. (1990). Pharmacologic approaches to the treatment of cocaine dependence. *Western Journal of Medicine, 152,* 573–578.

Teich, J. L. (2000). Monitoring change in behavioral health care. *Psychiatric Clinics of North America, 23,* 297–308.

Telenti, A., & Iseman, M. (2000). Drug-resistant tuberculosis. *Drugs, 59* (2), 171–179.

Terwilliger, E. G. (1995). Biology of HIV-1 and treatment strategies. *Emergency Medicine Clinics of North America, 13,* 27–42.

Thomas, D. L. (1997). *HIV/AIDS and hepatitis C.* Paper presented at NIDA conference: Heroin use and addiction. Washington, DC, September 29–30.

Thornton, J. (1990). Pharm aid: 10 new medicines you should know about. *Men's Health, 5* (4), 73–78.

Thorpe, L. E., Ouellet, L. J., Levy, J. R., Williams, I. T., & Monterroso, E. R. (2000). Hepatitis C virus infection: Prevalence, risk factors and prevention opportunities among young injection drug users in Chicago, 1997–1999. *Journal of Infectious Diseases, 182,* 1588–1594.

Timko, C., Moos, R. H., Finney, J. W., & Lesar, M. D. (2000). Long-term outcomes of alcohol use disorders: Comparing untreated individuals with those in Alcoholics Anonymous and formal treatment. *Journal of Studies on Alcohol, 61,* 529–540.

Tinsley, J. A., Finlayson, R. E., & Morse, R. M. (1998). Developments in the treatment of alcoholism. *Mayo Clinic Proceedings, 73,* 857–863.

Tobin, J. W. (1992). Is A.A. "treatment"? You bet. *Addiction & Recovery, 12* (3), 40.

Toneatto, T., Sobell, L. C., Sobell, M. B., & Leo, G. I. (1991). Psychoactive substance use disorder (Alcohol). In *Adult psychopathology & diagnosis* (2nd ed.) (Hersen, M., & Turner, S. M., eds.). New York: Wiley.

Toneatto, T., Sobell, L. C., Sobell, M. B., & Rubel, E. (1999). Natural recovery from cocaine dependence. *Psychology of Addictive Behaviors, 13,* 259–268.

Tonigan, J. S., & Hiller-Sturmhofel, S. (1994). Alcoholics Anonymous: Who benefits? *Alcohol Health & Research World, 18,* 308–310.

Tonigan, J. S., & Toscova, R. T. (1998). Mutual-help groups. In *Treating addictive behaviors* (2nd ed.) (Miller, W. R., & Heather, N., eds.). New York: Plenum.

Torrens, M., San, L., & Cami, J. (1993). Buprenorphine versus heroin dependence: Comparison of toxicologic and psychopathologic characteristics. *American Journal of Psychiatry, 150,* 822–824.

Trabert, W., Caspari, D., Bernhard, P., & Biro, G. (1992). Inappropriate vasopressin secretion in severe alcohol withdrawal. *Acta Psychiatrica Scandinavica, 85,* 376–379.

Trachtenberg, M. C., & Blum, K. (1987). Alcohol and opioid peptides: Neuropharmacological rationale for physical craving of alcohol. *American Journal of Drug and Alcohol Abuse, 13* (3), 365–372.

Trachtenberg, M. C., & Blum, K. (1988). Improvement of cocaine-induced neuromodulator deficits by the neuronutrient Tropamine. *Journal of Psychoactive Drugs, 20* (3), 315–331.

Treadway, D. (1990). Codependency: Disease, metaphor, or fad? *Family Therapy Networker, 14* (1), 39–43.

Tresch, D. D., & Aronow, W. S. (1996). Smoking and coronary artery disease. *Clinics in Geriatric Medicine, 12,* 23–32.

Trevisan, L. A., Boutros, N., Petrakis, I. L., & Krystal, J. H. (1998). Complications of alcohol withdrawal. *Alcohol Health & Research World, 22* (1), 61–66.

Triangle of self-obsession, The. (1983). New York: Narcotics Anonymous World Service Office.

Trichopoulos, D., Mollo, F., Tomatis, L., Agapitos, E., Delsedime, L., Zavitsanos, X., Kalandidi, A., Katsouyanni, K., Riboli, E., & Saracci, R. (1992). Active and passive smoking and pathological indicators of lung cancer risk in an autopsy study. *Journal of the American Medical Association, 268,* 1697–1701.

Tronick, E. Z., & Beeghly, M. (1999). Prenatal cocaine exposure, child development, and the compromising effects of cumulative risk. *Clinics in Perinatology, 26,* 151–171.

Truog, R. D., Berde, C. B., Mitchell, C., & Grier, H. E. (1992). Barbiturates in the care of the terminally ill. *The New England Journal of Medicine, 327,* 1678–1682.

Tsai, G., Gastfriend, D. R., & Coyle, J. T. (1995). The glutamatergic basis of human alcoholism. *American Journal of Psychiatry, 152,* 332–340.

Tsuang, M. T., Lyons, M. J., Meyer, J., Doyle, T., Eisen, S. A., Goldberg, J., True, W., Lin, N. Toomey, R., & Eaves, L. (1998). Co-occurrence of abuse of different drugs in men. *Archives of General Psychiatry, 55,* 967–972.

Tucker, J. A., & Sobell, L. C. (1992). Influences on help-seeking for drinking problems and on natural recovery without treatment. *The Behavior Therapist, 15* (1), 12–14.

Tunnicliff, G. (1997). Sites of action of gamma-hydroxybutyrate (GHB)—a neuroactive drug with abuse potential. *Journal of Toxicology: Clinical Toxicology, 35* (6), 581–591.

Turbo, R. (1989). Drying out is just a start: Alcoholism. *Medical World News, 30* (3), 56–63.

Tweed, S. H. (1998). Intervening in adolescent substance abuse. *Nursing Clinics of North America, 33,* 29–45.

Tweed, S. H., & Ryff, C. D. (1991). Profiles of wellness amidst distress. *Journal of Studies on Alcohol, 52,* 133–141.

Twelve Steps and Twelve Traditions. (1981). New York: Alcoholics Anonymous World Services, Inc.

Twerski, A. J., (1983). Early intervention in alcoholism: Confrontational techniques. *Hospital & Community Psychiatry, 34,* 1027–1030.

Tyas, S., & Rush, B. (!993). The treatment of disabled persons with alcohol and drug problems: Results of a survey of addiction services. *Journal of Studies on Alcohol, 54,* 275–282.

Tyler, D. C. (1994). Pharmacology of pain management. *Pediatric Clinics of North America, 41,* 59–71.

Tyrer, P. (1993). Withdrawal from hypnotic drugs. *British Medical Journal, 306,* 706–708.

Uhde, T. W., & Trancer, M. E. (1995). Barbiturates. In *Comprehensive textbook of psychiatry* (6th ed.) (Kaplan, H. I., & Sadock, B. J., eds.). Baltimore: Williams & Wilkins.

Understanding anonymity. (1981). New York: Alcoholics Anonymous World Services, Inc.

Ungvarski, P. J., & Grossman, A. H. (1999). Health problems of gay and bisexual men. *Nursing Clinics of North America, 34,* 313–326.

United Nations. (1997). *World drug report.* New York: Oxford University Press.

United States Department of Health & Human Services. (1994). *Morbidity and Mortality Weekly Report, 43* (SS-3).

United States Department of Health & Human Services (1999). Tobacco use—United States, 1900–1999. *Morbidity and Mortality Weekly Report, 48* (43), 986–993.

United States Department of Health & Human Services (2000). Cigarette smoking among adults—United States, 1998. *Morbidity and Mortality Weekly Report, 49* (39), 1–2.

United States Pharmacopeial Convention, Inc. (1990). *Advice for the patient* (10th ed.). Rockville, MD: USPC Board of Trustees.

Urbano-Marquez, A., Estruch, R., Fernandez-Sala, J., Nicholas, J. M., Pare, C., & Rubin, E. (1995). The greater risk of alcoholic cardiomyopathy and myopathy in women compared with men. *Journal of the American Medical Association, 274,* 149–154.

U.S. News & World Report. (1991). The men who created crack. *111* (8), 44–53.

U.S. News & World Report. (1994). Take 2 aspirins and come back in 76 years. *117* (12), 24.

Uva, J. L. (1991). Alcoholics Anonymous: Medical recovery through a higher power. *Journal of the American Medical Association, 266,* 3065–3068.

Vail, B. A. (1997). Management of chronic viral hepatitis. *American Family Physician, 55,* 2749–2756.

Vaillant, G. E. (1983). *The natural history of alcoholism.* Cambridge, MA: Harvard University Press.

Vaillant, G. E. (1995). *The natural history of alcoholism* (rev. ed.). Cambridge, MA: Harvard University Press.

Vaillant, G. E. (1990). We should retain the disease concept of alcoholism. *The Harvard Medical School Mental Health Letter, 9* (6), 4–6.

Vaillant, G. E. (1996). A long-term follow-up of male alcohol abuse. *Archives of General Psychiatry, 53,* 243–249.

Vaillant, G. E. (2000). *Alcoholics Anonymous: Cult or magic bullet?* Symposium presented to the Dept. of Psychiatry at The Cambridge Hospital, Boston, MA, March 4.

Vaillant, G. E., & Hiller-Sturmhofel, S. (1996). The natural history of alcoholism. *Alcohol Health & Research World, 20,* 152–161.

Valenzuela, C. F., & Harris, R. A. (1997). Alcohol: Neurobiology. In *Substance abuse: A comprehensive textbook* (3rd ed.) (Lowinson, J. H., Ruiz, P., Millman, R. B., & Langrod, J. G., eds.). New York: Williams & Wilkins.

Vanable, P. A., King, A. C., & de Wit, H. (2000). Psychometric screening instruments. In *Handbook of alcoholism* (Zernig, G., Saria, A., Kurz, M., & O'Malley, S. S., eds.). New York: CRC Press.

Vandeputte, C. (1989). Why bother to treat older adults? The answer is compelling. *Professional Counselor, 4* (2), 34–38.

Van Etten, M. L., Neumark, Y. D., & Anthony, J. C. (1999). Male-female differences in the earliest stages of drug involvement. *Addiction, 94,* 1413–1419.

Verebey, K., Buchan, B. J., & Turner, C. E. (1998). Laboratory testing. In *Clinical textbook of addictive disorders* (2nd ed.) (Frances, R. J., & Miller, S. I., eds.). New York: Guilford.

Verebey, K. G., & Buchan, B. J. (1997). Diagnostic laboratory: Screening for drug abuse. In *Substance Abuse: A comprehensive textbook (3rd ed.)* (Lowinson, J. H., Ruiz, P., Millman, R. B., & Langrod, J. G., eds.). New York: Williams & Wilkins.

Victor, M. (1993). Persistent altered mentation due to ethanol. *Neurologic Clinics, 11,* 639–661.

Voelker, R. (1994). Medical marijuana: A trial of science and politics. *Journal of the American Medical Association, 271,* 1645–1648.

Volkow, N. D., Hitzemann, R., Wang, G. J., Fowler, J. S., Burr, G., Pascani, K., Dewey, S. L., & Wolf, A. P. (1992). Decreased brain metabolism in neurologically intact healthy alcoholics. *American Journal of Psychiatry, 149,* 1016–1022.

Volkow, N. D., Wang, G. J., Fowler, J. S., Gatley, S. J., Logan, J., Ding, Y. S., Hitzemann, R., & Pappas, N. (1998). Dopamine transporter occupancies in the human brain induced by therapeutic doses of oral methylphenidate. *American Journal of Psychiatry, 155,* 1325–1331.

Volkow, N. D., Wang, G. J., Fowler, J. S., Logan, J., Gatley, S. J., Gifford, A., Hitzemann, R., Ding, Y. S., & Pappas, N. (1999). Prediction of reinforcing responses to psychostimulants in humans by brain dopamine D_2 receptor levels. *American Journal of Psychiatry, 156*, 1440–1443.

Volpe, J. J. (1995). *Neurology of the newborn* (3rd ed.). Philadelphia: W. B. Saunders.

Volpicelli, J., Balaraman, G., Hahn, J., Wallace, H., & Bux, D. (1999). The role of uncontrolled trauma in the development of PTSD and alcohol addiction. *Alcohol Research & Health, 23*, 256–262.

Volpicelli, J. R., Rhines, K. C., Rhines, J. S., Volpicelli, L. A., Alterman, A. J., & O'Brien, C. P.(1997). Naltrexone and alcohol dependence. *Archives of General Psychiatry, 54*, 737–742.

Vourakis, C. (1998). Substance abuse concerns in the treatment of pain. *Nursing Clinics of North America, 33*, 47–60.

Wadler, G. I. (1994). Drug use update. *Medical Clinics of North America, 78*, 439–455.

Wakefield, J. C. (1992). The concept of mental disorder. *American Psychologist, 47*, 373–388.

Walker, J. D. (1993). The tobacco epidemic: How far have we come? *Canadian Medical Association Journal, 148*, 145–147.

Walker, S. (1996). *A dose of sanity.* New York: Wiley.

Wallace, J. (1996). Theory of 12-step oriented treatment. In *Treating substance abuse* (Rotgers, F., Keller, D. S., & Morgenstern, J., eds.). New York: Guilford.

Wallen, M. C., & Weiner, H. D. (1989). Impediments to effective treatment of the dually diagnosed patient. *Journal of Psychoactive Drugs, 21*, 161–168.

Walsh, D. C., Hingson, R. W., Merrigan, D. M., Levenson, S. M., Cupples, L. A., Herren, T., Coffman, G. A., Becker, C. A., Barker, T. A., Hamilton, S. A., McGuire, T. G., & Kelly, C. A. (1991). A randomized trial of treatment options for alcohol-abusing workers. *The New England Journal of Medicine, 325*, 775–782.

Walsh, J. K., Pollak, C. P., Scharf, M. B., Schweitzer, P. K., & Vogel, G. W. (2000). Lack of residual sedation following middle of the night Zaleplon administration in sleep maintenance insomnia. *Clinical Neuropharmacology, 23* (1), 17–21.

Walsh, K., & Alexander, G. (2000). Alcoholic liver disease. *Postgraduate Medicine, 76*, 280–286.

Walter, D. S., & Inturrisi, C. E. (1995). Absorption, distribution, metabolism, and excretion of buprenorphine in animals and humans. In *Buprenorphine* (Cowan, A., & Lewis, J. W., eds.) New York: Wiley Interscience.

Walters, G. D. (1994). The drug lifestyle: One pattern or several? *Psychology of Addictive Behaviors, 8*, 8–13.

Wannamethee, S. G., Shaper, A. G., Whincup, P. H., & Walker, M. (1995). Smoking cessation and the risk of stroke in middle-aged men. *Journal of the American Medical Association, 274*, 155–160.

Wareing, M., Risk, J. E., & Murphy, P. N. (2000). Working memory deficits in current and previous users of MDMA ("ecstasy"). *British Journal of Psychiatry, 91.* 181–188.

Warn, D. J. (1997). Recovery issues of substance-abusing gay men. In *Gender and addictions* (Straussner, S. L. A., & Zelvin, E., eds.). Northvale, NJ: Jason-Aronson.

Warner, E. A. (1995). Is your patient using cocaine? *Postgraduate Medicine, 98*, 173–180.

Warner, E. A., Kosten, T. R., & O'Connor, P. G. (1997). Pharmacotherapy for opioid and cocaine abuse. *Medical Clinics of North America, 81*, 909–925.

Warner, E. A., Greene, G. S., Buchsbaum, M. S., Cooper, D. S., & Robinson, B. E. (1998). Diabetic ketoacidosis associated with cocaine use. *Archives of Internal Medicine, 158*, 1799–1802.

Warner, L. A., Kessler, R. C., Hughes, M., Anthony, J. C., & Nelson, C. B. (1995). Prevalence and correlates of drug use and dependence in the United States. *Archives of General Psychiatry, 51*, 219–229.

Washton, A. M. (1990). Crack and other substance abuse in the suburbs. *Medical Aspects of Human Sexuality, 24*, (5) 54–58.

Washton, A. M. (1995). Clinical assessment of psychoactive substance use. In *Psychotherapy and substance abuse* (Washton, A. M., ed.). New York: Guilford.

Washton, A. M., & Rawson, R. A. (1999). Substance abuse treatment under managed care: a provider perspective. In *Textbook of substance abuse treatment* (2nd ed.). Washington, DC: American Psychiatric Association Press, Inc.

Washton, A. M., Stone, N. S., & Hendrickson, E. C. (1988). Cocaine abuse. In *Assessment of addictive behaviors* (Donovan, D. M., & Marlatt, G. A., eds.). New York: The Guilford Press.

Watson, C. G., Hancock, M., Gearhart, L. P., Mendez, C. M., Malovrh, P., & Raden, M. (1997). A comparative outcome study of frequent, moderate, occasional, and nonattenders of Alcoholics Anonymous. *Journal of Clinical Psychology, 53*, 209–214.

Watson, C. G., Hancock, M., Malovrh, P., Gearhart, L. P.,& Raden, M. (1996). A 48 week natural history follow-up of alcoholics who do and do not engage in limited drinking after treatment. *Journal of Nervous and Mental Disease, 184*, (10), 623–627.

Watson, J. M. (1984). Solvent abuse and adolescents. *The Practitioner, 228*, 487–490.

Watson, S. J., Benson, J. A., & Joy, J. E. (2000). Marijuana and medicine: Assessing the science base. *Archives of General Psychiatry, 57*, 547–552.

Weathermon, R., & Crabb, D. W. (1999). Alcohol and medication interactions. *Alcohol Research & Health, 23* (1), 40–54.

Weathers, W. T., Crane, M. M., Sauvain, K. J., & Blackhurst, D. W. (1993). Cocaine use in women from a defined population: prevalence at delivery and effects on growth in infants. *Pediatrics, 91*, 350–354.

Weaver, M. F., Jarvis, M. A. E., & Schnoll, S. H. (1999). Role of primary care physician in problems of substance abuse. *Archives of Internal Medicine, 159*, 913–924.

Webb, S. T. (1989). Some developmental issues of adolescent children of alcoholics. *Adolescent Counselor, 1* (6), 47–48, 67.

Wechsler, H., Davenport, A., Dowdall, G., Moeykens, B., & Castillo, S. (1994). Health and behavioral consequences of binge drinking in college. *Journal of the American Medical Association, 272*, 1672–1677.

Weddington, W. W. (1993). Cocaine. *Psychiatric Clinics of North America, 16*, 87–95.

Wegscheider-Cruse, S. (1985). *Choice-making*. Pompano Beach, FL: Health Communications.

Wegscheider-Cruse, S., & Cruse, J. R. (1990). *Understanding co-dependency*. Pompano Beach, FL: Health Communications.

Weil, A. (1986). *The natural mind*. Boston: Houghton-Mifflin Co.

Weiner, H. R. (1997). HIV: An update for primary care physicians. *Emergency Medicine, 29* (9), 52–62.

Weingardt, K. R., Baer, J. S., Kivlahan, D. R., Roberts, L. J., Miller, E. T., & Marlatt, G. A. (1998). Episodic heavy drinking among college students: Methodological issues and longitudinal perspectives. *Psychology of Addictive Behaviors, 12*, 155–167.

Weisner, C., & Schmidt, L. (1992). Gender disparities in treatment for alcohol problems. *Journal of the American Medical Association, 268*, 1872–1876.

Weiss, C. J., & Millman, R. B. (1998). Hallucinogens, phencyclidine, marijuana, inhalants. In *Clinical textbook of addictive disorders* (2nd ed.) (Frances, R. J., & Miller, S. I., eds.). New York: Guilford.

Weiss, R. D., Greenfield, S. H., & Mirin, S. M. (1994). Intoxication and withdrawal syndromes. In *Handbook of psychiatric emergencies* (3rd ed.) (Hyman, S. E., & Tesar, G. E., eds.). Boston: Little Brown & Co.

Weiss, R. D., Griffin, M. L., Gallop, R., Luborsky, L., Siqueland, L., Frank, A., Onken, L. S., Daley, D. C., & Gastfriend, D. R. (2000). Predictors of self-help group attendance in cocaine dependent patients. *Journal of Studies on Alcohol, 61*, 714–719.

Weiss, R. D., & Mirin, S. M. (1988). Intoxication and withdrawal syndromes. In *Handbook of psychiatric emergencies* (2nd ed.) (Hyman, S. E., ed.). Boston: Little, Brown & Co.

Wellness Letter, The. (1990). Is there an addictive personality? *6* (9), 1–2.

Wells-Parker, E. (1994). Mandated treatment. *Alcohol Health & Research World, 18*, 302–306.

Welsby, P. D. (1997). An HIV view of the human condition. *Postgraduate Medicine, 73*, 609–610.

Wender, P. H. (1995). *Attention-deficit hyperactivity disorder in adults*. New York Oxford University Press.

Werner, E. E. (1989a). Children of the garden island. *Scientific American, 260* (4), 106–111.

Werner, E. E. (1989b). High-risk children in young adulthood. A longitudinal study from birth to 32 years. *American Journal of Orthopsychiatry, 59*, 72–81.

Werner, M. J., Walker, L. S., & Greene, J. W. (1995). Relation of alcohol expectancies to changes in problem drinking among college students. *Archives of Pediatric and Adolescent Medicine, 149*, 733–739.

Werner, R. M., & Pearson, T. A. (1998). What's so passive about passive smoking? *Journal of the American Medical Association, 279*, 157–158.

Wesson, D. R., & Ling, W. (1996). Addiction medicine. *Journal of the American Medical Association, 275*, 1792–1793.

West, R., & Hajek, P. (1997). What happens to anxiety levels on giving up smoking? *American Journal of Psychiatry, 154*, 1589–1592.

Westermeyer, J. (1987). The psychiatrist and solvent-inhalant abuse: Recognition, assessment and treatment. *American Journal of Psychiatry, 144*, 903–907.

Westermeyer, J. (1995). Cultural aspects of substance abuse and alcoholism. *The Psychiatric Clinics of North America, 18*, 589–620.

Westermeyer, J., Eames, S. L., & Nugent, S. (1998). Comorbid dysthymia and substance disorder: Treatment history and cost. *American Journal of Psychiatry, 155*, 1556–1560.

Westman, E. C. (1995). Does smokeless tobacco cause hypertension? *Southern Medical Journal, 88*, 716–720.

Wetli, C. V. (1987). Fatal reactions to cocaine. In *Cocaine: A clinician's handbook*. (Washton, A. M., & Gold, M. S., eds.). New York: The Guilford Press.

Wetter, D. W., Fiore, M. C., Baker, T. B., & Young, T. B. (1995). Tobacco withdrawal and nicotine replacement influence objective measures of sleep. *Journal of Consulting and Clinical Psychology, 63*, 658–667.

Wetter, D. W., Young, T. B., Bidwell, T. R., Badr, M. S., & Palta, M. (1994). Smoking as a risk factor for sleep-disordered breathing. *Archives of Internal Medicine, 154*, 2219–2224.

Wexler, B. E., Gottschalk, C. H., Fulbright, R. K., Prohovnik, I., Lacadie, C. M., Rounsaville, B. J., & Gore, J. C. (2001). Functional magnetic resonance imaging of cocaine craving. *American Journal of Psychiatry, 158*, 86–95.

Wheeler, K., & Malmquist, J. (1987). Treatment approaches in adolescent chemical dependency. *The Pediatric Clinics of North America, 34*, (2), 437–447.

Whitcomb, D. C., & Block, G. D. (1994). Association of acetaminophen hepatotoxicity with fasting and ethanol use. *Journal of the American Medical Association, 272*, 1845–1850.

White, P. T. (1989) Coca. *National Geographic, 175* (1), 3–47.

White, R. J. (1993). Washington figuring out it has fought drug war on wrong fronts. *Minneapolis Star-Tribune, XI* (351), 23A.

Whitehead, R., Chillag, S., & Elliott, D. (1992). Anabolic steroid use among adolescents in a rural state. *Journal of Family Practice, 35*, 401–405.

Whitman, D., Friedman, D., & Thomas, L. (1990). The return of skid row. *U.S. News World Report, 108* (2), 27–30.

Whitworth, A. B., Fischer, F., Lesch, O. M., Nimmerrichter, A., Oberbauer, H., Platz, T., Potgieter, A., Walter, H., & Fleischhacker, W. W. (1996). Comparison of acamprosate and placebo in long-term treatment of alcohol dependence. *The Lancet, 347*, 1438–1442.

Wilbur, R. (1986). A drug to fight cocaine. *Science '86, 7* (2), 42–46.

Wilcox, C. M., Shalek, K. A., & Cotsonis, G. (1994). Striking prevalence of over-the-counter nonsteroidal anti-inflammatory drug use in patients with upper gastrointestinal hemorrhage. *Archives of Internal Medicine, 154,* 42–46.

Wild, T. C., Cunningham, J., & Hobdon, K. (1998). When do people believe that alcohol treatment is effective? The importance of perceived client and therapist motivation. *Psychology of Addictive Behaviors, 12,* 93–100.

Wilkinson, R. J., Liewelyn, M., Toossi, A., Patel, P., Pasvol, G., Lalvani, A., Wright, D. Latif, M., & Davidson, R. N. (2000). Influence of vitamin D deficiency and vitamin D receptor polymorphisms on tuberculosis among Gujarati Asians in West London: A case-control study. *The Lancet, 355,* 618–621.

Will, G. F. (1993). U.S. drug policy sets off slew of unintended consequences. *Minneapolis Star Tribune, XII* (84), 21A.

Williams, B. R., & Baer, C. L. (1994). *Essentials of clinical pharmacology in nursing* (2nd ed.). Springhouse, PA: Springhouse Corp.

Williams, E. (1989). Strategies for intervention. *The Nursing Clinics of North America, 24* (1), 95–107.

Williams, H., Dratcu, L., Taylor, R., Roberts, M., & Oyefeso, A. (1998). "Saturday night fever": Ecstasy related problems in a London accident and emergency department. *Journal of Accident and Emergency Medicine, 15,* 322–326.

Williams, T. (2000). High on hemp: Ditchweed digs in. *Utne Reader, 98,* 72–77.

Williamson, D. F., Madans, J., Anda, R., Kleinman, J. C., Giovino, G. A., & Byers, T. (1991). Smoking cessation and severity of weight gain in a national cohort. *The New England Journal of Medicine, 324,* 739–745.

Willoughby, A. (1984). *The alcohol troubled person: Known and unknown.* Chicago: Nelson-Hall.

Wills, T. A., McNamara, G., Vaccaro, D., & Hirky, A. E. (!996). Escalated substance use: A longitudinal grouping analysis from early to middle adolescence. *Journal of Abnormal Psychology, 105,* 166–180.

Wilsnack, S. C., & Wilsnack, R. W. (1995). Drinking and problem drinking in U.S. women. In *Recent developments in alcoholism* (Vol. 12) (Galanter, M., ed.). New York: Plenum Press.

Wilsnack, S. C., Wilsnack, R. W., & Hiller-Sturmhoffel, S. (1994). How women drink. *Alcohol Health & Research World, 18,* 173–181.

Wilson, F., & Kunsman, K. (1997). The saliva solution: New choices for alcohol testing. *Occupational Health & Safety, 66* (4), 40–43.

Wilson-Tucker, S., & Dash, J. (1995). Legal—but lethal: Fighting the newest health threat to our kids. *Family Circle, 108* (14), 21–24.

Winchester, J. F. (1990). Barbiturates, methaqualone and primidone. In *Clinical management of poisoning and drug overdose* (2nd ed.) (Haddad, L. M., & Winchester, J. F., eds.). Philadelphia: W. B. Saunders.

Windle, M., Windle, R. C., Scheidt, D. M., & Miller, G. B. (1995). Physical and sexual abuse and associated mental disorders among alcoholic inpatients. *American Journal of Psychiatry, 152,* 1322–1328.

Winecker, R. E., & Goldberger, B.A. (1998). Urine specimen suitability for drug testing. In *Drug abuse handbook* (Karch, S. B., editor-in-chief). New York: CRC Press.

Wing, D. M. (1995) Transcending alcoholic denial. *Image, 27,* 121–126.

Wisconsin State Journal (1996). Health spending criticized. *157* (260), 1A, 3A.

Wiseman, B. (1997). Confronting the breakdown of law and order. *USA Today, 125,* (2620), 32–34.

Wisneiwski, L. (1994). Use of household products as inhalants rising among young teens. *Minneapolis Star-Tribune, XIII* (9), 8Ex.

Witkin, G. (1995). A new drug gallops through the west. *U.S. News & World Report, 119* (19), 50–51.

Witkin, G., & Griffin, J. (1994). The New Opium Wars. *U.S. News & World Report, 117* (114), 39–44.

Woititz, J. G. (1983)., *Adult children of alcoholics.* Pompano Beach, FL: Health Communications, Inc.

Wolf-Reeve, B. S. (1990). A guide to the assessment of psychiatric symptoms in the addictions treatment setting. In *Managing the dually diagnosed patient* (O'Connell, D. F., ed.). New York: The Halworth Press.

Wolin, S. J., & Wolin, S. (1993). *The resilient self.* New York: Villard Books.

Wolin, S. J., & Wolin, S. (1995). Resilience among youth growing up in substance-abusing families. *Pediatric Clinics of North America, 42,* 415–429.

Wolkowitz, O. M., Rubinow, D., Doran, A. R., Breier, A., Berrettini, W. H., Kling, M. A., & Pickar, D. (1990). Prednisone effects on neurochemistry and behavior: Preliminary findings. *Archives of General Psychiatry, 47,* 963–968.

Woods, J. H., Katz, J. L., & Winger, G. (1988). Use and abuse of benzodiazepines. *Journal of the American Medical Association, 260* (23), 3476–3480.

Woods, J. H., & Winger, G. (1997). Abuse liability of flunitrazepam. *Journal of Psychopharmacology, 17* (Supplement #3), 1S-57S.

Woods, J. R. (1998). Maternal and transplacental effects of cocaine. *Annals of the New York Academy of Sciences, 846,* 1–11.

Woody, G. E., McLellan, A. T., & Bedrick, J. (1995). Dual diagnosis. In *Review of psychiatry* (Vol. 14) (Oldham, J. M., & Riba, M. B., eds.). Washington, DC: American Psychiatric Association Press, Inc.

Woolf, A. D., & Shannon, M. W. (1995). Clinical toxicology for the pediatrician. *Pediatric Clinics of North America, 42,* 317–333.

Work Group on HIV/AIDS (2000). Practice guideline for the treatment of patients with HIV/AIDS. *American Journal of Psychiatry, 157* (11), Supplement.

Wright, K. (1999). A shot of sanity. *Discover, 20* (6), 47–48.

Wuethrich, B. (2001). Getting stupid. *Discover, 22* (3), 5663.

Yablonsky, L. (1967). *Synanon: The tunnel back*. Baltimore: Penguin Books.

Yalom, I. D. (1985). *The theory and practice of group psychotherapy* (3rd ed.). New York: Basic Books.

Yancey, P. (2000). *Reaching for the invisible god*. Grand Rapids, MI: Zondervan Publishing Co.

Yesalis, C. E., Kennedy, N. J., Kopstein, A. N., & Bahrke, M. S. (1993). Anabolic-androgenic steroid use in the United States. *Journal of the American Medical Association, 270,* 1217–1221.

Yip, L., Dart, R. C., & Gabow, P. A. (1994). Concepts and controversies in salicylate toxicity. *Emergency Medical Clinics of North America, 12,* 351–364.

Yost, D. A. (1996). Alcohol withdrawal syndrome. *American Family Physician, 54,* 657–664.

Yost, J. H., & Morgan, G. J. (1994). Cardiovascular effects of NSAIDS. *Journal of Musculoskeletal Medicine, 11* (10), 22–34.

Youngstrom, N. (1990a). The drugs used to treat drug abuse. *APA Monitor, 21* (10), 19.

Youngstrom, N. (1990b). Debate rages on: In- or outpatient? *APA Monitor, 21* (10), 19.

Youngstrom, N. (1992). Fetal alcohol syndrome carries severe deficits. *APA Monitor, 23* (4), 32.

Yu, K., & Daar, E. S. (2000). Primary HIV infection. *Postgraduate Medicine, 107,* 114–122.

Zakhari, S. (1997). Alcohol and the cardiovascular system. *Alcohol Health & Research World, 21,* 21–29.

Zarek, D., Hawkins, D., & Rogers, P. D. (1987). Risk factors for adolescent substance abuse. *The Pediatric Clinics of North America, 34* (2), 481–493.

Zealberg, J. J., & Brady, K. T. (1999). Substance abuse and emergency psychiatry. *Psychiatric Clinics of North America, 22,* 803–817.

Zelentz, P. D., & Epstein, M. E. (1999). HIV in women. *Emergency Medicine, 31,* 14–37.

Zelvin, E. (1997). Codependency issues of substance-abusing women. In *Gender and addictions* (Straussner, S. L. A., & Zelvin, E., eds.). Northvale, NJ: Jason-Aronson.

Zernig, G., & Battista, H. J. (2000). Drug interactions. In *Handbook of alcoholism* (Zernig, G., Saria, A., Kurz, M., & O'Malley, S. S., eds.). New York: CRC Press.

Zerwekh, J., & Michaels, B. (1989). Co-dependency. *The Nursing Clinics of North America, 24* (1), 109–120.

Zevin, S., & Benowitz, N. L. (1998). Drug-related syndromes. In *Drug abuse handbook* (Karch, S. B., editor-in-chief). New York: CRC Press.

Zickler, P. (1999). NIDA studies clarify developmental effects of prenatal cocaine exposure. *NIDA Notes, 14* (3), 5–7.

Ziedonis, D., & Brady, K. (1997). Dual diagnosis in primary care. *Medical Clinics of North America, 81,* 1017–1036.

Zimberg, S. (1978). Psychosocial treatment of elderly alcoholics. In *Practical approaches to alcoholism psychotherapy* (Zimberg, S., Wallace, J., & Blume, S. B., eds.). New York: Plenum Press.

Zimberg, S. (1995). The elderly. In *Psychotherapy and substance abuse* (Washton, A. M., ed.). New York: Guilford.

Zimberg, S. (1996). Treating alcoholism: An age-specific intervention that works for older patients. *Geriatrics, 51* (10), 45–49.

Zisook, S., Heaton, R., Moranville, J., Kuck, J., Jernigan, T., & Braff, D. (1992). Past substance abuse and clinical course of schizophrenia. *American Journal of Psychiatry, 149,* 552–553.

Zito, J. M. (1994). *Psychotherapeutic drug manual* (3rd ed.). New York: John Wiley & Sons, Inc.

Zoldan, J. (2000). *The treatment of denial in recovery: Moving from denial of acceptance towards acceptance of denial.* Symposium presented to the Dept. of Psychiatry at The Cambridge Hospital, Boston, MA, March 4.

Zubaran, C., Fernandes, J. G., & Rodnight, R. (1997). Wernicke-Korsakoff syndrome. *Postgraduate Medical Journal, 73,* 27–31.

Zucker, R. A., & Gomberg, E. S. L. (1986). Etiology of alcoholism reconsidered: The case for a biopsychosocial process. *American Psychologist, 41,* 783–794.

Zuckerman, B., & Bresnahan, K. (1991). Developmental and behavioral consequences of prenatal drug and alcohol exposure. *Pediatric Clinics of North America, 38,* 1387–1406.

Zuger, A. (1994). Meningitis mystery. *Discover, 15* (3), 40–43.

Zukin, S. R., Sloboda, Z., & Javitt, D. C. (1997). Phencyclidine. In *Substance abuse: A comprehensive textbook* (3rd ed.) (Lowinson, J. H., Ruiz, P., Millman, R. B., & Langrod, J. G., eds.). New York: Williams & Wilkins.

Zukin, S. R., & Zukin, R. S. (1992). Phencyclidine. In *Substance abuse: A comprehensive textbook* (2nd ed.) (Lowinson, J. H., Ruiz, P., Millman, R. B., & Langrod, J. G., eds.). New York: Williams & Wilkins.

Zweben, J. E. (1995). Integrating psychotherapy and 12-step approaches. In *Psychotherapy and substance abuse* (Washton, A. M., ed.). New York: Guilford.

Zweig, C., & Wolf, S. (1997). *Romancing the shadow*. New York: Ballantine Books.

Index

AA. *See* Alcoholics Anonymous
absorption, of drugs into body, 58–59
Acamprosate, 393
accidental injury
    alcohol use as cause of, 78
    as sign of adolescent chemical abuse, 295
accommodation
    of family to alcoholism, 311–312
acetaldehyde
    as byproduct of alcohol metabolism, 73
    relationship to Antabuse, 390
    as byproduct of tobacco use, 233
acetaminophen
    alcohol as contraindication, 224
    analgesic, as, 217
    death caused by, 225
    dosage levels
        normal, 220
        overdose, 226
    end stage renal disease and, 226
    history of, 215
    kidney damage, as result of use of, 225
    liver damage caused by, 224, 225
    NSAID status, 216
    pharmacology of, 218, 220
    pregnancy, use during, 255
    prostaglandins, inhibition of, by acetaminophen, 218
    normal dosage levels, 220
    overdose of, 226
    suicide, use during attempts of, 226
acetylcholine
    marijuana use and, 154
    nicotine use and, 233

acetylsalicylic acid, 214. *See also* aspirin
ACOA. *See* Adult Children of Alcoholics
acupuncture, as treatment technique, 348–349
adaptation, of family to alcoholic. *See* accommodation
addiction
    percentage of population addicted to chemicals, 4–7
    alcohol addiction, 5–6, 79
    adolescents, as result of chemical abuse, 293–294
    amphetamines, 132
    benzodiazepine addiction, 108–109
    buspirone addiction, reports of, 116
    continuum, addiction as a, 12–13
    cocaine, 139–140
    criteria for, 16, 21–22
    defined, 13–14, 319
    elderly and, 263
    elements of, 16
    family and, 309–318
    growth of, 14–15
    heroin, 173, 177–178
    marijuana, 160
    narcotic analgesics, 176
    tobacco, 235–236
    steroids, 212
    spiritual disease, as expression of, 45
Addiction Severity Index, 322
adenylate cyclase, THC and, 154
ADH. *See* Alcohol dehydrogenase, 73
ADHD. *See* attention deficit-hyperactivity disorder
adinazolam, 106
adolescents
    alcohol use and, 285–286

chemical use as problem in this age group, 284–285
    inhalant abuse by, 200–201, 285
    reasons for chemical use by, 289–291
    signs of adolescent "at risk" for substance use problems, 296
    stages in adolescent substance use, 292–293
    steroid abuse by, 207
    tobacco use by, 231, 287–289
Adult Children of Alcoholics (ACOA)
    Growth in ACOA movement, 341–342
    reactions against concept of, 342–34
adulterants, added to illicit drugs, 439–444
aerosols. *See* inhalants
aftercare, defined, 351
aggression
    as result of amphetamine abuse, 131
    as result of alcohol ingestion, 75
    See also paradoxical rage reaction; rage; 'roid rage; violence
agonist, defined, 67
AIDS, 406–408, 410–411
    Kaposi's sarcoma and, 411
    suicide and, 410–411
    See also HIV-1
Al-Anon, 428–429
Al-ateen, 428–429
alcohol
    abuse of and addiction to, 4–6, 79–80
    accidental injury, factor in, 78
    acetaminophen as contraindication, 224
    amphetamine abuse, and, 131
    anxiety, relationship to abuse of, 89
    barbiturates, when mixed with, 100